The
Chambers
Paperback Thesaurus

CHAMBERS
An imprint of Chambers Harrap Publishers Ltd
338 Euston Road, London,
NW1 3BH

Previous editions published 1997, 2003 and 2007
This edition published by Chambers Harrap Publishers Ltd 2012

Chambers Harrap is an Hachette UK company

© Chambers Harrap Publishers Ltd 2012

A CIP catalogue record for this book is available from the British Library.

ISBN 9780550105516

Designed and typeset by Chambers Harrap Publishers Ltd, Edinburgh
and Sharon McTeir, Creative Publishing Services
Printed and bound by CPI Group (UK) Ltd, Croydon, CR0 4YY

Contents

Contributors to the last edition

Editors
Vicky Aldus
Ian Brookes
Pat Bulhosen
Lorna Gilmour
Alice Grandison
Andrew Holmes

Data Management
Patrick Gaherty

Prepress
Heather Macpherson

Contributors to this edition

Editorial Director
Sarah Cole

Commissioning Editor
Robert Williams

Editor
Martin Manser

Production Controller
Georgina Cope

Preface

A thesaurus is a book that contains lists of synonyms - that is, words that have a similar meaning to another word. A thesaurus allows you to look up a common word and find a range of words that have the same or nearly the same meaning. *The Chambers Paperback Thesaurus* is one of a series of thesauruses drawn from the extensive *Chambers Dictionary* database, and is the ideal companion to *The Chambers Paperback Dictionary*.

Looking up a word in this thesaurus may help you to find a more exact term for an essay or report, a livelier phrase for a speech, or a simpler expression for a letter. This will enable you to say what you have to say using the full range of words available to you. Moreover, browsing through a thesaurus also offers you a fascinating insight into the richness and variety of the English language.

But this book offers much more than lists of alternative words. It also contains lists of antonyms - words that have an opposite meaning. This allows you the further option of describing things in terms of their opposites. For example, you can describe something that is expensive not only as 'costly', but also as 'not cheap'.

Another useful feature is the inclusion of almost 200 panels containing lists of related words (hyponyms). These words answer the question, 'What kinds of … are there?' The hyponym panels cover both technical subjects (phobias, parts of the brain, architectural terms) and more general themes (breeds of dog, mythological creatures, types of cake). A complete index of these hyponym panels is given on pages viii and ix.

Included in this new editon is a good writing guide to help you develop your word power. It contains a wealth of information on commonly confused words, words to impress and foreign words in English.

These features combine to make *The Chambers Paperback Thesaurus* a mine of information. We hope that you enjoy using it.

How to use the thesaurus

The Chambers Paperback Thesaurus has been designed to allow you to find the information you are looking for quickly and easily. The entries are arranged in alphabetical order, so you can go straight to the word you are looking for without having to search in an index.

The lists of synonyms are arranged according to shades of meaning or in order from the most common to the least frequently used or the most specialized term.

Some synonyms are followed by a label which indicates that the word is restricted in use to certain occasions. Thus some words are only appropriate in informal contexts and should not be used in business correspondence or formal writing. Similarly, formal words might not be appropriate for more general use.

If the word you want can be used in a number of different senses, you will find these senses are clearly distinguished. Each sense is numbered and introduced either by a phrase in italics giving an example of the word in use, or by a 'key' synonym in capital letters. These features mean that it is easy for you to work out which sense of the word you are interested in.

Similarly, when a headword can be used as different parts of speech, each is treated separately, with a new part of speech within an entry indicated by the symbol ◇.

Antonyms or opposite words are introduced by the symbol ⊡. Where there are several senses of a word, the antonyms are numbered to indicate to which senses they apply. Where there is more than one part of speech in an entry, the antonyms are listed after the part of speech to which they apply.

Some entries include additional information, such as synonyms for related idioms and phrasal verbs (introduced by the symbol •) or panels of related words (hyponyms).

The diagram on the facing page shows how these features appear in the text.

Headwords are shown in bold letters at the beginning of each entry.

helper *n* assistant, deputy, auxiliary, subsidiary, attendant, right-hand man, PA, mate, partner, associate, colleague, collaborator, accomplice, ally, supporter, second.

Different meanings are shown in numbered sections, introduced either by a key synonym in capitals or by a phrase in italics showing the word in use.

helpful *adj* **1** USEFUL, practical, constructive, worthwhile, valuable, beneficial, profitable, advantageous. **2** *a helpful person*: co-operative, obliging, neighbourly, friendly, considerate, caring, kind, sympathetic, supportive.
⊨ **1** useless, futile.

Labels in italics show when synonyms are restricted to certain areas of language.

helping *n* serving, portion, share, ration, amount, plateful, piece, dollop (*infml*).

Synonyms or alternative words are listed with the most commonly used ones before less frequent and more specialized terms, or arranged by shades of meaning.

helpless *adj* weak, feeble, powerless, dependent, vulnerable, exposed, unprotected, defenceless, abandoned, friendless, destitute, forlorn, incapable, incompetent, infirm, disabled, paralysed.
⊨ strong, independent, competent.

Idioms and phrasal verbs are grouped alphabetically at the end of some entries. These are indicated by the symbol •.

hem *n* edge, border, margin, fringe, trimming.
• **hem in** surround, enclose, box in, confine, restrict.

Antonyms, words that mean the opposite of the headword, are introduced by the symbol ⊨.

henpecked *adj* dominated, subjugated, browbeaten, bullied, intimidated, meek, timid.
⊨ dominant.

Parts of speech, eg noun, verb, are shown by abbreviations. A new part of speech within an entry is indicated by the symbol ◇.

herald *n* messenger, courier, harbinger, forerunner, precursor, omen, token, signal, sign, indication.
◇ *v* announce, proclaim, broadcast, advertise, publicize, trumpet, pave the way, precede, usher in, show, indicate, promise.

herb

Lists of related words are shown in panels after some entries.

Herbs and spices include:
angelica, anise, basil, bay, bergamot, borage, camomile, chervil, chives, comfrey, dill, fennel, garlic, hyssop, lavender, lemon balm, lovage, marjoram, mint, oregano, parsley, rosemary, sage, savory, sorrel, tarragon, thyme; allspice, caraway seeds, cardamom, cayenne pepper, chilli, cinnamon, cloves, coriander, cumin, curry powder, garam masala, ginger, mace, mustard, nutmeg, paprika, pepper, saffron, star anise, turmeric, vanilla.

Index of hyponym panels

Lists of related words (hyponyms) appear in the thesaurus after the following entries:

Abbreviations and symbols

adj	adjective
adv	adverb
Aust	Australian
conj	conjunction
fml	formal
infml	informal
interj	interjection
n	noun
N Am	North American
prep	preposition
®	trademark
sl	slang
US	United States
v	verb
⧧	antonym(s)

Aa

abandon v **1** DESERT, leave, forsake, jilt, ditch (*sl*), dump (*sl*), leave in the lurch (*infml*), maroon, strand, leave behind, scrap. **2** *abandon ship*: vacate, evacuate, withdraw from, quit. **3** RENOUNCE, resign, give up, forgo, relinquish, surrender, yield, waive, drop.
⊜ **1** support, maintain, keep. **3** continue.

abandoned adj **1** DESERTED, unoccupied, derelict, neglected, forsaken, forlorn, desolate. **2** DISSOLUTE, wild, uninhibited, wanton, wicked.
⊜ **1** kept, occupied. **2** restrained.

abandonment n **1** DESERTION, leaving, forsaking, jilting, neglect, scrapping. **2** RENUNCIATION, resignation, giving up, stopping, relinquishment, surrender, sacrifice, waiver, dropping, discontinuation.

abashed adj **1** ASHAMED, shamefaced, embarrassed, mortified, humiliated, humbled. **2** CONFUSED, taken aback, bewildered, nonplussed, confounded, perturbed, discomposed, disconcerted, dumbfounded, floored (*infml*), dismayed.
⊜ **2** composed, at ease.

abate v **1** DECREASE, reduce, lessen, diminish, decline, sink, dwindle, taper off, fall off. **2** MODERATE, ease, relieve, alleviate, mitigate, remit, pacify, quell, subside, let up (*infml*), weaken, wane, slacken, slow, fade.
⊜ **1** increase. **2** strengthen.

abbey n monastery, priory, friary, seminary, convent, nunnery, cloister.

abbreviate v shorten, cut, trim, clip, truncate, curtail, abridge, summarize, précis, abstract, digest, condense, compress, reduce, lessen, shrink, contract.
⊜ extend, lengthen, expand, amplify.

abbreviation n shortening, clipping, curtailment, abridgement, summarization, summary, reduction, synopsis, résumé, précis, abstract, compression, digest, contraction.
⊜ extension, expansion, amplification.

abdicate v renounce, give up, relinquish, surrender, cede, yield, forgo, abandon, quit, vacate, retire, resign, step down (*infml*).

abdomen n belly, guts, stomach, tummy (*infml*), paunch, midriff.

abdominal adj ventral, intestinal, visceral, gastric.

abduct v carry off, run away with, run off with (*infml*), make off with, spirit away, seduce, kidnap, snatch, seize, appropriate.

aberration n deviation, straying, wandering, divergence, irregularity, nonconformity, anomaly, oddity, peculiarity, eccentricity, quirk, freak, lapse, defect.
⊜ conformity.

abhor v hate, detest, loathe, despise, abominate, shudder at, recoil from, shrink from, spurn.
⊜ love, adore.

abhorrence n hate, hatred, aversion, loathing, abomination,

horror, repugnance, revulsion, disgust, distaste.
⊞ love, adoration.

abhorrent *adj* detestable, odious, loathsome, abominable, execrable, heinous, obnoxious, hated, hateful, horrible, horrid, offensive, repugnant, repellent, repulsive, revolting, nauseating, disgusting, distasteful.
⊞ delightful, attractive.

abide *v* 1 BEAR, stand, endure, tolerate, put up with, stomach, accept. 2 REMAIN, last, endure, continue, persist.
• **abide by** 1 *abide by the rules*: obey, observe, follow, comply with, adhere to, conform to, submit to, go along with, agree to. 2 FULFIL, discharge, carry out, stand by, hold to, keep to.

ability *n* 1 CAPABILITY, capacity, faculty, facility, potentiality, power. 2 SKILL, dexterity, deftness, adeptness, competence, proficiency, qualification, aptitude, talent, gift, endowment, knack, flair, touch, expertise, know-how (*infml*), forte, genius, strength.
⊞ 1 inability. 2 incompetence, weakness.

abject *adj* 1 CONTEMPTIBLE, worthless, low, mean, ignoble, dishonourable, deplorable, despicable, vile, sordid, debased, degenerate, submissive, servile, grovelling, slavish.
2 MISERABLE, wretched, forlorn, hopeless, pitiable, pathetic, outcast, degraded.
⊞ 1 proud, exalted.

ablaze *adj* 1 BLAZING, flaming, burning, on fire, ignited, lighted, alight, illuminated, luminous, glowing, aglow, radiant, flashing, gleaming, sparkling, brilliant.
2 IMPASSIONED, passionate, fervent, ardent, fiery, enthusiastic, excited, exhilarated, stimulated, aroused, angry, furious, raging, incensed, frenzied.

able *adj* capable, fit, fitted,

dexterous, adroit, deft, adept, competent, proficient, qualified, practised, experienced, skilled, accomplished, clever, expert, masterly, skilful, ingenious, talented, gifted, strong, powerful, effective, efficient, adequate.
⊞ unable, incapable, incompetent, ineffective.

able-bodied *adj* fit, healthy, sound, strong, robust, hardy, tough, vigorous, powerful, hale, hearty, lusty, sturdy, strapping, stout, stalwart, staunch.
⊞ infirm, delicate.

abnormal *adj* odd, strange, singular, peculiar, curious, queer, weird, eccentric, paranormal, unnatural, uncanny, extraordinary, exceptional, unusual, uncommon, unexpected, irregular, anomalous, aberrant, erratic, wayward, deviant, divergent, different.
⊞ normal, regular, typical.

abnormality *n* oddity, peculiarity, singularity, eccentricity, strangeness, bizarreness, unnaturalness, unusualness, irregularity, exception, anomaly, deformity, flaw, aberration, deviation, divergence, difference.
⊞ normality, regularity.

abolish *v* do away with, annul, nullify, invalidate, quash, repeal, rescind, revoke, cancel, obliterate, blot out, suppress, destroy, eliminate, eradicate, get rid of (*infml*), stamp out, end, put an end to, terminate, subvert, overthrow, overturn.
⊞ create, retain, authorize, continue.

abolition *n* annulment, nullification, invalidation, quashing, repeal, ending, abrogation, cancellation, obliteration, suppression, eradication, extinction, termination, subversion, overturning, dissolution.
⊞ creation, retention, continuance.

abominable *adj* loathsome, detestable, hateful, horrid, horrible,

abhorrent, execrable, odious, repugnant, repulsive, repellent, disgusting, revolting, obnoxious, nauseating, foul, vile, heinous, atrocious, appalling, terrible, reprehensible, contemptible, despicable, wretched.
⊞ delightful, pleasant, desirable.

abominate v hate, loathe, detest, abhor, execrate, despise, condemn.
⊞ love, adore.

abomination n hate, hatred, aversion, loathing, abhorrence, repugnance, revulsion, disgust, distaste, hostility, offence, outrage, disgrace, anathema, horror, evil, curse, plague, torment, bête noire.
⊞ adoration, delight.

abort v miscarry, terminate, end, stop, arrest, halt, check, frustrate, thwart, nullify, call off, fail.
⊞ continue.

abortion n miscarriage, termination, frustration, failure, misadventure.
⊞ continuation, success.

abortive adj failed, unsuccessful, fruitless, unproductive, barren, sterile, vain, idle, futile, useless, ineffective, unavailing.
⊞ successful, fruitful.

abound v be plentiful, proliferate, flourish, thrive, swell, increase, superabound, swarm, teem, run riot, overflow.

about prep 1 REGARDING, concerning, relating to, referring to, connected with, concerned with, as regards, with regard to, with respect to, with reference to. 2 CLOSE TO, near, nearby, beside, adjacent to. 3 ROUND, around, surrounding, throughout, all over, encircling, encompassing.
◇ adv 1 about twenty: around, approximately, roughly, in the region of, more or less, almost, nearly, approaching, nearing. 2 run about: to and fro, here and there, from place to place.

• **about to** on the point of, on the verge of, all but, ready to, intending to, preparing to.

above prep over, higher than, on top of, superior to, in excess of, exceeding, surpassing, beyond, before, prior to.
⊞ below, under.
◇ adv overhead, aloft, on high, earlier.
⊞ below, underneath.
◇ adj above-mentioned, above-stated, foregoing, preceding, previous, earlier, prior.

above-board adj honest, legitimate, straight, on the level, fair, fair and square, square, true, open, frank, candid, guileless, straightforward, forthright, truthful, veracious, trustworthy, honourable, reputable, upright.
⊞ dishonest, shady (infml), underhand.

abrasion n graze, scratch, scrape, scratching, scraping, scouring, grating, grinding, abrading, chafing, chafe, friction, rubbing, erosion, wearing away, wearing down.

abrasive adj scratching, scraping, grating, rough, harsh, chafing, frictional, galling, irritating, annoying, sharp, biting, nasty, caustic, hurtful, unpleasant.
⊞ smooth, pleasant.

abreast adj acquainted, informed, knowledgeable, in the picture, up to speed (infml), au courant, up-to-date, in touch, au fait, conversant, familiar.
⊞ unaware, out of touch.

abridge v shorten, cut (down), prune, curtail, abbreviate, contract, reduce, decrease, lessen, summarize, précis, abstract, digest, condense, compress, concentrate.
⊞ expand, amplify, pad out.

abridgement n 1 SHORTENING, cutting, reduction, decrease, diminishing, concentration, contraction, restriction, limitation.

2 SUMMARY, synopsis, résumé, outline, précis, abstract, digest, epitome.
☒ **1** expansion, padding.

abroad adv **1** OVERSEAS, in foreign parts, out of the country, far and wide, widely, extensively. **2** AT LARGE, around, about, circulating, current.
☒ **1** at home.

abrupt adj **1** abrupt departure: sudden, unexpected, unforeseen, surprising, quick, rapid, swift, hasty, hurried, precipitate (fml). **2** SHEER, precipitous, steep, sharp. **3** BRUSQUE, curt, terse, short, brisk, snappy, gruff, rude, uncivil, impolite, blunt, direct.
☒ **1** gradual, slow, leisurely.
3 expansive, ceremonious, polite.

abscond v run away, run off, make off, decamp, flee, fly, escape, bolt, quit, clear out (infml), disappear, take French leave.

absence n **1** NON-ATTENDANCE, non-appearance, truancy, absenteeism, non-existence. **2** LACK, need, want, deficiency, dearth, scarcity, default unavailability, , omission, vacancy.
☒ **1** presence, attendance, appearance. **2** existence.

absent adj **1** MISSING, not present, away, out, unavailable, gone, lacking, truant. **2** INATTENTIVE, daydreaming, dreamy, faraway, elsewhere, absent-minded, vacant, vague, distracted, preoccupied, unaware, oblivious, unheeding.
☒ **1** present. **2** alert, aware.

absent-minded adj forgetful, scatterbrained, absent, abstracted, withdrawn, faraway, distracted, preoccupied, absorbed, engrossed, pensive, musing, dreaming, dreamy, inattentive, unaware, oblivious, unconscious, heedless, unheeding, unthinking, impractical.
☒ attentive, practical, matter-of-fact.

absolute adj **1** UTTER, total, complete, entire, full, thorough, exhaustive, supreme, consummate,

definitive, conclusive, final, categorical, definite, unequivocal, unquestionable, decided, decisive, positive, sure, certain, genuine, pure, perfect, sheer, unmixed, unqualified, downright, out-and-out, outright.
2 OMNIPOTENT, totalitarian, despotic, autocratic, tyrannical, dictatorial, sovereign, unlimited, unrestricted.

absolutely adv utterly, totally, dead, completely, entirely, fully, wholly, thoroughly, exhaustively, perfectly, supremely, unconditionally, conclusively, finally, categorically, definitely, positively, unequivocally, unambiguously, unquestionably, decidedly, decisively, certainly, surely, infallibly, genuinely, truly, purely, exactly, precisely.

absorb v **1** TAKE IN, ingest, drink in, imbibe, suck up, soak up, consume, devour, engulf, digest, assimilate, understand, receive, hold, retain.
2 ENGROSS, involve, fascinate, enthral, monopolize, preoccupy, occupy, fill (up).
☒ **1** exude.

absorbing adj interesting, amusing, entertaining, diverting, engrossing, preoccupying, intriguing, fascinating, captivating, enthralling, spellbinding, gripping, riveting, compulsive, unputdownable (infml).
☒ boring, off-putting.

abstain v refrain, decline, refuse, reject, resist, forbear, shun, avoid, keep from, stop, cease, desist, give up, renounce, forgo, go without, deny oneself.
☒ indulge.

abstemious adj abstinent, self-denying, self-disciplined, disciplined, sober, temperate, moderate, sparing, frugal, austere, ascetic, restrained.
☒ intemperate, gluttonous, luxurious.

abstinence n abstaining, abstention, abstemiousness, self-denial, non-indulgence, avoidance,

forbearance, refraining, refusal, restraint, self-restraint, self-control, self-discipline, sobriety, teetotalism, temperance, moderation, frugality, asceticism.
⊞ indulgence, self-indulgence.

abstract adj non-concrete, conceptual, notional, intellectual, hypothetical, theoretical, symbolic, unpractical, unrealistic, general, generalized, indefinite, metaphysical, philosophical, academic, complex, abstruse, deep, profound, subtle.
⊞ concrete, real, actual.
◇ n synopsis, outline, summary, recapitulation, résumé, précis, epitome, digest, abridgement, compression.
◇ v 1 SUMMARIZE, outline, précis, digest, condense, compress, abridge, abbreviate, shorten. 2 EXTRACT, remove, withdraw, isolate, detach, dissociate, separate.
⊞ 1 expand. 2 insert.

abstraction n 1 IDEA, notion, concept, thought, conception, theory, hypothesis, theorem, formula, generalization, generality. 2 INATTENTION, dream, dreaminess, absent-mindedness, distraction, pensiveness, preoccupation, absorption. 3 EXTRACTION, isolation, withdrawal, separation.

absurd adj ridiculous, ludicrous, preposterous, fantastic, incongruous, illogical, paradoxical, implausible, untenable, unreasonable, irrational, nonsensical, meaningless, senseless, foolish, silly, stupid, idiotic, crazy, daft (infml), farcical, comical, funny, humorous, laughable, risible, derisory.
⊞ logical, rational, sensible.

abundant adj plentiful, in plenty, full, filled, well-supplied, ample, generous, bountiful, rich, copious, profuse, lavish, exuberant, teeming, overflowing.
⊞ scarce, sparse.

abuse v 1 MISUSE, misapply, exploit,

take advantage of, oppress, wrong, ill-treat, maltreat, hurt, injure, molest, damage, spoil, harm. 2 INSULT, swear at, defame, libel, slander, smear, disparage, malign, revile, scold, upbraid.
⊞ 1 cherish, care for. 2 compliment, praise.
◇ n 1 MISUSE, misapplication, exploitation, imposition, oppression, wrong, ill-treatment, maltreatment, hurt, injury, molestation, damage, spoiling, harm. 2 INSULTS, swearing, cursing, offence, defamation, libel, slander, disparagement, reproach, scolding, upbraiding, tirade.
⊞ 1 care, attention. 2 compliment, praise.

abusive adj insulting, offensive, rude, scathing, hurtful, injurious, cruel, destructive, defamatory, libellous, slanderous, derogatory, disparaging, pejorative, vilifying, maligning, reviling, censorious, reproachful, scolding, upbraiding.
⊞ complimentary, polite.

abyss n gulf, chasm, crevasse, fissure, gorge, canyon, crater, pit, depth, void.

academic adj 1 SCHOLARLY, erudite, learned, well-read, studious, bookish, scholastic, pedagogical, educational, instructional, literary, highbrow. 2 THEORETICAL, hypothetical, conjectural, speculative, notional, abstract, impractical.
◇ n professor, don, master, fellow, lecturer, tutor, student, scholar, man of letters, woman of letters, pedant.

accelerate v quicken, speed, speed up, pick up speed, step up, expedite, hurry, hasten, precipitate, stimulate, facilitate, advance, further, promote, forward.
⊞ decelerate, slow down, delay.

accent n pronunciation, enunciation, articulation, brogue, twang (infml), tone, pitch, intonation, inflection, accentuation, stress, emphasis, intensity, force, cadence, rhythm, beat, pulse, pulsation.

accentuate v accent, stress, emphasize, underline, highlight, intensify, strengthen, deepen.
🖝 play down, weaken.

accept v 1 *accept a gift*: take, receive, obtain, acquire, gain, secure. 2 ACKNOWLEDGE, recognize, admit, allow, approve, agree to, consent to, take on, adopt. 3 TOLERATE, put up with, stand, bear, abide, face up to, yield to.
🖝 1 refuse, turn down. 2 reject.

acceptable adj satisfactory, tolerable, moderate, passable, adequate, all right, OK (*infml*), so-so (*infml*), unexceptionable, admissible, suitable, conventional, correct, desirable, pleasant, gratifying, welcome.
🖝 unacceptable, unsatisfactory, unwelcome.

acceptance n 1 TAKING, receipt, obtaining, getting, acquiring, gaining, securing. 2 ACKNOWLEDGEMENT, recognition, admission, concession, affirmation, concurrence, agreement, assent, consent, permission, ratification, approval, stamp of approval, OK (*infml*), adoption, undertaking, belief, credence.
🖝 1 refusal. 2 rejection, dissent.

accepted adj authorized, approved, ratified, sanctioned, agreed, acknowledged, recognized, admitted, confirmed, acceptable, correct, conventional, unorthodox, traditional, customary, time-honoured, established, received, universal, regular, standard, normal, usual, common.
🖝 unconventional, unorthodox, controversial.

access n admission, admittance, entry, entering, entrance, gateway, door, key, approach, passage, road, path, course.
🖝 exit, outlet.

accessible adj 1 REACHABLE, get-at-able (*infml*), attainable, achievable, possible, obtainable, available, on hand, ready, handy, convenient, near, nearby. 2 FRIENDLY, affable, approachable, sociable, informal.
🖝 1 inaccessible, remote. 2 unapproachable.

accessory n 1 EXTRA, supplement, addition, appendage, attachment, extension, component, fitting, accompaniment, decoration, adornment, frill, trimming. 2 ACCOMPLICE, partner, associate, colleague, confederate, assistant, helper, help, aid.

accident n 1 CHANCE, hazard, fortuity, luck, fortune, fate, serendipity, contingency, fluke. 2 MISFORTUNE, mischance, misadventure, mishap, casualty, blow, calamity, disaster. 3 *road accident*: collision, crash, shunt (*sl*), prang (*sl*), pile-up.

accidental adj unintentional, unintended, inadvertent, unplanned, uncalculated, unexpected, unlooked-for, unforeseen, chance, random, fortuitous, flukey, uncertain, haphazard, casual, incidental.
🖝 intentional, deliberate, calculated, premeditated.

acclaim v praise, commend, extol, exalt, honour, hail, salute, welcome, applaud, clap, cheer, celebrate.
◇ n acclamation, praise, homage, commendation, tribute, eulogy, exaltation, honour, welcome, approbation, approval, applause, ovation, clapping, cheers, cheering, shouting, celebration.
🖝 criticism, disapproval.

accommodate v 1 LODGE, board, put up, house, shelter. 2 OBLIGE, help, assist, aid, serve, provide, supply, comply, conform. 3 ADAPT, accustom, acclimatize, adjust, modify, fit, harmonize, reconcile, settle, compose.

accommodating *adj* obliging, indulgent, helpful, co-operative, willing, kind, considerate, unselfish, sympathetic, friendly, hospitable.
⊜ disobliging, selfish.

accommodation

Types of accommodation include: flat, apartment, bedsit, bedsitter, digs (*infml*), lodgings, hostel, halls of residence, dorm (*US*), rooms, residence, dwelling, shelter, pad (*infml*), squat (*infml*); bed and breakfast, board, guest-house, hotel, youth hostel, villa, time-share, self-catering, motel, inn, pension, boarding house; barracks, billet, married quarters. see also **house**; **room**.

accompany *v* 1 ESCORT, attend, convoy, chaperone, usher, conduct, follow. 2 COEXIST, coincide, belong to, go with, complement, supplement.

accomplice *n* assistant, helper, abettor, mate, henchman, conspirator, collaborator, ally, confederate, partner, associate, colleague, participator, accessory.

accomplish *v* achieve, attain, do, perform, carry out, execute, fulfil, discharge, finish, complete, conclude, consummate, realize, effect, bring about, engineer, produce, obtain.

accomplished *adj* skilled, professional, practised, proficient, gifted, talented, skilful, adroit, adept, expert, masterly, consummate, polished, cultivated.
⊜ unskilled, inexpert, incapable.

accomplishment *n*
1 *the accomplishment of a task*: achievement, attainment, doing, performance, carrying out, execution, fulfilment, discharge, finishing, completion, conclusion, consummation, perfection, fruition, realization, production. 2 SKILL, art,

aptitude, faculty, ability, capability, proficiency, gift, talent, forte.
3 EXPLOIT, feat, deed, stroke, triumph.

accord *v* 1 AGREE, concur, harmonize, match, conform, correspond, suit. 2 GIVE, tender, grant, allow, bestow, endow, confer.
⊜ 1 disagree. 2 deny.
◇ *n* accordance, agreement, assent, unanimity, concert, unity, correspondence, conformity, harmony, sympathy.
⊜ conflict, discord, disharmony.

accordingly *adv* in accordance, in accord with, correspondingly, so, as a result, consequently, in consequence, therefore, thus, hence, appropriately, properly, suitably.

according to *prep* in accordance with, in keeping with, obedient to, in conformity with, in line with, consistent with, commensurate with, in proportion to, in relation to, after, in the light of, in the manner of, after the manner of.

accost *v* approach, confront, buttonhole, waylay, stop, halt, detain, importune, solicit.

account *n* 1 *an account of what happened*: narrative, story, tale, chronicle, history, memoir, record, statement, report, communiqué, write-up, version, portrayal, sketch, description, presentation, explanation. 2 LEDGER, book, books, register, inventory, statement, bill, invoice, tab, charge, reckoning, computation, tally, score, balance.
● **account for** explain, elucidate, illuminate, clear up, rationalize, justify, vindicate, answer for.

accountable *adj* answerable, responsible, liable, amenable, obliged, bound.

accumulate *v* gather, assemble, collect, amass, aggregate, cumulate, accrue, grow, increase, multiply,

build up, pile up, hoard, stockpile, stash (*infml*), store.
⊞ disseminate.

accumulation *n* gathering, mass, assembly, collection, growth, gain, increase, build-up, conglomeration, heap, pile, stack, stock, store, reserve, hoard, stockpile.

accuracy *n* correctness, precision, exactness, authenticity, truth, veracity, closeness, faithfulness, fidelity, carefulness.
⊞ inaccuracy.

accurate *adj* correct, right, unerring, precise, exact, well-directed, spot-on (*infml*), faultless, perfect, word-perfect, sound, authentic, factual, nice, true, truthful, veracious, just, proper, close, faithful, well-judged, careful, rigorous, scrupulous, meticulous, strict, minute.
⊞ inaccurate, wrong, imprecise, inexact.

accusation *n* charge, allegation, imputation, indictment, denunciation, impeachment, recrimination, complaint, incrimination.

accuse *v* charge, indict, impugn, denounce, arraign, impeach, cite, allege, attribute, impute, blame, censure, recriminate, incriminate, inform against.

accustomed *adj* used, in the habit of, given to, confirmed, seasoned, hardened, inured, disciplined, trained, adapted, acclimatized, acquainted, familiar, wonted, habitual, routine, regular, normal, usual, ordinary, everyday, conventional, customary, traditional, established, fixed, prevailing, general.
⊞ unaccustomed, unusual.

ache *v* 1 HURT, be sore, pain, suffer, agonize, throb, pound, twinge, smart, sting. 2 YEARN, long, pine, hanker, desire, crave, hunger, thirst, itch.

◇ *n* 1 PAIN, hurt, soreness, suffering, anguish, agony, throb, throbbing, pounding, pang, twinge, smarting, stinging. 2 YEARNING, longing, craving, itch.

achieve *v* accomplish, attain, reach, get, obtain, acquire, procure, gain, earn, win, succeed, manage, do, perform, carry out, execute, fulfil, finish, complete, consummate, effect, bring about, realize, produce.
⊞ underachieve, miss, fail.

achievement *n* 1 *the achievement of our aims*: accomplishment, attainment, acquirement, performance, execution, fulfilment, completion, success, realization, fruition. 2 ACT, deed, exploit, feat, effort.

acid *adj* sour, bitter, tart, vinegary, sharp, pungent, acerbic, caustic, corrosive, stinging, biting, mordant, cutting, incisive, trenchant, harsh, hurtful.

acknowledge *v* 1 *acknowledge an error*: admit, confess, own up to, declare, recognize, accept, grant, allow, concede. 2 GREET, address, notice, recognize. 3 *acknowledge a letter*: answer, reply to, respond to, confirm.
⊞ 1 deny. 2 ignore.

acknowledged *adj* recognized, accepted, approved, accredited, declared, professed, attested, avowed, confirmed.

acknowledgement *n* 1 ADMISSION, confession, declaration, profession, recognition, acceptance. 2 GREETING, salutation, notice, recognition. 3 ANSWER, reply, response, reaction, affirmation. 4 GRATITUDE, thanks, appreciation, tribute.

acquaint *v* accustom, familiarize, tell, notify, advise, inform, brief, enlighten, divulge, disclose, reveal, announce.

acquaintance *n* 1 AWARENESS,

knowledge, understanding, experience, familiarity, intimacy, relationship, association, fellowship, companionship. **2** FRIEND, companion, colleague, associate, contact.

acquire v buy, purchase, procure, appropriate, obtain, get, cop (*sl*), receive, collect, pick up, gather, net, gain, secure, earn, win, achieve, attain, realize.
⊜ relinquish, forfeit.

acquisition n purchase, buy (*infml*), procurement, appropriation, gain, securing, achievement, attainment, accession, takeover, property, possession.

acquit v absolve, clear, reprieve, let off, exonerate, exculpate, excuse, vindicate, free, liberate, deliver, relieve, release, dismiss, discharge, settle, satisfy, repay.
⊜ convict.

acquittal n absolution, clearance, reprieve, exoneration, exculpation, excusing, vindication, freeing, liberation, deliverance, relief, release, dismissal, discharge.
⊜ conviction.

acrid adj pungent, sharp, stinging, acid, burning, caustic, acerbic, biting, cutting, incisive, trenchant, sarcastic, sardonic, acrimonious, bitter, virulent, harsh, vitriolic, nasty, malicious, venomous.

acrimonious adj bitter, biting, cutting, trenchant, sharp, virulent, severe, spiteful, censorious, abusive, ill-tempered.
⊜ peaceable, kindly.

acrimony n bitterness, rancour, resentment, ill-will, petulance, gall, ill temper, irascibility, trenchancy, sarcasm, astringency, acerbity, harshness, virulence.

act n **1** DEED, action, undertaking, enterprise, operation, manoeuvre, move, step, doing, execution,
accomplishment, achievement, exploit, feat, stroke. **2** *put on an act*: pretence, make-believe, sham, fake, feigning, dissimulation, affectation, show, front. **3** LAW, statute, canon, ordinance, edict, decree, resolution, measure, bill. **4** TURN, item, routine, sketch, performance, gig (*sl*).
◇ v **1** BEHAVE, conduct, exert, make, work, function, operate, do, execute, carry out. **2** PRETEND, feign, put on, assume, simulate, mimic, imitate, impersonate, portray, represent, mime, play, perform, enact.
• **act on 1** *act on orders*: carry out, fulfil, comply with, conform to, obey, follow, heed, take. **2** AFFECT, influence, alter, modify, change, transform.

acting adj temporary, provisional, interim, stopgap, supply, stand-by, substitute, reserve.
◇ n theatre, stagecraft, artistry, performing, performance, play-acting, melodrama, dramatics, theatricals, portrayal, characterization, impersonation, imitating.

action n **1** ACT, move, deed, exploit, feat, accomplishment, achievement, performance, effort, endeavour, enterprise, undertaking, proceeding, process, activity, liveliness, spirit, energy, vigour, power, exertion, exercise, force, work, functioning, operation, mechanism, movement, motion. **2** *killed in action*: warfare, battle, conflict, combat, fight, fray, engagement, skirmish, clash. **3** LITIGATION, lawsuit, suit, case, prosecution.

activate v start, initiate, trigger, set off, fire, kick-start (*infml*), switch on, set in motion, mobilize, propel, move, stir, rouse, arouse, stimulate, motivate, prompt, animate, energize, impel, excite, galvanize.
⊜ deactivate, stop, arrest.

active adj **1** BUSY, occupied, on the

go (*infml*), industrious, diligent, hard-working, forceful, spirited, vital, forward, enterprising, enthusiastic, devoted, engaged, involved, committed, militant, activist. **2** AGILE, nimble, sprightly, light-footed, quick, alert, animated, lively, energetic, vigorous. **3** IN OPERATION, functioning, working, running.
🖅 **1** passive. **2** inert, dormant. **3** inactive.

activity *n* **1** LIVELINESS, life, activeness, action, motion, movement, commotion, bustle, hustle, industry, labour, exertion, exercise. **2** OCCUPATION, job, work, act, deed, project, scheme, task, venture, enterprise, endeavour, undertaking, pursuit, hobby, pastime, interest.

actor *n* actress, play-actor, film-actor, movie-actor (*US*), comedian, tragedian, ham, player, performer, artist, impersonator, mime.

actual *adj* **1** REAL, existent, substantial, tangible, material, physical, concrete, positive, definite, absolute, certain, unquestionable, indisputable, confirmed, verified, factual, truthful, true, genuine, legitimate, bona fide, authentic, realistic. **2** CURRENT, present, present-day, prevailing, live, living.
🖅 **1** theoretical, apparent, imaginary.

actually *adv* in fact, as a matter of fact, as it happens, in truth, in reality, really, truly, indeed, absolutely.

acumen *n* astuteness, shrewdness, sharpness, keenness, quickness, penetration, insight, intuition, discrimination, discernment, judgement, perception, sense, wit, wisdom, intelligence, cleverness, ingenuity.

acute *adj* **1** SEVERE, intense, extreme, violent, dangerous, serious, grave, urgent, crucial, dire, vital, decisive, sharp, cutting, poignant, distressing.

2 *an acute mind*: sharp, keen, incisive, penetrating, astute, shrewd, judicious, discerning, observant, perceptive.
🖅 **1** mild, slight.

adamant *adj* hard, resolute, determined, set, firm, insistent, rigid, stiff, inflexible, unbending, unrelenting, intransigent, unyielding, stubborn, uncompromising, tough, fixed, immovable, unshakable.
🖅 hesitant, flexible, yielding.

adapt *v* alter, change, qualify, modify, adjust, convert, remodel, customize, fit, tailor, fashion, shape, harmonize, match, suit, conform, comply, prepare, familiarize, acclimatize.

adaptable *adj* alterable, changeable, variable, modifiable, adjustable, convertible, conformable, versatile, plastic, malleable, flexible, compliant, amenable, easy-going.
🖅 inflexible, refractory.

adaptation *n* alteration, change, shift, transformation, modification, adjustment, accommodation, conversion, remodelling, reworking, reshaping, refitting, revision, variation, version.

add *v* append, annex, affix, attach, tack on, join, combine, supplement, augment.
🖅 take away, remove.
• **add up 1** ADD, sum up, tot up, total, tally, count (up), reckon, compute. **2** AMOUNT, come to, constitute, include. **3** *it doesn't add up*: be consistent, hang together, fit, be plausible, be reasonable, make sense, mean, signify, indicate.
🖅 **1** subtract.

addict *n* **1** ENTHUSIAST, fan, buff (*infml*), fiend, freak, devotee, follower, adherent. **2** DRUG-ADDICT, user (*infml*), dope-fiend, druggie (*infml*), junkie (*infml*), tripper (*sl*), mainliner (*sl*).

addicted adj dependent, hooked, obsessed, absorbed, devoted, dedicated, fond, inclined, disposed, accustomed.

addiction n dependence, craving, habit, monkey (sl), obsession.

addition n 1 ADDING, annexation, accession, extension, enlargement, increasing, increase, gain. 2 ADJUNCT, supplement, additive, addendum, appendix, appendage, accessory, attachment, extra, increment. 3 SUMMING-UP, totting-up, totalling, counting, reckoning, inclusion.
☒ 1 removal. 3 subtraction.
• **in addition** additionally, too, also, as well, besides, moreover, further, furthermore, over and above.

additional adj added, extra, more, supplementary, spare, further, increased, other, new, fresh.

address n 1 RESIDENCE, dwelling, abode, house, home, lodging, direction, inscription, whereabouts, location, situation, place. 2 SPEECH, talk, lecture, sermon, discourse, dissertation.
◇ v lecture, speak to, talk to, greet, salute, hail, invoke, accost, approach, buttonhole.

adept adj skilled, accomplished, expert, masterly, experienced, versed, practised, proficient, able, adroit, deft, nimble.

adequate adj enough, sufficient, commensurate, requisite, suitable, fit, able, competent, capable, serviceable, acceptable, satisfactory, passable, tolerable, fair, respectable, presentable.
☒ inadequate, insufficient.

adhere v 1 STICK, glue, paste, cement, fix, fasten, attach, join, link, combine, coalesce, cohere, hold, cling, cleave to. 2 adhere to the agreement: observe, follow, abide by, comply with, fulfil, obey, keep, heed, respect, stand by.

adherent n supporter, upholder, advocate, partisan, follower, disciple, satellite, henchman, hanger-on (infml), votary, devotee, admirer, fan, enthusiast, freak (infml), nut (infml).

adhesion n adherence, adhesiveness, bond, attachment, grip, cohesion.

adhesive adj sticky, tacky, self-adhesive, gummed, gummy, gluey, adherent, adhering, sticking, clinging, holding, attaching, cohesive.
◇ n glue, gum, paste, cement.

adjacent adj adjoining, abutting, touching, contiguous, bordering, alongside, beside, juxtaposed, next-door, neighbouring, next, closest, nearest, close, near.
☒ remote, distant.

adjoin v abut, touch, meet, border, verge, neighbour, interconnect, link, connect, join, combine, unite, couple, attach, annex, add.

adjourn v interrupt, suspend, discontinue, break off, delay, stay, defer, postpone, put off, recess, retire.
☒ assemble, convene.

adjournment n interruption, suspension, discontinuation, break, pause, recess, delay, stay, deferment, deferral, postponement, putting off, dissolution.

adjudicate v judge, arbitrate, umpire, referee, settle, determine, decide, pronounce.

adjust v 1 MODIFY, change, adapt, alter, convert, dispose, shape, remodel, fit, accommodate, suit, measure, rectify, regulate, balance, temper, tune, fine-tune, fix, set, arrange, compose, settle, square. 2 ACCUSTOM, habituate, acclimatize, reconcile, harmonize, conform.
☒ 1 disarrange, upset.

adjustment n 1 MODIFICATION, change, adaptation, alteration, conversion, remodelling, shaping, fitting, accommodation, rectification, regulation, tuning, fixing, setting, arranging, arrangement, ordering, settlement. **2** HABITUATION, orientation, acclimatization, naturalization, reconciliation, harmonization, conforming.

ad-lib v improvise, extemporize, make up, invent.
◇ adj impromptu, improvised, extempore, extemporaneous, off the cuff, unprepared, unpremeditated, unrehearsed, spontaneous, made-up.
🔁 prepared.
◇ adv impromptu, extempore, extemporaneously, off the cuff, off the top of one's head, spontaneously, impulsively.

administer v **1** administer an organization: govern, rule, lead, head, preside over, officiate, manage, run, organize, direct, conduct, control, regulate, superintend, supervise, oversee. **2** GIVE, provide, supply, distribute, dole out, dispense, measure out, mete out, execute, impose, apply.

administration n **1** ADMINISTERING, governing, ruling, leadership, management, execution, running, organization, direction, control, superintendence, supervision, overseeing. **2** GOVERNING BODY, regime, government, ministry, leadership, directorship, management, executive, term of office.

administrative adj governmental, legislative, authoritative, directorial, managerial, management, executive, organizational, regulatory, supervisory.

admirable adj praiseworthy, commendable, laudable, creditable, deserving, worthy, respected, fine, excellent, superior, wonderful, exquisite, choice, rare, valuable.

🔁 contemptible, despicable, deplorable.

admiration n esteem, regard, respect, reverence, veneration, worship, adoration, affection, approval, praise, appreciation, pleasure, delight, astonishment, wonder, amazement, surprise.
🔁 contempt.

admire v esteem, respect, revere, venerate, worship, idolize, adore, approve, praise, laud, applaud, appreciate, value.
🔁 despise, censure.

admirer n follower, disciple, adherent, supporter, fan, groupie (*infml*), enthusiast, devotee, worshipper, idolizer, suitor, boyfriend, girlfriend, sweetheart, lover.
🔁 critic, opponent.

admissible adj acceptable, tolerable, tolerated, passable, allowable, permissible, allowed, permitted, lawful, legitimate, justifiable.
🔁 inadmissible, illegitimate.

admission n confession, granting, acknowledgement, recognition, acceptance, allowance, concession, affirmation, declaration, profession, disclosure, divulgence, revelation, exposé.
🔁 denial.

admit v **1** CONFESS, own (up), grant, acknowledge, recognize, accept, allow, concede, agree, affirm, declare, profess, disclose, divulge, reveal. **2** LET IN, allow to enter, give access, accept, receive, take in, introduce, initiate.
🔁 **1** deny. **2** shut out, exclude.

admittance n admitting, admission, letting in, access, entrance, entry, acceptance, reception, introduction, initiation.
🔁 exclusion.

adolescence n teens, youth,

puberty, minority, boyhood, girlhood, development, immaturity, youthfulness, boyishness, girlishness.

adolescent adj 1 an adolescent son: teenage, young, youthful, juvenile, boyish, girlish, growing, developing. 2 adolescent behaviour: immature, puerile, childish.
◇ n teenager, youth, juvenile, minor.

adopt v take on, accept, assume, take up, appropriate, embrace, follow, choose, select, take in, foster, support, maintain, back, endorse, ratify, approve.
⊜ repudiate, disown.

adorable adj lovable, dear, darling, precious, appealing, sweet, winsome, charming, enchanting, captivating, winning, delightful, pleasing, attractive, fetching.
⊜ hateful, abominable.

adore v love, cherish, dote on, admire, esteem, honour, revere, venerate, worship, idolize, exalt, glorify.
⊜ hate, abhor.

adorn v decorate, deck, bedeck, ornament, crown, trim, garnish, gild, enhance, embellish, doll up, sex up (sl), enrich, grace.

adult adj grown-up, of age, full-grown, fully grown, developed, mature, ripe, ripened.
⊜ immature.

adulterate v contaminate, pollute, taint, corrupt, defile, debase, dilute, water down, weaken, devalue, deteriorate.
⊜ purify.

advance v 1 PROCEED, go forward, move on, go ahead, progress, prosper, flourish, thrive, improve, push the envelope (infml).
2 ACCELERATE, speed, hasten, send forward. 3 FURTHER, promote, upgrade, foster, support, assist, benefit, facilitate, increase, grow.
4 advance an idea: present, submit,

suggest, allege, cite, bring forward, offer, provide, supply, furnish.
5 advance a sum of money: lend, loan, pay beforehand, pay, give.
⊜ 1 retreat. 2 retard. 3 impede.
◇ n 1 PROGRESS, forward movement, onward movement, headway, step, advancement, furtherance, breakthrough, development, growth, increase, improvement, amelioration. 2 DEPOSIT, prepayment, down payment, credit, loan.
⊜ 1 retreat, recession.
• in advance beforehand, previously, early, earlier, sooner, ahead, in front, in the lead, in the forefront.
⊜ later, behind.

advanced adj leading, foremost, cutting-edge, state-of-the-art, ahead, forward, precocious, progressive, forward-looking, avant-garde, ultra-modern, sophisticated, complex, higher.
⊜ backward, retarded, elementary.

advancement n furtherance, promotion, preferment, betterment, improvement, development, growth, rise, gain, advance, progress, headway.
⊜ demotion, retardation.

advantage n 1 ASSET, blessing, benefit, good, welfare, interest, service, help, aid, assistance, use, avail, convenience, usefulness, utility, profit, gain, start. 2 LEAD, edge, upper hand, superiority, precedence, pre-eminence, sway.
⊜ 1 disadvantage, drawback, hindrance.

advantageous adj beneficial, favourable, opportune, convenient, helpful, useful, worthwhile, valuable, profitable, gainful, remunerative, rewarding.
⊜ disadvantageous, adverse, damaging.

adventure n exploit, venture, undertaking, enterprise, risk, hazard, chance, speculation, experience, incident, occurrence.

adventurous *adj* daring, intrepid, bold, audacious, headstrong, impetuous, reckless, rash, risky, venturesome, enterprising.
☒ cautious, chary, prudent.

adverse *adj* hostile, antagonistic, opposing, opposite, counter, contrary, conflicting, counter-productive, negative, unfavourable, disadvantageous, inauspicious, unfortunate, unlucky, inopportune, detrimental, harmful, noxious, injurious, hurtful, unfriendly, uncongenial.
☒ advantageous, favourable.

adversity *n* misfortune, ill fortune, bad luck, ill luck, reverse, hardship, hard times, misery, wretchedness, affliction, suffering, distress, sorrow, woe, trouble, trial, tribulation, calamity, disaster, catastrophe.
☒ prosperity.

advertise *v* publicize, promote, push, plug (*infml*), praise, hype (*sl*), trumpet, blazon, herald, announce, declare, proclaim, broadcast, publish, display, make known, inform, notify.

advertisement *n* advert (*infml*), ad (*infml*), commercial, publicity, promotion, promo (*infml*), plug (*infml*), hype (*sl*), display, blurb, announcement, notice, poster, bill, placard, leaflet, handbill, circular, handout, flyer, propaganda.

advice *n* **1** WARNING, caution, do's and don'ts, injunction, instruction, counsel, help, guidance, direction, suggestion, recommendation, opinion, view. **2** NOTIFICATION, notice, memorandum, communication, information, intelligence.

advisable *adj* suggested, wise, recommended, sensible, prudent, judicious, sound, profitable, suitable, beneficial, desirable, appropriate, apt, fitting, fit, proper, correct.

☒ inadvisable, foolish.

advise *v* **1** COUNSEL, guide, warn, forewarn, caution, instruct, teach, tutor, suggest, urge, recommend, commend. **2** NOTIFY, inform, tell, acquaint, make known, report.

adviser *n* counsellor, consultant, authority, guide, teacher, tutor, instructor, coach, helper, aide, right-hand man, mentor, confidant(e), counsel, lawyer.

advocate *v* defend, champion, campaign for, press for, argue for, plead for, justify, urge, encourage, advise, recommend, propose, promote, endorse, support, uphold, patronize, adopt, subscribe to, favour, countenance.
☒ impugn, disparage, deprecate.
◇ *n* defender, supporter, upholder, champion, campaigner, pleader, vindicator, proponent, promoter, speaker, spokesperson.
☒ opponent, critic.

affable *adj* friendly, amiable, approachable, open, expansive, genial, good-humoured, good-natured, mild, benevolent, kindly, gracious, obliging, courteous, amicable, congenial, cordial, warm, sociable, pleasant, agreeable.
☒ unfriendly, reserved, reticent, cool.

affair *n* **1** BUSINESS, transaction, operation, proceeding, undertaking, activity, project, responsibility, interest, concern, matter, question, issue, subject, topic, circumstance, happening, occurrence, incident, episode, event. **2** *have an affair*: relationship, liaison, intrigue, love affair, romance, amour.

affect *v* **1** CONCERN, regard, involve, relate to, apply to, bear upon, impinge upon, act on, change, transform, alter, modify, influence, sway, prevail over, attack, strike, impress, interest, stir, move, touch, upset, disturb, perturb, trouble, overcome. **2** ADOPT, assume, put on, feign, simulate, imitate, fake, counterfeit, sham, pretend, profess, aspire to.

affectation *n* airs, pretentiousness, mannerism, pose, act, show, façade, appearance, pretence, sham, simulation, imitation, artificiality, insincerity.
⊡ artlessness, ingenuousness.

affected *adj* assumed, put-on, feigned, simulated, artificial, fake, counterfeit, sham, phoney (*infml*), contrived, studied, precious, mannered, pretentious, pompous, stiff, unnatural, insincere.
⊡ genuine, natural.

affection *n* fondness, attachment, devotion, love, tenderness, care, warmth, feeling, kindness, friendliness, goodwill, favour, liking, partiality, inclination, penchant, passion, desire.
⊡ dislike, antipathy.

affectionate *adj* fond, attached, devoted, doting, loving, tender, caring, warm, warm-hearted, kind, friendly, amiable, cordial.
⊡ cold, undemonstrative.

affirm *v* confirm, corroborate, endorse, ratify, certify, witness, testify, swear, maintain, assert, state, declare, pronounce.
⊡ refute, deny.

affirmative *adj* agreeing, concurring, approving, assenting, positive, confirming, corroborative, emphatic.
⊡ negative, dissenting.

afflict *v* strike, visit, trouble, burden, oppress, distress, grieve, pain, hurt, wound, harm, try, harass, beset, plague, torment, torture.
⊡ comfort, solace.

affliction *n* distress, grief, sorrow, misery, depression, suffering, pain, torment, disease, illness, sickness, plague, curse, cross, ordeal, trial,

tribulation, trouble, hardship, adversity, misfortune, calamity, disaster.
⊡ comfort, consolation, solace, blessing.

affluence *n* wealthiness, wealth, riches, fortune, substance, property, prosperity, opulence, abundance, profusion, plenty.
⊡ poverty.

affluent *adj* wealthy, rich, moneyed, loaded (*sl*), flush (*infml*), well-off, prosperous, well-to-do, opulent, comfortable.
⊡ poor, impoverished.

afford *v* **1** HAVE ENOUGH FOR, spare, allow, manage, sustain, bear. **2** PROVIDE, supply, furnish, give, grant, offer, impart, produce, yield, generate.

affront *v* offend, insult, abuse, snub, slight, provoke, displease, irritate, annoy, anger, vex, incense, outrage.
⊡ compliment, appease.
◇ *n* offence, insult, slur, rudeness, discourtesy, disrespect, indignity, snub, slight, wrong, injury, abuse, provocation, vexation, outrage.
⊡ compliment.

afraid *adj* frightened, scared, alarmed, terrified, fearful, timorous, daunted, intimidated, faint-hearted, cowardly, reluctant, apprehensive, anxious, nervous, timid, distrustful, suspicious.
⊡ unafraid, brave, bold, confident.

after *prep* following, subsequent to, in consequence of, as a result of, behind, below.
⊡ before.

again *adv* once more, once again, another time, over again, afresh, anew, encore.

against *prep* **1** *against the wall*: abutting, adjacent to, close up to, touching, in contact with, on. **2** OPPOSITE TO, facing, fronting, in the face of, confronting, opposing,

versus, opposed to, anti (*infml*), in opposition to, hostile to, resisting, in defiance of, in contrast to.
🔁 **2** for, pro.

age *n* **1** ERA, epoch, day, days, generation, date, time, period, duration, span, years, aeon. **2** OLD AGE, maturity, elderliness, seniority, dotage, senility, decline.
🔁 **2** youth.
◇ *v* grow old, mature, ripen, mellow, season, decline, deteriorate, degenerate.

agency *n* **1** *recruitment agency*: bureau, office, department, organization, business, work. **2** MEANS, medium, instrumentality, power, force, influence, effect, intervention, action, activity, operation, mechanism, workings.

agent *n* **1** SUBSTITUTE, deputy, delegate, envoy, emissary, proxy, representative, rep (*infml*), liaison, broker, middleman, go-between, intermediary, negotiator, mover, doer, performer, operator, operative, functionary, worker. **2** INSTRUMENT, vehicle, channel, means, agency, cause, force.

aggravate *v* **1** *aggravate a problem*: exacerbate, worsen, make worse, inflame, increase, intensify, heighten, magnify, exaggerate. **2** (*infml*) ANNOY, irritate, vex, irk, exasperate, incense, provoke, tease, pester, harass, bug (*infml*).
🔁 **1** improve, alleviate. **2** appease, mollify.

aggregate *n* total, sum, amount, whole, totality, entirety, generality, combination, business, accumulation, collection.
◇ *adj* cumulative, accumulated, collected, combined, united, added, total, complete, composite, mixed, collective.
🔁 individual, particular.

aggression *n* **1** ANTAGONISM, provocation, offence, injury, attack,

offensive, assault, onslaught, raid, incursion, invasion, intrusion. **2** AGGRESSIVENESS, militancy, belligerence, combativeness, hostility.
🔁 **1** peace, resistance. **2** passivity, gentleness.

aggressive *adj* argumentative, quarrelsome, contentious, hostile, belligerent, offensive, provocative, intrusive, invasive, bold, assertive, pushy, go-ahead, forceful, feisty (*infml*), vigorous, zealous, ruthless, destructive.
🔁 peaceable, friendly, submissive, timid.

aggrieved *adj* wronged, offended, hurt, injured, insulted, maltreated, ill-used, resentful, pained, distressed, saddened, unhappy, upset, annoyed.
🔁 pleased.

aghast *adj* shocked, appalled, horrified, horror-struck, stunned, thunderstruck, stupefied, amazed, astonished, astounded, startled, confounded, dismayed.

agile *adj* active, lively, nimble, spry, sprightly, mobile, flexible, limber, lithe, fleet, quick, swift, brisk, prompt, sharp, acute, alert, quick-witted, clever, adroit, deft.
🔁 clumsy, stiff.

agitate *v* **1** ROUSE, arouse, stir up, excite, stimulate, incite, inflame, ferment, work up, worry, trouble, upset, alarm, disturb, unsettle, disquiet, discompose, fluster, ruffle, flurry, unnerve, confuse, distract, disconcert. **2** SHAKE, rattle, rock, stir, beat, churn, toss, convulse.
🔁 **1** calm, tranquillize.

agitator *n* troublemaker, rabble-rouser, revolutionary, stirrer (*sl*), inciter, instigator.

agony *n* anguish, torment, torture, pain, spasm, throes, suffering, affliction, tribulation, distress, woe, misery, wretchedness.

agree v **1** CONCUR, see eye to eye, get on, settle, accord, match, suit, fit, tally, correspond, conform. **2** CONSENT, allow, permit, assent, accede, grant, admit, concede, yield, comply.
🔁 **1** disagree, differ, conflict. **2** refuse.

agreeable adj pleasant, congenial, likable, attractive, delightful, enjoyable, gratifying, satisfying, palatable, acceptable, proper, appropriate, suitable, fitting, in accord, consistent.
🔁 disagreeable, nasty, distasteful.

agreement n **1** SETTLEMENT, compact, covenant, treaty, pact, contract, deal, bargain, arrangement, understanding. **2** be in agreement: concurrence, accord, concord, unanimity, union, harmony, sympathy, affinity, compatibility, similarity, correspondence, consistency, conformity, compliance, adherence, acceptance.
🔁 **2** disagreement.

agricultural adj agronomic, agrarian, farming, farmed, cultivated, rural, pastoral, bucolic.

agriculture n agronomics, farming, husbandry, cultivation, culture, tillage.

ahead adv forward, onward, leading, at the head, in front, in the lead, winning, at an advantage, advanced, superior, to the fore, in the forefront, in advance, before, earlier on.

aid v help, assist, succour, rally round, relieve, support, subsidize, sustain, second, serve, oblige, accommodate, favour, promote, boost, encourage, expedite, facilitate, ease.
🔁 hinder, impede, obstruct.
◇ n help, assistance, prop, support, relief, benefit, subsidy, donation, contribution, funding, grant, sponsorship, patronage, favour,

encouragement, service.
🔁 hindrance, impediment, obstruction.

ailing adj unwell, ill, sick, poorly, indisposed, out of sorts (infml), under the weather (infml), off-colour, suffering, languishing, sickly, diseased, invalid, infirm, unsound, frail, weak, feeble, failing.
🔁 healthy, thriving, flourishing.

ailment n illness, sickness, complaint, malady, disease, infection, disorder, affliction, infirmity, disability, weakness.

aim v **1** POINT, direct, take aim, level, train, sight, zero in on (infml), target. **2** aim to achieve: aspire, want, wish, seek, resolve, purpose, intend, propose, mean, plan, design, strive, try, attempt, endeavour.
◇ n aspiration, ambition, hope, dream, desire, wish, plan, design, scheme, purpose, motive, end, intention, object, objective, target, mark, goal, direction, course.

aimless adj pointless, purposeless, unmotivated, irresolute, rambling, directionless, undirected, unguided, stray, chance, random, haphazard, erratic, unpredictable, wayward.
🔁 purposeful, positive, determined.

air n **1** ATMOSPHERE, oxygen, sky, heavens, breath, puff, waft, draught, breeze, wind, blast. **2** APPEARANCE, look, aspect, aura, bearing, manner, demeanour, character, effect, impression, feeling.
◇ v **1** air a room: ventilate, aerate, freshen. **2** air an opinion: utter, voice, express, give vent to, make known, communicate, tell, declare, reveal, disclose, divulge, expose, make public, broadcast, publish, circulate, disseminate, exhibit, display, parade, publicize.

aircraft

Types of aircraft include: aeroplane, plane, jet, jumbo,

Concorde, Airbus®, helicopter, monoplane, two-seater, air ambulance, freighter, aquaplane, seaplane, glider, hang-glider, microlight, hot-air balloon; fighter, Spitfire, bomber, jump jet, dive-bomber, chopper (*sl*), spyplane, delta-wing, swing-wing, troop-carrier, airship, turbojet, VTOL (vertical take-off and landing), warplane, zeppelin.

airless *adj* unventilated, stuffy, musty, stale, suffocating, stifling, sultry, muggy, close, heavy, oppressive.
⊜ airy, fresh.

airy *adj* **1** ROOMY, spacious, open, well-ventilated, draughty, breezy, blowy, windy, gusty. **2** CHEERFUL, happy, light-hearted, high-spirited, lively, nonchalant, offhand.
⊜ **1** airless, stuffy, close, heavy, oppressive.

aisle *n* gangway, corridor, passage, passageway, alleyway, walkway, path, lane.

alarm *v* frighten, scare, startle, put the wind up (*infml*), terrify, panic, unnerve, daunt, dismay, distress, agitate.
⊜ reassure, calm, soothe.
◇ *n* **1** FRIGHT, scare, fear, terror, panic, horror, shock, consternation, dismay, distress, anxiety, nervousness, apprehension, trepidation, uneasiness. **2** DANGER SIGNAL, alert, warning, distress signal, siren, bell, alarm-bell.
⊜ **1** calmness, composure.

alarming *adj* frightening, scary, startling, terrifying, unnerving, daunting, ominous, threatening, dismaying, disturbing, distressing, shocking, dreadful.
⊜ reassuring.

alcohol *n* drink, booze (*sl*), liquor, spirits, hard stuff (*sl*), intoxicant.

Alcoholic drinks include: ale, beer, cider, lager, shandy, stout, Guinness®; aquavit, Armagnac, bourbon, brandy, Calvados, Cognac, gin, pink gin, sloe gin, rum, grog, rye, vodka, whisky, hot toddy; wine, mead, perry; alcopop, absinthe, advocaat, Baileys®, Benedictine, Chartreuse, black velvet, bloody Mary, Buck's fizz, Campari®, cherry brandy, cocktail, Cointreau®, crème de menthe, daiquiri, eggnog, ginger wine, kirsch, limoncello, margarita, Marsala, Martini®, mojito, ouzo, Pernod®, piña colada, port, punch, retsina, sake, sambuca, sangria, schnapps, sherry, snowball, spritzer, tequila, Tom Collins, vermouth. see also **wine**.

alcoholic *adj* intoxicating, brewed, fermented, distilled, strong, hard.
◇ *n* drunk, drunkard, inebriate, hard drinker, dipsomaniac, wino (*sl*), alkie (*sl*).

alcove *n* niche, nook, recess, bay, corner, cubby-hole, compartment, cubicle, booth, carrel.

alert *adj* attentive, wide awake, watchful, vigilant, on the lookout, sharp-eyed, observant, perceptive, sharp-witted, on the ball (*infml*), active, lively, spirited, quick, brisk, agile, nimble, ready, prepared, careful, heedful, circumspect, wary.
⊜ slow, listless, unprepared.
◇ *v* warn, forewarn, notify, inform, tip off, signal, alarm.

alias *n* pseudonym, false name, assumed name, nom de guerre, nom de plume, pen name, stage name, nickname, sobriquet.
◇ *prep* also known as, also called, otherwise, formerly.

alibi *n* defence, justification, story, explanation, excuse, pretext, reason.

alien *adj* strange, unfamiliar, outlandish, incongruous, foreign,

exotic, extraterrestrial, extraneous, remote, estranged, separated, opposed, contrary, conflicting, antagonistic, incompatible.
⊠ akin.
◇ *n* foreigner, immigrant, newcomer, stranger, outsider.
⊠ native.

alight¹ *v* descend, get down, dismount, get off, disembark, land, touch down, come down, come to rest, settle, light, perch.
⊠ ascend, board.

alight² *adj* lighted, lit, ignited, on fire, burning, blazing, ablaze, flaming, fiery, lit up, illuminated, bright, radiant, shining, brilliant.
⊠ dark.

align *v* **1** STRAIGHTEN, range, line up, make parallel, even up, adjust, regulate, regularize, order, co-ordinate. **2** ALLY, side, sympathize, associate, affiliate, join, co-operate, agree.

alike *adj* similar, resembling, comparable, akin, analogous, corresponding, equivalent, equal, the same, identical, duplicate, parallel, even, uniform.
⊠ dissimilar, unlike, different.
◇ *adv* similarly, analogously, correspondingly, equally, in common.

alive *adj* **1** LIVING, having life, live, animate, breathing, existent, in existence, real. **2** LIVELY, animated, spirited, awake, alert, active, brisk, energetic, vigorous, zestful, vivacious, vibrant, vital.
⊠ **1** dead, extinct. **2** lifeless, apathetic.

all *adj* **1** EACH, every, each and every, every single, every one of, the whole of, every bit of. **2** COMPLETE, entire, full, total, utter, outright, perfect, greatest.
⊠ **1** no, none.
◇ *n* everything, sum, total, aggregate, total amount, whole amount, whole,

entirety, utmost, comprehensiveness, universality.
⊠ nothing, none.
◇ *adv* completely, entirely, wholly, fully, totally, utterly, altogether, wholesale.

• **all right**
adj **1** SATISFACTORY, passable, unobjectionable, acceptable, allowable, adequate, fair, average, OK (*infml*). **2** *are you all right?*: well, healthy, unhurt, uninjured, unharmed, unimpaired, whole, sound, safe, secure.
⊠ **1** unacceptable, inadequate.
adv satisfactorily, well enough, passably, unobjectionably, acceptably, suitably, appropriately, adequately, reasonably, OK (*infml*).
⊠ unsatisfactorily, unacceptably.

allay *v* alleviate, relieve, soothe, ease, smooth, calm, tranquillize, quiet, quell, pacify, mollify, soften, blunt, lessen, reduce, diminish, check, moderate.
⊠ exacerbate, intensify.

allegation *n* accusation, charge, claim, profession, assertion, affirmation, declaration, statement, testimony, plea.

allege *v* assert, affirm, declare, state, attest, maintain, insist, hold, contend, claim, profess, plead.

alleged *adj* supposed, reputed, putative, inferred, so-called, professed, declared, stated, claimed, described, designated, doubtful, dubious, suspect, suspicious.

allegiance *n* loyalty, fidelity, faithfulness, constancy, duty, obligation, obedience, devotion, support, adherence, friendship.
⊠ disloyalty, enmity.

allergic *adj* sensitive, hypersensitive, susceptible, affected, incompatible, averse, disinclined, opposed, hostile, antagonistic.
⊠ tolerant.

alleviate v relieve, soothe, ease, palliate, mitigate, soften, cushion, dull, deaden, allay, abate, lessen, reduce, diminish, check, moderate, temper, subdue.
⊞ aggravate.

alliance n confederation, federation, association, affiliation, coalition, league, bloc, cartel, conglomerate, consortium, syndicate, guild, union, partnership, marriage, agreement, compact, bond, pact, treaty, combination, connection.
⊞ enmity, hostility, separation, divorce, estrangement.

allocate v assign, designate, budget, allow, earmark, set aside, allot, apportion, share out, distribute, dispense, mete.

allocation n allotment, lot, apportionment, measure, share, portion, stint, ration, quota, budget, allowance, grant.

allot v divide, ration, apportion, share out, distribute, dispense, mete, dole out, allocate, assign, designate, budget, allow, grant, earmark, set aside.

allotment n division, partition, allocation, apportionment, measure, percentage, lot, portion, share, stint, ration, quota, allowance, grant.

all-out adj complete, full, total, undivided, comprehensive, exhaustive, thorough, intensive, thoroughgoing, wholesale, vigorous, powerful, full-scale, no-holds-barred, maximum, utmost, unlimited, unrestrained, resolute, determined.
⊞ perfunctory, half-hearted.

allow v 1 PERMIT, let, enable, authorize, sanction, approve, put up with, tolerate, endure, suffer. 2 ADMIT, confess, own, acknowledge, concede, grant. 3 *allow two hours for the journey*: allot, allocate, assign, apportion, afford, give, provide.
⊞ 1 forbid, prevent. 2 deny.

• **allow for** take into account, make provision for, make allowances for, provide for, foresee, plan for, arrange for, bear in mind, keep in mind, consider, include.
⊞ discount.

allowance n 1 ALLOTMENT, lot, amount, allocation, portion, share, ration, quota. 2 REBATE, reduction, deduction, discount, concession, subsidy, weighting. 3 PAYMENT, remittance, pocket money, grant, maintenance, stipend, pension, annuity.

alloy n blend, compound, composite, amalgam, combination, mixture, fusion, coalescence.

allure v lure, entice, seduce, lead on, tempt, coax, cajole, persuade, win over, disarm, charm, enchant, attract, interest, fascinate, captivate, entrance, beguile.
⊞ repel.
◊ n lure, enticement, seduction, temptation, appeal, attraction, magnetism, fascination, glamour, captivation, charm, enchantment.

allusion n mention, reference, citation, quotation, remark, observation, suggestion, hint, intimation, implication, insinuation.

ally n confederate, associate, leaguer, consort, partner, sidekick, colleague, co-worker, collaborator, helper, helpmate, accomplice, accessory, friend.
⊞ antagonist, enemy.
◊ v confederate, affiliate, league, associate, collaborate, join forces, band together, team up, fraternize, side, join, connect, link, marry, unite, unify, amalgamate, combine.
⊞ estrange, separate.

almighty adj 1 OMNIPOTENT, all-powerful, supreme, absolute, great, invincible. 2 ENORMOUS, severe, intense, overwhelming, overpowering, terrible, awful, desperate.

◨ **1** impotent, weak.

almost adv nearly, well-nigh, practically, virtually, just about, as good as, all but, close to, not far from, approaching, nearing, not quite, about, approximately.

alone adj only, sole, single, unique, solitary, separate, detached, unconnected, isolated, apart, by oneself, by itself, on one's own, lonely, lonesome, deserted, abandoned, forsaken, forlorn, desolate, unaccompanied, unescorted, unattended, solo, single-handed, unaided, unassisted, mere. ◨ together, accompanied, escorted.

aloof adj distant, remote, offish, standoffish, haughty, supercilious, unapproachable, inaccessible, detached, forbidding, cool, chilly, cold, sympathetic, unresponsive, indifferent, uninterested, reserved, unforthcoming, unfriendly, unsociable, formal. ◨ sociable, friendly, concerned.

aloud adv out loud, audibly, intelligibly, clearly, plainly, distinctly, loudly, resoundingly, sonorously, noisily, vociferously. ◨ silently.

alphabet

Alphabets and writing systems include: American Sign Language, Braille, British Sign Language, Byzantine, cuneiform, Cyrillic, devanagari, finger-alphabet, futhork (or futhark), Greek, Gurmukhi, hieroglyphs, hiragana, ideograph, initial teaching alphabet (i.t.a.), International Phonetic Alphabet (IPA), kana, kanji, katakana, Kufic, Latin, linear A, linear B, logograph, nagari, Neskhi (or Naskhi), ogam (or ogham), pictograph, Roman, runic, syllabary.

also adv too, as well, and, plus,

along with, including, as well as, additionally, in addition, besides, further, furthermore, moreover.

alter v change, vary, diversify, modify, qualify, shift, transpose, adjust, adapt, convert, turn, transmute, transform, reform, reshape, remodel, recast, revise, amend, emend. ◨ fix.

alteration n change, variation, variance, difference, diversification, shift, transposition, modification, adjustment, adaptation, conversion, transformation, transfiguration, metamorphosis, reformation, reshaping, remodelling, revision, amendment. ◨ fixity.

alternate v interchange, reciprocate, rotate, take turns, follow one another, replace each other, substitute, change, alter, vary, oscillate, fluctuate, intersperse. ◇ adj alternating, every other, every second, interchanging, reciprocal, rotating, alternative.

alternative n option, choice, selection, preference, other, recourse, substitute, back-up. ◇ adj substitute, second, another, other, different, unorthodox, unconventional, fringe, alternate.

altitude n height, elevation, loftiness, tallness, stature. ◨ depth.

altogether adv totally, completely, entirely, wholly, fully, utterly, quite, absolutely, perfectly, thoroughly, in all, all told, in toto, all in all, as a whole, on the whole, generally, in general.

altruistic adj unselfish, self-sacrificing, disinterested, public-spirited, philanthropic, charitable, humanitarian, benevolent, generous, considerate, humane. ◨ selfish.

always *adv* every time, consistently, invariably, without exception, unfailingly, regularly, repeatedly, continually, constantly, 24-7 (*infml*), perpetually, unceasingly, eternally, endlessly, evermore, forever, ever.
🔁 never.

amalgamate *v* merge, blend, mingle, commingle, intermix, homogenize, incorporate, alloy, integrate, compound, fuse, coalesce, synthesize, combine, unite, unify, ally.
🔁 separate.

amateur *n* non-professional, layman, ham (*infml*), dilettante, dabbler, enthusiast, fancier, buff (*infml*).
🔁 professional.
◇ *adj* non-professional, lay, unpaid, unqualified, untrained, amateurish, inexpert, unprofessional.
🔁 professional.

amaze *v* surprise, startle, astonish, astound, stun, stupefy, daze, stagger, floor (*infml*), dumbfound, flabbergast (*infml*), shock, dismay, disconcert, confound, bewilder.

amazement *n* surprise, shock, astonishment, dismay, confusion, perplexity, bewilderment, admiration, wonderment, wonder, marvel.

ambassador *n* emissary, envoy, legate, diplomat, consul, plenipotentiary, deputy, representative, agent, minister, apostle.

ambiguity *n* double meaning, double entendre, equivocality, equivocation, enigma, puzzle, confusion, obscurity, unclearness, vagueness, woolliness, dubiousness, doubt, doubtfulness, uncertainty.
🔁 clarity.

ambiguous *adj* double-meaning, equivocal, double-edged, back-handed, cryptic, enigmatic, puzzling, confusing, obscure, unclear, vague, indefinite, woolly, confused, dubious, doubtful, uncertain, inconclusive, indeterminate.
🔁 clear, definite.

ambition *n* **1** ASPIRATION, aim, goal, target, objective, intent, purpose, design, object, ideal, dream, hope, wish, desire, yearning, longing, hankering, craving, hunger.
2 *a woman of ambition*: enterprise, drive, push, thrust, striving, eagerness, commitment, zeal.
🔁 **2** apathy, diffidence.

ambitious *adj* **1** ASPIRING, hopeful, desirous, intent, purposeful, pushy, bold, assertive, go-ahead, enterprising, driving, energetic, enthusiastic, eager, keen, striving, industrious, zealous. **2** FORMIDABLE, hard, difficult, arduous, strenuous, demanding, challenging, exacting, impressive, grandiose, elaborate.
🔁 **1** lazy, unassuming. **2** modest, uninspiring.

ambivalent *adj* contradictory, conflicting, clashing, warring, opposed, inconsistent, mixed, confused, fluctuating, vacillating, wavering, hesitant, irresolute, undecided, unresolved, unsettled, uncertain, unsure, doubtful, debatable, inconclusive.

amble *v* walk, saunter, stroll, promenade, wander, drift, meander, ramble, toddle (*infml*).
🔁 stride, march.

ambush *n* waylaying, surprise attack, trap, snare, cover, hiding-place.
◇ *v* lie in wait, waylay, surprise, trap, ensnare.

amenable *adj* accommodating, flexible, open, agreeable, persuadable, compliant, tractable, submissive, responsive, susceptible, liable, responsible.
🔁 intractable.

amend v revise, correct, rectify, emend, fix, repair, mend, remedy, redress, reform, change, alter, adjust, modify, qualify, enhance, improve, ameliorate, better.
☒ impair, worsen.

amendment n revision, correction, rectification, emendation, repair, remedy, reform, change, alteration, adjustment, modification, qualification, clarification, addendum, addition, adjunct, improvement.
☒ impairment, deterioration.

amends n atonement, expiation, requital, satisfaction, recompense, compensation, indemnification, indemnity, reparation, redress, restoration, restitution.

amiable adj affable, friendly, approachable, genial, cheerful, good-tempered, good-natured, kind, obliging, charming, engaging, likable, pleasant, agreeable, congenial, companionable, sociable.
☒ unfriendly, curt, hostile.

amid prep amidst, midst, in the midst of, in the thick of, among, amongst, in the middle of, surrounded by.

amnesty n pardon, forgiveness, absolution, mercy, lenience, indulgence, reprieve, remission, dispensation, immunity, oblivion.

among prep amongst, between, in the middle of, surrounded by, amid, amidst, midst, in the midst of, in the thick of, with, together with.

amount n quantity, number, sum, total, sum total, whole, entirety, aggregate, lot, quota, supply, volume, mass, bulk, measure, magnitude, extent, expanse.
• **amount to** add up to, total, aggregate, come to, make, equal, mean, be tantamount to, be equivalent to, approximate to, become, grow.

amphibian

Amphibians include: frog, bullfrog, tree frog, toad, horned toad, midwife toad, natterjack, newt, salamander, conger eel, axolotl.

ample adj large, big, extensive, expansive, broad, wide, full, voluminous, roomy, spacious, commodious, great, considerable, substantial, handsome, generous, bountiful, munificent, liberal, lavish, copious, abundant, plentiful, plenty, unrestricted, profuse, rich.
☒ insufficient, inadequate, meagre.

amplify v enlarge, magnify, expand, dilate, fill out, bulk out, add to, supplement, augment, increase, extend, lengthen, widen, broaden, develop, elaborate, enhance, boost, intensify, strengthen, deepen, heighten, raise.
☒ reduce, decrease, abridge.

amputate v cut off, remove, sever, dissever, separate, dock, lop, curtail, truncate.

amuse v entertain, divert, regale, make laugh, tickle (infml), crease (infml), slay (infml), cheer (up), gladden, enliven, please, charm, delight, enthral, engross, absorb, interest, occupy, recreate, relax.
☒ bore, displease.

amusement n entertainment, diversion, distraction, fun, enjoyment, pleasure, delight, merriment, mirth, hilarity, laughter, joke, prank, game, sport, recreation, hobby, pastime, interest.
☒ boredom, monotony.

amusing adj funny, humorous, hilarious, comical, laughable, ludicrous, droll, witty, facetious, jocular, jolly, enjoyable, pleasant, charming, delightful, entertaining, interesting.
☒ dull, boring.

anaemic adj bloodless, ashen,

chalky, livid, pasty, pallid, sallow, whey-faced, pale, wan, colourless, insipid, weak, feeble, ineffectual, enervated, frail, infirm, sickly.
⊟ ruddy, sanguine, full-blooded.

anaesthetize v desensitize, numb, deaden, dull, drug, dope, stupefy.

analogy n comparison, simile, metaphor, likeness, resemblance, similarity, parallel, correspondence, equivalence, relation, correlation, agreement.

analyse v break down, separate, divide, take apart, dissect, anatomize, reduce, resolve, sift, investigate, study, examine, scrutinize, review, interpret, test, judge, evaluate, estimate, consider.

analysis n breakdown, separation, division, dissection, reduction, resolution, sifting, investigation, inquiry, study, examination, scrutiny, review, exposition, explication, explanation, interpretation, test, judgement, opinion, evaluation, estimation, reasoning.
⊟ synthesis.

analytic adj analytical, dissecting, detailed, in-depth, searching, critical, questioning, inquiring, inquisitive, investigative, diagnostic, systematic, methodical, logical, rational, interpretative, explanatory, expository, studious.

anarchic adj lawless, ungoverned, anarchistic, libertarian, nihilist, revolutionary, rebellious, mutinous, riotous, chaotic, disordered, confused, disorganized.
⊟ submissive, orderly.

anarchist n revolutionary, rebel, insurgent, libertarian, nihilist, terrorist.

anarchy n lawlessness, unrule, misrule, anarchism, revolution, rebellion, insurrection, mutiny, riot, pandemonium, chaos, disorder, confusion.

⊟ rule, control, order.

anathema n aversion, abhorrence, abomination, object of loathing, bête noire, bugbear, bane, curse, proscription, taboo.

anatomy

Anatomy terms include: aural, cardiac, cerebral, dental, dorsal, duodenal, gastric, gingival, hepatic, intercostal, jugular, lachrymal, lumbar, membral, nasal, neural, ocular, optical, pectoral, pedal, pulmonary, renal. see also **body**; **bone**; **brain**; **ear**; **eye**; **heart**.

---

ancestor n forebear, forefather, progenitor, predecessor, forerunner, precursor, antecedent.
⊟ descendant.

ancestral adj familial, parental, genealogical, lineal, hereditary, genetic.

ancestry n ancestors, forebears, forefathers, progenitors, parentage, family, lineage, line, descent, blood, race, stock, roots, pedigree, genealogy, extraction, derivation, origin, heritage, heredity.

anchor v moor, berth, tie up, make fast, fasten, attach, affix, fix.

ancient adj 1 OLD, aged, time-worn, age-old, antique, antediluvian, prehistoric, fossilized, primeval, immemorial. 2 OLD-FASHIONED, out-of-date, antiquated, archaic, obsolete, bygone, early, original.
⊟ 1 recent, contemporary.
2 modern, up-to-date.

anecdote n story, tale, yarn, sketch, reminiscence.

angel n 1 angel of God: archangel, cherub, seraph, divine messenger, principality. 2 DARLING, treasure, saint, paragon, ideal.
⊟ 1 devil, fiend.

The nine orders of angels are:

seraph, cherub, throne,
domination/dominion, virtue,
power, principality, archangel,
angel.

angelic adj cherubic, seraphic,
celestial, heavenly, divine, holy,
pious, saintly, pure, innocent,
unworldly, virtuous, lovely, adorable,
beautiful.
ⓔ devilish, fiendish.

anger n annoyance, irritation,
antagonism, displeasure, irritability,
temper, pique, vexation, ire, rage,
fury, wrath, exasperation, outrage,
indignation, gall, bitterness, rancour,
resentment.
ⓔ forgiveness, forbearance.
◇ v annoy, irritate, aggravate (infml),
wind up (infml), piss off (sl), vex,
irk, rile, miff (infml), needle, nettle,
bother, ruffle, provoke, antagonize,
offend, affront, gall, madden, enrage,
incense, infuriate, exasperate,
outrage.
ⓔ please, appease, calm.

angle n 1 CORNER, nook, bend,
flexure, hook, crook, elbow, knee,
crotch, edge, point. 2 ASPECT,
outlook, facet, side, approach,
direction, position, standpoint,
viewpoint, point of view, slant,
perspective.

angry adj annoyed, cross, irritated,
aggravated (infml), displeased,
uptight (infml), irate, mad (infml),
enraged, incensed, infuriated,
furious, raging, passionate, hot,
heated, exasperated, outraged,
indignant, bitter, resentful.
ⓔ content, happy, calm.

animal n creature, mammal, beast,
brute, barbarian, savage, monster,
cur, pig, swine.

Animals include: cat, dog, mouse,
rat, rabbit, fox, horse, pig, cow,
bull, goat, sheep, monkey, whale,
lion, tiger, wolf, deer, camel, bear,

giraffe, hippopotamus, rhinoceros,
elephant. see also **amphibian**;
bird; **cat**; **cattle**; **dog**; **fish**; **insect**;
mammal; **reptile**.

◇ adj bestial, brutish, inhuman,
savage, wild, instinctive, bodily,
physical, carnal, fleshly, sensual.

animate adj alive, living, live,
breathing, conscious.
ⓔ inanimate.

animated adj lively, spirited,
buoyant, vibrant, ebullient,
vivacious, alive, vital, quick,
brisk, vigorous, energetic, active,
passionate, impassioned, vehement,
ardent, fervent, glowing, radiant,
excited, enthusiastic, eager.
ⓔ lethargic, sluggish, inert.

animosity n ill feeling, ill-will,
acrimony, bitterness, rancour,
resentment, spite, malice, malignity,
malevolence, hate, hatred, loathing,
antagonism, hostility, enmity, feud.
ⓔ goodwill.

annex v 1 ADD, append, affix, attach,
fasten, adjoin, join, connect, unite,
incorporate. 2 ACQUIRE, appropriate,
seize, usurp, occupy, conquer, take
over.

annexe n wing, extension,
attachment, addition, supplement,
expansion.

annihilate v eliminate, eradicate,
obliterate, erase, wipe out, liquidate
(infml), murder, assassinate,
exterminate, extinguish, raze,
destroy, abolish.

anniversary

**Names of wedding anniversaries
include:** 1st paper, 2nd cotton, 3rd
leather, 4th flowers/fruit, 5th
wood, 6th iron/sugar, 7th copper/
wool, 8th bronze/pottery, 9th
pottery/willow, 10th tin/aluminium,
11th steel, 12th silk/linen, 13th
lace, 14th ivory, 15th crystal, 20th
china, 25th silver, 30th pearl, 35th

coral, 40th ruby, 45th sapphire, 50th gold, 55th emerald, 60th diamond, 70th platinum.

annotation n note, footnote, gloss, comment, commentary, exegesis, explanation, elucidation.

announce v declare, proclaim, report, state, reveal, disclose, divulge, make known, notify, intimate, promulgate, propound, publish, broadcast, advertise, publicize, blazon.
⊞ suppress.

announcement n declaration, proclamation, report, statement, communiqué, dispatch, bulletin, notification, intimation, revelation, disclosure, divulgence, publication, broadcast, advertisement.

announcer n broadcaster, newscaster, newsreader, compère, commentator, master of ceremonies, MC, town crier, herald, messenger.

annoy v irritate, rile, aggravate (*infml*), bug (*infml*), displease, anger, vex, irk, piss off (*sl*), madden, exasperate, tease, provoke, ruffle, trouble, disturb, bother, pester, plague, harass, molest.
⊞ please, gratify, comfort.

annoyance n 1 NUISANCE, pest, disturbance, bother, trouble, bore, bind (*sl*), pain (*infml*), headache (*infml*), tease, provocation. 2 *express one's annoyance*: irritation, aggravation (*infml*), displeasure, anger, vexation, exasperation, harassment.
⊞ 2 pleasure.

annoyed adj irritated, cross, displeased, angry, vexed, piqued, exasperated, provoked, harassed.
⊞ pleased.

annoying adj irritating, aggravating (*infml*), vexatious, irksome, trying, tiresome, troublesome, bothersome, maddening, exasperating, galling,

offensive, teasing, provoking, harassing.
⊞ pleasing, welcome.

annul v nullify, invalidate, void, rescind, abrogate, suspend, cancel, abolish, quash, repeal, revoke, countermand, negate, retract, recall, reverse.
⊞ enact, restore.

anoint v 1 OIL, grease, lubricate, embrocate, rub, smear, daub. 2 BLESS, consecrate, sanctify, dedicate.

anomalous adj abnormal, atypical, exceptional, irregular, inconsistent, incongruous, deviant, freakish, eccentric, peculiar, odd, unusual, singular, rare.
⊞ normal, regular, ordinary.

anomaly n abnormality, exception, irregularity, inconsistency, incongruity, aberration, deviation, divergence, departure, freak, misfit, eccentricity, peculiarity, oddity, rarity.

anonymous adj unnamed, nameless, unsigned, unspecified, unacknowledged, unidentified, unknown, incognito, faceless, impersonal, nondescript, unexceptional.
⊞ named, signed, identifiable, distinctive.

answer n 1 REPLY, acknowledgement, response, reaction, rejoinder, retort, riposte, comeback, retaliation, rebuttal, vindication, defence, plea. 2 SOLUTION, explanation.
◇ v 1 REPLY, acknowledge, respond, react, retort, retaliate, refute, solve. 2 *answer one's needs*: fulfil, fill, meet, satisfy, match up to, correspond, correlate, conform, agree, fit, suit, serve, pass.
• **answer back** talk back, retort, riposte, retaliate, contradict, disagree, argue, dispute, rebut.

answerable adj liable, responsible, accountable, chargeable, blameworthy, to blame.

antagonism n hostility, opposition, rivalry, antipathy, ill feeling, ill-will, animosity, friction, discord, dissension, contention, conflict.
🔁 rapport, sympathy, agreement.

antagonist n opponent, adversary, enemy, foe, rival, competitor, contestant, contender.
🔁 ally, supporter.

antagonistic adj conflicting, opposed, adverse, at variance, incompatible, hostile, belligerent, contentious, unfriendly, ill-disposed, averse.
🔁 sympathetic, friendly.

antagonize v alienate, estrange, disaffect, repel, embitter, offend, insult, provoke, annoy, irritate, anger, incense.
🔁 disarm.

anthem n hymn, song, chorale, psalm, canticle, chant.

anthology n selection, collection, compilation, compendium, digest, treasury, miscellany.

anticipate v 1 FORESTALL, pre-empt, intercept, prevent, obviate, preclude. 2 EXPECT, foresee, predict, forecast, look for, await, look forward to, hope for, bank on, count upon.

anticlimax n bathos, comedown, let-down, disappointment, fiasco.

antics n foolery, tomfoolery, silliness, buffoonery, clowning, frolics, capers, skylarking, playfulness, mischief, tricks, monkey-tricks, pranks, stunts, doings.

antidote n remedy, cure, counter-agent, antitoxin, neutralizer, countermeasure, corrective.

antipathy n aversion, dislike, hate, hatred, loathing, abhorrence, distaste, disgust, repulsion, antagonism, animosity, ill-will, bad blood, enmity, hostility, opposition, incompatibility.

🔁 sympathy, affection, rapport.

antique adj antiquarian, ancient, old, veteran, vintage, quaint, antiquated, old-fashioned, outdated, archaic, obsolete.
◇ n antiquity, relic, bygone, period piece, heirloom, curio, museum piece, curiosity, rarity.

antiquity n ancient times, time immemorial, distant past, olden days, age, old age, oldness, agedness.
🔁 modernity, novelty.

antiseptic adj disinfectant, medicated, aseptic, germ-free, clean, pure, unpolluted, uncontaminated, sterile, sterilized, sanitized, sanitary, hygienic.
◇ n disinfectant, germicide, bactericide, purifier, cleanser.

antisocial adj asocial, unacceptable, disruptive, disorderly, rebellious, belligerent, antagonistic, hostile, unfriendly, unsociable, uncommunicative, reserved, retiring, withdrawn, alienated, unapproachable.
🔁 sociable, gregarious.

anxiety n worry, concern, care, distress, nervousness, apprehension, dread, foreboding, misgiving, uneasiness, restlessness, fretfulness, impatience, suspense, tension, stress.
🔁 calm, composure, serenity.

anxious adj worried, concerned, nervous, apprehensive, afraid, fearful, uneasy, restless, fretful, impatient, tense, in suspense, on tenterhooks, taut, distressed, disturbed, troubled, tormented, tortured.
🔁 calm, composed.

apart adv 1 SEPARATELY, independently, individually, singly, alone, on one's own, by oneself, privately, aside, to one side, away, afar, distant, aloof, excluded, isolated, cut off, separated, divorced, separate, distinct. 2 *tear apart*: to

pieces, to bits, into parts, in pieces, in bits, piecemeal.
⊞ **1** connected. **2** together.

apathetic *adj* uninterested, uninvolved, indifferent, cool, cold, unemotional, emotionless, impassive, unmoved, unconcerned, unfeeling, numb, unresponsive, passive, listless, unambitious.
⊞ enthusiastic, involved, concerned, feeling, responsive.

apathy *n* uninterestedness, indifference, coolness, impassivity, unconcern, coldness, insensibility, passivity, listlessness, lethargy, sluggishness, torpor, inertia.
⊞ enthusiasm, interest, concern.

ape *v* copy, imitate, echo, mirror, parrot, mimic, take off, caricature, parody, mock, counterfeit, affect.
◇ *n* monkey.

aplomb *n* composure, calmness, equanimity, poise, balance, coolness, confidence, assurance, self-assurance, audacity.
⊞ discomposure.

apocryphal *adj* unauthenticated, unverified, unsubstantiated, unsupported, questionable, spurious, equivocal, doubtful, dubious, fabricated, concocted, fictitious, imaginary, legendary, mythical.
⊞ authentic, true.

apologetic *adj* sorry, repentant, penitent, contrite, remorseful, rueful, regretful, conscience-stricken.
⊞ unrepentant, impenitent, defiant.

apology *n* acknowledgement, confession, excuse, explanation, justification, vindication, defence, plea.
⊞ defiance.

appal *v* horrify, shock, outrage, disgust, dismay, disconcert, daunt, intimidate, unnerve, alarm, scare, frighten, terrify.
⊞ reassure, encourage.

appalling *adj* horrifying, horrific, harrowing, shocking, outrageous, atrocious, disgusting, awful, dreadful, frightful, terrible, dire, grim, hideous, ghastly, horrible, horrid, loathsome, daunting, intimidating, unnerving, alarming, frightening, terrifying.
⊞ reassuring, encouraging.

apparatus *n* machine, appliance, gadget, device, contraption, gear, equipment, tackle, outfit, tools, implements, utensils, materials, machinery, system, mechanism, means.

apparent *adj* seeming, outward, visible, evident, noticeable, perceptible, plain, clear, distinct, marked, unmistakable, obvious, manifest, patent, open, declared.
⊞ hidden, obscure.

apparently *adv* seemingly, ostensibly, outwardly, superficially, plainly, clearly, obviously, manifestly, patently.

apparition *n* ghost, spectre, phantom, spirit, chimera, vision, manifestation, materialization, presence.

appeal *n* **1** REQUEST, application, petition, suit, solicitation, plea, entreaty, supplication, prayer, invocation. **2** ATTRACTION, allure, interest, fascination, enchantment, charm, attractiveness, winsomeness, beauty, charisma, magnetism.
◇ *v* **1** *appeal for help*: ask, request, call, apply, address, petition, sue, solicit, plead, beg, beseech, implore, entreat, supplicate, pray, invoke, call upon. **2** ATTRACT, draw, allure, lure, tempt, entice, invite, interest, engage, fascinate, charm, please.

appear *v* **1** ARRIVE, enter, turn up, attend, materialize, develop, show (up), come into sight, come into view, loom, rise, surface, arise, occur, crop up, come to light, come out, emerge, issue, be published. **2** SEEM, look, turn out. **3** *appear in a show*: act, perform, play, take part.

☒ **1** disappear, vanish.

appearance *n* **1** APPEARING, arrival, advent, coming, rise, emergence, debut, introduction. **2** LOOK, aspect, expression, face, air, bearing, demeanour, manner, looks, figure, form, semblance, show, front, guise, illusion, impression, image.
☒ **1** disappearance.

appendix *n* addition, appendage, adjunct, addendum, supplement, epilogue, codicil, postscript, rider.

appetite *n* hunger, stomach, relish, zest, taste, propensity, inclination, liking, desire, longing, yearning, craving, eagerness, passion, zeal.
☒ distaste.

appetizing *adj* mouthwatering, tempting, inviting, appealing, palatable, tasty, delicious, scrumptious (*infml*), succulent, piquant, savoury.
☒ disgusting, distasteful.

applaud *v* clap, cheer, acclaim, compliment, congratulate, approve, commend, praise, laud, eulogize, extol.
☒ criticize, censure.

applause *n* ovation, clapping, cheering, cheers, acclaim, acclamation, accolade, congratulation, approval, commendation, praise.
☒ criticism, censure.

appliance *n* machine, device, contrivance, contraption, gadget, tool, implement, instrument, apparatus, mechanism.

applicable *adj* relevant, pertinent, apposite, apt, appropriate, fitting, suited, useful, suitable, fit, proper, valid, legitimate.
☒ inapplicable, inappropriate.

applicant *n* candidate, interviewee, contestant, competitor, aspirant, suitor, petitioner, inquirer.

application *n* **1** REQUEST,

appeal, petition, suit, claim, inquiry. **2** RELEVANCE, pertinence, function, purpose, use, value. **3** DILIGENCE, industry, assiduity, effort, commitment, dedication, perseverance, keenness, attentiveness.

apply *v* **1** REQUEST, ask for, requisition, put in for, appeal, petition, solicit, sue, claim, inquire. **2** *apply oneself to a task*: address, buckle down, settle down, commit, devote, dedicate, give, direct, concentrate, study, persevere. **3** USE, exercise, utilize, employ, bring into play, engage, harness, ply, wield, administer, execute, implement, assign, direct, bring to bear, practise, resort to. **4** REFER, relate, be relevant, pertain, fit, suit. **5** *apply ointment*: put on, spread on, lay on, cover with, paint, anoint, smear, rub.

appoint *v* **1** NAME, nominate, elect, install, choose, select, engage, employ, take on, commission, delegate, assign, allot, designate, command, direct, charge, detail. **2** DECIDE, determine, arrange, settle, fix, set, establish, ordain, decree, destine.
☒ **1** reject, dismiss, discharge.

appointment *n* **1** ARRANGEMENT, engagement, interview, meeting, date, rendezvous, consultation. **2** JOB, position, situation, post, office, place. **3** NAMING, nomination, election, choosing, choice, selection, commissioning, delegation.

appraisal *n* valuation, rating, survey, inspection, review, examination, once-over (*infml*), evaluation, assessment, estimate, estimation, judgement, reckoning, opinion, appreciation.

appreciate *v* **1** ENJOY, relish, savour, prize, treasure, value, cherish, admire, respect, regard, esteem, like, welcome, take kindly to. **2** *appreciate in value*: grow, increase,

rise, mount, inflate, gain, strengthen, improve, enhance. **3** UNDERSTAND, comprehend, perceive, realize, recognize, acknowledge, sympathize with, know.
🔁 **1** despise. **2** depreciate. **3** overlook.

appreciation n **1** ENJOYMENT, relish, admiration, respect, regard, esteem, gratitude, gratefulness, thankfulness, indebtedness, obligation, liking, sensitivity, responsiveness, valuation, assessment, estimation, judgement. **2** GROWTH, increase, rise, inflation, gain, improvement, enhancement. **3** UNDERSTANDING, comprehension, perception, awareness, realization, recognition, acknowledgement, sympathy, knowledge.
🔁 **1** ingratitude. **2** depreciation.

appreciative adj **1** GRATEFUL, thankful, obliged, indebted, pleased. **2** ADMIRING, encouraging, enthusiastic, respectful, sensitive, responsive, perceptive, knowledgeable, conscious, mindful.
🔁 **1** ungrateful.

apprehension n dread, foreboding, misgiving, qualm, uneasiness, anxiety, worry, concern, disquiet, alarm, fear, doubt, suspicion, mistrust.

apprehensive adj nervous, anxious, worried, concerned, uneasy, doubtful, suspicious, mistrustful, distrustful, alarmed, afraid.
🔁 assured, confident.

apprentice n trainee, probationer, student, pupil, learner, novice, beginner, starter, recruit, newcomer.
🔁 expert.

approach v **1** ADVANCE, move towards, draw near, near, gain on, catch up, reach, meet. **2** APPLY TO, appeal to, sound out. **3** BEGIN, commence, set about, undertake, introduce, mention. **4** RESEMBLE, be like, compare with, approximate, come close.

◇ n **1** the approach of winter: advance, coming, advent, arrival. **2** ACCESS, road, avenue, way, passage, entrance, doorway, threshold. **3** APPLICATION, appeal, overture, proposition, proposal. **4** ATTITUDE, manner, style, technique, procedure, method, means.

appropriate adj applicable, relevant, pertinent, to the point, well-chosen, apt, fitting, meet (fml), suitable, fit, befitting, becoming, proper, right, correct, spot-on (infml), well-timed, timely, seasonable, opportune.
🔁 inappropriate, irrelevant, unsuitable.
◇ v **1** SEIZE, take, expropriate, commandeer, requisition, confiscate, impound, assume, usurp. **2** STEAL, pocket, filch, pilfer, purloin, embezzle, misappropriate.

approval n **1** ADMIRATION, esteem, regard, respect, good opinion, liking, appreciation, approbation, favour, recommendation, praise, commendation, acclaim, acclamation, honour, applause. **2** AGREEMENT, concurrence, assent, consent, permission, leave, sanction, authorization, licence, mandate, go-ahead, green light (infml), blessing, OK (infml), certification, ratification, validation, confirmation, support.
🔁 **1** disapproval, condemnation.

approve v **1** ADMIRE, esteem, regard, like, appreciate, favour, recommend, praise, commend, acclaim, applaud. **2** approve a proposal: agree to, assent to, consent to, accede to, allow, permit, pass, sanction, authorize, mandate, bless, countenance, OK (infml), ratify, rubber-stamp (infml), validate, endorse, support, uphold, second, back, accept, adopt, confirm.
🔁 **1** disapprove, condemn.

approximate adj estimated, guessed, rough, inexact, loose,

close, near, like, similar, relative.
⊡ exact.
◇ v approach, border on, verge on,
be tantamount to, resemble.

approximately adv roughly,
around, about, circa, more or less,
loosely, approaching, close to,
nearly, just about.

apt adj 1 RELEVANT, applicable,
apposite, appropriate, fitting,
suitable, fit, seemly, proper,
correct, accurate, spot-on (infml),
timely, seasonable. 2 CLEVER, gifted,
talented, skilful, expert, intelligent,
quick, sharp. 3 LIABLE, prone, given,
disposed, likely, ready.
⊡ 1 inapt. 2 stupid.

aptitude n ability, capability,
capacity, faculty, gift, talent, flair,
facility, proficiency, cleverness,
intelligence, quickness, bent,
inclination, leaning, disposition,
tendency.
⊡ inaptitude.

arbitrary adj 1 RANDOM,
chance, capricious, inconsistent,
discretionary, subjective, instinctive,
unreasoned, illogical, irrational,
unreasonable. 2 DESPOTIC, tyrannical,
dictatorial, autocratic, absolute,
imperious, magisterial, domineering,
overbearing, high-handed, dogmatic.
⊡ 1 reasoned, rational,
circumspect.

arbitrate v judge, adjudicate,
referee, umpire, mediate, settle,
decide, determine.

arbitration n judgement,
adjudication, intervention,
mediation, negotiation, settlement,
decision, determination.

arbitrator n judge, adjudicator,
arbiter, referee, umpire, moderator,
mediator, negotiator, intermediary,
go-between.

arch n archway, bridge, span,
dome, vault, concave, bend, curve,
curvature, bow, arc, semicircle.

◇ v bend, curve, bow, arc, vault,
camber.

archaic adj antiquated, old-
fashioned, outmoded, old hat
(infml), passé, outdated, out-of-
date, obsolete, old, ancient, antique,
quaint, primitive.
⊡ modern, recent.

archetype n pattern, model,
standard, form, type, prototype,
original, precursor, classic, paradigm,
ideal.

architect n designer, planner,
master builder, prime mover,
originator, founder, instigator, creator,
author, inventor, engineer, maker,
constructor, shaper.

architecture

Architectural and building terms
include: alcove, annexe,
architrave, baluster, barge-board,
baroque, bas-relief, capstone,
casement window, classical,
copestone (or coping-stone),
Corinthian, cornerstone, cornice,
coving, dado, dogtooth, dome,
Doric, dormer, double-glazing,
dry-stone, duplex, Early English,
eaves, Edwardian, elevation,
Elizabethan, façade, fanlight,
fascia, festoon, fillet, finial, Flemish
bond, fluting, French window,
frieze, frontispiece, gable,
gargoyle, Georgian, Gothic, groin,
ground plan, half-timbered, Ionic,
jamb, lintel, mullion, Norman,
pagoda, pantile, parapet, pinnacle,
plinth, Queen Anne, rafters,
Regency, reveal, ridge, rococo,
Romanesque, roof, rotunda,
roughcast, scroll, soffit, stucco,
terrazzo, Tudor, Tuscan, wainscot.

archives n records, annals,
chronicles, memorials, papers,
documents, deeds, ledgers, registers,
roll.

ardent adj fervent, fiery, warm,

passionate, impassioned, fierce, vehement, intense, spirited, enthusiastic, eager, keen, dedicated, devoted, zealous.
⊟ apathetic, unenthusiastic.

arduous adj hard, difficult, tough, rigorous, severe, harsh, formidable, strenuous, tiring, taxing, fatiguing, exhausting, backbreaking, punishing, gruelling, uphill, laborious, onerous.
⊟ easy.

area n locality, neighbourhood, environment, environs, patch, terrain, district, region, zone, sector, department, province, domain, realm, territory, sphere, field, range, scope, compass, size, extent, expanse, width, breadth, stretch, tract, part, portion, section.

argue v 1 QUARREL, squabble, bicker, row, wrangle, haggle, remonstrate, join issue, fight, feud, fall out, disagree, dispute, question, debate, discuss. 2 REASON, assert, contend, hold, maintain, claim, plead, exhibit, display, show, manifest, demonstrate, indicate, denote, prove, evidence, suggest, imply.

argument n 1 QUARREL, squabble, row, wrangle, controversy, debate, discussion, dispute, disagreement, clash, conflict, fight, feud.
2 REASONING, reason, logic, assertion, contention, claim, demonstration, defence, case, synopsis, summary, theme.

argumentative adj quarrelsome, contentious, polemical, opinionated, belligerent, perverse, contrary.
⊟ complaisant.

arid adj 1 arid landscape: dry, parched, waterless, desiccated, torrid, barren, infertile, unproductive, desert, waste. 2 DULL, uninteresting, boring, monotonous, tedious, dry, sterile, dreary, colourless, lifeless, spiritless, uninspired.
⊟ 1 fertile. 2 lively.

arise v 1 ORIGINATE, begin, start, commence, derive, stem, spring, proceed, flow, emerge, issue, appear, come to light, crop up, occur, result, happen, ensue, follow. 2 RISE, get up, stand up, go up, ascend, climb, mount, lift, soar, tower.

aristocracy n upper class, gentry, nobility, peerage, ruling class, gentility, élite.
⊟ common people.

aristocrat n noble, patrician, nobleman, noblewoman, peer, peeress, lord, lady.
⊟ commoner.

aristocratic adj upper-class, high-born, well-born, noble, patrician, blue-blooded, titled, lordly, courtly, gentle, thoroughbred, élite.
⊟ plebeian, vulgar.

arm¹ n 1 with arms folded: limb, upper limb, appendage. 2 BRANCH, projection, extension, offshoot, section, division, detachment, department.

arm² v provide, supply, furnish, issue, equip, rig, outfit, ammunition, prime, prepare, forearm, gird, steel, brace, reinforce, strengthen, fortify, protect.

armed services

Units in the armed services include: task-force, militia, garrison; air force: wing, squadron, flight; army: patrol, troop, corps, platoon, squad, battery, company, brigade, battalion, regiment; marines: Royal Marines, commandos; navy: fleet, flotilla, squadron, convoy.

Ranks in the armed services include: air force: aircraftman, aircraftwoman, corporal, sergeant, warrant officer, pilot officer, flying officer, flight lieutenant, squadron leader, wing commander, group-captain, air-commodore, air vice-marshal, air-marshal, air chief-marshal, marshal of the Royal Air Force; *army*: private, lance corporal, corporal, sergeant, warrant officer, lieutenant, captain, major, lieutenant colonel, colonel, brigadier, major-general, lieutenant general, general, field marshal; *navy*: able seaman, rating, petty officer, chief petty officer, sublieutenant, lieutenant, lieutenant commander, commander, captain, commodore, rear admiral, vice-admiral, admiral, admiral of the fleet. *see also* **soldier**.

armoured *adj* armour-plated, steel-plated, iron-clad, reinforced, protected, bullet-proof, bomb-proof.

armoury *n* arsenal, ordnance depot, ammunition dump, magazine, depot, repository, stock, stockpile.

arms *n* 1 WEAPONS, weaponry, firearms, guns, artillery, instruments of war, armaments, ordnance, munitions, ammunition. 2 COAT OF ARMS, armorial bearings, insignia, heraldic device, escutcheon, shield, crest, heraldry, blazonry.

army *n* armed force, military, militia, land forces, soldiers, troops, legions, cohorts, multitude, throng, host, horde.

aroma *n* smell, odour, scent, perfume, fragrance, bouquet, savour.

aromatic *adj* perfumed, fragrant, sweet-smelling, balmy, redolent, savoury, spicy, pungent.

around *prep* 1 SURROUNDING, round, encircling, encompassing, enclosing, on all sides of, on every side of. 2 *around a dozen*: approximately, roughly, about, circa, more or less. ◇ *adv* 1 EVERYWHERE, all over, in all directions, on all sides, about, here and there, to and fro. 2 CLOSE, close by, near, nearby, at hand.

arouse *v* rouse, startle, wake up, waken, awaken, instigate, summon up, call forth, spark, kindle, inflame, whet, sharpen, quicken, animate, excite, prompt, provoke, stimulate, turn on (*sl*), galvanize, goad, spur, incite, agitate, stir up, whip up. ⊞ calm, lull, quieten.

arrange *v* 1 ORDER, tidy, range, array, marshal, dispose, distribute, position, set out, lay out, align, group, class, classify, categorize, sort (out), sift, file, systematize, methodize, regulate, adjust. 2 ORGANIZE, co-ordinate, prepare, fix, plan, project, design, devise, contrive, determine, settle. 3 *arrange music*: adapt, set, score, orchestrate, instrument, harmonize. ⊞ 1 untidy, disorganize, muddle.

arrangement *n* 1 ORDER, array, display, disposition, layout, line-up, grouping, classification, structure, system, method, set-up, organization, preparation, planning, plan, scheme, design, schedule. 2 AGREEMENT, settlement, contract, terms, compromise. 3 ADAPTATION, version, interpretation, setting, score, orchestration, instrumentation, harmonization.

array *n* arrangement, display, show, exhibition, exposition, assortment, collection, assemblage, muster, order, formation, line-up, parade. ◇ *v* 1 ARRANGE, order, range, dispose, group, line up, align, draw up, marshal, assemble, muster, parade, display, show, exhibit. 2 CLOTHE, dress, robe, deck, adorn, decorate.

arrest *v* 1 *arrest a criminal*: capture, catch, seize, nick (*infml*), run in, apprehend, detain. 2 STOP, stem, check, restrain, inhibit, halt, interrupt, stall, delay, slow, retard, block, obstruct, impede, hinder.

arrival *n* appearance, entrance, advent, coming, approach, occurrence.

⎅ departure.

arrive *v* reach, get to, appear, materialize, turn up, show up (*infml*), roll up (*infml*), enter, come, occur, happen.
⎅ depart, leave.

arrogant *adj* haughty, supercilious, disdainful, scornful, contemptuous, superior, condescending, patronizing, high and mighty, lordly, overbearing, high-handed, imperious, self-important, presumptuous, assuming, insolent, proud, conceited, boastful.
⎅ humble, unassuming, bashful.

art *n* **1** FINE ART, painting, sculpture, drawing, artwork, craft, artistry, draughtsmanship, craftsmanship. **2** SKILL, knack, technique, method, aptitude, facility, dexterity, finesse, ingenuity, mastery, expertise, profession, trade. **3** ARTFULNESS, cunning, craftiness, slyness, guile, deceit, trickery, astuteness, shrewdness.

Schools of art include: abstract, action painting, aestheticism, art deco, art nouveau, Barbizon, baroque, classicism, conceptual art, constructivism, cubism, Dadaism, expressionism, Fauvism, Florentine, folk art, futurism, Gothic, impressionism, Mannerism, minimal art, Modernism, the Nabis, naturalism, neoclassicism, neoexpressionism, Neo-Impressionism, Neo-Plasticism, op art, plastic art, pop art, Post-Impressionism, post-modernism, Pre-Raphaelitism, realism, Renaissance, rococo, Romanesque, romanticism, Suprematism, surrealism, symbolism, Venetian, vorticism.

Arts and crafts include: painting, oil painting, watercolour, fresco, portraiture; architecture, drawing, sketching, caricature, animation, illustration; graphics, film, video, digital design; sculpture, modelling, woodcarving, woodcraft, marquetry, metalwork, enamelling, cloisonné, engraving, etching, pottery, ceramics, mosaic, jewellery, stained glass, photography, lithography, calligraphy, collage, origami, spinning, weaving, batik, silk-screen printing, needlework, tapestry, embroidery, patchwork, crochet, knitting.

artful *adj* cunning, crafty, sly, foxy, wily, tricky, scheming, designing, deceitful, devious, subtle, sharp, shrewd, smart, clever, masterly, ingenious, resourceful, skilful, dexterous.
⎅ artless, naive, ingenuous.

article *n* **1** *article in a magazine*: feature, report, story, account, piece, review, commentary, composition, essay, paper. **2** ITEM, thing, object, commodity, unit, part, constituent, piece, portion, division.

articulate *adj* distinct, well-spoken, clear, lucid, intelligible, comprehensible, understandable, coherent, fluent, vocal, expressive, meaningful.
⎅ inarticulate, incoherent.
◇ *v* say, utter, speak, talk, express, voice, vocalize, verbalize, state, pronounce, enunciate, breathe.

articulation *n* saying, utterance, speaking, talking, expression, voicing, vocalization, verbalization, pronunciation, enunciation, diction, delivery.

artificial *adj* false, fake, bogus, counterfeit, spurious, phoney (*infml*), pseudo, specious, sham, insincere, assumed, affected, mannered, forced, contrived, made-up, feigned, pretended, simulated, imitation, mock, synthetic, plastic, man-

made, manufactured, non-natural, unnatural.
⊞ genuine, true, real, natural.

artisan *n* craftsman, craftswoman, artificer, journeyman, expert, skilled worker, mechanic, technician.

artist

Types of artist include: architect, graphic designer, designer, draughtsman, draughtswoman, graphic artist, illustrator, cartoonist, animator, photographer, printer, engraver, goldsmith, silversmith, blacksmith, carpenter, potter, embroiderer, weaver, sculptor, painter.

---

artiste *n* performer, entertainer, variety artist, vaudevillian, comic, comedian, comedienne, player, trouper, actor, actress.

artistic *adj* aesthetic, ornamental, decorative, beautiful, exquisite, elegant, stylish, graceful, harmonious, sensitive, tasteful, refined, cultured, cultivated, skilled, talented, creative, imaginative.
⊞ inelegant, tasteless.

artistry *n* craftsmanship, workmanship, skill, craft, talent, flair, brilliance, genius, finesse, style, mastery, expertise, proficiency, accomplishment, deftness, touch, sensitivity, creativity.
⊞ ineptitude.

as *conj, prep* **1** WHILE, when. **2** SUCH AS, for example, for instance, like, in the manner of. **3** BECAUSE, since, seeing that, considering that, inasmuch as, being.
• **as for** with reference to, as regards, with regard to, on the subject of, in connection with, in relation to, with relation to, with respect to.

ascend *v* rise, take off, lift off, go up, move up, slope upwards, climb, scale, mount, tower, float up, fly up, soar.

⊞ descend, go down.

ascent *n* **1** ASCENDING, ascension, climb, climbing, scaling, escalation, rise, rising, mounting. **2** SLOPE, gradient, incline, ramp, hill, elevation.
⊞ **1** descent.

ascertain *v* find out, learn, discover, determine, fix, establish, settle, locate, detect, identify, verify, confirm, make certain.

ascribe *v* attribute, credit, accredit, put down, assign, impute, charge, chalk up to.

ashamed *adj* sorry, apologetic, remorseful, contrite, guilty, conscience-stricken, sheepish, embarrassed, blushing, red-faced, mortified, humiliated, abashed, humbled, crestfallen, distressed, discomposed, confused, reluctant, hesitant, shy, self-conscious, bashful, modest, prudish.
⊞ shameless, proud, defiant.

aside *adv* apart, on one side, in reserve, away, out of the way, separately, in isolation, alone, privately, secretly.
◇ *n* digression, parenthesis, departure, soliloquy, stage whisper, whisper.

ask *v* **1** REQUEST, appeal, petition, sue, plead, beg, entreat, implore, clamour, beseech, pray, supplicate, crave, demand, order, bid, require, seek, solicit, invite, summon. **2** INQUIRE, query, question, interrogate, quiz, press.

asleep *adj* sleeping, napping, snoozing, fast asleep, sound asleep, dormant, resting, inactive, inert, unconscious, numb, dozing.

aspect *n* angle, direction, elevation, side, facet, feature, face, expression, countenance, appearance, look, air, manner, bearing, attitude, condition, situation, position, standpoint, point of view, view, outlook, prospect, scene.

aspiration n aim, intent, purpose, endeavour, object, objective, goal, ambition, hope, dream, ideal, wish, desire, yearning, longing, craving, hankering.

aspire v aim, intend, purpose, seek, pursue, hope, dream, wish, desire, yearn, long, crave, hanker.

aspiring adj would-be, aspirant, striving, endeavouring, ambitious, enterprising, keen, eager, hopeful, optimistic, wishful, longing.

assassin n murderer, killer, slayer, cut-throat, executioner, hatchet man (infml), gunman, hit-man (sl), liquidator (infml).

assassinate v murder, kill, slay, dispatch, hit (sl), eliminate (infml), liquidate (infml).

assault n 1 ATTACK, offensive, onslaught, blitz, strike, raid, invasion, incursion, storm, storming, charge. 2 charged with assault: battery, grievous bodily harm, GBH (infml), mugging (sl), rape, abuse.
◇ v attack, charge, invade, strike, hit, set upon, fall on, beat up (infml), mug (sl), rape, molest, abuse.

assemble v 1 GATHER, congregate, muster, rally, convene, meet, join up, flock, group, collect, accumulate, amass, bring together, round up, marshal, mobilize. 2 CONSTRUCT, build, put together, piece together, compose, make, fabricate, manufacture.
🖃 1 scatter, disperse. 2 dismantle.

assembly n 1 GATHERING, rally, meeting, convention, conference, convocation, congress, council, group, body, company, congregation, flock, crowd, multitude, throng, collection, assemblage. 2 CONSTRUCTION, building, fabrication, manufacture.

assert v affirm, attest, swear, testify to, allege, claim, contend, maintain, insist, stress, protest, defend, vindicate, uphold, promote, declare, profess, state, pronounce, lay down, advance.
🖃 deny, refute.

assertion n affirmation, attestation, word, allegation, claim, contention, insistence, vindication, declaration, profession, statement, pronouncement.
🖃 denial.

assertive adj bold, confident, self-assured, forward, pushy, insistent, emphatic, forceful, firm, decided, strong-willed, dogmatic, opinionated, presumptuous, assuming, overbearing, domineering, aggressive.
🖃 timid, diffident.

assess v gauge, estimate, evaluate, appraise, review, judge, consider, weigh, size up, compute, determine, fix, value, rate, tax, levy, impose, demand.

assessment n gauging, estimation, estimate, evaluation, appraisal, review, judgement, opinion, consideration, calculation, determination, valuation, rating, taxation.

asset n strength, resource, virtue, plus (infml), benefit, advantage, blessing, boon, help, aid.
🖃 liability.

assets n estate, property, possessions, goods, holdings, securities, money, wealth, capital, funds, reserves, resources, means.

assign v 1 ALLOCATE, apportion, grant, give, dispense, distribute, allot, consign, delegate, name, nominate, designate, appoint, choose, select, determine, set, fix, specify, stipulate. 2 ATTRIBUTE, accredit, ascribe, put down.

assignment n commission, errand, task, project, job, position, post, duty, responsibility, charge, appointment, delegation, designation, nomination, selection, allocation, consignment, grant, distribution.

assist v help, aid, abet, rally round, co-operate, collaborate, back, second, support, reinforce, sustain, relieve, benefit, serve, enable, facilitate, expedite, boost, further, advance.
☒ hinder, thwart.

assistance n help, aid, succour, co-operation, collaboration, backing, support, reinforcement, relief, benefit, service, boost, furtherance.
☒ hindrance, resistance.

assistant n helper, helpmate, aide, right-hand man, auxiliary, ancillary, subordinate, backer, second, supporter, accomplice, accessory, abettor, collaborator, colleague, partner, ally, confederate, associate.

associate v 1 AFFILIATE, confederate, ally, league, join, amalgamate, combine, unite, link, connect, correlate, relate, couple, pair, yoke. 2 associate with bad company: socialize, mingle, mix, fraternize, consort, hang around (infml).
◇ n partner, ally, confederate, affiliate, collaborator, co-worker, mate, colleague, peer, compeer, fellow, comrade, companion, friend, sidekick (infml), assistant, follower.

association n 1 ORGANIZATION, corporation, company, partnership, league, alliance, coalition, confederation, confederacy, federation, affiliation, consortium, cartel, syndicate, union, society, club, user group, fraternity, fellowship, clique, group, band. 2 BOND, tie, connection, correlation, relation, relationship, involvement, intimacy, friendship, companionship, familiarity.

assorted adj miscellaneous, mixed, varied, different, differing, heterogeneous, diverse, sundry, various, several, manifold.

assortment n miscellany, medley, pot-pourri, jumble, mixture, variety, diversity, collection, selection, choice, arrangement, grouping.

assume v 1 PRESUME, surmise, accept, take for granted, expect, understand, deduce, infer, guess, postulate, suppose, think, believe, imagine, fancy. 2 AFFECT, take on, feign, counterfeit, simulate, put on, pretend. 3 assume command: undertake, adopt, embrace, seize, arrogate, commandeer, appropriate, usurp, take over.

assumed adj false, bogus, counterfeit, fake, phoney (infml), sham, affected, feigned, simulated, pretended, made-up, fictitious, hypothetical.
☒ true, real, actual.

assumption n presumption, surmise, inference, supposition, guess, conjecture, theory, hypothesis, premise, postulate, idea, notion, belief, fancy.

assurance n 1 ASSERTION, declaration, affirmation, guarantee, pledge, promise, vow, word, oath. 2 CONFIDENCE, self-confidence, aplomb, boldness, audacity, courage, nerve, conviction, sureness, certainty.
☒ 2 shyness, doubt, uncertainty.

assure v affirm, guarantee, warrant, pledge, promise, vow, swear, tell, convince, persuade, encourage, hearten, reassure, soothe, comfort, boost, strengthen, secure, ensure, confirm.

assured adj 1 SURE, certain, indisputable, irrefutable, confirmed, positive, definite, settled, fixed, guaranteed, secure. 2 SELF-ASSURED, confident, self-confident, self-possessed, bold, audacious, assertive.
☒ 1 uncertain. 2 shy.

astonish v surprise, startle, amaze,

astound, stun, stupefy, daze, stagger, floor (*infml*), dumbfound, flabbergast (*infml*), shock, confound, bewilder.

astonishment *n* surprise, amazement, shock, dismay, consternation, confusion, bewilderment, wonder.

astounding *adj* surprising, startling, amazing, astonishing, stunning, breathtaking, jaw-dropping (*infml*), stupefying, overwhelming, staggering, shocking, bewildering.

astray *adv* adrift, off course, lost, amiss, wrong, off the rails (*infml*), awry, off the mark.

astute *adj* shrewd, prudent, sagacious, wise, canny, knowing, intelligent, sharp, penetrating, keen, perceptive, discerning, subtle, clever, crafty, cunning, sly, wily.
⧧ stupid, slow.

asylum *n* haven, sanctuary, refuge, shelter, retreat, safety.

asymmetric *adj* unsymmetrical, unbalanced, uneven, crooked, awry, unequal, disproportionate, irregular.
⧧ symmetrical.

atheism *n* unbelief, non-belief, disbelief, scepticism, irreligion, ungodliness, godlessness, impiety, infidelity, paganism, heathenism, free-thinking, rationalism.

atheist *n* unbeliever, non-believer, disbeliever, sceptic, infidel, pagan, heathen, free-thinker.

athlete *n* sportsman, sportswoman, competitor, contestant, contender, runner, gymnast.

athletic *adj* fit, energetic, vigorous, active, sporty, muscular, sinewy, brawny, strapping, robust, sturdy, strong, powerful, well-knit, well-proportioned, wiry.
⧧ puny, wimpy (*infml*).

athletics *n* sports, games, races, track events, field events, exercises, gymnastics.

atmosphere *n* **1** AIR, sky, aerospace, heavens, ether. **2** AMBIENCE, environment, surroundings, aura, feel, feeling, mood, spirit, tone, tenor, character, quality, flavour.

atom *n* molecule, particle, bit, morsel, crumb, grain, spot, speck, mite, shred, scrap, hint, trace, scintilla, jot, iota, whit.

atrocious *adj* shocking, appalling, abominable, dreadful, terrible, horrible, hideous, ghastly, heinous, grievous, savage, vicious, monstrous, fiendish, ruthless.
⧧ admirable, fine.

atrocity *n* outrage, abomination, enormity, horror, monstrosity, savagery, barbarity, brutality, cruelty, viciousness, evil, villainy, wickedness, vileness, heinousness, hideousness, atrociousness.

attach *v* **1** *attach a label*: affix, stick, adhere, fasten, fix, secure, tie, bind, weld, join, unite, connect, link, couple, add, annex. **2** ASCRIBE, attribute, impute, assign, put, place, associate, relate to, belong.
⧧ **1** detach, unfasten.

attachment *n* **1** ACCESSORY, fitting, fixture, extension, appendage, extra, supplement, addition, adjunct, codicil. **2** FONDNESS, affection, tenderness, love, liking, partiality, loyalty, devotion, friendship, affinity, attraction, bond, tie, link.

attack *n* **1** OFFENSIVE, blitz, bombardment, invasion, incursion, foray, raid, strike, charge, rush, onslaught, assault, battery, aggression, criticism, censure, abuse. **2** SEIZURE, fit, convulsion, paroxysm, spasm, stroke.
◇ *v* **1** INVADE, raid, strike, storm, charge, assail, assault, set about, set upon, fall on, lay into, do over (*sl*). **2** CRITICIZE, censure, blame, denounce, revile, malign, abuse.
⧧ **1** defend, protect.

attacker n assailant, mugger (sl), aggressor, invader, raider, critic, detractor, reviler, abuser, persecutor. ⊞ defender, supporter.

attain v accomplish, achieve, fulfil, complete, effect, realize, earn, reach, touch, arrive at, grasp, get, acquire, obtain, procure, secure, gain, win, net.

attainment n accomplishment, achievement, feat, fulfilment, completion, consummation, realization, success, competence, ability, capability, proficiency, skill, art, talent, gift, aptitude, facility, mastery.

attempt n try, endeavour, shot (infml), go (infml), stab (infml), bash (infml), push, effort, struggle, bid, undertaking, venture, trial, experiment.
◇ v try, endeavour, have a go (infml), aspire, seek, strive, undertake, tackle, venture, experiment.

attend v 1 attend a meeting: be present, go to, frequent, visit. 2 ESCORT, chaperone, accompany, usher, follow, guard, look after, take care of, care for, nurse, tend, minister to, help, serve, wait on. 3 PAY ATTENTION, listen, hear, heed, mind, mark, note, notice, observe.
• **attend to** deal with, see to, take care of, look after, manage, direct, control, oversee, supervise.

attendance n presence, appearance, turnout, audience, house, crowd, gate.

attendant n aide, helper, assistant, auxiliary, steward, waiter, servant, page, retainer, guide, marshal, usher, escort, companion, follower, guard, custodian.
◇ adj accompanying, attached, associated, related, incidental, resultant, consequent, subsequent.

attention n alertness, vigilance, concentration, heed, notice, observation, regard, mindfulness, awareness, recognition, thought, contemplation, consideration, concern, care, treatment, service.
⊞ inattention, disregard, carelessness.

attentive adj 1 ALERT, awake, vigilant, watchful, observant, concentrating, heedful, mindful, careful, conscientious. 2 CONSIDERATE, thoughtful, kind, obliging, accommodating, polite, courteous, devoted.
⊞ 1 inattentive, heedless. 2 inconsiderate.

attitude n feeling, disposition, mood, aspect, manner, bearing, pose, posture, stance, position, point of view, opinion, view, outlook, perspective, approach.

attract v pull, draw, lure, allure, entice, seduce, tempt, invite, induce, incline, appeal to, interest, engage, fascinate, enchant, charm, bewitch, captivate, excite.
⊞ repel, disgust.

attraction n pull, draw, lure, allure, magnetism, bait, enticement, inducement, seduction, temptation, invitation, appeal, interest, fascination, enchantment, charm, captivation.
⊞ repulsion.

attractive adj pretty, fair, fetching, good-looking, handsome, beautiful, gorgeous, stunning, glamorous, lovely, pleasant, pleasing, agreeable, appealing, winsome, winning, enticing, seductive, tempting, inviting, interesting, sexy (infml), engaging, fascinating, charming, captivating, magnetic.
⊞ unattractive, repellent.

attribute v ascribe, accredit, credit, impute, assign, put down, blame, charge, refer, apply.
◇ n property, quality, virtue, point, aspect, facet, feature, trait, characteristic, idiosyncrasy,

peculiarity, quirk, note, mark, sign, symbol.

auburn adj red, chestnut, tawny, russet, copper, Titian.

audible adj clear, distinct, recognizable, perceptible, discernible, detectable.
🔁 inaudible, silent, unclear.

audience n spectators, onlookers, house, auditorium, listeners, viewers, crowd, turnout, bums-on-seats (infml), gathering, assembly, congregation, fans, devotees, regulars, following, public.

audit n examination, inspection, check, verification, investigation, scrutiny, analysis, review, statement, balancing.

augment v add to, amplify, boost, enlarge, build up, put on, expand, extend, grow, increase, make greater, magnify, multiply, raise, inflate, enhance, heighten, intensify, reinforce, strengthen, swell.
🔁 decrease.

augur v bode, forebode, herald, presage, portend, prophesy, predict, promise, signify.

auspices n aegis, authority, patronage, sponsorship, backing, support, protection, charge, care, supervision, control, influence, guidance.

auspicious adj favourable, propitious, encouraging, cheerful, bright, rosy, promising, hopeful, optimistic, fortunate, lucky, opportune, happy, prosperous.
🔁 inauspicious, ominous.

austere adj 1 STARK, bleak, plain, simple, unadorned, grim, forbidding. 2 SEVERE, stern, strict, cold, formal, rigid, rigorous, exacting, hard, harsh, spartan, grave, serious, solemn, sober, abstemious, self-denying, restrained, economical, frugal, ascetic, self-disciplined, puritanical, chaste.
🔁 1 ornate, elaborate. 2 genial.

austerity n plainness, simplicity, severity, coldness, formality, hardness, harshness, solemnity, abstemiousness, abstinence, economy, asceticism, puritanism.
🔁 elaborateness, materialism.

authentic adj genuine, true, real, actual, certain, bona fide, legitimate, honest, valid, original, pure, factual, accurate, true-to-life, faithful, reliable, trustworthy.
🔁 false, fake, counterfeit, spurious.

authenticate v guarantee, warrant, vouch for, attest, authorize, accredit, validate, certify, endorse, confirm, verify, corroborate.

authenticity n genuineness, certainty, authoritativeness, validity, truth, veracity, truthfulness, honesty, accuracy, correctness, faithfulness, fidelity, reliability, dependability, trustworthiness.
🔁 spuriousness, invalidity.

author n 1 WRITER, novelist, dramatist, playwright, composer, pen, penman, penwoman. 2 CREATOR, founder, originator, initiator, parent, prime mover, mover, inventor, designer, architect, planner, maker, producer.

authoritarian adj strict, severe, disciplinarian, harsh, rigid, inflexible, unyielding, dogmatic, doctrinaire, absolute, autocratic, dictatorial, despotic, tyrannical, oppressive, domineering, imperious.
🔁 liberal.

authoritative adj scholarly, learned, official, authorized, legitimate, valid, approved, sanctioned, accepted, definitive, decisive, authentic, factual, true, truthful, accurate, faithful, convincing, sound, reliable, dependable, trustworthy.
🔁 unofficial, unreliable.

authority n 1 SOVEREIGNTY,

supremacy, rule, sway, control, dominion, influence, power, force, government, administration, officialdom. **2** AUTHORIZATION, permission, sanction, permit, warrant, licence, credentials, right, prerogative. **3** *an authority on antiques*: expert, pundit, connoisseur, specialist, professional, master, scholar.

authorization *n* authority, permission, consent, sanction, approval, mandate, validation, ratification, confirmation, licence, entitlement, empowering, commission, warrant, permit, leave, credentials, accreditation (*fml*), OK (*infml*), go-ahead (*infml*).

authorize *v* legalize, validate, ratify, confirm, license, entitle, accredit, empower, enable, commission, warrant, permit, allow, consent to, sanction, approve, give the go-ahead.

autocracy *n* absolutism, totalitarianism, dictatorship, despotism, tyranny, fascism, authoritarianism.
⌽ democracy.

autocrat *n* absolutist, totalitarian, dictator, despot, tyrant, authoritarian, (little) Hitler (*infml*), fascist.

autocratic *adj* absolute, all-powerful, totalitarian, despotic, tyrannical, authoritarian, dictatorial, domineering, overbearing, imperious.
⌽ democratic, liberal.

automatic *adj* **1** AUTOMATED, self-activating, mechanical, mechanized, programmed, self-regulating, computerized, push-button, robotic, self-propelling, unmanned. **2** SPONTANEOUS, reflex, knee-jerk (*infml*), involuntary, unwilled, unconscious, unthinking, natural, instinctive, routine, necessary, certain, inevitable, unavoidable, inescapable.

autonomy *n* self-government, self-rule, home rule, sovereignty, independence, self-determination, freedom, free will.
⌽ subjection, compulsion.

auxiliary *adj* ancillary, assistant, subsidiary, accessory, secondary, supporting, supportive, aiding, helping, assisting, extra, reserve, supplementary, spare, back-up, emergency, substitute.

available *adj* free, vacant, to hand, within reach, at hand, accessible, handy, convenient, on hand, ready, on tap, obtainable, off-the-shelf (*infml*).
⌽ unavailable.

avalanche *n* landslide, landslip, cascade, torrent, deluge, flood, inundation, barrage.

avant-garde *adj* innovative, innovatory, pioneering, experimental, unconventional, far-out (*sl*), way-out (*sl*), progressive, advanced, forward-looking, enterprising, inventive.
⌽ conservative.

avarice *n* covetousness, rapacity, acquisitiveness, greed, greediness, meanness.
⌽ generosity, liberality.

avaricious *adj* covetous, grasping, rapacious, acquisitive, greedy, mercenary, mean, miserly.
⌽ generous.

avenge *v* take revenge for, take vengeance for, punish, requite, repay, retaliate.

average *n* mean, mid-point, norm, standard, rule, par, medium, run.
⌽ extreme, exception.
◇ *adj* mean, medial, median, middle, intermediate, medium, moderate, satisfactory, fair, mediocre, middling, indifferent, so-so (*infml*), passable, tolerable, undistinguished, run-of-the-mill, ordinary, everyday, common, usual, normal, regular, standard, vanilla (*infml*), typical, unexceptional.

⚖ extreme, exceptional, remarkable.

averse adj reluctant, unwilling, loth, disinclined, ill-disposed, hostile, opposed, antagonistic, unfavourable.
⚖ willing, keen, sympathetic.

aversion n dislike, hate, hatred, loathing, detestation, abhorrence, abomination, horror, phobia, reluctance, unwillingness, disinclination, distaste, disgust, revulsion, repugnance, repulsion, hostility, opposition, antagonism.
⚖ liking, sympathy, desire.

avert v turn away, deflect, turn aside, parry, fend off, ward off, stave off, forestall, frustrate, prevent, obviate, avoid, evade.

aviation n aeronautics, flying, flight, aircraft industry.

avid adj eager, earnest, keen, enthusiastic, fanatical, devoted, dedicated, zealous, ardent, fervent, intense, passionate, insatiable, ravenous, hungry, thirsty, greedy, grasping, covetous.
⚖ indifferent.

avoid v evade, elude, sidestep, dodge, shirk, duck (infml), escape, get out of, bypass, circumvent, balk, prevent, avert, shun, abstain from, refrain from, steer clear of.

avoidable adj escapable, preventable.
⚖ inevitable.

avowed adj sworn, declared, professed, self-proclaimed, self-confessed, confessed, admitted, acknowledged, open, overt.

await v wait for, expect, hope for, look forward to, look for, be in store for, lie in wait.

awake v awaken, waken, wake, wake up, rouse, arouse.
◇ adj wakeful, wide awake, aroused, alert, vigilant, watchful, observant, attentive, conscious, aware, sensitive, alive.

awakening n awaking, wakening, waking, rousing, arousal, stimulation, animating, enlivening, activation, revival, birth.

award v give, present, distribute, dispense, bestow, confer, accord, endow, gift, grant, allot, apportion, assign, allow, determine.
◇ n prize, trophy, decoration, medal, presentation, dispensation, bestowal, conferral, endowment, gift, grant, allotment, allowance, adjudication, judgement, decision, order.

aware adj conscious, alive to, sensitive, appreciative, sentient, familiar, conversant, acquainted, informed, up to speed (infml), enlightened, au courant, knowing, knowledgeable, cognizant, mindful, heedful, attentive, observant, sharp, alert, on the ball (infml), clued-up (infml), sussed (infml), shrewd, sensible.
⚖ unaware, oblivious, insensitive.

awe n wonder, veneration, reverence, respect, admiration, amazement, astonishment, fear, terror, dread, apprehension.
⚖ contempt.

awe-inspiring adj wonderful, sublime, magnificent, stupendous, overwhelming, breathtaking, stupefying, stunning, astonishing, amazing, impressive, imposing, majestic, solemn, moving, awesome, formidable, daunting, intimidating, fearsome.
⚖ contemptible, tame.

awful adj terrible, dreadful, fearful, frightful, ghastly, unpleasant, nasty, horrible, hideous, ugly, gruesome, dire, abysmal, atrocious, horrific, shocking, appalling, alarming, spine-chilling.
⚖ wonderful, excellent.

awkward adj 1 CLUMSY, gauche, inept, inexpert, unskilful, bungling, ham-fisted, unco-ordinated, ungainly, graceless, ungraceful, inelegant, cumbersome, clunky (*infml*), unwieldy, inconvenient, difficult, fiddly, delicate, troublesome, perplexing. **2** *feeling awkward in their presence*: uncomfortable, ill at ease, embarrassed. **3** OBSTINATE, stubborn, unco-operative, irritable, touchy, prickly, rude, unpleasant. ⊞ **1** graceful, elegant, convenient, handy. **2** comfortable, relaxed. **3** amenable, pleasant.

awry *adv, adj* **1** *clothing left awry*: askew, asymmetrical, cock-eyed, crooked, misaligned, oblique, off-centre, skew-whiff (*infml*), twisted, uneven, wonky (*infml*). **2** *plans gone awry*: wrong, amiss.

⊞ **1** straight, symmetrical.

axe *n* hatchet, chopper, cleaver, tomahawk, battle-axe.
◇ *v* **1** CUT (DOWN), fell, hew, chop, cleave, split. **2** CANCEL, terminate, discontinue, remove, withdraw, eliminate, get rid of, throw out, dismiss, discharge, sack (*infml*), fire (*infml*).

axiom *n* principle, fundamental, truth, truism, precept, dictum, byword, maxim, adage, aphorism.

axis *n* centre-line, vertical, horizontal, pivot, hinge.

axle *n* shaft, spindle, rod, pin, pivot.

Bb

babble v 1 CHATTER, gabble, jabber, cackle, prate, mutter, mumble, murmur. 2 *the stream babbled*: burble, gurgle.
◇ n chatter, gabble, clamour, hubbub, gibberish, burble, murmur.

babe n baby, infant, suckling, child, tiny, toddler, rugrat (*sl*).

baby n babe, infant, suckling, child, tiny, toddler, rugrat (*sl*).
◇ adj miniature, small-scale, mini (*infml*), midget, small, little, tiny, minute, diminutive.

babyish adj childish, juvenile, puerile, infantile, silly, foolish, soft (*infml*), sissy (*infml*), baby, young, immature, naive.
⊜ mature, precocious.

back n rear, stern, end, tail, tail end, hind part, hindquarters, posterior, backside, reverse.
⊜ front, face.
◇ v 1 GO BACKWARDS, reverse, recede, regress, backtrack, retreat, retire, withdraw, back away, recoil. 2 SUPPORT, sustain, assist, side with, champion, advocate, encourage, promote, boost, favour, sanction, countenance, endorse, second, countersign, sponsor, finance, subsidize, underwrite.
⊜ 1 advance, approach. 2 discourage, weaken.
◇ adj rear, end, tail, posterior, hind, hindmost, reverse.
⊜ front.
• **back down** concede, yield, give in, surrender, submit, retreat, withdraw, back-pedal, do a U-turn (*infml*).
• **back out** abandon, give up, chicken out (*infml*), withdraw, pull out (*infml*), resign, recant, go back on, cancel.
• **back up** confirm, corroborate, substantiate, endorse, second, champion, support, reinforce, bolster, assist, aid.
⊜ let down.

backbone n 1 SPINE, spinal column, vertebrae, vertebral column, core, mainstay, support, foundation. 2 COURAGE, mettle, pluck, nerve, grit, determination, resolve, tenacity, steadfastness, toughness, stamina, strength, power.
⊜ 2 spinelessness, weakness.

backfire v recoil, rebound, ricochet, boomerang, miscarry, fail, flop.

background n 1 SETTING, surroundings, environment, context, circumstances. 2 HISTORY, record, credentials, experience, grounding, preparation, education, upbringing, breeding, culture, tradition.

backing n support, aid, assistance, accompaniment, helpers, championing, advocacy, encouragement, moral support, favour, sanction, promotion, endorsement, seconding, patronage, sponsorship, finance, funds, grant, subsidy.

backlash n reaction, response, repercussion, reprisal, retaliation, recoil, kickback, backfire, boomerang.

backlog n accumulation, stock, supply, resources, reserve, reserves, excess.

backsliding n lapse, relapse, apostasy, defection, desertion, defaulting.

backward adj **1** a backward step: retrograde, retrogressive, regressive. **2** SHY, bashful, reluctant, unwilling, hesitant, hesitating, wavering, slow, behind, behindhand, late, immature, underdeveloped, retarded, subnormal, stupid.
🗷 **1** forward. **2** precocious.

bacteria n germs, bugs (infml), viruses, microbes, micro-organisms, bacilli.

bad adj **1** UNPLEASANT, disagreeable, nasty, undesirable, unfortunate, distressing, adverse, detrimental, harmful, damaging, injurious, serious, grave, severe, harsh. **2** EVIL, wicked, sinful, criminal, corrupt, immoral, vile. **3** bad workmanship: poor, inferior, substandard, shoddy (infml), imperfect, faulty, defective, deficient, unsatisfactory, useless. **4** ROTTEN, mouldy, decayed, spoilt, putrid, rancid, sour, off, tainted, contaminated. **5** a bad child: naughty, mischievous, ill-behaved, disobedient.
🗷 **1** good, pleasant, mild, slight. **2** virtuous. **3** skilled. **4** fresh. **5** well-behaved.

badge n identification, emblem, device, insignia, sign, mark, token, stamp, brand, trademark, logo.

badly adv **1** GREATLY, extremely, exceedingly, intensely, deeply, acutely, bitterly, painfully, seriously, desperately, severely, critically, crucially. **2** WICKEDLY, criminally, immorally, shamefully, unfairly. **3** WRONG, wrongly, incorrectly, improperly, faultily, defectively, poorly, imperfectly, inadequately, unsatisfactorily, incompetently, negligently, carelessly. **4** UNFAVOURABLY, adversely, unfortunately, unsuccessfully.
🗷 **3** well.

bad-tempered adj irritable, cross, crotchety, crabbed, crabby, snappy, grumpy, querulous, petulant, fractious, stroppy (infml), arsey (sl).
🗷 good-tempered, genial, equable.

baffle v puzzle, perplex, mystify, bemuse, bewilder, confuse, confound, bamboozle (infml), flummox (infml), daze, upset, disconcert, foil, thwart, frustrate, hinder, check, defeat, stump (infml).
🗷 enlighten, help.

bag v **1** CATCH, capture, trap, land, kill, shoot. **2** OBTAIN, acquire, get, gain, corner, take, grab, appropriate, commandeer, reserve.
◇ n container, sack, case, suitcase, grip, carrier, hold-all, handbag, shoulder-bag, satchel, rucksack, haversack, pack.

baggage n luggage, suitcases, bags, belongings, things, equipment, gear, paraphernalia, impedimenta (fml).

baggy adj loose, slack, roomy, ill-fitting, billowing, bulging, floppy, sagging, droopy.
🗷 tight, firm.

bail n security, surety, pledge, bond, guarantee, warranty.

bait n lure, incentive, inducement, bribe, temptation, enticement, allurement, attraction.
🗷 disincentive.
◇ v tease, provoke, goad, irritate, annoy, irk, needle (infml), harass, persecute, torment.

balance v **1** STEADY, poise, stabilize, level, square, equalize, equate, match, counterbalance, counteract, neutralize, offset, adjust. **2** COMPARE, consider, weigh, estimate.
🗷 **1** unbalance, overbalance.
◇ n **1** EQUILIBRIUM, steadiness, stability, evenness, symmetry, equality, parity, equity, equivalence, correspondence. **2** COMPOSURE, self-possession, poise, equanimity. **3** REMAINDER, rest, residue, surplus, difference.
🗷 **1** imbalance, instability.

balcony n terrace, veranda, porch

(*US*), gallery, upper circle, gods.

bald *adj* **1** BALD-HEADED, hairless, smooth, uncovered. **2** BARE, naked, unadorned, plain, simple, severe, stark, barren, treeless. **3** *a bald statement*: forthright, direct, straight, outright, downright, straightforward.
⊟ 1 hairy, hirsute. **2** adorned.

bale *n* bundle, truss, pack, package, parcel.

balk, baulk *v* **1** FLINCH, recoil, shrink, jib, boggle, hesitate, refuse, resist, dodge, evade, shirk. **2** THWART, frustrate, foil, forestall, disconcert, baffle, hinder, obstruct, check, stall, bar, prevent, defeat, counteract.

ball¹ *n* sphere, globe, orb, globule, drop, conglomeration, pellet, pill, shot, bullet, slug (*infml*).

ball² *n* dance, dinner-dance, party, soirée, masquerade, carnival, assembly.

ballad *n* poem, song, folk song, shanty, carol, ditty.

ballet

Terms used in ballet include: à pointe, arabesque, attitude, ballerina, prima ballerina, ballon, barre, battement, batterie, capriole, chassé, choreography, company, corps de ballet, coryphée, divertissement, écarté, élévation, entrechat, five positions, fouetté, fouetté en tournant, glissade, jeté, grand jeté, leotard, pas de deux, pas seul, pirouette, plié, pointes, sur les pointes, port de bras, régisseur, point shoe, tutu.

ballot *n* poll, polling, vote, voting, election, referendum, plebiscite.

ban *v* forbid, prohibit, disallow, proscribe, bar, exclude, ostracize, outlaw, banish, suppress, restrict.
⊟ allow, permit, authorize.
◇ *n* prohibition, embargo, veto, boycott, stoppage, restriction, suppression, censorship, outlawry, proscription, condemnation, denunciation, curse, taboo.
⊟ permission, dispensation.

banal *adj* trite, commonplace, ordinary, everyday, humdrum, boring, unimaginative, hackneyed, clichéd, stock, stereotyped, corny (*infml*), stale, threadbare, tired, empty.
⊟ original, fresh, imaginative.

band¹ *n* strip, belt, ribbon, tape, bandage, binding, tie, ligature, bond, strap, cord, chain.

band² *n* **1** TROOP, gang, crew, group, herd, flock, party, body, association, company, society, club, clique. **2** *the band played on*: group, orchestra, ensemble.
◇ *v* group, gather, join, unite, ally, collaborate, consolidate, amalgamate, merge, affiliate, federate.
⊟ disband, disperse.

bandage *n* dressing, plaster, compress, ligature, tourniquet, swathe, swaddle.
◇ *v* bind, dress, cover, swathe, swaddle.

bandit *n* robber, thief, brigand, marauder, outlaw, highwayman, pirate, buccaneer, hijacker, cowboy, gunman, desperado, gangster.

bandy¹ *v* exchange, swap, trade, barter, interchange, reciprocate, pass, toss, throw.

bandy² *adj* bandy-legged, bow-legged, curved, bowed, bent, crooked.

bang *n* **1** BLOW, hit, knock, bump, crash, collision, smack, punch, thump, wallop (*infml*), stroke, whack (*infml*). **2** *a loud bang*: explosion, detonation, pop, boom, clap, peal, clang, clash, thud, thump, slam, noise, report, shot.
◇ *v* **1** STRIKE, hit, bash, knock, bump, rap, drum, hammer, pound, thump,

stamp. **2** EXPLODE, burst, detonate, boom, echo, resound, crash, slam, clatter, clang, peal, thunder.
◇ *adv* straight, directly, headlong, right, precisely, slap, smack, hard, noisily, suddenly, abruptly.

banish *v* expel, eject, evict, deport, transport, exile, outlaw, ban, bar, debar, exclude, shut out, ostracize, excommunicate, dismiss, oust, dislodge, remove, get rid of, discard, dispel, eliminate, eradicate.
☒ recall, welcome.

banishment *n* expulsion, eviction, deportation, expatriation, transportation, exile, outlawry, ostracism, excommunication.
☒ return, recall, welcome.

bank¹ *n* accumulation, fund, pool, reservoir, depository, repository, treasury, savings, reserve, store, stock, stockpile, hoard, cache.
◇ *v* deposit, save, keep, store, accumulate, stockpile.
☒ spend.

bank² *n* heap, pile, mass, mound, earthwork, ridge, embankment, rampart, side, slope, tilt, edge, shore.
◇ *v* **1** HEAP, pile, stack, mass, amass, accumulate, mound, drift. **2** SLOPE, incline, pitch, slant, tilt, tip.

bank³ *n* array, panel, bench, tier, group, rank, line, row, series, succession, sequence, train.

bankrupt *adj* in liquidation, insolvent, ruined, failed, beggared, destitute, impoverished, broke (*infml*), spent, exhausted, depleted, lacking.
☒ solvent, wealthy.
◇ *n* insolvent, debtor, pauper.

banner *n* flag, standard, colours, ensign, pennant, streamer.

banquet *n* feast, dinner, meal, repast (*fml*), treat.

banter *n* joking, jesting, pleasantry, badinage, repartee, word play, chaff, chaffing, kidding (*infml*), ribbing (*sl*),

derision, mockery, ridicule.

baptism *n* christening, dedication, beginning, initiation, introduction, debut, launch, launching, immersion, sprinkling, purification.

baptize *v* christen, name, call, term, style, title, introduce, initiate, enrol, recruit, immerse, sprinkle, purify, cleanse.

bar *n* **1** PUBLIC HOUSE, pub (*infml*), inn, tavern, saloon, lounge, counter. **2** SLAB, block, lump, chunk, wedge, ingot, nugget. **3** ROD, stick, shaft, pole, stake, stanchion, batten, crosspiece, rail, railing, paling, barricade. **4** OBSTACLE, impediment, hindrance, obstruction, barrier, stop, check, deterrent.
◇ *v* **1** EXCLUDE, debar, ban, forbid, prohibit, prevent, preclude, hinder, obstruct, restrain. **2** *bar the door*: barricade, lock, bolt, latch, fasten, secure.

barbarian *n* savage, brute, ruffian, hooligan, vandal, lout, oaf, boor, philistine, ignoramus, illiterate.

barbaric *adj* barbarous, primitive, wild, savage, fierce, ferocious, cruel, inhuman, brutal, brutish, uncivilized, uncouth, vulgar, coarse, crude, rude.
☒ humane, civilized, gracious.

barbarity *n* barbarousness, wildness, savagery, ferocity, viciousness, cruelty, inhumanity, brutality, brutishness, rudeness.
☒ civilization, humanity, civility.

barbed *adj* **1** PRICKLY, spiny, thorny, spiked, pronged, hooked, jagged, toothed, pointed. **2** *a barbed remark*: cutting, caustic, acid, hurtful, unkind, nasty, snide, hostile, critical.

bare *adj* **1** NAKED, nude, unclothed, undressed, stripped, denuded, uncovered, exposed. **2** PLAIN, simple, unadorned, unfurnished, empty, barren, bald, stark, basic, essential.
☒ **1** clothed. **2** decorated, detailed.

barely *adv* hardly, scarcely, only

just, just, almost.

bargain n **1** DEAL, transaction, contract, treaty, pact, promise, pledge, agreement, understanding, arrangement, negotiation. **2** DISCOUNT, reduction, snip, giveaway, special offer.
◇ v negotiate, haggle, deal, trade, traffic, barter, buy, sell, transact, contract, covenant, promise, agree.
• **bargain for** expect, anticipate, plan for, include, reckon on, look for, foresee, imagine, contemplate, consider.

barge v bump, hit, collide, impinge, shove, elbow, push (in), muscle in, butt in, interrupt, gatecrash, intrude, interfere.
◇ n canal-boat, flatboat, narrowboat, houseboat, lighter.

bark n yap, woof, yelp, snap, snarl, growl, bay, howl.
◇ v yap, woof, yelp, snap, snarl, growl, bay, howl.

baroque adj elaborate, ornate, rococo, florid, flamboyant, OTT (infml), exuberant, vigorous, bold, convoluted, overdecorated, overwrought, extravagant, fanciful, fantastic, grotesque.
⊡ plain, simple.

barracks n garrison, encampment, camp, guardhouse, quarters, billet, lodging, accommodation.

barrage n bombardment, shelling, gunfire, cannonade, broadside, volley, salvo, burst, assault, attack, onset, onslaught, deluge, torrent, stream, storm, hail, rain, shower, mass, profusion.

barrel n cask, keg, tun, butt, water-butt.

barren adj **1** ARID, dry, desert, desolate, waste, empty, flat, dull, uninteresting, uninspiring, uninformative, uninstructive, unrewarding, unproductive, profitless, unfruitful, fruitless,

pointless, useless, boring. **2** INFERTILE, sterile, childless, unprolific, unbearing.
⊡ **1** productive, fruitful, useful. **2** fertile.

barricade n blockade, obstruction, barrier, fence, stockade, bulwark, rampart, protection.
◇ v block, obstruct, bar, fortify, defend, protect.

barrier n **1** WALL, fence, railing, barricade, blockade, boom, rampart, fortification, ditch, frontier, boundary, bar, check. **2** a barrier to success: obstacle, hurdle, stumbling-block, impediment, obstruction, hindrance, handicap, limitation, restriction, drawback, difficulty.

bartender n barman, barmaid, barkeeper, publican.

barter v exchange, swap, trade, traffic, deal, negotiate, bargain, haggle.

base n **1** the base of the statue: bottom, foot, pedestal, plinth, stand, rest, support, foundation, bed, groundwork. **2** BASIS, fundamental, essential, principal, key, heart, core, essence, root, origin, source. **3** HEADQUARTERS, centre, post, station, camp, settlement, home, starting point.
◇ v establish, found, ground, locate, station, build, construct, derive, depend, hinge.

baseless adj groundless, unfounded, unsupported, unsubstantiated, unauthenticated, unconfirmed, unjustified, uncalled-for, gratuitous.
⊡ justifiable.

bashful adj shy, retiring, backward, reticent, reserved, unforthcoming, hesitant, shrinking, nervous, timid, coy, diffident, modest, inhibited, self-conscious, embarrassed, blushing, abashed, shamefaced, sheepish.
⊡ bold, confident, aggressive, in-your-face (infml).

basic adj fundamental, elementary,

primary, root, underlying, key, central, inherent, intrinsic, essential, indispensable, mission-critical (*infml*), vital, necessary, important. ⊟ inessential, minor, peripheral.

basically *adv* fundamentally, at bottom, at heart, inherently, intrinsically, essentially, primarily, principally.

basics *n* fundamentals, rudiments, principles, essentials, necessaries, practicalities, brass tacks (*infml*), grass roots, bedrock, rock bottom, core, facts.

basin *n* bowl, dish, sink, crater, cavity, hollow, depression, dip.

basis *n* base, bottom, footing, support, foundation, ground, groundwork, fundamental, premise, principle, essential, heart, core, thrust.

bask *v* sunbathe, lie, lounge, relax, laze, wallow, revel, delight in, enjoy, relish, savour.

basket *n* hamper, creel, pannier, punnet, bassinet.

bass *adj* deep, low, low-toned, grave, resonant.

bastion *n* stronghold, citadel, fortress, defence, bulwark, mainstay, support, prop, pillar, rock.

batch *n* lot, consignment, parcel, pack, bunch, set, assortment, collection, assemblage, group, contingent, amount, quantity.

bath *n* wash, scrub, soak, shower, douche, tub (*US*), Jacuzzi®.
◇ *v* bathe, wash, clean, soak, shower.

bathe *v* swim, bath, wet, moisten, immerse, wash, cleanse, rinse, soak, steep, flood, cover, suffuse.
◇ *n* swim, dip, paddle, wash, rinse, soak.

battalion *n* army, force, brigade, regiment, squadron, company, platoon, division, contingent, legion,

horde, multitude, throng, host, mass, herd.

batter *v* beat, pound, pummel, buffet, smash, dash, pelt, lash, thrash, wallop (*infml*), abuse, ill-treat, maltreat, manhandle, maul, assault, hurt, injure, bruise, disfigure, mangle, distress, crush, demolish, destroy, ruin, shatter.

battered *adj* beaten, abused, ill-treated, injured, bruised, weather-beaten, dilapidated, tumbledown, ramshackle, crumbling, damaged, crushed.

battle *n* war, warfare, hostilities, action, conflict, strife, combat, fight, engagement, encounter, fray, attack, skirmish, clash, struggle, contest, campaign, crusade, row, disagreement, dispute, debate, controversy.
◇ *v* fight, combat, war, feud, contend, struggle, strive, campaign, crusade, agitate, clamour, contest, argue, dispute.

battle-cry *n* war cry, war song, slogan, motto, watchword, catchword.

baulk *see* **balk**.

bay¹ *n* gulf, bight, arm, inlet, cove.

bay² *n* recess, alcove, niche, nook, opening, compartment, cubicle, booth, stall, carrel.

bay³ *v* howl, roar, bellow, bell, bawl, cry, holler (*infml*), bark.

bazaar *n* market, marketplace, mart, exchange, sale, fair, fête, bring-and-buy.

be *v* **1** EXIST, breathe, live, inhabit, reside, dwell. **2** STAY, remain, abide, last, endure, persist, continue, survive, stand, prevail, obtain. **3** HAPPEN, occur, arise, come about, take place, come to pass, befall, develop.

beach *n* sand, sands, shingle, shore, strand, seashore, seaside, water's edge, coast, seaboard.

beacon n signal, fire, watch fire, bonfire, light, beam, lighthouse, flare, rocket, sign.

bead n drop, droplet, drip, globule, glob (infml), blob, dot, bubble, pearl, jewel, pellet.

beaker n glass, tumbler, jar, cup, mug, tankard.

beam n 1 a beam of light: ray, shaft, gleam, glint, glimmer, glow. 2 PLANK, board, timber, rafter, joist, girder, spar, boom, bar, support.
◇ v 1 EMIT, broadcast, transmit, radiate, shine, glare, glitter, glow, glimmer. 2 SMILE, grin.

bear v 1 CARRY, convey, transport, move, take, bring. 2 HOLD, support, shoulder, uphold, sustain, maintain, harbour, cherish. 3 bear children: give birth to, breed, propagate, beget, engender, produce, generate, develop, yield, bring forth, give up. 4 TOLERATE, stand, put up with, endure, abide, suffer, permit, allow, admit.
• **bear on** refer to, relate to, affect, concern, involve.
• **bear out** confirm, endorse, support, uphold, prove, demonstrate, corroborate, substantiate, vindicate, justify.
• **bear up** persevere, soldier on, carry on, suffer, endure, survive, withstand.
• **bear with** tolerate, put up with, endure, suffer, forbear, be patient with, make allowances for.

bearable adj tolerable, endurable, sufferable, supportable, sustainable, acceptable, manageable.
⊞ unbearable, intolerable.

bearded adj unshaven, bristly, whiskered, tufted, hairy, hirsute, shaggy, bushy.
⊞ beardless, clean-shaven, smooth.

bearer n carrier, conveyor, porter, courier, messenger, runner, holder, possessor.

bearing n 1 have no bearing on the matter: relevance, significance, connection, relation, reference. 2 DEMEANOUR, manner, mien, air, aspect, attitude, behaviour, comportment, poise, deportment, carriage, posture.

bearings n orientation, position, situation, location, whereabouts, course, track, way, direction, aim.

beast n animal, creature, brute, monster, savage, barbarian, pig, swine, devil, fiend.

beat v 1 WHIP, flog, lash, tan (infml), cane, strap, thrash, lay into, hit, punch, strike, swipe, knock, bang, wham, bash, pound, hammer, batter, buffet, pelt, bruise. 2 PULSATE, pulse, throb, thump, race, palpitate, flutter, vibrate, quiver, tremble, shake, quake. 3 DEFEAT, trounce, best, worst, hammer (infml), slaughter (sl), conquer, overcome, overwhelm, vanquish, subdue, surpass, excel, outdo, outstrip, outrun.
◇ n 1 PULSATION, pulse, stroke, throb, thump, palpitation, flutter. 2 RHYTHM, time, tempo, metre, measure, rhyme, stress, accent. 3 a police officer's beat: round, rounds, territory, circuit, course, journey, way, path, route.
• **beat up** (infml) attack, assault, knock about, knock around, batter, do over (infml).

beaten adj 1 HAMMERED, stamped, forged, wrought, worked, formed, shaped, fashioned. 2 WHISKED, whipped, mixed, blended, frothy, foamy.

beating n 1 CORPORAL PUNISHMENT, chastisement, whipping, flogging, caning, thrashing. 2 DEFEAT, conquest, rout, ruin, downfall.

beautiful adj attractive, fair, pretty, lovely, good-looking, handsome, gorgeous, radiant, ravishing, stunning (infml), pleasing, appealing, alluring,

charming, delightful, fine, exquisite.
ⓔ ugly, plain, hideous.

beautify v embellish, enhance,
improve, grace, gild, garnish,
decorate, ornament, deck, bedeck,
adorn, array, glamorize, titivate
(*infml*), tart up (*sl*).
ⓔ disfigure, spoil.

beauty n attractiveness, fairness,
prettiness, loveliness, (good) looks,
handsomeness, glamour, appeal,
allure, charm, grace, elegance,
symmetry, excellence.
ⓔ ugliness, repulsiveness.

because *conj* as, for, since, owing
to, on account of, by reason of,
thanks to.

beckon v summon, motion, gesture,
signal, nod, wave, gesticulate, call,
invite, attract, pull, draw, lure, allure,
entice, tempt, coax.

become v 1 *become old-fashioned*:
turn, grow, get, change into, develop
into. 2 SUIT, befit, flatter, enhance,
grace, embellish, ornament, set off,
harmonize.

bed n 1 *lie down on the bed*:
divan, couch, bunk, berth, cot,
mattress, pallet, sack (*sl*). 2 LAYER,
stratum, substratum, matrix, base,
bottom, foundation, groundwork,
watercourse, channel. 3 *bed of
flowers*: garden, border, patch, plot.

Types of bed include: four-poster,
chaise-longue, day bed, bed-
settee, divan, camp bed, bunk,
water bed, cot, cradle.

---

bedclothes n bedding, bed-linen,
sheets, pillowcases, pillowslips,
covers, blankets, bedspreads,
coverlets, quilts, eiderdowns,
pillows.

bedraggled *adj* untidy, unkempt,
dishevelled, disordered, scruffy,
slovenly, messy, dirty, muddy,
muddied, soiled, wet, sodden,

drenched.
ⓔ neat, tidy, clean.

before *adv* ahead, in front, in
advance, sooner, earlier, formerly,
previously.
ⓔ after, later.

beforehand *adv* in advance,
preliminarily, already, before,
previously, earlier, sooner.

befriend v help, aid, assist,
succour, back, support, stand by,
uphold, sustain, comfort, encourage,
welcome, favour, benefit, take under
one's wing, make friends with, get
to know.
ⓔ neglect, oppose.

beg v request, require, desire, crave,
beseech, plead, entreat, implore,
pray, supplicate, petition, solicit,
cadge, scrounge, sponge.

beggar n mendicant, supplicant,
pauper, down-and-out, tramp,
vagrant, cadger, scrounger, sponger.

begin v start, commence, set about,
embark on, set in motion, kick in
(*infml*), activate, originate, initiate,
introduce, found, institute, instigate,
arise, spring, emerge, appear.
ⓔ end, finish, cease.

beginner n novice, tiro, starter,
learner, trainee, apprentice, student,
freshman, fresher, recruit, cub,
tenderfoot, fledgling.
ⓔ veteran, old hand, expert.

beginning n start, commencement,
onset, outset, opening, preface,
prelude, introduction, initiation,
establishment, inauguration, birth,
inception, starting point, dawn,
origin, source, fountainhead, root,
seed, emergence, rise.
ⓔ end, finish.

begrudge v resent, grudge, mind,
object to, envy, covet, stint.
ⓔ allow.

beguile v 1 CHARM, enchant,
bewitch, captivate, amuse, entertain,

divert, distract, occupy, engross.
2 DECEIVE, fool, hoodwink, dupe,
trick, cheat, delude, mislead.

behalf n sake, account, good,
interest, benefit, advantage, profit,
name, authority, side, support.

behave v act, react, respond, work,
function, run, operate, perform,
conduct oneself, acquit oneself,
comport oneself (fml).

behaviour n conduct, comportment
(fml), manner, manners, action,
actions, doings, dealings, ways,
habits, reaction, response, functioning,
operation, performance.

behead v decapitate, execute,
guillotine.

behind prep **1** FOLLOWING, after,
later than, causing, responsible for,
instigating, initiating. **2** SUPPORTING,
backing, for.
◇ adv after, following, next,
subsequently, behindhand, late,
overdue, in arrears, in debt.
◇ n rump, rear, posterior (infml),
buttocks, seat, bottom, backside
(infml), bum (sl), butt (US infml),
arse (sl), ass (US sl), tail (infml).

beige adj buff, fawn, mushroom,
camel, sandy, khaki, coffee, neutral.

being n **1** EXISTENCE, actuality, reality,
life, animation, essence, substance,
nature, soul, spirit. **2** CREATURE,
animal, beast, human being, mortal,
person, individual, thing, entity.

belated adj late, tardy, overdue,
delayed, behindhand, unpunctual.
⊞ punctual, timely.

belch v burp (infml), hiccup, emit,
discharge, disgorge, spew.
◇ n burp (infml), hiccup.

beleaguered adj harassed,
pestered, badgered, bothered,
worried, vexed, plagued, beset,
persecuted, surrounded, besieged.

belief n **1** CONVICTION, persuasion,
credit, trust, reliance, confidence,

assurance, certainty, sureness,
presumption, expectation, feeling,
intuition, impression, notion,
theory, view, opinion, judgement.
2 IDEOLOGY, faith, creed, doctrine,
dogma, tenet, principle.
⊞ **1** disbelief.

believable adj credible, imaginable,
conceivable, acceptable, plausible,
possible, likely, probable, reliable,
authoritative, trustworthy.
⊞ unbelievable, incredible,
unconvincing.

believe v accept, wear (infml),
swallow (infml), credit, trust, count
on, depend on, rely on, swear
by, hold, maintain, postulate,
assume, presume, gather, speculate,
conjecture, guess, imagine, think,
consider, reckon, suppose, deem,
judge.
⊞ disbelieve, doubt.

believer n convert, proselyte,
disciple, follower, adherent, devotee,
zealot, supporter, upholder.
⊞ unbeliever, sceptic.

belittle v minimize, play down,
dismiss, underrate, undervalue,
underestimate, lessen, diminish,
detract from, deprecate, decry,
disparage, run down, deride, scorn,
ridicule.
⊞ exaggerate, praise.

belligerent adj aggressive, militant,
argumentative, quarrelsome,
contentious, combative, violent,
pugnacious, bullying, antagonistic,
warring, warlike, bellicose.
⊞ peaceable.

bellow v roar, yell, shout, bawl, cry,
scream, shriek, howl, clamour.

belong v fit, go with, be part of,
attach to, link up with, tie up with,
be connected with, relate to.

belongings n possessions, property,
chattels, goods, effects, things, stuff
(infml), gear (infml), paraphernalia.

beloved adj loved, adored,

cherished, treasured, prized, precious, pet, favourite, dearest, dear, darling, admired, revered.

below adv beneath, under, underneath, down, lower, lower down.
⊡ above.
◇ prep 1 UNDER, underneath, beneath. 2 INFERIOR TO, lesser than, subordinate to, subject to.
⊡ above.

belt n 1 SASH, girdle, waistband, girth, strap. 2 STRIP, band, swathe, stretch, tract, area, region, district, zone, layer.

bemused adj confused, muddled, bewildered, puzzled, perplexed, dazed, befuddled, stupefied.
⊡ clear-headed, clear, lucid.

bench n 1 SEAT, form, settle, pew, ledge, counter, table, stall, workbench, worktable. 2 COURT, courtroom, tribunal, judiciary, judicature, judge, magistrate.

bend v curve, turn, deflect, swerve, veer, diverge, twist, contort, flex, shape, mould, buckle, bow, incline, lean, stoop, crouch.
⊡ straighten.
◇ n curvature, curve, arc, bow, loop, hook, crook, elbow, angle, corner, turn, twist, zigzag.

beneath adv below, under, underneath, lower, lower down.
◇ prep 1 UNDER, underneath, below, lower than. 2 UNWORTHY OF, unbefitting.

benefactor n philanthropist, patron, sponsor, angel (infml), backer, supporter, promoter, donor, contributor, subscriber, provider, helper, friend, well-wisher.
⊡ opponent, persecutor.

beneficial adj advantageous, favourable, useful, helpful, profitable, rewarding, valuable, improving, edifying, wholesome.
⊡ harmful, detrimental, useless.

beneficiary n payee, receiver, recipient, inheritor, legatee, heir, heiress, successor.

benefit n advantage, good, welfare, interest, favour, help, aid, assistance, service, use, avail, gain, profit, asset, blessing.
⊡ disadvantage, harm, damage.
◇ v help, aid, assist, serve, avail, advantage, profit, improve, enhance, better, further, advance, promote.
⊡ hinder, harm, undermine.

benevolent adj philanthropic, humanitarian, charitable, generous, liberal, munificent, altruistic, benign, humane, kind, kindly, well-disposed, compassionate, caring, considerate.
⊡ mean, selfish, malevolent.

benign adj 1 BENEVOLENT, good, gracious, gentle, kind, obliging, friendly, amiable, genial, sympathetic. 2 a benign tumour: curable, harmless. 3 FAVOURABLE, propitious, beneficial, temperate, mild, warm, refreshing, restorative, wholesome.
⊡ 1 hostile. 2 malignant. 3 harmful, unpleasant.

bent adj 1 ANGLED, curved, bowed, arched, folded, doubled, twisted, hunched, stooped. 2 (infml) DISHONEST, crooked (infml), illegal, criminal, corrupt, untrustworthy.
⊡ 1 straight, upright. 2 honest.
◇ n tendency, inclination, leaning, preference, ability, capacity, faculty, aptitude, facility, gift, talent, knack, flair, forte.
• bent on determined, resolved, set, fixed, inclined, disposed.

bequeath v will, leave, bestow, gift, endow, grant, settle, hand down, pass on, impart, transmit, assign, entrust, commit.

bequest n legacy, inheritance, heritage, trust, bestowal, endowment, gift, donation, estate, devisal, settlement.

bereavement n loss, deprivation, dispossession, death.

bereft adj deprived, robbed, stripped, destitute, devoid, lacking, wanting, minus.

berserk adj mad, crazy, demented, insane, deranged, frantic, frenzied, wild, raging, furious, violent, rabid, raving.
⊡ sane, calm.

berth n 1 BED, bunk, hammock, billet. 2 MOORING, anchorage, quay, wharf, dock, harbour, port.

beside prep alongside, abreast of, next to, adjacent, abutting, bordering, neighbouring, next door to, close to, near, overlooking.

besides adv also, as well, too, in addition, additionally, further, furthermore, moreover.
◇ prep apart from, other than, in addition to, over and above.

besiege v 1 LAY SIEGE TO, blockade, surround, encircle, confine.
2 TROUBLE, bother, importune, assail, beset, beleaguer, harass, pester, badger, nag, hound, plague.

besotted adj infatuated, doting, obsessed, smitten, hypnotized, spellbound, intoxicated.
⊡ indifferent, disenchanted.

best adj optimum, optimal, premium, first, foremost, leading, unequalled, unsurpassed, matchless, incomparable, supreme, greatest, highest, largest, finest, excellent, outstanding, superlative, first-rate, first-class, top-drawer (infml), blue-chip (infml), perfect.
⊡ worst.
◇ adv greatly, extremely, exceptionally, excellently, superlatively.
⊡ worst.
◇ n finest, cream, prime, élite, top, first, pick, choice, favourite.
⊡ worst.

bestow v award, present, grant, confer, endow, bequeath, commit, entrust, impart, transmit, allot, apportion, accord, give, donate, lavish.
⊡ withhold, deprive.

bet n wager, flutter (infml), gamble, speculation, risk, venture, stake, ante, bid, pledge.
◇ v wager, gamble, punt, speculate, risk, hazard, chance, venture, lay, stake, bid, pledge.

betray v 1 betray a friend: inform on, shop (sl), sell (out), double-cross, stab in the back, desert, abandon, forsake. 2 DISCLOSE, give away, tell, divulge, expose, reveal, show, manifest.
⊡ 1 defend, protect. 2 conceal, hide.

betrayal n treachery, treason, sell-out, disloyalty, backstabbing, unfaithfulness, double-dealing, duplicity, deception, trickery, falseness.
⊡ loyalty, protection.

betrayer n traitor, Judas, informer, grass (sl), supergrass (sl), double-crosser, backstabber, deceiver, conspirator, renegade, apostate.
⊡ protector, supporter.

better adj 1 SUPERIOR, bigger, larger, longer, greater, worthier, finer, surpassing, preferable. 2 IMPROVING, progressing, recovering, on the mend, fitter, healthier, stronger, recovered, restored.
⊡ 1 inferior. 2 worse.
◇ v 1 IMPROVE, ameliorate, enhance, raise, further, promote, forward, reform, mend, correct. 2 SURPASS, top, beat, outdo, outstrip, overtake.
⊡ 1 worsen, deteriorate.

between prep mid, amid, amidst, among, amongst.

beverage n drink, draught, liquor, liquid refreshment.

bevy n gathering, band, company, troupe, group, flock, gaggle, pack, bunch, crowd, throng.

beware v watch out, look out, mind, take heed, steer clear of, avoid, shun, guard against.

bewilder v confuse, muddle, disconcert, confound, bamboozle (*infml*), baffle, puzzle, perplex, mystify, daze, stupefy, disorient.

bewildered adj confused, muddled, uncertain, disoriented, nonplussed, bamboozled (*infml*), baffled, puzzled, perplexed, mystified, bemused, surprised, stunned.
✦ unperturbed, collected.

bewitch v charm, enchant, allure, beguile, spellbind, possess, captivate, enrapture, obsess, fascinate, entrance, hypnotize.

beyond prep past, further than, apart from, away from, remote from, out of range of, out of reach of, above, over, superior to.

bias n slant, angle, distortion, bent, leaning, inclination, tendency, propensity, partiality, favouritism, prejudice, one-sidedness, unfairness, bigotry, intolerance.
✦ impartiality, fairness.

biased adj slanted, angled, distorted, warped, twisted, loaded, weighted, influenced, swayed, predisposed, partial, prejudiced, one-sided, unfair, bigoted, blinkered, jaundiced.
✦ impartial, fair.

bicker v squabble, row, quarrel, wrangle, argue, scrap, spar, fight, clash, disagree, dispute.
✦ agree.

bicycle n cycle, bike (*infml*), two-wheeler, pushbike, racer, mountain bike, tandem, penny-farthing.

bid v 1 ASK, request, desire, instruct, direct, command, enjoin, require, charge, call, summon, invite, solicit. 2 *he bid more than the painting was worth*: offer, proffer, tender, submit, propose.
◇ n 1 OFFER, tender, sum, amount, price, advance, submission, proposal. 2 ATTEMPT, effort, try, go (*infml*), endeavour, venture.

big adj 1 LARGE, great, sizable, considerable, substantial, huge, enormous, immense, massive, colossal, gigantic, mammoth, burly, bulky, extensive, spacious, vast, voluminous. 2 IMPORTANT, significant, momentous, serious, main, principal, eminent, prominent, influential. 3 *that's big of you*: generous, magnanimous, gracious, unselfish.
✦ 1 small, little. 2 insignificant, unknown.

bigot n chauvinist, sectarian, racist, sexist, dogmatist, fanatic, zealot.
✦ liberal, humanitarian.

bigoted adj prejudiced, biased, intolerant, illiberal, narrow-minded, narrow, blinkered, closed, dogmatic, opinionated, obstinate.
✦ tolerant, liberal, broad-minded, enlightened.

bigotry n prejudice, discrimination, bias, injustice, unfairness, intolerance, narrow-mindedness, chauvinism, jingoism, sectarianism, racism, racialism, sexism, dogmatism, fanaticism.
✦ tolerance.

bilious adj 1 IRRITABLE, choleric, cross, grumpy, crotchety, testy, grouchy, peevish. 2 SICK, queasy, nauseated, sickly, out of sorts (*infml*).

bill n 1 INVOICE, statement, account, charges, reckoning, tally, score. 2 CIRCULAR, leaflet, handout, bulletin, handbill, broadsheet, advertisement, notice, poster, placard, playbill, programme. 3 *parliamentary bill*: proposal, measure, legislation.
◇ v invoice, charge, debit.

billet n 1 ACCOMMODATION, quarters, barracks, lodging, housing, berth. 2 EMPLOYMENT, post, occupation.

billow v swell, expand, bulge, puff

out, fill out, balloon, rise, heave, surge, roll, undulate.

bind v 1 ATTACH, fasten, secure, clamp, stick, tie, lash, truss, strap, bandage, cover, dress, wrap. 2 OBLIGE, force, compel, constrain, necessitate, restrict, confine, restrain, hamper.

binding adj obligatory, compulsory, mandatory, necessary, requisite, permanent, conclusive, irrevocable, unalterable, indissoluble, unbreakable, strict.
◊ n border, edging, trimming, tape, bandage, covering, wrapping.

biography n life story, life, history, autobiography, memoirs, recollections, curriculum vitae, account, record.

biology

Biology terms include: animal kingdom, bacillus, bacteria, cell, chromosome, class, clone, coccus, corpuscle, cytoplasm, deoxyribonucleic acid (DNA), diffusion, ecosystem, embryo, enzyme, evolution, excretion, flora and fauna, food chain, fossil, gene, genetic engineering, genetically modified, germ, hereditary, meiosis, membrane, metabolism, micro-organism, microbe, mitosis, molecule, mutation, natural selection, nucleus, nutrition, order, organism, osmosis, parasitism, photosynthesis, pollution, protein, protoplasm, reproduction, respiration, ribonucleic acid (RNA), ribosome, secretion, species, symbiosis, virus.

bird

Birds include: sparrow, thrush, starling, blackbird, blue tit, chaffinch, greenfinch, bullfinch, dunnock, robin, wagtail, swallow, tit, wren, martin, swift, crow, magpie, dove, pigeon, skylark, nightingale, linnet, warbler, jay, jackdaw, rook, raven, cuckoo, woodpecker, yellowhammer; duck, mallard, eider, teal, swan, goose, heron, stork, flamingo, pelican, kingfisher, moorhen, coot, lapwing, peewit, plover, curlew, snipe, avocet, seagull, guillemot, tern, petrel, crane, bittern, albatross, gannet, cormorant, auk, puffin, dipper; eagle, owl, hawk, sparrow-hawk, falcon, kestrel, osprey, buzzard, vulture, condor; emu, ostrich, kiwi, peacock, penguin; chicken, grouse, partridge, pheasant, quail, turkey; canary, budgerigar or budgie (infml), cockatiel, cockatoo, lovebird, parakeet, parrot, macaw, toucan, myna bird, mockingbird, kookaburra, bird of paradise.

birth n 1 CHILDBIRTH, parturition, confinement, delivery, nativity. 2 of noble birth: ancestry, family, parentage, descent, line, lineage, genealogy, pedigree, blood, stock, race, extraction, background, breeding. 3 BEGINNING, rise, emergence, origin, source, derivation.

birthplace n place of origin, native town, native country, fatherland, mother country, roots, provenance, source, fount.

bisect v halve, divide, separate, split, intersect, cross, fork, bifurcate.

bit n fragment, part, segment, piece, slice, crumb, morsel, scrap, atom, mite, whit, jot, iota, grain, speck.
• **bit by bit** gradually, little by little, step by step, piecemeal.
⊞ wholesale.

bitchy adj catty, snide, nasty, mean, spiteful, malicious, vindictive, backbiting, venomous, cruel, vicious.
⊞ kind.

bite v 1 CHEW, masticate, munch,

gnaw, nibble, champ, crunch, crush.
2 *the dog bit her hand*: nip, pierce,
wound, tear, rend. **3** SMART, sting,
tingle. **4** GRIP, hold, seize, pinch, take
effect.
◇ *n* **1** NIP, wound, sting, smarting,
pinch. **2** *a bite to eat*: snack,
refreshment, mouthful, morsel, taste.
3 PUNGENCY, piquancy, kick (*infml*),
punch.

biting *adj* **1** COLD, freezing, bitter,
harsh, severe. **2** CUTTING, incisive,
piercing, penetrating, raw, stinging,
sharp, tart, caustic, scathing, cynical,
hurtful.
▣ **1** mild. **2** bland.

bitter *adj* **1** SOUR, tart, sharp, acrid,
acid, vinegary, unsweetened.
2 RESENTFUL, embittered, jaundiced,
cynical, rancorous, acrimonious,
acerbic, hostile. **3** INTENSE, severe,
harsh, fierce, cruel, merciless,
savage, painful, stinging, biting,
freezing, raw.
▣ **1** sweet. **2** contented. **3** mild.

bizarre *adj* strange, odd, queer,
curious, weird, peculiar, eccentric,
way-out (*infml*), off-the-wall (*infml*),
left-field (*US infml*), outlandish,
ludicrous, ridiculous, fantastic,
extravagant, grotesque, freakish,
abnormal, deviant, unusual,
extraordinary.
▣ normal, ordinary.

black *adj* **1** JET-BLACK, coal-black,
jet, ebony, sable, inky, sooty, dusky,
swarthy. **2** DARK, unlit, moonless,
starless, overcast, dingy, gloomy,
sombre, funereal. **3** FILTHY, dirty,
soiled, grimy, grubby.
▣ **1** white. **2** bright. **3** clean.
◇ *v* boycott, blacklist, ban, bar,
taboo.
● **black out 1** FAINT, pass out,
collapse, flake out (*infml*). **2** DARKEN,
eclipse, cover up, conceal, suppress,
withhold, censor, gag.

blacken *v* **1** DARKEN, dirty, soil,
smudge, cloud. **2** DEFAME, malign,

slander, libel, vilify, revile, denigrate,
detract, smear, besmirch, sully,
stain, tarnish, taint, defile, discredit,
dishonour.
▣ **2** praise, enhance.

blackmail *n* extortion, chantage,
hush money (*infml*), intimidation,
protection, pay-off, ransom.
◇ *v* extort, bleed, milk, squeeze,
hold to ransom, threaten, lean
on (*infml*), force, compel, coerce,
demand.

blackout *n* **1** *a news blackout*:
suppression, censorship, cover-
up (*infml*), concealment, secrecy.
2 FAINT, coma, unconsciousness,
oblivion. **3** POWER CUT, power failure.

blade *n* edge, knife, dagger, sword,
scalpel, razor, vane.

blame *n* censure, criticism, stick
(*sl*), reprimand, reproof, reproach,
recrimination, condemnation,
accusation, charge, incrimination,
guilt, culpability, fault, responsibility,
accountability, liability, onus.
◇ *v* accuse, charge, tax, reprimand,
chide, reprove, upbraid, reprehend,
admonish, rebuke, reproach,
censure, criticize, find fault with,
disapprove, condemn.
▣ exonerate, vindicate.

blameless *adj* innocent, guiltless,
clear, faultless, perfect, unblemished,
stainless, virtuous, sinless, upright,
above reproach, irreproachable,
unblamable, unimpeachable,
squeaky clean (*infml*).
▣ guilty, blameworthy.

blanch *v* blench, whiten, pale, fade,
bleach.
▣ colour, blush, redden.

bland *adj* boring, monotonous,
humdrum, tedious, dull, uninspiring,
uninteresting, unexciting,
nondescript, characterless, flat,
insipid, tasteless, weak, mild,
smooth, soft, gentle, non-irritant.
▣ lively, stimulating, sharp.

blank adj **1** a blank page: empty, unfilled, void, clear, bare, unmarked, pristine, plain, clean, white. **2** EXPRESSIONLESS, deadpan, poker-faced, impassive, apathetic, glazed, vacant, uncomprehending.
◇ n space, gap, break, void, emptiness, vacancy, vacuity, nothingness, vacuum.

blanket n covering, coating, coat, layer, film, carpet, rug, cloak, mantle, cover, sheet, envelope, wrapper, wrapping.
◇ v cover, coat, eclipse, hide, conceal, mask, cloak, surround, muffle, deaden, obscure, cloud.

blare v trumpet, clamour, roar, blast, boom, resound, ring, peal, clang, hoot, toot, honk.

blasé adj nonchalant, offhand, unimpressed, unmoved, unexcited, jaded, weary, bored, uninterested, uninspired, apathetic, indifferent, cool, unconcerned.
⊡ excited, enthusiastic.

blaspheme v profane, desecrate, swear, curse, imprecate, damn, execrate, revile, abuse.

blasphemous adj profane, impious, sacrilegious, imprecatory, godless, ungodly, irreligious, irreverent.

blasphemy n profanity, curse, expletive, imprecation, cursing, swearing, execration, impiety, irreverence, sacrilege, desecration, violation, outrage.

blast n **1** EXPLOSION, detonation, bang, crash, clap, crack, volley, burst, outburst, discharge. **2** a blast of cold air: draught, gust, gale, squall, storm, tempest. **3** SOUND, blow, blare, roar, boom, peal, hoot, wail, scream, shriek.
◇ v **1** EXPLODE, blow up, burst, shatter, destroy, demolish, ruin, assail, attack. **2** SOUND, blare, roar, boom, peal, hoot, wail, scream, shriek.

blatant adj flagrant, brazen, barefaced, arrant, open, overt, undisguised, ostentatious, glaring, conspicuous, obtrusive, prominent, pronounced, obvious, sheer, outright, unmitigated.

blaze n fire, flames, conflagration, bonfire, flare-up, explosion, blast, burst, outburst, radiance, brilliance, glare, flash, gleam, glitter, glow, light, flame.
◇ v burn, flame, flare (up), erupt, explode, burst, fire, flash, gleam, glare, beam, shine, glow.

bleach v whiten, blanch, decolorize, fade, pale, lighten.

bleak adj **1** GLOOMY, sombre, leaden, grim, dreary, dismal, depressing, joyless, cheerless, comfortless, hopeless, discouraging, disheartening. **2** COLD, chilly, raw, weather-beaten, unsheltered, windy, windswept, exposed, open, barren, bare, empty, desolate, gaunt.
⊡ **1** bright, cheerful.

bleed v **1** HAEMORRHAGE, gush, spurt, flow, run, exude, weep, ooze, seep, trickle. **2** DRAIN, suck dry, exhaust, squeeze, milk, sap, reduce, deplete.

blemish n flaw, imperfection, defect, fault, disfigurement, deformity, birthmark, naevus, spot, mark, speck, smudge, blotch, blot, stain, taint.
◇ v flaw, deface, disfigure, spoil, mar, damage, impair, spot, mark, blot, blotch, stain, sully, taint, tarnish.

blend v **1** MERGE, amalgamate, coalesce, compound, synthesize, fuse, unite, combine, mix, mingle. **2** HARMONIZE, complement, fit, match.
⊡ **1** separate.
◇ n compound, composite, alloy, amalgam, amalgamation, synthesis, fusion, combination, union, mix, mixture, concoction.

bless v **1** ANOINT, consecrate, sanctify, hallow, dedicate, ordain.

2 PRAISE, extol, magnify, glorify, exalt, thank. **3** APPROVE, countenance, favour, grace, bestow, endow, provide.
€ **1** curse. **2** condemn.

blessed adj **1** HOLY, hallowed, sacred, sanctified, revered, adored, divine. **2** HAPPY, contented, glad, joyful, joyous, lucky, fortunate, prosperous, favoured, endowed.
€ **1** cursed.

blessing n **1** CONSECRATION, dedication, benediction, grace, thanksgiving, invocation. **2** BENEFIT, advantage, favour, godsend, windfall, gift, gain, profit, help, service. **3** give a proposal one's blessing: approval, concurrence, backing, support, authority, sanction, consent, permission, leave.
€ **2** curse, blight. **3** condemnation.

blight n curse, trouble, bane, evil, scourge, affliction, disease, cancer, canker, fungus, mildew, rot, decay, pollution, contamination, corruption, infestation.
€ blessing, boon.
◇ v spoil, mar, injure, undermine, ruin, wreck, crush, shatter, destroy, annihilate, blast, wither, shrivel, frustrate, disappoint.
€ bless.

blind adj **1** SIGHTLESS, visually impaired, unsighted, unseeing, eyeless, purblind, partially sighted. **2** IMPETUOUS, impulsive, hasty, rash, reckless, wild, mad, indiscriminate, careless, heedless, mindless, unthinking, unreasoning, irrational. **3** blind to their needs: ignorant, oblivious, unaware, unconscious, unobservant, inattentive, neglectful, indifferent, insensitive, thoughtless, inconsiderate. **4** CLOSED, obstructed, hidden, concealed, obscured.
€ **1** sighted. **2** careful, cautious. **3** aware, sensitive.
◇ n screen, cover, cloak, mask, camouflage, masquerade, front,

façade, distraction, smokescreen, cover-up (infml).

bliss n blissfulness, ecstasy, euphoria, rapture, joy, happiness, gladness, blessedness, paradise, heaven.
€ misery, hell, damnation.

blissful adj ecstatic, euphoric, elated, enraptured, rapturous, delighted, enchanted, joyful, joyous, happy.
€ miserable, wretched.

blister n sore, swelling, cyst, boil, abscess, ulcer, pustule, pimple, carbuncle.

blizzard n snowstorm, squall, storm, tempest.

bloated adj swollen, puffy, blown up, inflated, distended, dilated, expanded, enlarged, turgid, bombastic.
€ thin, shrunken, shrivelled.

blob n drop, droplet, globule, glob (infml), bead, pearl, bubble, dab, spot, gob, lump, mass, ball, pellet, pill.

block n **1** a block of stone: piece, lump, mass, chunk, hunk, square, cube, brick, bar. **2** OBSTACLE, bar, barrier, jam, blockage, stoppage, resistance, obstruction, impediment, hindrance, let, delay.
◇ v choke, clog, plug, stop up, dam up, close, bar, obstruct, impede, hinder, stonewall, stop, check, arrest, halt, thwart, scotch, deter.

blockade n barrier, barricade, siege, obstruction, restriction, stoppage, closure.

blockage n blocking, obstruction, stoppage, occlusion, block, clot, jam, log-jam, gridlock, congestion, hindrance, impediment.

blond, blonde adj fair, flaxen, golden, fair-haired, golden-haired, light-coloured, bleached.

blood n extraction, birth, descent,

lineage, family, kindred, relations, ancestry, descendants, kinship, relationship.

bloodcurdling adj horrifying, chilling, spine-chilling, hair-raising, white-knuckle (infml), terrifying, frightening, scary, dreadful, fearful, horrible, horrid, horrendous.

bloodshed n killing, murder, slaughter, massacre, bloodbath, butchery, carnage, gore, bloodletting.

bloodthirsty adj murderous, homicidal, warlike, savage, barbaric, barbarous, brutal, ferocious, vicious, cruel, inhuman, ruthless.

bloody adj bleeding, bloodstained, gory, sanguinary, murderous, savage, brutal, ferocious, fierce, cruel.

bloom n 1 BLOSSOM, flower, bud. 2 PRIME, heyday, perfection, blush, flush, glow, rosiness, beauty, radiance, lustre, health, vigour, freshness.
◇ v bud, sprout, grow, wax, develop, mature, blossom, flower, blow, open.
⊞ fade, wither.

blossom n bloom, flower, bud.
◇ v develop, mature, bloom, flower, blow, flourish, thrive, prosper, succeed.
⊞ fade, wither.

blot n spot, stain, smudge, blotch, smear, mark, speck, blemish, flaw, fault, defect, taint, disgrace.
◇ v spot, mark, stain, smudge, blur, sully, taint, tarnish, spoil, mar, disfigure, disgrace.
• **blot out** obliterate, cancel, delete, erase, expunge, darken, obscure, shadow, eclipse.

blotch n patch, splodge, splotch, splash, smudge, blot, spot, mark, stain, blemish.

blotchy adj spotty, spotted, patchy, uneven, smeary, blemished, reddened, inflamed.

blow¹ v 1 BREATHE, exhale, pant, puff, waft, fan, flutter, float, flow, stream, rush, whirl, whisk, sweep, fling, buffet, drive, blast. 2 blow a horn: play, sound, pipe, trumpet, toot, blare.
◇ n puff, draught, flurry, gust, blast, wind, gale, squall, tempest.
• **blow over** die down, subside, end, finish, cease, pass, vanish, disappear, dissipate, fizzle out, peter out.
• **blow up 1** EXPLODE, go off, detonate, burst, blast, bomb. 2 LOSE ONE'S TEMPER, blow one's top (infml), erupt, hit the roof (infml), rage, go mad (infml). 3 INFLATE, pump up, swell, fill (out), puff up, bloat, distend, dilate, expand, enlarge, magnify, exaggerate, overstate.

blow² n 1 a blow on the head: concussion, box, cuff, clip, clout, swipe, biff (infml), bash, slap, smack, whack (infml), wallop (infml), belt (infml), buffet, bang, clap, knock, rap, stroke, thump, punch. 2 MISFORTUNE, affliction, reverse, setback, comedown, disappointment, upset, jolt, shock, bombshell, calamity, catastrophe, disaster.

blowy adj breezy, windy, fresh, blustery, gusty, squally, stormy.

bludgeon v 1 BEAT, strike, club, batter, cosh (sl), cudgel. 2 FORCE, coerce, bulldoze, badger, hector, harass, browbeat, bully, terrorize, intimidate.

blue adj 1 AZURE, sapphire, cobalt, ultramarine, navy, indigo, aquamarine, turquoise, cyan. 2 DEPRESSED, low, down in the dumps (infml), dejected, downcast, dispirited, downhearted, despondent, gloomy, glum, dismal, sad, unhappy, miserable, melancholy, morose, fed up (infml). 3 a blue joke: obscene, offensive, indecent, improper, coarse, vulgar, lewd, dirty, pornographic, bawdy, smutty, near the bone, near the knuckle, risqué.

⊠ 2 cheerful, happy. 3 decent, clean.

blueprint n archetype, prototype, model, pattern, design, outline, draft, sketch, pilot, guide, plan, scheme, project.

bluff v lie, pretend, feign, sham, fake, deceive, delude, mislead, hoodwink, blind, bamboozle (infml), fool.
◇ n lie, idle boast, bravado, humbug, pretence, show, sham, fake, fraud, trick, scam (infml), subterfuge, deceit, deception.

blunder n mistake, error, solecism, howler (infml), bloomer (infml), boob (infml), clanger (infml), inaccuracy, slip, gaffe, indiscretion, faux pas, slip-up (infml), oversight, fault, cock-up (sl).
◇ v stumble, flounder, bumble, err, slip up (infml), miscalculate, misjudge, bungle, botch, fluff (infml), mismanage, cock up (sl).

blunt adj 1 UNSHARPENED, dull, worn, pointless, rounded, stubbed. 2 FRANK, candid, direct, forthright, unceremonious, explicit, honest, plain-spoken, downright, outspoken, tactless, insensitive, rude, impolite, uncivil, brusque, curt, abrupt.
⊠ 1 sharp, pointed. 2 subtle, tactful.
◇ v dull, take the edge off, dampen, soften, deaden, numb, anaesthetize, alleviate, allay, abate, weaken.
⊠ sharpen, intensify.

blur v smear, smudge, mist, fog, befog, cloud, becloud, blear, dim, darken, obscure, mask, conceal, soften.
◇ n smear, smudge, blotch, haze, mist, fog, cloudiness, fuzziness, indistinctness, muddle, confusion, dimness, obscurity.

blurred adj out of focus, fuzzy, unclear, indistinct, vague, ill-defined, faint, hazy, misty, foggy, cloudy, bleary, dim, obscure, confused.
⊠ clear, distinct.

blurt out v exclaim, cry, gush, spout, utter, tell, reveal, disclose, divulge, blab (infml), let out, leak, let slip, spill the beans (infml).
⊠ bottle up, hush up.

blush v flush, redden, colour, glow.
⊠ blanch.
◇ n flush, reddening, rosiness, ruddiness, colour, glow.

blushing adj flushed, red, rosy, glowing, confused, embarrassed, ashamed, modest.
⊠ pale, white, composed.

bluster v boast, brag, crow, talk big (infml), swagger, strut, vaunt, show off, rant, roar, storm, bully, hector.
◇ n boasting, crowing, bravado, bluff, swagger.

blustery adj windy, gusty, squally, stormy, tempestuous, violent, wild, boisterous.
⊠ calm.

board n 1 a wooden board: sheet, panel, slab, plank, beam, timber, slat. 2 COMMITTEE, council, panel, jury, commission, directorate, directors, trustees, advisers. 3 MEALS, food, provisions, rations.
◇ v get on, embark, mount, enter, catch.

boast v brag, crow, swank (infml), claim, exaggerate, talk big (infml), bluster, trumpet, vaunt, strut, swagger, show off, exhibit, possess.
⊠ belittle, deprecate.
◇ n brag, swank (infml), claim, vaunt, pride, joy, gem, treasure.

boastful adj proud, conceited, vain, swollen-headed, bigheaded (infml), puffed up, bragging, crowing, swanky (infml), cocky, swaggering.
⊠ modest, self-effacing, humble.

boat

Types of boat or ship include: canoe, dinghy, lifeboat, rowing boat, kayak, coracle, skiff, punt, sampan, dhow, gondola, pedalo,

catamaran, trimaran, yacht;
airboat, cabin cruiser, motorboat,
speedboat, swamp boat, trawler,
barge, narrowboat, houseboat,
dredger, junk, smack, wherry,
lugger, hovercraft, hydrofoil;
clipper, cutter, ketch, packet, brig,
schooner, square-rigger, galleon;
tug, ferry, paddle steamer, freighter,
liner, container ship, tanker;
warship, battleship, destroyer,
submarine, U-boat, frigate, aircraft-
carrier, cruiser, dreadnought,
corvette, minesweeper, man-of-
war.

bob *v* bounce, hop, skip, spring,
jump, leap, twitch, jerk, jolt, shake,
quiver, wobble, oscillate, nod, bow,
curtsy.
● **bob up** appear, emerge, arrive,
show up (*infml*), materialize, rise,
surface, pop up, spring up, crop up,
arise.

bodily *adj* physical, corporeal,
carnal, fleshly, real, actual, tangible,
substantial, concrete, material.
⊡ spiritual.
◇ *adv* altogether, en masse, as a
whole, collectively, completely, fully,
wholly, entirely, totally, in toto.
⊡ piecemeal.

body *n* **1** ANATOMY, physique,
build, figure, trunk, torso. **2** CORPSE,
cadaver, carcase, stiff (*sl*). **3** COMPANY,
association, society, corporation,
confederation, bloc, cartel,
syndicate, congress, collection,
group, band, crowd, throng,
multitude, mob, mass. **4** CONSISTENCY,
density, solidity, firmness, bulk,
mass, substance, essence, fullness,
richness.

Body parts include: biceps, bone,
cartilage, diaphragm, elbow,
epidermis, epiglottis, Fallopian
tubes, foreskin, funny bone,
genitalia, gristle, groin, gullet,
hamstring, hock, ligament,

mammary, muscle, oesophagus,
spine, tendon, triceps, umbilicus,
uterus, uvula, voice box, vulva,
windpipe, wisdom tooth, womb.
see also **anatomy**; **bone**; **brain**;
ear; **eye**; **heart**.

bodyguard *n* guard, protector,
minder (*infml*).

bog *n* marsh, swamp, fen, mire,
quagmire, quag, slough, morass,
quicksands, marshland, swampland,
wetlands.
● **bog down** encumber, hinder,
impede, overwhelm, deluge, sink,
stick, slow down, slow up, delay,
retard, halt, stall.

bogus *adj* false, fake, counterfeit,
forged, fraudulent, phoney (*infml*),
spurious, sham, pseudo, artificial,
imitation, dummy.
⊡ genuine, true, real, valid.

bohemian *adj* artistic, arty (*infml*),
unconventional, unorthodox,
nonconformist, alternative, eccentric,
offbeat, way-out (*sl*), bizarre, exotic.
⊡ bourgeois, conventional,
orthodox.
◇ *n* beatnik, hippie, drop-out, new-
ager, nonconformist.
⊡ bourgeois, conformist.

boil[1] *v* **1** SIMMER, stew, seethe, brew,
gurgle, bubble, fizz, effervesce,
froth, foam, steam. **2** *boil with anger*:
erupt, explode, rage, rave, storm,
fulminate, fume.
● **boil down** reduce, concentrate,
distil, condense, digest, abstract,
summarize, abridge.

boil[2] *n* pustule, abscess, gumboil,
ulcer, tumour, pimple, carbuncle,
blister, inflammation.

boiling *adj* **1** *boiling water*:
turbulent, gurgling, bubbling,
steaming. **2** HOT, baking, roasting,
scorching, blistering. **3** ANGRY,
indignant, incensed, infuriated,
enraged, furious, fuming, flaming.

boisterous *adj* exuberant, rumbustious (*infml*), rollicking, bouncy, turbulent, tumultuous, loud, noisy, clamorous, rowdy, rough, disorderly, riotous, wild, unrestrained, unruly, obstreperous.
ⓔ quiet, calm, restrained.

bold *adj* **1** FEARLESS, dauntless, daring, audacious, brave, courageous, valiant, heroic, gallant, intrepid, adventurous, venturesome, enterprising, plucky, spirited, confident, outgoing. **2** EYE-CATCHING, striking, conspicuous, prominent, strong, pronounced, bright, vivid, colourful, loud, flashy, showy, flamboyant. **3** BRAZEN, brash, forward, shameless, unabashed, cheeky (*infml*), impudent, insolent.
ⓔ **1** cautious, timid, shy. **2** faint, restrained.

bolt *n* bar, rod, shaft, pin, peg, rivet, fastener, latch, catch, lock.
◇ *v* **1** FASTEN, secure, bar, latch, lock. **2** ABSCOND, escape, flee, fly, run, sprint, rush, dash, hurtle. **3** *bolt one's food*: gulp, wolf, gobble, gorge, devour, cram, stuff.

bomb *n* atom bomb, petrol bomb, shell, bombshell, explosive, charge, grenade, mine, torpedo, rocket, missile, projectile.
◇ *v* bombard, shell, torpedo, attack, blow up, destroy.

bombard *v* attack, assault, assail, pelt, pound, strafe, blast, bomb, shell, blitz, besiege, hound, harass, pester.

bombardment *n* attack, assault, air-raid, bombing, shelling, blitz, barrage, cannonade, fusillade, salvo, fire, flak.

bombastic *adj* grandiloquent, magniloquent, grandiose, pompous, high-flown, inflated, bloated, windy, wordy, verbose.

bond *n* **1** CONNECTION, relation, link, tie, union, affiliation, attachment,

affinity. **2** CONTRACT, covenant, agreement, pledge, promise, word, obligation. **3** FETTER, shackle, manacle, chain, cord, band, binding.
◇ *v* connect, fasten, bind, unite, fuse, glue, gum, paste, stick, seal.

bondage *n* imprisonment, incarceration, captivity, confinement, restraint, slavery, enslavement, serfdom, servitude, subservience, subjection, subjugation, yoke.
ⓔ freedom, independence.

bone

Human bones include: breastbone, carpal, clavicle, coccyx, collar bone, femur, fibula, hip bone, humerus, ilium, ischium, mandible, maxilla, metacarpal, metatarsal, patella, pelvis, phalange, pubis, radius, rib, sacrum, scapula, shoulder blade, skull, sternum, stirrup bone, tarsal, temporal, thigh bone, tibia, ulna, vertebra.

bonus *n* advantage, benefit, plus (*infml*), extra, perk (*infml*), perquisite, commission, dividend, premium, prize, reward, honorarium, tip, gratuity, gift, handout.
ⓔ disadvantage, disincentive.

bony *adj* thin, lean, angular, lanky, gawky, gangling, skinny, scrawny, emaciated, rawboned, gaunt, drawn.
ⓔ fat, plump.

book *n* volume, tome, publication, work, booklet, tract.

Types of book include: hardback, paperback, softback, audio book, e-book, bestseller; fiction, novel, story, thriller, romantic novel; children's book, primer, picture book, annual; reference book, encyclopedia, dictionary, lexicon, thesaurus, concordance, anthology, compendium, omnibus, atlas, guidebook, gazetteer, directory, A to Z, handbook, manual, cookbook, yearbook, almanac, catalogue; notebook, exercise book, jotter, textbook, scrapbook, album, sketchbook, diary, Filofax®, journal, pad, ledger; libretto, manuscript, hymn-book, hymnal, prayer book, psalter, missal, lectionary. *see also* **literature**.

◇ *v* reserve, bag (*infml*), engage, charter, procure, order, arrange, organize, schedule, programme.
☒ cancel.

boom *v* **1** BANG, crash, roar, thunder, roll, rumble, resound, reverberate, blast, explode. **2** FLOURISH, thrive, prosper, succeed, develop, grow, increase, gain, expand, swell, escalate, intensify, strengthen, explode.
☒ **2** fail, collapse, slump.
◇ *n* **1** BANG, clap, crash, roar, thunder, rumble, reverberation, blast, explosion, burst. **2** INCREASE, growth, expansion, gain, upsurge, jump, spurt, boost, upturn, improvement, advance, escalation, explosion.
☒ **2** failure, collapse, slump, recession, depression.

boon *n* blessing, advantage, benefit, godsend, windfall, favour, kindness, gift, present, grant, gratuity.
☒ disadvantage, blight.

boorish *adj* uncouth, oafish, loutish, ill-mannered, rude, coarse, crude, vulgar, unrefined, uncivilized, uneducated, ignorant.
☒ polite, refined, cultured.

boost *n* improvement, enhancement, expansion, increase, rise, jump, increment, addition, supplement, booster, lift, hoist, heave, push, thrust, help, advancement, promotion, praise, encouragement, fillip, ego-trip (*sl*).
☒ setback, blow.
◇ *v* raise, elevate, improve, enhance, develop, enlarge, expand, amplify, increase, augment, heighten, lift,

hoist, jack up, heave, push, thrust, help, aid, assist, advance, further, promote, advertise, plug (*infml*), praise, talk up (*infml*), inspire, encourage, foster, support, sustain, bolster, supplement.
☒ hinder, undermine, talk down (*infml*).

boot *n* gumboot, wellington, welly (*infml*), galosh, overshoe, walking-boot, riding-boot, top-boot.

booth *n* kiosk, stall, stand, hut, box, compartment, cubicle, carrel.

booty *n* loot, plunder, pillage, spoils, swag (*sl*), haul, gains, takings, pickings, winnings.

border *n* **1** BOUNDARY, frontier, bound, bounds, confine, confines, limit, demarcation, borderline, margin, fringe, periphery, surround, perimeter, circumference, edge, rim, brim, verge, brink. **2** TRIMMING, frill, valance, skirt, hem, frieze.
● **border on 1** ADJOIN, abut, touch, impinge, join, connect, communicate with. **2** RESEMBLE, approximate, approach, verge on.

bore¹ *v* drill, mine, pierce, perforate, penetrate, sink, burrow, tunnel, undermine, sap.

bore² *v* tire, weary, fatigue, jade, trouble, bother, worry, irritate, annoy, vex, irk.
☒ interest, excite.
◇ *n* (*infml*) nuisance, bother, bind (*infml*), drag (*infml*), bummer (*sl*), pain (*infml*), headache (*infml*).
☒ pleasure, delight.

boredom *n* tedium, tediousness, monotony, dullness, apathy, listlessness, weariness, world-weariness.
☒ interest, excitement.

boring *adj* tedious, monotonous, routine, repetitious, uninteresting, unexciting, uneventful, dull, dreary, humdrum, commonplace, trite, unimaginative, uninspired,

dry, stale, flat, insipid.
🠴 interesting, exciting, stimulating, original.

borrow v steal, pilfer, filch, lift, plagiarize, crib, copy, imitate, mimic, echo, take, draw, derive, obtain, adopt, use, scrounge, cadge, sponge, appropriate, usurp.
🠴 lend.

bosom n 1 BUST, breasts, chest, breast. 2 HEART, core, centre, midst, protection, shelter, sanctuary.

boss n employer, governor, master, owner, captain, head, chief, leader, supremo, administrator, executive, director, manager, foreman, gaffer, superintendent, overseer, supervisor.
• **boss around** order around, order about, domineer, tyrannize, bully, bulldoze, browbeat, push around, dominate.

bossy adj authoritarian, autocratic, tyrannical, despotic, dictatorial, domineering, overbearing, oppressive, lordly, high-handed, imperious, insistent, assertive, demanding, exacting.
🠴 unassertive.

bother v disturb, inconvenience, harass, hassle (infml), pester, plague, nag, annoy, irritate, irk, molest, trouble, worry, concern, alarm, dismay, distress, upset, vex.
◇ n inconvenience, trouble, problem, difficulty, hassle (infml), fuss, bustle, flurry, nuisance, pest, annoyance, irritation, aggravation (infml), vexation, worry, strain.

bottle n phial, flask, carafe, decanter, flagon, demijohn.
• **bottle up** hide, conceal, restrain, curb, hold back, suppress, inhibit, restrict, enclose, contain.
🠴 unbosom, unburden.

bottleneck n hold-up, traffic jam, gridlock, snarl-up, congestion, clogging, blockage, obstruction, block, obstacle.

bottom n 1 UNDERSIDE, underneath, sole, base, foot, plinth, pedestal, support, foundation, substructure, ground, floor, bed, depths, nadir. 2 RUMP, rear, behind, posterior (infml), buttocks, seat, backside (infml), bum (sl), butt (US infml), arse (sl), ass (US sl), tail (infml).
🠴 1 top.

bottomless adj deep, profound, fathomless, unfathomed, unplumbed, immeasurable, measureless, infinite, boundless, limitless, unlimited, inexhaustible.
🠴 shallow, limited.

bounce v spring, jump, leap, bound, bob, ricochet, rebound, recoil.
◇ n 1 SPRING, bound, springiness, elasticity, give, resilience, rebound, recoil. 2 EBULLIENCE, exuberance, vitality, vivacity, energy, vigour, go (infml), zip (infml), animation, liveliness.

bound[1] adj 1 FASTENED, secured, fixed, tied (up), chained, held, restricted, bandaged. 2 LIABLE, committed, duty-bound, obliged, required, forced, compelled, constrained, destined, fated, doomed, sure, certain.

bound[2] v jump, leap, vault, hurdle, spring, bounce, bob, hop, skip, frisk, gambol, frolic, caper, prance.
◇ n jump, leap, vault, spring, bounce, bob, hop, skip, gambol, frolic, caper, dance, prance.

boundary n border, frontier, barrier, line, borderline, demarcation, bounds, confines, limits, margin, fringe, verge, brink, edge, perimeter, extremity, termination.

boundless adj unbounded, limitless, unlimited, unconfined, countless, untold, incalculable, vast, immense, measureless, immeasurable, infinite, endless, unending, interminable, inexhaustible, unflagging, indefatigable.

⊞ limited, restricted.

bounds n confines, limits, borders, marches, margins, fringes, periphery, circumference, edges, extremities.

bounty n 1 GENEROSITY, liberality, munificence, largess(e), almsgiving, charity, philanthropy, beneficence, kindness. 2 REWARD, recompense, premium, bonus, gratuity, gift, present, donation, grant, allowance.

bouquet n 1 bouquet of flowers: bunch, posy, nosegay, spray, corsage, buttonhole, wreath, garland. 2 AROMA, smell, odour, scent, perfume, fragrance.

bourgeois adj middle-class, materialistic, conservative, traditional, conformist, conventional, hidebound, unadventurous, dull, humdrum, banal, commonplace, trite, unoriginal, unimaginative. ⊞ bohemian, unconventional, original.

bout n 1 FIGHT, battle, engagement, encounter, struggle, set-to, match, contest, competition, round, heat. 2 PERIOD, spell, time, stint, turn, go (infml), term, stretch, run, course, session, spree, attack, fit.

bow v 1 bow one's head: incline, bend, nod, bob, curtsy, genuflect (fml), kowtow, salaam, stoop. 2 YIELD, give in, consent, surrender, capitulate, submit, acquiesce, concede, accept, comply, defer. 3 SUBDUE, overpower, conquer, vanquish, crush, subjugate. ◇ n inclination, bending, nod, bob, curtsy, genuflexion (fml), kowtow, salaam, obeisance (fml), salutation, acknowledgement. ● bow out withdraw, pull out, desert, abandon, defect, back out, chicken out (infml), retire, resign, quit, stand down, step down, give up.

bowels n 1 INTESTINES, viscera, entrails, guts, insides, innards (infml). 2 DEPTHS, interior, inside, middle, centre, core, heart.

bowl¹ n receptacle, container, vessel, dish, basin, sink.

bowl² v throw, hurl, fling, pitch, roll, spin, whirl, rotate, revolve. ● bowl over surprise, amaze, astound, astonish, stagger, stun, dumbfound, flabbergast (infml), floor (infml).

box¹ n container, receptacle, case, crate, carton, packet, pack, package, present, chest, coffer, trunk, coffin. ◇ v case, encase, package, pack, wrap. ● box in enclose, surround, circumscribe, cordon off, hem in, corner, trap, confine, restrict, imprison, cage, coop up, contain.

box² v fight, spar, punch, hit, strike, slap, buffet, cuff, clout, sock (sl), wallop (infml), whack (infml).

boxer n pugilist, fighter, prizefighter, sparring partner, flyweight, featherweight, lightweight, welterweight, middleweight, heavyweight.

boxing n pugilism, prizefighting, fisticuffs, sparring.

boy n son, lad, youngster, kid (infml), nipper (infml), stripling, youth, fellow.

boycott v refuse, reject, embargo, black, ban, prohibit, disallow, bar, exclude, blacklist, outlaw, ostracize, cold-shoulder, ignore, spurn. ⊞ encourage, support.

boyfriend n young man, man, fellow (infml), bloke (infml), admirer, date, sweetheart, lover, fiancé, partner.

brace n pair, couple, twosome, duo. ◇ v strengthen, reinforce, fortify, bolster, buttress, prop, shore (up), support, steady, tighten, fasten, tie, strap, bind, bandage.

bracing adj fresh, crisp, refreshing, reviving, strengthening, fortifying,

tonic, rousing, stimulating, exhilarating, invigorating, enlivening, energizing, brisk, energetic, vigorous.
▨ weakening, debilitating.

braid v plait, interweave, interlace, intertwine, weave, lace, twine, entwine, ravel, twist, wind.
▨ undo, unravel.

brain n 1 CEREBRUM, grey matter, head, mind, intellect, nous, brains (infml), intelligence, wit, reason, sense, common sense, shrewdness, understanding. 2 MASTERMIND, intellectual, highbrow, egghead (infml), scholar, expert, boffin, genius, prodigy.
▨ 2 simpleton.

Parts of the brain include: brain stem, cerebellum, cerebral cortex (grey matter), cerebrum, corpus callosum, frontal lobe, hippocampus, hypothalamus, medulla oblongata, mesencephalon, occipital lobe, parietal lobe, pineal body, pituitary gland, pons Varolii, temporal lobe, thalamus.

brainy adj intellectual, intelligent, clever, smart, bright, brilliant.
▨ dull.

brake n check, curb, rein, restraint, control, restriction, constraint, drag.
◇ v slow, decelerate, retard, drag, slacken, moderate, check, halt, stop, pull up.
▨ accelerate.

branch n 1 BOUGH, limb, sprig, shoot, offshoot, arm, wing, prong.
2 a different branch of the company: department, office, part, section, division, subsection, subdivision.
• **branch out** diversify, vary, develop, expand, enlarge, extend, broaden out, increase, multiply, proliferate, ramify.

brand n make, brand name, tradename, trademark, logo, mark, symbol, sign, emblem, label, stamp, hallmark, grade, quality, class, kind, type, sort, line, variety, species.
◇ v mark, stamp, label, type, stigmatize, burn, scar, stain, taint, disgrace, discredit, denounce, censure.

brandish v wave, flourish, shake, raise, swing, wield, flash, flaunt, exhibit, display, parade.

brash adj 1 BRAZEN, forward, impertinent, impudent, insolent, rude, cocky, assured, bold, audacious. 2 RECKLESS, rash, impetuous, impulsive, hasty, precipitate, foolhardy, incautious, indiscreet.
▨ 1 reserved. 2 cautious.

bravado n swagger, boasting, bragging, bluster, bombast, talk, boast, vaunting, showing off, parade, show, pretence.
▨ modesty, restraint.

brave adj courageous, plucky, unafraid, fearless, dauntless, undaunted, bold, audacious, daring, intrepid, stalwart, hardy, stoical, resolute, stout-hearted, valiant, gallant, heroic, indomitable, feisty (infml).
▨ cowardly, afraid, timid.
◇ v face, confront, defy, challenge, dare, stand up to, face up to, suffer, endure, bear, withstand.
▨ capitulate.

bravery n courage, pluck, guts (infml), fearlessness, dauntlessness, boldness, audacity, daring, intrepidity, stalwartness, hardiness, fortitude, resolution, stout-heartedness, valiance, valour, gallantry, heroism, indomitability, grit, mettle, spirit.
▨ cowardice, faint-heartedness, timidity.

brawl n fight, punch-up (infml), scrap, scuffle, dust-up (infml), mêlée, free-for-all, fray, affray, broil, fracas, rumpus, disorder, row, argument, quarrel, squabble, altercation, dispute, clash.

◇ v fight, scrap, scuffle, wrestle, tussle, row, argue, quarrel, squabble, wrangle, dispute.

brawny adj muscular, sinewy, athletic, well-built, burly, beefy, hunky (infml), hefty, solid, bulky, hulking, massive, strapping, strong, powerful, vigorous, sturdy, robust, hardy, stalwart.

⊜ slight, frail.

brazen adj blatant, flagrant, brash, brassy, bold, forward, in-your-face (infml), saucy, pert, barefaced, impudent, insolent, defiant, shameless, unashamed, unabashed, immodest.

⊜ shy, shamefaced, modest.

breach n 1 a breach of the rules: violation, contravention, infringement, trespass, disobedience, offence, transgression, lapse, disruption. 2 QUARREL, disagreement, dissension, difference, variance, schism, rift, rupture, split, division, separation, parting, estrangement, alienation, disaffection, dissociation. 3 BREAK, crack, rift, rupture, fissure, cleft, crevice, opening, aperture, gap, space, hole, chasm.

bread n loaf, roll, food, provisions, diet, fare, nourishment, nutriment, sustenance, subsistence, necessities.

Types of bread and rolls include: bagel, baguette, brioche, challah, chapati, ciabatta, cottage loaf, croissant, flatbread, focaccia, French bread, Granary®, milk bread, nan (or naan), pitta, puri (or poori), pumpernickel, roti, ryebread, soda bread, sourdough, wholemeal, wholewheat.

---

breadth n width, broadness, wideness, latitude, thickness, size, magnitude, measure, scale, range, reach, scope, compass, span, sweep, extent, expanse, spread, comprehensiveness, extensiveness, vastness.

break v 1 FRACTURE, crack, snap, split, sever, separate, divide, rend, smash, disintegrate, splinter, shiver, shatter, ruin, destroy, demolish. 2 break the law: violate, contravene, infringe, breach, disobey, flout. 3 PAUSE, halt, stop, discontinue, interrupt, suspend, rest. 4 SUBDUE, tame, weaken, enfeeble, impair, undermine, demoralize. 5 break the news: tell, inform, impart, divulge, disclose, reveal, announce. 6 break a record: exceed, beat, better, excel, surpass, outdo, outstrip.

⊜ 1 mend. 2 keep, observe, abide by. 4 strengthen.

◇ n 1 FRACTURE, crack, split, rift, rupture, schism, separation, tear, gash, fissure, cleft, crevice, opening, gap, hole, breach. 2 INTERVAL, intermission, interlude, interruption, pause, halt, lull, let-up (infml), respite, rest, breather (infml), time out, holiday. 3 OPPORTUNITY, chance, advantage, fortune, luck.

• **break away** separate, split, part company, detach, secede, leave, depart, quit, run away, escape, flee, fly.

• **break down 1** the van broke down: fail, stop, pack up (infml), conk out (sl), seize up, give way, collapse, crack up (infml). 2 ANALYSE, dissect, separate, itemize, detail.

• **break in 1** INTERRUPT, butt in, interpose, interject, intervene, intrude, encroach, impinge. 2 BURGLE, rob, raid, invade.

• **break off 1** DETACH, snap off, sever, separate, part, divide, disconnect. 2 PAUSE, interrupt, suspend, discontinue, halt, stop, cease, end, finish, terminate.

• **break out 1** START, begin, commence, arise, emerge, happen, occur, erupt, flare up, burst out. 2 ESCAPE, abscond, bolt, flee.

• **break up 1** DISMANTLE, take apart, demolish, destroy, disintegrate, splinter, sever, divide, split, part, separate, divorce. **2** DISBAND, disperse, dissolve, adjourn, suspend, stop, finish, terminate.

breakable *adj* brittle, fragile, delicate, flimsy, insubstantial, frail. ⊞ unbreakable, durable, sturdy.

breakdown *n* **1** FAILURE, collapse, disintegration, malfunction, interruption, stoppage. **2** ANALYSIS, dissection, itemization, classification, categorization.

break-in *n* burglary, housebreaking, robbery, raid, invasion, intrusion, trespass.

breakthrough *n* discovery, find, finding, invention, innovation, advance, progress, headway, step, leap, development, improvement.

break-up *n* divorce, separation, parting, split, rift, finish, termination, dissolution, dispersal, disintegration, crumbling.

breakwater *n* groyne, mole, jetty, pier, quay, wharf, dock.

breath *n* **1** AIR, breathing, respiration, inhalation, exhalation, sigh, gasp, pant, gulp. **2** BREEZE, puff, waft, gust. **3** AROMA, smell, odour, whiff. **4** HINT, suggestion, suspicion, undertone, whisper, murmur.

breathe *v* **1** RESPIRE, inhale, exhale, expire, sigh, gasp, pant, puff. **2** SAY, utter, express, voice, articulate, murmur, whisper, impart, tell. **3** INSTIL, imbue, infuse, inject, inspire.

breathless *adj* **1** SHORT-WINDED, out of breath, panting, puffing, puffed (out), exhausted, winded, gasping, wheezing, choking. **2** *breathless anticipation*: expectant, impatient, eager, agog, excited, feverish, anxious.

breathtaking *adj* impressive, awe-inspiring, magnificent, amazing, overwhelming, astonishing, jaw-dropping (*infml*), stunning, exciting, thrilling, stirring, moving.

breed *v* **1** REPRODUCE, procreate, multiply, propagate, hatch, bear, bring forth, rear, raise, bring up, educate, train, instruct. **2** PRODUCE, create, originate, arouse, cause, occasion, engender, generate, make, foster, nurture, nourish, cultivate, develop.
◇ *n* species, strain, variety, family, ilk, sort, kind, type, stamp, stock, race, progeny, line, lineage, pedigree.

breeding *n* **1** REPRODUCTION, procreation, nurture, development, rearing, raising, upbringing, education, training, background, ancestry, lineage, stock. **2** MANNERS, politeness, civility, gentility, urbanity, refinement, culture, polish. ⊞ **2** vulgarity.

breeze *n* wind, gust, flurry, waft, puff, breath, draught, air.

breezy *adj* **1** WINDY, blowing, fresh, airy, gusty, blustery, squally. **2** ANIMATED, lively, vivacious, jaunty, buoyant, blithe, debonair, carefree, cheerful, easy-going (*infml*), casual, informal, light, bright, exhilarating. ⊞ **1** still. **2** staid, serious.

brevity *n* briefness, shortness, terseness, conciseness, succinctness, pithiness, crispness, incisiveness, abruptness, curtness, impermanence, ephemerality, transience, transitoriness. ⊞ verbosity, permanence, longevity.

brew *v* **1** INFUSE, stew, boil, seethe, ferment, prepare, soak, steep, mix, cook. **2** PLOT, scheme, plan, project, devise, contrive, concoct, hatch, excite, foment, build up, gather, develop.
◇ *n* infusion, drink, beverage, liquor, potion, broth, gruel, stew, mixture, blend, concoction, preparation, fermentation, distillation.

bribe *n* incentive, inducement,

allurement, enticement, back-hander (*infml*), kickback, payola, refresher (*infml*), sweetener (*infml*), hush money (*infml*), protection money. ◇ *v* corrupt, suborn, buy off, reward.

bribery *n* corruption, graft (*sl*), palm-greasing, inducement, lubrication.

bric-à-brac *n* knick-knacks, ornaments, curios, antiques, trinkets, baubles.

bridal *adj* wedding, nuptial, marriage, matrimonial, marital, conjugal.

bridge *n* arch, span, causeway, link, connection, bond, tie.

Types of bridge include: suspension bridge, arch bridge, cantilever bridge, flying bridge, flyover, overpass, footbridge, railway bridge, viaduct, aqueduct, humpback bridge, toll bridge, pontoon bridge, Bailey bridge, rope bridge, drawbridge, swing bridge.

◇ *v* span, cross, traverse, fill, link, connect, couple, join, unite, bind.

bridle *v* check, curb, restrain, control, govern, master, subdue, moderate, repress, contain.

brief *adj* 1 SHORT, terse, succinct, concise, pithy, crisp, compressed, thumbnail, laconic, abrupt, sharp, brusque, blunt, curt, surly. 2 SHORT-LIVED, momentary, ephemeral, transient, fleeting, passing, transitory, temporary, limited, cursory, hasty, quick, swift, fast.
⊞ 1 long. 2 lengthy.
◇ *n* 1 ORDERS, instructions, directions, remit, mandate, directive, advice, briefing, data, information. 2 OUTLINE, summary, précis, dossier, case, defence, argument.
◇ *v* instruct, direct, explain, guide, advise, prepare, prime, inform, fill in

(*infml*), gen up (*sl*), get up to speed (*infml*).

briefing *n* meeting, conference, preparation, priming, filling-in (*infml*), gen (*sl*), low-down (*infml*), information, advice, guidance, directions, instructions, orders.

bright *adj* 1 LUMINOUS, illuminated, radiant, shining, beaming, flashing, gleaming, glistening, glittering, sparkling, twinkling, shimmering, glowing, brilliant, resplendent, glorious, splendid, dazzling, glaring, blazing, intense, vivid. 2 HAPPY, cheerful, glad, joyful, merry, jolly, lively, vivacious, upbeat (*infml*). 3 *the future looks bright*: promising, propitious, auspicious, favourable, rosy, optimistic, hopeful, encouraging. 4 CLEVER, brainy (*infml*), smart, intelligent, quick-witted, quick, sharp, acute, keen, astute, perceptive. 5 CLEAR, transparent, translucent, lucid. 6 *a bright day*: fine, sunny, cloudless, unclouded.
⊞ 1 dull. 2 sad. 3 depressing. 4 stupid. 5 muddy. 6 dark.

brighten *v* 1 LIGHT UP, illuminate, lighten, clear up. 2 POLISH, burnish, rub up, shine, gleam, glow. 3 CHEER UP, gladden, hearten, encourage, enliven, perk up.
⊞ 1 darken. 2 dull, tarnish.

brilliance *n* 1 TALENT, virtuosity, genius, greatness, distinction, excellence, aptitude, cleverness. 2 RADIANCE, brightness, sparkle, dazzle, intensity, vividness, gloss, lustre, sheen, glamour, glory, magnificence, splendour.

brilliant *adj* 1 *a brilliant pianist*: gifted, talented, accomplished, expert, skilful, masterly, exceptional, outstanding, superb, illustrious, famous, celebrated. 2 SPARKLING, glittering, scintillating, dazzling, glaring, blazing, intense, vivid, bright, shining, glossy, showy, glorious, magnificent, splendid.

3 CLEVER, brainy (*infml*), intelligent, quick, astute.
⊞ **1** undistinguished. **2** dull. **3** stupid.

brim *n* rim, perimeter, circumference, lip, edge, margin, border, brink, verge, top, limit.

bring *v* **1** CARRY, bear, convey, transport, fetch, take, deliver, escort, accompany, usher, guide, conduct, lead. **2** CAUSE, produce, engender, create, prompt, provoke, force, attract, draw.
• **bring about** cause, occasion, create, produce, generate, effect, accomplish, achieve, fulfil, realize, manage, engineer, manoeuvre, manipulate.
• **bring in** earn, net, gross, produce, yield, fetch, return, accrue, realize.
• **bring off** achieve, accomplish, fulfil, execute, discharge, perform, succeed, win.
• **bring on** cause, occasion, induce, lead to, give rise to, generate, inspire, prompt, provoke, precipitate, expedite, accelerate, advance.
⊞ inhibit.
• **bring out 1** EMPHASIZE, stress, highlight, enhance, draw out. **2** PUBLISH, print, issue, launch, introduce.
• **bring up 1** REAR, raise, foster, nurture, educate, teach, train, form. **2** *bring up a subject*: introduce, broach, mention, submit, propose. **3** VOMIT, regurgitate, throw up (*infml*).

brink *n* verge, threshold, edge, margin, fringe, border, boundary, limit, extremity, lip, rim, brim, bank.

brisk *adj* **1** ENERGETIC, vigorous, quick, snappy, lively, spirited, active, busy, bustling, agile, nimble, alert. **2** INVIGORATING, exhilarating, stimulating, bracing, refreshing, fresh, crisp.
⊞ **1** lazy, sluggish.

bristle *n* hair, whisker, stubble, spine, prickle, barb, thorn.

bristly *adj* bearded, whiskered, hairy, unshaven, stubbly, rough, spiny, prickly, spiky, thorny.
⊞ clean-shaven, smooth.

brittle *adj* breakable, fragile, delicate, frail, crisp, crumbly, crumbling, friable, shattery, shivery.
⊞ durable, resilient.

broad *adj* **1** WIDE, large, vast, roomy, spacious, capacious, ample, extensive, widespread. **2** WIDE-RANGING, far-reaching, encyclopedic, catholic, eclectic, all-embracing, inclusive, comprehensive, general, sweeping, universal, unlimited.
⊞ **1** narrow. **2** restricted.

broadcast *v* air, show, transmit, beam, relay, televise, report, announce, publicize, advertise, publish, circulate, promulgate, disseminate, spread.
◇ *n* transmission, programme, show.

broaden *v* widen, thicken, swell, spread, enlarge, expand, extend, stretch, increase, augment, develop, open up, branch out, diversify.

broad-minded *adj* liberal, tolerant, permissive, enlightened, free-thinking, open-minded, receptive, unbiased, unprejudiced.
⊞ narrow-minded, intolerant, biased.

brochure *n* leaflet, booklet, pamphlet, prospectus, broadsheet, handbill, circular, handout, flyer, folder.

broke *adj* insolvent, penniless, bankrupt, bust, ruined, impoverished, destitute.
⊞ solvent, rich, affluent.

broken *adj* **1** FRACTURED, burst, ruptured, severed, separated, faulty, defective, out of order, shattered, destroyed, demolished. **2** DISJOINTED, disconnected, fragmentary, discontinuous, interrupted, intermittent, spasmodic, erratic, hesitating, stammering, halting,

imperfect. **3** *a broken man*: beaten, defeated, crushed, demoralized, down, weak, feeble, exhausted, tamed, subdued, oppressed.
⊟ **1** mended. **2** fluent.

broken-down *adj* dilapidated, worn-out, ruined, collapsed, decayed, inoperative, out of order.

broken-hearted *adj* heartbroken, inconsolable, devastated, grief-stricken, desolate, despairing, miserable, wretched, mournful, sorrowful, sad, unhappy, dejected, despondent, crestfallen, disappointed.

brooch *n* badge, pin, clip, clasp.

brood *v* ponder, ruminate, meditate, muse, mull over, go over, rehearse, dwell on, agonize, fret, mope.
◇ *n* clutch, chicks, hatch, litter, young, offspring, issue, progeny, children, family.

brook *n* stream, rivulet, beck, burn, watercourse, channel.

brother *n* sibling, relation, relative, comrade, friend, mate, partner, colleague, associate, fellow, companion, monk, friar.

brotherhood *n* fraternity, society, association, league, confederation, confederacy, alliance, union, guild, fellowship, community, clique.

browbeat *v* bully, coerce, dragoon, bulldoze, awe, cow, intimidate, threaten, tyrannize, domineer, overbear, oppress, hound.
⊟ coax.

brown *adj* mahogany, chocolate, coffee, hazel, bay, chestnut, umber, sepia, tan, tawny, russet, rust, rusty, brunette, dark, dusky, sunburnt, tanned, bronzed, browned, toasted.

browse *v* **1** LEAF THROUGH, flick through, dip into, skim, survey, scan, peruse. **2** GRAZE, pasture, feed, eat, nibble.

bruise *v* discolour, blacken, mark,

blemish, pound, pulverize, crush, hurt, injure, insult, offend, grieve.
◇ *n* contusion, discoloration, black eye, shiner (*sl*), mark, blemish, injury.

brush¹ *n* broom, sweeper, besom.
◇ *v* **1** CLEAN, sweep, flick, burnish, polish, shine. **2** TOUCH, contact, graze, kiss, stroke, rub, scrape.
● **brush aside** dismiss, pooh-pooh, belittle, disregard, ignore, flout, override.
● **brush off** disregard, ignore, slight, snub, cold-shoulder, rebuff, dismiss, spurn, reject, repulse, disown, repudiate.
● **brush up 1** REVISE, relearn, improve, polish up, study, read up, swot (*infml*). **2** REFRESH, freshen up, clean, tidy.

brush² *n* scrub, thicket, bushes, shrubs, brushwood, undergrowth, ground cover.

brush³ *n* confrontation, encounter, clash, conflict, fight, scrap, skirmish, set-to, tussle, dust-up (*infml*), fracas.

brusque *adj* abrupt, sharp, short, terse, curt, gruff, surly, discourteous, impolite, uncivil, blunt, tactless, undiplomatic.
⊟ courteous, polite, tactful.

brutal *adj* animal, bestial, beastly, brutish, inhuman, savage, bloodthirsty, vicious, ferocious, cruel, inhumane, remorseless, pitiless, merciless, ruthless, callous, insensitive, unfeeling, heartless, harsh, gruff, rough, coarse, crude, rude, uncivilized, barbarous.
⊟ kindly, humane, civilized.

brutality *n* savagery, bloodthirstiness, viciousness, ferocity, cruelty, inhumanity, violence, atrocity, ruthlessness, callousness, roughness, coarseness, barbarism, barbarity.
⊟ gentleness, kindness.

brute *n* animal, beast, swine, fiend, creature, monster, ogre, devil, savage, sadist, bully, lout.

bubble n blister, vesicle, globule, ball, drop, droplet, bead.
◇ v effervesce, fizz, sparkle, froth, foam, seethe, boil, burble, gurgle.

bubbly adj 1 EFFERVESCENT, fizzy, sparkling, carbonated, frothy, foaming, sudsy. 2 LIVELY, bouncy, happy, merry, elated, excited, hyper (infml).
⊞ 1 flat, still. 2 lethargic.

bucket n pail, can, bail, scuttle, vessel.

buckle n clasp, clip, catch, fastener.
◇ v 1 buckle one's belt: fasten, clasp, catch, hook, hitch, connect, close, secure. 2 BEND, warp, twist, distort, bulge, cave in, fold, wrinkle, crumple, collapse.

bud n shoot, sprout, germ, embryo.
◇ v shoot, sprout, burgeon, develop, grow.
⊞ wither, waste away.

budding adj potential, promising, embryonic, burgeoning, developing, growing, flowering.

budge v move, stir, shift, remove, dislodge, push, roll, slide, propel, sway, influence, persuade, convince, change, bend, yield, give (way).

budget n finances, funds, resources, means, allowance, allotment, allocation, estimate.
◇ v plan, estimate, allow, allot, allocate, apportion, ration.

buff¹ adj yellowish-brown, straw, sandy, fawn, khaki.
◇ v polish, burnish, shine, smooth, rub, brush.

buff² n expert, connoisseur, enthusiast, fan, admirer, devotee, addict, fiend, freak.

buffer n shock absorber, bumper, fender, pad, cushion, pillow, intermediary, screen, shield.

buffet¹ n snack bar, counter, café, cafeteria.

buffet² v batter, hit, strike, knock, bang, bump, push, shove, pound, pummel, beat, thump, box, cuff, clout, slap.
◇ n blow, knock, bang, bump, jar, jolt, push, shove, thump, box, cuff, clout, slap, smack.

bug n 1 VIRUS, bacterium, germ, microbe, micro-organism, infection, disease. 2 FAULT, defect, flaw, blemish, imperfection, failing, error, gremlin (infml).
◇ v (infml) annoy, irritate, vex, irk, needle (infml), bother, disturb, harass, badger.

build v 1 ERECT, raise, construct, fabricate, make, form, constitute, assemble, knock together, develop, enlarge, extend, increase, augment, escalate, intensify. 2 BASE, found, establish, institute, inaugurate, initiate, begin.
⊞ 1 destroy, demolish, knock down, lessen.
◇ n physique, figure, body, form, shape, size, frame, structure.
• **build up** strengthen, reinforce, fortify, extend, expand, develop, amplify, increase, escalate, intensify, heighten, boost, improve, enhance, publicize, advertise, promote, plug (infml), hype (sl), talk up (infml).
⊞ weaken, lessen.

building n edifice, dwelling, erection, construction, fabrication, structure, architecture.

Types of building include: house, bungalow, cottage, block of flats, cabin, farmhouse, villa, mansion, château, castle, palace; church, chapel, cathedral, abbey, monastery, temple, synagogue, gurdwara, pagoda, mosque; shop, store, garage, factory, warehouse, silo, office block, tower block, skyscraper, high-rise, low-rise, theatre, cinema, multiplex, gymnasium, restaurant, café, hotel, pub (infml), public house, inn, school, college, museum, library, hospital, prison, power station, observatory; barracks, fort, fortress, monument, mausoleum; shed, barn, outhouse, stable, mill, lighthouse, pier, pavilion, boathouse, summerhouse, gazebo, windmill. *see also* **house**; **shop**.

Types of building material include: aluminium, ashlar, asphalt, bitumen, breeze block, brick, building block, cast iron, cement, chipboard, clay, concrete, reinforced concrete, fixings, flagstone, girder, glass, glass fibre, gravel, granite, grout, gypsum, hardboard, hard core, insulation, foam insulation, loose fill insulation, lagging, lintel, lumber (*US*), marble, mortar, paving stone, paviour, plaster, plasterboard, plastic, plywood, sand, sandstone, shingle, slate, stainless steel, steel, steel beam, stone, tarmac, thatch, tile, floor tile, roof tile, timber, wattle and daub, wood.

---

build-up *n* **1** ENLARGEMENT, expansion, growth, development, increase, gain, escalation. **2** ACCUMULATION, mass, load, heap, stack, store, stockpile.
⊜ **1** reduction, decrease.

bulge *n* **1** SWELLING, bump, lump, hump, distension, protuberance, projection. **2** RISE, increase, surge, upsurge, intensification.
◇ *v* swell, puff out, bulb, hump, dilate, expand, enlarge, distend, protrude, project.

bulk *n* size, magnitude, dimensions, extent, amplitude, bigness, largeness, immensity, volume, mass, weight, substance, body, preponderance, majority, most.

bulky *adj* substantial, big, large, huge, enormous, immense, mammoth, massive, colossal,

hulking, hefty, heavy, weighty, unmanageable, unwieldy, awkward, cumbersome.
⊜ insubstantial, small, handy.

bullet *n* shot, pellet, ball, slug (*infml*), missile, projectile.

bulletin *n* report, newsflash, dispatch, communiqué, statement, announcement, notification, communication, message.

bully *n* persecutor, tormentor, browbeater, intimidator, bully-boy, heavy (*sl*), ruffian, tough.
◇ *v* persecute, torment, terrorize, bulldoze, coerce, browbeat, bullyrag, intimidate, cow, tyrannize, domineer, overbear, oppress, push around.

bump *v* **1** HIT, strike, knock, bang, crash, collide (with). **2** JOLT, jerk, jar, jostle, rattle, shake, bounce.
◇ *n* **1** BLOW, hit, knock, bang, thump, thud, smash, crash, collision, impact, jolt, jar, shock. **2** LUMP, swelling, bulge, hump, protuberance.
• **bump into** meet, encounter, run into, chance upon, come across.
• **bump off** (*infml*) kill, murder, assassinate, eliminate (*sl*), liquidate (*sl*), do in (*sl*), top (*sl*).

bumper *adj* plentiful, abundant, large, great, enormous, massive, excellent, exceptional.
⊜ small.

bumptious *adj* self-important, pompous, officious, overbearing, pushy, assertive, over-confident, presumptuous, forward, impudent, arrogant, cocky, conceited, full of oneself, swaggering, boastful, egotistic.
⊜ humble, modest.

bumpy *adj* jerky, jolting, bouncy, choppy, rough, lumpy, knobbly, knobby, uneven, irregular.
⊜ smooth, even.

bunch *n* **1** BUNDLE, sheaf, tuft, clump, cluster, batch, lot, heap, pile, stack, mass, number, quantity, collection,

assortment. **2** *bunch of flowers*: bouquet, posy, spray. **3** GANG, band, troop, crew, team, party, gathering, flock, swarm, crowd, mob, multitude.
◇ *v* group, bundle, cluster, collect, assemble, congregate, gather, flock, herd, crowd, mass, pack, huddle.
⊡ disperse, scatter, spread out.

bundle *n* bunch, sheaf, roll, bale, truss, parcel, package, packet, carton, box, bag, pack, batch, consignment, group, set, collection, assortment, quantity, mass, accumulation, pile, stack, heap.
◇ *v* pack, wrap, bale, truss, bind, tie, fasten.

bungle *v* mismanage, cock up (*sl*), screw up (*sl*), foul up (*infml*), mess up (*infml*), ruin, spoil, mar, botch, fudge, blunder.

buoy *n* float, marker, signal, beacon.
• **buoy up** support, sustain, raise, lift, boost, encourage, cheer, hearten.
⊡ depress, discourage.

buoyant *adj* **1** *in buoyant mood*: light-hearted, carefree, bright, cheerful, happy, joyful, lively, animated, bouncy. **2** FLOATABLE, floating, afloat, light, weightless.
⊡ **1** depressed, despairing. **2** heavy.

burden *n* cargo, load, weight, dead-weight, encumbrance, millstone, onus, responsibility, obligation, duty, strain, stress, worry, anxiety, care, trouble, trial, affliction, sorrow.
◇ *v* load, weigh down, encumber, handicap, bother, worry, tax, strain, overload, lie heavy on, oppress, overwhelm.
⊡ unburden, relieve.

bureau *n* service, agency, office, branch, department, division, counter, desk.

bureaucracy *n* administration, government, ministry, civil service, the authorities, the system, officialdom, red tape, regulations.

burglar *n* housebreaker, robber, thief, pilferer, trespasser.

burglary *n* housebreaking, break-in, robbery, theft, stealing, trespass.

burial *n* burying, interment, entombment, funeral, obsequies.

burlesque *n* caricature, mock, mockery, parody, ridicule, satire, travesty, take-off (*infml*), send-up (*infml*), spoof (*infml*).
◇ *adj* comic, derisive, farcical, mocking, parodying, satirical, caricatural (*fml*).
⊡ serious.

burly *adj* big, well-built, hulking, hunky (*infml*), hefty, heavy, stocky, sturdy, brawny, beefy, muscular, athletic, strapping, strong, powerful.
⊡ small, puny, wimpy (*infml*), thin, slim.

burn *v* **1** FLAME, blaze, flare, flash, glow, flicker, smoulder, smoke, fume, simmer, seethe. **2** IGNITE, light, kindle, incinerate, cremate, consume, corrode. **3** SCALD, scorch, singe, char, parch, shrivel, toast, brand, sear, smart, sting, bite, hurt, tingle.

burning *adj* **1** ABLAZE, aflame, afire, fiery, flaming, blazing, flashing, gleaming, glowing, smouldering, alight, lit, illuminated. **2** HOT, scalding, scorching, searing, piercing, acute, smarting, stinging, prickling, tingling, biting, caustic, pungent. **3** *burning desire*: ardent, fervent, eager, earnest, intense, vehement, passionate, impassioned, frantic, frenzied, consuming.
4 *burning issue*: urgent, pressing, important, significant, crucial, essential, vital.
⊡ **2** cold. **3** apathetic.
4 unimportant.

burrow *n* warren, hole, earth, set, den, lair, retreat, shelter, tunnel.
◇ *v* tunnel, dig, delve, excavate, mine, undermine.

burst *v* puncture, rupture, tear,

split, crack, break, fragment, shatter, shiver, disintegrate, explode, blow up, erupt, gush, spout, rush, run.
◇ *n* **1** PUNCTURE, blow-out (*infml*), rupture, split, crack, break, breach, explosion, blast, bang, eruption. **2** DISCHARGE, gush, spurt, surge, rush, spate, torrent, outpouring, outburst, outbreak, fit.

bury *v* **1** *bury the dead*: inter, entomb, lay to rest, shroud. **2** SINK, submerge, immerse, plant, implant, embed, conceal, hide, cover, enshroud, engulf, enclose, engross, occupy, engage, absorb.
🔁 **1** disinter, exhume. **2** uncover.

bush *n* **1** SHRUB, hedge, thicket. **2** SCRUB, brush, scrubland, backwoods, wilds.

business *n* **1** TRADE, commerce, industry, manufacturing, dealings, transactions, bargaining, trading, buying, selling. **2** COMPANY, firm, corporation, establishment, organization, concern, enterprise, venture. **3** JOB, occupation, work, employment, trade, profession, line, calling, career, vocation, duty, task, responsibility. **4** AFFAIR, matter, issue, subject, topic, question, problem, point.

businesslike *adj* professional, efficient, thorough, systematic, methodical, organized, orderly, well-ordered, practical, matter-of-fact, precise, correct, formal, impersonal.
🔁 inefficient, disorganized.

businessman, businesswoman *n* entrepreneur, industrialist, trader, merchant, tycoon, magnate, capitalist, financier, employer, executive.

bust *n* **1** SCULPTURE, head, torso, statue. **2** BOSOM, breasts, chest, breast.

bustle *v* dash, rush, scamper, scurry, hurry, hasten, scramble, fuss.
◇ *n* activity, stir, commotion, tumult, agitation, excitement, fuss, ado, flurry, hurry, haste.

busy *adj* occupied, engaged, tied up (*infml*), employed, working, slaving, stirring, restless, tireless, diligent, industrious, active, lively, energetic, strenuous, tiring, full, crowded, swarming, teeming, bustling, hectic, eventful.
🔁 idle, lazy, quiet.
◇ *v* occupy, engage, engross, employ, absorb, immerse, interest, concern, bother.

busybody *n* meddler, intruder, nosey parker (*infml*), pry, gossip, eavesdropper, snoop, snooper, troublemaker.

butt[1] *n* stub, end, tip, tail, base, foot, shaft, stock, handle, haft.

butt[2] *n* target, mark, object, subject, victim, laughing-stock, dupe.

butt[3] *v*, *n* hit, bump, knock, buffet, push, shove, ram, thrust, punch, jab, prod, poke.
• **butt in** interrupt, cut in, interpose, intrude, meddle, interfere.

butterfly

Types of butterfly include: red admiral, white admiral, apollo, cabbage-white, brimstone, meadow-brown, Camberwell beauty, Cleopatra, comma, copper, fritillary, gate-keeper, grayling, hairstreak, monarch, orange-tip, painted lady, peacock, purple emperor, ringlet, skipper, swallow-tail, tortoiseshell. *see also* **moth**.

---

buttocks *n* rump, hindquarters, rear, posterior (*infml*), seat, bottom, behind, backside (*infml*), arse (*sl*), ass (*US sl*).

buttonhole *v* accost, waylay, catch, grab, nab, detain, importune.

buttress *n* support, prop, shore, stay, brace, pier, strut, stanchion, mainstay, reinforcement.

◇ *v* support, prop up, shore (up), hold up, brace, strengthen, reinforce, bolster up, sustain.
⊞ undermine, weaken.

buy *v* purchase, invest in (*infml*), pay for, procure, acquire, obtain, get.
⊞ sell.
◇ *n* purchase, acquisition, bargain, deal.

buyer *n* purchaser, shopper, consumer, customer, vendee, emptor.
⊞ seller, vendor.

buzz *v* **1** *bees buzzing round*: hum, whirr, drone, murmur, susurrate (*fml*), bombilate (*fml*). **2** *buzz with excitement*: hum, throb, pulse, bustle, race.
◇ *n* **1** *the buzz of bees*: hum, whirr, drone, murmur, purr, susurration

(*fml*), bombilation (*fml*). **2** *give someone a buzz*: ring, (phone) call. **3** *the latest buzz*: rumour, gossip, scandal, latest, hearsay. **4** THRILL, excitement, stimulation, kicks (*infml*), high (*infml*).

by *prep* near, next to, beside, along, over, through, via, past.
◇ *adv* near, close, handy, at hand, past, beyond, away, aside.

bypass *v* avoid, dodge, sidestep, skirt, circumvent, ignore, neglect, omit.
◇ *n* ring road, detour, diversion.

by-product *n* consequence, result, side effect, fallout (*infml*), repercussion, after-effect.

bystander *n* spectator, onlooker, looker-on, watcher, observer, witness, eye-witness, passer-by.

Cc

cabin n 1 BERTH, quarters, room, compartment. 2 HUT, shack, shanty, lodge, chalet, cottage, shed, shelter.

cabinet n cupboard, closet, dresser, case, locker.

cable n line, rope, cord, chain, wire, flex, lead.

cadge v scrounge, sponge, beg, hitch.

café n coffee shop, tea shop, tea room, coffee bar, cafeteria, snack bar, buffet, bistro, brasserie, restaurant.

cage v encage, coop up, shut up, confine, restrain, fence in, imprison, impound, incarcerate, lock up.
☒ release, let out, free, spring (sl).
◇ n aviary, coop, hutch, enclosure, pen, pound, corral.

cajole v coax, persuade, get round, wheedle, flatter, sweet-talk (infml), butter up (infml), tempt, lure, seduce, entice, beguile, mislead, dupe.
☒ bully, force, compel.

cake v coat, cover, encrust, dry, harden, solidify, consolidate, coagulate, congeal, thicken.
◇ n 1 tea and cakes: gâteau, fancy, bun, pie, flan. 2 LUMP, mass, bar, slab, block, loaf.

Types of cake include: angel-food cake, banana cake, Battenberg cake, birthday cake, Black Forest gâteau, brownie, carrot cake, Chelsea bun, chocolate cake, creamcake, Christmas cake, Danish pastry, doughnut, Dundee cake, Eccles cake, éclair, flapjack, fruitcake, gateau, Genoa cake, gingerbread, hot cross bun, lardy cake, Madeira cake, poppyseed cake, Sachertorte, sponge cake, sultana cake, Victoria sponge, yeast cake; French cake, madeleine, muffin, queen cake.

---

calamitous adj disastrous, catastrophic, ruinous, devastating, deadly, fatal, dire, ghastly, dreadful, tragic, woeful, grievous.
☒ good, fortunate, happy.

calamity n disaster, catastrophe, mishap, misadventure, mischance, misfortune, adversity, reverse, trial, tribulation, affliction, distress, tragedy, ruin, downfall.
☒ blessing, godsend.

calculate v compute, work out, count, enumerate, reckon, figure, determine, weigh, rate, value, estimate, gauge, judge, consider, plan, intend, aim.

calculating adj crafty, cunning, sly, devious, scheming, designing, contriving, sharp, shrewd.
☒ artless, naive.

calculation n sum, computation, answer, result, reckoning, figuring, estimate, forecast, judgement, planning, deliberation.

calibre n 1 DIAMETER, bore, gauge, size, measure. 2 candidates of the right calibre: talent, gifts, strength, worth, merit, quality, character, ability, capacity, faculty, stature, distinction.

call v 1 NAME, christen, baptize, title, entitle, dub, style, term, label,

designate. **2** SHOUT, yell, exclaim,
cry. **3** SUMMON, invite, bid, convene,
assemble. **4** TELEPHONE, phone, ring
(up), contact.
◇ *n* **1** CRY, exclamation, shout, yell,
scream. **2** VISIT, ring, summons,
invitation. **3** *there's no call for it*:
demand, need, occasion, cause,
excuse, justification, reason, grounds,
right. **4** APPEAL, request, plea, order,
command, claim, announcement,
signal.
● **call for 1** DEMAND, require, need,
necessitate, involve, entail, occasion,
suggest. **2** FETCH, collect, pick up.
● **call off** cancel, drop, abandon,
discontinue, break off, withdraw.

calling *n* mission, vocation, career,
profession, occupation, job, trade,
business, line, work, employment,
field, province, pursuit.

callous *adj* heartless, cold, hard-
hearted, indifferent, uncaring,
unsympathetic, unfeeling, insensitive,
hardened, thick-skinned.
⊜ kind, caring, sympathetic,
sensitive.

calm *adj* **1** COMPOSED, self-possessed,
collected, cool, dispassionate,
unemotional, impassive, unmoved,
placid, sedate, imperturbable,
unflappable, unexcitable, laid-
back (*infml*), relaxed, unexcited,
unruffled, unflustered, unperturbed,
undisturbed, untroubled,
unapprehensive. **2** *calm waters*:
smooth, still, windless, unclouded,
mild, tranquil, serene, peaceful,
quiet, uneventful, restful.
⊜ **1** excitable, worried, anxious.
2 rough, wild, stormy.
◇ *v* compose, soothe, relax, sedate,
tranquillize, hush, quieten, placate,
pacify.
⊜ excite, worry.
◇ *n* calmness, stillness, tranquillity,
serenity, peacefulness, peace, quiet,
hush, repose.
⊜ storminess, restlessness.

camera

Types of camera include:
advanced photo system (APS),
automatic, bellows, binocular, box
Brownie®, camera obscura, cine,
compact, daguerreotype, digital,
disc, disposable, Instamatic®,
miniature, subminiature,
panoramic, pinhole, plate,
Polaroid®, reflex, single-lens reflex
(SLR), twin-lens reflex (TLR),
security, sound, Steadicam®,
stereo, Super 8®, surveillance, TV,
video, view, camcorder, webcam.

Camera parts include: eye-cup,
eye-piece magnifier; flashbulb,
flashcube, flashgun, hot shoe; lens,
afocal lens, close-up lens, fisheye
lens, macro lens, telephoto lens,
teleconverter, wide-angle lens,
zoom lens, lens cap, lens hood,
lens shield, viewfinder, right-angle
finder. *see also* **photograph**.

camouflage *n* disguise, guise,
masquerade, mask, cloak, screen,
blind, front, cover, concealment,
deception.
◇ *v* disguise, mask, cloak, veil,
screen, cover, conceal, hide,
obscure.
⊜ uncover, reveal.

campaign *n* crusade, movement,
promotion, drive, push, offensive,
attack, battle, expedition, operation.
◇ *v* crusade, promote, push,
advocate, fight, battle.

cancel *v* call off, abort, abandon,
drop, abolish, annul, quash, rescind,
revoke, repeal, countermand, delete,
erase, obliterate, eliminate, offset,
compensate, redeem, neutralize,
nullify.

cancer *n* **1** EVIL, blight, canker,
pestilence, sickness, corruption,
rot. **2** TUMOUR, growth, malignancy,
carcinoma.

candid *adj* frank, open, truthful, honest, sincere, straightforward, forthright, ingenuous, guileless, simple, plain, clear, unequivocal, blunt, outspoken.
🖭 guarded, evasive, devious.

candidate *n* applicant, aspirant, contender, contestant, competitor, entrant, runner, possibility, nominee, claimant, pretender, suitor.

candour *n* frankness, openness, truthfulness, honesty, plain-dealing, sincerity, straightforwardness, directness, ingenuousness, guilelessness, naiveté, artlessness, simplicity, plainness, bluntness, unequivocalness, outspokenness.
🖭 evasiveness, deviousness.

canopy *n* awning, covering, shade, shelter, sunshade, umbrella.

cantankerous *adj* irritable, irascible, grumpy, grouchy, crusty, crotchety, crabbed, crabby, testy, bad-tempered, ill-humoured, cross, peevish, difficult, perverse, contrary, quarrelsome.
🖭 good-natured, easy-going (*infml*).

canvass *v* 1 ELECTIONEER, agitate, campaign, solicit, ask for, seek, poll. 2 EXAMINE, inspect, scrutinize, study, scan, investigate, analyse, sift, discuss, debate.
◇ *n* poll, survey, examination, scrutiny, investigation, inquiry.

canyon *n* gorge, ravine, gully, valley.

cap *v* exceed, surpass, transcend, better, beat, outdo, outstrip, eclipse, complete, finish, crown, top, cover.
◇ *n* 1 HAT, skullcap, beret, tam-o'-shanter, baseball cap. 2 LID, top, cover.

capability *n* ability, capacity, faculty, power, potential, means, facility, competence, qualification, skill, proficiency, talent.
🖭 inability, incompetence.

capable *adj* able, competent, efficient, qualified, experienced, accomplished, skilful, proficient, gifted, talented, masterly, clever, intelligent, fitted, suited, apt, liable, disposed.
🖭 incapable, incompetent, useless.

capacity *n* 1 VOLUME, space, room, size, dimensions, magnitude, extent, compass, range, scope. 2 CAPABILITY, ability, faculty, power, potential, competence, efficiency, skill, gift, talent, genius, cleverness, intelligence, aptitude, readiness. 3 *in her capacity as president*: role, function, position, office, post, appointment, job.

cape[1] *n* headland, head, promontory, point, ness, peninsula.

cape[2] *n* cloak, shawl, wrap, robe, poncho, coat.

capital *n* funds, finance, principal, money, cash, savings, investments, wealth, means, wherewithal, resources, assets, property, stock.

capitalize on *v* profit from, take advantage of, exploit, cash in on.

capitulate *v* surrender, throw in the towel, yield, give in, relent, submit, succumb.
🖭 fight on.

capsize *v* overturn, turn over, turn turtle, invert, keel over, upset.

capsule *n* 1 TABLET, pill, lozenge. 2 SHELL, sheath, pod.

captain *n* commander, master, skipper, pilot, head, chief, leader, boss, officer.

captivate *v* charm, enchant, bewitch, beguile, fascinate, enthral, hypnotize, mesmerize, lure, allure, seduce, win, attract, enamour, infatuate, enrapture, dazzle.
🖭 repel, disgust, appal.

captive *n* prisoner, hostage, slave, detainee, internee, convict.
◇ *adj* imprisoned, caged, confined,

restricted, secure, locked up, enchained, enslaved, ensnared. ⊜ free.

captivity n custody, detention, imprisonment, incarceration, internment, confinement, restraint, bondage, duress, slavery, servitude. ⊜ freedom.

capture v catch, trap, snare, take, seize, arrest, apprehend, imprison, secure.
◇ n catching, trapping, taking, seizure, arrest, imprisonment.

car n automobile, motor car, motor, vehicle.

Types of car include: saloon, hatchback, fastback, estate, sports car, cabriolet, convertible, limousine, limo (*infml*), jalopy (*infml*), Mini®, bubble car, coupé, station wagon, people carrier (*infml*), shooting brake, veteran car, vintage car, four-wheel drive, sport utility vehicle (or SUV), Jeep®, buggy, Land Rover®, Range Rover®, panda car, patrol car, taxi, cab.

---

carcase n body, corpse, cadaver, remains, relics, skeleton, shell, structure, framework, hulk.

care n 1 WORRY, anxiety, stress, strain, pressure, concern, trouble, distress, affliction, tribulation, vexation. 2 CAREFULNESS, caution, prudence, forethought, vigilance, watchfulness, pains, meticulousness, attention, heed, regard, consideration, interest. 3 *in their care*: keeping, custody, guardianship, protection, ward, charge, responsibility, control, supervision.
⊜ 2 carelessness, thoughtlessness, inattention, neglect.
◇ v worry, mind, bother.
• **care for** 1 LOOK AFTER, nurse, tend, mind, watch over, protect, minister to, attend. 2 LIKE, be fond of, love,

be keen on, enjoy, delight in, want, desire.

career n vocation, calling, life-work, occupation, pursuit, profession, trade, job, employment, livelihood.
◇ v rush, dash, tear, hurtle, race, run, gallop, speed, shoot, bolt.

carefree adj unworried, untroubled, unconcerned, blithe, breezy, happy-go-lucky, cheery, light-hearted, cheerful, happy, easy-going (*infml*), laid-back (*infml*).
⊜ worried, anxious, despondent.

careful adj 1 CAUTIOUS, prudent, circumspect, judicious, wary, chary, vigilant, watchful, alert, attentive, mindful. 2 METICULOUS, painstaking, conscientious, scrupulous, thorough, detailed, punctilious, particular, accurate, precise, thoughtful.
⊜ 1 careless, inattentive, thoughtless, reckless. 2 careless.

careless adj 1 UNTHINKING, thoughtless, inconsiderate, uncaring, unconcerned, heedless, unmindful, forgetful, remiss, negligent, reckless, irresponsible, unguarded. 2 *careless work*: inaccurate, messy, untidy, disorderly, sloppy, neglectful, lax, slipshod, slapdash, hasty, cursory, offhand, casual.
⊜ 1 thoughtful, prudent. 2 careful, accurate, meticulous.

caress v stroke, pet, fondle, cuddle, hug, embrace, kiss, touch, rub.
◇ n stroke, pat, fondle, cuddle, hug, embrace, kiss.

caretaker n janitor, porter, watchman, keeper, custodian, curator, warden, superintendent.

cargo n freight, load, pay-load, lading, tonnage, shipment, consignment, contents, goods, merchandise, baggage.

caricature n cartoon, parody, lampoon, burlesque, satire, send-up, take-off, imitation, representation, distortion, travesty.

◇ v parody, mock, ridicule, satirize, send up, take off, mimic, distort, exaggerate.

carnage n bloodshed, bloodbath, butchery, slaughter, killing, murder, massacre, holocaust.

carnival n festival, fiesta, gala, jamboree, fête, fair, holiday, jubilee, celebration, merrymaking, revelry.

carriage n 1 COACH, wagon, car, vehicle. 2 DEPORTMENT, posture, bearing, air, manner, mien, demeanour, behaviour, conduct. 3 CARRYING, conveyance, transport, transportation, delivery, postage.

carry v 1 BRING, convey, transport, haul, move, transfer, relay, release, conduct, take, fetch. 2 BEAR, shoulder, support, underpin, maintain, uphold, sustain, suffer, stand.
• **carry on 1** CONTINUE, proceed, last, endure, maintain, keep on, persist, persevere. 2 carry on a business: operate, run, manage, administer.
⊟ 1 stop, finish.
• **carry out** do, perform, undertake, discharge, conduct, execute, implement, fulfil, accomplish, achieve, realize, bring off.

cart n barrow, wheelbarrow, handcart, wagon, truck.
◇ v move, convey, transport, haul, lug (infml), hump (infml), bear, carry.

carton n box, packet, pack, case, container, package, parcel.

cartoon n comic strip, animation, sketch, drawing, caricature, parody.

cartridge n cassette, canister, cylinder, tube, container, case, capsule, shell, magazine, round, charge.

carve v cut, slice, hack, hew, chisel, chip, sculpt, sculpture, shape, form, fashion, mould, etch, engrave, incise, indent.

cascade n rush, gush, outpouring, flood, deluge, torrent, avalanche, cataract, waterfall, falls, fountain, shower.
⊟ trickle.
◇ v rush, gush, surge, flood, spill, overflow, tumble, fall, descend, shower, pour, plunge, pitch.

case¹ n container, receptacle, holder, suitcase, trunk, crate, box, carton, casket, chest, cabinet, showcase, casing, cartridge, shell, capsule, sheath, cover, jacket, wrapper.

case² n 1 CIRCUMSTANCES, context, state, condition, position, situation, contingency, occurrence, occasion, event, specimen, example, instance, illustration, point. 2 LAWSUIT, suit, trial, proceedings, action, process, cause, argument, dispute.

cash n money, hard money, ready money, banknotes, notes, coins, change, legal tender, currency, hard currency, bullion, funds, resources, wherewithal.
◇ v encash, exchange, realize, liquidate.

cashier n clerk, teller, treasurer, bursar, purser, banker, accountant.

cask n barrel, tun, hogshead, firkin, vat, tub, butt.

cast v 1 THROW, hurl, lob, pitch, fling, toss, sling, shy, launch, impel, drive, direct, project, shed, emit, diffuse, spread, scatter. 2 MOULD, shape, form, model, found.
◇ n 1 COMPANY, troupe, actors, players, performers, entertainers, characters, dramatis personae. 2 CASTING, mould, shape, form.
• **cast down** depress, discourage, dishearten, deject, sadden, crush, desolate.
⊟ cheer up, encourage.

castle n stronghold, fortress, citadel, keep, tower, château, palace, mansion, stately home, country house.

Parts of a castle include: approach,

arrow-slit, bailey, barbican, bartizan, bastion, battlements, berm, brattice, buttress, corbel, courtyard, crenel, crenellation, crosslet, donjon, drawbridge, dungeon, embrasure, foss (or fosse), gatehouse, inner wall, keep, loophole, merlon, moat, motte, mound, outer bailey, parados, parapet, portcullis, postern, rampart, scarp, stockade, tower, lookout tower, turret, ward, watchtower.

casual adj **1** a casual meeting: chance, fortuitous, accidental, unintentional, unpremeditated, unexpected, unforeseen, irregular, random, occasional, incidental, superficial, cursory. **2** NONCHALANT, blasé, lackadaisical, negligent, couldn't-care-less (infml), apathetic, indifferent, unconcerned, informal, offhand, relaxed, laid-back (infml).
⊞ **1** deliberate, planned. **2** formal.

casualty n injury, loss, death, fatality, victim, sufferer, injured, injured person, wounded, dead person.

cat

Breeds of cat include: Abyssinian, American shorthair, Balinese, Birman, Bombay, British shorthair, Burmese, Chinchilla, Cornish Rex, Devon Rex, domestic tabby, Egyptian Mau, Exotic, Havana, Himalayan, Japanese Bobtail, Korat, Maine Coon, Manx, Norwegian Forest, Persian, Rag-doll, Russian Blue, Scottish Fold, Siamese, Singapura, Somali, Tiffanie, Tonkinese, tortoiseshell, Turkish Angora, Turkish Van.

catalogue n list, inventory, roll, register, roster, schedule, record, table, index, directory, gazetteer, brochure, prospectus.
◊ v list, register, record, index,

classify, alphabetize, file.

catapult v hurl, fling, throw, pitch, toss, sling, launch, propel, shoot, fire.

cataract n waterfall, falls, rapids, force, cascade, downpour, torrent, deluge.

catastrophe n disaster, calamity, cataclysm, debacle, fiasco, failure, ruin, devastation, tragedy, blow, reverse, mischance, misfortune, adversity, affliction, trouble, upheaval.

catch v **1** SEIZE, grab, take, hold, grasp, grip, clutch, capture, trap, entrap, snare, ensnare, hook, net, arrest, apprehend. **2** HEAR, understand, perceive, recognize. **3** SURPRISE, expose, unmask, find (out), discover, detect, discern. **4** catch a cold: contract, get, develop, go down with.
⊞ **1** drop, release, free. **2** miss.
◊ n **1** FASTENER, clip, hook, clasp, hasp, latch, bolt. **2** DISADVANTAGE, drawback, snag, hitch, obstacle, problem.
• **catch up** gain on, draw level with, overtake.

catching adj infectious, contagious, communicable, transmittable.

catchword n catchphrase, slogan, motto, watchword, byword, password.

catchy adj memorable, haunting, popular, melodic, tuneful, attractive, captivating.
⊞ dull, boring.

categorical adj absolute, total, utter, unqualified, unreserved, unconditional, downright, positive, definite, emphatic, unequivocal, clear, explicit, express, direct.
⊞ tentative, qualified, vague.

categorize v class, classify, group, sort, grade, rank, order, list.

category n class, classification, group, grouping, sort, type, section, division, department, chapter, head, heading, grade, rank, order, list.

cater *v* provision, victual, provide, supply, furnish, serve, indulge, pander.

catholic *adj* broad, wide, wide-ranging, universal, global, general, comprehensive, inclusive, all-inclusive, all-embracing, liberal, tolerant, broad-minded.
🗷 narrow, limited, narrow-minded.

cattle *n* cows, bulls, oxen, livestock, stock, beasts.

Breeds of cattle include: Aberdeen Angus, Africander, Alderney, Ankole, Ayrshire, Blonde d'Aquitaine, brahmin, Brown Swiss, cattabu, cattalo, Charolais, Devon, dexter, Durham, Friesian, Galloway, Guernsey, Hereford, Highland, Holstein, Jersey, Limousin, longhorn, Luing, redpoll, Santa Gertrudis, Shetland, shorthorn, Simmental.

cause *n* 1 SOURCE, origin, beginning, root, basis, spring, originator, creator, producer, maker, agent, agency. 2 REASON, motive, grounds, motivation, stimulus, incentive, inducement, impulse. 3 *a worthy cause*: object, purpose, end, ideal, belief, conviction, movement, undertaking, enterprise.
🗷 1 effect, result, consequence.
◇ *v* begin, give rise to, lead to, result in, occasion, bring about, effect, produce, generate, create, precipitate, motivate, stimulate, provoke, incite, induce, force, compel.
🗷 stop, prevent.

caustic *adj* corrosive, acid, burning, stinging, biting, cutting, mordant, trenchant, keen, pungent, bitter, acrimonious, sarcastic, scathing, virulent, severe.
🗷 soothing, mild.

caution *n* 1 CARE, carefulness, prudence, vigilance, watchfulness, alertness, heed, forethought, discretion, deliberation, wariness. 2 WARNING, caveat, injunction, admonition, advice, counsel.
🗷 1 carelessness, recklessness.
◇ *v* warn, admonish, advise, urge.

cautious *adj* careful, prudent, circumspect, judicious, vigilant, watchful, alert, heedful, discreet, tactful, chary, wary, cagey (*infml*), guarded, tentative, softly-softly, unadventurous.
🗷 incautious, imprudent, heedless, reckless.

cavalcade *n* procession, parade, march-past, troop, array, retinue, train.

cavalier *n* horseman, equestrian, knight, gentleman, gallant, escort, partner.
◇ *adj* supercilious, condescending, lordly, haughty, lofty, arrogant, swaggering, insolent, scornful, disdainful, curt, offhand, free-and-easy.

cave *n* cavern, grotto, hole, pothole, hollow, cavity.
• **cave in** collapse, subside, give way, yield, fall, slip.

cavernous *adj* hollow, concave, gaping, yawning, echoing, resonant, deep, sunken.

cavity *n* hole, gap, dent, hollow, crater, pit, well, sinus, ventricle.

cavort *v* caper, frolic, gambol, prance, skip, dance, frisk, sport, romp.

cease *v* stop, desist, refrain, pack in (*sl*), halt, call a halt, break off, discontinue, finish, end, conclude, terminate, fail, die.
🗷 begin, start, commence.

ceaseless *adj* endless, unending, never-ending, eternal, everlasting, continuous, non-stop, incessant, interminable, constant, perpetual,

continual, persistent, untiring, unremitting.
⊞ occasional, irregular.

cede v surrender, give up, resign, abdicate, renounce, abandon, yield, relinquish, convey, transfer, hand over, grant, allow, concede.

celebrate v commemorate, remember, observe, keep, rejoice, toast, drink to, honour, exalt, glorify, praise, extol, eulogize, commend, bless, solemnize.

celebrated adj famous, well-known, famed, renowned, illustrious, glorious, eminent, distinguished, notable, prominent, outstanding, popular, acclaimed, exalted, revered.
⊞ unknown, obscure, forgotten.

celebration n commemoration, remembrance, observance, anniversary, jubilee, festival, gala, merrymaking, jollification, revelry, festivity, party, rave-up (infml).

Celebrations include: anniversary, banquet, baptism, bar mitzvah, bat mitzvah, birthday, centenary, christening, coming-of-age, confirmation, feast, festival, fête, gala, graduation, harvest festival, homecoming, Independence Day, jubilee, marriage, Mayday, name day, party, reception, retirement, reunion, saint's day, thanksgiving, wedding. see also **anniversary**; **party**.

celebrity n celeb (infml), personage, dignitary, VIP (infml), luminary, star, worthy, personality, name, big name, superstar, megastar.
⊞ nobody, nonentity.

celibacy n bachelorhood, spinsterhood, singleness, virginity, chastity, purity, abstinence, continence.

cell n dungeon, prison, room, cubicle, chamber, compartment, cavity, unit.

cellar n basement, crypt, vault, storeroom, wine cellar.

cement v stick, bond, weld, solder, join, unite, bind, combine.
◇ n plaster, mortar, concrete.

cemetery n burial-ground, graveyard, churchyard.

censor v cut, edit, blue-pencil, bowdlerize, expurgate.

censorious adj condemnatory, disapproving, disparaging, fault-finding, carping, cavilling, critical, hypercritical, severe.
⊞ complimentary, approving.

censure n condemnation, blame, disapproval, criticism, admonishment, admonition, reprehension, reproof, reproach, rebuke, reprimand, telling-off (infml).
⊞ praise, compliments, approval, brownie points (infml).
◇ v condemn, denounce, blame, criticize, castigate, admonish, reprehend, reprove, upbraid, reproach, rebuke, reprimand, scold, tell off (infml).
⊞ praise, compliment, approve.

central adj middle, mid, inner, interior, focal, main, chief, key, principal, primary, fundamental, vital, essential, important.
⊞ peripheral, minor, secondary.

centre n middle, mid-point, bull's-eye, heart, core, nucleus, pivot, hub, focus, crux.
⊞ edge, periphery, outskirts.
◇ v focus, concentrate, converge, gravitate, revolve, pivot, hinge.

ceremonial adj formal, official, stately, solemn, ritual, ritualistic.
⊞ informal, casual.
◇ n ceremony, formality, protocol, solemnity, ritual, rite.

ceremonious adj stately, dignified, grand, solemn, ritual, civil, polite, courteous, deferential, courtly, formal, stiff, starchy, exact, precise, punctilious.

⊞ unceremonious, informal, relaxed.

ceremony n 1 *wedding ceremony*: service, rite, commemoration, observance, celebration, function, custom, parade. 2 ETIQUETTE, protocol, decorum, propriety, formality, form, niceties, ceremonial, ritual, pomp, show.

certain *adj* 1 SURE, positive, assured, confident, convinced, undoubted, indubitable, unquestionable, incontrovertible, undeniable, irrefutable, plain, conclusive, absolute, convincing, true. 2 INEVITABLE, unavoidable, bound, destined, fated. 3 SPECIFIC, special, particular, individual, precise, express, fixed, established, settled, decided, definite. 4 DEPENDABLE, reliable, trustworthy, constant, steady, stable.
⊞ 1 uncertain, unsure, hesitant, doubtful. 2 unlikely. 4 unreliable.

certainly *adv* of course, naturally, definitely, for sure, undoubtedly, doubtlessly.

certainty n sureness, positiveness, assurance, confidence, conviction, faith, trust, truth, validity, fact, reality, inevitability.
⊞ uncertainty, doubt, hesitation.

certificate n document, award, diploma, qualification, credentials, testimonial, guarantee, endorsement, warrant, licence, authorization, pass, voucher.

certify v declare, attest, aver, assure, guarantee, endorse, corroborate, confirm, vouch, testify, witness, verify, authenticate, validate, authorize, license.

chain n 1 FETTER, manacle, restraint, bond, link, coupling, union. 2 *chain of events*: sequence, succession, progression, string, train, series, set.
◊ v tether, fasten, secure, bind, restrain, confine, fetter, shackle,

manacle, handcuff, enslave.
⊞ release, free.

chair

Types of chair include: easy chair, armchair, rocking chair, recliner, dining chair, carver, kitchen chair, stool, swivel chair, highchair.

chairman, chairwoman n chairperson, chair, president, convenor, organizer, director, master of ceremonies, MC, toastmaster, speaker.

challenge v 1 DARE, defy, throw down the gauntlet, confront, brave, accost, provoke, test, tax, try. 2 DISPUTE, question, query, protest, object to.
◊ n dare, defiance, confrontation, provocation, test, trial, hurdle, obstacle, problem, question, ultimatum.

champion n winner, victor, hero, conqueror, guardian, protector, defender, vindicator, patron, backer, supporter, upholder, advocate.
◊ v defend, stand up for, back, support, maintain, uphold, espouse, advocate, promote.

chance n 1 ACCIDENT, fortuity, coincidence, fluke (*infml*), luck, fortune, providence, fate, destiny, risk, gamble, speculation, possibility, prospect, probability, likelihood, odds. 2 *a second chance*: opportunity, opening, occasion, time.
⊞ 1 certainty.
◊ v 1 RISK, hazard, gamble, wager, stake, try, venture. 2 HAPPEN, occur.
◊ adj fortuitous, casual, accidental, inadvertent, unintentional, unintended, unforeseen, unlooked-for, random, haphazard, incidental.
⊞ deliberate, intentional, foreseen, certain.

change v alter, modify, convert, reorganize, reform, remodel,

restyle, transform, transfigure, metamorphose, mutate, vary, fluctuate, vacillate, shift, displace, swap, exchange, trade, switch, transpose, substitute, replace, alternate, interchange.
◇ *n* alteration, modification, conversion, transformation, metamorphosis, mutation, variation, fluctuation, shift, exchange, transposition, substitution, interchange, difference, diversion, novelty, innovation, variety, transition, revolution, upheaval.

changeable *adj* variable, mutable, fluid, kaleidoscopic, shifting, mobile, unsettled, uncertain, unpredictable, unreliable, erratic, irregular, inconstant, fickle, capricious, volatile, unstable, unsteady, wavering, vacillating.
🠪 constant, reliable.

channel *n* 1 DUCT, conduit, main, groove, furrow, trough, gutter, canal, flume, watercourse, waterway, strait, sound. 2 *channel of communication*: route, course, path, avenue, way, means, medium, approach, passage.
◇ *v* direct, guide, conduct, convey, send, transmit, force.

chant *n* plainsong, psalm, song, melody, chorus, refrain, slogan, war cry.
◇ *v* recite, intone, sing, chorus.

chaos *n* disorder, confusion, disorganization, anarchy, tumult, lawlessness, upheaval, pandemonium, bedlam.
🠪 order.

chaotic *adj* disordered, confused, disorganized, topsy-turvy, deranged, anarchic, lawless, riotous, tumultuous, unruly, uncontrolled.
🠪 ordered, organized.

chap *n* fellow, bloke (*infml*), guy (*infml*), man, boy, person, individual, character, sort, type.

chapter *n* part, section, division,

clause, topic, episode, period, phase, stage.

character *n* 1 PERSONALITY, nature, disposition, temperament, temper, constitution, make-up, individuality, peculiarity, feature, attributes, quality, type, stamp, calibre, reputation, status, position, trait. 2 LETTER, figure, symbol, sign, mark, type, cipher, rune, hieroglyph, ideograph. 3 INDIVIDUAL, person, sort, type, role, part.

characteristic *adj* distinctive, distinguishing, individual, idiosyncratic, peculiar, specific, special, typical, representative, symbolic, symptomatic.
🠪 uncharacteristic, untypical.
◇ *n* peculiarity, idiosyncrasy, mannerism, feature, trait, attribute, property, quality, hallmark, mark, symptom.

characterize *v* typify, mark, stamp, brand, identify, distinguish, indicate, represent, portray.

charge *v* 1 *charge a high price*: ask, demand, levy, exact, debit. 2 ACCUSE, indict, impeach, incriminate, blame. 3 ATTACK, assail, storm, rush.
◇ *n* 1 PRICE, cost, fee, rate, amount, expense, expenditure, outlay, payment. 2 ACCUSATION, indictment, allegation, imputation. 3 ATTACK, assault, onslaught, sortie, rush. 4 *in your charge*: custody, keeping, care, safekeeping, guardianship, ward, trust, responsibility, duty.

charitable *adj* philanthropic, humanitarian, benevolent, benign, kind, compassionate, sympathetic, understanding, considerate, generous, magnanimous, liberal, tolerant, broad-minded, lenient, forgiving, indulgent, gracious.
🠪 uncharitable, inconsiderate, unforgiving.

charity *n* 1 GENEROSITY, bountifulness, almsgiving, beneficence, philanthropy, unselfishness, altruism,

benevolence, benignity, kindness, goodness, humanity, compassion, tender-heartedness, love, affection, clemency, indulgence. **2** ALMS, gift, handout, aid, relief, assistance.
⊞ **1** selfishness, malice.

charm v please, delight, enrapture, captivate, fascinate, beguile, enchant, bewitch, mesmerize, attract, allure, cajole, win, enamour.
⊞ repel.
◇ n **1** ATTRACTION, allure, magnetism, appeal, desirability, fascination, enchantment, spell, sorcery, magic. **2** *lucky charm*: trinket, talisman, amulet, fetish, idol.

charming adj pleasing, delightful, pleasant, lovely, captivating, enchanting, attractive, fetching, appealing, sweet, winsome, seductive, winning, irresistible.
⊞ ugly, unattractive, repulsive.

chart n diagram, table, graph, map, plan, blueprint.
◇ v map, map out, sketch, draw, draft, outline, delineate, mark, plot, place.

charter n right, privilege, prerogative, authorization, permit, licence, franchise, concession, contract, indenture, deed, bond, document.
◇ v hire, rent, lease, commission, engage, employ, authorize, sanction, license.

chase v pursue, follow, hunt, track, drive, expel, rush, hurry.

chasm n gap, opening, gulf, abyss, void, hollow, cavity, crater, breach, rift, split, cleft, fissure, crevasse, canyon, gorge, ravine.

chaste adj pure, virginal, unsullied, undefiled, immaculate, abstinent, continent, celibate, virtuous, moral, innocent, wholesome, modest, decent, plain, simple, austere.
⊞ corrupt, lewd, vulgar, indecorous.

chasten v humble, humiliate, tame,

subdue, repress, curb, moderate, soften, discipline, punish, correct, chastise, castigate, reprove.

chastise v punish, discipline, correct, beat, flog, whip, lash, scourge, smack, spank, castigate, reprove, admonish, scold, upbraid, berate, censure.

chat n talk, conversation, natter (*infml*), gossip, chinwag (*infml*), tête-à-tête, heart-to-heart.
◇ v talk, crack, natter (*infml*), gossip, chatter, rabbit (on) (*infml*).

chatter v, n prattle, babble, chat, natter (*infml*), gossip, tattle.

chatty adj talkative, gossipy, newsy, friendly, informal, colloquial, familiar.
⊞ quiet.

cheap adj **1** INEXPENSIVE, reasonable, dirt-cheap, bargain, reduced, cut-price, knock-down, budget, economy, economical. **2** TAWDRY, tatty, cheapo (*sl*), shoddy, inferior, second-rate, worthless, vulgar, common, poor, paltry, mean, contemptible, despicable, low.
⊞ **1** expensive, costly. **2** superior, noble, admirable.

cheapen v devalue, degrade, lower, demean, depreciate, belittle, disparage, denigrate, downgrade.

cheat v defraud, swindle, diddle, short-change, do (*infml*), rip off (*sl*), fleece, con (*infml*), double-cross, mislead, deceive, dupe, fool, trick, hoodwink, bamboozle (*infml*), beguile.
◇ n cheater, dodger, fraud, swindler, shark (*infml*), con man (*infml*), extortioner, double-crosser, impostor, charlatan, deceiver, trickster, rogue.

check v **1** EXAMINE, inspect, scrutinize, give the once-over (*infml*), investigate, probe, test, monitor, study, research, compare, cross-check, confirm, verify. **2** *check an impulse*: curb, bridle, restrain,

control, limit, repress, inhibit, damp,
thwart, hinder, impede, obstruct, bar,
retard, delay, stop, arrest, halt.
◇ *n* **1** EXAMINATION, inspection,
scrutiny, once-over (*infml*), check-up,
investigation, audit, test, research.
2 CURB, restraint, control, limitation,
constraint, inhibition, damper, blow,
disappointment, reverse, setback,
frustration, hindrance, impediment,
obstruction, stoppage.

cheek *n* impertinence, impudence,
insolence, disrespect, effrontery,
brazenness, temerity, audacity, nerve
(*infml*), gall.

cheeky *adj* impertinent, impudent,
insolent, disrespectful, forward,
brazen, pert, saucy (*infml*),
audacious.
🖃 respectful, polite.

cheer *v* **1** ACCLAIM, hail, clap,
applaud. **2** COMFORT, console,
brighten, gladden, warm, uplift,
elate, exhilarate, encourage, hearten.
🖃 **1** boo, jeer. **2** dishearten.
◇ *n* acclamation, hurrah, bravo,
applause, ovation.
• **cheer up** encourage, hearten, take
heart, rally, buck up (*infml*), perk up
(*infml*).

cheerful *adj* happy, glad, contented,
joyful, joyous, blithe, carefree, light-
hearted, cheery, good-humoured,
sunny, optimistic, enthusiastic,
hearty, genial, jovial, jolly, merry,
lively, animated, bright, chirpy,
breezy, jaunty, buoyant, sparkling.
🖃 sad, dejected, depressed.

cheese

Varieties of cheese include: bel
paese, Bleu d'Auvergne, Blue
Vinny, Boursin®, Brie, caboc,
Caerphilly, Cambozola®,
Camembert, Cheddar, Cheshire,
cottage cheese, cream cheese,
crowdie, curd cheese, Danish blue,
Derby, dolcelatte, double
Gloucester, Dunlop, Edam,
Emmental, ewe-cheese, feta,
fontina, fromage frais, Gloucester,
goat's cheese, Gorgonzola, Gouda,
Gruyère, Jarlsberg®, Lancashire,
Leicester, Limburger, mascarpone,
Manchego, Monterey Jack,
mozzarella, Neufchâtel, Orkney,
Parmesan, pecorino, Pont-
L'Évêque, Port Salut, processed
cheese, provolone, quark, Red
Leicester, Red Windsor, ricotta,
Roquefort, sage Derby, smoked
cheese, Stilton®, stracchino,
Vacherin, Wensleydale.

chemical element

The chemical elements (with their
symbols) are: actinium (Ac),
aluminium (Al), americium (Am),
antimony (Sb), argon (Ar), arsenic
(As), astatine (At), barium (Ba),
berkelium (Bk), beryllium (Be),
bismuth (Bi), bohrium (Bh), boron
(B), bromine (Br), cadmium (Cd),
caesium (Cs), calcium (Ca),
californium (Cf), carbon (C),
cerium (Ce), chlorine (Cl),
chromium (Cr), cobalt (Co), copper
(Cu), curium (Cm), darmstadtium
(Ds), dubnium (Db), dysprosium
(Dy), einsteinium (Es), erbium (Er),
europium (Eu), fermium (Fm),
fluorine (F), francium (Fr),
gadolinium (Gd), gallium (Ga),
germanium (Ge), gold (Au),
hafnium (Hf), hassium (Hs), helium
(He), holmium (Ho), hydrogen (H),
indium (In), iodine (I), iridium (Ir),
iron (Fe), krypton (Kr), lanthanum
(La), lawrencium (Lr), lead (Pb),
lithium (Li), lutetium (Lu),
magnesium (Mg), manganese (Mn),
meitnerium (Mt), mendelevium
(Md), mercury (Hg), molybdenum
(Mo), neodymium (Nd), neon (Ne),
neptunium (Np), nickel (Ni),
niobium (Nb), nitrogen (N),
nobelium (No), osmium (Os),
oxygen (O), palladium (Pd),
phosphorus (P), platinum (Pt),

plutonium (Pu), polonium (Po), potassium (K), praseodymium (Pr), promethium (Pm), protactinium (Pa), radium (Ra), radon (Rn), rhenium (Re), rhodium (Rh), roentgenium (Rg), rubidium (Rb), ruthenium (Ru), rutherfordium (Rf), samarium (Sm), scandium (Sc), seaborgium (Sg), selenium (Se), silicon (Si), silver (Ag), sodium (Na), strontium (Sr), sulphur (S), tantalum (Ta), technetium (Tc), tellurium (Te), terbium (Tb), thallium (Tl), thorium (Th), thulium (Tm), tin (Sn), titanium (Ti), tungsten (W), uranium (U), vanadium (V), xenon (Xe), ytterbium (Yb), yttrium (Y), zinc (Zn), zirconium (Zr).

chemistry

Terms used in chemistry include: acid, alkali, analysis, atom, atomic number, atomic structure, base, bond, buffer, catalyst, chain reaction, combustion, compound, corrosion, covalent bond, crystal, diffusion, distillation, electrode, electrolysis, electron, element, emulsion, equation, formula, free radical, gas, halogen, hydrolysis, indicator, inert, ion, isomer, isotope, liquid, litmus paper, litmus test, mass, mixture, mole, molecule, neutron, noble gas, nucleus, oxidation, periodic table, pH, polymer, proton, radioactivity, reaction, reduction, salt, solid, solution, solvent, subatomic particle, substance, suspension, symbol, synthesis, valency.

cherish v foster, care for, look after, nurse, nurture, nourish, sustain, support, harbour, shelter, entertain, hold dear, value, prize, treasure.

chest n trunk, crate, box, case, casket, coffer, strongbox.

chew v masticate, gnaw, munch, champ, crunch, grind.

chief adj leading, foremost, uppermost, highest, supreme, grand, arch, premier, principal, key, main, central, prime, prevailing, predominant, pre-eminent, vital, outstanding, essential, primary, major.
⊡ minor, unimportant.
◇ n ruler, chieftain, lord, master, supremo, head, principal, leader, commander, captain, governor, boss, director, manager, superintendent, superior, ringleader.

chiefly adv mainly, mostly, for the most part, predominantly, principally, primarily, essentially, especially, generally, usually.

child n youngster, kid (infml), nipper (infml), brat (infml), baby, infant, toddler, tot (infml), rugrat (US infml), minor, juvenile, offspring, issue, progeny, descendant.

childhood n babyhood, infancy, boyhood, girlhood, schooldays, youth, adolescence, minority, immaturity.

childish adj babyish, boyish, girlish, infantile, puerile, juvenile, immature, silly, foolish, frivolous.
⊡ mature, sensible.

childlike adj innocent, naive, ingenuous, artless, guileless, credulous, trusting, trustful, simple, natural.

chill v 1 COOL, refrigerate, freeze, ice. 2 FRIGHTEN, terrify, dismay, dishearten, discourage, depress, dampen.
⊡ 1 warm, heat.
◇ n coolness, cold, coldness, iciness, frigidity, rawness, bite, nip, crispness.
⊡ warmth.

chilly adj 1 chilly weather: cold, fresh, brisk, crisp, nippy (infml), wintry. 2 a chilly response: cool, frigid, unsympathetic, unwelcoming, aloof, stony, unfriendly, hostile.
⊡ 1 warm. 2 friendly.

chime v sound, strike, toll, ring, peal, clang, dong, jingle, tinkle.

china adj porcelain, ceramic, pottery, earthenware, terracotta.

Chinese calendar

The animals representing the years in which people are born: rat, buffalo, tiger, rabbit (or hare), dragon, snake, horse, goat (or sheep), monkey, rooster, dog, pig.

---

chink n crack, rift, cleft, fissure, crevice, slot, opening, aperture, gap, space.

chip n 1 NOTCH, nick, scratch, dent, flaw. 2 FRAGMENT, scrap, wafer, sliver, flake, shaving, paring.
◇ v chisel, whittle, nick, notch, gash, damage.

chirp v, n chirrup, tweet, cheep, peep, twitter, warble, sing, pipe, whistle.

chivalrous adj gentlemanly, polite, courteous, gallant, heroic, valiant, brave, courageous, bold, noble, honourable.
⊠ ungallant, cowardly.

chivalry n gentlemanliness, politeness, courtesy, gallantry, bravery, courage, boldness.

choice n option, alternative, selection, variety, pick, preference, say, decision, dilemma, election, discrimination, choosing, opting.
◇ adj best, superior, prime, plum, excellent, fine, exquisite, exclusive, select, hand-picked, special, prize, valuable, precious.
⊠ inferior, poor.

choke v 1 THROTTLE, suffocate, strangle, asphyxiate, stifle, smother, suppress. 2 OBSTRUCT, constrict, congest, clog, block, dam, bar, close, stop. 3 COUGH, gag, retch.

choose v pick, select, single out, designate, predestine, opt for, plump for, vote for, settle on, fix on, adopt,
elect, prefer, wish, desire, see fit.

choosy adj selective, discriminating, picky (infml), fussy, particular, finicky, fastidious, exacting.
⊠ undemanding.

chop v cut, hack, hew, lop, sever, truncate, cleave, divide, split, slash.
• **chop up** cut (up), slice (up), divide, cube, dice, mince.

choppy adj rough, turbulent, tempestuous, stormy, squally, ruffled, wavy, uneven, broken.
⊠ calm, still.

chore n task, job, errand, duty, burden.

chorus n 1 REFRAIN, burden, response, call, shout. 2 CHOIR, choristers, singers, vocalists, ensemble.

christen v baptize, name, call, dub, title, style, term, designate, inaugurate, use.

Christmas n Xmas, Noel, Yule, Yuletide.

chronic adj 1 INCURABLE, deep-seated, recurring, incessant, persistent, inveterate, confirmed, habitual, ingrained, deep-rooted. 2 (infml) a chronic film: awful, terrible, dreadful, appalling, atrocious.
⊠ 1 acute, temporary.

chronological adj historical, consecutive, sequential, progressive, ordered.

chubby adj plump, podgy, fleshy, flabby, stout, portly, rotund, round, tubby, paunchy.
⊠ slim, skinny.

chuckle v laugh, giggle, titter, snigger, chortle, snort, crow.

chunk n lump, hunk, mass, wodge (infml), wedge, block, slab, piece, portion.

church n chapel, house of God, cathedral, minster, abbey, temple.

cinema n 1 *an admirer of German cinema*: films, pictures, movies (*infml*), flicks (*sl*), the big screen, the silver screen. 2 *working in a cinema*: movie theatre, multiplex, picture-house, picture-palace, fleapit (*infml*).

circle n 1 RING, loop, disc, cycle, turn, revolution, circuit, orbit, circumference, perimeter. 2 *circle of friends*: group, band, company, crowd, set, clique, coterie, club, society, fellowship, fraternity.
◇ v 1 RING, loop, encircle, surround, gird, encompass, enclose, hem in, circumscribe, circumnavigate. 2 ROTATE, revolve, pivot, gyrate, whirl, turn, coil, wind.

circuit n lap, orbit, revolution, tour, journey, course, route, track, round, beat, district, area, region, circumference, boundary, bounds, limit, range, compass, ambit.

circuitous adj roundabout, indirect, oblique, devious, tortuous, winding, meandering, rambling, labyrinthine, periphrastic (*fml*).
⊞ direct, straight.

circular adj round, annular, ring-shaped, hoop-shaped, disc-shaped.
◇ n handbill, leaflet, pamphlet, notice, announcement, advertisement, letter.

Circular things include: ball, coronet, crown, disc, discus, halo, hoop, saucer, sphere, tyre, wheel, wreath.

circulate v 1 *circulate information*: spread, diffuse, broadcast, publicize, publish, issue, propagate, pass round, distribute. 2 GO ROUND, rotate, revolve, gyrate, whirl, swirl, flow.

circulation n 1 BLOOD-FLOW, flow, motion, rotation, circling. 2 SPREAD, transmission, publication, dissemination, distribution.

circumference n circuit, perimeter, rim, edge, outline, boundary, border, bounds, limits, extremity, margin, verge, fringe, periphery.

circumstances n details, particulars, facts, items, elements, factors, conditions, state, state of affairs, situation, position, status, lifestyle, means, resources.

cistern n tank, reservoir, sink, basin.

citadel n fortress, stronghold, bastion, castle, keep, tower, fortification, acropolis.

cite v quote, adduce, name, specify, enumerate, mention, refer to, advance, bring up.

citizen n city-dweller, townsman, townswoman, inhabitant, denizen, resident, householder, taxpayer, subject.

city n metropolis, town, municipality, conurbation.

civic adj city, urban, municipal, borough, community, local, public, communal.

civil adj 1 POLITE, courteous, well-mannered, well-bred, courtly, refined, civilized, polished, urbane, affable, complaisant, obliging, accommodating. 2 *civil affairs*: domestic, home, national, internal, interior, state, municipal, civic.
⊞ 1 uncivil, discourteous, rude. 2 international, military.

civility n politeness, courteousness, courtesy, breeding, refinement, urbanity, graciousness, affability, amenity.
⊞ discourtesy, rudeness.

civilization n progress, advancement, development, education, enlightenment, cultivation, culture, refinement, sophistication, urbanity.
⊞ barbarity, primitiveness.

civilize v tame, humanize, educate, enlighten, cultivate, refine, polish, sophisticate, improve, perfect.

civilized adj advanced, developed,

educated, enlightened, cultured, refined, sophisticated, urbane, polite, sociable.

⊞ uncivilized, barbarous, primitive.

claim v 1 ALLEGE, pretend, profess, state, affirm, assert, maintain, contend, hold, insist. 2 *claim a refund*: ask, request, require, need, demand, exact, take, collect.
◇ n 1 ALLEGATION, pretension, affirmation, assertion, contention, insistence. 2 APPLICATION, petition, request, requirement, demand, call, right, privilege.

clairvoyant adj psychic, prophetic, visionary, telepathic, extra-sensory.
◇ n psychic, fortune-teller, prophet, prophetess, visionary, seer, oracle, soothsayer, augur, diviner, telepath.

clammy adj damp, moist, sweaty, sweating, sticky, slimy, dank, muggy, heavy, close.

clamp n vice, grip, press, brace, bracket, fastener.
◇ v fasten, secure, fix, clinch, grip, brace.

clan n tribe, family, house, race, society, brotherhood, fraternity, confraternity, sect, faction, group, band, set, clique, coterie.

clap v 1 APPLAUD, acclaim, cheer. 2 SLAP, smack, pat, wallop (*infml*), whack (*infml*), bang.

clarify v 1 EXPLAIN, throw light on, illuminate, elucidate, gloss, define, simplify, resolve, clear up. 2 REFINE, purify, filter, clear.
⊞ 1 obscure, confuse. 2 cloud.

clarity n clearness, transparency, lucidity, simplicity, intelligibility, comprehensibility, explicitness, unambiguousness, obviousness, definition, precision.
⊞ obscurity, vagueness, imprecision.

clash v 1 CRASH, bang, clank, clang, jangle, clatter, rattle, jar. 2 CONFLICT, disagree, quarrel, wrangle, grapple, fight, feud, war.

◇ n 1 CRASH, bang, jangle, clatter, noise. 2 *a clash with the police*: confrontation, showdown, conflict, disagreement, fight, brush.

clasp n 1 FASTENER, buckle, clip, pin, hasp, hook, catch. 2 HOLD, grip, grasp, embrace, hug.
◇ v 1 HOLD, grip, grasp, clutch, embrace, enfold, hug, squeeze, press. 2 FASTEN, connect, attach, grapple, hook, clip, pin.

class n 1 CATEGORY, classification, group, set, kind, section, division, department, sphere, grouping, order, league, rank, status, caste, quality, grade, type, genre, sort, species, genus, style. 2 *a French class*: lesson, lecture, seminar, tutorial, course.
◇ v categorize, classify, group, sort, rank, grade, rate, designate, brand.

classic adj typical, characteristic, standard, regular, usual, traditional, time-honoured, established, model, archetypal, exemplary, ideal, best, finest, first-rate, consummate, definitive, masterly, excellent, ageless, immortal, undying, lasting, enduring, abiding.
⊞ unrepresentative, second-rate.
◇ n standard, model, prototype, exemplar, masterwork, masterpiece, pièce de résistance.

classical adj elegant, refined, pure, traditional, excellent, well-proportioned, symmetrical, harmonious, restrained.
⊞ modern, inferior.

classification n categorization, taxonomy, sorting, grading, arrangement, systematization, codification, tabulation, cataloguing.

classify v categorize, class, group, pigeonhole, sort, grade, rank, arrange, dispose, distribute, systematize, codify, tabulate, file, catalogue.

clause n article, item, part, section, subsection, paragraph, heading, chapter, passage, condition, proviso, provision, specification, point.

claw n talon, nail, pincer, nipper, gripper.
◇ v scratch, scrabble, scrape, graze, tear, rip, lacerate, maul, mangle.

clean adj **1** WASHED, laundered, sterile, aseptic, antiseptic, hygienic, sanitary, sterilized, decontaminated, purified, pure, fresh, unpolluted, uncontaminated, unadulterated, immaculate, spotless, unspotted, unstained, unsoiled, unsullied, perfect, faultless, flawless, unblemished. **2** a clean life: innocent, guiltless, virtuous, upright, moral, honest, honourable, respectable, decent, chaste. **3** SMOOTH, regular, straight, neat, tidy.
🗷 **1** dirty, polluted. **2** dishonourable, indecent. **3** rough.
◇ v wash, bath, launder, rinse, wipe, sponge, scrub, scour, mop, swab, sweep, vacuum, dust, freshen, deodorize, cleanse, purge, purify, decontaminate, disinfect, sanitize, sterilize, clear, filter.
🗷 dirty, defile.

cleanser n soap, detergent, cleaner, soap powder, solvent, scourer, scouring powder, purifier, disinfectant.

clear adj **1** PLAIN, distinct, comprehensible, intelligible, coherent, lucid, explicit, precise, unambiguous, well-defined, apparent, evident, patent, obvious, manifest, conspicuous, unmistakable, unquestionable. **2** SURE, certain, positive, definite, convinced. **3** clear water: transparent, limpid, crystalline, glassy, see-through, clean, unclouded, colourless. **4** a clear day: cloudless, unclouded, fine, bright, sunny, light, luminous, undimmed. **5** UNOBSTRUCTED, unblocked, open, free, empty, unhindered, unimpeded. **6** AUDIBLE, perceptible, pronounced, distinct, recognizable.

🗷 **1** unclear, vague, ambiguous, confusing. **2** unsure, muddled. **3** opaque, cloudy. **4** dull. **5** blocked. **6** inaudible, indistinct.
◇ v **1** UNBLOCK, unclog, decongest, free, rid, extricate, disentangle, loosen. **2** CLEAN, wipe, erase, cleanse, refine, filter, tidy, empty, unload. **3** ACQUIT, exculpate, exonerate, absolve, vindicate, excuse, justify, free, liberate, release, let go.
🗷 **1** block. **2** dirty, defile. **3** condemn.
• **clear up 1** EXPLAIN, clarify, elucidate, unravel, solve, resolve, answer. **2** TIDY, order, sort, rearrange, remove.

clearance n **1** AUTHORIZATION, sanction, endorsement, permission, consent, leave, OK (infml), go-ahead, green light (infml). **2** SPACE, gap, headroom, margin, allowance.

clearing n space, gap, opening, glade, dell.

clergy n clergymen, churchmen, clerics, the church, the cloth, ministry, priesthood.

clergyman n churchman, cleric, ecclesiastic, divine, man of God, minister, priest, reverend, father, vicar, pastor, padre, parson, rector, canon, dean, deacon, chaplain, curate, presbyter, rabbi.

clerical adj **1** OFFICE, secretarial, white-collar, official, administrative. **2** ECCLESIASTICAL, pastoral, ministerial, priestly, episcopal, canonical, sacerdotal.

clever adj intelligent, brainy (infml), bright, smart, witty, gifted, expert, knowledgeable, adroit, apt, able, capable, quick, quick-witted, sharp, keen, shrewd, knowing, discerning, cunning, ingenious, inventive, resourceful, sensible, rational.
🗷 foolish, stupid, senseless, ignorant.

cliché n platitude, commonplace, banality, truism, bromide, chestnut, stereotype.

client n customer, patron, regular, buyer, shopper, consumer, user, patient, applicant.

cliff n bluff, face, rock-face, scar, scarp, escarpment, crag, overhang, precipice.

climate n weather, temperature, setting, milieu, environment, ambience, atmosphere, feeling, mood, temper, disposition, tendency, trend.

climax n culmination, height, high point, highlight, acme, zenith, peak, summit, top, head.
⊞ nadir.

climb v ascend, scale, shin up, clamber, mount, rise, soar, top.
• **climb down** retract, eat one's words, back down, retreat, do a U-turn.

cling v clasp, clutch, grasp, grip, stick, adhere, cleave, fasten, embrace, hug.

clip¹ v trim, snip, cut, prune, pare, shear, crop, dock, poll, truncate, curtail, shorten, abbreviate.

clip² v pin, staple, fasten, attach, fix, hold.

clipping n cutting, snippet, quotation, citation, passage, section, excerpt, extract, clip.

clique n circle, set, coterie, group, bunch, pack, gang, crowd, faction, clan.

cloak n cape, mantle, robe, wrap, coat, cover, shield, mask, front, pretext.
◇ v cover, veil, mask, screen, hide, conceal, obscure, disguise, camouflage.

clock

Types of clock or watch include: alarm clock, digital clock, mantel clock, bracket clock, carriage clock, cuckoo clock, longcase clock, grandfather clock, grandmother clock, speaking clock; wristwatch, fob-watch, chronograph, stopwatch; chronometer, sundial.

clog v block, choke, stop up, bung up, dam, congest, jam, obstruct, impede, hinder, hamper, burden.
⊞ unblock.

close¹ v 1 SHUT, fasten, secure, lock, bar, obstruct, block, clog, plug, cork, stop up, fill, seal, fuse, join, unite. 2 END, finish, complete, conclude, terminate, wind up, stop, cease.
⊞ 1 open, separate. 2 start.
◇ n end, finish, completion, conclusion, culmination, ending, finale, dénouement, termination, cessation, stop, pause.

close² adj 1 NEAR, nearby, at hand, neighbouring, adjacent, adjoining, impending, imminent. 2 INTIMATE, dear, familiar, attached, devoted, loving. 3 OPPRESSIVE, heavy, muggy, humid, sultry, sweltering, airless, stifling, suffocating, stuffy, unventilated. 4 MISERLY, mean, parsimonious, tight (infml), stingy, niggardly. 5 SECRETIVE, uncommunicative, taciturn, private, secret, confidential. 6 a close translation: exact, precise, accurate, strict, literal, faithful. 7 pay close attention: fixed, concentrated, intense, keen. 8 DENSE, solid, packed, cramped.
⊞ 1 far, distant. 2 cool, unfriendly. 3 fresh, airy. 4 generous. 5 open. 6 rough.

clot n lump, mass, thrombus, thrombosis, clotting, coagulation.
◇ v coalesce, curdle, coagulate, congeal, thicken, solidify, set, gel.

cloth n 1 FABRIC, material, stuff, textile. 2 RAG, face cloth, flannel, dishcloth, floorcloth, duster, towel.

clothe v dress, put on, robe, attire,

deck, outfit, rig, vest, invest, drape, cover.
🔄 undress, strip, disrobe.

clothes n clothing, garments, wear, attire, garb, gear (infml), togs (infml), outfit, get-up (infml), dress, costume, wardrobe.

Clothes include: suit, coat, dress, skirt, top, trousers, shorts; leotard, salopette; hat, scarf, glove, mitten, muffler, earmuffs, leg warmers, sock, tie, bow tie, cravat, stole, shawl, belt, braces, cummerbund, veil, yashmak. see also **coat; dress; hat; nightwear; shoe; skirt; suit; top; trousers; underwear**.

---

cloud n vapour, haze, mist, fog, gloom, darkness, obscurity.
◇ v mist, fog, blur, dull, dim, darken, shade, shadow, overshadow, eclipse, veil, shroud, obscure, muddle, confuse, obfuscate.
🔄 clear.

Types of cloud include: cirrus, cirrostratus, cirrocumulus, altocumulus, altostratus, cumulus, stratocumulus, nimbostratus, fractostratus, fractocumulus, cumulonimbus, stratus, mammatus.

---

cloudy adj nebulous, hazy, misty, foggy, blurred, blurry, opaque, milky, muddy, dim, indistinct, obscure, dark, murky, sombre, leaden, lowering, overcast, dull, sunless.
🔄 clear, bright, sunny, cloudless.

clown n buffoon, comic, comedian, joker, jester, fool, harlequin, pierrot.

club n 1 ASSOCIATION, society, company, league, guild, order, union, fraternity, group, set, circle, clique. 2 BAT, stick, mace, bludgeon, truncheon, cosh (sl), cudgel.
◇ v hit, strike, beat, bash, clout, clobber (sl), bludgeon, cosh (sl), batter, pummel.

clue n hint, tip, suggestion, idea,

notion, lead, tip-off, pointer, sign, indication, evidence, trace, suspicion, inkling, intimation.

clump n cluster, bundle, bunch, mass, tuft, thicket.
◇ v tramp, clomp, stamp, stomp, plod, lumber, thump, thud.

clumsy adj bungling, ham-fisted, unhandy, unskilful, inept, bumbling, blundering, lumbering, gauche, ungainly, gawky (infml), unco-ordinated, awkward, ungraceful, uncouth, rough, crude, ill-made, shapeless, unwieldy, heavy, bulky, cumbersome.
🔄 careful, graceful, elegant.

cluster n bunch, clump, batch, group, knot, mass, crowd, gathering, collection, assembly.
◇ v bunch, group, gather, collect, assemble, flock.

clutch v hold, clasp, grip, hang on to, grasp, seize, snatch, grab, catch, grapple, embrace.

clutter n litter, mess, jumble, untidiness, disorder, disarray, muddle, confusion.
◇ v litter, encumber, fill, cover, strew, scatter.

coach n trainer, instructor, tutor, teacher.
◇ v train, drill, instruct, teach, tutor, cram, prepare.

coagulate v clot, curdle, congeal, thicken, solidify, gel.
🔄 melt.

coalition n merger, amalgamation, combination, integration, fusion, alliance, league, bloc, compact, federation, confederation, confederacy, association, affiliation, union.

coarse adj 1 ROUGH, unpolished, unfinished, uneven, lumpy, unpurified, unrefined, unprocessed. 2 coarse humour: bawdy, ribald, earthy, smutty, vulgar, crude, offensive, foul-mouthed, boorish,

loutish, rude, impolite, indelicate,
improper, indecent, immodest.
⊠ **1** smooth, fine. **2** refined,
sophisticated, polite.

coast n coastline, seaboard, shore,
beach, seaside.
◇ v freewheel, glide, slide, sail,
cruise, drift.

coat n **1** FUR, hair, fleece, pelt, hide,
skin. **2** LAYER, coating, covering.

Types of coat, cloak and jacket
include: overcoat, greatcoat, car
coat, duffel coat, Afghan, frock-
coat, tail coat, bomber jacket,
dinner jacket, donkey jacket,
hacking jacket, reefer, pea jacket,
shooting jacket, sports jacket,
safari jacket, Eton jacket, matinee
jacket, tuxedo, blazer, raincoat,
trench coat, mackintosh, mac
(*infml*), Burberry®, parka, snorkel,
puffa jacket, anorak, cagoul,
windcheater, jerkin, blouson, cape,
cloak, poncho.

◇ v cover, paint, spread, smear,
plaster.

coating n covering, layer, dusting,
wash, coat, blanket, sheet,
membrane, film, glaze, varnish,
finish, veneer, lamination, overlay.

coax v persuade, cajole, wheedle,
sweet-talk (*infml*), soft-soap, flatter,
beguile, allure, entice, tempt.

cocky adj arrogant, bumptious, self-
important, conceited, vain, swollen-
headed, egotistical, swaggering,
brash, cocksure, self-assured, self-
confident, over-confident.
⊠ humble, modest, shy.

code n **1** ETHICS, rules, regulations,
principles, system, custom,
convention, etiquette, manners.
2 *written in code:* cipher, secret
language.

coerce v force, drive, compel,
constrain, pressurize, bully,
intimidate, browbeat, bludgeon,

bulldoze, dragoon, press-gang.

coercion n force, duress,
compulsion, constraint, pressure,
bullying, intimidation, threats,
browbeating.

coffee

Types of coffee include: black
coffee, white coffee, Americano,
cappuccino, espresso, latte,
macchiato; arabica, Blue
Mountain, Colombian, Costa
Rican, Java, Mocha, Kenyan; light
roast, dark roast, French roast;
filter, ground, instant, percolated;
decaffeinated, decaff (*infml*);
Fairtrade.

coffer n casket, case, box, chest,
trunk, strongbox, treasury,
repository.

cognition n perception, insight,
awareness, consciousness,
knowledge, apprehension,
discernment, comprehension,
understanding, intelligence,
reasoning.

cohere v **1** STICK, adhere, cling,
fuse, unite, bind, combine, coalesce,
consolidate. **2** *the argument does not
cohere:* agree, square, correspond,
harmonize, hold, hang together.
⊠ **1** separate.

coherent adj articulate, intelligible,
comprehensible, meaningful,
lucid, consistent, logical, reasoned,
rational, sensible, orderly, systematic,
organized.
⊠ incoherent, unintelligible,
meaningless.

coil v wind, spiral, convolute, curl,
loop, twist, writhe, snake, wreathe,
twine, entwine.
◇ n roll, curl, loop, ring, convolution,
spiral, corkscrew, helix, twist.

coin v invent, make up, think
up, conceive, devise, formulate,
originate, create, fabricate, produce,

mint, forge.
◇ *n* piece, bit, money, cash, change, small change, loose change, silver, copper.

coincide *v* coexist, synchronize, agree, concur, correspond, square, tally, accord, harmonize, match.

coincidence *n* 1 CHANCE, accident, eventuality, fluke (*infml*), luck, fortuity, synchronicity. 2 COEXISTENCE, conjunction, concurrence, correspondence, correlation.

coincidental *adj* 1 CHANCE, accidental, casual, unintentional, unplanned, flukey (*infml*), lucky, fortuitous. 2 COINCIDENT, coexistent, concurrent, simultaneous, synchronous.
☒ 1 deliberate, planned.

cold *adj* 1 UNHEATED, cool, chilled, chilly, chill, shivery, nippy, parky (*infml*), raw, biting, bitter, wintry, frosty, icy, glacial, freezing, frozen, arctic, polar. 2 UNSYMPATHETIC, unmoved, unfeeling, stony, frigid, unfriendly, distant, aloof, standoffish, reserved, undemonstrative, unresponsive, indifferent, lukewarm.
☒ 1 hot, warm. 2 friendly, responsive.
◇ *n* coldness, chill, chilliness, coolness, frigidity, iciness.
☒ warmth.

cold-blooded *adj* cruel, inhuman, brutal, savage, barbaric, barbarous, merciless, pitiless, callous, unfeeling, heartless.
☒ compassionate, merciful.

collaborate *v* conspire, collude, work together, co-operate, join forces, team up, participate.

collaboration *n* conspiring, collusion, association, alliance, partnership, teamwork, co-operation.

collaborator *n* co-worker, associate, partner, team-mate, colleague, assistant, accomplice,

traitor, turncoat.

collapse *v* 1 *collapse with exhaustion*: faint, pass out, crumple. 2 FALL, sink, founder, fail, fold (*infml*), fall apart, disintegrate, crumble, subside, cave in.
◇ *n* failure, breakdown, flop, debacle, downfall, ruin, disintegration, subsidence, cave-in, faint, exhaustion.

colleague *n* workmate, co-worker, team-mate, partner, collaborator, ally, associate, confederate, confrère, comrade, companion, aide, helper, assistant, auxiliary.

collect *v* gather, assemble, congregate, convene, muster, rally, converge, cluster, aggregate, accumulate, amass, heap, hoard, stockpile, save, acquire, obtain, secure.
☒ disperse, scatter.

collected *adj* composed, self-possessed, placid, serene, calm, unruffled, unperturbed, imperturbable, cool.
☒ anxious, worried, agitated.

collection *n* 1 GATHERING, assembly, convocation, congregation, crowd, group, cluster, accumulation, conglomeration, mass, heap, pile, hoard, stockpile, store. 2 SET, assemblage, assortment, job-lot, anthology, compilation.

collective *adj* united, combined, concerted, co-operative, joint, common, shared, corporate, democratic, composite, aggregate, cumulative.
☒ individual.

Collective nouns (by animal) include: shrewdness of *apes*, cete of *badgers*, sloth of *bears*, swarm of *bees*, herd of *buffaloes*, clowder of *cats*, drove or herd of *cattle*, murder of *crows*, herd of *deer*, pack of *dogs*, school of *dolphins*, dole of *doves*, team or paddling of

ducks, charm of *finches*, shoal of
fish, skulk of *foxes*, gaggle or skein
of *geese*, herd or tribe of *goats*,
down or husk of *hares*, cast of
hawks, brood of *hens*, string of
horses, pack of *hounds*, troop of
kangaroos, kindle of *kittens*,
exaltation of *larks*, leap of
leopards, pride of *lions*, swarm of
locusts, troop of *monkeys*, watch
of *nightingales*, parliament of *owls*,
covey of *partridges*, muster of
peacocks, rookery of *penguins*, nye
of *pheasants*, litter of *pigs*, school
of *porpoises*, bury of *rabbits*,
unkindness of *ravens*, building of
rooks, pod of *seals*, flock of *sheep*,
murmuration of *starlings*, school or
gam of *whales*, pack or rout of
wolves.

collector

**Names of collectors and
enthusiasts include:** zoophile
(*animals*), antiquary (*antiques*),
campanologist (*bellringing*),
ornithologist (*birds*), bibliophile
(*books*), audiophile (*broadcast and
recorded sound*), lepidopterist
(*butterflies*), cartophilist (*cigarette
cards*), numismatist (*coins/medals*),
gourmet (*good food*), gastronome
(*good-living*), discophile
(*gramophone records*), hippophile
(*horses*), entomologist (*insects*),
phillumenist (*matches/
matchboxes*), deltiologist
(*postcards*), arachnologist (*spiders/
arachnids*), philatelist (*stamps*),
arctophile (*teddy bears*).

collide *v* crash, bump, smash, clash,
conflict, confront, meet.

collision *n* impact, crash, bump,
smash, accident, pile-up, clash,
conflict, confrontation, opposition.

colloquial *adj* conversational,
informal, familiar, everyday,
vernacular, idiomatic.

⊡ formal.

collude *v* conspire, plot, connive,
collaborate, scheme, machinate,
intrigue.

colonist *n* colonial, settler,
immigrant, emigrant, pioneer.

colonize *v* settle, occupy, people,
populate.

colony *n* settlement, outpost,
dependency, dominion, possession,
territory, province.

colossal *adj* huge, enormous,
immense, vast, massive, gigantic,
mega (*infml*), mammoth, monstrous,
monumental.
⊡ tiny, minute.

colour *n* 1 HUE, shade, tinge, tone,
tincture, tint, dye, paint, wash,
pigment, pigmentation, coloration,
complexion. 2 VIVIDNESS, brilliance,
rosiness, ruddiness, glow, liveliness,
animation.

The range of colours includes: red,
crimson, scarlet, vermilion, cherry,
cerise, magenta, maroon,
burgundy, ruby; orange, tangerine,
apricot, coral, salmon, peach,
amber; brown, chestnut,
mahogany, bronze, auburn, rust,
copper, cinnamon, chocolate, tan,
sepia, taupe, beige, fawn; yellow,
lemon, canary, ochre, saffron,
topaz, gold; green, chartreuse, eau
de nil, emerald, jade, lime,
avocado, sage, khaki; blue,
turquoise, aquamarine, cobalt,
sapphire, indigo, navy; purple,
violet, mauve, plum, lavender,
lilac; pink, rose; white, magnolia,
cream, ecru; grey, silver, charcoal;
black, ebony, jet.

◇ *v* 1 PAINT, crayon, dye, tint,
stain, tinge. 2 BLUSH, flush, redden.
3 *colour one's judgement*: affect,
bias, prejudice, distort, pervert,
exaggerate, falsify.

colourful *adj* 1 MULTICOLOURED,

kaleidoscopic, variegated, parti-coloured, vivid, bright, brilliant, rich, intense. **2** *a colourful description*: vivid, graphic, picturesque, lively, stimulating, exciting, interesting.
≇ **1** colourless, drab.

colourless *adj* **1** TRANSPARENT, neutral, bleached, washed-out, faded, pale, ashen, sickly, anaemic. **2** INSIPID, lacklustre, dull, dreary, drab, plain, characterless, unmemorable, uninteresting, tame.
≇ **1** colourful. **2** bright, exciting.

column *n* **1** PILLAR, post, shaft, upright, support, obelisk. **2** LIST, line, row, rank, file, procession, queue, string.

comb *v* **1** *comb one's hair*: groom, neaten, tidy, untangle. **2** SEARCH, hunt, scour, sweep, sift, screen, rake, rummage, ransack.

combat *n* war, warfare, hostilities, action, battle, fight, skirmish, struggle, conflict, clash, encounter, engagement, contest, bout, duel.
◇ *v* fight, battle, strive, struggle, contend, contest, oppose, resist, withstand, defy.

combination *n* **1** BLEND, mix, mixture, composite, amalgam, synthesis, compound. **2** MERGER, amalgamation, unification, alliance, coalition, association, federation, confederation, confederacy, combine, consortium, syndicate, union, integration, fusion, coalescence, connection.

combine *v* merge, amalgamate, unify, blend, mix, integrate, incorporate, synthesize, compound, fuse, bond, bind, join, connect, link, marry, unite, pool, associate, co-operate.
≇ divide, separate, detach.

come *v* advance, move towards, approach, near, draw near, reach, attain, arrive, enter, appear, materialize, happen, occur.

≇ go, depart, leave.
• **come about** happen, occur, come to pass, transpire, result, arise.
• **come across** find, discover, chance upon, happen upon, bump into, meet, encounter, notice.
• **come along** develop, improve, progress.
• **come apart** disintegrate, fall to bits, break, separate, split, tear.
• **come between** separate, part, divide, split up, disunite, estrange, alienate.
• **come down** descend, fall, reduce, decline, deteriorate, worsen, degenerate.
• **come in** enter, appear, show up (*infml*), arrive, finish.
• **come off** happen, occur, take place, succeed.
• **come on** begin, appear, advance, proceed, progress, develop, improve, thrive, succeed.
• **come out** result, end, conclude, terminate.
• **come out with** say, state, affirm, declare, exclaim, disclose, divulge.
• **come round 1** *come round from the anaesthetic*: recover, wake, awake. **2** YIELD, relent, concede, allow, grant, accede.
• **come through** endure, withstand, survive, prevail, triumph, succeed, accomplish, achieve.
• **come up** rise, arise, happen, occur, crop up.

comeback *n* return, reappearance, resurgence, revival, recovery.

comedian *n* comic, clown, humorist, wit, joker, wag.

comedown *n* anticlimax, let-down, disappointment, deflation, blow, reverse, decline, descent, demotion, humiliation, degradation.

comedy *n* farce, slapstick, clowning, hilarity, drollery, humour, wit, joking, jesting, facetiousness.

comfort *v* ease, soothe, relieve, alleviate, assuage, console, cheer,

gladden, reassure, hearten, encourage, invigorate, strengthen, enliven, refresh.
◇ *n* **1** CONSOLATION, compensation, cheer, reassurance, encouragement, alleviation, relief, help, aid, support. **2** EASE, relaxation, luxury, snugness, cosiness, wellbeing, satisfaction, contentment, enjoyment.
⊞ **1** distress. **2** discomfort.

comfortable *adj* **1** SNUG, cosy, comfy (*infml*), relaxing, restful, easy, convenient, pleasant, agreeable, enjoyable, delightful. **2** AT EASE, relaxed, contented, happy. **3** AFFLUENT, well-off, well-to-do, prosperous.
⊞ **1** uncomfortable, unpleasant. **2** uneasy, nervous. **3** poor.

comic *adj* funny, hilarious, side-splitting, comical, droll, humorous, witty, amusing, entertaining, diverting, joking, facetious, light, farcical, ridiculous, ludicrous, absurd, laughable, priceless (*infml*), rich (*infml*).
⊞ tragic, serious.
◇ *n* comedian, comedienne, gagster (*infml*), joker, jester, clown, buffoon, humorist, wit, wag.

coming *adj* next, forthcoming, impending, imminent, approaching, due, near, future, aspiring, rising, up-and-coming.
◇ *n* advent, approach, arrival, accession.

command *v* **1** ORDER, bid, charge, enjoin, direct, instruct, require, demand, compel. **2** LEAD, head, rule, reign, govern, control, dominate, manage, supervise.
◇ *n* **1** COMMANDMENT, decree, edict, precept, mandate, order, bidding, charge, injunction, directive, direction, instruction, requirement. **2** *be in command*: power, authority, leadership, control, domination, dominion, rule, sway, government, management.

commander *n* leader, head, chief, boss, commander-in-chief, general, admiral, captain, commanding officer, officer.

commemorate *v* celebrate, solemnize, remember, memorialize, mark, honour, salute, immortalize, observe, keep.

commemoration *n* celebration, observance, remembrance, tribute, honouring, ceremony.

commence *v* begin, start, embark on, originate, initiate, inaugurate, open, launch.
⊞ finish, end, cease.

commend *v* **1** PRAISE, compliment, acclaim, extol, applaud, approve, recommend. **2** COMMIT, entrust, confide, consign, deliver, yield.
⊞ **1** criticize, censure.

comment *v* say, mention, interpose, interject, remark, observe, note, annotate, interpret, explain, elucidate, criticize.
◇ *n* statement, remark, observation, note, annotation, footnote, marginal note, explanation, elucidation, illustration, exposition, commentary, criticism.

commentary *n* narration, voice-over, analysis, description, review, critique, explanation, notes, treatise.

commentator *n* sportscaster, broadcaster, reporter, narrator, commenter, critic, annotator, interpreter.

commerce *n* trade, traffic, business, dealings, relations, dealing, trafficking, exchange, marketing, merchandising.

commercial *adj* trade, trading, business, sales, profit-making, profitable, sellable, saleable, popular, monetary, financial, mercenary, venal.

commission *n* **1** ASSIGNMENT, mission, errand, task, job, duty,

function, appointment, employment, mandate, warrant, authority, charge, trust. **2** COMMITTEE, board, delegation, deputation, representative.
3 *commission on a sale*: percentage, cut (*infml*), rake-off (*infml*), allowance, fee.
◇ *v* nominate, select, appoint, engage, employ, authorize, empower, delegate, depute, send, order, request, ask for.

commit *v* **1** *commit a crime*: do, perform, execute, enact, perpetrate.
2 ENTRUST, confide, commend, consign, deliver, hand over, give, deposit. **3** BIND, obligate, pledge, engage, involve.
• **commit oneself** decide, undertake, promise, pledge, bind oneself.

commitment *n* undertaking, guarantee, assurance, promise, word, pledge, vow, engagement, involvement, dedication, devotion, adherence, loyalty, tie, obligation, duty, responsibility, liability.
🔁 vacillation, wavering.

committee *n* council, board, panel, jury, commission, advisory group, think-tank, working party, task force.

common *adj* **1** FAMILIAR, customary, habitual, usual, daily, everyday, routine, regular, frequent, widespread, prevalent, general, universal, standard, average, ordinary, plain, simple, workaday, run-of-the-mill, undistinguished, unexceptional, conventional, accepted, popular, commonplace.
2 VULGAR, coarse, unrefined, crude, inferior, low, ill-bred, loutish, plebeian, proletarian. **3** COMMUNAL, public, shared, mutual, joint, collective.
🔁 **1** uncommon, unusual, rare, noteworthy. **2** tasteful, refined.

commonplace *adj* ordinary, everyday, common, humdrum, pedestrian, banal, trite, widespread, frequent, hackneyed, stock,

stale, obvious, worn out, boring, uninteresting, threadbare.
🔁 memorable, exceptional.

commonsense *adj* commonsensical, matter-of-fact, sensible, level-headed, sane, sound, reasonable, practical, down-to-earth, pragmatic, hard-headed, realistic, shrewd, astute, prudent, judicious.
🔁 foolish, unreasonable, unrealistic.

commotion *n* agitation, hurly-burly, turmoil, tumult, excitement, ferment, fuss, bustle, ado, to-do (*infml*), uproar, furore, ballyhoo (*infml*), hullabaloo (*infml*), racket, hubbub, rumpus, fracas, disturbance, bust-up (*infml*), disorder, riot.

communal *adj* public, community, shared, joint, collective, general, common.
🔁 private, personal.

commune *n* collective, co-operative, kibbutz, community, fellowship, colony, settlement.
◇ *v* converse, discourse, communicate, make contact.

communicate *v* **1** ANNOUNCE, declare, proclaim, report, reveal, disclose, divulge, impart, inform, acquaint, intimate, notify, publish, disseminate, spread, diffuse, transmit, convey. **2** TALK, converse, commune, correspond, write, phone, telephone, e-mail, contact.

communication *n* information, intelligence, intimation, disclosure, contact, connection, transmission, dissemination.

Forms of communication include: broadcasting, radio, wireless, television, TV, cable TV, digital TV, satellite, video, teletext; newspaper, press, news, magazine, journal, website, blog (*infml*), podcast, advertising, publicity, poster, leaflet, pamphlet, brochure, catalogue; post, dispatch, correspondence, letter, e-mail, snail mail (*infml*), postcard, aerogram, telegram, cable, wire (*infml*), chain letter, junk mail, mailshot; conversation, word, message, dialogue, speech, gossip, grapevine (*infml*); conference call, videoconference; notice, announcement, bulletin, communiqué, circular, memo, note, press release, report, statement, broadcast, webcast; telephone, mobile phone, cellphone, text message, SMS (short message service), intercom, answering machine, voice mail, walkie-talkie, pager, bleeper, Tannoy®, telex, teleprinter, facsimile, fax, Dictaphone®, PDA (personal digital assistant), BlackBerry®; megaphone, loudhailer; radar, Morse code, semaphore, Braille, sign language.

communicative *adj* talkative, voluble, expansive, informative, chatty, sociable, friendly, forthcoming, outgoing, extrovert, unreserved, free, open, frank, candid.
⊞ quiet, reserved, reticent, secretive.

community *n* district, locality, population, people, populace, public, residents, nation, state, colony, commune, kibbutz, society, association, fellowship, brotherhood, fraternity.

commute *v* 1 REDUCE, decrease, shorten, curtail, lighten, soften, mitigate, remit, adjust, modify, alter, change, exchange, alternate. 2 *commute by train*: travel, journey.

compact *adj* small, short, brief, terse, succinct, concise, condensed, compressed, close, dense, impenetrable, solid, firm.
⊞ large, rambling, diffuse.

companion *n* fellow, comrade, friend, ally, buddy (*infml*), crony

(*infml*), intimate, confidant(e), confederate, colleague, associate, partner, mate, consort, escort, chaperone, attendant, aide, assistant, accomplice, follower.

companionship *n* fellowship, comradeship, camaraderie, esprit de corps, support, friendship, company, togetherness, conviviality, sympathy, rapport.

company *n* 1 a *manufacturing company*: firm, business, concern, association, corporation, establishment, house, partnership, syndicate, cartel, consortium. 2 TROUPE, group, band, ensemble, set, circle, crowd, throng, body, troop, crew, party, assembly, gathering, community, society. 3 GUESTS, visitors, callers, society, companionship, fellowship, support, attendance, presence.

comparable *adj* similar, alike, related, akin, cognate, corresponding, analogous, equivalent, tantamount, proportionate, commensurate, parallel, equal.
⊞ dissimilar, unlike, unequal.

compare *v* liken, equate, contrast, juxtapose, balance, weigh, correlate, resemble, match, equal, parallel.

comparison *n* juxtaposition, analogy, parallel, correlation, relationship, likeness, resemblance, similarity, comparability, contrast, distinction.

compartment *n* section, division, subdivision, category, pigeonhole, cubby-hole, niche, alcove, bay, area, stall, booth, cubicle, locker, carrel, cell, chamber, berth, carriage.

compassion *n* kindness, tenderness, heart, fellow-feeling, humanity, mercy, pity, sympathy, commiseration, condolence, sorrow, concern, care.
⊞ cruelty, indifference.

compassionate adj kind-hearted, kindly, tender-hearted, tender, caring, warm-hearted, benevolent, humanitarian, humane, merciful, clement, lenient, pitying, sympathetic, understanding, supportive.
⊡ cruel, indifferent.

compatible adj harmonious, consistent, congruous, matching, consonant, accordant, suitable, reconcilable, adaptable, like-minded, conformable, sympathetic, well-matched, similar.
⊡ incompatible, antagonistic, contradictory.

compel v force, make, constrain, oblige, necessitate, drive, urge, impel, coerce, pressurize, hustle, browbeat, bully, strongarm, bulldoze, press-gang, dragoon.

compelling adj forceful, coercive, imperative, urgent, pressing, irresistible, overriding, powerful, cogent, persuasive, convincing, conclusive, incontrovertible, irrefutable, gripping, enthralling, spellbinding, mesmeric, compulsive.
⊡ weak, unconvincing, boring.

compensate v balance (out), counterbalance, cancel, neutralize, counteract, offset, redress, satisfy, requite, repay, refund, reimburse, indemnify, recompense, reward, remunerate, atone, redeem, make good, restore.

compensation n amends, redress, satisfaction, requital, repayment, refund, reimbursement, indemnification, indemnity, damages, reparation, recompense, reward, payment, remuneration, return, restoration, restitution, consolation, comfort.

compete v vie, contest, fight, battle, struggle, strive, oppose, challenge, rival, emulate, contend, participate, take part.

competent adj capable, able, adept, efficient, trained, qualified, well-qualified, skilled, experienced, proficient, expert, masterly, equal, fit, suitable, appropriate, satisfactory, adequate, sufficient.
⊡ incompetent, incapable, unable, inefficient.

competition n 1 CONTEST, championship, tournament, cup, event, race, match, game, quiz. 2 RIVALRY, opposition, challenge, contention, conflict, struggle, strife, competitiveness, combativeness. 3 COMPETITORS, rivals, opponents, challengers, field.

competitive adj combative, contentious, antagonistic, aggressive, pushy, ambitious, keen, cut-throat.

competitor n contestant, contender, entrant, candidate, challenger, opponent, adversary, antagonist, rival, emulator, competition, opposition.

compile v compose, put together, collect, gather, garner, cull, accumulate, amass, assemble, marshal, organize, arrange.

complacent adj smug, self-satisfied, gloating, triumphant, proud, self-righteous, unconcerned, serene, self-assured, pleased, gratified, contented, satisfied.
⊡ diffident, concerned, discontented.

complain v protest, grumble, grouse, gripe, beef, carp, fuss, lament, bemoan, bewail, moan, whine, whinge (infml), groan, growl.

complaint n 1 PROTEST, objection, grumble, grouse, gripe, beef, moan, grievance, dissatisfaction, annoyance, fault-finding, criticism, censure, accusation, charge. 2 a chest complaint: ailment, illness, sickness, disease, malady, malaise, indisposition, affliction, disorder, trouble, upset.

complementary *adj* reciprocal, interdependent, correlative, interrelated, corresponding, matching, twin, fellow, companion.
⊞ contradictory, incompatible.

complete *adj* **1** UTTER, total, absolute, downright, out-and-out, thorough, perfect. **2** FINISHED, ended, concluded, over, done, accomplished, achieved. **3** UNABRIDGED, unabbreviated, unedited, unexpurgated, integral, whole, entire, full, undivided, intact.
⊞ **1** partial. **2** incomplete. **3** abridged.
◊ *v* finish, end, close, conclude, wind up, terminate, finalize, settle, clinch, perform, discharge, execute, fulfil, realize, accomplish, achieve, consummate, crown, perfect.

completion *n* finish, end, close, conclusion, termination, finalization, settlement, discharge, closure, fulfilment, realization, accomplishment, achievement, attainment, fruition, culmination, consummation, perfection.

complex *adj* complicated, intricate, elaborate, involved, convoluted, circuitous, tortuous, devious, mixed, varied, diverse, multiple, composite, compound, ramified.
⊞ simple, easy.
◊ *n* **1** NETWORK, structure, system, scheme, organization, establishment, institute, development. **2** FIXATION, obsession, preoccupation, hang-up (*infml*), phobia.

complexion *n* **1** SKIN, colour, colouring, pigmentation. **2** LOOK, appearance, aspect, light, character, nature, type, kind.

complicate *v* compound, elaborate, involve, muddle, mix up, confuse, tangle, entangle.
⊞ simplify.

complicated *adj* complex, intricate, elaborate, involved, convoluted, tortuous, difficult, problematic, puzzling, perplexing.
⊞ simple, easy.

complication *n* difficulty, snag, drawback, obstacle, problem, ramification, repercussion, complexity, intricacy, elaboration, convolution, tangle, web, confusion, mixture.

compliment *n* flattery, admiration, favour, approval, congratulations, tribute, honour, accolade, bouquet, commendation, praise, eulogy.
⊞ insult, criticism.
◊ *v* flatter, admire, commend, praise, extol, congratulate, applaud, salute.
⊞ insult, condemn.

complimentary *adj* **1** FLATTERING, admiring, favourable, approving, appreciative, congratulatory, commendatory, eulogistic. **2** *complimentary ticket*: free, gratis, honorary, courtesy.
⊞ **1** insulting, unflattering, critical.

comply *v* agree, consent, assent, accede, yield, submit, defer, respect, observe, obey, fall in, conform, follow, perform, discharge, fulfil, satisfy, meet, oblige, accommodate.
⊞ defy, disobey.

component *n* part, constituent, ingredient, element, factor, item, unit, piece, bit, spare part.

compose *v* **1** CONSTITUTE, make up, form. **2** CREATE, invent, devise, write, arrange, produce, make, form, fashion, build, construct, frame. **3** CALM, soothe, quiet, still, settle, tranquillize, quell, pacify, control, regulate.

composed *adj* calm, tranquil, serene, relaxed, unworried, unruffled, level-headed, cool, self-possessed, collected, confident, imperturbable, unflappable, placid.
⊞ agitated, hyper (*infml*), worried, troubled.

composition *n* **1** MAKING,

production, formation, creation, invention, design, formulation, writing, compilation, proportion. **2** CONSTITUTION, make-up, mixture, combination, form, structure, configuration, layout, arrangement, organization, harmony, consonance, balance, symmetry. **3** *a musical composition*: work, opus, piece, study, exercise.

composure n calm, tranquillity, serenity, ease, coolness, self-possession, confidence, assurance, self-assurance, aplomb, poise, dignity, imperturbability, placidity, equanimity, dispassion, impassivity.
⊜ agitation, nervousness, discomposure.

compound v **1** COMBINE, unite, amalgamate, fuse, coalesce, synthesize, alloy, blend, mix, mingle, intermingle. **2** WORSEN, exacerbate, aggravate, complicate, intensify, heighten, magnify, increase, augment.
◇ n alloy, blend, mixture, medley, composite, amalgam, synthesis, fusion, composition, amalgamation, combination.
◇ adj composite, mixed, multiple, complex, complicated, intricate.

comprehend v **1** UNDERSTAND, conceive, see, grasp, get it (*infml*), fathom, penetrate, tumble to (*infml*), realize, appreciate, know, apprehend, perceive, discern, take in, assimilate. **2** INCLUDE, comprise, encompass, embrace, cover.
⊜ **1** misunderstand.

comprehensible adj clear, understandable, intelligible, coherent, explicit, lucid, plain, simple, straightforward.
⊜ incomprehensible, obscure.

comprehension n understanding, conception, grasp, realization, appreciation, knowledge, apprehension, perception, discernment, judgement, sense,

intelligence.
⊜ incomprehension, unawareness.

comprehensive adj thorough, exhaustive, full, complete, encyclopedic, compendious, broad, wide, extensive, sweeping, general, blanket, inclusive, all-inclusive, all-embracing, across-the-board.
⊜ partial, incomplete, selective.

compress v press, squeeze, crush, squash, flatten, jam, wedge, cram, stuff, compact, concentrate, condense, contract, telescope, shorten, abbreviate, summarize.
⊜ expand, diffuse.

comprise v consist of, include, contain, incorporate, embody, involve, encompass, embrace.

compromise v **1** NEGOTIATE, bargain, arbitrate, settle, agree, concede, make concessions, meet halfway, adapt, adjust. **2** *compromise one's principles*: undermine, weaken, expose, endanger, imperil, jeopardize, risk, prejudice. **3** DISHONOUR, discredit, embarrass, involve, implicate.
◇ n bargain, trade-off, settlement, agreement, concession, give-and-take, co-operation, accommodation, adjustment.
⊜ disagreement, intransigence.

compulsive adj **1** IRRESISTIBLE, overwhelming, overpowering, uncontrollable, compelling, driving, urgent. **2** *a compulsive gambler*: obsessive, hardened, incorrigible, irredeemable, incurable, hopeless.

compulsory adj obligatory, mandatory, imperative, forced, required, requisite, set, stipulated, binding, contractual.
⊜ optional, voluntary, discretionary.

computer n personal computer, PC, mainframe, processor, word processor, data processor, calculator, adding machine.

Computing terms include: mainframe, microcomputer, minicomputer, PC (personal computer), desktop, AppleMac®, Mac (*infml*), iMac®; hardware, CPU (central processing unit), disk drive, joystick, keyboard, laptop, light pen, microprocessor, modem, monitor, motherboard, mouse, mouse mat, touchpad, notebook, palmtop, peripheral, port, printer, scanner, screen, sound card, graphics card, VDU (visual display unit); software, program, shell program, abandonware, freeware, shareware; disk, magnetic disk, floppy disk, hard disk, optical disk, flash drive, magnetic tape; programming language, AWK, BASIC, C, COBOL, FORTRAN, Java®, Pascal, Perl, Python; memory, backing storage, RAM (Random Access Memory), ROM (Read Only Memory), CD-ROM (Compact Disc Read Only Memory), CD-R (Compact Disc Recordable), DVD (Digital Versatile Disk); access, ASCII (American Standard Code for Information Interchange), back-up, bit, boot, buffer, byte, kilobyte, megabyte, gigabyte, character, chip, silicon chip, computer game, computer graphics, terminal, cursor, data, databank, database, default, desktop publishing (DTP), digitizer, directory, DOS (disk operating system), e-mail, broadband, dial-up, file, firewall, format, FTP (File Transfer Protocol), function, graphics, hacking, icon, interface, intranet, Linux, Mac OS®, macro, menu, MSDOS (Microsoft® disk operating system), network, peripheral, pixel, scrolling, spellchecker, spreadsheet, template, toggle, toolbar, Unicode, Unix®, user-friendly, user interface, virtual reality, virus, virus-checker, window, Windows®, word-processing, workstation, worm. *see also* **Internet**.

con *v* trick, hoax, dupe, deceive, mislead, inveigle, hoodwink, bamboozle (*infml*), cheat, double-cross, swindle, defraud, rip off (*sl*), rook.
◊ *n* confidence trick, trick, bluff, deception, swindle, fraud.

concave *adj* hollow, hollowed, cupped, scooped, excavated, sunken, depressed.
☒ convex.

conceal *v* hide, obscure, disguise, camouflage, mask, screen, veil, cloak, cover, bury, submerge, smother, suppress, keep dark, keep quiet, hush up (*infml*).
☒ reveal, disclose, uncover.

concede *v* **1** ADMIT, confess, acknowledge, recognize, own, grant, allow, accept. **2** YIELD, give up, surrender, relinquish, forfeit, sacrifice.
☒ **1** deny.

conceit *n* conceitedness, vanity, boastfulness, swagger, egotism, self-love, self-importance, cockiness, self-satisfaction, complacency, pride, arrogance.
☒ modesty, diffidence.

conceited *adj* vain, boastful, swollen-headed, bigheaded (*infml*), egotistical, self-important, cocky, self-satisfied, complacent, smug, proud, arrogant, stuck-up (*infml*), toffee-nosed (*infml*).
☒ modest, self-effacing, diffident, humble.

conceivable *adj* imaginable, credible, believable, thinkable, tenable, possible, likely, probable.
☒ inconceivable, unimaginable.

conceive *v* **1** IMAGINE, envisage, visualize, see, grasp, understand, comprehend, realize, appreciate, believe, think, suppose. **2** INVENT, design, devise, formulate, create, originate, form, produce, develop.

concentrate v 1 FOCUS, converge, centre, cluster, crowd, congregate, gather, collect, accumulate. 2 APPLY ONESELF, think, pay attention, attend. 3 CONDENSE, evaporate, reduce, thicken, intensify.
⊞ 1 disperse. 3 dilute.

concentrated adj 1 concentrated liquid: condensed, evaporated, reduced, thickened, dense, rich, strong, undiluted. 2 INTENSE, intensive, all-out, concerted, hard, deep.
⊞ 1 diluted. 2 half-hearted.

concentration n 1 CONVERGENCE, centralization, cluster, crowd, grouping, collection, accumulation, agglomeration, conglomeration. 2 ATTENTION, heed, absorption, application, single-mindedness, intensity. 3 COMPRESSION, reduction, consolidation, denseness, thickness.
⊞ 1 dispersal. 2 distraction. 3 dilution.

concept n idea, notion, plan, theory, hypothesis, thought, abstraction, conception, conceptualization, visualization, image, picture, impression.

conception n 1 CONCEPT, idea, notion, thought. 2 KNOWLEDGE, understanding, appreciation, perception, visualization, image, picture, impression, inkling, clue. 3 INVENTION, design, birth, beginning, origin, outset, initiation, inauguration, formation. 4 from conception to birth: impregnation, insemination, fertilization.

concern v 1 UPSET, distress, trouble, disturb, bother, worry. 2 RELATE TO, refer to, regard, involve, interest, affect, touch.
◇ n 1 a cause for concern: anxiety, worry, unease, disquiet, care, sorrow, distress. 2 REGARD, consideration, attention, heed, thought. 3 it's not my concern: duty, responsibility,

charge, job, task, field, business, affair, matter, problem, interest, involvement. 4 COMPANY, firm, business, corporation, establishment, enterprise, organization.
⊞ 1 joy. 2 indifference.

concerned adj 1 ANXIOUS, worried, uneasy, apprehensive, upset, unhappy, distressed, troubled, disturbed, bothered, attentive, caring. 2 CONNECTED, related, involved, implicated, complicit, interested, affected.
⊞ 1 unconcerned, indifferent, apathetic.

concerning prep about, regarding, with regard to, as regards, respecting, with reference to, relating to, in the matter of.

concerted adj combined, united, joint, collective, shared, collaborative, co-ordinated, organized, prearranged, planned.
⊞ separate, unco-ordinated, disorganized.

concession n compromise, adjustment, grant, allowance, exception, privilege, favour, indulgence, permit, admission, acknowledgement.

concise adj short, brief, terse, succinct, pithy, compendious, compact, compressed, condensed, abridged, abbreviated, summary, synoptic.
⊞ diffuse, wordy.

conclude v 1 INFER, deduce, assume, surmise, suppose, reckon, judge. 2 END, close, finish, complete, consummate, cease, terminate, culminate. 3 SETTLE, resolve, decide, establish, determine, clinch.
⊞ 2 start, commence.

conclusion n 1 INFERENCE, deduction, assumption, opinion, conviction, judgement, verdict, decision, resolution, settlement, result, consequence, outcome,

upshot, answer, solution.
2 END, close, finish, completion, consummation, termination, culmination, finale.

conclusive adj final, ultimate, definitive, decisive, clear, convincing, definite, undeniable, irrefutable, indisputable, incontrovertible, unarguable, unanswerable, clinching.
☒ inconclusive, questionable.

concoct v fabricate, invent, devise, contrive, formulate, plan, plot, hatch, brew, prepare, develop.

concoction n brew, potion, preparation, mixture, blend, compound, creation, contrivance.

concrete adj real, actual, factual, solid, physical, material, substantial, tangible, touchable, perceptible, visible, firm, definite, specific, explicit.
☒ abstract, vague.

concurrent adj simultaneous, synchronous, contemporaneous, coinciding, coincident, concomitant, coexisting, coexistent.

condemn v disapprove, reprehend, reprove, upbraid, reproach, castigate, blame, disparage, revile, denounce, censure, slam (infml), slate (infml), damn, doom, convict.
☒ praise, approve.

condemnation n disapproval, reproof, reproach, castigation, blame, disparagement, denunciation, censure, thumbs-down (infml), damnation, conviction, sentence, judgement.
☒ praise, approval.

condensation n 1 condensation of liquid: distillation, liquefaction, precipitation, concentration, moisture, evaporation, reduction, consolidation. 2 ABRIDGEMENT, précis, synopsis, digest, contraction, compression, curtailment.

condense v 1 condense a book: shorten, curtail, abbreviate, abridge, précis, summarize, encapsulate, contract, compress, compact.
2 DISTIL, precipitate, concentrate, evaporate, reduce, thicken, solidify, coagulate.
☒ 1 expand. 2 dilute.

condescend v deign, see fit, stoop, bend, lower oneself, patronize, talk down.

condescending adj patronizing, disdainful, supercilious, snooty, snobbish, haughty, lofty, superior, lordly, imperious.
☒ gracious, humble.

condition n 1 CASE, state, circumstances, position, situation, predicament, plight. 2 REQUIREMENT, obligation, prerequisite, terms, stipulation, proviso, qualification, limitation, restriction, rule. 3 a heart condition: disorder, defect, weakness, infirmity, problem, complaint, disease. 4 out of condition: fitness, health, state, shape, form, fettle, nick (sl).
◇ v indoctrinate, brainwash, influence, mould, educate, train, groom, equip, prepare, prime, accustom, season, temper, adapt, adjust, tune.

conditional adj provisional, qualified, limited, restricted, tied, relative, dependent, contingent.
☒ unconditional, absolute.

conditions n surroundings, environment, milieu, setting, atmosphere, background, context, circumstances, situation, state.

condom n sheath, French letter (sl), johnnie (sl), rubber (sl), protective.

condone v forgive, pardon, excuse, overlook, ignore, disregard, tolerate, brook, allow.
☒ condemn, censure.

conducive adj leading, tending, contributory, productive, promoting, advantageous, beneficial, favourable, helpful, encouraging.

⊞ detrimental, adverse, unfavourable.

conduct n 1 good conduct: behaviour, comportment, actions, ways, manners, bearing, attitude. 2 ADMINISTRATION, management, direction, running, organization, operation, control, supervision, leadership, guidance.
◇ v 1 ADMINISTER, manage, run, organize, orchestrate, chair, control, handle, regulate. 2 ACCOMPANY, escort, usher, lead, guide, direct, pilot, steer. 3 conduct heat: convey, carry, bear, transmit. 4 conduct oneself: behave, acquit, comport, act.

confer v 1 DISCUSS, debate, deliberate, consult, talk, converse. 2 BESTOW, award, present, give, grant, accord, impart, lend.

conference n meeting, convention, congress, convocation, symposium, forum, discussion, debate, consultation.

confess v admit, confide, own (up), come clean (infml), grant, concede, acknowledge, recognize, affirm, assert, profess, declare, disclose, divulge, expose.
⊞ deny, conceal.

confession n admission, acknowledgement, affirmation, assertion, profession, declaration, disclosure, divulgence, revelation, unburdening.
⊞ denial, concealment.

confide v confess, admit, reveal, disclose, divulge, whisper, breathe, tell, impart, unburden.
⊞ hide, suppress.

confidence n certainty, faith, credence, trust, reliance, dependence, assurance, composure, calmness, self-possession, self-confidence, self-reliance, self-assurance, boldness, courage.
⊞ distrust, diffidence.

confident adj sure, certain, positive, convinced, assured, composed, self-possessed, cool, self-confident, self-reliant, self-assured, unselfconscious, bold, fearless, dauntless, unabashed.
⊞ doubtful, diffident.

confidential adj secret, top secret, classified, restricted, hush-hush (infml), off-the-record, private, personal, intimate, privy.

confine v enclose, circumscribe, bound, limit, restrict, cramp, constrain, imprison, incarcerate, intern, cage, shut up, immure, bind, shackle, trammel, restrain, repress, inhibit.
⊞ free.

confinement n 1 IMPRISONMENT, incarceration, internment, custody, detention, house arrest. 2 CHILDBIRTH, birth, labour, delivery.
⊞ 1 freedom, liberty.

confines n limits, bounds, border, boundary, frontier, circumference, perimeter, edge.

confirm v 1 ENDORSE, back, support, reinforce, strengthen, fortify, verify, validate, authenticate, corroborate, substantiate, prove, evidence. 2 ESTABLISH, fix, settle, clinch, ratify, sanction, approve.
⊞ 1 refute, deny.

confirmation n ratification, sanction, approval, assent, acceptance, agreement, endorsement, backing, support, validation, authentication, corroboration, substantiation, verification, proof, evidence, testimony, smoking gun (infml).
⊞ denial.

confirmed adj inveterate, entrenched, dyed-in-the-wool, rooted, established, long-established, long-standing, habitual, chronic, seasoned, hardened, incorrigible, incurable.

confiscate v seize, appropriate,

expropriate, remove, take away, impound, sequester, commandeer. ⊡ return, restore.

conflict n 1 DIFFERENCE, variance, discord, contention, disagreement, dissension, dispute, opposition, antagonism, hostility, friction, strife, unrest, confrontation. 2 BATTLE, war, warfare, combat, fight, contest, engagement, skirmish, set-to, fracas, brawl, quarrel, feud, encounter, clash.
⊡ 1 agreement, harmony, concord. ◇ v differ, clash, collide, disagree, contradict, oppose, contest, fight, combat, battle, war, strive, struggle, contend.
⊡ agree, harmonize.

conform v agree, accord, match, harmonize, correspond, tally, square, adapt, adjust, accommodate, comply, obey, follow.
⊡ differ, conflict, rebel.

conformity n conventionality, orthodoxy, traditionalism, compliance, observance, allegiance, affinity, agreement, consonance, harmony, correspondence, congruity, likeness, similarity, resemblance.
⊡ nonconformity, rebellion, difference.

confound v 1 CONFUSE, bewilder, baffle, perplex, mystify, bamboozle (infml), nonplus, surprise, amaze, astonish, astound, flabbergast (infml), dumbfound, stupefy. 2 confound their plans: thwart, upset, defeat, overwhelm, overthrow, destroy, demolish, ruin.

confront v face, meet, encounter, accost, address, oppose, challenge, defy, brave, beard.
⊡ evade.

confrontation n encounter, clash, collision, showdown, conflict, disagreement, fight, battle, quarrel, set-to, engagement, contest.

confuse v 1 PUZZLE, baffle, perplex,

mystify, confound, bewilder, disorient, disconcert, fluster, discompose, upset, embarrass, mortify. 2 MUDDLE, mix up, mistake, jumble, disarrange, disorder, tangle, entangle, involve, mingle.
⊡ 1 enlighten, clarify.

confused adj 1 MUDDLED, jumbled, disarranged, disordered, untidy, disorderly, higgledy-piggledy (infml), chaotic, disorganized. 2 PUZZLED, baffled, perplexed, flummoxed (infml), nonplussed, bewildered, disorientated.
⊡ 1 orderly.

confusion n 1 DISORDER, disarray, untidiness, mess, clutter, jumble, muddle, mix-up, disorganization, chaos, turmoil, commotion, upheaval. 2 MISUNDERSTANDING, puzzlement, perplexity, mystification, bewilderment.
⊡ 1 order. 2 clarity.

congeal v clot, curdle, coalesce, coagulate, thicken, stiffen, harden, solidify, set, gel, freeze.
⊡ dissolve, melt.

congested adj clogged, blocked, jammed, packed, stuffed, crammed, full, crowded, overcrowded, overflowing, teeming.
⊡ clear.

congestion n clogging, blockage, overcrowding, jam, traffic jam, snarl-up (infml), gridlock, bottleneck.

conglomeration n mass, agglomeration, aggregation, accumulation, collection, assemblage, composite, medley, hotchpotch.

congratulate v praise, felicitate, compliment, wish well.
⊡ commiserate.

congregate v gather, assemble, collect, muster, rally, rendezvous, meet, convene, converge, flock, crowd, throng, mass, accumulate, cluster, clump, conglomerate.

⊠ disperse.

congregation n assembly, crowd, throng, multitude, host, flock, parishioners, parish, laity, fellowship.

conical adj cone-shaped, pyramidal, tapering, tapered, pointed.

conjecture v speculate, theorize, hypothesize, guess, estimate, reckon, suppose, surmise, assume, infer, imagine, suspect.
◇ n speculation, theory, hypothesis, notion, guesswork, guess, estimate, supposition, surmise, assumption, presumption, conclusion, inference, extrapolation, projection.

conjure v summon, invoke, rouse, raise, bewitch, charm, fascinate, compel.
• **conjure up** evoke, create, produce, excite, awaken, recollect, recall.

connect v join, link, unite, couple, combine, fasten, affix, attach, relate, associate, ally.
⊠ disconnect, cut off, detach.

connected adj joined, linked, united, coupled, combined, related, akin, associated, affiliated, allied.
⊠ disconnected, unconnected.

connection n junction, coupling, fastening, attachment, bond, tie, link, association, alliance, relation, relationship, interrelation, contact, communication, correlation, correspondence, relevance.
⊠ disconnection.

connoisseur n authority, specialist, expert, judge, devotee, buff (infml), gourmet, epicure.

connotation n implication, hint, suggestion, nuance, undertone, overtone, colouring, association.

conquer v 1 DEFEAT, beat, overthrow, vanquish, rout, overrun, best, worst, get the better of, overcome, surmount, win, succeed, triumph, prevail, overpower, master, crush, subdue, quell, subjugate, humble.

2 SEIZE, take, annex, occupy, possess, acquire, obtain.
⊠ 1 surrender, yield, give in.

conqueror n victor, winner, champion, champ (infml), hero, vanquisher, master, lord.

conquest n victory, triumph, defeat, overthrow, coup, rout, mastery, subjugation, subjection, invasion, occupation, capture, appropriation, annexation, acquisition.

conscience n principles, standards, morals, ethics, scruples, qualms.

conscientious adj diligent, hard-working, scrupulous, painstaking, thorough, meticulous, punctilious, particular, careful, attentive, responsible, upright, honest, faithful, dutiful.
⊠ careless, irresponsible, unreliable.

conscious adj 1 AWAKE, alive, responsive, sentient, sensible, rational, reasoning, alert. 2 AWARE, self-conscious, heedful, mindful, knowing, deliberate, intentional, calculated, premeditated, studied, wilful, voluntary.
⊠ 1 unconscious. 2 unaware.

consciousness n awareness, sentience, sensibility, knowledge, intuition, realization, recognition.
⊠ unconsciousness.

consecrate v sanctify, hallow, bless, dedicate, devote, ordain, venerate, revere, exalt.

consecutive adj sequential, successive, continuous, unbroken, uninterrupted, following, succeeding, running.
⊠ discontinuous.

consent v agree, concur, accede, assent, approve, permit, allow, grant, admit, concede, acquiesce, yield, comply.
⊠ refuse, decline, oppose.
◇ n agreement, concurrence, assent, approval, permission, go-ahead, green light (infml), sanction,

concession, compliance.
🔄 disagreement, refusal, opposition.

consequence n 1 RESULT, outcome, issue, end, upshot, effect, side effect, repercussion. 2 *of no consequence*: importance, significance, concern, value, weight, note, eminence, distinction.
🔄 1 cause. 2 unimportance, insignificance.

consequent adj resultant, resulting, ensuing, subsequent, following, successive, sequential.

conservation n keeping, saving, safekeeping, custody, economy, husbandry, maintenance, upkeep, preservation, protection, safeguarding, ecology, environmentalism.
🔄 destruction.

conservative adj Tory, right-wing, hidebound, die-hard, reactionary, establishmentarian, unprogressive, conventional, traditional, moderate, middle-of-the-road, cautious, guarded, sober.
🔄 left-wing, liberal, radical, innovative.
◇ n Tory, right-winger, die-hard, stick-in-the-mud, reactionary, traditionalist, moderate.
🔄 left-winger, liberal, radical.

conservatory n greenhouse, glasshouse, hothouse.

conserve v keep, save, store up, hoard, maintain, preserve, protect, guard, safeguard.
🔄 use, waste, squander.

consider v 1 PONDER, deliberate, reflect, contemplate, meditate, muse, mull over, chew over, examine, study, weigh, respect, remember, take into account. 2 *consider it an honour*: regard, deem, think, believe, judge, rate, count.

considerable adj great, large, big, sizable, substantial, tidy (*infml*), ample, plentiful, abundant, lavish,

marked, noticeable, perceptible, appreciable, reasonable, tolerable, respectable, important, significant, noteworthy, distinguished, influential.
🔄 small, slight, insignificant, unremarkable.

considerate adj kind, thoughtful, caring, attentive, obliging, helpful, charitable, unselfish, altruistic, gracious, sensitive, tactful, discreet.
🔄 inconsiderate, thoughtless, selfish.

consideration n 1 THOUGHT, deliberation, reflection, contemplation, meditation, examination, analysis, scrutiny, review, attention, notice, regard. 2 KINDNESS, thoughtfulness, care, attention, regard, respect.
🔄 1 disregard. 2 thoughtlessness.

consign v entrust, commit, devote, hand over, transfer, deliver, convey, ship, banish, relegate.

consignment n cargo, shipment, load, batch, delivery, goods.

consistency n 1 *of the consistency of porridge*: viscosity, thickness, density, firmness. 2 STEADINESS, regularity, evenness, uniformity, sameness, identity, constancy, steadfastness. 3 AGREEMENT, accordance, correspondence, congruity, compatibility, harmony.
🔄 3 inconsistency.

consistent adj 1 STEADY, stable, regular, uniform, unchanging, undeviating, constant, persistent, unfailing, dependable. 2 AGREEING, accordant, consonant, congruous, compatible, harmonious, logical.
🔄 1 irregular, erratic. 2 inconsistent.

consist of v comprise, be composed of, contain, include, incorporate, embody, embrace, involve, amount to.

console v comfort, cheer, hearten, encourage, relieve, soothe, calm.
🔄 upset, agitate.

consolidate v reinforce, strengthen, secure, stabilize, unify, unite, join, combine, amalgamate, fuse, cement, compact, condense, thicken, harden, solidify.

conspicuous adj apparent, visible, noticeable, marked, clear, obvious, evident, patent, manifest, prominent, striking, blatant, flagrant, glaring, ostentatious, showy, flashy, garish.
⁐ inconspicuous, concealed, hidden.

conspiracy n plot, scheme, intrigue, machination, fix (infml), frame-up (infml), collusion, league, treason.

conspirator n conspirer, plotter, schemer, intriguer, traitor.

conspire v plot, scheme, intrigue, manoeuvre, connive, collude, hatch, devise.

constancy n 1 STABILITY, steadiness, permanence, firmness, regularity, uniformity, resolution, perseverance, tenacity. 2 LOYALTY, faithfulness, fidelity, devotion.
⁐ 1 change, irregularity.
2 fickleness.

constant adj 1 CONTINUOUS, unbroken, never-ending, non-stop, endless, interminable, ceaseless, incessant, eternal, everlasting, perpetual, continual, unremitting, relentless, persistent, resolute, persevering, unflagging, unwavering, stable, steady, unchanging, fixed, unvarying, changeless, immutable, invariable, unalterable, permanent, firm, even, regular, uniform.
2 a constant friend: loyal, faithful, staunch, steadfast, dependable, trustworthy, true, devoted.
⁐ 1 variable, irregular, fitful, occasional. 2 disloyal, fickle.

constituent adj component, integral, essential, basic, intrinsic, inherent.
◇ n ingredient, element, factor, principle, component, part, bit, section, unit.

⁐ whole.

constitute v represent, make up, compose, comprise, form, create, establish, set up, found.

constrain v 1 FORCE, compel, oblige, necessitate, drive, impel, urge.
2 LIMIT, confine, constrict, restrain, check, curb, bind.

constrained adj uneasy, embarrassed, inhibited, reticent, reserved, guarded, stiff, forced, unnatural.
⁐ relaxed, free.

constraint n 1 FORCE, duress, compulsion, coercion, pressure, necessity, deterrent. 2 RESTRICTION, limitation, hindrance, restraint, check, curb, damper.

constrict v squeeze, compress, pinch, cramp, narrow, tighten, contract, shrink, choke, strangle, inhibit, limit, restrict.
⁐ expand.

construct v build, erect, raise, elevate, make, manufacture, fabricate, assemble, put together, compose, form, shape, fashion, model, design, engineer, create, found, establish, formulate.
⁐ demolish, destroy.

construction n building, edifice, erection, structure, fabric, form, shape, figure, model, manufacture, fabrication, assembly, composition, constitution, formation, creation.
⁐ destruction.

constructive adj practical, productive, positive, helpful, useful, valuable, beneficial, advantageous.
⁐ destructive, negative, unhelpful.

consult v refer to, ask, question, interrogate, confer, discuss, debate, deliberate.

consultant n adviser, expert, authority, specialist.

consultation n discussion, deliberation, dialogue, conference, meeting, hearing, interview, examination, appointment, session.

consume v 1 EAT, drink, swallow, devour, gobble. 2 USE, absorb, spend, expend, deplete, drain, exhaust, use up, dissipate, squander, waste. 3 DESTROY, demolish, annihilate, devastate, ravage.

consumer n user, end-user, customer, buyer, purchaser, shopper.

consumption n use, utilization, spending, expenditure, depletion, exhaustion, waste.

contact n touch, impact, juxtaposition, contiguity, communication, meeting, junction, union, connection, association.
◇ v approach, apply to, reach, get hold of, get in touch with, telephone, phone, ring, call, notify.

contagious adj infectious, catching, communicable, transmissible, spreading, epidemic.

contain v 1 INCLUDE, comprise, incorporate, embody, involve, embrace, enclose, accommodate, hold, seat. 2 contain one's feelings: repress, stifle, restrain, control, check, curb, limit.
⊞ 1 exclude.

container n receptacle, vessel, holder.

contaminate v infect, pollute, adulterate, taint, soil, sully, defile, corrupt, deprave, debase, stain, tarnish.
⊞ purify.

contemplate v 1 MEDITATE, reflect on, ponder, mull over, deliberate, consider, regard, view, survey, observe, study, examine, inspect, scrutinize. 2 EXPECT, foresee, envisage, plan, design, propose, intend, mean.

contemporary adj 1 MODERN, current, present, present-day, recent, latest, up-to-date, fashionable,

up-to-the-minute, ultra-modern. 2 CONTEMPORANEOUS, coexistent, concurrent, synchronous, simultaneous.
⊞ 1 out-of-date, old-fashioned.

contempt n scorn, disdain, condescension, derision, ridicule, mockery, disrespect, dishonour, disregard, neglect, dislike, loathing, detestation.
⊞ admiration, regard.

contemptible adj despicable, shameful, ignominious, low, mean, vile, detestable, loathsome, abject, wretched, pitiful, paltry, worthless.
⊞ admirable, honourable.

contemptuous adj scornful, disdainful, sneering, supercilious, condescending, arrogant, haughty, high and mighty, cynical, derisive, insulting, disrespectful, insolent.
⊞ humble, respectful.

contend v 1 MAINTAIN, hold, argue, allege, assert, declare, affirm. 2 COMPETE, vie, contest, dispute, clash, wrestle, grapple, struggle, strive, cope.

content v satisfy, humour, indulge, gratify, please, delight, appease, pacify, placate.
⊞ displease.
◇ n 1 SUBSTANCE, matter, essence, gist, meaning, significance, text, subject matter, ideas, contents, load, burden. 2 CAPACITY, volume, size, measure.
◇ adj satisfied, fulfilled, contented, untroubled, pleased, happy, willing.
⊞ dissatisfied, troubled.

contented adj happy, glad, pleased, cheerful, comfortable, relaxed, content, satisfied.
⊞ discontented, unhappy, annoyed.

contentment n contentedness, happiness, gladness, pleasure, gratification, comfort, ease, complacency, peace, peacefulness, serenity, equanimity, content,

satisfaction, fulfilment.
⊞ unhappiness, discontent, dissatisfaction.

contents n 1 *the contents of the package*: constituents, parts, elements, ingredients, content, load, items. 2 CHAPTERS, divisions, subjects, topics, themes.

contest n competition, game, match, tournament, encounter, fight, battle, set-to, combat, conflict, struggle, dispute, debate, controversy.
◇ v 1 DISPUTE, debate, question, doubt, challenge, oppose, argue against, litigate, deny, refute. 2 COMPETE, vie, contend, strive, fight.
⊞ 1 accept.

contestant n competitor, contender, player, participant, entrant, candidate, aspirant, rival, opponent.

context n background, setting, surroundings, framework, frame of reference, situation, position, circumstances, conditions.

contingent n body, company, deputation, delegation, section, detachment, group, set, batch, quota, complement.

continual adj constant, perpetual, incessant, interminable, eternal, everlasting, regular, frequent, recurrent, repeated.
⊞ occasional, intermittent, temporary.

continuation n resumption, maintenance, prolongation, extension, development, furtherance, addition, supplement.
⊞ cessation, termination.

continue v resume, recommence, carry on, go on, proceed, persevere, stick at, persist, last, endure, survive, remain, abide, stay, rest, pursue, sustain, maintain, lengthen, prolong, extend, project.

⊞ discontinue, stop.

continuity n flow, progression, succession, sequence, linkage, interrelationship, connection, cohesion.
⊞ discontinuity.

continuous adj unbroken, uninterrupted, consecutive, non-stop, endless, ceaseless, unending, unceasing, constant, unremitting, prolonged, extended, continued, lasting.
⊞ discontinuous, broken, sporadic.

contort v twist, distort, warp, disfigure, deform, misshape, convolute, gnarl, knot, wrench, writhe, squirm, wriggle.

contour n outline, silhouette, shape, form, figure, curve, relief, profile, character, aspect.

contraception n birth control, family planning.

contract v 1 SHRINK, lessen, diminish, reduce, shorten, curtail, abbreviate, abridge, condense, compress, constrict, narrow, tighten, tense, shrivel, wrinkle. 2 *contract pneumonia*: catch, get, go down with, develop. 3 PLEDGE, promise, undertake, agree, stipulate, arrange, negotiate, bargain.
⊞ 1 expand, enlarge, lengthen.
◇ n bond, commitment, engagement, covenant, treaty, convention, pact, compact, agreement, transaction, deal, bargain, settlement, arrangement, understanding.

contradict v deny, disaffirm, confute, challenge, oppose, impugn, dispute, counter, negate, gainsay.
⊞ agree, confirm, corroborate.

contradictory adj contrary, opposite, paradoxical, conflicting, discrepant, inconsistent, incompatible, antagonistic, irreconcilable, opposed, repugnant.
⊞ consistent.

contraption n contrivance, device, gadget, apparatus, rig, machine, mechanism.

contrary adj 1 OPPOSITE, counter, reverse, conflicting, antagonistic, opposed, adverse, hostile. 2 PERVERSE, awkward, disobliging, difficult, wayward, obstinate, intractable, cantankerous, stroppy (infml).
⊜ 1 like. 2 obliging.
◇ n opposite, converse, reverse.

contrast n difference, dissimilarity, disparity, divergence, distinction, differentiation, comparison, foil, antithesis, opposition.
⊜ similarity.
◇ v compare, differentiate, distinguish, discriminate, differ, oppose, clash, conflict.

contravene v infringe, violate, break, breach, disobey, defy, flout, transgress.
⊜ uphold, observe, obey.

contribute v donate, subscribe, chip in (infml), add, give, bestow, provide, supply, furnish, help, lead, conduce.
⊜ withhold.

contribution n donation, gift, subscription, gratuity, handout, grant, offering, input, addition.

contributor n 1 DONOR, subscriber, giver, patron, benefactor, sponsor, backer, supporter. 2 WRITER, journalist, reporter, correspondent, freelance.

contrite adj sorry, regretful, remorseful, repentant, penitent, conscience-stricken, chastened, humble, ashamed.

contrivance n 1 INVENTION, device, contraption, gadget, implement, appliance, machine, mechanism, apparatus, equipment, gear.
2 STRATAGEM, ploy, trick, dodge, ruse, expedient, plan, design, project, scheme, plot, intrigue, machination.

contrived adj unnatural, artificial, false, forced, strained, laboured, mannered, elaborate, overdone.
⊜ natural, genuine.

control v 1 LEAD, govern, rule, command, direct, manage, oversee, supervise, superintend, run, operate. 2 control the temperature: regulate, adjust, monitor, verify. 3 control one's temper: restrain, check, curb, subdue, repress, hold back, contain.
◇ n 1 POWER, charge, authority, command, mastery, government, rule, direction, management, oversight, supervision, discipline, superintendence, guidance.
2 RESTRAINT, check, curb, repression. 3 INSTRUMENT, dial, switch, button, knob, lever.

controversial adj contentious, polemical, disputed, doubtful, questionable, debatable, disputable.

controversy n debate, discussion, war of words, polemic, dispute, disagreement, argument, quarrel, squabble, wrangle, strife, contention, dissension.
⊜ accord, agreement.

convenience n 1 ACCESSIBILITY, availability, handiness, usefulness, use, utility, serviceability, service, benefit, advantage, help, suitability, fitness. 2 all modern conveniences: facility, amenity, appliance.
⊜ 1 inconvenience.

convenient adj nearby, at hand, accessible, available, handy, useful, commodious, beneficial, helpful, labour-saving, adapted, fitted, suited, suitable, fit, appropriate, opportune, timely, well-timed.
⊜ inconvenient, awkward.

convention n 1 CUSTOM, tradition, practice, usage, protocol, etiquette, formality, matter of form, code.
2 ASSEMBLY, congress, conference, meeting, council, delegates, representatives.

conventional adj traditional, orthodox, formal, correct, proper, prevalent, prevailing, accepted, received, expected, unoriginal, ritual, routine, usual, customary, regular, standard, normal, ordinary, straight, stereotyped, hidebound, pedestrian, commonplace, common, run-of-the-mill.
⊞ unconventional, unusual, exotic.

converge v focus, concentrate, approach, merge, coincide, meet, join, combine, gather.
⊞ diverge, disperse.

convergence n concentration, approach, merging, confluence, blending, meeting, coincidence, junction, intersection, union.
⊞ divergence, separation.

conversation n talk, chat, gossip, discussion, discourse, dialogue, exchange, communication.

converse n opposite, reverse, contrary, antithesis, obverse.
◇ adj opposite, reverse, counter, contrary, reversed, transposed.

conversion n alteration, change, transformation, adaptation, modification, remodelling, reconstruction, reorganization, reformation, regeneration, rebirth.

convert v 1 ALTER, change, turn, transform, adapt, modify, remodel, restyle, revise, reorganize. 2 WIN OVER, convince, persuade, reform, proselytize.

convex adj rounded, bulging, protuberant.
⊞ concave.

convey v carry, bear, bring, fetch, move, transport, send, forward, deliver, transfer, conduct, guide, transmit, communicate, impart, tell, relate, reveal.

convict v condemn, sentence, imprison.
◇ n criminal, felon, culprit, prisoner.

conviction n assurance, confidence, fervour, earnestness, certainty, firmness, persuasion, view, opinion, belief, faith, creed, tenet, principle.

convince v assure, persuade, sway, win over, bring round, reassure, satisfy.

convincing adj persuasive, cogent, powerful, telling, impressive, credible, plausible, likely, probable, conclusive, incontrovertible.
⊞ unconvincing, improbable.

convoluted adj twisting, winding, meandering, tortuous, involved, complicated, complex, tangled.
⊞ straight, straightforward.

convoy n fleet, escort, guard, protection, attendance, train.

convulsion n 1 FIT, seizure, paroxysm, spasm, cramp, contraction, tic, tremor. 2 ERUPTION, outburst, furore, disturbance, commotion, tumult, agitation, turbulence, upheaval.

convulsive adj jerky, spasmodic, fitful, sporadic, uncontrolled, violent.

cook

Ways of cooking include: bake, barbecue, boil, braise, broil, casserole, chargrill, coddle, deep-fry, fry, grill, microwave, poach, pot-roast, roast, sauté, scramble, sear, simmer, spit-roast, steam, stew, stir-fry, toast, heat.

• **cook up** concoct, prepare, brew, invent, fabricate, contrive, devise, plan, plot, scheme.

cool adj 1 CHILLY, fresh, breezy, nippy, cold, chilled, iced, refreshing. 2 CALM, unruffled, unexcited, composed, self-possessed, level-headed, unemotional, quiet, relaxed, laid-back (infml). 3 a cool reception: unfriendly, unwelcoming, cold, frigid, lukewarm, unenthusiastic,

half-hearted, apathetic, uninterested, unresponsive, uncommunicative, reserved, distant, aloof, standoffish.
⊟ **1** warm, hot. **2** excited, angry. **3** friendly, welcoming.
◇ v **1** CHILL, refrigerate, ice, freeze, fan. **2** MODERATE, lessen, temper, dampen, quiet, abate, calm, allay, assuage.
⊟ **1** warm, heat. **2** excite.
◇ n coolness, calmness, collectedness, composure, poise, self-possession, self-discipline, self-control, control, temper.

co-operate v collaborate, work together, play ball (*infml*), help, assist, aid, contribute, participate, combine, unite, conspire.

co-operation n helpfulness, assistance, participation, collaboration, teamwork, unity, co-ordination, give-and-take.
⊟ opposition, rivalry, competition.

co-operative adj **1** HELPFUL, supportive, obliging, willing, accommodating. **2** COLLECTIVE, joint, shared, combined, united, concerted, co-ordinated.
⊟ **1** unco-operative, rebellious.

co-ordinate v organize, arrange, systematize, tabulate, integrate, mesh, synchronize, harmonize, match, correlate, regulate.

cope v manage, carry on, survive, get by, make do.
• **cope with** deal with, encounter, contend with, struggle with, grapple with, wrestle with, handle, manage, weather.

copious adj abundant, plentiful, inexhaustible, overflowing, profuse, rich, lavish, bountiful, liberal, full, ample, generous, extensive, great, huge.
⊟ scarce, meagre.

copy n duplicate, carbon copy, photocopy, Photostat®, Xerox®, facsimile, reproduction, print,

tracing, transcript, transcription, replica, clone, model, pattern, archetype, representation, image, likeness, counterfeit, forgery, fake, imitation, borrowing, plagiarism, crib.
⊟ original.
◇ v duplicate, photocopy, print, reproduce, trace, transcribe, forge, counterfeit, simulate, imitate, impersonate, mimic, ape, parrot, repeat, echo, mirror, follow, emulate, borrow, plagiarize, crib.

cord n string, twine, rope, line, cable, flex, connection, link, bond, tie.

core n kernel, nucleus, heart, centre, middle, nub, crux, essence, gist, nitty-gritty (*infml*).
⊟ surface, exterior.

corner n **1** *round the corner*: angle, joint, crook, bend, turning. **2** NOOK, cranny, niche, recess, cavity, hole, hideout, hideaway, retreat.

corporation n council, authorities, association, society, organization, company, firm, combine, conglomerate.

corpse n body, stiff (*sl*), carcase, skeleton, remains.

correct v **1** *correct an error*: rectify, put right, right, emend, remedy, cure, debug, redress, adjust, regulate, improve, amend. **2** PUNISH, discipline, reprimand, reprove, reform.
◇ adj **1** *the correct answer*: right, accurate, precise, exact, strict, true, truthful, word-perfect, faultless, flawless. **2** PROPER, acceptable, OK (*infml*), standard, regular, just, appropriate, fitting.
⊟ **1** incorrect, wrong, inaccurate.

correction n rectification, emendation, adjustment, alteration, modification, amendment, improvement.

correspond v **1** MATCH, fit, answer, conform, tally, square, agree, concur, coincide, correlate, accord,

harmonize, dovetail, complement.
2 COMMUNICATE, write.

correspondence n
1 COMMUNICATION, writing, letters, post, mail. 2 CONFORMITY, agreement, concurrence, coincidence, correlation, relation, analogy, comparison, comparability, similarity, resemblance, congruity, equivalence, harmony, match.
🔄 2 divergence, incongruity.

correspondent n journalist, reporter, contributor, writer.

corresponding adj matching, complementary, reciprocal, interrelated, analogous, equivalent, similar, identical.

corridor n aisle, passageway, passage, hallway, hall, lobby.

corroborate v confirm, prove, bear out, support, endorse, ratify, substantiate, validate, authenticate, document, underpin, sustain.
🔄 contradict.

corrode v erode, wear away, eat away, consume, waste, rust, oxidize, tarnish, impair, deteriorate, crumble, disintegrate.

corrosive adj corroding, acid, caustic, cutting, abrasive, erosive, wearing, consuming, wasting.

corrugated adj ridged, fluted, grooved, channelled, furrowed, wrinkled, crinkled, rumpled, creased.

corrupt adj rotten, unscrupulous, unprincipled, unethical, immoral, fraudulent, shady (infml), dishonest, untrustworthy, bent (infml), crooked (infml), depraved, degenerate, dissolute.
🔄 ethical, virtuous, upright, honest, trustworthy.
◇ v contaminate, pollute, adulterate, taint, defile, debase, pervert, deprave, lead astray, lure, bribe, suborn.
🔄 purify.

corruption n unscrupulousness,

immorality, impurity, depravity, degeneration, degradation, perversion, distortion, dishonesty, crookedness (infml), fraud, shadiness (infml), bribery, extortion, vice, wickedness, iniquity, evil.
🔄 honesty, virtue.

cosmetic adj superficial, surface.
🔄 essential.

cosmetics n make-up, grease paint.

Types of cosmetics include:
blusher, cleanser, concealer, exfoliant, eyebrow pencil, eyelash dye, eyeliner, eyeshadow, face cream, face mask, face pack, face powder, facial scrub, false eyelashes, foundation, kohl pencil, lip gloss, lip liner, lipstick, mascara, moisturizer, nail polish, nail varnish, rouge, toner.

cosmopolitan adj worldly, worldly-wise, well-travelled, sophisticated, urbane, international, universal.
🔄 insular, parochial, rustic.

cosset v coddle, mollycoddle, baby, pamper, indulge, spoil, pet, fondle, cuddle, cherish.

cost n 1 EXPENSE, outlay, payment, disbursement, expenditure, charge, price, rate, amount, figure, worth.
2 DETRIMENT, harm, injury, hurt, loss, deprivation, sacrifice, penalty, price.

costly adj 1 EXPENSIVE, dear, pric(e)y (infml), exorbitant, excessive, lavish, rich, splendid, valuable, precious, priceless. 2 HARMFUL, damaging, disastrous, catastrophic, loss-making.
🔄 1 cheap, inexpensive.

costume n outfit, uniform, livery, robes, vestments, dress, clothing, get-up (infml), fancy dress.

cosy adj snug, comfortable, comfy (infml), warm, sheltered, secure, homely, intimate.
🔄 uncomfortable, cold.

cottage *n* lodge, chalet, bungalow, hut, cabin, shack.

couch

Types of couch include: settee, sofa, chaise-longue, ottoman, studio couch, chesterfield.

council *n* committee, panel, board, cabinet, ministry, parliament, congress, assembly, convention, conference.

counsel *n* 1 ADVICE, suggestion, recommendation, guidance, direction, information, consultation, deliberation, consideration, forethought. 2 *counsel for the defence*: lawyer, advocate, solicitor, attorney, barrister.
◇ *v* advise, warn, caution, suggest, recommend, advocate, urge, exhort, guide, direct, instruct.

count *v* 1 NUMBER, enumerate, list, include, reckon, calculate, compute, tell, check, add, total, tot up, score. 2 MATTER, signify, qualify. 3 *count yourself lucky*: consider, regard, deem, judge, think, reckon, hold.
◇ *n* numbering, enumeration, poll, reckoning, calculation, computation, sum, total, tally.
• **count on** depend on, rely on, bank on, reckon on, expect, believe, trust.

counter *adv* against, in opposition, conversely.
◇ *adj* contrary, opposite, opposing, conflicting, contradictory, contrasting, opposed, against, adverse.
◇ *v* parry, resist, offset, answer, respond, retaliate, retort, return, meet.

counteract *v* neutralize, offset, counterbalance, countervail, act against, oppose, resist, hinder, check, thwart, frustrate, foil, defeat, undo, negate, annul, invalidate.
🗷 support, assist.

counterfeit *v* fake, forge, fabricate, copy, imitate, impersonate, pretend, feign, simulate, sham.
◇ *adj* fake, false, phoney (*infml*), forged, copied, fraudulent, bogus, pseudo, sham, spurious, imitation, artificial, simulated, feigned, pretended.
🗷 genuine, authentic, real.
◇ *n* fake, forgery, copy, reproduction, imitation, fraud, sham.

counterpart *n* equivalent, opposite number, complement, supplement, match, fellow, mate, twin, duplicate, copy.

countless *adj* innumerable, myriad, numberless, unnumbered, untold, incalculable, immeasurable, measureless, infinite, endless, limitless.
🗷 finite, limited.

country *n* 1 STATE, nation, people, kingdom, realm, principality. 2 COUNTRYSIDE, green belt, farmland, provinces, sticks (*infml*), boondocks (*US infml*), backwoods, wilds. 3 TERRAIN, land, territory, region, area, district.
🗷 2 town, city.
◇ *adj* rural, provincial, agricultural, agrarian, pastoral, rustic, bucolic, landed.
🗷 urban.

countryside *n* landscape, scenery, country, green belt, farmland, outdoors.

county *n* shire, province, region, area, district.

couple *n* pair, brace, twosome, duo.
◇ *v* pair, match, marry, wed, unite, join, link, connect, fasten, hitch, clasp, buckle, yoke.

coupon *n* voucher, token, slip, check, ticket, certificate.

courage *n* bravery, pluck, guts (*infml*), fearlessness, dauntlessness, heroism, gallantry, valour, boldness, audacity, nerve, daring, resolution, fortitude, spirit, mettle.

≣ cowardice, fear.

courageous *adj* brave, plucky, fearless, dauntless, indomitable, heroic, gallant, valiant, lion-hearted, hardy, bold, audacious, daring, intrepid, feisty (*infml*), resolute. ≣ cowardly, afraid.

course *n* 1 CURRICULUM, syllabus, classes, lessons, lectures, studies. 2 FLOW, movement, advance, progress, development, furtherance, order, sequence, series, succession, progression. 3 DURATION, time, period, term, passage. 4 DIRECTION, way, path, track, road, route, channel, trail, line, circuit, orbit, trajectory, flight path. 5 *course of action*: plan, schedule, programme, policy, procedure, method, mode.

court *n* 1 LAW-COURT, bench, bar, tribunal, trial, session. 2 COURTYARD, yard, quadrangle, square, cloister, forecourt, enclosure. 3 ENTOURAGE, attendants, retinue, suite, train, cortège.

courteous *adj* polite, civil, respectful, well-mannered, well-bred, ladylike, gentlemanly, gracious, obliging, considerate, attentive, gallant, courtly, urbane, debonair, refined, polished. ≣ discourteous, impolite, rude.

courtesy *n* politeness, civility, respect, manners, breeding, graciousness, consideration, attention, gallantry, urbanity. ≣ discourtesy, rudeness.

courtier *n* noble, nobleman, lord, lady, steward, page, attendant, follower, flatterer, sycophant, toady.

courtyard *n* yard, quadrangle, quad (*infml*), area, enclosure, court.

cove *n* bay, bight, inlet, estuary, firth, fiord, creek.

cover *v* 1 HIDE, conceal, obscure, shroud, veil, screen, mask, disguise, camouflage. 2 *covered with mud*: coat, spread, daub, plaster, encase,

wrap, envelop, clothe, dress. 3 SHELTER, protect, shield, guard, defend. 4 *cover a topic*: deal with, treat, consider, examine, investigate, encompass, embrace, incorporate, embody, involve, include, contain, comprise. ≣ 1 uncover. 2 strip. 3 expose. 4 exclude. ◇ *n* 1 COATING, covering, top, lid, cup, veil, screen, mask, front, façade, jacket, wrapper, case, envelope, clothing, dress, bedspread, canopy. 2 SHELTER, refuge, protection, shield, guard, defence, concealment, disguise, camouflage. • **cover up** (*infml*) conceal, hide, whitewash, dissemble, suppress, hush up, keep dark, repress. ≣ disclose, reveal.

covering *n* layer, coat, coating, blanket, film, veneer, skin, crust, shell, casing, housing, wrapping, clothing, protection, mask, overlay, cover, top, shelter, roof.

cover-up *n* concealment, whitewash, smokescreen, front, façade, pretence, conspiracy, complicity.

covet *v* envy, begrudge, crave, long for, yearn for, hanker for, want, desire, fancy (*infml*), lust after.

coward *n* craven, faint-heart, chicken (*infml*), scaredy-cat, yellow-belly (*sl*), wimp (*infml*), wuss (*sl*), renegade, deserter. ≣ hero.

cowardice *n* cowardliness, faint-heartedness, timorousness, spinelessness. ≣ courage, valour.

cowardly *adj* faint-hearted, craven, fearful, timorous, scared, unheroic, chicken-hearted, chicken-livered, chicken (*infml*), yellow-bellied (*sl*), yellow (*sl*), spineless, weak, weak-kneed, soft. ≣ brave, courageous, bold.

cower v crouch, grovel, skulk, shrink, flinch, cringe, quail, tremble, shake, shiver.

coy adj modest, demure, prudish, diffident, shy, bashful, timid, shrinking, backward, retiring, self-effacing, reserved, evasive, arch, flirtatious, coquettish, skittish, kittenish.
⊞ bold, forward.

crack v 1 SPLIT, burst, fracture, break, snap, shatter, splinter, chip. 2 EXPLODE, burst, pop, crackle, snap, crash, clap, slap, whack (infml). 3 crack a code: decipher, work out, solve.
◇ n 1 BREAK, fracture, split, rift, gap, crevice, fissure, chink, line, flaw, chip. 2 EXPLOSION, burst, pop, snap, crash, clap, blow, smack, slap, whack (infml). 3 JOKE, quip, witticism, gag (infml), wisecrack, gibe, dig.
◇ adj (infml) first-class, first-rate, top-notch (infml), excellent, superior, choice, hand-picked.
• crack down on clamp down on, end, stop, put a stop to, crush, suppress, check, repress, act against.
• crack up go mad, go to pieces, break down, collapse.

cradle n 1 COT, crib, bed. 2 SOURCE, origin, spring, wellspring, fount, fountainhead, birthplace, beginning.
◇ v hold, support, rock, lull, nurse, nurture, tend.

craft n 1 SKILL, expertise, mastery, talent, knack, ability, aptitude, dexterity, cleverness, art, handicraft, handiwork. 2 TRADE, business, calling, vocation, job, occupation, work, employment. 3 VESSEL, boat, ship, aircraft, spacecraft, spaceship.

craftsman, craftswoman n artisan, technician, master, maker, wright, smith.

craftsmanship n artistry, workmanship, technique, dexterity, expertise, mastery.

crafty adj sly, cunning, artful, wily, devious, subtle, scheming, calculating, designing, deceitful, fraudulent, sharp, shrewd, astute, canny.
⊞ artless, naive.

cram v stuff, jam, ram, force, press, squeeze, crush, compress, pack, crowd, overfill, glut, gorge.

cramp¹ v hinder, hamper, obstruct, impede, inhibit, handicap, thwart, frustrate, check, restrict, confine, shackle, tie.

cramp² n pain, ache, twinge, pang, contraction, convulsion, spasm, crick, stitch, pins and needles, stiffness.

cramped adj narrow, tight, small, uncomfortable, restricted, confined, crowded, packed, squashed, squeezed, overcrowded, jam-packed, congested.
⊞ spacious.

crash n 1 car crash: accident, collision, bump, smash, pile-up, smash-up (infml), wreck. 2 BANG, clash, clatter, clang, thud, thump, boom, thunder, racket, din. 3 stock-market crash: collapse, failure, ruin, downfall, bankruptcy, depression.
◇ v 1 COLLIDE, hit, knock, bump, bang. 2 BREAK, fracture, smash, dash, shatter, splinter, shiver, fragment, disintegrate. 3 FALL, topple, pitch, plunge, collapse, fail, fold (up), go under, go bust (infml).

crate n container, box, case, tea-chest, packing-box, packing-case.

crave v hunger for, thirst for, long for, yearn for, pine for, hanker after, fancy (infml), desire, want, need, require.
⊞ dislike.

craving n appetite, hunger, thirst, longing, yearning, hankering, lust, desire, urge.
⊞ dislike, distaste.

crawl v 1 CREEP, inch, edge, slither, wriggle. 2 GROVEL, cringe, toady, fawn, flatter, suck up (sl).

craze n fad, novelty, fashion, vogue, mode, trend, rage (*infml*), thing (*infml*), obsession, preoccupation, mania, frenzy, passion, infatuation, enthusiasm.

crazy adj 1 MAD, insane, lunatic, unbalanced, deranged, demented, crazed, potty (*infml*), barmy (*infml*), daft (*infml*), silly, foolish, idiotic, senseless, unwise, imprudent, nonsensical, absurd, ludicrous, ridiculous, preposterous, outrageous, half-baked, impracticable, irresponsible, wild, berserk. 2 (*infml*) *crazy about golf*: enthusiastic, fanatical, zealous, ardent, passionate, infatuated, enamoured, smitten, mad, wild.
⊟ 1 sane, sensible. 2 indifferent.

creak v squeak, groan, grate, scrape, rasp, scratch, grind, squeal, screech.

cream n 1 PASTE, emulsion, oil, lotion, ointment, salve, cosmetic. 2 BEST, pick, élite, prime.

creamy adj 1 CREAM-COLOURED, off-white, yellowish-white. 2 MILKY, buttery, oily, smooth, velvety, rich, thick.

crease v fold, pleat, wrinkle, pucker, crumple, rumple, crinkle, crimp, corrugate, ridge.
◇ n fold, line, pleat, tuck, wrinkle, pucker, ruck, crinkle, corrugation, ridge, groove.

create v invent, coin, formulate, compose, design, devise, concoct, hatch, originate, initiate, found, establish, set up, institute, cause, occasion, produce, generate, engender, make, form, appoint, install, invest, ordain.
⊟ destroy.

creation n 1 MAKING, formation, constitution, invention, concoction, origination, foundation, origin, establishment, institution, design, production, generation, procreation, conception, birth.

2 INVENTION, brainchild, concept, product, handiwork, chef d'oeuvre, achievement.
⊟ 1 destruction.

creative adj artistic, inventive, original, imaginative, inspired, visionary, talented, gifted, clever, ingenious, resourceful, fertile, productive.
⊟ unimaginative.

creator n maker, inventor, designer, architect, author, originator, initiator.

creature n animal, beast, bird, fish, organism, being, mortal, individual, person, man, woman, body, soul.

credentials n diploma, certificate, reference, testimonial, recommendation, accreditation, authorization, warrant, licence, permit, passport, identity card, papers, documents, deed, title.

credibility n integrity, reliability, trustworthiness, plausibility, probability.
⊟ implausibility.

credible adj believable, imaginable, conceivable, thinkable, tenable, plausible, likely, probable, possible, reasonable, persuasive, convincing, sincere, honest, trustworthy, reliable, dependable.
⊟ incredible, unbelievable, implausible, unreliable.

credit n acknowledgement, recognition, thanks, approval, commendation, praise, acclaim, tribute, glory, fame, prestige, distinction, honour, reputation, esteem, estimation.
⊟ discredit, shame.
◇ v believe, swallow (*infml*), accept, subscribe to, trust, rely on.
⊟ disbelieve.

creditable adj honourable, reputable, respectable, estimable, admirable, commendable, praiseworthy, good, excellent, exemplary, worthy, deserving.

⊠ shameful, blameworthy.

credulous *adj* naive, gullible, wide-eyed, trusting, unsuspecting, uncritical.
⊠ sceptical, suspicious.

creed *n* belief, faith, persuasion, credo, catechism, doctrine, principles, tenets, articles, canon, dogma.

creek *n* inlet, estuary, cove, bay, bight.

creep *v* inch, edge, tiptoe, steal, sneak, slink, crawl, slither, worm, wriggle, squirm, grovel, writhe.

creepy *adj* eerie, spooky, sinister, threatening, frightening, scary, terrifying, hair-raising, nightmarish, macabre, gruesome, horrible, unpleasant, disturbing.

crest *n* **1** *the crest of the hill*: ridge, crown, top, peak, summit, pinnacle, apex, head. **2** TUFT, tassel, plume, comb, mane. **3** INSIGNIA, device, symbol, emblem, badge.

crevice *n* crack, fissure, split, rift, cleft, slit, chink, cranny, gap, hole, opening, break.

crew *n* team, party, squad, troop, corps, company, gang, band, bunch, crowd, mob, set, lot.

crime *n* law-breaking, lawlessness, delinquency, illegal act, unlawful act, offence, felony, misdemeanour, misdeed, wrongdoing, misconduct, transgression, violation, sin, iniquity, vice, villainy, wickedness, atrocity, outrage.

Crimes include: theft, robbery, burglary, larceny, pilfering, mugging, poaching; assault, rape, grievous bodily harm *or* GBH (*infml*), battery, manslaughter, homicide, murder, assassination; fraud, bribery, corruption, embezzlement, extortion, blackmail; arson, treason, terrorism, hijack, piracy, kidnapping, sabotage, vandalism, hooliganism, drug-smuggling, forgery, counterfeiting, perjury, joyriding, drink-driving.

criminal *n* law-breaker, crook, felon, delinquent, offender, wrongdoer, miscreant, culprit, perpetrator, convict, prisoner.
◇ *adj* illegal, unlawful, illicit, lawless, wrong, culpable, indictable, crooked (*infml*), bent (*infml*), dishonest, corrupt, wicked, scandalous, deplorable.
⊠ legal, lawful, honest, upright.

cringe *v* shrink, recoil, shy, start, flinch, wince, quail, tremble, quiver, cower, crouch, bend, bow, stoop, grovel, crawl, creep.

cripple *v* lame, paralyse, disable, handicap, injure, maim, mutilate, damage, impair, spoil, ruin, destroy, sabotage, incapacitate, weaken, debilitate.

crippled *adj* lame, paralysed, disabled, handicapped, incapacitated.

crisis *n* emergency, extremity, crunch (*infml*), catastrophe, disaster, calamity, dilemma, quandary, predicament, difficulty, trouble, problem.

crisp *adj* **1** *a crisp biscuit*: crispy, crunchy, brittle, crumbly, firm, hard. **2** BRACING, invigorating, refreshing, fresh, brisk. **3** TERSE, pithy, snappy, brief, short, clear, incisive.
⊠ **1** soggy, limp, flabby. **2** muggy. **3** wordy, vague.

criterion *n* standard, norm, touchstone, benchmark, yardstick, measure, gauge, rule, principle, canon, test.

critic *n* reviewer, commentator, analyst, pundit, authority, expert, judge, censor, carper, fault-finder, attacker, knocker (*infml*).

critical *adj* **1** *at the critical moment*:

crucial, vital, essential, all-important, momentous, decisive, urgent, pressing, serious, grave, dangerous, perilous. **2** ANALYTICAL, diagnostic, penetrating, probing, discerning, perceptive. **3** UNCOMPLIMENTARY, derogatory, disparaging, disapproving, censorious, carping, fault-finding, cavilling, nit-picking (*infml*).
☒ **1** unimportant. **3** complimentary, appreciative.

criticism *n* **1** CONDEMNATION, disapproval, disparagement, fault-finding, censure, blame, brickbat, flak (*infml*). **2** REVIEW, critique, assessment, evaluation, appraisal, judgement, analysis, commentary, appreciation.
☒ **1** praise, commendation.

criticize *v* **1** CONDEMN, slate (*infml*), slam (*infml*), knock (*infml*), disparage, carp, find fault, censure, blame. **2** REVIEW, assess, evaluate, appraise, judge, analyse.
☒ **1** praise, commend.

critique *n* review, essay, assessment, evaluation, appraisal, judgement, analysis, commentary, write-up, appreciation, explanation, interpretation, exposition (*fml*), explication (*fml*).

croak *v* rasp, squawk, caw, wheeze, speak harshly, gasp, grunt.

crockery *n* dishes, tableware, china, porcelain, earthenware, stoneware, pottery.

Items of crockery include: cup, saucer, coffee cup, mug, beaker, plate, side plate, dinner plate, bowl, cereal bowl, soup bowl, salad bowl, sugar bowl, jug, milk jug, basin, pot, teapot, coffee pot, meat dish, butter dish, tureen, gravy boat, cruet, tea set, dinner service.

---

crook *n* criminal, thief, robber, swindler, cheat, shark (*infml*), rogue, villain.

crooked *adj* **1** ASKEW, skew-whiff (*infml*), awry, lopsided, asymmetric, irregular, uneven, off-centre, tilted, slanting, bent, angled, hooked, curved, bowed, warped, distorted, misshapen, deformed, twisted, tortuous, winding, zigzag. **2** (*infml*) ILLEGAL, unlawful, illicit, criminal, nefarious, dishonest, deceitful, bent (*infml*), corrupt, fraudulent, shady (*infml*), shifty, underhand, treacherous, unscrupulous, unprincipled, unethical.
☒ **1** straight. **2** honest.

crop *n* growth, yield, produce, fruits, harvest, vintage, gathering.
◇ *v* cut, snip, clip, shear, trim, pare, prune, lop, shorten, curtail.
● **crop up** arise, emerge, appear, arrive, occur, happen.

cross *adj* **1** IRRITABLE, annoyed, angry, vexed, shirty (*infml*), bad-tempered, ill-tempered, crotchety, grumpy, grouchy, irascible, crabby, short, snappy, snappish, sullen, surly, fractious, fretful, impatient. **2** TRANSVERSE, crosswise, oblique, diagonal, intersecting, opposite, reciprocal.
☒ **1** placid, pleasant.
◇ *v* **1** *cross the river*: go across, traverse, ford, bridge, span.
2 INTERSECT, meet, criss-cross, lace, intertwine. **3** CROSSBREED, interbreed, mongrelize, hybridize, cross-fertilize, cross-pollinate, blend, mix. **4** THWART, frustrate, foil, hinder, impede, block, obstruct, oppose.
◇ *n* **1** BURDEN, load, affliction, misfortune, trouble, worry, trial, tribulation, grief, misery, woe.
2 CROSSBREED, hybrid, mongrel, blend, mixture, amalgam, combination.

crouch *v* squat, kneel, stoop, bend, bow, hunch, duck, cower, cringe.

crowd *n* **1** THRONG, multitude, host,

mob, masses, populace, people, public, riff-raff, rabble, horde, swarm, flock, herd, pack, press, crush, squash, assembly, company, group, bunch, lot, set, circle, clique. **2** SPECTATORS, gate, attendance, audience.
◇ *v* gather, congregate, muster, huddle, mass, throng, swarm, flock, surge, stream, push, shove, elbow, jostle, press, squeeze, bundle, pile, pack, congest, cram, compress.

crowded *adj* full, filled, packed, jammed, jam-packed, congested, cramped, overcrowded, overpopulated, busy, teeming, swarming, overflowing.
⊞ empty, deserted.

crown *n* **1** CORONET, diadem, tiara, circlet, wreath, garland. **2** PRIZE, trophy, reward, honour, laurels. **3** SOVEREIGN, monarch, king, queen, ruler, sovereignty, monarchy, royalty. **4** TOP, tip, apex, crest, summit, pinnacle, peak, acme.
◇ *v* **1** ENTHRONE, anoint, adorn, festoon, honour, dignify, reward. **2** TOP, cap, complete, fulfil, consummate, perfect.

crucial *adj* urgent, pressing, vital, essential, key, pivotal, central, important, momentous, decisive, critical, trying, testing, searching.
⊞ unimportant, trivial.

crude *adj* **1** RAW, unprocessed, unrefined, rough, unfinished, unpolished, natural, primitive. **2** VULGAR, coarse, rude, indecent, obscene, gross, dirty, lewd.
⊞ **1** refined, finished. **2** polite, decent.

cruel *adj* fierce, ferocious, vicious, savage, barbarous, bloodthirsty, murderous, cold-blooded, sadistic, brutal, inhuman, inhumane, unkind, malevolent, spiteful, callous, harsh, heartless, unfeeling, merciless, pitiless, flinty, hard-hearted, stony-hearted, implacable, ruthless,

remorseless, relentless, unrelenting, inexorable, grim, hellish, atrocious, bitter, severe, cutting, painful, excruciating.
⊞ kind, compassionate, merciful.

cruelty *n* ferocity, viciousness, savagery, barbarity, bloodthirstiness, murderousness, violence, sadism, brutality, bestiality, inhumanity, spite, venom, callousness, heartlessness, hard-heartedness, mercilessness, ruthlessness, tyranny, harshness, severity.
⊞ kindness, compassion, mercy.

cruise *n* holiday, voyage, sail, journey, trip.
◇ *v* **1** *cruising round the Mediterranean*: sail, travel, journey. **2** *cruising along comfortably*: sail, coast, drift, freewheel, glide, slide, taxi.

crumb *n* piece, scrap, morsel, bit, titbit, particle, grain, atom, flake, speck, iota, jot, mite, shred, sliver, snippet, soupçon.

crumble *v* fragment, break up, decompose, disintegrate, decay, degenerate, deteriorate, collapse, crush, pound, grind, powder, pulverize.

crumple *v* crush, wrinkle, pucker, crinkle, rumple, crease, fold, collapse.

crunch *v* munch, chomp, champ, masticate, grind, crush.

crusade *n* campaign, drive, push, movement, cause, undertaking, expedition, holy war, jihad.

crush *v* **1** SQUASH, compress, squeeze, press, pulp, break, smash, pound, pulverize, grind, crumble, crumple, wrinkle. **2** *the rebels were crushed*: conquer, vanquish, demolish, devastate, overpower, overwhelm, overcome, quash, quell, subdue, put down, humiliate, shame, abash.

crust *n* surface, exterior, outside,

covering, coat, coating, layer, film, skin, rind, shell, scab, incrustation, caking, concretion.

crux n nub, heart, core, essence.

cry v **1** WEEP, sob, blubber, wail, bawl, whimper, snivel. **2** SHOUT, call, exclaim, roar, bellow, yell, scream, shriek, screech.
◇ n **1** WEEP, sob, blubber, wail, bawl, whimper, snivel. **2** SHOUT, call, plea, exclamation, roar, bellow, yell, scream, shriek.

cryptic adj enigmatic, ambiguous, equivocal, puzzling, perplexing, mysterious, strange, bizarre, secret, hidden, veiled, obscure, abstruse, esoteric, dark, occult.
☒ straightforward, clear, obvious.

cuddle v hug, embrace, clasp, hold, nurse, nestle, snuggle, pet, fondle, caress.

cuddly adj cuddlesome, lovable, huggable, plump, soft, warm, cosy.

cue n signal, sign, nod, hint, suggestion, reminder, prompt, incentive, stimulus.

cuff v hit, thump, box, clip, knock, biff (infml), buffet, slap, smack, strike, clout, clobber (sl), belt (infml), beat, whack (infml).

culminate v climax, end (up), terminate, close, conclude, finish, consummate.
☒ start, begin.

culmination n climax, height, peak, pinnacle, summit, top, crown, perfection, consummation, finale, conclusion, completion.
☒ start, beginning.

culpable adj to blame, wrong, in the wrong, at fault, responsible, guilty, liable, offending, answerable, blamable, blameworthy, censurable, reprehensible.
☒ blameless, innocent.

culprit n guilty party, offender, perpetrator, wrongdoer, miscreant, law-breaker, criminal, felon, delinquent.

cult n **1** SECT, denomination, school, movement, party, faction. **2** CRAZE, fad, fashion, vogue, trend.

cultivate v **1** FARM, till, work, plough, grow, sow, plant, tend, harvest. **2** FOSTER, nurture, cherish, help, aid, support, encourage, promote, further, work on, develop, train, prepare, polish, refine, improve, enrich.
☒ **2** neglect.

cultural adj artistic, aesthetic, liberal, civilizing, humanizing, enlightening, educational, edifying, improving, enriching, elevating.

culture n **1** CIVILIZATION, society, lifestyle, way of life, customs, mores, the arts. **2** CULTIVATION, taste, education, enlightenment, breeding, gentility, refinement, politeness, urbanity.

cultured adj cultivated, civilized, advanced, enlightened, educated, well-read, well-informed, scholarly, highbrow, well-bred, refined, polished, genteel, urbane.
☒ uncultured, uneducated, ignorant.

cumbersome adj awkward, inconvenient, bulky, unwieldy, unmanageable, burdensome, clunky (infml), onerous, heavy, weighty.
☒ convenient, manageable.

cunning adj crafty, sly, artful, wily, tricky, devious, subtle, deceitful, guileful, sharp, shrewd, astute, canny, knowing, deep, imaginative, ingenious, skilful, deft, dexterous.
☒ naive, ingenuous, gullible.
◇ n craftiness, slyness, artfulness, trickery, deviousness, subtlety, deceitfulness, guile, sharpness, shrewdness, astuteness, ingenuity, cleverness, adroitness.

cup n mug, tankard, beaker, goblet, chalice, trophy.

cupboard n cabinet, locker, closet,

wardrobe.

Types of cupboard, cabinet and chest include: china cabinet, Welsh dresser, sideboard, buffet, chest of drawers, tallboy, chiffonier, commode, ottoman, chest, coffer, blanket box.

curb v restrain, constrain, restrict, contain, control, check, moderate, bridle, muzzle, suppress, subdue, repress, inhibit, hinder, impede, hamper, retard.
⊜ encourage, foster.

curdle v coagulate, congeal, clot, thicken, turn, sour, ferment.

cure v 1 HEAL, remedy, correct, restore, repair, mend, relieve, ease, alleviate, help. 2 PRESERVE, dry, smoke, salt, pickle, kipper.
◇ n remedy, antidote, panacea, medicine, specific, corrective, restorative, healing, treatment, therapy, alleviation, recovery.

curiosity n 1 INQUISITIVENESS, nosiness, prying, snooping, interest. 2 CURIO, objet d'art, antique, bygone, novelty, trinket, knick-knack. 3 ODDITY, rarity, freak, phenomenon, spectacle.

curious adj 1 INQUISITIVE, nosey, prying, meddlesome, questioning, inquiring, interested. 2 a curious sight: odd, queer, funny (infml), strange, peculiar, bizarre, mysterious, puzzling, extraordinary, unusual, rare, unique, novel, exotic, unconventional, unorthodox, quaint.
⊜ 1 uninterested, indifferent. 2 ordinary, usual, normal.

curl v crimp, frizz, wave, ripple, bend, curve, meander, loop, turn, twist, wind, wreathe, twine, coil, spiral, corkscrew, scroll.
⊜ uncurl.
◇ n wave, kink, swirl, twist, ringlet, coil, spiral, whorl.

curly adj wavy, kinky, curling, spiralled, corkscrew, curled, crimped, permed, frizzy, fuzzy.
⊜ straight.

currency n 1 MONEY, legal tender, coinage, coins, notes, bills. 2 ACCEPTANCE, publicity, popularity, vogue, circulation, prevalence, exposure.

Currencies of the world include: baht (Thailand), bolivar (Venezuela), dinar (Iraq, Jordan, etc), dirham (Morocco, UAE), dollar (US, Canada, Australia, NZ, etc), dong (Vietnam), euro (most EU countries), forint (Hungary), franc (Switzerland, Liechtenstein, etc), hryvnia (Ukraine), koruna (Czech Republic, Slovakia), krona (Sweden), króna (Iceland), krone (Denmark, Norway), kuna (Croatia), kyat (Myanmar), lari (Georgia), lek (Albania), leu (Romania, Moldova), lev (Bulgaria), lira (Turkey, Malta), naira (Nigeria), peso (Mexico, Cuba, Argentina, Chile, etc), pound (UK, Egypt, etc), rand (S Africa), real (Brazil), rial (Iran, Oman), ringgit (Malaysia), riyal (Saudi Arabia, Yemen, Qatar), rouble (Russia, Belarus), rupee (India, Pakistan, etc), rupiah (Indonesia), shekel (Israel), shilling (Kenya, Uganda, etc), som (Uzbekistan, Kyrgyzstan), tolar (Slovenia), won (N Korea, S Korea), yen (Japan), yuan (China), zloty (Poland).

current adj present, on-going, existing, contemporary, present-day, modern, fashionable, up-to-date, up-to-the-minute, trendy (infml), popular, widespread, prevalent, common, general, prevailing, reigning, accepted.
⊜ obsolete, old-fashioned.
◇ n draught, stream, jet, flow, tide, drift, course, trend, tendency, undercurrent, mood, feeling.

curriculum n syllabus, national curriculum, subjects, course of study, discipline, course, module, educational programme, timetable.

curse n 1 SWEAR-WORD, oath, expletive, obscenity, profanity, blasphemy. 2 JINX, anathema, bane, evil, plague, scourge, affliction, trouble, torment, ordeal, calamity, disaster.
⊟ 2 blessing, advantage.
◇ v 1 SWEAR, blaspheme, damn, condemn, denounce, fulminate.
2 BLIGHT, plague, scourge, afflict, trouble, torment.
⊟ 2 bless.

curtail v shorten, truncate, cut, trim, abridge, abbreviate, lessen, decrease, reduce, restrict.
⊟ lengthen, extend, prolong.

curtain n blind, screen, backdrop, hanging, drapery, tapestry.

curve v bend, arch, arc, bow, bulge, hook, crook, turn, wind, twist, spiral, coil.
◇ n bend, turn, arc, trajectory, loop, camber, curvature.

curved adj bent, arched, bowed, rounded, humped, convex, concave, crooked, twisted, sweeping, sinuous, serpentine.
⊟ straight.

cushion n pad, buffer, shock absorber, bolster, pillow, headrest, hassock.
◇ v soften, deaden, dampen, absorb, muffle, stifle, suppress, lessen, mitigate, protect, bolster, buttress, support.

custody n 1 KEEPING, possession, charge, care, safekeeping, protection, preservation, custodianship, trusteeship, guardianship, supervision. 2 DETENTION, confinement, imprisonment, incarceration.

custom n tradition, usage, use, habit, routine, procedure, practice, policy, way, manner, style, form, convention, etiquette, formality, observance, ritual.

customary adj traditional, conventional, obligatory, accepted, established, habitual, routine, regular, usual, normal, ordinary, everyday, familiar, common, general, popular, fashionable, prevailing.
⊟ unusual, rare.

customer n client, patron, regular, punter (infml), consumer, shopper, buyer, purchaser, prospect.

cut v 1 CLIP, trim, crop, shear, mow, shave, pare, chop, hack, hew, slice, carve, divide, part, split, bisect, dock, lop, sever, prune, excise, incise, penetrate, pierce, stab, wound, nick, gash, slit, slash, lacerate, score, engrave, chisel, sculpt. 2 REDUCE, decrease, lower, shorten, curtail, abbreviate, abridge, condense, précis, edit, delete.
3 IGNORE, cold-shoulder, spurn, avoid, snub, slight, rebuff, insult.
◇ n 1 INCISION, wound, nick, gash, slit, slash, rip, laceration. 2 spending cuts: reduction, decrease, lowering, cutback, saving, economy.
• **cut down 1** cut down a tree: fell, hew, lop, level, raze. 2 REDUCE, decrease, lower, lessen, diminish.
• **cut in** interrupt, butt in, interject, interpose, intervene, intrude.
• **cut off 1** SEVER, amputate, separate, isolate, disconnect, block, obstruct, intercept. 2 STOP, end, halt, suspend, discontinue, disown, disinherit.
• **cut out** excise, extract, remove, delete, eliminate, exclude, debar, stop, cease.
• **cut up** chop, dice, mince, dissect, divide, carve, slice, slash.

Types of cutting tools and implements include: axe, billhook, blade, chisel, chopper, clippers, guillotine, hedge trimmer, knife, flick-knife, penknife, pocket knife, Stanley knife®, Swiss army knife, lopper, machete, mower, lawnmower, plane, razor, saw, chainsaw, fretsaw, hacksaw, jigsaw, scalpel, scissors, scythe, secateurs, shears, pinking shears, sickle, Strimmer®, sword.

cutback n cut, saving, economy, retrenchment, reduction, downsizing, decrease, lowering, lessening.

cutlery

Items of cutlery include: knife, butter knife, carving knife, fish knife, steak knife, cheese knife, bread knife, fork, carving fork, corn holders, spoon, dessertspoon, tablespoon, teaspoon, soupspoon, caddy spoon, apostle spoon, ladle, salad servers, fish slice, cake server, sugar tongs, chopsticks, canteen of cutlery.

cut-price adj reduced, sale, discount, bargain, cheap, low-priced.

cutting adj sharp, keen, pointed, trenchant, incisive, penetrating, piercing, wounding, stinging, biting, mordant, caustic, acid, scathing, sarcastic, malicious, bitter, raw, chill. ◇ n clipping, extract, piece.

cycle n circle, round, rotation, revolution, series, sequence, phase, period, era, age, epoch, aeon.

cylinder n column, barrel, drum, reel, bobbin, spool, spindle.

cynic n sceptic, doubter, pessimist, killjoy, spoilsport (infml), scoffer, knocker (infml).

cynical adj sceptical, doubtful, distrustful, pessimistic, negative, scornful, derisive, contemptuous, sneering, scoffing, mocking, sarcastic, sardonic, ironic.

cynicism n scepticism, doubt, disbelief, distrust, pessimism, scorn, sarcasm, irony.

Dd

dab *v* pat, tap, daub, swab, wipe.
◇ *n* **1** BIT, dollop (*infml*), drop, speck, spot, trace, smear, smudge, fleck.
2 TOUCH, pat, stroke, tap.

dabble *v* **1** TRIFLE, tinker, toy, dally, potter. **2** PADDLE, moisten, wet, sprinkle, splash.

dabbler *n* amateur, dilettante, trifler.
⊞ professional, expert.

daft *adj* **1** FOOLISH, crazy, silly, stupid, absurd, dotty (*infml*), idiotic, inane.
2 INSANE, mad, lunatic, simple, crazy, mental. **3** (*infml*) INFATUATED.
⊞ **1** sensible. **2** sane.

daily *adj* **1** REGULAR, routine, everyday, customary, common, commonplace, ordinary. **2** EVERYDAY, diurnal (*fml*).

dainty *adj* **1** DELICATE, exquisite, elegant, refined, fine, graceful, neat, charming, delectable. **2** FASTIDIOUS, fussy, particular, scrupulous, nice (*fml*).
⊞ **1** gross, clumsy.

dam *n* barrier, barrage, embankment, blockage, obstruction, hindrance.
◇ *v* block, confine, restrict, check, barricade, staunch, stem, obstruct.

damage *n* harm, injury, hurt, destruction, devastation, loss, suffering, mischief, mutilation, impairment, detriment.
⊞ repair.
◇ *v* harm, injure, hurt, spoil, ruin, impair, mar, wreck, deface, mutilate, weaken, tamper with, play havoc with, incapacitate.
⊞ mend, repair, fix.

damn *v* **1** CURSE, swear, blast, imprecate, blaspheme. **2** ABUSE, revile, denounce, criticize, censure, slate (*infml*), denunciate, execrate, castigate, slam (*infml*). **3** CONDEMN, doom, sentence.
⊞ **1** bless.

damnation *n* condemnation, doom, denunciation, perdition, excommunication, anathema.

damp *n* dampness, moisture, clamminess, dankness, humidity, wet, dew, drizzle, fog, mist, vapour.
⊞ dryness.
◇ *adj* moist, wet, clammy, dank, humid, dewy, muggy, drizzly, misty, soggy.
⊞ dry, arid.

dampen *v* **1** MOISTEN, wet, spray.
2 DISCOURAGE, dishearten, deter, dash, dull, deaden, restrain, check, depress, dismay, reduce, lessen, moderate, decrease, diminish, muffle, stifle, smother.
⊞ **1** dry. **2** encourage.

dance *n* ball, hop (*infml*), knees-up (*infml*), social, shindig (*infml*).

Dances include: waltz, quickstep, foxtrot, tango, polka, one-step, military two-step, veleta, lancers, rumba, merengue, samba, salsa, macarena, mambo, bossa nova, beguine, fandango, flamenco, mazurka, bolero, paso doble, salsa, macarena, merengue, cancan; rock 'n' roll, jive, twist, stomp, bop, jitterbug; black bottom, Charleston, cha-cha, turkey-trot; Paul Jones, jig, reel, quadrille, Highland fling, morris dance, clogdance, hoedown, hokey cokey, Lambeth Walk, conga, belly-dance; galliard, gavotte, minuet.

Types of dancing include: ballet, tap, ballroom, old-time, disco, folk, country, Irish, Highland, Latin-American, flamenco, clog dancing, stepdancing, line dancing, morris dancing, limbo dancing, robotics, breakdancing.

Dance functions include: disco, dance, social, tea dance, barn dance, ball, fancy dress ball, charity ball, hunt ball, hop (*infml*), knees-up (*sl*), shindig (*infml*), rave (*infml*), prom (*US*), ceilidh.

---

danger *n* **1** *in danger of falling*: insecurity, endangerment, jeopardy, precariousness, liability, vulnerability. **2** *the dangers of smoking*: risk, threat, peril, hazard, menace.
▣ **1** safety, security. **2** safety.

dangerous *adj* unsafe, insecure, risky, threatening, breakneck, hairy (*infml*), hazardous, perilous, precarious, reckless, treacherous, vulnerable, menacing, exposed, alarming, critical, severe, serious, grave, daring, nasty.
▣ safe, secure, harmless.

dangle *v* **1** HANG, droop, swing, sway, flap, trail. **2** TEMPT, entice, flaunt, flourish, lure, tantalize.

dank *adj* damp, moist, clammy, dewy, slimy, soggy.
▣ dry.

dappled *adj* speckled, mottled, spotted, stippled, dotted, flecked, freckled, variegated, bespeckled, piebald, checkered.

dare *v* **1** RISK, venture, brave, hazard, adventure, endanger, stake, gamble. **2** CHALLENGE, goad, provoke, taunt. **3** DEFY, presume.

◇ *n* challenge, provocation, taunt, gauntlet.

daredevil *n* adventurer, desperado, madcap.
▣ coward.

daring *adj* bold, adventurous, intrepid, fearless, brave, plucky, audacious, valiant, dauntless, reckless, rash, impulsive.
▣ cautious, timid, afraid.
◇ *n* boldness, fearlessness, courage, bravery, nerve, audacity, guts (*infml*), intrepidity, defiance, pluck, rashness, spirit, grit, gall, prowess.
▣ caution, timidity, cowardice.

dark *adj* **1** *a dark room*: unlit, overcast, black, dim, unilluminated, shadowy, murky, cloudy, dusky, dingy. **2** *a dark manner*: gloomy, grim, cheerless, dismal, bleak, forbidding, sombre, sinister, mournful, ominous, menacing. **3** *dark secrets*: hidden, mysterious, obscure, secret, unintelligible, enigmatic, cryptic, abstruse.
▣ **1** light. **2** bright, cheerful. **3** comprehensible.
◇ *n* **1** DARKNESS, dimness, night, night-time, nightfall, gloom, dusk, twilight, murkiness. **2** CONCEALMENT, secrecy, obscurity.
▣ **1** light. **2** openness.

darken *v* **1** DIM, obscure, blacken, cloud (over), shadow, overshadow, eclipse. **2** DEPRESS, sadden.
▣ **1** lighten. **2** brighten.

darling *n* beloved, dear, dearest, favourite, sweetheart, love, pet, angel, treasure.
◇ *adj* dear, beloved, adored, cherished, precious, treasured.

dart *v* **1** DASH, bound, sprint, flit, flash, fly, rush, run, race, spring, tear. **2** THROW, hurl, fling, shoot, sling, launch, propel, send.
◇ *n* bolt, arrow, barb, shaft.

dash *v* **1** RUSH, dart, hurry, race, sprint, run, bolt, tear. **2** FLING, throw, crash, hurl. **3** DISCOURAGE, disappoint,

dampen, confound, blight, ruin, destroy, spoil, frustrate, smash, shatter.
◇ *n* **1** DROP, pinch, touch, flavour, soupçon, suggestion, hint, bit, little. **2** SPRINT, dart, bolt, rush, spurt, race, run.

dashing *adj* **1** LIVELY, vigorous, spirited, gallant, daring, bold, plucky, exuberant. **2** SMART, stylish, elegant, debonair, showy, flamboyant.
⊞ **1** lethargic. **2** dowdy.

data *n* information, documents, facts, input, statistics, figures, details, materials.

date *n* **1** TIME, age, period, era, stage, epoch. **2** APPOINTMENT, engagement, assignation, meeting, rendezvous. **3** ESCORT, steady (*infml*), partner, friend.
● **out-of-date** old-fashioned, unfashionable, outdated, obsolete, dated, outmoded, antiquated, passé.
⊞ fashionable, modern.
● **up-to-date** fashionable, modern, current, contemporary.
⊞ old-fashioned, dated.

daunt *v* **1** DISCOURAGE, dishearten, put off, dispirit, deter. **2** INTIMIDATE, overawe, unnerve, alarm, dismay, frighten, scare.
⊞ **1** encourage.

dauntless *adj* fearless, undaunted, resolute, brave, courageous, bold, intrepid, daring, plucky, valiant.
⊞ discouraged, disheartened.

dawdle *v* delay, loiter, lag, hang about, dally, trail, potter, dilly-dally (*infml*).
⊞ hurry.

dawn *n* **1** SUNRISE, daybreak, morning, daylight. **2** BEGINNING, start, emergence, onset, origin, birth, advent.
⊞ **1** dusk. **2** end.
◇ *v* **1** BREAK, brighten, lighten, gleam, glimmer. **2** BEGIN, appear, emerge, open, develop, originate, rise.

day *n* **1** DAYTIME, daylight. **2** AGE, period, time, date, era, generation, epoch.
⊞ **1** night.
● **day after day** regularly, continually, endlessly, persistently, monotonously, perpetually, relentlessly.
● **day by day** gradually, progressively, slowly but surely, steadily.

daydream *n* fantasy, imagining, reverie, castles in the air, pipe dream, vision, musing, wish, dream, figment.
◇ *v* fantasize, imagine, muse, fancy, dream.

daze *v* **1** STUN, stupefy, shock. **2** DAZZLE, bewilder, blind, confuse, baffle, dumbfound, amaze, surprise, startle, perplex, astonish, flabbergast (*infml*), astound, stagger.
◇ *n* bewilderment, confusion, stupor, trance, shock, distraction.

dazzle *v* **1** DAZE, blind, confuse, blur. **2** SPARKLE, fascinate, impress, overwhelm, awe, overawe, scintillate, bedazzle, amaze, astonish, bewitch, stupefy.
◇ *n* sparkle, brilliance, magnificence, splendour, scintillation, glitter, glare.

dead *adj* **1** LIFELESS, deceased, inanimate, defunct, departed, late, gone. **2** UNRESPONSIVE, apathetic, dull, indifferent, insensitive, numb, cold, frigid, lukewarm, torpid. **3** EXHAUSTED, tired, worn out, dead-beat (*infml*). **4** EXACT, absolute, perfect, outright, unqualified, utter, complete, entire, total, downright.
⊞ **1** alive. **2** lively. **3** refreshed.

deaden *v* reduce, blunt, muffle, lessen, quieten, suppress, weaken, numb, diminish, stifle, alleviate, anaesthetize, desensitize, smother, check, abate, allay, dampen, hush, mute, paralyse.
⊞ heighten.

deadlock *n* standstill, stalemate, impasse, halt.

deadly adj 1 deadly poison:
lethal, fatal, dangerous, venomous,
destructive, pernicious, malignant,
murderous, mortal. 2 a deadly
lecture: dull, boring, uninteresting,
tedious, monotonous. 3 deadly aim:
unerring, effective, true.
🔁 1 harmless. 2 exciting.

deaf adj 1 HARD OF HEARING, stone-
deaf. 2 UNCONCERNED, indifferent,
unmoved, oblivious, heedless,
unmindful.
🔁 2 aware, conscious.

deafening adj piercing, ear-
splitting, booming, resounding,
thunderous, ringing, roaring.
🔁 quiet.

deal v 1 APPORTION, distribute, share,
dole out, divide, allot, dispense,
assign, mete out, give, bestow.
2 TRADE, negotiate, traffic, bargain,
treat.
◇ n 1 QUANTITY, amount, extent,
degree, portion, share. 2 AGREEMENT,
contract, understanding, pact,
transaction, bargain, buy. 3 ROUND,
hand, distribution.
• **deal with** attend to, concern, see
to, manage, handle, cope with, treat,
consider, oversee.

dealer n trader, seller, merchant,
wholesaler, marketer, merchandizer.

dear adj 1 LOVED, beloved, valued,
treasured, cherished, precious,
favourite, esteemed, intimate, close,
darling, familiar. 2 EXPENSIVE, high-
priced, costly, overpriced, pric(e)y
(infml).
🔁 1 disliked, hated. 2 cheap.
◇ n beloved, loved one, precious,
darling, treasure.

dearly adv 1 he loves her dearly:
fondly, affectionately, lovingly,
devotedly, tenderly. 2 I wish it dearly:
greatly, extremely, profoundly.

dearth n scarcity, shortage,
insufficiency, inadequacy, deficiency,
lack, want, absence, scantiness,

sparsity, need, paucity, poverty,
famine.
🔁 excess, abundance.

death n 1 DECEASE, end, finish, loss,
demise, departure, fatality, cessation,
passing, expiration, dissolution.
2 DESTRUCTION, ruin, undoing, end,
annihilation, downfall, extermination,
extinction, obliteration, eradication.
🔁 1 life, birth.

deathly adj 1 ASHEN, grim, haggard,
pale, pallid, ghastly, wan. 2 FATAL,
deadly, mortal, intense.

debase v 1 DEGRADE, demean,
devalue, disgrace, dishonour, shame,
humble, humiliate, lower, reduce,
abase, defile. 2 CONTAMINATE, pollute,
corrupt, adulterate, taint.
🔁 1 elevate. 2 purify.

debatable adj questionable,
uncertain, disputable, contestable,
controversial, arguable, open to
question, doubtful, contentious,
undecided, unsettled, problematical,
dubious, moot.
🔁 unquestionable, certain,
incontrovertible.

debate v 1 DISPUTE, argue, discuss,
contend, wrangle. 2 CONSIDER,
deliberate, ponder, reflect, meditate
on, mull over, weigh.
◇ n discussion, argument,
controversy, disputation,
deliberation, consideration,
contention, dispute, reflection,
polemic.

debauchery n depravity,
intemperance, overindulgence,
dissipation, licentiousness,
dissoluteness, excess, decadence,
wantonness, lewdness, carousal,
orgy, revel, lust, riot.
🔁 restraint, temperance.

debilitate v weaken, enervate,
undermine, sap, incapacitate, wear
out, exhaust, impair.
🔁 strengthen, invigorate, energize.

debris n remains, ruins, rubbish,

waste, wreck, wreckage, litter, fragments, rubble, trash, pieces, bits, sweepings, drift.

debt n indebtedness, obligation, due, debit, arrears, liability, duty, bill, commitment, claim, score.
⊠ credit, asset.

debtor n borrower, bankrupt, insolvent, defaulter, mortgagor.
⊠ creditor.

debunk v expose, deflate, show up, ridicule, mock, explode, lampoon.

debut n introduction, launching, beginning, entrance, presentation, inauguration, première, appearance, initiation.

decadent adj 1 CORRUPT, debased, debauched, depraved, dissolute, immoral, degenerate, degraded, self-indulgent. 2 DECAYING, declining.
⊠ 1 moral.

decay v 1 ROT, go bad, putrefy, decompose, spoil, perish, mortify. 2 DECLINE, deteriorate, disintegrate, corrode, crumble, waste away, degenerate, wear away, dwindle, shrivel, wither, sink.
⊠ 2 flourish, grow.
◇ n 1 ROT, decomposition, rotting, perishing. 2 DECLINE, deterioration, disintegration, degeneration, collapse, decadence, wasting, failing, withering, fading.

decease n death, dying, demise, departure, passing, dissolution.

deceased adj dead, departed, former, late, lost, defunct, expired, gone, finished, extinct.
◇ n dead, departed.

deceit n deception, pretence, cheating, misrepresentation, fraud, duplicity, trickery, fraudulence, double-dealing, underhandedness, fake, guile, sham, subterfuge, swindle, treachery, hypocrisy, artifice, ruse, cunning, slyness, craftiness, stratagem, wile, imposition, feint, shift, abuse.

⊠ honesty, openness, frankness.

deceitful adj dishonest, deceptive, deceiving, false, insincere, untrustworthy, double-dealing, fraudulent, two-faced (infml), treacherous, duplicitous, guileful, tricky (infml), underhand, sneaky, counterfeit, crafty, hypocritical, designing, illusory, knavish.
⊠ honest, open.

deceive v mislead, delude, cheat, betray, fool, take in (infml), trick, dissemble, hoax, con (infml), have on (infml), take for a ride (infml), double-cross (infml), dupe, kid (infml), swindle, impose upon, bamboozle (infml), two-time (infml), lead on, outwit, hoodwink, beguile, ensnare, camouflage, abuse, befool, gull.

decency n propriety, courtesy, modesty, decorum, respectability, civility, correctness, fitness, etiquette, helpfulness.
⊠ impropriety, discourtesy.

decent adj 1 RESPECTABLE, proper, fitting, decorous, chaste, seemly, suitable, modest, appropriate, presentable, pure, fit, becoming, befitting, nice. 2 KIND, obliging, courteous, helpful, generous, polite, gracious. 3 ADEQUATE, acceptable, satisfactory, reasonable, sufficient, tolerable, competent.
⊠ 1 indecent. 2 disobliging.

deception n deceit, pretence, trick, cheat, fraud, imposture, lie, dissembling, deceptiveness, insincerity, con (infml), sham, subterfuge, artifice, hypocrisy, bluff, treachery, hoax, fraudulence, duplicity, ruse, snare, stratagem, leg-pull (infml), illusion, wile, guile, craftiness, cunning.
⊠ openness, honesty.

deceptive adj dishonest, false, fraudulent, misleading, unreliable, illusive, fake, illusory, spurious, mock, fallacious, ambiguous, specious.

⊞ genuine, artless, open.

decide v choose, determine, resolve, reach a decision, settle, elect, opt, judge, adjudicate, conclude, fix, purpose, decree.

decided adj 1 DEFINITE, certain, undeniable, indisputable, absolute, clear-cut, undisputed, unmistakable, unquestionable, positive, distinct, unambiguous, categorical, emphatic. 2 RESOLUTE, decisive, determined, firm, unhesitating, deliberate, forthright.
⊞ 1 inconclusive. 2 irresolute.

decipher v decode, unscramble, crack, construe, interpret, make out (infml), figure out (infml), understand, transliterate.
⊞ encode.

decision n 1 RESULT, conclusion, outcome, verdict, settlement, finding, judgement, arbitration, ruling. 2 DETERMINATION, decisiveness, firmness, resolve, purpose.

decisive adj 1 CONCLUSIVE, definite, definitive, absolute, final. 2 DETERMINED, resolute, decided, positive, firm, forceful, forthright, strong-minded. 3 SIGNIFICANT, critical, crucial, influential, momentous, fateful.
⊞ 1 inconclusive. 2 indecisive. 3 insignificant.

declaration n 1 AFFIRMATION, acknowledgement, assertion, statement, testimony, attestation, disclosure, profession, revelation. 2 ANNOUNCEMENT, notification, edict, pronouncement, proclamation, manifesto, promulgation.

declare v 1 AFFIRM, assert, claim, profess, maintain, state, attest, certify, confess, confirm, disclose, reveal, show, aver, swear, testify, witness, validate. 2 ANNOUNCE, proclaim, pronounce, decree, broadcast.

decline v 1 REFUSE, reject, deny, forgo, avoid, balk. 2 DIMINISH, lessen,

decrease, dwindle, fall, sink, wane. 3 DECAY, deteriorate, worsen, degenerate. 4 DESCEND, sink, slope, dip, slant.
⊞ 3 improve. 4 rise.
◇ n 1 DETERIORATION, dwindling, lessening, decay, degeneration, weakening, worsening, failing, downturn, diminution, falling-off, recession, slump, abatement. 2 DESCENT, dip, declivity, declination, hill, slope, incline, divergence, deviation.
⊞ 1 improvement. 2 rise.

decode v decipher, interpret, unscramble, translate, transliterate, uncipher.
⊞ encode.

decompose v disintegrate, rot, decay, putrefy, break down, break up, crumble, spoil, dissolve, separate, fester.

décor n decoration, furnishings, colour scheme, ornamentation, scenery.

decorate v 1 ORNAMENT, adorn, beautify, embellish, trim, deck, tart up (sl), grace, enrich, prettify, trick out. 2 RENOVATE, do up (infml), paint, paper, colour, refurbish. 3 HONOUR, crown, cite, garland, bemedal.

decoration n 1 ORNAMENT, adornment, ornamentation, trimming, embellishment, garnish, beautification, flourish, enrichment, elaboration, frill, scroll, bauble. 2 AWARD, medal, order, badge, garland, crown, colours, ribbon, laurel, star, emblem.

decorative adj ornamental, fancy, adorning, beautifying, embellishing, non-functional, pretty, ornate, enhancing.
⊞ plain.

decorum n propriety, seemliness, etiquette, good manners, respectability, protocol, behaviour, decency, dignity, deportment,

restraint, politeness, modesty, grace, breeding.
≆ impropriety, indecorum, bad manners.

decoy *n* lure, trap, enticement, inducement, ensnarement, pretence, attraction, bait.
◇ *v* bait, lure, entrap, entice, ensnare, allure, tempt, deceive, attract, seduce, lead, draw.

decrease *v* lessen, lower, diminish, dwindle, decline, fall off, reduce, subside, abate, cut down, contract, drop, ease, shrink, taper, wane, slim, slacken, peter out, curtail.
≆ increase.
◇ *n* lessening, reduction, decline, falling-off, dwindling, diminution, loss, abatement, cutback, ebb, contraction, downturn, shrinkage, subsidence, step-down.
≆ increase.

decree *n* order, command, law, ordinance, regulation, ruling, statute, act, enactment, edict, proclamation, mandate, precept, interlocution.
◇ *v* order, command, rule, lay down, dictate, decide, determine, ordain, prescribe, proclaim, pronounce, enact.

decrepit *adj* dilapidated, run-down, rickety, broken-down, worn-out, tumbledown.

dedicate *v* 1 DEVOTE, commit, assign, give over to, pledge, offer, present, sacrifice, surrender. 2 CONSECRATE, bless, sanctify, set apart, hallow. 3 *dedicate a book*: inscribe, address.

dedicated *adj* devoted, committed, enthusiastic, single-minded, whole-hearted, single-hearted, zealous, given over to, purposeful.
≆ uncommitted, apathetic.

dedication *n* 1 COMMITMENT, devotion, single-mindedness, whole-heartedness, allegiance, attachment, adherence, faithfulness, loyalty, self-sacrifice. 2 CONSECRATION, hallowing, presentation. 3 INSCRIPTION, address.
≆ 1 apathy.

deduce *v* derive, infer, gather, conclude, reason, surmise, understand, draw, glean.

deduct *v* subtract, take away, remove, reduce by, decrease by, knock off (*infml*), withdraw.
≆ add.

deduction *n* 1 INFERENCE, reasoning, finding, conclusion, corollary, assumption, result. 2 SUBTRACTION, reduction, decrease, diminution, abatement, withdrawal, discount, allowance.
≆ 2 addition, increase.

deed *n* 1 ACTION, act, achievement, performance, exploit, feat, fact, truth, reality. 2 DOCUMENT, contract, record, title, transaction, indenture (*fml*).

deep *adj* 1 PROFOUND, bottomless, unplumbed, fathomless, yawning, immersed. 2 OBSCURE, mysterious, difficult, recondite, abstruse, esoteric. 3 WISE, perceptive, learned, discerning, profound, astute. 4 INTENSE, serious, earnest, extreme. 5 LOW, bass, resonant, booming.
≆ 1 shallow, open. 3 clear, plain, open. 3 superficial. 4 light. 5 high.

deepen *v* 1 INTENSIFY, grow, increase, strengthen, reinforce, magnify. 2 HOLLOW, scoop out.

deep-seated *adj* ingrained, entrenched, deep-rooted, fixed, confirmed, deep, settled.
≆ eradicable, temporary.

deface *v* damage, spoil, disfigure, blemish, impair, mutilate, mar, sully, tarnish, vandalize, deform, obliterate, injure, destroy.
≆ repair.

defamation *n* vilification, aspersion (*fml*), slander, libel, disparagement, slur, smear, innuendo, scandal.
≆ commendation, praise.

defamatory adj vilifying, slanderous, libellous, denigrating, disparaging, pejorative, insulting, injurious, derogatory.
🔁 complimentary, appreciative.

default n failure, absence, neglect, non-payment, omission, deficiency, lapse, fault, want, lack, defect.
◇ v fail, evade, defraud, neglect, dodge, swindle, backslide.

defaulter n non-payer, offender.

defeat v 1 CONQUER, beat, overpower, subdue, overthrow, worst, repel, subjugate, overwhelm, rout, ruin, thump (infml), quell, vanquish (fml). 2 FRUSTRATE, confound, balk, get the better of, disappoint, foil, thwart, baffle, checkmate.
◇ n 1 CONQUEST, beating, overthrow, rout, subjugation, vanquishment (fml). 2 FRUSTRATION, failure, setback, reverse, disappointment, checkmate.

defeatist n pessimist, quitter, prophet of doom.
🔁 optimist.
◇ adj pessimistic, resigned, fatalistic, despondent, helpless, hopeless, despairing, gloomy.
🔁 optimistic.

defect n imperfection, fault, flaw, deficiency, failing, mistake, inadequacy, blemish, error, bug (infml), shortcoming, want, weakness, frailty, lack, spot, absence, taint.
◇ v desert, break faith, rebel, apostatize (fml), revolt, renege.

defective adj faulty, imperfect, out of order, flawed, deficient, broken, abnormal.
🔁 in order, operative.

defence n 1 PROTECTION, resistance, security, fortification, cover, safeguard, shelter, guard, shield, deterrence, barricade, bastion, immunity, bulwark, rampart, buttress. 2 JUSTIFICATION, explanation,

excuse, argument, exoneration, plea, vindication, apologia (fml), pleading, alibi, case.
🔁 1 attack, assault. 2 accusation.

defenceless adj unprotected, undefended, unarmed, unguarded, vulnerable, exposed, helpless, powerless.
🔁 protected, guarded.

defend v 1 PROTECT, guard, safeguard, shelter, fortify, secure, shield, screen, cover, contest. 2 SUPPORT, stand up for, stand by, uphold, endorse, vindicate, champion, argue for, speak up for, justify, plead.
🔁 1 attack. 2 accuse.

defendant n accused, offender, prisoner, respondent.

defender n 1 PROTECTOR, guard, bodyguard. 2 SUPPORTER, advocate, vindicator, champion, patron, sponsor, counsel.
🔁 1 attacker. 2 accuser.

defensive adj 1 PROTECTIVE, defending, safeguarding, protecting, wary, opposing, cautious, watchful. 2 SELF-JUSTIFYING, apologetic.

defer[1] v delay, postpone, put off, adjourn, hold over, shelve, suspend, procrastinate, prorogue (fml), protract, waive.

defer[2] v yield, give way, comply, submit, accede, capitulate, respect, bow.

deference n 1 SUBMISSION, submissiveness, compliance, acquiescence, obedience, yielding. 2 RESPECT, regard, honour, esteem, reverence, courtesy, civility, politeness, consideration.
🔁 1 resistance. 2 contempt.

defiance n opposition, resistance, confrontation, challenge, contempt, disobedience, rebelliousness, insubordination, disregard, insolence.
🔁 compliance, acquiescence, submissiveness.

defiant *adj* challenging, resistant, antagonistic, aggressive, rebellious, insubordinate, disobedient, intransigent, bold, contumacious (*fml*), insolent, obstinate, unco-operative, provocative.
⊜ compliant, acquiescent, submissive.

deficiency *n* **1** SHORTAGE, lack, inadequacy, scarcity, insufficiency, dearth, want, scantiness, absence, deficit. **2** IMPERFECTION, shortcoming, weakness, fault, defect, flaw, failing, frailty.
⊜ **1** excess, surfeit. **2** perfection.

deficient *adj* **1** INADEQUATE, insufficient, lacking, wanting, scarce, short, meagre, scanty, skimpy, incomplete. **2** IMPERFECT, impaired, flawed, faulty, defective, unsatisfactory, inferior, weak.
⊜ **1** excessive. **2** perfect.

deficit *n* shortage, shortfall, lack, deficiency, loss, arrears, default.
⊜ excess.

defile *v* pollute, violate, contaminate, degrade, dishonour, desecrate, debase, soil, stain, sully, tarnish, taint, profane, corrupt, disgrace.

define *v* **1** *define the boundaries*: bound, limit, delimit, demarcate, mark out. **2** *define the meaning*: explain, characterize, describe, interpret, expound, determine, designate, specify, spell out, detail.

definite *adj* **1** CERTAIN, settled, sure, positive, fixed, decided, determined, assured, guaranteed. **2** CLEAR, clear-cut, exact, precise, specific, explicit, particular, obvious, marked.
⊜ **1** indefinite. **2** vague.

definitely *adv* positively, surely, unquestionably, absolutely, certainly, categorically, undeniably, clearly, doubtless, unmistakably, plainly, obviously, indeed, easily.

definition *n* **1** DELINEATION, demarcation, delimitation. **2** EXPLANATION, meaning, significance, sense, description, interpretation, exposition, clarification, elucidation, determination. **3** DISTINCTNESS, clarity, precision, clearness, focus, contrast, sharpness.

definitive *adj* decisive, conclusive, final, authoritative, standard, correct, ultimate, reliable, exhaustive, perfect, exact, absolute, complete.
⊜ interim.

deflate *v* **1** FLATTEN, puncture, collapse, exhaust, squash, empty, contract, void, shrink, squeeze. **2** DEBUNK, humiliate, put down (*infml*), dash, dispirit, humble, mortify, disconcert. **3** DECREASE, devalue, reduce, lessen, lower, diminish, depreciate, depress.
⊜ **1** inflate. **2** boost. **3** increase.

deflect *v* deviate, diverge, turn (aside), swerve, veer, sidetrack, twist, avert, wind, glance off, bend, ricochet.

deform *v* distort, contort, disfigure, warp, mar, pervert, ruin, spoil, twist.

deformed *adj* distorted, misshapen, contorted, disfigured, crooked, bent, twisted, warped, buckled, defaced, mangled, maimed, marred, ruined, mutilated, perverted, corrupted.

deformity *n* distortion, misshapenness, malformation, disfigurement, abnormality, irregularity, imperfection, misproportion, defect, corruption.

defraud *v* cheat, swindle, dupe, fleece, sting (*infml*), rip off (*infml*), do (*infml*), diddle (*infml*), rob, trick, con (*infml*), rook, deceive, delude, embezzle, beguile.

deft *adj* adept, handy, dexterous, nimble, skilful, adroit, agile, expert, nifty, proficient, able, neat, clever.
⊜ clumsy, awkward.

defunct *adj* **1** DEAD, deceased, departed, gone, expired, extinct.

2 OBSOLETE, invalid, inoperative, expired.
☒ 1 alive, live. 2 operative.

defy v 1 *defy the authorities*: challenge, confront, resist, dare, brave, face, repel, spurn, beard, flout, withstand, disregard, scorn, despise, defeat, provoke, thwart.
2 *her writings defy categorization*: elude, frustrate, baffle, foil.
☒ 1 obey. 2 permit.

degenerate adj dissolute, debauched, depraved, degraded, debased, base, low, decadent, corrupt, immoral, mean, perverted, deteriorated.
☒ moral, upright.
◇ v decline, deteriorate, sink, decay, rot, slip, worsen, regress, fall off, lapse.
☒ improve.

degradation n 1 DETERIORATION, degeneration, decline, downgrading, demotion. 2 ABASEMENT, humiliation, mortification, dishonour, disgrace, shame, ignominy, decadence.
☒ 1 virtue. 2 enhancement.

degrade v 1 DISHONOUR, disgrace, debase, abase, shame, humiliate, humble, discredit, demean, lower, weaken, impair, deteriorate, cheapen, adulterate, corrupt.
2 DEMOTE, depose, downgrade, deprive, cashier.
☒ 1 exalt. 2 promote.

degree n 1 GRADE, class, rank, order, position, standing, status. 2 EXTENT, measure, range, stage, step, level, intensity, standard. 3 LEVEL, limit, unit, mark.

deify v exalt, elevate, worship, glorify, idolize, extol, venerate, immortalize, ennoble, idealize.

deign v condescend, stoop, lower oneself, consent, demean oneself.

deity n god, goddess, divinity, godhead, idol, demigod, demigoddess, power, immortal.

dejected adj downcast, depressed, despondent, down, downhearted, disheartened, low, melancholy, disconsolate, sad, miserable, cast down, gloomy, glum, crestfallen, dismal, wretched, doleful, morose, spiritless.
☒ cheerful, high-spirited, happy.

delay v 1 OBSTRUCT, hinder, impede, hold up, check, hold back, set back, stop, halt, detain. 2 DEFER, put off, postpone, procrastinate, suspend, shelve, hold over, stall. 3 DAWDLE, linger, lag, loiter, dilly-dally (*infml*), tarry.
☒ 1 accelerate. 2 bring forward.
3 hurry.
◇ n 1 OBSTRUCTION, hindrance, impediment, hold-up, check, setback, stay, stoppage. 2 DEFERMENT, postponement, procrastination, suspension. 3 DAWDLING, lingering, tarrying. 4 INTERRUPTION, lull, interval, wait.
☒ 1 hastening. 3 hurry.
4 continuation.

delegate n representative, agent, envoy, messenger, deputy, ambassador, commissioner.
◇ v authorize, appoint, depute, charge, commission, assign, empower, entrust, devolve, consign, designate, nominate, name, hand over.

delegation n 1 DEPUTATION, commission, legation, mission, contingent, embassy.
2 AUTHORIZATION, commissioning, assignment.

delete v erase, remove, cross out, cancel, rub out, strike out, obliterate, edit (out), blot out, efface.
☒ add, insert.

deliberate v consider, ponder, reflect, think, cogitate, meditate, mull over, debate, discuss, weigh, consult.
◇ adj 1 INTENTIONAL, planned, calculated, prearranged,

premeditated, willed, conscious, designed, considered, advised. **2** CAREFUL, unhurried, thoughtful, methodical, cautious, circumspect, studied, prudent, slow, ponderous, measured, heedful.
⊞ **1** unintentional, accidental. **2** hasty.

deliberation n **1** CONSIDERATION, reflection, thought, calculation, forethought, meditation, rumination, study, debate, discussion, consultation, speculation. **2** CARE, carefulness, caution, circumspection, prudence.

delicacy n **1** DAINTINESS, fineness, elegance, exquisiteness, lightness, precision. **2** REFINEMENT, sensitivity, subtlety, finesse, discrimination, tact, niceness. **3** TITBIT, dainty, taste, sweetmeat, savoury, relish.
⊞ **1** coarseness, roughness. **2** tactlessness.

delicate adj **1** FINE, fragile, dainty, exquisite, flimsy, elegant, graceful. **2** FRAIL, weak, ailing, faint. **3** SENSITIVE, scrupulous, discriminating, careful, accurate, precise. **4** SUBTLE, muted, pastel, soft.
⊞ **1** coarse, clumsy. **2** healthy.

delicious adj **1** ENJOYABLE, pleasant, agreeable, delightful. **2** APPETIZING, palatable, tasty, delectable, scrumptious (infml), yummy (infml), mouthwatering, succulent, savoury.
⊞ **1** unpleasant. **2** unpalatable, yucky (infml).

delight n bliss, happiness, joy, ecstasy, pleasure, gladness, enjoyment, contentment, rapture, transport, gratification, jubilation.
⊞ disgust, displeasure.
◇ v please, charm, gratify, enchant, tickle, thrill, ravish.
⊞ displease, dismay.
• **delight in** enjoy, relish, like, love, appreciate, revel in, take pride in, glory in, savour.
⊞ dislike, hate.

delighted adj charmed, elated, happy, pleased, enchanted, captivated, ecstatic, thrilled, overjoyed, jubilant, joyous.
⊞ disappointed, dismayed.

delightful adj charming, enchanting, captivating, enjoyable, pleasant, thrilling, agreeable, pleasurable, engaging, attractive, pleasing, gratifying, entertaining, fascinating.
⊞ nasty, unpleasant.

delinquency n crime, offence, wrongdoing, misbehaviour, misconduct, law-breaking, misdemeanour, criminality.

delinquent n offender, criminal, wrongdoer, law-breaker, hooligan, culprit, miscreant (fml).

delirious adj demented, raving, incoherent, beside oneself, deranged, frenzied, light-headed, wild, mad, frantic, insane, crazy, ecstatic.
⊞ sane.

deliver v **1** deliver a parcel: convey, bring, send, give, carry, supply. **2** SURRENDER, hand over, relinquish, yield, transfer, grant, entrust, commit. **3** UTTER, speak, proclaim, pronounce. **4** ADMINISTER, inflict, direct. **5** SET FREE, liberate, release, emancipate.

delivery n **1** CONVEYANCE, consignment, dispatch, transmission, transfer, surrender. **2** ARTICULATION, enunciation, speech, utterance, intonation, elocution. **3** CHILDBIRTH, labour, confinement.

delude v deceive, mislead, beguile, dupe, take in, trick, hoodwink, hoax, cheat, misinform.

deluge n flood, inundation, downpour, torrent, spate, rush.
◇ v flood, inundate, drench, drown, overwhelm, soak, swamp, engulf, submerge.

delusion n illusion, hallucination, fancy, misconception, misapprehension, deception, misbelief, fallacy.

demand v 1 ASK, request, call for, insist on, solicit, claim, exact, inquire, question, interrogate. 2 NECESSITATE, need, require, involve. ◇ n 1 REQUEST, question, claim, order, inquiry, desire, interrogation. 2 NEED, necessity, call.

demanding adj hard, difficult, challenging, exacting, taxing, tough, exhausting, wearing, backbreaking, insistent, pressing, urgent, trying. 🗷 easy, undemanding, easy-going.

demean v lower, humble, degrade, humiliate, debase, abase, descend, stoop, condescend. 🗷 exalt, enhance.

demeanour n bearing, manner, deportment, conduct, behaviour, air.

demented adj mad, insane, lunatic, out of one's mind, crazy, loony (sl), deranged, unbalanced, frenzied. 🗷 sane.

demise n 1 DEATH, decease, end, passing, departure, termination, expiration. 2 DOWNFALL, fall, collapse, failure, ruin. 3 TRANSFER, conveyance, inheritance, transmission, alienation.

democracy n self-government, commonwealth, autonomy, republic.

democratic adj self-governing, representative, elected, egalitarian, autonomous, popular, populist, republican.

demolish v 1 DESTROY, dismantle, knock down, pull down, flatten, bulldoze, raze, tear down, level. 2 RUIN, defeat, destroy, annihilate, wreck, overturn, overthrow. 🗷 1 build up.

demolition n destruction, dismantling, levelling, razing.

demon n 1 DEVIL, fiend, evil spirit, fallen angel, imp. 2 VILLAIN, devil, rogue, monster.

demonstrable adj verifiable, provable, arguable, attestable, self-evident, obvious, evident, certain, clear, positive. 🗷 unverifiable.

demonstrate v 1 SHOW, display, prove, establish, exhibit, substantiate, manifest, testify to, indicate. 2 EXPLAIN, illustrate, describe, teach. 3 PROTEST, march, parade, rally, picket, sit in.

demonstration n 1 DISPLAY, exhibition, manifestation, proof, confirmation, affirmation, indication, substantiation, validation, evidence, testimony, expression. 2 EXPLANATION, illustration, description, exposition, presentation, test, trial. 3 PROTEST, march, demo (infml), rally, picket, sit-in, parade.

demonstrative adj affectionate, expressive, expansive, emotional, open, loving. 🗷 reserved, cold, restrained.

demoralize v 1 DISCOURAGE, dishearten, dispirit, undermine, depress, deject, crush, lower, disconcert. 2 CORRUPT, deprave, debase. 🗷 1 encourage. 2 improve.

demote v downgrade, degrade, relegate, reduce, cashier. 🗷 promote, upgrade.

demur v disagree, dissent, object, take exception, refuse, protest, dispute, balk, scruple, doubt, hesitate.

demure adj modest, reserved, reticent, prim, coy, shy, retiring, prissy, grave, prudish, sober, staid, strait-laced. 🗷 wanton, forward.

den n lair, hideout, hole, retreat, study, hideaway, shelter, sanctuary, haunt.

denial n 1 CONTRADICTION, negation, dissent, repudiation, disavowal, disclaimer, dismissal, renunciation. 2 REFUSAL, rebuff, rejection, prohibition, veto.

denigrate v disparage, run down, slander, revile, defame, malign, vilify, decry, besmirch, impugn, belittle, abuse, assail, criticize.
⊞ praise, acclaim.

denomination n 1 CLASSIFICATION, category, class, kind, sort. 2 RELIGION, persuasion, sect, belief, faith, creed, communion, school.

denote v indicate, stand for, signify, represent, symbolize, mean, express, designate, typify, mark, show, imply.

dénouement n culmination, climax, conclusion, outcome, upshot, pay-off (*infml*), finale, resolution, finish, solution, close.

denounce v condemn, censure, accuse, revile, decry, attack, inform against, betray, impugn, vilify, fulminate.
⊞ acclaim, praise.

dense adj 1 COMPACT, thick, compressed, condensed, close, close-knit, heavy, solid, opaque, impenetrable, packed, crowded. 2 STUPID, thick (*infml*), crass, dull, slow, slow-witted.
⊞ 1 thin, sparse. 2 quick-witted, clever.

dent n hollow, depression, dip, concavity, indentation, crater, dimple, dint, pit.
◇ v depress, gouge, push in, indent.

denude v strip, divest, expose, uncover, bare, deforest.
⊞ cover, clothe.

denunciation n condemnation, denouncement, censure, accusation, incrimination, invective, criticism.
⊞ praise.

deny v 1 *deny God's existence*: contradict, oppose, refute, disagree with, disaffirm, disprove. 2 *deny one's parentage*: disown, disclaim, renounce, repudiate, recant. 3 *deny their human rights*: refuse, turn down, forbid, reject, withhold, rebuff, veto.

⊞ 1 admit. 3 allow.

depart v 1 GO, leave, withdraw, exit, make off, quit, decamp, take one's leave, absent oneself, set off, remove, retreat, migrate, escape, disappear, retire, vanish. 2 DEVIATE, digress, differ, diverge, swerve, veer.
⊞ 1 arrive, return. 2 keep to.

departed adj dead, deceased, gone, late, expired.

department n 1 DIVISION, branch, subdivision, section, sector, office, station, unit, region, district. 2 SPHERE, realm, province, domain, field, area, concern, responsibility, speciality, line.

departure n 1 EXIT, going, leave-taking, removal, withdrawal, retirement, exodus. 2 DEVIATION, digression, divergence, variation, innovation, branching (out), difference, change, shift, veering.
⊞ 1 arrival, return.

dependable adj reliable, trustworthy, responsible, steady, trusty, faithful, unfailing, sure, honest, conscientious, certain.
⊞ unreliable, fickle.

dependence n 1 RELIANCE, confidence, faith, trust, need, expectation. 2 SUBORDINATION, attachment, subservience, helplessness, addiction.
⊞ 2 independence.

dependent adj 1 RELIANT, helpless, weak, immature, subject, subordinate, vulnerable. 2 CONDITIONAL, contingent, determined by, relative.
⊞ 1 independent.

depend on v 1 RELY UPON, count on, bank on (*infml*), calculate on, reckon on (*infml*), build upon, trust in, lean on, expect. 2 HINGE ON, rest on, revolve around, be contingent upon, hang on.

depict v portray, illustrate, delineate, sketch, outline, draw, picture, paint, trace, describe, characterize, detail.

deplete v empty, drain, exhaust, evacuate, use up, expend, run down, reduce, lessen, decrease.

deplorable adj 1 GRIEVOUS, lamentable, pitiable, regrettable, unfortunate, wretched, distressing, sad, miserable, heartbreaking, melancholy, disastrous, dire, appalling. 2 REPREHENSIBLE, disgraceful, scandalous, shameful, dishonourable, disreputable.
☒ 1 excellent. 2 commendable.

deplore v 1 GRIEVE FOR, lament, mourn, regret, bemoan, rue. 2 CENSURE, condemn, denounce, deprecate.
☒ 2 extol.

deploy v dispose, arrange, position, station, use, utilize, distribute.

deport v expel, banish, exile, oust, extradite, transport, expatriate, ostracize.

depose v demote, dethrone, unseat, downgrade, dismiss, topple, disestablish, displace, oust.

deposit v 1 LAY, drop, place, put, settle, dump (infml), park, precipitate, sit, locate. 2 SAVE, store, hoard, bank, amass, consign, entrust, lodge, file.
◇ n 1 SEDIMENT, accumulation, dregs, precipitate, lees, silt. 2 SECURITY, stake, down payment, pledge, retainer, instalment, part payment, money.

depot n 1 military depot: store, storehouse, warehouse, depository, repository, arsenal. 2 bus depot: station, garage, terminus.

deprave v corrupt, debauch, debase, degrade, pervert, subvert, infect, demoralize, seduce.
☒ improve, reform.

depraved adj corrupt, debauched, degenerate, perverted, debased, dissolute, immoral, base, shameless, licentious, wicked, sinful, vile, evil.

☒ moral, upright.

depreciate v 1 DEVALUE, deflate, downgrade, decrease, reduce, lower, drop, fall, lessen, decline, slump. 2 DISPARAGE, belittle, undervalue, underestimate, underrate, slight.
☒ 1 appreciate. 2 overrate.

depreciation n 1 DEVALUATION, deflation, depression, slump, fall. 2 DISPARAGEMENT, belittlement, underestimation.

depress v 1 DEJECT, sadden, dishearten, discourage, oppress, upset, daunt, burden, overburden. 2 WEAKEN, undermine, sap, tire, drain, exhaust, weary, impair, reduce, lessen, press, lower, level. 3 DEVALUE, bring down, lower.
☒ 1 cheer. 2 fortify. 3 increase, raise.

depressed adj 1 DEJECTED, low-spirited, melancholy, dispirited, sad, unhappy, low, down, downcast, disheartened, fed up (infml), miserable, moody, cast down, discouraged, glum, downhearted, distressed, despondent, morose, crestfallen, pessimistic. 2 POOR, disadvantaged, deprived, destitute. 3 SUNKEN, recessed, concave, hollow, indented, dented.
☒ 1 cheerful. 2 affluent. 3 convex, protuberant.

depressing adj dismal, bleak, gloomy, dejecting, saddening, cheerless, dreary, disheartening, sad, melancholy, sombre, grey, black, daunting, discouraging, heartbreaking, distressing, hopeless.
☒ cheerful, encouraging.

depression n 1 DEJECTION, despair, despondency, melancholy, low spirits, sadness, gloominess, doldrums, blues (infml), glumness, dumps (infml), hopelessness. 2 RECESSION, slump, stagnation, hard times, decline, inactivity. 3 INDENTATION, hollow, dip, concavity, dent, dimple, valley, pit, sink, dint,

bowl, cavity, basin, impression, dish, excavation.
🔁 **1** cheerfulness. **2** prosperity, boom. **3** convexity, protuberance.

deprive *v* **1** DISPOSSESS, strip, divest, denude, bereave, expropriate, rob. **2** DENY, withhold, refuse.
🔁 **1** endow. **2** provide.

deprived *adj* poor, needy, destitute, underprivileged, disadvantaged, impoverished, lacking, bereft.
🔁 prosperous.

depth *n* **1** DEEPNESS, profoundness, extent, measure, drop. **2** MIDDLE, midst, abyss, deep, gulf. **3** WISDOM, insight, discernment, penetration. **4** INTENSITY, strength.
🔁 **1** shallowness. **2** surface.

deputation *n* commission, delegation, embassy, mission, representatives, legation.

deputize *v* **1** REPRESENT, stand in for, substitute, replace, understudy, double. **2** DELEGATE, commission.

deputy *n* representative, agent, delegate, proxy, substitute, second-in-command, ambassador, assistant, commissioner, lieutenant, surrogate, subordinate, locum.

deranged *adj* disordered, demented, crazy, mad, lunatic, insane, unbalanced, disturbed, confused, frantic, delirious, distraught, berserk.
🔁 sane, calm.

derelict *adj* abandoned, neglected, deserted, forsaken, desolate, discarded, dilapidated, ruined.

deride *v* ridicule, mock, scoff, scorn, jeer, sneer, satirize, knock (*infml*), gibe, disparage, insult, belittle, disdain, taunt.
🔁 respect, praise.

derision *n* ridicule, mockery, scorn, contempt, scoffing, satire, sneering, disrespect, insult, disparagement, disdain.

🔁 respect, praise.

derisive *adj* mocking, scornful, contemptuous, disrespectful, irreverent, jeering, disdainful, taunting.
🔁 respectful, flattering.

derivation *n* source, origin, root, beginning, etymology, extraction, foundation, genealogy, ancestry, basis, descent, deduction, inference.

derivative *adj* unoriginal, acquired, copied, borrowed, derived, imitative, obtained, second-hand, secondary, plagiarized, cribbed (*infml*), trite, hackneyed.
◇ *n* derivation, offshoot, by-product, development, branch, outgrowth, spin-off, product, descendant.

derive *v* **1** GAIN, obtain, get, draw, extract, receive, procure, acquire, borrow. **2** ORIGINATE, arise, spring, flow, emanate, descend, proceed, stem, issue, follow, develop. **3** INFER, deduce, trace, gather, glean.

derogatory *adj* insulting, pejorative, offensive, disparaging, depreciative, critical, defamatory, injurious.
🔁 flattering.

descend *v* **1** DROP, go down, fall, plummet, plunge, tumble, swoop, sink, arrive, alight, dismount, dip, slope, subside. **2** DEGENERATE, deteriorate. **3** CONDESCEND, deign, stoop. **4** ORIGINATE, proceed, spring, stem.
🔁 **1** ascend, rise.

descendants *n* offspring, children, issue, progeny, successors, lineage, line, seed (*fml*).

descent *n* **1** FALL, drop, plunge, dip, decline, incline, slope. **2** COMEDOWN, debasement, degradation. **3** ANCESTRY, parentage, heredity, family tree, genealogy, lineage, extraction, origin.
🔁 **1** ascent, rise.

describe *v* portray, depict, delineate, illustrate, characterize, specify, draw, define, detail, explain, express, tell, narrate, outline, relate, recount, present, report, sketch, mark out, trace.

description n 1 PORTRAYAL, representation, characterization, account, delineation, depiction, sketch, presentation, report, outline, explanation, exposition, narration. 2 SORT, type, kind, variety, specification, order.

descriptive adj illustrative, explanatory, expressive, detailed, graphic, colourful, pictorial, vivid.

desert[1] n wasteland, wilderness, wilds, void.
◇ adj bare, barren, waste, wild, uninhabited, uncultivated, dry, arid, infertile, desolate, sterile, solitary.

desert[2] v abandon, forsake, leave, maroon, strand, decamp, defect, give up, renounce, relinquish, jilt, abscond, quit.
⊜ stand by, support.

desert[3] n 1 DUE, right, reward, deserts, retribution, come-uppance (infml), return, payment, recompense, remuneration. 2 WORTH, merit, virtue.

deserted adj abandoned, forsaken, empty, derelict, desolate, neglected, god-forsaken, underpopulated, stranded, isolated, bereft, vacant, betrayed, lonely, solitary, unoccupied.
⊜ populous.

deserter n runaway, absconder, escapee, truant, renegade, defector, rat (infml), traitor, fugitive, betrayer, apostate, backslider, delinquent.

deserve v earn, be worthy of, merit, be entitled to, warrant, justify, win, rate, incur.

deserved adj due, earned, merited, justifiable, warranted, right, rightful, well-earned, suitable, proper, fitting, fair, just, appropriate, apt, legitimate, apposite, meet (fml).

⊜ gratuitous, undeserved.

deserving adj worthy, estimable, exemplary, praiseworthy, admirable, commendable, laudable, righteous.
⊜ undeserving, unworthy.

design n 1 BLUEPRINT, draft, pattern, plan, prototype, sketch, drawing, outline, model, guide. 2 STYLE, shape, form, figure, structure, organization, arrangement, composition, construction, motif. 3 AIM, intention, goal, purpose, plan, end, object, objective, scheme, plot, project, meaning, target, undertaking.
◇ v 1 PLAN, plot, intend, devise, purpose, aim, scheme, shape, project, propose, tailor, mean. 2 SKETCH, draft, outline, draw (up). 3 INVENT, originate, conceive, create, think up, develop, construct, fashion, form, model, fabricate, make.

designation n 1 NAME, title, label, epithet, nickname. 2 INDICATION, specification, description, definition, classification, category. 3 NOMINATION, appointment, selection.

designer n deviser, originator, maker, stylist, inventor, creator, contriver, fashioner, architect, author.

designing adj artful, crafty, scheming, conspiring, devious, intriguing, plotting, tricky, wily, sly, deceitful, cunning, guileful, underhand, sharp, shrewd.
⊜ artless, naive.

desirable adj 1 ADVANTAGEOUS, profitable, worthwhile, advisable, appropriate, expedient, beneficial, preferable, sensible, eligible, good, pleasing. 2 ATTRACTIVE, alluring, sexy (infml), seductive, fetching, tempting.
⊜ 1 undesirable. 2 unattractive.

desire v 1 ASK, request, petition, solicit. 2 WANT, wish for, covet, long for, need, crave, hunger for, yearn for, fancy (infml), hanker after.

◇ *n* **1** WANT, longing, wish, need, yearning, craving, hankering, appetite, aspiration. **2** LUST, passion, concupiscence (*fml*), ardour. **3** REQUEST, petition, appeal, supplication.

desist *v* stop, cease, leave off, refrain, discontinue, end, break off, give up, halt, abstain, suspend, pause, peter out, remit, forbear (*fml*).
⊜ continue, resume.

desolate *adj* **1** DESERTED, uninhabited, abandoned, unfrequented, barren, bare, arid, bleak, gloomy, dismal, dreary, lonely, god-forsaken, forsaken, waste, depressing. **2** FORLORN, bereft, depressed, dejected, forsaken, despondent, distressed, miserable, melancholy, lonely, gloomy, disheartened, dismal, downcast, solitary, wretched.
⊜ **1** populous. **2** cheerful.
◇ *v* devastate, lay waste, destroy, despoil, spoil, wreck, denude, depopulate, ruin, waste, ravage, plunder, pillage.

desolation *n* **1** DESTRUCTION, ruin, devastation, ravages. **2** DEJECTION, despair, despondency, gloom, misery, sadness, melancholy, sorrow, unhappiness, anguish, grief, distress, wretchedness. **3** BARRENNESS, bleakness, emptiness, forlornness, loneliness, isolation, solitude, wildness.

despair *v* lose heart, lose hope, give up, give in, collapse, surrender.
⊜ hope.
◇ *n* despondency, hopelessness, gloom, desperation, anguish, inconsolableness, melancholy, misery, wretchedness.
⊜ cheerfulness, resilience.

despairing *adj* despondent, distraught, inconsolable, desolate, desperate, heartbroken, suicidal, grief-stricken, hopeless, disheartened, dejected, miserable, wretched, sorrowful, dismayed, downcast.
⊜ cheerful, hopeful.

despatch *see* **dispatch**.

desperado *n* bandit, criminal, brigand, gangster, hoodlum (*infml*), outlaw, ruffian, thug, cut-throat, law-breaker.

desperate *adj* **1** HOPELESS, wretched, inconsolable, despondent, abandoned. **2** RECKLESS, rash, impetuous, audacious, daring, dangerous, do-or-die, foolhardy, risky, hazardous, hasty, precipitate, wild, violent, frantic, frenzied, determined. **3** CRITICAL, acute, serious, severe, extreme, urgent.
⊜ **1** hopeful. **2** cautious.

desperately *adv* dangerously, critically, gravely, hopelessly, seriously, severely, badly, dreadfully, fearfully, frightfully.

desperation *n* **1** DESPAIR, anguish, despondency, hopelessness, misery, agony, distress, pain, sorrow, trouble, worry, anxiety. **2** RECKLESSNESS, rashness, frenzy, madness, hastiness.

despicable *adj* contemptible, vile, worthless, detestable, disgusting, mean, wretched, disgraceful, disreputable, shameful, reprobate.
⊜ admirable, noble.

despise *v* scorn, deride, look down on, disdain, condemn, spurn, undervalue, slight, revile, deplore, dislike, detest, loathe.
⊜ admire.

despite *prep* in spite of, regardless of, notwithstanding, in the face of, undeterred by, against, defying.

despondent *adj* depressed, dejected, disheartened, downcast, down, low, gloomy, discouraged, glum, miserable, melancholy, sad, sorrowful, doleful, despairing, heartbroken, inconsolable, mournful, wretched.
⊜ cheerful, heartened, hopeful.

despot n autocrat, tyrant, dictator, oppressor, absolutist, boss.

despotic adj autocratic, tyrannical, imperious, oppressive, dictatorial, authoritarian, domineering, absolute, overbearing, arbitrary, arrogant.
⊜ democratic, egalitarian, liberal, tolerant.

despotism n autocracy, tyranny, totalitarianism, dictatorship, absolutism, oppression, repression.
⊜ democracy, egalitarianism, liberalism, tolerance.

dessert

Types of dessert include: ice cream, charlotte russe, mousse, cheesecake, cranachan, crème caramel, egg custard, fruit salad, fruit cocktail, gateau, millefeuille, pavlova, profiterole, Sachertorte, soufflé, summer pudding, Bakewell tart, banoffee pie, trifle, yogurt, sundae, syllabub, queen of puddings, Christmas pudding, tapioca, rice pudding, roly-poly pudding, spotted dick, tiramisu, zabaglione.

destination n 1 GOAL, objective, aim, object, purpose, target, end, intention, aspiration, design, ambition. 2 JOURNEY'S END, terminus, station, stop.

destined adj 1 FATED, doomed, inevitable, predetermined, certain, ordained, foreordained, meant, unavoidable, inescapable, intended, designed, appointed. 2 BOUND, directed, en route, headed, heading, scheduled, assigned, booked.

destiny n fate, doom, fortune, karma, lot (fml), portion (fml), predestination, kismet.

destitute adj 1 LACKING, needy, wanting, devoid of, bereft, innocent of, deprived, deficient, depleted. 2 POOR, penniless, poverty-stricken, impoverished, down and out (infml), distressed, bankrupt.
⊜ 2 prosperous, rich.

destroy v 1 DEMOLISH, ruin, shatter, wreck, devastate, smash, break, crush, overthrow, sabotage, undo, dismantle, thwart, undermine, waste, gut, level, ravage, raze, torpedo, unshape. 2 KILL, annihilate, eliminate, extinguish, eradicate, dispatch, slay (fml), nullify.
⊜ 1 build up. 2 create.

destruction n 1 RUIN, devastation, shattering, crushing, wreckage, demolition, defeat, downfall, overthrow, ruination, desolation, undoing, wastage, havoc, ravagement. 2 ANNIHILATION, extermination, eradication, end, elimination, extinction, slaughter, massacre, liquidation, nullification.
⊜ 2 creation.

destructive adj 1 destructive storms: devastating, damaging, catastrophic, disastrous, deadly, harmful, fatal, disruptive, lethal, ruinous, detrimental, hurtful, malignant, mischievous, nullifying, slaughterous. 2 destructive criticism: adverse, hostile, negative, discouraging, disparaging, contrary, undermining, subversive, vicious.
⊜ 1 creative. 2 constructive.

desultory adj random, erratic, aimless, disorderly, haphazard, irregular, spasmodic, inconsistent, undirected, unco-ordinated, fitful, unsystematic, unmethodical, disconnected, loose, capricious.
⊜ systematic, methodical.

detach v separate, disconnect, unfasten, disjoin, cut off, disengage, remove, undo, uncouple, sever, dissociate, isolate, loosen, free, unfix, unhitch, segregate, divide, disentangle, estrange.
⊜ attach.

detached adj 1 SEPARATE, disconnected, dissociated, severed, free, loose, divided, discrete.

2 ALOOF, dispassionate, impersonal, neutral, impartial, independent, disinterested, objective.
⊠ 1 connected. 2 involved.

detachment n 1 ALOOFNESS, remoteness, coolness, unconcern, indifference, impassivity, disinterestedness, neutrality, impartiality, objectivity, fairness. 2 SEPARATION, disconnection, disunion, disengagement. 3 SQUAD, unit, force, corps, brigade, patrol, task force.

detail n particular, item, factor, element, aspect, component, feature, point, specific, ingredient, attribute, count, respect, technicality, complication, intricacy, triviality, fact, thoroughness, elaboration, meticulousness, refinement, nicety.
◇ v 1 LIST, enumerate, itemize, specify, catalogue, recount, relate. 2 ASSIGN, appoint, charge, delegate, commission.

detailed adj comprehensive, exhaustive, full, blow-by-blow (infml), thorough, minute, exact, specific, particular, itemized, intricate, elaborate, complicated, complex, meticulous, descriptive.
⊠ cursory, general.

detain v 1 DELAY, hold (up), hinder, impede, check, retard, slow, stay, stop. 2 CONFINE, arrest, intern, hold, restrain, keep.
⊠ 2 release.

detect v 1 NOTICE, ascertain, note, observe, perceive, recognize, discern, distinguish, identify, sight, spot, spy. 2 UNCOVER, catch, discover, disclose, expose, find, track down, unmask, reveal.

detective n investigator, private eye (infml), gumshoe (US sl), sleuth (infml), sleuth-hound (infml).

detention n 1 DETAINMENT, custody, confinement, imprisonment,

restraint, incarceration, constraint, quarantine. 2 DELAY, hindrance, holding back.
⊠ 1 release.

deter v discourage, put off, inhibit, intimidate, dissuade, daunt, turn off (infml), check, caution, warn, restrain, hinder, frighten, disincline, prevent, prohibit, stop.
⊠ encourage.

deteriorate v 1 WORSEN, decline, degenerate, depreciate, go downhill (infml), fail, fall off, lapse, slide, relapse, slip. 2 DECAY, disintegrate, decompose, weaken, fade.
⊠ 1 improve. 2 progress.

determination n 1 RESOLUTENESS, tenacity, firmness, willpower, perseverance, persistence, purpose, backbone, guts (infml), grit (infml), steadfastness, single-mindedness, will, insistence, conviction, dedication, drive, fortitude. 2 DECISION, judgement, settlement, resolution, conclusion.
⊠ 1 irresolution.

determine v 1 DECIDE, settle, resolve, make up one's mind, choose, conclude, fix on, elect, clinch, finish. 2 DISCOVER, establish, find out, ascertain, identify, check, detect, verify. 3 AFFECT, influence, govern, control, dictate, direct, guide, regulate, ordain.

determined adj resolute, firm, purposeful, strong-willed, single-minded, persevering, persistent, strong-minded, steadfast, tenacious, dogged, insistent, intent, fixed, convinced, decided, unflinching.
⊠ irresolute, wavering.

deterrent n hindrance, impediment, obstacle, repellent, check, bar, discouragement, obstruction, curb, restraint, difficulty.
⊠ incentive, encouragement.

detest v hate, abhor, loathe, abominate, execrate (fml), dislike,

recoil from, deplore, despise.
⊟ adore, love.

detestable *adj* hateful, loathsome,
abhorrent, abominable, repellent,
obnoxious, execrable (*fml*),
despicable, revolting, repulsive,
repugnant, offensive, vile, disgusting,
accursed (*fml*), heinous, shocking,
sordid.
⊟ adorable, admirable.

detour *n* deviation, diversion,
indirect route, circuitous route,
roundabout route, digression,
byroad, byway, bypath, bypass.

detract (from) *v* diminish, subtract
from, take away from, reduce, lessen,
lower, devaluate, depreciate, belittle,
disparage.
⊟ add to, enhance, praise.

detriment *n* damage, harm,
hurt, disadvantage, loss, ill, injury,
disservice, evil, mischief, prejudice.
⊟ advantage, benefit.

detrimental *adj* damaging, harmful,
hurtful, adverse, disadvantageous,
injurious, prejudicial, mischievous,
destructive.
⊟ advantageous, favourable,
beneficial.

devastate *v* **1** DESTROY, desolate,
lay waste, demolish, spoil, despoil,
wreck, ruin, ravage, waste, ransack,
plunder, level, raze, pillage, sack.
2 DISCONCERT, overwhelm, take
aback, confound, shatter (*infml*),
floor (*infml*), nonplus, discomfit.

devastating *adj* **1** *devastating
storms*: destructive, disastrous.
2 *a devastating argument*: effective,
incisive, overwhelming, stunning.

devastation *n* destruction,
desolation, havoc, ruin, wreckage,
ravages, demolition, annihilation,
pillage, plunder, spoliation.

develop *v* **1** ADVANCE, evolve,
expand, progress, foster, flourish,
mature, prosper, branch out.
2 ELABORATE, amplify, argument,

enhance, unfold. **3** ACQUIRE, contract,
begin, generate, create, invent.
4 RESULT, come about, grow, ensue,
arise, follow, happen.

development *n* **1** GROWTH,
evolution, advance, blossoming,
elaboration, furtherance, progress,
unfolding, expansion, extension,
spread, increase, improvement,
maturity, promotion, refinement,
issue. **2** OCCURRENCE, happening,
event, change, outcome, situation,
result, phenomenon.

deviate *v* diverge, veer, turn (aside),
digress, swerve, vary, differ, depart,
stray, yaw, wander, err, go astray, go
off the rails (*infml*), drift, part.

deviation *n* divergence, aberration,
departure, abnormality, irregularity,
variance, variation, digression,
eccentricity, anomaly, deflection,
alteration, disparity, discrepancy,
detour, fluctuation, change, quirk,
shift, freak.
⊟ conformity, regularity.

device *n* **1** TOOL, implement,
appliance, gadget, contrivance,
contraption (*infml*), apparatus,
utensil, instrument, machine.
2 SCHEME, ruse, strategy, plan, plot,
gambit, manoeuvre, wile, trick,
dodge (*infml*), machination. **3** EMBLEM,
symbol, motif, logo (*infml*), design,
insignia, crest, badge, shield.

devil *n* **1** DEMON, Satan, fiend, evil
spirit, arch-fiend, Lucifer, imp, Evil
One, Prince of Darkness, Adversary,
Beelzebub, Mephistopheles, Old
Nick (*infml*), Old Harry (*infml*).
2 BRUTE, rogue, monster, ogre.

devious *adj* **1** UNDERHAND, deceitful,
dishonest, disingenuous, double-
dealing, scheming, tricky (*infml*),
insidious, insincere, calculating,
cunning, evasive, wily, sly, slippery
(*infml*), surreptitious, treacherous,
misleading. **2** INDIRECT, circuitous,
rambling, roundabout, wandering,
winding, tortuous, erratic.

⮹ straightforward.

devise v invent, contrive, plan, plot, design, conceive, arrange, formulate, imagine, scheme, construct, concoct, forge, frame, project, shape, form.

devoid adj lacking, wanting, without, free, bereft, destitute, deficient, deprived, barren, empty, vacant, void.
⮹ endowed.

devote v dedicate, consecrate, commit, give oneself, set apart, set aside, reserve, apply, allocate, allot, sacrifice, enshrine, assign, appropriate, surrender, pledge.

devoted adj dedicated, ardent, committed, loyal, faithful, devout, loving, staunch, steadfast, true, constant, fond, unswerving, tireless, concerned, attentive, caring.
⮹ indifferent, disloyal.

devotee n enthusiast, fan (infml), fanatic, addict, aficionado, follower, supporter, zealot, adherent, admirer, disciple, buff (infml), freak (infml), merchant (infml), fiend (infml), hound.

devotion n 1 DEDICATION, commitment, consecration, ardour, loyalty, allegiance, adherence, zeal, support, love, passion, fervour, fondness, attachment, adoration, affection, faithfulness, reverence, steadfastness, regard, earnestness. 2 DEVOUTNESS, piety, godliness, faith, holiness, spirituality. 3 PRAYER, worship.
⮹ 1 inconstancy. 2 irreverence.

devour v 1 EAT, consume, guzzle, gulp, gorge, gobble, bolt, wolf down, swallow, stuff (infml), cram, polish off (infml), gormandize, feast on, relish, revel in. 2 DESTROY, consume, absorb, engulf, ravage, dispatch.

devout adj 1 SINCERE, earnest, devoted, fervent, genuine, staunch, steadfast, ardent, passionate, serious, whole-hearted, constant, faithful, intense, heartfelt, zealous, unswerving, deep, profound. 2 PIOUS, godly, religious, reverent, prayerful, saintly, holy, orthodox.
⮹ 1 insincere. 2 irreligious.

dexterous adj deft, adroit, agile, able, nimble, proficient, skilful, clever, expert, nifty, nippy, handy, facile, nimble-fingered, neat-handed.
⮹ clumsy, inept, awkward.

diabolical adj devilish, fiendish, demonic, hellish, damnable, evil, infernal, wicked, vile, dreadful, outrageous, shocking, disastrous, excruciating, atrocious.

diagnose v identify, determine, recognize, pinpoint, distinguish, analyse, explain, isolate, interpret, investigate.

diagnosis n identification, verdict, explanation, conclusion, answer, interpretation, analysis, opinion, investigation, examination, scrutiny.

diagonal adj oblique, slanting, cross, crosswise, sloping, crooked, angled, cornerways.

diagram n plan, sketch, chart, drawing, figure, representation, schema, illustration, outline, graph, picture, layout, table.

dial n circle, disc, face, clock, control.
◇ v phone, ring, call (up).

dialect n idiom, language, regionalism, patois, provincialism, vernacular, argot, jargon, accent, lingo (infml), speech, diction.

dialectic adj dialectical, logical, rational, argumentative, analytical, rationalistic, logistic, polemical, inductive, deductive.
◇ n dialectics, logic, reasoning, rationale, disputation, analysis, debate, argumentation, contention, discussion, polemics, induction, deduction.

dialogue n 1 CONVERSATION,

interchange, discourse, talk, communication, exchange, discussion, converse, debate, conference. **2** LINES, script.

diametric *adj* diametrical, opposed, opposite, contrary, contrasting, counter, antithetical.

diary *n* journal, daybook, logbook, chronicle, year-book, appointment book, engagement book.

diatribe *n* tirade, invective, abuse, harangue, attack, onslaught, denunciation, criticism, insult, reviling, upbraiding.
⊞ praise, eulogy.

dictate *v* **1** SAY, speak, utter, announce, pronounce, transmit. **2** COMMAND, order, direct, decree, instruct, rule.
◇ *n* command, decree, precept, principle, rule, direction, injunction, edict, order, ruling, statute, law, requirement, ordinance, bidding, mandate, ultimatum, word.

dictator *n* despot, autocrat, tyrant, supremo (*infml*), Big Brother (*infml*).

dictatorial *adj* tyrannical, despotic, totalitarian, authoritarian, autocratic, oppressive, imperious, domineering, bossy (*infml*), absolute, repressive, overbearing, arbitrary, dogmatic.
⊞ democratic, egalitarian, liberal.

diction *n* speech, articulation, language, elocution, enunciation, intonation, pronunciation, inflection, fluency, delivery, expression, phrasing.

dictionary *n* lexicon, glossary, thesaurus, vocabulary, wordbook, encyclopedia, concordance.

dictum *n* pronouncement, ruling, maxim, decree, dictate, edict, fiat (*fml*), precept, axiom, command, order, utterance.

didactic *adj* instructive, educational, educative, pedagogic, prescriptive, pedantic, moralizing, moral.

die *v* **1** DECEASE, perish, pass away, expire, depart, breathe one's last, peg out (*infml*), snuff it (*sl*), bite the dust (*infml*), kick the bucket (*sl*). **2** DWINDLE, fade, ebb, sink, wane, wilt, wither, peter out, decline, decay, finish, lapse, end, disappear, vanish, subside. **3** LONG FOR, pine for, yearn, desire.
⊞ **1** live.

die-hard *n* reactionary, intransigent, hardliner, blimp (*infml*), old fogey (*infml*), ultra-conservative, stick-in-the-mud (*infml*), rightist, fanatic.

diet *n* **1** FOOD, nutrition, provisions, sustenance, rations, foodstuffs, subsistence. **2** FAST, abstinence, regimen.
◇ *v* lose weight, slim, fast, reduce, abstain, weight-watch (*infml*).

differ *v* **1** VARY, diverge, deviate, depart from, contradict, contrast. **2** DISAGREE, argue, conflict, oppose, dispute, dissent, be at odds with, clash, quarrel, fall out, debate, contend, take issue.
⊞ **1** conform. **2** agree.

difference *n* **1** DISSIMILARITY, unlikeness, discrepancy, diversity, variation, variety, distinctness, distinction, deviation, divergence, differentiation, contrast, disparity, singularity, exception. **2** DISAGREEMENT, clash, dispute, conflict, contention, controversy. **3** REMAINDER, rest.
⊞ **1** conformity. **2** agreement.

different *adj* **1** DISSIMILAR, unlike, contrasting, divergent, inconsistent, deviating, clashing, at odds, opposed. **2** VARIED, various, diverse, miscellaneous, assorted, disparate, many, numerous, several, sundry, other. **3** UNUSUAL, unconventional, unique, distinct, distinctive, extraordinary, individual, original, special, strange, separate, peculiar, rare, bizarre, anomalous.
⊞ **1** similar. **2** same. **3** conventional.

differentiate v distinguish, tell apart, discriminate, contrast, separate, mark off, individualize, particularize.

difficult adj 1 HARD, laborious, demanding, arduous, strenuous, tough, wearisome, uphill, formidable. 2 COMPLEX, complicated, intricate, involved, abstruse, obscure, dark, knotty, thorny, problematical, perplexing, abstract, baffling, intractable. 3 UNMANAGEABLE, perverse, troublesome, trying, unco-operative, tiresome, stubborn, obstinate, intractable.
☞ 1 easy. 2 straightforward. 3 manageable.

difficulty n 1 HARDSHIP, trouble, labour, arduousness, painfulness, trial, tribulation, awkwardness. 2 PROBLEM, predicament, dilemma, quandary, perplexity, embarrassment, plight, distress, fix (infml), mess (infml), jam (infml), spot (infml), hiccup (infml), hang-up. 3 OBSTACLE, hindrance, hurdle, impediment, objection, opposition, block, complication, pitfall, protest, stumbling-block.
☞ 1 ease.

diffidence n unassertiveness, modesty, shyness, timidity, self-consciousness, self-effacement, insecurity, reserve, bashfulness, humility, inhibition, meekness, self-distrust, self-doubt, hesitancy, reluctance, backwardness.
☞ confidence.

diffident adj unassertive, modest, shy, timid, self-conscious, self-effacing, insecure, meek, bashful, abashed, reserved, withdrawn, tentative, shrinking, inhibited, hesitant, reluctant, unsure, shamefaced.
☞ assertive, confident.

diffuse adj 1 diffuse outbreaks of rain: scattered, unconcentrated, diffused, dispersed, disconnected.

2 a diffuse prose style: verbose, imprecise, wordy, rambling, long-winded, waffling (infml), vague, discursive.
☞ 1 concentrated. 2 succinct.
◇ v spread, scatter, disperse, distribute, propagate, dispense, disseminate, circulate, dissipate.
☞ concentrate.

dig v 1 EXCAVATE, penetrate, burrow, mine, quarry, scoop, tunnel, till, gouge, delve, pierce. 2 POKE, prod. 3 INVESTIGATE, probe, go into, research, search.
◇ n gibe, jeer, sneer, taunt, crack, insinuation, insult, wisecrack.
☞ compliment.
● **dig up** discover, unearth, uncover, disinter, expose, extricate, exhume, find, retrieve, track down.
☞ bury, obscure.

digest v 1 ABSORB, assimilate, incorporate, process, dissolve. 2 TAKE IN, absorb, understand, assimilate, grasp, study, consider, contemplate, meditate, ponder. 3 SHORTEN, summarize, condense, compress, reduce.
◇ n summary, abridgement, abstract, précis, synopsis, résumé, reduction, abbreviation, compression, compendium.

dignified adj stately, solemn, imposing, majestic, noble, august, lordly, lofty, exalted, formal, distinguished, grave, impressive, reserved, honourable.
☞ undignified, lowly.

dignitary n worthy, notable, VIP (infml), high-up, personage, bigwig (infml).

dignity n stateliness, propriety, solemnity, decorum, courtliness, grandeur, loftiness, majesty, honour, eminence, importance, nobility, self-respect, self-esteem, standing, poise, respectability, greatness, status, pride.

digress v diverge, deviate, stray,

wander, go off at a tangent, drift, depart, ramble.

dilapidated *adj* ramshackle, shabby, broken-down, neglected, tumbledown, uncared-for, rickety, decrepit, crumbling, run-down, worn-out, ruined, decayed, decaying.

dilate *v* distend, enlarge, expand, spread, broaden, widen, increase, extend, stretch, swell.
⊟ contract.

dilatory *adj* procrastinating, delaying, slow, tardy, tarrying, sluggish, lingering, lackadaisical, slack.
⊟ prompt.

dilemma *n* quandary, conflict, predicament, problem, catch-22 (*infml*), difficulty, puzzle, embarrassment, perplexity, plight.

diligent *adj* assiduous, industrious, busy, hard-working, conscientious, painstaking, attentive, tireless, careful, meticulous, persevering, persistent, studious.
⊟ negligent, lazy.

dilute *v* adulterate, water down, thin (out), attenuate, weaken, diffuse, diminish, decrease, lessen, reduce, temper, mitigate.
⊟ concentrate.

dim *adj* **1** DARK, dull, dusky, cloudy, shadowy, gloomy, sombre, dingy, lacklustre, feeble, imperfect.
2 INDISTINCT, blurred, hazy, ill-defined, obscure, misty, unclear, foggy, fuzzy, vague, faint, weak.
3 STUPID, dense, obtuse, thick (*infml*), doltish.
⊟ **1** bright. **2** distinct. **3** bright, intelligent.
◇ *v* darken, dull, obscure, cloud, blur, fade, tarnish, shade.
⊟ brighten, illuminate.

dimension(s) *n* measurement, measure, size, extent, scope, magnitude, largeness, capacity, mass, scale, range, bulk, importance, greatness.

diminish *v* **1** DECREASE, lessen, reduce, lower, contract, decline, dwindle, shrink, recede, taper off, wane, weaken, abate, fade, sink, subside, ebb, slacken, cut. **2** BELITTLE, disparage, deprecate, devalue.
⊟ **1** increase. **2** exaggerate.

diminutive *adj* undersized, small, tiny, little, miniature, minute, infinitesimal, wee, petite, midget, mini (*infml*), teeny (*infml*), teeny-weeny (*infml*), Lilliputian, dinky (*infml*), pint-size(d) (*infml*), pocket, pocket-sized, pygmy.
⊟ big, large, oversized.

din *n* noise, row, racket, clash, clatter, clamour, pandemonium, uproar, commotion, crash, hubbub, hullabaloo (*infml*), outcry, shout, babble.
⊟ quiet, calm.

dine *v* eat, feast, sup, lunch, banquet, feed.

dingy *adj* dark, drab, grimy, murky, faded, dull, dim, shabby, soiled, discoloured, dirty, dreary, gloomy, seedy, sombre, obscure, run-down, colourless, dusky, worn.
⊟ bright, clean.

dinner *n* meal, supper, tea (*infml*), banquet, feast, spread, repast (*fml*).

dinosaur

Dinosaurs include: allosaurus, ankylosaurus, apatosaurus, brachiosaurus, brontosaurus, camptosaurus, compsognathus, corythosaurus, diplodocus, heterodontosaurus, iguanodon, microraptor, ornithomimus, pachycephalosaurus, parasaurolophus, plateosaurus, stegosaurus, styracosaurus, triceratops, tyrannosaurus, velociraptor.

dip v 1 PLUNGE, immerse, submerge, duck, dunk, bathe, douse, sink. 2 DESCEND, decline, drop, fall, subside, slump, sink, lower.
◇ n 1 HOLLOW, basin, decline, hole, concavity, incline, depression, fall, slope, slump, lowering. 2 BATHE, immersion, plunge, soaking, ducking, swim, drenching, infusion, dive.

diplomacy n 1 TACT, tactfulness, finesse, delicacy, discretion, savoir-faire, subtlety, skill, craft. 2 STATECRAFT, statesmanship, politics, negotiation, manoeuvring.

diplomat n go-between, mediator, negotiator, ambassador, envoy, conciliator, peacemaker, moderator, politician.

diplomatic adj tactful, politic, discreet, judicious, subtle, sensitive, prudent, discreet.
⊠ tactless.

dire adj 1 DISASTROUS, dreadful, awful, appalling, calamitous, catastrophic. 2 DESPERATE, urgent, grave, drastic, crucial, extreme, alarming, ominous.

direct v 1 CONTROL, manage, run, administer, organize, lead, govern, regulate, superintend, supervise. 2 INSTRUCT, command, order, charge. 3 GUIDE, lead, conduct, point. 4 AIM, point, focus, turn.
◇ adj 1 STRAIGHT, undeviating, through, uninterrupted. 2 STRAIGHTFORWARD, outspoken, blunt, frank, unequivocal, sincere, candid, honest, explicit. 3 IMMEDIATE, first-hand, face-to-face, personal.
⊠ 1 circuitous. 2 equivocal. 3 indirect.

direction n 1 CONTROL, administration, management, government, supervision, guidance, leadership. 2 ROUTE, way, line, road.

directions n instructions, guidelines, orders, briefing, guidance, recommendations, indication, plan.

directive n command, instruction, order, regulation, ruling, imperative, dictate, decree, charge, mandate, injunction, ordinance, edict, fiat, notice.

directly adv 1 IMMEDIATELY, instantly, promptly, right away, speedily, forthwith, instantaneously, quickly, soon, presently, straight away, straight. 2 FRANKLY, bluntly, candidly, honestly.

director n manager, head, boss, chief, controller, executive, principal, governor, leader, organizer, supervisor, administrator, producer, conductor.

dirt n 1 EARTH, soil, clay, dust, mud. 2 FILTH, grime, muck, mire, excrement, stain, smudge, slime, tarnish. 3 INDECENCY, impurity, obscenity, pornography.

dirty adj 1 FILTHY, grimy, grubby, mucky, soiled, unwashed, foul, messy, muddy, polluted, squalid, dull, miry, scruffy, shabby, sullied, clouded, dark. 2 INDECENT, obscene, filthy, smutty, sordid, salacious, vulgar, pornographic, corrupt.
⊠ 1 clean. 2 decent.
◇ v pollute, soil, stain, foul, mess up, defile, smear, smirch, spoil, smudge, sully, muddy, blacken.
⊠ clean, cleanse.

disability n handicap, impairment, disablement, disorder, inability, incapacity, infirmity, defect, unfitness, disqualification, affliction, ailment, complaint, weakness.

disable v cripple, incapacitate, damage, handicap, impair, debilitate, disqualify, weaken, immobilize, invalidate, paralyse, prostrate.

disabled adj handicapped, incapacitated, impaired, infirm, crippled, lame, immobilized, maimed, weak, weakened,

paralysed, wrecked.
⊟ able, able-bodied.

disadvantage n 1 HARM, damage, detriment, hurt, injury, loss, prejudice. 2 DRAWBACK, snag, hindrance, handicap, impediment, inconvenience, flaw, nuisance, weakness, trouble.
⊟ 2 advantage, benefit.

disadvantaged adj deprived, underprivileged, poor, impoverished, handicapped, struggling.
⊟ privileged.

disadvantageous adj harmful, detrimental, inopportune, adverse, unfavourable, prejudicial, damaging, hurtful, injurious, inconvenient, ill-timed.
⊟ advantageous, auspicious.

disaffected adj disloyal, hostile, estranged, alienated, antagonistic, rebellious, dissatisfied, disgruntled, discontented.
⊟ loyal.

disaffection n disloyalty, hostility, alienation, discontentment, ill-will, resentment, dissatisfaction, animosity, coolness, unfriendliness, antagonism, disharmony, discord, disagreement, aversion, dislike.
⊟ loyalty, contentment.

disagree v 1 DISSENT, oppose, quarrel, argue, bicker, fall out (infml), wrangle, fight, squabble, contend, dispute, contest, object. 2 CONFLICT, clash, diverge, contradict, counter, differ, deviate, depart, run counter to, vary.
⊟ 1 agree. 2 correspond.

disagreeable adj 1 a disagreeable old man: bad-tempered, difficult, ill-humoured, peevish, rude, surly, churlish, irritable, contrary, cross, brusque. 2 a disagreeable taste: disgusting, offensive, repulsive, repellent, obnoxious, unsavoury, objectionable, nasty.
⊟ 1 amiable, pleasant. 2 agreeable.

disagreement n 1 DISPUTE, argument, conflict, altercation (fml), quarrel, clash, dissent, falling-out, contention, strife, misunderstanding, squabble, tiff (infml), wrangle. 2 DIFFERENCE, variance, unlikeness, disparity, discrepancy, deviation, discord, dissimilarity, incompatibility, divergence, diversity, incongruity.
⊟ 1 agreement, harmony. 2 similarity.

disappear v 1 VANISH, wane, recede, fade, evaporate, dissolve, ebb. 2 GO, depart, withdraw, retire, flee, fly, escape, scarper (infml), hide. 3 END, expire, perish, pass.
⊟ 1 appear. 3 emerge.

disappearance n vanishing, fading, evaporation, departure, loss, going, passing, melting, desertion, flight.
⊟ appearance, manifestation.

disappoint v fail, dissatisfy, let down, disillusion, dash, dismay, disenchant, sadden, thwart, vex, frustrate, foil, dishearten, disgruntle, disconcert, hamper, hinder, deceive, defeat, delude.
⊟ satisfy, please, delight.

disappointed adj let down, frustrated, thwarted, disillusioned, dissatisfied, miffed (infml), upset, discouraged, disgruntled, disheartened, distressed, downhearted, saddened, despondent, depressed.
⊟ pleased, satisfied.

disappointment n 1 FRUSTRATION, dissatisfaction, failure, disenchantment, disillusionment, displeasure, discouragement, distress, regret. 2 FAILURE, let-down, setback, comedown, blow, misfortune, fiasco, disaster, calamity, wash-out (infml), damp squib (infml), swiz (infml), swizzle (infml).
⊟ 1 pleasure, satisfaction, delight. 2 success.

disapproval n censure, disapprobation (fml), condemnation,

criticism, displeasure, reproach, objection, dissatisfaction, denunciation, dislike.
☒ approbation (fml), approval.

disapprove of v censure, condemn, blame, take exception to, object to, deplore, denounce, disparage, dislike, reject, spurn.
☒ approve of.

disarm v 1 DISABLE, unarm, demilitarize, demobilize, deactivate, disband. 2 APPEASE, conciliate, win, mollify, persuade.
☒ 1 arm.

disarray n disorder, confusion, chaos, mess, muddle, shambles (infml), disorganization, clutter, untidiness, unruliness, jumble, indiscipline, tangle, upset.
☒ order.

disaster n calamity, catastrophe, misfortune, reverse, tragedy, blow, accident, act of God, cataclysm, debacle, mishap, failure, flop (infml), fiasco, ruin, stroke, trouble, mischance, ruination.
☒ success, triumph.

disastrous adj dreadful, dire, terrible, destructive, calamitous, catastrophic, cataclysmic, devastating, ruinous, tragic, ill-fated, unfortunate, fatal, miserable.
☒ successful, auspicious.

disband v disperse, break up, scatter, dismiss, demobilize, part company, separate, dissolve.
☒ assemble, muster.

disbelief n unbelief, incredulity, doubt, scepticism, suspicion, distrust, mistrust, rejection.
☒ belief.

disbelieve v discount, discredit, repudiate, reject, mistrust, suspect.
☒ believe, trust.

disc n 1 CIRCLE, face, plate, ring. 2 RECORD, album, LP, CD, MiniDisc®. 3 DISK, diskette, hard disk, floppy disk, CD-ROM, DVD.

discard v reject, abandon, dispose of, get rid of, jettison, dispense with, cast aside, ditch (infml), dump (infml), drop, scrap, shed, remove, relinquish.
☒ retain, adopt.

discern v 1 PERCEIVE, make out, observe, detect, recognize, see, ascertain, notice, determine, discover, descry. 2 DISCRIMINATE, distinguish, differentiate, judge.

discernible adj perceptible, noticeable, detectable, appreciable, distinct, observable, recognizable, visible, apparent, clear, obvious, plain, patent, manifest, discoverable.
☒ imperceptible.

discerning adj discriminating, perceptive, astute, clear-sighted, sensitive, shrewd, wise, sharp, subtle, sagacious, penetrating, acute, piercing, critical, eagle-eyed.
☒ dull, obtuse.

discharge v 1 LIBERATE, free, pardon, release, clear, absolve, exonerate, acquit, relieve, dismiss. 2 EXECUTE, carry out, perform, fulfil, dispense. 3 FIRE, shoot, let off, detonate, explode. 4 EMIT, sack (infml), fire (infml), remove, expel, oust, eject.
☒ 1 detain. 2 neglect. 4 appoint.
◇ n 1 LIBERATION, release, acquittal, exoneration. 2 EMISSION, secretion, ejection. 3 EXECUTION, accomplishment, fulfilment.
☒ 1 confinement, detention. 2 absorption. 3 neglect.

disciple n follower, convert, proselyte, adherent, believer, devotee, supporter, learner, pupil, student.

disciplinarian n authoritarian, taskmaster, autocrat, stickler, despot, tyrant.

discipline n 1 TRAINING, exercise, drill, practice. 2 PUNISHMENT, chastisement, correction. 3 STRICTNESS, restraint, regulation, self-

control, orderliness.
⊡ **3** indiscipline.
◇ v **1** TRAIN, instruct, drill, educate,
exercise, break in. **2** CHECK, control,
correct, restrain, govern. **3** PUNISH,
chastise, chasten, penalize,
reprimand, castigate.

disclaim v deny, disown, repudiate,
abandon, renounce, reject, abjure
(fml).
⊡ accept, confess.

disclose v **1** DIVULGE, make known,
reveal, tell, confess, let slip, relate,
publish, communicate, impart, leak
(infml). **2** EXPOSE, reveal, uncover, lay
bare, unveil, discover.
⊡ conceal.

disclosure n divulgence, exposure,
exposé, revelation, uncovering,
publication, leak (infml), discovery,
admission, acknowledgement,
announcement, declaration.

discomfort n ache, pain,
uneasiness, malaise, trouble,
distress, disquiet, hardship, vexation,
irritation, annoyance.
⊡ comfort, ease.

disconcerting adj disturbing,
confusing, upsetting, unnerving,
alarming, bewildering, off-putting
(infml), distracting, embarrassing,
awkward, baffling, perplexing,
dismaying, bothersome.

disconnect v cut off, disengage,
uncouple, sever, separate, detach,
unplug, unhook, part, divide.
⊡ attach, connect.

disconnected adj confused,
incoherent, rambling, unco-
ordinated, unintelligible, loose,
irrational, disjointed, illogical,
jumbled.
⊡ coherent, connected.

disconsolate adj desolate,
dejected, dispirited, sad, melancholy,
unhappy, wretched, miserable,
gloomy, forlorn, inconsolable,
crushed, heavy-hearted, hopeless.

⊡ cheerful, joyful.

discontent n uneasiness, disquiet,
dissatisfaction, restlessness,
fretfulness, unrest, impatience,
vexation, regret.
⊡ content.

discontented adj dissatisfied, fed
up (infml), disgruntled, unhappy,
browned off (infml), cheesed off
(infml), disaffected, miserable,
exasperated, complaining.
⊡ contented, satisfied.

discontinue v stop, end, finish,
cease, break off, terminate, halt,
drop, suspend, abandon, cancel,
interrupt.
⊡ continue.

discord n **1** DISSENSION, disunity,
disagreement, discordance, clashing,
incompatibility, conflict, difference,
dispute, contention, friction,
division, opposition, strife, split,
wrangling. **2** DISSONANCE, disharmony,
cacophony (fml), jangle, jarring,
harshness.
⊡ **1** concord, agreement. **2** harmony.

discordant adj **1** DISAGREEING,
conflicting, at odds, clashing,
contradictory, incongruous,
incompatible, inconsistent.
2 DISSONANT, cacophonous (fml),
grating, jangling, jarring, harsh.
⊡ **1** harmonious. **2** harmonious.

discount[1] v **1** DISREGARD, ignore,
overlook, disbelieve, gloss over.
2 REDUCE, deduct, mark down, knock
off (infml).

discount[2] n reduction, rebate,
allowance, cut, concession,
deduction, mark-down.

discourage v **1** DISHEARTEN, dampen,
dispirit, depress, demoralize, dismay,
unnerve, deject, disappoint. **2** DETER,
dissuade, hinder, put off, restrain,
prevent.
⊡ **1** hearten. **2** encourage.

discouragement n
1 DOWNHEARTEDNESS, despondency,

pessimism, dismay, depression, dejection, despair, disappointment. **2** DETERRENT, damper, setback, impediment, obstacle, opposition, hindrance, restraint, rebuff.
🗷 **1** encouragement. **2** incentive.

discourse n **1** CONVERSATION, dialogue, chat, communication, talk, converse, discussion. **2** SPEECH, address, oration (fml), lecture, sermon, essay, treatise, dissertation, homily.
◇ v converse, talk, discuss, debate, confer, lecture.

discourteous adj rude, bad-mannered, ill-mannered, impolite, boorish, disrespectful, ill-bred, uncivil, unceremonious, insolent, offhand, curt, brusque, abrupt.
🗷 courteous, polite.

discover v **1** FIND, uncover, unearth, dig up, disclose, reveal, light on, locate. **2** ASCERTAIN, determine, realize, notice, recognize, perceive, see, find out, spot, discern, learn, detect. **3** ORIGINATE, invent, pioneer.
🗷 **1** miss. **2** conceal, cover (up).

discovery n **1** BREAKTHROUGH, find, origination, introduction, innovation, invention, exploration. **2** DISCLOSURE, detection, revelation, location.

discredit v **1** DISBELIEVE, distrust, doubt, question, mistrust, challenge. **2** DISPARAGE, dishonour, degrade, defame, disgrace, slander, slur, smear, reproach, vilify.
🗷 **1** believe. **2** honour.
◇ n **1** DISBELIEF, distrust, doubt, mistrust, scepticism, suspicion. **2** DISHONOUR, disrepute, censure, aspersion, disgrace, blame, shame, reproach, slur, smear, scandal.
🗷 **1** belief. **2** credit.

discreditable adj dishonourable, disreputable, reprehensible, disgraceful, scandalous, blameworthy, shameful, infamous, degrading, improper.
🗷 creditable.

discreet adj tactful, careful, diplomatic, politic, prudent, cautious, delicate, judicious, reserved, wary, sensible.
🗷 tactless, indiscreet.

discrepancy n difference, disparity, variance, variation, inconsistency, dissimilarity, discordance, conflict, divergence, disagreement, inequality.

discretion n **1** TACT, diplomacy, judiciousness, caution, prudence, wisdom, circumspection, judgement, discernment, care, carefulness, consideration, wariness. **2** CHOICE, freedom, preference, will, wish.
🗷 **1** indiscretion.

discriminate v distinguish, tell apart, differentiate, discern, make a distinction, segregate, separate.
🗷 confuse, confound.
• **discriminate (against)** be prejudiced, be biased, victimize.

discriminating adj discerning, fastidious, selective, critical, perceptive, particular, tasteful, astute, sensitive, cultivated.

discrimination n **1** BIAS, prejudice, intolerance, unfairness, bigotry, favouritism, inequity, racism, sexism. **2** DISCERNMENT, judgement, acumen, perception, acuteness, insight, penetration, subtlety, keenness, refinement, taste.

discursive adj rambling, digressing, wandering, meandering, long-winded, wide-ranging, circuitous.
🗷 terse.

discuss v debate, talk about, confer, argue, consider, deliberate, converse, consult, examine.

discussion n debate, conference, argument, conversation, dialogue, exchange, consultation, discourse, deliberation, consideration, analysis, review, examination, scrutiny, seminar, symposium.

disdain n scorn, contempt, arrogance, haughtiness, derision,

sneering, dislike, snobbishness.
⊜ admiration, respect.

disdainful adj scornful,
contemptuous, derisive, haughty,
aloof, arrogant, supercilious,
sneering, superior, proud, insolent.
⊜ respectful.

disease n illness, sickness, ill health,
infirmity, complaint, ailment, disorder,
indisposition, malady, condition,
affliction, infection, epidemic.
⊜ health.

diseased adj sick, ill, unhealthy,
ailing, unsound, contaminated,
infected.
⊜ healthy.

disembark v land, arrive, alight,
debark.
⊜ embark.

disembodied adj incorporeal (fml),
bodiless, ghostly, phantom, spiritual,
immaterial, intangible.

disengage v disconnect, detach,
loosen, free, extricate, undo, release,
liberate, separate, disentangle, untie,
withdraw.
⊜ connect, engage.

disentangle v 1 LOOSE, free,
extricate, disconnect, untangle,
disengage, detach, unravel, separate,
unfold. 2 RESOLVE, clarify, simplify.
⊜ 1 entangle.

disfigure v deface, blemish, mar,
mutilate, scar, deform, distort,
damage, spoil.
⊜ adorn, embellish.

disgrace n shame, ignominy,
disrepute, dishonour, disfavour,
humiliation, defamation, discredit,
scandal, reproach, slur, stain.
⊜ honour, esteem.
◇ v shame, dishonour, abase,
defame, humiliate, disfavour, stain,
discredit, reproach, slur, sully, taint,
stigmatize.
⊜ honour, respect.

disgraceful adj shameful,

dishonourable, disreputable,
ignominious, scandalous, shocking,
unworthy, dreadful, appalling.
⊜ honourable, respectable.

disguise v 1 CONCEAL, cover,
camouflage, mask, hide, dress up,
cloak, screen, veil, shroud. 2 FALSIFY,
deceive, dissemble, misrepresent,
fake, fudge.
⊜ 1 reveal, expose.
◇ n concealment, camouflage, cloak,
cover, costume, mask, front, façade,
masquerade, deception, pretence,
travesty, screen, veil.

disgust v offend, displease,
nauseate, revolt, sicken, repel,
outrage, put off.
⊜ delight, please.
◇ n revulsion, repulsion, repugnance,
distaste, aversion, abhorrence, nausea,
loathing, detestation, hatred.

disgusted adj repelled, repulsed,
revolted, offended, appalled,
outraged.
⊜ attracted, delighted.

disgusting adj repugnant,
repellent, revolting, offensive,
sickening, nauseating, odious, foul,
unappetizing, unpleasant, vile,
obscene, abominable, detestable,
objectionable, nasty.
⊜ delightful, pleasant.

dish n plate, bowl, platter, food,
recipe.
• **dish out** distribute, give out, hand
out, hand round, dole out, allocate,
mete out, inflict.
• **dish up** serve, present, ladle,
spoon, dispense, scoop.

dishearten v discourage, dispirit,
dampen, cast down, depress, dismay,
dash, disappoint, deject, daunt,
crush, deter.
⊜ encourage, hearten.

dishevelled adj tousled, unkempt,
uncombed, untidy, bedraggled,
messy, ruffled, slovenly, disordered.
⊜ neat, tidy.

dishonest *adj* untruthful, fraudulent, deceitful, false, lying, deceptive, double-dealing, cheating, crooked (*infml*), treacherous, unprincipled, swindling, shady (*infml*), corrupt, disreputable.
🔁 honest, trustworthy, scrupulous.

dishonesty *n* deceit, falsehood, falsity, fraudulence, fraud, criminality, insincerity, treachery, cheating, crookedness (*infml*), corruption, unscrupulousness, trickery.
🔁 honesty, truthfulness.

dishonour *v* disgrace, shame, humiliate, debase, defile, degrade, defame, discredit, demean, debauch.
🔁 honour.
◇ *n* disgrace, abasement, humiliation, shame, degradation, discredit, disrepute, indignity, ignominy, reproach, slight, slur, scandal, insult, disfavour, outrage, aspersion, abuse, discourtesy.
🔁 honour.

disillusioned *adj* disenchanted, disabused, undeceived, disappointed.

disinclined *adj* averse, reluctant, resistant, indisposed, loath, opposed, hesitant.
🔁 inclined, willing.

disinfect *v* sterilize, fumigate, sanitize, decontaminate, cleanse, purify, purge, clean.
🔁 contaminate, infect.

disinfectant *n* sterilizer, antiseptic, sanitizer.

disintegrate *v* break up, decompose, fall apart, crumble, rot, moulder, separate, splinter.

disinterest *n* disinterestedness, impartiality, neutrality, detachment, unbiasedness, dispassionateness, fairness.

disinterested *adj* unbiased, neutral, impartial, unprejudiced, dispassionate, detached, uninvolved, open-minded, equitable, even-handed, unselfish.
🔁 biased, concerned.

disjointed *adj* **1** DISCONNECTED, dislocated, divided, separated, disunited, displaced, broken, fitful, split, disarticulated. **2** INCOHERENT, aimless, confused, disordered, loose, unconnected, bitty, rambling, spasmodic.
🔁 **2** coherent.

dislike *n* aversion, hatred, repugnance, hostility, distaste, disinclination, disapproval, disapprobation, displeasure, animosity, antagonism, enmity, detestation, disgust, loathing.
🔁 liking, predilection.
◇ *v* hate, detest, object to, loathe, abhor, abominate, disapprove, shun, despise, scorn.
🔁 like, favour.

dislocate *v* disjoint, displace, misplace, disengage, put out (*infml*), disorder, shift, disconnect, disrupt, disunite.

dislodge *v* displace, eject, remove, oust, extricate, shift, move, uproot.

disloyal *adj* treacherous, faithless, false, traitorous, two-faced (*infml*), backstabbing, unfaithful, apostate, unpatriotic.
🔁 loyal, trustworthy.

dismal *adj* dreary, gloomy, depressing, bleak, cheerless, dull, drab, low-spirited, melancholy, sad, sombre, lugubrious, forlorn, despondent, dark, sorrowful, long-faced (*infml*), hopeless, discouraging.
🔁 cheerful, bright.

dismantle *v* demolish, take apart, disassemble, strip.
🔁 assemble, put together.

dismay *v* alarm, daunt, frighten, unnerve, unsettle, scare, put off, dispirit, distress, disconcert, dishearten, discourage, disillusion, depress, horrify, disappoint.
🔁 encourage, hearten.

◇ *n* consternation, alarm, distress, apprehension, agitation, dread, fear, trepidation, fright, horror, terror, discouragement, disappointment.
⊞ boldness, encouragement.

dismember *v* disjoint, amputate, dissect, dislocate, divide, mutilate, sever.
⊞ assemble, join.

dismiss *v* **1** *the class was dismissed*: discharge, free, let go, release, send away, remove, drop, discord, banish. **2** *dismiss employees*: sack (*infml*), make redundant, lay off, fire (*infml*), relegate. **3** *dismiss it from your mind*: discount, disregard, reject, repudiate, set aside, shelve, spurn.
⊞ **1** retain. **2** appoint. **3** accept.

disobey *v* contravene, infringe, violate, transgress, flout, disregard, defy, ignore, resist, rebel.
⊞ obey.

disorder *n* **1** CONFUSION, chaos, muddle, disarray, mess, untidiness, shambles (*infml*), clutter, disorganization, jumble. **2** DISTURBANCE, tumult, riot, confusion, commotion, uproar, fracas, brawl, fight, clamour, quarrel. **3** ILLNESS, complaint, disease, sickness, disability, ailment, malady, affliction.
⊞ **1** neatness, order. **2** law and order, peace.
◇ *v* disturb, mess up, disarrange, mix up, muddle, upset, disorganize, confuse, confound, clutter, jumble, discompose, scatter, unsettle.
⊞ arrange, organize.

disorderly *adj* **1** DISORGANIZED, confused, chaotic, irregular, messy, untidy. **2** UNRULY, undisciplined, unmanageable, obstreperous, rowdy, turbulent, rebellious, lawless.
⊞ **1** neat, tidy. **2** well-behaved.

disorganize *v* disorder, disrupt, disturb, disarrange, muddle, upset, confuse, discompose, jumble, play havoc with, unsettle, break up, destroy.
⊞ organize.

disorganized *adj* **1** CONFUSED, disordered, haphazard, jumbled, muddled, chaotic, unsorted, unsystematized, topsy-turvy, shambolic (*infml*). **2** UNMETHODICAL, unorganized, unstructured, unsystematic, careless, muddled, untogether (*infml*).
⊞ **1** organized, tidy. **2** organized, methodical.

disown *v* repudiate, renounce, disclaim, deny, cast off, disallow, reject, abandon.
⊞ accept, acknowledge.

disparaging *adj* derisive, derogatory, mocking, scornful, critical, insulting, snide (*infml*).
⊞ flattering, praising.

dispassionate *adj* detached, objective, impartial, neutral, disinterested, impersonal, fair, cool, calm, composed.
⊞ biased, emotional.

dispatch, despatch *v* **1** SEND, express, transmit, forward, consign, expedite, accelerate. **2** DISPOSE OF, finish, perform, discharge, conclude. **3** KILL, murder, execute.
⊞ **1** receive.
◇ *n* **1** COMMUNICATION, message, report, bulletin, communiqué, news, letter, account. **2** PROMPTNESS, speed, alacrity, expedition, celerity, haste, rapidity, swiftness.
⊞ **2** slowness.

dispense *v* **1** DISTRIBUTE, give out, apportion, allot, allocate, assign, share, mete out. **2** ADMINISTER, apply, implement, enforce, discharge, execute, operate.
• **dispense with** dispose of, get rid of, abolish, discard, omit, disregard, cancel, forgo, ignore, waive.

disperse *v* scatter, dispel, spread, distribute, diffuse, dissolve, break up, dismiss, separate.
⊞ gather.

displace *v* **1** DISLODGE, move, shift,

misplace, disturb, dislocate. **2** DEPOSE, oust, remove, replace, dismiss, discharge, supplant, eject, evict, succeed, supersede.

display v **1** SHOW, present, demonstrate, exhibit. **2** BETRAY, disclose, reveal, show, expose. **3** SHOW OFF, flourish, parade, flaunt.
⊞ **1** conceal. **2** disguise.
◊ n show, exhibition, demonstration, presentation, parade, spectacle, revelation.

displease v offend, annoy, irritate, anger, upset, put out (*infml*), infuriate, exasperate, incense.
⊞ please.

displeasure n offence, annoyance, disapproval, irritation, resentment, disfavour, anger, indignation, wrath.
⊞ pleasure.

disposal n **1** ARRANGEMENT, grouping, order. **2** CONTROL, direction, command. **3** REMOVAL, riddance, discarding, jettisoning.

disposed adj liable, inclined, predisposed, prone, likely, apt, minded, subject, ready, willing.
⊞ disinclined.

dispose of v **1** DEAL WITH, decide, settle. **2** GET RID OF, discard, scrap, destroy, dump (*infml*), ditch (*infml*), jettison.
⊞ **2** keep.

disposition n character, nature, temperament, inclination, make-up, bent, leaning, predisposition, constitution, habit, spirit, tendency, proneness.

disproportionate adj unequal, uneven, incommensurate, excessive, unreasonable.
⊞ balanced.

disprove v refute, rebut, confute, discredit, invalidate, contradict, expose.
⊞ confirm, prove.

dispute v argue, debate, question,

contend, challenge, discuss, doubt, contest, contradict, deny, quarrel, clash, wrangle, squabble.
⊞ agree.
◊ n argument, debate, disagreement, controversy, conflict, contention, quarrel, wrangle, feud, squabble, strife.
⊞ agreement, settlement.

disqualify v **1** INCAPACITATE, disable, invalidate. **2** DEBAR, preclude, rule out, disentitle, eliminate, prohibit.
⊞ **2** qualify, accept.

disquiet n anxiety, concern, worry, nervousness, uneasiness, restlessness, alarm, distress, fretfulness, fear, disturbance, trouble.
⊞ calm, reassurance.

disregard v **1** IGNORE, overlook, discount, neglect, pass over, disobey, make light of, turn a blind eye to (*infml*), brush aside. **2** SLIGHT, snub, despise, disdain, disparage.
⊞ **1** heed, pay attention to.
2 respect.
◊ n neglect, negligence, inattention, oversight, indifference, disrespect, contempt, disdain, brush-off (*infml*).
⊞ attention, heed.

disrepair n dilapidation, decay, deterioration, collapse, ruin, shabbiness.
⊞ good repair.

disreputable adj **1** DISGRACEFUL, discreditable, dishonourable, unrespectable, notorious, infamous, scandalous, shameful, shady, louche, base, contemptible, low, mean, shocking. **2** SCRUFFY, shabby, seedy, unkempt.
⊞ **1** respectable. **2** smart.

disrespectful adj discourteous, rude, impertinent, impolite, impudent, insolent, uncivil, unmannerly, cheeky, insulting, irreverent, contemptuous.
⊞ polite, respectful.

disrupt v disturb, disorganize,

confuse, interrupt, break up, unsettle, intrude, upset.

dissatisfaction n discontent, displeasure, dislike, discomfort, disappointment, frustration, annoyance, irritation, exasperation, regret, resentment.
⊞ satisfaction.

dissect v 1 DISMEMBER, anatomize. 2 ANALYSE, investigate, scrutinize, examine, inspect, pore over.

dissension n disagreement, discord, dissent, dispute, contention, conflict, strife, friction, quarrel.
⊞ agreement.

dissent v disagree, differ, protest, object, refuse, quibble.
⊞ assent.
◇ n disagreement, difference, dissension, discord, resistance, opposition, objection.
⊞ agreement, conformity.

disservice n disfavour, injury, wrong, bad turn, harm, unkindness, injustice.
⊞ favour.

dissident adj disagreeing, differing, dissenting, discordant, nonconformist, heterodox (fml).
⊞ acquiescent, orthodox.
◇ n dissenter, protester, rebel, nonconformist, agitator, schismatic, revolutionary, recusant.
⊞ assenter.

dissimilar adj unlike, different, divergent, disparate, unrelated, incompatible, mismatched, diverse, various, heterogeneous.
⊞ similar, like.

dissipate v 1 he dissipated his inheritance: spend, waste, squander, expend, consume, deplete, fritter away, burn up. 2 the clouds dissipated: disperse, vanish, disappear, dispel, diffuse, evaporate, dissolve.
⊞ 1 accumulate. 2 appear.

dissociate v separate, detach, break

off, disunite, disengage, disconnect, cut off, disband, divorce, disrupt, isolate, segregate.
⊞ associate, join.

dissolute adj dissipated, debauched, degenerate, depraved, wanton, abandoned, corrupt, immoral, licentious, lewd, wild.
⊞ restrained, virtuous.

dissolution n 1 DISINTEGRATION, decomposition, separation, resolution, division. 2 ENDING, termination, conclusion, finish, discontinuation, divorce, dismissal, dispersal, destruction, overthrow. 3 EVAPORATION, disappearance.

dissolve v 1 EVAPORATE, disintegrate, liquefy, melt. 2 DECOMPOSE, disintegrate, disperse, break up, disappear, crumble. 3 END, terminate, separate, sever, divorce.

dissuade v deter, discourage, put off, disincline.
⊞ persuade.

distance n 1 SPACE, interval, gap, extent, range, reach, length, width. 2 ALOOFNESS, reserve, coolness, coldness, remoteness.
⊞ 1 closeness. 2 approachability.

distant adj 1 FAR, faraway, far-flung, out-of-the-way, remote, outlying, abroad, dispersed. 2 ALOOF, cool, reserved, standoffish (infml), formal, cold, restrained, stiff.
⊞ 1 close. 2 approachable.

distaste n dislike, aversion, repugnance, disgust, revulsion, loathing, abhorrence.
⊞ liking.

distasteful adj disagreeable, offensive, unpleasant, objectionable, repulsive, obnoxious, repugnant, unsavoury, loathsome, abhorrent.
⊞ pleasing.

distinct adj 1 SEPARATE, different, detached, individual, dissimilar. 2 CLEAR, plain, evident, obvious, apparent, marked, definite,

noticeable, recognizable.
≠ **2** indistinct, vague.

distinction n **1** DIFFERENTIATION, discrimination, discernment, separation, difference, dissimilarity, contrast. **2** CHARACTERISTIC, peculiarity, individuality, feature, quality, mark. **3** RENOWN, fame, celebrity, prominence, eminence, importance, reputation, greatness, honour, prestige, repute, superiority, worth, merit, excellence, quality.
≠ **3** unimportance, obscurity.

distinctive adj characteristic, distinguishing, individual, peculiar, different, unique, singular, special, original, extraordinary, idiosyncratic.
≠ ordinary, common.

distinguish v **1** DIFFERENTIATE, tell apart, discriminate, determine, categorize, characterize, classify. **2** DISCERN, perceive, identify, ascertain, make out, recognize, see, discriminate.

distinguished adj famous, eminent, celebrated, well-known, acclaimed, illustrious, notable, noted, renowned, famed, honoured, outstanding, striking, marked, extraordinary, conspicuous.
≠ insignificant, obscure, unimpressive.

distort v **1** DEFORM, contort, bend, misshape, disfigure, twist, warp. **2** FALSIFY, misrepresent, pervert, slant, colour, garble.

distract v **1** DIVERT, sidetrack, deflect. **2** CONFUSE, disconcert, bewilder, confound, disturb, perplex, puzzle. **3** AMUSE, occupy, divert, engross.

distraught adj agitated, anxious, overwrought, upset, distressed, distracted, beside oneself, worked up, frantic, hysterical, raving, mad, wild, crazy.
≠ calm, untroubled.

distress n **1** ANGUISH, grief, misery, sorrow, heartache, affliction, suffering, torment, wretchedness, sadness, worry, anxiety, desolation, pain, agony. **2** ADVERSITY, hardship, poverty, need, privation, destitution, misfortune, trouble, difficulties, trial.
≠ **1** content. **2** comfort, ease.
◇ v upset, afflict, grieve, disturb, trouble, sadden, worry, torment, harass, harrow, pain, agonize, bother.
≠ comfort.

distribute v **1** DISPENSE, allocate, dole out, dish out, share, deal, divide, apportion. **2** DELIVER, hand out, spread, issue, circulate, diffuse, disperse, scatter.
≠ **2** collect.

distribution n **1** ALLOCATION, apportionment, division, sharing. **2** CIRCULATION, spreading, scattering, delivery, dissemination, supply, dealing, handling. **3** ARRANGEMENT, grouping, classification, organization.
≠ **2** collection.

district n region, area, quarter, neighbourhood, locality, sector, precinct, parish, locale, community, vicinity, ward.

distrust v mistrust, doubt, disbelieve, suspect, question.
≠ trust.
◇ n mistrust, doubt, disbelief, suspicion, misgiving, wariness, scepticism, question, qualm.
≠ trust.

disturb v **1** DISRUPT, interrupt, distract. **2** AGITATE, unsettle, upset, distress, worry, fluster, annoy, bother. **3** DISARRANGE, disorder, confuse, upset.
≠ **2** reassure. **3** order.

disturbance n **1** DISRUPTION, agitation, interruption, intrusion, upheaval, upset, confusion, annoyance, bother, trouble, hindrance. **2** DISORDER, uproar, commotion, tumult, turmoil, fray, fracas, brawl, riot.
≠ **1** peace. **2** order.

disturbed adj 1 disturbed by the news: anxious, apprehensive, bothered, concerned, troubled, worried, confused, discomposed, upset, uneasy, flustered. 2 emotionally disturbed: maladjusted, neurotic, unbalanced, psychotic, mentally ill, paranoid, upset, screwed-up (infml), hung-up (infml).
⊞ 1 calm.

disuse n neglect, desuetude (fml), abandonment, discontinuance, decay.
⊞ use.

ditch n trench, dyke, channel, gully, furrow, moat, drain, level, watercourse.

dither v hesitate, shilly-shally (infml), waver, vacillate.

dive v plunge, plummet, dip, submerge, jump, leap, nose-dive, fall, drop, swoop, descend, pitch.
◇ n 1 PLUNGE, lunge, header, jump, leap, nose-dive, swoop, dash, spring. 2 (infml) BAR, club, saloon.

diverge v 1 DIVIDE, branch, fork, separate, spread, split. 2 DEVIATE, digress, stray, wander. 3 DIFFER, vary, disagree, dissent, conflict.
⊞ 1 converge. 3 agree.

diverse adj various, varied, varying, sundry, different, differing, assorted, dissimilar, miscellaneous, discrete, separate, several, distinct.
⊞ similar, identical.

diversify v vary, change, expand, branch out, spread out, alter, mix, assort.

diversion n 1 DEVIATION, detour. 2 AMUSEMENT, entertainment, distraction, pastime, recreation, relaxation, play, game. 3 ALTERATION, change.

diversity n variety, dissimilarity, difference, variance, assortment, range, medley.
⊞ similarity, likeness.

divert v 1 DEFLECT, redirect, reroute, sidetrack, avert, distract, switch. 2 AMUSE, entertain, occupy, distract, interest.

divide v 1 SPLIT, separate, part, cut, break up, detach, bisect, disconnect. 2 DISTRIBUTE, share, allocate, deal out, allot, apportion. 3 DISUNITE, separate, estrange, alienate. 4 CLASSIFY, group, sort, grade, segregate.
⊞ 1 join. 2 collect. 3 unite.

divine adj 1 GODLIKE, superhuman, supernatural, celestial, heavenly, angelic, spiritual. 2 HOLY, sacred, sanctified, consecrated, transcendent, exalted, glorious, religious, supreme.
⊞ 1 human. 2 mundane.

divinity n god, goddess, deity, godliness, holiness, sanctity, godhead, spirit.

division n 1 SEPARATION, detaching, parting, cutting, disunion. 2 BREACH, rupture, split, schism, disunion, estrangement, disagreement, feud. 3 DISTRIBUTION, sharing, allotment, apportionment. 4 SECTION, sector, segment, part, department, category, class, compartment, branch.
⊞ 1 union. 2 unity. 3 collection. 4 whole.

divorce n dissolution, annulment, break-up, split-up, rupture, separation, breach, disunion.
◇ v separate, part, annul, split up, sever, dissolve, divide, dissociate.
⊞ marry, unite.

divulge v disclose, reveal, communicate, tell, leak (infml), impart, confess, betray, uncover, let slip, expose, publish, proclaim.

dizzy adj 1 GIDDY, faint, light-headed, woozy (infml), shaky, reeling. 2 CONFUSED, bewildered, dazed, muddled.

do v 1 PERFORM, carry out, execute, accomplish, achieve, fulfil, implement, complete, undertake,

work, put on, present, conclude, end, finish. **2** BEHAVE, act, conduct oneself. **3** FIX, prepare, organize, arrange, deal with, look after, manage, produce, make, create, cause, proceed. **4** SUFFICE, satisfy, serve.
◇ *n* (*infml*) function, affair, event, gathering, party, occasion.
● **do away with** get rid of, dispose of, exterminate, eliminate, abolish, discontinue, remove, destroy, discard, kill, murder.
● **do up 1** FASTEN, tie, lace, pack. **2** RENOVATE, restore, decorate, redecorate, modernize, repair.
● **do without** dispense with, abstain from, forgo, give up, relinquish.

docile *adj* tractable, co-operative, manageable, submissive, obedient, amenable, controlled, obliging.
⊟ truculent, unco-operative.

dock¹ *n* harbour, wharf, quay, boat-yard, pier, waterfront, marina.
◇ *v* anchor, moor, drop anchor, land, berth, put in, tie up.

dock² *v* crop, clip, cut, shorten, curtail, deduct, reduce, lessen, withhold, decrease, subtract, diminish.

doctor *n* physician, medic (*infml*), doc (*infml*), quack (*infml*), clinician.

Types of medical doctor include: general practitioner (GP), family doctor, family practitioner, locum, hospital doctor, houseman, intern, resident, registrar, consultant, medical officer (MO), dentist, veterinary surgeon *or* vet (*infml*).

◇ *v* **1** ALTER, tamper with, falsify, misrepresent, pervert, adulterate, change, disguise, dilute. **2** REPAIR, fix, patch up.

doctrine *n* dogma, creed, belief, tenet, principle, teaching, precept, conviction, opinion, canon.

document *n* paper, certificate, deed, record, report, form, instrument (*fml*).
◇ *v* **1** RECORD, report, chronicle, list, detail, cite. **2** SUPPORT, prove, corroborate, verify.

dodge *v* avoid, elude, evade, swerve, side-step, shirk, shift.
◇ *n* trick, ruse, ploy, wile, scheme, stratagem, machination, manoeuvre.

dog *n* hound, cur, mongrel, canine, puppy, pup, bitch, mutt (*infml*), pooch (*infml*).

Breeds of dog include: Afghan hound, Alsatian, Australian terrier, basset hound, beagle, Border collie, borzoi, bulldog, bull mastiff, bull terrier, cairn terrier, chihuahua, chow, cocker spaniel, collie, corgi, dachshund, Dalmatian, Doberman pinscher, foxhound, fox-terrier, German shepherd, golden retriever, Great Dane, greyhound, husky, Irish setter, Irish wolfhound, Jack Russell, King Charles spaniel, komondor, Labrador, lhasa apso, lurcher, Maltese, Norfolk terrier, Old English sheepdog, Pekingese, pit bull terrier, pointer, poodle, pug, Rottweiler, saluki, sausage dog (*infml*), schnauzer, Scottish terrier *or* Scottie (*infml*), Sealyham, setter, sheltie, shih tzu, springer spaniel, St Bernard, terrier, whippet, West Highland terrier *or* Westie (*infml*), wolfhound, Yorkshire terrier.

◇ *v* pursue, follow, trail, track, tail, hound, shadow, plague, harry, haunt, trouble, worry.

dogged *adj* determined, resolute, persistent, persevering, intent, tenacious, firm, steadfast, staunch, single-minded, indefatigable, steady, unshakable, stubborn, obstinate, relentless, unyielding.
⊟ irresolute, apathetic.

dogma *n* doctrine, creed, belief, precept, principle, article (of faith), credo, tenet, conviction, teaching, opinion.

dogmatic adj opinionated, assertive, authoritative, positive, doctrinaire, dictatorial, doctrinal, categorical, emphatic, overbearing, arbitrary.

dole out v distribute, allocate, hand out, dish out, apportion, allot, mete out, share, divide, deal, issue, ration, dispense, administer, assign.

domain n 1 DOMINION, kingdom, realm, territory, region, empire, lands, province. 2 FIELD, area, speciality, concern, department, sphere, discipline, jurisdiction.

domestic adj 1 HOME, family, household, home-loving, stay-at-home, homely, house-trained, tame, pet, private. 2 INTERNAL, indigenous, native.
◇ n servant, maid, charwoman, char, daily help, daily, au pair.

domesticate v tame, house-train, break, train, accustom, familiarize.

dominant adj 1 AUTHORITATIVE, controlling, governing, ruling, powerful, assertive, influential. 2 PRINCIPAL, main, outstanding, chief, important, predominant, primary, prominent, leading, pre-eminent, prevailing, prevalent, commanding.
⊡ 1 submissive. 2 subordinate.

dominate v 1 CONTROL, domineer, govern, rule, direct, monopolize, master, lead, overrule, prevail, overbear, tyrannize. 2 OVERSHADOW, eclipse, dwarf.

domineering adj overbearing, authoritarian, imperious, autocratic, bossy (infml), dictatorial, despotic, masterful, high-handed, oppressive, tyrannical, arrogant.
⊡ meek, servile.

dominion n 1 POWER, authority, domination, command, control, rule, sway, jurisdiction, government, lordship, mastery, supremacy,

sovereignty. 2 DOMAIN, country, territory, province, colony, realm, kingdom, empire.

donate v give, contribute, present, bequeath, cough up (infml), fork out (infml), bestow (fml), confer (fml), subscribe.
⊡ receive.

donation n gift, present, offering, grant, gratuity, largess(e), contribution, presentation, alms, subscription, benefaction (fml), bequest.

done adj 1 FINISHED, over, completed, ended, concluded, settled, realized, accomplished, executed. 2 CONVENTIONAL, acceptable, proper. 3 COOKED, ready.

donor n giver, donator, benefactor, contributor, philanthropist, provider, fairy godmother (infml).
⊡ beneficiary.

doom n 1 FATE, fortune, destiny, portion, lot. 2 DESTRUCTION, catastrophe, downfall, ruin, death, death-knell. 3 CONDEMNATION, judgement, sentence, verdict.
◇ v condemn, damn, consign, judge, sentence, destine.

doomed adj condemned, damned, fated, ill-fated, ill-omened, cursed, destined, hopeless, luckless, ill-starred.

door n opening, entrance, entry, exit, doorway, portal, hatch.

dope n 1 NARCOTIC, drugs, marijuana, cannabis, opiate, hallucinogen. 2 FOOL, dolt, idiot, half-wit (infml), dimwit (infml), dunce, simpleton, clot (infml), blockhead. 3 INFORMATION, facts, low-down (infml), details.
◇ v drug, sedate, anaesthetize, stupefy, medicate, narcotize, inject, doctor.

dormant adj 1 INACTIVE, asleep, sleeping, inert, resting, slumbering, sluggish, torpid, hibernating, fallow, comatose. 2 LATENT, unrealized,

potential, undeveloped, undisclosed.
⊞ **1** active, awake. **2** realized,
developed.

dose *n* measure, dosage, amount,
portion, quantity, draught, potion,
prescription, shot.
◊ *v* medicate, administer, prescribe,
dispense, treat.

dot *n* point, spot, speck, mark, fleck,
circle, pinpoint, atom, decimal point,
full stop, iota, jot.
◊ *v* spot, sprinkle, stud, dab,
punctuate.

dote on *v* adore, idolize, treasure,
admire, indulge.

double *adj* dual, twofold, twice,
duplicate, twin, paired, doubled,
coupled.
⊞ single, half.
◊ *v* duplicate, enlarge, increase,
repeat, multiply, fold, magnify.
◊ *n* twin, duplicate, copy, clone,
replica, doppelgänger, look-alike,
spitting image (*infml*), ringer (*infml*),
image, counterpart, impersonator.
• **at the double** immediately, at once,
quickly, without delay.

double-cross *v* cheat, swindle,
defraud, trick, con (*infml*), hoodwink,
betray, two-time (*infml*), mislead.

doubt *v* **1** DISTRUST, mistrust,
query, question, suspect, fear. **2** BE
UNCERTAIN, be dubious, hesitate,
vacillate, waver.
⊞ **1** believe, trust.
◊ *n* **1** DISTRUST, suspicion, mistrust,
scepticism, reservation, misgiving,
incredulity, apprehension, hesitation.
2 UNCERTAINTY, difficulty, confusion,
ambiguity, problem, indecision,
perplexity, dilemma, quandary.
⊞ **1** trust, faith. **2** certainty, belief.

doubtful *adj* **1** *doubtful about his
future*: uncertain, unsure, undecided,
suspicious, irresolute, wavering,
hesitant, vacillating, tentative,
sceptical. **2** *writing of doubtful
origin*: dubious, questionable,

unclear, ambiguous, vague, obscure,
debatable.
⊞ **1** certain, decided. **2** definite,
settled.

doubtless *adv* **1** CERTAINLY, without
doubt, undoubtedly, unquestionably,
indisputably, no doubt, clearly,
surely, of course, truly, precisely.
2 PROBABLY, presumably, most likely,
seemingly, supposedly.

dour *adj* **1** GLOOMY, dismal,
forbidding, grim, morose, unfriendly,
dreary, austere, sour, sullen. **2** HARD,
inflexible, unyielding, rigid, severe,
rigorous, strict, obstinate.
⊞ **1** cheerful, bright. **2** easy-going.

douse, dowse *v* **1** SOAK, saturate,
steep, submerge, immerse, dip, duck,
drench, dunk, plunge. **2** EXTINGUISH,
put out, blow out, smother, snuff.

dowdy *adj* unfashionable, ill-
dressed, frumpy, drab, shabby, tatty
(*infml*), frowsy, tacky (*infml*), dingy,
old-fashioned, slovenly.
⊞ fashionable, smart.

down *v* **1** KNOCK DOWN, fell, floor,
prostrate, throw, topple. **2** SWALLOW,
drink, gulp, swig (*infml*), knock back
(*infml*).
• **down and out** destitute,
impoverished, penniless, derelict,
ruined.

downcast *adj* dejected, depressed,
despondent, down, sad, unhappy,
miserable, low, disheartened,
dispirited, blue (*infml*), fed up
(*infml*), discouraged, disappointed,
crestfallen, dismayed.
⊞ cheerful, happy, elated.

downfall *n* fall, ruin, failure,
collapse, destruction, disgrace,
debacle, undoing, overthrow.

downgrade *v* **1** DEGRADE, demote,
lower, humble. **2** DISPARAGE,
denigrate, belittle, run down, decry.
⊞ **1** upgrade, improve. **2** praise.

downhearted *adj* depressed,
dejected, despondent, downcast,

discouraged, disheartened, low-spirited, sad, unhappy, gloomy, glum, dismayed.
⊜ cheerful, enthusiastic.

downpour n cloudburst, deluge, rainstorm, flood, inundation, torrent.

downright adj, adv absolute(ly), outright, plain(ly), utter(ly), clear(ly), complete(ly), out-and-out, frank(ly), explicit(ly).

down-trodden adj oppressed, subjugated, subservient, exploited, trampled on, abused, tyrannized, victimized, helpless.

downward adj descending, declining, downhill, sliding, slipping.
⊜ upward.

dowse see **douse**.

doze v sleep, nod off, drop off, snooze (infml), kip (infml), zizz (sl).
◇ n nap, catnap, siesta, snooze (infml), forty winks (infml), kip (infml), shut-eye (infml), zizz (sl).

drab adj dull, dingy, dreary, dismal, gloomy, flat, grey, lacklustre, cheerless, sombre, shabby.
⊜ bright, cheerful.

draft¹ v draw (up), outline, sketch, plan, design, formulate, compose.
◇ n outline, sketch, plan, delineation, abstract, rough, blueprint, protocol (fml).

draft² n bill of exchange, cheque, money order, letter of credit, postal order.

drag v 1 DRAW, pull, haul, lug, tug, trail, tow. 2 GO SLOWLY, creep, crawl, lag.
◇ n (infml) bore, annoyance, nuisance, pain (infml), bother.

drain v 1 EMPTY, remove, evacuate, draw off, strain, dry, milk, bleed. 2 DISCHARGE, trickle, flow out, leak, ooze. 3 EXHAUST, consume, sap, use up, deplete, drink up, swallow.
⊜ 1 fill.
◇ n 1 CHANNEL, conduit, culvert,

duct, outlet, trench, ditch, pipe, sewer. 2 DEPLETION, exhaustion, sap, strain.

drama n 1 PLAY, acting, theatre, show, spectacle, stagecraft, scene, melodrama. 2 EXCITEMENT, crisis, turmoil.

Forms of drama include: comedy, black comedy, comedy of manners, commedia dell'arte, duologue, farce, fringe theatre, Grand Guignol, kabuki, kitchen-sink, legitimate drama, masque, melodrama, mime, miracle play, monologue, morality play, mummers' play, mystery play, Noh, pantomime, play, theatre-in-the-round, theatre of the absurd, theatre of cruelty, tragedy.

dramatic adj 1 EXCITING, striking, stirring, thrilling, marked, significant, expressive, impressive. 2 HISTRIONIC, exaggerated, melodramatic, flamboyant.

dramatize v 1 STAGE, put on, adapt. 2 ACT, play-act, exaggerate, overdo, overstate.

drape v cover, wrap, hang, fold, drop, suspend.

drastic adj extreme, radical, strong, forceful, severe, harsh, far-reaching, desperate, dire.
⊜ moderate, cautious.

draught n 1 PUFF, current, influx, flow. 2 DRINK, potion, quantity. 3 PULLING, traction.

draw v 1 ATTRACT, allure, entice, bring in, influence, persuade, elicit. 2 PULL, drag, haul, tow, tug. 3 DELINEATE, map out, sketch, portray, trace, pencil, depict, design. 4 TIE, be equal, be even.
⊜ 1 repel. 2 push.
◇ n 1 ATTRACTION, enticement, lure, appeal, bait, interest. 2 TIE, stalemate, dead heat.
• **draw out** protract, extend, prolong,

drag out, spin out, elongate, stretch, lengthen, string out.
🗷 shorten.
• **draw up 1** DRAFT, compose, formulate, prepare, frame, write out.
2 PULL UP, stop, halt, run in.

drawback n disadvantage, snag, hitch, obstacle, impediment, hindrance, difficulty, flaw, fault, fly in the ointment (*infml*), catch, stumbling-block, nuisance, trouble, defect, handicap, deficiency, imperfection.
🗷 advantage, benefit.

drawing n sketch, picture, outline, representation, delineation, portrayal, illustration, cartoon, graphic, portrait.

dread v fear, shrink from, quail, cringe at, flinch, shy, shudder, tremble.
◇ n fear, apprehension, misgiving, trepidation, dismay, alarm, horror, terror, fright, disquiet, worry, qualm.
🗷 confidence, security.

dreadful adj awful, terrible, frightful, horrible, appalling, dire, shocking, ghastly, horrendous, tragic, grievous, hideous, tremendous.
🗷 wonderful, comforting.

dream n **1** VISION, illusion, reverie, trance, fantasy, daydream, nightmare, hallucination, delusion, imagination.
2 ASPIRATION, wish, hope, ambition, desire, pipe dream, ideal, goal, design, speculation.
◇ v imagine, envisage, fancy, fantasize, daydream, hallucinate, conceive, visualize, conjure up, muse.
• **dream up** invent, devise, conceive, think up, imagine, concoct, hatch, create, spin, contrive.

dreamer n idealist, visionary, fantasizer, romancer, daydreamer, star-gazer, theorizer.
🗷 realist, pragmatist.

dreamy adj **1** FANTASTIC, unreal,

imaginary, shadowy, vague, misty.
2 IMPRACTICAL, fanciful, daydreaming, romantic, visionary, faraway, absent, musing, pensive.
🗷 **1** real. **2** practical, down-to-earth.

dreary adj **1** a *dreary job*: boring, tedious, uneventful, dull, humdrum, routine, monotonous, wearisome, commonplace, colourless, lifeless.
2 a *dreary landscape*: gloomy, depressing, drab, dismal, bleak, sombre, sad, mournful.
🗷 **1** interesting. **2** cheerful.

dregs n **1** SEDIMENT, deposit, residue, lees, grounds, scum, dross, trash, waste. **2** OUTCASTS, rabble, riff-raff, scum, down-and-outs.

drench v soak, saturate, steep, wet, douse, souse, immerse, inundate, duck, flood, imbue, drown.

dress n **1** FROCK, gown, robe.
2 CLOTHES, clothing, garments, outfit, costume, garb, get-up (*infml*), gear (*infml*), togs (*infml*).

Types of dress include: evening dress, cocktail dress, pinafore dress, wedding dress, shirtwaister, caftan, kimono, sari.

◇ v **1** CLOTHE, put on, garb, rig, robe, wear, don, decorate, deck, garnish, trim, adorn, fit, drape. **2** ARRANGE, adjust, dispose, prepare, groom, straighten. **3** BANDAGE, tend, treat.
🗷 **1** strip, undress.
• **dress up** beautify, adorn, embellish, improve, deck, doll up, tart up (*infml*), sex up (*sl*), gild, disguise.

dribble v **1** TRICKLE, drip, leak, run, seep, drop, ooze. **2** DROOL, slaver, slobber, drivel.

drift v **1** WANDER, waft, stray, float, freewheel, coast. **2** GATHER, accumulate, pile up, drive.
◇ n **1** ACCUMULATION, mound, pile, bank, mass, heap. **2** TREND, tendency, course, direction, flow, movement, current, rush, sweep. **3** MEANING,

intention, implication, gist, tenor, thrust, significance, aim, design, scope.

drill v 1 TEACH, train, instruct, coach, practise, school, rehearse, exercise, discipline. 2 BORE, pierce, penetrate, puncture, perforate.
◇ n 1 INSTRUCTION, training, practice, coaching, exercise, repetition, tuition, preparation, discipline. 2 BORER, awl, bit, gimlet.

drink v 1 IMBIBE, swallow, sip, drain, down, gulp, swig (*infml*), knock back (*infml*), sup, quaff, absorb, guzzle, partake of (*fml*), swill. 2 GET DRUNK, booze (*infml*), tipple (*infml*), indulge, carouse, revel, tank up (*infml*).
◇ n 1 BEVERAGE, liquid refreshment, draught, sip, swallow, swig (*infml*), gulp. 2 ALCOHOL, spirits, booze (*infml*), liquor, tipple (*infml*), tot, the bottle (*infml*), stiffener (*infml*).

drip v drop, dribble, trickle, plop, drizzle, splash, sprinkle, weep.
◇ n 1 DROP, trickle, dribble, leak, bead, tear. 2 (*infml*) WEAKLING, wimp (*infml*), softy (*infml*), bore, wet (*infml*), ninny (*infml*).

drive v 1 DIRECT, control, manage, operate, run, handle, motivate. 2 FORCE, compel, impel, coerce, constrain, press, push, urge, dragoon, goad, guide, oblige. 3 STEER, motor, propel, ride, travel.
◇ n 1 ENERGY, enterprise, ambition, initiative, get-up-and-go (*infml*), vigour, motivation, determination. 2 CAMPAIGN, crusade, appeal, effort, action. 3 EXCURSION, outing, journey, ride, spin, trip, jaunt. 4 URGE, instinct, impulse, need, desire.
• **drive at** imply, allude to, intimate, mean, suggest, hint, get at, intend, refer to, signify, insinuate, indicate.

driving adj compelling, forceful, vigorous, dynamic, energetic, forthright, heavy, violent, sweeping.

drizzle n mist, mizzle, rain, spray, shower.

◇ v spit, spray, sprinkle, rain, spot, shower.

droop v 1 HANG (DOWN), dangle, sag, bend. 2 LANGUISH, decline, flag, falter, slump, lose heart, wilt, wither, drop, faint, fall down, fade, slouch.
☒ 1 straighten. 2 flourish, rise.

drop n 1 DROPLET, bead, tear, drip, bubble, globule, trickle. 2 DASH, pinch, spot, sip, trace, dab. 3 FALL, decline, falling-off, lowering, downturn, decrease, reduction, slump, plunge, deterioration. 4 DESCENT, precipice, slope, chasm, abyss.
◇ v 1 FALL, sink, decline, plunge, plummet, tumble, dive, descend, lower, droop, depress, diminish. 2 ABANDON, forsake, desert, give up, relinquish, reject, jilt, leave, renounce, throw over, repudiate, cease, discontinue, quit.
☒ 1 rise.
• **drop off 1** NOD OFF, doze, snooze (*infml*), have forty winks (*infml*). 2 DECLINE, fall off, decrease, dwindle, lessen, diminish, slacken. 3 DELIVER, set down, leave.
☒ 1 wake up. 2 increase. 3 pick up.
• **drop out** back out, abandon, cry off, withdraw, forsake, leave, quit.

drought n dryness, aridity, parchedness, dehydration, desiccation, shortage, want.

drove n herd, horde, gathering, crowd, multitude, swarm, throng, flock, company, mob, press.

drown v 1 SUBMERGE, immerse, inundate, go under, flood, sink, deluge, engulf, drench. 2 OVERWHELM, overpower, overcome, swamp, wipe out, extinguish.

drowsy adj sleepy, tired, lethargic, nodding, dreamy, dozy, somnolent (*fml*).
☒ alert, awake.

drudge n toiler, menial, dogsbody (*infml*), hack, servant, slave, factotum, worker, skivvy (*infml*),

galley-slave, lackey.
◇ v plod, toil, work, slave, plug away
(infml), grind (infml), labour, beaver
(infml).
🔁 idle, laze.

drudgery n labour, donkey-work
(infml), hack-work, slog (infml),
grind (infml), slavery, sweat, sweated
labour, toil, skivvying, chore.

drug n medication, medicine,
remedy, potion.

Types of drug include: anaesthetic,
analgesic, antibiotic,
antidepressant, antihistamine,
barbiturate, hallucinogenic,
narcotic, opiate, sedative, steroid,
stimulant, tranquillizer; aspirin,
codeine, paracetamol, morphine,
penicillin, diazepam, temazepam,
Valium®, Prozac®, Viagra®,
cortisone, insulin, digitalis,
laudanum, quinine, cannabis,
marijuana, LSD, acid, ecstasy,
E (sl), heroin, smack (sl), opium,
cocaine, crack, dope (infml). see
also **medicine**.

◇ v medicate, sedate, tranquillize,
dope (infml), anaesthetize, dose,
knock out (infml), stupefy, deaden,
numb.

drum v beat, pulsate, tap, throb,
thrum, tattoo, reverberate, rap.
• **drum up** obtain, round up, collect,
gather, solicit, canvass, petition,
attract.

drunk adj inebriated, intoxicated,
under the influence, drunken,
stoned (sl), legless (sl), paralytic
(infml), sloshed (infml), merry (infml),
tight (infml), tipsy (infml), tanked
up (infml), tiddly (infml), plastered
(infml), loaded (infml), lit up (infml),
sozzled (infml), well-oiled (infml),
canned (sl), blotto (sl).
🔁 sober, temperate, abstinent,
teetotal.

drunkard n drunk, inebriate,

alcoholic, dipsomaniac, boozer
(infml), wino (infml), tippler (infml),
soak (infml), lush (infml), sot (infml).

dry adj 1 ARID, parched, thirsty,
dehydrated, desiccated, barren.
2 BORING, dull, dreary, tedious,
monotonous. 3 dry humour: ironic,
cynical, droll, deadpan, sarcastic,
cutting.
🔁 1 wet. 2 interesting.
◇ v dehydrate, parch, desiccate,
drain, shrivel, wither.
🔁 soak.

dual adj double, twofold, duplicate,
duplex, binary, combined, paired,
twin, matched.

dubious adj 1 DOUBTFUL, uncertain,
undecided, unsure, wavering,
unsettled, suspicious, sceptical,
hesitant. 2 QUESTIONABLE, debatable,
unreliable, ambiguous, suspect,
obscure, fishy (infml), shady (infml).
🔁 1 certain. 2 trustworthy.

duck v 1 CROUCH, stoop, bob,
bend. 2 AVOID, dodge, evade, shirk,
sidestep. 3 DIP, immerse, plunge,
dunk, dive, submerge, douse, souse,
wet, lower.

due adj 1 OWED, owing, payable,
unpaid, outstanding, in arrears.
2 RIGHTFUL, fitting, appropriate,
proper, merited, deserved, justified,
suitable. 3 ADEQUATE, enough,
sufficient, ample, plenty of.
4 EXPECTED, scheduled.
🔁 1 paid. 3 inadequate.
◇ adv exactly, direct(ly), precisely,
straight, dead (infml).

duel n affair of honour, combat,
contest, fight, clash, competition,
rivalry, encounter.

dull adj 1 BORING, uninteresting,
unexciting, flat, dreary, monotonous,
tedious, uneventful, humdrum,
unimaginative, dismal, lifeless, plain,
insipid, heavy. 2 DARK, gloomy,
drab, murky, indistinct, grey,
cloudy, lacklustre, opaque, dim,

overcast. **3** UNINTELLIGENT, dense, dim, dimwitted (*infml*), thick (*infml*), stupid, slow.
⊞ **1** interesting, exciting. **2** bright. **3** intelligent, clever.
◇ *v* **1** BLUNT, alleviate, mitigate, moderate, lessen, relieve, soften. **2** DEADEN, numb, paralyse. **3** DISCOURAGE, dampen, subdue, sadden. **4** DIM, obscure, fade.

dumb *adj* silent, mute, soundless, speechless, tongue-tied, inarticulate, mum (*infml*).

dumbfounded *adj* astonished, amazed, astounded, overwhelmed, speechless, taken aback, thrown (*infml*), startled, overcome, confounded, flabbergasted (*infml*), staggered, confused, bowled over, dumb, floored (*infml*), paralysed.

dummy *n* **1** COPY, duplicate, imitation, counterfeit, substitute. **2** MODEL, lay-figure, mannequin, figure, form. **3** TEAT, pacifier.
◇ *adj* **1** ARTIFICIAL, fake, imitation, false, bogus, mock, sham, phoney. **2** SIMULATED, practice, trial.

dump *v* **1** DEPOSIT, drop, offload, throw down, let fall, unload, empty out, discharge, park. **2** GET RID OF, scrap, throw away, dispose of, ditch, tip, jettison.
◇ *n* **1** RUBBISH TIP, junkyard, rubbish heap, tip. **2** HOVEL, slum, shack, shanty, hole (*infml*), joint (*infml*), pigsty, mess.

dungeon *n* cell, prison, jail, gaol, cage, lock-up, keep, oubliette, vault.

dupe *n* victim, sucker (*infml*), fool, gull, mug (*infml*), pushover (*infml*), fall guy (*infml*), pawn, puppet, instrument, stooge (*infml*), simpleton.
◇ *v* deceive, delude, fool, trick, outwit, con (*infml*), cheat, hoax, swindle, rip off (*infml*), take in, hoodwink, defraud, bamboozle (*infml*).

duplicate *adj* identical, matching,

twin, twofold, corresponding, matched.
◇ *n* copy, replica, clone, reproduction, photocopy, carbon (copy), match, facsimile.
◇ *v* copy, reproduce, repeat, photocopy, double, clone, echo.

durable *adj* lasting, enduring, long-lasting, hard-wearing, strong, sturdy, tough, unfading, substantial, sound, reliable, dependable, stable, resistant, persistent, constant, abiding, permanent, firm, fixed, fast.
⊞ perishable, weak, fragile.

duress *n* constraint, coercion, compulsion, pressure, restraint, threat, force.

dusk *n* twilight, sunset, nightfall, evening, sundown, gloaming, darkness, dark, gloom, shadows, shade.
⊞ dawn, brightness.

dust *n* powder, particles, dirt, earth, soil, ground, grit, grime.

dusty *adj* **1** DIRTY, grubby, filthy. **2** POWDERY, granular, crumbly, chalky, sandy.
⊞ **1** clean. **2** solid, hard.

dutiful *adj* obedient, respectful, conscientious, devoted, filial, reverential, submissive.

duty *n* **1** OBLIGATION, responsibility, assignment, calling, charge, role, task, job, business, function, work, office, service. **2** OBEDIENCE, respect, loyalty. **3** TAX, toll, tariff, levy, customs, excise.
• **on duty** at work, engaged, busy.

dwarf *n* **1** PERSON OF RESTRICTED GROWTH, midget, pygmy, Tom Thumb, Lilliputian. **2** GNOME, goblin.
◇ *adj* miniature, small, tiny, pocket, mini (*infml*), diminutive, petite, Lilliputian, baby.
⊞ large.
◇ *v* **1** STUNT, retard, check. **2** OVERSHADOW, tower over, dominate.

dwell *v* live, inhabit, reside, stay,

settle, populate, people, lodge, rest, abide (*fml*).

dwindle *v* diminish, decrease, decline, lessen, subside, ebb, fade, weaken, taper off, tail off, shrink, peter out, fall, wane, waste away, die out, wither, shrivel, disappear.
⊜ increase, grow.

dye *n* colour, colouring, stain, pigment, tint, tinge.
◇ *v* colour, tint, stain, pigment, tinge, imbue.

dying *adj* moribund, passing, final, going, mortal, not long for this world, perishing, failing, fading, vanishing.
⊜ reviving.

dynamic *adj* forceful, powerful, energetic, vigorous, go-ahead, high-powered, driving, self-starting, spirited, vital, lively, active.
⊜ inactive, apathetic.

dynasty *n* house, line, succession, dominion, regime, government, rule, empire, sovereignty.

Ee

eager adj 1 KEEN, enthusiastic, fervent, intent, earnest, zealous. 2 LONGING, yearning.
⊟ 1 unenthusiastic, indifferent.

ear n 1 ATTENTION, heed, notice, regard. 2 *an ear for language*: perception, sensitivity, discrimination, appreciation, hearing, skill, ability.

Parts of the ear include: anvil (incus), auditory canal, auditory nerve, auricle, cochlea, concha, eardrum, eustachian tube, hammer (malleus), helix, labyrinth, lobe, pinna, semicircular canal, stirrup (stapes), tragus, tympanum, vestibule.

early adj 1 *early symptoms*: forward, advanced, premature, untimely, undeveloped. 2 *early theatre*: primitive, ancient, primeval.
◇ adv ahead of time, in good time, beforehand, in advance, prematurely.
⊟ late.

earn v 1 *earn a good salary*: receive, obtain, make, get, draw, bring in (*infml*), gain, realize, gross, reap. 2 *earn one's reputation*: deserve, merit, warrant, win, rate.
⊟ 1 spend, lose.

earnest adj 1 RESOLUTE, devoted, ardent, conscientious, intent, keen, fervent, firm, fixed, eager, enthusiastic, steady. 2 SERIOUS, sincere, solemn, grave, heartfelt.
⊟ 1 apathetic. 2 frivolous, flippant.

earnings n pay, income, salary, wages, profits, gain, proceeds, reward, receipts, return, revenue, remuneration, stipend.
⊟ expenditure, outgoings.

earth n 1 WORLD, planet, globe, sphere. 2 LAND, ground, soil, clay, loam, sod, humus.

earthenware n pottery, ceramics, crockery, pots.

earthly adj 1 *our earthly life*: material, physical, human, worldly, mortal, mundane, fleshly, secular, sensual, profane, temporal. 2 *no earthly explanation*: possible, likely, conceivable, slightest.
⊟ 1 spiritual, heavenly.

earthy adj crude, coarse, vulgar, bawdy, rough, raunchy (*infml*), down-to-earth, ribald, robust.
⊟ refined, modest.

ease n 1 FACILITY, effortlessness, skilfulness, deftness, dexterity, naturalness, cleverness. 2 COMFORT, contentment, peace, affluence, repose, leisure, relaxation, rest, quiet, happiness.
⊟ 1 difficulty. 2 discomfort.
◇ v 1 *ease the pain*: alleviate, moderate, lessen, lighten, relieve, mitigate, abate, relent, allay, assuage, relax, comfort, calm, soothe, facilitate, smooth. 2 *ease it into position*: inch, steer, slide, still.
⊟ 1 aggravate, intensify, worsen.

easily adv 1 EFFORTLESSLY, comfortably, readily, simply. 2 BY FAR, undoubtedly, indisputably, definitely, certainly, doubtlessly, clearly, far and away, undeniably, simply, surely, probably, well.
⊟ 1 laboriously.

easy adj 1 EFFORTLESS, simple,

uncomplicated, undemanding, straightforward, manageable, cushy (*infml*). 2 RELAXED, carefree, easy-going, comfortable, informal, calm, natural, leisurely.
⊞ 1 difficult, demanding, exacting. 2 tense, uneasy.

easy-going *adj* relaxed, tolerant, laid-back (*infml*), amenable, happy-go-lucky (*infml*), carefree, calm, even-tempered, serene.
⊞ strict, intolerant, critical.

eat *v* 1 CONSUME, feed, swallow, devour, chew, scoff (*infml*), munch, dine. 2 CORRODE, erode, wear away, decay, rot, crumble, dissolve.

eatable *adj* edible, palatable, good, wholesome, shading, comestible (*fml*), harmless.
⊞ inedible, unpalatable.

eavesdrop *v* listen in, spy, overhear, snoop (*infml*), tap (*infml*), bug (*infml*), monitor.

eccentric *adj* odd, peculiar, abnormal, unconventional, strange, quirky, weird, way-out (*infml*), queer, outlandish, idiosyncratic, bizarre, freakish, erratic, singular, dotty.
⊞ conventional, orthodox, normal.
◇ *n* nonconformist, oddball (*infml*), oddity, crank (*infml*), freak (*infml*), character (*infml*).

eccentricity *n* unconventionality, nonconformity, strangeness, peculiarity, abnormality, oddity, weirdness, idiosyncrasy, capriciousness, singularity, quirk, freakishness, aberration, anomaly.
⊞ conventionality, ordinariness.

ecclesiastical *adj* church, churchly, religious, clerical, priestly, divine, spiritual.

echo *v* 1 REVERBERATE, resound, repeat, reflect, reiterate, ring. 2 IMITATE, copy, reproduce, mirror, resemble, mimic.
◇ *n* 1 REVERBERATION, reiteration, repetition, reflection. 2 IMITATION,

copy, reproduction, mirror image, image, parallel.

eclipse *v* 1 BLOT OUT, obscure, cloud, veil, darken, dim. 2 OUTDO, overshadow, outshine, surpass, transcend.
◇ *n* 1 OBSCURATION, overshadowing, darkening, shading, dimming. 2 DECLINE, failure, fall, loss.

economic *adj* 1 COMMERCIAL, business, industrial. 2 FINANCIAL, budgetary, fiscal, monetary. 3 PROFITABLE, profit-making, money making, productive, cost-effective, viable.

economical *adj* 1 THRIFTY, careful, prudent, saving, sparing, frugal. 2 CHEAP, inexpensive, low-priced, reasonable, cost-effective, modest, efficient.
⊞ 1 wasteful. 2 expensive, uneconomical.

economize *v* save, cut back, tighten one's belt (*infml*), cut costs.
⊞ waste, squander.

economy *n* thrift, saving, restraint, prudence, frugality, parsimony, providence, husbandry.
⊞ extravagance.

ecstasy *n* delight, rapture, bliss, elation, joy, euphoria, frenzy, exaltation, fervour.
⊞ misery, torment.

ecstatic *adj* elated, blissful, joyful, rapturous, overjoyed, euphoric, delirious, frenzied, fervent.
⊞ downcast.

eddy *n* whirlpool, swirl, vortex, twist.
◇ *v* swirl, whirl.

edge *n* 1 BORDER, rim, boundary, limit, brim, threshold, brink, fringe, margin, outline, side, verge, line, perimeter, periphery, lip. 2 ADVANTAGE, superiority, force. 3 SHARPNESS, acuteness, keenness, incisiveness, pungency, zest.
◇ *v* creep, inch, ease, sidle.

edgy *adj* on edge, nervous, tense, anxious, ill at ease, keyed up, touchy, irritable.
✹ calm.

edible *adj* eatable, fit to eat, palatable, digestible, wholesome, good, harmless.
✹ inedible.

edict *n* command, order, proclamation, law, decree, rule, regulation, pronouncement, ruling, mandate, statute, fiat, injunction, manifesto.

edifice *n* building, construction, structure, erection.

edify *v* instruct, improve, enlighten, inform, guide, educate, nurture, teach.

edit *v* correct, emend, revise, rewrite, reorder, rearrange, adapt, check, compile, rephrase, select, polish, annotate, censor.

edition *n* copy, volume, impression, printing, issue, version, number.

educate *v* teach, train, instruct, tutor, coach, school, inform, cultivate, edify, drill, improve, discipline, develop.

educated *adj* learned, taught, schooled, trained, knowledgeable, informed, instructed, lettered, cultured, civilized, tutored, refined, well-bred.
✹ uneducated, uncultured.

education *n* teaching, training, schooling, tuition, tutoring, coaching, guidance, instruction, cultivation, culture, scholarship, improvement, enlightenment, knowledge, nurture, development.

Educational terms include: A-level, AS level, assisted place, A2, baccalaureate, bursar, campus, catchment area, classroom, coeducation, Common Entrance, course, curriculum, degree, diploma, eleven-plus, examination, exercise book, final exam, finals, further education, GCSE (General Certificate of Secondary Education), graduation, half-term, head boy, head girl, head teacher, Higher, Advanced Higher, higher education, homework, intake, invigilator, lecture, literacy, matriculation, mixed-ability, modular course, National Curriculum, NVQ (national vocational qualification), numeracy, PTA (parent teacher association), playground, playtime, prefect, primary education, proctor, professor, pupil, qualification, refresher course, register, report, SAT (Student Aptitude Test, Standard Assessment Task), SCE (Scottish Certificate of Education), scholarship, term, secondary education, statemented, streaming, student, student grant, student loan, study, subject, syllabus, teacher, teacher training, tertiary education, test paper, textbook, thesis, timetable, truancy, university entrance, work experience, YTS (Youth Training Scheme). *see also* **school**.

eerie *adj* weird, strange, uncanny, spooky (*infml*), creepy, frightening, scary, spine-chilling.

effect *n* **1** OUTCOME, result, conclusion, consequence, upshot, aftermath, issue. **2** POWER, force, impact, efficacy, impression, strength. **3** MEANING, significance, import.
◇ *v* cause, execute, create, achieve, accomplish, perform, produce, make, initiate, fulfil, complete.
● **in effect** in fact, actually, really, in reality, to all intents and purposes, for all practical purposes, essentially, effectively, virtually.
● **take effect** be effective, become operative, come into force, come into operation, kick in (*infml*), be

implemented, begin, work.

effective adj 1 EFFICIENT, efficacious, productive, adequate, capable, useful. 2 OPERATIVE, in force, functioning, current, active. 3 STRIKING, impressive, forceful, cogent, powerful, persuasive, convincing, telling.
⊜ 1 ineffective, powerless.

effects n belongings, possessions, property, goods, gear (infml), movables, chattels (fml), things, trappings.

effeminate adj unmanly, womanly, womanish, feminine, sissy (infml), delicate.
⊜ manly.

effervescent adj 1 BUBBLY, sparkling, fizzy, frothy, carbonated, foaming. 2 LIVELY, ebullient, vivacious, animated, buoyant, exhilarated, enthusiastic, exuberant, excited, vital.
⊜ 1 flat. 2 dull.

efficiency n effectiveness, competence, proficiency, skill, expertise, skilfulness, capability, ability, productivity.
⊜ inefficiency, incompetence.

efficient adj effective, competent, proficient, skilful, capable, able, productive, well-organized, businesslike, powerful, well-conducted.
⊜ inefficient, incompetent.

effort n 1 EXERTION, strain, application, struggle, trouble, energy, toil, striving, pains, travail (fml). 2 ATTEMPT, try, go (infml), endeavour, shot, stab. 3 ACHIEVEMENT, accomplishment, feat, exploit, production, creation, deed, product, work.

effortless adj easy, simple, facile, undemanding, painless, smooth.
⊜ difficult.

effrontery n audacity, impertinence, insolence, cheek

(infml), impudence, temerity, boldness, brazenness, cheekiness, gall, nerve, presumption, disrespect, arrogance, brashness.
⊜ respect, timidity.

effusive adj fulsome, gushing, unrestrained, expansive, ebullient, demonstrative, profuse, overflowing, enthusiastic, exuberant, extravagant, lavish, talkative, voluble.
⊜ reserved, restrained.

egotism n egoism, egomania, self-centredness, self-importance, conceitedness, self-regard, self-love, self-conceit, narcissism, self-admiration, vanity, bigheadedness (infml).
⊜ humility.

egotistic adj egoistic, egocentric, self-centred, self-important, vain, conceited, swollen-headed (infml), bigheaded (infml), boasting, bragging.
⊜ humble.

ejaculate v 1 DISCHARGE, eject, spurt, emit. 2 EXCLAIM, call, blurt (out), cry, shout, yell, utter, scream.

eject v 1 EMIT, expel, discharge, spout, spew, evacuate, vomit. 2 OUST, evict, throw out, drive out, turn out, expel, remove, banish, deport, dismiss, exile, kick out, fire (infml), sack (infml).

elaborate adj 1 elaborate plans: detailed, careful, thorough, exact, extensive, painstaking, precise, perfected, minute, laboured, studied. 2 elaborate design: intricate, complex, complicated, involved, ornamental, ornate, fancy, decorated, ostentatious, showy, fussy.
⊜ 2 simple, plain.
◇ v amplify, develop, enlarge, expand, flesh out, polish, improve, refine, devise, explain.
⊜ précis, simplify.

elapse v pass, lapse, go by, slip away.

elastic *adj* 1 PLIABLE, flexible, stretchable, supple, resilient, yielding, springy, rubbery, pliant, plastic, bouncy, buoyant. 2 ADAPTABLE, accommodating, flexible, tolerant, adjustable.
⊞ 1 rigid. 2 inflexible.

elasticity *n* 1 PLIABILITY, flexibility, resilience, stretch, springiness, suppleness, give, plasticity, bounce, buoyancy. 2 ADAPTABILITY, flexibility, tolerance, adjustability.
⊞ 1 rigidity. 2 inflexibility.

elated *adj* exhilarated, euphoric, excited, ecstatic, exultant, jubilant, overjoyed, joyful.
⊞ despondent, downcast.

elbow *v* jostle, nudge, push, shove, bump, crowd, knock, shoulder.

elder *adj* older, senior, first-born, ancient.
⊞ younger.

elderly *adj* aging, aged, old, hoary, senile.
⊞ young, youthful.

elect *v* choose, pick, opt for, select, vote for, prefer, adopt, designate, appoint, determine.
◇ *adj* choice, élite, chosen, designated, designate, picked, prospective, selected, -to-be, preferred, hand-picked.

election *n* choice, selection, voting, ballot, poll, appointment, determination, decision, preference.

elector *n* selector, voter, constituent.

electric *adj* electrifying, exciting, stimulating, thrilling, charged, dynamic, stirring, tense, rousing.
⊞ unexciting, flat.

electrify *v* thrill, excite, shock, invigorate, animate, stimulate, stir, rouse, fire, jolt, galvanize, amaze, astonish, astound, stagger.
⊞ bore.

elegant *adj* stylish, chic, fashionable, modish, smart, refined, polished, genteel, smooth, tasteful, fine, exquisite, beautiful, graceful, handsome, delicate, neat, artistic.
⊞ inelegant, unrefined, unfashionable.

elegy *n* dirge, lament, requiem, plaint.

element *n* factor, component, constituent, ingredient, member, part, piece, fragment, feature, trace.
⊞ whole.

elementary *adj* basic, fundamental, rudimentary, principal, primary, introductory, straightforward, clear, easy, uncomplicated, simple.
⊞ advanced.

elements *n* basics, fundamentals, foundations, principles, rudiments, essentials.

elevate *v* 1 LIFT, raise, hoist, heighten, intensify, magnify. 2 EXALT, advance, promote, aggrandize, upgrade. 3 UPLIFT, rouse, boost, brighten.
⊞ 1 lower. 2 downgrade.

elevated *adj* raised, lofty, exalted, high, grand, noble, dignified, sublime.
⊞ base.

elevation *n* 1 RISE, promotion, advancement, preferment, aggrandizement. 2 EXALTATION, loftiness, grandeur, eminence, nobility. 3 HEIGHT, altitude, hill, rise.
⊞ 1 demotion. 3 dip.

elicit *v* evoke, draw out, derive, extract, obtain, exact, extort, cause.

eligible *adj* qualified, fit, appropriate, suitable, acceptable, worthy, proper, desirable.
⊞ ineligible.

eliminate *v* remove, get rid of, cut out, take out, exclude, delete, dispense with, rub out, omit, reject, disregard, dispose of, drop, do away with, eradicate, expel, extinguish,

stamp out, exterminate, knock out, kill, murder.
⊜ include, accept.

élite n best, elect, aristocracy, upper classes, nobility, gentry, crème de la crème, top drawer, establishment, high society.
◇ adj choice, best, exclusive, selected, first-class, top-notch, aristocratic, noble, upper-class.

elocution n delivery, articulation, diction, enunciation, pronunciation, oratory, rhetoric, speech, utterance.

elongated adj lengthened, extended, prolonged, protracted, stretched, long.

elope v run off, run away, decamp, bolt, abscond, do a bunk (infml), escape, steal away, leave, disappear.

eloquent adj articulate, fluent, well-expressed, glib, expressive, vocal, voluble, persuasive, moving, forceful, graceful, plausible, stirring, vivid.
⊜ inarticulate, tongue-tied.

elucidate v explain, clarify, clear up, interpret, spell out, illustrate, unfold.
⊜ confuse.

elude v 1 AVOID, escape, evade, dodge, shirk, duck (infml), flee. 2 PUZZLE, frustrate, baffle, confound, thwart, stump, foil.

elusive adj 1 INDEFINABLE, intangible, unanalysable, subtle, puzzling, baffling, transient, transitory. 2 EVASIVE, shifty, slippery, tricky.

emaciated adj thin, gaunt, lean, haggard, wasted, scrawny, skeletal, pinched, attenuated, meagre, lank.
⊜ plump, well-fed.

emanate v 1 ORIGINATE, proceed, arise, derive, issue, spring, stem, flow, come, emerge. 2 DISCHARGE, send out, emit, give out, give off, radiate.

emancipate v free, liberate, release, set free, enfranchise, deliver,

discharge, loose, unchain, unshackle, unfetter.
⊜ enslave.

embankment n causeway, dam, rampart, levee, earthwork.

embargo n restriction, ban, prohibition, restraint, proscription, bar, barrier, interdiction (fml), impediment, check, hindrance, blockage, stoppage, seizure.

embark v board (ship), go aboard, take ship.
⊜ disembark.
• **embark on** begin, start, commence, set about, launch, undertake, enter, initiate, engage.
⊜ complete, finish.

embarrass v disconcert, mortify, show up, discompose, fluster, humiliate, shame, distress.

embarrassment n 1 SELF-CONSCIOUSNESS, discomposure, chagrin, mortification, humiliation, shame, awkwardness, confusion, bashfulness. 2 DIFFICULTY, constraint, predicament, distress, discomfort.

embellish v adorn, ornament, decorate, deck, dress up, sex up (sl), beautify, gild, garnish, festoon, elaborate, embroider, enrich, exaggerate, enhance, varnish, grace.
⊜ simplify, denude.

embellishment n adornment, ornament, ornamentation, decoration, elaboration, garnish, trimming, gilding, enrichment, enhancement, embroidery, exaggeration.

embezzle v steal, appropriate, misappropriate, pilfer, filch, pinch (infml).

embezzlement n appropriation, misappropriation, pilfering, fraud, stealing, theft, filching.

embittered adj bitter, disaffected, sour, disillusioned.

emblem n symbol, sign, token,

representation, logo, insignia, device, crest, mark, badge, figure.

embodiment n incarnation, personification, exemplification, expression, epitome, example, incorporation, realization, representation, manifestation, concentration.

embody v 1 PERSONIFY, exemplify, represent, stand for, symbolize, incorporate, express, manifest. 2 INCLUDE, contain, integrate.

embrace v 1 HUG, clasp, cuddle, hold, grasp, squeeze. 2 INCLUDE, encompass, incorporate, contain, comprise, cover, involve. 3 ACCEPT, take up, welcome. ◇ n hug, cuddle, clasp, clinch (infml).

embroil v involve, implicate, entangle, enmesh, mix up, incriminate.

embryo n nucleus, germ, beginning, root.

embryonic adj undeveloped, rudimentary, immature, early, germinal, primary. ⊞ developed.

emerge v 1 ARISE, rise, surface, appear, develop, crop up (infml), transpire, turn up, materialize. 2 EMANATE, issue, proceed. ⊞ 1 disappear.

emergence n appearance, rise, advent, coming, dawn, development, arrival, disclosure, issue. ⊞ disappearance.

emergency n crisis, danger, predicament, difficulty, exigency (fml), plight, pinch, strait, quandary.

emigrate v migrate, relocate, move, depart.

eminence n distinction, fame, pre-eminence, prominence, renown, reputation, greatness, importance, esteem, note, prestige, rank.

eminent adj distinguished, famous, prominent, illustrious, outstanding, notable, pre-eminent, prestigious, celebrated, renowned, noteworthy, conspicuous, esteemed, important, well-known, elevated, respected, great, high-ranking, grand, superior. ⊞ unknown, obscure, unimportant.

emissary n ambassador, agent, envoy, messenger, delegate, herald, courier, representative, scout, deputy, spy.

emission n discharge, issue, ejection, emanation, ejaculation, diffusion, transmission, exhalation, radiation, release, exudation, vent.

emit v discharge, issue, eject, emanate, exude, give out, give off, diffuse, radiate, release, shed, vent. ⊞ absorb.

emotion n feeling, passion, sense, sensation, sentiment, ardour, fervour, warmth, reaction, vehemence, excitement.

emotional adj 1 FEELING, passionate, sensitive, responsive, ardent, tender, warm, roused, demonstrative, excitable, enthusiastic, fervent, impassioned, moved, sentimental, zealous, hot-blooded, heated, tempestuous, overcharged, temperamental, fiery. 2 EMOTIVE, moving, poignant, thrilling, touching, stirring, heart-warming, exciting, pathetic. ⊞ 1 unemotional, cold, detached, calm.

emotive adj controversial, delicate, inflammatory, sensitive, awkward, touchy.

emphasis n stress, weight, significance, importance, priority, underscoring, accent, force, power, prominence, pre-eminence, attention, intensity, strength, urgency, positiveness, insistence, mark, moment.

emphasize v stress, accentuate, underline, highlight, accent, feature, dwell on, weight, point up, spotlight,

play up, insist on, press home, intensify, strengthen, punctuate.
⊞ play down, understate.

emphatic adj forceful, positive, insistent, certain, definite, decided, unequivocal, absolute, categorical, earnest, marked, pronounced, significant, strong, striking, vigorous, distinct, energetic, forcible, important, impressive, momentous, powerful, punctuated, telling, vivid, graphic, direct.
⊞ tentative, hesitant, understated.

empire n 1 SUPREMACY, sovereignty, rule, authority, command, government, jurisdiction, control, power, sway. 2 DOMAIN, dominion, kingdom, realm, commonwealth, territory.

employ v 1 ENGAGE, hire, take on, recruit, enlist, commission, retain, fill, occupy, take up. 2 USE, utilize, make use of, apply, bring to bear, ply, exercise.

employee n worker, member of staff, job-holder, hand, wage-earner.

employer n boss, proprietor, owner, manager, gaffer (infml), management, company, firm, business, establishment.

employment n 1 JOB, work, occupation, situation, business, calling, profession, line (infml), vocation, trade, pursuit, craft.
2 ENLISTMENT, employ, engagement, hire.
⊞ 1 unemployment.

empower v authorize, warrant, enable, license, sanction, permit, entitle, commission, delegate, qualify.

emptiness n 1 VACUUM, vacantness, void, hollowness, hunger, bareness, barrenness, desolation. 2 FUTILITY, meaninglessness, worthlessness, aimlessness, ineffectiveness, unreality.
⊞ 1 fullness.

empty adj 1 VACANT, void, unoccupied, uninhabited, unfilled, deserted, bare, hollow, desolate, blank, clear. 2 FUTILE, aimless, meaningless, senseless, trivial, vain, worthless, useless, insubstantial, ineffective, insincere. 3 VACUOUS, inane, expressionless, blank, vacant.
⊞ 1 full. 2 meaningful.
◇ v drain, exhaust, discharge, clear, evacuate, vacate, pour out, unload, void, gut.
⊞ fill.

empty-headed adj inane, silly, frivolous, scatter-brained (infml), feather-brained (infml), ditzy (infml).

emulate v match, copy, mimic, follow, imitate, echo, compete with, contend with, rival, vie with.

enable v equip, qualify, empower, authorize, sanction, warrant, allow, permit, prepare, fit, facilitate, license, commission, endue.
⊞ prevent, inhibit, forbid.

enact v 1 DECREE, ordain, order, authorize, command, legislate, sanction, ratify, pass, establish.
2 ACT (OUT), perform, play, portray, represent, depict.
⊞ 1 repeal, rescind.

enamoured adj charmed, infatuated, in love with, enchanted, captivated, entranced, smitten, keen, taken, fascinated, fond.

enchant v 1 CAPTIVATE, charm, fascinate, enrapture, attract, allure, appeal, delight, thrill. 2 ENTRANCE, enthral, bewitch, spellbind, hypnotize, mesmerize.
⊞ 1 repel.

enclose v encircle, encompass, surround, fence, hedge, hem in, bound, encase, embrace, envelop, hold, shut in, wrap, pen, cover, circumscribe, incorporate, include, insert, contain, comprehend.

enclosure n pen, pound,

compound, paddock, fold, stockade, sty, arena, corral, court, ring, cloister.

encompass v 1 ENCIRCLE, circle, ring, surround, gird, envelop, circumscribe, hem in, enclose, hold. 2 INCLUDE, cover, embrace, contain, comprise, admit, incorporate, involve, embody, comprehend.

encounter v 1 MEET, come across, run into (infml), happen on, chance upon, run across, confront, face, experience. 2 FIGHT, clash with, combat, cross swords with (infml), engage, grapple with, struggle, strive, contend.
◇ n 1 MEETING, brush, confrontation. 2 CLASH, fight, combat, conflict, contest, battle, set-to (infml), dispute, engagement, action, skirmish, run-in, collision.

encourage v 1 HEARTEN, exhort, stimulate, spur, reassure, rally, inspire, incite, egg on (infml), buoy up, cheer, urge, rouse, comfort, console. 2 PROMOTE, advance, aid, boost, forward, further, foster, support, help, strengthen.
⊞ 1 discourage, depress. 2 discourage.

encouragement n 1 REASSURANCE, inspiration, cheer, exhortation, incitement, pep talk (infml), urging, stimulation, consolation, succour (fml). 2 PROMOTION, help, aid, boost, shot in the arm (infml), incentive, support, stimulus.
⊞ 1 discouragement, disapproval.

encouraging adj heartening, promising, hopeful, reassuring, stimulating, uplifting, auspicious, cheering, comforting, bright, rosy, cheerful, satisfactory.
⊞ discouraging.

encroach v intrude, invade, impinge, trespass, infringe, usurp, overstep, make inroads, muscle in (infml).

encumber v burden, overload,

weigh down, saddle, oppress, handicap, hamper, hinder, impede, slow down, obstruct, inconvenience, prevent, retard, cramp.

encumbrance n burden, cumbrance, load, cross, millstone, albatross, difficulty, handicap, impediment, obstruction, obstacle, inconvenience, hindrance, liability.

end n 1 FINISH, conclusion, close, termination, completion, cessation, culmination, dénouement.
2 EXTREMITY, boundary, edge, limit, tip. 3 REMAINDER, tip, butt, leftover, remnant, stub, scrap, fragment. 4 AIM, object, objective, purpose, intention, goal, point, reason, design. 5 RESULT, outcome, consequence, upshot. 6 DEATH, demise, destruction, extermination, downfall, doom, ruin, dissolution.
⊞ 1 beginning, start. 6 birth.
◇ v 1 FINISH, close, cease, conclude, stop, terminate, complete, culminate, wind up. 2 DESTROY, annihilate, exterminate, extinguish, ruin, abolish, dissolve.
⊞ 1 begin, start.

endanger v imperil, hazard, jeopardize, risk, expose, threaten, compromise.
⊞ protect.

endearing adj lovable, charming, appealing, attractive, winsome, delightful, enchanting.

endeavour n attempt, effort, go (infml), try, shot (infml), stab (infml), undertaking, enterprise, aim, venture.
◇ v attempt, try, strive, aim, aspire, undertake, venture, struggle, labour, take pains.

ending n end, close, finish, completion, termination, conclusion, culmination, climax, resolution, consummation, dénouement, finale, epilogue.
⊞ beginning, start.

endless adj 1 INFINITE, boundless,

unlimited, measureless.
2 EVERLASTING, ceaseless, perpetual, constant, continual, continuous, undying, eternal, interminable, monotonous.
≠ **1** finite, limited. **2** temporary.

endorse v **1** APPROVE, sanction, authorize, support, back, affirm, ratify, confirm, vouch for, advocate, warrant, recommend, subscribe to, sustain, adopt. **2** SIGN, countersign.

endorsement n **1** APPROVAL, sanction, authorization, support, backing, affirmation, ratification, confirmation, advocacy, warrant, recommendation, commendation, seal of approval, testimonial, OK (infml). **2** SIGNATURE, countersignature.

endow v bestow, bequeath, leave, will, give, donate, endue (fml), confer, grant, present, award, finance, fund, support, make over, furnish, provide, supply.

endowment n **1** BEQUEST, legacy, award, grant, fund, gift, provision, settlement, donation, bestowal, benefaction, dowry, income, revenue. **2** TALENT, attribute, faculty, gift, ability, quality, flair, genius, qualification.

endurance n fortitude, patience, staying power, stamina, resignation, stoicism, tenacity, perseverance, resolution, stability, persistence, strength, toleration.

endure v **1** endure hardship: bear, stand, put up with, tolerate, weather, brave, cope with, face, go through, experience, submit to, suffer, sustain, swallow, undergo, withstand, stick, stomach, allow, permit, support. **2** a peace that will endure for ever: last, abide (fml), remain, live, survive, stay, persist, hold, prevail.

enemy n adversary, opponent, foe (fml), rival, antagonist, the opposition, competitor, opposer, other side.

≠ friend, ally.

energetic adj lively, vigorous, active, animated, dynamic, forceful, potent, powerful, strenuous, high-powered.
≠ lethargic, sluggish, inactive, idle.

energy n liveliness, vigour, activity, animation, drive, dynamism, get-up-and-go (infml), life, spirit, verve, vivacity, vitality, zest, zeal, ardour, fire, efficiency, force, forcefulness, zip (infml), strength, power, intensity, exertion, stamina.
≠ lethargy, inertia, weakness.

enforce v impose, administer, implement, apply, execute, discharge, insist on, compel, oblige, urge, carry out, constrain, require, coerce, prosecute, reinforce.

engage v **1** PARTICIPATE, take part, embark on, take up, practise, involve. **2** ATTRACT, allure, draw, captivate, charm, catch. **3** OCCUPY, engross, absorb, busy, tie up, grip. **4** EMPLOY, hire, appoint, take on, enlist, enrol, commission, recruit, contract. **5** INTERLOCK, mesh, interconnect, join, interact, attach. **6** FIGHT, battle with, attack, take on, encounter, assail, combat.
≠ **2** repel. **4** dismiss, discharge. **5** disengage.

engaged adj **1** engaged in his work: occupied, busy, engrossed, immersed, absorbed, preoccupied, involved, employed. **2** engaged to be married: promised, betrothed (fml), pledged, spoken for, committed. **3** the phone is engaged: busy, tied up, unavailable.

engagement n **1** APPOINTMENT, meeting, date, arrangement, assignation, fixture, rendezvous. **2** PROMISE, pledge, betrothal (fml), commitment, obligation, assurance, vow, troth (fml). **3** FIGHT, battle, combat, conflict, action, encounter, confrontation, contest.

engaging adj charming, attractive, appealing, captivating, pleasing, delightful, winsome, lovable, likable, pleasant, fetching, fascinating, agreeable.
⊠ repulsive, repellent.

engine n motor, mechanism, machine, appliance, contraption, apparatus, device, instrument, tool, locomotive, dynamo.

Types of engine include: diesel, donkey, dynamo, fuel-injection, internal-combustion, jet, petrol, steam, turbine, turbojet, turboprop, twin-cam, V-engine.

---

engineer n 1 MECHANIC, technician, engine driver. 2 DESIGNER, originator, planner, inventor, deviser, mastermind, architect.
◇ v plan, contrive, devise, manoeuvre, cause, manipulate, control, bring about, mastermind, originate, orchestrate, effect, plot, scheme, manage, create, rig.

engrave v 1 INSCRIBE, cut, carve, chisel, etch, chase. 2 *engraved on her mind*: imprint, impress, fix, stamp, lodge, ingrain.

engraving n print, impression, inscription, carving, etching, woodcut, plate, block, cutting, chiselling, mark.

engross v absorb, occupy, engage, grip, hold, preoccupy, rivet, fascinate, captivate, enthral, arrest, involve, intrigue.
⊠ bore.

enhance v heighten, intensify, increase, improve, elevate, magnify, swell, exalt, raise, lift, boost, strengthen, reinforce, embellish.
⊠ reduce, minimize.

enigma n mystery, riddle, puzzle, conundrum, problem, poser (*infml*), brain-teaser.

enigmatic adj mysterious, puzzling, cryptic, obscure, strange, perplexing.
⊠ simple, straightforward.

enjoy v take pleasure in, delight in, appreciate, like, relish, revel in, be fond of, rejoice in, savour.
⊠ dislike, hate.
• **enjoy oneself** have a good time, have fun, make merry.

enjoyable adj pleasant, agreeable, delightful, pleasing, gratifying, entertaining, amusing, fun, delicious, good, satisfying.
⊠ disagreeable.

enjoyment n 1 PLEASURE, delight, amusement, gratification, entertainment, relish, joy, fun, happiness, diversion, indulgence, recreation, zest, satisfaction.
2 POSSESSION, use, advantage, benefit.
⊠ 1 displeasure.

enlarge v increase, expand, augment, add to, grow, extend, magnify, inflate, swell, wax, stretch, multiply, develop, amplify, blow up, widen, broaden, lengthen, heighten, elaborate.
⊠ diminish, shrink.

enlighten v instruct, edify, educate, inform, illuminate, teach, counsel, apprise, advise.
⊠ confuse.

enlightened adj informed, aware, knowledgeable, educated, civilized, cultivated, refined, sophisticated, conversant, wise, reasonable, liberal, open-minded, literate.
⊠ ignorant, confused.

enlist v engage, enrol, register, sign up, recruit, conscript, employ, volunteer, join (up), gather, muster, secure, obtain, procure, enter.

enmity n animosity, hostility, antagonism, discord, strife, feud, antipathy, acrimony, bitterness, hatred, aversion, ill-will, bad blood, rancour, malevolence, malice, venom.
⊠ friendship.

enormity n atrocity, outrage, iniquity, horror, evil, crime, abomination, monstrosity, wickedness, vileness, depravity, atrociousness, viciousness.

enormous adj huge, immense, vast, gigantic, massive, colossal, gross, gargantuan, monstrous, mammoth, jumbo (infml), tremendous, prodigious.
€ small, tiny.

enough adj sufficient, adequate, ample, plenty, abundant.
◇ n sufficiency, adequacy, plenty, abundance.
◇ adv sufficiently, adequately, reasonably, tolerably, passably, moderately, fairly, satisfactorily, amply.

enquire see inquire.

enquiry see inquiry.

enrage v incense, infuriate, anger, madden, provoke, incite, inflame, exasperate, irritate, rile.
€ calm, placate.

enrich v 1 ENDOW, enhance, improve, refine, develop, cultivate, augment. 2 ADORN, ornament, beautify, embellish, decorate, grace.
€ 1 impoverish.

enrol v 1 REGISTER, enlist, sign on, sign up, join (up), recruit, engage, admit. 2 RECORD, list, note, inscribe.

enrolment n registration, recruitment, enlistment, admission, acceptance.

ensemble n 1 WHOLE, total, entirety, sum, aggregate, set, collection. 2 OUTFIT, costume, get-up (infml), rig-out (infml). 3 GROUP, band, company, troupe, chorus.

ensign n banner, standard, flag, colours, pennant, jack, badge.

enslave v subjugate, subject, dominate, bind, enchain, yoke.
€ free, emancipate.

ensue v follow, issue, proceed, succeed, result, arise, happen, turn out, befall, flow, derive, stem.
€ precede.

ensure v 1 CERTIFY, guarantee, warrant. 2 PROTECT, guard, safeguard, secure.

entail v involve, necessitate, need, occasion, require, demand, cause, give rise to, lead to, result in.

entangle v enmesh, ensnare, embroil, involve, implicate, snare, tangle, entrap, trap, catch, mix up, knot, ravel, muddle.
€ disentangle.

enter v 1 COME IN, go in, arrive, insert, introduce, board, penetrate. 2 RECORD, log, note, register, take down, inscribe. 3 JOIN, embark upon, enrol, enlist, set about, sign up, participate, commence, start, begin.
€ 1 depart. 2 delete.

enterprise n 1 UNDERTAKING, venture, project, plan, effort, operation, programme, endeavour. 2 INITIATIVE, resourcefulness, drive, adventurousness, boldness, get-up-and-go (infml), push, energy, enthusiasm, spirit. 3 BUSINESS, company, firm, establishment, concern.
€ 2 apathy.

enterprising adj venturesome, adventurous, bold, daring, go-ahead, imaginative, resourceful, self-reliant, enthusiastic, energetic, keen, ambitious, aspiring, spirited, active.
€ unenterprising, lethargic.

entertain v 1 AMUSE, divert, please, delight, cheer. 2 RECEIVE, have guests, accommodate, put up, treat. 3 HARBOUR, countenance, contemplate, consider, imagine, conceive.
€ 1 bore. 3 reject.

entertainer

Entertainers include: acrobat, actor, actress, busker, chat-show host, clown, comedian, comic, conjuror, dancer, disc jockey, DJ (*infml*), escapologist, game-show host, hypnotist, ice-skater, impressionist, jester, juggler, magician, mimic, mind-reader, minstrel, musician, presenter, singer, song-and-dance act, stand-up comedian, stripper (*infml*), striptease-artist, trapeze-artist, tight-rope walker, ventriloquist; performer, artiste. *see also* **musician**; **singer**.

---

entertaining *adj* amusing, fun, diverting, delightful, interesting, pleasant, pleasing, humorous, witty.
🔁 boring.

entertainment *n* **1** AMUSEMENT, diversion, recreation, enjoyment, play, pastime, fun, sport, distraction, pleasure. **2** SHOW, spectacle, performance, extravaganza.

Forms of entertainment include: cinema, cartoon, video, DVD, radio, television, theatre, pantomime; chat show, documentary, docusoap, game show, reality television, sitcom, soap opera; dance, disco, discothèque, concert, recital, musical, opera, variety show, music hall, revue, karaoke, cabaret, nightclub, casino; magic show, puppet show, Punch-and-Judy show, circus, gymkhana, waxworks, zoo, rodeo, carnival, pageant, fête, festival, fireworks.

---

enthral *v* captivate, entrance, enchant, fascinate, charm, beguile, thrill, intrigue, hypnotize, mesmerize, engross.
🔁 bore.

enthusiasm *n* zeal, ardour, fervour, passion, keenness, eagerness, vehemence, warmth, frenzy, excitement, earnestness, relish, spirit,

devotion, craze, mania, rage.
🔁 apathy.

enthusiast *n* devotee, zealot, admirer, fan (*infml*), supporter, follower, buff (*infml*), freak (*infml*), fanatic, fiend (*infml*), lover.

enthusiastic *adj* keen, ardent, eager, fervent, vehement, passionate, warm, whole-hearted, zealous, vigorous, spirited, earnest, devoted, avid, excited, exuberant.
🔁 unenthusiastic, apathetic.

entice *v* tempt, lure, attract, seduce, lead on, draw, coax, persuade, induce, sweet-talk (*infml*).

entire *adj* complete, whole, total, full, intact, perfect.
🔁 incomplete, partial.

entirely *adv* completely, wholly, totally, fully, utterly, unreservedly, absolutely, in toto, thoroughly, altogether, perfectly, solely, exclusively, every inch.
🔁 partially.

entitle *v* **1** AUTHORIZE, qualify, empower, enable, allow, permit, license, warrant. **2** NAME, call, term, title, style, christen, dub, label, designate.

entity *n* being, existence, thing, body, creature, individual, organism, substance.

entrance¹ *n* **1** ACCESS, admission, admittance, entry, entrée. **2** ARRIVAL, appearance, debut, initiation, introduction, start. **3** OPENING, way in, door, doorway, gate.
🔁 **2** departure. **3** exit.

entrance² *v* charm, enchant, enrapture, captivate, bewitch, spellbind, fascinate, delight, ravish, transport, hypnotize, mesmerize.
🔁 repel.

entrant *n* **1** NOVICE, beginner, newcomer, initiate, convert, probationer. **2** COMPETITOR, candidate, contestant, contender, entry, participant, player.

entreat v beg, implore, plead with, beseech, crave, supplicate, pray, invoke, ask, petition, request, appeal to.

entreaty n appeal, plea, prayer, petition, supplication, invocation, suit, cry, solicitation, request.

entrench v establish, fix, embed, dig in, ensconce, install, lodge, root, ingrain, settle, seat, plant, anchor, set. ⊠ dislodge.

entrust v trust, commit, confide, consign, authorize, charge, assign, turn over, commend, depute, invest, delegate, deliver.

entry n 1 ENTRANCE, appearance, admittance, admission, access, entrée, introduction. 2 OPENING, entrance, door, doorway, access, threshold, way in, passage, gate. 3 RECORD, item, minute, note, memorandum, statement, account. 4 ENTRANT, competitor, contestant, candidate, participant, player. ⊠ 2 exit.

enumerate v list, name, itemize, cite, detail, specify, count, number, relate, recount, spell out, tell, mention, calculate, quote, recite, reckon.

enunciate v 1 ARTICULATE, express, pronounce, vocalize, voice, say, speak, utter, sound. 2 STATE, declare, proclaim, announce, propound.

envelop v wrap, enfold, enwrap, encase, cover, swathe, shroud, engulf, enclose, encircle, encompass, surround, cloak, veil, blanket, conceal, obscure, hide.

envelope n wrapper, wrapping, cover, case, casing, sheath, covering, shell, skin, jacket, coating.

enviable adj desirable, privileged, favoured, blessed, fortunate, lucky, advantageous, sought-after, excellent, fine. ⊠ unenviable.

envious adj covetous, jealous, resentful, green (with envy), dissatisfied, grudging, jaundiced, green-eyed (infml).

environment n surroundings, conditions, circumstances, milieu, atmosphere, habitat, situation, element, medium, background, ambience, setting, context, territory, domain.

envisage v visualize, imagine, picture, envision, conceive of, preconceive, predict, anticipate, foresee, image, see, contemplate.

envoy n agent, representative, ambassador, diplomat, messenger, legate, emissary, minister, delegate, deputy, courier, intermediary.

envy n covetousness, jealousy, resentfulness, resentment, dissatisfaction, grudge, ill-will, malice, spite. ◇ v covet, resent, begrudge, grudge, crave.

epidemic adj widespread, prevalent, rife, rampant, pandemic, sweeping, wide-ranging, prevailing. ◇ n plague, outbreak, spread, rash, upsurge, wave.

epilogue n afterword, postscript, coda, conclusion. ⊠ foreword, prologue, preface.

episode n 1 INCIDENT, event, occurrence, happening, occasion, circumstance, experience, adventure, matter, business. 2 INSTALMENT, part, chapter, passage, section, scene.

epitome n 1 PERSONIFICATION, embodiment, representation, model, archetype, type, essence. 2 SUMMARY, abstract, abridgement, digest.

epoch n age, era, period, time, date.

equable adj 1 an equable person: even-tempered, placid, calm, serene, unexcitable, tranquil, unflappable, composed, level-headed, easy-going. 2 an equable climate: uniform,

even, consistent, constant, regular, temperate, unvarying, steady, stable, smooth.
🗷 **1** excitable. **2** variable.

equal *adj* **1** IDENTICAL, the same, alike, like, equivalent, corresponding, commensurate, comparable. **2** EVEN, uniform, regular, unvarying, balanced, matched. **3** COMPETENT, able, adequate, fit, capable, suitable.
🗷 **1** different. **2** unequal. **3** unsuitable.
◇ *n* peer, counterpart, equivalent, coequal, match, parallel, twin, fellow.
◇ *v* match, parallel, correspond to, balance, square with, tally with, equalize, equate, rival, level, even.

equality *n* **1** UNIFORMITY, evenness, equivalence, correspondence, balance, parity, par, symmetry, proportion, identity, sameness, likeness. **2** IMPARTIALITY, fairness, justice, egalitarianism.
🗷 **2** inequality.

equalize *v* level, even up, match, equal, equate, draw level, balance, square, standardize, compensate, smooth.

equate *v* compare, liken, match, pair, correspond to, correspond with, balance, parallel, equalize, offset, square, agree, tally, juxtapose.

equation *n* correspondence, equality, equivalence, balancing, agreement, parallel, pairing, comparison, match, likeness, juxtaposition.

equilibrium *n* **1** BALANCE, poise, symmetry, evenness, stability. **2** EQUANIMITY, self-possession, composure, calmness, coolness, serenity.
🗷 **1** imbalance.

equip *v* provide, fit out, supply, furnish, prepare, arm, fit up, kit out, stock, endow, rig, dress, array, deck out.

equipment *n* apparatus, gear, supplies, tackle, rig-out (*infml*), tools, material, furnishings, baggage, outfit, paraphernalia, stuff, things, accessories, furniture.

equivalence *n* identity, parity, correspondence, agreement, likeness, interchangeability, similarity, substitutability, correlation, parallel, conformity, sameness.
🗷 unlikeness, dissimilarity.

equivalent *adj* equal, same, similar, substitutable, corresponding, alike, comparable, interchangeable, even, tantamount, twin.
🗷 unlike, different.

equivocal *adj* ambiguous, vague, uncertain, obscure, evasive, oblique, misleading, dubious, confusing, indefinite.
🗷 unequivocal, clear.

equivocate *v* prevaricate, evade, dodge, fence, beat about the bush (*infml*), hedge, mislead.

era *n* age, epoch, period, date, day, days, time, aeon, stage, century.

eradicate *v* eliminate, annihilate, get rid of, remove, root out, suppress, destroy, exterminate, extinguish, weed out, stamp out, abolish, erase, obliterate.

erase *v* obliterate, rub out, expunge (*fml*), delete, blot out, cancel, efface, get rid of, remove, eradicate.

erect *adj* upright, straight, vertical, upstanding, standing, raised, rigid, stiff.
◇ *v* build, construct, put up, establish, set up, elevate, assemble, found, form, institute, initiate, raise, rear, lift, mount, pitch, create.

erode *v* wear away, eat away, wear down, corrode, abrade, consume, grind down, disintegrate, deteriorate, spoil.

erosion *n* wear, corrosion, abrasion, attrition, denudation, disintegration, deterioration, destruction, undermining.

erotic *adj* aphrodisiac, seductive, sexy, sensual, titillating, suggestive, pornographic, lascivious, stimulating, amorous, amatory, venereal, carnal, lustful, voluptuous.

err *v* **1** MAKE A MISTAKE, be wrong, miscalculate, mistake, misjudge, slip up (*infml*), blunder, misunderstand. **2** DO WRONG, sin, misbehave, go astray, offend, transgress, deviate.

errand *n* commission, charge, mission, assignment, message, task, job, duty.

erratic *adj* changeable, variable, fitful, fluctuating, inconsistent, irregular, unstable, shifting, inconstant, unpredictable, unreliable, aberrant, abnormal, eccentric, desultory, meandering.
⊞ steady, consistent, stable.

erroneous *adj* incorrect, wrong, mistaken, false, untrue, inaccurate, inexact, invalid, illogical, unfounded, faulty, flawed.
⊞ correct, right.

error *n* mistake, inaccuracy, slip, blunder, gaffe, faux pas, solecism, lapse, miscalculation, misunderstanding, misconception, misapprehension, misprint, howler (*infml*), oversight, omission, slip-up (*infml*), fallacy, flaw, fault, wrong.

erudite *adj* learned, scholarly, well-educated, knowledgeable, lettered, educated, well-read, literate, academic, cultured, wise, highbrow, profound.
⊞ illiterate, ignorant.

erupt *v* break out, explode, belch, discharge, burst, gush, spew, spout, eject, expel, emit, flare up, vomit, break.

eruption *n* **1** OUTBURST, discharge, ejection, emission, explosion, flare-up. **2** RASH, outbreak, inflammation.

escalate *v* increase, intensify, grow, accelerate, rise, step up, heighten, raise, spiral, magnify, enlarge, expand, extend, mount, ascend, climb, amplify.
⊞ decrease, diminish.

escapade *n* adventure, exploit, fling, prank, caper, romp, spree, lark (*infml*), antic, stunt, trick.

escape *v* **1** GET AWAY, break free, run away, bolt, abscond, flee, fly, decamp, break loose, break out, do a bunk (*infml*), flit, slip away, shake off, slip. **2** AVOID, evade, elude, dodge, skip, shun. **3** LEAK, seep, flow, drain, gush, issue, discharge, ooze, trickle, pour forth, pass.
◇ *n* **1** GETAWAY, flight, bolt, flit, break-out, decampment, jail-break. **2** AVOIDANCE, evasion. **3** LEAK, seepage, leakage, outflow, gush, drain, discharge, emission, spurt, outpour, emanation. **4** ESCAPISM, diversion, distraction, recreation, relaxation, pastime, safety valve.

escapist *n* dreamer, daydreamer, fantasizer, wishful thinker, non-realist, ostrich (*infml*).
⊞ realist.

escort *n* **1** COMPANION, chaperone, partner, attendant, aide, squire, guide, bodyguard, protector. **2** ENTOURAGE, company, retinue, suite, train, guard, convoy, cortège.
◇ *v* accompany, partner, chaperone, guide, lead, usher, conduct, guard, protect.

esoteric *adj* recondite, obscure, abstruse, cryptic, inscrutable, mysterious, mystic, mystical, occult, hidden, secret, confidential, private, inside.
⊞ well-known, familiar.

especially *adv* **1** CHIEFLY, mainly, principally, primarily, pre-eminently, above all. **2** PARTICULARLY, specially, markedly, notably, exceptionally, outstandingly, expressly, supremely, uniquely, unusually, strikingly, very.

essay n composition, dissertation, paper, article, assignment, thesis, piece, commentary, critique, discourse, treatise, review, leader, tract.

essence n 1 NATURE, being, quintessence, substance, soul, spirit, core, centre, heart, meaning, quality, significance, life, entity, crux, kernel, marrow, pith, character, characteristics, attributes, principle. 2 CONCENTRATE, extract, distillation, spirits.

essential adj 1 FUNDAMENTAL, basic, intrinsic, inherent, principal, main, key, characteristic, definitive, typical, constituent. 2 CRUCIAL, indispensable, necessary, vital, requisite, required, needed, important.
☒ 1 incidental. 2 dispensable, inessential.
◇ n necessity, prerequisite, must, requisite, sine qua non (fml), requirement, basic, fundamental, necessary, principle.
☒ inessential.

establish v 1 SET UP, found, start, form, institute, create, organize, inaugurate, introduce, install, plant, settle, secure, lodge, base. 2 PROVE, substantiate, demonstrate, authenticate, ratify, verify, validate, certify, confirm, affirm.
☒ 1 uproot. 2 refute.

establishment n 1 FORMATION, setting up, founding, creation, foundation, installation, institution, inauguration. 2 BUSINESS, company, firm, institute, organization, concern, institution, enterprise. 3 RULING CLASS, the system, the authorities, the powers that be.

estate n 1 POSSESSIONS, effects, assets, belongings, holdings, property, goods, lands. 2 AREA, development, land, manor. 3 (fml) STATUS, standing, situation, position, class, place, condition, state, rank.

estimate v assess, reckon, evaluate, calculate, gauge, guess, value, conjecture, consider, judge, think, number, count, compute, believe.
◇ n reckoning, valuation, judgement, guess, approximation, assessment, estimation, evaluation, computation, opinion.

estimation n 1 JUDGEMENT, opinion, belief, consideration, estimate, view, evaluation, assessment, reckoning, conception, calculation, computation. 2 RESPECT, regard, appreciation, esteem, credit.

estranged adj divided, separate, alienated, disaffected, antagonized.
☒ reconciled, united.

estuary n inlet, mouth, firth, fjord, creek, arm, sea-loch.

eternal adj 1 eternal bliss: unending, endless, ceaseless, everlasting, never-ending, infinite, limitless, immortal, undying, imperishable. 2 eternal truths: unchanging, timeless, enduring, lasting, perennial, abiding. 3 (infml) eternal quarrelling: constant, continuous, perpetual, incessant, interminable.
☒ 1 ephemeral, temporary. 2 changeable.

eternity n 1 EVERLASTINGNESS, endlessness, forever, everlasting, imperishability, infinity, timelessness, perpetuity, immutability, ages, age, aeon. 2 AFTERLIFE, hereafter, immortality, heaven, paradise, next world, world to come.

ethical adj moral, principled, just, right, proper, virtuous, honourable, fair, upright, righteous, seemly, honest, good, correct, commendable, fitting, noble, meet (fml).
☒ unethical.

ethics n moral values, morality, principles, standards, code, moral philosophy, rules, beliefs, propriety, conscience, equity.

ethnic adj racial, native, indigenous,

traditional, tribal, folk, cultural, national, aboriginal.

ethos n attitude, beliefs, standards, manners, ethics, morality, code, principles, spirit, tenor, rationale, character, disposition.

etiquette n code, formalities, standards, correctness, conventions, customs, protocol (fml), rules, manners, politeness, courtesy, civility, decorum, ceremony, decency.

euphemism n evasion, polite term, substitution, politeness, understatement.

euphoria n elation, ecstasy, bliss, rapture, high spirits, wellbeing, high (infml), exhilaration, exultation, joy, intoxication, jubilation, transport, glee, exaltation, enthusiasm, cheerfulness.
⊞ depression, despondency.

evacuate v 1 LEAVE, depart, quit, withdraw, remove, retire from, clear (out) (infml), abandon, desert, forsake, vacate, decamp, relinquish. 2 EMPTY, eject, void, expel, discharge, eliminate, defecate, purge.

evacuation n 1 DEPARTURE, withdrawal, retreat, exodus, removal, quitting, desertion, abandonment, clearance, relinquishment, retirement, vacation. 2 EMPTYING, expulsion, ejection, discharge, elimination, defecation, urination.

evade v 1 evade one's duties: elude, avoid, escape, dodge, shirk, steer clear of, shun, sidestep, duck (infml), balk, skive (infml), fend off, chicken out (infml), cop out (infml). 2 evade a question: prevaricate, equivocate, fence, fudge, parry, quibble, hedge.
⊞ 1 confront, face.

evaluate v value, assess, appraise, estimate, reckon, calculate, gauge, judge, rate, size up, weigh, compute, rank.

evaluation n valuation, appraisal, assessment, estimation, estimate, judgement, reckoning, calculation, opinion, computation.

evaporate v 1 DISAPPEAR, dematerialize, vanish, melt (away), dissolve, disperse, dispel, dissipate, fade. 2 VAPORIZE, dry, dehydrate, exhale.

evasion n avoidance, escape, dodge, equivocation, excuse, prevarication, put-off, trickery, subterfuge, shirking.
⊞ frankness, directness.

evasive adj equivocating, indirect, prevaricating, devious, shifty (infml), unforthcoming, slippery (infml), misleading, deceitful, deceptive, cagey (infml), oblique, secretive, tricky, cunning.
⊞ direct, frank.

eve n day before, verge, brink, edge, threshold.

even adj 1 LEVEL, flat, smooth, horizontal, flush, parallel, plane. 2 STEADY, unvarying, constant, regular, uniform. 3 EQUAL, balanced, matching, same, similar, like, level, symmetrical, fifty-fifty, side by side, neck and neck (infml), even-stevens (infml). 4 EVEN-TEMPERED, calm, placid, serene, tranquil, composed, unruffled. 5 EVEN-HANDED, balanced, equitable, fair, impartial.
⊞ 1 uneven. 3 unequal.
◇ v smooth, flatten, level, match, regularize, balance, equalize, align, square, stabilize, steady, straighten.

evening n nightfall, dusk, eve, eventide, twilight, sunset, sundown.

event n 1 HAPPENING, occurrence, incident, occasion, affair, circumstance, episode, eventuality, experience, matter, case, adventure, business, fact, possibility, milestone. 2 CONSEQUENCE, result, outcome, conclusion, end, effect, issue, termination. 3 GAME, match, competition, contest, tournament, engagement.

even-tempered adj calm, level-headed, placid, stable, tranquil, serene, composed, cool, steady, peaceful, peaceable.
☞ excitable, erratic.

eventful adj busy, exciting, lively, active, full, interesting, remarkable, significant, memorable, momentous, notable, noteworthy, unforgettable, action-packed (infml).
☞ dull, ordinary.

eventual adj final, ultimate, resulting, concluding, ensuing, future, later, subsequent, prospective, projected, planned, impending.

eventually adv finally, ultimately, at last, in the end, after all, at length, subsequently, sooner or later.

ever adv 1 ALWAYS, evermore, forever, perpetually, constantly, at all times, continually, endlessly. 2 AT ANY TIME, in any case, in any circumstances, at all, on any account.
☞ 1 never.

everlasting adj eternal, undying, never-ending, endless, immortal, infinite, imperishable, constant, permanent, perpetual, indestructible, timeless.
☞ temporary, transient.

everyday adj ordinary, common, commonplace, day-to-day, familiar, run-of-the-mill, regular, plain, routine, usual, workaday, common-or-garden (infml), normal, customary, stock, accustomed, conventional, daily, habitual, monotonous, frequent, simple, informal.
☞ unusual, exceptional, special.

everyone n everybody, one and all, each one, all and sundry, the whole world.

everything n all, all things, each thing, the lot, the whole lot, the entirety, the sum, the total, lock, stock and barrel, the aggregate (fml),

the whole caboodle (infml), the whole shooting-match (infml), the whole bag of tricks (infml).

everywhere adv all around, all over, throughout, far and near, far and wide, high and low, ubiquitous, left, right and centre (infml).

evict v expel, eject, dispossess, put out, turn out, turf out (infml), kick out (infml), force out, remove, cast out, chuck out (infml), oust, dislodge, expropriate.

evidence n 1 PROOF, verification, confirmation, affirmation, grounds, substantiation, documentation, data. 2 TESTIMONY, declaration. 3 INDICATION, manifestation, suggestion, sign, mark, hint, demonstration, token.

evident adj clear, obvious, manifest, apparent, plain, patent, visible, conspicuous, noticeable, clear-cut, unmistakable, perceptible, distinct, discernible, tangible, incontestable, indisputable, incontrovertible.

evidently adv clearly, apparently, plainly, patently, manifestly, obviously, seemingly, undoubtedly, doubtlessly, indisputably.

evil adj 1 WICKED, wrong, sinful, bad, immoral, vicious, vile, malevolent, iniquitous, cruel, base, corrupt, heinous, malicious, malignant, devilish, depraved, mischievous. 2 HARMFUL, pernicious, destructive, deadly, detrimental, hurtful, poisonous. 3 DISASTROUS, ruinous, calamitous, catastrophic, adverse, dire, inauspicious. 4 OFFENSIVE, noxious, foul.
◇ n 1 WICKEDNESS, wrongdoing, wrong, immorality, badness, sin, sinfulness, vice, viciousness, iniquity, depravity, baseness, corruption, malignity, mischief, heinousness. 2 ADVERSITY, affliction, calamity, disaster, misfortune, suffering, sorrow, ruin, catastrophe, blow, curse, distress, hurt, harm, ill, injury, misery, woe.

evoke v summon (up), call, elicit, invoke, arouse, stir, raise, stimulate, call forth, call up, conjure up, awaken, provoke, excite, recall. ⊞ suppress.

evolution n development, growth, progression, progress, expansion, increase, ripening, derivation, descent.

evolve v develop, grow, increase, mature, progress, unravel, expand, enlarge, emerge, descend, derive, result, elaborate.

exact adj 1 PRECISE, accurate, correct, faithful, literal, flawless, faultless, right, true, veracious, definite, explicit, detailed, specific, strict, unerring, close, factual, identical, express, word-perfect, blow-by-blow (infml). 2 CAREFUL, scrupulous, particular, rigorous, methodical, meticulous, orderly, painstaking. ⊞ 1 inexact, imprecise.
◇ v extort, extract, claim, insist on, wrest, wring, compel, demand, command, force, impose, require, squeeze, milk (infml).

exacting adj demanding, difficult, hard, laborious, arduous, rigorous, taxing, tough, harsh, painstaking, severe, strict, unsparing. ⊞ easy.

exactly adv 1 PRECISELY, accurately, literally, faithfully, correctly, specifically, rigorously, scrupulously, veraciously, verbatim, carefully, faultlessly, unerringly, strictly, to the letter, particularly, methodically, explicitly, expressly, dead (infml). 2 ABSOLUTELY, definitely, precisely, indeed, certainly, truly, quite, just, unequivocally. ⊞ 1 inaccurately, roughly.

exaggerate v overstate, overdo, magnify, overemphasize, emphasize, embellish, embroider, enlarge, amplify, oversell, pile it on (infml). ⊞ understate.

examination n 1 INSPECTION, inquiry, scrutiny, study, survey, search, analysis, exploration, investigation, probe, appraisal, observation, research, review, scan, once-over (infml), perusal, check, check-up, audit, critique. 2 TEST, exam, quiz, questioning, cross-examination, cross-questioning, trial, inquisition, interrogation, viva.

examine v 1 INSPECT, investigate, scrutinize, study, survey, analyse, explore, inquire, consider, probe, review, scan, check (out), ponder, pore over, sift, vet, weigh up, appraise, assay, audit, peruse, case (sl). 2 TEST, quiz, question, cross-examine, cross-question, interrogate, grill (infml), catechize (fml).

example n instance, case, case in point, illustration, exemplification, sample, specimen, model, pattern, ideal, archetype, prototype, standard, type, lesson, citation.

exasperate v infuriate, annoy, anger, incense, irritate, madden, provoke, get on someone's nerves, enrage, irk, rile, rankle, rouse, get to (infml), goad, vex. ⊞ appease, pacify.

excavate v dig (out), dig up, hollow, burrow, tunnel, delve, unearth, gouge, scoop, mine, quarry, disinter, exhume, uncover.

excavation n hole, hollow, pit, quarry, mine, dugout, dig, diggings, burrow, cavity, crater, trench, trough, shaft, ditch, cutting.

exceed v surpass, outdo, outstrip, beat, better, pass, overtake, top, outshine, eclipse, outreach, outrun, transcend, cap, overdo, overstep.

excel v 1 SURPASS, outdo, beat, outclass, outperform, outrank, eclipse, better. 2 BE EXCELLENT, succeed, shine, stand out, predominate.

excellence n superiority, pre-eminence, distinction, merit, supremacy, quality, worth, fineness, eminence, goodness, greatness, virtue, perfection, purity.

excellent *adj* superior, first-class, first-rate, prime, superlative, unequalled, outstanding, surpassing, remarkable, distinguished, great, good, exemplary, select, superb, admirable, commendable, top-notch (*infml*), splendid, noteworthy, notable, fine, wonderful, worthy, stellar (*infml*).
🗷 inferior, second-rate.

except *prep* excepting, but, apart from, other than, save, omitting, not counting, leaving out, excluding, except for, besides, bar, minus, less.
◇ *v* leave out, omit, bar, exclude, reject, rule out.

exception *n* oddity, anomaly, deviation, abnormality, irregularity, peculiarity, inconsistency, rarity, special case, quirk.

exceptional *adj* 1 ABNORMAL, unusual, anomalous, strange, odd, irregular, extraordinary, peculiar, special, rare, uncommon. 2 OUTSTANDING, remarkable, phenomenal, prodigious, notable, noteworthy, superior, unequalled, marvellous.
🗷 1 normal. 2 mediocre.

excerpt *n* extract, passage, portion, section, selection, quote, quotation, part, citation, scrap, fragment.

excess *n* 1 SURFEIT, overabundance, surplus, glut, plethora, superfluity, superabundance, overflow, overkill, remainder, leftover. 2 OVERINDULGENCE, dissipation, immoderateness, intemperance, extravagance, unrestraint, debauchery.
🗷 1 deficiency. 2 restraint.
◇ *adj* extra, surplus, spare, redundant, remaining, residual, leftover, additional, superfluous, supernumerary.
🗷 inadequate.

excessive *adj* immoderate, inordinate, extreme, undue, uncalled-for, disproportionate, unnecessary, unneeded, superfluous, unreasonable, exorbitant, steep (*infml*), extravagant, OTT (*infml*).
🗷 insufficient.

exchange *v* barter, change, trade, swap, switch, replace, interchange, convert, commute, substitute, reciprocate, bargain, bandy.
◇ *n* 1 CONVERSATION, discussion, chat. 2 TRADE, commerce, dealing, market, traffic, barter, bargain. 3 INTERCHANGE, swap, switch, replacement, substitution, reciprocity.

excitable *adj* temperamental, volatile, passionate, emotional, highly-strung, fiery, hot-headed, hasty, nervous, hot-tempered, irascible, quick-tempered, sensitive, susceptible.
🗷 calm, stable.

excite *v* 1 MOVE, agitate, disturb, upset, touch, stir up, thrill, elate, turn on (*infml*), impress. 2 AROUSE, rouse, animate, awaken, fire, inflame, kindle, motivate, stimulate, engender, inspire, instigate, incite, induce, ignite, galvanize, generate, provoke, sway, quicken, evoke.
🗷 1 calm.

excited *adj* aroused, roused, stimulated, stirred, thrilled, elated, enthusiastic, eager, moved, high (*infml*), worked up, wrought-up, overwrought, restless, frantic, frenzied, wild, hyper (*infml*).
🗷 calm, apathetic.

excitement *n* 1 UNREST, ado, action, activity, commotion, fuss, tumult, flurry, furore, adventure. 2 DISCOMPOSURE, agitation, passion, thrill, animation, elation, enthusiasm, restlessness, kicks (*infml*), ferment, fever, eagerness, stimulation.
🗷 1 calm. 2 apathy.

exciting *adj* stimulating, stirring, intoxicating, exhilarating, thrilling,

rousing, moving, enthralling, electrifying, nail-biting (*infml*), white-knuckle (*infml*), action-packed (*infml*), cliff-hanging (*infml*), striking, sensational, provocative, inspiring, interesting.
⊞ dull, unexciting.

exclaim v cry (out), declare, blurt (out), call, yell, shout, proclaim, utter.

exclamation n cry, call, yell, shout, expletive, interjection, ejaculation, outcry, utterance.

exclude v 1 BAN, bar, prohibit, disallow, veto, proscribe, forbid, blacklist. 2 OMIT, leave out, keep out, refuse, reject, ignore, shut out, rule out, ostracize, eliminate. 3 EXPEL, eject, evict, excommunicate.
⊞ 1 admit. 2 include.

exclusive adj 1 SOLE, single, unique, only, undivided, unshared, whole, total, peculiar. 2 RESTRICTED, limited, closed, private, narrow, restrictive, choice, select, discriminative, cliquey, chic, classy (*infml*), elegant, fashionable, posh (*infml*), snobbish.

excruciating adj agonizing, painful, severe, tormenting, unbearable, insufferable, acute, intolerable, intense, sharp, piercing, extreme, atrocious, racking, harrowing, savage, burning, bitter.

excursion n outing, trip, jaunt, expedition, day trip, awayday, journey, tour, airing, breather, junket (*infml*), ride, drive, walk, ramble.

excuse v 1 FORGIVE, pardon, overlook, absolve, acquit, exonerate, tolerate, ignore, indulge. 2 RELEASE, free, discharge, liberate, let off, relieve, spare, exempt. 3 CONDONE, explain, mitigate, justify, vindicate, defend, apologize for.
⊞ 1 criticize. 2 punish.
◇ n justification, explanation, vindication, grounds, defence, plea, alibi, reason, apology, pretext, pretence, exoneration, evasion, cop-

out (*infml*), shift, substitute.

execute v 1 PUT TO DEATH, kill, liquidate, hang, electrocute, shoot, guillotine, decapitate, behead. 2 CARRY OUT, perform, do, accomplish, achieve, fulfil, complete, discharge, effect, enact, deliver, enforce, finish, implement, administer, consummate, realize, dispatch, expedite, validate, serve, render, sign.

execution n 1 DEATH PENALTY, capital punishment, killing, hanging, electrocution, firing squad, shooting, guillotining, decapitation, beheading. 2 ACCOMPLISHMENT, operation, performance, completion, achievement, administration, effect, enactment, implementation, realization, discharge, dispatch, consummation, enforcement. 3 STYLE, technique, rendition, delivery, performance, manner, mode.

executive n 1 ADMINISTRATION, management, government, leadership, hierarchy.
2 ADMINISTRATOR, manager, organizer, leader, controller, director, governor, official, chairperson.
◇ adj administrative, managerial, controlling, supervisory, regulating, decision-making, governing, organizing, directing, directorial, organizational, leading, guiding.

exemplary adj 1 MODEL, ideal, perfect, admirable, excellent, faultless, flawless, correct, good, commendable, praiseworthy, worthy, laudable, estimable, honourable.
2 CAUTIONARY, warning.
⊞ 1 imperfect, unworthy.

exemplify v illustrate, demonstrate, show, instance, represent, typify, manifest, embody, epitomize, exhibit, depict, display.

exempt v excuse, release, relieve, let off, free, absolve, discharge, dismiss, liberate, spare.
◇ adj excused, not liable, immune,

free, released, spared, absolved, discharged, excluded, liberated, clear.
☒ liable.

exercise v 1 USE, utilize, employ, apply, exert, practise, wield, try, discharge. 2 TRAIN, drill, practise, work out, keep fit. 3 WORRY, disturb, trouble, upset, burden, distress, vex, annoy, agitate, afflict.
◇ n 1 TRAINING, drill, practice, effort, exertion, task, lesson, work, discipline, activity, physical jerks (infml), work-out, aerobics, labour. 2 USE, utilization, employment, application, implementation, practice, operation, discharge, assignment, fulfilment, accomplishment.

exert v use, utilize, employ, apply, exercise, bring to bear, wield, expend.
• **exert oneself** strive, struggle, strain, make every effort, take pains, toil, labour, work, sweat (infml), endeavour, apply oneself.

exertion n 1 EFFORT, industry, labour, toil, work, struggle, diligence, assiduousness, perseverance, pains, endeavour, attempt, strain, travail (fml), trial. 2 USE, utilization, employment, application, exercise, operation, action.
☒ 1 idleness, rest.

exhaust v 1 CONSUME, empty, deplete, drain, sap, spend, waste, squander, dissipate, impoverish, use up, finish, dry, bankrupt. 2 TIRE (OUT), weary, fatigue, tax, strain, weaken, overwork, wear out.
☒ 1 renew. 2 refresh.
◇ n emission, exhalation, discharge, fumes.

exhausted adj 1 EMPTY, finished, depleted, spent, used up, drained, dry, worn out, void. 2 TIRED (OUT), dead tired, dead-beat (infml), all in (infml), done in (infml), fatigued, weak, washed-out, whacked (infml),

knackered (infml), jaded.
☒ 1 fresh. 2 vigorous.

exhausting adj tiring, strenuous, taxing, gruelling, arduous, hard, laborious, backbreaking, draining, severe, testing, punishing, formidable, debilitating.
☒ refreshing.

exhaustion n fatigue, tiredness, weariness, debility, feebleness, jet lag.
☒ freshness, liveliness.

exhaustive adj comprehensive, all-embracing, all-inclusive, far-reaching, complete, extensive, encyclopedic, full-scale, thorough, full, in-depth, intensive, detailed, definitive, all-out, sweeping.
☒ incomplete, restricted.

exhibit v display, show, present, demonstrate, manifest, expose, parade, reveal, express, disclose, indicate, air, flaunt, offer.
☒ conceal.
◇ n display, exhibition, show, illustration, model.

exhibition n display, show, demonstration, demo (infml), exhibit, presentation, manifestation, spectacle, exposition, expo (infml), showing, fair, performance, airing, representation, showcase.

exhilarate v thrill, excite, elate, animate, enliven, invigorate, vitalize, stimulate.
☒ bore.

exile n 1 BANISHMENT, deportation, expatriation, expulsion, ostracism, transportation. 2 EXPATRIATE, refugee, émigré, deportee, outcast.
◇ v banish, expel, deport, expatriate, drive out, ostracize, oust.

exist v 1 BE, live, abide, continue, endure, have one's being, breathe, prevail. 2 SUBSIST, survive. 3 BE PRESENT, occur, happen, be available, remain.

existence n 1 BEING, life, reality,

actuality, continuance, continuation, endurance, survival, breath, subsistence. **2** CREATION, the world. **3** (*fml*) ENTITY, creature, thing.
⊞ **1** death, non-existence.

exit *n* **1** DEPARTURE, going, retreat, withdrawal, leave-taking, retirement, farewell, exodus. **2** DOOR, way out, doorway, gate, vent.
⊞ **1** entrance, arrival. **2** entrance.
◇ *v* depart, leave, go, retire, retreat, withdraw, take one's leave, issue.
⊞ arrive, enter.

exonerate *v* **1** ABSOLVE, acquit, clear, vindicate, exculpate (*fml*), justify, pardon, discharge. **2** EXEMPT, excuse, spare, let off, release, relieve.
⊞ **1** incriminate.

exorbitant *adj* excessive, unreasonable, unwarranted, undue, inordinate, immoderate, extravagant, extortionate, enormous, preposterous.
⊞ reasonable, moderate.

exorcize *v* cast out, drive out, free, expel, purify, adjure (*fml*).

exotic *adj* **1** FOREIGN, alien, imported, introduced. **2** UNUSUAL, striking, different, unfamiliar, extraordinary, bizarre, curious, strange, fascinating, colourful, peculiar, outlandish.
⊞ **1** native. **2** ordinary.

expand *v* **1** STRETCH, swell, widen, lengthen, thicken, magnify, multiply, inflate, broaden, blow up, open out, fill out, fatten. **2** INCREASE, grow, extend, enlarge, develop, amplify, spread, branch out, diversify, elaborate.
⊞ **1** contract.

expanse *n* extent, space, area, breadth, range, stretch, sweep, field, plain, tract.

expansive *adj* **1** FRIENDLY, genial, outgoing, open, affable, sociable, talkative, warm, communicative, effusive. **2** EXTENSIVE, broad, comprehensive, wide-ranging, all-

embracing, thorough.
⊞ **1** reserved, cold. **2** restricted, narrow.

expect *v* **1** *expect the money soon*: anticipate, await, look forward to, hope for, look for, bank on, bargain for, envisage, predict, forecast, contemplate, project, foresee. **2** *expect you to comply*: require, want, wish, insist on, demand, rely on, count on. **3** *expect you're right*: suppose, surmise, assume, believe, think, presume, imagine, reckon, guess (*infml*), trust.

expectant *adj* **1** AWAITING, anticipating, hopeful, in suspense, ready, apprehensive, anxious, watchful, eager, curious. **2** PREGNANT, expecting (*infml*), with child (*fml*).

expedition *n* **1** JOURNEY, excursion, trip, voyage, tour, exploration, trek, safari, hike, sail, ramble, raid, quest, pilgrimage, mission, crusade. **2** (*fml*) PROMPTNESS, speed, alacrity, haste.

expel *v* **1** DRIVE OUT, eject, evict, banish, throw out, ban, bar, oust, exile, expatriate. **2** DISCHARGE, evacuate, void, cast out.
⊞ **1** welcome.

expend *v* **1** SPEND, pay, disburse (*fml*), fork out (*infml*). **2** CONSUME, use up, dissipate, exhaust, employ.
⊞ **1** save. **2** conserve.

expenditure *n* spending, expense, outlay, outgoings, disbursement (*fml*), payment, output.
⊞ income.

expense *n* spending, expenditure, disbursement (*fml*), outlay, payment, loss, cost, charge.

expensive *adj* dear, high-priced, costly, exorbitant, extortionate, steep (*infml*), extravagant, lavish.
⊞ cheap, inexpensive.

experience *n* **1** KNOWLEDGE, familiarity, know-how, involvement, participation, practice, training, understanding. **2** INCIDENT, event,

episode, happening, encounter, occurrence, adventure.
⊠ **1** inexperience.
◇ *v* undergo, go through, live through, suffer, feel, endure, encounter, face, meet, know, try, perceive, sustain.

experienced *adj* **1** PRACTISED, knowledgeable, familiar, capable, competent, well-versed, expert, accomplished, qualified, skilled, tried, trained, professional. **2** MATURE, seasoned, wise, veteran.
⊠ **1** inexperienced, unskilled.

experiment *n* trial, test, investigation, experimentation, research, examination, trial run, venture, trial and error, attempt, procedure, proof.
◇ *v* try, test, investigate, examine, research, sample, verify.

experimental *adj* trial, test, exploratory, empirical (*fml*), tentative, provisional, speculative, pilot, preliminary, trial-and-error.

expert *n* specialist, connoisseur, authority, professional, pro (*infml*), dab hand (*infml*), maestro, virtuoso.
◇ *adj* proficient, adept, skilled, skilful, knowledgeable, experienced, able, practised, professional, masterly, specialist, qualified, virtuoso.
⊠ amateurish, novice.

expertise *n* expertness, proficiency, skill, skilfulness, know-how, knack (*infml*), knowledge, mastery, dexterity, virtuosity.
⊠ inexperience.

expire *v* end, cease, finish, stop, terminate, close, conclude, discontinue, run out, lapse, die, depart, decease, perish.
⊠ begin.

explain *v* **1** INTERPRET, clarify, describe, define, make clear, elucidate, simplify, resolve, solve, spell out, translate, unfold, unravel,

untangle, illustrate, demonstrate, disclose, expound, teach. **2** JUSTIFY, excuse, account for, rationalize.
⊠ **1** obscure, confound.

explanation *n* **1** INTERPRETATION, clarification, definition, elucidation, illustration, demonstration, account, description, exegesis (*fml*). **2** JUSTIFICATION, excuse, warrant, rationalization. **3** ANSWER, meaning, motive, reason, key, sense, significance.

explanatory *adj* descriptive, interpretive, explicative, demonstrative, expository (*fml*), justifying.

explicit *adj* **1** CLEAR, distinct, exact, categorical, absolute, certain, positive, precise, specific, unambiguous, express, definite, declared, detailed, stated.
2 OPEN, direct, frank, outspoken, straightforward, unreserved, plain.
⊠ **1** implicit, unspoken, vague.

explode *v* **1** BLOW UP, burst, go off, set off, detonate, discharge, blast, erupt. **2** DISCREDIT, disprove, give the lie to, debunk, invalidate, refute, rebut, repudiate.
⊠ **2** prove, confirm.

exploit *n* deed, feat, adventure, achievement, accomplishment, attainment, stunt.
◇ *v* **1** USE, utilize, capitalize on, profit by, turn to account, take advantage of, cash in on, make capital out of. **2** MISUSE, abuse, oppress, ill-treat, impose on, manipulate, rip off (*infml*), fleece (*infml*).

exploration *n* **1** INVESTIGATION, examination, inquiry, research, scrutiny, study, inspection, analysis, probe. **2** EXPEDITION, survey, reconnaissance, search, trip, tour, voyage, travel, safari.

explore *v* **1** INVESTIGATE, examine, inspect, research, scrutinize, probe, analyse. **2** TRAVEL, tour, search, reconnoitre, prospect, scout, survey.

explosion n detonation, blast, burst, outburst, discharge, eruption, bang, outbreak, clap, crack, fit, report.

explosive adj unstable, volatile, sensitive, tense, fraught, charged, touchy, overwrought, dangerous, hazardous, perilous, stormy.
⊜ stable, calm.

exponent n 1 ADVOCATE, promoter, supporter, upholder, defender, backer, adherent, spokesman, spokeswoman, spokesperson, champion, proponent (fml).
2 PRACTITIONER, adept, expert, master, specialist, player, performer.

export v trade, deal with, sell abroad/overseas, traffic in, transport.
◇ n exported product/commodity/goods, transfer, trade, foreign trade, international trade.

expose v 1 REVEAL, show, exhibit, display, disclose, uncover, bring to light, present, manifest, detect, divulge, unveil, unmask, denounce.
2 ENDANGER, jeopardize, imperil, risk, hazard.
⊜ 1 conceal. 2 cover up.

exposed adj bare, open, revealed, laid bare, unprotected, vulnerable, exhibited, on display, on show, on view, shown, susceptible.
⊜ covered, sheltered.

exposure n 1 REVELATION, uncovering, disclosure, exposé, showing, unmasking, unveiling, display, airing, exhibition, presentation, publicity, discovery, manifestation, divulgence.
2 FAMILIARITY, experience, knowledge, contact. 3 JEOPARDY, danger, hazard, risk, vulnerability.

express v 1 ARTICULATE, verbalize, utter, voice, say, speak, state, communicate, pronounce, tell, assert, declare, put across, formulate, intimate, testify, convey. 2 SHOW, manifest, exhibit, disclose, divulge,

reveal, indicate, denote, depict, embody. 3 SYMBOLIZE, stand for, represent, signify, designate.
◇ adj 1 SPECIFIC, explicit, exact, definite, clear, categorical, precise, distinct, clear-cut, certain, plain, manifest, particular, stated, unambiguous. 2 FAST, speedy, rapid, quick, high-speed, non-stop.
⊜ 1 vague.

expression n 1 LOOK, air, aspect, countenance, appearance, mien (fml). 2 REPRESENTATION, manifestation, demonstration, indication, exhibition, embodiment, show, sign, symbol, style. 3 UTTERANCE, verbalization, communication, articulation, statement, assertion, announcement, declaration, pronouncement, speech.
4 TONE, intonation, delivery, diction, enunciation, modulation, wording.
5 PHRASE, term, turn of phrase, saying, set phrase, idiom.

expressionless adj dull, blank, deadpan, impassive, straight-faced, poker-faced (infml), inscrutable, empty, vacuous, glassy.
⊜ expressive.

expressive adj eloquent, meaningful, forceful, telling, revealing, informative, indicative, communicative, demonstrative, emphatic, moving, poignant, lively, striking, suggestive, significant, thoughtful, vivid, sympathetic.

expulsion n ejection, eviction, exile, banishment, removal, discharge, exclusion, dismissal.

exquisite adj 1 BEAUTIFUL, attractive, dainty, delicate, charming, elegant, delightful, lovely, pleasing. 2 PERFECT, flawless, fine, excellent, choice, precious, rare, outstanding. 3 REFINED, discriminating, meticulous, sensitive, impeccable. 4 INTENSE, keen, sharp, poignant.
⊜ 1 ugly. 2 flawed. 3 unrefined.

extend v 1 SPREAD, stretch, reach, continue. 2 ENLARGE, increase,

expand, develop, amplify, lengthen, widen, elongate, draw out, protract, prolong, spin out, unwind. **3** OFFER, give, grant, hold out, impart, present, bestow, confer.
🔁 **2** contract, shorten. **3** withhold.

extension _n_ **1** ENLARGEMENT, increase, stretching, broadening, widening, lengthening, expansion, elongation, development, enhancement, protraction, continuation. **2** ADDITION, supplement, appendix, annexe, addendum (_fml_). **3** DELAY, postponement.

extensive _adj_ **1** BROAD, far-reaching, comprehensive, large-scale, thorough, widespread, universal, extended, all-inclusive, general, pervasive, prevalent. **2** LARGE, huge, roomy, spacious, vast, voluminous, long, lengthy, wide.
🔁 **1** restricted, narrow. **2** small.

extent _n_ **1** DIMENSION(S), amount, magnitude, expanse, size, area, bulk, degree, breadth, quantity, spread, stretch, volume, width, measure, duration, term, time. **2** LIMIT, bounds, lengths, range, reach, scope, compass, sphere, play, sweep.

exterior _n_ outside, surface, covering, coating, face, façade, shell, skin, finish, externals, appearance.
🔁 inside, interior.
◇ _adj_ outer, outside, outermost, surface, external, superficial, surrounding, outward, peripheral, extrinsic.
🔁 inside, interior.

exterminate _v_ annihilate, eradicate, destroy, eliminate, massacre, abolish, wipe out.

external _adj_ outer, surface, outside, exterior, superficial, outward, outermost, apparent, visible, extraneous, extrinsic, extramural, independent.
🔁 internal.

extinct _adj_ **1** DEFUNCT, dead, gone, obsolete, ended, exterminated, terminated, vanished, lost, abolished. **2** EXTINGUISHED, quenched, inactive, out.
🔁 **1** living.

extinction _n_ annihilation, extermination, death, eradication, obliteration, destruction, abolition, excision.

extinguish _v_ **1** PUT OUT, blow out, snuff out, stifle, smother, douse, quench. **2** ANNIHILATE, exterminate, eliminate, destroy, kill, eradicate, erase, expunge, abolish, remove, end, suppress.

extort _v_ extract, wring, exact, coerce, force, milk (_infml_), blackmail, squeeze, bleed (_infml_), bully.

extortionate _adj_ exorbitant, excessive, grasping, exacting, immoderate, rapacious, unreasonable, oppressive, blood-sucking (_infml_), rigorous, severe, hard, harsh, inordinate.

extra _adj_ **1** ADDITIONAL, added, auxiliary, supplementary, new, more, further, ancillary, fresh, other. **2** EXCESS, spare, superfluous, supernumerary, surplus, unused, unneeded, leftover, reserve, redundant.
🔁 **1** integral. **2** essential.
◇ _n_ addition, supplement, extension, accessory, appendage, bonus, complement, adjunct, addendum (_fml_), attachment.
◇ _adv_ especially, exceptionally, extraordinarily, particularly, unusually, remarkably, extremely.

extract _v_ **1** REMOVE, take out, draw out, exact, uproot, withdraw. **2** DERIVE, draw, distil, obtain, get, gather, glean, wrest, wring, elicit. **3** CHOOSE, select, cull, abstract, cite, quote.
🔁 **1** insert.
◇ _n_ **1** DISTILLATION, essence, juice. **2** EXCERPT, passage, selection, clip,

cutting, quotation, abstract, citation.

extraordinary adj remarkable, unusual, exceptional, notable, noteworthy, outstanding, unique, special, strange, peculiar, rare, uncommon, surprising, amazing, astounding, wonderful, unprecedented, marvellous, fantastic, significant, particular.
⊡ commonplace, ordinary.

extravagance n 1 OVERSPENDING, profligacy, squandering, waste, imprudence. 2 EXCESS, immoderation, recklessness, profusion, outrageousness, folly, wildness, lavishness, splurge. 3 LUXURY, extra, treat.
⊡ 1 thrift. 2 moderation.

extravagant adj 1 PROFLIGATE, prodigal, spendthrift, thriftless, wasteful, reckless. 2 IMMODERATE, flamboyant, preposterous, outrageous, ostentatious, pretentious, lavish, ornate, flashy (infml), fanciful, fantastic, wild. 3 OVERPRICED, exorbitant, expensive, excessive, costly.
⊡ 1 thrifty. 2 moderate. 3 reasonable.

extreme adj 1 INTENSE, great, immoderate, inordinate, utmost, utter, out-and-out, maximum, acute, downright, extraordinary, exceptional, greatest, highest, unreasonable, remarkable.
2 FARTHEST, far-off, faraway, distant, endmost, outermost, remotest, uttermost, final, last, terminal, ultimate. 3 RADICAL, zealous, extremist, fanatical. 4 DRASTIC, dire, uncompromising, stern, strict, rigid, severe, harsh.
⊡ 1 mild. 3 moderate.
◇ n extremity, limit, maximum, ultimate, utmost, excess, top, pinnacle, peak, height, end, climax, depth, edge, termination.

extremely adv exceedingly, excessively, very, really,

exceptionally, extraordinarily, intensely, thoroughly, remarkably, utterly, greatly, highly, unusually, unreasonably, immoderately, uncommonly, inordinately, acutely, severely, decidedly, awfully (infml), terribly (infml), dreadfully (infml), frightfully (infml), terrifically (infml), majorly (sl).

extremist n fanatic, hardliner, fundamentalist, militant, radical, zealot, diehard, ultra.
⊡ moderate.

extremity n 1 EXTREME, limit, boundary, brink, verge, bound, border, apex, height, tip, top, edge, excess, end, acme, termination, peak, pinnacle, margin, terminal, terminus, ultimate, pole, maximum, minimum, frontier, depth. 2 CRISIS, danger, emergency, plight, hardship.

extricate v disentangle, clear, disengage, free, deliver, liberate, release, rescue, relieve, remove, withdraw.
⊡ involve.

extroverted adj outgoing, friendly, sociable, amicable, amiable, exuberant.
⊡ introverted.

exuberant adj 1 LIVELY, vivacious, spirited, zestful, high-spirited, effervescent, ebullient, enthusiastic, sparkling, excited, exhilarated, effusive, cheerful, fulsome.
2 PLENTIFUL, lavish, overflowing, plenteous.
⊡ 1 apathetic. 2 scarce.

exude v 1 exude confidence: radiate, ooze, display, show, emanate, emit, exhibit, manifest (fml). 2 DISCHARGE, issue, flow out, bleed, excrete, leak, secrete, seep, perspire, sweat, trickle, weep, well.

exult v rejoice, revel, delight, glory, celebrate, relish, crow, gloat, triumph.

eye n 1 APPRECIATION, discrimination,

discernment, perception, recognition. **2** VIEWPOINT, opinion, judgement, mind. **3** WATCH, observation, lookout.

Parts of the eye include: aqueous humour, blind spot, choroid, ciliary body, cone, conjunctiva, cornea, eyelash, eyelid, fovea, iris, lachrymal duct, lens, ocular muscle, optic nerve, pupil, retina, rod, sclera, suspensory ligament, vitreous humour.

◇ *v* look at, watch, regard, observe, stare at, gaze at, glance at, view, scrutinize, scan, examine, peruse, study, survey, inspect, contemplate.

eyesight *n* vision, sight, perception, observation, view.

eyesore *n* ugliness, blemish, monstrosity, blot on the landscape, carbuncle (*infml*), disfigurement, horror, blight, atrocity, mess.

eye-witness *n* witness, observer, spectator, looker-on, onlooker, bystander, viewer, passer-by.

Ff

fable *n* allegory, parable, story, tale, yarn, myth, legend, fiction, fabrication, invention, lie, untruth, falsehood, tall story, old wives' tale.

fabric *n* **1** CLOTH, material, textile, stuff, web, texture. **2** STRUCTURE, framework, construction, make-up, constitution, organization, infrastructure, foundations.

Fabrics include: alpaca, angora, astrakhan, barathea, bouclé, cashmere, chenille, duffel, felt, flannel, Harris tweed®, mohair, paisley, pashmina, serge, Shetland wool, tweed, vicuña, wool, worsted; brocade, buckram, calico, cambric, candlewick, canvas, chambray, cheesecloth, chino, chintz, cord, corduroy, cotton, crêpe, denim, drill, jean, flannelette, fleece, gaberdine, gingham, jersey, lawn, linen, lisle, madras, moleskin, muslin, needlecord, piqué, poplin, sateen, seersucker, terry, ticking, Viyella®, webbing, winceyette; grosgrain, damask, lace, Chantilly, chiffon, georgette, gossamer, voile, organza, organdie, tulle, net, crêpe de Chine, silk, satin, taffeta, shantung, velvet, velour; polycotton, polyester, rayon, nylon, Crimplene®, Terylene®, Lurex®, Lycra®, lamé; hessian, horsehair, sharkskin.

fabricate *v* **1** FAKE, falsify, forge, invent, make up, trump up, concoct, spin. **2** MAKE, manufacture, construct, assemble, build, erect, form, shape, fashion, create, devise.

⊜ **2** demolish, destroy.

fabulous *adj* **1** WONDERFUL, marvellous, fantastic, great, superb, breathtaking, spectacular, phenomenal, amazing, astounding, unbelievable, incredible, magic, inconceivable. **2** *a fabulous beast*: mythical, legendary, fabled, fantastic, fictitious, invented, imaginary.
⊜ **2** real.

face *n* **1** FEATURES, countenance, visage, physiognomy. **2** EXPRESSION, look, appearance, air. **3** *pull a face*: grimace, frown, scowl, pout. **4** EXTERIOR, outside, surface, cover, front, façade, aspect, side.
◇ *v* **1** BE OPPOSITE, give on to, front, overlook. **2** CONFRONT, face up to, deal with, cope with, tackle, brave, defy, oppose, encounter, meet, experience. **3** COVER, coat, dress, clad, overlay, veneer.
• **face to face** opposite, eye to eye, eyeball to eyeball, in confrontation.
• **face up to** accept, come to terms with, acknowledge, recognize, cope with, deal with, confront, meet head-on, stand up to.

facet *n* surface, plane, side, face, aspect, angle, point, feature, characteristic.

facetious *adj* flippant, frivolous, playful, jocular, jesting, tongue-in-cheek, funny, amusing, humorous, comical, witty.
⊜ serious.

facile *adj* easy, simple, simplistic, ready, quick, hasty, glib, fluent, smooth, slick, plausible, shallow, superficial.

≡ complicated, profound.

facilitate v ease, help, assist, further, promote, forward, expedite, speed up.

facilities n amenities, services, conveniences, resources, equipment, prerequisites, mod cons (*infml*), means, opportunities.

facility n ease, effortlessness, readiness, quickness, fluency, proficiency, skill, skilfulness, talent, gift, knack, ability.

fact n 1 *facts and figures*: datum, information, detail, particular, specific, point, item, circumstance, event, incident, occurrence, happening, act, deed, fait accompli. 2 REALITY, actuality, truth.
≡ 2 fiction.
• **in fact** actually, in actual fact, in point of fact, as a matter of fact, in reality, really, indeed.

faction n splinter group, ginger group, minority, division, section, contingent, party, camp, set, clique, coterie, cabal, junta, lobby, pressure group.

factor n cause, influence, circumstance, determinant, contingency, consideration, element, ingredient, component, part, point, aspect, fact, item, detail.

factory n works, plant, mill, shop floor, assembly line, manufactory.

factual adj true, historical, actual, real, genuine, authentic, correct, accurate, precise, exact, literal, faithful, close, detailed, unbiased, objective.
≡ false, fictitious, imaginary, fictional.

faculties n wits, senses, intelligence, reason, powers, capabilities.

faculty n ability, capability, capacity, power, facility, knack, gift, talent, skill, aptitude, bent.

fad n craze, rage (*infml*), mania,

fashion, mode, vogue, trend, whim, fancy, affectation.

fade v 1 DISCOLOUR, bleach, blanch, blench, pale, whiten, dim, dull. 2 DECLINE, fall, diminish, dwindle, ebb, wane, disappear, vanish, flag, weaken, droop, wilt, wither, shrivel, perish, die.

fail v 1 GO WRONG, miscarry, misfire, flop, miss, flunk (*sl*), underachieve, fall through, come to grief, collapse, fold (*infml*), go bankrupt, go bust, go under, founder, sink, decline, fall, weaken, dwindle, fade, wane, peter out, cease, die. 2 *fail to pay a bill*: omit, neglect, forget. 3 LET DOWN, disappoint, leave, desert, abandon, forsake.
≡ 1 succeed, prosper.

failing n weakness, foible, fault, defect, imperfection, flaw, blemish, drawback, deficiency, shortcoming, failure, lapse, error.
≡ strength, advantage.

failure n 1 MISCARRIAGE, flop, wash-out (*infml*), fiasco, disappointment, loss, defeat, downfall, decline, decay, deterioration, ruin, bankruptcy, crash, collapse, breakdown, stoppage. 2 OMISSION, slip-up (*infml*), neglect, negligence, failing, shortcoming, deficiency.
≡ 1 success, prosperity.

faint adj 1 SLIGHT, weak, feeble, soft, low, hushed, muffled, subdued, faded, bleached, light, pale, dull, dim, hazy, indistinct, vague. 2 *I feel faint*: dizzy, giddy, woozy (*infml*), light-headed, weak, feeble, exhausted.
≡ 1 strong, clear.
◇ v black out, pass out, swoon, collapse, flake out (*infml*), keel over (*infml*), drop.
◇ n blackout, swoon, collapse, unconsciousness.

fair¹ adj 1 JUST, equitable, square, even-handed, dispassionate, impartial, objective, disinterested,

unbiased, unprejudiced, right, proper, lawful, legitimate, honest, trustworthy, upright, honourable. **2** FAIR-HAIRED, fair-headed, blond(e), light. **3** *fair weather*: fine, dry, sunny, bright, clear, cloudless, unclouded. **4** AVERAGE, moderate, middling, not bad, all right, OK (*infml*), satisfactory, adequate, acceptable, tolerable, reasonable, passable, mediocre, so-so (*infml*).
⊞ **1** unfair. **2** dark. **3** inclement, cloudy. **4** excellent, poor.

fair² *n* show, exhibition, exposition, expo (*infml*), market, bazaar, fête, festival, carnival, gala.

faith *n* **1** BELIEF, credit, trust, reliance, dependence, conviction, confidence, assurance. **2** RELIGION, denomination, persuasion, church, creed, dogma. **3** FAITHFULNESS, fidelity, loyalty, allegiance, honour, sincerity, honesty, truthfulness.
⊞ **1** mistrust. **3** unfaithfulness, treachery.

faithful *adj* **1** LOYAL, devoted, staunch, steadfast, constant, trusty, reliable, dependable, true. **2** *a faithful description*: accurate, precise, exact, strict, close, true, truthful.
⊞ **1** disloyal, treacherous. **2** inaccurate, vague.

fake *v* forge, fabricate, counterfeit, copy, imitate, simulate, feign, sham, pretend, put on, affect, assume.
◇ *n* forgery, copy, reproduction, replica, imitation, simulation, sham, hoax, fraud, phoney (*infml*), impostor, charlatan.
◇ *adj* forged, counterfeit, false, spurious, phoney (*infml*), pseudo, bogus, assumed, affected, sham, artificial, simulated, mock, imitation, reproduction.
⊞ genuine.

fall *v* **1** TUMBLE, stumble, trip, topple, keel over, collapse, slump, crash. **2** DESCEND, go down, drop, slope, incline, slide, sink, dive,

plunge, plummet, nose-dive, pitch. **3** DECREASE, lessen, decline, diminish, dwindle, fall off, subside.
⊞ **2** rise. **3** increase.
◇ *n* **1** TUMBLE, descent, slope, incline, dive, plunge, decrease, reduction, lessening, drop, decline, dwindling, slump, crash. **2** *the fall of Rome*: defeat, conquest, overthrow, downfall, collapse, surrender, capitulation.
● **fall apart** break, go to pieces, shatter, disintegrate, crumble, decompose, decay, rot.
● **fall asleep** drop off, doze off, nod off (*infml*).
● **fall back on** resort to, have recourse to, use, turn to, look to.
● **fall behind** lag, trail, drop back.
● **fall in** cave in, come down, collapse, give way, subside, sink.
● **fall in with** agree with, assent to, go along with, accept, comply with, co-operate with.
● **fall off** decrease, lessen, drop, slump, decline, deteriorate, worsen, slow, slacken.
● **fall out** quarrel, argue, squabble, bicker, fight, clash, disagree, differ.
⊞ agree.
● **fall through** come to nothing, fail, miscarry, founder, collapse.
⊞ come off, succeed.

fallacy *n* misconception, delusion, mistake, error, flaw, inconsistency, falsehood.
⊞ truth.

fallow *adj* uncultivated, unplanted, unsown, undeveloped, unused, idle, inactive, dormant, resting.

false *adj* **1** INCORRECT, wrong, mistaken, erroneous, inaccurate, inexact, misleading, faulty, fallacious, invalid. **2** UNREAL, artificial, synthetic, imitation, simulated, mock, fake, counterfeit, forged, feigned, pretended, sham, bogus, assumed, fictitious. **3** *false friends*: disloyal, unfaithful, faithless, lying, deceitful, insincere, hypocritical, two-faced

(*infml*), double-dealing, treacherous, unreliable.
⊟ **1** true, correct, right. **2** real, genuine. **3** faithful, reliable.

falsehood *n* untruth, lie, fib, story, fiction, fabrication, perjury, untruthfulness, deceit, deception, dishonesty.
⊟ truth, truthfulness.

falsify *v* alter, cook (*infml*), tamper with, doctor, distort, pervert, misrepresent, misstate, forge, counterfeit, fake.

falter *v* totter, stumble, stammer, stutter, hesitate, waver, vacillate, flinch, quail, shake, tremble, flag, fail.

fame *n* renown, celebrity, stardom, prominence, eminence, illustriousness, glory, honour, esteem, reputation, name.

familiar *adj* **1** EVERYDAY, routine, household, common, ordinary, well-known, recognizable. **2** INTIMATE, close, confidential, friendly, informal, free, free-and-easy, relaxed.
3 *familiar with the procedure*: aware, acquainted, abreast, knowledgeable, versed, conversant.
⊟ **1** unfamiliar, strange. **2** formal, reserved. **3** unfamiliar, ignorant.

familiarity *n* **1** INTIMACY, liberty, closeness, friendliness, sociability, openness, naturalness, informality.
2 AWARENESS, acquaintance, experience, knowledge, grasp, understanding.

familiarize *v* accustom, acclimatize, school, train, coach, instruct, prime, brief.

family *n* **1** RELATIVES, relations, kin, kindred, kinsmen, people, folk (*infml*), ancestors, forebears, children, offspring, issue, progeny, descendants. **2** CLAN, tribe, race, dynasty, house, pedigree, ancestry, parentage, descent, line, lineage, extraction, blood, stock, birth.
3 CLASS, group, classification.

Members of a family include:
ancestor, forebear, forefather, descendant, offspring, heir; husband, wife, spouse, parent, father, mother, grandparent, grandfather, grandmother, grandchild, grandson, granddaughter, child, son, daughter, brother, half-brother, sister, half-sister, sibling, uncle, aunt, nephew, niece, cousin, godparent, godchild, stepfather, stepmother, stepchild, foster-parent, foster-child.

• **family tree** ancestry, pedigree, genealogy, line, lineage, extraction.

famine *n* starvation, hunger, destitution, want, scarcity, dearth.
⊟ plenty.

famous *adj* well-known, famed, renowned, celebrated, noted, great, distinguished, illustrious, eminent, honoured, acclaimed, glorious, legendary, remarkable, notable, prominent, signal.
⊟ unheard-of, unknown, obscure.

fan¹ *v* **1** COOL, ventilate, air, air-condition, air-cool, blow, refresh.
2 INCREASE, provoke, stimulate, rouse, arouse, excite, agitate, stir up, work up, whip up.
◇ *n* extractor fan, ventilator, air-conditioner, blower, propeller, vane.

fan² *n* enthusiast, admirer, supporter, follower, adherent, devotee, lover, buff (*infml*), fiend, freak.

fanatic *n* zealot, devotee, enthusiast, addict, fiend, freak, visionary, maniac, bigot, radical, extremist, militant, activist.

fanatical *adj* overenthusiastic, extreme, passionate, zealous, fervent, burning, mad, wild, frenzied, rabid, obsessive, single-minded, bigoted, visionary.
⊟ moderate, unenthusiastic.

fanaticism *n* extremism,

monomania, single-mindedness, obsessiveness, madness, infatuation, bigotry, zeal, fervour, enthusiasm, dedication.
⊠ moderation.

fanciful adj imaginary, mythical, fabulous, fantastic, visionary, romantic, fairytale, airy-fairy, vaporous, whimsical, wild, extravagant, curious.
⊠ real, ordinary.

fancy v 1 LIKE, be attracted to, take a liking to, take to, go for, prefer, favour, desire, wish for, long for, yearn for. 2 THINK, conceive, imagine, dream of, picture, conjecture, believe, suppose, reckon, guess.
⊠ 1 dislike.
◇ n 1 DESIRE, craving, hankering, urge, liking, fondness, inclination, preference. 2 NOTION, thought, impression, imagination, dream, fantasy.
⊠ 1 dislike, aversion. 2 fact, reality.
◇ adj elaborate, ornate, decorated, ornamented, rococo, baroque, elegant, extravagant, fantastic, fanciful, far-fetched.
⊠ plain.

fantasize v imagine, daydream, dream, hallucinate, invent, romance, build castles in the air (infml), live in a dream (infml).

fantastic adj 1 WONDERFUL, marvellous, sensational, superb, excellent, first-rate, tremendous, terrific, great, incredible, unbelievable, overwhelming, enormous, extreme. 2 STRANGE, weird, odd, exotic, outlandish, fanciful, fabulous, imaginative, visionary.
⊠ 1 ordinary. 2 real.

fantasy n dream, daydream, reverie, pipe dream, nightmare, vision, hallucination, illusion, mirage, apparition, invention, fancy, flight of fancy, delusion, misconception,

imagination, unreality.
⊠ reality.

far adv a long way, a good way, miles (infml), much, greatly, considerably, extremely, decidedly, incomparably.
⊠ near, close.
◇ adj distant, far-off, faraway, far-flung, outlying, remote, out-of-the-way, god-forsaken, removed, far-removed, further, opposite, other.
⊠ nearby, close.

farce n 1 COMEDY, slapstick, satire, buffoonery, burlesque. 2 TRAVESTY, sham, parody, joke, mockery, ridiculousness, absurdity, nonsense.

fare n 1 pay one's fare: charge, cost, price, fee, passage. 2 FOOD, eatables (infml), provisions, rations, sustenance, meals, diet, menu, board, table.

far-fetched adj implausible, improbable, unlikely, dubious, incredible, unbelievable, fantastic, preposterous, crazy, unrealistic.
⊠ plausible.

farm n ranch, farmstead, grange, homestead, station, land, holding, acreage, acres.

Types of farm include: arable farm, cattle ranch, dairy farm, free-range farm, mixed farm, organic farm, sheep station, croft, smallholding, estate, plantation, wind farm.

◇ v cultivate, till, work the land, plant, operate.

farmer n agriculturist, crofter, smallholder, husbandman, yeoman.

farming n agriculture, cultivation, husbandry, crofting.

far-reaching adj broad, extensive, widespread, sweeping, important, significant, momentous.
⊠ insignificant.

fascinate v absorb, engross, intrigue, delight, charm, captivate,

spellbind, enthral, rivet, transfix, hypnotize, mesmerize.
🔁 bore, repel.

fascinating adj intriguing, gripping, exciting, interesting, engaging, engrossing, irresistible, compelling, alluring, bewitching, captivating, enchanting, riveting, enticing, seductive, tempting, charming, absorbing, stimulating, delightful, mesmerizing.
🔁 boring, uninteresting.

fascination n interest, attraction, lure, magnetism, pull, charm, enchantment, spell, sorcery, magic.
🔁 boredom, repulsion.

fashion n 1 MANNER, way, method, mode, style, shape, form, pattern, line, cut, look, appearance, type, sort, kind. 2 VOGUE, trend, mode, style, fad, craze, rage (infml), latest (infml), custom, convention.
◇ v create, form, shape, mould, model, design, fit, tailor, alter, adjust, adapt, suit.

fashionable adj chic, smart, elegant, stylish, modish, à la mode, in vogue, trendy (infml), in, all the rage (infml), popular, prevailing, current, latest, up-to-the-minute, contemporary, modern, up-to-date.
🔁 unfashionable.

fast¹ adj 1 QUICK, swift, rapid, brisk, accelerated, speedy, nippy (infml), hasty, hurried, flying. 2 FASTENED, secure, fixed, immovable, immobile, firm, tight.
🔁 1 slow, unhurried. 2 loose.
◇ adv quickly, swiftly, rapidly, speedily, like a flash, like a shot, hastily, hurriedly, apace, presto.
🔁 slowly, gradually.

fast² v go hungry, diet, starve, abstain.
◇ n fasting, diet, starvation, abstinence.
🔁 gluttony, self-indulgence.

fasten v fix, attach, clamp, grip,

anchor, rivet, nail, seal, close, shut, lock, bolt, secure, tie, bind, chain, link, interlock, connect, join, unite, do up, button, lace, buckle.
🔁 unfasten, untie.

fat adj plump, obese, tubby, stout, corpulent, portly, round, rotund, paunchy, pot-bellied, overweight, heavy, beefy, solid, chubby, podgy, fleshy, flabby, gross.
🔁 thin, slim, poor.
◇ n fatness, obesity, overweight, corpulence, paunch, pot (belly), blubber, flab (infml).

fatal adj deadly, lethal, mortal, killing, incurable, terminal, final, malignant, destructive, calamitous, catastrophic, disastrous.
🔁 harmless.

fatality n death, mortality, loss, casualty, deadliness, lethality, disaster.

fate n destiny, providence, chance, future, fortune, horoscope, stars, lot, doom, end, outcome, ruin, destruction, death.

fated adj destined, predestined, preordained, foreordained, doomed, unavoidable, inevitable, inescapable, certain, sure.
🔁 avoidable.

fateful adj crucial, critical, decisive, important, momentous, significant, fatal, lethal, disastrous.
🔁 unimportant.

father n 1 PARENT, begetter, procreator, progenitor, sire (fml), papa, dad (infml), daddy (infml), old man (infml), patriarch, elder, forefather, ancestor, forebear, predecessor. 2 FOUNDER, creator, originator, inventor, maker, architect, author, patron, leader, prime mover. 3 PRIEST, padre, abbé, curé.
◇ v beget, procreate, sire, produce.

fathom v 1 MEASURE, gauge, plumb, sound, probe, penetrate. 2 UNDERSTAND, comprehend, grasp, see, work out, get to the bottom of, interpret.

fatigue n tiredness, weariness, exhaustion, lethargy, listlessness, lassitude, weakness, debility.
⊟ energy.
◇ v tire, wear out, weary, exhaust, drain, weaken, debilitate.

fatten v feed, nourish, build up, overfeed, cram, stuff, bloat, swell, fill out, spread, expand, thicken.

fatty adj fat, greasy, oily.

fault n 1 DEFECT, flaw, blemish, imperfection, deficiency, shortcoming, weakness, failing, foible, negligence, omission, oversight. 2 ERROR, mistake, blunder, slip-up (infml), slip, lapse, misdeed, offence, wrong, sin. 3 it's your fault: responsibility, accountability, liability, culpability.
◇ v find fault with, pick holes in, criticize, knock (infml), impugn, censure, blame, call to account.
⊟ praise.
● at fault (in the) wrong, to blame, blameworthy, responsible, guilty, culpable.

faultless adj perfect, flawless, pure, unblemished, spotless, immaculate, unsullied, blameless, exemplary, model, correct, accurate.
⊟ faulty, imperfect, flawed.

faulty adj imperfect, defective, flawed, blemished, damaged, impaired, out of order, broken, wrong.
⊟ faultless.

favour n 1 APPROVAL, esteem, support, backing, sympathy, goodwill, patronage, favouritism, preference, partiality. 2 he did me a favour: kindness, service, good turn, courtesy.
⊟ 1 disapproval.
◇ v 1 PREFER, choose, opt for, like, approve, support, back, advocate, champion. 2 HELP, assist, aid, benefit,

promote, encourage, pamper, spoil.
⊟ 1 dislike. 2 mistreat.
● in favour of for, supporting, on the side of.
⊟ against.

favourable adj beneficial, advantageous, helpful, fit, suitable, convenient, timely, opportune, good, fair, promising, auspicious, hopeful, positive, encouraging, complimentary, enthusiastic, friendly, amicable, well-disposed, kind, sympathetic, understanding, reassuring.
⊟ unfavourable, unhelpful, negative.

favourite adj preferred, favoured, pet, best-loved, dearest, beloved, esteemed, chosen.
⊟ hated.
◇ n preference, choice, pick, pet, blue-eyed boy, teacher's pet, the apple of one's eye, darling, idol.
⊟ bête noire, pet hate.

favouritism n nepotism, preferential treatment, preference, partiality, one-sidedness, bias, partisanship, injustice.
⊟ impartiality.

fear n alarm, fright, terror, horror, panic, agitation, worry, anxiety, consternation, concern, dismay, distress, uneasiness, qualms, misgivings, apprehension, dread, trepidation, foreboding, awe, phobia, nightmare.
⊟ courage, bravery, confidence.
◇ v take fright, shrink from, dread, shudder at, tremble, worry, suspect, anticipate, expect, foresee, respect, venerate.

fearful adj 1 FRIGHTENED, afraid, scared, alarmed, nervous, anxious, tense, uneasy, apprehensive, hesitant, nervy, panicky. 2 TERRIBLE, fearsome (fml), dreadful, awful, frightful, atrocious, shocking, appalling, monstrous, gruesome, hideous, ghastly, horrible.
⊟ 1 brave, courageous, fearless.

2 wonderful, delightful.

feasible *adj* practicable, practical, workable, achievable, attainable, realizable, viable, reasonable, possible, likely.
⊟ impossible.

feast *n* 1 BANQUET, dinner, spread, blow-out (*sl*), binge (*infml*), beano (*infml*), junket. 2 FESTIVAL, holiday, gala, fête, celebration, revels.
◇ *v* gorge, binge (*infml*), pig out (*sl*), eat one's fill, wine and dine, treat, entertain.

feat *n* exploit, deed, action, act, accomplishment, achievement, attainment, performance, undertaking.

feature *n* 1 ASPECT, facet, point, factor, attribute, quality, property, trait, lineament, characteristic, peculiarity, mark, hallmark, speciality, highlight. 2 *a magazine feature*: column, article, report, story, piece, item, comment.
◇ *v* 1 EMPHASIZE, highlight, spotlight, play up, promote, show, present. 2 APPEAR, figure, participate, act, perform, star.

fee *n* charge, terms, bill, account, pay, remuneration, payment, retainer, subscription, reward, recompense, hire, toll.

feeble *adj* 1 WEAK, faint, exhausted, frail, delicate, puny, sickly, infirm, powerless, helpless. 2 INADEQUATE, lame, poor, thin, flimsy, ineffective, incompetent, indecisive.
⊟ 1 strong, powerful.

feed *v* nourish, cater for, provide for, supply, sustain, suckle, nurture, foster, strengthen, fuel, graze, pasture, eat, dine.
◇ *n* food, fodder, forage, pasture, silage.
• **feed on** eat, consume, devour, live on, exist on.

feel *v* 1 EXPERIENCE, go through, undergo, suffer, endure, enjoy.

2 TOUCH, finger, handle, manipulate, hold, stroke, caress, fondle, paw, fumble, grope. 3 *feel soft*: seem, appear. 4 THINK, believe, consider, reckon, judge. 5 SENSE, perceive, notice, observe, know.
◇ *n* texture, surface, finish, touch, knack, sense, impression, feeling, quality.
• **feel for** pity, sympathize (with), empathize (with), commiserate (with), be sorry for.
• **feel like** fancy, want, desire.

feeling *n* 1 SENSATION, perception, sense, instinct, hunch, suspicion, inkling, impression, idea, notion, opinion, view, point of view. 2 EMOTION, passion, intensity, warmth, compassion, sympathy, understanding, pity, concern, affection, fondness, sentiment, sentimentality, susceptibility, sensibility, sensitivity, appreciation. 3 AIR, aura, atmosphere, mood, quality.

fell *v* cut down, hew, knock down, strike down, floor, level, flatten, raze, demolish.

fellow *n* 1 PERSON, man, boy, chap (*infml*), bloke (*infml*), guy (*infml*), individual, character. 2 PEER, compeer, equal, partner, associate, colleague, co-worker, companion, comrade, friend, counterpart, match, mate, twin, double.
◇ *adj* co-, associate, associated, related, like, similar.

fellowship *n* 1 COMPANIONSHIP, camaraderie, communion, familiarity, intimacy. 2 ASSOCIATION, league, guild, society, club, fraternity, brotherhood, sisterhood, order.

female *adj* feminine, she-, girlish, womanly.
⊟ male.

feminine *adj* 1 FEMALE, womanly, ladylike, graceful, gentle, tender. 2 EFFEMINATE, unmanly, womanish, girlish, girly, sissy.

⊞ **1** masculine. **2** manly.

feminism n women's movement, women's lib(eration), female emancipation, women's rights.

fence n barrier, railing, paling, wall, hedge, windbreak, guard, defence, barricade, stockade, rampart.
◇ v **1** SURROUND, encircle, bound, hedge, wall, enclose, pen, coop, confine, restrict, separate, protect, guard, defend, fortify. **2** PARRY, dodge, evade, hedge, equivocate, quibble, pussyfoot, stonewall.

fencing

Fencing terms include: appel, coquille, en garde, épée, feint, foible, foil, forte, lunge, parry, counter-parry, pink, piste, plastron, remise, riposte, counter-riposte, sabre, tac-au-tac, thrust, touché, volt.

fend for v look after, take care of, shift for, support, maintain, sustain, provide for.

fend off v ward off, beat off, parry, deflect, avert, resist, repel, repulse, hold at bay, keep off, shut out.

ferment v **1** BUBBLE, effervesce, froth, foam, boil, seethe, smoulder, fester, brew, rise. **2** ROUSE, stir up, excite, work up, agitate, foment, incite, provoke, inflame, heat.
◇ n unrest, agitation, turbulence, stir, excitement, turmoil, disruption, commotion, tumult, hubbub, uproar, furore, frenzy, fever, glow.
⊞ calm.

ferocious adj vicious, savage, fierce, wild, barbarous, barbaric, brutal, inhuman, cruel, sadistic, murderous, bloodthirsty, violent, merciless, pitiless, ruthless.
⊞ gentle, mild, tame.

ferocity n viciousness, savagery, fierceness, wildness, barbarity, brutality, inhumanity, cruelty,

sadism, bloodthirstiness, violence, ruthlessness.
⊞ gentleness, mildness.

ferry n ferry-boat, car ferry, ship, boat, vessel.
◇ v transport, ship, convey, carry, take, shuttle, taxi, drive, run, move, shift.

fertile adj fruitful, productive, rich, generative, yielding, prolific, teeming, abundant, plentiful, lush, luxuriant, fat.
⊞ infertile, barren, sterile, unproductive.

fertilize v **1** IMPREGNATE, inseminate, pollinate. **2** fertilize land: enrich, feed, dress, compost, manure, dung.

fertilizer n dressing, compost, manure, dung.

fervent adj ardent, earnest, eager, enthusiastic, whole-hearted, excited, energetic, vigorous, fiery, spirited, intense, vehement, passionate, full-blooded, zealous, devout, heartfelt, impassioned, emotional, warm.
⊞ cool, indifferent, apathetic.

fervour n ardour, eagerness, enthusiasm, excitement, animation, energy, vigour, spirit, verve, intensity, vehemence, passion, zeal, warmth.
⊞ apathy.

fester v ulcerate, gather, suppurate, discharge, putrefy, rot, decay, rankle, smoulder.

festival n celebration, holiday, commemoration, anniversary, jubilee, feast, gala, fête, carnival, fiesta, party, merrymaking, entertainment, festivities.

festive adj celebratory, festal, holiday, gala, carnival, happy, joyful, merry, hearty, cheery, jolly, jovial, cordial, convivial.
⊞ gloomy, sombre, sober.

festivity n celebration, jubilation, feasting, banqueting, fun, enjoyment, pleasure, entertainment, sport, amusement, merriment, merrymaking, revelry, jollity, joviality, conviviality.

festoon v adorn, deck, bedeck, garland, wreathe, drape, hang, swathe, decorate, garnish.

fetch v 1 *fetch a bucket*: get, collect, bring, carry, transport, deliver, escort. 2 SELL FOR, go for, bring in, yield, realize, make, earn.

fetching adj attractive, pretty, sweet, cute, charming, enchanting, fascinating, captivating.
⊞ repellent.

fête n fair, bazaar, sale of work, garden party, gala, carnival, festival.
◇ v entertain, treat, regale, welcome, honour, lionize.

feud n vendetta, quarrel, row, argument, disagreement, dispute, conflict, strife, discord, animosity, ill-will, bitterness, enmity, hostility, antagonism, rivalry.
⊞ agreement, peace.

fever n 1 FEVERISHNESS, (high) temperature, delirium. 2 EXCITEMENT, agitation, turmoil, unrest, heat, restlessness, passion, ecstasy.

feverish adj 1 DELIRIOUS, hot, burning, flushed. 2 EXCITED, impatient, agitated, overwrought, restless, nervous, frenzied, frantic, hectic, hasty, hurried.
⊞ 1 cool. 2 calm.

few adj scarce, rare, uncommon, sporadic, infrequent, sparse, thin, scant, scanty, meagre, inconsiderable, inadequate, insufficient, in short supply.
⊞ many.
◇ pron not many, hardly any, one or two, a couple, scattering, sprinkling, handful, some.
⊞ many.

fibre n 1 FILAMENT, strand, thread, nerve, sinew, pile, texture. 2 *moral fibre*: character, calibre, backbone, strength, stamina, toughness,

courage, resolution, determination.

fickle adj inconstant, disloyal, unfaithful, faithless, treacherous, unreliable, unpredictable, changeable, capricious, mercurial, irresolute, vacillating.
⊞ constant, steady, stable.

fiction n 1 FANTASY, fancy, imagination, figment, invention, fabrication, concoction, untruth, improvisation, story-telling. 2 NOVEL, romance, story, tale, yarn, fable, parable, legend, myth, lie.
⊞ 2 non-fiction, fact, truth.

fictional adj literary, invented, made-up, imaginary, make-believe, legendary, mythical, mythological, fabulous, non-existent, unreal.
⊞ factual, real.

fictitious adj false, untrue, invented, made-up, fabricated, apocryphal, imaginary, non-existent, bogus, counterfeit, spurious, assumed, supposed.
⊞ true, genuine.

fiddle v 1 *fiddling with her necklace*: play, tinker, toy, trifle, tamper, mess around, meddle, interfere, fidget. 2 CHEAT, swindle, diddle, cook the books (*infml*), juggle, manoeuvre, racketeer, graft (*sl*).
◇ n swindle, con (*infml*), scam (*infml*), rip-off (*sl*), fraud, racket, sharp practice, graft (*sl*).

fiddling adj trifling, petty, trivial, insignificant, negligible, paltry.
⊞ important, significant.

fidelity n 1 FAITHFULNESS, loyalty, allegiance, devotion, constancy, reliability. 2 ACCURACY, exactness, precision, closeness, adherence.
⊞ 1 infidelity, inconstancy, treachery. 2 inaccuracy.

fidget v squirm, wriggle, shuffle, twitch, jerk, jump, fret, fuss, bustle, fiddle, mess about, play around.

fidgety adj restless, impatient, uneasy, nervous, agitated, jittery,

jumpy, twitchy, on edge.
⊜ still.

field n **1** GRASSLAND, meadow, pasture, paddock, playing-field, ground, pitch, green, lawn. **2** RANGE, scope, bounds, limits, confines, territory, area, province, domain, sphere, environment, department, discipline, speciality, line, forte. **3** PARTICIPANTS, entrants, contestants, competitors, contenders, runners, candidates, applicants, opponents, opposition, competition.

fiend n **1** EVIL SPIRIT, demon, devil, monster. **2** a health fiend: enthusiast, fanatic, addict, devotee, freak (infml), nut (infml).

fiendish adj devilish, diabolical, infernal, wicked, malevolent, cunning, cruel, inhuman, savage, monstrous, unspeakable.

fierce adj ferocious, vicious, savage, cruel, brutal, merciless, aggressive, dangerous, murderous, frightening, menacing, threatening, stern, grim, relentless, raging, wild, passionate, intense, strong, powerful.
⊜ gentle, kind, calm.

fiery adj **1** BURNING, afire, flaming, aflame, blazing, ablaze, red-hot, glowing, aglow, flushed, hot, torrid, sultry. **2** PASSIONATE, inflamed, ardent, fervent, impatient, excitable, impetuous, impulsive, hot-headed, fierce, violent, heated.
⊜ **1** cold. **2** impassive.

fight v **1** WRESTLE, box, fence, joust, brawl, scrap, scuffle, tussle, skirmish, combat, battle, do battle, war, wage war, clash, cross swords, engage, grapple, struggle, strive, contend. **2** QUARREL, argue, dispute, squabble, bicker, wrangle. **3** OPPOSE, contest, campaign against, resist, withstand, defy, stand up to.
◇ n **1** BOUT, contest, duel, combat, action, battle, war, hostilities, brawl, scrap, scuffle, tussle, struggle, skirmish, set-to, clash, engagement,

brush, encounter, conflict, fray, free-for-all, fracas, riot. **2** QUARREL, row, argument, dispute, dissension.
• **fight back 1** RETALIATE, defend oneself, resist, put up a fight, retort, reply. **2** fight back the tears: hold back, restrain, curb, control, repress, bottle up, contain, suppress.
• **fight off** hold off, keep at bay, ward off, stave off, resist, repel, rebuff, beat off, rout, put to flight.

fighter n combatant, contestant, contender, disputant, boxer, wrestler, pugilist, prizefighter, soldier, trouper, mercenary, warrior, man-at-arms, swordsman, gladiator.

figurative adj metaphorical, symbolic, emblematic, allegorical, representative, parabolic, descriptive, pictorial.
⊜ literal.

figure n **1** NUMBER, numeral, digit, integer, sum, amount. **2** SHAPE, form, outline, silhouette, body, frame, build, physique. **3** public figure: dignitary, celebrity, personality, character, person. **4** DIAGRAM, illustration, picture, drawing, sketch, image, representation, symbol.
◇ v **1** RECKON, guess, estimate, judge, think, believe. **2** FEATURE, appear, crop up.
• **figure out** work out, calculate, compute, reckon, puzzle out, resolve, fathom, understand, see, make out, decipher.

figurehead n mouthpiece, front man, name, dummy, puppet.

filament n fibre, strand, thread, hair, whisker, wire, string, pile.

file¹ v rub (down), sand, abrade, scour, scrape, grate, rasp, hone, whet, shave, plane, smooth, polish.

file² n folder, dossier, portfolio, binder, case, record, documents, data, information.
◇ v record, register, note, enter, process, store, classify, categorize,

pigeonhole, catalogue.

file³ *n* line, queue, column, row, procession, cortège, train, string, stream, trail.
◇ *v* march, troop, parade, stream, trail.

fill *v* **1** REPLENISH, stock, supply, furnish, satisfy, pack, crowd, cram, stuff, congest, block, clog, plug, bung, cork, stop, close, seal. **2** PERVADE, imbue, permeate, soak, impregnate. **3** *fill a post*: take up, hold, occupy, discharge, fulfil.
⊟ **1** empty, drain.
● *fill in* **1** *fill in a form*: complete, fill out, answer. **2** (*infml*) STAND IN, deputize, understudy, substitute, replace, represent, act for. **3** (*infml*) BRIEF, inform, advise, acquaint, bring up to date, bring up to speed (*infml*).

filling *n* contents, inside, stuffing, padding, wadding, filler.
◇ *adj* satisfying, nutritious, square, solid, substantial, heavy, large, big, generous, ample.
⊟ insubstantial.

film *n* **1** MOTION PICTURE, picture, movie (*infml*), video, feature film, short, documentary. **2** LAYER, covering, dusting, coat, coating, glaze, skin, membrane, tissue, sheet, veil, screen, cloud, mist, haze.
◇ *v* photograph, shoot, video, videotape.

filter *v* strain, sieve, sift, screen, refine, purify, clarify, percolate, ooze, seep, leak, trickle, dribble.
◇ *n* strainer, sieve, sifter, colander, mesh, gauze, membrane.

filth *n* **1** DIRT, grime, muck, dung, excrement, faeces, sewage, refuse, rubbish, garbage, trash, slime, sludge, effluent, pollution, contamination, corruption, impurity, uncleanness, foulness, sordidness, squalor. **2** OBSCENITY, pornography, smut, indecency, vulgarity, coarseness.
⊟ **1** cleanness, cleanliness, purity.

filthy *adj* **1** DIRTY, soiled, unwashed, grimy, grubby, mucky, muddy, slimy, sooty, unclean, impure, foul, gross, sordid, squalid, vile, low, mean, base, contemptible, despicable. **2** OBSCENE, pornographic, smutty, bawdy, suggestive, indecent, offensive, foul-mouthed, vulgar, coarse, corrupt, depraved.
⊟ **1** clean, pure. **2** decent.

final *adj* last, latest, closing, end, concluding, finishing, ultimate, terminal, dying, last-minute, eventual, conclusive, definitive, decisive, definite, incontrovertible.
⊟ first, initial.

finale *n* climax, dénouement, culmination, crowning glory, end, conclusion, close, curtain, epilogue.

finalize *v* conclude, finish, round off, complete, resolve, settle, agree, decide, close, clinch, sew up (*infml*), wrap up (*infml*).

finally *adv* lastly, in conclusion, ultimately, eventually, at last, at length, in the end, conclusively, once and for all, forever, irreversibly, irrevocably, definitely.

finance *n* economics, money management, accounting, banking, investment, stock market, business, commerce, trade, money, funding, sponsorship, subsidy.
◇ *v* pay for, fund, sponsor, back, support, underwrite, guarantee, subsidize, capitalize, float, set up.

finances *n* accounts, affairs, budget, bank account, income, revenue, liquidity, resources, assets, capital, wealth, money, cash, funds, wherewithal.

financial *adj* monetary, money, pecuniary, economic, fiscal, budgetary, commercial.

financier *n* financialist, banker, stockbroker, money-maker, investor, speculator, venture capitalist.

find *v* **1** DISCOVER, locate, track down,

trace, retrieve, recover, unearth, uncover, expose, reveal, come across, chance on, stumble on, meet, encounter, detect, recognize, notice, observe, perceive, realize, learn. **2** ATTAIN, achieve, win, reach, gain, obtain, get. **3** *find it difficult*: consider, think, judge, declare. ⊞ **1** lose.

● **find out 1** LEARN, ascertain, discover, detect, note, observe, perceive, realize. **2** UNMASK, expose, show up, uncover, reveal, disclose, catch, suss out (*sl*), rumble (*sl*), tumble to (*infml*).

finding *n* **1** FIND, discovery, breakthrough. **2** DECISION, conclusion, judgement, verdict, pronouncement, decree, recommendation, award.

fine¹ *adj* **1** EXCELLENT, outstanding, exceptional, superior, exquisite, splendid, magnificent, brilliant, beautiful, handsome, attractive, elegant, lovely, nice, good. **2** THIN, slender, sheer, gauzy, powdery, flimsy, fragile, delicate, dainty. **3** SATISFACTORY, acceptable, all right, OK (*infml*). **4** *fine weather*: bright, sunny, clear, cloudless, dry, fair. ⊞ **1** mediocre. **2** thick, coarse. **4** cloudy.

fine² *n* penalty, punishment, forfeit, forfeiture, damages.

finger *v* touch, handle, manipulate, feel, stroke, caress, fondle, paw, fiddle with, toy with, play about with, meddle with.

finicky *adj* **1** PARTICULAR, finickety, pernickety, fussy, choosy (*infml*), fastidious, meticulous, scrupulous, critical, hypercritical, nit-picking. **2** FIDDLY, intricate, tricky, difficult, delicate. ⊞ **1** easy-going. **2** easy.

finish *v* **1** END, terminate, stop, cease, complete, accomplish, achieve, fulfil, discharge, deal with, do, conclude, close, wind up, settle, round off, culminate, perfect.

2 DESTROY, ruin, exterminate, get rid of, annihilate, defeat, overcome, rout, overthrow. **3** USE UP, consume, devour, eat, drink, exhaust, drain, empty. ⊞ **1** begin, start. ◇ *n* **1** END, termination, completion, conclusion, close, ending, finale, culmination. **2** SURFACE, appearance, texture, grain, polish, shine, gloss, lustre, smoothness. ⊞ **1** beginning, start, initiation, commencement.

finite *adj* limited, restricted, bounded, demarcated, terminable, definable, fixed, measurable, calculable, countable, numbered. ⊞ infinite.

fire *n* **1** FLAMES, blaze, bonfire, conflagration, inferno, burning, combustion. **2** PASSION, feeling, excitement, enthusiasm, spirit, intensity, heat, radiance, sparkle. ◇ *v* **1** IGNITE, light, kindle, set fire to, set on fire, set alight. **2** *fire a missile*: shoot, launch, set off, let off, detonate, explode. **3** DISMISS, discharge, sack (*infml*), eject. **4** EXCITE, whet, enliven, galvanize, electrify, stir, arouse, rouse, stimulate, inspire, incite, spark off, trigger off. ● **on fire** burning, alight, ignited, flaming, in flames, aflame, blazing, ablaze, fiery.

firm¹ *adj* **1** *firm ground*: dense, compressed, compact, concentrated, set, solid, hard, unyielding, stiff, rigid, inflexible. **2** FIXED, embedded, fast, tight, secure, fastened, anchored, immovable, motionless, stationary, steady, stable, sturdy, strong. **3** ADAMANT, unshakable, resolute, determined, dogged, unwavering, strict, constant, steadfast, staunch, dependable, true, sure, convinced, definite, settled, committed. ⊞ **1** soft, flabby. **2** unsteady. **3** hesitant.

firm² *n* company, corporation,

business, enterprise, concern, house, establishment, institution, organization, association, partnership, syndicate, conglomerate.

first *adj* **1** INITIAL, opening, introductory, preliminary, basic, elementary, primary, fundamental. **2** ORIGINAL, earliest, earlier, prior, primitive, primeval, oldest, eldest, senior. **3** CHIEF, main, key, cardinal, principal, head, leading, ruling, sovereign, highest, uppermost, paramount, prime, predominant, pre-eminent.
🔁 **1** last, final.
◇ *adv* initially, to begin with, to start with, at the outset, beforehand, originally, in preference, rather, sooner.
• **first name** forename, Christian name, baptismal name, given name.

first-rate *adj* first-class, A1, second-to-none, matchless, peerless, top, top-notch (*infml*), top-flight, leading, supreme, superior, prime, excellent, outstanding, superlative, exceptional, splendid, superb, fine, admirable.
🔁 inferior.

fish

Types of fish include: bass, bream, brill, brisling, carp, catfish, chub, cod, coley, conger eel, dab, dace, dogfish, dory, Dover sole, eel, flounder, goldfish, guppy, haddock, hake, halibut, herring, hoki, ling, mackerel, marlin, minnow, monkfish, mullet, perch, pike, pilchard, piranha, plaice, pollock, rainbow trout, ray, roach, roughy, salmon, sardine, shark, skate, snapper, sole, sprat, stickleback, stingray, sturgeon, swordfish, tench, trout, tuna, turbot, whitebait, whiting.

v angle, trawl, delve, hunt, seek, invite, solicit.
• **fish out** produce, take out, extract, find, come up with, dredge up, haul up.

fishing *n* angling, trawling.

fit[1] *adj* **1** SUITABLE, appropriate, apt, fitting, correct, right, proper, ready, prepared, able, capable, competent, qualified, eligible, worthy. **2** HEALTHY, well, able-bodied, in good form, in good shape, sound, sturdy, strong, robust, hale and hearty.
🔁 **1** unsuitable, unworthy. **2** unfit.
◇ *v* **1** MATCH, correspond, conform, follow, agree, concur, tally, suit, harmonize, go, belong, dovetail, interlock, join, meet, arrange, place, position, accommodate. **2** ALTER, modify, change, adjust, adapt, tailor, shape, fashion.
• **fit out** equip, rig out, kit out, outfit, provide, supply, furnish, prepare, arm.

fit[2] *n* seizure, convulsion, spasm, paroxysm, attack, outbreak, bout, spell, burst, surge, outburst, eruption, explosion.

fitful *adj* sporadic, intermittent, occasional, spasmodic, erratic, irregular, uneven, broken, disturbed.
🔁 steady, regular.

fitted *adj* **1** *fitted wardrobe*: built-in, permanent. **2** EQUIPPED, rigged out, provided, furnished, appointed, prepared, armed. **3** SUITED, right, suitable, fit, qualified.

fitting *adj* apt, appropriate, suitable, fit, correct, right, proper, seemly, meet (*fml*), desirable, deserved.
🔁 unsuitable, improper.
◇ *n* connection, attachment, accessory, part, unit, component, piece, fitment.

fittings *n* equipment, furnishings, furniture, fixtures, installations, fitments, accessories, extras.

fix *v* **1** FASTEN, secure, tie, bind, attach, join, connect, link, couple, anchor, pin, nail, rivet, stick, glue, cement, set, harden, solidify, stiffen,

stabilize, plant, root, implant, embed, establish, install, place, locate, position. **2** *fix a date*: arrange, set, specify, define, agree on, decide, determine, settle, resolve, finalize. **3** MEND, repair, correct, rectify, adjust, restore.
☒ **1** move, shift. **3** damage.
◇ *n* (*infml*) dilemma, quandary, predicament, plight, difficulty, hole (*infml*), corner, spot (*infml*), mess, muddle.
• **fix up** arrange, organize, plan, lay on, provide, supply, furnish, equip, settle, sort out, produce, bring about.

fixation *n* preoccupation, obsession, mania, fetish, infatuation, thing (*infml*), compulsion, hang-up (*infml*), complex.

fixed *adj* decided, settled, established, definite, arranged, planned, set, firm, rigid, inflexible, steady, secure, fast, rooted, permanent.
☒ variable.

fizz *v* effervesce, sparkle, bubble, froth, foam, fizzle, hiss, sizzle, sputter, spit.

fizzy *adj* effervescent, sparkling, aerated, carbonated, gassy, bubbly, bubbling, frothy, foaming.

flabbergasted *adj* amazed, confounded, astonished, astounded, staggered, dumbfounded, speechless, stunned, dazed, overcome, overwhelmed, bowled over.

flabby *adj* fleshy, soft, yielding, flaccid, limp, floppy, drooping, hanging, sagging, slack, loose, lax, weak, feeble.
☒ firm, strong.

flag¹ *v* lessen, diminish, decline, fall (off), abate, subside, sink, slump, dwindle, peter out, fade, fail, slow, weaken, falter, tire, weary, wilt, droop, sag, flop, faint, die.
☒ revive.

flag² *n* ensign, jack, pennant,

colours, standard, banner, streamer.
◇ *v* **1** SIGNAL, wave, salute, motion.
2 MARK, indicate, label, tag, note.

flail *v* thresh, thrash, beat, whip.

flair *n* skill, ability, aptitude, faculty, gift, talent, facility, knack, mastery, genius, feel, taste, discernment, acumen, style, elegance, stylishness, panache.
☒ inability, ineptitude.

flake *n* scale, peeling, paring, shaving, sliver, wafer, chip, splinter.
◇ *v* scale, peel, chip, splinter.

flamboyant *adj* showy, flashy, gaudy, ostentatious, colourful, brilliant, dazzling, striking, extravagant, rich, elaborate, ornate, florid.
☒ modest, restrained.

flame *v* burn, flare, blaze, glare, flash, beam, shine, glow, radiate.
◇ *n* **1** FIRE, blaze, light, brightness, heat, warmth. **2** PASSION, ardour, fervour, enthusiasm, zeal, intensity, radiance.

flaming *adj* **1** *a flaming torch*: burning, alight, aflame, blazing, fiery, brilliant, scintillating, red-hot, glowing, smouldering. **2** INTENSE, vivid, aroused, impassioned, hot, raging, frenzied.

flammable *adj* inflammable, ignitable, combustible.
☒ non-flammable, incombustible, flameproof, fire-resistant.

flank *n* side, edge, quarter, wing, loin, hip, thigh.
◇ *v* edge, fringe, skirt, line, border, bound, confine, wall, screen.

flap *v* flutter, vibrate, wave, agitate, shake, wag, swing, swish, thrash, beat.
◇ *n* **1** FOLD, fly, lapel, tab, lug, tag, tail, skirt, aileron. **2** (*infml*) PANIC, state (*infml*), fuss, commotion, fluster, agitation, flutter, dither, tizzy (*infml*).

flare *v* **1** FLAME, burn, blaze, glare,

flash, flicker, burst, explode, erupt.
2 BROADEN, widen, flare out, spread
out, splay.
◇ *n* **1** FLAME, blaze, glare, flash,
flicker, burst. **2** BROADENING,
widening, splay.
• **flare up** erupt, break out, explode,
blow up.

flash *v* **1** BEAM, shine, light up, flare,
blaze, glare, gleam, glint, flicker,
twinkle, sparkle, glitter, shimmer.
2 *the train flashed past*: streak, fly,
dart, race, dash.
◇ *n* beam, ray, shaft, spark, blaze,
flare, burst, streak, gleam, glint,
flicker, twinkle, sparkle, shimmer.

flashy *adj* showy, ostentatious,
flamboyant, glamorous, bold, loud,
garish, gaudy, jazzy, flash, tawdry,
cheap, vulgar, tasteless.
⊞ plain, tasteful.

flat¹ *adj* **1** LEVEL, plane, even, smooth,
uniform, unbroken, horizontal,
outstretched, prostrate, prone,
recumbent, reclining, low. **2** DULL,
boring, monotonous, tedious,
uninteresting, unexciting, stale,
lifeless, dead, spiritless, lacklustre,
vapid, insipid, weak, watery, empty,
pointless. **3** *a flat refusal*: absolute,
utter, total, unequivocal, categorical,
positive, unconditional, unqualified,
point-blank, direct, straight, explicit,
plain, final. **4** *a flat tyre*: punctured,
burst, deflated, collapsed.
⊞ **1** bumpy, vertical. **2** exciting, full.
3 equivocal.
• **flat out** at top speed, at full speed,
all out, for all one is worth.

flat² *n* apartment, penthouse, rooms,
maisonette, tenement, flatlet, suite,
bed-sit(ter).

flatten *v* **1** SMOOTH, iron, press, roll,
crush, squash, compress, level, even
out. **2** KNOCK DOWN, prostrate, floor,
fell, demolish, raze, overwhelm,
subdue.

flatter *v* praise, compliment, sweet-
talk (*infml*), adulate, fawn, butter up

(*infml*), wheedle, humour, play up to,
court, curry favour with.
⊞ criticize.

flattering *adj* complimentary, kind,
favourable, enhancing, gratifying,
becoming, adulatory, ingratiating,
fawning, fulsome, effusive, servile,
smooth-spoken, smooth-tongued,
honeyed, honey-tongued, sugared,
sugary.
⊞ candid, uncompromising,
unflattering.

flattery *n* adulation, eulogy, sweet
talk (*infml*), soft soap (*infml*), flannel
(*infml*), blarney, cajolery, fawning,
toadyism, sycophancy, ingratiation,
servility.
⊞ criticism.

flavour *n* **1** TASTE, tang, smack,
savour, relish, zest, zing (*infml*),
aroma, odour. **2** QUALITY, property,
character, style, aspect, feeling, feel,
atmosphere. **3** HINT, suggestion,
touch, tinge, tone.
◇ *v* season, spice, ginger up, infuse,
imbue.

flavouring *n* seasoning, zest,
essence, extract, additive.

flaw *n* defect, imperfection, fault,
blemish, spot, mark, speck, crack,
crevice, fissure, cleft, split, rift, break,
fracture, weakness, shortcoming,
failing, fallacy, lapse, slip, error,
mistake.

flawed *adj* imperfect, defective,
faulty, blemished, marked, damaged,
spoilt, marred, cracked, chipped,
broken, unsound, fallacious,
erroneous.
⊞ flawless, perfect.

flawless *adj* perfect, faultless,
unblemished, spotless, immaculate,
stainless, sound, intact, whole,
unbroken, undamaged.
⊞ flawed, imperfect.

fleck *v* dot, spot, mark, speckle,
dapple, mottle, streak, sprinkle,
dust.

◇ *n* dot, point, spot, mark, speck, speckle, streak.

flee *v* run away, bolt, fly, take flight, take off, make off, cut and run, escape, get away, decamp, abscond, leave, depart, withdraw, retreat, vanish, disappear.
⊟ stay.

fleet *n* flotilla, armada, navy, task force, squadron.

fleeting *adj* short, brief, flying, short-lived, momentary, ephemeral, transient, transitory, passing, temporary.
⊟ lasting, permanent.

flesh *n* body, tissue, fat, muscle, brawn, skin, meat, pulp, substance, matter, physicality.

flex *v* bend, bow, curve, angle, ply, double up, tighten, contract.
⊟ straighten, extend.
◇ *n* cable, wire, lead, cord.

flexible *adj* **1** BENDABLE, bendy (*infml*), pliable, pliant, plastic, malleable, mouldable, elastic, stretchy, springy, yielding, supple, lithe, limber, double-jointed, mobile. **2** ADAPTABLE, adjustable, amenable, accommodating, variable, open.
⊟ **1** inflexible, rigid.

flick *v* hit, strike, rap, tap, touch, dab, flip, jerk, whip, lash.
◇ *n* rap, tap, touch, dab, flip, jerk, click.
• **flick through** flip through, thumb through, leaf through, glance at, skim, scan.

flicker *v* flash, blink, wink, twinkle, sparkle, glimmer, shimmer, gutter, flutter, vibrate, quiver, waver.
◇ *n* flash, gleam, glint, twinkle, glimmer, spark, trace, drop, iota, atom, indication.

flight¹ *n* **1** FLYING, aviation, air transport, air travel, aeronautics. **2** JOURNEY, trip, voyage.

flight² *n* fleeing, escape, getaway, breakaway, exit, departure, exodus, retreat.

flimsy *adj* thin, fine, light, slight, insubstantial, ethereal, fragile, delicate, shaky, rickety, makeshift, weak, feeble, meagre, inadequate, shallow, superficial, trivial, poor, unconvincing, implausible.
⊟ sturdy.

flinch *v* wince, start, cringe, cower, quail, tremble, shake, quake, duck, shudder, shiver, shrink, recoil, draw back, balk, shy away, shirk, withdraw, retreat, flee.

fling *v* throw, hurl, pitch, lob, toss, chuck (*infml*), cast, sling, catapult, launch, propel, send, let fly, heave, jerk.

flip *v* flick, spin, twirl, twist, turn, toss, throw, cast, pitch, jerk, flap.
◇ *n* flick, spin, twirl, twist, turn, toss, jerk, flap.

flippant *adj* facetious, light-hearted, frivolous, superficial, offhand, flip, glib, pert, saucy (*infml*), cheeky (*infml*), impudent, impertinent, rude, disrespectful, irreverent.
⊟ serious, respectful.

flirt *v* chat up, make up to, lead on, philander, dally.
• **flirt with** consider, entertain, toy with, play with, trifle with, dabble in, try.

flit *v* dart, speed, flash, fly, wing, flutter, whisk, skim, slip, pass, bob, dance.

float *v* **1** GLIDE, sail, swim, bob, drift, waft, hover, hang. **2** LAUNCH, initiate, set up, promote.
⊟ **1** sink.

floating *adj* **1** AFLOAT, buoyant, unsinkable, sailing, swimming, bobbing, drifting. **2** VARIABLE, fluctuating, movable, migratory, transitory, wandering, unattached, free, uncommitted.
⊟ **1** sinking. **2** fixed.

flock v herd, swarm, troop, converge, mass, bunch, cluster, huddle, crowd, throng, group, gather, collect, congregate.
◇ n herd, pack, crowd, throng, multitude, mass, bunch, cluster, group, gathering, assembly, congregation.

flog v beat, whip, lash, flagellate, scourge, birch, cane, flay, drub, thrash, whack (infml), chastise, punish.

flogging n beating, whipping, lashing, flagellation, scourging, birching, caning, flaying, thrashing, hiding.

flood v 1 DELUGE, inundate, soak, drench, saturate, fill, overflow, immerse, submerge, engulf, swamp, overwhelm, drown. 2 FLOW, pour, stream, rush, surge, gush.
◇ n deluge, inundation, downpour, torrent, flow, tide, stream, rush, spate, outpouring, overflow, glut, excess, abundance, profusion.
⊟ drought, trickle, dearth.

floor n 1 FLOORING, ground, base, basis. 2 on the third floor: storey, level, stage, landing, deck, tier.
◇ v (infml) defeat, overwhelm, beat, stump (infml), frustrate, confound, perplex, baffle, puzzle, bewilder, disconcert, throw.

flop v 1 DROOP, hang, dangle, sag, drop, fall, topple, tumble, slump, collapse. 2 FAIL, misfire, fall flat, founder, fold.
◇ n failure, non-starter, fiasco, debacle, wash-out (infml), disaster.

floppy adj droopy, hanging, dangling, sagging, limp, loose, baggy, soft, flabby.
⊟ firm.

florid adj 1 FLOWERY, ornate, elaborate, fussy, overelaborate, baroque, rococo, flamboyant, grandiloquent. 2 a florid complexion: ruddy, red, flushed, purple.

⊟ 1 plain, simple. 2 pale.

flotsam n jetsam, wreckage, debris, rubbish, junk, oddments.

flounder v wallow, struggle, grope, fumble, blunder, stagger, stumble, falter.

flourish v 1 THRIVE, grow, wax, increase, flower, blossom, bloom, develop, progress, get on, do well, prosper, succeed, boom. 2 BRANDISH, wave, shake, twirl, swing, display, wield, flaunt, parade, vaunt.
⊟ 1 decline, languish, fail.
◇ n display, parade, show, gesture, wave, sweep, fanfare, ornament, decoration, panache, pizzazz (infml).

flourishing adj thriving, blooming, prosperous, successful, booming.

flout v defy, disobey, violate, break, disregard, spurn, reject, scorn, jeer at, scoff at, mock, ridicule.
⊟ obey, respect, regard.

flow v 1 CIRCULATE, ooze, trickle, ripple, bubble, well, spurt, squirt, gush, spill, run, pour, cascade, rush, stream, teem, flood, overflow, surge, sweep, move, drift, slip, slide, glide, roll, swirl. 2 ORIGINATE, derive, arise, spring, emerge, issue, result, proceed, emanate.
◇ n course, flux, tide, current, drift, outpouring, stream, deluge, cascade, spurt, gush, flood, spate, abundance, plenty.

flower n 1 BLOOM, blossom, bud, floret. 2 BEST, cream, pick, choice, élite.

Flowers include: African violet, alyssum, anemone, aster, aubrieta, azalea, begonia, bluebell, busy Lizzie (impatiens), calendula, candytuft, carnation, chrysanthemum, cornflower, cowslip, crocus, cyclamen, daffodil, dahlia, daisy, delphinium, forget-me-not, foxglove (digitalis), freesia, fuchsia, gardenia, geranium, gladiolus, hollyhock, hyacinth, iris (flag), lily, lily of the valley, lobelia, lupin, marigold, narcissus, nasturtium, orchid, pansy, petunia, pink (dianthus), phlox, poinsettia, polyanthus, poppy, primrose, primula, rose, salvia, snapdragon (antirrhinum), snowdrop, stock, sunflower, sweetpea, sweet william, tulip, verbena, violet, wallflower, zinnia. *see also* **plant**; **shrub**.

Parts of a flower include: anther, calyx, capitulum, carpel, corolla, corymb, dichasium, filament, gynoecium, monochasium, nectary, ovary, ovule, panicle, pedicel, petal, pistil, raceme, receptacle, sepal, spadix, spike, stalk, stamen, stigma, style, thalamus, torus, umbel.

◇ *v* bud, burgeon, bloom, blossom, open, come out.

flowery *adj* florid, ornate, elaborate, fancy, baroque, rhetorical.
⊞ plain, simple.

fluctuate *v* vary, change, alter, shift, rise and fall, seesaw, ebb and flow, alternate, swing, sway, oscillate, vacillate, waver.

fluent *adj* flowing, smooth, easy, effortless, articulate, eloquent, voluble, glib, ready.
⊞ broken, inarticulate, tongue-tied.

fluff *n* down, nap, pile, fuzz, floss, lint, dust.

fluffy *adj* furry, fuzzy, downy, feathery, fleecy, woolly, hairy, shaggy, velvety, silky, soft.

fluid *adj* 1 LIQUID, liquefied, aqueous, watery, running, runny, melted, molten. 2 *a fluid situation:* variable, changeable, unstable, inconstant, shifting, mobile, flexible, adjustable, adaptable, open. 3 *fluid movements:* flowing, smooth, graceful.

⊞ 1 solid. 2 stable. 3 erratic.
◇ *n* liquid, solution, liquor, juice, gas, vapour.

flurry *n* 1 BURST, outbreak, spell, spurt, gust, blast, squall.
2 BUSTLE, hurry, fluster, fuss, to-do, commotion, tumult, whirl, disturbance, stir, flap (*infml*).

flush¹ *v* 1 BLUSH, go red, redden, crimson, colour, burn, glow, suffuse.
2 CLEANSE, wash, rinse, hose, swab, clear, empty, evacuate.
◇ *adj* 1 ABUNDANT, lavish, generous, full, overflowing, rich, prosperous, wealthy, moneyed, well-off, well-heeled, well-to-do. 2 LEVEL, even, smooth, flat, plane, square, true.

flush² *v* start, rouse, disturb, drive out, force out, expel, eject, run to earth, discover, uncover.

fluster *v* bother, upset, embarrass, disturb, perturb, agitate, ruffle, discompose, confuse, confound, unnerve, disconcert, rattle (*infml*), put off, distract.
⊞ calm.
◇ *n* flurry, bustle, commotion, disturbance, turmoil, state (*infml*), agitation, embarrassment, flap (*infml*), dither, tizzy (*infml*).
⊞ calm.

fluted *adj* grooved, furrowed, channelled, corrugated, ribbed, ridged.

flutter *v* flap, wave, beat, bat, flicker, vibrate, palpitate, agitate, shake, tremble, quiver, shiver, ruffle, ripple, twitch, toss, waver, fluctuate.
◇ *n* flapping, beat, flicker, vibration, palpitation, tremble, tremor, quiver, shiver, shudder, twitch.

flux *n* fluctuation, instability, change, alteration, modification, fluidity, flow, movement, motion, transition, development.
⊞ stability, rest.

fly *v* 1 TAKE OFF, rise, ascend, mount, soar, glide, float, hover, flit, wing.

2 RACE, sprint, dash, tear, rush, hurry, speed, zoom, shoot, dart, career.
• **fly at** attack, go for, fall upon.

foam n froth, lather, suds, head, bubbles, effervescence.
◇ v froth, lather, bubble, effervesce, fizz, boil, seethe.

fob off v foist, pass off, palm off (*infml*), get rid of, dump, unload, inflict, impose, deceive, put off.

focus n focal point, target, centre, heart, core, nucleus, kernel, crux, hub, axis, linchpin, pivot, hinge.
◇ v converge, meet, join, centre, concentrate, aim, direct, fix, spotlight, home in, zoom in, zero in (*infml*).

fog n **1** MIST, haze, cloud, gloom, murkiness, smog, pea-souper.
2 PERPLEXITY, puzzlement, confusion, bewilderment, daze, trance, vagueness, obscurity.
◇ v mist, steam up, cloud, dull, dim, darken, obscure, blur, confuse, muddle.

foggy adj misty, hazy, smoggy, cloudy, murky, dark, shadowy, dim, indistinct, obscure.
🗶 clear.

foil[1] v defeat, outwit, frustrate, thwart, baffle, counter, nullify, stop, check, obstruct, block, circumvent, elude.
🗶 abet.

foil[2] n setting, background, relief, contrast, complement, balance.

fold v **1** BEND, ply, double, overlap, tuck, pleat, crease, crumple, crimp, crinkle. **2** (*infml*) *the business folded*: fail, go bust, shut down, collapse, crash. **3** ENFOLD, embrace, hug, clasp, envelop, wrap (up), enclose, entwine, intertwine.
◇ n bend, turn, layer, ply, overlap, tuck, pleat, crease, knife-edge, line, wrinkle, furrow, corrugation.

folder n file, binder, folio, portfolio, envelope, holder.

folk n people, society, nation, race, tribe, clan, family, kin, kindred.
◇ adj ethnic, national, traditional, native, indigenous, tribal, ancestral.

follow v **1** *night follows day*: come after, succeed, come next, replace, supersede, supplant. **2** CHASE, pursue, go after, hunt, track, trail, shadow, tail, hound, catch. **3** ACCOMPANY, go (along) with, escort, attend. **4** RESULT, ensue, develop, emanate, arise. **5** OBEY, comply with, adhere to, heed, mind, observe, conform to, carry out, practise. **6** GRASP, understand, comprehend, fathom.
🗶 **1** precede. **3** abandon, desert. **5** disobey.
• **follow through** continue, pursue, see through, finish, complete, conclude, fulfil, implement.
• **follow up** investigate, check out, continue, pursue, reinforce, consolidate.

follower n attendant, retainer, helper, companion, sidekick (*infml*), apostle, disciple, pupil, imitator, emulator, adherent, hanger-on, believer, convert, backer, supporter, admirer, fan, devotee, freak (*infml*), buff (*infml*).
🗶 leader, opponent.

following adj subsequent, next, succeeding, successive, resulting, ensuing, consequent, later.
🗶 previous.
◇ n followers, suite, retinue, entourage, circle, fans, admirers, supporters, support, backing, patronage, clientèle, audience, public.

folly n foolishness, stupidity, senselessness, rashness, recklessness, irresponsibility, indiscretion, lunacy, craziness, madness, insanity, idiocy, imbecility, silliness, absurdity, nonsense.
🗶 wisdom, prudence, sanity.

fond adj affectionate, warm, tender, caring, loving, adoring, devoted,

doting, indulgent.
• **fond of** partial to, attached to, enamoured of, keen on, addicted to, hooked on.

fondle v caress, stroke, pat, pet, cuddle.

food n foodstuffs, comestibles, eatables (*infml*), provisions, stores, rations, eats (*infml*), grub (*sl*), nosh (*sl*), scran (*infml*), refreshment, sustenance, nourishment, nutrition, nutriment, subsistence, feed, fodder, diet, fare, cooking, cuisine, menu, board, table, larder.

Types of food include: biscuit, bread, cake, cheese, fish, fruit, meat, egg, nut, soup, vegetable; chips, French fries; pasta, cannelloni, fettuccine, ravioli, spaghetti bolognese, tortellini, lasagne; fish and chips, fish cake, fish pie, fish finger, kedgeree, kipper, pickled herring, scampi, prawn cocktail, caviar; casserole, cassoulet, hotpot, shepherd's pie, cottage pie, chilli con carne; balti, biriyani, chop suey, enchilada, moussaka, paella, pakora, pizza, ragout, risotto, rissole, samosa, smorgasbord, stovies, stroganoff, taco, tandoori, vindaloo, Wiener schnitzel; French toast, welsh rarebit; brawn, faggot, haggis, black pudding, pâté, sausage, salami, frankfurter, hot dog, fritter, beefburger, hamburger, Big Mac®; omelette, quiche, tofu, Quorn®, Yorkshire pudding, toad-in-the-hole; gingerbread, shortbread, scone, macaroon, muffin; sauce, dip, dressing, gravy. *see also* **bread**; **cake**; **cheese**; **dessert**; **fish**; **fruit**; **meat**; **nut**; **pasta**; **pastry**; **sauce**; **soup**; **sweet**; **vegetable**.

---

fool n blockhead, fat-head, butthead (*sl*), nincompoop (*infml*), ass (*infml*), chump (*infml*), ninny (*infml*), clot (*infml*), dope (*infml*), twit (*infml*), nitwit (*infml*), nit (*infml*), dunce, dimwit, simpleton, halfwit, idiot, imbecile, moron, dupe, sucker (*infml*), mug (*infml*), stooge, clown, buffoon, jester.
◇ v deceive, take in, delude, mislead, dupe, gull, hoodwink, put one over on, trick, hoax, con (*infml*), cheat, swindle, diddle (*infml*), string along (*infml*), have on (*infml*), kid (*infml*), tease, joke, jest.
• **fool about** lark about, horse around (*sl*), play about, mess about (*infml*), mess around (*infml*).

foolhardy adj rash, reckless, imprudent, ill-advised, irresponsible.
🔁 cautious, prudent.

foolish adj stupid, senseless, unwise, ill-advised, ill-considered, short-sighted, half-baked, daft (*infml*), crazy, mad, insane, idiotic, moronic, hare-brained, halfwitted, simple-minded, simple, unintelligent, inept, inane, silly, absurd, ridiculous, ludicrous, nonsensical.
🔁 wise, prudent.

foolproof adj idiot-proof, infallible, fail-safe, sure, certain, sure-fire (*infml*), guaranteed.
🔁 unreliable.

footing n base, foundation, basis, ground, relations, relationship, terms, conditions, state, standing, status, grade, rank, position, balance, foothold, purchase.

footprint n footmark, track, trail, trace, vestige.

forage n fodder, pasturage, feed, food, foodstuffs.
◇ v rummage, search, cast about, scour, hunt, scavenge, ransack, plunder, raid.

forbid v prohibit, disallow, ban, proscribe, interdict, veto, refuse, deny, outlaw, debar, exclude, rule out, preclude, prevent, block, hinder, inhibit.
🔁 allow, permit, approve.

forbidden *adj* prohibited, banned, proscribed, taboo, vetoed, outlawed, out of bounds.

forbidding *adj* stern, formidable, awesome, daunting, off-putting, uninviting, menacing, threatening, ominous, sinister, frightening.
⊡ approachable, congenial.

force *n* **1** COMPULSION, impulse, influence, coercion, constraint, pressure, duress, violence, aggression. **2** POWER, might, strength, intensity, effort, energy, vigour, drive, dynamism, stress, emphasis. **3** ARMY, troop, body, corps, regiment, squadron, battalion, division, unit, detachment, patrol.
⊡ **2** weakness.
◇ *v* **1** COMPEL, make, oblige, urge, necessitate, coerce, constrain, press, pressurize, lean on (*infml*), press-gang, bulldoze, drive, propel, push, thrust. **2** PRISE, wrench, wrest, extort, exact, wring.

forced *adj* unnatural, stiff, wooden, stilted, laboured, strained, false, artificial, contrived, feigned, affected, insincere.
⊡ spontaneous, sincere.

forceful *adj* strong, mighty, powerful, potent, effective, compelling, convincing, persuasive, cogent, telling, weighty, urgent, emphatic, vehement, forcible, dynamic, energetic, vigorous.
⊡ weak, feeble.

forebear *n* ancestor, forefather, father, predecessor, forerunner, antecedent.
⊡ descendant.

foreboding *n* misgiving, anxiety, worry, apprehension, dread, fear, omen, sign, token, premonition, warning, prediction, prognostication, intuition, feeling.

forecast *v* predict, prophesy, foretell, foresee, anticipate, expect, estimate, calculate.

◇ *n* prediction, prophecy, expectation, prognosis, outlook, projection, guess, guesstimate (*infml*).

forefront *n* front, front line, firing line, van, vanguard, lead, fore, avant-garde.
⊡ rear.

foregoing *adj* preceding, above, antecedent, previous, earlier, former, prior.
⊡ following.

foreign *adj* alien, immigrant, imported, international, external, outside, overseas, exotic, faraway, distant, remote, strange, unfamiliar, unknown, uncharacteristic, odd, incongruous, extraneous, borrowed.
⊡ native, indigenous.

foreigner *n* alien, immigrant, incomer, stranger, newcomer, visitor.
⊡ native.

foremost *adj* first, leading, front, chief, main, principal, primary, cardinal, paramount, central, highest, uppermost, supreme, prime, pre-eminent.

forerunner *n* predecessor, ancestor, antecedent, precursor, harbinger, herald, envoy, sign, token.
⊡ successor, follower.

foresee *v* envisage, anticipate, expect, forecast, predict, prophesy, prognosticate, foretell, forebode, divine.

foreshadow *v* prefigure, presage, augur, predict, prophesy, signal, indicate, promise.

foresight *n* anticipation, planning, forethought, far-sightedness, vision, caution, prudence, circumspection, care, readiness, preparedness, provision, precaution.
⊡ improvidence.

forestall *v* pre-empt, anticipate, preclude, obviate, avert, head off, ward off, parry, balk, frustrate, thwart, hinder, prevent.

foretaste n preview, trailer, sample, specimen, example, whiff, indication, warning, premonition.

foretell v prophesy, forecast, predict, prognosticate, augur, presage, signify, foreshadow, forewarn.

forethought n preparation, planning, forward planning, provision, precaution, anticipation, foresight, far-sightedness, circumspection, prudence, caution. ⊜ improvidence, carelessness.

forever adv continually, constantly, 24-7 (infml), persistently, incessantly, perpetually, endlessly, eternally, always, evermore, for all time, permanently.

foreword n preface, introduction, prologue. ⊜ appendix, postscript, epilogue.

forfeit n loss, surrender, confiscation, sequestration, penalty, fine, damages. ◇ v lose, give up, surrender, relinquish, sacrifice, forgo, renounce, abandon.

forge v 1 MAKE, mould, cast, shape, form, fashion, beat out, hammer out, work, create, invent. 2 forge a document: fake, counterfeit, falsify, copy, imitate, simulate, feign.

forgery n fake, counterfeit, copy, replica, reproduction, imitation, dud (infml), phoney (infml), sham, fraud. ⊜ original.

forget v omit, fail, neglect, let slip, overlook, disregard, ignore, lose sight of, dismiss, think no more of, unlearn. ⊜ remember, recall, recollect.

forgetful adj absent-minded, dreamy, inattentive, oblivious, negligent, lax, heedless. ⊜ attentive, heedful.

forgive v pardon, absolve, excuse, exonerate, exculpate, acquit, remit, let off, overlook, condone. ⊜ punish, censure.

forgiveness n pardon, absolution, exoneration, acquittal, remission, amnesty, mercy, clemency, leniency. ⊜ punishment, censure, blame.

forgiving adj merciful, clement, lenient, tolerant, forbearing, indulgent, kind, humane, compassionate, soft-hearted, mild. ⊜ merciless, censorious, harsh.

forgo v give up, yield, surrender, relinquish, sacrifice, forfeit, waive, renounce, abandon, resign, pass up, do without, abstain from, refrain from. ⊜ claim, indulge in.

fork v split, divide, part, separate, diverge, branch (off).

forlorn adj deserted, abandoned, forsaken, forgotten, bereft, friendless, lonely, lost, homeless, destitute, desolate, hopeless, unhappy, miserable, wretched, helpless, pathetic, pitiable. ⊜ cheerful.

form v 1 SHAPE, mould, model, fashion, make, manufacture, produce, create, found, establish, build, construct, assemble, put together, arrange, organize. 2 COMPRISE, constitute, make up, compose. 3 APPEAR, take shape, materialize, crystallize, grow, develop. ◇ n 1 APPEARANCE, shape, mould, cast, cut, outline, silhouette, figure, build, frame, structure, format, model, pattern, design, arrangement, organization, system. 2 a form of punishment: type, kind, sort, order, species, variety, genre, style, manner, nature, character, description. 3 CLASS, year, grade, stream. 4 on top form: health, fitness, fettle, condition, spirits. 5 ETIQUETTE, protocol, custom, convention, ritual, behaviour, manners. 6 QUESTIONNAIRE, document, paper, sheet.

formal *adj* **1** OFFICIAL, ceremonial, stately, solemn, conventional, orthodox, correct, fixed, set, regular. **2** PRIM, starchy, stiff, strict, rigid, precise, exact, punctilious, ceremonious, stilted, reserved.
⊜ **2** informal, casual.

formality *n* custom, convention, ceremony, ritual, procedure, matter of form, bureaucracy, red tape, protocol, etiquette, form, correctness, propriety, decorum, politeness.
⊜ informality.

formation *n* **1** STRUCTURE, construction, composition, order, constitution, configuration, format, organization, arrangement, grouping, pattern, design, figure. **2** CREATION, generation, production, manufacture, appearance, development, establishment.

former *adj* past, ex-, one-time, sometime, late, departed, old, old-time, ancient, bygone, earlier, prior, previous, preceding, antecedent, foregoing, above.
⊜ current, present, future, following.

formerly *adv* once, previously, earlier, before, at one time, lately.
⊜ currently, now, later.

formidable *adj* daunting, challenging, intimidating, threatening, frightening, terrifying, terrific, frightful, fearful, great, huge, tremendous, prodigious, impressive, awesome, overwhelming, staggering.

formula *n* recipe, prescription, proposal, blueprint, code, wording, rubric, rule, principle, procedure, technique, method, form, way.

formulate *v* create, invent, originate, found, form, devise, work out, plan, design, draw up, frame, define, express, state, specify, detail, develop, evolve.

forsake *v* desert, abandon, jilt, throw over, discard, jettison, reject, disown, leave, quit, give up, surrender, relinquish, renounce, forgo.

fort *n* fortress, castle, tower, citadel, stronghold, fortification, garrison, station, camp.

forthcoming *adj* **1** *their forthcoming wedding*: impending, imminent, approaching, coming, future, prospective, projected, expected. **2** COMMUNICATIVE, talkative, chatty, conversational, sociable, informative, expansive, open, frank, direct.
⊜ **2** reticent, reserved.

forthright *adj* direct, blunt, straightforward, frank, candid, plain, open, bold, outspoken, in-your-face (*infml*).
⊜ devious, secretive.

fortify *v* **1** STRENGTHEN, reinforce, brace, shore (up), buttress, garrison, defend, protect, secure. **2** INVIGORATE, sustain, support, boost, encourage, hearten, cheer, reassure.
⊜ **1** weaken.

fortitude *n* courage, bravery, valour, grit, pluck, resolution, determination, perseverance, firmness, strength of mind, willpower, hardihood, endurance, stoicism.
⊜ cowardice, fear.

fortuitous *adj* accidental, chance, random, arbitrary, casual, incidental, unforeseen, lucky, fortunate, providential.
⊜ intentional, planned.

fortunate *adj* lucky, providential, happy, felicitous, prosperous, successful, well-off, timely, well-timed, opportune, convenient, propitious, advantageous, favourable, auspicious.
⊜ unlucky, unfortunate, unhappy.

fortune *n* **1** WEALTH, riches, treasure, mint (*infml*), pile (*infml*), income, means, assets, estate, property, possessions, affluence, prosperity, success. **2** LUCK, chance, accident, providence, fate, destiny, doom, lot, portion, life, history, future.

forward *adj* **1** FIRST, head, front, fore, foremost, leading, onward, progressive, go-ahead, forward-looking, enterprising. **2** CONFIDENT, assertive, pushy, bold, audacious, brazen, brash, barefaced, cheeky (*infml*), impudent, impertinent, fresh (*sl*), familiar, presumptuous. **3** EARLY, advance, precocious, premature, advanced, well-advanced, well-developed.
⊟ **1** backward, retrograde. **2** shy, modest. **3** late, retarded.
◇ *adv* forwards, ahead, on, onward, out, into view.
◇ *v* advance, promote, further, foster, encourage, support, back, favour, help, assist, aid, facilitate, accelerate, speed, hurry, hasten, expedite, dispatch, send (on), post, transport, ship.
⊟ impede, obstruct, hinder, slow.

foster *v* raise, rear, bring up, nurse, care for, take care of, nourish, feed, sustain, support, promote, advance, encourage, stimulate, cultivate, nurture, cherish, entertain, harbour.
⊟ neglect, discourage.

foul *adj* **1** DIRTY, filthy, unclean, tainted, polluted, contaminated, rank, fetid, stinking, smelly, putrid, rotten, nauseating, offensive, repulsive, revolting, disgusting, squalid. **2** *foul language*: obscene, lewd, smutty, indecent, coarse, vulgar, gross, blasphemous, abusive. **3** NASTY, disagreeable, wicked, vicious, vile, base, abhorrent, disgraceful, shameful. **4** *foul weather*: bad, unpleasant, rainy, wet, stormy, rough.
⊟ **1** clean. **4** fine.
◇ *v* **1** DIRTY, soil, stain, sully, defile, taint, pollute, contaminate. **2** BLOCK, obstruct, clog, choke, foul up. **3** ENTANGLE, catch, snarl, twist,

ensnare.
⊟ **1** clean. **2** clear. **3** disentangle.

found *v* **1** START, originate, create, initiate, institute, inaugurate, set up, establish, endow, organize. **2** BASE, ground, bottom, rest, settle, fix, plant, raise, build, erect, construct.

foundation *n* **1** BASE, foot, bottom, ground, bedrock, substance, basis, footing. **2** SETTING UP, establishment, institution, inauguration, endowment, organization, groundwork.

founder[1] *n* originator, initiator, father, mother, benefactor, creator, author, architect, designer, inventor, maker, builder, constructor, organizer.

founder[2] *v* sink, go down, subside, submerge, collapse, break down, fall, come to grief, fail, misfire, miscarry, abort, fall through, come to nothing.

fountain *n* **1** SPRAY, jet, spout, spring, well, wellspring, reservoir, waterworks. **2** SOURCE, origin, fount, font, fountainhead, wellhead.

fracture *n* break, crack, fissure, cleft, rupture, split, rift, rent, schism, breach, gap, opening.
◇ *v* break, crack, rupture, split, splinter, chip.
⊟ join.

fragile *adj* brittle, breakable, frail, delicate, flimsy, dainty, fine, slight, insubstantial, weak, feeble, infirm.
⊟ robust, tough, durable.

fragment *n* piece, bit, part, portion, fraction, particle, crumb, morsel, scrap, remnant, shred, chip, splinter, shiver, sliver, shard.
◇ *v* break, shatter, splinter, shiver, crumble, disintegrate, come to pieces, come apart, break up, divide, split (up), disunite.
⊟ hold together, join.

fragmentary *adj* bitty, piecemeal, scrappy, broken, disjointed, disconnected, separate, scattered,

sketchy, partial, incomplete.
 whole, complete.

fragrance *n* perfume, scent, smell, odour, aroma, bouquet.

fragrant *adj* perfumed, scented, sweet-smelling, sweet, balmy, aromatic, odorous.
 unscented.

frail *adj* delicate, brittle, breakable, fragile, flimsy, insubstantial, puny, slight, weak, feeble, infirm, vulnerable.
 robust, tough, strong.

frailty *n* weakness, foible, failing, deficiency, shortcoming, fault, defect, flaw, blemish, imperfection, fallibility, susceptibility.
 strength, robustness, toughness.

frame *v* **1** COMPOSE, formulate, conceive, devise, contrive, concoct, cook up, plan, map out, sketch, draw up, draft, shape, form, model, fashion, mould, forge, assemble, put together, build, construct, fabricate, make. **2** SURROUND, enclose, box in, case, mount. **3** *I've been framed*: set up, fit up (*sl*), trap.
◇ *n* **1** STRUCTURE, fabric, framework, skeleton, carcase, shell, casing, chassis, construction, bodywork, body, build, form. **2** MOUNT, mounting, setting, surround, border, edge.
• **frame of mind** state of mind, mindset, mood, humour, temper, disposition, spirit, outlook, attitude.

framework *n* structure, fabric, bare bones, skeleton, shell, frame, outline, plan, foundation, groundwork.

franchise *n* concession, licence, charter, authorization, privilege, right, liberty, freedom, immunity, exemption.

frank *adj* honest, truthful, sincere, candid, blunt, open, free, plain, direct, forthright, straight, straightforward, downright, outspoken.
 insincere, evasive.

frankly *adv* to be frank, to be honest, in truth, honestly, candidly, bluntly, openly, freely, plainly, directly, straight.
 insincerely, evasively.

frantic *adj* agitated, overwrought, fraught, desperate, beside oneself, furious, raging, mad, wild, raving, frenzied, berserk, hectic.
 calm, composed.

fraternize *v* mix, mingle, socialize, consort, associate, affiliate, unite, sympathize.
 shun, ignore.

fraud *n* **1** DECEIT, deception, guile, cheating, swindling, double-dealing, sharp practice, fake, counterfeit, forgery, sham, hoax, trick. **2** (*infml*) CHARLATAN, impostor, pretender, phoney (*infml*), bluffer, hoaxer, cheat, swindler, double-dealer, con man (*infml*).

fraudulent *adj* dishonest, crooked (*infml*), criminal, deceitful, deceptive, false, bogus, phoney (*infml*), sham, counterfeit, swindling, double-dealing.
 honest, genuine.

fray *n* brawl, scuffle, dust-up (*infml*), free-for-all, set-to, clash, conflict, fight, combat, battle, quarrel, row, rumpus, disturbance, riot.

frayed *adj* ragged, tattered, worn, threadbare, unravelled.

freak *n* **1** MONSTER, mutant, monstrosity, malformation, deformity, irregularity, anomaly, abnormality, aberration, oddity, curiosity, quirk, caprice, vagary, twist, turn. **2** ENTHUSIAST, fanatic, addict, devotee, fan, buff (*infml*), fiend (*infml*), nut (*infml*).
◇ *adj* abnormal, atypical, unusual, exceptional, odd, queer, bizarre, aberrant, capricious, unpredictable, erratic, unexpected, surprise, chance, fortuitous, flukey.
 normal, common.

free adj 1 AT LIBERTY, at large, loose, unattached, unrestrained, liberated, emancipated, independent, democratic, self-governing. 2 free time: spare, available, idle, unemployed, unoccupied, vacant, empty. 3 free tickets: gratis, without charge, free of charge, complimentary, on the house. 4 CLEAR, unobstructed, unimpeded, open. 5 GENEROUS, liberal, open-handed, lavish, charitable, hospitable.
⊡ 1 imprisoned, confined, restricted. 2 busy, occupied.
◇ v release, let go, loose, turn loose, set free, untie, unbind, unchain, unleash, liberate, emancipate, rescue, deliver, save, ransom, disentangle, disengage, extricate, clear, rid, relieve, unburden, exempt, absolve, acquit.
⊡ imprison, confine.
● free of lacking, devoid of, without, unaffected by, immune to, exempt from, safe from.

freedom n 1 LIBERTY, emancipation, deliverance, release, exemption, immunity, impunity. 2 INDEPENDENCE, autonomy, self-government, home rule. 3 RANGE, scope, play, leeway, latitude, licence, privilege, power, free rein, free hand, opportunity, informality.
⊡ 1 captivity, confinement. 3 restriction.

freely adv 1 READILY, willingly, voluntarily, spontaneously, easily. 2 give freely: generously, liberally, lavishly, extravagantly, amply, abundantly. 3 speak freely: frankly, candidly, unreservedly, openly, plainly.
⊡ 2 grudgingly. 3 evasively, cautiously.

freeze v 1 ICE OVER, ice up, glaciate, congeal, solidify, harden, stiffen. 2 DEEP-FREEZE, ice, refrigerate, chill, cool. 3 STOP, suspend, fix, immobilize, hold.

◇ n 1 FROST, freeze-up. 2 STOPPAGE, halt, standstill, shutdown, suspension, interruption, postponement, stay, embargo, moratorium.

freezing adj icy, frosty, glacial, arctic, polar, Siberian, wintry, raw, bitter, biting, cutting, penetrating, numbing, cold, chilly.
⊡ hot, warm.

freight n cargo, load, lading, pay-load, contents, goods, merchandise, consignment, shipment, haulage, transportation, conveyance, carriage.

frenzied adj frantic, frenetic, hectic, feverish, desperate, furious, wild, uncontrolled, mad, demented, hysterical.
⊡ calm, composed.

frenzy n 1 TURMOIL, agitation, distraction, derangement, madness, lunacy, mania, hysteria, delirium, fever. 2 BURST, fit, spasm, paroxysm, convulsion, seizure, outburst, transport, passion, rage, fury.
⊡ 1 calm, composure.

frequent adj 1 NUMEROUS, countless, incessant, constant, continual, persistent, repeated, recurring, regular. 2 COMMON, commonplace, everyday, familiar, usual, customary.
⊡ 1 infrequent.
◇ v visit, patronize, attend, haunt, hang out at (infml), associate with, hang about with (infml), hang out with (infml).

fresh adj 1 ADDITIONAL, extra, supplementary, more, further, other. 2 NEW, novel, innovative, original, different, unconventional, modern, up-to-date, recent, latest. 3 REFRESHING, bracing, invigorating, brisk, crisp, keen, cool, fair, bright, clear, pure. 4 fresh fruit: raw, natural, unprocessed, crude. 5 REFRESHED, revived, restored, renewed, rested, invigorated, energetic, vigorous, lively, alert. 6 PERT, saucy (infml), cheeky (infml), disrespectful,

impudent, insolent, bold, brazen, forward, familiar, presumptuous.
⊡ **2** old, hackneyed. **3** stale. **4** processed. **5** tired.

freshen v **1** AIR, ventilate, purify. **2** REFRESH, restore, revitalize, reinvigorate, liven, enliven, spruce up, tart up (infml).
⊡ **2** tire.

fret v **1** WORRY, agonize, brood, pine. **2** VEX, irritate, nettle, bother, trouble, torment.

friction n **1** DISAGREEMENT, dissension, dispute, disharmony, conflict, antagonism, hostility, opposition, rivalry, animosity, ill feeling, bad blood, resentment. **2** RUBBING, chafing, irritation, abrasion, scraping, grating, rasping, erosion, wearing away, resistance.

friend n mate (infml), pal (infml), chum (infml), buddy (infml), crony (infml), homeboy (sl), intimate, confidant(e), bosom friend, soul mate, comrade, ally, partner, associate, companion, playmate, pen friend, acquaintance, well-wisher, supporter.
⊡ enemy, opponent.

friendly adj **1** AMIABLE, affable, genial, kind, kindly, neighbourly, helpful, sympathetic, affectionate, fond, familiar, intimate, close, matey (infml), pally (infml), chummy (infml), companionable, sociable, outgoing, approachable, receptive, comradely, amicable, peaceable, well-disposed, favourable. **2** a friendly atmosphere: convivial, congenial, cordial, welcoming, warm.
⊡ **1** hostile, unsociable. **2** cold.

friendship n closeness, intimacy, familiarity, affinity, rapport, attachment, affection, fondness, love, harmony, concord, goodwill, friendliness, alliance, fellowship, comradeship.
⊡ enmity, animosity.

fright n shock, scare, alarm, consternation, dismay, dread, apprehension, trepidation, fear, terror, horror, panic.

frighten v alarm, daunt, unnerve, dismay, intimidate, terrorize, scare, startle, scare stiff, terrify, petrify, horrify, appal, shock.
⊡ reassure, calm.

frightening adj alarming, daunting, formidable, fearsome, terrifying, scary, hair-raising, bloodcurdling, spine-chilling, petrifying, traumatic.

frightful adj unpleasant, disagreeable, awful, dreadful, fearful, terrible, appalling, shocking, harrowing, unspeakable, dire, grim, ghastly, hideous, horrible, horrid, grisly, macabre, gruesome.
⊡ pleasant, agreeable.

frigid adj **1** UNFEELING, unresponsive, passionless, unloving, cool, aloof, passive, lifeless. **2** FROZEN, icy, frosty, glacial, arctic, cold, chill, chilly, wintry.
⊡ **1** responsive. **2** hot.

frilly adj ruffled, crimped, gathered, frilled, trimmed, lacy, fancy, ornate.
⊡ plain.

fringe n **1** MARGIN, periphery, outskirts, edge, perimeter, limits, borderline. **2** BORDER, edging, trimming, tassel, frill, valance.
◇ adj unconventional, unorthodox, unofficial, alternative, avant-garde.
⊡ conventional, mainstream.

frisk v jump, leap, skip, hop, caper, bounce, dance, gambol, frolic, romp, play, sport.

frisky adj lively, spirited, high-spirited, frolicsome, playful, romping, rollicking, bouncy.
⊡ quiet.

fritter v waste, squander, dissipate, idle, misspend, blow (sl).

frivolity n fun, gaiety, flippancy, facetiousness, jest, light-heartedness,

levity, triviality, superficiality,
silliness, folly, nonsense.
▣ seriousness.

frivolous *adj* trifling, trivial,
unimportant, shallow, superficial,
light, flippant, jocular, light-hearted,
juvenile, puerile, foolish, silly, idle,
vain, pointless.
▣ serious, sensible.

frolic *v* gambol, caper, romp, play,
lark around, rollick, make merry,
frisk, prance, cavort, dance.
◇ *n* fun, amusement, sport, gaiety,
jollity, merriment, revel, romp, prank,
lark, caper, high jinks, antics.

front *n* **1** *at the front*: face, aspect,
frontage, façade, outside, exterior,
facing, cover, obverse, top, head,
lead, vanguard, forefront, front
line, foreground, forepart, bow.
2 PRETENCE, show, air, appearance,
look, expression, manner, façade,
cover, mask, disguise, pretext, cover-
up.
▣ **1** back, rear.
◇ *adj* fore, leading, foremost, head,
first.
▣ back, rear, last.
• **in front** ahead, leading, first, in
advance, before, preceding.
▣ behind.

frontier *n* border, boundary,
borderline, limit, edge, perimeter,
confines, marches, bounds, verge.

frosty *adj* **1** ICY, frozen, freezing,
frigid, wintry, cold, chilly.
2 UNFRIENDLY, unwelcoming, cool,
aloof, standoffish, stiff, discouraging.
▣ warm.

froth *n* bubbles, effervescence,
foam, lather, suds, head, scum.
◇ *v* foam, lather, ferment, fizz,
effervesce, bubble.

frown *v* scowl, glower, lour, glare,
grimace.
◇ *n* scowl, glower, dirty look (*infml*),
glare, grimace.
• **frown on** disapprove of, object to,

dislike, discourage.
▣ approve of.

frozen *adj* iced, chilled, icy,
icebound, ice-covered, arctic,
ice-cold, frigid, freezing, numb,
solidified, stiff, rigid, fixed.
▣ warm.

frugal *adj* thrifty, penny-wise,
parsimonious, careful, provident,
saving, economical, sparing, meagre.
▣ wasteful, generous.

fruit

Varieties of fruit include: apple,
crab-apple, pear, orange,
mandarin, minneola, clementine,
satsuma, tangerine, kumquat;
apricot, peach, plum, nectarine,
cherry, sloe, damson, greengage,
grape, gooseberry, physalis,
rhubarb, tomato; banana,
pineapple, olive, lemon, lime,
Ugli®, star fruit, lychee, date, fig,
grapefruit, kiwi fruit, mango,
papaya, guava, passion fruit,
dragon fruit, avocado; melon,
watermelon; strawberry, raspberry,
blackberry, bilberry, loganberry,
elderberry, blueberry, boysenberry,
cranberry; redcurrant,
blackcurrant, whitecurrant.

fruitful *adj* **1** FERTILE, rich,
teeming, plentiful, abundant,
prolific, productive. **2** REWARDING,
profitable, advantageous, beneficial,
worthwhile, well-spent, useful,
successful.
▣ **1** barren. **2** fruitless.

fruition *n* realization, fulfilment,
attainment, achievement,
completion, maturity, ripeness,
consummation, perfection, success,
enjoyment.

fruitless *adj* unsuccessful, abortive,
useless, futile, pointless, vain, idle,
hopeless, barren, sterile.
▣ fruitful, successful, profitable.

frustrate *v* **1** THWART, foil, balk,

baffle, block, check, spike, defeat, circumvent, forestall, counter, nullify, neutralize, inhibit. **2** DISAPPOINT, discourage, dishearten, depress.
☲ **1** further, promote. **2** encourage.

fuel n **1** a tax on fuel: combustible, propellant, motive power. **2** PROVOCATION, incitement, encouragement, ammunition, material.

Fuels include: gas, Calor Gas®, propane, butane, methane, acetylene, electricity, coal, coke, anthracite, charcoal, oil, petrol, gasoline, diesel, derv, paraffin, kerosene, methylated spirit, wood, logs, peat, nuclear power.

◇ v incite, inflame, fire, encourage, fan, feed, nourish, sustain, stoke up.
☲ discourage, damp down.

fugitive n escapee, runaway, deserter, refugee.
◇ adj fleeting, transient, transitory, passing, short, brief, flying, temporary, ephemeral, elusive.
☲ permanent.

fulfil v complete, finish, conclude, consummate, perfect, realize, achieve, accomplish, perform, execute, discharge, implement, carry out, comply with, observe, keep, obey, conform to, satisfy, fill, answer.
☲ fail, break.

fulfilment n completion, perfection, consummation, realization, achievement, accomplishment, success, performance, execution, discharge, implementation, observance, satisfaction.
☲ failure.

full adj **1** FILLED, loaded, packed, crowded, crammed, stuffed, jammed. **2** ENTIRE, whole, intact, total, complete, unabridged, unexpurgated. **3** THOROUGH, comprehensive, exhaustive, all-inclusive, broad, vast, extensive,

ample, generous, abundant, plentiful, copious, profuse. **4** a full sound: rich, resonant, loud, deep, clear, distinct. **5** at full speed: maximum, top, highest, greatest, utmost.
☲ **1** empty. **2** partial, incomplete. **3** superficial.

full-grown adj adult, grown-up, of age, mature, ripe, developed, full-blown, full-scale.
☲ young, undeveloped.

fully adv completely, totally, utterly, wholly, entirely, thoroughly, altogether, quite, positively, without reserve, perfectly.
☲ partly.

fumble v grope, feel, bungle, botch, mishandle, mismanage.

fume v **1** SMOKE, smoulder, boil, steam. **2** RAGE, storm, rant, rave, seethe.

fumes n exhaust, smoke, gas, vapour, haze, fog, smog, pollution.

fumigate v deodorize, disinfect, sterilize, purify, cleanse.

fun n enjoyment, pleasure, amusement, entertainment, diversion, distraction, recreation, play, sport, game, foolery, tomfoolery, horseplay, skylarking, romp, merrymaking, mirth, craic (Irish), jollity, jocularity, joking, jesting.
● **make fun of** rag, jeer at, ridicule, laugh at, mock, taunt, tease, rib (sl).

function n **1** ROLE, part, office, duty, charge, responsibility, concern, job, task, occupation, business, activity, purpose, use. **2** RECEPTION, party, gathering, affair, do (infml), dinner, luncheon.
◇ v work, operate, run, go, serve, act, perform, behave.

functional adj working, operational, practical, useful, utilitarian, utility, plain, hard-wearing.
☲ useless, decorative.

fund n pool, kitty, treasury, repository, storehouse, store, reserve, stock, hoard, cache, stack, mine, well, source, supply.
◊ v finance, capitalize, endow, subsidize, underwrite, sponsor, back, support, promote, float.

fundamental adj basic, primary, first, rudimentary, elementary, underlying, integral, central, principal, cardinal, prime, main, key, essential, mission-critical (infml), indispensable, vital, necessary, crucial, important.

funds n money, finance, backing, capital, resources, savings, wealth, cash.

funeral n burial, interment, entombment, cremation, obsequies, wake.

fungus

Types of fungus include: blight, botrytis, candida, mildew, ergot, mould, mushroom, penicillium, potato blight, rust, scab, smut, toadstool, yeast. see also **mushroom**.

funnel v channel, direct, convey, move, transfer, pass, pour, siphon, filter.

funny adj **1** HUMOROUS, amusing, entertaining, comic, comical, hilarious, witty, facetious, droll, farcical, laughable, ridiculous, absurd, silly. **2** ODD, strange, peculiar, curious, queer, weird, unusual, remarkable, puzzling, perplexing, mysterious, suspicious, dubious.
⊵ **1** serious, solemn, sad. **2** normal, ordinary, usual.

furious adj **1** ANGRY, mad (infml), up in arms (infml), livid, enraged, infuriated, incensed, raging, fuming, boiling. **2** VIOLENT, wild, fierce, intense, vigorous, frantic, boisterous, stormy, tempestuous.
⊵ **1** calm, pleased.

furnish v equip, fit out, decorate, rig, stock, provide, supply, afford, grant, give, offer, present.
⊵ divest.

furniture n equipment, appliances, furnishings, fittings, fitments, household goods, movables, possessions, effects, things.

Types of furniture include: table, chair, suite, couch, pouffe, footstool, beanbag, bed, desk, bureau, secretaire, bookcase, cabinet, cupboard, dumb-waiter, fireplace, overmantel, fender, firescreen, hallstand, umbrella stand, mirror, magazine rack, wardrobe, armoire, vanity unit, washstand. see also **bed**; **chair**; **couch**; **cupboard**; **table**.

furrow n groove, channel, trench, hollow, rut, track, line, crease, wrinkle.
◊ v seam, flute, corrugate, groove, crease, wrinkle, draw together, knit.

further adj more, additional, supplementary, extra, fresh, new, other.
◊ v advance, forward, promote, champion, push, encourage, foster, help, aid, assist, ease, facilitate, speed, hasten, accelerate, expedite.
⊵ stop, frustrate.

furthermore adv moreover, what's more, in addition, further, besides, also, too, as well, additionally.

furthest adj farthest, furthermost, remotest, outermost, outmost, extreme, ultimate, utmost, uttermost.
⊵ nearest.

furtive adj surreptitious, sly, stealthy, secretive, underhand, hidden, covert, secret.
⊵ open.

fury n anger, rage, wrath, frenzy, madness, passion, vehemence, fierceness, ferocity, violence, wildness, turbulence, power.

▣ calm, peacefulness.

fusion *n* melting, smelting, welding, union, synthesis, blending, coalescence, amalgamation, integration, conflation, merger, federation.

fuss *n* bother, trouble, hassle (*infml*), palaver, to-do (*infml*), hoo-ha (*infml*), furore, squabble, row, commotion, stir, fluster, confusion, upset, worry, agitation, flap (*infml*), excitement, bustle, flurry, hurry.
▣ calm.
◇ *v* complain, grumble, fret, worry, flap (*infml*), take pains, bother, bustle, fidget.

fussy *adj* 1 PARTICULAR, fastidious, scrupulous, finicky, pernickety, difficult, hard to please, choosy (*infml*), discriminating. 2 FANCY, elaborate, ornate, cluttered.
▣ 1 casual, uncritical. 2 plain.

futile *adj* pointless, useless, worthless, vain, idle, wasted, fruitless, profitless, unavailing, unsuccessful, abortive, unprofitable, unproductive, ineffective, barren, empty, hollow, forlorn.
▣ fruitful, profitable.

futility *n* pointlessness, uselessness, worthlessness, vanity, emptiness, hollowness, aimlessness.
▣ use, purpose.

future *n* hereafter, tomorrow, outlook, prospects, expectations.
▣ past.
◇ *adj* prospective, designate, to be, fated, destined, to come, forthcoming, in the offing, impending, coming, approaching, expected, planned, unborn, later, subsequent, eventual.
▣ past.

fuzzy *adj* 1 FRIZZY, fluffy, furry, woolly, fleecy, downy, velvety, napped. 2 BLURRED, unfocused, ill-defined, unclear, vague, faint, hazy, shadowy, woolly, muffled, distorted.
▣ 2 clear, distinct.

Gg

gadget *n* tool, appliance, device, contrivance, contraption, thing, thingumajig (*infml*), invention, novelty, gimmick.

gag¹ *v* muffle, muzzle, silence, quiet, stifle, throttle, suppress, curb, check, still.

gag² *n* (*infml*) joke, jest, quip, crack, wisecrack, one-liner, pun, witticism, funny (*infml*).

gaiety *n* happiness, glee, cheerfulness, joie de vivre, jollity, merriment, mirth, hilarity, fun, merrymaking, revelry, festivity, celebration, joviality, good humour, high spirits, light-heartedness, liveliness, brightness, brilliance, sparkle, colour, colourfulness, show, showiness.
⊞ sadness, drabness.

gaily *adv* happily, joyfully, merrily, blithely, brightly, brilliantly, colourfully, flamboyantly.
⊞ sadly, dully.

gain *v* 1 EARN, make, produce, gross, net, clear, profit, yield, bring in, reap, harvest, win, capture, secure, obtain, acquire, procure. 2 REACH, arrive at, come to, get to, attain, achieve, realize. 3 *gain speed*: increase, pick up, gather, collect, advance, progress, improve.
⊞ 1, 3 lose.
◇ *n* earnings, proceeds, income, revenue, winnings, profit, return, yield, dividend, growth, increase, increment, rise, advance, progress, headway, improvement, advantage, benefit, attainment, achievement, acquisition.
⊞ loss.

• **gain on** close with, narrow the gap, approach, catch up (with), level with, overtake, outdistance, leave behind.

gala *n* festivity, celebration, festival, carnival, jubilee, jamboree, fête, fair, pageant, procession.

gale *n* 1 WIND, squall, storm, hurricane, tornado, typhoon, cyclone. 2 BURST, outburst, outbreak, fit, eruption, explosion, blast.

gallant *adj* chivalrous, gentlemanly, courteous, polite, gracious, courtly, noble, dashing, heroic, valiant, brave, courageous, fearless, dauntless, bold, daring.
⊞ ungentlemanly, cowardly.

gallery *n* art gallery, museum, arcade, passage, walk, balcony, circle, gods (*infml*), spectators.

gallop *v* bolt, run, sprint, race, career, fly, dash, tear, speed, zoom, shoot, dart, rush, hurry, hasten.
⊞ amble.

galvanize *v* electrify, shock, jolt, prod, spur, provoke, stimulate, stir, move, arouse, excite, fire, invigorate, vitalize.

gamble *v* bet, wager, have a flutter (*infml*), try one's luck, punt, play, game, stake, chance, take a chance, risk, hazard, venture, speculate, back.
◇ *n* bet, wager, flutter (*infml*), punt, lottery, chance, risk, venture, speculation.

gambler *n* better, punter.

gambol *v* caper, frolic, frisk, skip, jump, bound, hop, bounce.

game[1] n 1 RECREATION, play, sport, pastime, diversion, distraction, entertainment, amusement, fun, frolic, romp, joke, jest. 2 COMPETITION, contest, match, round, tournament, event, meeting. 3 GAME BIRDS, animals, meat, flesh, prey, quarry, bag, spoils.

Types of indoor game include: board game, backgammon, chess, Chinese checkers, Cluedo®, draughts, halma, ludo, mah-jong, Monopoly®, nine men's morris, Scrabble®, snakes and ladders, Trivial Pursuit®; card game, baccarat, beggar-my-neighbour, bezique, blackjack, brag, bridge, canasta, chemin de fer, crib (infml), cribbage, faro, gin rummy, rummy, happy families, old maid, patience, Pelmanism, piquet, poker, pontoon, vingt-et-un, snap, solitaire, twenty-one, whist; bagatelle, pinball, billiards, pool, snooker, bowling, tenpin bowling, bowls, darts, dice, craps, dominoes, roulette, shove-halfpenny, table tennis, Ping-Pong®.

Types of children's game include: battleships, blindman's buff, charades, Chinese whispers, consequences, five-stones, forfeits, hangman, hide-and-seek, I-spy, jacks, jack-straws, musical chairs, noughts and crosses, pass the parcel, piggy-in-the-middle, pin the tail on the donkey, postman's knock, sardines, Simon says, spillikins, spin the bottle, tiddlywinks.

---

game[2] adj (infml) 1 game for anything: willing, inclined, ready, prepared, eager. 2 BOLD, daring, intrepid, brave, courageous, fearless, resolute, spirited.
⊡ 1 unwilling. 2 cowardly.

gamut n scale, series, range, sweep, scope, compass, spectrum, field, area.

gang n group, band, ring, pack, herd, mob, crowd, circle, clique, coterie, set, lot, team, crew, squad, shift, party.

gangster n mobster, goodfella (N Am), desperado, hoodlum, ruffian, rough, tough, thug, heavy (sl), racketeer, bandit, brigand, robber, criminal, crook (infml).

gaol see **jail**.

gaoler see **jailer**.

gap n 1 SPACE, blank, void, hole, opening, crack, chink, crevice, cleft, breach, rift, divide, divergence, difference. 2 INTERRUPTION, break, recess, pause, lull, interlude, intermission, interval.

gape v 1 STARE, gaze, gawp (infml), goggle, gawk (infml). 2 OPEN, yawn, part, split, crack.

gaping adj open, yawning, broad, wide, vast, cavernous.
⊡ tiny.

garage n lock-up, petrol station, gas station (US), service station.

garble v confuse, muddle, jumble, scramble, mix up, twist, distort, pervert, slant, misrepresent, falsify.
⊡ decipher.

garden n yard, backyard, plot, allotment, orchard, park.

garish adj gaudy, lurid, loud, vulgar, glaring, flashy, showy, tawdry, tasteless.
⊡ quiet, tasteful.

garland n wreath, festoon, decoration, flowers, laurels, honours.
◇ v wreathe, festoon, deck, adorn, crown.

garments n clothes, clothing, wear, attire, gear (infml), togs (infml), outfit, get-up (infml), dress, costume, uniform.

garnish v decorate, adorn, trim, ornament, embellish, enhance, grace, set off.
⊞ divest.
◇ n decoration, ornament, trimming, embellishment, enhancement, relish.

gash v cut, wound, slash, slit, incise, lacerate, tear, rend, split, score, gouge.
◇ n cut, wound, slash, slit, incision, laceration, tear, rent, split, score, gouge.

gasp v pant, puff, blow, breathe, wheeze, choke, gulp.
◇ n pant, puff, blow, breath, gulp, exclamation.

gate n barrier, door, doorway, gateway, opening, entrance, exit, access, passage.

gather v 1 CONGREGATE, convene, muster, rally, round up, assemble, collect, group, amass, accumulate, hoard, stockpile, heap, pile up, build. 2 INFER, deduce, conclude, surmise, assume, understand, learn, hear. 3 FOLD, pleat, tuck, pucker. 4 *gather flowers*: pick, pluck, cull, select, reap, harvest, glean.
⊞ 1 scatter, dissipate.

gathering n assembly, convocation, convention, meeting, round-up, rally, get-together, jamboree, party, group, company, congregation, mass, crowd, throng, turnout.

gaudy adj bright, brilliant, glaring, garish, loud, flashy, showy, ostentatious, tinselly, glitzy (*infml*), tawdry, vulgar, tasteless.
⊞ drab, plain.

gauge v estimate, guess, judge, assess, evaluate, value, rate, reckon, figure, calculate, compute, count, measure, weigh, determine, ascertain.
◇ n 1 STANDARD, norm, criterion, benchmark, yardstick, rule, guideline, indicator, measure, meter, test, sample, example, model,

pattern. 2 SIZE, magnitude, measure, capacity, bore, calibre, thickness, width, span, extent, scope, height, depth, degree.

gaunt adj 1 HAGGARD, hollow-eyed, angular, bony, thin, lean, lank, skinny, scraggy, scrawny, skeletal, emaciated, wasted. 2 BLEAK, stark, bare, desolate, forlorn, dismal, dreary, grim, harsh.
⊞ 1 plump.

gawky adj awkward, clumsy, maladroit, gauche, inept, oafish, ungainly, gangling, unco-ordinated, graceless.
⊞ graceful.

gay adj 1 HAPPY, joyful, jolly, merry, cheerful, blithe, sunny, carefree, debonair, fun-loving, pleasure-seeking, vivacious, lively, animated, playful, light-hearted. 2 *gay colours*: vivid, rich, bright, brilliant, sparkling, festive, colourful, gaudy, garish, flashy, showy, flamboyant. 3 HOMOSEXUAL, lesbian, queer (*sl*), pink (*infml*).
⊞ 1 sad, gloomy. 3 heterosexual, straight (*sl*).
◇ n homosexual, homo (*sl*), queer (*sl*), poof (*sl*), lesbian, dike (*sl*).
⊞ heterosexual.

gaze v stare, contemplate, regard, watch, view, look, gape, wonder.
◇ n stare, look.

gear n 1 EQUIPMENT, kit, outfit, tackle, apparatus, tools, instruments, accessories. 2 GEARWHEEL, cogwheel, cog, gearing, mechanism, machinery, works. 3 (*infml*) BELONGINGS, possessions, things, stuff, baggage, luggage, paraphernalia. 4 (*infml*) CLOTHES, clothing, garments, attire, dress, garb (*infml*), togs (*infml*), get-up (*infml*).

gel, jell v set, congeal, coagulate, crystallize, harden, thicken, solidify, materialize, come together, finalize, form, take shape.

gelatinous adj jelly-like, jellied, congealed, rubbery, glutinous, gummy, gluey, gooey (infml), sticky, viscous.

gem n gemstone, precious stone, stone, jewel, treasure, prize, masterpiece, pièce de résistance.

Gems and gemstones include: diamond, zircon, marcasite, rhinestone, pearl, moonstone, onyx, opal, mother-of-pearl, amber, citrine, topaz, agate, tiger's eye, jasper, morganite, ruby, garnet, rose quartz, beryl, cornelian, coral, amethyst, sapphire, turquoise, lapis lazuli, emerald, aquamarine, bloodstone, jade, peridot, tourmaline, jet.

genealogy n family tree, pedigree, lineage, ancestry, descent, derivation, extraction, family, line.

general adj 1 a general statement: broad, sweeping, blanket, all-inclusive, comprehensive, universal, global, total, across-the-board, widespread, prevalent, extensive, overall, panoramic. 2 VAGUE, ill-defined, indefinite, imprecise, inexact, approximate, loose, unspecific. 3 USUAL, regular, normal, typical, ordinary, everyday, customary, conventional, common, public.
⊞ 1 particular, limited. 2 specific. 3 rare.

generally adv usually, normally, as a rule, by and large, on the whole, mostly, mainly, chiefly, broadly, commonly, universally.

generate v produce, engender, whip up, arouse, cause, bring about, give rise to, create, originate, initiate, make, form, breed, propagate.
⊞ prevent.

generation n 1 AGE GROUP, age, era, epoch, period, time. 2 PRODUCTION, creation, origination, formation,

genesis, procreation, reproduction, propagation, breeding.

generosity n liberality, munificence, open-handedness, bounty, charity, magnanimity, philanthropy, kindness, big-heartedness, benevolence, goodness.
⊞ meanness, selfishness.

generous adj 1 LIBERAL, free, bountiful, open-handed, unstinting, unsparing, lavish. 2 MAGNANIMOUS, charitable, philanthropic, public-spirited, unselfish, kind, big-hearted, benevolent, good, high-minded, noble. 3 AMPLE, full, plentiful, abundant, copious, overflowing.
⊞ 1 mean, miserly. 2 selfish. 3 meagre.

genial adj affable, amiable, friendly, convivial, cordial, kindly, kind, warm-hearted, warm, hearty, jovial, jolly, cheerful, happy, good-natured, easy-going (infml), agreeable, pleasant.
⊞ cold.

genius n 1 VIRTUOSO, maestro, master, past master, expert, adept, egghead (infml), intellectual, mastermind, brain, intellect. 2 INTELLIGENCE, brightness, brilliance, ability, aptitude, gift, talent, flair, knack, bent, inclination, propensity, capacity, faculty.

gentle adj 1 KIND, kindly, amiable, tender, soft-hearted, compassionate, sympathetic, merciful, mild, placid, calm, tranquil. 2 a gentle slope: gradual, slow, easy, smooth, moderate, slight, light, imperceptible. 3 SOOTHING, peaceful, serene, quiet, soft, balmy.
⊞ 1 unkind, rough, harsh, wild.

genuine adj real, actual, natural, pure, original, authentic, veritable, true, bona fide, legitimate, honest, sincere, frank, candid, earnest.
⊞ artificial, false, insincere.

germ n 1 MICRO-ORGANISM, microbe,

bacterium, bacillus, virus, bug (*infml*). **2** BEGINNING, start, origin, source, cause, spark, rudiment, nucleus, root, seed, embryo, bud, sprout.

germinate *v* bud, sprout, shoot, develop, grow, swell.

gesticulate *v* wave, signal, gesture, indicate, sign.

gesture *n* act, action, movement, motion, indication, sign, signal, wave, gesticulation.
◇ *v* indicate, sign, motion, beckon, point, signal, wave, gesticulate.

get *v* **1** OBTAIN, acquire, procure, come by, receive, earn, gain, win, secure, achieve, realize. **2** *it's getting dark*: become, turn, go, grow. **3** *get him to help*: persuade, coax, induce, urge, influence, sway. **4** MOVE, go, come, reach, arrive. **5** FETCH, collect, pick up, take, catch, capture, seize, grab. **6** CONTRACT, catch, pick up, develop, come down with.
⊟ **1** lose. **4** leave.
• **get across** communicate, transmit, convey, impart, put across, bring home to.
• **get ahead** advance, progress, get on, go places (*infml*), thrive, flourish, prosper, succeed, make good, make it, get there (*infml*).
⊟ fall behind, fail.
• **get along 1** COPE, manage, get by, survive, fare, progress, develop. **2** AGREE, harmonize, get on, hit it off.
• **get at 1** REACH, attain, find, discover. **2** (*infml*) BRIBE, suborn, corrupt, influence. **3** (*infml*) MEAN, intend, imply, insinuate, hint, suggest. **4** (*infml*) CRITICIZE, find fault with, pick on, attack, make fun of.
• **get away** escape, get out, break out, break away, run away, flee, depart, leave.
• **get back** recover, regain, recoup, repossess, retrieve.
• **get down 1** DEPRESS, sadden, dishearten, dispirit. **2** DESCEND, dismount, disembark, alight, get off.

⊟ **1** encourage. **2** board.
• **get in** enter, penetrate, infiltrate, arrive, come, land, embark.
• **get off 1** *get off a train*: alight, disembark, dismount, descend. **2** REMOVE, detach, separate, shed, get down.
⊟ **1** get on. **2** put on.
• **get on 1** BOARD, embark, mount, ascend. **2** COPE, manage, fare, get along, make out, prosper, succeed. **3** CONTINUE, proceed, press on, advance, progress.
⊟ **1** get off.
• **get out 1** ESCAPE, flee, break out, extricate oneself, free oneself, leave, quit, vacate, evacuate, clear out, clear off (*infml*). **2** *she got out a pen*: take out, produce.
• **get over 1** RECOVER FROM, shake off, survive. **2** SURMOUNT, overcome, defeat, deal with. **3** COMMUNICATE, get across, convey, put over, impart, explain.
• **get round 1** CIRCUMVENT, bypass, evade, avoid. **2** PERSUADE, win over, talk round, coax, prevail upon.
• **get together** assemble, collect, gather, congregate, rally, meet, join, unite, collaborate.
• **get up** stand (up), arise, rise, ascend, climb, mount, scale.

ghastly *adj* awful, dreadful, frightful, terrible, grim, gruesome, hideous, horrible, horrid, loathsome, repellent, shocking, appalling.
⊟ delightful, attractive.

ghost *n* spectre, phantom, spook (*infml*), apparition, visitant, spirit, wraith, soul, shade, shadow.

ghostly *adj* eerie, spooky (*infml*), creepy, supernatural, unearthly, ghostlike, spectral, wraith-like, phantom, illusory.

giant *n* monster, titan, colossus, Goliath, Hercules.
◇ *adj* gigantic, colossal, titanic, mammoth, jumbo (*infml*), king-size, huge, enormous, immense, vast, large.

gibe, jibe n jeer, sneer, mockery, ridicule, taunt, derision, scoff, dig (*infml*), crack (*infml*), poke, quip.

giddy adj 1 DIZZY, faint, light-headed, unsteady, reeling, vertiginous. 2 SILLY, flighty, wild.

gift n 1 PRESENT, offering, donation, contribution, bounty, largess(e), gratuity, tip, bonus, freebie (*sl*), legacy, bequest, endowment. 2 TALENT, genius, flair, aptitude, knack, power, faculty, attribute, ability, bent, capability, capacity.

gifted adj talented, skilful, adept, expert, masterly, skilled, accomplished, able, capable, clever, intelligent, bright, brilliant.

gigantic adj huge, enormous, immense, vast, giant, colossal, mega (*infml*), titanic, mammoth, gargantuan, Brobdingnagian. ⊞ tiny, Lilliputian, nano-.

giggle v, n titter, snigger, chuckle, chortle, laugh.

gilded adj gilt, gold, golden, gold-plated.

gimmick n attraction, ploy, ruse, stratagem, scheme, trick, stunt, dodge, device, contrivance, gadget.

gingerly adv tentatively, hesitantly, warily, cautiously, carefully, delicately. ⊞ boldly, carelessly.

gipsy see gypsy.

girdle n belt, sash, band, waistband, corset.

girl n lass, young woman, girlfriend, sweetheart, daughter.

girth n 1 CIRCUMFERENCE, perimeter, measure, size, bulk. 2 STRAP, band.

gist n pith, essence, marrow, substance, matter, meaning, significance, import, sense, idea, drift, direction, point, nub, core, quintessence.

give v 1 PRESENT, award, confer, offer, lend, donate, contribute, provide, supply, furnish, grant, bestow, endow, gift, make over, hand over, deliver, entrust, commit, devote. 2 *give news*: communicate, transmit, impart, utter, announce, declare, pronounce, publish, set forth. 3 CONCEDE, allow, admit, yield, give way, surrender. 4 *give trouble*: cause, occasion, make, produce, do, perform. 5 SINK, yield, bend, give (way), break, collapse, fall. ⊞ 1 take, withhold. 5 withstand.

• **give away** betray, inform on, expose, uncover, divulge, let slip, disclose, reveal, leak, let out.

• **give in** surrender, capitulate, submit, yield, give way, concede, give up, quit. ⊞ hold out.

• **give off** emit, discharge, release, give out, send out, throw out, pour out, exhale, exude, produce.

• **give out 1** DISTRIBUTE, hand out, dole out, deal. **2** ANNOUNCE, declare, broadcast, publish, disseminate, communicate, transmit, impart, notify, advertise.

• **give up 1** STOP, cease, quit, resign, abandon, renounce, relinquish, waive. **2** SURRENDER, capitulate, give in. ⊞ 1 start. 2 hold out.

given adj 1 *a given number*: specified, particular, definite. 2 INCLINED, disposed, likely, liable, prone.

glad adj 1 PLEASED, delighted, gratified, contented, happy, joyful, merry, cheerful, cheery, bright. 2 WILLING, eager, keen, ready, inclined, disposed. ⊞ 1 sad, unhappy. 2 unwilling, reluctant.

glamorous adj smart, elegant, attractive, beautiful, gorgeous, enchanting, captivating, alluring, appealing, fascinating, exciting, dazzling, glossy, colourful. ⊞ plain, drab, boring.

glamour n attraction, allure, appeal, fascination, charm, magic, beauty, elegance, glitter, prestige.

glance v peep, peek, glimpse, view, look, scan, skim, leaf, flip, thumb, dip, browse.
◇ n peep, peek, glimpse, look.

glare v 1 GLOWER, look daggers, frown, scowl, stare. 2 DAZZLE, blaze, flame, flare, shine, reflect.
◇ n 1 BLACK LOOK, dirty look (infml), frown, scowl, stare, look. 2 BRIGHTNESS, brilliance, blaze, flame, dazzle, spotlight.

glaring adj blatant, flagrant, open, conspicuous, manifest, patent, obvious, outrageous, gross.
⊡ hidden, concealed, minor.

glassy adj 1 GLASSLIKE, smooth, slippery, icy, shiny, glossy, transparent, clear. 2 a glassy stare: expressionless, blank, empty, vacant, dazed, fixed, glazed, cold, lifeless, dull.

glaze v coat, enamel, gloss, varnish, lacquer, polish, burnish.
◇ n coat, coating, finish, enamel, varnish, lacquer, polish, shine, lustre, gloss.

gleam n glint, flash, beam, ray, flicker, glimmer, shimmer, sparkle, glitter, gloss, glow.
◇ v glint, flash, glance, flare, shine, glisten, glimmer, glitter, sparkle, shimmer, glow.

glib adj fluent, easy, facile, quick, ready, talkative, plausible, insincere, smooth, slick, suave, smooth-tongued.
⊡ tongue-tied, implausible.

glide v slide, slip, skate, skim, fly, float, drift, sail, coast, roll, run, flow.

glimmer v glow, shimmer, glisten, glitter, sparkle, twinkle, wink, blink, flicker, gleam, shine.
◇ n 1 GLOW, shimmer, sparkle, twinkle, flicker, glint, gleam. 2 TRACE, hint, suggestion, grain.

glimpse n peep, peek, squint, glance, look, sight, sighting, view.
◇ v spy, espy, spot, catch sight of, sight, view.

glint v flash, gleam, shine, reflect, glitter, sparkle, twinkle, glimmer.
◇ n flash, gleam, shine, reflection, glitter, sparkle, twinkle, glimmer.

glisten v shine, gleam, glint, glitter, sparkle, twinkle, glimmer, shimmer.

glitter v sparkle, spangle, scintillate, twinkle, shimmer, glimmer, glisten, glint, gleam, flash, shine.
◇ n sparkle, coruscation, scintillation, twinkle, shimmer, glimmer, glint, gleam, flash, shine, lustre, sheen, brightness, radiance, brilliance, splendour, showiness, glamour, tinsel.

gloat v triumph, glory, exult, rejoice, revel in, relish, crow, boast, vaunt, rub it in (infml).

global adj universal, worldwide, international, general, all-encompassing, total, thorough, exhaustive, comprehensive, all-inclusive, encyclopedic, wide-ranging.
⊡ parochial, limited.

globe n world, earth, planet, sphere, ball, orb, round.

gloom n 1 DEPRESSION, low spirits, despondency, dejection, sadness, unhappiness, glumness, melancholy, misery, desolation, despair. 2 DARK, darkness, shade, shadow, dusk, twilight, dimness, obscurity, cloud, cloudiness, dullness.
⊡ 1 cheerfulness, happiness. 2 brightness.

gloomy adj 1 DEPRESSED, down, low, despondent, dejected, downcast, dispirited, downhearted, sad, miserable, glum, morose, pessimistic, cheerless, dismal, depressing. 2 DARK, sombre, shadowy, dim, obscure, overcast, dull, dreary.
⊡ 1 cheerful. 2 bright.

glorious adj 1 ILLUSTRIOUS, eminent, distinguished, famous, renowned, noted, great, noble, splendid, magnificent, grand, majestic, triumphant. 2 FINE, bright, radiant, shining, brilliant, dazzling, superb, beautiful, gorgeous, excellent, wonderful, marvellous, delightful, heavenly.
⊞ 1 unknown.

glory n 1 FAME, renown, celebrity, illustriousness, greatness, eminence, distinction, honour, prestige, kudos, triumph. 2 PRAISE, homage, tribute, worship, veneration, adoration, exaltation, blessing, thanksgiving, gratitude. 3 BRIGHTNESS, radiance, brilliance, beauty, splendour, resplendence, magnificence, grandeur, majesty, dignity.

gloss¹ n 1 POLISH, varnish, lustre, sheen, shine, brightness, brilliance. 2 SHOW, appearance, semblance, surface, front, façade, veneer, window-dressing.
• **gloss over** conceal, hide, veil, mask, disguise, camouflage, cover up, whitewash, explain away.

gloss² n annotation, note, footnote, explanation, elucidation, interpretation, translation, definition, comment, commentary.
◇ v annotate, define, explain, elucidate, interpret, construe, translate, comment.

glossy adj shiny, sheeny, lustrous, sleek, silky, smooth, glassy, polished, burnished, glazed, enamelled, bright, shining, brilliant.
⊞ matt.

glow n 1 LIGHT, gleam, glimmer, radiance, luminosity, brightness, vividness, brilliance, splendour. 2 ARDOUR, fervour, intensity, warmth, passion, enthusiasm, excitement. 3 FLUSH, blush, rosiness, redness, burning.
◇ v 1 SHINE, radiate, gleam, glimmer, burn, smoulder. 2 *their faces glowed*: flush, blush, colour, redden.

glower v glare, look daggers, frown, scowl.
◇ n glare, black look, dirty look (*infml*), frown, scowl, stare, look.

glowing adj 1 BRIGHT, luminous, vivid, vibrant, rich, warm, flushed, red, flaming. 2 *a glowing review*: complimentary, enthusiastic, ecstatic, rhapsodic, rave (*infml*).
⊞ 1 dull, colourless. 2 restrained.

glue n adhesive, gum, paste, size, cement.
◇ v stick, affix, gum, paste, seal, bond, cement, fix.

glut n surplus, excess, superfluity, surfeit, overabundance, superabundance, saturation, overflow.
⊞ scarcity, lack.

glutton n gourmand, gormandizer, guzzler, gorger, gobbler, pig.
⊞ ascetic.

gluttony n gourmandise, gourmandism, greed, greediness, voracity, insatiability, piggishness.
⊞ abstinence, asceticism.

gnarled adj gnarly, knotted, knotty, twisted, contorted, distorted, rough, rugged, weather-beaten.

gnaw v 1 BITE, nibble, munch, chew, eat, devour, consume, erode, wear, haunt. 2 WORRY, niggle, fret, trouble, plague, nag, prey.

go v 1 MOVE, pass, advance, progress, proceed, make for, travel, journey, start, begin, depart, leave, take one's leave, retreat, withdraw, disappear, vanish. 2 OPERATE, function, work, run, act, perform. 3 EXTEND, spread, stretch, reach, span, continue, unfold. 4 *time goes quickly*: pass, elapse, lapse, roll on.
⊞ 2 break down, fail.
◇ n (*infml*) 1 *have a go*: attempt, try, shot (*infml*), bash (*infml*), stab (*infml*), turn. 2 ENERGY, get-up-and-go (*infml*), vitality, life, spirit, dynamism, effort.

• **go about** approach, begin, set about, address, tackle, attend to, undertake, engage in, perform.

• **go ahead** begin, proceed, carry on, continue, advance, progress, move.

• **go away** depart, leave, clear off (*infml*), withdraw, retreat, disappear, vanish.

• **go back** return, revert, backslide, retreat.

• **go by 1** PASS, elapse, flow. **2** *go by the rules*: observe, follow, comply with, heed.

• **go down** descend, sink, set, fall, drop, decrease, decline, deteriorate, degenerate, fail, founder, go under, collapse, fold (*infml*).

• **go for 1** (*infml*) CHOOSE, prefer, favour, like, admire, enjoy. **2** ATTACK, assail, set about, lunge at.

• **go in for** enter, take part in, participate in, engage in, take up, embrace, adopt, undertake, practise, pursue, follow.

• **go into** discuss, consider, review, examine, study, scrutinize, investigate, inquire into, check out, probe, delve into, analyse, dissect.

• **go off 1** DEPART, leave, quit, abscond, vanish, disappear. **2** EXPLODE, blow up, detonate. **3** *the milk has gone off*: deteriorate, turn, sour, go bad, rot.

• **go on 1** CONTINUE, carry on, proceed, persist, stay, endure, last. **2** CHATTER, rabbit (*infml*), witter (*infml*), ramble on. **3** HAPPEN, occur, take place.

• **go out** exit, depart, leave.

• **go over** examine, peruse, study, revise, scan, read, inspect, check, review, repeat, rehearse, list.

• **go through 1** SUFFER, undergo, experience, bear, tolerate, endure, withstand. **2** INVESTIGATE, check, examine, look, search, hunt, explore. **3** USE, consume, exhaust, spend, squander.

• **go together** match, harmonize, accord, fit.

• **go with 1** MATCH, harmonize, co-ordinate, blend, complement, suit, fit, correspond. **2** ACCOMPANY, escort, take, usher.
⊠ **1** clash.

• **go without** abstain, forgo, manage without, do without, lack, want.

goad *v* prod, prick, spur, impel, push, drive, provoke, incite, instigate, arouse, stimulate, prompt, urge, nag, hound, harass, annoy, irritate, vex.

go-ahead *n* permission, clearance, authorization, green light (*infml*), sanction, assent, consent, OK (*infml*), agreement.
⊠ ban, veto, embargo.
◇ *adj* enterprising, pioneering, progressive, ambitious, up-and-coming, dynamic, energetic.
⊠ unenterprising, sluggish.

goal *n* target, mark, objective, aim, intention, object, purpose, end, ambition, aspiration.

gobble *v* bolt, guzzle, gorge, cram, stuff, devour, consume, put away (*infml*), swallow, gulp.

go-between *n* intermediary, mediator, liaison, contact, broker, middleman, dealer, agent, messenger, medium.

God *n* Supreme Being, Creator, Providence, Lord, Almighty, Holy One, Jehovah, Yahweh, Allah, Brahma, Zeus.

god, goddess *n* deity, divinity, idol, spirit, power.

god-forsaken *adj* remote, isolated, lonely, bleak, desolate, abandoned, deserted, forlorn, dismal, dreary, gloomy, miserable, wretched, depressing.

godless *adj* ungodly, atheistic, heathen, pagan, irreligious, unholy, impious, sacrilegious, profane, irreverent, bad, evil, wicked.
⊠ godly, pious.

godly *adj* religious, holy, pious, devout, God-fearing, righteous,

good, virtuous, pure, innocent.
🔁 godless, impious.

godsend n blessing, boon, stroke of luck, windfall, miracle.
🔁 blow, setback.

golden adj 1 GOLD, gilded, gilt, yellow, blond(e), fair, bright, shining, lustrous, resplendent. 2 PROSPEROUS, successful, glorious, excellent, happy, joyful, favourable, auspicious, promising, rosy.

good adj 1 ACCEPTABLE, satisfactory, pleasant, agreeable, nice, enjoyable, pleasing, commendable, excellent, great (infml), super (infml), first-class, first-rate, superior, advantageous, beneficial, favourable, auspicious, helpful, useful, worthwhile, profitable, appropriate, suitable, fitting. 2 good at her job: competent, proficient, skilled, expert, accomplished, professional, skilful, clever, talented, gifted, fit, able, capable, dependable, reliable. 3 KIND, considerate, gracious, benevolent, charitable, philanthropic. 4 VIRTUOUS, exemplary, moral, upright, honest, trustworthy, worthy, righteous. 5 WELL-BEHAVED, obedient, well-mannered.
6 THOROUGH, complete, whole, substantial, considerable.
🔁 1 bad, poor. 2 incompetent. 3 unkind, inconsiderate. 4 wicked, immoral. 5 naughty, disobedient.
◇ n 1 VIRTUE, morality, goodness, righteousness, right. 2 USE, purpose, avail, advantage, profit, gain, worth, merit, usefulness, service. 3 for your own good: welfare, wellbeing, interest, sake, behalf, benefit, convenience.

good-bye n farewell, adieu, au revoir, valediction, leave-taking, parting.

good-humoured adj cheerful, happy, jovial, genial, affable, amiable, friendly, congenial, pleasant, good-tempered, approachable.
🔁 ill-humoured.

good-looking adj attractive, handsome, beautiful, fair, pretty, personable, presentable.
🔁 ugly, plain.

good-natured adj kind, kindly, kind-hearted, sympathetic, benevolent, helpful, neighbourly, gentle, good-tempered, approachable, friendly, tolerant, patient.
🔁 ill-natured.

goodness n virtue, uprightness, rectitude, honesty, probity, kindness, compassion, graciousness, goodwill, benevolence, unselfishness, generosity, friendliness, helpfulness.
🔁 badness, wickedness.

goods n 1 PROPERTY, chattels, effects, possessions, belongings, paraphernalia, stuff, things, gear (infml). 2 MERCHANDISE, wares, commodities, stock, freight.

goodwill n benevolence, kindness, generosity, favour, friendliness, friendship, zeal.
🔁 ill-will.

gore v pierce, penetrate, stab, spear, stick, impale, wound.

gorge n canyon, ravine, gully, defile, chasm, abyss, cleft, fissure, gap, pass.
◇ v feed, guzzle, gobble, devour, bolt, wolf, gulp, swallow, cram, stuff, fill, sate, surfeit, glut, overeat.
🔁 fast.

gorgeous adj magnificent, splendid, grand, glorious, superb, fine, rich, sumptuous, luxurious, brilliant, dazzling, showy, glamorous, attractive, beautiful, handsome, good-looking, delightful, pleasing, lovely, enjoyable, good.
🔁 dull, plain.

gory adj bloody, sanguinary, bloodstained, blood-soaked, grisly, brutal, savage, murderous.

gossip n 1 IDLE TALK, prattle, chitchat,

tittle-tattle, rumour, hearsay, report, scandal. **2** GOSSIP-MONGER, scandalmonger, whisperer, prattler, babbler, chatterbox, nosey parker (*infml*), busybody, talebearer, tell-tale, tattler.
◇ *v* talk, chat, natter, chatter, gabble, prattle, tattle, tell tales, whisper, rumour.

gouge *v* chisel, cut, hack, incise, score, groove, scratch, claw, gash, slash, dig, scoop, hollow, extract.

gourmet *n* gastronome, epicure, epicurean, connoisseur, bon vivant.

govern *v* **1** RULE, reign, direct, manage, superintend, supervise, oversee, preside, lead, head, command, influence, guide, conduct, steer, pilot. **2** *govern one's temper*: dominate, master, control, regulate, curb, check, restrain, contain, quell, subdue, tame, discipline.

government *n* **1** *blame the government*: administration, executive, ministry, Establishment, authorities, powers that be, state, regime. **2** RULE, sovereignty, sway, direction, management, superintendence, supervision, surveillance, command, charge, authority, guidance, conduct, domination, dominion, control, regulation, restraint.

Government systems include: absolutism, autocracy, commonwealth, communism, democracy, despotism, dictatorship, empire, federation, hierocracy, junta, kingdom, monarchy, plutocracy, republic, theocracy, triumvirate. *see also* **parliament**.

governor *n* ruler, commissioner, administrator, executive, director, manager, leader, head, chief, commander, superintendent, supervisor, overseer, controller, boss.

gown *n* robe, dress, frock, dressing-gown, habit, costume.

grab *v* seize, snatch, take, nab (*infml*), pluck, snap up, catch hold of, grasp, clutch, grip, catch, bag, capture, collar (*infml*), commandeer, appropriate, usurp, annex.

grace *n* **1** GRACEFULNESS, poise, beauty, attractiveness, loveliness, shapeliness, elegance, tastefulness, refinement, polish, breeding, manners, etiquette, decorum, decency, courtesy, charm. **2** KINDNESS, kindliness, compassion, consideration, goodness, virtue, generosity, charity, benevolence, goodwill, favour, forgiveness, indulgence, mercy, leniency, pardon, reprieve. **3** *say grace*: blessing, benediction, thanksgiving, prayer.
▣ **2** cruelty, harshness.
◇ *v* favour, honour, dignify, distinguish, embellish, enhance, set off, trim, garnish, decorate, ornament, adorn.
▣ spoil, detract from.

graceful *adj* easy, flowing, smooth, supple, agile, deft, natural, slender, fine, tasteful, elegant, beautiful, charming, suave.
▣ graceless, awkward, clumsy, ungainly.

gracious *adj* elegant, refined, polite, courteous, considerate, kind, well-mannered, sweet, obliging, accommodating, compassionate, kindly, benevolent, generous, magnanimous, charitable, hospitable, forgiving, indulgent, lenient, mild, clement, merciful.
▣ ungracious.

grade *n* rank, status, standing, station, place, position, level, stage, degree, step, rung, notch, mark, brand, quality, standard, condition, size, order, group, class, category.
◇ *v* sort, arrange, categorize, order, group, class, rate, size, rank, range, classify, evaluate, assess, value, mark,

brand, label, pigeonhole, type.

gradient *n* slope, incline, hill, bank, rise, declivity.

gradual *adj* slow, leisurely, unhurried, easy, gentle, moderate, regular, even, measured, steady, continuous, progressive, step by step.
☒ sudden, precipitate.

gradually *adv* little by little, bit by bit, imperceptibly, inch by inch, step by step, progressively, by degrees, piecemeal, slowly, gently, cautiously, gingerly, moderately, evenly, steadily.

graduate *v* 1 *graduate from medical school*: pass, qualify. 2 CALIBRATE, mark off, measure out, proportion, grade, arrange, range, order, rank, sort, group, classify.

graft *n* implant, implantation, splice, transplant, bud, sprout, shoot, scion.
◇ *v* engraft, implant, insert, transplant, join, splice.

grain *n* 1 BIT, piece, fragment, scrap, morsel, crumb, granule, particle, molecule, atom, jot, iota, mite, speck, modicum, trace. 2 SEED, kernel, corn, cereals. 3 TEXTURE, fibre, weave, pattern, marking, surface.

grand *adj* 1 MAJESTIC, regal, stately, splendid, magnificent, glorious, superb, sublime, fine, excellent, outstanding, first-rate, impressive, imposing, striking, monumental, large, noble, lordly, lofty, pompous, pretentious, grandiose, ambitious. 2 SUPREME, pre-eminent, leading, head, chief, arch, highest, senior, great, illustrious.
☒ 1 humble, common, poor.

grandeur *n* majesty, stateliness, pomp, state, dignity, splendour, magnificence, nobility, greatness, illustriousness, importance.
☒ humbleness, lowliness, simplicity.

grandiose *adj* pompous, pretentious, high-flown, lofty, ambitious, extravagant, ostentatious, showy, flamboyant, grand, majestic,

stately, magnificent, impressive, imposing, monumental.
☒ unpretentious.

grant *v* 1 GIVE, donate, present, award, confer, bestow, impart, transmit, dispense, apportion, assign, allot, allocate, provide, supply. 2 ADMIT, acknowledge, concede, allow, permit, consent to, agree to, accede to.
☒ 1 withhold. 2 deny.
◇ *n* allowance, subsidy, concession, award, bursary, scholarship, gift, donation, endowment, bequest, annuity, pension, honorarium.

granular *adj* grainy, granulated, gritty, sandy, lumpy, rough, crumbly, friable.

graph *n* diagram, chart, table, grid.

graphic *adj* vivid, descriptive, expressive, striking, telling, lively, realistic, explicit, clear, lucid, specific, detailed, blow-by-blow, visual, pictorial, diagrammatic, illustrative.
☒ vague, impressionistic.

grapple *v* seize, grasp, snatch, grab, grip, clutch, clasp, hold, wrestle, tussle, struggle, contend, fight, combat, clash, engage, encounter, face, confront, tackle, deal with, cope with.
☒ release, avoid, evade.

grasp *v* 1 HOLD, clasp, clutch, grip, grapple, seize, snatch, grab, catch. 2 *grasp a concept*: understand, comprehend, get (*infml*), follow, see, realize.
◇ *n* 1 GRIP, clasp, hold, embrace, clutches, possession, control, power. 2 UNDERSTANDING, comprehension, apprehension, mastery, familiarity, knowledge.

grasping *adj* avaricious, greedy, rapacious, acquisitive, mercenary, mean, selfish, miserly, close-fisted, tight-fisted, parsimonious.
☒ generous.

grass n turf, lawn, green, grassland, field, meadow, pasture, prairie, pampas, savanna, steppe.

Types of grass include: bamboo, barley, beard-grass, bent, bluegrass, cane, cocksfoot, corn, couch grass, esparto, fescue, kangaroo-grass, knotgrass, maize, marram, meadow foxtail, meadow-grass, millet, oats, paddy, pampas grass, papyrus, rattan, reed, rice, rye, rye grass, sorghum, squirrel-tail grass, sugar cane, twitch grass, wheat, wild oat.

grate v 1 GRIND, shred, mince, pulverize, rub, rasp, scrape. 2 JAR, set one's teeth on edge, annoy, irritate, aggravate (infml), get on one's nerves, vex, irk, exasperate.

grateful adj thankful, appreciative, indebted, obliged, obligated, beholden.
⊡ ungrateful.

gratify v satisfy, fulfil, indulge, pander to, humour, favour, please, gladden, delight, thrill.
⊡ frustrate, thwart.

grating¹ adj harsh, rasping, scraping, squeaky, strident, discordant, jarring, annoying, irritating, unpleasant, disagreeable.
⊡ harmonious, pleasing.

grating² n grate, grill, grid, lattice, trellis.

gratitude n gratefulness, thankfulness, thanks, appreciation, acknowledgement, recognition, indebtedness, obligation.
⊡ ingratitude, ungratefulness.

gratuitous adj unnecessary, wanton, needless, superfluous, unwarranted, unjustified, groundless, undeserved, unprovoked, uncalled-for, unasked-for, unsolicited, voluntary, free, gratis, complimentary.
⊡ justified, provoked.

gratuity n tip, bonus, perk (infml), gift, present, donation, reward, recompense.

grave¹ n burial-place, tomb, vault, crypt, sepulchre, mausoleum, pit, barrow, tumulus, cairn.

grave² adj 1 a grave mistake: important, significant, weighty, momentous, serious, critical, vital, crucial, urgent, acute, severe, dangerous, hazardous. 2 SOLEMN, dignified, sober, sedate, serious, thoughtful, pensive, grim, long-faced, quiet, reserved, subdued, restrained.
⊡ 1 trivial, light, slight. 2 cheerful.

graveyard n cemetery, burial-ground, churchyard.

gravity n 1 IMPORTANCE, significance, seriousness, urgency, acuteness, severity, danger. 2 SOLEMNITY, dignity, sobriety, seriousness, thoughtfulness, sombreness, reserve, restraint. 3 GRAVITATION, attraction, pull, weight, heaviness.
⊡ 1 triviality. 2 levity.

graze v scratch, scrape, skin, abrade, rub, chafe, shave, brush, skim, touch. ◊ n scratch, scrape, abrasion.

grease n oil, lubrication, fat, lard, dripping, tallow.

greasy adj oily, fatty, lardy, buttery, smeary, slimy, slippery, smooth, waxy.

great adj 1 LARGE, big, huge, enormous, massive, colossal, gigantic, mammoth, immense, vast, impressive. 2 with great care: considerable, pronounced, extreme, excessive, inordinate. 3 FAMOUS, renowned, celebrated, illustrious, eminent, distinguished, prominent, noteworthy, notable, remarkable, outstanding, grand, glorious, fine. 4 IMPORTANT, significant, serious, major, principal, primary, main, chief, leading. 5 (infml) EXCELLENT, first-rate, superb, wonderful, marvellous, tremendous, terrific,

fantastic, fabulous.
🔁 **1** small. **2** slight. **3** unknown.
4 unimportant, insignificant.

greed n **1** HUNGER, ravenousness, gluttony, gourmandism, voracity, insatiability. **2** ACQUISITIVENESS, covetousness, desire, craving, longing, eagerness, avarice, selfishness.
🔁 **1** abstemiousness, self-restraint.

greedy adj **1** HUNGRY, starving, ravenous, gluttonous, gormandizing, voracious, insatiable. **2** ACQUISITIVE, covetous, desirous, craving, eager, impatient, avaricious, grasping, selfish.
🔁 **1** abstemious.

green adj **1** GRASSY, leafy, verdant, unripe, unseasoned, tender, fresh, budding, blooming, flourishing.
2 green with envy: envious, covetous, jealous, resentful.
3 IMMATURE, naive, unsophisticated, ignorant, inexperienced, untrained, raw, new, recent, young.
4 ECOLOGICAL, environmental, eco-friendly, environmentally aware.
◇ n common, lawn, grass, turf.

greenhouse n glasshouse, hothouse, conservatory, pavilion, vinery, orangery.

greet v hail, salute, acknowledge, address, accost, meet, receive, welcome.
🔁 ignore.

greeting n salutation, wave, hallo, acknowledgement, the time of day, address, reception, welcome.

greetings n regards, respects, compliments, salutations, best wishes, good wishes, love.

gregarious adj sociable, outgoing, extrovert, friendly, affable, social, convivial, cordial, warm.
🔁 unsociable.

grey adj **1** NEUTRAL, colourless, pale, ashen, leaden, dull, cloudy, overcast, dim, dark, murky. **2** GLOOMY, dismal,

cheerless, depressing, dreary, bleak.

grief n sorrow, sadness, unhappiness, depression, dejection, desolation, distress, misery, woe, heartbreak, mourning, bereavement, heartache, anguish, agony, pain, suffering, affliction, trouble, regret, remorse.
🔁 happiness, delight.

grievance n complaint, moan (infml), grumble (infml), resentment, objection, protest, charge, wrong, injustice, injury, damage, trouble, affliction, hardship, trial, tribulation.

grieve v **1** SORROW, mope, lament, mourn, wail, cry, weep. **2** SADDEN, upset, dismay, distress, afflict, pain, hurt, wound.
🔁 **1** rejoice. **2** please, gladden.

grim adj **1** UNPLEASANT, horrible, horrid, ghastly, gruesome, grisly, sinister, frightening, fearsome, terrible, shocking. **2** STERN, severe, harsh, dour, forbidding, surly, sullen, morose, gloomy, depressing, unattractive.
🔁 **1** pleasant. **2** attractive.

grimace n frown, scowl, pout, smirk, sneer, face.
◇ v make a face, pull a face, frown, scowl, pout, smirk, sneer.

grime n dirt, muck, filth, soot, dust.

grimy adj dirty, mucky, grubby, soiled, filthy, sooty, smutty, dusty, smudgy.
🔁 clean.

grind v crush, pound, pulverize, powder, mill, grate, scrape, gnash, rut, abrade, sand, file, smooth, polish, sharpen, whet.

grip n hold, grasp, clasp, embrace, clutches, control, power.
◇ v **1** HOLD, grasp, clasp, clutch, seize, grab, catch. **2** FASCINATE, thrill, enthral, spellbind, mesmerize, hypnotize, rivet, engross, absorb, involve, engage, compel.

grisly *adj* gruesome, gory, grim, macabre, horrid, horrible, ghastly, awful, frightful, terrible, dreadful, abominable, appalling, shocking.
⊜ delightful.

grit *n* gravel, pebbles, shingle, sand, dust.
◇ *v* clench, gnash, grate, grind.

groan *n* moan, sigh, cry, whine, wail, lament, complaint, objection, protest, outcry.
⊜ cheer.
◇ *v* moan, sigh, cry, whine, wail, lament, complain, object, protest.
⊜ cheer.

groom *v* 1 SMARTEN, neaten, tidy, spruce up, clean, brush, curry, preen, dress. 2 *groomed for her new post*: prepare, train, school, educate, drill.

groove *n* furrow, rut, track, slot, channel, gutter, trench, hollow, indentation, score.
⊜ ridge.

grope *v* feel, fumble, scrabble, flounder, cast about, fish, search, probe.

gross *adj* 1 *gross misconduct*: serious, grievous, blatant, flagrant, glaring, obvious, plain, sheer, utter, outright, shameful, shocking. 2 OBSCENE, lewd, improper, indecent, offensive, rude, coarse, crude, vulgar, tasteless. 3 FAT, obese, overweight, big, large, huge, colossal, hulking, bulky, heavy. 4 *gross earnings*: inclusive, all-inclusive, total, entire, aggregate, complete, whole.
⊜ 3 slight. 4 net.

grotesque *adj* bizarre, odd, weird, unnatural, freakish, monstrous, hideous, ugly, unsightly, misshapen, deformed, distorted, twisted, fantastic, fanciful, extravagant, absurd, surreal, macabre.
⊜ normal, graceful.

ground *n* 1 BOTTOM, foundation, surface, land, terrain, dry land, terra firma, earth, soil, clay, loam, dirt,

dust. 2 *football ground*: field, pitch, stadium, arena, park.
◇ *v* 1 BASE, found, establish, set, fix, settle. 2 PREPARE, introduce, initiate, familiarize with, acquaint with, inform, instruct, teach, train, drill, coach, tutor.

groundless *adj* baseless, unfounded, unsubstantiated, unsupported, empty, imaginary, false, unjustified, unwarranted, unprovoked, uncalled-for.
⊜ well-founded, reasonable, justified.

grounds¹ *n* land, terrain, holding, estate, property, territory, domain, gardens, park, campus, surroundings, fields, acres.

grounds² *n* base, foundation, justification, excuse, vindication, reason, motive, inducement, cause, occasion, call, score, account, argument, principle, basis.

group *n* band, gang, pack, team, crew, troop, squad, detachment, party, faction, set, circle, clique, club, society, association, organization, company, gathering, congregation, crowd, flock, collection, bunch, clump, cluster, conglomeration, constellation, knot, batch, lot, combination, formation, grouping, class, classification, category, genus, species.
◇ *v* 1 GATHER, collect, assemble, congregate, mass, cluster, clump, bunch. 2 *group them according to size*: sort, range, arrange, marshal, organize, order, class, classify, categorize, band, link, associate.

grovel *v* crawl, creep, ingratiate oneself, toady, suck up (*sl*), flatter, fawn, cringe, cower, kowtow, defer, demean oneself.

grow *v* 1 INCREASE, rise, expand, enlarge, swell, spread, extend, stretch, develop, proliferate, mushroom. 2 ORIGINATE, arise, issue, spring, germinate, shoot, sprout, bud,

flower, mature, develop, progress, thrive, flourish, prosper. **3** CULTIVATE, farm, produce, propagate, breed, raise. **4** *grow cold*: become, get, go, turn.
🗷 **1** decrease, shrink.

growl *v* snarl, snap, yap, rumble, roar.

grown-up *adj* adult, mature, of age, full-grown, fully-fledged.
🗷 young, immature.
◇ *n* adult, man, woman.
🗷 child.

growth *n* **1** INCREASE, rise, extension, enlargement, expansion, spread, proliferation, development, evolution, progress, advance, improvement, success, prosperity. **2** TUMOUR, lump, swelling, protuberance, outgrowth.
🗷 **1** decrease, decline, failure.

grub *v* dig, burrow, delve, probe, root, rummage, forage, ferret, hunt, search, scour, explore.
◇ *n* maggot, worm, larva, pupa, caterpillar, chrysalis.

grubby *adj* dirty, soiled, unwashed, mucky, grimy, filthy, squalid, seedy, scruffy.
🗷 clean.

grudge *n* resentment, bitterness, envy, jealousy, spite, malice, enmity, antagonism, hate, dislike, animosity, ill-will, hard feelings, grievance.
🗷 favour.
◇ *v* begrudge, resent, envy, covet, dislike, take exception to, object to, mind.

grudging *adj* reluctant, unwilling, hesitant, half-hearted, unenthusiastic, resentful, envious, jealous.

gruelling *adj* hard, difficult, taxing, demanding, tiring, exhausting, laborious, arduous, strenuous, backbreaking, harsh, severe, tough, punishing.
🗷 easy.

gruesome *adj* horrible, disgusting,

repellent, repugnant, repulsive, hideous, grisly, macabre, grim, ghastly, awful, terrible, horrific, shocking, monstrous, abominable.
🗷 pleasant.

gruff *adj* **1** CURT, brusque, abrupt, blunt, rude, surly, sullen, grumpy, bad-tempered. **2** *a gruff voice*: rough, harsh, rasping, guttural, throaty, husky, hoarse.
🗷 **1** friendly, courteous.

grumble *v* complain, moan, whine, bleat, grouch, gripe, mutter, murmur, carp, find fault.

grumpy *adj* bad-tempered, ill-tempered, churlish, cantankerous, crotchety, crabbed, cross, irritable, surly, sullen, sulky, grouchy, discontented.
🗷 contented.

guarantee *n* warranty, insurance, assurance, promise, word of honour, pledge, oath, bond, security, collateral, surety, endorsement, testimonial.
◇ *v* assure, promise, pledge, swear, vouch for, answer for, warrant, certify, underwrite, endorse, secure, protect, insure, ensure, make sure, make certain.

guard *v* protect, safeguard, save, preserve, shield, screen, shelter, cover, defend, patrol, police, escort, supervise, oversee, watch, look out, mind, beware.
◇ *n* **1** PROTECTOR, defender, custodian, warder, escort, bodyguard, minder (*sl*), watchman, lookout, sentry, picket, patrol, security. **2** PROTECTION, safeguard, defence, wall, barrier, screen, shield, bumper, buffer, pad.

guarded *adj* cautious, wary, careful, watchful, discreet, non-committal, reticent, reserved, secretive, cagey (*infml*).
🗷 communicative, frank.

guardian *n* trustee, curator, steward, custodian, keeper, warden, protector, preserver, defender, champion, guard, warder, escort, attendant.

guess v speculate, conjecture, predict, estimate, judge, reckon, work out, suppose, assume, surmise, think, believe, imagine, fancy, feel, suspect.
◇ n prediction, estimate, speculation, conjecture, supposition, assumption, belief, fancy, idea, notion, theory, hypothesis, opinion, feeling, suspicion, intuition.

guesswork n speculation, conjecture, estimation, reckoning, supposition, assumption, surmise, intuition.

guest n visitor, caller, boarder, lodger, resident, patron, regular.

guidance n leadership, direction, management, control, teaching, instruction, advice, counsel, counselling, help, instructions, directions, guidelines, indications, pointers, recommendations.

guide v lead, conduct, direct, navigate, point, steer, pilot, manoeuvre, usher, escort, show, accompany, attend, control, govern, manage, preside over, oversee, supervise, superintend, advise, counsel, influence, educate, teach, instruct, train.
◇ n 1 LEADER, courier, navigator, pilot, helmsman, steersman, usher, escort, chaperone, attendant, companion, adviser, counsellor, mentor, guru, teacher, instructor. 2 MANUAL, handbook, guidebook, user guide, catalogue, directory. 3 GUIDELINE, example, model, standard, criterion, indication, pointer, signpost, sign, marker.

guideline n instruction, recommendation, suggestion, direction, advice, information, indication, rule, regulation, standard, criterion, measure, benchmark, yardstick, touchstone, framework, parameter, constraint,

procedure, principle, terms.

guild n organization, association, alliance, federation, society, club, union, fellowship, league, order, company, chapel, brotherhood, lodge, fraternity, sorority, corporation.

guilt n 1 he confessed his guilt: culpability, responsibility, blame, disgrace, dishonour. 2 a feeling of guilt: guilty conscience, conscience, shame, self-condemnation, self-reproach, regret, remorse, contrition.
🖃 1 innocence, righteousness. 2 shamelessness.

guilty adj 1 CULPABLE, responsible, blamable, blameworthy, offending, wrong, sinful, wicked, criminal, convicted. 2 CONSCIENCE-STRICKEN, ashamed, shamefaced, sheepish, sorry, regretful, remorseful, contrite, penitent, repentant.
🖃 1 innocent, guiltless, blameless. 2 shameless.

gulf n bay, bight, basin, gap, opening, separation, rift, split, breach, cleft, chasm, gorge, abyss, void.

gullible adj credulous, suggestible, impressionable, trusting, naive, unsuspecting, foolish, green, unsophisticated, innocent.
🖃 astute.

gully n channel, watercourse, gutter, ditch, ravine.

gulp v swallow, swig, swill, knock back (infml), bolt, wolf (infml), gobble, guzzle, devour, stuff.
🖃 sip, nibble.
◇ n swallow, swig, draught, mouthful.

gum n adhesive, glue, paste, cement.
◇ v stick, glue, paste, fix, cement, seal, clog.

gun n firearm, handgun, pistol, revolver, shooter (sl), shooting iron (sl), rifle, shotgun, machine gun, sub-machine gun, Uzi, bazooka, howitzer, cannon.

gurgle v bubble, babble, burble, murmur, ripple, lap, splash, crow.
◇ n babble, murmur, ripple.

gush v 1 FLOW, run, pour, stream, cascade, flood, rush, burst, spurt, spout, jet. 2 ENTHUSE, chatter, babble, jabber, go on (*infml*), drivel.
◇ n flow, outflow, stream, torrent, cascade, flood, tide, rush, burst, outburst, spurt, spout, jet.

gust n blast, burst, rush, flurry, blow, puff, breeze, wind, gale, squall.

gusto n zest, relish, appreciation, enjoyment, pleasure, delight, élan, enthusiasm, exuberance, verve, zeal.
⊜ distaste, apathy.

gut v 1 *gut fish*: disembowel, draw, clean (out). 2 STRIP, clear, empty, rifle, ransack, plunder, loot, sack, ravage.

guts n 1 INTESTINES, bowels, viscera, entrails, insides, innards (*infml*), belly, stomach. 2 (*infml*) COURAGE, bravery, pluck, grit, nerve, mettle.

gutter n drain, sluice, ditch, trench, trough, channel, duct, conduit, passage, pipe, tube.

guy n fellow, bloke (*infml*), chap (*infml*), man, boy, youth, person, individual.

Gypsy n Roma, Romany, Traveller.

gypsy, gipsy n traveller, wanderer, nomad, tinker.

gyrate v turn, revolve, rotate, twirl, pirouette, spin, whirl, wheel, circle, spiral.

Hh

habit *n* custom, usage, practice, routine, rule, second nature, way, manner, mode, wont, inclination, tendency, bent, mannerism, quirk, addiction, dependence, fixation, obsession, weakness.

habitat *n* home, abode, domain, element, environment, surroundings, locality, territory, terrain.

habitual *adj* **1** CUSTOMARY, usual, traditional, wonted, routine, ordinary, common, natural, normal, standard, regular, recurrent, fixed, established, familiar. **2** *habitual drinker*: confirmed, inveterate, hardened, addicted, dependent, persistent.
⊜ **1** occasional, infrequent.

hack¹ *v* cut, chop, hew, notch, gash, slash, lacerate, mutilate, mangle.

hack² *n* scribbler, journalist, drudge, slave.

hackneyed *adj* stale, overworked, tired, worn-out, time-worn, corny (*infml*), threadbare, unoriginal, clichéd, stereotyped, stock, banal, trite, commonplace, common, pedestrian, uninspired.
⊜ original, new, fresh.

hag *n* crone, witch, battle-axe (*infml*), shrew, termagant, vixen.

haggard *adj* drawn, gaunt, careworn, thin, wasted, pinched, shrunken, pale, wan, ghastly.
⊜ hale.

haggle *v* bargain, negotiate, barter, wrangle, squabble, bicker, quarrel, dispute.

hail¹ *n* barrage, bombardment, volley, torrent, shower, rain, storm.

◇ *v* pelt, bombard, shower, rain, batter, attack, assail.

hail² *v* greet, address, acknowledge, salute, wave, signal to, flag down, shout, call, acclaim, cheer, applaud, honour, welcome.

hair *n* locks, tresses, shock, mop, mane, barnet (*infml*).

hairdresser *n* hairstylist, stylist, barber, coiffeur, coiffeuse.

hairless *adj* bald, bald-headed, shorn, tonsured, shaven, clean-shaven, beardless.
⊜ hairy, hirsute.

hair-raising *adj* frightening, scary, terrifying, horrifying, shocking, bloodcurdling, spine-chilling, white-knuckle (*infml*), eerie, alarming, startling, thrilling.

hairstyle *n* style, coiffure, hairdo (*infml*), cut, haircut, set, perm (*infml*).

Hairstyles include: Afro, bangs, beehive, bob, bouffant, braid, bun, bunches, buzzcut, chignon, combover, cornrows, crew cut, dreadlocks, Eton crop, French pleat, fringe, Marcel wave, mohican, mullet, pageboy, perm, pigtail, plait, pompadour, ponytail, pouffe, quiff, ringlets, shingle, short back and sides, skinhead, tonsure, topknot, updo.

hairy *adj* hirsute, bearded, shaggy, bushy, fuzzy, furry, woolly.
⊜ bald, clean-shaven.

half *n* fifty per cent, bisection, hemisphere, semicircle, section, segment, portion, share, fraction.

◇ *adj* semi-, halved, divided, part, partial, fractional, incomplete, moderate, limited.
⊡ whole.
◇ *adv* partly, partially, incompletely, moderately, slightly.
⊡ completely.

half-hearted *adj* lukewarm, cool, weak, feeble, passive, apathetic, uninterested, indifferent, neutral.
⊡ whole-hearted, enthusiastic.

halfway *adv* midway, in the middle, centrally.
◇ *adj* middle, central, equidistant, mid, midway, intermediate.

hall *n* hallway, corridor, passage, passageway, entrance hall, foyer, vestibule, lobby, concert hall, auditorium, chamber, assembly room.

hallmark *n* stamp, mark, trademark, brand name, sign, indication, symbol, emblem, device, badge.

hallucinate *v* dream, imagine, see things, daydream, fantasize, freak out (*sl*), trip (*sl*).

hallucination *n* illusion, mirage, vision, apparition, dream, daydream, fantasy, figment, delusion, freak-out (*sl*), trip (*sl*).

halt *v* stop, draw up, pull up, pause, wait, rest, break off, discontinue, cease, desist, quit, end, terminate, check, stem, curb, obstruct, impede.
⊡ start, continue.
◇ *n* stop, stoppage, interruption, arrest, break, pause, rest, standstill, end, close, termination.
⊡ start, continuation.

halting *adj* hesitant, stuttering, stammering, faltering, stumbling, broken, imperfect, laboured, awkward.
⊡ fluent.

halve *v* bisect, cut in half, split in two, divide, split, share, cut down, reduce, lessen.

hammer *v* hit, strike, beat, drum, bang, bash, pound, batter, knock, drive, shape, form, make.
◇ *n* mallet, gavel.
● **hammer out** settle, sort out, negotiate, thrash out, produce, bring about, accomplish, complete, finish.

hamper *v* hinder, impede, slow down, obstruct, hold up, frustrate, thwart, prevent, handicap, hamstring, shackle, cramp, restrict, curb, restrain.
⊡ aid, facilitate.

hand *n* **1** FIST, palm, paw (*infml*), mitt (*sl*). **2** *give me a hand*: help, aid, assistance, support, participation, part, influence. **3** WORKER, employee, operative, workman, labourer, farm hand, hireling.
◇ *v* give, pass, offer, submit, present, yield, deliver, transmit, conduct, convey.
● **at hand** near, close, to hand, handy, accessible, available, ready, imminent.
● **hand down** bequeath, will, pass on, transfer, give, grant.
● **hand out** distribute, deal out, give out, share out, dish out (*infml*), mete out, dispense.
● **hand over** yield, relinquish, turn over, surrender, deliver, release, give, donate, present.
⊡ keep, retain.

handbook *n* manual, instruction book, guide, guidebook, user guide, companion.

handful *n* few, sprinkling, scattering, smattering.
⊡ a lot, many.

handicap *n* obstacle, block, barrier, impediment, stumbling-block, hindrance, drawback, disadvantage, restriction, limitation, penalty, disability, impairment, defect, shortcoming.
⊡ assistance, advantage.
◇ *v* impede, hinder, disadvantage, hold back, retard, hamper, burden,

encumber, restrict, limit, disable.
⊡ help, assist.

handicraft n craft, art, craftwork,
handwork, handiwork.

handiwork n work, doing,
responsibility, achievement, product,
result, design, invention, creation,
production, skill, workmanship,
craftsmanship, artisanship.

handle n grip, handgrip, knob,
stock, shaft, hilt.
◇ v 1 TOUCH, finger, feel, fondle, pick
up, hold, grasp. 2 handle a situation:
tackle, treat, deal with, manage,
cope with, control, supervise.

handout n 1 CHARITY, alms, dole,
largess(e), share, issue, free sample,
freebie (sl). 2 LEAFLET, flyer, circular,
bulletin, statement, press release,
literature.

hands n care, custody, possession,
charge, authority, command, power,
control, supervision.

handsome adj 1 GOOD-LOOKING,
attractive, fair, personable, fine,
elegant. 2 GENEROUS, liberal, large,
considerable, ample.
⊡ 1 ugly, unattractive. 2 mean.

handwriting n writing, script,
hand, fist (infml), penmanship,
calligraphy.

handy adj 1 AVAILABLE, to hand,
ready, at hand, near, accessible,
convenient, practical, useful, helpful.
2 SKILFUL, proficient, expert, skilled,
clever, practical.
⊡ 1 inconvenient. 2 clumsy.

hang v 1 SUSPEND, dangle, swing,
drape, drop, flop, droop, sag, trail.
2 FASTEN, attach, fix, stick. 3 hang
in the air: float, drift, hover, linger,
remain, cling.
• **hang about** hang around, linger,
loiter, dawdle, waste time, associate
with, frequent, haunt.
• **hang back** hold back, demur,
hesitate, shy away, recoil.
• **hang on 1** WAIT, hold on, remain,

hold out, endure, continue, carry on,
persevere, persist. 2 GRIP, grasp, hold
fast. 3 DEPEND ON, hinge on, turn on.
⊡ 1 give up.

hanger-on n follower, minion,
lackey, toady, sycophant, parasite,
sponger, dependant.

hang-up n inhibition, difficulty,
problem, obsession, preoccupation,
thing (infml), block, mental block.

hanker for v hanker after, crave,
hunger for, thirst for, want, wish for,
desire, covet, yearn for, long for, pine
for, itch for.

hankering n craving, hunger, thirst,
wish, desire, yearning, longing, itch,
urge.

haphazard adj random, chance,
casual, arbitrary, hit-or-miss,
unsystematic, disorganized,
disorderly, careless, slapdash,
slipshod.
⊡ methodical, orderly.

happen v occur, take place, arise,
crop up, develop, materialize (infml),
come about, result, ensue, follow,
turn out, transpire.

happening n occurrence,
phenomenon, event, incident,
episode, occasion, adventure,
experience, accident, chance,
circumstance, case, affair.

happiness n joy, joyfulness,
gladness, cheerfulness, contentment,
pleasure, delight, glee, elation, bliss,
ecstasy, euphoria.
⊡ unhappiness, sadness.

happy adj 1 JOYFUL, jolly, merry,
cheerful, glad, pleased, delighted,
thrilled, elated, satisfied, content,
contented. 2 a happy coincidence:
lucky, fortunate, felicitous,
favourable, appropriate, apt, fitting.
⊡ 1 unhappy, sad, discontented.
2 unfortunate, inappropriate.

harangue n diatribe, tirade, lecture,
speech, address.

◇ *v* lecture, preach, hold forth, spout, declaim, address.

harass *v* pester, badger, harry, plague, torment, persecute, exasperate, vex, annoy, irritate, bother, disturb, hassle (*infml*), trouble, worry, stress, tire, wear out, exhaust, fatigue.

harbour *n* port, dock, quay, wharf, marina, mooring, anchorage, haven, shelter.
◇ *v* **1** HIDE, conceal, protect, shelter. **2** *harbour a feeling*: hold, retain, cling to, entertain, foster, nurse, nurture, cherish, believe, imagine.

hard *adj* **1** SOLID, firm, unyielding, tough, strong, dense, impenetrable, stiff, rigid, inflexible. **2** DIFFICULT, arduous, strenuous, laborious, tiring, exhausting, backbreaking, complex, complicated, involved, knotty, baffling, puzzling, perplexing. **3** HARSH, severe, strict, callous, unfeeling, unsympathetic, cruel, pitiless, merciless, ruthless, unrelenting, distressing, painful, unpleasant.
☒ **1** soft, yielding. **2** easy, simple. **3** kind, pleasant.
◇ *adv* industriously, diligently, assiduously, doggedly, steadily, laboriously, strenuously, earnestly, keenly, intently, strongly, violently, intensely, energetically, vigorously.
• **hard up** poor, broke (*infml*), penniless, impoverished, in the red, bankrupt, bust, short, lacking.
☒ rich.

harden *v* solidify, set, freeze, bake, stiffen, strengthen, reinforce, fortify, buttress, brace, steel, nerve, toughen, season, accustom, train.
☒ soften, weaken.

hard-headed *adj* shrewd, astute, businesslike, level-headed, clear-thinking, sensible, realistic, pragmatic, practical, hard-boiled, tough, unsentimental.
☒ unrealistic.

hard-hearted *adj* callous, unfeeling, cold, hard, stony, heartless, unsympathetic, cruel, inhuman, pitiless, merciless.
☒ soft-hearted, kind, merciful.

hard-hitting *adj* condemnatory, critical, unsparing, no-holds-barred, vigorous, forceful, tough.
☒ mild.

hardly *adv* barely, scarcely, just, only just, not quite, not at all, by no means.

hardship *n* misfortune, adversity, trouble, difficulty, affliction, distress, suffering, trial, tribulation, want, need, privation, austerity, poverty, destitution, misery.
☒ ease, comfort, prosperity.

hard-wearing *adj* durable, lasting, strong, tough, sturdy, stout, rugged, resilient.
☒ delicate.

hard-working *adj* industrious, diligent, assiduous, conscientious, zealous, busy, energetic.
☒ idle, lazy.

hardy *adj* strong, tough, sturdy, robust, vigorous, fit, sound, healthy.
☒ weak, unhealthy.

harm *n* damage, loss, injury, hurt, detriment, ill, misfortune, wrong, abuse.
☒ benefit.
◇ *v* damage, impair, blemish, spoil, mar, ruin, hurt, injure, wound, ill-treat, maltreat, abuse, misuse.
☒ benefit, improve.

harmful *adj* damaging, detrimental, pernicious, noxious, unhealthy, unwholesome, injurious, dangerous, hazardous, poisonous, toxic, destructive.
☒ harmless.

harmless *adj* safe, innocuous, non-toxic, inoffensive, gentle, innocent.
☒ harmful, dangerous, destructive.

harmonious *adj* **1** MELODIOUS,

tuneful, musical, sweet-sounding.
2 MATCHING, co-ordinated, balanced, compatible, like-minded, agreeable, cordial, amicable, friendly, sympathetic.
⊞ **1** discordant.

harmonize *v* match, co-ordinate, balance, fit in, suit, tone, blend, correspond, agree, reconcile, accommodate, adapt, arrange, compose.
⊞ clash.

harmony *n* **1** TUNEFULNESS, tune, melody, euphony. **2** *live in harmony*: agreement, unanimity, accord, concord, unity, compatibility, like-mindedness, peace, goodwill, rapport, sympathy, understanding, amicability, friendliness, co-operation, co-ordination, balance, symmetry, correspondence, conformity.
⊞ **1** discord. **2** conflict.

harness *n* tackle, gear, equipment, reins, straps, tack.
◇ *v* control, channel, use, utilize, exploit, make use of, employ, mobilize, apply.

harrowing *adj* distressing, upsetting, heart-rending, disturbing, alarming, frightening, terrifying, nerve-racking, traumatic, agonizing, excruciating.

harry *v* badger, pester, nag, chivvy, harass, plague, torment, persecute, annoy, vex, worry, trouble, bother, hassle (*infml*), disturb, molest.

harsh *adj* **1** SEVERE, strict, Draconian, unfeeling, cruel, hard, pitiless, austere, Spartan, bleak, grim, comfortless. **2** *a harsh sound*: rough, coarse, rasping, croaking, guttural, grating, jarring, discordant, strident, raucous, sharp, shrill, unpleasant. **3** BRIGHT, dazzling, glaring, gaudy, lurid.
⊞ **1** lenient. **2** soft.

harvest *n* **1** HARVEST-TIME,

ingathering, reaping, collection.
2 CROP, yield, return, produce, fruits, result, consequence.
◇ *v* reap, mow, pick, gather, collect, accumulate, amass.

hash *n* mess, botch, muddle, mix-up, jumble, confusion, hotchpotch, mishmash.

haste *n* hurry, rush, hustle, bustle, speed, velocity, rapidity, swiftness, quickness, briskness, urgency, rashness, recklessness, impetuosity.
⊞ slowness.

hasten *v* hurry, rush, make haste, run, sprint, dash, tear, race, fly, bolt, accelerate, speed (up), quicken, expedite, dispatch, precipitate, urge, press, advance, step up.
⊞ dawdle, delay.

hasty *adj* hurried, rushed, impatient, headlong, rash, reckless, heedless, thoughtless, impetuous, impulsive, hot-headed, fast, quick, rapid, swift, speedy, brisk, prompt, short, brief, cursory.
⊞ slow, careful, deliberate.

hat

Hats include: trilby, bowler, fedora, top hat, Homburg, derby (*US*), pork-pie hat, flat cap, beret, bonnet, Tam o' Shanter, tammy, deerstalker, stovepipe hat, Stetson®, ten-gallon hat, boater, sunhat, panama, straw hat, picture hat, pillbox, cloche, beanie (*US*), poke bonnet, mob cap, turban, fez, sombrero, sou'wester, glengarry, bearskin, busby, peaked cap, sailor hat, baseball cap, jockey cap, Balaclava, hood, snood, toque, helmet, mortarboard, skullcap, yarmulka, mitre, biretta.

hatch *v* **1** INCUBATE, brood, breed.
2 CONCOCT, formulate, originate, think up, dream up, conceive, devise, contrive, plot, scheme, design, plan, project.

hate v dislike, despise, detest, loathe, abhor, abominate, execrate.
⊜ like, love.
◇ n hatred, aversion, loathing, dislike, abhorrence, abomination.
⊜ liking, love.

hatred n hate, aversion, dislike, detestation, loathing, repugnance, revulsion, abhorrence, abomination, execration, animosity, ill-will, antagonism, hostility, enmity, antipathy.
⊜ liking, love.

haughty adj lofty, imperious, high and mighty, supercilious, cavalier, snooty (infml), contemptuous, disdainful, scornful, superior, snobbish, arrogant, proud, stuck-up (infml), conceited.
⊜ humble, modest.

haul v pull, heave, tug, draw, tow, drag, trail, move, transport, convey, carry, cart, lug, hump (infml).
⊜ push.
◇ n loot, booty, plunder, swag (sl), spoils, takings, gain, yield, find.

haunt v 1 FREQUENT, patronize, visit. 2 memories haunted her: plague, torment, trouble, disturb, recur, prey on, beset, obsess, possess.
◇ n resort, hangout (infml), stamping-ground, den, meeting-place, rendezvous.

haunting adj memorable, unforgettable, persistent, recurrent, evocative, nostalgic, poignant.
⊜ unmemorable.

have v 1 OWN, possess, get, obtain, gain, acquire, procure, secure, receive, accept, keep, hold. 2 FEEL, experience, enjoy, suffer, undergo, endure, put up with. 3 CONTAIN, include, comprise, incorporate, consist of. 4 have a baby: give birth to, bear.
⊜ 1 lack.
• **have to** must, be forced, be compelled, be obliged, be required, ought, should.

haven n harbour, port, anchorage, shelter, refuge, sanctuary, asylum, retreat.

havoc n chaos, confusion, disorder, disruption, damage, destruction, ruin, wreck, rack and ruin, devastation, waste, desolation.

haywire adj wrong, tangled, out of control, crazy, mad, wild, chaotic, confused, disordered, disorganized, topsy-turvy.

hazard n risk, danger, peril, threat, jeopardy, deathtrap, accident, chance.
⊜ safety.
◇ v 1 RISK, endanger, jeopardize, expose. 2 CHANCE, gamble, stake, venture, suggest, speculate.

hazardous adj risky, dangerous, unsafe, perilous, precarious, insecure, chancy, difficult, tricky.
⊜ safe, secure.

haze n mist, fog, cloud, steam, vapour, film, mistiness, smokiness, dimness, obscurity.

hazy adj misty, foggy, clouded, cloudy, milky, fuzzy, blurred, smoky, ill-defined, veiled, obscure, dim, faint, unclear, indistinct, vague, indefinite, uncertain.
⊜ clear, bright, definite.

head n 1 SKULL, cranium, brain, mind, mentality, brains (infml), intellect, intelligence, understanding, thought. 2 TOP, peak, summit, crown, tip, apex, height, climax, front, fore, lead. 3 LEADER, chief, captain, commander, boss, director, manager, superintendent, principal, head teacher, ruler.
⊜ 1 foot, tail. 2 base, foot. 3 subordinate.
◇ adj leading, front, foremost, first, chief, main, prime, principal, top, highest, supreme, premier, dominant, pre-eminent.
◇ v lead, rule, govern, command, direct, manage, run, superintend,

oversee, supervise, control, guide, steer.

● **head for** make for, go towards, direct towards, aim for, point to, turn for, steer for.

● **head off** forestall, intercept, intervene, interpose, deflect, divert, fend off, ward off, avert, prevent, stop.

heading n title, name, headline, rubric, caption, section, division, category, class.

headland n promontory, cape, head, point, foreland.

headlong adj hasty, precipitate, impetuous, impulsive, rash, reckless, dangerous, breakneck, head-first. ◇ adv head first, hurriedly, hastily, precipitately, rashly, recklessly, heedlessly, thoughtlessly, wildly.

headquarters n HQ, base (camp), head office, nerve centre.

headstrong adj stubborn, obstinate, intractable, pigheaded, wilful, self-willed, perverse, contrary. ✣ tractable, docile.

headway n advance, progress, way, improvement.

heady adj intoxicating, strong, stimulating, exhilarating, thrilling, exciting.

heal v cure, remedy, mend, restore, treat, soothe, salve, settle, reconcile, patch up.

health n fitness, constitution, form, shape, trim, fettle, condition, tone, state, healthiness, good condition, wellbeing, welfare, soundness, robustness, strength, vigour. ✣ illness, infirmity.

healthy adj 1 WELL, fit, good, fine, in condition, in good shape, in fine fettle, sound, sturdy, robust, strong, vigorous, hale and hearty, blooming, flourishing, thriving. 2 healthy food: wholesome, nutritious, nourishing, bracing, invigorating, healthful.

✣ 1 ill, sick, infirm.

heap n pile, stack, mountain, mound, lot, mass, accumulation, collection, hoard, stockpile, store. ◇ v pile, stack, mound, bank, build, amass, accumulate, collect, gather, hoard, stockpile, store, load.

hear v 1 LISTEN, catch, pick up, overhear, eavesdrop, heed, pay attention. 2 LEARN, ascertain, find out, discover, understand, gather. 3 JUDGE, try, examine, investigate.

hearing n 1 EARSHOT, sound, range, reach, ear, perception. 2 TRIAL, inquiry, investigation, inquest, audition, interview, audience.

hearsay n rumour, word-of-mouth, talk, gossip, tittle-tattle, report, buzz (infml).

heart n 1 SOUL, mind, character, disposition, nature, temperament, feeling, emotion, sentiment, love, tenderness, compassion, sympathy, pity. 2 lose heart: courage, bravery, boldness, spirit, resolution, determination. 3 CENTRE, middle, core, kernel, nucleus, nub, crux, essence. ✣ 2 cowardice. 3 periphery. ● **by heart** by rote, parrot-fashion, pat, off pat, word for word, verbatim.

Parts of the heart include: aortic valve, aorta, bicuspid valve, carotid artery, vena cava, atrium, pulmonary artery, pulmonary veins, ventricle, mitral valve, myocardium, pulmonary valve, tricuspid valve, ventricular septum.

---

heartbreaking adj distressing, sad, tragic, harrowing, heart-rending, pitiful, agonizing, grievous, bitter, disappointing. ✣ heartwarming, heartening.

heartbroken adj broken-hearted, desolate, sad, miserable, dejected, despondent, downcast, crestfallen,

disappointed, dispirited, grieved, crushed.
☒ delighted, elated.

hearten v comfort, console, cheer (up), reassure, buck up (infml), encourage, boost, inspire, stimulate, rouse, pep up (infml).
☒ dishearten, depress, dismay.

heartfelt adj deep, profound, sincere, honest, genuine, earnest, ardent, fervent, whole-hearted, warm.
☒ insincere, false.

heartless adj unfeeling, uncaring, cold, hard, hard-hearted, callous, unkind, cruel, inhuman, brutal, pitiless, merciless.
☒ kind, considerate, sympathetic, merciful.

heart-rending adj harrowing, heartbreaking, agonizing, pitiful, piteous, pathetic, tragic, sad, distressing, moving, affecting, poignant.

heartwarming adj pleasing, gratifying, satisfying, cheering, heartening, encouraging, touching, moving, affecting.
☒ heartbreaking.

hearty adj 1 ENTHUSIASTIC, whole-hearted, unreserved, heartfelt, sincere, genuine, warm, friendly, cordial, jovial, cheerful, ebullient, exuberant, boisterous, energetic, vigorous. 2 a hearty breakfast: large, sizable, substantial, filling, ample, generous.
☒ 1 half-hearted, cool, cold. 2 light.

heat n 1 HOTNESS, warmth, sultriness, closeness, high temperature, fever. 2 ARDOUR, fervour, fieriness, passion, intensity, vehemence, fury, excitement, impetuosity, earnestness, zeal.
☒ 1 cold(ness). 2 coolness.
◊ v warm, boil, toast, cook, bake, roast, reheat, warm up, inflame,

excite, animate, rouse, stimulate, flush, glow.
☒ cool, chill.

heated adj angry, furious, raging, passionate, fiery, stormy, tempestuous, bitter, fierce, intense, vehement, violent, frenzied.
☒ calm.

heave v 1 PULL, haul, drag, tug, raise, lift, hitch, hoist, lever, rise, surge. 2 THROW, fling, hurl, cast, toss, chuck, let fly. 3 RETCH, vomit, throw up (infml), spew.

heaven n sky, firmament, next world, hereafter, afterlife, paradise, utopia, ecstasy, rapture, bliss, happiness, joy.
☒ hell.

heavenly adj 1 BLISSFUL, wonderful, glorious, beautiful, lovely, delightful, out of this world. 2 CELESTIAL, unearthly, supernatural, spiritual, divine, godlike, angelic, immortal, sublime, blessed.
☒ 1 hellish. 2 infernal.

heavy adj 1 WEIGHTY, hefty, ponderous, burdensome, massive, large, bulky, solid, dense, stodgy. 2 heavy work: hard, difficult, tough, arduous, laborious, strenuous, demanding, taxing, harsh, severe. 3 OPPRESSIVE, intense, serious, dull, tedious.
☒ 1 light. 2 easy.

heavy-handed adj clumsy, awkward, unsubtle, tactless, insensitive, thoughtless, oppressive, overbearing, domineering, autocratic.

hectic adj busy, frantic, frenetic, chaotic, fast, feverish, excited, heated, furious, wild.
☒ leisurely.

hedge n hedgerow, screen, windbreak, barrier, fence, dike, boundary.
◊ v 1 SURROUND, enclose, hem in, confine, restrict, fortify, guard, shield,

protect, safeguard, cover. **2** STALL, temporize, equivocate, dodge, sidestep, evade, duck.

heed v listen, pay attention, mind, note, regard, observe, follow, obey.
⊠ ignore, disregard.

heedless adj oblivious, unthinking, careless, negligent, rash, reckless, inattentive, unobservant, thoughtless, unconcerned.
⊠ heedful, mindful, attentive.

hefty adj heavy, weighty, big, large, burly, hulking, beefy, brawny, strong, powerful, vigorous, robust, strapping, solid, substantial, massive, colossal, bulky, unwieldy.
⊠ slight, small.

height n **1** HIGHNESS, altitude, elevation, tallness, loftiness, stature. **2** TOP, summit, peak, pinnacle, apex, crest, crown, zenith, apogee, culmination, climax, extremity, maximum, limit, ceiling.
⊠ **1** depth.

heighten v raise, elevate, increase, add to, magnify, intensify, strengthen, sharpen, improve, enhance.
⊠ lower, decrease, diminish.

hell n **1** heaven and hell: inferno, underworld, Hades, lower regions, nether world, abyss. **2** SUFFERING, anguish, agony, torment, ordeal, nightmare, misery.
⊠ **1** heaven.

hellish adj infernal, devilish, diabolical, fiendish, accursed, damnable, monstrous, abominable, atrocious, dreadful.
⊠ heavenly.

helm n tiller, wheel, driving seat, reins, saddle, command, control, leadership, direction.

help v **1** AID, assist, lend a hand, serve, be of use, collaborate, co-operate, back, stand by, support. **2** IMPROVE, ameliorate, relieve, alleviate, mitigate, ease, facilitate.
⊠ **1** hinder. **2** worsen.

◇ n aid, assistance, collaboration, co-operation, support, advice, guidance, service, use, utility, avail, benefit.
⊠ hindrance.

helper n assistant, deputy, auxiliary, subsidiary, attendant, right-hand man, PA, mate, partner, associate, colleague, collaborator, accomplice, ally, supporter, second.

helpful adj **1** USEFUL, practical, constructive, worthwhile, valuable, beneficial, profitable, advantageous. **2** a helpful person: co-operative, obliging, neighbourly, friendly, considerate, caring, kind, sympathetic, supportive.
⊠ **1** useless, futile.

helping n serving, portion, share, ration, amount, plateful, piece, dollop (infml).

helpless adj weak, feeble, powerless, dependent, vulnerable, exposed, unprotected, defenceless, abandoned, friendless, destitute, forlorn, incapable, incompetent, infirm, disabled, paralysed.
⊠ strong, independent, competent.

hem n edge, border, margin, fringe, trimming.
● **hem in** surround, enclose, box in, confine, restrict.

henpecked adj dominated, subjugated, browbeaten, bullied, intimidated, meek, timid.
⊠ dominant.

herald n messenger, courier, harbinger, forerunner, precursor, omen, token, signal, sign, indication.
◇ v announce, proclaim, broadcast, advertise, publicize, trumpet, pave the way, precede, usher in, show, indicate, promise.

herb

Herbs and spices include: angelica, anise, basil, bay, bergamot, borage, camomile,

chervil, chives, comfrey, dill,
fennel, garlic, hyssop, lavender,
lemon balm, lovage, marjoram,
mint, oregano, parsley, rosemary,
sage, savory, sorrel, tarragon,
thyme; allspice, caraway seeds,
cardamom, cayenne pepper, chilli,
cinnamon, cloves, coriander,
cumin, curry powder, garam
masala, ginger, mace, mustard,
nutmeg, paprika, pepper, saffron,
star anise, turmeric, vanilla.

herd n drove, flock, swarm, pack,
press, crush, mass, horde, throng,
multitude, crowd, mob, the masses,
rabble.
◇ v 1 FLOCK, congregate, gather,
collect, assemble, rally. 2 LEAD,
guide, shepherd, round up, drive,
force.

hereditary adj bequeathed,
inherited, handed down, family,
ancestral, inborn, inbred, innate,
natural, congenital, genetic.

heresy n heterodoxy, unorthodoxy,
free-thinking, apostasy, dissidence,
schism, blasphemy.
⊞ orthodoxy.

heretic n free-thinker, apostate,
nonconformist, dissident, dissenter,
unbeliever, atheist, agnostic,
revisionist, separatist, schismatic,
sectarian, renegade.
⊞ conformist.

heretical adj heterodox,
unorthodox, free-thinking,
rationalistic, schismatic,
impious, irreverent, iconoclastic,
blasphemous.
⊞ orthodox, conventional,
conformist.

heritage n 1 INHERITANCE, legacy,
bequest, endowment, lot, portion,
share, birthright, due. 2 HISTORY, past,
tradition, culture.

hermit n recluse, solitary, monk,
ascetic, anchorite.

hero n protagonist, lead, celebrity,
star, superstar, idol, paragon, goody
(infml), champion, conqueror.

heroic adj brave, courageous,
fearless, dauntless, undaunted, lion-
hearted, stout-hearted, valiant, bold,
daring, intrepid, adventurous, gallant,
chivalrous, noble, selfless.
⊞ cowardly, timid.

heroism n bravery, courage,
valour, boldness, daring, intrepidity,
gallantry, prowess, selflessness.
⊞ cowardice, timidity.

hesitant adj hesitating, reluctant,
half-hearted, uncertain, unsure,
indecisive, irresolute, vacillating,
wavering, tentative, wary, shy, timid,
halting, stammering, stuttering.
⊞ decisive, resolute, confident,
fluent.

hesitate v pause, delay, wait, be
reluctant, be unwilling, think twice,
hold back, shrink from, scruple,
boggle, demur, vacillate, waver, be
uncertain, dither, shilly-shally, falter,
stumble, halt, stammer, stutter.
⊞ decide.

hesitation n pause, delay, holding-
back, reluctance, unwillingness,
hesitance, scruples, qualms,
misgivings, doubt, second thoughts,
vacillation, uncertainty, indecision,
irresolution, faltering, stumbling,
stammering, stuttering.
⊞ eagerness, assurance.

hew v cut, fell, axe, lop, chop, hack,
sever, split, carve, sculpt, sculpture,
fashion, model, form, shape, make.

heyday n peak, prime, flush, bloom,
flowering, golden age, boom time.

hidden adj 1 a hidden door:
concealed, covered, shrouded,
veiled, disguised, camouflaged,
unseen, secret. 2 OBSCURE, dark,
occult, secret, covert, close, cryptic,
mysterious, abstruse, mystical, latent,
ulterior.
⊞ 1 showing, apparent. 2 obvious.

hide¹ v 1 CONCEAL, cover, cloak, shroud, veil, screen, mask, disguise, camouflage, obscure, shadow, eclipse, bury, stash (*infml*), secrete, withhold, keep dark, suppress. 2 TAKE COVER, shelter, lie low, go to ground, hole up (*infml*).
☒ 1 reveal, show, display.

hide² n skin, pelt, fell, fur, leather.

hidebound adj set, rigid, entrenched, narrow-minded, strait-laced, conventional, ultra-conservative.
☒ liberal, progressive.

hideous adj ugly, repulsive, grotesque, monstrous, horrid, ghastly, awful, dreadful, frightful, terrible, grim, gruesome, macabre, terrifying, shocking, appalling, disgusting, revolting, horrible.
☒ beautiful, attractive.

hiding¹ n beating, flogging, whipping, caning, spanking, thrashing, walloping (*infml*).

hiding² n concealment, cover, veiling, screening, disguise, camouflage.

hiding-place n hideaway, hideout, lair, den, hole, hide, cover, refuge, haven, sanctuary, retreat.

hierarchy n pecking order, ranking, grading, scale, series, ladder, echelons, strata.

high adj 1 TALL, lofty, elevated, soaring, towering. 2 GREAT, strong, intense, extreme. 3 IMPORTANT, influential, powerful, eminent, distinguished, prominent, chief, leading, senior. 4 HIGH-PITCHED, soprano, treble, sharp, shrill, piercing. 5 *a high price*: expensive, dear, costly, exorbitant, excessive.
☒ 1 low, short. 3 lowly. 4 deep. 5 cheap.

high-born adj noble, aristocratic, blue-blooded, thoroughbred.
☒ low-born.

highbrow n intellectual, egghead (*infml*), scholar, academic.
◇ adj intellectual, sophisticated, cultured, cultivated, academic, deep, bookish, brainy (*infml*), serious, classical.
☒ low-brow.

high-class adj upper-class, posh (*infml*), classy (*infml*), top-class, top-flight, high-quality, quality, de luxe, superior, excellent, first-rate, choice, select, exclusive.
☒ ordinary, mediocre.

high-flown adj florid, extravagant, exaggerated, elaborate, flamboyant, ostentatious, pretentious, high-standing, grandiose, pompous, bombastic, turgid, artificial, stilted, affected, lofty, highfalutin, la-di-da (*infml*), supercilious.

high-handed adj overbearing, domineering, bossy (*infml*), imperious, dictatorial, autocratic, despotic, tyrannical, oppressive, arbitrary.

highlight n high point, high spot, peak, climax, best, cream.
◇ v underline, emphasize, stress, accentuate, play up, point up, set off, spotlight, illuminate, show up, focus on, feature.

highly adv very, greatly, extremely, considerably, decidedly, immensely, tremendously, exceptionally, extraordinarily, enthusiastically, warmly, well.

highly-strung adj sensitive, neurotic, nervy, jumpy, edgy, temperamental, excitable, restless, nervous, tense.
☒ calm.

high-minded adj lofty, noble, moral, ethical, principled, idealistic, virtuous, upright, righteous, honourable, worthy.
☒ immoral, unscrupulous.

high-powered adj powerful, forceful, driving, aggressive, dynamic, go-ahead, enterprising, energetic, vigorous.

high-spirited *adj* boisterous, bouncy, exuberant, effervescent, frolicsome, ebullient, sparkling, vibrant, vivacious, lively, energetic, spirited, dashing, bold, daring.
🖃 quiet, sedate.

hijack *v* commandeer, expropriate, skyjack, seize, take over.

hike *v* ramble, walk, trek, tramp, trudge, plod.
◇ *n* ramble, walk, trek, tramp, march.

hilarious *adj* funny, amusing, comical, side-splitting, hysterical (*infml*), uproarious, noisy, rollicking, merry, jolly, jovial.
🖃 serious, grave.

hilarity *n* mirth, laughter, fun, amusement, levity, frivolity, merriment, jollity, conviviality, high spirits, boisterousness, exuberance, exhilaration.
🖃 seriousness, gravity.

hill *n* **1** HILLOCK, knoll, mound, prominence, eminence, elevation, foothill, down, fell, mountain, height. **2** *a steep hill*: slope, incline, gradient, ramp, rise, ascent, acclivity, drop, descent, declivity.

hinder *v* hamper, obstruct, impede, encumber, handicap, hamstring, hold up, delay, retard, slow down, hold back, check, curb, stop, prevent, frustrate, thwart, oppose.
🖃 help, aid, assist.

hindrance *n* obstruction, impediment, handicap, obstacle, encumbrance, stumbling-block, barrier, bar, check, restraint, restriction, limitation, difficulty, drag, snag, hitch, drawback, disadvantage, inconvenience, deterrent.
🖃 help, aid, assistance.

hinge *v* centre, turn, revolve, pivot, hang, depend, rest.

hint *n* **1** TIP, advice, suggestion,

help, clue, inkling, suspicion, tip-off, reminder, indication, sign, pointer, mention, allusion, intimation, insinuation, implication, innuendo. **2** *a hint of garlic*: touch, trace, tinge, taste, dash, soupçon, speck.
◇ *v* suggest, prompt, tip off, indicate, imply, insinuate, intimate, allude, mention.

hire *v* rent, let, lease, charter, commission, book, reserve, employ, take on, sign up, engage, appoint, retain.
🖃 dismiss, fire.
◇ *n* rent, rental, fee, charge, cost, price.

hiss *v* **1** WHISTLE, shrill, whizz, sizzle. **2** JEER, mock, ridicule, deride, boo, hoot.

historic *adj* momentous, important, consequential, significant, epoch-making, notable, remarkable, outstanding, extraordinary, celebrated, renowned, famed, famous.
🖃 unimportant, insignificant, unknown.

historical *adj* real, actual, authentic, factual, documented, recorded, attested, verifiable.
🖃 legendary, fictional.

history *n* **1** PAST, olden days, days of old, antiquity. **2** CHRONICLE, record, annals, archives, chronology, account, narrative, story, tale, saga, biography, life, autobiography, memoirs.

hit *v* **1** STRIKE, knock, tap, smack, slap, thrash, whack (*infml*), bash, thump, clout, punch, belt (*infml*), wallop (*infml*), beat, batter. **2** BUMP, collide with, bang, crash, smash, damage, harm.
◇ *n* **1** STROKE, shot, blow, knock, tap, slap, smack, bash, bump, collision, impact, crash, smash. **2** SUCCESS, triumph, winner (*sl*).
🖃 **2** failure.
• **hit back** retaliate, reciprocate,

counter-attack, strike back.

• **hit on** chance on, stumble on, light on, discover, invent, realize, arrive at, guess.

• **hit out** lash out, assail, attack, rail, denounce, condemn, criticize.

hitch v 1 FASTEN, attach, tie, harness, yoke, couple, connect, join, unite. 2 PULL, heave, yank (infml), tug, jerk, hoist, hike (up) (infml).
🔁 1 unhitch, unfasten.
◇ n delay, hold-up, trouble, problem, difficulty, mishap, setback, hiccup, drawback, snag, catch, impediment, hindrance.

hoard n collection, accumulation, mass, heap, pile, fund, reservoir, supply, reserve, store, stockpile, cache, treasure-trove.
◇ v collect, gather, accumulate, amass, save, put by, lay up, store, stash away (infml), stockpile, keep, treasure.
🔁 use, spend, squander.

hoarse adj husky, croaky, throaty, guttural, gravelly, gruff, growling, rough, harsh, rasping, grating, raucous, discordant.
🔁 clear, smooth.

hoax n trick, prank, practical joke, put-on, joke, leg-pull (infml), spoof, fake, fraud, deception, bluff, humbug, cheat, swindle, con (infml).
◇ v trick, deceive, take in, fool, dupe, gull, delude, have on (infml), pull someone's leg (infml), con (infml), swindle, take for a ride (infml), cheat, hoodwink, bamboozle (infml), bluff.

hobble v limp, stumble, falter, stagger, totter, dodder, shuffle.

hobby n pastime, diversion, recreation, relaxation, pursuit, sideline.

Hobbies include: aerobics, astronomy, ballet, ballroom dancing, beekeeping, birdwatching, bridge, bungee jumping, camping, chess, climbing, collecting, computer games, cooking, crochet, crosswords, darts, diving, DIY, extreme sports, gardening, hillwalking, horse-riding, jigsaws, kite-flying, knitting, martial arts, model railways, orienteering, origami, paintball, patchwork, photography, pottery, quilting, skateboarding, snooker, sports, wargaming, wine-tasting, woodwork, yoga. see also **dance**; **martial art**; **sport**.

hoist v lift, elevate, raise, erect, jack up, winch up, heave, rear, uplift.
◇ n jack, winch, crane, tackle, lift, elevator.

hold v 1 GRIP, grasp, clutch, clasp, embrace, have, own, possess, keep, retain. 2 hold a meeting: conduct, carry on, continue, call, summon, convene, assemble. 3 CONSIDER, regard, deem, judge, reckon, think, believe, maintain. 4 BEAR, support, sustain, carry, comprise, contain, accommodate. 5 IMPRISON, detain, stop, arrest, check, curb, restrain. 6 CLING, stick, adhere, stay.
🔁 1 drop. 5 release, free, liberate.
◇ n 1 GRIP, grasp, clasp, embrace. 2 INFLUENCE, power, sway, mastery, dominance, authority, control, leverage.

• **hold back 1** CONTROL, curb, check, restrain, suppress, stifle, retain, withhold, repress, inhibit. 2 HESITATE, delay, desist, refrain, shrink, refuse.
🔁 1 release.

• **hold forth** speak, talk, lecture, discourse, orate, preach, declaim.

• **hold off 1** FEND OFF, ward off, stave off, keep off, repel, rebuff. 2 PUT OFF, postpone, defer, delay, wait.

• **hold out 1** OFFER, give, present, extend. 2 LAST, continue, persist, endure, persevere, stand fast, hang on.
🔁 2 give in, yield.

● **hold up 1** SUPPORT, sustain, brace, shore (up), lift, raise. **2** DELAY, detain, retard, slow, hinder, impede.

● **hold with** agree with, go along with, approve of, countenance, support, subscribe to, accept.

holder n **1** *holders of British passports*: bearer, owner, possessor, proprietor, keeper, custodian, occupant, incumbent. **2** CONTAINER, receptacle, case, housing, cover, sheath, rest, stand.

hold-up n **1** DELAY, wait, hitch, setback, snag, difficulty, trouble, obstruction, stoppage, (traffic) jam, bottleneck. **2** ROBBERY, heist (*sl*), stick-up (*sl*).

hole n aperture, opening, orifice, pore, puncture, perforation, eyelet, tear, split, vent, outlet, shaft, slot, gap, breach, break, crack, fissure, fault, defect, flaw, dent, dimple, depression, hollow, cavity, crater, pit, excavation, cavern, cave, chamber, pocket, niche, recess, burrow, nest, lair, retreat.

holiday n vacation, recess, leave, time off, day off, break, rest, half-term, bank-holiday, feast-day, festival, celebration, anniversary.

holiness n sacredness, sanctity, spirituality, divinity, devoutness, piety, godliness, saintliness, virtuousness, righteousness, purity. ⊞ impiety.

hollow adj **1** CONCAVE, indented, depressed, sunken, deep, cavernous, empty, vacant, unfilled. **2** FALSE, artificial, deceptive, insincere, meaningless, empty, vain, futile, fruitless, worthless. ⊞ **1** solid. **2** real. ◇ n hole, pit, well, cavity, crater, excavation, cavern, cave, depression, concavity, basin, bowl, cup, dimple, dent, indentation, groove, channel, trough, valley. ◇ v dig, excavate, burrow, tunnel, scoop, gouge, channel, groove,

furrow, pit, dent, indent.

holy adj **1** *holy ground*: sacred, hallowed, consecrated, sanctified, dedicated, blessed, venerated, revered, spiritual, divine, evangelical. **2** PIOUS, religious, devout, godly, God-fearing, saintly, virtuous, good, righteous, faithful, pure, perfect. ⊞ **1** unsanctified. **2** impious, irreligious.

homage n acknowledgement, recognition, tribute, honour, praise, adulation, admiration, regard, esteem, respect, deference, reverence, adoration, awe, veneration, worship, devotion.

home n residence, domicile, dwelling-place, abode, base, house, pied-à-terre, hearth, fireside, birthplace, home town, home ground, territory, habitat, element. ◇ adj domestic, household, family, internal, local, national, inland. ⊞ foreign, international.

● **at home 1** COMFORTABLE, relaxed, at ease. **2** FAMILIAR, knowledgeable, experienced, skilled.

homeland n native land, native country, fatherland, motherland.

homeless adj itinerant, travelling, nomadic, wandering, vagrant, rootless, unsettled, displaced, dispossessed, evicted, exiled, outcast, abandoned, forsaken, destitute, down-and-out. ◇ n travellers, vagabonds, vagrants, tramps, down-and-outs, dossers (*sl*), squatters.

homely adj homelike, homey, comfortable, cosy, snug, relaxed, informal, friendly, intimate, familiar, everyday, ordinary, domestic, natural, plain, simple, modest, unassuming, unpretentious, unsophisticated, folksy, homespun. ⊞ grand, formal.

homicide n murder, manslaughter, assassination, killing, bloodshed.

homogeneous *adj* uniform, consistent, unvarying, identical, similar, alike, akin, kindred, analogous, comparable, harmonious, compatible.
⊞ different.

homosexual *n* gay, queer (*sl*), poof (*sl*), homo (*sl*), lesbian, dike (*sl*).
⊞ heterosexual, straight (*sl*).
◇ *adj* gay, queer (*sl*), lesbian.

hone *v* sharpen, whet, point, edge, grind, file, polish.

honest *adj* 1 TRUTHFUL, sincere, frank, candid, blunt, outspoken, direct, straight, outright, forthright, straightforward, plain, simple, open, above-board, legitimate, legal, lawful, on the level (*infml*), fair, just, impartial, objective. 2 LAW-ABIDING, virtuous, upright, ethical, moral, high-minded, scrupulous, honourable, reputable, respectable, reliable, trustworthy, true, genuine, real.
⊞ 1 dishonest. 2 dishonourable.

honestly *adv* truly, really, truthfully, sincerely, frankly, directly, outright, plainly, openly, legitimately, legally, lawfully, on the level, fairly, justly, objectively, honourably, in good faith.
⊞ dishonestly, dishonourably.

honesty *n* 1 TRUTHFULNESS, sincerity, frankness, candour, bluntness, outspokenness, straightforwardness, plain-speaking, explicitness, openness, legitimacy, legality, equity, fairness, justness, objectivity, even-handedness. 2 VIRTUE, uprightness, honour, integrity, morality, scrupulousness, trustworthiness, genuineness, veracity.
⊞ 1 dishonesty.

honorary *adj* unpaid, unofficial, titular, nominal, in name only, honorific, formal.
⊞ paid.

honour *n* 1 REPUTATION, good name, repute, renown, distinction, esteem, regard, respect, credit, dignity, self-respect, pride, integrity, morality, decency, rectitude, probity. 2 AWARD, accolade, commendation, acknowledgement, recognition, tribute, privilege. 3 PRAISE, acclaim, homage, admiration, reverence, worship, adoration.
⊞ 1 dishonour, disgrace.
◇ *v* 1 PRAISE, acclaim, exalt, glorify, pay homage to, decorate, crown, celebrate, commemorate, remember, admire, esteem, respect, revere, worship, prize, value. 2 *honour a promise*: keep, observe, respect, fulfil, carry out, discharge, execute, perform.
⊞ 1 dishonour, disgrace.

honourable *adj* great, eminent, distinguished, renowned, respected, worthy, prestigious, trusty, reputable, respectable, virtuous, upright, upstanding, straight, honest, trustworthy, true, sincere, noble, high-minded, principled, moral, ethical, fair, just, right, proper, decent.
⊞ dishonourable, unworthy, dishonest.

hoodwink *v* deceive, dupe, fool, take in, delude, bamboozle (*infml*), have on (*infml*), mislead, hoax, trick, cheat, con (*infml*), rook, gull, swindle.

hook *n* crook, sickle, peg, barb, trap, snare, catch, fastener, clasp, hasp.
◇ *v* 1 BEND, crook, curve, curl. 2 CATCH, capture, bag, grab, trap, snare, ensnare, entangle. 3 FASTEN, clasp, hitch, fix, secure.

hooligan *n* ruffian, rowdy, hoodlum, mobster, bovver boy (*sl*), thug, tough, lout, yob (*sl*), vandal, delinquent.

hoop *n* ring, circle, round, loop, wheel, band, girdle, circlet.

hoot *n, v* call, cry, shout, shriek, whoop, toot, beep, whistle, boo, jeer, laugh, howl.

hop v jump, leap, spring, bound, vault, skip, dance, prance, frisk, limp, hobble.
◇ n jump, leap, spring, bound, vault, bounce, step, skip, dance.

hope n hopefulness, optimism, ambition, aspiration, wish, desire, longing, dream, expectation, anticipation, prospect, promise, belief, confidence, assurance, conviction, faith.
⊠ pessimism, despair.
◇ v aspire, wish, desire, long, expect, await, look forward, anticipate, contemplate, foresee, believe, trust, rely, reckon on, assume.
⊠ despair.

hopeful adj 1 OPTIMISTIC, bullish (infml), confident, assured, expectant, sanguine, cheerful, buoyant. 2 a hopeful sign: encouraging, heartening, reassuring, favourable, auspicious, promising, rosy, bright.
⊠ 1 pessimistic, despairing. 2 discouraging.

hopeless adj 1 PESSIMISTIC, defeatist, negative, despairing, demoralized, downhearted, dejected, despondent, forlorn, wretched. 2 UNATTAINABLE, unachievable, impracticable, impossible, vain, foolish, futile, useless, pointless, worthless, poor, helpless, lost, irremediable, irreparable, incurable.
⊠ 1 hopeful, optimistic. 2 curable.

horde n band, gang, pack, herd, drove, flock, swarm, crowd, mob, throng, multitude, host.

horizon n skyline, vista, prospect, compass, range, scope, perspective.

horizontal adj level, flat, plane, smooth, levelled, on its side, supine (fml).

horrible adj unpleasant, nasty, disagreeable, unkind, horrid, disgusting, revolting, offensive, repulsive, hideous, grim, ghastly, awful, dreadful, frightful, fearful, terrible, abominable, shocking, appalling, horrific.
⊠ pleasant, agreeable, lovely, attractive.

horrific adj horrifying, shocking, appalling, awful, dreadful, ghastly, gruesome, terrifying, frightening, scary, harrowing, bloodcurdling.

horrify v shock, outrage, scandalize, appal, disgust, sicken, dismay, alarm, startle, scare, frighten, terrify.
⊠ please, delight.

horror n 1 recoil in horror: shock, outrage, disgust, revulsion, repugnance, abhorrence, loathing, dismay, consternation, alarm, fright, fear, terror, panic, dread, apprehension. 2 GHASTLINESS, awfulness, frightfulness, hideousness.
⊠ 1 approval, delight.

horseman, horsewoman n equestrian, rider, jockey, cavalryman, hussar.

horseplay n clowning, buffoonery, foolery, tomfoolery, skylarking, pranks, capers, high jinks, fun and games, rough-and-tumble.

hospitable adj friendly, sociable, welcoming, receptive, cordial, amicable, congenial, convivial, genial, kind, gracious, generous, liberal.
⊠ inhospitable, unfriendly, hostile.

hospitality n friendliness, sociability, welcome, accommodation, entertainment, conviviality, warmth, cheer, generosity, open-handedness.
⊠ unfriendliness.

host¹ n 1 COMPÈRE, master of ceremonies, presenter, announcer, anchorman, anchorwoman, linkman. 2 PUBLICAN, innkeeper, landlord, proprietor.
◇ v present, introduce, compère.

host² n multitude, myriad, array, army, horde, crowd, throng, swarm, pack, band.

hostage n prisoner, captive, pawn, surety, security, pledge.

hostel n youth hostel, residence, dosshouse (sl), boarding house, guest-house, hotel, inn.

hostile adj belligerent, warlike, ill-disposed, unsympathetic, unfriendly, inhospitable, inimical, antagonistic, opposed, adverse, unfavourable, contrary, opposite.
≢ friendly, welcoming, favourable.

hostilities n war, warfare, battle, fighting, conflict, strife, bloodshed.

hostility n opposition, aggression, belligerence, enmity, estrangement, antagonism, animosity, ill-will, malice, resentment, hate, hatred, dislike, aversion, abhorrence.
≢ friendliness, friendship.

hot adj 1 WARM, heated, fiery, burning, scalding, blistering, scorching, roasting, baking, boiling, steaming, sizzling, sweltering, sultry, torrid, tropical. 2 SPICY, peppery, piquant, sharp, pungent, strong.
≢ 1 cold, cool. 2 mild.

hotchpotch n mishmash, medley, miscellany, collection, mix, mixture, jumble, confusion, mess.

hotel n boarding house, guest-house, pension, motel, inn, public house, pub (infml), hostel.

hotheaded adj headstrong, impetuous, impulsive, hasty, rash, reckless, fiery, volatile, hot-tempered, quick-tempered.
≢ cool, calm.

hothouse n greenhouse, orangery, glasshouse, conservatory, vinery.

hound v chase, pursue, hunt (down), drive, goad, prod, chivvy, nag, pester, badger, harry, harass, persecute.

house n 1 BUILDING, dwelling,

residence, home. 2 DYNASTY, family, clan, tribe.

Types of house include: semi-detached, semi (infml), detached, terraced, town house, council house, cottage, bungalow; flat, bedsit (or bedsitter), apartment, studio flat, maisonette, penthouse, granny flat, duplex (US), condominium (US); manor, hall, lodge, grange, villa, mansion, rectory, vicarage, parsonage, manse, croft, farmhouse, homestead, ranchhouse, chalet, log cabin, shack, shanty, hut, igloo, hacienda.

◇ v 1 LODGE, quarter, billet, board, accommodate, put up, take in, shelter, harbour. 2 HOLD, contain, protect, cover, sheathe, place, keep, store.

household n family, family circle, house, home, ménage, establishment, set-up.
◇ adj domestic, home, family, ordinary, plain, everyday, common, familiar, well-known, established.

householder n resident, tenant, occupier, occupant, owner, landlady, freeholder, leaseholder, proprietor, landlord, home-owner, head of the household.

housing n 1 ACCOMMODATION, houses, homes, dwellings, habitation, shelter. 2 CASING, case, container, holder, covering, cover, sheath, protection.

hovel n shack, shanty, cabin, hut, shed, dump, hole (infml).

hover v 1 HANG, poise, float, drift, fly, flutter, flap. 2 he hovered by the door: pause, linger, hang about, hesitate, waver, fluctuate, seesaw.

however conj nevertheless, nonetheless, still, yet, even so, notwithstanding, though, anyhow.

howl n, v wail, cry, shriek, scream,

shout, yell, roar, bellow, bay, yelp, hoot, moan, groan.

hub n centre, middle, focus, focal point, axis, pivot, linchpin, nerve centre, core, heart.

hubbub n noise, racket, din, clamour, commotion, disturbance, riot, uproar, hullabaloo, rumpus, confusion, disorder, tumult, hurly-burly, chaos, pandemonium.
⊡ peace, quiet.

huddle n 1 CLUSTER, clump, knot, mass, crowd, muddle, jumble. 2 CONCLAVE, conference, meeting.
◇ v cluster, gravitate, converge, meet, gather, congregate, crowd, flock, throng, press, cuddle, snuggle, nestle, curl up, crouch, hunch.
⊡ disperse.

hue n colour, shade, tint, dye, tinge, nuance, tone, complexion, aspect, light.

huff n pique, sulks, mood, bad mood, anger, rage, passion.

hug v embrace, cuddle, squeeze, enfold, hold, clasp, clutch, grip, cling to, enclose.
◇ n embrace, cuddle, squeeze, clasp, hold, clinch.

huge adj immense, vast, enormous, massive, colossal, titanic, giant, gigantic, mammoth, monumental, tremendous, great, big, large, bulky, unwieldy.
⊡ tiny, minute.

hulking adj massive, unwieldy, heavy, bulky, awkward, ungainly.
⊡ small, delicate.

hull n body, frame, framework, structure, casing, covering.

hullabaloo n fuss, palaver, to-do (infml), outcry, furore, hue and cry, uproar, pandemonium, rumpus, disturbance, commotion, hubbub.
⊡ calm, peace.

hum v buzz, whirr, purr, drone, thrum, croon, sing, murmur,

mumble, throb, pulse, vibrate.
◇ n buzz, whirr, purring, drone, murmur, mumble, throb, pulsation, vibration.

human adj 1 MORTAL, fallible, susceptible, reasonable, rational. 2 KIND, considerate, understanding, humane, compassionate.
⊡ 2 inhuman.
◇ n human being, mortal, homo sapiens, man, woman, child, person, individual, body, soul.

humane adj kind, compassionate, sympathetic, understanding, kind-hearted, good-natured, gentle, tender, loving, mild, lenient, merciful, forgiving, forbearing, kindly, benevolent, charitable, humanitarian, good.
⊡ inhumane, cruel.

humanitarian adj benevolent, charitable, philanthropic, public-spirited, compassionate, humane, altruistic, unselfish.
⊡ selfish, self-seeking.
◇ n philanthropist, benefactor, good Samaritan, do-gooder, altruist.
⊡ egoist, self-seeker.

humanity n 1 HUMAN RACE, humankind, mankind, womankind, mortality, people. 2 HUMANENESS, kindness, compassion, fellow-feeling, understanding, tenderness, benevolence, generosity, goodwill.
⊡ 2 inhumanity.

humanize v domesticate, tame, civilize, cultivate, educate, enlighten, edify, improve, better, polish, refine.

humble adj 1 MEEK, submissive, unassertive, self-effacing, polite, respectful, deferential, servile, subservient, sycophantic, obsequious. 2 LOWLY, low, mean, insignificant, unimportant, common, commonplace, ordinary, plain, simple, modest, unassuming, unpretentious, unostentatious.
⊡ 1 proud, assertive. 2 important, pretentious.

◇ *v* bring down, lower, bring low, abase, demean, sink, discredit, disgrace, shame, humiliate, mortify, chasten, crush, deflate, subdue.
⊟ exalt.

humbug *n* **1** DECEPTION, pretence, sham, fraud, swindle, trick, hoax, deceit, trickery. **2** NONSENSE, rubbish, baloney (*sl*), bunkum (*infml*), claptrap (*infml*), eye-wash (*infml*), bluff, cant, hypocrisy.

humdrum *adj* boring, tedious, monotonous, routine, dull, dreary, uninteresting, uneventful, ordinary, mundane, everyday, commonplace.
⊟ lively, unusual, exceptional.

humid *adj* damp, moist, dank, clammy, sticky, muggy, sultry, steamy.
⊟ dry.

humiliate *v* mortify, embarrass, confound, crush, break, deflate, chasten, shame, disgrace, discredit, degrade, demean, humble, bring low.
⊟ dignify, exalt.

humiliation *n* mortification, embarrassment, shame, disgrace, dishonour, ignominy, abasement, deflation, put-down, snub, rebuff, affront.
⊟ gratification, triumph.

humility *n* meekness, deference, submissiveness, self-abasement, servility, humbleness, lowliness, modesty, unpretentiousness.
⊟ pride, arrogance, assertiveness.

humorist *n* wit, satirist, comedian, comic, joker, wag, jester, clown.

humorous *adj* funny, amusing, comic, entertaining, witty, satirical, jocular, facetious, playful, waggish, droll, whimsical, comical, farcical, zany (*infml*), ludicrous, absurd, hilarious, side-splitting.
⊟ serious, humourless.

humour *n* **1** WIT, drollery, jokes, jesting, badinage, repartee, facetiousness, satire, comedy, farce, fun, amusement. **2** *in a bad humour*: mood, temper, frame of mind, spirits, disposition, temperament.
◇ *v* go along with, comply with, accommodate, gratify, indulge, pamper, spoil, favour, please, mollify, flatter.

humourless *adj* boring, tedious, dull, dry, solemn, serious, glum, morose.
⊟ humorous, witty.

hump *n* hunch, lump, knob, bump, projection, protuberance, bulge, swelling, mound, prominence.

hunch *n* premonition, presentiment, intuition, suspicion, feeling, impression, idea, guess.
◇ *v* hump, bend, curve, arch, stoop, crouch, squat, huddle, draw in, curl up.

hunger *n* **1** HUNGRINESS, emptiness, starvation, malnutrition, famine, appetite, ravenousness, voracity, greed, greediness. **2** *hunger for power*: desire, craving, longing, yearning, itch, thirst.
◇ *v* starve, want, wish, desire, crave, hanker, long, yearn, pine, ache, itch, thirst.

hungry *adj* **1** STARVING, underfed, undernourished, peckish (*infml*), empty, hollow, famished, ravenous, greedy. **2** *hungry for knowledge*: desirous, craving, longing, aching, thirsty, eager, avid.
⊟ **1** satisfied, full.

hunk *n* chunk, lump, piece, block, slab, wedge, mass, clod.

hunt *v* **1** CHASE, pursue, hound, dog, stalk, track, trail. **2** SEEK, look for, search, scour, rummage, forage, investigate.
◇ *n* chase, pursuit, search, quest, investigation.

hurdle *n* jump, fence, wall, hedge, barrier, barricade, obstacle, obstruction, stumbling-block, hindrance, impediment, handicap, problem, snag, difficulty, complication.

hurl v throw, toss, fling, sling, fire, catapult, project, propel, launch, send.

hurricane n gale, tornado, typhoon, cyclone, whirlwind, squall, storm, tempest.

hurried adj rushed, hectic, hasty, precipitate, speedy, quick, swift, rapid, passing, brief, short, cursory, superficial, shallow, careless, slapdash.
🠶 leisurely.

hurry v rush, dash, fly, get a move on (infml), hasten, quicken, speed up, hustle, push.
🠶 slow down, delay.
◇ n rush, haste, quickness, speed, urgency, hustle, bustle, flurry, commotion.
🠶 leisureliness, calm.

hurt v 1 my leg hurts: ache, pain, throb, sting. 2 INJURE, wound, maltreat, ill-treat, bruise, cut, burn, torture, maim, disable. 3 DAMAGE, impair, harm, mar, spoil. 4 UPSET, sadden, grieve, distress, afflict, offend, annoy.
◇ n pain, soreness, discomfort, suffering, injury, wound, damage, harm, distress, sorrow.
◇ adj 1 INJURED, wounded, bruised, grazed, cut, scarred, maimed.
2 UPSET, sad, saddened, distressed, aggrieved, annoyed, offended, affronted.

hurtful adj 1 UPSETTING, wounding, vicious, cruel, mean, unkind, nasty, malicious, spiteful, catty, derogatory, scathing, cutting. 2 HARMFUL, damaging, injurious, pernicious, destructive.
🠶 1 kind.

hurtle v dash, tear, race, fly, shoot, speed, rush, charge, plunge, dive, crash, rattle.

husband n spouse, partner, mate,

better half, hubby (infml), groom, married man.

husbandry n 1 FARMING, agriculture, cultivation, tillage, land management, farm management, conservation, agribusiness, agronomics, agronomy.
2 MANAGEMENT, saving, thrift, thriftiness, frugality, economy, good housekeeping.
🠶 2 wastefulness, squandering.

hush v quieten, silence, shush, still, settle, compose, calm, soothe, subdue.
🠶 disturb, rouse.
◇ n quietness, silence, peace, stillness, repose, calm, calmness, tranquillity, serenity.
🠶 noise, clamour.
◇ interj quiet, hold your tongue, shut up, not another word.
• **hush up** keep dark, suppress, conceal, cover up, stifle, gag.
🠶 publicize.

hush-hush adj secret, confidential, classified, restricted, under wraps (infml), top secret.
🠶 open, public.

husk n covering, case, shell, pod, hull, rind, bran, chaff.

husky adj hoarse, croaky, croaking, low, throaty, guttural, gruff, rasping, rough, harsh.

hustle v hasten, rush, hurry, bustle, force, push, shove, thrust, bundle, elbow, jostle.

hut n cabin, shack, shanty, booth, shed, lean-to, shelter, den.

hybrid n cross, crossbreed, half-breed, mongrel, composite, combination, mixture, amalgam, compound.
◇ adj crossbred, mongrel, composite, combined, mixed, heterogeneous, compound.
🠶 pure-bred.

hygiene n sanitariness, sanitation, sterility, disinfection, cleanliness, purity, wholesomeness.
🠶 insanitariness.

hygienic *adj* sanitary, sterile, aseptic, germ-free, disinfected, clean, pure, salubrious, healthy, wholesome.
⊠ unhygienic, insanitary.

hype *n* publicity, advertisement, advertising, promotion, build-up, racket, fuss, plugging (*infml*).
◇ *v* promote, publicize, advertise, build up, plug (*infml*).

hyperbole *n* overstatement, exaggeration, magnification, extravagance.
⊠ understatement.

hypnotic *adj* mesmerizing, sleep-inducing, soporific, spellbinding, fascinating, compelling, irresistible, magnetic.

hypnotism *n* hypnosis, mesmerism, suggestion.

hypnotize *v* mesmerize, spellbind, bewitch, enchant, entrance, fascinate, captivate, magnetize.

hypocrisy *n* insincerity, double-talk, double-dealing, falsity, deceit, deception, pretence.
⊠ sincerity.

hypocritical *adj* insincere, two-faced, self-righteous, double-dealing, false, hollow, deceptive, spurious, deceitful, dissembling, pharisaic(al).
⊠ sincere, genuine.

hypothesis *n* theory, thesis, premise, postulate, proposition, supposition, conjecture, speculation.

hypothetical *adj* theoretical, imaginary, supposed, assumed, proposed, conjectural, speculative.
⊠ real, actual.

hysteria *n* agitation, frenzy, panic, hysterics, neurosis, mania, madness.
⊠ calm, composure.

hysterical *adj* **1** FRANTIC, frenzied, berserk, uncontrollable, mad, raving, crazed, demented, overwrought, neurotic, hyper (*infml*). **2** (*infml*) HILARIOUS, uproarious, side-splitting, priceless (*infml*), rich (*infml*).
⊠ **1** calm, composed, self-possessed.

Ii

ice *n* frost, rime, icicle, glacier, iciness, frostiness, coldness, chill.
◇ *v* freeze, refrigerate, chill, cool, frost.

icon *n* idol, portrait, image, representation, symbol.

icy *adj* **1** ICE-COLD, arctic, polar, glacial, freezing, frozen, raw, bitter, biting, cold, chill, chilly. **2** *icy roads*: frosty, slippery, glassy, frozen, icebound, frostbound. **3** HOSTILE, cold, stony, cool, indifferent, aloof, distant, formal.
☒ **1** hot. **3** friendly, warm.

idea *n* **1** THOUGHT, concept, notion, theory, hypothesis, guess, conjecture, belief, opinion, view, viewpoint, judgement, conception, vision, image, impression, fancy, perception, interpretation, clue, understanding, inkling, suspicion. **2** *a good idea*: brainwave, suggestion, proposal, proposition, recommendation, plan, scheme, design. **3** AIM, intention, purpose, reason, point, object.

ideal *n* perfection, epitome, acme, paragon, exemplar, example, model, pattern, archetype, prototype, type, image, criterion, standard.
◇ *adj* **1** PERFECT, dream, utopian, best, optimum, optimal, supreme, highest, model, archetypal. **2** UNREAL, imaginary, theoretical, hypothetical, unattainable, impractical, idealistic.

idealist *n* perfectionist, romantic, visionary, dreamer, optimist.
☒ realist, pragmatist.

idealistic *adj* perfectionist, utopian, visionary, romantic, quixotic, starry-eyed, optimistic, unrealistic,

impractical, impracticable.
☒ realistic, pragmatic.

idealize *v* utopianize, romanticize, glamorize, glorify, exalt, worship, idolize.
☒ caricature.

identical *adj* same, selfsame, indistinguishable, interchangeable, twin, duplicate, like, alike, corresponding, matching, equal, equivalent.
☒ different.

identification *n* **1** RECOGNITION, detection, diagnosis, naming, labelling, classification. **2** EMPATHY, association, involvement, rapport, relationship, sympathy, fellow-feeling. **3** IDENTITY CARD, documents, papers, credentials.

identify *v* recognize, know, pick out, single out, distinguish, perceive, make out, discern, notice, detect, diagnose, name, label, tag, specify, pinpoint, place, catalogue, classify.
• **identify with** empathize with, relate to, associate with, respond to, sympathize with, feel for.

identity *n* **1** INDIVIDUALITY, particularity, singularity, uniqueness, self, personality, character, existence. **2** SAMENESS, likeness.

ideology *n* philosophy, world-view, ideas, principles, tenets, doctrine(s), convictions, belief(s), faith, creed, dogma.

idiocy *n* folly, stupidity, silliness, senselessness, lunacy.
☒ wisdom, sanity.

idiom *n* phrase, expression,

colloquialism, language, turn of phrase, phraseology, style, usage, jargon, vernacular.

idiosyncrasy n characteristic, peculiarity, singularity, oddity, eccentricity, freak, quirk, habit, mannerism, trait, feature.

idiosyncratic adj personal, individual, characteristic, distinctive, peculiar, singular, odd, eccentric, quirky.
⊜ general, common.

idiot n fool, blockhead, ass (infml), nitwit (infml), dimwit, halfwit, imbecile, moron, cretin, simpleton, dunce, ignoramus.

idiotic adj foolish, stupid, silly, absurd, senseless, daft (infml), lunatic, insane, foolhardy, hare-brained, halfwitted, moronic, cretinous, crazy.
⊜ sensible, sane.

idle adj 1 INACTIVE, inoperative, unused, unoccupied, unemployed, jobless, redundant. 2 LAZY, work-shy, indolent. 3 idle talk: empty, trivial, casual, futile, vain, pointless, unproductive.
⊜ 1 active. 2 busy.
◇ v do nothing, laze, lounge, take it easy, kill time, potter, loiter, dawdle, fritter, waste, loaf, slack, skive (infml).
⊜ work.

idol n icon, effigy, image, graven image, god, deity, fetish, favourite, darling, hero, heroine, pin-up.

idolize v hero-worship, lionize, exalt, glorify, worship, venerate, revere, admire, adore, love, dote on.
⊜ despise.

idyllic adj perfect, idealized, heavenly, delightful, charming, picturesque, pastoral, rustic, unspoiled, peaceful, happy.
⊜ unpleasant.

ignite v set fire to, set alight, catch fire, flare up, burn, conflagrate, fire,

kindle, touch off, spark off.
⊜ quench.

ignoble adj low, mean, petty, base, vulgar, wretched, contemptible, despicable, vile, heinous, infamous, disgraceful, dishonourable, shameless.
⊜ noble, worthy, honourable.

ignominious adj humiliating, mortifying, degrading, undignified, shameful, dishonourable, disreputable, disgraceful, despicable, scandalous.
⊜ triumphant, honourable.

ignorance n unintelligence, illiteracy, unawareness, unconsciousness, oblivion, unfamiliarity, inexperience, innocence, naiveté.
⊜ knowledge, wisdom.

ignorant adj uneducated, illiterate, unread, untaught, untrained, inexperienced, stupid, clueless (infml), uninitiated, unenlightened, uninformed, ill-informed, unwitting, unaware, unconscious, oblivious.
⊜ educated, knowledgeable, clever, wise.

ignore v disregard, take no notice of, shut one's eyes to, overlook, pass over, neglect, omit, reject, snub, cold-shoulder.
⊜ notice, observe.

ill adj 1 SICK, poorly, unwell, indisposed, laid up, ailing, off-colour, out of sorts (infml), under the weather (infml), seedy, queasy, diseased, unhealthy, infirm, frail. 2 an ill omen: bad, evil, damaging, harmful, injurious, detrimental, adverse, unfavourable, inauspicious, unpromising, sinister, ominous, threatening, unlucky, unfortunate, difficult, harsh, severe, unkind, unfriendly, antagonistic.
⊜ 1 well. 2 good, favourable, fortunate.

ill-advised adj imprudent,

injudicious, unwise, foolish, ill-considered, thoughtless, hasty, rash, short-sighted, misguided, inappropriate.
☒ wise, sensible, well-advised.

ill-bred *adj* bad-mannered, ill-mannered, discourteous, impolite, rude, coarse, indelicate.
☒ well-bred, polite.

illegal *adj* unlawful, illicit, criminal, wrong, forbidden, prohibited, banned, outlawed, unauthorized, under-the-counter, black-market, unconstitutional, wrongful.
☒ legal, lawful.

illegible *adj* indecipherable, unreadable, scrawled, obscure, faint, indistinct.
☒ legible.

illegitimate *adj* 1 *an illegitimate child*: natural, bastard, born out of wedlock (*fml*). 2 ILLEGAL, unlawful, illicit, unauthorized, unwarranted, improper, incorrect, inadmissible, spurious, invalid, unsound.
☒ 1 legitimate. 2 legal.

ill-fated *adj* doomed, ill-starred, ill-omened, unfortunate, unlucky, luckless, unhappy.
☒ lucky.

illicit *adj* illegal, unlawful, criminal, wrong, illegitimate, improper, forbidden, prohibited, unauthorized, unlicensed, black-market, ill-gotten, contraband, under-the-counter, furtive, clandestine.
☒ legal, permissible.

illness *n* disease, disorder, complaint, ailment, sickness, ill health, ill-being, indisposition, infirmity, disability, affliction.

illogical *adj* unreasonable, irrational, unscientific, invalid, unsound, faulty, fallacious, specious, sophistical, inconsistent, senseless, meaningless, absurd.
☒ logical.

ill-treat *v* maltreat, abuse, injure,

harm, damage, neglect, mistreat, mishandle, misuse, wrong, oppress.

illuminate *v* 1 LIGHT, light up, brighten, decorate. 2 ENLIGHTEN, edify, instruct, elucidate, illustrate, explain, clarify, clear up.
☒ 1 darken. 2 mystify.

illumination *n* light, lights, lighting, beam, ray, brightness, radiance, decoration, ornamentation.
☒ darkness.

illusion *n* apparition, mirage, hallucination, figment, fantasy, fancy, delusion, misapprehension, misconception, error, fallacy.
☒ reality, truth.

illusory *adj* illusive, deceptive, misleading, apparent, seeming, deluding, delusive, unsubstantial, unreal, sham, false, fallacious, untrue, mistaken.
☒ real.

illustrate *v* draw, sketch, depict, picture, show, exhibit, demonstrate, exemplify, explain, interpret, clarify, elucidate, illuminate, decorate, ornament, adorn.

illustration *n* 1 PICTURE, plate, half-tone, photograph, drawing, sketch, figure, representation, decoration. 2 EXAMPLE, specimen, instance, case, analogy, demonstration, explanation, interpretation.

illustrious *adj* great, noble, eminent, distinguished, celebrated, famous, famed, renowned, noted, prominent, outstanding, remarkable, notable, brilliant, excellent, splendid, magnificent, glorious, exalted.
☒ ignoble, inglorious.

ill-will *n* hostility, antagonism, bad blood, enmity, unfriendliness, malevolence, malice, spite, animosity, ill feeling, resentment, hard feelings, grudge, dislike, aversion, hatred.
☒ goodwill, friendship.

image *n* 1 IDEA, notion, concept,

impression, perception.
2 REPRESENTATION, likeness, picture, portrait, icon, effigy, figure, statue, idol, replica, reflection.

imaginable *adj* conceivable, thinkable, believable, credible, plausible, likely, possible.
⊜ unimaginable.

imaginary *adj* imagined, fanciful, illusory, hallucinatory, visionary, pretend, make-believe, unreal, non-existent, fictional, fabulous, legendary, mythological, made-up, invented, fictitious, assumed, supposed, hypothetical.
⊜ real.

imagination *n* imaginativeness, creativity, inventiveness, originality, inspiration, insight, ingenuity, resourcefulness, enterprise, wit, vision, mind's eye, fancy, illusion.
⊜ unimaginativeness, reality.

imaginative *adj* creative, inventive, innovative, original, inspired, visionary, ingenious, clever, resourceful, enterprising, fanciful, fantastic, vivid.
⊜ unimaginative.

imagine *v* **1** PICTURE, visualize, envisage, conceive, fancy, fantasize, pretend, make believe, conjure up, dream up, think up, invent, devise, create, plan, project. **2** *I imagine so*: think, believe, judge, suppose, guess, conjecture, assume, take it, gather.

imbalance *n* unevenness, inequality, disparity, disproportion, unfairness, partiality, bias.
⊜ balance, parity.

imbecile *n* idiot, halfwit, simpleton, moron, cretin, fool, blockhead, bungler.

imbue *v* permeate, impregnate, pervade, suffuse, fill, saturate, steep, inculcate, instil, tinge, tint.

imitate *v* copy, emulate, follow, ape, mimic, impersonate, take off,

caricature, parody, send up, spoof, mock, parrot, repeat, echo, mirror, duplicate, reproduce, simulate, counterfeit, forge.

imitation *n* **1** MIMICRY, impression, impersonation, take-off, caricature, parody, send-up, spoof, mockery, travesty. **2** COPY, duplicate, reproduction, replica, simulation, counterfeit, fake, forgery, sham, likeness, resemblance, reflection, dummy.
◇ *adj* artificial, synthetic, man-made, ersatz, fake, phoney (*infml*), mock, pseudo, reproduction, simulated, sham, dummy.
⊜ genuine.

imitative *adj* copying, mimicking, parrot-like, unoriginal, derivative, plagiarized, second-hand, simulated, mock.

imitator *n* mimic, impersonator, impressionist, parrot, copycat (*infml*), copier, emulator, follower.

immaculate *adj* perfect, unblemished, flawless, faultless, impeccable, spotless, clean, spick and span, pure, unsullied, undefiled, untainted, stainless, blameless, innocent.
⊜ blemished, stained, contaminated.

immaterial *adj* irrelevant, insignificant, unimportant, minor, trivial, trifling, inconsequential.
⊜ relevant, important.

immature *adj* young, under-age, adolescent, juvenile, childish, puerile, infantile, babyish, raw, crude, callow, inexperienced, green, unripe, undeveloped.
⊜ mature.

immeasurable *adj* vast, immense, infinite, limitless, unlimited, boundless, unbounded, endless, bottomless, inexhaustible, incalculable, inestimable.
⊜ limited.

immediate *adj* **1** INSTANT,

instantaneous, direct, prompt, swift, current, present, existing, urgent, pressing. **2** NEAREST, next, adjacent, near, close, recent.
⊞ **1** delayed. **2** distant.

immediately adv now, straight away, right away, at once, instantly, directly, forthwith, without delay, promptly, unhesitatingly.
⊞ eventually, never.

immense adj vast, great, huge, enormous, massive, giant, gigantic, tremendous, monumental.
⊞ tiny, minute.

immensity n magnitude, bulk, expanse, vastness, greatness, hugeness, enormousness, massiveness.
⊞ minuteness.

immerse v plunge, submerge, submerse, sink, duck, dip, douse, bathe.

immigrant n incomer, settler, newcomer, alien.
⊞ emigrant.

imminent adj impending, in the offing, forthcoming, approaching, coming, near, close, looming, menacing, threatening, brewing, in the air.
⊞ remote, far-off.

immobile adj stationary, still, motionless, unmoving, stock-still, static, immovable, rooted, fixed, frozen, rigid, stiff.
⊞ mobile, moving.

immobilize v stop, halt, fix, freeze, transfix, paralyse, cripple, disable.
⊞ mobilize.

immodest adj indecent, revealing, shameless, forward, improper, immoral, obscene, lewd, coarse, risqué.

immoral adj unethical, wrong, bad, sinful, evil, wicked, unscrupulous, unprincipled, dishonest, corrupt, depraved, degenerate, dissolute,

lewd, indecent, pornographic, obscene, impure.
⊞ moral, right, good.

immortal adj undying, eternal, imperishable, everlasting, perpetual, endless, ceaseless, lasting, enduring, abiding, timeless, ageless.
⊞ mortal.

immortalize v celebrate, commemorate, memorialize, perpetuate, enshrine.

immovable adj fixed, rooted, immobile, stuck, fast, secure, stable, constant, firm, set, determined, resolute, adamant, unshakable, obstinate, unyielding.
⊞ movable.

immune adj invulnerable, insusceptible, resistant, proof, protected, safe, exempt, free, clear.
⊞ susceptible.

immunity n resistance, protection, exemption, indemnity, impunity, exoneration, freedom, liberty, licence, franchise, privilege, right.
⊞ susceptibility.

immunize v vaccinate, inoculate, inject, protect, safeguard.

impact n **1** *the impact of the reforms*: effect, consequences, repercussions, impression, power, influence, significance, meaning. **2** COLLISION, crash, smash, bang, bump, blow, knock, contact, jolt, shock, brunt.

impair v damage, harm, injure, hinder, mar, spoil, worsen, undermine, weaken, reduce, lessen, diminish, blunt.
⊞ improve, enhance.

impale v pierce, puncture, perforate, run through, spear, lance, spike, skewer, spit, stick, transfix.

impart v tell, relate, communicate, make known, disclose, divulge, reveal, convey, pass on, give, grant, confer, offer, contribute, lend.

⊞ withhold.

impartial adj objective, detached, dispassionate, disinterested, neutral, non-partisan, unbiased, unprejudiced, open-minded, fair, just, equitable, even-handed, equal.
⊞ biased, prejudiced.

impasse n deadlock, stalemate, dead end, cul-de-sac, blind alley, halt, standstill.

impassive adj expressionless, calm, composed, unruffled, unconcerned, cool, unfeeling, unemotional, unmoved, imperturbable, unexcitable, stoical, indifferent, dispassionate.
⊞ responsive, moved.

impatience n eagerness, keenness, restlessness, agitation, anxiety, nervousness, irritability, intolerance, shortness, brusqueness, haste, rashness.
⊞ patience.

impatient adj eager, keen, restless, fidgety, fretful, edgy, irritable, snappy, hot-tempered, quick-tempered, intolerant, brusque, abrupt, impetuous, hasty, precipitate, headlong.
⊞ patient.

impeach v accuse, charge, indict, arraign, denounce, impugn, disparage, criticize, censure, blame.

impeccable adj perfect, faultless, precise, exact, flawless, unblemished, stainless, immaculate, pure, irreproachable, blameless, innocent.
⊞ faulty, flawed, corrupt.

impede v hinder, hamper, obstruct, block, clog, slow, retard, hold up, delay, check, curb, restrain, thwart, disrupt, stop, bar.
⊞ aid, promote, further.

impediment n hindrance, obstacle, obstruction, barrier, bar, block, stumbling-block, snag, difficulty, handicap, check, curb, restraint,

restriction.
⊞ aid.

impel v urge, force, oblige, compel, constrain, drive, propel, push, spur, goad, prompt, stimulate, excite, instigate, motivate, inspire, move.
⊞ deter, dissuade.

impending adj imminent, forthcoming, approaching, coming, close, near, looming, menacing, threatening.
⊞ remote.

impenetrable adj 1 *impenetrable jungle*: solid, thick, dense, impassable. 2 UNINTELLIGIBLE, incomprehensible, unfathomable, baffling, mysterious, cryptic, enigmatic, obscure, dark, inscrutable.
⊞ 2 accessible, understandable.

imperative adj compulsory, obligatory, mandatory, essential, vital, crucial, pressing, urgent.
⊞ optional, unimportant.

imperceptible adj inappreciable, indiscernible, inaudible, faint, slight, negligible, infinitesimal, microscopic, minute, tiny, small, fine, subtle, gradual.
⊞ perceptible.

imperfect adj faulty, flawed, defective, damaged, broken, chipped, deficient, incomplete.
⊞ perfect.

imperfection n fault, flaw, defect, blemish, deficiency, shortcoming, weakness, failing.
⊞ perfection.

imperial adj sovereign, supreme, royal, regal, majestic, grand, magnificent, great, noble.

imperil v endanger, jeopardize, risk, hazard, expose, compromise, threaten.

imperious adj overbearing, domineering, autocratic, despotic, tyrannical, dictatorial, high-handed, commanding, arrogant, haughty.

⇨ humble.

impersonal *adj* formal, official, businesslike, bureaucratic, faceless, aloof, remote, distant, detached, neutral, objective, dispassionate, cold, frosty, glassy.
⇨ informal, friendly.

impersonate *v* imitate, mimic, take off, parody, caricature, mock, masquerade as, pose as, act, portray.

impertinence *n* rudeness, impoliteness, disrespect, insolence, impudence, cheek (*infml*), brass (*sl*), effrontery, nerve (*infml*), audacity, boldness, brazenness, forwardness, presumption.
⇨ politeness, respect.

impertinent *adj* rude, impolite, ill-mannered, discourteous, disrespectful, insolent, impudent, cheeky (*infml*), saucy (*infml*), pert, bold, brazen, forward, presumptuous, fresh.
⇨ polite, respectful.

imperturbable *adj* unexcitable, unflappable (*infml*), calm, tranquil, composed, collected, self-possessed, cool, unmoved, unruffled.

impervious *adj* **1** IMPERMEABLE, waterproof, damp-proof, watertight, hermetic, closed, impenetrable, sealed. **2** *impervious to criticism*: immune, invulnerable, untouched, unaffected, unmoved, resistant.
⇨ **1** porous, pervious. **2** responsive, vulnerable.

impetuous *adj* impulsive, spontaneous, unpremeditated, unplanned, hasty, precipitate, rash, reckless, thoughtless, unthinking.
⇨ cautious, wary, circumspect.

impetus *n* impulse, momentum, force, energy, power, drive, boost, push, spur, stimulus, incentive, motivation.

impinge *v* hit, touch (on), affect, influence, encroach, infringe, intrude, trespass, invade.

implacable *adj* inexorable, relentless, remorseless, merciless, pitiless, cruel, ruthless, intransigent, inflexible.
⇨ compassionate.

implant *v* graft, engraft, embed, sow, plant, fix, root, insert, instil, inculcate.

implausible *adj* improbable, unlikely, far-fetched, dubious, suspect, unconvincing, weak, flimsy, thin, transparent.
⇨ plausible, likely, reasonable.

implement *n* tool, instrument, utensil, gadget, device, apparatus, appliance.
◇ *v* enforce, effect, bring about, carry out, execute, discharge, perform, do, fulfil, complete, accomplish, realize.

implicate *v* involve, embroil, entangle, incriminate, compromise, include, concern, connect, associate.
⇨ exonerate.

implication *n* **1** INFERENCE, insinuation, suggestion, meaning, significance, ramification, repercussion. **2** INVOLVEMENT, entanglement, incrimination, connection, association.

implicit *adj* **1** IMPLIED, inferred, insinuated, indirect, unsaid, unspoken, tacit, understood. **2** *implicit belief*: unquestioning, utter, total, full, complete, absolute, unqualified, unreserved, whole-hearted.
⇨ **1** explicit. **2** half-hearted.

imply *v* suggest, insinuate, hint, intimate, mean, signify, point to, indicate, involve, require.
⇨ state.

impolite *adj* rude, discourteous, bad-mannered, ill-mannered, ill-bred, disrespectful, insolent, rough, coarse, vulgar, abrupt.
⇨ polite, courteous.

import *n* **1** *exports and imports*:

imported product/commodity/
goods, foreign product/commodity/
goods, foreign trade. **2** IMPORTANCE,
consequence, significance,
weight, substance. **3** CONTENT,
sense, substance, nub, meaning,
implication, intention, thrust,
message, drift, essence, gist, purport
(*fml*).
◇ *v* betoken, bring in, imply,
indicate, introduce, mean, purport,
signify.

importance *n* momentousness,
significance, consequence,
substance, matter, concern, interest,
usefulness, value, worth, weight,
influence, mark, prominence,
eminence, distinction, esteem,
prestige, status, standing.
🔁 unimportance.

important *adj* **1** MOMENTOUS,
noteworthy, significant, meaningful,
relevant, material, salient, urgent,
vital, essential, key, primary, major,
substantial, valuable, seminal,
weighty, serious, grave, far-reaching.
2 LEADING, foremost, high-level, high-
ranking, influential, powerful, pre-
eminent, prominent, outstanding,
eminent, noted.
🔁 **1** unimportant, insignificant,
trivial.

impose *v* **1** INTRODUCE, institute,
enforce, promulgate, exact, levy, set,
fix, put, place, lay, inflict, burden,
encumber, saddle. **2** INTRUDE, butt in,
encroach, trespass, obtrude, force
oneself, presume, take liberties.

imposing *adj* impressive, striking,
grand, stately, majestic, dignified.
🔁 unimposing, modest.

imposition *n* **1** INTRODUCTION,
infliction, exaction, levying.
2 INTRUSION, encroachment, liberty,
burden, constraint, charge, duty,
task, punishment.

impossible *adj* hopeless,
impracticable, unworkable,
unattainable, unachievable,

unobtainable, insoluble,
unreasonable, unacceptable,
inconceivable, unthinkable,
preposterous, absurd, ludicrous,
ridiculous.
🔁 possible.

impostor *n* fraud, fake, phoney
(*infml*), quack, charlatan, sham,
impersonator, pretender, con man
(*infml*), swindler, cheat, rogue.

impotent *adj* powerless, helpless,
unable, incapable, ineffective,
incompetent, inadequate, weak,
feeble, frail, infirm, disabled,
incapacitated, paralysed.
🔁 potent, strong.

impoverished *adj* poor, needy,
impecunious, poverty-stricken,
destitute, bankrupt, ruined.
🔁 rich.

impracticable *adj* unworkable,
unfeasible, unattainable,
unachievable, impossible, non-
viable, useless, unserviceable,
inoperable.
🔁 practicable.

impractical *adj* unrealistic,
idealistic, romantic, starry-eyed,
impracticable, unworkable,
impossible, awkward, inconvenient.
🔁 practical, realistic, sensible.

imprecise *adj* inexact, inaccurate,
approximate, estimated, rough,
loose, indefinite, vague, woolly,
hazy, ill-defined, sloppy, ambiguous,
equivocal.
🔁 precise, exact.

impregnable *adj* impenetrable,
unconquerable, invincible,
unbeatable, unassailable, inviolable,
indestructible, fortified, strong, solid,
secure, safe, invulnerable.
🔁 vulnerable.

impregnate *v* **1** SOAK, steep,
saturate, fill, permeate, pervade,
suffuse, imbue. **2** INSEMINATE, fertilize.

impress *v* **1** *I'm not impressed*:
strike, move, touch, affect, influence,

stir, inspire, excite, grab (*sl*). **2** STAMP, imprint, mark, indent, instil, inculcate.

impression *n* **1** FEELING, awareness, consciousness, sense, illusion, idea, notion, opinion, belief, conviction, suspicion, hunch, memory, recollection. **2** STAMP, mark, print, dent, outline. **3** IMPERSONATION, imitation, take-off, parody, send-up. **4** *make a good impression*: effect, impact, influence.

impressionable *adj* naive, gullible, susceptible, vulnerable, sensitive, responsive, open, receptive.

impressive *adj* striking, imposing, grand, powerful, effective, stirring, exciting, moving, touching.
☒ unimpressive, uninspiring.

imprint *n* print, mark, stamp, impression, sign, logo.
◇ *v* print, mark, brand, stamp, impress, engrave, etch.

imprison *v* jail, incarcerate, intern, detain, send down (*infml*), put away (*infml*), lock up, cage, confine, shut in.
☒ release, free.

imprisonment *n* incarceration, internment, detention, custody, confinement.
☒ freedom, liberty.

improbable *adj* uncertain, questionable, doubtful, unlikely, dubious, implausible, unconvincing, far-fetched, preposterous, unbelievable, incredible.
☒ probable, likely, convincing.

impromptu *adj* improvised, extempore, ad-lib, off the cuff, unscripted, unrehearsed, unprepared, spontaneous.
☒ rehearsed.
◇ *adv* extempore, ad lib, off the cuff, off the top of one's head, spontaneously, on the spur of the moment.

improper *adj* wrong, incorrect,

irregular, unsuitable, inappropriate, inopportune, incongruous, out of place, indecent, rude, vulgar, unseemly, unbecoming, shocking.
☒ proper, appropriate, decent.

improve *v* better, ameliorate, enhance, polish, touch up, mend, rectify, correct, amend, reform, upgrade, increase, rise, pick up, develop, look up, advance, progress, get better, recover, recuperate, rally, perk up, mend one's ways, turn over a new leaf.
☒ worsen, deteriorate, decline.

improvement *n* betterment, amelioration, enhancement, rectification, correction, amendment, reformation, increase, rise, upswing, gain, development, advance, progress, furtherance, recovery, rally.
☒ deterioration, decline.

improvise *v* **1** CONTRIVE, devise, concoct, invent, throw together, make do. **2** EXTEMPORIZE, ad-lib, play by ear, vamp.

imprudent *adj* unwise, ill-advised, foolish, short-sighted, rash, reckless, hasty, irresponsible, careless, heedless, impolitic, indiscreet.
☒ prudent, wise, cautious.

impudence *n* impertinence, cheek (*infml*), effrontery, nerve (*infml*), face (*infml*), boldness, insolence, rudeness, presumption.
☒ politeness.

impudent *adj* impertinent, cheeky (*infml*), saucy (*infml*), bold, forward, shameless, cocky, insolent, rude, presumptuous, fresh.
☒ polite.

impulse *n* **1** URGE, wish, desire, inclination, whim, notion, instinct, feeling, passion. **2** IMPETUS, momentum, force, pressure, drive, thrust, push, incitement, stimulus, motive.

impulsive *adj* impetuous, rash, reckless, hasty, quick, spontaneous,

automatic, instinctive, intuitive.
⊜ cautious, premeditated.

impure *adj* 1 UNREFINED, adulterated, diluted, contaminated, polluted, tainted, infected, corrupt, debased, unclean, dirty, foul. 2 OBSCENE, indecent, immodest.
⊜ 1 pure. 2 chaste, decent.

impurity *n* contamination, adulteration, pollution, taint, infection, corruption, dirtiness, contaminant, dirt, filth, foreign body, mark, spot.
⊜ purity.

inability *n* incapability, incapacity, powerlessness, impotence, inadequacy, weakness, handicap, disability.
⊜ ability.

inaccessible *adj* isolated, remote, unfrequented, unapproachable, unreachable, unget-at-able (*infml*), unattainable.
⊜ accessible.

inaccuracy *n* mistake, error, miscalculation, slip, blunder, fault, defect, imprecision, inexactness, unreliability.
⊜ accuracy, precision.

inaccurate *adj* incorrect, wrong, erroneous, mistaken, faulty, flawed, defective, imprecise, inexact, loose, unreliable, unfaithful, untrue.
⊜ accurate, correct.

inaction *n* inactivity, immobility, inertia, rest, idleness, lethargy, torpor, stagnation.
⊜ action.

inactive *adj* immobile, inert, idle, unused, inoperative, dormant, passive, sedentary, lazy, lethargic, sluggish, torpid, sleepy.
⊜ active, working, busy.

inadequacy *n* 1 INSUFFICIENCY, lack, shortage, dearth, want, deficiency, scantiness, meagreness, defectiveness, ineffectiveness, inability, incompetence. 2 *the*

inadequacies of the system: fault, defect, imperfection, weakness, failing, shortcoming.
⊜ 1 adequacy.

inadequate *adj* 1 INSUFFICIENT, short, wanting, deficient, scanty, sparse, meagre, niggardly. 2 INCOMPETENT, incapable, unequal, unqualified, ineffective, faulty, defective, imperfect, unsatisfactory.
⊜ 1 adequate. 2 satisfactory.

inadmissible *adj* unacceptable, irrelevant, immaterial, inappropriate, disallowed, prohibited.
⊜ admissible.

inadvertent *adj* accidental, chance, unintentional, unintended, unplanned, unpremeditated, careless.
⊜ deliberate, conscious, careful.

inadvisable *adj* unwise, imprudent, injudicious, foolish, silly, ill-advised, misguided, indiscreet.
⊜ advisable, wise.

inane *adj* senseless, foolish, stupid, unintelligent, silly, idiotic, fatuous, frivolous, trifling, puerile, mindless, vapid, empty, vacuous, vain, worthless, futile.
⊜ sensible.

inanimate *adj* lifeless, dead, defunct, extinct, unconscious, inactive, inert, dormant, immobile, stagnant, spiritless, dull.
⊜ animate, living, alive.

inappropriate *adj* unsuitable, inapt, ill-suited, ill-fitted, irrelevant, incongruous, out of place, untimely, ill-timed, tactless, improper, unseemly, unbecoming, unfitting.
⊜ appropriate, suitable.

inarticulate *adj* incoherent, unintelligible, incomprehensible, unclear, indistinct, hesitant, faltering, halting, tongue-tied, speechless, dumb.
⊜ articulate.

inattention *n* carelessness,

negligence, disregard, absent-mindedness, forgetfulness, daydreaming, preoccupation.

inattentive adj distracted, dreamy, daydreaming, preoccupied, absent-minded, unmindful, heedless, regardless, careless, negligent.
⊜ attentive.

inaudible adj silent, noiseless, imperceptible, faint, indistinct, muffled, muted, low, mumbled.
⊜ audible, loud.

inaugural adj introductory, opening, first, initial.

inaugurate v institute, originate, begin, commence, start, set up, open, launch, introduce, usher in, initiate, induct, ordain, invest, install, commission, dedicate, consecrate.

inauspicious adj unfavourable, bad, unlucky, unfortunate, unpromising, discouraging, threatening, ominous, black.
⊜ auspicious, promising.

inborn adj innate, inherent, natural, native, congenital, inbred, hereditary, inherited, ingrained, instinctive, intuitive.
⊜ learned.

incalculable adj countless, untold, inestimable, limitless, unlimited, immense, vast.
⊜ limited, restricted.

incapable adj unable, powerless, impotent, helpless, weak, feeble, unfit, unsuited, unqualified, incompetent, inept, inadequate, ineffective.
⊜ capable.

incapacitate v disable, cripple, paralyse, immobilize, disqualify, put out of action, lay up, scupper (infml).

incapacity n incapability, inability, disability, powerlessness, impotence, ineffectiveness, weakness, feebleness, inadequacy,

incompetency.
⊜ capability.

incarnation n personification, embodiment, manifestation, impersonation.

incautious adj careless, imprudent, injudicious, ill-judged, unthinking, thoughtless, inconsiderate, rash, reckless, hasty, impulsive.
⊜ cautious, careful.

incense v anger, enrage, infuriate, madden, exasperate, irritate, rile, provoke, excite.
⊜ calm.

incentive n bait, lure, enticement, carrot (infml), sweetener (sl), reward, encouragement, inducement, reason, motive, impetus, spur, stimulus, motivation.
⊜ disincentive, discouragement, deterrent.

incessant adj ceaseless, unceasing, endless, never-ending, interminable, continual, persistent, constant, perpetual, eternal, everlasting, continuous, unbroken, unremitting, non-stop.
⊜ intermittent, sporadic, periodic, temporary.

incidence n frequency, extent, commonness, prevalence, range, amount, degree, rate, occurrence.

incident n 1 OCCURRENCE, happening, event, episode, adventure, affair, occasion, instance. 2 CONFRONTATION, clash, fight, skirmish, commotion, disturbance, scene, upset, mishap.

incidental adj accidental, chance, random, minor, non-essential, secondary, subordinate, subsidiary, ancillary, supplementary, accompanying, attendant, related, contributory.
⊜ important, essential.

incinerate v burn, cremate, reduce to ashes, torch (infml).

incision *n* cut, opening, slit, gash, notch.

incisive *adj* cutting, keen, sharp, acute, trenchant, piercing, penetrating, biting, caustic, acid, astute, perceptive.
🠲 vague.

incite *v* prompt, instigate, rouse, foment, stir up, whip up, work up, excite, animate, provoke, stimulate, spur, goad, impel, drive, urge, encourage, egg on (*infml*).
🠲 restrain.

incitement *n* prompting, instigation, agitation, provocation, spur, goad, impetus, stimulus, motivation, encouragement, inducement, incentive.
🠲 discouragement.

inclement *adj* intemperate, harsh, severe, stormy, tempestuous, rough.
🠲 fine.

inclination *n* **1** LIKING, fondness, taste, predilection, preference, partiality, bias, tendency, trend, disposition, propensity, leaning. **2** *an inclination of 45 degrees*: angle, slope, gradient, incline, pitch, slant, tilt, bend, bow, nod.
🠲 **1** disinclination, dislike.

incline *v* **1** DISPOSE, influence, persuade, affect, bias, prejudice. **2** LEAN, slope, slant, tilt, tip, bend, bow, tend, veer.
◇ *n* slope, gradient, ramp, hill, rise, ascent, acclivity, dip, descent, declivity.

inclined *adj* liable, likely, given, apt, disposed, of a mind, willing.

include *v* comprise, incorporate, embody, comprehend, contain, enclose, embrace, encompass, cover, subsume, take in, add, allow for, take into account, involve, rope in.
🠲 exclude, omit, eliminate.

inclusion *n* incorporation, involvement, addition, insertion.
🠲 exclusion.

inclusive *adj* comprehensive, full, all-in, all-inclusive, all-embracing, blanket, across-the-board, general, catch-all, overall, sweeping.
🠲 exclusive, narrow.

incognito *adj* in disguise, disguised, masked, veiled, unmarked, unidentified, unrecognizable, unknown.
🠲 undisguised.

incoherent *adj* unintelligible, incomprehensible, inarticulate, rambling, stammering, stuttering, unconnected, disconnected, broken, garbled, scrambled, confused, muddled, jumbled, disordered.
🠲 coherent, intelligible.

income *n* revenue, returns, proceeds, gains, profits, interest, takings, receipts, earnings, pay, salary, wages, means.
🠲 expenditure, expenses.

incoming *adj* arriving, entering, approaching, coming, homeward, returning, ensuing, succeeding, next, new.
🠲 outgoing.

incomparable *adj* matchless, unmatched, unequalled, unparalleled, unrivalled, peerless, supreme, superlative, superb, brilliant.
🠲 ordinary, run-of-the-mill, poor.

incompatible *adj* irreconcilable, contradictory, conflicting, at variance, inconsistent, clashing, mismatched, unsuited.
🠲 compatible.

incompetent *adj* incapable, unable, unfit, inefficient, inexpert, unskilful, bungling, stupid, useless, ineffective.
🠲 competent, able.

incomplete *adj* deficient, lacking, short, unfinished, abridged, partial, part, fragmentary, broken, imperfect, defective.
🠲 complete, exhaustive.

incomprehensible *adj*
unintelligible, impenetrable,
unfathomable, above one's head,
puzzling, perplexing, baffling,
mysterious, inscrutable, obscure,
opaque.
🔁 comprehensible, intelligible.

inconceivable *adj* unthinkable,
unimaginable, mind-boggling (*infml*),
staggering, unheard-of, unbelievable,
incredible, implausible.
🔁 conceivable.

inconclusive *adj* unsettled,
undecided, open, uncertain,
indecisive, ambiguous, vague,
unconvincing, unsatisfying.
🔁 conclusive.

incongruous *adj* inappropriate,
unsuitable, out of place, out of
keeping, inconsistent, conflicting,
incompatible, irreconcilable,
contradictory, contrary.
🔁 consistent, compatible.

inconsequential *adj* minor, trivial,
trifling, unimportant, insignificant,
immaterial.
🔁 important.

inconsiderable *adj* small, slight,
negligible, trivial, petty, minor,
unimportant, insignificant.
🔁 considerable, large.

inconsiderate *adj* unkind,
uncaring, unconcerned, selfish,
self-centred, intolerant, insensitive,
tactless, rude, thoughtless,
unthinking, careless, heedless.
🔁 considerate.

inconsistent *adj* **1** CONFLICTING,
at variance, at odds, incompatible,
contradictory, contrary, incongruous,
discordant. **2** CHANGEABLE, variable,
irregular, unpredictable, varying,
unstable, unsteady, inconstant, fickle.
🔁 **2** constant.

inconsolable *adj* heartbroken,
broken-hearted, devastated,
desolate, despairing, wretched.

inconspicuous *adj* hidden,

concealed, camouflaged, plain,
ordinary, unobtrusive, discreet, low-
key, modest, unassuming, quiet,
retiring, insignificant.
🔁 conspicuous, noticeable,
obtrusive.

incontrovertible *adj* indisputable,
unquestionable, irrefutable,
undeniable, certain, clear, self-
evident.
🔁 questionable, uncertain.

inconvenience *n* awkwardness,
difficulty, annoyance, nuisance,
hindrance, drawback, bother,
trouble, fuss, upset, disturbance,
disruption.
🔁 convenience.
◇ *v* bother, disturb, disrupt, put out,
trouble, upset, irk.

inconvenient *adj* awkward, ill-
timed, untimely, inopportune,
unsuitable, difficult, embarrassing,
annoying, troublesome, unwieldy,
unmanageable.
🔁 convenient.

incorporate *v* include, embody,
contain, subsume, take in, absorb,
assimilate, integrate, combine, unite,
merge, blend, mix, fuse, coalesce,
consolidate.
🔁 separate.

incorrect *adj* wrong, mistaken,
erroneous, inaccurate, imprecise,
inexact, false, untrue, faulty,
ungrammatical, improper,
illegitimate, inappropriate,
unsuitable.
🔁 correct.

incorrigible *adj* irredeemable,
incurable, inveterate, hardened,
hopeless.

incorruptible *adj* honest, straight,
upright, moral, honourable,
trustworthy, unbribable, just.
🔁 corruptible.

increase *v* raise, boost, add to,
improve, enhance, advance, step up,
intensify, strengthen, heighten, grow,

develop, build up, wax, enlarge, extend, prolong, expand, spread, swell, magnify, multiply, proliferate, rise, mount, soar, escalate.
⊡ decrease, reduce, decline.
◇ n rise, surge, upsurge, upturn, gain, boost, addition, increment, advance, step-up, intensification, growth, development, enlargement, extension, expansion, spread, proliferation, escalation.
⊡ decrease, reduction, decline.

incredible adj unbelievable, improbable, implausible, far-fetched, preposterous, absurd, impossible, inconceivable, unthinkable, unimaginable, extraordinary, amazing, astonishing, astounding.
⊡ credible, believable.

incredulity n unbelief, disbelief, scepticism, doubt, distrust, mistrust.
⊡ credulity.

incredulous adj unbelieving, disbelieving, unconvinced, sceptical, doubting, distrustful, suspicious, dubious, doubtful, uncertain.
⊡ credulous.

incriminate v inculpate, implicate, involve, accuse, charge, impeach, indict, point the finger at, blame.
⊡ exonerate.

incur v suffer, sustain, provoke, arouse, bring upon oneself, expose oneself to, meet with, run up, gain, earn.

incurable adj 1 an incurable disease: terminal, fatal, untreatable, inoperable, hopeless. 2 INCORRIGIBLE, inveterate, hardened, dyed-in-the-wool.
⊡ 1 curable.

indebted adj obliged, grateful, thankful.

indecency n immodesty, indecorum, impurity, obscenity, pornography, lewdness, vulgarity, coarseness, crudity, foulness, grossness.

⊡ decency, modesty.

indecent adj improper, immodest, impure, indelicate, offensive, obscene, pornographic, lewd, licentious, vulgar, coarse, crude, dirty, filthy, foul, gross, outrageous, shocking.
⊡ decent, modest.

indecision n indecisiveness, irresolution, vacillation, wavering, hesitation, hesitancy, ambivalence, uncertainty, doubt.
⊡ decisiveness, resolution.

indecisive adj undecided, irresolute, undetermined, vacillating, wavering, in two minds, hesitating, faltering, tentative, uncertain, unsure, doubtful, inconclusive, indefinite, indeterminate, unclear.
⊡ decisive.

indeed adv really, actually, in fact, certainly, positively, truly, undeniably, undoubtedly, to be sure.

indefensible adj unjustifiable, inexcusable, unforgivable, unpardonable, insupportable, untenable, wrong, faulty.
⊡ defensible, excusable.

indefinite adj unknown, uncertain, unsettled, unresolved, undecided, undetermined, undefined, ill-defined, unspecified, unlimited, vague, indistinct, unclear, obscure, ambiguous, imprecise, inexact, loose, general.
⊡ definite, limited, clear.

indefinitely adv forever, eternally, endlessly, continually, ad infinitum.

indelible adj lasting, enduring, permanent, fast, ineffaceable, ingrained, indestructible.
⊡ erasable.

indemnity n compensation, reimbursement, remuneration, reparation, insurance, guarantee, security, protection, immunity, amnesty.

indentation n notch, nick, cut, serration, dent, groove, furrow, depression, dip, hollow, pit, dimple.

independence n autonomy, self-government, self-determination, self-rule, home rule, sovereignty, freedom, liberty, individualism, separation.
⊜ dependence.

independent adj 1 AUTONOMOUS, self-governing, self-determining, sovereign, absolute, non-aligned, neutral, impartial, unbiased.
2 FREE, liberated, unconstrained, individualistic, unconventional, self-sufficient, self-supporting, self-reliant, unaided. 3 INDIVIDUAL, self-contained, separate, unconnected, unrelated.
⊜ 1 dependent.

indescribable adj indefinable, inexpressible, unutterable, unspeakable.
⊜ describable.

indestructible adj unbreakable, durable, tough, strong, lasting, enduring, abiding, permanent, eternal, everlasting, immortal, imperishable.
⊜ breakable, mortal.

indeterminate adj unspecified, unstated, undefined, unfixed, imprecise, inexact, indefinite, vague, open-ended, undecided, undetermined, uncertain.
⊜ known, specified, fixed.

index n 1 index of names: table, key, list, catalogue, directory, guide. 2 INDICATOR, pointer, needle, hand, sign, token, mark, indication, clue.

indicate v register, record, show, reveal, display, manifest, point to, designate, specify, point out, mark, signify, mean, denote, express, suggest, imply.

indication n mark, sign, manifestation, evidence, symptom, signal, warning, omen, intimation, suggestion, hint, clue, note, explanation.

indicator n pointer, needle, marker, sign, symbol, token, signal, display, dial, gauge, meter, index, guide, signpost.

indict v charge, accuse, arraign, impeach, summon, summons, prosecute, incriminate.
⊜ exonerate.

indifference n apathy, unconcern, coldness, coolness, inattention, disregard, negligence, neutrality, disinterestedness.
⊜ interest, concern.

indifferent adj 1 UNINTERESTED, unenthusiastic, unexcited, apathetic, unconcerned, unmoved, uncaring, unsympathetic, cold, cool, distant, aloof, detached, uninvolved, neutral, disinterested. 2 MEDIOCRE, average, middling, passable, moderate, fair, ordinary.
⊜ 1 interested, caring. 2 excellent.

indigenous adj native, aboriginal, original, local, home-grown.
⊜ non-indigenous, foreign.

indignant adj annoyed, angry, irate, heated, fuming, livid, furious, incensed, infuriated, exasperated, outraged.
⊜ pleased, delighted.

indignation n annoyance, anger, ire, wrath, rage, fury, exasperation, outrage, scorn, contempt.
⊜ pleasure, delight.

indirect adj 1 ROUNDABOUT, circuitous, wandering, rambling, winding, meandering, zigzag, tortuous. 2 an indirect effect: secondary, incidental, unintended, subsidiary, ancillary.
⊜ 1 direct. 2 primary.

indiscreet adj tactless, undiplomatic, impolitic, injudicious, imprudent, unwise, foolish, rash, reckless, hasty, careless, heedless, unthinking.

⊞ discreet, cautious.

indiscretion n mistake, error, slip, boob (*infml*), faux pas, gaffe, tactlessness, rashness, recklessness, foolishness, folly.

indiscriminate adj general, sweeping, wholesale, random, haphazard, hit-or-miss, aimless, unsystematic, unmethodical, mixed, motley, miscellaneous.
⊞ selective, specific, precise.

indispensable adj vital, essential, basic, key, crucial, imperative, required, requisite, needed, necessary.
⊞ dispensable, unnecessary.

indisposed adj ill, sick, unwell, poorly, ailing, laid up.
⊞ well.

indisputable adj incontrovertible, unquestionable, irrefutable, undeniable, absolute, undisputed, definite, positive, certain, sure.
⊞ doubtful.

indistinct adj unclear, ill-defined, blurred, fuzzy, misty, hazy, shadowy, obscure, dim, faint, muffled, confused, unintelligible, vague, woolly, ambiguous, indefinite.
⊞ distinct, clear.

individual n person, being, party, creature, body, soul, character, fellow.
◇ adj distinctive, characteristic, idiosyncratic, peculiar, singular, unique, exclusive, special, personal, own, proper, respective, several, separate, distinct, specific, personalized, particular, single.
⊞ collective, shared, general.

individuality n character, personality, distinctiveness, peculiarity, singularity, uniqueness, separateness, distinction.
⊞ sameness.

indoctrinate v brainwash, teach, instruct, school, ground, train, drill.

induce v 1 CAUSE, effect, bring about, occasion, give rise to, lead to, incite, instigate, prompt, provoke, produce, generate. 2 COAX, prevail upon, encourage, press, persuade, talk into, move, influence, draw, tempt.
⊞ 2 discourage, deter.

inducement n lure, bait, attraction, enticement, encouragement, incentive, reward, spur, stimulus, motive, reason.
⊞ disincentive.

indulge v gratify, satisfy, humour, pander to, go along with, give in to, yield to, favour, pet, cosset, pamper, mollycoddle, spoil, treat, regale.

indulgence n extravagance, luxury, excess, immoderation, intemperance, favour, tolerance.

indulgent adj tolerant, easy-going (*infml*), lenient, permissive, generous, liberal, kind, fond, tender, understanding, patient.
⊞ strict, harsh.

industrialist n manufacturer, producer, magnate, tycoon, baron, captain of industry, capitalist, financier.

industrious adj busy, productive, hard-working, diligent, assiduous, conscientious, zealous, active, energetic, tireless, persistent, persevering.
⊞ lazy, idle.

industry n 1 *the steel industry*: business, trade, commerce, manufacturing, production. 2 INDUSTRIOUSNESS, diligence, application, effort, labour, toil, persistence, perseverance, determination.

inebriated adj drunk, intoxicated, tipsy, merry.
⊞ sober.

inedible adj uneatable, unpalatable, indigestible, harmful, noxious,

poisonous, deadly.
🗶 edible.

ineffective adj useless, worthless, vain, idle, futile, unavailing, fruitless, unproductive, unsuccessful, powerless, impotent, ineffectual, inadequate, weak, feeble, inept, incompetent.
🗶 effective, effectual.

inefficient adj uneconomic, wasteful, money-wasting, time-wasting, incompetent, inexpert, unworkmanlike, slipshod, sloppy, careless, negligent.
🗶 efficient.

inelegant adj graceless, ungraceful, clumsy, awkward, laboured, ugly, unrefined, crude, unpolished, rough, unsophisticated, uncultivated, uncouth.
🗶 elegant.

ineligible adj disqualified, ruled out, unacceptable, undesirable, unworthy, unsuitable, unfit, unqualified, unequipped.
🗶 eligible.

inept adj awkward, clumsy, bungling, incompetent, unskilful, inexpert, foolish, stupid.
🗶 competent, skilful.

inequality n unequalness, imbalance, difference, diversity, dissimilarity, disparity, unevenness, disproportion, bias, prejudice.
🗶 equality.

inert adj immobile, motionless, unmoving, still, inactive, inanimate, lifeless, dead, passive, unresponsive, apathetic, dormant, idle, lazy, lethargic, sluggish, torpid, sleepy.
🗶 lively, animated.

inertia n immobility, inaction, stillness, inactivity, passivity, unresponsiveness, apathy, idleness, laziness, lethargy, torpor.
🗶 activity, liveliness.

inescapable adj inevitable, unavoidable, destined, fated, certain,

sure, irrevocable, unalterable.
🗶 escapable.

inevitable adj unavoidable, inescapable, necessary, definite, certain, sure, decreed, ordained, destined, fated, automatic, assured, fixed, unalterable, irrevocable, inexorable.
🗶 avoidable, uncertain, alterable.

inexcusable adj indefensible, unforgivable, unpardonable, intolerable, unacceptable, outrageous, shameful, blameworthy, reprehensible.
🗶 excusable, justifiable.

inexhaustible adj 1 an inexhaustible supply: unlimited, limitless, boundless, unbounded, infinite, endless, never-ending, abundant. 2 INDEFATIGABLE, tireless, untiring, unflagging, unwearied, unwearying.
🗶 1 limited.

inexpensive adj cheap, low-priced, reasonable, modest, bargain, budget, low-cost, economical.
🗶 expensive, dear.

inexperience n inexpertness, ignorance, unfamiliarity, strangeness, newness, rawness, naiveté, innocence.
🗶 experience.

inexperienced adj inexpert, untrained, unskilled, amateur, probationary, apprentice, unacquainted, unfamiliar, unaccustomed, new, fresh, raw, callow, young, immature, naive, unsophisticated, innocent.
🗶 experienced, mature.

inexplicable adj unexplainable, unaccountable, strange, mystifying, puzzling, baffling, mysterious, enigmatic, unfathomable, incomprehensible, incredible, unbelievable, miraculous.
🗶 explicable.

inexpressive adj unexpressive,

expressionless, deadpan, inscrutable, blank, vacant, empty, emotionless, impassive.
⊜ expressive.

infallible adj accurate, unerring, unfailing, foolproof, fail-safe, sure-fire (infml), certain, sure, reliable, dependable, trustworthy, sound, perfect, faultless, impeccable.
⊜ fallible.

infamous adj notorious, ill-famed, disreputable, disgraceful, shameful, shocking, outrageous, scandalous, wicked, iniquitous.
⊜ illustrious, glorious.

infamy n notoriety, disrepute, disgrace, shame, dishonour, discredit, ignominy, wickedness.
⊜ glory.

infancy n 1 BABYHOOD, childhood, youth. 2 BEGINNING, start, commencement, inception, outset, birth, dawn, genesis, emergence, origins, early stages.
⊜ 1 adulthood.

infant n baby, toddler, tot (infml), rugrat (infml), child, babe (fml), babe in arms (fml).
⊜ adult.
◇ adj newborn, baby, young, youthful, juvenile, immature, growing, developing, rudimentary, early, initial, new.
⊜ adult, mature.

infantile adj babyish, childish, puerile, juvenile, young, youthful, adolescent, immature.
⊜ adult, mature.

infatuated adj besotted, obsessed, enamoured, smitten (infml), crazy (infml), spellbound, mesmerized, captivated, fascinated, enraptured, ravished.
⊜ indifferent, disenchanted.

infatuation n besottedness, obsession, fixation, passion, crush (sl), love, fondness, fascination.
⊜ indifference, disenchantment.

infect v contaminate, pollute, defile, taint, blight, poison, corrupt, pervert, influence, affect, touch, inspire.

infection n illness, disease, virus, epidemic, contagion, pestilence, contamination, pollution, defilement, taint, blight, poison, corruption, influence.

infectious adj contagious, communicable, transmissible, infective, catching, spreading, epidemic, virulent, deadly, contaminating, polluting, defiling, corrupting.

infer v derive, extrapolate, deduce, conclude, assume, presume, surmise, gather, understand.

inference n deduction, conclusion, corollary, consequence, assumption, presumption, surmise, conjecture, extrapolation, construction, interpretation, reading.

inferior adj 1 LOWER, lesser, minor, secondary, junior, subordinate, subsidiary, second-class, low, humble, menial. 2 inferior work: substandard, second-rate, mediocre, bad, poor, unsatisfactory, slipshod, shoddy.
⊜ 1 superior. 2 excellent.
◇ n subordinate, junior, underling (infml), minion, vassal, menial.
⊜ superior.

inferiority n 1 SUBORDINATION, subservience, humbleness, lowliness, meanness, insignificance. 2 MEDIOCRITY, imperfection, inadequacy, slovenliness, shoddiness.
⊜ 1 superiority. 2 excellence.

infernal adj hellish, satanic, devilish, diabolical, fiendish, accursed, damned.
⊜ heavenly.

infertile adj barren, sterile, childless, unproductive, unfruitful, arid, parched, dried up.
⊜ fertile, fruitful.

infest v swarm, teem, throng, flood,

overrun, invade, infiltrate, penetrate, permeate, pervade, ravage.

infidelity *n* adultery, unfaithfulness, faithlessness, disloyalty, duplicity, treachery, betrayal, cheating, falseness.
☒ fidelity, faithfulness.

infiltrate *v* penetrate, enter, creep into, insinuate, intrude, pervade, permeate, filter, percolate.

infinite *adj* limitless, unlimited, boundless, unbounded, endless, never-ending, inexhaustible, bottomless, uncountable, countless, innumerable, numberless, untold, incalculable, inestimable, immeasurable, unfathomable, vast, immense, enormous, huge, absolute, total.
☒ finite, limited.

infinitesimal *adj* tiny, minute, microscopic, minuscule, inconsiderable, insignificant, negligible, inappreciable, imperceptible.
☒ great, large, enormous.

infinity *n* eternity, perpetuity, limitlessness, boundlessness, endlessness, inexhaustibility, countlessness, immeasurableness, vastness, immensity.
☒ finiteness, limitation.

infirm *adj* weak, feeble, frail, ill, unwell, poorly, sickly, failing, faltering, unsteady, shaky, wobbly, doddery, lame.
☒ healthy, strong.

inflame *v* anger, enrage, infuriate, incense, exasperate, madden, provoke, stimulate, excite, rouse, arouse, agitate, foment, kindle, ignite, fire, heat, fan, fuel, increase, intensify, worsen, aggravate.
☒ cool, quench.

inflamed *adj* sore, swollen, septic, infected, poisoned, red, hot, heated, fevered, feverish.

inflammable *adj* flammable, combustible, burnable.
☒ non-flammable, incombustible, flameproof.

inflammation *n* soreness, painfulness, tenderness, swelling, abscess, infection, redness, heat, rash, sore, irritation.

inflate *v* blow up, pump up, blow out, puff out, swell, distend, bloat, expand, enlarge, increase, boost, exaggerate.
☒ deflate.

inflation *n* expansion, increase, rise, escalation, hyperinflation.
☒ deflation.

inflexible *adj* rigid, stiff, hard, solid, set, fixed, fast, immovable, firm, strict, stringent, unbending, unyielding, adamant, resolute, relentless, implacable, stubborn, uncompromising, obstinate, intransigent, entrenched, dyed-in-the-wool.
☒ flexible, yielding, adaptable.

inflict *v* impose, enforce, perpetrate, wreak, administer, apply, deliver, deal, mete out, lay, burden, exact, levy.

influence *n* power, sway, rule, authority, domination, mastery, hold, control, direction, guidance, bias, prejudice, pull, pressure, effect, impact, weight, importance, prestige, standing.
◇ *v* dominate, control, manipulate, direct, guide, manoeuvre, change, alter, modify, affect, impress, move, stir, arouse, rouse, sway, persuade, induce, incite, instigate, prompt, motivate, dispose, incline, bias, prejudice, predispose.

influential *adj* dominant, controlling, leading, authoritative, charismatic, persuasive, convincing, compelling, inspiring, moving, powerful, potent, effective, telling, strong, weighty, momentous, important, significant, instrumental, guiding.

⊑ ineffective, unimportant.

influx n inflow, inrush, invasion, arrival, stream, flow, rush, flood, inundation.

inform v tell, advise, notify, tip off, communicate, impart, leak, acquaint, fill in (infml), brief, instruct, enlighten, illuminate.
• **inform on** betray, incriminate, shop (sl), tell on (infml), squeal (sl), blab, grass (sl), denounce.

informal adj unofficial, casual, unceremonious, relaxed, easy, free, natural, simple, unpretentious, familiar, colloquial.
⊑ formal, solemn.

information n facts, data, input, gen (infml), bumf (sl), intelligence, news, report, bulletin, communiqué, message, word, advice, notice, briefing, instruction, knowledge, dossier, database, databank, clues, evidence.

informative adj educational, instructive, edifying, enlightening, illuminating, revealing, forthcoming, communicative, chatty, gossipy, newsy, helpful, useful, constructive.
⊑ uninformative.

informed adj 1 we'll keep you informed: familiar, conversant, acquainted, enlightened, briefed, primed, posted, up-to-date, abreast, au fait, in the know (infml). 2 an informed opinion: well-informed, authoritative, expert, versed, well-read, erudite, learned, knowledgeable, well-researched.
⊑ 1 ignorant, unaware.

informer n informant, grass (sl), supergrass (sl), betrayer, traitor, Judas, tell-tale, sneak, spy, mole (infml).

infringe v 1 BREAK, violate, contravene, transgress, overstep, disobey, defy, flout, ignore. 2 INTRUDE, encroach, trespass, invade.

infuriate v anger, vex, enrage, incense, exasperate, madden, provoke, rouse, annoy, irritate, rile, antagonize.
⊑ calm, pacify.

ingenious adj clever, shrewd, cunning, crafty, skilful, masterly, imaginative, creative, inventive, resourceful, original, innovative.
⊑ unimaginative.

ingenuous adj artless, guileless, innocent, honest, sincere, frank, open, plain, simple, unsophisticated, naive, trusting.
⊑ artful, sly.

ingrained adj fixed, rooted, deep-rooted, deep-seated, entrenched, immovable, ineradicable, permanent, inbuilt, inborn, inbred.

ingratiate v curry favour, flatter, creep, crawl, grovel, fawn, get in with.

ingratitude n ungratefulness, thanklessness, unappreciativeness, ungraciousness.
⊑ gratitude, thankfulness.

ingredient n constituent, element, factor, component, part.

inhabit v live, dwell, reside, occupy, possess, colonize, settle, people, populate, stay.

inhabitant n resident, dweller, citizen, native, occupier, occupant, inmate, tenant, lodger.

inherent adj inborn, inbred, innate, inherited, hereditary, native, natural, inbuilt, built-in, intrinsic, ingrained, essential, fundamental, basic.

inherit v succeed to, accede to, assume, come into, be left, receive.

inheritance n legacy, bequest, heritage, birthright, heredity, descent, succession.

inheritor n heir, heiress, successor, beneficiary, recipient.

inhibit v discourage, repress, hold back, suppress, curb, check, restrain, hinder, impede, obstruct, interfere

with, frustrate, thwart, prevent, stop, stanch, stem.
☒ encourage, assist.

inhibited adj repressed, self-conscious, shy, reticent, withdrawn, reserved, guarded, subdued.
☒ uninhibited, open, relaxed.

inhibition n repression, hang-up (sl), self-consciousness, shyness, reticence, reserve, restraint, curb, check, hindrance, impediment, obstruction, bar.
☒ freedom.

inhuman adj barbaric, barbarous, animal, bestial, vicious, savage, sadistic, cold-blooded, brutal, cruel, inhumane.
☒ human.

inhumane adj unkind, insensitive, callous, unfeeling, heartless, cold-hearted, hard-hearted, pitiless, ruthless, cruel, brutal, inhuman.
☒ humane, kind, compassionate.

initial adj first, beginning, opening, introductory, inaugural, original, primary, early, formative.
☒ final, last.

initially adv at first, at the beginning, to begin with, to start with, originally, first, firstly, first of all.
☒ finally, in the end.

initiate v begin, start, commence, originate, pioneer, institute, set up, introduce, launch, open, inaugurate, instigate, activate, trigger, prompt, stimulate, cause.

initiation n admission, reception, entrance, entry, debut, introduction, enrolment, induction, investiture, installation, inauguration, inception.

initiative n 1 ENERGY, drive, dynamism, get-up-and-go (infml), ambition, enterprise, resourcefulness, inventiveness, originality, innovativeness. 2 SUGGESTION, recommendation, action, lead, first move, first step.

inject v 1 inject drugs: inoculate, vaccinate, shoot (sl). 2 INTRODUCE, insert, add, bring, infuse, instil.

injection n inoculation, vaccination, jab (infml), shot (infml), fix (sl), dose, insertion, introduction.

injunction n command, order, directive, ruling, mandate, direction, instruction, precept.

injure v hurt, harm, damage, impair, spoil, mar, ruin, disfigure, deface, mutilate, wound, cut, break, fracture, maim, disable, cripple, lame, ill-treat, maltreat, abuse, offend, wrong, upset, put out.

injury n wound, cut, lesion, fracture, trauma, hurt, mischief, ill, harm, damage, impairment, ruin, disfigurement, mutilation, ill-treatment, abuse, insult, offence, wrong, injustice.

injustice n unfairness, inequality, disparity, discrimination, oppression, bias, prejudice, one-sidedness, partisanship, partiality, favouritism, wrong, iniquity.
☒ justice, fairness.

inkling n suspicion, idea, notion, faintest (infml), glimmering, clue, hint, intimation, suggestion, allusion, indication, sign, pointer.

inlet n bay, cove, creek, fiord, opening, entrance, passage.

inn n public house, pub (infml), local (infml), tavern, hostelry, hotel.

innate adj inborn, inbred, inherent, intrinsic, native, natural, instinctive, intuitive.
☒ acquired, learnt.

inner adj internal, interior, inside, inward, innermost, central, middle, concealed, hidden, secret, private, personal, intimate, mental, psychological, spiritual, emotional.
☒ outer, outward.

innocence n 1 GUILTLESSNESS, blamelessness, honesty, virtue,

righteousness, purity, chastity, virginity, incorruptibility, harmlessness, innocuousness. 2 ARTLESSNESS, guilelessness, naiveté, inexperience, ignorance, naturalness, simplicity, unsophistication, unworldliness, credulity, gullibility, trustfulness.
⊞ 1 guilt. 2 experience.

innocent adj 1 innocent of the crime: guiltless, blameless, irreproachable, unimpeachable, honest, upright, virtuous, righteous, sinless, faultless, impeccable, stainless, spotless, immaculate, unsullied, untainted, uncontaminated, pure, chaste, virginal, incorrupt, inoffensive, harmless, innocuous. 2 ARTLESS, guileless, ingenuous, naive, green, inexperienced, fresh, natural, simple, unsophisticated, unworldly, childlike, credulous, gullible, trusting.
⊞ 1 guilty. 2 experienced.

innocuous adj harmless, safe, inoffensive, unobjectionable, innocent.
⊞ harmful.

innovation n newness, novelty, neologism, modernization, progress, reform, change, alteration, variation, departure.

innovative adj new, fresh, original, groundbreaking, creative, imaginative, inventive, resourceful, enterprising, go-ahead, progressive, reforming, bold, daring, adventurous.
⊞ conservative, unimaginative.

innuendo n insinuation, aspersion, slur, whisper, hint, intimation, suggestion, implication.

innumerable adj numberless, unnumbered, untold, countless, uncountable, incalculable, infinite, numerous, many.

inoculation n vaccination, immunization, protection, injection, shot (infml), jab (infml).

inoffensive adj harmless, innocuous, innocent, peaceable, mild, unobtrusive, unassertive, quiet, retiring.
⊞ offensive, harmful, provocative.

inordinate adj excessive, immoderate, unwarranted, undue, unreasonable, disproportionate, great.
⊞ moderate, reasonable.

inquire, enquire v ask, question, quiz, query, investigate, look into, probe, examine, inspect, scrutinize, search, explore.

inquiry, enquiry n question, query, investigation, inquest, hearing, inquisition, examination, inspection, scrutiny, study, survey, poll, search, probe, exploration.

inquisitive adj curious, questioning, probing, searching, prying, peeping, snooping, nosey, interfering, meddlesome, intrusive.

insane adj 1 MAD, crazy, mentally ill, lunatic, mental (sl), demented, deranged, unhinged, disturbed. 2 FOOLISH, stupid, senseless, impractical.
⊞ 1 sane. 2 sensible.

insanity n madness, craziness, lunacy, mental illness, neurosis, psychosis, mania, dementia, derangement, folly, stupidity, senselessness, irresponsibility.
⊞ sanity.

insatiable adj unquenchable, unsatisfiable, ravenous, voracious, immoderate, inordinate.

inscribe v engrave, etch, carve, cut, incise, imprint, impress, stamp, print, write, sign, autograph, dedicate.

inscription n engraving, epitaph, caption, legend, lettering, words, writing, signature, autograph, dedication.

inscrutable adj incomprehensible, unfathomable, impenetrable, deep,

inexplicable, unexplainable, baffling, mysterious, enigmatic, cryptic, hidden.
⊞ comprehensible, expressive.

insect

Insects include: fly, gnat, midge, mosquito, tsetse fly, locust, dragonfly, cranefly, daddy-long-legs (*infml*), horsefly, mayfly, butterfly, moth, bee, bumblebee, wasp, hornet, aphid, black fly, greenfly, whitefly, ladybird, ladybug (*US*), water boatman, lacewing; beetle, cockroach, roach (*US*), earwig, stick insect, grasshopper, cricket, cicada, flea, louse, nit, termite, glow-worm, woodworm, weevil, woodlouse.

Parts of an insect include: abdomen, antenna, cercus, compound eye, forewing, head, hindwing, mandible, mouthpart, ocellus, ovipositor, spiracle, thorax.

insecure *adj* **1** ANXIOUS, worried, nervous, uncertain, unsure, afraid. **2** UNSAFE, dangerous, hazardous, perilous, precarious, unsteady, shaky, loose, unprotected, defenceless, exposed, vulnerable.
⊞ **1** confident, self-assured. **2** secure, safe.

insensible *adj* numb, anaesthetized, dead, cold, insensitive, unresponsive, blind, deaf, unconscious, unaware, oblivious, unmindful.
⊞ conscious.

insensitive *adj* hardened, tough, resistant, impenetrable, impervious, immune, unsusceptible, thick-skinned, unfeeling, impassive, indifferent, unaffected, unmoved, untouched, uncaring, unconcerned, callous, thoughtless, tactless, crass.
⊞ sensitive.

inseparable *adj* indivisible, indissoluble, inextricable, close,

intimate, bosom, devoted.
⊞ separable.

insert *v* put, place, put in, stick in, push in, introduce, implant, embed, engraft, set, inset, let in, interleave, intercalate, interpolate, interpose.
◇ *n* insertion, enclosure, inset, notice, advertisement, supplement, addition.

inside *n* interior, content, contents, middle, centre, heart, core.
⊞ outside.
◇ *adv* within, indoors, internally, inwardly, secretly, privately.
⊞ outside.
◇ *adj* interior, internal, inner, innermost, inward, secret, classified, confidential, private.

insides *n* entrails, guts, intestines, bowels, innards (*infml*), organs, viscera, belly, stomach.

insidious *adj* subtle, sly, crafty, cunning, wily, deceptive, devious, stealthy, surreptitious, furtive, sneaking, treacherous.
⊞ direct, straightforward.

insight *n* awareness, knowledge, comprehension, understanding, grasp, apprehension, perception, intuition, sensitivity, discernment, judgement, acumen, penetration, observation, vision, wisdom, intelligence.

insignificant *adj* unimportant, irrelevant, meaningless, trivial, inconsequential, minor, trifling, petty, paltry, small, tiny, insubstantial, inconsiderable, negligible, non-essential.
⊞ significant, important.

insincere *adj* hypocritical, two-faced, double-dealing, lying, untruthful, dishonest, deceitful, devious, unfaithful, faithless, untrue, false, feigned, pretended, phoney (*infml*), hollow.
⊞ sincere.

insinuate *v* imply, suggest, allude,

hint, intimate, get at (*infml*), indicate.

insipid *adj* tasteless, flavourless, unsavoury, unappetizing, watery, weak, bland, wishy-washy (*infml*), colourless, drab, dull, monotonous, boring, uninteresting, tame, flat, lifeless, spiritless, characterless, trite, unimaginative, dry.
🖝 tasty, spicy, piquant, appetizing.

insist *v* demand, require, urge, stress, emphasize, repeat, reiterate, dwell on, harp on, assert, maintain, claim, contend, hold, vow, swear, persist, stand firm.

insistence *n* demand, entreaty, exhortation, urging, stress, emphasis, repetition, reiteration, assertion, claim, contention, persistence, determination, resolution, firmness.

insistent *adj* demanding, importunate, emphatic, forceful, pressing, urgent, dogged, tenacious, persistent, persevering, relentless, unrelenting, unremitting, incessant.

insolent *adj* rude, abusive, insulting, disrespectful, cheeky (*infml*), impertinent, impudent, saucy (*infml*), bold, forward, fresh, presumptuous, arrogant, defiant, insubordinate.
🖝 polite, respectful.

insoluble *adj* unsolvable, unexplainable, inexplicable, incomprehensible, unfathomable, impenetrable, obscure, mystifying, puzzling, perplexing, baffling.
🖝 explicable.

insolvent *adj* bankrupt, bust, failed, ruined, broke (*infml*), penniless, destitute.
🖝 solvent.

inspect *v* check, vet, look over, examine, search, investigate, scan, scrutinize, study, survey, superintend, supervise, oversee, visit.

inspection *n* check, check-up, examination, scrutiny, scan, study, survey, review, search, investigation, supervision, visit.

inspector *n* supervisor, overseer, superintendent, surveyor, controller, scrutineer, checker, tester, examiner, investigator, reviewer, critic.

inspiration *n* **1** CREATIVITY, genius, imagination, muse, influence, encouragement, stimulation, motivation, spur, stimulus. **2** IDEA, brainwave, insight, illumination, revelation, awakening.

inspire *v* encourage, hearten, influence, impress, animate, enliven, quicken, galvanize, fire, kindle, stir, arouse, trigger, spark off, prompt, spur, motivate, provoke, stimulate, excite, exhilarate, thrill, enthral, enthuse, imbue, infuse.

inspiring *adj* encouraging, heartening, uplifting, invigorating, stirring, rousing, stimulating, exciting, exhilarating, thrilling, enthralling, moving, affecting, memorable, impressive.
🖝 uninspiring, dull.

instability *n* unsteadiness, shakiness, vacillation, wavering, irresolution, unpredictability, uncertainty, changeableness, variability, fluctuation, volatility, capriciousness, fickleness, fitfulness, inconstancy, unreliability, insecurity, unsafeness, unsoundness.
🖝 stability.

install *v* fix, fit, lay, put, place, position, locate, site, situate, station, plant, settle, establish, set up, introduce, institute, inaugurate, invest, induct, ordain.

instalment *n* **1** *pay in instalments*: payment, repayment, portion. **2** EPISODE, chapter, part, section, division.

instant *n* flash, twinkling, trice, moment, tick (*infml*), split second, second, minute, time, occasion.
◇ *adj* instantaneous, immediate, on-the-spot, direct, prompt, urgent,

unhesitating, quick, fast, rapid, swift.
≠ slow.

instead adv alternatively, preferably, rather.
• **instead of** in place of, in lieu of, on behalf of, in preference to, rather than.

instigate v initiate, set on, start, begin, cause, generate, inspire, move, influence, encourage, urge, spur, prompt, provoke, stimulate, incite, stir up, whip up, foment, rouse, excite.

instil v infuse, imbue, insinuate, introduce, inject, implant, inculcate, impress, din into (infml).

instinct n intuition, sixth sense, gut reaction (infml), impulse, urge, feeling, hunch, flair, knack, gift, talent, feel, faculty, ability, aptitude, predisposition, tendency.

instinctive adj natural, native, inborn, innate, inherent, intuitive, impulsive, involuntary, automatic, mechanical, reflex, spontaneous, immediate, unthinking, gut (infml), unpremeditated, visceral.
≠ conscious, voluntary, deliberate.

institute v originate, initiate, introduce, enact, begin, start, commence, create, establish, set up, organize, found, inaugurate, open, launch, appoint, install, invest, induct, ordain.
≠ cancel, discontinue, abolish.
◇ n school, college, academy, conservatory, foundation, institution.

institution n 1 CUSTOM, tradition, usage, practice, ritual, convention, rule, law. 2 ORGANIZATION, association, society, guild, concern, corporation, foundation, establishment, institute, hospital, home. 3 INITIATION, introduction, enactment, inception, creation, establishment, formation, founding, foundation, installation.

instruct v 1 TEACH, educate, tutor,

coach, train, drill, ground, school, discipline. 2 ORDER, command, direct, mandate, tell, inform, notify, advise, counsel, guide.

instruction n 1 follow the instructions: direction, guidance, recommendation, advice, information, order, command, injunction, mandate, directive, ruling. 2 EDUCATION, schooling, lessons, tuition, teaching, training, coaching, drilling, grounding, preparation.

instructive adj informative, educational, edifying, enlightening, illuminating, helpful, useful.
≠ unenlightening.

instructor n teacher, master, mistress, tutor, coach, trainer, demonstrator, exponent, adviser, mentor, guide, guru.

instrument n 1 TOOL, implement, utensil, appliance, gadget, contraption, device, contrivance, apparatus, mechanism. 2 AGENT, agency, vehicle, organ, medium, factor, channel, way, means.

instrumental adj active, involved, complicit, contributory, conducive, influential, useful, helpful, auxiliary, subsidiary.
≠ obstructive, unhelpful.

insufferable adj intolerable, unbearable, detestable, loathsome, dreadful, impossible.
≠ pleasant, tolerable.

insufficiency n inadequacy, shortage, deficiency, lack, scarcity, dearth, want, need, poverty.
≠ sufficiency, excess.

insufficient adj inadequate, short, deficient, lacking, sparse, scanty, scarce.
≠ sufficient, excessive.

insular adj parochial, provincial, cut off, detached, isolated, remote, withdrawn, inward-looking, blinkered, closed, narrow-minded, narrow, limited, petty.

insulate v cushion, pad, lag, cocoon, protect, shield, shelter, isolate, separate, cut off.

insult v abuse, call names, revile, disparage, libel, slander, slight, snub, injure, affront, offend, outrage.
☒ compliment, praise.
◇ n abuse, rudeness, insolence, defamation, libel, slander, slight, snub, affront, indignity, offence, outrage.
☒ compliment, praise.

insurance n cover, protection, safeguard, security, provision, assurance, indemnity, guarantee, warranty, policy, premium.

insure v cover, protect, assure, underwrite, indemnify, guarantee, warrant.

insurmountable adj insuperable, unconquerable, invincible, overwhelming, hopeless, impossible.
☒ surmountable.

insurrection n rising, uprising, insurgence, riot, rebellion, mutiny, revolt, revolution, coup, putsch.

intact adj unbroken, all in one piece, whole, complete, integral, entire, perfect, sound, undamaged, unhurt, uninjured.
☒ broken, incomplete, damaged.

intangible adj insubstantial, imponderable, elusive, fleeting, airy, shadowy, vague, indefinite, abstract, unreal, invisible.
☒ tangible, real.

integral adj 1 an integral part: intrinsic, constituent, elemental, basic, fundamental, necessary, essential, indispensable. 2 COMPLETE, entire, full, whole, undivided.
☒ 1 extra, additional, unnecessary.

integrate v assimilate, merge, join, unite, combine, amalgamate, incorporate, coalesce, fuse, knit,

mesh, mix, blend, harmonize.
☒ divide, separate.

integrity n 1 HONESTY, uprightness, probity, incorruptibility, purity, morality, principle, honour, virtue, goodness, righteousness.
2 COMPLETENESS, wholeness, unity, coherence, cohesion.
☒ 1 dishonesty. 2 incompleteness.

intellect n mind, brain(s), brainpower, intelligence, genius, reason, understanding, sense, wisdom, judgement.
☒ stupidity.

intellectual adj academic, scholarly, intelligent, studious, thoughtful, cerebral, mental, highbrow, cultural.
☒ low-brow.
◇ n thinker, academic, highbrow, egghead, mastermind, genius.
☒ low-brow.

intelligence n 1 INTELLECT, reason, wit(s), brain(s) (infml), brainpower, cleverness, brightness, aptitude, quickness, alertness, discernment, perception, understanding, comprehension. 2 INFORMATION, facts, data, low-down (infml), knowledge, findings, news, report, warning, tip-off.
☒ 1 stupidity, foolishness.

intelligent adj clever, bright, smart, brainy (infml), quick, alert, quick-witted, sharp, acute, knowing, knowledgeable, well-informed, thinking, rational, sensible.
☒ unintelligent, stupid, foolish.

intend v aim, have a mind, contemplate, mean, propose, plan, project, scheme, plot, design, purpose, resolve, determine, destine, mark out, earmark, set apart.

intense adj great, deep, profound, strong, powerful, forceful, fierce, harsh, severe, acute, sharp, keen, eager, earnest, ardent, fervent, fervid, passionate, vehement, energetic,

violent, intensive, concentrated, heightened.
☒ moderate, mild, weak.

intensify v increase, step up, escalate, heighten, hot up (infml), fire, boost, fuel, aggravate, add to, strengthen, reinforce, sharpen, whet, quicken, deepen, concentrate, emphasize, enhance.
☒ reduce, weaken.

intensive adj concentrated, thorough, exhaustive, detailed, comprehensive, in-depth, thoroughgoing, all-out, intense.
☒ superficial.

intent adj determined, resolved, resolute, set, bent, concentrated, eager, earnest, committed, steadfast, fixed, alert, attentive, concentrating, preoccupied, engrossed, wrapped up, absorbed, occupied.
☒ absent-minded, distracted.

intention n aim, purpose, object, end, point, target, goal, objective, idea, plan, design, view, intent, meaning.

intentional adj designed, wilful, conscious, planned, deliberate, prearranged, premeditated, calculated, studied, intended, meant.
☒ unintentional, accidental.

intercede v mediate, arbitrate, intervene, plead, entreat, beseech, speak.

intercept v head off, ambush, interrupt, cut off, stop, arrest, catch, take, seize, check, block, obstruct, delay, frustrate, thwart.

interchangeable adj reciprocal, equivalent, similar, identical, the same, synonymous, standard.
☒ different.

interest n 1 IMPORTANCE, significance, note, concern, care, attention, notice, curiosity, involvement, participation. 2 leisure interests: activity, pursuit, pastime, hobby, diversion, amusement.

3 ADVANTAGE, benefit, profit, gain.
☒ 1 boredom.
◇ v concern, involve, touch, move, attract, appeal to, divert, amuse, occupy, engage, absorb, engross, fascinate, intrigue.
☒ bore.

interested adj 1 ATTENTIVE, curious, absorbed, engrossed, fascinated, enthusiastic, keen, attracted. 2 CONCERNED, involved, affected.
☒ 1 uninterested, indifferent, apathetic. 2 disinterested, unaffected.

interesting adj attractive, appealing, entertaining, engaging, absorbing, engrossing, fascinating, intriguing, compelling, gripping, stimulating, thought-provoking, curious, unusual.
☒ uninteresting, boring, monotonous, tedious.

interfere v 1 INTRUDE, poke one's nose in, pry, butt in, interrupt, intervene, meddle, tamper. 2 HINDER, hamper, obstruct, block, impede, handicap, cramp, inhibit, conflict, clash.
☒ 2 assist.

interference n 1 INTRUSION, prying, interruption, intervention, meddling. 2 OBSTRUCTION, opposition, conflict, clashing.
☒ 2 assistance.

interim adj temporary, provisional, stopgap, makeshift, improvised, stand-in, acting, caretaker.
◇ n meantime, meanwhile, interval.

interior adj 1 INTERNAL, inside, inner, central, inward, mental, spiritual, private, secret, hidden. 2 HOME, domestic, inland, up-country, remote.
☒ 1 exterior, external.
◇ n inside, centre, middle, core, heart, depths.
☒ exterior, outside.

interjection n exclamation,

ejaculation, cry, shout, call, interpolation.

intermediary n mediator, go-between, middleman, broker, agent.

intermediate adj midway, halfway, in-between, middle, mid, median, mean, intermediary, intervening, transitional.
⊜ extreme.

interminable adj endless, never-ending, ceaseless, perpetual, limitless, unlimited, long, long-winded, long-drawn-out, dragging, wearisome.
⊜ limited, brief.

intermission n interval, interlude, break, recess, rest, respite, breather (infml), breathing-space, pause, lull, let-up (infml), remission, suspension, interruption, halt, stop, stoppage, cessation.

intermittent adj occasional, erratic, periodic, sporadic, spasmodic, fitful, irregular, broken.
⊜ continuous, constant.

internal adj 1 INSIDE, inner, interior, inward. 2 INTIMATE, private, personal. 3 DOMESTIC, in-house.
⊜ 1 external, outside, outer.

international adj global, worldwide, intercontinental, cosmopolitan, universal, general.
⊜ national, local, parochial.

Internet

Internet terms include: the Net (infml), the World Wide Web, the Information Superhighway; HTML (Hypertext Markup Language), XML (Extensible Markup Language), XSL (Extensible Style Language), CSS (Cascading Style Sheet), javascript; applet, bot, broadband account, browser, cache, CGI (Common Gateway Interface), cookie, dial-up account, domain hosting, domain name, dotcom, download, e-commerce, e-mail, frame, FTP (File Transfer Protocol), gateway, GIF (Graphics Interchange Format), home page, http (Hypertext Transfer Protocol), ISP (Internet Service Provider), JPEG (Joint Photographic Experts Group), MP3, navigation bar, online, plug-in, PNG (Portable Network Graphics), podcast, portal, search engine, site map, spider, stylesheet, surfing, troll, up-time, W3C (World Wide Web Consortium), web authoring, web bug, webcam, webcast, webmaster, webpage, web server, website.

interplay n exchange, interchange, interaction, reciprocation, give-and-take.

interpose v insert, introduce, interject, interpolate, put in, thrust in, interrupt, intrude, interfere, come between, intervene, step in, mediate.

interpret v explain, expound, elucidate, clarify, throw light on, define, paraphrase, translate, render, decode, decipher, solve, make sense of, understand, construe, read, take.

interpretation n explanation, clarification, analysis, translation, rendering, version, performance, reading, understanding, sense, meaning.

interrogate v question, quiz, examine, cross-examine, grill, give the third degree, pump, debrief.

interrogation n questioning, cross-questioning, examination, cross-examination, grilling, third degree, inquisition, inquiry, inquest.

interrupt v intrude, barge in (infml), butt in, interject, break in, heckle, disturb, disrupt, interfere, obstruct, check, hinder, hold up, stop, halt, suspend, discontinue, cut off, disconnect, punctuate, separate, divide, cut, break.

interruption *n* intrusion, interjection, disturbance, disruption, obstruction, impediment, obstacle, hitch, pause, break, halt, stop, stoppage, suspension, discontinuance, disconnection, separation, division.

intersect *v* cross, criss-cross, cut across, bisect, divide, meet, converge.

intersection *n* junction, interchange, crossroads, crossing.

intertwine *v* entwine, interweave, interlace, interlink, twist, twine, cross, weave.

interval *n* interlude, intermission, break, rest, pause, delay, wait, interim, meantime, meanwhile, gap, opening, space, distance, period, spell, time, season.

intervene *v* 1 STEP IN, mediate, arbitrate, interfere, interrupt, intrude. 2 OCCUR, happen, elapse, pass.

intervention *n* involvement, interference, intrusion, mediation, agency, intercession.

interview *n* audience, consultation, talk, dialogue, meeting, conference, press conference, oral examination, viva.
◇ *v* question, interrogate, examine, vet.

intestines *n* bowels, guts, entrails, insides, innards (*infml*), offal, viscera, vitals.

intimacy *n* friendship, closeness, familiarity, confidentiality, confidence, privacy.
⊜ distance.

intimate¹ *v* hint, insinuate, imply, suggest, indicate, communicate, impart, tell, state, declare, announce.

intimate² *adj* friendly, informal, familiar, cosy, warm, affectionate, dear, bosom, close, near, confidential, secret, private, personal, internal, innermost, deep, penetrating, detailed, exhaustive.
⊜ unfriendly, cold, distant.
◇ *n* friend, bosom friend, confidant(e), associate.
⊜ stranger.

intimidate *v* daunt, cow, overawe, appal, dismay, alarm, scare, frighten, terrify, threaten, menace, terrorize, bully, browbeat, bulldoze, coerce, pressure, pressurize, lean on (*sl*).

intolerable *adj* unbearable, unendurable, insupportable, unacceptable, insufferable, impossible.
⊜ tolerable.

intolerant *adj* impatient, prejudiced, bigoted, narrow-minded, small-minded, opinionated, dogmatic, illiberal, uncharitable.
⊜ tolerant, liberal.

intonation *n* modulation, tone, accentuation, inflection.

intoxicated *adj* 1 DRUNK, drunken, inebriated, tipsy. 2 EXCITED, elated, exhilarated, thrilled.
⊜ 1 sober.

intoxicating *adj* 1 *intoxicating liquor*: alcoholic, strong. 2 EXCITING, stimulating, heady, exhilarating, thrilling.
⊜ 2 sobering.

intoxication *n* 1 DRUNKENNESS, inebriation, tipsiness. 2 EXCITEMENT, elation, exhilaration, euphoria.
⊜ 1 sobriety.

intrepid *adj* bold, daring, brave, courageous, plucky, valiant, lion-hearted, fearless, dauntless, undaunted, stout-hearted, stalwart, gallant, heroic.
⊜ cowardly, timid.

intricate *adj* elaborate, fancy, ornate, rococo, complicated, complex, sophisticated, involved, convoluted, tortuous, tangled, entangled, knotty, perplexing, difficult.
⊜ simple, plain, straightforward.

intrigue n 1 PLOT, scheme, conspiracy, collusion, machination, manoeuvre, stratagem, ruse, wile, trickery, double-dealing, sharp practice. 2 ROMANCE, liaison, affair, amour, intimacy.
◇ v 1 FASCINATE, rivet, puzzle, tantalize, attract, charm, captivate. 2 PLOT, scheme, conspire, connive, machinate, manoeuvre.
🔄 1 bore.

introduce v 1 INSTITUTE, begin, start, commence, establish, found, inaugurate, launch, open, bring in, announce, present, acquaint, familiarize, initiate. 2 PUT FORWARD, advance, submit, offer, propose, suggest.
🔄 1 end, conclude. 2 remove, take away.

introduction n 1 INSTITUTION, beginning, start, commencement, establishment, inauguration, launch, presentation, debut, initiation. 2 FOREWORD, preface, preamble, prologue, preliminaries, overture, prelude, lead-in, opening.
🔄 1 removal, withdrawal. 2 appendix, conclusion.

introductory adj preliminary, preparatory, opening, inaugural, first, initial, early, elementary, basic.

introspective adj inward-looking, contemplative, meditative, pensive, thoughtful, brooding, introverted, self-centred, reserved, withdrawn.
🔄 outward-looking.

introverted adj introspective, inward-looking, self-centred, withdrawn, shy, reserved, quiet.
🔄 extroverted.

intrude v interrupt, butt in, meddle, interfere, violate, infringe, encroach, trespass.
🔄 withdraw, stand back.

intruder n trespasser, prowler, burglar, raider, invader, infiltrator, interloper, gatecrasher.

intrusion n interruption, interference, violation, infringement, encroachment, trespass, invasion, incursion.
🔄 withdrawal.

intuition n instinct, sixth sense, perception, discernment, insight, hunch, feeling, gut feeling (infml).
🔄 reasoning.

intuitive adj spontaneous, instinctive, involuntary, innate, untaught.
🔄 reasoned.

inundate v flood, deluge, swamp, engulf, submerge, immerse, drown, bury, overwhelm, overrun.

invade v enter, penetrate, infiltrate, burst in, descend on, attack, raid, seize, occupy, overrun, swarm over, infest, pervade, encroach, infringe, violate.
🔄 withdraw, evacuate.

invalid¹ adj sick, ill, poorly, ailing, sickly, weak, feeble, frail, infirm, disabled, bedridden.
🔄 healthy.
◇ n patient, convalescent.

invalid² adj 1 FALSE, fallacious, unsound, ill-founded, unfounded, baseless, illogical, irrational, unscientific, wrong, incorrect. 2 ILLEGAL, null, void, worthless.
🔄 1 valid. 2 legal.

invaluable adj priceless, inestimable, incalculable, precious, valuable, useful.
🔄 worthless, cheap.

invariable adj fixed, set, unvarying, unchanging, unchangeable, permanent, constant, steady, unwavering, uniform, rigid, inflexible, habitual, regular.
🔄 variable.

invariably adv always, without exception, without fail, unfailingly, consistently, regularly, habitually.
🔄 never.

invasion n attack, offensive, onslaught, raid, incursion, foray, breach, penetration, infiltration, intrusion, encroachment, infringement, violation.
≢ withdrawal, evacuation.

invent v conceive, think up, design, discover, create, originate, formulate, frame, devise, contrive, improvise, fabricate, make up, concoct, cook up, trump up, imagine, dream up.

invention n 1 *her latest invention*: design, creation, brainchild, discovery, development, device, gadget. 2 LIE, falsehood, deceit, fabrication, fiction, tall story, fantasy, figment. 3 INVENTIVENESS, imagination, creativity, innovation, originality, ingenuity, inspiration, genius.
≢ 2 truth.

inventive adj imaginative, creative, innovative, original, ingenious, resourceful, fertile, inspired, gifted, clever.

inventor n designer, discoverer, creator, originator, author, architect, maker, scientist, engineer.

inverse adj inverted, upside down, transposed, reversed, opposite, contrary, reverse, converse.

invert v upturn, turn upside down, overturn, capsize, upset, transpose, reverse.
≢ right.

invertebrate

Invertebrates include: *sponges*: calcareous, glass, horny; *jellyfish, corals and sea anemones*: Portuguese man-of-war, box jellyfish, dead men's fingers, sea gooseberry, Venus's girdle; *echinoderms*: sea lily, feather star, starfish, crown-of-thorns starfish, brittlestar, sea urchin, sand dollar, sea cucumber; *worms*: annelid, arrow worm, bristle worm, earthworm, eelworm, flatworm, fluke, hookworm, leech, liver fluke, lugworm, ragworm, ribbon worm, roundworm, sea mouse, tapeworm, threadworm; *crustaceans*: acorn-barnacle, barnacle, brine shrimp, crab, crayfish, daphnia, fiddler crab, fish louse, goose-barnacle, hermit crab, king prawn, krill, lobster, mantis shrimp, pill bug, prawn, sand hopper, shrimp, spider crab, spiny lobster, water flea, woodlouse; centipede, millipede; *arachnids*: spider, black widow, tarantula, scorpion, mite, tick.

invest v 1 SPEND, lay out, put in, sink. 2 PROVIDE, supply, endow, vest, empower, authorize, sanction.

investigate v inquire into, look into, consider, examine, study, inspect, scrutinize, analyse, go into, probe, explore, search, sift.

investigation n inquiry, inquest, hearing, examination, study, research, survey, review, inspection, scrutiny, analysis, probe, exploration, search.

investigator n examiner, reviewer, researcher, detective, sleuth (*infml*), private detective, private eye (*infml*).

investment n asset, speculation, venture, stake, contribution, outlay, expenditure, transaction.

invigorate v vitalize, energize, animate, enliven, liven up, quicken, strengthen, fortify, brace, stimulate, inspire, exhilarate, perk up, refresh, freshen, revitalize, rejuvenate.
≢ tire, weary, dishearten.

invincible adj unbeatable, unconquerable, insuperable, insurmountable, indomitable, unassailable, impregnable, impenetrable, invulnerable, indestructible.
≢ beatable.

invisible adj unseen, out of sight,

hidden, concealed, disguised, inconspicuous, indiscernible, imperceptible, infinitesimal, microscopic, imaginary, non-existent.
⊜ visible.

invitation n request, solicitation, call, summons, appeal, temptation, enticement, allurement, come-on (*infml*), encouragement, inducement, provocation, incitement, challenge.

invite v ask, call, summon, welcome, encourage, lead, draw, attract, tempt, entice, allure, bring on, provoke, ask for, request, solicit, seek.

inviting adj welcoming, appealing, attractive, tempting, seductive, enticing, alluring, pleasing, delightful, captivating, fascinating, intriguing, tantalizing.
⊜ uninviting, unappealing.

invoke v call upon, conjure, appeal to, petition, solicit, implore, entreat, beg, beseech, supplicate, pray.

involuntary adj spontaneous, unconscious, automatic, mechanical, reflex, instinctive, conditioned, impulsive, unthinking, blind, uncontrolled, unintentional.
⊜ deliberate, intentional.

involve v 1 REQUIRE, necessitate, mean, imply, entail, include, incorporate, embrace, cover, take in, affect, concern. 2 IMPLICATE, incriminate, inculpate, draw in, mix up, embroil, associate. 3 ENGAGE, occupy, absorb, engross, preoccupy, hold, grip, rivet.
⊜ 1 exclude.

involved adj 1 CONCERNED, implicated, complicit, mixed up, caught up, in on (*sl*), participating. 2 *an involved explanation*: complicated, complex, intricate, elaborate, tangled, knotty, tortuous, confusing.
⊜ 1 uninvolved. 2 simple.

involvement n concern, interest, responsibility, association, connection, participation, implication, entanglement.

invulnerable adj safe, secure, unassailable, impenetrable, invincible, indestructible.
⊜ vulnerable.

inward adj incoming, entering, inside, interior, internal, inner, innermost, inmost, personal, private, secret, confidential.
⊜ outward, external.

iota n scrap, bit, mite, jot, speck, trace, hint, grain, particle, atom.

irate adj annoyed, irritated, indignant, up in arms, angry, enraged, mad (*infml*), furious, infuriated, incensed, worked up, fuming, livid, exasperated.
⊜ calm, composed.

iron adj rigid, inflexible, adamant, determined, hard, steely, tough, strong.
⊜ pliable, weak.
◇ v press, smooth, flatten.
• **iron out** resolve, settle, sort out, straighten out, clear up, put right, reconcile, deal with, get rid of, eradicate, eliminate.

ironic adj ironical, sarcastic, sardonic, scornful, contemptuous, derisive, sneering, scoffing, mocking, satirical, wry, paradoxical.

irony n sarcasm, mockery, satire, paradox, contrariness, incongruity.

irrational adj unreasonable, unsound, illogical, absurd, crazy, wild, foolish, silly, senseless, unwise.
⊜ rational.

irreconcilable adj incompatible, opposed, conflicting, clashing, contradictory, inconsistent.
⊜ reconcilable.

irrefutable adj undeniable, incontrovertible, indisputable, incontestable, unquestionable, unanswerable, certain, sure.

irregular adj 1 ROUGH, bumpy, uneven, crooked. 2 VARIABLE, fluctuating, wavering, erratic, fitful, intermittent, sporadic, spasmodic, occasional, random, haphazard, disorderly, unsystematic. 3 ABNORMAL, unconventional, unorthodox, improper, unusual, exceptional, anomalous.
⊞ 1 smooth, level. 2 regular. 3 conventional.

irrelevant adj immaterial, beside the point, inapplicable, inappropriate, unrelated, unconnected, inconsequent, peripheral, tangential.
⊞ relevant.

irreplaceable adj indispensable, essential, vital, unique, priceless, peerless, matchless, unmatched.
⊞ replaceable.

irrepressible adj ebullient, bubbly, uninhibited, buoyant, resilient, boisterous, uncontrollable, ungovernable, unstoppable.

irreproachable adj blameless, irreprehensible, innocent, beyond reproach, unimpeachable, faultless, impeccable, perfect, unblemished, immaculate, stainless, spotless, pure.
⊞ blameworthy, culpable.

irresistible adj overwhelming, overpowering, unavoidable, inevitable, inescapable, uncontrollable, potent, compelling, imperative, pressing, urgent, tempting, seductive, ravishing, enchanting, charming, fascinating.
⊞ resistible, avoidable.

irresponsible adj unreliable, untrustworthy, careless, negligent, thoughtless, heedless, ill-considered, rash, reckless, wild, carefree, light-hearted, immature.
⊞ responsible, cautious.

irreverent adj 1 IMPIOUS, godless, irreligious, profane, sacrilegious,

blasphemous. 2 DISRESPECTFUL, discourteous, rude, impudent, impertinent, mocking, flippant.
⊞ 1 reverent. 2 respectful.

irreversible adj irrevocable, unalterable, final, permanent, lasting, irreparable, irremediable, irretrievable, incurable, hopeless.
⊞ reversible, remediable, curable.

irrevocable adj unalterable, unchangeable, changeless, invariable, immutable, final, fixed, settled, predetermined, irreversible, irretrievable.
⊞ alterable, flexible, reversible.

irrigate v water, flood, inundate, wet, moisten, dampen.

irritable adj cross, bad-tempered, ill-tempered, crotchety, crusty, cantankerous, crabby, testy, short-tempered, snappish, snappy, short, impatient, touchy, edgy, thin-skinned, hypersensitive, prickly, peevish, fretful, fractious.
⊞ good-tempered, cheerful.

irritate v 1 ANNOY, get on one's nerves, aggravate (infml), bug (infml), bother, harass, rouse, provoke, rile, anger, enrage, infuriate, incense, exasperate, peeve, piss off (sl), put out. 2 INFLAME, chafe, rub, tickle, itch.
⊞ 1 please, gratify.

irritation n displeasure, dissatisfaction, annoyance, aggravation, provocation, anger, vexation, indignation, fury, exasperation, irritability, crossness, testiness, snappiness, impatience.
⊞ pleasure, satisfaction, delight.

isolate v set apart, sequester, seclude, keep apart, segregate, quarantine, insulate, cut off, detach, remove, disconnect, separate, divorce, alienate, shut out, ostracize, exclude.
⊞ assimilate, incorporate.

isolated adj 1 REMOTE, out-of-the-way, outlying, god-forsaken, deserted, unfrequented, secluded, detached, cut off, lonely, solitary, single. **2** *an isolated occurrence*: unique, special, exceptional, atypical, unusual, freak, abnormal, anomalous.

⊞ **1** populous. **2** typical.

isolation *n* quarantine, solitude, solitariness, loneliness, remoteness, seclusion, retirement, withdrawal, exile, segregation, insulation, separation, detachment, disconnection, dissociation, alienation.

issue *n* **1** MATTER, affair, concern, problem, point, subject, topic, question, debate, argument, dispute, controversy. **2** PUBLICATION, release, distribution, supply, delivery, circulation, promulgation, broadcast, announcement. **3** *last week's issue*: copy, number, instalment, edition, impression, printing.
◇ *v* **1** PUBLISH, release, distribute, supply, deliver, give out, deal out, circulate, promulgate, broadcast,

announce, put out, emit, produce. **2** ORIGINATE, stem, spring, rise, emerge, burst forth, gush, flow, proceed, emanate, arise.

itch *v* tickle, irritate, tingle, prickle, crawl.
◇ *n* **1** ITCHINESS, tickle, irritation, prickling. **2** EAGERNESS, keenness, desire, longing, yearning, hankering, craving.

item *n* **1** OBJECT, article, thing, piece, component, ingredient, element, factor, point, detail, particular, aspect, feature, consideration, matter. **2** *an item in the local paper*: article, piece, report, account, notice, entry, paragraph.

itinerant *adj* travelling, peripatetic, roving, roaming, wandering, rambling, nomadic, migratory, rootless, unsettled.
⊞ stationary, settled.

itinerary *n* route, course, journey, tour, circuit, plan, programme, schedule.

Jj

jab *v* poke, prod, dig, nudge, stab, push, elbow, lunge, punch, tap, thrust.

jackpot *n* prize, winnings, kitty, pool, pot, reward, award, big time (*infml*), bonanza, stakes.

jaded *adj* fatigued, exhausted, dulled, played-out, tired, tired out, weary, spent, bored, fagged (*infml*).
⊟ fresh, refreshed.

jagged *adj* uneven, irregular, rough, notched, indented, serrated, saw-edged, toothed, ragged, pointed, ridged, craggy, barbed, broken.
⊟ even, smooth.

jail, gaol *n* prison, jailhouse, custody, lock-up, penitentiary, pen (*US sl*), guardhouse, inside (*infml*), nick (*sl*), clink (*sl*).
◇ *v* imprison, incarcerate, lock up, put away, send down, confine, detain, intern, impound, immure.

jailer, gaoler *n* prison officer, warden, warder, guard, screw (*sl*), keeper, captor.

jam¹ *v* **1** CRAM, pack, wedge, squash, squeeze, press, crush, crowd, ram, congest, stuff, confine, force.
2 BLOCK, clog, obstruct, stall, stick.
◇ *n* **1** CRUSH, crowd, press, congestion, pack, mob, throng, bottleneck, traffic jam.
2 PREDICAMENT, trouble, quandary, plight, fix (*infml*).

jam² *n* conserve, preserve, jelly, spread, marmalade.

jangle *v* clank, clash, jar, clatter, jingle, chime, rattle, vibrate.
◇ *n* clang, clash, rattle, jar, racket, cacophony, dissonance, din, discord, reverberation.
⊟ euphony.

jar¹ *n* pot, container, vessel, receptacle, crock, pitcher, urn, vase, flagon, jug, mug.

jar² *v* **1** JOLT, agitate, rattle, shake, vibrate, jangle, rock, disturb, discompose. **2** ANNOY, irritate, grate, nettle (*infml*), offend, upset, irk.
3 BICKER, quarrel, clash, disagree.

jargon *n* **1** PARLANCE, cant, argot, vernacular, idiom. **2** NONSENSE, gobbledegook (*infml*), mumbo-jumbo (*infml*), gibberish.

jarring *adj* discordant, jangling, harsh, grating, irritating, cacophonous, rasping, strident, upsetting, disturbing, jolting.

jaundiced *adj* **1** BITTER, cynical, pessimistic, sceptical, distrustful, disbelieving, envious, jealous, hostile, jaded, suspicious, resentful.
2 DISTORTED, biased, prejudiced, preconceived.

jaunty *adj* sprightly, lively, perky, breezy, buoyant, high-spirited, self-confident, carefree, airy, cheeky, debonair, dapper, smart, showy, spruce.
⊟ depressed, dowdy.

jealous *adj* **1** ENVIOUS, covetous, grudging, resentful, green (*infml*), green-eyed (*infml*). **2** SUSPICIOUS, wary, distrustful, anxious, possessive, protective.
⊟ **1** contented, satisfied.

jealousy *n* **1** ENVY, covetousness, grudge, resentment, spite, ill-will. **2** SUSPICION, distrust, mistrust, possessiveness.

jeer v mock, scoff, taunt, gibe, ridicule, sneer, deride, make fun of, chaff, barrack, twit, knock (*infml*), heckle, banter.
◇ n mockery, derision, ridicule, taunt, gibe, sneer, scoff, abuse, catcall, dig (*infml*), hiss, hoot.

jell *see* gel.

jeopardize v endanger, imperil, risk, hazard, venture, gamble, chance, threaten, menace, expose, stake.
⊡ protect, safeguard.

jeopardy n danger, peril, risk, hazard, endangerment, venture, vulnerability, precariousness, insecurity, exposure, liability.
⊡ safety, security.

jerk n jolt, tug, twitch, jar, jog, yank, wrench, pull, pluck, lurch, throw, thrust, shrug.
◇ v jolt, tug, twitch, jog, yank, wrench, pull, jiggle, lurch, pluck, thrust, shrug, throw, bounce.

jerky adj fitful, twitchy, spasmodic, jumpy, jolting, bumpy, bouncy, convulsive, disconnected, shaky, rough, unco-ordinated, uncontrolled, incoherent.
⊡ smooth.

jest n joke, quip, wisecrack (*infml*), witticism, crack (*infml*), banter, fooling, gag (*infml*), prank, kidding (*infml*), leg-pull (*infml*), trick, hoax, practical joke.
◇ v joke, quip, fool, kid (*infml*), tease, mock, jeer.

jet¹ n gush, spurt, spout, spray, spring, sprinkler, sprayer, fountain, flow, stream, squirt.

jet² adj black, pitch-black, ebony, sable, sooty.

jetty n breakwater, pier, dock, groyne, quay, wharf.

jewel n **1** GEM, precious stone,

gemstone, ornament, rock (*sl*).
2 TREASURE, find, prize, rarity, paragon, pearl.

jewellery

Types of jewellery include: bangle, bracelet, charm bracelet, anklet, cuff link, tiepin, lapel pin, brooch, cameo, ear cuff, earring, nose ring, toe ring, ring, signet ring, necklace, necklet, choker, pendant, locket, chain, beads, power beads, amulet, torque, tiara, coronet, diadem; body jewel, nail jewel, tooth jewel, bindi.

Jewish calendar

The Jewish calendar and its Gregorian equivalents: Tishri (September-October), Heshvan (October-November), Kislev (November-December), Tevet (December-January), Shebat or Shevat (January-February), Adar (February-March), Adar Sheni (leap years only), Nisan (March-April), Iyyar or Iyar (April-May), Sivan (May-June), Tammuz (June-July), Ab or Av (July-August), Elul (August-September).

jibe *see* gibe.

jig v jerk, prance, caper, hop, jump, twitch, skip, bounce, bob, wiggle, shake, wobble.

jilt v abandon, reject, desert, discard, ditch (*infml*), drop, spurn, betray.

jingle v clink, tinkle, ring, chime, chink, jangle, clatter, rattle.
◇ n **1** CLINK, tinkle, ringing, clang, rattle, clangour. **2** RHYME, verse, song, tune, ditty, doggerel, melody, poem, chant, chorus.

jingoism n chauvinism, flag-waving, patriotism, nationalism, imperialism, warmongering, insularity.

jinx n spell, curse, evil eye, hex, voodoo, hoodoo, black magic,

gremlin (*infml*), charm, plague.
◇ *v* curse, bewitch, bedevil, doom, plague.

job *n* **1** *she has a good job*: work, employment, occupation, position, post, situation, profession, career, calling, vocation, trade, métier, capacity, business, livelihood. **2** *it's a difficult job*: task, chore, duty, responsibility, charge, commission, mission, activity, affair, concern, proceeding, project, enterprise, office, pursuit, role, undertaking, venture, province, part, place, share, errand, function, contribution, stint, assignment, consignment.

jobless *adj* unemployed, out of work, laid off, on the dole, inactive, redundant.
🗵 employed.

jocular *adj* joking, jesting, funny, jocose (*fml*), humorous, jovial, amusing, comical, entertaining, facetious, droll, whimsical, teasing, witty.
🗵 serious.

jog *v* **1** JOLT, jar, bump, jostle, jerk, joggle, nudge, poke, shake, prod, bounce, push, rock. **2** PROMPT, remind, stir, arouse, activate, stimulate. **3** RUN, trot.
◇ *n* **1** JOLT, bump, jerk, nudge, shove, push, poke, prod, shake. **2** RUN, trot.

join *v* **1** UNITE, connect, combine, conjoin, attach, link, amalgamate, fasten, merge, marry, couple, yoke, tie, splice, knit, cement, add, adhere, annex. **2** ABUT, adjoin, border (on), verge on, touch, meet, coincide, march with. **3** ASSOCIATE, affiliate, accompany, ally, enlist, enrol, enter, sign up, team.
🗵 **1** divide, separate. **3** leave.

joint *n* junction, connection, union, juncture, intersection, hinge, knot, articulation, seam.
◇ *adj* combined, communal, common, joined, shared, united, collective, amalgamated, mutual, co-operative, co-ordinated, consolidated, concerted.

joke *n* **1** JEST, quip, crack (*infml*), gag (*infml*), witticism, wisecrack (*infml*), one-liner (*infml*), pun, hoot, whimsy, yarn. **2** TRICK, jape, lark, prank, spoof, fun.
◇ *v* jest, quip, clown, fool, pun, wisecrack (*infml*), kid (*infml*), tease, banter, mock, laugh, frolic, gambol.

joker *n* comedian, comedienne, comic, wit, humorist, jester, trickster, wag, clown, buffoon, kidder, droll, card (*infml*), character, sport.

jolly *adj* jovial, merry, cheerful, playful, hearty, happy, exuberant.
🗵 sad.

jolt *v* **1** JAR, jerk, jog, bump, jostle, knock, bounce, shake, push. **2** UPSET, startle, shock, surprise, stun, discompose, disconcert, disturb.
◇ *n* **1** JAR, jerk, jog, bump, blow, impact, lurch, shake. **2** SHOCK, surprise, reversal, setback, start.

jostle *v* push, shove, jog, bump, elbow, hustle, jolt, crowd, shoulder, joggle, shake, squeeze, throng.

jot down *v* write down, take down, note, list, record, scribble, register, enter.

journal *n* newspaper, periodical, magazine, fanzine, e-zine, paper, publication, review, weekly, monthly, register, chronicle, diary, weblog, blog (*infml*), vlog, gazette, day book, log, record.

journalist *n* reporter, news-writer, hack, correspondent, editor, columnist, feature-writer, commentator, broadcaster, contributor.

journey *n* voyage, trip, travel, expedition, passage, trek, tour, ramble, outing, wanderings, safari, progress.
◇ *v* travel, voyage, go, trek, tour, roam, rove, proceed, wander, tramp, ramble, range, gallivant.

jovial *adj* jolly, cheery, merry, affable, cordial, genial.
⊟ gloomy.

joy *n* happiness, gladness, delight, pleasure, bliss, ecstasy, elation, joyfulness, exultation, gratification, rapture.
⊟ despair, grief.

joyful *adj* happy, pleased, delighted, glad, elated, ecstatic, triumphant.
⊟ sorrowful.

jubilant *adj* joyful, rejoicing, overjoyed, delighted, elated, triumphant, exuberant, excited, euphoric, thrilled.

jubilee *n* celebration, anniversary, commemoration, festival, festivity, gala, fête, carnival.

judge *n* 1 JUSTICE, Law Lord, magistrate, arbiter, adjudicator, arbitrator, mediator, moderator, referee, umpire, beak (*sl*).
2 CONNOISSEUR, authority, expert, evaluator, assessor, critic.
◇ *v* 1 ADJUDICATE, arbitrate, try, referee, umpire, decree, mediate, examine, sentence, review, rule, find. 2 ASCERTAIN, determine, decide, assess, appraise, evaluate, estimate, value, distinguish, discern, reckon, believe, think, consider, conclude, rate. 3 CONDEMN, criticize, doom.

judgement *n* 1 VERDICT, sentence, ruling, decree, conclusion, decision, arbitration, finding, result, mediation, order. 2 DISCERNMENT, discrimination, understanding, wisdom, prudence, common sense, sense, intelligence, taste, shrewdness, penetration, enlightenment. 3 ASSESSMENT, evaluation, appraisal, estimate, opinion, view, belief, diagnosis.
4 CONVICTION, damnation, punishment, retribution, doom, fate, misfortune.

judicial *adj* legal, forensic, official, discriminating, critical, impartial.

judicious *adj* wise, prudent,

careful, cautious, astute, discerning, informed, shrewd, thoughtful, reasonable, sensible, sound, well-judged, well-advised, considered.
⊟ injudicious.

jug *n* pitcher, carafe, ewer, flagon, urn, jar, vessel, container.

juggle *v* alter, change, manipulate, falsify, rearrange, rig, doctor (*infml*), cook (*infml*), disguise.

juice *n* liquid, fluid, extract, essence, sap, secretion, nectar, liquor.

juicy *adj* 1 SUCCULENT, moist, lush, watery. 2 (*infml*) INTERESTING, colourful, sensational, racy, risqué, suggestive, lurid.
⊟ 1 dry.

jumble *v* disarrange, confuse, disorganize, mix (up), muddle, shuffle, tangle.
⊟ order.
◇ *n* disorder, disarray, confusion, mess, chaos, mix-up, muddle, clutter, mixture, hotchpotch, mishmash (*infml*), medley.

jump *v* 1 LEAP, spring, bound, vault, clear, bounce, skip, hop, prance, frolic, gambol. 2 START, flinch, jerk, recoil, jump out of one's skin (*infml*), wince, quail. 3 OMIT, leave out, miss, skip, pass over, bypass, disregard, ignore, avoid, digress.
4 RISE, increase, gain, appreciate, ascend, escalate, mount, advance, surge, spiral.
◇ *n* 1 LEAP, spring, bound, vault, hop, skip, bounce, prance, frisk, frolic, pounce. 2 START, jerk, jolt, jar, lurch, shock, spasm, quiver, shiver, twitch.
3 BREAK, gap, interruption, lapse, omission, interval, breach, switch.
4 RISE, increase, escalation, boost, advance, increment, upsurge, upturn, mounting. 5 HURDLE, fence, gate, hedge, barricade, obstacle.

jumpy *adj* nervous, anxious, agitated, apprehensive, jittery, tense, edgy, fidgety, shaky.

⊡ calm, composed.

junction n joint, join, joining, connection, juncture, union, intersection, linking, coupling, meeting-point, confluence.

junior adj younger, minor, lesser, lower, subordinate, secondary, subsidiary, inferior.
⊡ senior.

junk n rubbish, refuse, trash, litter, debris, garbage, waste, scrap, clutter, oddments, rummage, dregs, wreckage.

jurisdiction n power, authority, control, influence, dominion, province, sovereignty, command, domination, rule, prerogative (fml), sway, orbit, bounds, area, field, scope, range, reach, sphere, zone.

just adj 1 a just ruler: fair, equitable, impartial, unbiased, unprejudiced, objective, fair-minded, even-handed, righteous, upright, virtuous, honourable, good, honest, irreproachable. 2 a just punishment: deserved, merited, fitting, well-deserved, appropriate, suitable, due, proper, reasonable, rightful, lawful, legitimate.
⊡ 1 unjust. 2 undeserved.

justice n 1 FAIRNESS, equity, impartiality, objectivity, justness, equitableness, legitimacy, honesty, right, rightfulness, rightness, justifiableness, reasonableness,

rectitude. 2 LEGALITY, law, penalty, recompense, reparation, satisfaction. 3 JUDGE, Justice of the Peace, JP, magistrate.
⊡ 1 injustice, unfairness.

justifiable adj defensible, excusable, warranted, reasonable, justified, lawful, legal, legitimate, acceptable, explainable, forgivable, pardonable, understandable, sound, valid, well-founded, right, proper, explicable, fit, tenable.
⊡ unjustifiable.

justification n defence, plea, mitigation, apology, explanation, excuse, vindication, warrant, rationalization, reason, grounds.

justify v vindicate, exonerate, warrant, substantiate, defend, acquit, absolve, excuse, forgive, explain, pardon, validate, uphold, sustain, support, maintain, establish.

jut out v project, protrude, stick out, overhang, extend.
⊡ recede.

juvenile n child, youth, minor, young person, youngster, adolescent, teenager, boy, girl, kid (infml), infant.
◇ adj young, youthful, immature, childish, puerile, infantile, adolescent, babyish, unsophisticated.
⊡ mature.

juxtaposition n contiguity, proximity, nearness, closeness, contact, vicinity, immediacy.

Kk

keel over v 1 OVERTURN, capsize, founder, collapse, upset. 2 FAINT, pass out, swoon, fall, drop, stagger, topple over.

keen adj 1 EAGER, avid, fervent, enthusiastic, earnest, devoted, diligent, industrious. 2 ASTUTE, shrewd, clever, perceptive, wise, discerning, quick, deep, sensitive. 3 SHARP, piercing, penetrating, incisive, acute, pointed, intense, pungent, trenchant.
⊞ 1 apathetic. 2 superficial. 3 dull.

keep v 1 RETAIN, hold, preserve, hold on to, hang on to, store, stock, possess, amass, accumulate, collect, stack, conserve, deposit, heap, pile, place, maintain, furnish. 2 CARRY ON, keep on, continue, persist, remain. 3 LOOK AFTER, tend, care for, have charge of, have custody of, maintain, provide for, subsidize, support, sustain, be responsible for, foster, mind, protect, shelter, guard, defend, watch (over), shield, safeguard, feed, nurture, manage. 4 DETAIN, delay, retard, check, hinder, hold (up), impede, obstruct, prevent, block, curb, interfere with, restrain, limit, inhibit, deter, hamper, keep back, control, constrain, arrest, withhold. 5 OBSERVE, comply with, respect, obey, fulfil, adhere to, recognize, keep up, keep faith with, commemorate, celebrate, hold, maintain, perform, perpetuate, mark, honour.
◇ n 1 SUBSISTENCE, board, livelihood, living, maintenance, support, upkeep, means, food, nourishment, nurture. 2 FORT, fortress, tower, castle, citadel, stronghold, dungeon.

• **keep back** 1 RESTRAIN, check, constrain, curb, impede, limit, prohibit, retard, stop, control, delay. 2 HOLD BACK, restrict, suppress, withhold, conceal, censor, hide, hush up, stifle, reserve, retain.

• **keep in** 1 REPRESS, keep back, inhibit, bottle up, conceal, stifle, suppress, hide, control, restrain, quell, stop up. 2 CONFINE, detain, shut in, coop up.
⊞ 1 declare. 2 release.

• **keep on** continue, carry on, endure, persevere, persist, keep at it, last, remain, stay, stay the course, soldier on (infml), hold on, retain, maintain.

• **keep up** 1 KEEP PACE, equal, contend, compete, vie, rival, match, emulate. 2 CONTINUE, maintain, persevere, support, sustain, preserve.

keeper n guard, custodian, curator, caretaker, attendant, guardian, overseer, steward, warder, jailer, gaoler, warden, supervisor, minder (infml), inspector, conservator (fml), defender, governor, superintendent, surveyor.

keepsake n memento, souvenir, remembrance, relic, reminder, token, pledge, emblem.

kernel n core, grain, seed, nucleus, heart, nub, essence, germ, marrow, substance, nitty-gritty (infml), gist.

key n 1 CLUE, cue, indicator, pointer, explanation, sign, answer, solution, interpretation, means, secret. 2 GUIDE, glossary, translation, legend, code, table, index.
◇ adj important, essential, vital, crucial, necessary, principal,

Develop your word power

Contents

1

Powerful words

You can use these words in context to make your writing more effective.

accomplished — expert or skilled; professional

affirm — to show approval of and acknowledge as good or worthy

appreciate — to be grateful or thankful for someone or something

array — a large and impressive number, display or collection; well-ordered arrangement

aspire — to have a strong desire to achieve or reach (an objective or ambition)

authentic — genuine; reliable; trustworthy; true to the original

authoritative — accepted as a reliable source of knowledge; having authority

breathtaking — very surprising, exciting or impressive

buoyant — (of a person) cheerful; (of sales, profits, etc) tending to rise; (of a business, etc) having increasing trade or rising profits

champion — to strongly support or defend (a person or cause)

cogent — (of arguments, reasons, etc) strong; persuasive; convincing

consolidate — to make or become solid or strong; (of businesses, etc) combine or merge into one

decisive — most important and therefore bringing a result, so ending doubt or dispute

definitive — settling a matter once and for all; most complete or authoritative

distinctive — easily recognized because very individual; special

effective — having the power to produce, or producing, a desired result; producing a pleasing effect; impressive; striking

eminent — famous and admired; distinguished; outstanding

energetic	having or displaying energy; lively, forceful or vigorous
enterprising	showing boldness and initiative; adventurous; imaginative
far-reaching	having wide validity, scope or influence
far-sighted	wise; prudent; forward-looking
forward-looking	planning ahead; progressive, enterprising or go-ahead
fresh	(of an approach) original; different and innovative
genuine	authentic, not artificial or fake; honest; sincere
go-ahead	energetically ambitious and far-sighted
impetus	the force or energy with which something moves; momentum; driving force; incentive or encouragement
impressive	producing admiration, wonder or approval
incisive	clear and sharp; to the point
innovative	introducing new ideas, methods, etc; fresh, original, creative, imaginative
integrity	honest and firm adherence to moral values and principles; uprightness
landmark	an important occasion, event or development, especially one that is significant in the history or progress of something
masterpiece	an extremely skilful piece of work, especially the greatest work of an artist or writer
nurture	to encourage the development of (a project, idea or feeling, etc)
opportune	(of a time) suitable; proper; convenient or advantageous
optimistic	tending to take a bright, hopeful view of things and expect the best possible outcome
pioneer	to explore the unknown or break new ground in anything; be innovative; try out, originate or develop (a new technique, etc)
pivotal	crucially important; critical

3

potential	the range of capabilities that someone or something has; powers or resources not yet developed or made use of
proficient	fully trained and competent; expert; able, accomplished
refreshing	giving new strength, energy and enthusiasm; (of an attitude) particularly pleasing because different, unexpected or new
resilient	(of a person) strong and able to recover quickly from, or to deal readily with, illness, sudden, unexpected difficulties, hardship, etc
resonate	to appeal; be attractive, interesting, pleasing, etc
resourceful	skilled in finding ways of solving difficulties, problems, etc; ingenious
rigorous	showing strict precision or exactitude, eg of thought
robust	(of an opinion) strong, forceful and vigorous; straightforward and direct
significant	important; worth noting or considering; having a special meaning; indicating or implying something
spearhead	to lead (a movement, campaign, attack, etc)
special	distinct from, and usually better than, others of the same or a similar kind; not common; exceptional; designed for a particular purpose
trenchant	incisive; penetrating; forthright; vigorous
unique	being the only one of its kind; without equal; unparalleled, especially in excellence
unparalleled	so remarkable as to have no equal or parallel; incomparable, unprecedented
versatile	adapting easily to different tasks; flexible; all-round
vibrant	extremely lively or exciting; made strikingly animated or energetic
visionary	showing or marked by great foresight or imagination; far-sighted
vital	essential; of the greatest importance; crucial

Foreign words and phrases

ab initio (Latin) 'from the beginning'

à bon marché (French) 'good market'; at a good bargain, cheap

ab ovo (Latin) 'from the egg'; from the beginning

a cappella (Italian) 'in the style of the chapel'; sung without instrumental accompaniment

Achtung (German) 'Look out! Take care!'

à deux (French) 'for two'; often denotes a dinner or conversation of a romantic nature

ad hoc (Latin) 'towards this'; for this special purpose

ad infinitum (Latin) 'to infinity'; denotes endless repetition

ad nauseam (Latin) 'to the point of sickness'; disgustingly endless or repetitive

ad valorem (Latin) 'to value'; 'according to what it is worth'; often used of taxes etc

advocatus diaboli (Latin) 'devil's advocate'; person opposing an argument in order to expose any flaws in it

aficionado (Spanish) 'amateur'; an ardent follower; a 'fan'

a fortiori (Latin) 'from the stronger' (argument); denotes the validity and stronger reason of a proposition

agent provocateur (French) 'provocative agent'; someone who incites others, by pretended sympathy, to commit crimes

aide-de-camp (French) 'assistant on the field'; an officer who acts as a confidential personal assistant for an officer of higher rank

aide-mémoire (French) 'help-memory'; a reminder; memorandum-book; a written summary of a diplomatic agreement

à la carte (French) 'from the menu'; each dish individually priced

à la mode (French) 'in fashion, fashionable'; also in cooking, of meat braised and stewed with vegetables; with ice cream (American English)

al fresco (Italian) 'fresh'; painting on fresh or moist plaster; in the fresh, cool or open air

alma mater (Latin) 'bountiful mother'; one's former school, college, or university; official college or university song (American English)

amour-propre (French) 'own love, self-love'; legitimate self-esteem, sometimes exaggerated; vanity, conceit

ancien régime (French) 'old regime'; a superseded and outdated political system or ruling élite

angst (German) 'anxiety'; an unsettling feeling produced by awareness of the uncertainties and paradoxes inherent in the state of being human

anno Domini (Latin) 'in the year of the Lord'; used in giving dates of the Christian era, counting forward from the year of Christ's birth

annus mirabilis (Latin) 'year of wonders'; a remarkably successful or auspicious year

Anschluss (German) 'joining together'; union, especially the political union of Germany and Austria in 1938

ante meridiem (Latin) 'before midday'; between midnight and noon, abbreviated to am

a posteriori (Latin) 'from the later'; applied to reasoning from experience, from effect to cause; inductive reasoning

après-ski (French) 'after-ski'; pertaining to the evening's amusements after skiing

a priori (Latin) 'from the previous'; denotes argument from the cause to the effect; deductive reasoning

au contraire (French) 'on the contrary'

au fait (French) 'to the point'; highly skilled; knowledgeable or familiar with something

au fond (French) 'at the bottom'; fundamentally

au naturel (French) 'in the natural state'; naked; also as a culinary term: cooked plainly, raw, or without dressing

au pair (French) 'on an equal basis'; originally an arrangement of mutual service without payment; now used of a girl (usually foreign) who performs domestic duties for board, lodging and pocket money

auto-da-fé (Portuguese) 'act of the faith'; the public declaration or carrying out of a sentence imposed on heretics in Spain and Portugal by the Inquisition, eg burning at the stake

avant-garde (French) 'front guard'; applied to those in the forefront of an artistic movement

babushka (Russian) 'grandmother'; granny; a triangular

headscarf worn under the chin

bain-marie (French) 'bath of Mary'; a water-bath; a vessel of boiling water in which another is placed for slow and gentle cooking, or for keeping food warm

baksheesh (Persian) a gift or present of money, particularly in the East (India, Turkey, Egypt, etc)

batik (Javanese) 'painted'; method of producing patterns on fabric by drawing with wax before dyeing

bête noire (French) 'black beast'; a bugbear; something one especially dislikes

blitzkrieg (German) 'lightning war'; a sudden overwhelming attack by ground and air forces; a burst of intense activity

bona fides (Latin) 'good faith'; genuineness

bonne-bouche (French) 'good mouth'; a delicious morsel eaten at the end of a meal

bonsai (Japanese) art of growing miniature trees in pots; a dwarf tree grown by this method

bon vivant (French) 'good living (person)'; one who lives well, particularly enjoying good food and wine; a jovial companion

bon voyage (French) have a safe and pleasant journey

carpe diem (Latin) 'seize the day'; enjoy the pleasures of the present moment while they last

carte blanche (French) 'blank sheet of paper'; freedom of action

casus belli (Latin) 'occasion of war'; whatever sparks off or justifies a war or quarrel

cause célèbre (French) a very notable or famous trial; a notorious controversy

caveat emptor (Latin) 'let the buyer beware'; warns the buyer to examine carefully the article about to be purchased

c'est la vie (French) 'that's life'; denotes fatalistic resignation

chacun à son goût (French) 'each to his own taste'; implies surprise at another's choice

chambré (French) 'put into a room'; (of red wine) at room temperature

chargé-d'affaires (French) a diplomatic agent of lesser rank; an ambassador's deputy

chef d'oeuvre (French) a masterpiece; the best piece of work by a particular artist, writer, etc

7

chutzpah (Yiddish) 'effrontery'; nerve to do or say outrageous things

cinéma vérité (French) 'cinema truth'; realism in films usually sought by photographic scenes of real life

circa (Latin) 'surrounding'; of dates and numbers: approximately

cliché (French) 'stereotype printing block'; the impression made by a die in any soft metal; a hackneyed phrase or concept

cognoscente (Italian) 'one who knows'; one who professes critical knowledge of art, music, etc; a connoisseur

coitus interruptus (Latin) 'interrupted intercourse'; coitus intentionally interrupted by withdrawal before semen is ejaculated

comme il faut (French) 'as it is necessary'; correct; genteel

compos mentis (Latin) 'having control of one's mind'; sane

cordon bleu (French) 'blue ribbon'; denotes food cooked to a very high standard

coup de grâce (French) 'blow of mercy'; a finishing blow to end pain; a decisive action which ends a troubled enterprise

coup d'état (French) 'blow of state'; a violent overthrow of a government or subversive stroke of state policy

coupé (French) 'cut'; (usually) two-door motor-car with sloping roof

crème de la crème (French) 'cream of the cream'; the very best

cul-de-sac (French) 'bottom of the bag'; a road closed at one end

curriculum vitae (Latin) 'course of life'; denotes a summary of someone's educational qualifications and work experience for presenting to a prospective employer

décolleté (French) 'with bared neck and shoulders'; with neck uncovered; (of dress) low-cut

de facto (Latin) 'from the fact'; in fact; actually; irrespective of what is legally recognized

déjà vu (French) 'already seen'; in any of the arts: unoriginal material; an illusion of having experienced something before; something seen so often it has become tedious

de jure (Latin) 'according to law'; denotes the legal or theoretical position, which may not correspond with reality

Deo volente (Latin) 'God willing'; a sort of good-luck talisman

de rigueur (French) 'of strictness'; compulsory; required by strict etiquette

derrière (French) 'behind'; the buttocks

déshabillé (French) 'undressed'; state of being only partially dressed, or of being casually dressed

de trop (French) 'of too much'; superfluous; in the way

deus ex machina (Latin) 'a god from a machine'; a contrived solution to a difficulty in a plot

distingué (French) 'distinguished'; having an aristocratic or refined demeanour; striking

doppelgänger (German) 'double goer'; a ghostly duplicate of a living person; a wraith; someone who looks exactly like someone else

double entendre (French) 'double meaning'; ambiguity (normally with indecent connotations)

echt (German) 'real, genuine'; denotes authenticity, typicality

élan (French) 'dash, rush, bound'; flair; flamboyance

El Dorado (Spanish) 'the gilded man'; the golden land (or city) imagined by the Spanish conquerors of America; any place which offers the opportunity of acquiring fabulous wealth

embarras de richesse (French) 'embarrassment of wealth'; a perplexing amount of wealth or an abundance of any kind

emeritus (Latin) 'having served one's time'; eg of a retired professor, honourably discharged from a public duty; holding a position on an honorary basis only

éminence grise (French) 'grey eminence'; someone exerting power through their influence over a superior

enfant terrible (French) 'terrible child'; a precocious child whose sayings embarrass its parents; a person whose behaviour is indiscreet, embarrassing to his associates

ennui (French) 'boredom'; world-weary listlessness

en passant (French) 'in passing'; by the way; incidentally; applied in chess to the taking of a pawn that has just moved two squares as if it had moved only one

9

en route (French) 'on the way, on the road'; let us go

entente (French) 'understanding'; a friendly agreement between nations

erratum *plural* **errata** (Latin) an error in writing or printing

ersatz (German) 'replacement, substitute'; connotes a second-rate substitute; a supplementary reserve from which waste can be made good

et al (Latin) et alii 'and other things'; used to avoid giving a complete and possibly over-lengthy list of all items eg of authors

Et tu, Brute? (Latin) 'You too, Brutus?' (Caesar's alleged exclamation when he saw Brutus among his assassins)

eureka (Greek) *heureka* 'I have found!'; cry of triumph at a discovery

ex cathedra (Latin) 'from the seat'; from the chair of office; authoritatively; judicially

ex gratia (Latin) 'from favour'; of a payment; one that is made as a favour, without any legal obligation and without admitting legal liability

ex officio (Latin) 'from office, by virtue of office'; used as a reason for membership of a body

fait accompli (French) 'accomplished fact'; already done or settled, and therefore irreversible

fatwa (Arabic) 'the statement of a formal legal opinion'; a formal legal opinion delivered by an Islamic religious leader

faux ami (French) 'false friend'; a word in a foreign language that does not mean what it appears to

faux pas (French) 'false step'; a social blunder

femme fatale (French) 'fatal woman'; an irresistibly attractive woman who brings difficulties or disasters on men; a siren

film noir (French) 'black film'; a bleak and pessimistic film

fin de siècle (French) 'end of the century'; of the end of the 19th century in Western culture or of an era; decadent

floruit (Latin) 'he or she flourished'; denotes a period during which a person lived

fons et origo (Latin) 'the source and origin'

force majeure (French) 'superior force'; an unforeseeable or uncontrollable course of events, excusing one from fulfilling a contract; a legal term

Führer (German) 'leader, guide'; an insulting term for anyone bossily asserting authority

Gastarbeiter (German) 'guest-worker'; an immigrant worker, especially one who does menial work

gemütlich (German) amiable; comfortable; cosy

gestalt (German) 'form, shape'; original whole or unit, more than the sum of its parts

Gesundheit (German) 'health', 'your health'; said to someone who has just sneezed

glasnost (Russian) 'publicity'; the policy of openness and forthrightness followed by the Soviet government, initiated by Mikhail Gorbachev

goy (Hebrew) non-Jewish, a gentile

grand mal (French) 'large illness'; a violently convulsive form of epilepsy

grand prix (French) 'great prize'; any of several international motor races; any competition of similar importance in other sports

gran turismo (Italian) 'great touring, touring on a grand scale'; a motor car designed for high speed touring in luxury (abbreviation GT)

gratis (Latin) gratiis 'kindness, favour'; free of charge

gringo (Mexican-Spanish) 'foreigner'

guru (Hindi) a spiritual leader; a revered instructor or mentor

habeas corpus (Latin) 'you should have the body'; a writ to a jailer to produce a prisoner in person, and to state the reasons for detention; maintains the right of the subject to protection from unlawful imprisonment

haiku (Japanese) 'amusement poem'; a Japanese poem consisting of only three lines, containing respectively five, seven, and five syllables

hajj (Arabic) 'pilgrimage'; the Muslim pilgrimage to Mecca

haka (Maori) a Maori ceremonial war dance; a similar dance performed by New Zealanders eg before a rugby game

halal (Arabic) 'lawful'; meat from an animal killed in strict accordance with Islamic law

haute couture (French) 'higher tailoring'; fashionable, expensive dress designing and tailoring

haut monde (French) 'high world'; high society; fashionable society; composed of the aristocracy and the wealthy

hoi polloi (Greek) 'the many'; the rabble; the vulgar

honoris causa (Latin) 'for the sake of honour'; a token of respect; used to designate honorary university degrees

ibidem (Latin) 'in the same place'; used in footnotes to indicate that the same book (or chapter) has been cited previously

id (Latin) 'it'; the sum total of the primitive instinctive forces in an individual

idée fixe (French) 'a fixed idea'; an obsession

idem (Latin) 'the same'

in absentia (Latin) 'in absence'; used for occasions, such as the receiving of a degree award, when the recipient would normally be present

in camera (Latin) 'in the room'; in a private room; in secret

incommunicado (Spanish) 'unable to communicate'; deprived of the right to communicate with others

in extremis (Latin) 'in the last'; at the point of death; in desperate circumstances

in flagrante delicto (Latin) 'with the crime blazing'; in the very act of committing the crime

infra dig (Latin) 'below dignity'; below one's dignity

in loco parentis (Latin) 'in place of a parent'

in Shallah (Arabic) 'if God wills'

inter alia (Latin) 'among other things'; used to show that a few examples have been chosen from many possibilities

in vitro (Latin) 'in glass'; in the test tube

ipso facto (Latin) 'by the fact itself'; thereby

je ne sais quoi (French) 'I do not know what'; an indefinable something

jihad (Arabic) 'struggle'; a holy war undertaken by Muslims against unbelievers

kamikaze (Japanese) 'divine wind'; Japanese pilots making a suicide attack; any reckless, potentially self- destructive act

karaoke (Japanese) 'empty orchestra'; in bars, clubs, etc members of the public sing a solo to a recorded backing

karma (Sanskrit) 'act'; the concept that the actions in a life determine the future condition of an individual

kibbutz (Hebrew) a Jewish communal agricultural settlement in Israel

kitsch (German) 'rubbish'; work in any of the arts that is pretentious and inferior or in bad taste

la dolce vita (Italian) 'the sweet life'; the name of a film made by Federico Fellini in 1960 showing a life of wealth, pleasure and self-indulgence

laissez-faire (French) 'let do'; a general principle of non-interference

Lebensraum (German) 'life space'; room to live; used by Hitler to justify his acquisition of land for Germany

leitmotiv (German) 'leading motive'; a recurrent theme

lèse-majesté (French) 'injured majesty'; offence against the sovereign power; treason

lingua franca (Italian) 'Frankish language'; originally a mixed Italian trading language used in the Levant, subsequently any language chosen as a means of communication among speakers of different languages

locum tenens (Latin) 'place holder'; a deputy or substitute, especially for a doctor or a clergyman

macho (Mexican-Spanish) 'male'; originally a positive term denoting masculinity or virility, it has come in English to describe an ostentatious virility

magnum opus (Latin) 'great work'; a person's greatest achievement, especially a literary work

maharishi (Sanskrit) a Hindu sage or spiritual leader; a guru

mañana (Spanish) 'tomorrow'; an unspecified time in the future

mea culpa (Latin) 'through my fault'; originally part of the Latin mass; an admission of fault and an expression of repentance

ménage à trois (French) 'household of three'; a household comprising a husband and wife and the lover of one of them

mens sana in corpore sano (Latin) 'a sound mind in a sound body'; the guiding rule of the 19th-century English educational system

modus operandi (Latin) 'mode of working'; the characteristic methods employed by a particular criminal

modus vivendi (Latin) 'mode of living'; an arrangement or compromise by means of which those who differ may get on together for a time

mot juste (French) 'exact word'; the word which fits the context exactly

multum in parvo (Latin) 'much in little'; a large amount in a small space

mutatis mutandis (Latin) 'with the necessary changes made'

ne plus ultra (Latin) 'not more beyond'; extreme perfection

netsuke (Japanese) a small Japanese carved ornament used to fasten small objects, eg a purse, tobacco pouch, or medicine box, to the sash of a kimono. They are now collectors' pieces

noblesse oblige (French) 'nobility obliges'; rank imposes obligations

non sequitur (Latin) 'it does not follow'; a conclusion that does not follow logically from the premise; a remark that has no relation to what has gone before

nota bene (Latin) 'observe well, note well'; often abbreviated NB

nouveau riche (French) 'new rich'; one who has only lately acquired wealth (without acquiring good taste)

nouvelle cuisine (French) 'new cooking'; a style of simple French cookery that aims to produce dishes that are light and healthy, utilizing fresh fruit and vegetables, and avoiding butter and cream

obiter dictum (Latin) 'something said in passing'; originally a legal term for something said by a trial judge that was incidental to the case in question

origami (Japanese) 'paper-folding'; Japanese art of folding paper to make shapes suggesting birds, boats, etc

O tempora! O mores! (Latin) 'O the times! O the manners!'; a condemnation of present times, as contrasted with a past which is seen as golden

outré (French) 'gone to excess'; beyond what is customary or proper; eccentric

pace (Latin) 'peace'; by your leave (indicating polite disagreement)

passim (Latin) 'everywhere, throughout'; dispersed through a book

per capita (Latin) 'by heads'; per head of the population in statistical contexts

perestroika (Russian) 'reconstruction'; restructuring of an organization

persona non grata (Latin) one who is not welcome or favoured (originally a term in diplomacy)

pied-à-terre (French) 'foot to the ground'; a flat, small house etc kept for temporary or occasional accommodation

plus ça change (French) abbreviated form of *plus ça change, plus c'est la même chose* 'the more things change, the more they stay the same'; a comment on the unchanging nature of the world

post meridiem (Latin) 'after midday, after noon'; abbreviated to pm

post mortem (Latin) 'after death'; an examination of a body in order to determine the cause of death; an after-the-event discussion

pour encourager les autres (French) 'to encourage the others'; exemplary punishment

prêt-à-porter (French) 'ready to wear'; refers to 'designer' clothes that are made in standard sizes as opposed to made-to-measure clothes

prima donna (Italian) 'first lady'; leading female singer in an opera; a person who is temperamental and hard to please

prima facie (Latin) 'at first sight'; a legal term for evidence that is assumed to be true unless disproved by other evidence

primus inter pares (Latin) 'first among equals'

prix fixe (French) 'fixed price'; used of a meal in a restaurant offered at a set price for a restricted choice. Compare **table d'hôte**

pro bono publico (Latin) 'for the public good'; something done for no fee

quid pro quo (Latin) 'something for something'; something given or taken as equivalent to another, often as retaliation

quod erat demonstrandum (Latin) 'which was to be shown'; often used in its abbreviated form QED

raison d'être (French) 'reason for existence'

rara avis (Latin) 'rare bird'; something or someone remarkable and unusual

realpolitik (German) 'politics of realism'; practical politics based on the realities and necessities of life, rather than moral or ethical ideas

recherché (French) 'sought out'; carefully chosen; particularly choice; rare or exotic

reductio ad absurdum (Latin) 'reduction to absurdity'; originally used in logic to mean the proof of a proposition by proving the falsity of its contradictory; the application of a principle so strictly that it is carried to absurd lengths

répondez, s'il vous plaît (French) 'reply, please'; in English mainly in its abbreviated form, RSVP, on invitations

revenons à nos moutons (French) 'let us return to our sheep'; let us get back to our subject

risqué (French) 'risky, hazardous'; audaciously bordering on the unseemly

sanctum sanctorum (Latin) 'holy of holies'; the innermost chamber of the temple, where the Ark of the Covenant was kept; any private room reserved for personal use

sangfroid (French) 'cold blood'; self-possession; coolness under stress

savoir faire (French) 'knowing what to do'; knowing what to do and how to do it in any situation

schadenfreude (German) 'hurt joy'; pleasure in others' misfortunes

schlimazel (Yiddish) 'bad luck'; a persistently unlucky person

schlock (Yiddish) 'broken or damaged goods'; inferior; shoddy

schmaltz (Yiddish) 'melted fat, grease'; showy sentimentality, particularly in writing, music, art, etc

schmuck (Yiddish) 'penis'; a (male) stupid person

shogun (Japanese) 'leader of the army'; ruler of feudal Japan

sic (Latin) 'so, thus'; used in brackets within printed matter to show that the original is faithfully reproduced even if incorrect

sic transit gloria mundi (Latin) 'so passes away earthly glory'

sine qua non (Latin) 'without which not'; an indispensable condition

sotto voce (Italian) 'below the voice'; in an undertone; aside

status quo (Latin) 'the state in which'; the existing condition

sub judice (Latin) 'under a judge'; under consideration by a judge or a court of law

subpoena (Latin) 'under penalty'; a writ commanding attendance in court

sub rosa (Latin) 'under the rose'; in secret; privately

summa cum laude (Latin) 'with the highest praise'; with great distinction; the highest class of degree award that can be gained by a US college student

summum bonum (Latin) 'the chief good'

table d'hôte (French) 'host's table'; a set meal at a fixed price. Compare **prix fixe**

tabula rasa (Latin) 'scraped table'; a cleaned tablet; a mind not yet influenced by outside impressions and experience

t'ai chi (Chinese) 'great art of boxing'; a system of exercise and self-defence in which good use of balance and co-ordination allows effort to be minimized

tempus fugit (Latin) 'time flies'; delay cannot be tolerated

terra incognita (Latin) 'unknown land'; an unknown land (so marked on early maps); an area of study about which very little is known

touché (French) 'touched'; claiming or acknowledging a hit made in fencing; claiming or acknowledging a point scored in an argument

tour de force (French) 'turning movement'; feat of strength or skill

trompe l'oeil (French) 'deceives the eye'; an appearance of reality achieved by the use of perspective and detail in painting, architecture, etc

tsunami (Japanese) 'wave in harbour'; a wave generated by movement of the earth's surface underwater; commonly (and erroneously) called a 'tidal wave'

Übermensch (German) 'over-person'; superman

ultra vires (Latin) 'beyond strength, beyond powers'; beyond one's power or authority

urbi et orbi (Latin) 'to the city and the world'; used of the Pope's pronouncements; to everyone

vade-mecum (Latin) 'go with me'; a handbook; pocket companion

vin du pays (French) 'wine of the country'; a locally

produced wine for everyday consumption

vis-à-vis (French) 'face to face'; one who faces or is opposite another; in relation to

viva voce (Latin) 'with the living voice'; in speech, orally; an oral examination, particularly at a university (commonly 'viva' alone)

volte-face (French) 'turn-face'; a sudden and complete change in opinion or in views expressed

vox populi (Latin) 'voice of the people'; public or popular opinion

Weltschmerz (German) 'world pain'; sympathy with universal misery; thoroughgoing pessimism

wunderkind (German) 'wonder-child'; a 'child prodigy'; one who shows great talent and/or achieves great success at an early (or comparatively early) age

zeitgeist (German) 'time-spirit'; the spirit of the age

Roots of words

Root	Meaning	Example
amble-	walk	amble, perambulator
-anim-	life	animal, animate
-cred-	belief	credible, creed
-demos-	people	democracy
-derma-	skin	epidermis
-dorm-	sleep	dormant, dormitory
-duct-	lead, carry	viaduct, conduct
-graph-	writing	autograph, graphics
-grat-	please	gratify, gratitude
-helio-	sun	heliotrope
-hippo-	horse	hippodrome
-leg-	read, speak	legible, lecture
-log-	word, speak, talk	dialogue, monologue
-mal-	evil	malicious, malevolent
-man(u)-	hand	manuscript
-mort-	death	mortal, mortuary
-oner-	burden	onerous, exonerate
-path-	feeling	pathos, empathy
-pyro-	fire	pyrometer
-scienc-	knowledge	science, omniscient
-scop-	see	telescope, microscope
-script-	write	manuscript
-terra-	earth	terrace
-tra-	drag, pull	tractor, extract
-urb-	city	urban, suburban
-vers-	against	versus, adversary
-vict-	conquer, defeat	victor, victory, victorious

Common prefixes

Prefix	Meaning	Example
a-, an-	without, not	asexual, amoral, anarchy, anachronism
ab-	away, from, off	absent, abnormal, abduct
ad-	toward, make, against	adhere, admit, adumbrate
aero-	aircraft	aerodrome, aeronautics
agri-	field	agriculture
amphi-, ambi-	around, both sides	amphitheatre, ambidextrous, ambivalent
ante-	before	anteroom, antecedent
anthropo-	human	anthropology
anti-	against	antibiotic, antitank
aqua-	water	aquarium, aquarobics
arch-	chief	archduke, archenemy
astro-	stars	astronomy, astrology, astronaut
audio-	hear	audiotypist, audiovisual
auto-	self	autograph, autobiography, automatic
bi-	two	bicycle, biannual, bisexual
biblio-	book	bibliography, bibliophile
bio-	life	biology, biorhythm, biosphere
cardio-	heart	cardiac
centi-	one hundredth; one hundred	centimetre, centipede
chromo-	colour	chromatology
chron-	time	chronology, chronometer
circum-	around	circumference, circumnavigate
co-	together	cooperate, coenzyme

Prefix	Meaning	Example
com-	with, together, in association	combine, commemorate, commiserate
contra-	against	contradict, contraflow, contraception
de-	separation, away, opposite of, reduce	decouple, depart, deactivate, decrease
deca-	ten	decade
di-	two, double	dialogue, diphthong
dis-	opposite, apart, away, not	disagree, disperse, disinherit
ego-	self	egocentric, egomania
electro-	electricity	electrolysis, electroplate
en-	cause to be, put in or on	enclose, envelope
epi-	upon, over	epidermis, epidemic
equi-	equal	equidistant
ex-	from, out of, apart, away, former	exhale, exterior, extraneous, ex-wife
extra-	outside	extraterrestrial
fore-	front, before	foreword, foretell
frater-	brother	fraternal
geo-	earth	geography, geology
graph-	write, record	graphics, graphology
haemo-	blood	haemorrhage
hecto-	one hundred	hectometre
hemi-	half	hemisphere
hepta-	seven	heptagon
hetero-	mixed, unlike	heterosexual
hexa-	eight	hexagon
homo-	same, alike	homogenous, homosexual
hydro-	water	hydrant, hydroelectricity, hydrofoil

Prefix	Meaning	Example
hyper-	over, excessive	hyperactive, hypermarket, hypertension
hypo-	under, inadequate	hypoallergenic, hypochondriac, hypocrisy
ideo-	idea	ideology, ideal
il-	not	illogical, illiterate
im-	not	impossible, immoral
in-	not, the opposite, the reverse	injustice, incredible
in-	into, in, within	inhale, incorporate, incarcerate
infra-	below	infrared, infra-molecular
inter-	between	international, intergalactic, interact
intra-	inside	intravenous
ir-	not	irresolute, irresponsible
kilo-	one thousand	kilometre, kilogram
macro-	great, long, big, large	macrobiotic, macroeconomics
magni-	great	magnify
mal-	bad	malfunction, malware
mater-	mother	maternal
mega-	million, big	megawatt, megaphone
micro-	small	microfilm, microscope
milli-	one thousandth	millimetre
mini-	small	minibus, miniskirt
mis-	wrongly, badly	misbehave, mismanage
mono-	single	monocle, monogamy
multi-	many	multicoloured, multistorey
neo-	new	neoclassical, neologism
neuro-	mind or nerves	neurosis, neurotic
non-	not	nonstop

Prefix	Meaning	Example
octo-, octa-	eight	octopus, octagon, octave
omni-	all	omnipotent, omnipresent
ortho-	right	orthodox
out-	greater than, outside	outlast, outlive, outbuilding
over-	above, too much	overhang, overdo
pater-	father	paternal, paternity
ped-	foot	pedal, pedestrian, pedicure
penta-	five	pentagon
peri-	around	perimeter, peripatetic, periscope
phil-	love	philanthropy, philosophy
photo-	light	photography, photosynthesis
physio-	nature	physiology
poly-	many	polygamy, polygon
post-	after	posterior, postnatal, postscript
pre-	before	preschool, preview, pre-war
pro-	before, in favour of, substitute	proceed, proactive, projection, pronoun
proto-	first, original	prototype
pseudo-	not real, pretender	pseudonym
psycho-	soul, mind	psychiatric, psychoanalyse, psychology
quad-	four	quadruplet
quin-	five	quintet
re-	again	recapture, revisit
retro-	back	retrograde
self-	oneself	self-confident, self-harm
semi-	half	semiquaver, semicircle

Prefix	Meaning	Example
sept-	seven	septet
sex-	six	sextet
socio-	society	sociology
sub-	under	submarine, subsoil, subterfuge
super-	above, beyond, greater	superfluous, superhero, supervisor
syn-	with	synchronize, synod, synthesis
techno-	practical skill and science	technology
tele-	distant	telecommunication, teleconference
theo-	God	theology
thermo-	heat	thermometer, thermodynamic
trans-	across	transport, transcend, transsexual
tri-	three	triangle, tricycle
ultra-	beyond	ultraviolet
un-	not	unattractive, unnecessary, unplanned
under-	below, too little	underground, undergrowth, underdeveloped
uni-	one	unity, union
vice-	assistant	vice-president

Common suffixes

Suffix	Meaning	Example
-able, -ible	able, capable	breakable, debatable, lovable
-ade	result of an action	blockade
-age	act, state, result of	damage, storage, wreckage
-al	relating to	manual, natural usual
-algia	pain	neuralgia, nostalgia
-an, -ian	native of, relating to	American, Georgian, thespian
-ance, -ancy	action, process, state	assistance, allowance, defiance
-ant, -ent	(a person or thing) that does something	pleasant, student
-ate	salt; cause to have or become	carbonate, hyphenate
-ation	quality or act of	admiration, examination
-cian	skill or art of	magician, optician
-cide	killing	germicide, homicide, suicide
-cracy	rule	autocracy, bureaucracy, democracy
-cy	action, function of	captaincy, hesitancy
-dom	quality, realm	freedom, kingdom
-ee	receiver of	employee, lessee, refugee
-en	made of	silken, woollen
-ence, -ency	action, state, quality	agency, confidence, urgency
-er, -or	one who, that which	baker, instructor, fastener
-ese	native to, the language of	Chinese, Maltese
-ess	female of	baroness, lioness

Suffix	Meaning	Example
-ette	small	cigarette
-fic	making, causing	scientific, specific
-fold	having a certain number of parts	fourfold
-ful	full of	careful, hopeful, painful
-fy	make	liquefy, magnify, purify
-gon	having a certain number of angles	polygon
-hood	quality, condition	childhood, widowhood
-ic, -ical	like, in the nature of	atomic, biological, poetic
-ics	science, subject, activities	physics, politics, acrobatics
-ide	chemical compound	chloride
-ine	like or consisting of	crystalline
-ion	act, result, state of	corruption, exhaustion, oppression
-ish	resembling	faddish, whitish
-ism	manner, condition, system	alcoholism, Catholicism, mannerism
-ist	one who	optometrist, florist
-ite	group of people, follower, mineral	Canaanite, pre-Raphaelite, graphite
-itis	disease, inflammation	appendicitis
-ity, -ty	state of, quality	cruelty, oddity, purity
-ive	causing	abortive, exhaustive
-ize, -ise	make	Americanize, legalize, popularize
-less	without	careless, painless, thoughtless
-logy	study, science of	meteorology, pathology
-ly	like, in that manner	easily, mainly, quickly
-man	person	salesman, chairman
-ment	act, state or result of	amazement, payment, retirement

Suffix	Meaning	Example
-meter	measure	diameter
-most	furthest	northernmost
-ness	state of	darkness, deafness, kindness
-oid	resembling	anthropoid, rhomboid
-ory	place; action, quality	dormitory, depository, contributory
-ous	full of	humorous, poisonous
-phile	liking very much	Francophile
-phobia	fear	agoraphobia
-pod	foot	tripod
-proof	resistant	fireproof
-ship	state of, office	companionship, governorship
-some	like, apt	fulsome, wholesome
-tude	state, condition	aptitude, solitude
-ward	in a direction	downward, homeward
-ways	direction	sideways
-wise	direction or manner, relevance	clockwise, weatherwise
-y	resembling, inclined to	bushy, panicky

Words to impress

Words that will add colour and conviction to your expression.

abstruse difficult to understand

aficionado an amateur who is very interested in a subject, knows a lot about it and devotes a lot of time to it

alacrity a willingness or eagerness to act quickly

ambivalent having two opposite or conflicting views or feelings about someone or something

analogous (of two things) having similar characteristics to or functioning in the same way as another

antithesis the exact opposite of a person or thing

apposite particularly appropriate under the circumstances or for the purpose

assiduous energetic and devoted in continuing to do something for a long time without tiring

auspicious suggesting that someone or something is going to be successful

axiomatic so obviously true that it does not need to be proved or explained

benign (of someone, behaviour or appearance) kind and gentle

capricious (of a person) subject to sudden changes in behaviour, mood or opinions, often for no good reason

caveat a warning that something is only true within certain limitations

circumspect cautious; prudent

circumvent to get round, outwit, avoid

commensurate (of two things) in proportion to each other

concomitant (of an event or situation) accompanying another, happening at the same time as another, usually because of it or as a result of it

conspicuous easy to spot, usually because of being different

contiguous touching; adjoining

corollary a natural or obvious consequence or result of something

disparate very different

eclectic (of a collection or range) containing material or ideas from a wide range of sources

efficacy power to produce the effect that something is supposed to produce

empirical known through practical experience

endemic regularly found among a particular people or in a particular district

ephemeral short-lived or fleeting

epitomize the most typical example of someone or something

esoteric understood only by a few people who have the necessary knowledge

evocative (of a smell, sound or picture) making you remember a particular memory or time

exemplary (of behaviour or work) so good that it should be used as an example by others

expedient profitable or convenient rather than fair or just

expedite to hasten, speed up

exponential (of an increase) happening at an increasingly rapid rate over a period of time

heuristic serving or leading to find out

hiatus a break in something that should be continuous

hubris over-confidence; arrogance that brings about disaster

iconoclastic opposed to or attacking traditional beliefs or customs

incipient just beginning to happen

inherent (of a quality) existing as an essential, natural or permanent part of something

integral (of a part, feature or aspect of something) essential to the thing for it to be complete

intrinsic belonging to someone or something as a natural and essential part of their nature

juxtaposition the act of putting people or things beside each other to show the differences or similarities between them

lacuna a gap or space where something is missing, especially in a printed text or manuscript

laudable (of an action, statement or idea) deserving praise

magnanimous (of a person or action) showing a willingness to behave generously, fairly and forgivingly

mandatory required by a law or rule

paradigm a typical example, model or pattern of something

perspicacity the ability to analyse and understand people and situations

plethora a large, especially excessive, amount of something

pragmatic (of a person or approach) practical, sensible and realistic

pristine (of a place such as forest or beach) still in its natural state and unspoilt by human activity

propound to suggest (an idea or theory) for consideration or discussion by other people

purport to claim or appear to be someone or do something

putative commonly supposed to be, but not necessarily

quintessential being an absolutely perfect example of a particular type of person or thing

ramification a complicated consequence of something

refulgent beaming

repudiate to refuse to accept (something, such as a policy or treaty)

salient prominent, striking

salubrious pleasant, respectable, clean

sanguine confident and inclined to hopefulness

serendipity the state of frequently making lucky or beneficial finds

specious plausible, but wrong or inaccurate in reality

spurious (of a claim, charge or explanation) false, counterfeit or untrue

sycophantic (of a person or way of behaving) excessive and insincere in the way they flatter someone in power or authority to gain an advantage

symbiosis a mutually beneficial relationship between two people or groups

tangential involving only a slight connection and relatively unimportant

temerity extremely confident or bold behaviour

tendentious deliberately and forcefully biased and controversial

truculence discourtesy; aggression

ubiquitous seeming to be everywhere at the same time

unconscionable outrageous and completely unacceptable

virulent with extremely rapid and harmful effects

Clichés

Overused phrases, with suggestions for alternatives in plain English.

at the end of the day ultimately; in the end
at this moment in time now; just now; at the moment
can of worms complex problem; difficult situation; unpredictable situation
emotional rollercoaster difficult/trying/emotional experience
hold your hands up to admit/take responsibility
in a very real sense [This can be omitted without loss of meaning.]
... is the new ... ... has become fashionable, etc
move the goalposts to change the conditions/requirements
not rocket science simple; easy; requiring little intelligence
push the envelope to push the boundaries; challenge the limits
score an own goal to make a mistake; make a move to your own disadvantage
set out your stall to make your aims/intentions clear
sing from the same hymn sheet to agree; be in agreement
step up to the plate to put yourself forward; take on responsibility
take your eye off the ball to lose focus; lose sight of your priorities; become distracted from your aims
the bottom line to what is most important
the complete package have all the necessary talents
the fact of the matter the fact; the truth; the reality
think outside the box to be imaginative or creative, disregarding conventional thinking
tick all the boxes to fulfil all the requirements

Overused words

Overused words, with suggestions for alternatives in plain English.

110% meaning 'very much'
actually used unnecessarily to mean 'in fact'
basically used unnecessarily to mean 'really'
closure meaning 'resolution, acceptance'
dynamic as a noun referring to the relationship between things
factor meaning 'a component, element, part or feature'
hard-hitting used to describe anything frankly critical
individual as a noun meaning 'a person'
joined-up co-ordinated; organized
journey meaning a set of personal experiences, progress
on-message/off-message following/not following an accepted policy or view
quality meaning good, excellent
quantum leap an advance
quasi- combined with anything to mean 'in appearance only'
roadmap a plan
scenario meaning 'any imagined or projected situation'
sea change a big change
slam as a verb meaning 'to criticize'
solutions any services or products a company sells
step change a fundamental change
synergy the phenomenon in which the combined action of two or more actions is greater than the sum of their individual effects
time bomb referring to anything that might have a negative future effect
tragedy referring to a sad or shocking event
transparency meaning 'openness, honesty'
tsar referring to an expert, authority or adviser
veritable intensifier used for anything at all
vision referring to one's intention or hope
witch-hunt referring to any persecution

Commonly confused words

advice or **advise?** *Advice* is the noun, as in: *My advice to you is put the money in the bank immediately*. *Advise* (which should not be spelt with ending '-ize') is the verb, as in: *I advise you to put the money in the bank immediately*.

affect or **effect?** *Affect* is always a verb and has two main senses. The first sense means 'to influence, make a difference to', as in: *The changes won't affect the staff in this branch*. The second sense is rather formal and means 'to pretend', as in: *Though she affected indifference, I knew she was really very upset*. *Effect* can be a noun or a verb. As a noun it means 'result, consequence', as in: *I was still suffering from the effects of the journey*. The verb *effect* is more formal and means 'to cause, to bring about', as in: *His aim was to effect a radical change in the party structure*.

alternate or **alternative?** *Alternate* as a verb is pronounced /**awl**-ter-nayt/ and means 'to switch between two things repeatedly' as in: *Her mood alternates between elation and deep despair*. As an adjective, *alternate* is pronounced /awl-**ter**-nit/ and refers to things that come after each other by turns, or which happen on every second occasion, as in: *She visits her parents on alternate Saturdays*. Notice that in American English the adjective *alternate* is used where British English would use the adjective *alternative*, as in: (American English) *an alternate route;* (British English) *an alternative route*. *Alternative* is pronounced /awl-**ter**-na-tiv/. As a noun, it means 'one of several possibilities or choices', as in: *There are several equally attractive alternatives*. As an adjective, *alternative* refers to something that offers a choice between two possibilities, as in: *an alternative method of payment*.

complement or **compliment?** A *complement* is something that completes or perfects: *A dry white wine is an ideal complement to fish*. In grammar, *complement* denotes a word or phrase added after the verb to complete the predicate of a sentence. A *compliment* is an expression of praise or regard, as in: *My compliments to the chef*.

comprise, compose or **consist?** *Comprise* is used for the parts that make up a whole, and for the whole, as in: *The three countries that comprise Great Britain are England, Scotland and Wales. Great Britain comprises England, Scotland and Wales.* **Compose** is used of all the parts that make up a whole, as in: *The three countries that compose Great Britain are England, Scotland and Wales. Great Britain is composed of three countries – England, Scotland and Wales.* **Constitute** is used of the elements that added together make something up, without the mixing or creating of a new substance or entity implied by *compose*, as in: *A balanced diet and regular exercise constitute a healthy lifestyle.*

continual or **continuous?** *Continual* means 'constantly repeated or very frequent', as in: *How can I be expected to concentrate when there are continual interruptions?* **Continuous** means 'never stopping', as in: *We've had three weeks of continuous rain.*

council or **counsel?** A *council* is a group of people who organize, control, take decisions or advise. **Counsel** is a rather formal word meaning 'advice'. It also means 'a lawyer or lawyers'.

councillor or **counsellor?** A *councillor* is an elected member of a council. A **counsellor** is someone who gives advice.

currant or **current?** A *currant* is a dried fruit. When **current** is a noun it means 'flow', as in: *an electric current; The current carried the boat out to sea.* As an adjective, **current** describes things that are happening now: *current affairs; What's the current cost of a TV licence?*

defuse or **diffuse?** *Defuse* is a verb and is pronounced /dee-**fewz**/. Its literal meaning is 'to remove the fuse from (a bomb)'. It also means 'to make (a situation) less tense'. **Diffuse** as a verb is pronounced /di-**fewz**/ and means 'to spread in all directions'. As an adjective it is pronounced /di-**fews**/.

dependant or **dependent?** *Dependant* is a noun and

means 'a person who depends on another for money, food, etc', as in: *As a young man without dependants, he was free to spend his money as he pleased.* **Dependent** is an adjective, as in: *He's still dependent on state benefit.*

discreet or **discrete?** *Discreet* means 'not saying or doing anything that may cause trouble or embarrassment', as in: *This is a very delicate matter: can we rely on you to be discreet?* *Discrete* means 'separate, not connected or attached to others', as in: *On closer examination, we find that the pattern is formed from thousands of discrete dots of colour.*

economic or **economical?** *Economic* means 'relating to economics, the study of money' or 'giving a reasonable profit', as in: *an economic survey of Scotland; Without generous subsidies many smaller farms just wouldn't be economic.* *Economical* means 'careful with money or other resources, not wasteful', as in: *He's had to learn to be more economical now that his only income is a small pension.*

envelop or **envelope?** *Envelop* is the verb meaning 'to completely surround or cover' and is pronounced /en-**vel**-up/. *Envelope* is the noun and is pronounced /**en**-vel-ope/, as in: *Don't forget to put a stamp on the envelope.*

fatal or **fateful?** *Fatal* means 'causing death or disaster', as in: *a fatal accident; He made a fatal mistake.* *Fateful* means 'crucial, significant, deciding one's fate', as in: *On that one fateful day in October, millions of pounds were wiped off the value of shares.*

fewer or **less?** *Fewer* is used with plural countable nouns, as in: *There are fewer fruits on the apple tree this year. If fewer people smoked there would be fewer cases of heart disease. I might not be so fat if I ate fewer cakes. There were fewer than 20 people at the meeting.* *Less* is used with uncountable nouns, as in: *There is less fruit on the apple tree this year. If fewer people smoked there would be less heart disease. I might not be so fat if I ate less chocolate.*

I or **me?** *I* is used before a verb when you are the subject of the clause or sentence, as in: *I love old movies. Jane and I like* *gardening*. **Me** is used after a verb: *He gave me a lift home. She gave Alan and me a lift home. He sends Mum and Dad and me a present every Christmas.* Another common error is to use *I* instead of **me** after a preposition, as in: *Janey sat between Robbie and me* [not: I].

imply or **infer**? *Imply* means 'to suggest or express (something) indirectly', as in: *Are you implying that I'm a liar? Infer* means 'to draw a conclusion from what appears to be suggested or from what one knows', as in: *Am I to infer from what you say that you think I'm not up to the job?*

it's or **its**? Note that adding an apostrophe changes the meaning, so take care to use the correct form in writing. *It's* (with an apostrophe) is the informal short form of 'it is' or 'it has', as in: *It's* [= It is] *nice to meet you. It's* [= It has] *gone dark all of a sudden. Its* (without an apostrophe) is the possessive form of 'it', as in: *The moorhen makes its nest in the vegetation close to the water's edge. The car is old and its bodywork is rusting.*

lay or **lie**? *Lay* means 'to put down carefully or in a flat, horizontal or prone position', as in: *Lay the map out on the grass and hold the corners down with stones.* The past tense and past participle of *lay* is **laid**. *She carried the sleeping child upstairs and laid him down gently on the bed.* Note that where *lay* is the verb, there must be an object, because it is a transitive verb.
Lie means 'to be or move into a flat, horizontal or prone position', as in: *He lies on that bed all day staring at the ceiling.* Note that *lie* is an intransitive verb, and therefore does not have an object. Do not use *lay* instead of *lie*: *Surely you're not going to lie* [not: lay] *in bed all day again?*
The past tense of *lie* is *lay*, and the past participle is *lain*: *He lay down and tried to get some sleep. If you hadn't lain in bed all morning, you wouldn't have missed all the fun.*

licence and **license**? In British English, *licence* is the noun and *license* is the verb. In American English, *license* is both the noun and the verb.

lightening or **lightning?** *Lightening* is the present participle of the verb *lighten*, as in: *He smiled, lightening the tension that had grown between them. Lightning* is a sudden bright flash of electricity in the sky, usually followed by the sound of thunder.

loose or **lose?** *Loose* means 'not tight or not firmly attached', as in: *When the weather is hot, it is more comfortable to wear loose cotton clothing. Holly's front tooth is loose.* To *lose* means 'to mislay', as in: *If you don't do something about that loose button on your jacket you'll lose it.*

practice or **practise?** In British English, the form with the *c* is the noun and the form with the *s* is the verb. In American English *practice* is used for both the noun and the verb.

principal or **principle?** *Principal* is an adjective as well as a noun. It means 'main or most important', as in: *He gave as the principal reason for his resignation lack of cooperation from colleagues. Principle* is a noun meaning 'rule' or 'theory', as in: *the principles of English grammar; I'm not going to sacrifice my principles for money.*

their, **there** or **they're?** *Their* means 'belonging to them', as in: *They can do what they like in their own home. There* means 'at, in or to that place', as in: *There they can do as they please; it is their retreat from the world. They're* is the short form of 'they are', as in: *They're moving their desks over there.*

theirs and **there's?** Remember that *theirs* [= belonging to them] does not have an apostrophe, and *there's* (the short form of 'there is') has an apostrophe.

who's or **whose?** *Who's* is the short form of 'who is' or 'who has', as in: *Who's that at the door? Who's eaten all the chocolates?* Remember not to use this shortened form in formal writing. *Whose* is the possessive form of 'who', as in: *This is the boy whose mother was injured in the accident. Whose dirty socks are these? Whose* is also correctly used to mean 'of which', as in: *The tree, whose branches were home to many small creatures, blew down in the storm.*

your or **you're?** *Your* is the possessive form of 'you', as in: *Are those your CDs?*

You're is the short form of 'you are', as in: *Come on, Isabel, you're next*. Try to avoid using this shortened form in formal business correspondence.

decisive, central, chief, main, major, leading, basic, fundamental.

keynote n core, centre, heart, substance, theme, gist, essence, emphasis, accent, stress.

keystone n cornerstone, core, crux, base, basis, linchpin, foundation, ground, principle, root, mainspring, source, spring, motive.

kick v 1 BOOT, hit, strike, jolt. 2 (infml) GIVE UP, quit, stop, leave off, abandon, desist from, break. ◇ n 1 BLOW, recoil, jolt, striking. 2 (infml) STIMULATION, thrill, excitement.
• **kick off** begin, commence, start, open, get under way, open the proceedings, set the ball rolling, introduce, inaugurate, initiate.
• **kick out** eject, evict, expel, oust, remove, chuck out (infml), discharge, dismiss, get rid of, sack (infml), throw out, reject.

kid¹ n child, youngster, youth, juvenile, infant, girl, boy, teenager, lad, nipper (infml), tot (infml).

kid² v tease, joke, have on (infml), hoax, fool, pull someone's leg (infml), pretend, trick, delude, dupe, con (infml), jest, hoodwink, humbug, bamboozle.

kidnap v abduct, capture, seize, hold to ransom, snatch, hijack, steal.

kill v 1 SLAUGHTER, murder, slay, put to death, exterminate, assassinate, do to death, do in (infml), bump off (infml), finish off, massacre, smite (fml), execute, eliminate (sl), destroy, dispatch (infml), annihilate, do away with, butcher, liquidate (sl), knock off (infml), rub out (sl). 2 STIFLE, deaden, smother, quash, quell, suppress.

killer n murderer, assassin, executioner, destroyer, slaughterer, exterminator, butcher (infml), cut-throat, gunman, hatchet man (sl), hit-man (sl).

killing n 1 SLAUGHTER, murder, massacre, homicide, assassination, execution, slaying, manslaughter, extermination, carnage, bloodshed, elimination, fatality, liquidation. 2 (infml) GAIN, fortune, windfall, profit, lucky break, coup, clean-up (infml), success, stroke of luck, bonanza (infml), hit, big hit. ◇ adj (infml) 1 FUNNY, hilarious, comical, amusing, side-splitting (infml), ludicrous. 2 EXHAUSTING, hard, taxing, arduous.

kind n sort, type, class, category, set, variety, character, genus, genre, style, brand, family, breed, race, nature, persuasion, description, species, stamp, temperament, manner. ◇ adj benevolent, kind-hearted, kindly, good-hearted, good-natured, helpful, obliging, humane, generous, compassionate, charitable, amiable, friendly, congenial, soft-hearted, thoughtful, warm, warm-hearted, considerate, courteous, sympathetic, tender-hearted, understanding, lenient, mild, hospitable, gentle, indulgent, neighbourly, tactful, giving, good, loving, gracious. ⊡ cruel, inconsiderate, unhelpful.

kindle v 1 IGNITE, light, set alight, set on fire. 2 INFLAME, fire, stir, thrill, stimulate, rouse, arouse, awaken, excite, fan, incite, inspire, induce, provoke.

kindly adj benevolent, kind, compassionate, charitable, good-natured, helpful, warm, generous, cordial, favourable, giving, indulgent, pleasant, sympathetic, tender, gentle, mild, patient, polite. ⊡ cruel, uncharitable.

kindness n 1 BENEVOLENCE, kindliness, charity, magnanimity, compassion, generosity, hospitality, humanity, loving-kindness (fml), courtesy, friendliness, goodwill, goodness, grace, indulgence, tolerance, understanding, gentleness.

2 FAVOUR, good turn, assistance, help, service.
◉ 1 cruelty, inhumanity.
2 disservice.

king n monarch, ruler, sovereign, majesty, emperor, chief, chieftain, prince, supremo, leading light (infml).

kingdom n monarchy, sovereignty, reign, realm, empire, dominion, commonwealth, nation, principality, state, country, domain, dynasty, province, sphere, territory, land, division.

kink n 1 CURL, twist, bend, dent, indentation, knot, loop, crimp, coil, tangle, wrinkle. 2 QUIRK, eccentricity, idiosyncrasy, foible, perversion.

kinship n 1 KIN, family, blood, relation. 2 AFFINITY, similarity, association, alliance, connection, correspondence, relationship, tie, community, conformity.

kiosk n booth, stall, stand, news-stand, bookstall, cabin, box, counter.

kiss v 1 CARESS, peck (infml), smooch (infml), neck (infml), snog (sl).
2 TOUCH, graze, glance, brush, lick, scrape, fan.
◇ n peck (infml), smack (infml), smacker (sl).

kit n equipment, gear, apparatus, supplies, tackle, provisions, outfit, implements, set, tools, trappings, rig, instruments, paraphernalia, utensils, effects, luggage, baggage.
• **kit out** equip, fit out, outfit, supply, fix up, furnish, prepare, arm, deck out, dress.

knack n flair, faculty, facility, hang (infml), bent, skill, talent, genius, gift, trick, propensity, ability, expertise, skilfulness, forte, capacity, handiness, dexterity, quickness, turn.

knapsack n bag, pack, haversack, rucksack, backpack.

knead v manipulate, press, massage, work, ply, squeeze, shape, rub,

form, mould, knuckle.

knell n toll, ringing, chime, peel, knoll.

knick-knack n trinket, trifle, bauble, gewgaw, gimcrack, bric-à-brac, plaything.

knife n blade, cutter, carver, dagger, pen-knife, pocket-knife, switchblade, jack-knife, flick-knife, machete.
◇ v cut, rip, slash, stab, pierce, wound.

knit v 1 JOIN, unite, secure, connect, tie, fasten, link, mend, interlace, intertwine. 2 KNOT, loop, crochet, weave. 3 WRINKLE, furrow.

knock v hit, strike, rap, thump, pound, slap, smack.
◇ n blow, box, rap, thump, cuff, clip, pounding, hammering, slap, smack.
• **knock about** 1 WANDER, travel, roam, rove, saunter, traipse, ramble, range. 2 ASSOCIATE, go around. 3 BEAT UP, batter, abuse, mistreat, hurt, hit, bash, damage, maltreat, manhandle, bruise, buffet.
• **knock down** demolish, destroy, fell, floor, level, wreck, raze, pound, batter, clout, smash, wallop.
• **knock off** 1 (infml) FINISH, cease, stop, pack (it) in, clock off, clock out, terminate. 2 (infml) STEAL, rob, pilfer, pinch (infml), nick (infml), filch. 3 DEDUCT, take away. 4 (sl) KILL, murder, slay, assassinate, do away with, bump off (infml), do in (infml), waste (sl).

knockout n success, triumph, hit, sensation, smash (infml), smash-hit (infml), winner, stunner (infml).
◉ flop, loser.

knot v tie, secure, bind, entangle, tangle, knit, entwine, ravel, weave.
◇ n 1 TIE, bond, joint, fastening, loop, splice, hitch. 2 BUNCH, cluster, clump, group.

Types of knot include: bend, Blackwall hitch, bow, bowline, running bowline, carrick bend, clove hitch, Englishman's tie (or knot), figure of eight, fisherman's bend, fisherman's knot, granny knot, half-hitch, hangman's knot, hitch, loop knot, overhand knot (or thumb knot), reef knot (or square knot), rolling hitch, sheepshank, sheet bend, slipknot, surgeon's knot, swab hitch, timber hitch, Turk's head, wall knot, weaver's knot, Windsor knot.

know v **1** *she knows French*: understand, comprehend, apprehend, perceive, notice, be aware, fathom, experience, realize, see, undergo. **2** *I know George*: be acquainted with, be familiar with, recognize, identify. **3** *know a good wine*: distinguish, discriminate, discern, differentiate, make out, tell.

knowledge n **1** LEARNING, scholarship, erudition, education, schooling, instruction, tuition, information, enlightenment, know-how. **2** ACQUAINTANCE, familiarity, awareness, cognizance, intimacy, consciousness. **3** UNDERSTANDING, comprehension, cognition, apprehension, recognition, judgement, discernment, ability, grasp, wisdom, intelligence.
⊠ **1** ignorance. **2** unawareness.

knowledgeable adj **1** EDUCATED, scholarly, learned, well-informed, lettered, intelligent. **2** AWARE, acquainted, conscious, familiar, au fait, in the know (*infml*), conversant, experienced.
⊠ **1** ignorant.

known adj acknowledged, recognized, well-known, noted, obvious, patent, plain, admitted, familiar, avowed, commonplace, published, confessed, celebrated, famous.

kowtow v defer, cringe, fawn, grovel, pander, suck up (*infml*), brown-nose (*US sl*), toady (*infml*), flatter, kneel.

Ll

label n **1** TAG, ticket, docket, mark, marker, sticker, trademark. **2** DESCRIPTION, categorization, identification, characterization, classification, badge, brand.
◇ v **1** TAG, mark, stamp. **2** DEFINE, describe, classify, categorize, characterize, identify, class, designate, brand, call, dub, name.

laborious adj **1** HARD, arduous, difficult, strenuous, backbreaking, tough, wearisome, tiresome, uphill, onerous, heavy, toilsome. **2** HARD-WORKING, industrious, painstaking, indefatigable, diligent.
🖃 **1** easy, effortless. **2** lazy.

labour n **1** WORK, task, job, chore, toil, effort, exertion, drudgery, grind (infml), slog (infml), sweat (infml). **2** WORKERS, employees, workforce, labourers. **3** CHILDBIRTH, birth, delivery, labour pains, contractions.
🖃 **1** ease, leisure. **2** management.
◇ v **1** WORK, toil, drudge, slave, strive, endeavour, struggle, grind (infml), sweat (infml), plod, travail (fml). **2** TOSS, pitch, roll. **3** OVERDO, overemphasize, dwell on, elaborate, overstress, strain.
🖃 **1** laze, idle, lounge.

labourer n manual worker, blue-collar worker, navvy, hand, worker, drudge, hireling.

labyrinth n maze, complexity, intricacy, complication, puzzle, riddle, windings, tangle, jungle.

lace n **1** NETTING, mesh-work, open-work, tatting, crochet. **2** STRING, cord, thong, tie, shoelace, bootlace.
◇ v **1** TIE, do up, fasten, thread,
close, bind, attach, string, intertwine, interweave. **2** ADD TO, mix in, spike (infml), fortify.

lacerate v tear, rip, rend, cut, gash, slash, wound, claw, mangle, maim, torture, torment, distress, afflict.

lack n need, want, scarcity, shortage, insufficiency, dearth, deficiency, absence, scantiness, vacancy, void, privation, deprivation, destitution, emptiness.
🖃 abundance, profusion.
◇ v need, want, require, miss.

lacking adj needing, wanting, without, short of, missing, minus, inadequate, deficient, defective, flawed.

lacklustre adj drab, dull, flat, boring, leaden, lifeless, dim, unimaginative.
🖃 brilliant, inspired.

laconic adj terse, succinct, pithy, concise, crisp, taciturn, short, curt, brief.
🖃 verbose, wordy.

lad n boy, youth, youngster, kid (infml), schoolboy, chap, guy (infml), fellow.

lag v dawdle, loiter, hang back, linger, straggle, trail, saunter, delay, shuffle, tarry, idle.
🖃 hurry, lead.

lair n den, burrow, hole, nest, earth, form, roost, retreat, hideout, refuge, sanctuary, stronghold.

lake n lagoon, reservoir, loch, mere, tarn.

lame adj **1** DISABLED, handicapped, crippled, limping, hobbling.

2 WEAK, feeble, flimsy, inadequate, unsatisfactory, poor.
⊞ **1** able-bodied. **2** convincing.

lament v mourn, bewail, bemoan, grieve, sorrow, weep, wail, complain, deplore, regret.
⊞ rejoice, celebrate.
◇ n lamentation, dirge, elegy, requiem, threnody (fml), complaint, moan, wail.

lamentable adj **1** DEPLORABLE, regrettable, mournful, distressing, tragic, unfortunate, sorrowful. **2** MEAGRE, low, inadequate, insufficient, mean, unsatisfactory, pitiful, miserable, poor, disappointing.

lampoon n satire, skit, caricature, parody, send-up (infml), spoof, take-off, burlesque.
◇ v satirize, caricature, parody, send up, take off, spoof, make fun of, ridicule, mock, burlesque.

land n **1** EARTH, ground, soil, terra firma. **2** PROPERTY, grounds, estate, real estate, country, countryside, farmland, tract. **3** COUNTRY, nation, region, territory, province.
◇ v **1** ALIGHT, disembark, dock, berth, touch down, come to rest, arrive, deposit, wind up, end up, drop, settle, turn up. **2** OBTAIN, secure, gain, get, acquire, net, capture, achieve, win.

landlord n owner, proprietor, host, publican, innkeeper, hotelier, restaurateur, hotel-keeper, freeholder.
⊞ tenant.

landmark n feature, monument, signpost, turning-point, watershed, milestone, beacon, cairn.

landscape n scene, scenery, view, panorama, outlook, vista, prospect, countryside, aspect.

landslide n landslip, rock-fall, avalanche.
◇ adj overwhelming, decisive,

emphatic, runaway.

language n **1** SPEECH, vocabulary, terminology, parlance. **2** TALK, conversation, discourse. **3** WORDING, style, phraseology, phrasing, expression, utterance, diction.

Language terms include: brogue, dialect, idiom, patois, tongue, pidgin, creole, lingua franca, vernacular, argot, cant, jargon, double speak, gobbledegook, buzzword, journalese, lingo (infml), patter, slang, rhyming slang; etymology, lexicography, linguistics, phonetics, semantics, syntax, usage, grammar, orthography, sociolinguistics.

Languages of the world include: Afrikaans, Amharic, Arabic, Armenian, Bantu, Basque, Belorussian, Bengali, Burmese, Catalan, Chinese, Cornish, Czech, Danish, Dari, Dutch, English, Esperanto, Estonian, Farsi, Finnish, Flemish, French, Gaelic, German, Greek, Hawaiian, Hebrew, Hindi, Hungarian, Icelandic, Indonesian, Inuit, Irish, Italian, Japanese, Korean, Kurdish, Lapp, Latin, Latvian, Lithuanian, Magyar, Malay, Maltese, Mandarin, Manx, Maori, Nahuatl, Norwegian, Pashto, Persian, Polish, Portuguese, Punjabi, Quechua, Romanian, Romany, Russian, Sanskrit, Serbo-Croat, Sinhalese, Slovak, Slovene, Somali, Spanish, Swahili, Swedish, Tamil, Thai, Tibetan, Tupí, Turkish, Ukrainian, Urdu, Vietnamese, Volapök, Welsh, Yiddish, Zulu.

---

languish v **1** WILT, droop, fade, fail, flag, wither, waste away, weaken, sink, faint, decline, mope, waste, grieve, sorrow, sigh, sicken. **2** PINE, yearn, want, long, desire, hanker, hunger.
⊞ **1** flourish.

lanky *adj* gaunt, gangling, scrawny, tall, thin, scraggy, weedy.
⊜ short, squat.

lap¹ *v* drink, sip, sup, lick.

lap² *n* circuit, round, orbit, tour, loop, course, circle, distance.
◇ *v* wrap, fold, envelop, enfold, swathe, surround, cover, swaddle, overlap.

lapse *n* **1** ERROR, slip, mistake, negligence, omission, oversight, fault, failing, indiscretion, aberration, backsliding, relapse. **2** FALL, descent, decline, drop, deterioration. **3** BREAK, gap, interval, lull, interruption, intermission, pause.
◇ *v* **1** DECLINE, fall, sink, drop, slide, slip, deteriorate, fail, worsen, degenerate, backslide. **2** EXPIRE, run out, end, stop, terminate.

large *adj* **1** BIG, huge, immense, massive, vast, sizable, great, giant, gigantic, bulky, enormous, king-sized, broad, considerable, monumental, substantial. **2** FULL, extensive, generous, liberal, roomy, plentiful, spacious, grand, sweeping, grandiose.
⊜ **1** small, tiny.
• **at large** free, at liberty, on the loose, on the run, independent.

largely *adv* mainly, principally, chiefly, generally, predominantly, primarily, mostly, considerably, by and large, widely, extensively, greatly.

lark *n* escapade, antic, fling, prank, romp, skylark (*infml*), revel, mischief, frolic, caper, game.

lash¹ *n* blow, whip, stroke, swipe, hit.
◇ *v* **1** WHIP, flog, beat, hit, thrash, strike, scourge. **2** ATTACK, criticize, lay into, scold.

lash² *v* tie, bind, fasten, secure, make fast, join, affix, rope, tether, strap.

last¹ *adj* final, ultimate, closing, latest, rearmost, terminal, furthest, concluding, remotest, utmost, extreme, conclusive, definitive.
⊜ first, initial.
◇ *adv* finally, ultimately, behind, after.
⊜ first, firstly.
• **at last** eventually, finally, in the end, in due course, at length.

last² *v* continue, endure, remain, persist, keep (on), survive, hold out, carry on, wear, stay, hold on, stand up, abide (*fml*).
⊜ cease, stop, fade.

lasting *adj* enduring, unchanging, unceasing, unending, continuing, permanent, perpetual, lifelong, long-standing, long-term.
⊜ brief, fleeting, short-lived.

latch *n* fastening, catch, bar, bolt, lock, hook, hasp.

late *adj* **1** OVERDUE, behind, delayed, behind hand, slow, unpunctual, last-minute. **2** FORMER, previous, departed, dead, deceased, past, preceding, old. **3** RECENT, up-to-date, current, fresh, new.
⊜ **1** early, punctual.

lately *adv* recently, of late, latterly.

latent *adj* potential, dormant, undeveloped, unrealized, lurking, unexpressed, unseen, secret, concealed, hidden, invisible, underlying, veiled.
⊜ active, conspicuous.

later *adv* next, afterwards, after, subsequently, successively.
⊜ earlier.

lateral *adj* sideways, side, oblique, sideward, edgeways, marginal, flanking.

lather *n* **1** FOAM, suds, soap-suds, froth, bubbles, soap, shampoo. **2** AGITATION, fluster, fuss, dither, state (*infml*), flutter, flap (*infml*), fever.
◇ *v* foam, froth, soap, shampoo, whip up.

latitude *n* **1** SCOPE, range, room, space, play, clearance, breadth, width, spread, sweep, reach, span, field, extent. **2** FREEDOM, liberty, licence, leeway, indulgence.

latter *adj* last-mentioned, last, later, closing, concluding, ensuing, succeeding, successive, second.
⊜ former.

laugh *v* chuckle, giggle, guffaw, snigger, titter, chortle, split one's sides, fall about (*infml*), crease up (*infml*).
◇ *n* giggle, chuckle, snigger, titter, guffaw, chortle, lark, scream (*infml*), hoot (*infml*), joke.
• **laugh at** mock, ridicule, deride, jeer, make fun of, scoff at, scorn, taunt.

laughable *adj* **1** FUNNY, amusing, comical, humorous, hilarious, droll, farcical, diverting. **2** RIDICULOUS, absurd, ludicrous, preposterous, nonsensical, derisory, derisive.
⊜ **1** serious.

laughing-stock *n* figure of fun, butt, victim, target, fair game.

laughter *n* laughing, giggling, chuckling, chortling, guffawing, tittering, hilarity, amusement, merriment, mirth, glee, convulsions.

launch *v* **1** PROPEL, dispatch, discharge, send off, project, float, set in motion, throw, fire. **2** BEGIN, commence, start, embark on, establish, found, open, initiate, inaugurate, introduce, instigate.

lavatory *n* toilet, loo (*infml*), WC, bathroom, cloakroom, washroom, rest room (*N Am*), water-closet, public convenience, Ladies (*infml*), Gents (*infml*), bog (*sl*), john (*US sl*), urinal, powder room.

lavish *adj* **1** ABUNDANT, lush, luxuriant, plentiful, profuse, unlimited, prolific. **2** GENEROUS, liberal, open-handed, extravagant, thriftless, prodigal, immoderate, intemperate, unstinting.
⊜ **1** scant. **2** frugal, thrifty.

law *n* **1** RULE, act, decree, edict, order, statute, regulation, command, ordinance, charter, constitution, enactment. **2** PRINCIPLE, axiom, criterion, standard, precept, formula, code, canon. **3** JURISPRUDENCE, legislation, litigation.

law-abiding *adj* obedient, upright, orderly, lawful, honest, honourable, decent, good.
⊜ lawless.

lawful *adj* legal, permissible, legitimate, legalized, authorized, allowable, warranted, valid, proper, rightful.
⊜ illegal, unlawful, illicit.

lawless *adj* disorderly, rebellious, anarchic(al), unruly, riotous, mutinous, unrestrained, chaotic, wild, reckless.
⊜ law-abiding.

lawsuit *n* litigation, suit, action, proceedings, case, prosecution, dispute, process, trial, argument, contest, cause.

lawyer *n* solicitor, barrister, QC, advocate, attorney, counsel.

lax *adj* **1** CASUAL, careless, easy-going, slack, lenient, negligent, remiss. **2** IMPRECISE, inexact, indefinite, loose.
⊜ **1** strict. **2** exact.

lay¹ *v* **1** PUT, place, deposit, set down, settle, lodge, plant, set, establish, leave. **2** ARRANGE, position, set out, locate, work out, devise, prepare, present, submit. **3** ATTRIBUTE, ascribe, assign, charge.
• **lay in** store (up), stock up, amass, accumulate, hoard, stockpile, gather, collect, build up, glean.
• **lay into** (*infml*) attack, assail, pitch into, set about, tear into, let fly at, hit out at.
• **lay off 1** DISMISS, discharge, make redundant, sack (*infml*), pay off, let go. **2** (*infml*) GIVE UP, drop, stop, quit, cease, desist, leave off, leave alone, let up.

● **lay on** provide, supply, cater, furnish, give, set up.

● **lay out 1** DISPLAY, set out, spread out, exhibit, arrange, plan, design. **2** (*infml*) KNOCK OUT, fell, flatten, demolish. **3** (*infml*) SPEND, pay, shell out (*infml*), fork out (*infml*), give, invest.

● **lay up** store (up), hoard, accumulate, amass, keep, save, put away.

lay² *adj* **1** LAIC, secular. **2** AMATEUR, non-professional, non-specialist.
▣ **1** clergy. **2** expert.

layer *n* **1** COVER, coating, coat, covering, film, blanket, mantle, sheet, lamina. **2** STRATUM, seam, thickness, tier, bed, plate, row, ply.

layman *n* **1** LAYPERSON, parishioner. **2** AMATEUR, outsider.
▣ **1** clergyman. **2** expert.

layout *n* arrangement, design, outline, plan, sketch, draft, map.

laze *v* idle, loaf (*infml*), lounge, sit around, lie around, loll.

lazy *adj* idle, slothful, slack, work-shy, inactive, lethargic.
▣ industrious.

lead *v* **1** GUIDE, conduct, escort, steer, pilot, usher. **2** RULE, govern, head, preside over, direct, supervise. **3** INFLUENCE, persuade, incline. **4** SURPASS, outdo, excel, outstrip, transcend. **5** PASS, spend, live, undergo.
▣ **1** follow.
◇ *n* **1** PRIORITY, precedence, start, first place, van, vanguard, advantage, edge, margin. **2** LEADERSHIP, guidance, direction, example, model. **3** CLUE, hint, indication, guide, tip, suggestion. **4** TITLE ROLE, starring part, principal.

● **lead off** begin, commence, open, get going, start (off), inaugurate, initiate, kick off (*infml*), start the ball rolling.

● **lead on** entice, lure, seduce, tempt, draw on, beguile, persuade, string along, deceive, trick.

● **lead to** cause, result in, produce, bring about, bring on, contribute to, tend towards.

● **lead up to** prepare (the way) for, approach, introduce, make overtures, pave the way.

leader *n* head, chief, director, ruler, principal, commander, captain, boss (*infml*), superior, chieftain, ringleader, guide, conductor.
▣ follower.

leadership *n* direction, control, command, management, authority, guidance, domination, pre-eminence, premiership, administration, sway, directorship.

leading *adj* main, principal, chief, primary, first, supreme, outstanding, foremost, dominant, ruling, superior, greatest, highest, governing, pre-eminent, number one.
▣ subordinate.

leaflet *n* pamphlet, booklet, brochure, circular, handout.

league *n* **1** ASSOCIATION, union, confederation, alliance, federation, confederacy, coalition, combination, band, syndicate, guild, consortium, cartel, combine, partnership, fellowship, compact. **2** CATEGORY, class, level, group.

● **in league** allied, collaborating, conspiring.

leak *n* **1** CRACK, hole, opening, puncture, crevice, chink. **2** LEAKAGE, leaking, seepage, drip, oozing, percolation. **3** DISCLOSURE, divulgence.
◇ *v* **1** SEEP, drip, ooze, escape, spill, trickle, percolate, exude, discharge. **2** DIVULGE, disclose, reveal, let slip, make known, make public, tell, give away, pass on.

leaky *adj* leaking, holey, perforated, punctured, split, cracked, porous, permeable.

lean¹ *v* **1** SLANT, slope, bend, tilt, list, tend. **2** RECLINE, prop, rest. **3** INCLINE, favour, prefer.

lean² adj 1 THIN, skinny, bony, gaunt, lank, angular, slim, scraggy, scrawny, emaciated. 2 SCANTY, inadequate, bare, barren.
⊜ 1 fat.

leaning n tendency, inclination, propensity, partiality, liking, bent, bias, disposition, aptitude.

leap v 1 JUMP (OVER), bound, spring, vault, clear, skip, hop, bounce, caper, gambol. 2 SOAR, surge, increase, rocket, escalate, rise.
⊜ 2 drop, fall.
◇ n 1 JUMP, bound, spring, vault, hop, skip, caper. 2 INCREASE, upsurge, upswing, surge, rise, escalation.

learn v 1 GRASP, comprehend, understand, master, acquire, pick up, gather, assimilate, discern. 2 MEMORIZE, learn by heart. 3 DISCOVER, find out, ascertain, hear, detect, determine.

learned adj scholarly, erudite, well-informed, well-read, cultured, academic, lettered, literate, intellectual, versed.
⊜ uneducated, illiterate.

learner n novice, beginner, student, trainee, pupil, scholar, apprentice.

learning n scholarship, erudition, education, schooling, knowledge, information, letters, study, wisdom, tuition, culture, edification, research.

lease v let, loan, rent, hire, sublet, charter.

least adj smallest, lowest, minimum, fewest, slightest, poorest.
⊜ most.

leave¹ v 1 DEPART, go, go away, set out, take off, decamp, exit, move, quit, retire, withdraw, disappear, do a bunk (infml). 2 ABANDON, desert, forsake, give up, drop, relinquish, renounce, pull out, surrender, desist, cease. 3 ASSIGN, commit, entrust, consign, bequeath, will, hand down, leave behind, give over, transmit.
⊜ 1 arrive. 3 receive.

• **leave off** stop, cease, discontinue, desist, abstain, refrain, lay off, quit, terminate, break off, end, halt, give over.

• **leave out** omit, exclude, overlook, ignore, except, disregard, count out, pass over, cut (out), eliminate, neglect, reject, cast aside, bar.

leave² n 1 PERMISSION, authorization, consent, allowance, sanction, warrant, concession, dispensation, indulgence, liberty, freedom. 2 HOLIDAY, time off, vacation, sabbatical, furlough.
⊜ 1 refusal, rejection.

lecture n 1 DISCOURSE, address, lesson, speech, talk, instruction. 2 REPRIMAND, scolding, rebuke, reproof, scolding, harangue, censure, chiding, telling-off (infml), talking-to (infml), dressing-down (infml).
◇ v 1 TALK, teach, hold forth, speak, expound, address. 2 REPRIMAND, reprove, scold, admonish, harangue, chide, censure, tell off (infml).

ledge n shelf, sill, mantle, ridge, projection, step.

leeway n space, room, latitude, elbow-room, play, scope.

left adj 1 LEFT-HAND, port, sinistral. 2 LEFT-WING, socialist, radical, progressive, revolutionary, liberal, communist, red (infml).
⊜ 1 right. 2 right-wing.

left-overs n leavings, remainder, remains, remnants, residue, surplus, scraps, sweepings, refuse, dregs, excess.

leg n 1 LIMB, member, shank, pin (infml), stump (infml). 2 SUPPORT, prop, upright, brace. 3 STAGE, part, section, portion, stretch, segment, lap.

legacy n bequest, endowment, gift, heritage, inheritance, birthright, estate, heirloom.

legal adj 1 LAWFUL, legitimate, permissible, sanctioned, allowed,

authorized, allowable, legalized, constitutional, valid, warranted, above-board, proper, rightful.
2 JUDICIAL, forensic.
⊟ **1** illegal.

Legal terms include: *courts*: county court, courthouse, courtroom, Court of Appeal, Court of Protection, Court of Session, Crown Court, European Court of Human Rights, European Court of Justice, High Court of Justice, House of Lords, International Court of Justice, juvenile court, magistrates' court, Old Bailey, sheriff court, small claims court, Supreme Court (*N Am*); *criminal law*: acquittal, age of consent, alibi, arrest, bail, caution, charge, confession, contempt of court, dock, fine, guilty, indictment, innocent, malice aforethought, pardon, parole, plead guilty, plead not guilty, prisoner, probation, remand, reprieve, sentence; *marriage and divorce*: adultery, alimony, annulment, bigamy, decree absolute, decree nisi, divorce, maintenance, settlement; *people*: accessory, accomplice, accused, advocate, Attorney-General, barrister, brief (*infml*), clerk of the court, client, commissioner of oaths, convict, coroner, criminal, defendant, Director of Public Prosecutions, DPP, executor, felon, judge, jury, Justice of the Peace, JP, juvenile, Law Lord, lawyer, Lord Advocate, Lord Chancellor, Lord Chief Justice, liquidator, magistrate, notary public, offender, plaintiff, procurator fiscal, receiver, Queen's Counsel, QC, sheriff, solicitor, witness, young offender; *property or ownership*: asset, conveyance, copyright, deed, easement, endowment, estate, exchange of contracts, fee simple, foreclosure, freehold, inheritance, intestacy, lease, leasehold, legacy, mortgage, patent, tenancy, title, trademark, will; *miscellaneous*: act of God, act of parliament, adjournment, affidavit, agreement, allegation, amnesty, appeal, arbitration, bar, bill of rights, bench, brief, bylaw, charter, civil law, claim, codicil, common law, constitution, court case, court martial, cross-examine, custody, damages, defence, equity, eviction, evidence, extradition, hearing, hung jury, indemnity, injunction, inquest, inquiry, judgement, judiciary, lawsuit, legal aid, liability, mandate, misadventure, miscarriage of justice, oath, party, penalty, power of attorney, precedent, probate, proceedings, proof, proxy, public inquiry, repeal, sanction, settlement, statute, subpoena, sue, summons, testimony, trial, tribunal, verdict, waiver, ward of court, warrant, will, writ. *see also* **crime**.

---

legalize *v* legitimize, license, permit, sanction, allow, authorize, warrant, validate, approve.

legend *n* **1** MYTH, story, tale, folk-tale, fable, fiction, narrative.
2 INSCRIPTION, caption, key, motto.

legendary *adj* **1** MYTHICAL, fabulous, story-book, fictitious, traditional.
2 FAMOUS, celebrated, renowned, well-known, illustrious.

legible *adj* readable, intelligible, decipherable, clear, distinct, neat.
⊟ illegible.

legislate *v* enact, ordain, authorize, codify, constitutionalize, prescribe, establish.

legislation *n* **1** LAW, statute, regulation, bill, act, charter, authorization, ruling, measure.
2 LAW-MAKING, enactment, codification.

legislative *adj* law-making, law-giving, judicial, parliamentary, congressional, senatorial.

legislator *n* law-maker, law-giver, member of parliament, parliamentarian.

legislature *n* assembly, chamber, house, parliament, congress, senate.

legitimate *adj* 1 LEGAL, lawful, authorized, statutory, rightful, proper, correct, real, acknowledged. 2 REASONABLE, sensible, admissible, acceptable, justifiable, warranted, well-founded, valid, true.
⊜ 1 illegal. 2 invalid.

leisure *n* relaxation, rest, spare time, time off, ease, freedom, liberty, recreation, retirement, holiday, vacation.
⊜ work.

leisurely *adj* unhurried, slow, relaxed, comfortable, easy, unhasty, tranquil, restful, gentle, carefree, laid-back (*infml*), lazy, loose.
⊜ rushed, hectic.

lend *v* 1 LOAN, advance. 2 GIVE, grant, bestow, provide, furnish, confer, supply, impart, contribute.
⊜ 1 borrow.

length *n* 1 EXTENT, distance, reach, measure, piece, portion, section, segment. 2 DURATION, period, term, stretch, space, span.

lengthen *v* stretch, extend, draw out, elongate, prolong, protract, spin out, eke out, pad out, increase, expand, continue.
⊜ reduce, shorten.

lengthy *adj* long, prolonged, protracted, extended, lengthened, overlong, long-drawn-out, long-winded, rambling, diffuse, verbose, drawn-out, interminable.
⊜ brief, concise.

lenient *adj* tolerant, forbearing, sparing, indulgent, merciful, kind, forgiving, soft-hearted, mild, gentle, compassionate.
⊜ strict, severe.

lessen *v* decrease, reduce, diminish, lower, ease, abate, contract, die down, dwindle, lighten, slow down, weaken, shrink, abridge, de-escalate, erode, minimize, narrow, moderate, slack, flag, fail, deaden, impair.
⊜ grow, increase.

lesser *adj* lower, secondary, inferior, smaller, subordinate, slighter, minor.
⊜ greater.

lesson *n* 1 CLASS, period, instruction, lecture, tutorial, teaching, coaching. 2 ASSIGNMENT, exercise, homework, practice, task, drill. 3 EXAMPLE, model, warning, deterrent.

let *v* 1 PERMIT, allow, give leave, give permission, authorize, consent to, agree to, sanction, grant, OK, enable, tolerate. 2 LEASE, hire, rent.
⊜ 1 prohibit, forbid.
• **let in** admit, accept, receive, take in, include, incorporate, welcome.
⊜ prohibit, bar, forbid.
• **let off** 1 EXCUSE, absolve, pardon, exempt, forgive, acquit, exonerate, spare, ignore, liberate, release. 2 DISCHARGE, detonate, fire, explode, emit.
⊜ 1 punish.
• **let out** 1 FREE, release, let go, discharge, leak (*infml*). 2 REVEAL, disclose, make known, utter, betray, let slip.
⊜ 1 keep in.
• **let up** abate, subside, ease (up), moderate, slacken, diminish, decrease, stop, end, cease, halt.
⊜ continue.

let-down *n* disappointment, anticlimax, disillusionment, setback, betrayal, desertion, wash-out (*infml*).

lethal *adj* fatal, deadly, deathly, mortal, dangerous, poisonous, noxious, destructive, devastating.
⊜ harmless, safe.

lethargy *n* lassitude, listlessness, sluggishness, torpor, dullness, inertia, slowness, apathy, inaction,

indifference, sleepiness, drowsiness, stupor.
⊜ liveliness.

letter *n* **1** NOTE, message, line, missive, epistle (*fml*), dispatch, communication, acknowledgement, chit. **2** CHARACTER, symbol, sign, grapheme.

level *adj* **1** FLAT, smooth, even, flush, horizontal, aligned, plane. **2** EQUAL, balanced, even, on a par, neck and neck (*infml*), even-stevens (*infml*), matching, uniform.
⊜ **1** uneven. **2** unequal.
◇ *v* **1** DEMOLISH, destroy, devastate, flatten, knock down, raze, pull down, bulldoze, tear down, lay low. **2** EVEN OUT, flush, plane, smooth, equalize. **3** DIRECT, point.
◇ *n* **1** HEIGHT, elevation, altitude. **2** POSITION, rank, status, class, degree, grade, standard, standing, plane, echelon, layer, stratum, storey, stage, zone.

level-headed *adj* calm, balanced, even-tempered, sensible, steady, reasonable, composed, cool, unflappable, sane, self-possessed, dependable.

lever *n* bar, crowbar, jemmy, handle, joystick.
◇ *v* force, prise, pry, raise, dislodge, jemmy, shift, move, heave.

levity *n* light-heartedness, frivolity, facetiousness, flippancy, irreverence, triviality, silliness.
⊜ seriousness.

levy *v* tax, impose, exact, demand, charge.
◇ *n* tax, toll, subscription, fee, contribution, duty, tariff, collection.

lewd *adj* obscene, smutty, indecent, bawdy, pornographic, salacious, licentious, lascivious, impure, vulgar, unchaste, lustful.
⊜ decent, chaste.

liability *n* **1** ACCOUNTABILITY, duty, obligation, responsibility, onus.

2 DEBT, arrears, indebtedness. **3** DRAWBACK, disadvantage, hindrance, impediment, drag (*infml*).

liable *adj* **1** INCLINED, likely, apt, disposed, prone, tending, susceptible. **2** RESPONSIBLE, answerable, accountable, amenable.

liaison *n* **1** CONTACT, connection, go-between, link. **2** LOVE AFFAIR, affair, romance, intrigue, amour, entanglement.

liar *n* falsifier, perjurer, deceiver, fibber (*infml*).

libel *n* defamation, slur, smear, slander, vilification, aspersion, calumny.
◇ *v* defame, slur, smear, slander, vilify, malign.

libellous *adj* defamatory, vilifying, slanderous, derogatory, maligning, injurious, scurrilous, untrue.

liberal *adj* **1** BROAD-MINDED, open-minded, tolerant, lenient. **2** PROGRESSIVE, reformist, moderate. **3** GENEROUS, ample, bountiful, lavish, plentiful, handsome.
⊜ **1** narrow-minded. **2** conservative. **3** mean, miserly.

liberate *v* free, emancipate, release, let loose, let go, let out, set free, deliver, unchain, discharge, rescue, ransom.
⊜ imprison, enslave.

liberty *n* **1** FREEDOM, emancipation, release, independence, autonomy. **2** LICENCE, permission, sanction, right, authorization, dispensation, franchise. **3** FAMILIARITY, disrespect, overfamiliarity, presumption, impertinence, impudence.
⊜ **1** imprisonment. **3** respect.
● **at liberty** free, unconstrained, unrestricted, not confined.

licence *n* **1** PERMISSION, permit, leave, warrant, authorization, authority, certificate, charter, right, imprimatur, entitlement, privilege, dispensation, carte blanche, freedom, liberty,

exemption, independence.
2 ABANDON, dissipation, excess, immoderation, indulgence, lawlessness, unruliness, anarchy, disorder, debauchery, dissoluteness, impropriety, irresponsibility.
🔁 **1** prohibition, restriction.
2 decorum, moderation.

license v permit, allow, authorize, certify, warrant, entitle, empower, sanction, commission, accredit.
🔁 ban, prohibit.

licentious adj debauched, depraved, decadent, dissolute, profligate, lascivious, immoral, abandoned, lewd, promiscuous, libertine, impure, lax, lustful, disorderly, wanton, unchaste.
🔁 modest, chaste.

lick v touch, lap, dart, flick, flicker, play over.

lie¹ v perjure, misrepresent, fabricate, falsify, fib (infml), invent, equivocate, prevaricate, forswear oneself (fml).
◊ n falsehood, untruth, falsification, fabrication, invention, fiction, deceit, fib (infml), falsity, white lie, prevarication, whopper (infml), porkie (infml).
🔁 truth.

lie² v be, exist, dwell, belong, extend, remain.
• **lie down** repose, rest, recline, stretch out, lounge, couch, laze.

life n **1** BEING, existence, animation, breath, viability, entity, soul.
2 DURATION, course, span, career.
3 LIVELINESS, vigour, vitality, vivacity, verve, zest, energy, élan, spirit, sparkle, activity.

lifeless adj **1** DEAD, deceased, cold, defunct, unconscious, inanimate, insensible, stiff. **2** LETHARGIC, listless, sluggish, dull, apathetic, passive, insipid, colourless, slow. **3** BARREN, bare, empty, desolate, arid.
🔁 **1** alive. **2** lively.

lifelike adj realistic, true-to-life,

real, true, vivid, natural, authentic, faithful, exact, graphic.
🔁 unrealistic, unnatural.

lifelong adj lifetime, long-lasting, long-standing, persistent, lasting, enduring, abiding, permanent, constant.
🔁 impermanent, temporary.

lift v **1** she lifted the chair: raise, elevate, hoist, upraise. **2** he lifted their spirits: uplift, exalt, buoy up, boost. **3** the ban has been lifted: revoke, cancel, relax.
🔁 **1** drop. **2** lower.

light¹ n **1** ILLUMINATION, brightness, brilliance, luminescence, radiance, glow, ray, shine, glare, gleam, glint, lustre, flash, blaze. **2** LAMP, lantern, lighter, match, torch, candle, bulb, beacon. **3** DAY, daybreak, daylight, daytime, dawn, sunrise.
4 ENLIGHTENMENT, explanation, elucidation, understanding.
🔁 **1** darkness. **3** night.
◊ v **1** IGNITE, fire, set alight, set fire to, kindle. **2** ILLUMINATE, light up, lighten, brighten, animate, cheer, switch on, turn on, put on.
🔁 **1** extinguish. **2** darken.
◊ adj **1** ILLUMINATED, bright, brilliant, luminous, glowing, shining, well-lit, sunny. **2** PALE, pastel, fair, blond(e), bleached, faded, faint.
🔁 **1** dark. **2** black.

light² adj **1** WEIGHTLESS, airy, insubstantial, delicate, buoyant, flimsy, feathery, slight.
2 TRIVIAL, inconsiderable, trifling, inconsequential, worthless.
3 CHEERFUL, cheery, carefree, lively, merry, blithe. **4** ENTERTAINING, funny, amusing, humorous, frivolous, witty, pleasing.
🔁 **1** heavy, weighty. **2** important, serious. **3** solemn. **4** serious.

lighten¹ v illuminate, illumine, brighten, light up, shine.
🔁 darken.

lighten² v **1** EASE, lessen, unload, lift,

relieve, reduce, mitigate, alleviate.
2 BRIGHTEN, cheer, encourage,
hearten, inspirit, uplift, gladden,
revive, elate, buoy up, inspire.
▣ **1** burden. **2** depress.

light-headed adj **1** FAINT, giddy,
dizzy, woozy (infml), delirious.
2 FLIGHTY, scatter-brained (infml),
ditzy (infml), foolish, frivolous, silly,
superficial, shallow, feather-brained
(infml), flippant, vacuous, trifling.
▣ **2** level-headed, solemn.

light-hearted adj cheerful, jolly,
joyful, happy-go-lucky, bright,
carefree, untroubled, merry, sunny,
glad, elated, jovial, playful.
▣ sad, unhappy, serious.

likable adj loveable, pleasing,
appealing, agreeable, charming,
engaging, winsome, pleasant,
amiable, congenial, attractive,
sympathetic.
▣ unpleasant, disagreeable.

like¹ adj similar, resembling, same,
alike, identical, equivalent, akin,
corresponding, related, relating,
parallel, allied, analogous,
approximating.
▣ unlike, dissimilar.

like² v **1** ENJOY, delight in, care for,
admire, appreciate, love, adore, hold
dear, esteem, cherish, prize, relish,
revel in, approve, take (kindly) to.
2 PREFER, choose, select, feel inclined,
go for (infml), desire, want, wish.
▣ **1** dislike. **2** reject.

likelihood n likeliness, probability,
possibility, chance, prospect, liability.
▣ improbability, unlikeliness.

likely adj **1** PROBABLE, possible,
anticipated, expected, liable, prone,
tending, predictable, odds-on (infml),
inclined, foreseeable. **2** CREDIBLE,
believable, plausible, feasible,
reasonable. **3** PROMISING, hopeful,
pleasing, appropriate, proper,
suitable.
▣ **1** unlikely. **3** unsuitable.

◇ adv probably, presumably, like
as not, in all probability, no doubt,
doubtlessly.

liken v compare, equate, match,
parallel, relate, juxtapose, associate,
set beside.

likeness n **1** SIMILARITY, resemblance,
affinity, correspondence.
2 REPRESENTATION, image, copy,
reproduction, replica, facsimile,
effigy, picture, portrait, photograph,
counterpart. **3** SEMBLANCE, guise,
appearance, form.
▣ **1** dissimilarity, unlikeness.

likewise adv moreover, furthermore,
in addition, similarly, also, further,
besides, by the same token, too.

liking n fondness, love, affection,
preference, partiality, affinity,
predilection, penchant, taste,
attraction, appreciation, proneness,
propensity, inclination, tendency,
bias, desire, weakness, fancy, soft
spot.
▣ dislike, aversion, hatred.

limb n **1** ARM, leg, member,
appendage. **2** BRANCH, projection,
offshoot, wing, fork, extension, part,
spur, extremity, bough.

limber up v loosen up, warm up,
work out, exercise, prepare.

limelight n fame, celebrity,
spotlight, stardom, recognition,
renown, attention, prominence,
publicity, public eye.

limit n **1** BOUNDARY, bound,
border, frontier, confines, edge,
brink, threshold, verge, brim, end,
perimeter, rim, compass, termination,
ultimate, utmost, terminus, extent.
2 CHECK, curb, restraint, restriction,
limitation, ceiling, maximum, cut-off
point, saturation point, deadline.
◇ v check, curb, restrict, restrain,
constrain, confine, demarcate,
delimit, bound, hem in, ration,
specify, hinder.

limitation n **1** CHECK, restriction,

curb, control, constraint, restraint,
delimitation, demarcation, block.
2 INADEQUACY, shortcoming,
disadvantage, drawback, condition,
qualification, reservation.
⊒ **1** extension.

limited adj restricted, controlled,
circumscribed, constrained, confined,
checked, defined, finite, fixed,
minimal, narrow, inadequate,
insufficient.
⊒ limitless.

limitless adj unlimited, unbounded,
boundless, undefined, immeasurable,
incalculable, infinite, countless,
endless, never-ending, unending,
inexhaustible, untold, vast.
⊒ limited.

limp¹ v hobble, falter, stumble, hop,
shuffle, shamble.

limp² adj **1** FLABBY, drooping, flaccid,
floppy, loose, slack, relaxed, lax,
soft, flexible, pliable, limber. **2** TIRED,
weary, exhausted, spent, weak, worn
out, lethargic, debilitated, enervated.
⊒ **1** stiff. **2** vigorous.

line¹ n **1** STROKE, band, bar, stripe,
mark, strip, rule, dash, strand, streak,
underline, score, scratch. **2** ROW,
rank, queue, file, column, sequence,
series, procession, chain, trail. **3** LIMIT,
boundary, border, borderline, edge,
frontier, demarcation. **4** STRING, rope,
cord, cable, thread, filament, wire.
5 PROFILE, contour, outline, silhouette,
figure, formation, configuration.
6 CREASE, wrinkle, furrow, groove,
corrugation. **7** COURSE, direction,
path, track, route, axis. **8** APPROACH,
avenue, course (of action), belief,
ideology, policy, system, position,
practice, procedure, method,
scheme. **9** OCCUPATION, business,
trade, profession, vocation, job,
activity, interest, employment,
department, calling, field, province,
forte, area, pursuit, specialization,
specialism, speciality. **10** ANCESTRY,
family, descent, extraction, lineage,

pedigree, stock, race, breed.
• **line up 1** ALIGN, range, straighten,
marshal, order, regiment, queue up,
form ranks, fall in, array, assemble.
2 ORGANIZE, lay on, arrange, prepare,
produce, procure, secure, obtain.

line² v encase, cover, fill, pad, stuff,
reinforce.

lineage n (fml) ancestry, descent,
extraction, genealogy, family, line,
pedigree, race, stock, birth, breed,
house, heredity, ancestors, forebears,
descendants, offspring, succession.

lined adj **1** RULED, feint. **2** WRINKLED,
furrowed, wizened, worn.
⊒ **1** unlined. **2** smooth.

line-up n array, arrangement,
queue, row, selection, cast, team,
bill.

linger v loiter, delay, dally, tarry,
wait, remain, stay, hang on, lag,
procrastinate, dawdle, dilly-dally
(infml), idle, stop, endure, hold out,
last, persist, survive.
⊒ leave, rush.

lining n inlay, interfacing, padding,
backing, encasement, stiffening.

link n **1** CONNECTION, bond, tie,
association, joint, relationship, tie-
up, union, knot, liaison, attachment,
communication. **2** PART, piece,
element, member, constituent,
component, division.
◇ v connect, join, couple, tie, fasten,
unite, bind, amalgamate, merge,
associate, ally, bracket, identify,
relate, yoke, attach, hook up, join
forces, team up.
⊒ separate, unfasten.

lip n edge, brim, border, brink, rim,
margin, verge.

liquid n liquor, fluid, juice, drink,
sap, solution, lotion.
◇ adj fluid, flowing, liquefied,
watery, wet, runny, melted, molten,
thawed, clear, smooth.
⊒ solid.

liquidate v **1** ANNIHILATE, terminate, do away with, dissolve, kill, murder, massacre, assassinate, destroy, dispatch, abolish, eliminate, exterminate, remove, finish off, rub out (*infml*). **2** PAY (OFF), close down, clear, discharge, wind up, sell.

liquor n alcohol, intoxicant, strong drink, spirits, drink, hard stuff (*infml*), booze (*infml*).

list¹ n catalogue, roll, inventory, register, enumeration, schedule, index, listing, record, file, directory, table, tabulation, tally, series, syllabus, invoice.
◇ v enumerate, register, itemize, catalogue, index, tabulate, record, file, enrol, enter, note, bill, book, set down, write down.

list² v lean, incline, tilt, slope, heel (over), tip.

listen v hark, attend, pay attention, hear, heed, hearken, hang on (someone's) words, prick up one's ears, take notice, lend an ear, eavesdrop, overhear, give ear.

listless adj sluggish, lethargic, languid, torpid, enervated, spiritless, limp, lifeless, dull, inert, inactive, impassive, indifferent, uninterested, vacant, apathetic, indolent, depressed, bored, heavy.
⊟ energetic, enthusiastic.

literal adj **1** VERBATIM, word for word, strict, close, actual, precise, faithful, exact, accurate, factual, true, genuine, unexaggerated. **2** PROSAIC, unimaginative, uninspired, matter-of-fact, down-to-earth, humdrum.
⊟ **1** imprecise, loose. **2** imaginative.

literary adj educated, well-read, bookish, learned, erudite, scholarly, lettered, literate, cultured, cultivated, refined, formal.
⊟ ignorant, illiterate.

literature n **1** WRITINGS, letters, paper(s). **2** INFORMATION, leaflet(s), pamphlet(s), circular(s), brochure(s), hand-out(s), bumf (*infml*).

Types of literature include: Aga saga, allegory, anti-novel, autobiography, belles-lettres (*fml*), biography, children's literature, classic novel, crime fiction, criticism, drama, epic, epistle, essay, fiction, fan fiction, fantasy, graphic novel, Gothic novel, historical novel, horror, interactive fiction, lampoon, libretto, magnum opus, non-fiction, novel, novelization, novella, parody, pastiche, penny dreadful (*infml*), picaresque novel, poetry, polemic, prose, pulp fiction, roman novel, saga, satire, science fiction, thesis, thriller, tragedy, treatise, triad, trilogy, verse. *see also* **poem**; **story**.

litigation n lawsuit, action, suit, case, prosecution, process, contention.

litter n **1** RUBBISH, debris, refuse, waste, mess, disorder, clutter, confusion, disarray, untidiness, junk (*infml*), muck, jumble, fragments, shreds. **2** OFFSPRING, young, progeny (*fml*), brood, family.
◇ v strew, scatter, mess up, disorder, clutter.
⊟ tidy.

little adj **1** SMALL, short, tiny, minute, wee (*infml*), teeny (*infml*), diminutive, miniature, infinitesimal, mini, microscopic, petite, pint-size(d) (*infml*), slender. **2** SHORT-LIVED, brief, fleeting, passing, transient. **3** INSUFFICIENT, sparse, scant, meagre, paltry, skimpy. **4** INSIGNIFICANT, inconsiderable, negligible, trivial, petty, trifling, unimportant.
⊟ **1** big. **2** lengthy. **3** ample.
4 considerable.
◇ adv barely, hardly, scarcely, rarely, seldom, infrequently, not much.
⊟ frequently.
◇ n bit, dash, pinch, spot, trace, drop, dab, speck, touch, taste,

particle, hint, fragment, modicum, trifle.
🄴 lot.

live[1] v **1** BE, exist, breathe, draw breath. **2** LAST, endure, continue, remain, persist, survive. **3** DWELL, inhabit, reside, lodge, abide. **4** PASS, spend, lead.
🄴 **1** die. **2** cease.

live[2] adj **1** ALIVE, living, existent. **2** LIVELY, vital, active, energetic, dynamic, alert, vigorous. **3** BURNING, glowing, blazing, ignited. **4** RELEVANT, current, topical, pertinent, controversial.
🄴 **1** dead. **2** apathetic.

livelihood n occupation, job, employment, living, means, income, maintenance, work, support, subsistence, sustenance.

lively adj **1** ANIMATED, alert, active, energetic, spirited, vivacious, vigorous, sprightly, spry, agile, nimble, quick, keen. **2** CHEERFUL, blithe, merry, frisky, perky, breezy, chirpy (infml), frolicsome. **3** BUSY, bustling, brisk, crowded, eventful, exciting, buzzing. **4** VIVID, bright, colourful, stimulating, stirring, invigorating, racy, refreshing, sparkling.
🄴 **1** moribund, apathetic. **3** inactive.

liven up v enliven, vitalize, put life into, rouse, invigorate, animate, energize, brighten, stir (up), buck up (infml), pep up (infml), perk up (infml), hot up (infml).
🄴 dishearten.

livery n uniform, costume, regalia, dress, clothes, clothing, apparel (fml), attire, vestments, suit, garb, habit.

livid adj **1** LEADEN, black-and-blue, bruised, discoloured, greyish, purple. **2** PALE, pallid, ashen, blanched, bloodless, wan, waxy, pasty. **3** (infml) ANGRY, furious, infuriated, irate, outraged, enraged, raging, fuming,

indignant, incensed, exasperated, mad (infml).
🄴 **3** calm.

living adj alive, breathing, existing, live, current, extant, operative, strong, vigorous, active, lively, vital, animated.
🄴 dead, sluggish.
◇ n **1** BEING, life, animation, existence. **2** LIVELIHOOD, maintenance, support, income, subsistence, sustenance, work, job, occupation, profession, benefice, way of life.

load n **1** BURDEN, onus, weight, encumbrance, pressure, oppression, millstone. **2** CARGO, consignment, shipment, goods, lading, freight.
◇ v **1** BURDEN, weigh down, encumber, overburden, oppress, trouble, weight, saddle with. **2** PACK, pile, heap, freight, fill, stack.

loaded adj burdened, charged, laden, full, weighted.

loafer n (infml) idler, layabout (infml), shirker, skiver (infml), sluggard, wastrel, lounger, ne'er-do-well, lazybones (infml), couch potato (infml).

loan n advance, credit, mortgage, allowance.
◇ v lend, advance, credit, allow.

loathe v hate, detest, abominate, abhor, despise, dislike.
🄴 adore, love.

loathing n hatred, detestation, abhorrence, abomination, repugnance, revulsion, repulsion, dislike, disgust, aversion, horror.
🄴 affection, love.

loathsome adj detestable, abhorrent, odious, repulsive, abominable, hateful, repugnant, repellent, offensive, horrible, disgusting, vile, revolting, nasty.

lobby v campaign for, press for, demand, persuade, call for, urge, push for, influence, solicit, pressure, promote.

◇ *n* **1** VESTIBULE, foyer, porch, anteroom, hall, hallway, waiting room, entrance hall, corridor, passage. **2** PRESSURE GROUP, campaign, ginger group.

local *adj* regional, provincial, community, district, neighbourhood, parochial, vernacular, small-town, limited, narrow, restricted.
☒ national.
◇ *n* **1** INHABITANT, citizen, resident, native. **2** (*infml*) PUB.

locality *n* neighbourhood, vicinity, district, area, locale, region, position, place, site, spot, scene, setting.

locate *v* **1** FIND, discover, unearth, run to earth (*infml*), track down, detect, lay one's hands on (*infml*), pinpoint, identify. **2** SITUATE, settle, fix, establish, place, put, set, seat.

location *n* position, situation, place, locus, whereabouts, venue, site, locale, bearings, spot, point.

lock *n* fastening, bolt, clasp, padlock.
◇ *v* **1** FASTEN, secure, bolt, latch, seal, shut. **2** JOIN, unite, engage, link, mesh, entangle, entwine, clench. **3** CLASP, hug, embrace, grasp, encircle, enclose, clutch, grapple.
☒ **1** unlock.
• **lock out** shut out, refuse admittance to, keep out, exclude, bar, debar.
• **lock up** imprison, jail, confine, shut in, shut up, incarcerate, secure, cage, pen, detain, close up.
☒ free.

lodge *n* hut, cabin, cottage, chalet, shelter, retreat, den, gatehouse, house, hunting-lodge, meeting-place, club, haunt.
◇ *v* **1** ACCOMMODATE, put up (*infml*), quarter, board, billet, shelter. **2** LIVE, stay, reside. **3** FIX, imbed, implant, get stuck. **4** DEPOSIT, place, put, submit, register.

lodger *n* boarder, paying guest, resident, tenant, roomer, inmate, guest.

lodgings *n* accommodation, digs (*infml*), dwelling, quarters, billet, abode, boarding-house, rooms, pad (*infml*), residence.

log *n* **1** TIMBER, trunk, block, chunk. **2** RECORD, diary, journal, weblog, blog (*infml*), logbook, day book, account, tally.
◇ *v* record, register, write up, note, book, chart, tally.

logic *n* reasoning, reason, sense, deduction, rationale, argumentation.

logical *adj* reasonable, rational, reasoned, coherent, consistent, valid, sound, well-founded, clear, sensible, deducible, methodical, well-organized.
☒ illogical, irrational.

loiter *v* dawdle, hang about, idle, linger, dally, dilly-dally (*infml*), delay, mooch (*infml*), lag, saunter.

lone *adj* single, sole, alone, one, only, isolated, solitary, separate, separated, unattached, unaccompanied, unattended.
☒ accompanied.

loneliness *n* aloneness, isolation, lonesomeness, solitariness, solitude, seclusion, desolation.

lonely *adj* **1** ALONE, friendless, lonesome, solitary, abandoned, forsaken, companionless, destitute, unaccompanied. **2** ISOLATED, uninhabited, remote, out-of-the-way, unfrequented, secluded, abandoned, deserted, forsaken, desolate.
☒ **1** popular. **2** crowded, populous.

long *adj* lengthy, extensive, extended, expanded, prolonged, protracted, stretched, spread out, sustained, expansive, far-reaching, long-drawn-out, interminable, slow.
☒ brief, short, fleeting, abbreviated.
• **long for** yearn for, crave, want, wish, desire, dream of, hanker for, pine, thirst for, lust after, covet, itch for, yen for (*infml*).

longing *n* craving, desire, yearning,

hungering, hankering, yen, thirst, wish, urge, coveting, aspiration, ambition.

long-lasting *adj* permanent, imperishable, enduring, unchanging, unfading, continuing, abiding, long-standing, prolonged, protracted.
⊜ short-lived, ephemeral, transient.

long-standing *adj* established, long-established, long-lived, long-lasting, enduring, abiding, time-honoured, traditional.

long-suffering *adj* uncomplaining, forbearing, forgiving, tolerant, easy-going, patient, stoical.

long-winded *adj* lengthy, overlong, prolonged, diffuse, verbose, wordy, voluble, long-drawn-out, discursive, repetitious, rambling, tedious.
⊜ brief, terse.

look *v* 1 WATCH, see, observe, view, survey, regard, gaze, study, stare, examine, inspect, scrutinize, glance, contemplate, scan, peep, gawp (*infml*). 2 SEEM, appear, show, exhibit, display.
◇ *n* 1 VIEW, survey, inspection, examination, observation, sight, review, once-over (*infml*), glance, glimpse, gaze, peek. 2 APPEARANCE, aspect, manner, semblance, face, mien, expression, bearing, complexion.
● **look after** take care of, mind, care for, attend to, take charge of, tend, keep an eye on, watch over, protect, supervise, guard.
⊜ neglect.
● **look down on** despise, scorn, sneer at, hold in contempt, disdain, look down one's nose at (*infml*), turn one's nose up at (*infml*).
⊜ esteem, approve.
● **look forward to** anticipate, await, expect, hope for, long for, envisage, envision, count on, wait for, look for.
● **look into** investigate, probe, research, study, go into, examine, enquire about, explore, check out,

inspect, scrutinize, look over, plumb, fathom.
● **look out** pay attention, watch out, beware, be careful, keep an eye out.
● **look over** inspect, examine, check, give a once-over (*infml*), cast an eye over, look through, scan, view.
● **look up 1** SEARCH FOR, research, hunt for, find, track down. **2** VISIT, call on, drop in on, look in on, pay a visit to, stop by, drop by. **3** IMPROVE, get better, pick up, progress, come on.
● **look up to** admire, esteem, respect, revere, honour, have a high opinion of.

look-alike *n* double, replica, twin, spitting image (*infml*), living image, clone, spit (*infml*), ringer (*infml*), doppelgänger.

lookout *n* 1 GUARD, sentry, watch, watch-tower, watchman, sentinel, tower, post. **2** (*infml*) CONCERN, affair, responsibility, worry, business, problem.

loom *v* appear, emerge, take shape, menace, threaten, impend, hang over, dominate, tower, overhang, rise, soar, overshadow, overtop.

loop *n* hoop, ring, circle, noose, coil, eyelet, loophole, spiral, curve, curl, kink, twist, whorl, twirl, turn, bend.
◇ *v* coil, encircle, roll, bend, circle, curve round, turn, twist, spiral, connect, join, knot, fold, braid.

loophole *n* let-out, escape, evasion, excuse, pretext, plea, pretence.

loose *adj* 1 FREE, unfastened, untied, movable, unattached, insecure, wobbly. **2** SLACK, lax, baggy, hanging. **3** IMPRECISE, vague, inexact, ill-defined, indefinite, inaccurate, indistinct.
⊜ **1** firm, secure. **2** tight. **3** precise.

loosen *v* 1 EASE, relax, loose, undo, slacken, unbind, untie, unfasten. **2** FREE, set free, release, let go, let out, deliver.
⊜ **1** tighten.

loot n spoils, booty, plunder, haul, swag (infml), prize.
◇ v plunder, pillage, rob, sack, rifle, raid, maraud, ransack, ravage.

lop-sided adj asymmetrical, unbalanced, askew, off balance, uneven.
☞ balanced, symmetrical.

lord n 1 PEER, noble, earl, duke, count, baron. 2 MASTER, ruler, superior, overlord, leader, commander, governor, king.

lordly adj 1 NOBLE, dignified, aristocratic. 2 PROUD, arrogant, disdainful, haughty, imperious, condescending, high-handed, domineering, overbearing.
☞ 1 low(ly). 2 humble.

lore n knowledge, wisdom, learning, erudition, scholarship, traditions, teaching, beliefs, sayings.

lose v 1 MISLAY, misplace, forget, miss, forfeit. 2 WASTE, squander, dissipate, use up, exhaust, expend, drain. 3 FAIL, fall short, suffer defeat.
☞ 1 gain. 2 make. 3 win.

loser n failure, also-ran, runner-up, flop (infml), no-hoper.
☞ winner.

loss n 1 DEPRIVATION, disadvantage, defeat, failure, losing, bereavement, damage, destruction, ruin, hurt. 2 WASTE, depletion, disappearance, deficiency, deficit.
☞ 1 gain.

lost adj 1 MISLAID, missing, vanished, disappeared, misplaced, astray. 2 CONFUSED, disoriented, bewildered, puzzled, baffled, perplexed, preoccupied. 3 WASTED, squandered, ruined, destroyed.
☞ 1 found.

lot n 1 COLLECTION, batch, assortment, quantity, group, set, crowd. 2 SHARE, portion, allowance, ration, quota, part, piece, parcel.

lotion n ointment, balm, cream, salve.

lottery n 1 DRAW, raffle, sweepstake. 2 SPECULATION, venture, risk, gamble, crapshoot (N Am).

loud adj 1 NOISY, deafening, booming, resounding, ear-piercing, ear-splitting, piercing, thundering, blaring, clamorous, vociferous. 2 GARISH, gaudy, glaring, flashy, brash, showy, ostentatious, tasteless.
☞ 1 quiet. 2 subdued.

lounge v relax, loll, idle, laze, waste time, kill time, lie about, take it easy, sprawl, recline, lie back, slump.
◇ n sitting room, living room, drawing room, day-room, parlour.

lovable adj adorable, endearing, winsome, captivating, charming, engaging, attractive, fetching, sweet, lovely, pleasing, delightful.
☞ detestable, hateful.

love v 1 he loves his wife: adore, cherish, dote on, treasure, hold dear, idolize, worship. 2 I love macaroons: like, take pleasure in, enjoy, delight in, appreciate, desire, fancy.
☞ detest, hate.
◇ n adoration, affection, fondness, attachment, regard, liking, ardour, amorousness, devotion, adulation, passion, rapture, tenderness, warmth, inclination, infatuation, delight, enjoyment, soft spot (infml), weakness, taste, friendship.
☞ detestation, hate, loathing.

lovely adj beautiful, charming, delightful, attractive, enchanting, pleasing, pleasant, pretty, adorable, agreeable, enjoyable, sweet, winning, exquisite.
☞ ugly, hideous.

lover n beloved, admirer, boyfriend, girlfriend, sweetheart, suitor, mistress, fiancé(e), flame (infml).

loving adj amorous, affectionate, devoted, doting, fond, ardent, passionate, warm, warm-hearted, tender.

low adj 1 SHORT, small, stunted, squat, little, shallow, deep, depressed, sunken. 2 INADEQUATE, deficient, poor, sparse, meagre, paltry, scant, insignificant. 3 UNHAPPY, depressed, downcast, gloomy. 4 BASE, coarse, vulgar, mean, contemptible. 5 CHEAP, inexpensive, reasonable. 6 SUBDUED, muted, soft.
⊟ 1 high. 2 high. 3 cheerful. 4 honourable. 5 exorbitant. 6 loud.

lower adj inferior, subordinate, lesser, secondary, minor, second-class, low-level, lowly, junior.
⊟ higher.
◇ v 1 DROP, depress, sink, descend, let down. 2 REDUCE, decrease, cut, lessen, diminish.
⊟ 1 raise. 2 increase.

lowly adj humble, low-born, obscure, poor, plebeian, plain, simple, modest, ordinary, inferior, meek, mild, mean, submissive, subordinate.
⊟ lofty, noble.

low-spirited adj depressed, gloomy, heavy-hearted, low, down, downhearted, despondent, fed up (infml), sad, unhappy, miserable, moody.
⊟ high-spirited, cheerful.

loyal adj true, faithful, steadfast, staunch, devoted, trustworthy, sincere, patriotic.
⊟ disloyal, treacherous.

loyalty n allegiance, faithfulness, fidelity, devotion, steadfastness, constancy, trustworthiness, reliability, patriotism.
⊟ disloyalty, treachery.

lubricate v oil, grease, smear, wax, lard.

luck n 1 CHANCE, fortune, accident, fate, fortuity (fml), fluke (infml), destiny. 2 GOOD FORTUNE, success, break (infml), godsend.
⊟ 1 design. 2 misfortune.

luckily adv fortunately, happily, providentially.
⊟ unfortunately.

lucky adj fortunate, favoured, auspicious, successful, prosperous, timely.
⊟ unlucky.

lucrative adj profitable, well-paid, remunerative, advantageous.
⊟ unprofitable.

ludicrous adj absurd, ridiculous, preposterous, nonsensical, silly, laughable, farcical, comical, funny, outlandish, crazy (infml).
⊟ serious.

lug v pull, drag, haul, carry, tow, heave, hump.

luggage

Types of luggage include: case, suitcase, vanity case, bag, holdall, portmanteau, valise, overnight bag, kitbag, flight bag, hand-luggage, tote bag, travel bag, Gladstone bag, grip, rucksack, bergen, knapsack, haversack, backpack, bum bag, fanny pack (US), money belt, briefcase, attaché-case, portfolio, satchel, basket, hamper, trunk, chest, box, pet carrier.

lukewarm adj cool, half-hearted, apathetic, tepid, indifferent, unenthusiastic, uninterested, unresponsive, unconcerned.

lull v soothe, subdue, calm, hush, pacify, quieten down, quiet, quell, compose.
⊟ agitate.
◇ n calm, peace, quiet, tranquillity, stillness, let-up, pause, hush, silence.
⊟ agitation.

lumber¹ n clutter, jumble, rubbish, bits and pieces, odds and ends, junk.

lumber² v clump, shamble, plod, shuffle, stump, trundle.

luminous adj glowing, illuminated, lit, lighted, radiant, shining, fluorescent, brilliant, lustrous, bright.

lump n 1 MASS, cluster, clump, clod, ball, bunch, piece, chunk, cake, hunk, nugget, wedge. 2 SWELLING, growth, bulge, bump, protuberance, protrusion, tumour.
◇ v collect, mass, gather, cluster, combine, coalesce, group, consolidate, unite.

lunacy n madness, insanity, aberration, derangement, mania, craziness (infml), idiocy, imbecility, folly, absurdity, stupidity.
⊞ sanity.

lunatic n psychotic, psychopath, madman, maniac, loony (infml), nutcase (infml), nutter (infml), fruitcake (infml).
◇ adj mad, insane, deranged, psychotic, irrational, crazy (infml), bonkers (infml).
⊞ sane.

lunge v thrust, jab, stab, pounce, plunge, pitch into, charge, dart, dash, dive, poke, strike (at), fall upon, grab (at), hit (at), leap.
◇ n thrust, stab, pounce, charge, jab, pass, cut, spring.

lurch v roll, rock, pitch, sway, stagger, reel, list.

lure v tempt, entice, draw, attract, allure, seduce, ensnare, lead on.
◇ n temptation, enticement, attraction, bait, inducement.

lurid adj 1 SENSATIONAL, shocking, startling, graphic, exaggerated. 2 MACABRE, gruesome, gory, ghastly, grisly. 3 BRIGHTLY COLOURED, garish, glaring, loud, vivid.

lurk v skulk, prowl, lie in wait, crouch, lie low, hide, snoop.

luscious adj delicious, juicy, succulent, mouthwatering, appetizing, sweet, tasty, savoury, desirable.

lush adj 1 FLOURISHING, luxuriant, abundant, prolific, overgrown, green, verdant. 2 SUMPTUOUS, opulent, ornate, plush, rich.

lust n 1 SENSUALITY, libido, lechery, licentiousness, lewdness. 2 CRAVING, desire, appetite, longing, passion, greed, covetousness.
• **lust after** desire, crave, yearn for, want, need, hunger for, thirst for.

lustre n 1 SHINE, gloss, sheen, gleam, glow, brilliance, brightness, radiance, sparkle, resplendence, burnish, glitter, glint. 2 GLORY, honour, prestige, illustriousness.

lusty adj robust, strong, sturdy, vigorous, hale, hearty, healthy, gutsy (infml), energetic, strapping, rugged, powerful.

luxurious adj sumptuous, opulent, lavish, de luxe, plush, magnificent, splendid, expensive, costly, self-indulgent, pampered.
⊞ austere, spartan.

luxury n sumptuousness, opulence, hedonism, splendour, affluence, richness, magnificence, pleasure, indulgence, gratification, comfort, extravagance, satisfaction.
⊞ austerity.

lying adj deceitful, dishonest, false, untruthful, double-dealing, two-faced (infml).
⊞ honest, truthful.
◇ n dishonesty, untruthfulness, deceit, falsity, fibbing (infml), perjury, duplicity, fabrication, double-dealing.
⊞ honesty, truthfulness.

Mm

macabre *adj* gruesome, grisly, grim, horrible, frightful, dreadful, ghostly, eerie.

machine *n* 1 INSTRUMENT, device, contrivance, tool, mechanism, engine, apparatus, appliance. 2 AGENCY, organization, structure, system.

machinery *n* 1 INSTRUMENTS, mechanism, tools, apparatus, equipment, tackle, gear. 2 ORGANIZATION, channels, structure, system, procedure.

mad *adj* 1 INSANE, lunatic, unbalanced, psychotic, deranged, demented, out of one's mind, crazy (*infml*), nuts (*infml*), barmy (*infml*), bonkers (*infml*). 2 (*infml*) ANGRY, furious, enraged, infuriated, incensed. 3 IRRATIONAL, illogical, unreasonable, absurd, preposterous, foolish. 4 FANATICAL, enthusiastic, infatuated, ardent.
🔁 1 sane. 2 calm. 3 sensible. 4 apathetic.

madden *v* anger, enrage, infuriate, incense, exasperate, provoke, annoy, irritate.
🔁 calm, pacify.

madly *adv* 1 *he rolled his eyes madly*: insanely, dementedly, hysterically, wildly. 2 *madly cleaning up*: excitedly, frantically, furiously, recklessly, violently, energetically, rapidly, hastily, hurriedly. 3 *madly in love*: intensely, extremely, exceedingly, fervently, devotedly.

madman, madwoman *n* lunatic, psychotic, psychopath, maniac, loony (*infml*), nutcase (*infml*), fruitcake (*infml*).

magazine *n* 1 JOURNAL, periodical, paper, weekly, monthly, quarterly. 2 ARSENAL, storehouse, ammunition dump, depot, ordnance.

magic *n* 1 SORCERY, enchantment, occultism, black art, witchcraft, wicca, spell. 2 CONJURING, illusion, sleight of hand, trickery. 3 CHARM, fascination, glamour, allure.
◇ *adj* charming, enchanting, bewitching, fascinating, spellbinding.

magician *n* sorcerer, miracle-worker, conjuror, enchanter, wizard, witch, warlock, spellbinder, wonder-worker.

magnanimous *adj* generous, liberal, open-handed, benevolent, selfless, charitable, big-hearted, kind, noble, unselfish, ungrudging.
🔁 mean.

magnate *n* tycoon, captain of industry, industrialist, mogul, entrepreneur, plutocrat, baron, personage, notable.

magnetic *adj* attractive, alluring, fascinating, charming, mesmerizing, seductive, irresistible, entrancing, captivating, gripping, absorbing, charismatic.
🔁 repellent, repulsive.

magnetism *n* attraction, allure, fascination, charm, lure, appeal, drawing power, draw, pull, hypnotism, mesmerism, charisma, grip, spell.

magnificent *adj* splendid, grand, imposing, impressive, glorious, gorgeous, brilliant, excellent,

majestic, superb, sumptuous, noble, elegant, fine, rich.
☒ modest, humble, poor.

magnify v enlarge, amplify, increase, expand, intensify, boost, enhance, greaten, heighten, deepen, build up, talk up, exaggerate, dramatize, overemphasize, overplay, overstate, overdo, blow up (*infml*).
☒ belittle, play down.

magnitude n 1 SIZE, extent, measure, amount, expanse, dimensions, mass, proportions, quantity, volume, bulk, largeness, space, strength, amplitude. 2 IMPORTANCE, consequence, significance, weight, greatness, moment, intensity.

maiden n girl, virgin, lass, lassie, damsel (*fml*), miss.

mail n post, letters, correspondence, packages, parcels, delivery.
◇ v post, send, dispatch, forward.

maim v mutilate, wound, injure, incapacitate, disable, hurt, impair, cripple, lame.

main adj principal, chief, leading, first, foremost, predominant, pre-eminent, primary, prime, supreme, paramount, central, cardinal, outstanding, essential, critical, crucial, necessary, vital.
☒ minor, unimportant, insignificant.
◇ n pipe, duct, conduit, channel, cable, line.

mainly adv primarily, principally, chiefly, in the main, mostly, on the whole, for the most part, generally, in general, especially, as a rule, above all, largely, overall.

mainstay n support, buttress, bulwark, linchpin, prop, pillar, backbone, foundation.

maintain v 1 CARRY ON, continue, keep (up), sustain, retain. 2 CARE FOR, conserve, look after, take care of, preserve, support, finance, supply.

3 ASSERT, affirm, claim, contend, declare, hold, state, insist, believe, fight for.
☒ 2 neglect. 3 deny.

maintenance n 1 CONTINUATION, continuance, perpetuation. 2 CARE, conservation, preservation, support, repairs, protection, upkeep, running. 3 KEEP, subsistence, living, livelihood, allowance, alimony.
☒ 2 neglect.

majestic adj magnificent, grand, dignified, noble, royal, stately, splendid, imperial, impressive, exalted, imposing, regal, sublime, superb, lofty, monumental, pompous.
☒ lowly, unimpressive, unimposing.

majesty n grandeur, glory, dignity, magnificence, nobility, royalty, resplendence, splendour, stateliness, pomp, exaltedness, impressiveness, loftiness.

major adj greater, chief, main, larger, bigger, higher, leading, outstanding, notable, supreme, uppermost, significant, crucial, important, key, keynote, great, senior, older, superior, pre-eminent, vital, weighty.
☒ minor, unimportant, trivial.

majority n 1 BULK, mass, most, preponderance, greater part. 2 ADULTHOOD, maturity, manhood, womanhood, years of discretion.
☒ 1 minority.

make v 1 CREATE, manufacture, fabricate, construct, build, produce, put together, originate, compose, form, shape. 2 CAUSE, bring about, effect, accomplish, occasion, give rise to, generate, render, perform. 3 COERCE, force, oblige, constrain, compel, prevail upon, pressurize, press, require. 4 APPOINT, elect, designate, nominate, ordain, install. 5 EARN, gain, net, obtain, acquire. 6 CONSTITUTE, compose, comprise, add up to, amount to.
☒ 1 dismantle. 5 spend.

◇ *n* brand, sort, type, style, variety, manufacture, model, mark, kind, form, structure.

• **make off** run off, run away, depart, bolt, leave, fly, cut and run (*infml*), beat a hasty retreat (*infml*), clear off (*infml*).

• **make out 1** DISCERN, perceive, decipher, distinguish, recognize, see, detect, discover, understand, work out, grasp, follow, fathom. **2** DRAW UP, complete, fill in, write out. **3** MAINTAIN, imply, claim, assert, describe, demonstrate, prove. **4** MANAGE, get on, progress, succeed, fare (*fml*).

• **make up 1** CREATE, invent, devise, fabricate, construct, originate, formulate, dream up, compose, spin. **2** COMPLETE, fill, supply, meet, supplement. **3** COMPRISE, constitute, compose, form. **4** BE RECONCILED, make peace, settle differences, bury the hatchet (*infml*), forgive and forget, call it quits (*infml*).

• **make up for** compensate for, make good, make amends for, redress, recompense, redeem, atone for.

make-believe *n* pretence, imagination, fantasy, unreality, play-acting, role-play, dream, charade.
⊞ reality.

maker *n* creator, manufacturer, constructor, builder, producer, director, architect, author.

makeshift *adj* temporary, improvised, rough and ready, provisional, substitute, stopgap, expedient, make-do.
⊞ permanent.

make-up *n* **1** COSMETICS, paint, powder, maquillage, war paint (*infml*). **2** CONSTITUTION, nature, composition, character, construction, form, format, formation, style, arrangement, organization, structure, assembly.

maladjusted *adj* disturbed, unstable, confused, alienated,

neurotic, estranged.
⊞ well-adjusted.

male *adj* masculine, manly, virile, boyish, laddish (*infml*), he-.
⊞ female.

malevolent *adj* malicious, malign, spiteful, vindictive, ill-natured, hostile, vicious, venomous, evil-minded.
⊞ benevolent, kind.

malformation *n* irregularity, deformity, distortion, warp.

malformed *adj* misshapen, irregular, deformed, distorted, twisted, warped, crooked, bent.
⊞ perfect.

malfunction *n* fault, defect, failure, breakdown.
◇ *v* break down, go wrong, fail.

malice *n* malevolence, enmity, animosity, ill-will, hatred, hate, spite, vindictiveness, bitterness.
⊞ love.

malicious *adj* malevolent, ill-natured, malign, spiteful, venomous, vicious, vengeful, evil-minded, bitter, resentful.
⊞ kind, friendly.

malign *adj* malignant, malevolent, bad, evil, harmful, hurtful, injurious, destructive, hostile.
⊞ benign.
◇ *v* defame, slander, libel, disparage, abuse, run down (*infml*), harm, injure.
⊞ praise.

malignant *adj* **1** MALEVOLENT, malicious, spiteful, evil, hostile, vicious, venomous, destructive, harmful, hurtful, pernicious. **2** FATAL, deadly, incurable, dangerous, cancerous, uncontrollable, virulent.
⊞ **1** kind. **2** benign.

malpractice *n* misconduct, mismanagement, negligence, impropriety, dereliction of duty (*fml*), abuse, misdeed.

maltreat v ill-treat, mistreat, misuse, abuse, injure, harm, damage, hurt.
⊞ care for.

mammal

Mammals include: aardvark, anteater, antelope, armadillo, baboon, badger, bat, bear, bush-baby, camel, cat, chimpanzee, cow, deer, dog, dolphin, duck-billed platypus, dugong, echidna, elephant, ferret, flying lemur, fox, gibbon, giraffe, goat, gorilla, hedgehog, hippopotamus, horse, human being, hyena, leopard, lion, manatee, meerkat, mole, monkey, orang utan, otter, pig, porpoise, raccoon, rhinoceros, sea cow, seal, sea lion, sheep, shrew, sloth, tapir, tiger, walrus, weasel, whale, wolf, zebra. see also **cat**; **cattle**; **dog**; **marsupial**; **monkey**; **rodent**.

mammoth adj enormous, huge, vast, colossal, gigantic, giant, massive, immense, monumental, mighty.
⊞ tiny, minute.

man n 1 MALE, gentleman, gent (infml), fellow, bloke (infml), chap (infml), guy (infml). 2 HUMAN BEING, person, individual, adult, human. 3 HUMANITY, humankind, mankind, human race, people, Homo sapiens, mortals. 4 MANSERVANT, servant, worker, employee, hand, soldier, valet, houseman, houseboy.
◇ v staff, crew, take charge of, operate, occupy.

manacle v handcuff, shackle, put in chains, restrain, fetter, chain, bind, curb, check, hamper, inhibit.
⊞ free, unshackle.

manage v 1 ACCOMPLISH, succeed, bring about, bring off, effect. 2 ADMINISTER, direct, run, command, govern, preside over, rule, supervise, superintend, oversee, conduct. 3 CONTROL, influence, deal with,

handle, operate, manipulate, guide. 4 COPE, fare, survive, get by, get along, get on, make do.
⊞ 1 fail. 2 mismanage.

manageable adj tractable, governable, controllable, amenable, submissive, docile.
⊞ unmanageable.

management n 1 ADMINISTRATION, direction, control, government, command, running, superintendence, supervision, charge, care, handling. 2 MANAGERS, directors, directorate, executive, executives, governors, board, bosses (infml), supervisors.
⊞ 1 mismanagement. 2 workers.

manager n director, executive, administrator, controller, supervisor, superintendent, overseer, governor, organizer, head, boss (infml).

mandate n order, command, decree, edict, injunction, charge, directive, warrant, authorization, authority, instruction, commission, sanction.

mandatory adj obligatory, compulsory, binding, required, necessary, requisite, essential.
⊞ optional.

mangle v mutilate, disfigure, mar, maim, spoil, butcher, destroy, deform, wreck, twist, maul, distort, crush, cut, hack, tear, rend.

mangy adj seedy, shabby, scruffy, scabby, tatty (infml), shoddy, moth-eaten, dirty, mean.

manhandle v 1 the porters manhandled the baggage: haul, heave, hump, pull, push, shove, tug. 2 the police manhandled the demonstrators: maul, mistreat, maltreat, misuse, abuse, knock about (infml), rough up (infml).

manhood n 1 ADULTHOOD, maturity. 2 MASCULINITY, virility, manliness, manfulness, machismo (infml).

mania n 1 MADNESS, insanity, lunacy,

psychosis, derangement, disorder, aberration, craziness (*infml*), frenzy. **2** PASSION, craze, rage, obsession, compulsion, enthusiasm, fad (*infml*), infatuation, fixation, craving.

Manias include: dipsomania (*alcohol*), bibliomania (*books*), ailuromania (*cats*), ablutomania (*cleanliness*), necromania (*dead bodies*), thanatomania (*death*), cynomania (*dogs*), pyromania (*fire-raising*), anthomania (*flowers*), hippomania (*horses*), mythomania (*lying and exaggerating*), egomania (*oneself*), hedonomania (*pleasure*), megalomania (*power*), theomania (*religion*), nymphomania (*sex*), monomania (*single idea or thing*), kleptomania (*stealing*), logomania (*talking*), ergomania (*work*). *see also* **phobia**; supplement **Words Grouped by Ending**.

maniac *n* **1** LUNATIC, madman, madwoman, psychotic, psychopath, loony (*infml*). **2** ENTHUSIAST, fan (*infml*), fanatic, fiend (*infml*), freak (*infml*).

manifest *adj* obvious, evident, clear, apparent, plain, open, patent, noticeable, conspicuous, unmistakable, visible, unconcealed.
▣ unclear.
◇ *v* show, exhibit, demonstrate, display, reveal, set forth, expose, prove, illustrate, establish.
▣ conceal.

manifestation *n* display, show, exhibition, demonstration, revelation, exposure, disclosure, appearance, expression, sign, indication.

manifesto *n* statement, declaration, policies, platform.

manifold *adj* (*fml*) many, numerous, varied, various, diverse, multiple, kaleidoscopic, abundant, copious.

manipulate *v* **1** HANDLE, control, wield, operate, use, manoeuvre,

influence, engineer, guide, direct, steer, negotiate, work. **2** FALSIFY, rig, juggle with, doctor (*infml*), cook (*infml*), fiddle (*infml*).

mankind *n* humankind, humanity, human race, man, Homo sapiens, people.

manly *adj* masculine, male, virile, manful, macho (*infml*), robust.

man-made *adj* manufactured, synthetic, simulated, imitation, artificial.
▣ natural.

manner *n* **1** WAY, method, means, fashion, style, procedure, process, form. **2** BEHAVIOUR, conduct, bearing, demeanour, air, appearance, look, character.

mannerism *n* idiosyncrasy, peculiarity, characteristic, quirk, trait, feature, foible, habit.

manners *n* behaviour, conduct, demeanour, etiquette, politeness, bearing, courtesy, formalities, social graces, p's and q's.

manoeuvre *n* move, movement, operation, action, exercise, plan, ploy, plot, ruse, stratagem, machination, gambit, tactic, trick, scheme, dodge (*infml*).
◇ *v* **1** MOVE, manipulate, handle, guide, pilot, steer, navigate, jockey, direct, drive, exercise. **2** CONTRIVE, engineer, plot, scheme, wangle (*infml*), pull strings (*infml*), manipulate, manage, plan, devise, negotiate.

mantle *n* cloak, cover, covering, cape, hood, blanket, shawl, veil, wrap, shroud, screen.

manual *n* handbook, guide, guidebook, instructions, Bible, vade mecum, directions.
◇ *adj* hand-operated, by hand, physical, human.

manufacture *v* **1** MAKE, produce, construct, build, fabricate, create,

assemble, mass-produce, turn out, process, forge, form. **2** INVENT, make up, concoct, fabricate, think up.
◇ *n* production, making, construction, fabrication, mass-production, assembly, creation, formation.

manufacturer *n* maker, producer, industrialist, constructor, factory-owner, builder, creator.

manure *n* fertilizer, compost, muck, dung.

many *adj* numerous, countless, lots of (*infml*), manifold (*fml*), various, varied, sundry, diverse, umpteen (*infml*).
🗷 few.

map *n* chart, plan, street plan, atlas, graph, plot.

mar *v* spoil, impair, harm, hurt, damage, deface, disfigure, mutilate, injure, maim, scar, detract from, mangle, ruin, wreck, tarnish.
🗷 enhance.

marauder *n* bandit, brigand, robber, raider, plunderer, pillager, pirate, buccaneer, outlaw, ravager, predator.

march *v* walk, stride, parade, pace, file, tread, stalk.
◇ *n* **1** STEP, pace, stride. **2** WALK, trek, hike, footslog (*infml*). **3** PROCESSION, parade, demonstration, demo (*infml*). **4** ADVANCE, development, progress, evolution, passage.

margin *n* **1** BORDER, edge, boundary, bound, periphery, perimeter, rim, brink, limit, confine, verge, side, skirt. **2** ALLOWANCE, play, leeway, latitude, scope, room, space, surplus, extra.

marginal *adj* borderline, peripheral, negligible, minimal, insignificant, minor, slight, doubtful, low, small.
🗷 central, core.

marine *adj* sea, maritime, naval, nautical, seafaring, sea-going,
ocean-going, saltwater.

mariner *n* sailor, seaman, seafarer, deckhand, navigator, tar (*infml*), sea-dog (*infml*), salt (*infml*).

marital *adj* conjugal, matrimonial, married, wedded, nuptial (*fml*), connubial (*fml*).

maritime *adj* marine, nautical, naval, seafaring, sea, seaside, oceanic, coastal.

mark *n* **1** SPOT, stain, blemish, blot, blotch, smudge, dent, impression, scar, scratch, bruise, line. **2** SYMBOL, sign, indication, emblem, brand, stamp, token, characteristic, feature, proof, evidence, badge. **3** TARGET, goal, aim, objective, purpose.
◇ *v* **1** STAIN, blemish, blot, smudge, dent, scar, scratch, bruise. **2** BRAND, label, stamp, characterize, identify, distinguish. **3** EVALUATE, assess, correct, grade. **4** HEED, listen, mind, note, observe, regard, notice, take to heart.

marked *adj* **1** NOTICEABLE, obvious, conspicuous, evident, pronounced, distinct, decided, considerable, emphatic, remarkable, apparent, glaring. **2** SUSPECTED, watched, doomed.
🗷 **1** unnoticeable, slight.

market *n* mart, marketplace, bazaar, fair, exchange, outlet.
◇ *v* sell, retail, hawk, peddle.
🗷 buy.

maroon *v* abandon, cast away, desert, put ashore, strand, leave, isolate.

marriage *n* **1** MATRIMONY, wedlock, wedding, nuptials (*fml*). **2** UNION, alliance, partnership, merger, coupling, amalgamation, link, association, confederation.
🗷 **1** divorce. **2** separation.

marrow *n* essence, heart, nub, kernel, core, soul, spirit, substance, quick, stuff, gist.

marry v **1** WED, join in matrimony, lead up the aisle, tie the knot (*infml*), get hitched (*infml*), get spliced (*infml*). **2** UNITE, ally, join, merge, match, link, knit.
⊟ **1** divorce. **2** separate.

marsh n marshland, bog, swamp, fen, morass, quagmire, slough.

marshal v **1** ARRANGE, dispose, order, line up, align, array, rank, organize, assemble, gather, muster, group, collect, draw up, deploy. **2** GUIDE, lead, escort, conduct, usher.

marsupial

Marsupials include: bandicoot, cuscus, kangaroo, rat-kangaroo, tree kangaroo, wallaroo, koala, marsupial mole, marsupial mouse, opossum, pademelon, phalanger, Tasmanian devil, Tasmanian wolf, wallaby, wombat.

martial adj warlike, military, army, belligerent, soldierly, militant, heroic, brave.

martial art

Martial arts include: *unarmed*: aikido, capoeira, judo, ju-jitsu, karate, kempo, kick boxing, kung fu, tae kwon do, t'ai chi, wushu; *weapons*: bojutsu, kendo, kenjutsu, kumdo, kyodo.

marvel n wonder, miracle, suprise, phenomenon, prodigy, spectacle, sensation, genius.
◇ v wonder, gape, gaze, be amazed at.

marvellous adj **1** WONDERFUL, excellent, splendid, superb, magnificent, terrific (*infml*), super, fantastic (*infml*). **2** EXTRAORDINARY, amazing, astonishing, astounding, miraculous, remarkable, surprising, unbelievable, incredible, glorious.
⊟ **1** terrible, awful. **2** ordinary, run-of-the-mill.

masculine adj **1** MALE, man-like, manly, mannish, virile, macho, laddish (*infml*). **2** VIGOROUS, strong, strapping, robust, powerful, red-blooded, muscular, bold, brave, gallant, resolute, stout-hearted.
⊟ **1** feminine.

mash v crush, pulp, beat, pound, pulverize, pummel, grind, smash.

mask n disguise, camouflage, façade, front, concealment, cover-up, cover, guise, pretence, semblance, cloak, veil, blind, show, veneer, visor.
◇ v disguise, camouflage, cover, conceal, cloak, veil, hide, obscure, screen, shield.
⊟ expose, uncover.

masquerade n **1** MASQUE, masked ball, costume ball, fancy dress party. **2** DISGUISE, counterfeit, cover-up, cover, deception, front, pose, pretence, guise, cloak.
◇ v disguise, impersonate, pose, pass oneself off, mask, play, pretend, profess, dissimulate.

mass n **1** HEAP, pile, collection, load, accumulation, aggregate, conglomeration, combination, entirety, totality, sum, lot, group, batch, bunch. **2** QUANTITY, multitude, throng, troop, crowd, band, horde, mob. **3** MAJORITY, body, bulk. **4** SIZE, dimension, magnitude, immensity. **5** LUMP, piece, chunk, block, hunk.
◇ adj widespread, large-scale, extensive, comprehensive, general, indiscriminate, popular, across-the-board, sweeping, wholesale, blanket.
⊟ limited, small-scale.
◇ v collect, gather, assemble, crowd, congregate, rally, cluster, muster, swarm, throng.
⊟ separate.

massacre n slaughter, murder, extermination, carnage, butchery, holocaust, bloodbath, annihilation, killing.
◇ v slaughter, butcher, murder, mow down, wipe out, exterminate,

annihilate, kill, decimate.

massage n manipulation, kneading, rubbing, rub-down.
◇ v manipulate, knead, rub (down).

massive adj huge, immense, enormous, vast, colossal, big, gigantic, mega (infml), bulky, monumental, solid, substantial, heavy, large-scale, extensive.
🖭 tiny, small.

master n 1 RULER, chief, governor, head, lord, captain, boss (infml), employer, commander, controller, director, manager, superintendent, overseer, principal, overlord, owner. 2 EXPERT, genius, virtuoso, past master, maestro, dab hand (infml), ace (infml), pro (infml). 3 TEACHER, tutor, instructor, schoolmaster, guide, guru, preceptor (fml).
🖭 1 servant, underling. 2 amateur. 3 learner, pupil.
◇ adj 1 CHIEF, principal, main, leading, foremost, prime, great, predominant, controlling, grand. 2 EXPERT, masterly, skilled, skilful, proficient.
🖭 1 subordinate. 2 inept.
◇ v 1 CONQUER, defeat, subdue, subjugate, vanquish, triumph over, overcome, quell, rule, control. 2 LEARN, grasp, acquire, get the hang of (infml), manage.

masterful adj 1 ARROGANT, authoritative, domineering, bossy (infml), overbearing, high-handed, despotic, dictatorial, autocratic, tyrannical, powerful. 2 EXPERT, masterly, skilful, skilled, dexterous, first-rate, professional.
🖭 1 humble. 2 inept, unskilful.

masterly adj expert, skilled, skilful, dexterous, adept, adroit, first-rate, ace (infml), excellent, superb, superior, supreme.
🖭 inept, clumsy.

masterpiece n masterwork, magnum opus, pièce de résistance, chef d'oeuvre, jewel.

mastery n 1 PROFICIENCY, skill, ability, command, expertise, virtuosity, knowledge, know-how, dexterity, familiarity, grasp. 2 CONTROL, command, domination, supremacy, upper hand, dominion, authority.
🖭 1 incompetence. 2 subjugation.

match n 1 CONTEST, competition, bout, game, test, trial. 2 EQUAL, equivalent, peer, counterpart, fellow, mate, rival, copy, double, replica, look-alike, twin, duplicate. 3 MARRIAGE, alliance, union, partnership, affiliation.
◇ v 1 EQUAL, compare, measure up to, rival, compete, oppose, contend, vie, pit against. 2 FIT, go with, accord, agree, suit, correspond, harmonize, tally, co-ordinate, blend, adapt, go together, relate, tone with, accompany. 3 JOIN, marry, unite, mate, link, couple, combine, ally, pair, yoke, team.
🖭 2 clash. 3 separate.

matching adj corresponding, comparable, equivalent, like, identical, co-ordinating, similar, duplicate, same, twin.
🖭 clashing.

matchless adj unequalled, peerless, incomparable, unmatched, unparalleled, unsurpassed, unrivalled, inimitable, unique.

mate n 1 FRIEND, companion, comrade, pal (infml), colleague, partner, fellow-worker, co-worker, associate. 2 SPOUSE, husband, wife. 3 ASSISTANT, helper, subordinate. 4 MATCH, fellow, twin.
◇ v 1 COUPLE, pair, breed, copulate. 2 JOIN, match, marry, wed.

material n 1 STUFF, substance, body, matter. 2 FABRIC, textile, cloth. 3 INFORMATION, facts, data, evidence, constituents, work, notes.
◇ adj 1 PHYSICAL, concrete, tangible, substantial. 2 RELEVANT, significant, important, meaningful, pertinent, essential, vital, indispensable, serious.

⊞ **1** abstract. **2** irrelevant.

materialize v appear, arise, take shape, turn up, happen, occur.
⊞ disappear.

mathematics

Mathematical terms include: acute angle, addition, algebra, angle, area, average, axis, Cartesian co-ordinates, coefficient, concentric, constant, co-ordinate, cosine, cube, cube root, decimal, degree, denominator, diameter, division, equation, exponential, factor, formula, fraction, function, geometry, gradient, integer, irrational number, locus, mean, median, minus, mode, multiplication, natural number, negative, number, numerator, origin, parallel, percentage, perimeter, perpendicular, pi, plane, plus, positive, prime number, probability, product, Pythagoras's theorem, quadrant, quadratic, quadrilateral, quotient, radius, ratio, rational number, real number, reciprocal, recurring decimal, reflex angle, remainder, right-angle, scalar, set, sine, square, square root, symmetry, tangent, total, trigonometry, vector, volume, zero.

matrimonial adj marital, nuptial, marriage, wedding, married, wedded, conjugal.

matter n **1** SUBJECT, issue, case, topic, question, affair, business, concern, event, episode, incident. **2** IMPORTANCE, significance, consequence, note. **3** TROUBLE, problem, difficulty, worry. **4** SUBSTANCE, stuff, material, body, content.
◇ v count, be important, be relevant, carry weight, make a difference, mean something.

matter-of-fact adj unemotional, prosaic, emotionless, straightforward, sober, unimaginative, flat, deadpan (infml).
⊞ emotional.

mature adj **1** ADULT, grown-up, grown, full-grown, fully-fledged, complete, perfect, perfected, well-thought-out. **2** RIPE, ripened, seasoned, mellow, ready.
⊞ **1** childish. **2** immature.
◇ v grow up, come of age, develop, mellow, ripen, perfect, age, bloom, fall due.

maturity n **1** ADULTHOOD, majority, womanhood, manhood, wisdom, experience. **2** RIPENESS, readiness, mellowness, perfection.
⊞ **1** childishness. **2** immaturity.

maul v abuse, ill-treat, manhandle, maltreat, molest, paw, beat (up), knock about, rough up, claw, lacerate, batter.

maxim n saying, proverb, adage, axiom, aphorism, epigram, motto, byword, precept, rule.

maximum adj greatest, highest, largest, biggest, most, utmost, supreme.
⊞ minimum.
◇ n most, top (point), utmost, upper limit, peak, pinnacle, summit, height, ceiling, extremity, zenith (fml).
⊞ minimum.

maybe adv perhaps, possibly, perchance (fml).
⊞ definitely.

maze n labyrinth, network, tangle, web, complex, confusion, puzzle, intricacy.

meadow n field, grassland, pasture, lea.

meagre adj **1** SCANTY, inadequate, sparse, deficient, skimpy, paltry, negligible, poor. **2** THIN, puny, insubstantial, bony, emaciated, scrawny, slight.
⊞ **1** ample. **2** fat.

meal

Meals include: breakfast, wedding breakfast, elevenses (*infml*), brunch, lunch, luncheon, tea, tea party, tiffin, afternoon tea, cream tea, high tea, evening meal, dinner, TV dinner, supper, harvest supper, fork supper, banquet, feast, barbecue, barbie (*infml*), buffet, cold table, picnic, snack, takeaway.

mean[1] *adj* 1 MISERLY, niggardly, parsimonious, selfish, tight (*infml*), tight-fisted, stingy (*infml*), penny-pinching (*infml*). 2 UNKIND, unpleasant, nasty, bad-tempered, cruel. 3 LOWLY, base, poor, humble, wretched.
⊞ 1 generous. 2 kind. 3 splendid.

mean[2] *v* 1 SIGNIFY, represent, denote, stand for, symbolize, suggest, indicate, imply. 2 INTEND, propose, aim, design. 3 CAUSE, give rise to, involve, entail.

mean[3] *adj* average, intermediate, middle, halfway, median, normal.
⊞ extreme.
◇ *n* average, middle, mid-point, norm, median, compromise, middle course, middle way, happy medium.
⊞ extreme.

meander *v* 1 WIND, zigzag, turn, twist, snake, curve. 2 WANDER, stray, amble, ramble, stroll.

meaning *n* 1 SIGNIFICANCE, sense, import, implication, gist, trend, explanation, interpretation. 2 AIM, intention, purpose, object, idea. 3 VALUE, worth, point.

meaningful *adj* 1 IMPORTANT, significant, relevant, valid, useful, worthwhile, material, purposeful, serious. 2 EXPRESSIVE, speaking, suggestive, warning, pointed.
⊞ 1 unimportant, worthless.

meaningless *adj* 1 SENSELESS, pointless, purposeless, useless, insignificant, aimless, insubstantial, futile, trifling, trivial. 2 EMPTY, hollow, vacuous, vain, worthless, nonsensical, absurd.
⊞ 1 important, meaningful.
2 worthwhile.

means *n* 1 METHOD, mode, way, medium, course, agency, process, instrument, channel, vehicle.
2 RESOURCES, funds, money, income, wealth, riches, substance, wherewithal, fortune, affluence.

measure *n* 1 PORTION, ration, share, allocation, quota. 2 SIZE, quantity, magnitude, amount, degree, extent, range, scope, proportion. 3 RULE, gauge, scale, standard, criterion, norm, touchstone, yardstick, test, meter. 4 STEP, course, action, deed, procedure, method, act, bill, statute.
◇ *v* quantify, evaluate, assess, weigh, value, gauge, judge, sound, fathom, determine, calculate, estimate, plumb, survey, compute, measure out, measure off.
• **measure up to** equal, meet, match, compare with, touch, rival, make the grade.

measured *adj* deliberate, planned, reasoned, slow, unhurried, steady, studied, well-thought-out, calculated, careful, considered, precise.

measurement *n* 1 DIMENSION, size, extent, amount, magnitude, area, capacity, height, depth, length, width, weight, volume. 2 ASSESSMENT, evaluation, estimation, computation, calculation, calibration, gauging, judgement, appraisal, appreciation, survey.

SI base units include: ampere, candela, kelvin, kilogram, metre, mole, second.

SI derivatives and other measurements include: acre, angstrom, atmosphere, bar, barrel, becquerel, bushel, cable, calorie, centimetre, century, chain, coulomb, cubic centimetre, cubic foot, cubic inch, cubic metre, cubic yard, day, decade, decibel, degree, dyne, erg, farad, fathom, fluid ounce, fresnel, foot, foot-pound, furlong, gallon, gill, gram, hand, hectare, hertz, horsepower, hour, hundredweight, inch, joule, kilometre, knot, league, litre, lumen, micrometre, mile, millennium, millibar, millilitre, minute, month, nautical mile, newton, ohm, ounce, pascal, peck, pint, pound, radian, rod, siemens, span, square centimetre, square foot, square inch, square kilometre, square metre, square mile, square yard, steradian, stone, therm, ton, tonne, volt, watt, week, yard, year.

meat *n* **1** FLESH. **2** (*infml*) FOOD, rations, provisions, nourishment, sustenance, subsistence, eats (*infml*).

Kinds of meat include: bacon, beef, pork, lamb, mutton, ham, gammon, chicken, turkey, goose, duck, rabbit, hare, venison, pheasant, grouse, partridge, pigeon, quail; offal, liver, heart, tongue, kidney, brains, pig's knuckle, trotters, oxtail, sweetbread, tripe; steak, mince.

Cuts of meat include: shoulder, collar, loin, hock, leg, chop, shin, knuckle, rib, spare rib, breast, brisket, chine, cutlet, fillet, rump, scrag, silverside, topside, sirloin, flank, escalope, neck, saddle.

mechanical *adj* automatic, involuntary, instinctive, routine, habitual, impersonal, emotionless, cold, matter-of-fact, unfeeling, perfunctory, lifeless, dead, dull. ⊠ conscious.

mechanism *n* **1** MACHINE, machinery, engine, appliance, instrument, tool, motor, works,

workings, gadget, device, apparatus, contrivance, gears, components. **2** MEANS, method, agency, process, procedure, system, technique, medium, structure, operation, functioning, performance.

meddle *v* interfere, intervene, pry, snoop (*infml*), intrude, butt in, tamper.

meddlesome *adj* interfering, meddling, prying, intrusive, intruding, mischievous.

mediate *v* arbitrate, conciliate, intervene, referee, umpire, intercede, moderate, reconcile, negotiate, resolve, settle, step in.

mediator *n* arbitrator, referee, umpire, intermediary, negotiator, go-between, interceder, judge, moderator, intercessor, conciliator, peacemaker, Ombudsman.

medical

Medical terms include: abortion, allergy, amniocentesis, amputation, analgesic, antibiotic, antiseptic, bandage, barium meal, biopsy, blood bank, blood count, blood donor, blood group, blood pressure, blood test, caesarean, cardiopulmonary resuscitation (CPR), case history, casualty, cauterization, cervical smear, check-up, childbirth, circulation, circumcision, clinic, complication, compress, consultant, consultation, contraception, convulsion, cure, diagnosis, dialysis, dislocate, dissection, doctor, donor, dressing, enema, examination, gene, hormone replacement therapy (HRT), hospice, hospital, immunization, implantation, incubation, infection, inflammation, injection, injury, inoculation, intensive care, keyhole surgery, in vitro fertilization (IVF), labour, laser treatment, microsurgery, miscarriage, mouthto-mouth, nurse, ointment, operation, paraplegia, post-mortem, pregnancy, prescription, prognosis, prosthesis, psychosomatic, quarantine, radiotherapy, recovery, rehabilitation, relapse, remission, respiration, resuscitation, scan, side effect, sling, smear test, specimen, splint, sterilization, steroid, surgery, suture, symptom, syndrome, therapy, tourniquet, tranquillizer, transfusion, transplant, trauma, treatment, tumour, ultrasound scanning, vaccination, vaccine, virus, X-ray.

medicinal *adj* therapeutic, healing, remedial, curative, restorative, medical.

medicine *n* medication, drug, cure, remedy, medicament, prescription, pharmaceutical, panacea.

Types of medicine include: tablet, capsule, pill, pain-killer, lozenge, pastille, gargle, linctus, tonic, laxative, suppository, antacid, ointment, eye-drops, eardrops, nasal spray, inhaler, antibiotic, penicillin, emetic, gripe water. *see also* **drug**.

Forms of alternative medicine include: acupressure, acupuncture, aromatherapy, ayurveda, Chinese medicine, chiropractic, craniosacral therapy, herbalism, homeopathy, hypnotherapy, iridology, naturopathy, osteopathy, reflexology, reiki, Rolfing, shiatsu.

mediocre *adj* ordinary, average, middling, medium, indifferent, unexceptional, undistinguished, so-so (*infml*), run-of-the-mill, bog-standard (*infml*), commonplace, insignificant, second-rate, inferior, uninspired.

⊞ exceptional, extraordinary, distinctive.

mediocrity *n* **1** ORDINARINESS, unimportance, insignificance, poorness, inferiority, indifference. **2** NONENTITY, nobody.

meditate *v* **1** REFLECT, ponder, ruminate, contemplate, muse, brood, think. **2** THINK OVER, consider, deliberate, mull over, study, speculate, scheme, plan, devise, intend.

medium *adj* average, middle, median, mean, medial, intermediate, middling, midway, standard, fair. ◇ *n* **1** AVERAGE, middle, mid-point, middle ground, compromise, centre, happy medium, golden mean. **2** MEANS, agency, channel, vehicle, instrument, way, mode, form, avenue, organ. **3** PSYCHIC, spiritualist, spiritist, clairvoyant.

medley *n* assortment, mixture, miscellany, pot-pourri, hotchpotch, hodge-podge, collection, jumble.

meek *adj* modest, long-suffering, forbearing, humble, docile, patient, unassuming, unpretentious, resigned, gentle, peaceful, tame, timid, submissive, spiritless. ⊞ arrogant, assertive, rebellious.

meet *v* **1** ENCOUNTER, come across, run across, run into, chance on, bump into (*infml*). **2** EXPERIENCE, encounter, face, go through, undergo, endure. **3** GATHER, collect, assemble, congregate, convene. **4** FULFIL, satisfy, match, answer, measure up to, equal, discharge, perform. **5** JOIN, converge, come together, connect, cross, intersect, touch, abut, unite. ⊞ **3** scatter. **5** diverge.

meeting *n* **1** ENCOUNTER, confrontation, rendezvous, engagement, assignation, introduction, tryst (*fml*). **2** ASSEMBLY, gathering, congregation, conference,

convention, rally, get-together, forum, conclave, session.
3 CONVERGENCE, confluence, junction, intersection, union.

melancholy adj depressed, dejected, down, downhearted, downcast, gloomy, low, low-spirited, heavy-hearted, sad, unhappy, despondent, dispirited, miserable, mournful, dismal, sorrowful, moody. ☒ cheerful, elated, joyful.
◇ n depression, dejection, gloom, despondency, low spirits, blues (infml), sadness, unhappiness, sorrow.
☒ elation, joy.

mellow adj **1** MATURE, ripe, juicy, full-flavoured, sweet, tender, mild. **2** GENIAL, cordial, affable, pleasant, relaxed, placid, serene, tranquil, cheerful, happy, jolly. **3** SMOOTH, melodious, rich, rounded, soft.
☒ **1** unripe. **2** cold. **3** harsh.
◇ v mature, ripen, improve, sweeten, soften, temper, season, perfect.

melodious adj tuneful, musical, melodic, harmonious, dulcet, sweet-sounding, euphonious (fml), silvery.
☒ discordant, grating, harsh.

melodramatic adj histrionic, theatrical, overdramatic, exaggerated, overemotional, sensational, hammy (infml).

melody n tune, music, song, refrain, harmony, theme, air, strain.

melt v liquefy, dissolve, thaw, fuse, deliquesce (fml).
☒ freeze, solidify.
● **melt away** disappear, vanish, fade, evaporate, dissolve, disperse.

member n adherent, associate, subscriber, representative, comrade, fellow.

memento n souvenir, keepsake, remembrance, reminder, token, memorial, record, relic.

memoirs n reminiscences, life story, recollections, autobiography, diary,

chronicles, annals, journals, records, confessions, experiences.

memorable adj unforgettable, remarkable, significant, impressive, notable, noteworthy, extraordinary, important, outstanding, momentous.
☒ forgettable, trivial, unimportant.

memorial n remembrance, monument, souvenir, memento, record, stone, plaque, mausoleum.
◇ adj commemorative, celebratory.

memorize v learn, learn by heart, commit to memory, remember.
☒ forget.

memory n recall, retention, recollection, remembrance, reminiscence, commemoration.
☒ forgetfulness.

menace v threaten, frighten, alarm, intimidate, terrorize, loom.
◇ n **1** INTIMIDATION, threat, terrorism, warning. **2** DANGER, peril, hazard, jeopardy, risk. **3** NUISANCE, annoyance, pest.

mend v **1** REPAIR, renovate, restore, refit, fix, patch, cobble, darn, heal. **2** RECOVER, get better, improve. **3** REMEDY, correct, rectify, reform, revise.
☒ **1** break. **2** deteriorate. **3** destroy.

menial adj low, lowly, humble, base, dull, humdrum, routine, degrading, demeaning, ignominious, unskilled, subservient, servile, slavish.
◇ n servant, domestic, labourer, minion, attendant, drudge, slave, underling, skivvy (infml), dogsbody (infml).

mental adj **1** INTELLECTUAL, abstract, conceptual, cognitive, cerebral, theoretical, rational. **2** (infml) MAD, insane, lunatic, crazy, unbalanced, deranged, psychotic, disturbed, loony (infml).
☒ **1** physical. **2** sane.

mentality n **1** INTELLECT, brains, understanding, faculty, rationality.

2 FRAME OF MIND, character, disposition, personality, psychology, outlook.

mention v refer to, speak of, allude to, touch on, name, cite, namecheck, acknowledge, bring up, report, make known, impart, declare, communicate, broach, divulge, disclose, intimate, point out, reveal, state, hint at, quote.
◇ n reference, allusion, citation, observation, recognition, remark, acknowledgement, announcement, notification, tribute, indication.

mercenary adj **1** GREEDY, avaricious, covetous, grasping, acquisitive, materialistic. **2** HIRED, paid, venal.

merchandise n goods, stock, commodities, produce, products, wares, cargo, freight, shipment.

merchant n trader, dealer, broker, trafficker, wholesaler, retailer, seller, shopkeeper, vendor.

merciful adj compassionate, forgiving, forbearing, humane, lenient, sparing, tender-hearted, pitying, gracious, humanitarian, kind, liberal, sympathetic, generous, mild.
⊜ hard-hearted, merciless.

merciless adj pitiless, relentless, unmerciful, ruthless, hard-hearted, hard, heartless, implacable, cruel, inhumane, unforgiving, remorseless, unpitying, unsparing, severe, callous, inhuman.
⊜ compassionate, merciful.

mercy n **1** COMPASSION, clemency, forgiveness, forbearance, leniency, pity, humanitarianism, kindness, grace. **2** BLESSING, godsend, good luck, relief.
⊜ **1** cruelty, harshness.

mere adj sheer, plain, simple, bare, utter, pure, absolute, complete, stark, unadulterated, common, paltry, petty.

merge v join, unite, combine, converge, amalgamate, blend, coalesce, mix, intermix, mingle, melt into, fuse, meet, meld, incorporate, consolidate.

merger n amalgamation, union, fusion, combination, coalition, consolidation, confederation, incorporation.

merit n worth, excellence, value, quality, good, goodness, virtue, asset, credit, advantage, strong point, talent, justification, due, claim.
⊜ fault.
◇ v deserve, be worthy of, earn, justify, warrant.

merriment n fun, jollity, mirth, hilarity, laughter, conviviality, craic (Irish), festivity, amusement, revelry, frolic, liveliness, joviality.
⊜ gloom, seriousness.

merry adj jolly, light-hearted, mirthful, joyful, happy, convivial, festive, cheerful, glad.
⊜ gloomy, melancholy, sober.

mesh n net, network, netting, lattice, web, tangle, entanglement, snare, trap.
◇ v engage, interlock, dovetail, fit, connect, harmonize, co-ordinate, combine, come together.

mess n **1** CHAOS, untidiness, disorder, disarray, confusion, muddle, jumble, clutter, disorganization, mix-up, shambles (infml). **2** DIFFICULTY, trouble, predicament, fix (infml).
⊜ **1** order, tidiness.
• **mess about** mess around, fool around, play, play around, play about, muck about (infml), interfere, tamper, trifle.
• **mess up 1** DISARRANGE, jumble, muddle, tangle, dishevel, disrupt. **2** BOTCH, bungle, spoil, muck up (infml).

message n **1** COMMUNICATION, bulletin, dispatch, communiqué, report, missive (fml), errand, letter, memorandum, note, notice, cable, e-mail, text. **2** MEANING, idea, point, theme, moral.

messenger n courier, emissary (fml), envoy, go-between, herald, runner, carrier, bearer, harbinger, agent, ambassador.

messy adj untidy, unkempt, dishevelled, disorganized, chaotic, sloppy, slovenly, confused, dirty, grubby, muddled, cluttered.
⊡ neat, ordered, tidy.

metamorphosis n change, alteration, transformation, rebirth, regeneration, transfiguration, conversion, modification.

metaphor n figure of speech, allegory, analogy, symbol, picture, image.

metaphorical adj figurative, allegorical, symbolic.

meteoric adj rapid, speedy, swift, sudden, overnight, instantaneous, momentary, brief, spectacular, brilliant, dazzling.

mete out v allot, apportion, deal out, dole out, hand out, measure out, share out, ration out, portion, distribute, dispense, divide out, assign, administer.

method n 1 WAY, approach, means, course, manner, mode, fashion, process, procedure, route, technique, style, plan, scheme, programme. 2 ORGANIZATION, order, structure, system, pattern, form, planning, regularity, routine.

methodical adj systematic, structured, organized, ordered, orderly, tidy, regular, planned, efficient, disciplined, businesslike, deliberate, neat, scrupulous, precise, meticulous, painstaking.
⊡ chaotic, irregular, confused.

meticulous adj precise, scrupulous, exact, punctilious, fussy, detailed, accurate, thorough, fastidious, painstaking, strict.
⊡ careless, slapdash.

metropolis n capital, city, municipality, megalopolis.

mettle n 1 CHARACTER, temperament, disposition. 2 SPIRIT, courage, nerve, vigour, boldness, daring, resolve, indomitability, pluck, valour, bravery, fortitude.

microbe n micro-organism, bacterium, bacillus, germ, virus, pathogen, bug (infml).

microscopic adj minute, tiny, minuscule, infinitesimal, indiscernible, imperceptible, negligible.
⊡ huge, enormous.

middle adj central, halfway, mean, median, intermediate, inner, inside, intervening.
◇ n centre, halfway point, mid-point, mean, heart, core, midst, inside, bull's-eye.
⊡ extreme, end, edge, beginning, border.

middle-class adj conventional, suburban, professional, white-collar, gentrified, bourgois.

middling adj mediocre, medium, ordinary, moderate, average, fair, unexceptional, unremarkable, run-of-the-mill, indifferent, modest, passable, tolerable, so-so (infml), OK (infml).

midget n person of restricted growth, pygmy, dwarf, Tom Thumb, gnome.
⊡ giant.
◇ adj tiny, small, miniature, little, pocket, pocket-sized.
⊡ giant.

midst n middle, centre, mid-point, heart, hub, interior.

migrant n traveller, wanderer, itinerant, emigrant, immigrant, rover, nomad, globetrotter, drifter, gypsy, tinker, vagrant.

migrate v move, resettle, relocate, emigrate, wander, roam, rove, trek, journey, travel, voyage, drift.

mild adj 1 mild manners: gentle, calm, peaceable, placid, tender, soft, good-natured, kind, amiable, lenient, compassionate. 2 mild weather: calm, temperate, warm, balmy, fair, clement, pleasant. 3 mild coffee: bland, mellow, smooth, subtle, soothing.
⊜ 1 harsh, fierce. 2 stormy. 3 strong.

militant adj aggressive, belligerent, vigorous, fighting, warring.
⊜ pacifist, peaceful.
◇ n activist, combatant, fighter, struggler, warrior, aggressor, belligerent.

military adj martial, armed, soldierly, warlike, service.
◇ n army, armed forces, soldiers, forces, services.

militate against v oppose, counter, counteract, count against, tell against, weigh against, contend, resist.

milk v drain, bleed, tap, extract, draw off, exploit, use, express, press, pump, siphon, squeeze, wring.

milky adj white, milk-white, chalky, opaque, clouded, cloudy.

mill n 1 FACTORY, plant, workshop, works, foundry, quern, roller. 2 GRINDER, crusher, quern, roller.
◇ v grind, pulverize, powder, pound, crush, roll, press, grate.

mime n dumb show, pantomime, gesture, mimicry.
◇ v gesture, signal, act out, represent, simulate, impersonate, mimic.

mimic v imitate, parody, caricature, take off, ape, parrot, impersonate, echo, mirror, simulate, look like.
◇ n imitator, impersonator, impressionist, caricaturist, copycat (infml), copy.

mimicry n imitation, imitating, impersonation, copying, parody, impression, caricature, take-off, burlesque.

mince v 1 CHOP, cut, hash, dice, grind, crumble. 2 DIMINISH, suppress, play down, tone down, hold back, moderate, weaken, soften, spare.

mind n 1 INTELLIGENCE, intellect, brains, reason, sense, understanding, wits, mentality, thinking, thoughts, grey matter (infml), head, genius, concentration, attention, spirit, psyche. 2 MEMORY, remembrance, recollection. 3 OPINION, view, point of view, belief, attitude, judgement, feeling, sentiment. 4 INCLINATION, disposition, tendency, will, wish, intention, desire.
◇ v 1 CARE, object, take offence, resent, disapprove, dislike. 2 REGARD, heed, pay attention, pay heed to, note, obey, listen to, comply with, follow, observe, be careful, watch. 3 LOOK AFTER, take care of, watch over, guard, have charge of, keep an eye on (infml).
• **bear in mind** consider, remember, note.
• **make up one's mind** decide, choose, determine, settle, resolve.

mindful adj aware, conscious, alive to, alert, attentive, careful, watchful, wary.
⊜ heedless, inattentive.

mindless adj 1 THOUGHTLESS, senseless, illogical, irrational, stupid, foolish, gratuitous, negligent. 2 MECHANICAL, automatic, tedious.
⊜ 1 thoughtful, intelligent.

mine n 1 PIT, colliery, coalfield, excavation, vein, seam, shaft, trench, deposit. 2 SUPPLY, source, stock, store, reserve, fund, hoard, treasury, wealth.
◇ v excavate, dig for, dig up, delve, quarry, extract, unearth, tunnel, remove, undermine.

mineral

Minerals include: alabaster, albite, anhydrite, asbestos, aventurine, azurite, bentonite, bloodstone, blue john, borax, cairngorm, calamine, calcite, calcspar, cassiterite, chalcedony, chlorite, chrysoberyl, cinnabar, corundum, dolomite, emery, feldspar, fluorite, fluorspar, fool's gold, galena, graphite, gypsum, haematite, halite, hornblende, hyacinth, idocrase, jacinth, jargoon, kaolinite, lapis lazuli, lazurite, magnetite, malachite, mica, microcline, montmorillonite, orthoclase, plumbago, pyrites, quartz, rock salt, rutile, sanidine, silica, smithsonite, sodalite, sphalerite, spinel, talc, uralite, uranite, vesuvianite, wurtzite, zircon.

mingle v 1 MIX, intermix, combine, blend, merge, unite, alloy, coalesce, join, compound. 2 ASSOCIATE, socialize, circulate, hobnob (infml), rub shoulders (infml).

miniature adj tiny, small, scaled-down, minute, diminutive, baby, pocket, pocket-sized, pint-size(d) (infml), little, mini (infml).
⊞ giant.

minimal adj least, smallest, minimum, slightest, littlest, negligible, minute, token.

minimize v 1 REDUCE, decrease, diminish. 2 BELITTLE, make light of, make little of, disparage, deprecate, discount, play down, underestimate, underrate.
⊞ 1 maximize.

minimum n least, lowest point, slightest, bottom.
⊞ maximum.
◇ adj minimal, least, lowest, slightest, smallest, littlest, tiniest.
⊞ maximum.

minion n 1 ATTENDANT, follower, underling, lackey, hireling. 2 DEPENDANT, hanger-on, favourite, darling, sycophant, yes-man (infml), bootlicker (infml).

minister n 1 OFFICIAL, office-holder, politician, dignitary, diplomat, ambassador, delegate, envoy, consul, cabinet minister, agent, aide, administrator, executive. 2 MEMBER OF THE CLERGY, churchman, churchwoman, cleric, parson, priest, pastor, vicar, preacher, ecclesiastic (fml), divine.
◇ v attend, serve, tend, take care of, wait on, cater to, accommodate, nurse.

ministry n 1 GOVERNMENT, cabinet, department, office, administration, bureau. 2 THE CHURCH, holy orders, the priesthood.

minor adj lesser, secondary, smaller, inferior, subordinate, subsidiary, junior, younger, insignificant, inconsiderable, negligible, petty, trivial, trifling, second-class, unclassified, slight, light.
⊞ major, significant, important.

mint v coin, stamp, strike, cast, forge, punch, make, manufacture, produce, construct, devise, fashion, invent, make up.
◇ adj perfect, brand-new, fresh, immaculate, unblemished, excellent, first-class.

minute[1] n moment, second, instant, flash, jiffy (infml), tick (infml).

minute[2] adj 1 TINY, infinitesimal, minuscule, microscopic, miniature, inconsiderable, negligible, small. 2 DETAILED, precise, meticulous, painstaking, close, critical, exhaustive.
⊞ 1 gigantic, huge. 2 cursory, superficial.

minutes n proceedings, record(s), notes, memorandum, transcript, transactions, details, tapes.

miracle n wonder, marvel, prodigy, phenomenon.

miraculous adj wonderful, marvellous, phenomenal, amazing, extraordinary, astounding,

astonishing, unbelievable, supernatural, incredible, inexplicable, unaccountable, superhuman.
⊞ natural, normal.

mirage n illusion, optical illusion, hallucination, fantasy, phantasm.

mirror n 1 GLASS, looking-glass, reflector. 2 REFLECTION, likeness, image, double, copy.
◇ v reflect, echo, imitate, copy, represent, show, depict, mimic.

mirth n merriment, hilarity, gaiety, fun, laughter, jollity, jocularity, amusement, revelry, glee, cheerfulness.
⊞ gloom, melancholy.

misapprehension n misunderstanding, misconception, misinterpretation, misreading, error, mistake, fallacy, delusion.

misappropriate v steal, embezzle, peculate, pocket, swindle (infml), misspend, misuse, misapply, abuse, pervert.

misbehave v offend, transgress, trespass, get up to mischief, mess about, muck about (infml), play up, act up (infml).

misbehaviour n misconduct, misdemeanour, impropriety, disobedience, naughtiness, insubordination.

miscalculate v misjudge, get wrong, slip up (infml), blunder, err, boob (infml), miscount, overestimate, underestimate.

miscarriage n failure, breakdown, abortion, mishap, mismanagement, error, ruination, disappointment.
⊞ success.

miscarry v fail, abort, come to nothing, fall through, misfire, founder, come to grief.
⊞ succeed.

miscellaneous adj mixed, varied, various, assorted, diverse, diversified, sundry, motley, jumbled, indiscriminate.

miscellany n mixture, variety, assortment, collection, anthology, medley, mixed bag, pot-pourri, hotchpotch, jumble, diversity.

mischief n 1 TROUBLE, harm, evil, damage, injury, disruption. 2 MISBEHAVIOUR, naughtiness, impishness, pranks.

mischievous adj 1 MALICIOUS, evil, spiteful, vicious, wicked, pernicious, destructive, injurious. 2 NAUGHTY, impish, rascally, roguish, playful, teasing.
⊞ 1 kind. 2 well-behaved, good.

misconception n misapprehension, misunderstanding, misreading, error, fallacy, delusion, the wrong end of the stick (infml).

misconduct n misbehaviour, impropriety, misdemeanour, malpractice, mismanagement, wrongdoing.

miser n niggard, skinflint, penny-pincher (infml), Scrooge.
⊞ spendthrift.

miserable adj 1 UNHAPPY, sad, dejected, despondent, downcast, heartbroken, wretched, distressed, crushed. 2 CHEERLESS, depressing, dreary, impoverished, shabby, gloomy, dismal, forlorn, joyless, squalid. 3 CONTEMPTIBLE, despicable, ignominious, detestable, disgraceful, deplorable, shameful. 4 MEAGRE, paltry, niggardly, worthless, pathetic, pitiful.
⊞ 1 cheerful, happy. 2 pleasant. 4 generous.

miserly adj mean, niggardly, tight, stingy (infml), sparing, parsimonious, cheese-paring, beggarly, penny-pinching (infml), mingy (infml).
⊞ generous, spendthrift.

misery n 1 UNHAPPINESS, sadness, suffering, distress, depression, despair, gloom, grief, wretchedness,

affliction. **2** PRIVATION, hardship, deprivation, poverty, want, oppression, destitution. **3** (*infml*) SPOILSPORT, pessimist, killjoy, wet blanket (*infml*), party pooper (*infml*).
⊜ 1 contentment. **2** comfort.

misfire *v* miscarry, go wrong, abort, fail, fall through, flop (*infml*), founder, fizzle out, come to grief.
⊜ succeed.

misfit *n* individualist, nonconformist, eccentric, maverick, drop-out, loner, lone wolf.
⊜ conformist.

misfortune *n* bad luck, mischance, mishap, ill luck, setback, reverse, calamity, catastrophe, disaster, blow, accident, tragedy, trouble, hardship, trial, tribulation.
⊜ luck, success.

misgiving *n* doubt, uncertainty, hesitation, qualm, reservation, apprehension, scruple, suspicion, second thoughts, niggle, anxiety, worry, fear.
⊜ confidence.

misguided *adj* misconceived, misled, ill-considered, ill-advised, ill-judged, imprudent, rash, misplaced, deluded, foolish, erroneous.
⊜ sensible, wise.

mishap *n* misfortune, ill fortune, misadventure, accident, setback, calamity, disaster, adversity.

misinterpret *v* misconstrue, misread, misunderstand, mistake, distort, garble.

misjudge *v* miscalculate, mistake, misinterpret, misconstrue, misunderstand, overestimate, underestimate.

mislay *v* lose, misplace, miss, lose sight of.

mislead *v* misinform, misdirect, deceive, delude, lead astray, fool.

misleading *adj* deceptive, confusing, unreliable, ambiguous,

biased, loaded, evasive, tricky (*infml*).
⊜ unequivocal, authoritative, informative.

mismanage *v* mishandle, botch, bungle, make a mess of, mess up, misrule, misspend, misjudge, foul up, mar, waste.

misprint *n* mistake, error, erratum, literal, typo (*infml*).

misrepresent *v* distort, falsify, slant, pervert, twist, garble, misquote, exaggerate, minimize, misconstrue, misinterpret.

miss *v* **1** FAIL, miscarry, lose, let slip, let go, omit, overlook, pass over, slip, leave out, mistake, trip, misunderstand, err. **2** AVOID, escape, evade, dodge, forego, skip, bypass, circumvent. **3** PINE FOR, long for, yearn for, regret, grieve for, mourn, sorrow for, want, wish, need, lament.
◇ *n* failure, error, blunder, mistake, omission, oversight, fault, flop (*infml*), fiasco.

misshapen *adj* deformed, distorted, twisted, malformed, warped, contorted, crooked, crippled, grotesque, ugly, monstrous.
⊜ regular, shapely.

missile *n* projectile, shot, guided missile, arrow, shaft, dart, rocket, bomb, shell, flying bomb, grenade, torpedo, weapon.

missing *adj* absent, lost, lacking, gone, mislaid, unaccounted-for, wanting, disappeared, astray, strayed, misplaced.
⊜ found, present.

mission *n* **1** TASK, undertaking, assignment, operation, campaign, crusade, business, errand. **2** CALLING, duty, purpose, vocation, raison d'être, aim, charge, office, job, work. **3** COMMISSION, ministry, delegation, deputation, legation, embassy.

missionary *n* evangelist, campaigner, preacher, proselytizer, apostle, crusader, propagandist, champion, promoter, emissary, envoy, ambassador.

mist n haze, fog, vapour, smog, cloud, condensation, film, spray, drizzle, dew, steam, veil, dimness.
• **mist over** cloud over, fog, dim, blur, steam up, obscure, veil.
⊜ clear.

mistake n error, inaccuracy, slip, slip-up (*infml*), oversight, lapse, blunder, clanger (*infml*), boob (*infml*), gaffe, fault, faux pas, solecism (*fml*), indiscretion, misjudgement, miscalculation, misunderstanding, misprint, misspelling, misreading, mispronunciation, howler (*infml*).
◇ v misunderstand, misapprehend, misconstrue, misjudge, misread, miscalculate, confound, confuse, slip up (*infml*), blunder, err, boob (*infml*).

mistaken adj wrong, incorrect, erroneous, inaccurate, inexact, untrue, inappropriate, ill-judged, inauthentic, false, deceived, deluded, misinformed, misled, faulty.
⊜ correct, right.

mistreat v abuse, ill-treat, ill-use, maltreat, harm, hurt, batter, injure, knock about, molest.

mistress n 1 LOVER, live-in lover, kept woman, concubine, courtesan, girlfriend, paramour, woman, lady-love. 2 TEACHER, governess, tutor.

mistrust n distrust, doubt, suspicion, wariness, misgiving, reservations, qualm, hesitancy, chariness, caution, uncertainty, scepticism, apprehension.
⊜ trust.
◇ v distrust, doubt, suspect, be wary of, beware, have reservations, fear.
⊜ trust.

misty adj hazy, foggy, cloudy, blurred, fuzzy, murky, smoky, unclear, dim, indistinct, obscure, opaque, vague, veiled.
⊜ clear.

misunderstand v misapprehend, misconstrue, misinterpret, misjudge, mistake, get wrong, miss the point, mishear, get hold of the wrong end of the stick (*infml*).
⊜ understand.

misunderstanding n
1 MISTAKE, error, misapprehension, misconception, misjudgement, misinterpretation, misreading, mix-up. 2 DISAGREEMENT, argument, dispute, conflict, clash, difference, breach, quarrel, discord, rift.
⊜ 1 understanding. 2 agreement.

misuse n mistreatment, maltreatment, mishandling, abuse, harm, ill-treatment, misapplication, misappropriation, waste, perversion, corruption, exploitation.
◇ v abuse, misapply, misemploy, ill-use, ill-treat, harm, mistreat, wrong, distort, injure, corrupt, pervert, waste, squander, misappropriate, exploit, dissipate.

mitigating adj extenuating, justifying, vindicating, modifying, qualifying.

mix v 1 COMBINE, blend, mingle, intermingle, intermix, amalgamate, compound, homogenize, synthesize, merge, join, unite, coalesce, fuse, incorporate, fold in. 2 ASSOCIATE, consort, fraternize, socialize, mingle, join, hobnob (*infml*).
⊜ 1 divide, separate.
◇ n mixture, blend, amalgam, assortment, combination, conglomerate, compound, fusion, synthesis, medley, composite, mishmash (*infml*).
• **mix up** confuse, bewilder, muddle, perplex, puzzle, confound, mix, jumble, complicate, garble, involve, implicate, disturb, upset, snarl up.

mixed adj 1 *mixed race*: combined, hybrid, mingled, crossbred, mongrel, blended, composite, compound, incorporated, united, alloyed, amalgamated, fused.

2 *mixed biscuits*: assorted, varied, miscellaneous, diverse, diversified, motley. **3** *mixed feelings*: ambivalent, equivocal, conflicting, contradicting, uncertain.

mixture *n* mix, blend, combination, amalgamation, amalgam, compound, conglomeration, composite, alloy, coalescence, brew, synthesis, union, fusion, concoction, cross, hybrid, assortment, variety, miscellany, medley, mélange, mixed bag, pot-pourri, jumble, hotchpotch.

moan *n* lament, lamentation, sob, wail, howl, whimper, whine, grumble, complaint, grievance, groan.
◇ *v* **1** LAMENT, wail, sob, weep, howl, groan, whimper, mourn, grieve. **2** (*infml*) COMPLAIN, grumble, whine, whinge (*infml*), gripe (*infml*), carp.
⊞ **1** rejoice.

mob *n* **1** CROWD, mass, throng, multitude, horde, host, swarm, gathering, group, collection, flock, herd, pack, set, tribe, troop, company, crew, gang. **2** POPULACE, rabble, masses, hoi polloi, plebs (*infml*), riff-raff (*infml*).
◇ *v* crowd, crowd round, surround, swarm round, jostle, overrun, set upon, besiege, descend on, throng, pack, pester, charge.

mobile *adj* **1** MOVING, movable, portable, peripatetic, travelling, roaming, roving, itinerant, wandering, migrant. **2** FLEXIBLE, agile, active, energetic, nimble. **3** CHANGING, changeable, ever-changing, expressive, lively.
⊞ **1** immobile.

mobilize *v* assemble, marshal, rally, conscript, muster, enlist, activate, galvanize, organize, prepare, ready, summon, animate.

mock *v* **1** RIDICULE, jeer, make fun of, laugh at, disparage, deride, scoff, sneer, taunt, scorn, tease. **2** IMITATE,

simulate, mimic, ape, caricature, satirize.
◇ *adj* imitation, counterfeit, artificial, sham, simulated, synthetic, false, fake, forged, fraudulent, bogus, phoney (*infml*), pseudo, spurious, feigned, faked, pretended, dummy.

mockery *n* **1** RIDICULE, jeering, scoffing, scorn, derision, contempt, disdain, disrespect, sarcasm. **2** PARODY, satire, sham, travesty.

mocking *adj* scornful, derisive, contemptuous, sarcastic, satirical, taunting, scoffing, sardonic, snide (*infml*), insulting, irreverent, impudent, disrespectful, disdainful, cynical.

model *n* **1** COPY, representation, replica, facsimile, imitation, mock-up. **2** EXAMPLE, exemplar, pattern, standard, ideal, mould, prototype, template. **3** DESIGN, style, type, version, mark. **4** MANNEQUIN, dummy, sitter, subject, poser.
◇ *adj* exemplary, perfect, typical, ideal.
◇ *v* **1** MAKE, form, fashion, mould, sculpt, carve, cast, shape, work, create, design, plan. **2** DISPLAY, wear, show off.

moderate *adj* **1** MEDIOCRE, medium, ordinary, fair, indifferent, average, middle-of-the-road. **2** REASONABLE, restrained, sensible, calm, controlled, cool, mild, well-regulated.
⊞ **1** exceptional. **2** immoderate.
◇ *v* control, regulate, decrease, lessen, soften, restrain, tone down, play down, diminish, ease, curb, calm, check, modulate, repress, subdue, soft-pedal, tame, subside, pacify, mitigate, allay, alleviate, abate, dwindle.

moderately *adv* somewhat, quite, rather, fairly, slightly, reasonably, passably, to some extent.
⊞ extremely.

moderation *n* **1** DECREASE, reduction. **2** RESTRAINT, self-control, caution, control, composure, sobriety, abstemiousness, temperance, reasonableness.

modern *adj* current, contemporary, up-to-date, new, fresh, latest, late, novel, present, present-day, recent, up-to-the-minute, newfangled (*infml*), advanced, avant-garde, progressive, modernistic, innovative, inventive, state-of-the-art, go-ahead, fashionable, stylish, in vogue, in style, modish, trendy (*infml*).
🔁 old-fashioned, old, out-of-date, antiquated, oldfangled (*infml*).

modernize *v* renovate, refurbish, rejuvenate, regenerate, streamline, revamp, renew, update, improve, do up, redesign, reform, remake, remodel, refresh, transform, modify, progress.
🔁 regress.

modest *adj* **1** UNASSUMING, humble, self-effacing, quiet, reserved, retiring, unpretentious, discreet, bashful, shy. **2** MODERATE, ordinary, unexceptional, fair, reasonable, limited, small.
🔁 **1** immodest, conceited. **2** exceptional, excessive.

modesty *n* humility, humbleness, self-effacement, reticence, reserve, quietness, decency, propriety, demureness, shyness, bashfulness, coyness.
🔁 immodesty, vanity, conceit.

modify *v* **1** CHANGE, alter, redesign, revise, vary, adapt, adjust, transform, reform, convert, improve, reorganize. **2** MODERATE, reduce, temper, tone down, limit, soften, qualify.

modulate *v* modify, adjust, balance, alter, soften, lower, regulate, vary, harmonize, inflect, tune.

moist *adj* damp, clammy, humid, wet, dewy, rainy, muggy, marshy, drizzly, watery, soggy.
🔁 dry, arid.

moisten *v* moisturize, dampen,

damp, wet, water, lick, irrigate.
🔁 dry.

moisture *n* water, liquid, wetness, wateriness, damp, dampness, dew, dankness, mugginess, humidity, vapour, condensation, steam, spray.
🔁 dryness.

molest *v* **1** ANNOY, disturb, bother, harass, irritate, persecute, pester, plague, tease, torment, hound, upset, worry, trouble, badger. **2** ATTACK, accost, assail, hurt, ill-treat, maltreat, mistreat, abuse, harm, injure.

mollusc

Molluscs include: abalone, clam, cockle, cowrie, cuttlefish, limpet, mussel, nautilus, nudibranch, octopus, oyster, periwinkle, scallop, slug, snail, squid, tusk shell, whelk.

---

moment *n* second, instant, minute, split second, trice, jiffy (*infml*), tick (*infml*).

momentary *adj* brief, short, short-lived, temporary, transient, transitory, fleeting, ephemeral, hasty, quick, passing.
🔁 lasting, permanent.

momentous *adj* significant, important, critical, crucial, decisive, weighty, grave, serious, vital, fateful, historic, earth-shaking, epoch-making, eventful, major.
🔁 insignificant, unimportant, trivial.

momentum *n* impetus, force, energy, impulse, drive, power, thrust, speed, velocity, impact, incentive, stimulus, urge, strength, push.

monarch *n* sovereign, crowned head, ruler, king, queen, emperor, empress, prince, princess, tsar, potentate.

monarchy *n* **1** KINGDOM, empire, principality, realm, dominion, domain. **2** ROYALISM, sovereignty, autocracy, monocracy, absolutism, despotism, tyranny.

monastery n friary, priory, abbey, cloister, charterhouse.

monastic adj reclusive, withdrawn, secluded, cloistered, austere, ascetic, celibate, contemplative.
⊞ secular, worldly.

monetary adj financial, fiscal, pecuniary (fml), budgetary, economic, capital, cash.

money n currency, cash, legal tender, banknotes, coin, funds, capital, dough (infml), dosh (infml), riches, wealth.

mongrel n cross, crossbreed, hybrid, half-breed.
◇ adj crossbred, hybrid, half-breed, bastard, mixed, ill-defined.
⊞ pure-bred, pedigree.

monitor n 1 SCREEN, display, VDU, recorder, scanner. 2 SUPERVISOR, watchdog, overseer, invigilator, adviser, prefect.
◇ v check, watch, keep track of, keep under surveillance, keep an eye on, follow, track, supervise, observe, note, survey, trace, scan, record, plot, detect.

monkey n 1 PRIMATE, simian, ape. 2 (infml) SCAMP, imp, urchin, brat, rogue, scallywag (infml), rascal.

Monkeys include: baboon, capuchin, colobus monkey, douroucouli, drill, guenon, guereza, howler monkey, langur, macaque, mandrill, mangabey, marmoset, proboscis monkey, rhesus monkey, saki, spider monkey, squirrel monkey, tamarin, titi, toque, uakari, woolly monkey.

---

monopolize v dominate, take over, appropriate, corner, control, hog (infml), engross, occupy, preoccupy, take up, tie up.
⊞ share.

monotonous adj boring, dull, tedious, uninteresting, tiresome, wearisome, unchanging, uneventful, unvaried, uniform, toneless, flat, colourless, repetitive, routine, plodding, humdrum, soul-destroying.
⊞ lively, varied, colourful.

monotony n tedium, dullness, boredom, sameness, tiresomeness, uneventfulness, flatness, wearisomeness, uniformity, routine, repetitiveness.
⊞ liveliness, colour.

monster n 1 BEAST, fiend, brute, barbarian, savage, villain, giant, ogre, ogress, troll, mammoth. 2 FREAK, monstrosity, mutant.
◇ adj huge, gigantic, giant, colossal, enormous, immense, massive, vast, monstrous, jumbo, mammoth, tremendous.
⊞ tiny, minute.

monstrous adj 1 WICKED, evil, vicious, cruel, criminal, heinous, outrageous, scandalous, disgraceful, atrocious, abhorrent, dreadful, frightful, horrible, horrifying, terrible. 2 UNNATURAL, inhuman, freakish, grotesque, hideous, deformed, malformed, misshapen. 3 HUGE, enormous, colossal, gigantic, vast, immense, massive, mammoth.

monument n memorial, cenotaph, headstone, gravestone, tombstone, shrine, mausoleum, cairn, barrow, cross, marker, obelisk, pillar, statue, relic, remembrance, commemoration, testament, reminder, record, memento, evidence, token.

monumental adj 1 IMPRESSIVE, imposing, awe-inspiring, awesome, overwhelming, significant, important, epoch-making, historic, magnificent, majestic, memorable, notable, outstanding, abiding, immortal, lasting, classic. 2 HUGE, immense, enormous, colossal, vast, tremendous, massive, great.

3 COMMEMORATIVE, memorial.
⊡ **1** insignificant, unimportant.

mood n **1** DISPOSITION, frame of mind, state of mind, temper, humour, spirit, tenor, whim. **2** BAD TEMPER, sulk, the sulks, pique, melancholy, depression, blues (infml), doldrums, dumps (infml).

moody adj temperamental, unpredictable, changeable, capricious, irritable, short-tempered, crabby (infml), crotchety, crusty (infml), testy, touchy, morose, angry, broody, mopy, sulky, sullen, gloomy, melancholy, miserable, downcast, doleful, glum, impulsive, fickle, flighty.
⊡ equable, cheerful.

moon v idle, loaf, mooch, languish, pine, mope, brood, daydream, dream, fantasize.

moor¹ v fasten, secure, tie up, drop anchor, anchor, berth, dock, make fast, fix, hitch, bind.
⊡ loose.

moor² n moorland, heath, fell, upland.

mop n head of hair, shock, mane, tangle, thatch, mass.
◇ v swab, sponge, wipe, clean, wash, absorb, soak.

mope v brood, fret, sulk, languish, droop, pine, despair, grieve, idle.

moral adj ethical, virtuous, good, right, principled, honourable, decent, upright, upstanding, straight, righteous, high-minded, honest, incorruptible, proper, blameless, chaste, clean-living, pure, just, noble.
⊡ immoral.
◇ n lesson, message, teaching, dictum, meaning, maxim, adage, precept, saying, proverb, aphorism, epigram.

morale n confidence, spirits, esprit de corps, self-esteem, state of mind, heart, mood.

morality n ethics, morals, ideals, principles, standards, virtue, rectitude, righteousness, decency, goodness, honesty, integrity, justice, uprightness, propriety, conduct, manners.
⊡ immorality.

morals n morality, ethics, principles, standards, ideals, integrity, scruples, behaviour, conduct, habits, manners.

morbid adj **1** GHOULISH, ghastly, gruesome, macabre, hideous, horrid, grim. **2** GLOOMY, pessimistic, melancholy, sombre. **3** SICK, unhealthy, unwholesome, insalubrious.

more adj further, extra, additional, added, new, fresh, increased, other, supplementary, repeated, alternative, spare.
⊡ less.
◇ adv further, longer, again, besides, moreover, better.
⊡ less.

moreover adv furthermore, further, besides, in addition, as well, also, additionally, what is more.

morning n daybreak, daylight, dawn, sunrise, break of day, before noon.

morose adj ill-tempered, bad-tempered, moody, sullen, sulky, surly, gloomy, grim, gruff, sour, taciturn, glum, grouchy (infml), crabby (infml), saturnine.
⊡ cheerful, communicative.

morsel n bit, scrap, piece, crumb, bite, mouthful, nibble, taste, soupçon, titbit, fragment, slice, fraction, modicum, grain, atom, part.

mortal adj **1** WORLDLY, earthly, bodily, human, perishable, temporal. **2** FATAL, lethal, deadly. **3** EXTREME, great, severe, intense, grave, awful.
⊡ **1** immortal.
◇ n human being, human, individual, person, being, body, creature.
⊡ immortal, god.

mortality n 1 HUMANITY, death, impermanence, perishability. 2 FATALITY, death rate.
⊞ 1 immortality.

mortified adj humiliated, shamed, ashamed, humbled, embarrassed, crushed.

mostly adv mainly, on the whole, principally, chiefly, generally, usually, largely, for the most part, as a rule.

moth

Types of moth include: brown-tail, buff-tip, burnet, carpet, cinnabar, clothes, death's-head, emperor, gypsy, hawk-moth, Kentish glory, lackey, lappet, leopard, lobster, magpie, oak-egger, peach-blossom, peppered, puss, red underwing, silkworm, silver-Y, swallow-tail, tiger, turnip, tussock, wax, winter. see also **butterfly**.

mother n 1 PARENT, procreator (fml), progenitress (fml), birth mother, dam, mamma, mum (infml), mummy (infml), mom (US infml), matriarch, ancestor, matron, old woman (infml). 2 ORIGIN, source.
◇ v 1 BEAR, produce, nurture, raise, rear, nurse, care for, cherish. 2 PAMPER, spoil, baby, indulge, overprotect, fuss over.

motherly adj maternal, caring, comforting, affectionate, kind, loving, protective, warm, tender, gentle, fond.
⊞ neglectful, uncaring.

motif n theme, idea, topic, concept, pattern, design, figure, form, logo, shape, device, ornament, decoration.

motion n 1 MOVEMENT, action, mobility, moving, activity, locomotion, travel, transit, passage, passing, progress, change, flow, inclination. 2 GESTURE, gesticulation, signal, sign, wave, nod. 3 PROPOSAL, suggestion, recommendation, proposition.

◇ v signal, gesture, gesticulate, sign, wave, nod, beckon, direct, usher.

motionless adj unmoving, still, stationary, static, immobile, at a standstill, fixed, halted, at rest, resting, standing, paralysed, inanimate, lifeless, frozen, rigid, stagnant.
⊞ active, moving.

motivate v prompt, incite, impel, spur, provoke, stimulate, drive, lead, stir, urge, push, propel, persuade, move, inspire, encourage, cause, trigger, induce, kindle, draw, arouse, bring.
⊞ deter, discourage.

motive n grounds, cause, reason, purpose, motivation, object, intention, influence, rationale, thinking, incentive, impulse, stimulus, inspiration, incitement, urge, encouragement, design, desire, consideration.
⊞ deterrent, disincentive.

mottled adj speckled, dappled, blotchy, flecked, piebald, stippled, streaked, tabby, spotted, freckled, variegated.
⊞ monochrome, uniform.

motto n saying, slogan, maxim, watchword, catchword, byword, precept, proverb, adage, formula, rule, golden rule, dictum.

mould¹ n 1 CAST, form, die, template, pattern, matrix. 2 SHAPE, form, format, pattern, structure, style, type, build, construction, cut, design, kind, model, sort, stamp, arrangement, brand, frame, character, nature, quality, line, make.
◇ v 1 FORGE, cast, shape, stamp, make, form, create, design, construct, sculpt, model, work. 2 INFLUENCE, direct, control.

mould² n mildew, fungus, mouldiness, mustiness, blight.

mouldy adj mildewed, blighted, musty, decaying, corrupt, rotten,

fusty, putrid, bad, spoiled, stale.
☒ fresh, wholesome.

mound n **1** HILL, hillock, hummock,
rise, knoll, bank, dune, elevation,
ridge, embankment, earthwork.
2 HEAP, pile, stack.

mount v **1** PRODUCE, put on, set
up, prepare, stage, exhibit, display,
launch. **2** INCREASE, grow, accumulate,
multiply, rise, intensify, soar, swell.
3 CLIMB, ascend, get up, go up, get
on, clamber up, scale, get astride.
☒ **2** decrease, diminish, subside.
3 descend, dismount, go down.
◇ n horse, steed, support, mounting.

mountain n **1** HEIGHT, elevation,
mount, peak, mound, alp, tor, massif.
2 HEAP, pile, stack, mass, abundance,
backlog.

mountainous adj **1** CRAGGY, rocky,
hilly, high, highland, upland, alpine,
soaring, steep. **2** HUGE, towering,
enormous, immense.
☒ **1** flat. **2** tiny.

mourn v grieve, lament, sorrow,
bemoan, miss, regret, deplore, weep,
wail.
☒ rejoice.

mournful adj sorrowful, sad,
unhappy, desolate, grief-stricken,
heavy-hearted, heartbroken,
broken-hearted, cast down,
downcast, miserable, tragic, woeful,
melancholy, sombre, depressed,
dejected, gloomy, dismal.
☒ joyful.

mourning n bereavement, grief,
grieving, lamentation, sadness,
sorrow, desolation, weeping.
☒ rejoicing.

mouth n **1** LIPS, jaws, trap (infml),
gob (sl). **2** OPENING, aperture, orifice,
cavity, entrance, gateway, inlet,
estuary.
◇ v enunciate, articulate, utter,
pronounce, whisper, form.

movable adj mobile, portable,
transportable, changeable, alterable,

adjustable, flexible, transferable.
☒ fixed, immovable.

move v **1** STIR, go, advance, budge,
change, proceed, progress, make
strides. **2** TRANSPORT, carry, transfer.
3 DEPART, go away, leave, decamp,
migrate, remove, move house,
relocate. **4** PROMPT, stimulate, urge,
impel, drive, propel, motivate, incite,
persuade, induce, inspire. **5** AFFECT,
touch, agitate, stir, impress, excite.
◇ n **1** MOVEMENT, motion, step,
manoeuvre, action, device,
stratagem. **2** REMOVAL, relocation,
migration, transfer.

movement n **1** REPOSITIONING, move,
moving, relocation, activity, act,
action, agitation, stirring, transfer,
passage. **2** CHANGE, development,
advance, evolution, current, drift,
flow, shift, progress, progression,
trend, tendency. **3** CAMPAIGN, crusade,
drive, group, organization, party,
faction.

moving adj **1** MOBILE, active, in
motion. **2** TOUCHING, affecting,
poignant, impressive, emotive,
arousing, stirring, inspiring,
inspirational, exciting, thrilling,
persuasive, stimulating.
☒ **1** immobile. **2** unemotional.

mow v cut, trim, crop, clip, shear,
scythe.

much adv greatly, considerably, a
lot, frequently, often.
◇ adj copious, plentiful, ample, a
lot, considerable, abundant, great,
substantial.
◇ n plenty, a lot, lots (infml), loads
(infml), heaps (infml), lashings
(infml).
☒ little.

muck n dirt, dung, manure, mire,
filth, mud, sewage, slime, gunge
(infml), ordure, scum, sludge.
• **muck up** ruin, wreck, spoil, mess
up, make a mess of, botch, bungle,
screw up (infml), cock up (sl).

mud n clay, mire, ooze, dirt, sludge, silt.

muddle v 1 DISORGANIZE, disorder, mix up, mess up, jumble, scramble, tangle. 2 CONFUSE, bewilder, bemuse, perplex.
◇ n chaos, confusion, disorder, mess, mix-up, jumble, clutter, tangle.

muddy adj 1 DIRTY, foul, miry, mucky, marshy, boggy, swampy, quaggy, grimy. 2 CLOUDY, indistinct, obscure, opaque, murky, hazy, blurred, fuzzy, dull.
⊞ 1 clean. 2 clear.

muffle v 1 WRAP, envelop, cloak, swathe, cover. 2 DEADEN, dull, quieten, silence, stifle, dampen, muzzle, suppress.
⊞ 2 amplify.

mug¹ n cup, beaker, pot, tankard.

mug² v set upon, attack, assault, waylay, steal from, rob, beat up, jump (on).

muggy adj humid, sticky, stuffy, sultry, close, clammy, oppressive, sweltering, moist, damp.
⊞ dry.

mull over v reflect on, ponder, contemplate, think over, think about, ruminate, consider, weigh up, chew over, meditate, study, examine, deliberate.

multiple adj many, numerous, manifold, various, several, sundry, collective.

multiply v increase, proliferate, expand, spread, reproduce, propagate, breed, accumulate, intensify, extend, build up, augment, boost.
⊞ decrease, lessen.

multitude n crowd, throng, horde, swarm, mob, mass, herd, congregation, host, lot, lots, legion, public, people, populace.
⊞ few, scattering.

munch v eat, chew, crunch, masticate (fml).

mundane adj banal, ordinary, everyday, commonplace, prosaic, humdrum, workaday, routine.
⊞ extraordinary.

municipal adj civic, city, town, urban, borough, community, public.

murder n homicide, killing, manslaughter, slaying, assassination, massacre, bloodshed.
◇ v kill, slaughter, slay, assassinate, butcher, massacre.

murderer n killer, homicide, slayer, slaughterer, assassin, butcher, cut-throat.

murderous adj 1 HOMICIDAL, brutal, barbarous, bloodthirsty, bloody, cut-throat, killing, lethal, cruel, savage, ferocious, deadly. 2 (infml) DIFFICULT, exhausting, strenuous, unpleasant, dangerous.

murky adj dark, dismal, gloomy, dull, overcast, misty, foggy, dim, cloudy, obscure, veiled, grey.
⊞ bright, clear.

murmur n mumble, muttering, whisper, undertone, humming, rumble, drone, grumble.
◇ v mutter, mumble, whisper, buzz, hum, rumble, purr, burble.

muscular adj brawny, beefy (infml), sinewy, athletic, powerfully built, strapping, hefty, powerful, husky, robust, stalwart, vigorous, strong.
⊞ puny, flabby, weak.

mushroom

Types of mushroom and toadstool include: amanita, beefsteak fungus, blewits, boletus, chestnut mushroom, button mushroom, cep, champignon, chanterelle, death cap, destroying angel, elf cup, fairy ring, false morel, fly agaric, honey fungus, horn of plenty, horse mushroom, ink-cap, lawyer's wig, meadow mushroom, milk cap, morel, oyster mushroom, parasol mushroom, penny-bun, porcini, saffron milk cap, shaggy ink-cap, shiitake, sulphur tuft, truffle.

music

Types of music include: acid house, adult-oriented rock (AOR), ambient, Americana, ballet, Big Beat, bluegrass, blues, boogie-woogie, Cajun, calypso, chamber, choral, classical, country-and-western, dance, dancehall, disco, Dixieland, doo-wop, drum and bass, electronic, emo, folk, folk rock, funk, fusion, gangsta, garage, glam rock, gospel, grunge, hard-core, heavy metal, hip-hop, honky-tonk, house, incidental, instrumental, jazz, jazz-funk, jazz-rock, jive, jungle, lovers' rock, middle-of-the-road (MOR), nu-metal, operatic, orchestral, pop, punk rock, ragtime, rap, reggae, rhythm and blues (R & B), rock, rock and roll, salsa, samba, ska, skiffle, soul, swing, techno, thrash metal, trance, trip hop.

musical *adj* tuneful, melodious, melodic, harmonious, dulcet, sweet-sounding, lyrical.
🄴 discordant, unmusical.

Musical instruments include:
stringed: balalaika, banjo, cello, clarsach, double bass, erhu, guitar, harp, hurdy-gurdy, lute, lyre, mandolin, oud, sitar, spinet, ukulele, viola, violin, fiddle (*infml*), zither; *keyboard*: accordion, concertina, clavichord, harmonium, harpsichord, keyboard, melodeon, organ, Wurlitzer®, piano, grand piano, Pianola®, player piano, synthesizer, virginals; *wind*: bagpipes, bassoon, bugle, clarinet, cor anglais, cornet, didgeridoo, euphonium, fife, flugelhorn, flute,

French horn, gaita, harmonica, horn, kazoo, mouth organ, oboe, Pan-pipes, piccolo, recorder, saxophone, sousaphone, trombone, trumpet, tuba, uillean pipes; *percussion*: castanets, cymbal, glockenspiel, maracas, marimba, mbira, rainstick, tambourine, triangle, tubular bells, xylophone; *drums*: bass drum, bodhran, bongo, kettledrum, snare drum, steel drum, tabla, tenor drum, timpani, tom-tom.

Musical terms include:
accompaniment, alto, arpeggio, arrangement, bar, baritone, bass, beat, cadence, chord, clef, bass clef, treble clef, coda, contralto, counterpoint, crotchet, descant, downbeat, encore, ensemble, finale, flat, harmony, key, medley, melody, middle C, minim, natural, note, octave, orchestra, pitch, quaver, rest, rhythm, scale, score, semibreve, semiquaver, semitone, sharp, solo, soprano, stave, syncopation, tempo, tenor, timbre, time signature, tone, tonic sol-fa, treble, tremolo, tuning, unison, up-beat, vibrato, virtuoso.

Musical directions include: a cappella, accelerando, adagio, ad lib, affettuoso, agitato, alla breve, allargando, allegretto, allegro, amoroso, andante, animato, arco, a tempo, cantabile, con brio, con fuoco, con moto, crescendo, da capo, decrescendo, diminuendo, dolce, doloroso, fine, forte, fortissimo, glissando, grave, larghetto, largo, legato, lento, maestoso, marcato, mezza voce, mezzo-forte, moderato, molto, non troppo, obbligato, pianissimo, piano, pizzicato, presto, rallentando, ritenuto, semplice, sempre, senza, sforzando, smorzando, sostenuto, sotto voce, spiritoso, staccato, subito, tacet, tanto, tenuto, tutti, vigoroso, vivace.

musician

Musicians include: instrumentalist, accompanist, player; bugler, busker, cellist, clarinettist, drummer, fiddler, flautist, guitarist, harpist, lutenist, oboist, organist, percussionist, pianist, piper, soloist, trombonist, trumpeter, violinist; singer, vocalist, balladeer, diva, prima donna; conductor; band, orchestra, group, backing group, ensemble, chamber orchestra, choir, duo, duet, trio, quartet, quintet, sextet, septet, octet, nonet.

must *n* necessity, prerequisite, obligation, requirement, stipulation, essential, fundamental, imperative, duty, basic, provision, sine qua non, requisite (*fml*).

muster *v* assemble, convene, gather, call together, mobilize, round up, marshal, come together, congregate, collect, group, meet, rally, mass, throng, call up, summon, enrol.

musty *adj* mouldy, mildewy, stale, stuffy, fusty, dank, airless, decayed, smelly.

mutation *n* change, alteration, variation, deviation, modification, transformation, anomaly, evolution.

mute *adj* silent, dumb, voiceless, wordless, speechless, mum (*infml*), unspoken, noiseless, unexpressed, unpronounced.
☒ vocal, talkative.
◇ *v* tone down, subdue, muffle, lower, moderate, dampen, deaden, soften, silence.

mutilate *v* 1 MAIM, injure, dismember, disable, disfigure, lame, mangle, cut to pieces, cut up,

butcher. 2 SPOIL, mar, damage, cut, censor.

mutinous *adj* rebellious, insurgent, insubordinate, disobedient, seditious, revolutionary, riotous, subversive, bolshie (*infml*), unruly.
☒ obedient, compliant.

mutiny *n* rebellion, insurrection, revolt, revolution, rising, uprising, insubordination, disobedience, defiance, resistance, riot, strike.
◇ *v* rebel, revolt, rise up, resist, protest, disobey, strike.

mutter *v* 1 MUMBLE, murmur, rumble. 2 COMPLAIN, grumble, grouse (*infml*).

mutual *adj* reciprocal, shared, common, joint, interchangeable, interchanged, exchanged, complementary.

muzzle *v* restrain, stifle, suppress, gag, mute, silence, censor, choke.

myopic *adj* 1 *myopic vision*: short-sighted, near-sighted, purblind. 2 *myopic attitudes*: short-sighted, unwise, ill-considered, thoughtless, narrow, narrow-minded, localized, parochial, short-term, imprudent (*fml*), uncircumspect (*fml*).
☒ 2 far-sighted.

myriad *adj* countless, innumerable, limitless, immeasurable, incalculable, untold, boundless, mulitudinous (*fml*).
◇ *n* multitude, throng, horde, army, flood, host, swarm, sea, scores, thousands, millions, mountain.

mysterious *adj* enigmatic, cryptic, mystifying, inexplicable, incomprehensible, puzzling, perplexing, obscure, strange, unfathomable, mystical, baffling, curious, hidden, insoluble, secret, weird, secretive, veiled, dark, furtive.
☒ straightforward, comprehensible.

mystery *n* 1 ENIGMA, puzzle, secret, riddle, conundrum, question. 2 OBSCURITY, secrecy, ambiguity.

mystical *adj* occult, arcane, mystic, esoteric, supernatural, paranormal, transcendental, metaphysical, hidden, mysterious.

mystify *v* puzzle, bewilder, baffle, perplex, confound, confuse.

mystique *n* mystery, secrecy, fascination, glamour, magic, spell, charm, appeal, charisma, awe.

myth *n* legend, fable, fairy tale, allegory, parable, saga, story, fiction, tradition, fancy, fantasy, superstition.

mythical *adj* **1** MYTHOLOGICAL, legendary, fabled, fairytale. **2** FICTITIOUS, imaginary, made-up, invented, make-believe, non-existent, unreal, pretended, fanciful.
⊠ **1** historical. **2** actual, real.

mythology *n* legend, myths, lore, tradition(s), folklore, folk-tales, tales.

Mythological creatures and spirits include: abominable snowman (or yeti), afrit, basilisk, bigfoot, brownie, bunyip, centaur, Cerberus, chimera, cockatrice, Cyclops, dragon, dryad, elf, Erinyes (or Furies), fairy, faun, genie, gnome, goblin, golem, Gorgon, griffin, harpy, hippocampus, hippogriff, hobgoblin, imp, kelpie, kraken, lamia, leprechaun, Loch Ness monster, mermaid, merman, Minotaur, naiad, nereid, nymph, ogre, ogress, orc, oread, Pegasus, phoenix, pixie, roc, salamander, sasquatch, satyr, sea serpent, silkie, siren, Sphinx, sylph, troll, unicorn, vampire, werewolf, wyvern.

Nn

nag *v* scold, berate, irritate, annoy, pester, badger, plague, torment, harass, earbash (*infml*), henpeck (*infml*), harry, vex, upbraid, goad.

nail *v* fasten, attach, secure, pin, tack, fix, join.
◇ *n* 1 FASTENER, pin, tack, spike, skewer. 2 TALON, claw.

naive *adj* unsophisticated, ingenuous, innocent, unaffected, artless, guileless, simple, frank, natural, childlike, open, trusting, unsuspecting, gullible, credulous, wide-eyed.
🠮 experienced, sophisticated.

naiveté *n* ingenuousness, innocence, inexperience, naturalness, simplicity, openness, frankness, gullibility, credulity.
🠮 experience, sophistication.

naked *adj* 1 NUDE, bare, undressed, unclothed, uncovered, stripped, stark-naked, disrobed, denuded, in the altogether (*infml*). 2 OPEN, unadorned, undisguised, unqualified, plain, stark, overt, blatant, exposed.
🠮 1 clothed, covered. 2 concealed.

name *n* 1 TITLE, appellation (*fml*), designation, label, term, epithet, handle (*infml*). 2 REPUTATION, character, repute, renown, esteem, eminence, fame, honour, distinction, note.
◇ *v* 1 CALL, christen, baptize, term, title, entitle, dub, label, style.
2 DESIGNATE, nominate, cite, choose, select, specify, classify, commission, appoint.

nameless *adj* 1 UNNAMED, anonymous, unidentified, unknown, obscure. 2 INEXPRESSIBLE, indescribable, unutterable, unspeakable, unmentionable, unheard-of.
🠮 1 named.

namely *adv* that is, ie, specifically, viz, that is to say.

nap *v* doze, sleep, snooze (*infml*), nod off, drop off, rest, kip (*infml*).
◇ *n* rest, sleep, siesta, catnap, forty winks (*infml*), kip (*infml*).

narcotic *n* drug, opiate, sedative, tranquillizer, pain-killer.
◇ *adj* soporific, hypnotic, sedative, analgesic, pain-killing, numbing, dulling, calming, stupefying.

narrate *v* tell, relate, report, recount, describe, unfold, recite, state, detail.

narrative *n* story, tale, chronicle, account, history, report, detail, statement.

narrator *n* storyteller, chronicler, reporter, raconteur, commentator, writer.

narrow *adj* 1 TIGHT, confined, constricted, cramped, slim, slender, thin, fine, tapering, close. 2 LIMITED, restricted, circumscribed. 3 NARROW-MINDED, biased, bigoted, exclusive, dogmatic.
🠮 1 wide. 2 broad. 3 broad-minded, tolerant.
◇ *v* constrict, limit, tighten, reduce, diminish, simplify.
🠮 broaden, widen, increase.

narrow-minded *adj* illiberal, biased, bigoted, prejudiced, reactionary, small-minded,

conservative, intolerant, insular, petty.
⊞ broad-minded.

nasty adj **1** UNPLEASANT, repellent, repugnant, repulsive, objectionable, offensive, disgusting, sickening, horrible, filthy, foul, polluted, obscene. **2** MALICIOUS, mean, spiteful, vicious, malevolent.
⊞ **1** agreeable, pleasant, decent. **2** benevolent, kind.

nation n country, people, race, state, realm, population, community, society.

national adj countrywide, civil, domestic, nationwide, state, internal, general, governmental, public, widespread, social.
◇ n citizen, native, subject, inhabitant, resident.

nationalism n patriotism, loyalty, allegiance, chauvinism, xenophobia, jingoism.

nationality n race, nation, ethnic group, birth, tribe, clan.

native adj **1** LOCAL, indigenous, domestic, vernacular, home, aboriginal, autochthonous (fml), mother, original. **2** INBORN, inherent, innate, inbred, hereditary, inherited, congenital, instinctive, natural, intrinsic, natal.
◇ n inhabitant, resident, national, citizen, dweller, aborigine, autochthon (fml).
⊞ foreigner, outsider, stranger.

natural adj **1** ORDINARY, normal, common, regular, standard, usual, typical. **2** INNATE, inborn, instinctive, intuitive, inherent, congenital, native, indigenous. **3** GENUINE, pure, authentic, unrefined, unprocessed, unmixed, real. **4** SINCERE, unaffected, genuine, artless, ingenuous, guileless, simple, unsophisticated, open, candid, spontaneous.
⊞ **1** unnatural. **2** acquired. **3** artificial. **4** affected, disingenuous.

naturalistic adj natural, realistic, true-to-life, representational, lifelike, graphic, real-life, photographic.

naturally adv **1** OF COURSE, as a matter of course, simply, obviously, logically, typically, certainly, absolutely. **2** NORMALLY, genuinely, instinctively, spontaneously.

nature n **1** ESSENCE, quality, character, features, disposition, attributes, personality, make-up, constitution, temperament, mood, outlook, temper. **2** KIND, sort, type, description, category, variety, style, species. **3** UNIVERSE, world, creation, earth, environment. **4** COUNTRYSIDE, country, landscape, scenery, natural history.

naughty adj **1** BAD, badly behaved, mischievous, disobedient, wayward, exasperating, playful, roguish. **2** INDECENT, obscene, bawdy, risqué, smutty.
⊞ **1** good, well-behaved. **2** decent.

nausea n **1** VOMITING, sickness, retching, queasiness, biliousness. **2** DISGUST, revulsion, loathing, repugnance.

nauseate v sicken, disgust, revolt, repel, offend, turn one's stomach (infml).

nautical adj naval, marine, maritime, sea-going, seafaring, sailing, oceanic, boating.

navigate v steer, drive, direct, pilot, guide, handle, manoeuvre, cruise, sail, skipper, voyage, journey, cross, helm, plot, plan.

navigation n sailing, steering, cruising, voyaging, seamanship, helmsmanship.

navy n fleet, ships, flotilla, armada, warships.

near adj **1** NEARBY, close, bordering, adjacent, adjoining, alongside, neighbouring. **2** IMMINENT, impending, forthcoming, coming,

approaching. **3** DEAR, familiar, close, related, intimate, akin.
⊞ **1** far. **2** distant. **3** remote.

nearby adj near, neighbouring, adjoining, adjacent, accessible, convenient, handy.
⊞ faraway.
◊ adv near, within reach, at close quarters, close at hand, not far away.

nearly adv almost, practically, virtually, closely, approximately, more or less, as good as, just about, roughly, well-nigh.
⊞ completely, totally.

neat adj **1** TIDY, orderly, smart, spruce, trim, clean, spick and span, shipshape. **2** DEFT, clever, adroit, skilful, expert. **3** UNDILUTED, unmixed, unadulterated, straight, pure.
⊞ **1** untidy. **3** clumsy. **3** diluted.

nebulous adj vague, hazy, imprecise, indefinite, indistinct, cloudy, misty, obscure, uncertain, unclear, dim, ambiguous, confused, fuzzy, shapeless, amorphous.
⊞ clear.

necessary adj needed, required, essential, compulsory, indispensable, vital, mission-critical, imperative, mandatory, obligatory, needful, unavoidable, inevitable, inescapable, inexorable, certain.
⊞ unnecessary, inessential, unimportant.

necessitate v require, call for, involve, entail, demand, oblige, force, constrain, compel.

necessity n **1** REQUIREMENT, obligation, prerequisite, need, essential, fundamental, want, compulsion, demand. **2** INDISPENSABILITY, inevitability, needfulness. **3** POVERTY, destitution, hardship.

need v miss, lack, want, require, demand, call for, necessitate, have need of, have to, crave.
◊ n **1** a need for caution: call,
demand, obligation, requirement.
2 the country's needs: essential, necessity, requisite, prerequisite, desideratum. **3** a need for equipment: want, lack, insufficiency, inadequacy, neediness, shortage.

needless adj unnecessary, gratuitous, uncalled-for, unwanted, redundant, superfluous, useless, pointless, purposeless.
⊞ necessary, essential.

needy adj poor, destitute, in need, impoverished, penniless, disadvantaged, deprived, poverty-stricken, underprivileged.
⊞ affluent, wealthy, well-off.

negate v **1** NULLIFY, annul, cancel, invalidate, undo, countermand, abrogate (fml), neutralize, quash, retract, reverse, revoke, rescind, wipe out, void, repeal. **2** DENY, contradict, oppose, disprove, refute, repudiate.
⊞ **2** affirm.

negative adj **1** CONTRADICTORY, contrary, denying, opposing, invalidating, neutralizing, nullifying, annulling. **2** UNCO-OPERATIVE, cynical, pessimistic, unenthusiastic, uninterested, unwilling.
⊞ **1** affirmative, positive.
2 constructive, positive.
◊ n contradiction, denial, opposite, refusal.

neglect v **1** DISREGARD, ignore, leave alone, abandon, pass by, rebuff, scorn, disdain, slight, spurn.
2 FORGET, fail (in), omit, overlook, let slide, shirk, skimp.
⊞ **1** cherish, appreciate.
2 remember.
◊ n negligence, disregard, carelessness, failure, inattention, indifference, slackness, dereliction of duty, forgetfulness, heedlessness, oversight, slight, disrespect.
⊞ care, attention, concern.

negligence n inattentiveness, carelessness, laxity, neglect, slackness, thoughtlessness,

forgetfulness, indifference, omission, oversight, disregard, failure, default.
☒ attentiveness, care, regard.

negligent adj neglectful, inattentive, remiss, thoughtless, casual, lax, careless, indifferent, offhand, nonchalant, slack, uncaring, forgetful.
☒ attentive, careful, scrupulous.

negligible adj unimportant, insignificant, small, imperceptible, trifling, trivial, minor, minute.
☒ significant.

negotiate v 1 CONFER, deal, mediate, arbitrate, bargain, arrange, transact, work out, manage, settle, consult, contract. 2 GET ROUND, cross, surmount, traverse, pass.

negotiation n mediation, arbitration, debate, discussion, diplomacy, bargaining, transaction.

negotiator n arbitrator, go-between, mediator, intermediary, moderator, intercessor, adjudicator, broker, ambassador, diplomat.

neighbourhood n district, locality, vicinity, community, locale, environs, confines, surroundings, region, proximity.

neighbouring adj adjacent, bordering, near, nearby, adjoining, connecting, next, surrounding.
☒ distant, remote.

neighbourly adj sociable, friendly, amiable, kind, helpful, genial, hospitable, obliging, considerate, companionable.

nerve n 1 COURAGE, bravery, mettle, pluck, guts (infml), spunk (infml), spirit, vigour, intrepidity, daring, fearlessness, firmness, resolution, fortitude, steadfastness, will, determination, endurance, force.
2 (infml) AUDACITY, impudence, cheek (infml), effrontery, brazenness, boldness, chutzpah (infml), impertinence, insolence.
☒ 1 weakness. 2 timidity.

nerve-racking adj harrowing, distressing, trying, stressful, tense, maddening, worrying, difficult, frightening.

nerves n nervousness, tension, stress, anxiety, worry, strain, fretfulness.

nervous adj highly-strung, excitable, anxious, agitated, nervy (infml), on edge, edgy, jumpy (infml), jittery (infml), tense, fidgety, apprehensive, neurotic, shaky, uneasy, worried, flustered, fearful.
☒ calm, relaxed.

nest n 1 BREEDING-GROUND, den, roost, eyrie, lair. 2 RETREAT, refuge, haunt, hideaway.

nestle v snuggle, huddle, cuddle, curl up.

net¹ n mesh, web, network, netting, open-work, lattice, lace.
◊ v catch, trap, capture, bag, ensnare, entangle, nab (infml).

net² adj nett, clear, after tax, final, lowest.
◊ v bring in, clear, earn, make, realize, receive, gain, obtain, accumulate.

network n system, organization, arrangement, structure, complex, interconnections, grid, net, maze, mesh, labyrinth, channels, circuitry, convolution, grill, tracks.

neurosis n disorder, affliction, abnormality, disturbance, instability, derangement, deviation, obsession, phobia.

neurotic adj disturbed, maladjusted, anxious, nervous, overwrought, unstable, unhealthy, deviant, abnormal, compulsive, obsessive.

neuter v castrate, emasculate, doctor, geld, spay.

neutral adj 1 IMPARTIAL, uncommitted, unbiased, non-aligned, disinterested, unprejudiced, undecided, non-partisan, non-

committal, objective, indifferent, dispassionate, even-handed. **2** DULL, nondescript, colourless, drab, expressionless, indistinct.
⊞ **1** biased, partisan. **2** colourful.

neutralize v counteract, counterbalance, offset, negate, cancel, nullify, invalidate, undo, frustrate.

never-ending adj everlasting, eternal, non-stop, perpetual, endless, unceasing, uninterrupted, unremitting, interminable, incessant, unbroken, permanent, persistent, unchanging, relentless.
⊞ fleeting, transitory.

nevertheless adv nonetheless, notwithstanding, still, anyway, even so, yet, however, anyhow, but, regardless.

new adj **1** NOVEL, original, fresh, different, unfamiliar, unusual, brand-new, mint, unknown, unused, virgin, newborn. **2** MODERN, contemporary, current, latest, recent, up-to-date, up-to-the-minute, topical, trendy (infml), ultra-modern, advanced, newfangled (infml). **3** CHANGED, altered, modernized, improved, renewed, restored, redesigned. **4** ADDED, additional, extra, more, supplementary.
⊞ **1** usual. **2** outdated, out-of-date. **3** old.

newcomer n immigrant, alien, foreigner, incomer, colonist, settler, arrival, outsider, stranger, novice, beginner.

news n report, account, information, intelligence, dispatch, communiqué, bulletin, gossip, hearsay, rumour, statement, story, word, tidings, latest, release, scandal, revelation, low-down (infml), exposé, disclosure, gen (infml), advice.

next adj **1** ADJACENT, adjoining, neighbouring, nearest, closest. **2** FOLLOWING, subsequent,

succeeding, ensuing, later.
⊞ **2** previous, preceding.
◊ adv afterwards, subsequently, later, then.

nibble n bite, morsel, taste, titbit, bit, crumb, snack, piece.
◊ v bite, eat, peck, pick at, gnaw.

nice adj **1** PLEASANT, agreeable, delightful, charming, likable, attractive, good, kind, friendly, well-mannered, polite, respectable. **2** SUBTLE, delicate, fine, fastidious, discriminating, scrupulous, precise, exact, accurate, careful, strict.
⊞ **1** nasty, disagreeable, unpleasant. **2** careless.

nicety n **1** DELICACY, refinement, subtlety, distinction, nuance. **2** PRECISION, meticulousness, accuracy, scrupulousness, minuteness, finesse.

niche n **1** RECESS, alcove, hollow, nook, cubby-hole, corner, opening. **2** POSITION, place, vocation, calling, métier, slot.

nick n **1** NOTCH, indentation, chip, cut, groove, dent, scar, scratch, mark. **2** (sl) PRISON, jail, police station.
◊ v **1** NOTCH, cut, dent, indent, chip, score, scratch, scar, mark, damage, snick. **2** (sl) STEAL, pilfer, knock off (infml), pinch (infml).

nickname n pet name, sobriquet, epithet, diminutive.

night n night-time, darkness, dark, dead of night.
⊞ day, daytime.

nightfall n sunset, dusk, twilight, evening, gloaming.
⊞ dawn, sunrise.

nightmare n **1** BAD DREAM, hallucination. **2** ORDEAL, horror, torment, trial.

nightwear

Types of **nightwear** include:
nightdress, nightie (infml), pyjamas,

bed-jacket, bedsocks, dressing-gown, housecoat, negligee.

nil *n* nothing, zero, none, nought, naught, love, duck, zilch (*sl*).

nimble *adj* agile, active, lively, sprightly, spry, smart, quick, brisk, nippy (*infml*), deft, alert, light-footed, prompt, ready, swift, quick-witted.
🠪 clumsy, slow.

nip¹ *v* bite, pinch, squeeze, snip, clip, tweak, catch, grip, nibble.

nip² *n* dram, draught, shot, swallow, mouthful, drop, sip, taste, portion.

nobility *n* **1** NOBLENESS, dignity, grandeur, illustriousness, stateliness, majesty, magnificence, eminence, excellence, superiority, uprightness, honour, virtue, worthiness. **2** ARISTOCRACY, peerage, nobles, gentry, élite, lords, high society.
🠪 **1** baseness. **2** proletariat.

Titles of the nobility include:
baron, baroness, baronet, count, countess, dame, dowager, duchess, duke, earl, grand duke, knight, lady, laird, life peer, lord, marchioness, marquess, marquis, peer, peeress, seigneur, squire, thane, viscount, viscountess.

noble *n* aristocrat, peer, lord, lady, nobleman, noblewoman.
🠪 commoner.
◇ *adj* **1** ARISTOCRATIC, high-born, titled, high-ranking, patrician, blue-blooded (*infml*). **2** MAGNIFICENT, magnanimous, splendid, stately, generous, dignified, distinguished, eminent, grand, great, honoured, honourable, imposing, impressive, majestic, virtuous, worthy, excellent, elevated, fine, gentle.
🠪 **1** low-born. **2** ignoble, base, contemptible.

nobody *n* no-one, nothing, nonentity, menial, cipher.
🠪 somebody.

nod *v* **1** GESTURE, indicate, sign, signal, salute, acknowledge. **2** AGREE, assent. **3** SLEEP, doze, drowse, nap.
◇ *n* gesture, indication, sign, signal, salute, greeting, beck, acknowledgement.

noise *n* sound, din, racket, row, clamour, clash, clatter, commotion, outcry, hubbub, uproar, cry, blare, talk, pandemonium, tumult, babble.
🠪 quiet, silence.
◇ *v* report, rumour, publicize, announce, circulate.

noiseless *adj* silent, inaudible, soundless, quiet, mute, still, hushed.
🠪 loud, noisy.

noisy *adj* loud, deafening, ear-splitting, clamorous, piercing, vocal, vociferous, tumultuous, boisterous, obstreperous.
🠪 quiet, silent, peaceful.

nomad *n* traveller, wanderer, itinerant, rambler, roamer, rover, migrant.

nominal *adj* **1** TITULAR, supposed, purported, professed, ostensible, so-called, theoretical, self-styled, puppet, symbolic. **2** TOKEN, minimal, trifling, trivial, insignificant, small.
🠪 **1** actual, genuine, real.

nominate *v* propose, choose, select, name, designate, submit, suggest, recommend, put up, present, elect, appoint, assign, commission, elevate, term.

nomination *n* proposal, choice, selection, submission, suggestion, recommendation, designation, election, appointment.

nominee *n* candidate, entrant, contestant, appointee, runner, assignee.

nonchalant *adj* unconcerned, detached, dispassionate, offhand, blasé, indifferent, casual, cool, collected, apathetic, careless, insouciant.
🠪 concerned, careful.

non-committal *adj* guarded, unrevealing, cautious, wary, reserved, ambiguous, discreet, equivocal, evasive, circumspect, careful, neutral, indefinite, politic, tactful, tentative, vague.

nonconformist *n* dissenter, rebel, individualist, dissident, radical, protester, heretic, iconoclast, eccentric, maverick, secessionist.
⊒ conformist.

nondescript *adj* featureless, indeterminate, undistinctive, undistinguished, unexceptional, ordinary, commonplace, plain, dull, bland, uninspiring, uninteresting, unclassified.
⊒ distinctive, remarkable.

none *pron* no-one, not any, not one, nobody, nil, zero.

nonplussed *adj* disconcerted, confounded, taken aback, stunned, bewildered, astonished, astounded, dumbfounded, perplexed, stumped, flabbergasted, flummoxed, puzzled, baffled, dismayed, embarrassed.

nonsense *n* rubbish, trash, drivel, balderdash, gibberish, gobbledygook, senselessness, stupidity, silliness, foolishness, folly, rot (*infml*), blather, twaddle, ridiculousness, claptrap (*infml*), cobblers (*sl*).
⊒ sense, wisdom.

nonsensical *adj* ridiculous, meaningless, senseless, foolish, inane, irrational, stupid, silly, incomprehensible, ludicrous, absurd, fatuous, crazy (*infml*).
⊒ reasonable, sensible, logical.

non-stop *adj* never-ending, uninterrupted, continuous, incessant, constant, endless, interminable, unending, unbroken, round-the-clock, on-going.
⊒ intermittent, occasional.

nook *n* recess, alcove, corner, cranny, niche, cubby-hole, hideout, retreat, shelter, cavity.

norm *n* average, mean, standard, rule, pattern, criterion, model, yardstick, benchmark, measure, reference.

normal *adj* usual, standard, general, common, ordinary, conventional, average, regular, routine, typical, mainstream, natural, accustomed, well-adjusted, straight, rational, reasonable.
⊒ abnormal, irregular, peculiar.

normality *n* usualness, commonness, ordinariness, regularity, routine, conventionality, balance, adjustment, typicality, naturalness, reason, rationality.
⊒ abnormality, irregularity, peculiarity.

normally *adv* ordinarily, usually, as a rule, typically, commonly, characteristically.
⊒ abnormally, exceptionally.

nose *n* **1** *the animal's nose*: bill, neb, proboscis (*fml*), beak, hooter (*infml*), schnozzle (*infml*), snitch (*infml*), snout (*infml*), snoot (*infml*), conk (*sl*). **2** *a nose for a good story*: sense, flair, feel, perception, instinct.
◇ *v* nudge, inch, edge, ease, push.
● **nose around** poke around, search, pry, snoop (*infml*), rubberneck (*infml*), poke one's nose in (*infml*).
● **nose out** discover, detect, find out, uncover, reveal, inquire, sniff out (*infml*).

nosedive *v* plummet, dive, drop, plunge, decline, get worse, go down, submerge, swoop.
◇ *n* plummet, dive, drop, plunge, swoop, header.

nosegay *n* bouquet, posy, spray, bunch.

nosey *adj* inquisitive, meddlesome, prying, interfering, snooping, curious, eavesdropping.

nostalgia *n* yearning, longing, regretfulness, remembrance, reminiscence, homesickness, pining.

nostalgic *adj* yearning, longing, wistful, emotional, regretful, sentimental, homesick.

notable *adj* noteworthy, remarkable, noticeable, striking, extraordinary, impressive, outstanding, marked, unusual, celebrated, distinguished, famous, eminent, well-known, notorious, renowned, rare.
🗷 ordinary, commonplace, usual.
◇ *n* celebrity, notability, VIP, personage, somebody, dignitary, luminary, worthy.
🗷 nobody, nonentity.

notably *adv* markedly, noticeably, particularly, remarkably, strikingly, conspicuously, distinctly, especially, impressively, outstandingly, eminently.

notation *n* symbols, characters, code, signs, alphabet, system, script, noting, record, shorthand.

notch *n* cut, nick, indentation, incision, score, groove, cleft, mark, snip, degree, grade, step.
◇ *v* cut, nick, score, scratch, indent, mark.

note *n* **1** COMMUNICATION, letter, message, memorandum, reminder, memo (*infml*), line, jotting, record. **2** ANNOTATION, comment, gloss, remark. **3** INDICATION, signal, token, mark, symbol. **4** EMINENCE, distinction, consequence, fame, renown, reputation. **5** HEED, attention, regard, notice, observation.
◇ *v* **1** NOTICE, observe, perceive, heed, detect, mark, remark, mention, see, witness. **2** RECORD, register, write down, enter.

noted *adj* famous, well-known, renowned, notable, celebrated, eminent, prominent, acclaimed, great, illustrious, distinguished, respected, recognized.
🗷 obscure, unknown.

notes *n* jottings, record, impressions,

report, sketch, outline, synopsis, draft.

noteworthy *adj* remarkable, significant, important, notable, memorable, exceptional, unusual, extraordinary, outstanding.
🗷 commonplace, unexceptional, ordinary.

nothing *n* nought, zero, zilch (*sl*), nothingness, nullity, non-existence, emptiness, void, nobody, nonentity.
🗷 something.

notice *v* note, remark, perceive, observe, mind, see, discern, distinguish, mark, detect, heed, spot.
🗷 ignore, overlook.
◇ *n* **1** NOTIFICATION, announcement, information, declaration, communication, intelligence, news, warning, instruction. **2** ADVERTISEMENT, poster, sign, bill. **3** REVIEW, comment, criticism. **4** ATTENTION, observation, awareness, note, regard, consideration, heed.

noticeable *adj* perceptible, observable, appreciable, unmistakable, conspicuous, evident, manifest, clear, distinct, significant, striking, plain, obvious, measurable.
🗷 inconspicuous, unnoticeable.

notification *n* announcement, information, notice, declaration, advice, warning, intelligence, message, publication, statement, communication.

notify *v* inform, tell, advise, announce, declare, warn, acquaint, alert, publish, disclose, reveal.

notion *n* **1** IDEA, thought, concept, conception, belief, impression, view, opinion, understanding, apprehension. **2** INCLINATION, wish, whim, fancy, caprice.

notional *adj* theoretical, abstract, imaginary, hypothetical, illusory, conceptual, speculative, fanciful, fancied, unfounded, unreal,

visionary, thematic.
⊠ real.

notoriety n infamy, disrepute, dishonour, disgrace, scandal.

notorious adj infamous, disreputable, scandalous, dishonourable, disgraceful, ignominious, flagrant, well-known.

nought n zero, nil, zilch, naught, nothing, nothingness.

nourish v 1 NURTURE, feed, foster, care for, provide for, sustain, support, tend, nurse, maintain, cherish.
2 STRENGTHEN, encourage, promote, cultivate, stimulate.

nourishment n nutrition, food, sustenance, diet.

novel adj new, original, fresh, innovative, unfamiliar, unusual, uncommon, different, imaginative, unconventional, strange.
⊠ hackneyed, familiar, ordinary.
◇ n fiction, story, tale, narrative, romance.

novelty n 1 NEWNESS, originality, freshness, innovation, unfamiliarity, uniqueness, difference, strangeness.
2 GIMMICK, gadget, trifle, memento, knick-knack, curiosity, souvenir, trinket, bauble, gimcrack.

novice n beginner, tiro, learner, pupil, trainee, probationer, apprentice, neophyte (fml), amateur, newcomer.
⊠ expert.

now adv 1 IMMEDIATELY, at once, directly, instantly, straight away, promptly, next. 2 AT PRESENT, nowadays, these days.

noxious adj harmful, poisonous, pernicious, toxic, injurious, unhealthy, deadly, destructive, noisome, foul.
⊠ innocuous, wholesome.

nuance n subtlety, suggestion, shade, hint, suspicion, gradation, distinction, overtone, refinement, touch, trace, tinge, degree, nicety.

nub n centre, heart, core, nucleus, kernel, crux, gist, pith, point, essence.

nucleus n centre, heart, nub, core, focus, kernel, pivot, basis, crux.

nude adj naked, bare, undressed, unclothed, stripped, stark-naked, uncovered, starkers (infml), in one's birthday suit (infml).
⊠ clothed, dressed.

nudge v, n poke, prod, shove, dig, jog, prompt, push, elbow, bump.

nuisance n annoyance, bother, inconvenience, irritation, pest, pain (infml), drag (infml), bore, problem, trial, trouble, drawback.

null adj void, invalid, ineffectual, useless, vain, worthless, powerless, inoperative.
⊠ valid.

nullify v annul, revoke, cancel, invalidate, abrogate, abolish, negate, rescind, quash, repeal, counteract.
⊠ validate.

numb adj benumbed, insensible, unfeeling, deadened, insensitive, frozen, immobilized.
⊠ sensitive.
◇ v deaden, anaesthetize, freeze, immobilize, paralyse, dull, stun.
⊠ sensitize.

number n 1 FIGURE, numeral, digit, integer, unit. 2 TOTAL, sum, aggregate, collection, amount, quantity, several, many, company, crowd, multitude, throng, horde. 3 COPY, issue, edition, impression, volume, printing.
◇ v count, calculate, enumerate, reckon, total, add, compute, include.

numberless adj innumerable, countless, endless, uncounted, many, unnumbered, unsummed, infinite, untold, myriad, immeasurable, multitudinous (fml).

numeral n number, figure, digit, integer, unit, character, cipher.

numerous *adj* many, abundant, several, plentiful, copious, profuse, sundry.
⊜ few.

nurse *v* **1** TEND, care for, look after, treat. **2** BREAST-FEED, feed, suckle, nurture, nourish. **3** PRESERVE, sustain, support, cherish, encourage, keep, foster, promote.
◇ *n* sister, matron, nursemaid, nanny.

nurture *n* **1** FOOD, nourishment. **2** REARING, upbringing, training, care, cultivation, development, education, discipline.
◇ *v* **1** FEED, nourish, nurse, tend, care for, foster, support, sustain. **2** BRING UP, rear, cultivate, develop, educate, instruct, train, school, discipline.

nut

Varieties of nut include: almond, beech nut, Brazil nut, cashew, chestnut, cobnut, coconut, filbert, hazelnut, macadamia, monkey nut, peanut, pecan, pine nut, pistachio, walnut.

---

nutrition *n* food, nourishment, sustenance.

nutritious *adj* nourishing, nutritive, wholesome, healthful, health-giving, good, beneficial, strengthening, substantial, invigorating.
⊜ bad, unwholesome.

Oo

oasis *n* 1 SPRING, watering-hole.
2 REFUGE, haven, island, sanctuary,
retreat.

oath *n* 1 VOW, pledge, promise,
word, affirmation, assurance, word
of honour. 2 CURSE, imprecation,
swear-word, profanity, expletive,
blasphemy.

obedient *adj* compliant, docile,
acquiescent, submissive, tractable,
yielding, dutiful, law-abiding,
deferential, respectful, subservient,
observant.
⊒ disobedient, rebellious, wilful.

obesity *n* fatness, overweight,
corpulence, stoutness, grossness,
plumpness, portliness, bulk.
⊒ thinness, slenderness, skinniness.

obey *v* 1 COMPLY, submit, surrender,
yield, be ruled by, bow to, take
orders from, defer (to), give way,
follow, observe, abide by, adhere to,
conform, heed, keep, mind, respond.
2 CARRY OUT, discharge, execute, act
upon, fulfil, perform.
⊒ 1 disobey.

object¹ *n* 1 THING, entity, article,
body. 2 AIM, objective, purpose,
goal, target, intention, motive, end,
reason, point, design. 3 TARGET,
recipient, butt, victim.

object² *v* protest, oppose, demur,
take exception, disapprove, refuse,
complain, rebut, repudiate.
⊒ agree, acquiesce.

objection *n* protest, dissent,
disapproval, opposition, demur,
complaint, challenge, scruple.
⊒ agreement, assent.

objectionable *adj* unacceptable,
unpleasant, offensive, obnoxious,
repugnant, disagreeable, abhorrent,
detestable, deplorable, despicable.
⊒ acceptable.

objective *adj* impartial, unbiased,
detached, unprejudiced, open-
minded, equitable, dispassionate,
even-handed, neutral, disinterested,
just, fair.
⊒ subjective.
◇ *n* object, aim, goal, end, purpose,
ambition, mark, target, intention,
design.

obligation *n* duty, responsibility,
onus, charge, commitment, liability,
requirement, bond, contract, debt,
burden, trust.

obligatory *adj* compulsory,
mandatory, statutory, required,
binding, essential, necessary,
enforced.
⊒ optional.

oblige *v* 1 COMPEL, constrain, coerce,
require, make, necessitate, force,
bind. 2 HELP, assist, accommodate, do
a favour, serve, gratify, please.

obliging *adj* accommodating,
co-operative, helpful, considerate,
agreeable, friendly, kind, civil.
⊒ unhelpful.

oblique *adj* slanting, sloping,
inclined, angled, tilted.

obliterate *v* eradicate, destroy,
annihilate, delete, blot out, wipe out,
erase.

oblivion *n* obscurity, nothingness,
unconsciousness, void, limbo.
⊒ awareness.

oblivious *adj* unconscious, unaware, inattentive, careless, heedless, blind, insensible, negligent.
🔁 aware.

obnoxious *adj* unpleasant, disagreeable, disgusting, loathsome, nasty, horrid, odious, repulsive, revolting, repugnant, sickening, nauseating.
🔁 pleasant.

obscene *adj* indecent, improper, immoral, impure, filthy, dirty, bawdy, lewd, licentious, pornographic, scurrilous, suggestive, disgusting, foul, shocking, shameless, offensive.
🔁 decent, wholesome.

obscenity *n* 1 INDECENCY, immodesty, impurity, impropriety, lewdness, licentiousness, suggestiveness, pornography, dirtiness, filthiness, foulness, grossness, indelicacy, coarseness.
2 ATROCITY, evil, outrage, offence.
3 PROFANITY, expletive, swear-word, four-letter word.

obscure *adj* 1 UNKNOWN, unimportant, little-known, unheard-of, undistinguished, nameless, inconspicuous, humble, minor.
2 INCOMPREHENSIBLE, enigmatic, cryptic, recondite, esoteric, arcane, mysterious, deep, abstruse, confusing. 3 INDISTINCT, unclear, indefinite, shadowy, blurred, cloudy, faint, hazy, dim, misty, shady, vague, murky, gloomy, dusky.
🔁 1 famous, renowned.
2 intelligible, straightforward. 3 clear, definite.
◇ *v* conceal, cloud, obfuscate, hide, cover, blur, disguise, mask, overshadow, shadow, shade, cloak, veil, shroud, darken, dim, eclipse, screen, block out.
🔁 clarify, illuminate.

obsequious *adj* servile, ingratiating, grovelling, fawning, sycophantic, cringing, deferential, flattering, smarmy (*infml*), unctuous, oily,

submissive, subservient, slavish.

observance *n* 1 ADHERENCE, compliance, observation, performance, obedience, fulfilment, honouring, notice, attention.
2 RITUAL, custom, ceremony, practice, celebration.

observant *adj* attentive, alert, vigilant, watchful, perceptive, eagle-eyed, wide awake, heedful.
🔁 unobservant.

observation *n* 1 ATTENTION, notice, examination, inspection, scrutiny, monitoring, study, watching, consideration, discernment.
2 REMARK, comment, utterance, thought, statement, pronouncement, reflection, opinion, finding, note.

observe *v* 1 WATCH, see, study, notice, contemplate, keep an eye on, perceive. 2 REMARK, comment, say, mention. 3 ABIDE BY, comply with, honour, keep, fulfil, celebrate, perform.
🔁 1 miss. 3 break, violate.

observer *n* watcher, spectator, viewer, witness, looker-on, onlooker, eye-witness, commentator, bystander, beholder.

obsess *v* preoccupy, dominate, rule, monopolize, haunt, grip, plague, prey on, possess.

obsession *n* preoccupation, fixation, idée fixe, ruling passion, compulsion, fetish, hang-up (*infml*), infatuation, mania, enthusiasm.

obsessive *adj* consuming, compulsive, gripping, fixed, haunting, tormenting, maddening.

obsolete *adj* outmoded, disused, out-of-date, old-fashioned, passé, dated, outworn, old, antiquated, antique, dead, extinct.
🔁 modern, current, up-to-date.

obstacle *n* barrier, bar, obstruction, impediment, hurdle, hindrance, check, snag, stumbling-block,

drawback, difficulty, hitch, catch, stop, interference, interruption.
🔁 advantage, help.

obstinate adj stubborn, inflexible, immovable, intractable, pigheaded, unyielding, intransigent, persistent, dogged, headstrong, bloody-minded (sl), strong-minded, self-willed, steadfast, firm, determined, wilful.
🔁 flexible, tractable.

obstruct v block, impede, hinder, prevent, check, frustrate, hamper, clog, choke, bar, barricade, stop, stall, retard, restrict, thwart, inhibit, hold up, curb, arrest, slow down, interrupt, interfere with, shut off, cut off, obscure.
🔁 assist, further.

obstruction n barrier, blockage, bar, barricade, hindrance, check, impediment, stop, stoppage, difficulty.
🔁 help.

obstructive adj hindering, delaying, blocking, stalling, unhelpful, awkward, difficult, restrictive, inhibiting.
🔁 co-operative, helpful.

obtain v 1 ACQUIRE, get, gain, come by, attain, procure, secure, earn, achieve. 2 PREVAIL, exist, hold, be in force, be the case, stand, reign, rule, be prevalent.

obtrusive adj 1 PROMINENT, protruding, noticeable, obvious, blatant, forward. 2 INTRUSIVE, interfering, prying, meddling, nosey (infml), pushy (infml).
🔁 1 unobtrusive.

obtuse adj slow, stupid, thick (infml), dull, dense, crass, dumb (infml), stolid, dull-witted, thick-skinned.
🔁 bright, sharp.

obvious adj evident, self-evident, manifest, patent, clear, plain, distinct, transparent, undeniable, unmistakable, conspicuous, glaring, apparent, open, unconcealed,

visible, noticeable, perceptible, pronounced, recognizable, self-explanatory, straightforward, prominent.
🔁 unclear, indistinct, obscure.

obviously adv plainly, clearly, evidently, manifestly, undeniably, unmistakably, without doubt, certainly, distinctly, of course.

occasion n 1 EVENT, occurrence, incident, time, instance, chance, case, opportunity. 2 REASON, cause, excuse, justification, grounds. 3 CELEBRATION, function, affair, party.

occasional adj periodic, intermittent, irregular, sporadic, infrequent, uncommon, incidental, odd, rare, casual.
🔁 frequent, regular, constant.

occasionally adv sometimes, on occasion, from time to time, at times, at intervals, now and then, now and again, irregularly, periodically, every so often, once in a while, off and on, infrequently.
🔁 frequently, often, always.

occult adj mystical, supernatural, magical, esoteric, mysterious, concealed, arcane, recondite, obscure, secret, hidden, veiled.

occupant n occupier, holder, inhabitant, resident, householder, tenant, user, lessee, squatter, inmate.

occupation n 1 JOB, profession, work, vocation, employment, trade, post, calling, business, line, pursuit, craft, walk of life, activity. 2 INVASION, seizure, conquest, control, takeover. 3 OCCUPANCY, possession, holding, tenancy, tenure, residence, habitation, use.

occupy v 1 INHABIT, live in, possess, reside in, stay in, take possession of, own. 2 ABSORB, take up, engross, engage, hold, involve, preoccupy, amuse, busy, interest. 3 INVADE, seize, capture, overrun, take over. 4 FILL, take up, use.

occur v happen, come about, take place, transpire, chance, come to pass, materialize, befall, develop, crop up, arise, appear, turn up, obtain, result, exist, be present, be found.

occurrence n **1** INCIDENT, event, happening, affair, circumstance, episode, instance, case, action, development. **2** INCIDENCE, existence, appearance, manifestation.

odd adj **1** UNUSUAL, strange, uncommon, peculiar, abnormal, exceptional, curious, atypical, different, queer, bizarre, eccentric, remarkable, unconventional, weird, irregular, extraordinary, outlandish, rare. **2** OCCASIONAL, incidental, irregular, random, casual. **3** UNMATCHED, unpaired, single, spare, surplus, leftover, remaining, sundry, various, miscellaneous.
🖃 **1** normal, usual. **2** regular.

oddity n **1** ABNORMALITY, peculiarity, rarity, eccentricity, idiosyncrasy, phenomenon, quirk. **2** CURIOSITY, character, freak, misfit.

oddment n bit, scrap, leftover, fragment, offcut, end, remnant, shred, snippet, patch.

odds n **1** LIKELIHOOD, probability, chances. **2** ADVANTAGE, edge, lead, superiority.

odious adj offensive, loathsome, unpleasant, obnoxious, disgusting, hateful, repulsive, revolting, repugnant, foul, execrable, detestable, abhorrent, horrible, horrid, abominable.
🖃 pleasant.

odour n smell, scent, fragrance, aroma, perfume, redolence, stench, stink (infml).

off adj **1** ROTTEN, bad, sour, turned, rancid, mouldy, decomposed. **2** CANCELLED, postponed. **3** AWAY, absent, gone. **4** SUBSTANDARD, below par, disappointing, unsatisfactory, slack.

◇ adv away, elsewhere, out, at a distance, apart, aside.

off-colour adj indisposed, off form, under the weather, unwell, sick, out of sorts, ill, poorly.

offence n **1** MISDEMEANOUR, transgression, violation, wrong, wrongdoing, infringement, crime, misdeed, sin, trespass. **2** AFFRONT, insult, injury. **3** RESENTMENT, indignation, pique, umbrage, outrage, hurt, hard feelings.

offend v **1** HURT, insult, injure, affront, wrong, wound, displease, snub, upset, annoy, outrage. **2** DISGUST, repel, sicken. **3** TRANSGRESS, sin, violate, err.
🖃 **1** please.

offender n transgressor, wrongdoer, culprit, perpetrator, criminal, miscreant, guilty party, law-breaker, delinquent.

offensive adj **1** DISAGREEABLE, unpleasant, objectionable, displeasing, disgusting, odious, obnoxious, repellent, repugnant, revolting, loathsome, vile, nauseating, nasty, detestable, abominable. **2** INSOLENT, abusive, rude, insulting, impertinent.
🖃 **1** pleasant. **2** polite.
◇ n attack, assault, onslaught, invasion, raid, sortie.

offer v **1** PRESENT, make available, advance, extend, put forward, submit, suggest, hold out, provide, sell. **2** PROFFER, propose, bid, tender. **3** VOLUNTEER, come forward, show willing (infml).
◇ n proposal, bid, submission, tender, suggestion, proposition, overture, approach, attempt, presentation.

offering n present, gift, donation, contribution, subscription.

offhand adj casual, unconcerned, uninterested, take-it-or-leave-it (infml), brusque, abrupt, perfunctory,

informal, cavalier, careless.
☒ calculated, planned.
◇ *adv* impromptu, off the cuff,
extempore (*fml*), off the top of one's
head.

office *n* **1** RESPONSIBILITY, duty,
obligation, charge, commission,
occupation, situation, employment,
post, function, appointment,
business, role, service. **2** WORKPLACE,
workroom, bureau.

officer *n* official, office-holder,
public servant, functionary,
dignitary, bureaucrat, administrator,
representative, executive, agent,
appointee.

official *adj* authorized, authoritative,
legitimate, formal, licensed,
accredited, certified, approved,
authenticated, authentic, bona fide,
proper.
☒ unofficial.
◇ *n* office-bearer, functionary,
bureaucrat, executive, representative,
agent.

officiate *v* preside, superintend,
conduct, chair, manage, oversee,
run.

officious *adj* obtrusive, dictatorial,
intrusive, bossy (*infml*), interfering,
meddlesome, over-zealous, self-
important, pushy (*infml*), forward,
bustling, importunate (*fml*).

offload *v* unburden, unload,
jettison, dump, drop, deposit, get rid
of, discharge.

off-putting *adj* intimidating,
daunting, disconcerting,
discouraging, disheartening,
formidable, unnerving, unsettling,
demoralizing, disturbing.

offset *v* counterbalance, compensate
for, cancel out, counteract, make up
for, balance out, neutralize.

offshoot *n* branch, outgrowth, limb,
arm, development, spin-off, by-
product, appendage.

offspring *n* child, children, young,
issue, progeny (*fml*), brood, heirs,
successors, descendants.
☒ parent(s).

often *adv* frequently, repeatedly,
regularly, generally, again and again,
time after time, time and again,
much.
☒ rarely, seldom, never.

ogre *n* giant, monster, fiend,
bogeyman, demon, devil, troll.

oil *v* grease, lubricate, anoint.

oily *adj* **1** GREASY, fatty. **2** UNCTUOUS,
smooth, obsequious, ingratiating,
smarmy (*infml*), glib, flattering.

ointment *n* salve, balm, cream,
lotion, liniment, embrocation.

OK *adj* acceptable, all right, fine,
permitted, in order, fair, satisfactory,
cushty (*sl*), reasonable, tolerable,
passable, not bad, good, adequate,
convenient, correct, accurate.
◇ *n* authorization, approval, go-
ahead, endorsement, permission,
green light, consent, agreement.
◇ *v* approve, authorize, pass, give
the go-ahead to, give the green light
to (*infml*), rubber-stamp, agree to.
◇ *interj* all right, fine, very well,
agreed, right, yes.

old *adj* **1** AGED, elderly, advanced in
years, grey, senile. **2** ANCIENT, original,
primitive, antiquated, mature.
3 LONG-STANDING, long-established,
time-honoured, traditional.
4 OBSOLETE, old-fashioned, out-of-
date, worn-out, decayed, decrepit.
5 FORMER, previous, earlier, one-time,
ex-.
☒ **1** young. **2** new. **4** modern.
5 current.

old-fashioned *adj* outmoded,
out-of-date, outdated, dated,
unfashionable, obsolete, behind the
times, antiquated, archaic, passé,
obsolescent, oldfangled (*infml*).
☒ modern, up-to-date.

omen *n* portent, sign, warning,

premonition, foreboding, augury, indication.

ominous adj portentous, sinister, inauspicious, foreboding, menacing, fateful, unpromising, threatening. ⊞ auspicious, favourable.

omission n exclusion, gap, oversight, failure, lack, neglect, default, avoidance.

omit v leave out, exclude, miss out, pass over, overlook, drop, skip, eliminate, forget, neglect, leave undone, fail, disregard, edit (out). ⊞ include.

once adv formerly, previously, in the past, at one time, long ago, in times past, once upon a time, in the old days.
• **at once 1** IMMEDIATELY, instantly, directly, right away, straight away, without delay, now, promptly, forthwith. **2** SIMULTANEOUSLY, together, at the same time.

oncoming adj approaching, advancing, upcoming, looming, onrushing, gathering.

one adj **1** SINGLE, solitary, lone, individual, only. **2** UNITED, harmonious, like-minded, whole, entire, complete, equal, identical, alike.

onerous adj oppressive, tiring, burdensome, demanding, laborious, hard, taxing, difficult, troublesome, exacting, exhausting, heavy, weighty. ⊞ easy, light.

one-sided adj **1** UNBALANCED, unequal, lopsided. **2** UNFAIR, unjust, prejudiced, biased, partial, partisan. **3** UNILATERAL, independent. ⊞ **1** balanced. **2** impartial. **3** bilateral, multilateral.

on-going adj **1** CONTINUING, continuous, unbroken, uninterrupted, constant. **2** DEVELOPING, evolving, progressing, growing, in progress, unfinished, unfolding.

onlooker n bystander, observer, spectator, looker-on, eye-witness, witness, watcher, viewer.

only adv just, at most, merely, simply, purely, barely, exclusively, solely.
◇ adj sole, single, solitary, lone, unique, exclusive, individual.

onset n **1** BEGINNING, start, commencement, inception, outset, outbreak. **2** ASSAULT, attack, onslaught, onrush. ⊞ **1** end, finish.

onslaught n attack, assault, offensive, charge, bombardment, blitz.

onus n burden, responsibility, load, obligation, duty, liability, task.

onward(s) adv forward, on, ahead, in front, beyond, forth. ⊞ backward(s).

ooze v seep, exude, leak, percolate, escape, dribble, trickle, drip, drop, discharge, bleed, secrete, emit, overflow with, filter, drain.

opaque adj **1** CLOUDY, clouded, murky, dull, dim, hazy, muddied, muddy, turbid. **2** OBSCURE, unclear, impenetrable, incomprehensible, unintelligible, enigmatic, difficult. ⊞ **1** transparent. **2** clear, obvious.

open adj **1** UNCLOSED, ajar, gaping, uncovered, unfastened, unlocked, unsealed, yawning, lidless. **2** UNRESTRICTED, free, unobstructed, clear, accessible, exposed, unprotected, unsheltered, vacant, wide, available. **3** OVERT, obvious, plain, evident, manifest, noticeable, flagrant, conspicuous. **4** UNDECIDED, unresolved, unsettled, debatable, problematic, moot. **5** FRANK, candid, honest, guileless, natural, ingenuous, unreserved. ⊞ **1** shut. **2** restricted. **3** hidden. **4** decided. **5** reserved.
◇ v **1** UNFASTEN, undo, unlock, uncover, unseal, unblock, uncork,

clear, expose. **2** EXPLAIN, divulge, disclose, lay bare. **3** EXTEND, spread (out), unfold, separate, split. **4** BEGIN, start, commence, inaugurate, initiate, set in motion, launch.
⊞ **1** close, shut. **2** hide. **4** end, finish.

open-air adj outdoor, alfresco.
⊞ indoor.

opening n **1** APERTURE, breach, gap, orifice, break, chink, crack, fissure, cleft, chasm, hole, split, vent, rupture. **2** START, onset, beginning, inauguration, inception, birth, dawn, launch. **3** OPPORTUNITY, chance, occasion, break (infml), place, vacancy.
⊞ **2** close, end.
◇ adj beginning, commencing, starting, first, inaugural, introductory, initial, early, primary.
⊞ closing.

openly adv overtly, frankly, plainly, candidly, bluntly, blatantly, flagrantly, unashamedly, unreservedly, glaringly, in public, in full view, shamelessly.
⊞ secretly, slyly.

operate v **1** it operates on batteries: function, act, perform, run, work, go. **2** she can operate that machine: control, handle, manage, use, utilize, manoeuvre.

operation n **1** FUNCTIONING, action, running, movement, motion, performance, working. **2** INFLUENCE, manipulation, handling, management, use, utilization. **3** UNDERTAKING, enterprise, affair, procedure, proceeding, process, business, deal, transaction, effort. **4** CAMPAIGN, action, task, manoeuvre, exercise.

operational adj working, in working order, usable, functional, going, viable, workable, ready, prepared, in service.
⊞ out of order.

operative adj **1** OPERATIONAL, in operation, in force, functioning,

active, effective, efficient, in action, workable, viable, serviceable, functional. **2** KEY, crucial, important, relevant, significant.
⊞ **1** inoperative, out of service.

opinion n belief, judgement, view, point of view, idea, perception, stance, theory, impression, feeling, sentiment, estimation, assessment, conception, mind, notion, way of thinking, persuasion, attitude.

opinionated adj dogmatic, doctrinaire, dictatorial, arrogant, inflexible, obstinate, stubborn, uncompromising, single-minded, prejudiced, biased, bigoted.
⊞ open-minded.

opponent n adversary, enemy, antagonist, foe, competitor, contestant, challenger, opposer, opposition, rival, objector, dissident.
⊞ ally.

opportunity n chance, opening, break (infml), occasion, possibility, hour, moment.

oppose v **1** RESIST, withstand, counter, attack, combat, contest, stand up to, take a stand against, take issue with, confront, defy, face, fight, fly in the face of, hinder, obstruct, bar, check, prevent, thwart. **2** COMPARE, contrast, match, offset, counterbalance, play off.
⊞ **1** defend, support.

opposed adj in opposition, against, hostile, conflicting, opposing, opposite, antagonistic, clashing, contrary, incompatible, anti.
⊞ in favour.

opposite adj **1** FACING, fronting, corresponding. **2** OPPOSED, antagonistic, conflicting, contrary, hostile, adverse, contradictory, antithetical, irreconcilable, unlike, reverse, inconsistent, different, contrasted, differing.
⊞ **2** same.
◇ n reverse, converse, contrary,

antithesis, contradiction, inverse.
⊒ same.

opposition n **1** ANTAGONISM, hostility, resistance, obstructiveness, unfriendliness, disapproval.
2 OPPONENT, antagonist, rival, foe, other side.
⊒ **1** co-operation, support. **2** ally, supporter.

oppress v **1** BURDEN, afflict, lie heavy on, harass, depress, sadden, torment, vex. **2** SUBJUGATE, suppress, subdue, overpower, overwhelm, crush, trample, tyrannize, persecute, maltreat, abuse.

oppression n tyranny, subjugation, subjection, repression, despotism, suppression, injustice, cruelty, brutality, abuse, persecution, maltreatment, harshness, hardship.

oppressive adj **1** AIRLESS, stuffy, close, stifling, suffocating, sultry, muggy, heavy. **2** TYRANNICAL, despotic, overbearing, overwhelming, repressive, harsh, unjust, inhuman, cruel, brutal, burdensome, onerous, intolerable.
⊒ **1** airy. **2** just, gentle.

oppressor n tyrant, bully, taskmaster, slave-driver, despot, dictator, persecutor, tormentor, intimidator, autocrat.

optimistic adj confident, assured, sanguine, hopeful, positive, cheerful, buoyant, bright, idealistic, expectant.
⊒ pessimistic.

optimum adj best, ideal, perfect, optimal, superlative, top, choice.
⊒ worst.

option n choice, alternative, preference, possibility, selection.

optional adj voluntary, elective, discretionary, free, unforced.
⊒ compulsory.

oral adj verbal, spoken, unwritten, vocal.
⊒ written.

orbit n **1** CIRCUIT, cycle, circle, course, path, trajectory, track, revolution, rotation. **2** RANGE, scope, domain, influence, sphere of influence, compass.
◇ v revolve, circle, encircle, circumnavigate.

ordeal n trial, test, tribulation(s), affliction, trouble(s), suffering, anguish, agony, pain, persecution, torture, nightmare.

order n **1** COMMAND, directive, decree, injunction, instruction, direction, edict, ordinance, mandate, regulation, rule, precept, law. **2** REQUISITION, request, booking, commission, reservation, application, demand. **3** ARRANGEMENT, organization, grouping, disposition, sequence, categorization, classification, method, pattern, plan, system, array, layout, line-up, structure. **4** PEACE, quiet, calm, tranquillity, harmony, law and order, discipline. **5** ASSOCIATION, society, community, fraternity, brotherhood, sisterhood, lodge, guild, company, organization, denomination, sect, union. **6** CLASS, kind, sort, type, rank, species, hierarchy, family.
⊒ **3** confusion, disorder. **4** anarchy.
◇ v **1** COMMAND, instruct, direct, bid, decree, require, authorize. **2** REQUEST, reserve, book, apply for, requisition.
3 ARRANGE, organize, dispose, classify, group, marshal, sort out, lay out, manage, control, catalogue.
● **out of order 1** BROKEN, broken-down, not working, inoperative.
2 DISORDERED, disorganized, out of sequence. **3** UNSEEMLY, improper, uncalled-for, incorrect, wrong.

orderly adj **1** ORDERED, systematic, neat, tidy, regular, methodical, in order, well-organized, well-regulated. **2** WELL-BEHAVED, controlled, disciplined, law-abiding.
⊒ **1** chaotic. **2** disorderly.

ordinary adj common,

commonplace, regular, routine, standard, average, everyday, run-of-the-mill, bog-standard (*infml*), usual, unexceptional, unremarkable, typical, normal, customary, common-or-garden, plain, familiar, habitual, simple, conventional, modest, mediocre, indifferent, pedestrian, prosaic, undistinguished.
⊞ extraordinary, unusual.

organ *n* 1 DEVICE, instrument, implement, tool, element, process, structure, unit, member. 2 MEDIUM, agency, forum, vehicle, voice, mouthpiece, publication, newspaper, periodical, journal.

organic *adj* natural, biological, living, animate.

organization *n* 1 ASSOCIATION, institution, society, company, firm, corporation, federation, group, league, club, confederation, consortium. 2 ARRANGEMENT, system, classification, methodology, order, formation, grouping, method, plan, structure, pattern, composition, configuration, design.

organize *v* 1 STRUCTURE, co-ordinate, arrange, order, group, marshal, classify, systematize, tabulate, catalogue. 2 ESTABLISH, found, set up, develop, form, frame, construct, shape, run.
⊞ 1 disorganize.

orgy *n* debauch, carousal, revelry, bout, bacchanalia, indulgence, excess, spree.

orientation *n* 1 SITUATION, bearings, location, direction, position, alignment, placement, attitude. 2 INITIATION, training, acclimatization, familiarization, adaptation, adjustment, settling in.

origin *n* 1 SOURCE, spring, fount, foundation, base, cause, derivation, provenance, roots, wellspring. 2 BEGINNING, commencement, start, inauguration, launch, dawning,

creation, emergence. 3 ANCESTRY, descent, extraction, heritage, family, lineage, parentage, pedigree, birth, paternity, stock.
⊞ 2 end, termination.

original *adj* 1 FIRST, early, earliest, initial, primary, archetypal, rudimentary, embryonic, starting, opening, commencing, first-hand. 2 NOVEL, innovative, new, creative, fresh, imaginative, inventive, unconventional, unusual, unique.
⊞ 1 latest. 2 hackneyed, unoriginal.
◇ *n* prototype, master, paradigm, model, pattern, archetype, standard, type.

originate *v* 1 RISE, arise, spring, stem, issue, flow, proceed, derive, come, evolve, emerge, be born. 2 CREATE, invent, inaugurate, introduce, give birth to, develop, discover, establish, begin, commence, start, set up, launch, pioneer, conceive, form, produce, generate.
⊞ 1 end, terminate.

ornament *n* decoration, adornment, embellishment, garnish, trimming, accessory, frill, trinket, bauble, jewel.
◇ *v* decorate, adorn, embellish, garnish, trim, beautify, brighten, dress up, deck, gild.

ornamental *adj* decorative, embellishing, adorning, attractive, showy.

ornate *adj* elaborate, ornamented, fancy, decorated, baroque, rococo, florid, flowery, fussy, busy, sumptuous.
⊞ plain.

orthodox *adj* conformist, conventional, accepted, official, traditional, usual, well-established, established, received, customary, conservative, recognized, authoritative.
⊞ nonconformist, unorthodox.

ostensible *adj* alleged, apparent,

presumed, seeming, supposed, so-called, professed, outward, pretended, superficial.
🄔 real.

ostentatious adj showy, flashy, pretentious, vulgar, loud, garish, gaudy, flamboyant, conspicuous, extravagant, OTT (infml).
🄔 restrained.

ostracize v exclude, banish, exile, expel, excommunicate, reject, segregate, send to Coventry, shun, snub, boycott, blacklist, blackball, avoid, cold-shoulder (infml), cut.
🄔 accept, welcome.

other adj 1 DIFFERENT, dissimilar, unlike, separate, distinct, contrasting. 2 MORE, further, extra, additional, supplementary, spare, alternative.

oust v expel, eject, depose, displace, turn out, throw out, overthrow, evict, drive out, unseat, dispossess, disinherit, replace, topple.
🄔 install, settle.

out adj 1 AWAY, absent, elsewhere, not at home, gone, outside, abroad. 2 REVEALED, exposed, disclosed, public, evident, manifest. 3 FORBIDDEN, unacceptable, impossible, disallowed, excluded. 4 OUT-OF-DATE, unfashionable, old-fashioned, dated, passé, antiquated. 5 EXTINGUISHED, finished, expired, dead, used up.
🄔 1 in. 2 concealed. 3 allowed. 4 up-to-date.

outbreak n eruption, outburst, explosion, flare-up, upsurge, flash, rash, burst, epidemic.

outburst n outbreak, eruption, explosion, flare-up, outpouring, burst, fit, gush, surge, storm, spasm, seizure, gale, attack, fit of temper.

outcast n castaway, exile, pariah, outsider, untouchable, refugee, reject, persona non grata.

outcome n result, consequence, upshot, conclusion, effect, end result.

outcry n protest, complaint, protestation, objection, dissent, indignation, uproar, cry, exclamation, clamour, row, commotion, noise, hue and cry, hullabaloo (infml), outburst.

outdated adj out-of-date, old-fashioned, dated, unfashionable, outmoded, behind the times, obsolete, obsolescent, antiquated, oldfangled (infml), archaic.
🄔 fashionable, modern.

outdo v surpass, exceed, beat, excel, outstrip, outshine, get the better of, overcome, outclass, outdistance.

outdoor adj out-of-door(s), outside, open-air.
🄔 indoor.

outer adj 1 EXTERNAL, exterior, outside, outward, surface, superficial, peripheral. 2 OUTLYING, distant, remote, further.
🄔 1 internal. 2 inner.

outfit n 1 CLOTHES, costume, ensemble, get-up (infml), togs (infml), garb. 2 EQUIPMENT, gear (infml), kit, rig, trappings, paraphernalia. 3 (infml) ORGANIZATION, firm, business, corporation, company, group, team, unit, set, set-up, crew, gang, squad.

outgoing adj 1 SOCIABLE, friendly, unreserved, amiable, warm, approachable, expansive, open, extrovert, cordial, easy-going, communicative, demonstrative, sympathetic. 2 DEPARTING, retiring, former, last, past, ex-.
🄔 1 reserved. 2 incoming.

outing n excursion, expedition, jaunt, pleasure trip, awayday, trip, spin, picnic.

outlandish adj unconventional, unfamiliar, bizarre, strange, odd, weird, eccentric, alien, exotic, barbarous, foreign, extraordinary.
🄔 familiar, ordinary.

outlaw n bandit, brigand, robber, desperado, highwayman, criminal, marauder, pirate, fugitive.

◇ *v* ban, disallow, forbid, prohibit, exclude, embargo, bar, debar, banish, condemn.
⊞ allow, legalize.

outlay *n* expenditure, expenses, outgoings, disbursement (*fml*), cost, spending.
⊞ income.

outlet *n* **1** EXIT, way out, vent, egress, escape, opening, release, safety valve, channel. **2** RETAILER, shop, store, market.
⊞ **1** entry, inlet.

outline *n* **1** SUMMARY, synopsis, précis, bare facts, sketch, thumbnail sketch, abstract. **2** PROFILE, form, contour, silhouette, shape.
◇ *v* sketch, summarize, draft, trace, rough out.

outlook *n* **1** VIEW, viewpoint, point of view, attitude, perspective, frame of mind, angle, slant, standpoint, opinion. **2** EXPECTATIONS, future, forecast, prospect, prognosis.

outlying *adj* distant, remote, far-off, faraway, far-flung, outer, provincial.
⊞ inner.

out-of-the-way *adj* remote, isolated, far-flung, far-off, faraway, distant, inaccessible, little-known, obscure, unfrequented.

output *n* production, productivity, product, yield, manufacture, achievement.

outrage *n* **1** ANGER, fury, rage, indignation, shock, affront, horror. **2** ATROCITY, offence, injury, enormity, barbarism, crime, violation, evil, scandal.
◇ *v* anger, infuriate, affront, incense, enrage, madden, disgust, injure, offend, shock, scandalize.

outrageous *adj* **1** ATROCIOUS, abominable, shocking, scandalous, offensive, disgraceful, monstrous, heinous, unspeakable, horrible. **2** EXCESSIVE, exorbitant, immoderate, unreasonable, extortionate,

inordinate, preposterous.
⊞ **2** acceptable, reasonable.

outright *adj* total, utter, absolute, complete, downright, out-and-out, unqualified, unconditional, perfect, pure, thorough, direct, definite, categorical, straightforward.
⊞ ambiguous, indefinite.
◇ *adv* **1** TOTALLY, absolutely, completely, utterly, thoroughly, openly, without restraint, straightforwardly, positively, directly, explicitly. **2** *killed outright*: instantaneously, at once, there and then, instantly, immediately.

outset *n* start, beginning, opening, inception, commencement, inauguration, kick-off (*infml*).
⊞ end, conclusion.

outside *adj* **1** EXTERNAL, exterior, outer, surface, superficial, outward, extraneous, outdoor, outermost, extreme. **2** *an outside chance*: remote, marginal, distant, faint, slight, slim, negligible.
⊞ **1** inside.
◇ *n* exterior, façade, front, surface, face, appearance, cover.
⊞ inside.

outsider *n* stranger, intruder, alien, non-member, non-resident, foreigner, newcomer, visitor, interloper, misfit, odd man out.

outskirts *n* suburbs, vicinity, periphery, fringes, borders, boundary, edge, margin.
⊞ centre.

outspoken *adj* candid, frank, forthright, blunt, unreserved, plain-spoken, direct, explicit.
⊞ diplomatic, reserved.

outstanding *adj* **1** EXCELLENT, distinguished, eminent, pre-eminent, celebrated, exceptional, superior, remarkable, prominent, superb, great, notable, impressive, striking, superlative, important, noteworthy, memorable, special, extraordinary.

2 OWING, unpaid, due, unsettled, unresolved, uncollected, pending, payable, remaining, on-going, leftover.
⊞ **1** ordinary, unexceptional. **2** paid, settled.

outstrip v surpass, exceed, better, outdo, beat, top, transcend, outshine, pass, gain on, leave behind, leave standing, outrun, outdistance, overtake, eclipse.

outward adj external, exterior, outer, outside, surface, superficial, visible, apparent, observable, evident, supposed, professed, public, obvious, ostensible.
⊞ inner, private.

outwardly adv apparently, to all appearances, externally, visibly, superficially, supposedly, seemingly, on the surface, at first sight.

outweigh v override, prevail over, overcome, take precedence over, cancel out, make up for, compensate for, predominate.

outwit v outsmart, outthink, get the better of, trick, better, beat, dupe, cheat, deceive, defraud, swindle.

outworn adj outdated, out-of-date, outmoded, stale, discredited, defunct, old-fashioned, hackneyed, rejected, obsolete, disused, exhausted.
⊞ fresh, new.

oval adj egg-shaped, elliptical, ovoid, ovate.

ovation n applause, acclaim, acclamation, praises, plaudits (fml), tribute, clapping, cheering, bravos.
⊞ abuse, catcalls.

over adj finished, ended, done with, concluded, past, gone, completed, closed, in the past, settled, up, forgotten, accomplished.
◇ adv **1** ABOVE, beyond, overhead, on high. **2** EXTRA, remaining, surplus, superfluous, left, unclaimed, unused, unwanted, in excess, in addition.

◇ prep **1** ABOVE, on, on top of, upon, in charge of, in command of. **2** EXCEEDING, more than, in excess of.

overact v overplay, exaggerate, overdo, ham (infml).
⊞ underact, underplay.

overall adj total, all-inclusive, all-embracing, comprehensive, inclusive, general, universal, global, broad, blanket, complete, all-over.
⊞ narrow, specific.
◇ adv in general, on the whole, by and large, broadly, generally speaking.

overbearing adj imperious, domineering, arrogant, dictatorial, tyrannical, high-handed, haughty, bossy (infml), cavalier, autocratic, oppressive.
⊞ meek, unassertive.

overcast adj cloudy, grey, dull, dark, sombre, sunless, hazy, lowering.
⊞ bright, clear.

overcharge v surcharge, short-change, cheat, extort, rip off (infml), sting (infml), do (infml), diddle (infml).
⊞ undercharge.

overcome v conquer, defeat, beat, surmount, triumph over, vanquish, rise above, master, overpower, overwhelm, overthrow, subdue.

overcrowded adj congested, packed (out), jam-packed, crammed full, chock-full, overpopulated, overloaded, swarming.
⊞ deserted, empty.

overdo v exaggerate, go too far, carry to excess, go overboard (infml), lay it on thick (infml), overindulge, overstate, overact, overplay, overwork.

overdue adj late, behindhand, behind schedule, delayed, owing, unpunctual, slow.
⊞ early.

overeat v gorge, binge, overindulge, guzzle, stuff oneself, make a pig of

oneself, pig out (infml), gormandize.
⊜ abstain, starve.

overflow v spill, overrun, run over, pour over, well over, brim over, bubble over, surge, flood, inundate, deluge, shower, submerge, soak, swamp, teem.
◇ n overspill, spill, inundation, flood, overabundance, surplus.

overhang v jut, project, bulge, protrude, stick out, extend.

overhaul v 1 RENOVATE, repair, service, recondition, mend, examine, inspect, check, survey, re-examine, fix. 2 OVERTAKE, pull ahead of, outpace, outstrip, gain on, pass.
◇ n reconditioning, renovation, repair, check, service, examination, inspection, going-over (infml).

overhead adv above, up above, on high, upward.
⊜ below, underfoot.
◇ adj elevated, aerial, overhanging, raised.

overjoyed adj delighted, elated, euphoric, ecstatic, in raptures, enraptured, thrilled, jubilant, over the moon (infml).
⊜ sad, disappointed.

overload v burden, oppress, strain, tax, weigh down, overcharge, encumber.

overlook v 1 FRONT ON TO, face, look on to, look over, command a view of. 2 MISS, disregard, ignore, omit, neglect, pass over, let pass, let ride, slight. 3 EXCUSE, forgive, pardon, condone, wink at, turn a blind eye to.
⊜ 2 notice. 3 penalize.

overpower v overcome, conquer, overwhelm, vanquish, defeat, beat, subdue, overthrow, quell, master, crush, immobilize, floor.

overpowering adj overwhelming, powerful, strong, forceful, irresistible, uncontrollable, compelling, extreme, oppressive, suffocating, unbearable, nauseating, sickening.

overrate v overestimate, overvalue, overpraise, magnify, blow up, make too much of.
⊜ underrate.

overrule v overturn, override, reject, countermand, revoke, rescind, reverse, invalidate, cancel, vote down.

overrun v 1 INVADE, occupy, infest, overwhelm, inundate, run riot, spread over, swamp, swarm over, surge over, ravage, overgrow. 2 EXCEED, overshoot, overstep, overreach.

overseer n supervisor, boss (infml), chief, foreman, forewoman, manager, superintendent.

overshadow v 1 OBSCURE, cloud, darken, dim, spoil, veil. 2 OUTSHINE, eclipse, excel, surpass, dominate, dwarf, put in the shade, rise above, tower above.

oversight n 1 LAPSE, omission, fault, error, slip-up (infml), mistake, blunder, carelessness, neglect. 2 SUPERVISION, responsibility, care, charge, control, custody, keeping, administration, management, direction.

overt adj open, manifest, plain, evident, observable, obvious, apparent, public, professed, unconcealed.
⊜ covert, secret.

overtake v 1 PASS, catch up with, outdistance, outstrip, draw level with, pull ahead of, overhaul. 2 COME UPON, befall, happen, strike, engulf.

overthrow v depose, oust, bring down, topple, unseat, displace, dethrone, conquer, vanquish, beat, defeat, crush, overcome, overpower, overturn, overwhelm, subdue, master, abolish, upset.
⊜ install, protect, reinstate, restore.
◇ n ousting, unseating, defeat, deposition, dethronement, fall, rout, undoing, suppression, downfall, end,

humiliation, destruction, ruin.

overtone n suggestion, intimation, nuance, hint, undercurrent, insinuation, connotation, association, feeling, implication, sense, flavour.

overture n **1** APPROACH, advance, offer, invitation, proposal, proposition, suggestion, signal, move, motion. **2** PRELUDE, opening, introduction, opening move, (opening) gambit.

overturn v **1** CAPSIZE, upset, upturn, tip over, topple, overbalance, keel over, knock over, spill. **2** OVERTHROW, repeal, rescind, reverse, annul, abolish, destroy, quash, set aside.

overwhelm v **1** OVERCOME, overpower, destroy, defeat, crush, rout, devastate. **2** OVERRUN, inundate, snow under, submerge, swamp, engulf. **3** CONFUSE, bowl over, stagger, floor.

overwork v overstrain, overload, exploit, exhaust, overuse, overtax, strain, wear out, oppress, burden, weary.

overwrought adj tense, agitated, keyed up, on edge, worked up, wound up, frantic, overcharged, overexcited, excited, beside oneself, uptight (infml), hyper (infml). ⊜ calm.

owing adj unpaid, due, owed, in arrears, outstanding, payable, unsettled, overdue.
• **owing to** because of, as a result of, on account of, thanks to.

own adj personal, individual, private, particular, idiosyncratic.
◇ v possess, have, hold, retain, keep, enjoy.
• **own up** admit, confess, come clean (infml), tell the truth, acknowledge.

owner n possessor, holder, landlord, landlady, proprietor, proprietress, master, mistress, freeholder.

Pp

pace n **1** STEP, stride, walk, gait, tread. **2** SPEED, rate, velocity, celerity, quickness, rapidity, tempo.
◇ v step, stride, walk, march, tramp, pound, patrol, mark out, measure.

pacifist n peace-lover, conscientious objector, peacemaker, peace-monger, dove.
⊞ warmonger, hawk.

pacify v appease, conciliate, placate, mollify, calm, compose, soothe, assuage, allay, moderate, soften, lull, still, quiet, silence, quell, crush, put down, tame, subdue.
⊞ anger.

pack n **1** PACKET, box, carton, parcel, package, bundle, burden, load, backpack, rucksack, haversack, knapsack, kitbag. **2** GROUP, company, troop, herd, flock, band, crowd, gang, mob.
◇ v **1** WRAP, parcel, package, bundle, stow, store. **2** FILL, load, charge, cram, stuff, crowd, throng, press, ram, wedge, compact, compress.

package n parcel, pack, packet, box, carton, bale, consignment.
◇ v parcel (up), wrap (up), pack (up), box, batch.

packed adj filled, full, jam-packed, chock-a-block, crammed, crowded, congested.
⊞ empty, deserted.

packet n pack, carton, box, bag, package, parcel, case, container, wrapper, wrapping, packing.

pact n treaty, convention, covenant, bond, alliance, cartel, contract, deal, bargain, compact, agreement, arrangement, understanding.

⊞ disagreement, quarrel.

pad n **1** CUSHION, pillow, wad, buffer, padding, protection. **2** WRITING PAD, notepad, jotter, block.
◇ v fill, stuff, wad, pack, wrap, line, cushion, protect.
• **pad out** expand, inflate, fill out, augment, amplify, elaborate, flesh out, lengthen, stretch, protract, spin out.

padding n **1** FILLING, stuffing, wadding, packing, protection. **2** VERBIAGE, verbosity, wordiness, waffle (*infml*), bombast, hot air.

paddle¹ n oar, scull.
◇ v row, oar, scull, propel, steer.

paddle² v wade, splash, slop, dabble.

pagan n heathen, atheist, unbeliever, infidel, idolater.
⊞ believer.
◇ adj heathen, irreligious, atheistic, godless, infidel, idolatrous.

page¹ n leaf, sheet, folio, side.

page² n pageboy, attendant, messenger, bellboy, footman, servant.
◇ v call, send for, summon, bid, announce.

pageant n procession, parade, show, display, tableau, scene, play, spectacle, extravaganza.

pageantry n pomp, ceremony, grandeur, magnificence, splendour, glamour, glitter, spectacle, parade, display, show, extravagance, theatricality, drama, melodrama.

pain n **1** HURT, ache, throb, cramp, spasm, twinge, pang, stab, sting,

smart, soreness, tenderness, discomfort, distress, suffering, affliction, trouble, anguish, agony, torment, torture. **2** (*infml*) NUISANCE, bother, bore (*infml*), annoyance, vexation, burden, headache (*infml*).
◇ *v* hurt, afflict, torment, torture, agonize, distress, upset, sadden, grieve.
🗷 please, delight, gratify.

pained *adj* hurt, injured, wounded, stung, offended, aggrieved, upset, distressed, saddened, grieved.
🗷 pleased, gratified.

painful *adj* **1** SORE, tender, aching, throbbing, smarting, stabbing, agonizing, excruciating. **2** *a painful experience*: unpleasant, disagreeable, distressing, upsetting, saddening, harrowing, traumatic. **3** HARD, difficult, laborious, tedious.
🗷 **1** painless, soothing. **2** pleasant, agreeable. **3** easy.

pain-killer *n* analgesic, anodyne, anaesthetic, palliative, sedative, drug, remedy.

painless *adj* pain-free, trouble-free, effortless, easy, simple, undemanding.
🗷 painful, difficult.

pains *n* trouble, bother, effort, labour, care, diligence.

painstaking *adj* careful, meticulous, scrupulous, thorough, conscientious, diligent, assiduous, industrious, hard-working, dedicated, devoted, persevering.
🗷 careless, negligent.

paint *n* colour, colouring, pigment, dye, tint, stain.

Paints include: acrylic, colourwash, distemper, eggshell, emulsion, enamel, gloss, gouache, matt, oil paint, oils, pastel, poster paint, primer, undercoat, watercolour, whitewash.

◇ *v* **1** COLOUR, dye, tint, stain,

lacquer, varnish, glaze, apply, daub, coat, cover, decorate. **2** PORTRAY, depict, describe, recount, picture, represent.

painting *n* oil painting, oil, watercolour, picture, portrait, landscape, still life, miniature, illustration, fresco, mural.

pair *n* couple, brace, twosome, duo, twins, two of a kind.
◇ *v* match (up), twin, team, mate, marry, wed, splice, join, couple, link, bracket, put together.
🗷 separate, part.

palace *n* castle, château, mansion, stately home, basilica, dome.

palatable *adj* tasty, appetizing, eatable, edible, acceptable, satisfactory, pleasant, agreeable, enjoyable, attractive.
🗷 unpalatable, unacceptable, unpleasant, disagreeable.

palate *n* taste, appreciation, liking, relish, enjoyment, appetite, stomach, heart.

palatial *adj* grand, magnificent, splendid, majestic, regal, stately, grandiose, imposing, luxurious, de luxe, sumptuous, opulent, plush, spacious.

pale *adj* **1** PALLID, livid, ashen, ashy, white, chalky, pasty, pasty-faced, waxen, waxy, wan, sallow, anaemic. **2** *pale blue*: light, pastel, faded, washed-out, bleached, colourless, insipid, vapid, weak, feeble, faint, dim.
🗷 **1** ruddy. **2** dark.
◇ *v* whiten, blanch, bleach, fade, dim.
🗷 colour, blush.

pall¹ *n* shroud, veil, mantle, cloak, cloud, shadow, gloom, damper.

pall² *v* tire, weary, jade, sate, satiate, cloy, sicken.

palm *n* hand, paw (*infml*), mitt (*sl*).
◇ *v* take, grab, snatch, appropriate.

• **palm off** foist, impose, fob off, offload, unload, pass off.

palpable adj solid, substantial, material, real, touchable, tangible, visible, apparent, clear, plain, obvious, evident, manifest, conspicuous, blatant, unmistakable.
⊞ impalpable, imperceptible, intangible, elusive.

palpitate v flutter, quiver, tremble, shiver, vibrate, beat, pulsate, pound, thump, throb.

paltry adj meagre, derisory, mean, contemptible, low, miserable, wretched, poor, sorry, small, slight, trifling, inconsiderable, negligible, trivial, minor, petty, unimportant, insignificant, worthless.
⊞ substantial, significant, valuable.

pamper v cosset, coddle, mollycoddle, humour, gratify, indulge, overindulge, spoil, pet, fondle.
⊞ neglect, ill-treat.

pamphlet n leaflet, brochure, booklet, folder, circular, handout, notice.

pan n saucepan, frying pan, pot, casserole, container, vessel.

panache n flourish, flamboyance, ostentation, style, flair, élan, dash, spirit, enthusiasm, zest, energy, vigour, verve.

pandemonium n chaos, disorder, confusion, commotion, rumpus, turmoil, turbulence, tumult, uproar, din, bedlam, hubbub, hullabaloo, hue and cry, to-do (infml).
⊞ order, calm, peace.

pander to v humour, indulge, pamper, please, gratify, satisfy, fulfil, provide, cater to.

panel n board, committee, jury, team.

pang n pain, ache, twinge, stab, sting, prick, stitch, gripe, spasm, throe, agony, anguish, discomfort, distress.

panic n agitation, flap (infml), alarm, dismay, consternation, fright, fear, horror, terror, frenzy, hysteria.
⊞ calmness, confidence.
◇ v lose one's nerve, lose one's head, go to pieces, flap (infml), overreact.
⊞ relax.

panic-stricken adj alarmed, frightened, horrified, terrified, petrified, scared stiff, in a cold sweat, panicky, frantic, frenzied, hysterical.
⊞ relaxed, confident.

panorama n view, vista, prospect, scenery, landscape, scene, spectacle, perspective, overview, survey.

panoramic adj scenic, wide, sweeping, extensive, far-reaching, widespread, overall, general, universal.
⊞ narrow, restricted, limited.

pant v puff, blow, gasp, wheeze, breathe, sigh, heave, throb, palpitate.

pants n 1 UNDERPANTS, drawers, panties, briefs, knickers (infml), Y-fronts, boxer shorts, boxers (infml), trunks, shorts. 2 TROUSERS, slacks, jeans.

paper n 1 NEWSPAPER, daily, broadsheet, tabloid, rag (sl), journal, organ. 2 DOCUMENT, credential, authorization, identification, certificate, deed. 3 a paper on alternative medicine: essay, composition, dissertation, thesis, treatise, article, report.

Types of paper include: acid-free paper, art paper, bank paper, blotting paper, bond, carbon paper, cartridge paper, crêpe paper, greaseproof paper, graph paper, manila, notepaper, parchment paper, rag paper, recycled paper, rice paper, silver paper, tissue paper, toilet paper, tracing paper, vellum, wallpaper, wrapping paper, writing paper; A5, A4, A3, foolscap, legal (US), letter

(*US*), quarto, atlas, crown.

parable *n* fable, allegory, lesson, moral tale, story.

parade *n* procession, cavalcade, motorcade, march, column, file, train, review, ceremony, spectacle, pageant, show, display, exhibition.
◇ *v* 1 MARCH, process, file past.
2 SHOW, display, exhibit, show off, vaunt, flaunt, brandish.

paradise *n* heaven, Utopia, Shangri-La, Elysium, Eden, bliss, delight.
⊟ hell, Hades.

paradox *n* contradiction, inconsistency, incongruity, absurdity, oddity, anomaly, mystery, enigma, riddle, puzzle.

paradoxical *adj* self-contradictory, contradictory, conflicting, absurd, inconsistent, incongruous, illogical, improbable, impossible, mysterious, enigmatic, puzzling, baffling.

paragon *n* ideal, exemplar, epitome, quintessence, model, pattern, archetype, prototype, standard, criterion.

paragraph *n* passage, section, part, portion, subsection, subdivision, clause, item.

parallel *adj* equidistant, aligned, coextensive, alongside, analogous, equivalent, corresponding, matching, like, similar, resembling.
⊟ divergent, different.
◇ *n* 1 MATCH, equal, twin, duplicate, analogue, equivalent, counterpart.
2 SIMILARITY, resemblance, likeness, correspondence, correlation, equivalence, analogy, comparison.
◇ *v* match, echo, conform, agree, correspond, correlate, compare, liken.
⊟ diverge, differ.

paralyse *v* cripple, lame, disable, incapacitate, immobilize, anaesthetize, numb, deaden, freeze, transfix, halt, stop.

paralysed *adj* paralytic, paraplegic, quadriplegic, crippled, lame, disabled, incapacitated, immobilized, numb.
⊟ able-bodied.

paralysis *n* paraplegia, quadriplegia, palsy, numbness, deadness, immobility, halt, standstill, stoppage, shutdown.

parameter *n* variable, guideline, indication, criterion, specification, limitation, restriction, limit, boundary.

paramount *adj* supreme, highest, topmost, predominant, pre-eminent, prime, principal, main, chief, cardinal, primary, first, foremost.
⊟ lowest, last.

paraphernalia *n* equipment, gear, tackle, apparatus, accessories, trappings, bits and pieces, odds and ends, belongings, effects, stuff, things, baggage.

paraphrase *n* rewording, rephrasing, restatement, version, interpretation, rendering, translation.
◇ *v* reword, rephrase, restate, interpret, render, translate.

parasite *n* sponger, scrounger, cadger, hanger-on, leech, bloodsucker.

parcel *n* package, packet, pack, box, carton, bundle.
◇ *v* package, pack, wrap, bundle, tie up.
• **parcel out** divide, carve up, apportion, allocate, allot, share out, distribute, dispense, dole out, deal out, mete out.

parch *v* dry (up), desiccate, dehydrate, bake, burn, scorch, sear, blister, wither, shrivel.

parched *adj* 1 ARID, waterless, dry, dried up, dehydrated, scorched, withered, shrivelled. 2 (*infml*) THIRSTY, gasping (*infml*).

pardon *v* forgive, condone,

overlook, excuse, vindicate, acquit, absolve, remit, let off, reprieve, free, liberate, release.
⊞ punish, discipline.
◇ *n* forgiveness, mercy, clemency, indulgence, amnesty, excuse, acquittal, absolution, reprieve, release, discharge.
⊞ punishment, condemnation.

pardonable *adj* forgivable, excusable, justifiable, warrantable, understandable, allowable, permissible, minor, venial.
⊞ inexcusable.

pare *v* peel, skin, shear, clip, trim, crop, cut, dock, lop, prune, cut back, reduce, decrease.

parent *n* father, mother, dam, sire, progenitor, begetter, procreator, guardian.

parish *n* district, community, parishioners, church, churchgoers, congregation, flock, fold.

park *n* grounds, estate, parkland, gardens, woodland, reserve, pleasure ground.
◇ *v* put, position, deposit, leave.

parliament *n* legislature, senate, congress, house, assembly, convocation, council, diet.

Names of parliaments and political assemblies include:
House of Representatives, Senate (*Australia*); Nationalrat, Bundesrat (*Austria*); Narodno Sobraniye (*Bulgaria*); House of Commons, Senate (*Canada*); National People's Congress (*China*); Folketing (*Denmark*); People's Assembly (*Egypt*); Eduskunta (*Finland*); Assemblée nationale, Sénat (*France*); Bundesrat, Bundestag, Landtag (*Germany*); Althing (*Iceland*); Lok Sabha, Rajya Sabha (*India*); Majlis (*Iran*); Dáil Eireann, Seanad (*Republic of Ireland*); Knesset (*Israel*); Camera dei Deputati, Senato (*Italy*); House of

Representatives, House of Councillors (*Japan*); Tweede Kamer, Eerste Kamer (*Netherlands*); House of Representatives (*New Zealand*); Northern Ireland Assembly (*Northern Ireland*); Odelsting, Lagting (*Norway*); Sejm, Senate (*Poland*); Cortes (*Portugal*); State Duma, Federation Council (*Russia*); Scottish Parliament (*Scotland*); National Council of Provinces, National Assembly (*South Africa*); Congreso de los Diputados, Senado (*Spain*); Riksdag (*Sweden*); Nationalrat, Ständerat (*Switzerland*); Porte (*Turkey*); House of Commons, House of Lords (*UK*); House of Representatives, Senate (*US*); National Assembly (*Vietnam*), National Assembly for Wales (*Wales*).

parliamentary *adj* governmental, senatorial, congressional, legislative, law-making.

parochial *adj* insular, provincial, parish-pump, petty, small-minded, narrow-minded, inward-looking, blinkered, limited, restricted, confined.
⊞ national, international.

parody *n* caricature, lampoon, burlesque, satire, send-up, spoof, skit, mimicry, imitation, take-off, travesty, distortion.
◇ *v* caricature, lampoon, burlesque, satirize, send up, spoof, mimic, imitate, ape, take off.

paroxysm *n* fit, seizure, spasm, convulsion, attack, outbreak, outburst, explosion.

parry *v* ward off, fend off, repel, repulse, field, deflect, block, avert, avoid, evade, duck, dodge, sidestep, shun.

parson *n* vicar, rector, minister, priest, pastor, preacher, clergyman, reverend, cleric, churchman.

part *n* **1** COMPONENT, constituent, element, factor, piece, bit, particle, fragment, scrap, segment, fraction, portion, share, section, division, department, branch, sector, district, region, territory. **2** ROLE, character, duty, task, responsibility, office, function, capacity.
⊞ **1** whole, totality.
◇ *v* separate, detach, disconnect, sever, split, tear, break, break up, take apart, dismantle, come apart, split up, divide, disband, disunite, part company, disperse, scatter, leave, depart, withdraw, go away.
• **part with** relinquish, let go of, give up, yield, surrender, renounce, forgo, abandon, discard, jettison.

partial *adj* **1** *a partial victory*: incomplete, limited, restricted, imperfect, fragmentary, unfinished. **2** BIASED, prejudiced, partisan, one-sided, discriminatory, unfair, unjust, predisposed, coloured, affected.
⊞ **1** complete, total. **2** impartial, disinterested, unbiased, fair.
• **partial to** fond of, keen on, crazy about (*infml*), mad about (*infml*).

partiality *n* liking, fondness, predilection (*fml*), proclivity, inclination, preference, predisposition.

participant *n* entrant, contributor, participator, member, party, co-operator, helper, worker.

participate *v* take part, join in, contribute, engage, be involved, enter, share, partake.

participation *n* involvement, sharing, partnership, co-operation, contribution, assistance.

particle *n* bit, piece, fragment, scrap, shred, sliver, speck, morsel, crumb, iota, whit, jot, tittle, atom, grain, drop.

particular *adj* **1** *on that particular day*: specific, precise, exact, distinct, special, peculiar. **2** EXCEPTIONAL,

remarkable, notable, marked, thorough, unusual, uncommon. **3** FUSSY, discriminating, choosy (*infml*), finicky, fastidious.
⊞ **1** general.
◇ *n* detail, specific, point, feature, item, fact, circumstance.

particularly *adv* **1** EXCEPTIONALLY, remarkably, notably, extraordinarily, unusually, uncommonly, surprisingly. **2** IN PARTICULAR, especially, specifically, explicitly, distinctly.

parting *n* **1** DEPARTURE, going, leave-taking, farewell, goodbye, adieu. **2** DIVERGENCE, separation, division, partition, rift, split, rupture, breaking.
⊞ **1** meeting. **2** convergence.
◇ *adj* departing, farewell, last, dying, final, closing, concluding.
⊞ first.

partisan *n* devotee, adherent, follower, disciple, backer, supporter, champion, stalwart, guerrilla, irregular.
◇ *adj* biased, prejudiced, partial, predisposed, discriminatory, one-sided, factional, sectarian.
⊞ impartial.

partition *n* **1** DIVIDER, barrier, wall, panel, screen, room-divider. **2** DIVISION, break-up, splitting, separation, parting, severance.
◇ *v* **1** SEPARATE, divide, subdivide, wall off, fence off, screen. **2** SHARE, divide, split up, parcel out.

partly *adv* somewhat, to some extent, to a certain extent, up to a point, slightly, fractionally, moderately, relatively, in part, partially, incompletely.
⊞ completely, totally.

partner *n* associate, team-mate, ally, confederate, colleague, collaborator, accomplice, helper, mate, sidekick (*infml*), opposite number (*infml*), companion, comrade, consort, spouse, husband, wife, other half (*infml*).

partnership n 1 ALLIANCE, confederation, affiliation, combination, union, syndicate, co-operative, association, society, corporation, company, firm, fellowship, fraternity, brotherhood. 2 COLLABORATION, co-operation, participation, sharing.

party n 1 CELEBRATION, festivity, social, do (infml), knees-up (sl), rave-up (sl), get-together, gathering, reunion, function, reception, at-home, housewarming. 2 a search party: team, squad, crew, gang, band, group, company, detachment. 3 a political party: faction, side, league, cabal, alliance, association, grouping, combination. 4 PERSON, individual, litigant, plaintiff, defendant.

Types of party include: acid-house party, baby shower (N Am), barbecue, beanfeast (infml), beano (infml), birthday party, bridal shower (N Am), bun fight (infml), ceilidh, dinner party, disco, discotheque, fancy dress party, garden party, Hallowe'en party, hen night, hen party, hooley, hootenanny (N Am infml), house-warming, orgy, picnic, potluck supper (N Am), pyjama party, rave, sleepover, slumber party (US infml), social, soirée, stag night, stag party, tea party, toga party, welcoming party, wrap party.

---

pass¹ v 1 SURPASS, exceed, go beyond, outdo, outstrip, overtake, leave behind. 2 pass time: spend, while away, fill, occupy. 3 GO PAST, go by, elapse, lapse, proceed, roll, flow, run, move, go, disappear, vanish. 4 GIVE, hand, transfer, transmit. 5 ENACT, ratify, validate, adopt, authorize, sanction, approve. 6 pass an exam: succeed, get through, qualify, graduate.
◊ n 1 THROW, kick, move,

lunge, swing. 2 PERMIT, passport, identification, ticket, licence, authorization, warrant, permission.
• **pass away** die, pass on, expire, decease, give up the ghost.
• **pass off** 1 FEIGN, counterfeit, fake, palm off. 2 HAPPEN, occur, take place, go off.
• **pass out** 1 FAINT, black out, lose consciousness, collapse, flake out, keel over (infml), drop. 2 GIVE OUT, hand out, dole out, distribute, deal out, share out.
• **pass over** disregard, ignore, overlook, miss, omit, leave, neglect.

pass² n col, defile, gorge, ravine, canyon, gap, passage.

passable adj 1 SATISFACTORY, acceptable, allowable, tolerable, average, ordinary, unexceptional, moderate, fair, adequate, all right, OK (infml), mediocre. 2 CLEAR, unobstructed, unblocked, open, navigable.
⊡ 1 unacceptable, excellent.
2 obstructed, blocked, impassable.

passage n 1 PASSAGEWAY, aisle, corridor, hall, hallway, lobby, vestibule, doorway, opening, entrance, exit. 2 THOROUGHFARE, way, route, road, avenue, path, lane, alley. 3 EXTRACT, excerpt, quotation, text, paragraph, section, piece, clause, verse. 4 JOURNEY, voyage, trip, crossing.

passenger n traveller, voyager, commuter, rider, fare, hitch-hiker.

passer-by n bystander, witness, looker-on, onlooker, spectator.

passing adj ephemeral, transient, short-lived, temporary, momentary, fleeting, brief, short, cursory, hasty, quick, slight, superficial, shallow, casual, incidental.
⊡ lasting, permanent.

passion n feeling, emotion, love, adoration, infatuation, fondness, affection, lust, itch, desire, craving,

fancy, mania, obsession, craze, eagerness, keenness, avidity, zest, enthusiasm, fanaticism, ardour, zeal, fervour, warmth, heat, fire, spirit, intensity, vehemence, anger, indignation, fury, rage, outburst.
🔄 coolness, indifference, self-possession.

passionate adj 1 ARDENT, fervent, eager, keen, avid, enthusiastic, fanatical, zealous, warm, hot, fiery, inflamed, aroused, excited, impassioned, intense, strong, fierce, vehement, violent, stormy, tempestuous, wild, frenzied.
2 EMOTIONAL, excitable, hot-headed, impetuous, impulsive, quick-tempered, irritable. 3 LOVING, affectionate, lustful, erotic, sexy, sensual, sultry.
🔄 1 phlegmatic, laid-back (infml).
3 frigid.

passive adj receptive, unassertive, submissive, docile, unresisting, non-violent, patient, resigned, long-suffering, indifferent, apathetic, lifeless, inert, inactive, non-participating.
🔄 active, lively, responsive, involved.

past adj 1 OVER, ended, finished, completed, done, over and done with. 2 FORMER, previous, preceding, foregoing, late, recent. 3 ANCIENT, bygone, olden, early, gone, no more, extinct, defunct, forgotten.
🔄 2 future.
◇ n 1 in the past: history, former times, olden days, antiquity. 2 LIFE, background, experience, track record.
🔄 1 future.

pasta

Forms and shapes of pasta include: agnolotti, anelli, bucatini, cannelloni, cappelletti, conchiglie, ditali, elbow macaroni, farfalle, fedelini, fettuccine, fusilli, lasagne, linguini, lumache, macaroni, noodles, penne, ravioli, rigatoni, spaghetti, tagliarini, tagliatelle, tortellini, vermicelli, ziti.

paste n adhesive, glue, gum, mastic, putty, cement.
◇ v stick, glue, gum, cement, fix.

pastel adj delicate, soft, soft-hued, light, pale, subdued, faint.

pastime n hobby, activity, game, sport, recreation, play, fun, amusement, entertainment, diversion, distraction, relaxation.
🔄 work, employment.

pastoral adj 1 RURAL, country, rustic, bucolic, agricultural, agrarian, idyllic.
2 ECCLESIASTICAL, clerical, priestly, ministerial.
🔄 1 urban.

pastry

Types of pastry include: biscuit-crumb pastry, choux, filo pastry, flaky pastry, flan pastry, hot-water crust pastry, pâte à savarin, pâte brisée, pâte sablée, pâte sucrée, puff pastry, rough puff-pastry, shortcrust pastry, short pastry, suetcrust pastry, sweet pastry, wholemeal pastry.

pasture n grass, grassland, meadow, field, paddock, pasturage, grazing.

pasty adj pale, pallid, wan, anaemic, pasty-faced, sickly, unhealthy.
🔄 ruddy, healthy.

pat v tap, dab, slap, touch, stroke, caress, fondle, pet.
◇ n tap, dab, slap, touch, stroke, caress.
◇ adv precisely, exactly, perfectly, flawlessly, faultlessly, fluently.
🔄 imprecisely, inaccurately, wrongly.
◇ adj glib, fluent, smooth, slick, ready, easy, facile, simplistic.

patch n piece, bit, scrap, spot, area,

stretch, tract, plot, lot, parcel.
◇ *v* mend, repair, fix, cover,
reinforce.

patchy *adj* uneven, inconsistent,
irregular, variable, random, fitful,
erratic, sketchy, bitty, spotty, blotchy.
☞ even, uniform, regular, consistent.

patent *adj* obvious, evident,
conspicuous, manifest, clear,
transparent, apparent, visible,
palpable, unequivocal, open, overt,
blatant, flagrant, glaring.
☞ hidden, opaque.

path *n* route, course, direction,
way, passage, road, avenue, lane,
footpath, bridleway, trail, track, walk.

pathetic *adj* 1 PITIABLE, poor,
sorry, lamentable, miserable, sad,
distressing, moving, touching,
poignant, plaintive, heart-rending,
heartbreaking. 2 (*infml*) CONTEMPTIBLE,
derisory, deplorable, useless,
worthless, inadequate, meagre,
feeble.
☞ 1 cheerful. 2 admirable, excellent,
valuable.

patience *n* calmness, composure,
self-control, restraint, tolerance,
forbearance, endurance, fortitude,
long-suffering, submission,
resignation, stoicism, persistence,
perseverance, diligence.
☞ impatience, intolerance,
exasperation.

patient *adj* calm, composed, self-
possessed, self-controlled, restrained,
even-tempered, mild, lenient,
indulgent, understanding, forgiving,
tolerant, accommodating, forbearing,
long-suffering, uncomplaining,
submissive, resigned, philosophical,
stoical, persistent, persevering.
☞ impatient, restless, intolerant,
exasperated.
◇ *n* invalid, sufferer, case, client.

patriotic *adj* nationalistic,
chauvinistic, jingoistic, loyal, flag-
waving.

patrol *n* 1 GUARD, sentry, sentinel,
watchman. 2 *on patrol*: watch,
surveillance, policing, protection,
defence.
◇ *v* police, guard, protect, defend, go
the rounds, tour, inspect.

patron *n* 1 BENEFACTOR,
philanthropist, sponsor, backer,
supporter, sympathizer, advocate,
champion, defender, protector,
guardian, helper. 2 CUSTOMER, client,
frequenter, regular, shopper, buyer,
purchaser, subscriber.

patronage *n* custom, business,
trade, sponsorship, backing, support.

patronize *v* 1 SPONSOR, fund,
back, support, maintain, help,
assist, promote, foster, encourage.
2 FREQUENT, shop at, buy from, deal
with.

patronizing *adj* condescending,
stooping, overbearing, high-
handed, haughty, superior, snobbish,
supercilious, disdainful.
☞ humble, lowly.

patter *v* tap, pat, pitter-patter, beat,
pelt, scuttle, scurry.
◇ *n* 1 PATTERING, tapping, pitter-
patter, beating. 2 *a salesman's patter*:
chatter, gabble, jabber, line, pitch,
spiel (*sl*), jargon, lingo (*infml*).

pattern *n* 1 SYSTEM, method, order,
plan. 2 DECORATION, ornamentation,
ornament, figure, motif, design, style.
3 MODEL, template, stencil, guide,
original, prototype, standard,
norm.

patterned *adj* decorated,
ornamented, figured, printed.
☞ plain.

paunch *n* abdomen, belly, pot-belly,
beer belly, corporation (*infml*).

pause *v* halt, stop, cease,
discontinue, break off, interrupt, take
a break, rest, wait, delay, hesitate.
◇ *n* halt, stoppage, interruption,
break, rest, breather (*infml*), lull,
let-up (*infml*), respite, gap, interval,

interlude, intermission, wait, delay, hesitation.

pave v flag, tile, floor, surface, cover, asphalt, tarmac, concrete.

paw v maul, manhandle, mishandle, molest.
◇ n foot, pad, forefoot, hand.

pawn¹ n dupe, puppet, tool, instrument, toy, plaything.

pawn² v deposit, pledge, stake, mortgage, hock (sl), pop (sl).

pay v 1 REMIT, settle, discharge, reward, remunerate, recompense, reimburse, repay, refund, spend, pay out. 2 BENEFIT, profit, pay off, bring in, yield, return. 3 ATONE, make amends, compensate, answer, suffer.
◇ n remuneration, wages, salary, earnings, income, fee, stipend, honorarium, emoluments, payment, reward, recompense, compensation, reimbursement.
• **pay back** 1 REPAY, refund, reimburse, recompense, settle, square.
2 RETALIATE, get one's own back, take revenge, get even with, reciprocate, counter-attack.
• **pay off** 1 DISCHARGE, settle, square, clear. 2 DISMISS, fire, sack (infml), lay off. 3 the preparations paid off: succeed, work.
• **pay out** spend, disburse, hand over, fork out (infml), shell out (infml), lay out.

payable adj owed, owing, unpaid, outstanding, in arrears, due, mature.

payment n remittance, settlement, discharge, premium, outlay, advance, deposit, instalment, contribution, donation, allowance, reward, remuneration, pay, fee, hire, fare, toll.

peace n 1 SILENCE, quiet, hush, stillness, rest, relaxation, tranquillity, calm, calmness, composure, contentment. 2 ARMISTICE, truce, ceasefire, conciliation, concord, harmony, agreement, treaty.

≢ 1 noise, disturbance. 2 war, disagreement.

peaceable adj pacific, peace-loving, unwarlike, non-violent, conciliatory, friendly, amicable, inoffensive, gentle, placid, easy-going (infml), mild.
≢ belligerent, aggressive.

peaceful adj quiet, still, restful, relaxing, tranquil, serene, calm, placid, unruffled, undisturbed, untroubled, friendly, amicable, peaceable, pacific, gentle.
≢ noisy, disturbed, troubled, violent.

peacemaker n appeaser, conciliator, mediator, arbitrator, intercessor, peace-monger, pacifist.

peak n top, summit, pinnacle, crest, crown, zenith, height, maximum, climax, culmination, apex, tip, point.
≢ nadir, trough.
◇ v climax, culminate, come to a head.

peal n chime, carillon, toll, knell, ring, clang, ringing, reverberation, rumble, roar, crash, clap.
◇ v chime, toll, ring, clang, resonate, reverberate, resound, rumble, roll, roar, crash.

peasant n rustic, provincial, yokel, bumpkin, oaf, boor, lout.

peculiar adj 1 a peculiar sound: strange, odd, curious, funny, weird, bizarre, extraordinary, unusual, abnormal, exceptional, unconventional, offbeat, eccentric, way-out (sl), outlandish, exotic.
2 CHARACTERISTIC, distinctive, specific, particular, special, individual, personal, idiosyncratic, unique, singular.
≢ 1 ordinary, normal. 2 general.

peculiarity n oddity, bizarreness, abnormality, exception, eccentricity, quirk, mannerism, feature, trait, mark, quality, attribute, characteristic, distinctiveness, particularity, idiosyncrasy.

pedantic *adj* stilted, fussy, purist, particular, precise, exact, punctilious, hair-splitting, nit-picking, finical, academic, bookish, erudite.
⊉ imprecise, informal, casual.

peddle *v* sell, vend, flog (*infml*), hawk, tout, push, trade, traffic, market.

pedestal *n* plinth, stand, support, mounting, foot, base, foundation, platform, podium.

pedestrian *n* walker, foot-traveller.
◇ *adj* dull, boring, flat, uninspired, banal, mundane, run-of-the-mill, commonplace, ordinary, mediocre, indifferent, prosaic, stodgy, plodding.
⊉ exciting, imaginative.

pedigree *n* genealogy, family tree, lineage, ancestry, descent, line, family, parentage, derivation, extraction, race, breed, stock, blood.

peel *v* pare, skin, strip, scale, flake (off).
◇ *n* skin, rind, zest, peeling.

peep *v* look, peek, glimpse, spy, squint, peer, emerge, issue, appear.
◇ *n* look, peek, glimpse, glance, squint.

peephole *n* spyhole, keyhole, pinhole, hole, opening, aperture, slit, chink, crack, fissure, cleft, crevice.

peer¹ *v* look, gaze, scan, scrutinize, examine, inspect, spy, snoop, peep, squint.

peer² *n* **1** ARISTOCRAT, noble, nobleman, lord, duke, marquess, marquis, earl, count, viscount, baron. **2** EQUAL, counterpart, equivalent, match, fellow.

peerage *n* aristocracy, nobility, upper crust.

peeress *n* aristocrat, noble, lady, noblewoman, dame, duchess, marchioness, countess, viscountess, baroness.

peevish *adj* petulant, querulous, fractious, fretful, touchy, irritable, cross, grumpy, ratty (*infml*), crotchety, ill-tempered, crabbed, cantankerous, crusty, snappy, short-tempered, surly, sullen, sulky.
⊉ good-tempered.

peg *v* **1** FASTEN, secure, fix, attach, join, mark. **2** *peg prices*: control, stabilize, limit, freeze, fix, set.
◇ *n* pin, dowel, hook, knob, marker, post, stake.

pejorative *adj* derogatory, disparaging, belittling, slighting, unflattering, uncomplimentary, unpleasant, bad, negative.
⊉ complimentary.

pelt *v* **1** THROW, hurl, bombard, shower, assail, batter, beat, hit, strike. **2** POUR, teem, rain cats and dogs (*infml*). **3** RUSH, hurry, charge, belt (*infml*), tear, dash, speed, career.

pen¹ *n* fountain pen, ballpoint, rollerball, Biro®, felt-tip pen, light pen, mouse pen.
◇ *v* write, compose, draft, scribble, jot down.

pen² *n* enclosure, fold, stall, sty, coop, cage, hutch.
◇ *v* enclose, fence, hedge, hem in, confine, cage, coop, shut up.

penalize *v* punish, discipline, correct, fine, handicap.
⊉ reward.

penalty *n* punishment, retribution, fine, forfeit, handicap, disadvantage.
⊉ reward.

penance *n* atonement, reparation, punishment, penalty, mortification.

pendant *n* medallion, locket, necklace.

pending *adj* impending, in the offing, forthcoming, imminent, undecided, in the balance.
⊉ finished, settled.

penetrate *v* pierce, stab, prick, puncture, probe, sink, bore, enter, infiltrate, permeate, seep, pervade, suffuse.

penetrating adj piercing, stinging, biting, incisive, sharp, keen, acute, shrewd, discerning, perceptive, observant, profound, deep, searching, probing.
⊞ blunt.

penitence n repentance, contrition, remorse, regret, shame, self-reproach.

penitent adj repentant, contrite, sorry, apologetic, remorseful, regretful, conscience-stricken, shamefaced, humble.
⊞ unrepentant, hard-hearted, callous.

penniless adj poor, poverty-stricken, impoverished, destitute, bankrupt, ruined, bust, broke (infml), stony-broke (sl).
⊞ rich, wealthy, affluent.

pension n annuity, superannuation, allowance, benefit.

pensive adj thoughtful, reflective, contemplative, meditative, ruminative, absorbed, preoccupied, absent-minded, wistful, solemn, serious, sober.
⊞ carefree.

pent-up adj repressed, inhibited, restrained, bottled-up, suppressed, stifled.

people n persons, individuals, humans, human beings, mankind, humanity, folk, public, general public, populace, rank and file, population, inhabitants, citizens, community, society, race, nation.
◇ v populate, inhabit, occupy, settle, colonize.

pep n energy, vigour, verve, spirit, vitality, liveliness, get-up-and-go (infml), exuberance, high spirits.
• **pep up** (infml) invigorate, vitalize, liven up, quicken, stimulate, excite, exhilarate, inspire.
⊞ tone down.

perceive v 1 SEE, discern, make out, detect, discover, spot, catch sight of, notice, observe, view, remark, note, distinguish, recognize. 2 SENSE, feel, apprehend, learn, realize, appreciate, be aware of, know, grasp, understand, gather, deduce, conclude.

perceptible adj perceivable, discernible, detectable, appreciable, distinguishable, observable, noticeable, obvious, evident, conspicuous, clear, plain, apparent, visible.
⊞ imperceptible, inconspicuous.

perception n sense, feeling, impression, idea, conception, apprehension, awareness, consciousness, observation, recognition, grasp, understanding, insight, discernment, taste.

perceptive adj discerning, observant, sensitive, responsive, aware, alert, quick, sharp, astute, shrewd.
⊞ unobservant.

perch v land, alight, settle, sit, roost, balance, rest.

percolate v filter, strain, seep, ooze, leak, drip, penetrate, permeate, pervade.

peremptory adj imperious, commanding, dictatorial, autocratic, authoritative, assertive, high-handed, overbearing, domineering, bossy (infml), abrupt, curt, summary, arbitrary.

perennial adj lasting, enduring, everlasting, eternal, immortal, undying, imperishable, unceasing, incessant, never-ending, constant, continual, uninterrupted, perpetual, persistent, unfailing.

perfect adj 1 FAULTLESS, impeccable, flawless, immaculate, spotless, blameless, pure, superb, excellent, matchless, incomparable. 2 EXACT, precise, accurate, right, correct, true. 3 IDEAL, model, exemplary, ultimate, consummate, expert, accomplished,

experienced, skilful. **4** *perfect strangers*: utter, absolute, sheer, complete, entire, total.
⊜ **1** imperfect, flawed, blemished. **2** inaccurate, wrong. **3** inexperienced, unskilled.
◇ *v* fulfil, consummate, complete, finish, polish, refine, elaborate.
⊜ spoil, mar.

perfection *n* faultlessness, flawlessness, excellence, superiority, ideal, model, paragon, crown, pinnacle, acme, consummation, completion.
⊜ imperfection, flaw.

perfectionist *n* idealist, purist, pedant, stickler.

perfectly *adv* **1** UTTERLY, absolutely, quite, thoroughly, completely, entirely, wholly, totally, fully. **2** FAULTLESSLY, flawlessly, impeccably, ideally, exactly, correctly.
⊜ **1** partially. **2** imperfectly, badly.

perforate *v* hole, punch, drill, bore, pierce, prick, stab, puncture, penetrate.

perforation *n* hole, bore, prick, puncture, dotted line.

perform *v* **1** DO, carry out, execute, discharge, fulfil, satisfy, complete, achieve, accomplish, bring off, pull off, effect, bring about. **2** *perform a play*: stage, put on, present, enact, represent, act, play, appear as. **3** FUNCTION, work, operate, behave, produce.

performance *n* **1** SHOW, act, play, appearance, gig (*sl*), presentation, production, interpretation, rendition, representation, portrayal, acting. **2** ACTION, deed, doing, carrying out, execution, implementation, discharge, fulfilment, completion, achievement, accomplishment. **3** FUNCTIONING, operation, behaviour, conduct.

performer *n* actor, actress, player, artiste, entertainer.

perfume *n* scent, fragrance, smell, odour, aroma, bouquet, sweetness, balm, essence, cologne, toilet water, incense.

perhaps *adv* maybe, possibly, conceivably, feasibly.

peril *n* danger, hazard, risk, jeopardy, uncertainty, insecurity, threat, menace.
⊜ safety, security.

perilous *adj* dangerous, unsafe, hazardous, risky, chancy, precarious, insecure, unsure, vulnerable, exposed, menacing, threatening, dire.
⊜ safe, secure.

perimeter *n* circumference, edge, border, boundary, frontier, limit, bounds, confines, fringe, margin, periphery.
⊜ middle, centre, heart.

period *n* era, epoch, age, eon, generation, date, years, time, term, season, stage, phase, stretch, turn, session, interval, space, span, spell, cycle.

periodic *adj* occasional, infrequent, sporadic, intermittent, recurrent, repeated, regular, periodical, seasonal.

periodical *n* magazine, journal, publication, weekly, monthly, quarterly.

peripheral *adj* **1** MINOR, secondary, incidental, unimportant, irrelevant, unnecessary, marginal, borderline, surface, superficial. **2** OUTLYING, outer, outermost.
⊜ **1** major, crucial. **2** central.

perish *v* rot, decay, decompose, disintegrate, crumble, collapse, fall, die, expire, pass away.

perishable *adj* destructible, biodegradable, decomposable, short-lived.
⊜ imperishable, durable.

perk *n* perquisite, fringe benefit,

benefit, bonus, dividend, gratuity, tip, extra, plus (*infml*).

• **perk up** (*infml*) brighten, cheer up, buck up (*infml*), revive, liven up, pep up (*infml*), rally, recover, improve, look up.

permanence *n* fixedness, stability, imperishability, perpetuity, constancy, endurance, durability.
⊜ impermanence, transience.

permanent *adj* fixed, stable, unchanging, imperishable, indestructible, unfading, eternal, everlasting, lifelong, perpetual, constant, steadfast, perennial, long-lasting, lasting, enduring, durable.
⊜ temporary, ephemeral, fleeting.

permeable *adj* porous, absorbent, absorptive, penetrable.
⊜ impermeable, watertight.

permeate *v* pass through, soak through, filter through, seep through, penetrate, infiltrate, pervade, imbue, saturate, impregnate, fill.

permissible *adj* permitted, allowable, allowed, admissible, all right, acceptable, proper, authorized, sanctioned, lawful, legal, legitimate.
⊜ prohibited, banned, forbidden.

permission *n* consent, assent, agreement, approval, go-ahead, green light (*infml*), authorization, sanction, leave, warrant, permit, licence, dispensation, freedom, liberty.
⊜ prohibition.

permissive *adj* liberal, broad-minded, tolerant, forbearing, lenient, easy-going (*infml*), indulgent, overindulgent, lax, free.
⊜ strict, rigid.

permit *v* allow, let, consent, agree, admit, grant, authorize, sanction, warrant, license.
⊜ prohibit, forbid.
◇ *n* pass, passport, visa, licence, warrant, authorization, sanction, permission.

⊜ prohibition.

perpendicular *adj* vertical, upright, erect, straight, sheer, plumb.
⊜ horizontal.

perpetrate *v* commit, carry out, execute, do, perform, inflict, wreak.

perpetual *adj* eternal, everlasting, infinite, endless, unending, never-ending, interminable, ceaseless, unceasing, incessant, continuous, uninterrupted, constant, persistent, continual, repeated, recurrent, perennial, permanent, lasting, enduring, abiding, unchanging.
⊜ intermittent, temporary, ephemeral, transient.

perpetuate *v* continue, keep up, maintain, preserve, keep alive, immortalize, commemorate.

perplex *v* puzzle, baffle, mystify, stump, confuse, muddle, confound, bewilder, dumbfound.

persecute *v* hound, pursue, hunt, bother, worry, annoy, pester, harass, molest, abuse, ill-treat, maltreat, oppress, tyrannize, victimize, martyr, distress, afflict, torment, torture, crucify.
⊜ pamper, spoil.

persecution *n* harassment, molestation, abuse, maltreatment, discrimination, oppression, subjugation, suppression, tyranny, punishment, torture, martyrdom.

perseverance *n* persistence, determination, resolution, doggedness, tenacity, diligence, assiduity, dedication, commitment, constancy, steadfastness, stamina, endurance, indefatigability.

persevere *v* continue, carry on, stick at it (*infml*), keep going, soldier on, persist, plug away (*infml*), remain, stand firm, stand fast, hold on, hang on.
⊜ give up, quit, stop, discontinue.

persist *v* remain, linger, last, endure,

abide, continue, carry on, keep at it, persevere, insist.
⊒ desist, stop.

persistent *adj* 1 INCESSANT, endless, never-ending, interminable, continuous, unrelenting, relentless, unremitting, constant, steady, continual, repeated, perpetual, lasting, enduring. 2 *persistent effort*: persevering, determined, resolute, dogged, tenacious, stubborn, obstinate, steadfast, zealous, tireless, unflagging, indefatigable.

person *n* individual, being, human being, human, man, woman, body, soul, character, type.

personal *adj* own, private, confidential, intimate, special, particular, individual, exclusive, idiosyncratic, distinctive.
⊒ public, general, universal.

personality *n* 1 CHARACTER, nature, disposition, temperament, individuality, psyche, traits, make-up. 2 CELEBRITY, celeb (*infml*), notable, personage, public figure, VIP (*infml*), star.

personify *v* embody, epitomize, typify, exemplify, symbolize, represent, mirror.

personnel *n* staff, workforce, workers, employees, crew, human resources, manpower, people, members.

perspective *n* aspect, angle, slant, attitude, standpoint, viewpoint, point of view, view, vista, scene, prospect, outlook, proportion, relation.

perspiration *n* sweat, secretion, moisture, wetness.

perspire *v* sweat, exude, secrete, swelter, drip.

persuade *v* coax, prevail upon, lean on, cajole, wheedle, inveigle, talk into, induce, bring round, win over, convince, convert, sway, influence, lead on, incite, prompt, urge.

⊒ dissuade, deter, discourage.

persuasion *n* 1 COAXING, cajolery, wheedling, inducement, enticement, pull, power, influence, conviction, conversion. 2 OPINION, school (of thought), party, faction, side, conviction, faith, belief, denomination, sect.

persuasive *adj* convincing, plausible, cogent, sound, valid, influential, forceful, weighty, effective, telling, potent, compelling, moving, touching.
⊒ unconvincing.

pertinent *adj* appropriate, suitable, fitting, apt, apposite, relevant, to the point, material, applicable.
⊒ inappropriate, unsuitable, irrelevant.

perturb *v* disturb, bother, trouble, upset, worry, alarm, disconcert, unsettle, discompose, ruffle, fluster, agitate, vex, rattle (*infml*).
⊒ reassure, compose.

peruse *v* study, pore over, read, browse, look through, scan, scrutinize, examine, inspect, check.

pervade *v* affect, penetrate, permeate, percolate, charge, fill, imbue, infuse, suffuse, saturate, impregnate.

pervasive *adj* prevalent, common, extensive, widespread, general, universal, inescapable, omnipresent, ubiquitous.

perverse *adj* contrary, wayward, wrong-headed, wilful, headstrong, stubborn, obstinate, unyielding, intransigent, disobedient, rebellious, troublesome, unmanageable, ill-tempered, cantankerous, unreasonable, incorrect, improper.
⊒ obliging, co-operative, reasonable.

perversion *n* 1 CORRUPTION, depravity, debauchery, immorality, vice, wickedness, deviance, kinkiness (*infml*), abnormality. 2 TWISTING, distortion, misrepresentation, travesty, misinterpretation, aberration, deviation, misuse, misapplication.

pervert v 1 *pervert the truth*: twist, warp, distort, misrepresent, falsify, garble, misinterpret. 2 CORRUPT, lead astray, deprave, debauch, debase, degrade, abuse, misuse, misapply.
◇ n deviant, debauchee, degenerate, weirdo (*infml*), perv (*infml*).

perverted adj twisted, warped, distorted, deviant, kinky (*infml*), pervy (*infml*), unnatural, abnormal, unhealthy, corrupt, depraved, debauched, debased, immoral, evil, wicked.
🖅 natural, normal.

pessimistic adj negative, cynical, fatalistic, defeatist, resigned, hopeless, despairing, despondent, dejected, downhearted, glum, morose, melancholy, depressed, dismal, gloomy, bleak.
🖅 optimistic.

pest n nuisance, bother, annoyance, irritation, vexation, trial; curse, scourge, bane, blight, bug.

pester v nag, badger, hound, hassle (*infml*), harass, plague, torment, provoke, worry, bother, disturb, annoy, irritate, pick on, get at (*infml*).

pet n favourite, darling, idol, treasure, jewel.
◇ adj favourite, favoured, preferred, dearest, cherished, special, particular, personal.
◇ v stroke, caress, fondle, cuddle, kiss, neck (*sl*), snog (*sl*).

peter out v dwindle, taper off, fade, wane, ebb, fail, cease, stop.

petition n appeal, round robin, application, request, solicitation, plea, entreaty, prayer, supplication, invocation.
◇ v appeal, call upon, ask, crave, solicit, bid, urge, press, implore, beg, plead, entreat, beseech, supplicate, pray.

petrify v terrify, horrify, appal, paralyse, numb, stun, dumbfound.

petty adj 1 MINOR, unimportant, insignificant, trivial, secondary, lesser, small, little, slight, trifling, paltry, inconsiderable, negligible.
2 SMALL-MINDED, mean, ungenerous, grudging, spiteful.
🖅 1 important, significant.
2 generous.

petulant adj fretful, peevish, cross, irritable, snappish, bad-tempered, ill-humoured, moody, sullen, sulky, sour, ungracious.

phantom n ghost, spectre, spirit, apparition, vision, hallucination, illusion, figment.

phase n stage, step, time, period, spell, season, chapter, position, point, aspect, state, condition.
• **phase out** wind down, run down, ease off, taper off, eliminate, dispose of, get rid of, remove, withdraw, close, terminate.

phenomenal adj marvellous, sensational, stupendous, amazing, remarkable, extraordinary, exceptional, unusual, unbelievable, incredible.

phenomenon n 1 OCCURRENCE, happening, event, incident, episode, fact, appearance, sight. 2 WONDER, marvel, miracle, prodigy, rarity, curiosity, spectacle, sensation.

philanthropic adj humanitarian, public-spirited, altruistic, unselfish, benevolent, kind, charitable, liberal, almsgiving, generous, open-handed.
🖅 misanthropic.

philanthropist n humanitarian, benefactor, patron, sponsor, giver, donor, contributor, altruist.
🖅 misanthrope.

philanthropy n humanitarianism, public-spiritedness, altruism, unselfishness, benevolence, kind-

heartedness, charity, almsgiving, patronage, generosity, liberality, open-handedness.
☒ misanthropy.

philosophical adj 1 a philosophical discussion: metaphysical, abstract, theoretical, analytical, rational, logical, erudite, learned, wise, thoughtful. 2 RESIGNED, patient, stoical, unruffled, calm, composed.

philosophy n reason, thought, thinking, wisdom, knowledge, ideology, world-view, doctrine, beliefs, convictions, values, principles, attitude, viewpoint.

Philosophical terms include: absolutism, a posteriori, a priori, atomism, deduction, deontology, determinism, dialectical materialism, dualism, egoism, empiricism, Epicureanism, epistemology, ethics, existentialism, fatalism, hedonism, humanism, idealism, identity, induction, instrumentalism, interactionism, intuition, libertarianism, logic, logical positivism, materialism, metaphysics, monism, naturalism, nihilism, nominalism, objectivism, ontology, phenomenalism, phenomenology, positivism, pragmatism, prescriptivism, rationalism, realism, reductionism, relativism, scepticism, scholasticism, sensationalism, solipsism, stoicism, structuralism, subjectivism, syllogism, teleology, utilitarianism.

phlegmatic adj placid, stolid, impassive, calm, cool, unemotional, unconcerned, indifferent, matter-of-fact, stoical.
☒ emotional, passionate.

phobia n fear, terror, dread, anxiety, neurosis, obsession, hang-up (infml), thing (infml), aversion, dislike, hatred, horror, loathing, revulsion, repulsion.

☒ love, liking.

Phobias (by name of object feared) include: zoophobia (animals), apiphobia (bees), ailurophobia (cats), necrophobia (corpses), scotophobia (darkness), cynophobia (dogs), claustrophobia (enclosed places), pantophobia (everything), pyrophobia (fire), xenophobia (foreigners), phasmophobia (ghosts), acrophobia (high places), hippophobia (horses), entomophobia (insects), astraphobia (lightning), autophobia (loneliness), agoraphobia (open spaces), toxiphobia (poison), herpetophobia (reptiles), ophidiophobia (snakes), tachophobia (speed), arachnophobia (spiders), triskaidekaphobia (thirteen), brontophobia (thunder), hydrophobia (water). see also: supplement **Words Grouped by Ending**

phone v telephone, ring (up), call (up), dial, contact, get in touch, give a buzz (infml), give a tinkle (infml).

phoney adj fake, counterfeit, forged, bogus, trick, false, spurious, assumed, affected, put-on, sham, pseudo, imitation.
☒ real, genuine.

photocopy v copy, duplicate, Photostat®, Xerox®, print, run off.
◇ n copy, duplicate, Photostat®, Xerox®.

photograph n photo, snap, snapshot, print, shot, slide, transparency, picture, image, likeness.
◇ v snap, take, film, shoot, video, record.

Photographic equipment includes: camera, camcorder; cable release, remote control; battery, stand, tripod, flash umbrella, boom arm; film, cartridge film, cassette film, disc film; filter, colour filter, heat filter, polarizing filter; memory card, memory reader; light meter, exposure meter, spot meter; diffuser, barn doors, parabolic reflector, snoot; developing bath, developing tank, dry mounting press, enlarger, fixing bath, focus magnifier, light box, negative carrier, print washer, contact printer, safelight, stop bath, Vertoscope®, viewer; slide mount, slide viewer, slide projector, film projector, screen; cassette adaptor, tele-cine converter. *see also* **camera**.

phrase *n* construction, clause, idiom, expression, saying, utterance, remark.
◇ *v* word, formulate, frame, couch, present, put, express, say, utter, pronounce.

physical *adj* bodily, corporeal, fleshy, incarnate, mortal, earthly, material, concrete, solid, substantial, tangible, visible, real, actual.
⊟ mental, spiritual.

physician *n* doctor, medical practitioner, medic (*infml*), general practitioner, GP, houseman, intern, registrar, consultant, specialist, healer.

physics

Terms used in physics include: absolute zero, acceleration, atom, Big Bang theory, boiling point, centre of gravity, centrifugal force, charge, circuit, critical mass, current, density, diffraction, discharge, dynamics, electricity, electromagnetic, electron, energy, equilibrium, evaporation, field, force, freezing point, frequency, friction, gamma ray, grand unified theory (GUT), gravity, half-life, inertia, infrared, interference, ion, kinetic energy, laser, latent heat, lens, longitudinal wave, magnetic field, magnetism, mass, microwave, molecule, moment, momentum, motion, neutron, nuclear fission, nuclear fusion, nucleus, oscillation, particle, photon, polarity, potential energy, pressure, proton, quantum, radiation, radioactivity, radio wave, reflection, refraction, relativity, resistance, semiconductor, SI unit, sound wave, spectrum, superstring theory, surface tension, transverse wave, ultrasound, ultraviolet, velocity, viscosity, volume, wave, X-ray.

physique *n* body, figure, shape, form, build, frame, structure, constitution, make-up.

pick *v* 1 SELECT, choose, opt for, decide on, settle on, single out.
2 GATHER, collect, pluck, harvest, cull.
◇ *n* 1 CHOICE, selection, option, decision, preference. 2 BEST, cream, flower, élite, elect.
● **pick on** bully, torment, persecute, nag, get at (*infml*), needle (*infml*), bait.
● **pick out** spot, notice, perceive, recognize, distinguish, tell apart, separate, single out, hand-pick, choose, select.
● **pick up 1** LIFT, raise, hoist. 2 *I'll pick you up at eight*: call for, fetch, collect. 3 LEARN, master, grasp, gather. 4 IMPROVE, rally, recover, perk up (*infml*). 5 BUY, purchase. 6 OBTAIN, acquire, gain. 7 *pick up an infection*: catch, contract, get.

picket *n* picketer, protester, demonstrator, striker.
◇ *v* protest, demonstrate, boycott, blockade, enclose, surround.

pickle *v* preserve, conserve, souse, marinade, steep, cure, salt.

pictorial *adj* graphic, diagrammatic, schematic, representational, vivid, striking, expressive, illustrated, picturesque, scenic.

picture n 1 PAINTING, portrait, landscape, drawing, sketch, illustration, engraving, photograph, print, representation, likeness, image, effigy. 2 DEPICTION, portrayal, description, account, report, impression. 3 *the picture of health*: embodiment, personification, epitome, archetype, essence. 4 FILM, movie (*infml*), motion picture.
◇ v 1 IMAGINE, envisage, envision, conceive, visualize, see. 2 DEPICT, describe, represent, show, portray, draw, sketch, paint, photograph, illustrate.

picturesque adj 1 ATTRACTIVE, beautiful, pretty, charming, quaint, idyllic, scenic. 2 DESCRIPTIVE, graphic, vivid, colourful, striking.
⊞ 1 unattractive. 2 dull.

piece n 1 FRAGMENT, bit, scrap, morsel, mouthful, bite, lump, chunk, slice, sliver, snippet, shred, offcut, sample, component, constituent, element, part, segment, section, division, fraction, share, portion, quantity. 2 ARTICLE, item, study, work, composition, creation, specimen, example.

pier n 1 JETTY, breakwater, landing-stage, quay, wharf. 2 SUPPORT, upright, pillar, post.

pierce v penetrate, enter, stick into, puncture, drill, bore, probe, perforate, punch, prick, stab, lance, bayonet, run through, spear, skewer, spike, impale, transfix.

piercing adj 1 *a piercing cry*: shrill, high-pitched, loud, ear-splitting, sharp. 2 PENETRATING, probing, searching. 3 COLD, bitter, raw, biting, keen, fierce, severe, wintry, frosty, freezing. 4 PAINFUL, agonizing, excruciating, stabbing, lacerating.

piety n piousness, devoutness, godliness, saintliness, holiness,

sanctity, religion, faith, devotion, reverence.
⊞ impiety, irreligion.

pig n 1 SWINE, hog, sow, boar, animal, beast, brute. 2 GLUTTON, gourmand.

pigeonhole n compartment, niche, slot, cubby-hole, cubicle, locker, box, place, section.
◇ v compartmentalize, label, classify, sort, file, catalogue.

pigment n colour, hue, tint, dye, stain, paint, colouring, tincture.

pile¹ n stack, heap, mound, mountain, mass, accumulation, collection, assortment, hoard, stockpile.
◇ v stack, heap, mass, amass, accumulate, build up, gather, assemble, collect, hoard, stockpile, store, load, pack, jam, crush, crowd, flock, flood, stream, rush, charge.

pile² n post, column, upright, support, bar, beam, foundation.

pile³ n nap, shag, plush, fur, hair, fuzz, down.

pilfer v steal, pinch (*infml*), nick (*infml*), knock off (*sl*), filch, lift, shoplift, rob, thieve.

pilgrim n crusader, traveller, wanderer.

pilgrimage n crusade, mission, expedition, journey, trip, tour.

pill n tablet, capsule, pellet.

pillar n 1 COLUMN, shaft, post, mast, pier, upright, pile, support, prop. 2 MAINSTAY, bastion, tower of strength.

pilot n 1 FLYER, aviator, airman. 2 NAVIGATOR, steersman, helmsman, coxswain, captain, leader, director, guide.
◇ v fly, drive, steer, direct, control, handle, manage, operate, run, conduct, lead, guide, navigate.
◇ adj experimental, trial, test, model.

pimple n spot, zit (*sl*), blackhead,

boil, swelling.

pin v tack, nail, fix, affix, attach, join, staple, clip, fasten, secure, hold down, restrain, immobilize.
◇ n tack, nail, screw, spike, rivet, bolt, peg, fastener, clip, staple, brooch.
• **pin down 1** PINPOINT, identify, determine, specify. **2** FORCE, make, press, pressurize.

pinch v **1** SQUEEZE, compress, crush, press, tweak, nip, hurt, grip, grasp. **2** (infml) STEAL, nick, pilfer, filch, snatch.
◇ n **1** SQUEEZE, tweak, nip. **2** DASH, soupçon, taste, bit, speck, jot, mite. **3** EMERGENCY, crisis, predicament, difficulty, hardship, pressure, stress.

pine v long, yearn, ache, sigh, grieve, mourn, wish, desire, crave, hanker, hunger, thirst.

pinnacle n **1** PEAK, summit, top, cap, crown, crest, apex, vertex, acme, zenith, height, eminence. **2** SPIRE, steeple, turret, pyramid, cone, obelisk, needle.

pinpoint v identify, spot, locate, distinguish, place, home in on, zero in on (infml), pin down, determine, specify, define.

pioneer n colonist, settler, frontiersman, frontierswoman, explorer, developer, pathfinder, trail-blazer, leader, innovator, inventor, discoverer, founder.
◇ v invent, discover, originate, create, initiate, instigate, begin, start, launch, institute, found, establish, set up, develop, open up.

pious adj **1** DEVOUT, godly, saintly, holy, spiritual, religious, reverent, good, virtuous, righteous, moral. **2** SANCTIMONIOUS, holier-than-thou, self-righteous, goody-goody (infml), hypocritical.
⊡ **1** impious, irreligious, irreverent.

pipe n tube, hose, piping, tubing, pipeline, line, main, flue, duct,
conduit, channel, passage, conveyor.
◇ v **1** CHANNEL, funnel, siphon, carry, convey, conduct, transmit, supply, deliver. **2** WHISTLE, chirp, tweet, cheep, peep, twitter, sing, warble, trill, play, sound.

piquant adj **1** piquant sauce: spicy, tangy, savoury, salty, peppery, pungent, sharp, biting, stinging. **2** LIVELY, spirited, stimulating, provocative, interesting, sparkling.
⊡ **1** bland, insipid. **2** dull, banal.

pique n annoyance, irritation, vexation, displeasure, offence, huff (infml), resentment, grudge.

piqued adj annoyed, irritated, vexed, riled, angry, displeased, offended, miffed (infml), peeved (infml), put out, resentful.

pirate n **1** BUCCANEER, brigand, freebooter, filibuster, corsair, marauder, raider, rover, picaroon, sea robber, sea rover, sea wolf, sea rat, water rat, marque. **2** INFRINGER, plagiarist, plagiarizer.
◇ v copy, reproduce illegally, steal, pinch, (infml), plagiarize, poach, appropriate (fml), borrow (infml), crib (infml), lift (infml), nick (sl).

pit n mine, coalmine, excavation, trench, ditch, hollow, depression, indentation, dent, hole, cavity, crater, pothole, gulf, chasm, abyss.

pitch v **1** THROW, fling, toss, chuck (infml), lob, bowl, hurl, heave, sling, fire, launch, aim, direct. **2** PLUNGE, dive, plummet, drop, fall headlong, tumble, lurch, roll, wallow. **3** pitch camp: erect, put up, set up, place, station, settle, plant, fix.
◇ n **1** cricket pitch: ground, field, playing-field, arena, stadium. **2** SOUND, tone, timbre, modulation, frequency, level. **3** GRADIENT, incline, slope, tilt, angle, degree, steepness.

piteous adj poignant, moving, touching, distressing, heart-rending, plaintive, mournful, sad, sorrowful, woeful, wretched, pitiful, pitiable, pathetic.

pitfall n danger, peril, hazard, trap, snare, stumbling-block, catch, snag, drawback, difficulty.

pith n importance, significance, moment, weight, consequence, substance, matter, marrow, meat, gist, essence, crux, nub, heart, core, kernel.

pithy adj succinct, concise, compact, terse, short, brief, pointed, trenchant, forceful, cogent, telling.
☒ wordy, verbose.

pitiful adj 1 CONTEMPTIBLE, despicable, low, mean, vile, shabby, deplorable, lamentable, woeful, inadequate, hopeless, pathetic (infml), insignificant, paltry, worthless. 2 PITEOUS, doleful, mournful, distressing, heart-rending, pathetic, pitiable, sad, miserable, wretched, poor, sorry.

pitiless adj merciless, cold-hearted, unsympathetic, unfeeling, uncaring, hard-hearted, callous, cruel, inhuman, brutal, cold-blooded, ruthless, relentless, unremitting, inexorable, harsh.
☒ merciful, compassionate, kind, gentle.

pittance n modicum, crumb, drop (in the ocean), chicken-feed (infml), peanuts (sl), trifle.

pitted adj dented, holey, potholed, pockmarked, blemished, scarred, marked, notched, indented, rough.

pity n 1 SYMPATHY, commiseration, regret, understanding, fellow-feeling, compassion, kindness, tenderness, mercy, forbearance. 2 what a pity!: shame, misfortune, bad luck.
☒ 1 cruelty, anger, scorn.
◇ v feel sorry for, feel for, sympathize with, commiserate with, grieve for, weep for.

pivot n axis, hinge, axle, spindle, kingpin, linchpin, swivel, hub, focal

point, centre, heart.
◇ v 1 SWIVEL, turn, spin, revolve, rotate, swing. 2 DEPEND, rely, hinge, hang, lie.

placard n poster, bill, notice, sign, advertisement.

placate v appease, pacify, conciliate, mollify, calm, assuage, soothe, lull, quiet.
☒ anger, enrage, incense, infuriate.

place n 1 SITE, locale, venue, location, situation, spot, point, position, seat, space, room. 2 CITY, town, village, locality, neighbourhood, district, area, region. 3 BUILDING, property, dwelling, residence, house, flat, apartment, home.
◇ v put, set, plant, fix, position, locate, situate, rest, settle, lay, stand, deposit, leave.
• **in place of** instead of, in lieu of, as a replacement for, as a substitute for, as an alternative to.
• **out of place** inappropriate, unsuitable, unfitting, unbecoming, unseemly.
• **take place** happen, occur, come about.

placid adj calm, composed, unruffled, untroubled, cool, self-possessed, level-headed, easy-going, imperturbable, mild, gentle, equable, even-tempered, serene, tranquil, still, quiet, peaceful, restful.
☒ excitable, agitated, disturbed.

plagiarize v crib, copy, reproduce, imitate, counterfeit, pirate, infringe copyright, poach, steal, lift, appropriate, borrow.

plague n 1 PESTILENCE, epidemic, disease, infection, contagion, infestation. 2 NUISANCE, annoyance, curse, scourge, trial, affliction, torment, calamity.
◇ v annoy, vex, bother, disturb, trouble, distress, upset, pester, harass, hound, haunt, bedevil, afflict, torment, torture, persecute.

plain adj 1 *plain cookery*: ordinary, basic, simple, vanilla (*infml*), unpretentious, modest, unadorned, unelaborate, restrained. 2 OBVIOUS, evident, patent, clear, understandable, apparent, visible, unmistakable. 3 FRANK, candid, blunt, outspoken, direct, forthright, straightforward, unambiguous, plain-spoken, open, honest, truthful. 4 UNATTRACTIVE, ugly, unprepossessing, unlovely. 5 *plain fabric*: unpatterned, unvariegated, uncoloured, self-coloured.
⊠ 1 fancy, elaborate. 2 unclear, obscure. 3 devious, deceitful. 4 attractive, good-looking. 5 patterned.
◇ *n* grassland, prairie, steppe, lowland, flat, plateau, tableland.

plaintive adj doleful, mournful, melancholy, wistful, sad, sorrowful, grief-stricken, piteous, heart-rending, high-pitched.

plan *n* 1 BLUEPRINT, layout, diagram, chart, map, drawing, sketch, representation, design. 2 IDEA, suggestion, proposal, proposition, project, scheme, plot, system, method, procedure, strategy, programme, schedule, scenario.
◇ *v* 1 PLOT, scheme, design, invent, devise, contrive, formulate, frame, draft, outline, prepare, organize, arrange. 2 AIM, intend, propose, contemplate, envisage, foresee.

planet

Planets within the Earth's solar system (nearest the sun shown first) are: Mercury, Venus, Earth, Mars, Jupiter, Saturn, Uranus, Neptune.

plant *n* factory, works, foundry, mill, shop, yard, workshop, machinery, apparatus, equipment, gear.
◇ *v* 1 SOW, seed, bury, transplant. 2 INSERT, put, place, set, fix, lodge, root, settle, found, establish.

Plants include: annual, biennial, perennial, herbaceous plant, evergreen, succulent, cultivar, hybrid, house plant, pot plant; flower, herb, shrub, bush, tree, vegetable, grass, vine, weed, cereal, wild flower, air plant, water plant, cactus, fern, moss, algae, lichen, fungus; bulb, corm, seedling, sapling, bush, climber. *see also* **flower**; **fungus**; **grass**; **shrub**; **tree**.

plaster *n* sticking-plaster, dressing, bandage, plaster of Paris, mortar, stucco.
◇ *v* daub, smear, coat, cover, spread.

plastic adj soft, pliable, flexible, supple, malleable, mouldable, ductile, receptive, impressionable, manageable.
⊠ rigid, inflexible.

plate *n* 1 DISH, platter, salver, helping, serving, portion. 2 ILLUSTRATION, picture, print, lithograph.
◇ *v* coat, cover, overlay, veneer, laminate, electroplate, anodize, galvanize.

platform *n* 1 STAGE, podium, dais, rostrum, stand. 2 POLICY, party line, principles, tenets, manifesto, programme, objectives.

platitude *n* banality, commonplace, truism, cliché, chestnut.

plausible adj credible, believable, reasonable, logical, likely, possible, probable, convincing, persuasive, smooth-talking, glib.
⊠ implausible, unlikely, improbable.

play *v* 1 AMUSE ONESELF, have fun, enjoy oneself, revel, sport, romp, frolic, caper. 2 PARTICIPATE, take part, join in, compete. 3 *France played Italy*: oppose, vie with, challenge, take on. 4 ACT, perform, portray, represent, impersonate.
⊠ 1 work.
◇ *n* 1 FUN, amusement,

entertainment, diversion, recreation, sport, game, hobby, pastime. **2** DRAMA, tragedy, comedy, farce, show, performance. **3** MOVEMENT, action, flexibility, give, leeway, latitude, margin, scope, range, room, space.
⊠ **1** work.

• **play down** minimize, make light of, gloss over, underplay, understate, undervalue, underestimate.
⊠ exaggerate.

• **play on** exploit, take advantage of, turn to account, profit by, trade on, capitalize on.

• **play up 1** EXAGGERATE, highlight, spotlight, accentuate, emphasize, stress. **2** MISBEHAVE, malfunction, trouble, bother, annoy, hurt.

playboy *n* philanderer, womanizer, ladies' man, rake, libertine.

player *n* **1** CONTESTANT, competitor, participant, sportsman, sportswoman. **2** PERFORMER, entertainer, artiste, actor, actress, musician, instrumentalist.

playful *adj* sportive, frolicsome, lively, spirited, mischievous, roguish, impish, puckish, kittenish, good-natured, jesting, teasing, humorous, tongue-in-cheek.
⊠ serious.

playwright *n* dramatist, scriptwriter, screenwriter.

plea *n* **1** APPEAL, petition, request, entreaty, supplication, prayer, invocation. **2** DEFENCE, justification, excuse, explanation, claim.

plead *v* **1** BEG, implore, beseech, entreat, appeal, petition, ask, request. **2** *plead ignorance*: assert, maintain, claim, allege.

pleasant *adj* agreeable, nice, fine, lovely, delightful, charming, likable, amiable, friendly, affable, good-humoured, cheerful, congenial, enjoyable, amusing, pleasing, gratifying, satisfying, acceptable,

welcome, refreshing.
⊠ unpleasant, nasty, unfriendly.

please *v* **1** DELIGHT, charm, captivate, entertain, amuse, cheer, gladden, humour, indulge, gratify, satisfy, content, suit. **2** WANT, will, wish, desire, like, prefer, choose, think fit.
⊠ **1** displease, annoy, anger, sadden.

pleased *adj* contented, satisfied, gratified, glad, happy, delighted, thrilled, euphoric.
⊠ displeased, annoyed.

pleasing *adj* gratifying, satisfying, acceptable, good, pleasant, nice, agreeable, delightful, charming, attractive, engaging, winning.
⊠ unpleasant, disagreeable.

pleasure *n* amusement, entertainment, recreation, fun, enjoyment, gratification, satisfaction, contentment, happiness, joy, delight, comfort, solace.
⊠ sorrow, pain, trouble, displeasure.

pleat *v* tuck, fold, crease, flute, crimp, gather, pucker.

pledge *n* **1** PROMISE, vow, word of honour, oath, bond, covenant, guarantee, warrant, assurance, undertaking. **2** DEPOSIT, security, surety, bail.
◇ *v* promise, vow, swear, contract, engage, undertake, vouch, guarantee, secure.

plentiful *adj* ample, abundant, profuse, copious, overflowing, lavish, generous, liberal, bountiful, fruitful, productive.
⊠ scarce, scanty, rare.

plenty *n* abundance, profusion, plethora, lots (*infml*), loads (*infml*), masses (*infml*), heaps (*infml*), piles (*infml*), stacks (*infml*), enough, sufficiency, quantity, mass, volume, fund, mine, store.
⊠ scarcity, lack, want, need.

pliable *adj* **1** FLEXIBLE, pliant, bendable, bendy (*infml*), supple, lithe, malleable, plastic, yielding.

2 ADAPTABLE, accommodating, manageable, tractable, docile, compliant, biddable, persuadable, responsive, receptive, impressionable, susceptible.
⊞ **2** rigid, inflexible, headstrong.

plight n predicament, quandary, dilemma, extremity, trouble, difficulty, straits, state, condition, situation, circumstances, case.

plod v **1** TRUDGE, tramp, stump, lumber, plough through. **2** DRUDGE, labour, toil, grind, slog, persevere, soldier on.

plot n **1** CONSPIRACY, intrigue, machination, scheme, plan, stratagem. **2** STORY, narrative, subject, theme, storyline, thread, outline, scenario. **3** plot of land: patch, tract, area, allotment, lot, parcel.
◇ v **1** CONSPIRE, intrigue, machinate, scheme, hatch, lay, cook up, devise, contrive, plan, project, design, draft. **2** CHART, map, mark, locate, draw, calculate.

plotter n conspirator, intriguer, machinator, schemer.

ploy n manoeuvre, stratagem, tactic, move, device, contrivance, scheme, game, trick, artifice, dodge, wile, ruse, subterfuge.

pluck n courage, bravery, spirit, mettle, nerve (infml), guts (infml), grit, backbone, fortitude, resolution, determination.
⊞ cowardice.
◇ v **1** PULL, draw, tug, snatch, pull off, remove, pick, collect, gather, harvest. **2** pluck a guitar: pick, twang, strum.

plucky adj brave, courageous, bold, daring, intrepid, heroic, valiant, feisty (infml), spirited.
⊞ cowardly, weak, feeble.

plug n **1** STOPPER, bung, cork, spigot. **2** (infml) ADVERTISEMENT, publicity, mention, puff.
◇ v **1** STOP (UP), bung, cork, block,

choke, close, seal, fill, pack, stuff. **2** (infml) ADVERTISE, publicize, promote, push, mention.

plumb adv **1** VERTICALLY, perpendicularly. **2** PRECISELY, exactly, dead, slap (infml), bang (infml).
◇ v sound, fathom, measure, gauge, penetrate, probe, search, explore.

plummet v plunge, dive, nose-dive, descend, drop, fall, tumble.
⊞ soar.

plump adj fat, obese, dumpy, tubby, stout, round, rotund, portly, chubby, podgy, fleshy, full, ample, buxom.
⊞ thin, skinny.

plump for v opt for, choose, select, favour, back, support.

plunder v loot, pillage, ravage, devastate, sack, raid, ransack, rifle, steal, rob, strip.
◇ n loot, pillage, booty, swag (sl), spoils, pickings, ill-gotten gains, prize.

plunge v **1** DIVE, jump, nose-dive, swoop, dive-bomb, plummet, descend, go down, sink, drop, fall, pitch, tumble, hurtle, career, charge, dash, rush, tear. **2** IMMERSE, submerge, dip.
◇ n dive, jump, swoop, descent, drop, fall, tumble, immersion, submersion.

ply n layer, fold, thickness, strand, sheet, leaf.

poach v steal, pilfer, appropriate, trespass, encroach, infringe.

pocket n pouch, bag, envelope, receptacle, compartment, hollow, cavity.
◇ adj small, little, mini (infml), concise, compact, portable, miniature.
◇ v take, appropriate, help oneself to, lift, pilfer, filch, steal, nick (infml), pinch (infml).

pod n shell, husk, case, hull.

poem

Types of poem include: ballad, elegy, epic, haiku, idyll, lay, limerick, lyric, madrigal, nursery rhyme, ode, pastoral, roundelay, sonnet, tanka.

poet *n* versifier, rhymer, rhymester, lyricist, bard, minstrel.

poetic *adj* poetical, lyrical, moving, artistic, graceful, flowing, metrical, rhythmical, versified, rhyming.
⊞ prosaic.

poignant *adj* moving, touching, affecting, tender, distressing, upsetting, heartbreaking, heart-rending, piteous, pathetic, sad, painful, agonizing.

point *n* 1 FEATURE, attribute, aspect, facet, detail, particular, item, subject, topic. 2 *what's the point?*: use, purpose, motive, reason, object, intention, aim, end, goal, objective. 3 ESSENCE, crux, core, pith, gist, thrust, meaning, drift, burden. 4 PLACE, position, situation, location, site, spot. 5 MOMENT, instant, juncture, stage, time, period. 6 DOT, spot, mark, speck, full stop.
◇ *v* 1 *point a gun*: aim, direct, train, level. 2 INDICATE, signal, show, signify, denote, designate.
• **point out** show, indicate, draw attention to, point to, reveal, identify, specify, mention, bring up, allude to, remind.

point-blank *adj* direct, forthright, straightforward, plain, explicit, open, unreserved, blunt, frank, candid.
◇ *adv* directly, forthrightly, plainly, straightforwardly, explicitly, openly, bluntly, frankly, candidly.

pointed *adj* sharp, keen, edged, barbed, cutting, incisive, trenchant, biting, penetrating, telling.

pointer *n* 1 ARROW, indicator, needle, hand. 2 TIP, recommendation, suggestion, hint, guide, indication, advice, warning, caution.

pointless *adj* useless, futile, vain, fruitless, unproductive, unprofitable, worthless, senseless, absurd, meaningless, aimless.
⊞ useful, profitable, meaningful.

poise *n* calmness, composure, self-possession, presence of mind, coolness, equanimity, aplomb, assurance, dignity, elegance, grace, balance, equilibrium.
◇ *v* balance, position, hover, hang, suspend.

poised *adj* 1 DIGNIFIED, graceful, calm, composed, unruffled, collected, self-possessed, cool, self-confident, assured. 2 *poised for action*: prepared, ready, set, waiting, expectant.

poison *n* toxin, venom, bane, blight, cancer, malignancy, contagion, contamination, corruption.
◇ *v* infect, contaminate, pollute, taint, adulterate, corrupt, deprave, pervert, warp.

poisonous *adj* toxic, venomous, lethal, deadly, fatal, mortal, noxious, pernicious, malicious.

poke *v* prod, stab, jab, stick, thrust, push, shove, nudge, elbow, dig, butt, hit, punch.
◇ *n* prod, jab, thrust, shove, nudge, dig, butt, punch.

pole¹ *n* bar, rod, stick, shaft, spar, upright, post, stake, mast, staff.

pole² *n* antipode, extremity, extreme, limit.
• **poles apart** irreconcilable, worlds apart, incompatible, like chalk and cheese.

police *n* police force, constabulary, the Law (*infml*), the Bill (*sl*), the fuzz (*sl*).
◇ *v* check, control, regulate, monitor, watch, observe, supervise, oversee, patrol, guard, protect, defend, keep the peace.

policeman, policewoman n
officer, constable, PC, cop (sl),
copper (infml), bobby (infml), bizzy (sl).

policy n 1 CODE OF PRACTICE, rules,
guidelines, procedure, method,
practice, custom, protocol.
2 COURSE OF ACTION, line, course,
plan, programme, scheme, stance,
position.

polish v 1 SHINE, brighten, smooth,
rub, buff, burnish, clean, wax.
2 IMPROVE, enhance, brush up, touch
up, finish, perfect, refine, cultivate.
⊟ 1 tarnish, dull.
◇ n 1 a tin of polish: wax, varnish.
2 SHINE, gloss, sheen, lustre,
brightness, brilliance, sparkle,
smoothness, finish, glaze, veneer.
3 REFINEMENT, cultivation, class,
breeding, sophistication, finesse,
style, elegance, grace, poise.
⊟ 2 dullness. 3 clumsiness.

polished adj 1 SHINING, shiny,
glossy, lustrous, gleaming, burnished,
smooth, glassy, slippery. 2 FAULTLESS,
flawless, impeccable, perfect,
outstanding, superlative, masterly,
expert, professional, skilful,
accomplished, perfected. 3 REFINED,
cultivated, genteel, well-bred, polite,
sophisticated, urbane, suave, elegant,
graceful.
⊟ 1 tarnished. 2 inexpert. 3 gauche.

polite adj courteous, well-
mannered, respectful, civil, well-
bred, refined, cultured, gentlemanly,
ladylike, gracious, obliging,
thoughtful, considerate, tactful,
diplomatic.
⊟ impolite, discourteous, rude.

politician n Member of
Parliament, MP, minister, statesman,
stateswoman, legislator.

politics n public affairs, civics,
affairs of state, statecraft,
government, diplomacy,
statesmanship, political science.

Terms used in politics include:
alliance, apartheid, ballot, bill,
blockade, cabinet, campaign,
coalition, constitution, council,
coup d'état, détente, election,
electoral register, ethnic cleansing,
general election, glasnost, go to
the country, green paper, Hansard,
left wing, lobby, local government,
majority, mandate, manifesto,
nationalization, parliament, party,
party line, perestroika, prime
minister's question time,
privatization, propaganda,
proportional representation,
rainbow coalition, referendum,
right wing, sanction, shadow
cabinet, sovereignty, state, summit,
summit conference, term of office,
trade union, veto, vote, welfare
state, whip, three-line whip, white
paper.

Political ideologies include:
absolutism, anarchism,
authoritarianism, Bolshevism,
Christian democracy, collectivism,
communism, conservatism,
democracy, egalitarianism, fascism,
federalism, holism, imperialism,
individualism, liberalism, liberal
democracy, Maoism, Marxism,
nationalism, Nazism,
neocolonialism, neoconservatism,
neo-fascism, neo-Nazism,
pluralism, republicanism, social
democracy, socialism, syndicalism,
theocracy, totalitarianism,
unilateralism, Trotskyism,
Whiggism. see also **government**;
parliament.

poll n ballot, vote, voting, plebiscite,
referendum, straw-poll, sampling,
canvass, opinion poll, survey, census,
count, tally.

pollute v contaminate, infect,
poison, taint, adulterate, debase,
corrupt, dirty, foul, soil, defile, sully,
stain, mar, spoil.

pollution n impurity, contamination, infection, taint, adulteration, corruption, dirtiness, foulness, defilement.
🖭 purification, purity, cleanness.

pomp n ceremony, ceremonial, ritual, solemnity, formality, ceremoniousness, state, grandeur, splendour, magnificence, pageantry, show, display, parade, ostentation, flourish.
🖭 austerity, simplicity.

pompous adj self-important, arrogant, grandiose, supercilious, overbearing, imperious, magisterial, bombastic, high-flown, overblown, windy, affected, pretentious, ostentatious.
🖭 unassuming, modest, simple, unaffected.

pool[1] n puddle, pond, lake, mere, tarn, watering hole, paddling pool, swimming pool.

pool[2] n **1** FUND, reserve, bank, kitty, purse, pot, accumulation, jackpot. **2** SYNDICATE, cartel, ring, combine, consortium, collective, group, team.
◇ v contribute, chip in (infml), combine, amalgamate, merge, share, muck in (infml).

poor adj **1** IMPOVERISHED, poverty-stricken, badly off, hard-up, broke (infml), stony-broke (sl), skint (sl), bankrupt, penniless, destitute, miserable, wretched, distressed, straitened, needy, lacking, deficient, insufficient, scanty, skimpy, meagre, sparse, depleted, exhausted. **2** BAD, substandard, unsatisfactory, inferior, mediocre, below par, low-grade, second-rate, third-rate, shoddy, imperfect, faulty, weak, feeble, pathetic (infml), sorry, worthless, fruitless. **3** UNFORTUNATE, unlucky, luckless, ill-fated, unhappy, miserable, pathetic, pitiable, pitiful.
🖭 **1** rich, wealthy, affluent. **2** superior, impressive. **3** fortunate, lucky.

poorly adj ill, sick, unwell, ailing, indisposed, sickly, off-colour, below par, out of sorts (infml), under the weather (infml), seedy, groggy, rotten (infml).
🖭 well, healthy.

pop v burst, explode, go off, bang, crack, snap.
◇ n bang, crack, snap, burst, explosion.

popular adj well-liked, favourite, liked, favoured, approved, in demand, sought-after, fashionable, modish, trendy (infml), prevailing, current, accepted, conventional, standard, stock, common, prevalent, widespread, universal, general, household, famous, well-known, celebrated, idolized.
🖭 unpopular.

popularize v spread, propagate, universalize, democratize, simplify.

popularly adv commonly, widely, universally, generally, usually, customarily, conventionally, traditionally.

populate v people, occupy, settle, colonize, inhabit, live in, overrun.

population n inhabitants, natives, residents, citizens, occupants, community, society, people, folk.

populous adj crowded, packed, swarming, teeming, crawling, overpopulated.
🖭 deserted.

pornographic adj obscene, indecent, dirty, filthy, blue, risqué, bawdy, coarse, gross, lewd, erotic, titillating.

porous adj permeable, pervious, penetrable, absorbent, spongy, honeycombed, pitted.
🖭 impermeable, impervious.

portable adj movable, transportable, compact, lightweight, manageable, handy, convenient.
🖭 fixed, immovable.

porter¹ n bearer, carrier, baggage attendant, baggage handler.

porter² n doorman, commissionaire, doorkeeper, gatekeeper, janitor, caretaker, concierge.

portion n share, allocation, allotment, parcel, allowance, ration, quota, measure, part, section, division, fraction, percentage, bit, fragment, morsel, piece, segment, slice, serving, helping.

portly adj stout, corpulent, rotund, round, fat, plump, obese, overweight, heavy, large.
⊜ slim, thin, slight.

portrait n picture, painting, drawing, sketch, caricature, miniature, icon, photograph, likeness, image, representation, vignette, profile, characterization, description, depiction, portrayal.

portray v draw, sketch, paint, illustrate, picture, represent, depict, describe, evoke, play, impersonate, characterize, personify.

portrayal n representation, characterization, depiction, description, evocation, presentation, performance, interpretation, rendering.

pose v 1 MODEL, sit, position. 2 PRETEND, feign, affect, put on an act, masquerade, pass oneself off, impersonate. 3 pose a question: set, put forward, submit, present.
◊ n 1 POSITION, stance, air, bearing, posture, attitude. 2 PRETENCE, sham, affectation, façade, front, masquerade, role, act.

poser¹ n puzzle, riddle, conundrum, brain-teaser, mystery, enigma, problem, vexed question.

poser² n poseur, posturer, attitudinizer, exhibitionist, show-off, pseud (infml), phoney (infml).

posh adj smart, stylish, fashionable, high-class, upper-class, la-di-da (sl),

grand, luxurious, lavish, swanky (infml), luxury, de luxe, up-market, exclusive, select, classy (infml), swish (infml).
⊜ inferior, cheap.

position n 1 PLACE, situation, location, site, spot, point. 2 POSTURE, stance, pose, arrangement, disposition. 3 JOB, post, occupation, employment, office, duty, function, role. 4 RANK, grade, level, status, standing. 5 OPINION, point of view, belief, view, outlook, viewpoint, standpoint, stand.
◊ v put, place, set, fix, stand, arrange, dispose, lay out, deploy, station, locate, situate, site.

positive adj 1 SURE, certain, convinced, confident, assured. 2 positive criticism: helpful, constructive, practical, useful, optimistic, hopeful, promising. 3 DEFINITE, decisive, conclusive, clear, unmistakable, explicit, unequivocal, express, firm, emphatic, categorical, undeniable, irrefutable, indisputable, incontrovertible. 4 ABSOLUTE, utter, sheer, complete, perfect.
⊜ 1 uncertain. 2 negative. 3 indefinite, vague.

possess v 1 OWN, have, hold, enjoy, be endowed with. 2 SEIZE, take, obtain, acquire, take over, occupy, control, dominate, bewitch, haunt.

possession n ownership, title, tenure, occupation, custody, control, hold, grip.

possessions n belongings, property, things, paraphernalia, effects, goods, chattels, movables, assets, estate, wealth, riches.

possessive adj selfish, clinging, overprotective, domineering, dominating, jealous, covetous, acquisitive, grasping.
⊜ unselfish, sharing.

possibility n likelihood, probability, odds, chance, risk, danger, hope,

prospect, potentiality, conceivability, practicability, feasibility.
⊠ impossibility, impracticability.

possible *adj* potential, promising, likely, probable, imaginable, viable, conceivable, practicable, feasible, tenable, workable, achievable, attainable, accomplishable, realizable.
⊠ impossible, unthinkable, impracticable, unattainable.

possibly *adv* perhaps, maybe, hopefully (*infml*), by any means, at all, by any chance.

post¹ *n* pole, stake, picket, pale, pillar, column, shaft, support, baluster, upright, stanchion, strut, leg.
◇ *v* display, stick up, pin up, advertise, publicize, announce, make known, report, publish.

post² *n* office, job, employment, position, situation, place, vacancy, appointment, assignment, station, beat.
◇ *v* station, locate, situate, position, place, put, appoint, assign, second, transfer, move, send.

post³ *n* mail, letters, e-mail, dispatch, collection, delivery.
◇ *v* mail, e-mail, send, dispatch, transmit.

poster *n* notice, bill, sign, placard, sticker, advertisement, flyer, announcement.

posterity *n* descendants, future generations, successors, progeny, issue, offspring, children.

postpone *v* put off, defer, put back, hold over, delay, adjourn, suspend, shelve, pigeonhole, freeze, put on ice.
⊠ advance, forward.

postscript *n* PS (*infml*), addition, supplement, afterthought, addendum, codicil, appendix, afterword, epilogue.
⊠ introduction, prologue.

postulate *v* theorize, hypothesize, suppose, assume, propose, advance, lay down, stipulate.

posture *n* position, stance, pose, attitude, disposition, bearing, carriage, deportment.

posy *n* bouquet, spray, buttonhole, corsage.

pot *n* receptacle, vessel, teapot, coffee pot, urn, jar, vase, bowl, basin, pan, cauldron, crucible.

potent *adj* powerful, mighty, strong, intoxicating, pungent, effective, impressive, cogent, convincing, persuasive, compelling, forceful, dynamic, vigorous, authoritative, commanding, dominant, influential, overpowering.
⊠ impotent, weak.

potential *adj* possible, likely, probable, prospective, future, aspiring, would-be, promising, budding, embryonic, undeveloped, dormant, latent, hidden, concealed, unrealized.
◇ *n* possibility, ability, capability, capacity, aptitude, talent, powers, resources.

potion *n* mixture, concoction, brew, beverage, drink, draught, dose, medicine, tonic, elixir.

pot-pourri *n* medley, mixture, jumble, hotchpotch, miscellany, collection.

potter *v* tinker, fiddle, mess about (*infml*), dabble, loiter, fritter.

pottery *n* ceramics, crockery, china, porcelain.

Terms used in pottery include: basalt, blanc-de-chine, celadon, china clay, cloisonné, crackleware, crazing, creamware, delft, earthenware, enamel, faïence, fairing, figure, firing, flambé, flatback, glaze, ground, ironstone, jasper, kiln, lustre, majolica, maker's mark, monogram, overglaze, raku, saggar, sgraffito, slip, slip-cast, spongeware, Staffordshire, stoneware, terracotta, underglaze, willow pattern.

pounce v fall on, dive on, swoop, drop, attack, strike, ambush, spring, jump, leap, snatch, grab.

pound¹ v 1 STRIKE, thump, beat, drum, pelt, hammer, batter, bang, bash, smash. 2 PULVERIZE, powder, grind, mash, crush. 3 *his heart was pounding*: throb, pulsate, palpitate, thump, thud.

pound² n enclosure, compound, corral, yard, pen, fold.

pour v 1 *pour a drink*: serve, decant, tip. 2 SPILL, issue, discharge, flow, stream, run, rush, spout, spew, gush, cascade, crowd, throng, swarm.

pout v scowl, glower, grimace, pull a face, sulk, mope.
☒ grin, smile.
◇ n scowl, glower, grimace, long face.
☒ grin, smile.

poverty n poorness, impoverishment, insolvency, bankruptcy, pennilessness, penury, destitution, distress, hardship, privation, need, necessity, want, lack, deficiency, shortage, inadequacy, insufficiency, depletion, scarcity, meagreness, paucity, dearth.
☒ wealth, richness, affluence, plenty.

powdery adj dusty, sandy, grainy, granular, powdered, pulverized, ground, fine, loose, dry, crumbly, friable, chalky.

power n 1 COMMAND, authority, sovereignty, rule, dominion, control, influence. 2 RIGHT, privilege, prerogative, authorization, warrant. 3 POTENCY, strength, intensity, force, vigour, energy. 4 ABILITY, capability, capacity, potential, faculty, competence.
☒ 1 subjection. 3 weakness. 4 inability.

powerful adj dominant, prevailing, leading, influential, high-powered, authoritative, commanding, potent, effective, strong, mighty, robust, muscular, energetic, forceful, telling, impressive, convincing, persuasive, compelling, winning, overwhelming.
☒ impotent, ineffective, weak.

powerless adj impotent, incapable, ineffective, weak, feeble, frail, infirm, incapacitated, disabled, paralysed, helpless, vulnerable, defenceless, unarmed.
☒ powerful, potent, able.

practicable adj possible, feasible, performable, achievable, attainable, viable, workable, practical, realistic.
☒ impracticable.

practical adj 1 REALISTIC, sensible, commonsense, practicable, workable, feasible, down-to-earth, matter-of-fact, pragmatic, hardnosed (*infml*), hard-headed, businesslike, experienced, trained, qualified, skilled, accomplished, proficient, hands on, applied. 2 USEFUL, handy, serviceable, utilitarian, functional, working, everyday, ordinary.
☒ 1 impractical, unskilled, theoretical.

practically adv 1 ALMOST, nearly, well-nigh, virtually, pretty well, all but, just about, in principle, in effect, essentially, fundamentally, to all intents and purposes. 2 REALISTICALLY, sensibly, reasonably, rationally, pragmatically.

practice n 1 CUSTOM, tradition, convention, usage, habit, routine, shtick (*sl*), way, method, system, procedure, policy. 2 REHEARSAL, run-through, dry run, dummy run, try-out, training, drill, exercise, work-out, study, experience. 3 *in practice*: effect, reality, actuality, action, operation, performance, use,

application.
⊜ **3** theory, principle.

practise v **1** DO, perform, execute, implement, carry out, apply, put into practice, follow, pursue, engage in, undertake. **2** REHEARSE, run through, repeat, drill, exercise, train, study, perfect.

practised adj experienced, seasoned, veteran, trained, qualified, accomplished, skilled, versed, knowledgeable, able, proficient, expert, masterly, consummate, finished.
⊜ unpractised, inexperienced, inexpert.

pragmatic adj practical, realistic, sensible, matter-of-fact, businesslike, efficient, hard-headed, hardnosed (infml), unsentimental.
⊜ unrealistic, idealistic, romantic.

praise n approval, admiration, commendation, congratulation, compliment, flattery, adulation, eulogy, applause, ovation, cheering, acclaim, recognition, testimonial, tribute, accolade, homage, honour, glory, worship, adoration, devotion, thanksgiving.
⊜ criticism, revilement.
◇ v commend, congratulate, admire, compliment, flatter, talk up (infml), eulogize, wax lyrical, rave over (infml), extol, promote, applaud, cheer, acclaim, hail, recognize, acknowledge, pay tribute to, honour, laud, glorify, magnify, exalt, worship, adore, bless.
⊜ criticize, revile, talk down (infml).

praiseworthy adj commendable, fine, excellent, admirable, worthy, deserving, honourable, reputable, estimable, sterling.
⊜ blameworthy, dishonourable, ignoble.

prank n trick, practical joke, joke, stunt, caper, frolic, lark, antic, escapade.

pray v invoke, call on, supplicate, entreat, implore, plead, beg, beseech, petition, ask, request, crave, solicit.

prayer n collect, litany, devotion, communion, invocation, supplication, entreaty, plea, appeal, petition, request.

preach v address, lecture, harangue, pontificate, sermonize, evangelize, moralize, exhort, urge, advocate.

precarious adj unsafe, dangerous, treacherous, risky, hazardous, chancy, uncertain, unsure, dubious, doubtful, unpredictable, unreliable, unsteady, unstable, shaky, wobbly, insecure, vulnerable.
⊜ safe, certain, stable, secure.

precaution n safeguard, security, protection, insurance, providence, forethought, caution, prudence, foresight, anticipation, preparation, provision.

precautionary adj safety, protective, preventive, provident, cautious, prudent, judicious, preparatory, preliminary.

precede v come before, lead, come first, go before, take precedence, introduce, herald, usher in.
⊜ follow, succeed.

precedence n priority, preference, pride of place, superiority, pre-eminence, supremacy, lead, first place, seniority, rank.

precedent n example, instance, pattern, model, standard, criterion.

precinct n **1** ZONE, area, district, quarter, sector, division, section. **2** BOUNDARY, limit, bound, confine.

precious adj **1** VALUED, treasured, prized, cherished, beloved, dearest, darling, favourite, loved, adored, idolized. **2** VALUABLE, expensive, costly, dear, priceless, inestimable, rare, choice, fine.

precipitate v hasten, hurry, speed,

accelerate, quicken, expedite, advance, further, bring on, induce, trigger, cause, occasion.
◇ *adj* sudden, unexpected, abrupt, quick, swift, rapid, brief, hasty, hurried, headlong, breakneck, frantic, violent, impatient, hot-headed, impetuous, impulsive, rash, reckless, heedless, indiscreet.
🗲 cautious, careful.

precipitous *adj* steep, sheer, perpendicular, vertical, high.
🗲 gradual.

precise *adj* exact, accurate, right, punctilious, correct, factual, faithful, authentic, literal, word for word, express, definite, explicit, unequivocal, unambiguous, clear-cut, distinct, detailed, blow-by-blow, minute, nice, particular, specific, fixed, rigid, strict, careful, meticulous, scrupulous, fastidious.
🗲 imprecise, inexact, ambiguous, careless.

precisely *adv* exactly, absolutely, just so, accurately, correctly, literally, verbatim, word for word, strictly, minutely, clearly, distinctly.

precision *n* exactness, accuracy, correctness, faithfulness, explicitness, distinctness, detail, particularity, rigour, care, meticulousness, scrupulousness, neatness.
🗲 imprecision, inaccuracy.

precocious *adj* forward, ahead, advanced, early, premature, mature, developed, gifted, clever, bright, smart, quick, fast.
🗲 backward.

preconceive *v* presuppose, assume, presume, anticipate, project, imagine, conceive, envisage, expect, visualize, picture.

preconception *n* presupposition, presumption, assumption, conjecture, anticipation, expectation, prejudgement, bias, prejudice.

precondition *n* condition,

stipulation, requirement, prerequisite, essential, necessity, must.

precursor *n* antecedent, forerunner, sign, indication, herald, harbinger, messenger, usher, pioneer, trail-blazer.
🗲 follower, successor.

predecessor *n* ancestor, forefather, forebear, antecedent, forerunner, precursor.
🗲 successor, descendant.

predestination *n* destiny, fate, lot, doom, predetermination, foreordination.

predetermined *adj* 1 PREDESTINED, destined, fated, doomed, ordained, foreordained. 2 PREARRANGED, arranged, agreed, fixed, set.

predicament *n* situation, plight, trouble, mess, fix, spot (*infml*), quandary, dilemma, impasse, crisis, emergency.

predict *v* foretell, prophesy, foresee, forecast, prognosticate, project.

predictable *adj* foreseeable, expected, anticipated, likely, probable, imaginable, foreseen, foregone, certain, sure, reliable, dependable.
🗲 unpredictable, uncertain.

prediction *n* prophecy, forecast, prognosis, augury, divination, fortune-telling, soothsaying.

predispose *v* dispose, incline, prompt, induce, make, sway, influence, affect, bias, prejudice.

predominant *adj* dominant, prevailing, preponderant, chief, main, principal, primary, capital, paramount, supreme, sovereign, ruling, controlling, leading, powerful, potent, prime, important, influential, forceful, strong.
🗲 minor, lesser, weak.

pre-eminent *adj* supreme, unsurpassed, unrivalled, unequalled, unmatched, matchless,

incomparable, inimitable, chief, foremost, leading, distinguished, eminent, renowned, famous, prominent, outstanding, exceptional, excellent, superlative, transcendent, superior.
⊡ inferior, unknown.

preface n foreword, introduction, preamble, prologue, prelude, preliminaries.
⊡ epilogue, postscript.
◇ v precede, prefix, lead up to, introduce, launch, open, begin, start.
⊡ end, finish, complete.

prefer v favour, like better, would rather, would sooner, want, wish, desire, choose, select, pick, opt for, go for, plump for, single out, advocate, recommend, back, support, fancy, elect, adopt.
⊡ reject.

preferable adj better, superior, nicer, preferred, favoured, chosen, desirable, advantageous, advisable, recommended.
⊡ inferior, undesirable.

preference n 1 FAVOURITE, first choice, choice, pick, selection, option, wish, desire. 2 LIKING, fancy, inclination, predilection, partiality, favouritism, preferential treatment.

preferential adj better, superior, favoured, privileged, special, favourable, advantageous.
⊡ equal.

pregnant adj 1 a pregnant woman: expectant, expecting, with child (fml), in the club (sl), up the spout (sl). 2 a pregnant pause: meaningful, significant, eloquent, expressive, suggestive, charged, loaded, full.

prejudice n 1 BIAS, partiality, partisanship, discrimination, unfairness, injustice, intolerance, narrow-mindedness, bigotry, chauvinism, racism, sexism. 2 HARM, damage, impairment, hurt, injury, detriment, disadvantage, loss, ruin.

⊡ 1 fairness, tolerance. 2 benefit, advantage.
◇ v 1 BIAS, predispose, incline, sway, influence, condition, colour, slant, distort, load, weight. 2 HARM, damage, impair, hinder, undermine, hurt, injure, mar, spoil, ruin, wreck.
⊡ 2 benefit, help, advance.

prejudiced adj biased, partial, predisposed, subjective, partisan, one-sided, discriminatory, unfair, unjust, loaded, weighted, intolerant, narrow-minded, bigoted, chauvinist, racist, sexist, jaundiced, distorted, warped, influenced, conditioned.
⊡ impartial, fair, tolerant.

prejudicial adj harmful, damaging, hurtful, injurious, detrimental, disadvantageous, unfavourable, inimical.
⊡ beneficial, advantageous.

preliminaries n preparation, groundwork, foundations, basics, rudiments, formalities, introduction, preface, prelude, opening, beginning, start.

preliminary adj preparatory, prior, advance, exploratory, experimental, trial, test, pilot, early, earliest, first, initial, primary, qualifying, inaugural, introductory, opening.
⊡ final, closing.

prelude n overture, introduction, preface, foreword, preamble, prologue, opening, opener, preliminary, preparation, beginning, start, commencement, precursor, curtain raiser.
⊡ finale, epilogue.

premature adj early, immature, green, unripe, embryonic, half-formed, incomplete, undeveloped, abortive, hasty, ill-considered, rash, untimely, inopportune, ill-timed.
⊡ late, tardy.

premeditated adj planned, intended, intentional, deliberate,

wilful, conscious, cold-blooded, calculated, considered, contrived, preplanned, prearranged, predetermined.
⊟ unpremeditated, spontaneous.

première n first performance, opening, opening night, first night, debut.

premise n proposition, statement, assertion, postulate, thesis, argument, basis, supposition, hypothesis, presupposition, assumption.

premises n building, property, establishment, office, grounds, estate, site, place.

premonition n presentiment, feeling, intuition, hunch, idea, suspicion, foreboding, misgiving, fear, apprehension, anxiety, worry, warning, omen, sign.

preoccupation n 1 OBSESSION, fixation, hang-up (infml), concern, interest, enthusiasm, hobby-horse. 2 DISTRACTION, absent-mindedness, reverie, obliviousness, oblivion.

preoccupied adj 1 OBSESSED, intent, immersed, engrossed, engaged, taken up, wrapped up, involved. 2 DISTRACTED, abstracted, absent-minded, daydreaming, absorbed, faraway, heedless, oblivious, pensive.

preparation n 1 READINESS, provision, precaution, safeguard, foundation, groundwork, spadework, basics, rudiments, preliminaries, plans, arrangements. 2 MIXTURE, compound, concoction, potion, medicine, lotion, application.

preparatory adj preliminary, introductory, opening, initial, primary, basic, fundamental, rudimentary, elementary.

prepare v 1 GET READY, warm up, train, coach, study, make ready, adapt, adjust, plan, organize, arrange, pave the way. 2 prepare a meal: make, produce, construct, assemble, concoct, contrive, devise,

draft, draw up, compose. 3 PROVIDE, supply, equip, fit out, rig out.
• **prepare oneself** brace oneself, steel oneself, gird oneself, fortify oneself.

prepared adj ready, waiting, set, fit, inclined, disposed, willing, planned, organized, arranged.
⊟ unprepared, unready.

preponderant adj greater, larger, superior, predominant, prevailing, overriding, overruling, controlling, foremost, important, significant.

preposterous adj incredible, unbelievable, absurd, ridiculous, ludicrous, foolish, crazy, nonsensical, unreasonable, monstrous, shocking, outrageous, intolerable, unthinkable, impossible.
⊟ sensible, reasonable, acceptable.

prerequisite n precondition, condition, proviso, qualification, requisite, requirement, imperative, necessity, essential, must.
⊟ extra.

prescribe v ordain, decree, dictate, rule, command, order, require, direct, assign, specify, stipulate, lay down, set, appoint, impose, fix, define, limit.

prescription n 1 INSTRUCTION, direction, formula. 2 MEDICINE, drug, preparation, mixture, remedy, treatment.

presence n 1 ATTENDANCE, company, occupancy, residence, existence. 2 AURA, air, demeanour, bearing, carriage, appearance, poise, self-assurance, personality, charisma. 3 NEARNESS, closeness, proximity, vicinity.
⊟ 1 absence. 3 remoteness.

present¹ adj 1 ATTENDING, here, there, near, at hand, to hand, available, ready. 2 at the present time: current, contemporary, present-day, immediate, instant, existent, existing.
⊟ 1 absent. 2 past, out-of-date.

present² v **1** SHOW, display, exhibit, demonstrate, mount, stage, put on, introduce, announce. **2** AWARD, confer, bestow, grant, give, donate, hand over, entrust, extend, hold out, offer, tender, submit.

present³ n gift, prezzie (*infml*), offering, donation, grant, endowment, benefaction, bounty, largess(e), gratuity, tip, favour.

presentable adj neat, tidy, clean, respectable, decent, proper, suitable, acceptable, satisfactory, tolerable.
⊕ unpresentable, untidy, shabby.

presentation n **1** SHOW, performance, production, staging, representation, display, exhibition, demonstration, talk, delivery, appearance, arrangement. **2** AWARD, conferral, bestowal, investiture.

present-day adj current, present, existing, living, contemporary, modern, up-to-date, fashionable.
⊕ past, future.

presently adv **1** SOON, shortly, in a minute, before long, by and by. **2** CURRENTLY, at present, now.

preserve v **1** PROTECT, safeguard, guard, defend, shield, shelter, care for, maintain, uphold, sustain, continue, perpetuate, keep, retain, conserve, save, store. **2** *preserve food*: bottle, tin, can, pickle, salt, cure, dry.
⊕ **1** destroy, ruin.
◇ n **1** *home-made preserves*: conserve, jam, marmalade, jelly, pickle. **2** DOMAIN, realm, sphere, area, field, speciality. **3** RESERVATION, sanctuary, game reserve, safari park.

preside v chair, officiate, conduct, direct, manage, administer, control, run, head, lead, govern, rule.

press v **1** CRUSH, squash, squeeze, compress, stuff, cram, crowd, push, depress. **2** *press clothes*: iron, smooth, flatten. **3** HUG, embrace, clasp, squeeze. **4** URGE, plead, petition, campaign, demand, insist on, compel, constrain, force, pressure, pressurize, harass.
◇ n **1** CROWD, throng, multitude, mob, horde, swarm, pack, crush, push. **2** JOURNALISTS, reporters, correspondents, the media, newspapers, papers, Fleet Street, fourth estate.

pressing adj urgent, high-priority, burning, crucial, vital, essential, imperative, serious, important.
⊕ unimportant, trivial.

pressure n **1** FORCE, power, load, burden, weight, heaviness, compression, squeezing, stress, strain. **2** DIFFICULTY, problem, demand, constraint, obligation, urgency.

pressurize v force, compel, constrain, oblige, drive, bulldoze, coerce, press, pressure, lean on (*infml*), browbeat, bully.

prestige n status, reputation, standing, stature, eminence, distinction, esteem, regard, importance, authority, influence, fame, renown, kudos, credit, honour.
⊕ humbleness, unimportance.

prestigious adj esteemed, respected, reputable, important, influential, great, eminent, prominent, illustrious, renowned, celebrated, exalted, imposing, impressive, up-market.
⊕ humble, modest.

presume v **1** ASSUME, take it, think, believe, suppose, surmise, infer, presuppose, take for granted, count on, rely on, depend on, bank on, trust. **2** *presume to criticize*: dare, make so bold, go so far, venture, undertake.

presumption n **1** ASSUMPTION, belief, opinion, hypothesis, presupposition, supposition, surmise, conjecture, guess, likelihood, probability. **2** PRESUMPTUOUSNESS, boldness, audacity, impertinence,

cheek (*infml*), nerve (*infml*), impudence, insolence, forwardness, assurance.
≠ **2** humility.

presumptuous *adj* audacious, bold, impertinent, impudent, insolent, over-familiar, forward, pushy, arrogant, over-confident, conceited.
≠ humble, modest.

pretence *n* show, display, appearance, cover, front, façade, veneer, cloak, veil, mask, guise, sham, feigning, faking, simulation, deception, trickery, wile, ruse, excuse, pretext, bluff, falsehood, deceit, fabrication, invention, make-believe, charade, acting, play-acting, posturing, posing, affectation, pretension, pretentiousness.
≠ honesty, openness.

pretend *v* **1** AFFECT, put on, assume, feign, sham, counterfeit, fake, simulate, bluff, impersonate, pass oneself off, act, play-act, mime, go through the motions. **2** CLAIM, allege, profess, purport. **3** IMAGINE, make believe, suppose.

pretender *n* claimant, aspirant, candidate.

pretension *n* **1** PRETENTIOUSNESS, pomposity, self-importance, airs, conceit, vanity, snobbishness, affectation, pretence, show, showiness, ostentation. **2** CLAIM, profession, demand, aspiration, ambition.
≠ **1** modesty, humility, simplicity.

pretentious *adj* pompous, self-important, conceited, immodest, snobbish, affected, mannered, showy, ostentatious, extravagant, over-the-top, exaggerated, magniloquent, high-sounding, inflated, grandiose, OTT (*infml*), ambitious, overambitious.
≠ modest, humble, simple, straightforward.

pretext *n* excuse, ploy, ruse, cover,

cloak, mask, guise, semblance, appearance, pretence, show.

pretty *adj* attractive, good-looking, beautiful, fair, lovely, bonny, cute, winsome, appealing, charming, dainty, graceful, elegant, fine, delicate, nice.
≠ plain, unattractive, ugly.
◇ *adv* fairly, somewhat, rather, quite, reasonably, moderately, tolerably.

prevail *v* **1** PREDOMINATE, preponderate, abound. **2** WIN, triumph, succeed, overcome, overrule, reign, rule.
≠ **2** lose.
• **prevail upon** persuade, talk into, prompt, induce, incline, sway, influence, convince, win over.

prevailing *adj* predominant, preponderant, main, principal, dominant, controlling, powerful, compelling, influential, reigning, ruling, current, fashionable, popular, mainstream, accepted, established, set, usual, customary, common, prevalent, widespread.
≠ minor, subordinate.

prevalent *adj* widespread, extensive, rampant, rife, frequent, general, customary, usual, universal, ubiquitous, common, everyday, popular, current, prevailing.
≠ uncommon, rare.

prevaricate *v* hedge, equivocate, quibble, cavil, dodge, evade, shift, shuffle, lie, deceive.

prevent *v* stop, avert, avoid, head off, ward off, stave off, intercept, forestall, anticipate, frustrate, thwart, check, restrain, inhibit, hinder, hamper, impede, obstruct, block, bar.
≠ cause, help, foster, encourage, allow.

prevention *n* avoidance, frustration, check, hindrance, impediment, obstruction, obstacle, bar, elimination, precaution,

safeguard, deterrence.
☞ cause, help.

preventive adj preventative, anticipatory, pre-emptive, inhibitory, obstructive, precautionary, protective, counteractive, deterrent.
☞ causative.

previous adj preceding, foregoing, earlier, prior, past, former, ex-, one-time, sometime, erstwhile.
☞ following, subsequent, later.

previously adv formerly, once, earlier, before, beforehand.
☞ later.

prey n quarry, victim, game, kill.
• **prey on 1** HUNT, kill, devour, feed on, live off, exploit. **2** prey on one's mind: haunt, trouble, distress, worry, burden, weigh down, oppress.

price n value, worth, cost, expense, outlay, expenditure, fee, charge, levy, toll, rate, bill, assessment, valuation, estimate, quotation, figure, amount, sum, payment, reward, penalty, forfeit, sacrifice, consequences.
◇ v value, rate, cost, evaluate, assess, estimate.

priceless adj **1** INVALUABLE, inestimable, incalculable, expensive, costly, dear, precious, valuable, prized, treasured, irreplaceable.
2 (infml) FUNNY, amusing, comic, hilarious, riotous, side-splitting, killing (infml), rich (infml).
☞ **1** cheap, run-of-the-mill.

prick v pierce, puncture, perforate, punch, jab, stab, sting, bite, prickle, itch, tingle.
◇ n puncture, perforation, pinhole, stab, pang, twinge, sting, bite.

prickle n thorn, spine, barb, spur, point, spike, needle.
◇ v tingle, itch, smart, sting, prick.

prickly adj **1** THORNY, brambly, spiny, barbed, spiky, bristly, rough, scratchy. **2** IRRITABLE, edgy, touchy, grumpy, short-tempered.
☞ **1** smooth. **2** relaxed, easy-going

(infml), laid-back (infml).

pride n **1** CONCEIT, vanity, egotism, bigheadedness, boastfulness, smugness, arrogance, self-importance, presumption, haughtiness, superciliousness, snobbery, pretentiousness. **2** DIGNITY, self-respect, self-esteem, honour.
3 SATISFACTION, gratification, pleasure, delight.
☞ **1** humility, modesty. **2** shame.

priest n minister, vicar, padre, father, man of God, woman of God, man of the cloth, clergywoman, clergyman, churchman, churchwoman.

priggish adj smug, self-righteous, goody-goody (infml), sanctimonious, holier-than-thou, puritanical, prim, prudish, narrow-minded.
☞ broad-minded.

prim adj prudish, strait-laced, formal, demure, proper, priggish, prissy, fussy, particular, precise, fastidious.
☞ informed, relaxed, easy-going (infml), laid-back (infml).

primarily adv chiefly, principally, mainly, mostly, fundamentally, basically, especially, particularly, essentially.

primary adj **1** FIRST, earliest, original, initial, introductory, beginning, basic, fundamental, essential, radical, rudimentary, elementary, simple.
2 CHIEF, principal, main, dominant, leading, foremost, supreme, cardinal, capital, paramount, greatest, highest, ultimate.
☞ **2** secondary, subsidiary, minor.

prime adj best, choice, select, quality, first-class, first-rate, excellent, top, supreme, pre-eminent, superior, senior, leading, ruling, chief, principal, main, predominant, primary.
☞ second-rate, secondary.
◇ n height, peak, zenith, heyday, flower, bloom, maturity, perfection.

primeval adj earliest, first, original,

primordial, early, old, ancient, prehistoric, primitive, instinctive.
⊞ modern.

primitive adj 1 CRUDE, rough, unsophisticated, uncivilized, barbarian, savage. 2 EARLY, elementary, rudimentary, primary, first, original, earliest.
⊞ 1 advanced, sophisticated, civilized.

princely adj 1 SOVEREIGN, imperial, royal, regal, majestic, stately, grand, noble. 2 princely sum: generous, liberal, lavish, sumptuous, magnificent, handsome.

principal adj main, chief, key, essential, cardinal, primary, first, foremost, leading, dominant, prime, paramount, pre-eminent, supreme, highest.
⊞ minor, subsidiary, lesser, least.
◇ n head, head teacher, headmaster, headmistress, chief, leader, boss, director, manager, superintendent.

principally adv mainly, mostly, chiefly, primarily, predominantly, above all, particularly, especially.

principle n 1 RULE, formula, law, canon, axiom, dictum, precept, maxim, truth, tenet, doctrine, creed, dogma, code, standard, criterion, proposition, fundamental, essential. 2 a man of principle: honour, integrity, rectitude, uprightness, virtue, decency, morality, morals, ethics, standards, scruples, conscience.

print v mark, stamp, imprint, impress, engrave, copy, reproduce, run off, publish, issue.
◇ n 1 LETTERS, characters, lettering, type, typescript, typeface, fount. 2 MARK, impression, fingerprint, footprint. 3 COPY, reproduction, picture, engraving, lithograph, photograph, photo.

prior adj earlier, preceding, foregoing, previous, former.

⊞ later.
• **prior to** before, preceding, earlier than.
⊞ after, following.

priority n right of way, precedence, seniority, rank, superiority, pre-eminence, supremacy, the lead, first place, urgency.
⊞ inferiority.

prison n jail, nick (sl), clink (sl), cooler (sl), penitentiary, cell, lock-up, cage, dungeon, imprisonment, confinement, detention, custody.

prisoner n captive, hostage, convict, con (sl), jail-bird (infml), inmate, internee, detainee.

privacy n secrecy, confidentiality, independence, solitude, isolation, seclusion, concealment, retirement, retreat.

private adj secret, classified, hush-hush (infml), off-the-record, unofficial, confidential, intimate, personal, individual, own, exclusive, particular, special, separate, independent, solitary, isolated, secluded, hidden, concealed, reserved, withdrawn.
⊞ public, open.
• **in private** privately, in confidence, secretly, in secret, behind closed doors, in camera.
⊞ publicly, openly.

privilege n advantage, benefit, concession, birthright, title, due, right, prerogative, entitlement, freedom, liberty, franchise, licence, sanction, authority, immunity, exemption.
⊞ disadvantage.

privileged adj favoured, advantaged, special, sanctioned, authorized, immune, exempt, élite, honoured, ruling, powerful.
⊞ disadvantaged, underprivileged.

prize n reward, trophy, medal, award, winnings, jackpot, purse, premium, stakes, honour, accolade.

◇ *adj* best, top, first-rate, excellent, outstanding, champion, winning, prize-winning, award-winning.
⊟ second-rate.

◇ *v* treasure, value, appreciate, esteem, revere, cherish, hold dear.
⊟ despise.

probability *n* likelihood, odds, chances, expectation, prospect, chance, possibility.
⊟ improbability.

probable *adj* likely, odds-on, expected, credible, believable, plausible, feasible, possible, apparent, seeming.
⊟ improbable, unlikely.

probation *n* apprenticeship, trial period, trial, test.

probe *v* prod, poke, pierce, penetrate, sound, plumb, explore, examine, scrutinize, investigate, go into, look into, search, sift, test.
◇ *n* **1** BORE, drill. **2** INQUIRY, inquest, investigation, exploration, examination, test, scrutiny, study, research.

problem *n* **1** TROUBLE, worry, predicament, quandary, dilemma, difficulty, complication, snag.
2 QUESTION, poser, puzzle, brain-teaser, conundrum, riddle, enigma.
◇ *adj* difficult, unmanageable, uncontrollable, unruly, delinquent.
⊟ well-behaved, manageable.

procedure *n* routine, process, method, system, technique, custom, practice, policy, formula, course, scheme, strategy, plan of action, move, step, action, conduct, operation, performance.

proceed *v* **1** *permission to proceed*: advance, go ahead, move on, progress, continue, carry on, press on. **2** ORIGINATE, derive, flow, start, stem, spring, arise, issue, result, ensue, follow, come.
⊟ **1** stop, retreat.

proceedings *n* **1** MATTERS, affairs,

business, dealings, transactions, report, account, minutes, records, archives, annals. **2** EVENTS, happenings, deeds, doings, moves, steps, measures, action, course of action.

proceeds *n* revenue, income, returns, receipts, takings, earnings, gain, profit, yield, produce.
⊟ expenditure, outlay.

process *n* **1** PROCEDURE, operation, practice, method, system, technique, means, manner, mode, way, stage, step. **2** COURSE, progression, advance, progress, development, evolution, formation, growth, movement, action, proceeding.
◇ *v* deal with, handle, treat, prepare, refine, transform, convert, change, alter.

procession *n* march, parade, cavalcade, motorcade, cortège, file, column, train, succession, series, sequence, course, run.

proclaim *v* announce, declare, pronounce, affirm, give out, publish, advertise, make known, profess, testify, show, indicate.

proclamation *n* announcement, declaration, pronouncement, affirmation, publication, promulgation, notice, notification, manifesto, decree, edict.

procrastinate *v* defer, put off, postpone, delay, retard, stall, play for time, temporize, dally, dilly-dally (*infml*), drag one's feet, prolong, protract.
⊟ advance, proceed.

procure *v* acquire, buy, purchase, get, obtain, find, come by, pick up, lay hands on, earn, gain, win, secure, appropriate, requisition.
⊟ lose.

prod *v* poke, jab, dig, elbow, nudge, push, shove, goad, spur, urge, egg on (*infml*), prompt, stimulate, motivate.
◇ *n* poke, jab, dig, elbow, nudge,

push, shove, prompt, reminder, stimulus, motivation.

prodigy n genius, virtuoso, wonder, marvel, miracle, phenomenon, sensation, freak, curiosity, rarity, child genius, wonder child, whizz kid (infml).

produce v 1 CAUSE, occasion, give rise to, provoke, bring about, result in, effect, create, originate, invent, make, manufacture, fabricate, build, construct, compose, generate, yield, bear, deliver. 2 ADVANCE, put forward, present, offer, give, supply, provide, furnish, bring out, bring forth, show, exhibit, demonstrate. 3 produce a play: direct, stage, mount, put on.
◇ n crop, harvest, yield, output, product.

product n 1 COMMODITY, goods, merchandise, end-product, artefact, work, creation, invention, production, output, yield, produce, fruit, return. 2 RESULT, consequence, outcome, issue, upshot, offshoot, spin-off, by-product, legacy.
⊞ 2 cause.

production n 1 MAKING, manufacture, fabrication, building, construction, assembly, creation, origination, preparation, formation. 2 an amateur production: staging, presentation, direction, management.
⊞ 1 consumption.

productive adj fruitful, profitable, rewarding, valuable, worthwhile, useful, constructive, creative, inventive, fertile, rich, teeming, busy, energetic, vigorous, efficient, effective.
⊞ unproductive, fruitless, useless.

productivity n productiveness, yield, output, work rate, efficiency.

profane adj secular, temporal, lay, unconsecrated, unhallowed, unsanctified, unholy, irreligious, impious, sacrilegious, blasphemous, ungodly, irreverent, disrespectful,

abusive, crude, coarse, foul, filthy, unclean.
⊞ sacred, religious, respectful.
◇ v desecrate, pollute, contaminate, defile, debase, pervert, abuse, misuse.
⊞ revere, honour.

profess v admit, confess, own, acknowledge, confirm, certify, declare, announce, proclaim, state, assert, affirm, maintain, claim, allege, make out, pretend.

profession n 1 CAREER, job, occupation, employment, business, line (of work), trade, vocation, calling, métier, craft, office, position. 2 ADMISSION, confession, acknowledgement, declaration, announcement, statement, testimony, assertion, affirmation, claim.

professional adj qualified, licensed, trained, experienced, practised, skilled, expert, masterly, proficient, competent, businesslike, efficient.
⊞ amateur, unprofessional.
◇ n expert, authority, specialist, pro (infml), master, virtuoso, dab hand (infml).
⊞ amateur.

proficiency n skill, skilfulness, expertise, mastery, talent, knack, dexterity, finesse, aptitude, ability, competence.
⊞ incompetence.

proficient adj able, capable, skilled, qualified, trained, experienced, accomplished, expert, masterly, gifted, talented, clever, skilful, competent, efficient.
⊞ unskilled, incompetent.

profile n 1 SIDE VIEW, outline, contour, silhouette, shape, form, figure, sketch, drawing, diagram, chart, graph. 2 BIOGRAPHY, curriculum vitae, thumbnail sketch, vignette, portrait, study, analysis, examination, survey, review.

profit n gain, surplus, excess, bottom line, revenue, return, yield, proceeds, receipts, takings, earnings, winnings, interest, advantage, benefit, use, avail, value, worth.
⊜ loss.
◇ v gain, make money, pay, serve, avail, benefit.
⊜ lose.
• **profit by, profit from** exploit, take advantage of, use, utilize, turn to advantage, capitalize on, cash in on, reap the benefit of.

profitable adj cost-effective, economic, commercial, lucrative, moneymaking, remunerative, paying, rewarding, successful, fruitful, productive, advantageous, beneficial, useful, valuable, worthwhile.
⊜ unprofitable, loss-making, non-profit-making.

profound adj 1 DEEP, great, intense, extreme, heartfelt, marked, far-reaching, extensive, exhaustive.
2 a profound remark: serious, weighty, penetrating, thoughtful, philosophical, wise, learned, erudite, abstruse.
⊜ 1 shallow, slight, mild.

profuse adj ample, abundant, plentiful, copious, generous, liberal, lavish, rich, luxuriant, excessive, immoderate, extravagant, overabundant, superabundant, overflowing.
⊜ inadequate, sparse.

profusion n abundance, plenty, wealth, multitude, plethora, glut, excess, surplus, superfluity, extravagance.
⊜ inadequacy, scarcity.

programme n 1 SCHEDULE, agenda, timetable, calendar, order of events, listing, line-up, plan, scheme, project, syllabus, curriculum. 2 radio programme: broadcast, transmission, show, performance, production, presentation.

progress n movement, progression, passage, journey, way, advance, headway, step forward, breakthrough, development, evolution, growth, increase, improvement, betterment, promotion.
⊜ recession, deterioration, decline.
◇ v proceed, advance, go forward, forge ahead, make progress, make headway, come on, develop, grow, mature, blossom, improve, better, prosper, increase.
⊜ deteriorate, decline.

progression n cycle, chain, string, succession, series, sequence, order, course, advance, headway, progress, development.

progressive adj 1 MODERN, avant-garde, advanced, forward-looking, enlightened, liberal, radical, revolutionary, reformist, dynamic, enterprising, go-ahead, up-and-coming. 2 ADVANCING, continuing, developing, growing, increasing, intensifying.
⊜ 1 regressive.

prohibit v forbid, ban, bar, veto, proscribe, outlaw, rule out, preclude, prevent, stop, hinder, hamper, impede, obstruct, restrict.
⊜ permit, allow, authorize.

project n assignment, contract, task, job, work, occupation, activity, enterprise, undertaking, venture, plan, scheme, programme, design, proposal, idea, conception.
◇ v 1 PREDICT, forecast, extrapolate, estimate, reckon, calculate.
2 THROW, fling, hurl, launch, propel.
3 PROTRUDE, stick out, bulge, jut out, overhang.

projection n 1 PROTUBERANCE, bulge, overhang, ledge, sill, shelf, ridge.
2 PREDICTION, forecast, extrapolation, estimate, reckoning, calculation, computation.

proliferate v multiply, reproduce, breed, increase, build up, intensify, escalate, mushroom, snowball,

spread, expand, flourish, thrive.
⊞ dwindle.

prolific adj productive, fruitful,
fertile, profuse, copious, abundant.
⊞ unproductive.

prolong v lengthen, extend, stretch,
protract, draw out, spin out, drag
out, delay, continue, perpetuate.
⊞ shorten.

prominence n 1 FAME, celebrity,
renown, eminence, distinction,
greatness, importance, reputation,
name, standing, rank, prestige.
2 BULGE, protuberance, bump,
hump, lump, mound, rise, elevation,
projection, process, headland,
promontory, cliff, crag.
⊞ 1 unimportance, insignificance.

prominent adj 1 NOTICEABLE,
conspicuous, obvious, unmistakable,
striking, eye-catching. 2 BULGING,
protuberant, projecting, jutting,
protruding, obtrusive. 3 a prominent
writer: famous, well-known,
celebrated, renowned, noted,
eminent, distinguished, respected,
leading, foremost, chief, main,
important, popular, outstanding.
⊞ 1 inconspicuous. 3 unknown,
unimportant, insignificant.

promiscuity n looseness, laxity,
permissiveness, wantonness,
immorality, licentiousness,
debauchery, depravity.
⊞ chastity, morality.

promiscuous adj 1 LOOSE, immoral,
licentious, dissolute. 2 CASUAL,
random, haphazard, indiscriminate.
⊞ 1 chaste, moral.

promise v 1 VOW, pledge, swear,
take an oath, contract, undertake,
give one's word, vouch, warrant,
guarantee, assure. 2 AUGUR, presage,
indicate, suggest, hint at.
◇ n 1 VOW, pledge, oath, word of
honour, bond, compact, covenant,
guarantee, assurance, undertaking,
engagement, commitment.

2 POTENTIAL, ability, capability,
aptitude, talent.

promising adj auspicious,
propitious, favourable, rosy, bright,
encouraging, hopeful, talented,
gifted, budding, up-and-coming.
⊞ unpromising, inauspicious,
discouraging.

promote v 1 ADVERTISE, plug (infml),
publicize, hype (sl), popularize,
market, sell, push, recommend,
advocate, champion, endorse,
sponsor, support, back, help,
aid, assist, foster, nurture, further,
forward, encourage, boost, stimulate,
urge. 2 UPGRADE, advance, move up,
raise, elevate, exalt, honour.
⊞ 1 disparage, hinder. 2 demote.

promotion n 1 ADVANCEMENT,
upgrading, rise, preferment,
elevation, exaltation. 2 ADVERTISING,
plugging (infml), publicity, hype
(sl), campaign, propaganda,
marketing, pushing, support,
backing, furtherance, development,
encouragement, boosting.
⊞ 1 demotion. 2 disparagement,
obstruction.

prompt¹ adj punctual, on time,
immediate, instantaneous, instant,
direct, quick, swift, rapid, speedy,
unhesitating, willing, ready, alert,
responsive, timely, early.
⊞ slow, hesitant, late.
◇ adv promptly, punctually, exactly,
on the dot, to the minute, sharp.

prompt² v cause, give rise to, result
in, occasion, produce, instigate, call
forth, elicit, provoke, incite, urge,
encourage, inspire, move, stimulate,
motivate, spur, prod, remind.
⊞ deter, dissuade.
◇ n reminder, cue, hint, help, jolt,
prod, spur, stimulus.

prone adj 1 LIKELY, given, inclined,
disposed, predisposed, bent,
apt, liable, subject, susceptible,
vulnerable. 2 she lay prone: face
down, prostrate, flat, horizontal, full-

length, stretched, recumbent.
⊜ **1** unlikely, immune. **2** upright, supine.

pronounce v **1** SAY, utter, speak, express, voice, vocalize, sound, enunciate, articulate, stress. **2** DECLARE, announce, proclaim, decree, judge, affirm, assert.

pronounced adj clear, distinct, definite, positive, decided, marked, noticeable, conspicuous, evident, obvious, striking, unmistakable, strong, broad.
⊜ faint, vague.

pronunciation n speech, diction, elocution, enunciation, articulation, delivery, accent, stress, inflection, intonation, modulation.

proof n evidence, documentation, demonstration, verification, confirmation, corroboration, substantiation, smoking gun (infml).

prop v **1** SUPPORT, sustain, uphold, maintain, shore, stay, buttress, bolster, underpin, set. **2** propped against the wall: lean, rest, stand.
◇ n support, stay, mainstay, strut, buttress, brace, truss.

propaganda n advertising, publicity, hype (sl), indoctrination, brainwashing, disinformation, spin (infml).

propagate v **1** SPREAD, transmit, broadcast, diffuse, disseminate, circulate, publish, promulgate, publicize, promote. **2** INCREASE, multiply, proliferate, generate, produce, breed, beget, spawn, procreate, reproduce.

propel v move, drive, impel, force, thrust, push, shove, launch, shoot, send.
⊜ stop.

proper adj **1** RIGHT, correct, accurate, exact, precise, true, genuine, real, actual. **2** ACCEPTED, correct, suitable, appropriate, fitting, decent, respectable, polite, formal.

⊜ **1** wrong. **2** improper, indecent.

property n **1** ESTATE, land, real estate, acres, premises, buildings, house(s), wealth, riches, resources, means, capital, assets, holding(s), belongings, possessions, effects, goods, chattels. **2** FEATURE, trait, quality, attribute, characteristic, idiosyncrasy, peculiarity, mark.

prophecy n prediction, augury, forecast, prognosis.

prophesy v predict, foresee, augur, foretell, forewarn, forecast.

prophet n seer, soothsayer, foreteller, forecaster, oracle, clairvoyant, fortune-teller.

proportion n **1** PERCENTAGE, fraction, part, division, share, quota, amount. **2** RATIO, relationship, correspondence, symmetry, balance, distribution.
⊜ **2** disproportion, imbalance.

proportional adj proportionate, relative, commensurate, consistent, corresponding, analogous, comparable, equitable, even.
⊜ disproportionate.

proportions n dimensions, measurements, size, magnitude, volume, capacity.

proposal n proposition, suggestion, recommendation, motion, plan, scheme, project, design, programme, manifesto, presentation, bid, offer, tender, terms.

propose v **1** SUGGEST, recommend, move, advance, put forward, introduce, bring up, table, submit, present, offer, tender. **2** INTEND, mean, aim, purpose, plan, design. **3** NOMINATE, put up.
⊜ **1** withdraw.

proprietor, proprietress n landlord, landlady, title-holder, freeholder, leaseholder, landowner, owner, possessor.

prosecute v accuse, indict, sue,

prefer charges, take to court, litigate, summon, put on trial, try.
🄔 defend.

prospect n chance, odds, probability, likelihood, possibility, hope, expectation, anticipation, outlook, future.
🄔 unlikelihood.

prospective adj future, -to-be, intended, designate, destined, forthcoming, approaching, coming, imminent, awaited, expected, anticipated, likely, possible, probable, potential, aspiring, would-be.
🄔 current.

prospectus n plan, scheme, programme, syllabus, manifesto, outline, synopsis, pamphlet, leaflet, brochure, catalogue, list.

prosper v boom, thrive, flourish, flower, bloom, succeed, get on, advance, progress, grow rich.
🄔 fail.

prosperity n boom, plenty, affluence, wealth, riches, fortune, wellbeing, luxury, the good life, success, good fortune.
🄔 adversity, poverty.

prosperous adj booming, thriving, flourishing, blooming, successful, fortunate, lucky, rich, wealthy, affluent, well-off, well-to-do.
🄔 unfortunate, poor.

prostrate adj flat, horizontal, prone, fallen, overcome, overwhelmed, crushed, paralysed, powerless, helpless, defenceless.
🄔 triumphant.
◇ v lay low, overcome, overwhelm, crush, overthrow, tire, wear out, fatigue, exhaust, drain, ruin.
🄔 strengthen.
• **prostrate oneself** bow down, kneel, kowtow, submit, grovel, cringe, abase oneself.

protagonist n hero, heroine, lead, principal, leader, prime mover,

champion, advocate, supporter, proponent, exponent.

protect v safeguard, defend, guard, escort, cover, screen, shield, secure, watch over, look after, care for, support, shelter, harbour, keep, conserve, preserve, save.
🄔 attack, neglect.

protection n 1 *protection of the environment*: care, custody, charge, guardianship, safekeeping, conservation, preservation, safety, safeguard. 2 BARRIER, buffer, bulwark, defence, guard, shield, armour, screen, cover, shelter, refuge, security, insurance.
🄔 1 neglect, negligence, attack.

protective adj 1 POSSESSIVE, defensive, motherly, maternal, fatherly, paternal, watchful, vigilant, careful. 2 *protective clothing*: waterproof, fireproof, windproof, Gore-Tex®, insulating.
🄔 1 aggressive, threatening.

protest n objection, disapproval, opposition, dissent, complaint, protestation, outcry, appeal, demonstration.
🄔 acceptance.
◇ v 1 OBJECT, take exception, complain, appeal, demonstrate, oppose, disapprove, disagree, argue. 2 *protest one's innocence*: assert, maintain, contend, insist, profess.
🄔 1 accept.

protester n demonstrator, agitator, rebel, dissident, dissenter.

protocol n procedure, formalities, convention, custom, etiquette, manners, good form, propriety.

protracted adj long, lengthy, prolonged, extended, drawn-out, long-drawn-out, overlong, interminable.
🄔 brief, shortened.

protrude v stick out, poke out, come through, bulge, jut out, project, extend, stand out, obtrude.

proud *adj* **1** CONCEITED, vain, egotistical, bigheaded, boastful, smug, complacent, arrogant, self-important, cocky, presumptuous, haughty, high and mighty, overbearing, supercilious, snooty (*infml*), snobbish, toffee-nosed (*infml*), stuck-up (*infml*). **2** SATISFIED, contented, gratified, pleased, delighted, honoured. **3** DIGNIFIED, noble, honourable, worthy, self-respecting.
◨ **1** humble, modest, unassuming. **2** ashamed. **3** deferential, ignoble.

prove *v* show, demonstrate, attest, verify, confirm, corroborate, substantiate, bear out, document, certify, authenticate, validate, justify, establish, determine, ascertain, try, test, check, examine, analyse.
◨ disprove, discredit, falsify.

proverb *n* saying, adage, aphorism, maxim, byword, dictum, precept.

proverbial *adj* axiomatic, accepted, conventional, traditional, customary, time-honoured, famous, well-known, legendary, notorious, typical, archetypal.

provide *v* **1** SUPPLY, furnish, stock, equip, outfit, prepare for, cater, serve, present, give, contribute, yield, lend, add, bring. **2** PLAN FOR, allow, make provision, accommodate, arrange for, take precautions. **3** STATE, specify, stipulate, lay down, require.
◨ **1** take, remove.

providence *n* **1** FATE, destiny, divine intervention, God's will, fortune, luck. **2** PRUDENCE, far-sightedness, foresight, caution, care, thrift.
◨ **2** improvidence.

provident *adj* prudent, far-sighted, judicious, cautious, careful, thrifty, economical, frugal.
◨ improvident.

providential *adj* timely, opportune, convenient, fortunate, lucky, happy, welcome, heaven-sent.

◨ untimely.

providing *conj* provided, with the proviso, given, as long as, on condition, on the understanding.

province *n* **1** REGION, area, district, zone, county, shire, department, territory, colony, dependency. **2** RESPONSIBILITY, concern, duty, office, role, function, field, sphere, domain, department, line.

provincial *adj* regional, local, rural, rustic, country, home-grown, small-town, parish-pump, parochial, insular, inward-looking, limited, narrow, narrow-minded, small-minded.
◨ national, cosmopolitan, urban, sophisticated.

provision *n* **1** PLAN, arrangement, preparation, measure, precaution. **2** STIPULATION, specification, proviso, condition, term, requirement.

provisional *adj* temporary, interim, transitional, stopgap, makeshift, conditional, tentative.
◨ permanent, fixed, definite.

provisions *n* food, foodstuff, groceries, sustenance, rations, supplies, stocks, stores.

proviso *n* condition, term, requirement, stipulation, qualification, reservation, restriction, limitation, provision, clause, rider.

provocation *n* cause, grounds, justification, reason, motive, stimulus, motivation, incitement, instigation, annoyance, aggravation (*infml*), vexation, grievance, offence, insult, affront, injury, taunt, challenge, dare.

provocative *adj* **1** ANNOYING, aggravating (*infml*), galling, outrageous, offensive, insulting, abusive. **2** STIMULATING, exciting, challenging. **3** EROTIC, titillating, arousing, sexy, seductive, alluring, tempting, inviting, tantalizing, teasing, suggestive.

⊞ **1** conciliatory.

provoke v **1** ANNOY, irritate, rile, aggravate (*infml*), offend, insult, anger, enrage, infuriate, incense, madden, exasperate, tease, taunt. **2** CAUSE, occasion, give rise to, produce, generate, induce, elicit, evoke, excite, inspire, move, stir, prompt, stimulate, motivate, incite, instigate.
⊞ **1** please, pacify. **2** result.

prowess n accomplishment, attainment, ability, aptitude, skill, expertise, mastery, command, talent, genius.

proximity n closeness, nearness, vicinity, neighbourhood, adjacency, juxtaposition.
⊞ remoteness.

proxy n agent, factor, deputy, stand-in, substitute, representative, delegate, attorney.

prudent adj wise, sensible, politic, judicious, shrewd, discerning, careful, cautious, wary, vigilant, circumspect, discreet, provident, far-sighted, thrifty.
⊞ imprudent, unwise, careless, rash.

pry v meddle, interfere, poke one's nose in, intrude, peep, peer, snoop, nose, ferret, dig, delve.
⊞ mind one's own business.

pseudonym n false name, assumed name, alias, incognito, pen name, nom de plume, stage name.

psychic adj spiritual, supernatural, occult, mystic(al), clairvoyant, extra-sensory, telepathic, mental, psychological, intellectual, cognitive.

psychological adj mental, cerebral, intellectual, cognitive, emotional, subjective, subconscious, unconscious, psychosomatic, irrational, unreal.
⊞ physical, real.

puberty n pubescence, adolescence, teens, youth, growing up, maturity.
⊞ childhood, immaturity, old age.

public adj **1** *public buildings*: state, national, civil, community, social, collective, communal, common, general, universal, open, unrestricted. **2** KNOWN, well-known, recognized, acknowledged, overt, open, exposed, published.
⊞ **1** private, personal. **2** secret.
◇ n people, nation, country, population, populace, masses, citizens, society, community, voters, electorate, followers, supporters, fans, audience, patrons, clientèle, customers, buyers, consumers.

publication n **1** BOOK, newspaper, magazine, periodical, booklet, leaflet, pamphlet, handbill. **2** ANNOUNCEMENT, declaration, notification, disclosure, release, issue, printing, publishing.

publicity n advertising, plug (*infml*), hype (*sl*), promotion, build-up, boost, attention, limelight, splash.

publicize v advertise, plug (*infml*), hype (*sl*), promote, push, spotlight, broadcast, make known, blaze.

publish v **1** ANNOUNCE, declare, communicate, make known, divulge, disclose, reveal, release, publicize, advertise. **2** *publish a book*: produce, print, issue, bring out, distribute, circulate, spread, diffuse.

pucker v gather, ruffle, wrinkle, shrivel, crinkle, crumple, crease, furrow, purse, screw up, contract, compress.

puerile adj childish, babyish, infantile, juvenile, immature, irresponsible, silly, foolish, inane, trivial.
⊞ mature.

puff n **1** BREATH, waft, whiff, draught, flurry, gust, blast. **2** *a puff on a cigarette*: pull, drag.
◇ v **1** BREATHE, pant, gasp, gulp, wheeze, blow, waft, inflate, expand,

swell. **2** *puff a cigarette*: smoke, pull, drag, draw, suck.

puffy *adj* inflated, swollen, bloated, distended, enlarged.

pugnacious *adj* hostile, aggressive, belligerent, contentious, disputatious, argumentative, quarrelsome, hot-tempered.
🗲 peaceable.

pull *v* **1** TOW, drag, haul, draw, tug, jerk, yank (*infml*). **2** REMOVE, take out, extract, pull out, pluck, uproot, pull up, rip, tear. **3** ATTRACT, draw, lure, allure, entice, tempt, magnetize.
4 DISLOCATE, sprain, wrench, strain.
🗲 **1** push, press. **3** repel, deter, discourage.
◇ *n* **1** TOW, drag, tug, jerk, yank (*infml*). **2** ATTRACTION, lure, allurement, drawing power, magnetism, influence, weight.
• **pull apart** separate, dismantle, part, dismember, take to pieces.
🗲 join.
• **pull down** destroy, demolish, knock down, bulldoze.
🗲 build, erect, put up.
• **pull off 1** ACCOMPLISH, achieve, bring off, succeed, manage, carry out. **2** DETACH, remove.
🗲 **1** fail. **2** attach.
• **pull out** retreat, withdraw, leave, depart, quit, move out, evacuate, desert, abandon.
🗲 join, arrive.
• **pull through** recover, rally, recuperate, survive, weather.
• **pull together** co-operate, work together, collaborate, team up.
🗲 fight.
• **pull up 1** STOP, halt, park, draw up, pull in, pull over, brake. **2** REPRIMAND, tell off (*infml*), tick off (*infml*), take to task, rebuke, criticize.

pulp *n* flesh, marrow, paste, purée, mash, mush, pap.
◇ *v* crush, squash, pulverize, mash, purée, liquidize.

pulsate *v* pulse, beat, throb, pound, hammer, drum, thud, thump, vibrate, oscillate, quiver.

pulse *n* beat, stroke, rhythm, throb, pulsation, beating, pounding, drumming, vibration, oscillation.

pulverize *v* **1** CRUSH, pound, grind, mill, powder. **2** DEFEAT, destroy, demolish, annihilate.

pump *v* push, drive, force, inject, siphon, draw, drain.
• **pump up** blow up, inflate, fill.

pun *n* play on words, double entendre, witticism, quip.

punch¹ *v* hit, strike, pummel, jab, bash, clout, cuff, box, thump, sock (*sl*), wallop (*infml*).
◇ *n* **1** BLOW, jab, bash, clout, thump, wallop (*infml*). **2** FORCE, impact, effectiveness, drive, vigour, verve, panache.

punch² *v* perforate, pierce, puncture, prick, bore, drill, stamp, cut.

punctilious *adj* scrupulous, conscientious, meticulous, careful, exact, precise, strict, formal, proper, particular, finicky, fussy.
🗲 lax, informal.

punctual *adj* prompt, on time, on the dot, exact, precise, early, in good time.
🗲 unpunctual, late.

punctuation

Punctuation marks include:
comma, full stop, period, ellipsis, colon, semicolon, brackets, parentheses, square brackets, inverted commas, quotation marks, quotes (*infml*), exclamation mark, question mark, apostrophe, asterisk, at sign, star, hashmark, hyphen, dash, oblique stroke, solidus, backslash, smiley, emoticon.

puncture *n* **1** FLAT TYRE, flat (*infml*), blow-out. **2** LEAK, hole, perforation,

cut, nick.
◇ v prick, pierce, penetrate, perforate, hole, cut, nick, burst, rupture, flatten, deflate.

pungent adj 1 a pungent taste: strong, hot, peppery, spicy, aromatic, tangy, piquant, sour, bitter, acrid, sharp. 2 pungent comments: caustic, stinging, biting, cutting, incisive, pointed, piercing, penetrating, sarcastic, scathing.
☒ 1 mild, bland, tasteless.

punish v penalize, discipline, correct, chastise, castigate, scold, beat, flog, lash, cane, spank, fine, imprison.
☒ reward.

punishment n discipline, correction, chastisement, beating, flogging, penalty, fine, imprisonment, sentence, deserts, retribution, revenge.
☒ reward.

punitive adj penal, disciplinary, retributive, retaliatory, vindictive, punishing.

puny adj weak, feeble, frail, sickly, undeveloped, underdeveloped, stunted, undersized, diminutive, little, tiny, insignificant.
☒ strong, sturdy, large, important.

pupil n student, scholar, schoolboy, schoolgirl, learner, apprentice, beginner, novice, disciple, protégé(e).
☒ teacher.

purchase v buy, pay for, invest in (infml), procure, acquire, obtain, get, secure, gain, earn, win.
☒ sell.
◇ n acquisition, buy (infml), investment, asset, possession, property.
☒ sale.

purchaser n buyer, consumer, shopper, customer, client.
☒ seller, vendor.

pure adj 1 pure gold: unadulterated, unalloyed, unmixed, undiluted,

neat, solid, simple, natural, real, authentic, genuine, true. 2 STERILE, uncontaminated, unpolluted, germ-free, aseptic, antiseptic, disinfected, sterilized, hygienic, sanitary, clean, immaculate, spotless, clear. 3 SHEER, utter, complete, total, thorough, absolute, perfect, unqualified. 4 CHASTE, virginal, undefiled, unsullied, moral, upright, virtuous, blameless, innocent. 5 pure mathematics: theoretical, abstract, conjectural, speculative, academic.
☒ 1 impure, adulterated.
2 contaminated, polluted. 4 immoral.
5 applied.

purely adv 1 UTTERLY, completely, totally, entirely, wholly, thoroughly, absolutely. 2 ONLY, simply, merely, just, solely, exclusively.

purge v 1 PURIFY, cleanse, clean out, scour, clear, absolve. 2 OUST, remove, get rid of, eject, expel, root out, eradicate, exterminate, wipe out, kill.
◇ n removal, ejection, expulsion, witch hunt, eradication, extermination.

purify v refine, filter, clarify, clean, cleanse, decontaminate, sanitize, disinfect, sterilize, fumigate, deodorize.
☒ contaminate, pollute, defile.

purist n pedant, literalist, formalist, stickler, quibbler, nit-picker.

puritanical adj puritan, moralistic, disciplinarian, ascetic, abstemious, austere, severe, stern, strict, strait-laced, prim, proper, prudish, disapproving, stuffy, stiff, rigid, narrow-minded, bigoted, fanatical, zealous.
☒ hedonistic, liberal, indulgent, broad-minded.

purity n 1 CLEARNESS, clarity, cleanness, cleanliness, untaintedness, wholesomeness. 2 SIMPLICITY, authenticity, genuineness, truth. 3 CHASTITY, decency, morality, integrity, rectitude, uprightness,

virtue, innocence, blamelessness.
≠ **1** impurity. **3** immorality.

purpose *n* **1** INTENTION, aim, objective, end, goal, target, plan, design, vision, idea, point, object, reason, motive, rationale, principle, result, outcome. **2** DETERMINATION, resolve, resolution, drive, single-mindedness, dedication, devotion, constancy, steadfastness, persistence, tenacity, zeal. **3** USE, function, application, good, advantage, benefit, value.
• **on purpose** purposely, deliberately, intentionally, consciously, knowingly, wittingly, wilfully.
≠ accidentally, impulsively, spontaneously.

purposeful *adj* determined, decided, resolved, resolute, single-minded, constant, steadfast, persistent, persevering, tenacious, strong-willed, positive, firm, deliberate.
≠ purposeless, aimless.

purse *n* **1** MONEY-BAG, wallet, pouch. **2** MONEY, means, resources, finances, funds, coffers, treasury, exchequer. **3** REWARD, award, prize.
◇ *v* pucker, wrinkle, draw together, close, tighten, contract, compress.

pursue *v* **1** *pursue an activity*: perform, engage in, practise, conduct, carry on, continue, keep on, keep up, maintain, persevere in, persist in, hold to, aspire to, aim for, strive for, try for. **2** CHASE, go after, follow, track, trail, shadow, tail, dog, harass, harry, hound, hunt, seek, search for, investigate, inquire into.

pursuit *n* **1** CHASE, hue and cry, tracking, stalking, trail, hunt, quest, search, investigation. **2** ACTIVITY, interest, hobby, pastime, occupation, trade, craft, line, speciality, vocation.

push *v* **1** PROPEL, thrust, ram, shove, jostle, elbow, prod, poke, press, depress, squeeze, squash, drive, force, constrain. **2** PROMOTE, advertise, publicize, boost, encourage, urge, egg on (*infml*), incite, spur, influence, persuade, pressurize, bully.
≠ **1** pull. **2** discourage, dissuade.
◇ *n* **1** KNOCK, shove, nudge, jolt, prod, poke, thrust. **2** ENERGY, vigour, vitality, go (*infml*), drive, effort, dynamism, enterprise, initiative, ambition, determination.

pushy *adj* assertive, self-assertive, ambitious, forceful, aggressive, over-confident, forward, bold, brash, arrogant, presumptuous, assuming, bossy (*infml*), in-your-face (*infml*).
≠ unassertive, unassuming.

put *v* **1** PLACE, lay, deposit, plonk (*infml*), set, fix, settle, establish, stand, position, dispose, situate, station, post. **2** APPLY, impose, inflict, levy, assign, subject. **3** WORD, phrase, formulate, frame, couch, express, voice, utter, state. **4** *put a suggestion*: submit, present, offer, suggest, propose.
• **put across** put over, communicate, convey, express, explain, spell out, bring home to, get through to.
• **put aside** put by, set aside, keep, retain, save, reserve, store, stow, stockpile, stash (*infml*), hoard, salt away.
• **put away** (*infml*) **1** CONSUME, devour, eat, drink. **2** IMPRISON, jail, lock up, commit, certify.
• **put back 1** DELAY, defer, postpone, reschedule. **2** REPLACE, return.
≠ **1** bring forward.
• **put down 1** WRITE DOWN, transcribe, enter, log, register, record, note. **2** CRUSH, quash, suppress, defeat, quell, silence, snub, slight, squash, deflate, humble, take down a peg, shame, humiliate, mortify. **3** *put down a sick dog*: kill, put to sleep. **4** ASCRIBE, attribute, blame, charge.
• **put forward** advance, suggest, recommend, nominate, propose, move, table, introduce, present, submit, offer, tender.

• **put in** insert, enter, input, submit, install, fit.

• **put off 1** DELAY, defer, postpone, reschedule. **2** DETER, dissuade, discourage, dishearten, demoralize, daunt, dismay, intimidate, disconcert, confuse, distract.
⊞ **2** encourage.

• **put on 1** ATTACH, affix, apply, place, add, impose. **2** PRETEND, feign, sham, fake, simulate, affect, assume. **3** STAGE, mount, produce, present, do, perform.

• **put out 1** PUBLISH, announce, broadcast, circulate. **2** EXTINGUISH, quench, douse, smother, switch off, turn off. **3** INCONVENIENCE, impose on, bother, disturb, trouble, upset, hurt, offend, annoy, irritate, irk, anger, exasperate.
⊞ **2** light.

• **put through** accomplish, achieve, complete, conclude, finalize, execute, manage, bring off.

• **put up 1** ERECT, build, construct, assemble. **2** ACCOMMODATE, house, lodge, shelter. **3** *put up prices*: raise, increase. **4** PAY, invest, give, advance, float, provide, supply, pledge, offer.

• **put up to** prompt, incite, encourage, egg on (*infml*), urge, goad.
⊞ discourage, dissuade.

• **put up with** stand, bear, abide, stomach, endure, suffer, tolerate, allow, accept, stand for, take, take lying down.

⊞ object to, reject.

putrid *adj* rotten, decayed, decomposed, mouldy, off, bad, rancid, addled, corrupt, contaminated, tainted, polluted, foul, rank, fetid, stinking.
⊞ fresh, wholesome.

put-upon *adj* imposed on, taken advantage of, exploited, used, abused, maltreated, persecuted.

puzzle *v* **1** BAFFLE, mystify, perplex, confound, stump (*infml*), floor (*infml*), confuse, bewilder, flummox (*infml*). **2** THINK, ponder, meditate, consider, mull over, deliberate, figure, rack one's brains.
◇ *n* question, poser, brain-teaser, mind-bender, crossword, rebus, anagram, riddle, conundrum, mystery, enigma, paradox.

• **puzzle out** solve, work out, figure out, decipher, decode, crack, unravel, untangle, sort out, resolve, clear up.

puzzled *adj* baffled, mystified, perplexed, confounded, at a loss, beaten, stumped (*infml*), confused, bewildered, nonplussed, lost, at sea, flummoxed (*infml*).
⊞ clear.

pyromaniac *n* arsonist, incendiary, fire-raiser, firebug (*infml*), torch (*US sl*).

Qq

quagmire *n* bog, marsh, quag, fen, swamp, morass, mire, quicksand.

quail *v* recoil, back away, shy away, shrink, flinch, cringe, cower, tremble, quake, shudder, falter.

quaint *adj* picturesque, charming, twee (*infml*), old-fashioned, antiquated, old-world, olde-worlde (*infml*), unusual, strange, odd, curious, bizarre, fanciful, whimsical.
⊞ modern.

quake *v* shake, tremble, shudder, quiver, shiver, quail, vibrate, wobble, rock, sway, move, convulse, heave.

qualification *n* **1** CERTIFICATE, diploma, training, skill, competence, ability, capability, capacity, aptitude, suitability, fitness, eligibility. **2** RESTRICTION, limitation, reservation, exception, exemption, condition, caveat, provision, proviso, stipulation, modification.

qualified *adj* **1** CERTIFIED, chartered, licensed, professional, trained, experienced, practised, skilled, accomplished, expert, knowledgeable, skilful, talented, proficient, competent, efficient, able, capable, fit, eligible. **2** *qualified praise*: reserved, guarded, cautious, restricted, limited, bounded, contingent, conditional, provisional, equivocal.
⊞ **1** unqualified. **2** unconditional, whole-hearted.

qualify *v* **1** TRAIN, prepare, equip, fit, pass, graduate, certify, empower, entitle, authorize, sanction, permit. **2** MODERATE, reduce, lessen, diminish, temper, soften, weaken, mitigate, ease, adjust, modify, restrain, restrict, limit, delimit, define, classify.
⊞ **1** disqualify.

quality *n* **1** PROPERTY, characteristic, peculiarity, attribute, aspect, feature, trait, mark. **2** *of poor quality*: standard, grade, class, kind, sort, nature, character, calibre, status, rank, value, worth, merit, condition. **3** EXCELLENCE, superiority, pre-eminence, distinction, refinement.

qualm *n* misgiving, apprehension, fear, anxiety, worry, disquiet, uneasiness, scruple, hesitation, reluctance, uncertainty, doubt.

quandary *n* dilemma, predicament, impasse, perplexity, bewilderment, confusion, mess, fix, hole (*infml*), problem, difficulty.

quantity *n* amount, number, sum, total, aggregate, mass, lot, share, portion, quota, allotment, measure, dose, proportion, part, content, capacity, volume, weight, bulk, size, magnitude, expanse, extent, length, breadth.

quarrel *n* row, argument, slanging match (*infml*), wrangle, squabble, tiff, misunderstanding, disagreement, dispute, dissension, controversy, difference, contention, conflict, clash, strife, fight, scrap, brawl, feud, vendetta, schism.
⊞ agreement, harmony.
◇ *v* row, argue, bicker, squabble, wrangle, be at loggerheads, fall out, disagree, dispute, dissent, differ, be at variance, clash, contend, fight, scrap, feud.
⊞ agree.

quarrelsome *adj* argumentative, disputatious, contentious, belligerent, ill-tempered, irritable.
⊞ peaceable, placid.

quarry *n* prey, victim, object, goal, target, game, kill, prize.

quarter *n* district, sector, zone, neighbourhood, locality, vicinity, area, region, province, territory, division, section, part, place, spot, point, direction, side.
◇ *v* station, post, accommodate, billet, put up, lodge, board, house, shelter.

quarters *n* accommodation, lodgings, billet, digs (*infml*), residence, dwelling, habitation, domicile, rooms, barracks, station, post.

quash *v* annul, revoke, rescind, overrule, cancel, nullify, void, invalidate, reverse, set aside, squash, crush, quell, suppress, subdue, defeat, overthrow.
⊞ confirm, vindicate, reinstate.

quaver *v* shake, tremble, quake, shudder, quiver, vibrate, pulsate, oscillate, flutter, flicker, trill, warble.

quay *n* wharf, pier, jetty, dock, harbour.

queasy *adj* sick, ill, unwell, queer, groggy, green, nauseated, sickened, bilious, squeamish, faint, dizzy, giddy.

queen *n* monarch, sovereign, ruler, majesty, princess, empress, consort.

queer *adj* **1** ODD, mysterious, strange, unusual, uncommon, weird, unnatural, bizarre, eccentric, peculiar, funny, puzzling, curious, remarkable. **2** *I feel queer*: unwell, ill, sick, queasy, light-headed, faint, giddy, dizzy. **3** SUSPECT, suspicious, shifty, dubious, shady (*infml*). **4** (*sl*) HOMOSEXUAL, gay, lesbian.
⊞ **1** ordinary, usual, common. **2** well. **4** straight (*sl*).

quell *v* subdue, quash, crush, squash, suppress, put down, overcome, conquer, defeat, overpower, moderate, mitigate, allay, alleviate, soothe, calm, pacify, hush, quiet, silence, stifle, extinguish.

quench *v* **1** *quench one's thirst*: slake, satisfy, sate, cool. **2** EXTINGUISH, douse, put out, snuff out.

querulous *adj* peevish, fretful, fractious, cantankerous, cross, irritable, complaining, grumbling, discontented, dissatisfied, critical, carping, captious, fault-finding, fussy.
⊞ placid, uncomplaining, contented.

query *v* ask, inquire, question, challenge, dispute, quarrel with, doubt, suspect, distrust, mistrust, disbelieve.
⊞ accept.
◇ *n* question, inquiry, problem, uncertainty, doubt, suspicion, scepticism, reservation, hesitation.

quest *n* search, hunt, pursuit, investigation, inquiry, mission, crusade, enterprise, undertaking, venture, journey, voyage, expedition, exploration, adventure.

question *v* interrogate, quiz, grill, pump, interview, examine, cross-examine, debrief, ask, inquire, investigate, probe, query, challenge, dispute, doubt, disbelieve.
◇ *n* **1** QUERY, inquiry, poser, problem, difficulty. **2** ISSUE, matter, subject, topic, point, proposal, proposition, motion, debate, dispute, controversy.

questionable *adj* debatable, disputable, unsettled, undetermined, unproven, uncertain, arguable, controversial, vexed, doubtful, dubious, suspicious, suspect, shady (*infml*), fishy (*infml*), iffy (*sl*).
⊞ unquestionable, indisputable, certain.

questionnaire *n* quiz, test, survey, opinion poll.

queue *n* line, tailback, file, crocodile, procession, train, string, succession, series, sequence, order.

quibble v carp, cavil, split hairs, nit-pick, equivocate, prevaricate.
◇ n complaint, objection, criticism, query.

quick adj 1 FAST, swift, rapid, speedy, express, hurried, hasty, cursory, fleeting, brief, prompt, ready, immediate, instant, instantaneous, sudden, brisk, nimble, sprightly, agile. 2 CLEVER, intelligent, quick-witted, smart, sharp, keen, shrewd, astute, discerning, perceptive, responsive, receptive.
🗵 1 slow, sluggish, lethargic.
2 unintelligent, dull.

quicken v 1 ACCELERATE, speed, hurry, hasten, precipitate, expedite, dispatch, advance. 2 ANIMATE, enliven, invigorate, energize, galvanize, activate, rouse, arouse, stimulate, excite, inspire, revive, refresh, reinvigorate, reactivate.
🗵 1 slow, retard. 2 dull.

quiet adj 1 SILENT, noiseless, inaudible, hushed, soft, low.
2 PEACEFUL, still, tranquil, serene, calm, composed, undisturbed, untroubled, placid. 3 SHY, reserved, reticent, uncommunicative, taciturn, unforthcoming, retiring, withdrawn, thoughtful, subdued, meek. 4 a quiet spot: isolated, unfrequented, lonely, secluded, private.
🗵 1 noisy, loud. 2 excitable.
3 extrovert.
◇ n quietness, silence, hush, peace, lull, stillness, tranquillity, serenity, calm, rest, repose.
🗵 noise, loudness, disturbance, bustle.

quieten v 1 SILENCE, hush, mute, soften, lower, diminish, reduce, stifle, muffle, deaden, dull. 2 SUBDUE, pacify, quell, quiet, still, smooth, calm, soothe, compose, sober.
🗵 2 disturb, agitate.

quilt n bedcover, coverlet, bedspread, counterpane, eiderdown, duvet.

quip n joke, jest, crack, gag (infml), witticism, riposte, retort, gibe.

quirk n freak, eccentricity, curiosity, oddity, peculiarity, idiosyncrasy, mannerism, habit, trait, foible, whim, caprice, turn, twist.

quit v 1 LEAVE, depart, go, exit, decamp, desert, forsake, abandon, renounce, relinquish, surrender, give up, resign, retire, withdraw.
2 quit smoking: stop, cease, end, discontinue, desist, drop, give up, pack in (sl).

quite adv 1 MODERATELY, rather, somewhat, fairly, comparatively, relatively. 2 UTTERLY, absolutely, totally, completely, entirely, wholly, fully, perfectly, exactly, precisely.

quiver v shake, tremble, shudder, shiver, quake, quaver, vibrate, palpitate, flutter, flicker, oscillate, wobble.
◇ n shake, tremble, shudder, shiver, tremor, vibration, palpitation, flutter, flicker, oscillation, wobble.

quiz n questionnaire, test, examination, competition.
◇ v question, interrogate, grill, pump, examine, cross-examine.

quizzical adj questioning, inquiring, curious, amused, humorous, teasing, mocking, satirical, sardonic, sceptical.

quota n ration, allowance, allocation, assignment, share, portion, part, slice, cut (infml), percentage, proportion.

quotation n 1 CITATION, quote (infml), extract, excerpt, passage, piece, cutting, reference. 2 ESTIMATE, quote (infml), tender, figure, price, cost, charge, rate.

quote v cite, refer to, mention, name, reproduce, echo, repeat, recite, recall, recollect.

Rr

rabble *n* crowd, throng, horde, herd, mob, masses, populace, riff-raff.

rabble-rouser *n* agitator, troublemaker, incendiary, demagogue, ringleader.

race¹ *n* competition, contest, contention, rivalry, chase, pursuit, quest.
◇ *v* run, sprint, dash, tear, fly, gallop, speed, career, dart, zoom, rush, hurry, hasten.

Types of race and famous races include: criterium, cycle race, cyclo-cross, road race, time trial, Tour de France; greyhound race, Greyhound Derby; horse race, Cheltenham Gold Cup, the Classics (Derby, Oaks, One Thousand Guineas, St. Leger, Two Thousand Guineas), Grand National, Kentucky Derby, Breeders' Cup, Melbourne Cup, Prix de l'Arc de Triomphe, steeplechase, trotting race, harness race; motorcycle race, motocross, scramble, speedway, Isle of Man Tourist Trophy (TT); motor race, Grand Prix, Indianapolis 500, Le Mans, Monte Carlo Rally, RAC Rally, stock car race; rowing, regatta, Boat Race; running, cross-country, dash (*N Am*), hurdles, marathon, London Marathon, half marathon, relay, sprint, steeplechase, track event; ski race, downhill, slalom, giant slalom, super giant slalom; swimming race; walking race; yacht race, Admiral's Cup, America's Cup; egg-and-spoon race, three-legged race, sack

race, wheelbarrow race.

---

race² *n* nation, people, tribe, clan, house, dynasty, family, kindred, ancestry, line, blood, stock, genus, species, breed.

racecourse *n* racetrack, course, track, circuit, lap, turf, speedway.

racial *adj* national, tribal, ethnic, folk, genealogical, ancestral, inherited, genetic.

racism *n* racialism, xenophobia, chauvinism, jingoism, discrimination, prejudice, bias.

rack *n* shelf, stand, support, structure, frame, framework.

racket *n* **1** NOISE, din, uproar, row, fuss, outcry, clamour, commotion, disturbance, pandemonium, hurly-burly, hubbub. **2** SWINDLE, con (*infml*), scam (*infml*), fraud, fiddle, deception, trick, dodge, scheme, business, game.

racy *adj* **1** RIBALD, bawdy, risqué, naughty, indecent, indelicate, suggestive. **2** LIVELY, animated, spirited, energetic, dynamic, buoyant, boisterous.

radiance *n* light, luminosity, incandescence, radiation, brightness, brilliance, shine, lustre, gleam, glow, glitter, resplendence, splendour.

radiant *adj* **1** BRIGHT, luminous, shining, gleaming, glowing, beaming, glittering, sparkling, brilliant, resplendent, splendid, glorious.
2 HAPPY, joyful, delighted, ecstatic.
⊞ **1** dull. **2** miserable.

radiate *v* shine, gleam, glow, beam,

shed, pour, give off, emit, emanate, diffuse, issue, disseminate, scatter, spread (out), diverge, branch.

radical *adj* **1** BASIC, fundamental, primary, essential, natural, native, innate, intrinsic, deep-seated, profound. **2** *radical changes*: drastic, comprehensive, thorough, sweeping, far-reaching, thoroughgoing, complete, total, entire. **3** FANATICAL, militant, extreme, extremist, revolutionary.
⊞ **1** superficial. **3** moderate.
◇ *n* fanatic, militant, extremist, revolutionary, reformer, reformist, fundamentalist.

raffle *n* draw, lottery, sweepstake, sweep, tombola.

rage *n* **1** ANGER, wrath, fury, frenzy, tantrum, temper. **2** (*infml*) *all the rage*: craze, fad, thing (*infml*), fashion, vogue, style, passion, enthusiasm, obsession.
◇ *v* fume, seethe, rant, rave, storm, thunder, explode, rampage.

ragged *adj* **1** *ragged clothes*: frayed, torn, ripped, tattered, worn-out, threadbare, tatty, shabby, scruffy, unkempt, down-at-heel. **2** JAGGED, serrated, indented, notched, rough, uneven, irregular, fragmented, erratic, disorganized.

raid *n* attack, onset, onslaught, invasion, inroad, incursion, foray, sortie, strike, blitz, swoop, bust (*sl*), robbery, break-in, hold-up.
◇ *v* loot, pillage, plunder, ransack, rifle, maraud, attack, descend on, invade, storm.

raider *n* attacker, invader, looter, plunderer, ransacker, marauder, robber, thief, brigand, pirate.

railing *n* fence, paling, barrier, parapet, rail, balustrade.

railway *n* track, line, rails, railroad (*N Am*), monorail, underground, tube (*infml*), subway, metro.

rain *n* rainfall, precipitation,

raindrops, drizzle, shower, cloudburst, downpour, deluge, torrent, storm, thunderstorm, squall.
◇ *v* spit, drizzle, shower, pour, teem, pelt, bucket (*infml*), deluge.

rainy *adj* wet, damp, showery, drizzly.
⊞ dry.

raise *v* **1** LIFT, elevate, hoist, jack up, erect, build, construct. **2** INCREASE, augment, escalate, magnify, heighten, strengthen, intensify, amplify, boost, enhance. **3** *raise funds*: get, obtain, collect, gather, assemble, rally, muster, recruit.
4 BRING UP, rear, breed, propagate, grow, cultivate, develop. **5** *raise a subject*: bring up, broach, introduce, present, put forward, moot, suggest.
⊞ **1** lower. **2** decrease, reduce.
5 suppress.

rake in *v* collect, accumulate, amass.

rally *v* **1** GATHER, collect, assemble, congregate, convene, muster, summon, round up, unite, marshal, organize, mobilize, reassemble, regroup, reorganize. **2** RECOVER, recuperate, revive, improve, pick up.
◇ *n* **1** GATHERING, assembly, convention, convocation, conference, meeting, jamboree, reunion, march, demonstration.
2 RECOVERY, recuperation, revival, comeback, improvement, resurgence, renewal.

ram *v* **1** HIT, strike, butt, hammer, pound, drum, crash, smash, slam.
2 FORCE, drive, thrust, cram, stuff, pack, crowd, jam, wedge.

ramble *v* **1** WALK, hike, trek, tramp, traipse, stroll, amble, saunter, straggle, wander, roam, rove, meander, wind, zigzag. **2** CHATTER, babble, rabbit (on) (*infml*), witter (on) (*infml*), expatiate, digress, drift.
◇ *n* walk, hike, trek, tramp, stroll, saunter, tour, trip, excursion.

rambler n hiker, walker, stroller, rover, roamer, wanderer, wayfarer.

rambling adj 1 SPREADING, sprawling, straggling, trailing. 2 CIRCUITOUS, roundabout, digressive, wordy, long-winded, long-drawn-out, disconnected, incoherent. ⊠ 2 direct.

ramification n branch, offshoot, development, complication, result, consequence, upshot, implication.

ramp n slope, incline, gradient, rise.

rampage v run wild, run amok, run riot, rush, tear, storm, rage, rant, rave. ◇ n rage, fury, frenzy, storm, uproar, violence, destruction. • on the rampage wild, amok, berserk, violent, out of control.

rampant adj unrestrained, uncontrolled, unbridled, unchecked, wanton, excessive, fierce, violent, raging, wild, riotous, rank, profuse, rife, widespread, prevalent.

ramshackle adj dilapidated, tumbledown, broken-down, crumbling, ruined, derelict, jerry-built, unsafe, rickety, shaky, flimsy, unsteady, tottering, decrepit. ⊠ solid, stable.

rancid adj sour, off, bad, musty, stale, rank, foul, fetid, putrid, rotten. ⊠ sweet.

random adj arbitrary, chance, fortuitous, casual, incidental, haphazard, irregular, unsystematic, unplanned, accidental, aimless, purposeless, indiscriminate, stray. ⊠ systematic, deliberate.

range n 1 SCOPE, compass, scale, gamut, spectrum, sweep, spread, extent, distance, reach, span, limits, bounds, parameters, area, field, domain, province, sphere, orbit. 2 a range of fittings: variety, diversity, assortment, selection, sort, kind, class, order, series, string, chain. ◇ v 1 EXTEND, stretch, reach, spread, vary, fluctuate. 2 ALIGN, arrange, order, rank, classify, catalogue.

rank¹ n 1 GRADE, degree, class, caste, status, standing, position, station, condition, estate, echelon, level, stratum, tier, classification, sort, type, group, division. 2 ROW, line, range, column, file, series, order, formation. ◇ v grade, class, rate, place, position, range, sort, classify, categorize, order, arrange, organize, marshal.

rank² adj 1 UTTER, total, complete, absolute, unmitigated, thorough, sheer, downright, out-and-out, arrant, gross, flagrant, glaring, outrageous. 2 FOUL, repulsive, disgusting, revolting, stinking, putrid, rancid, stale.

rankle v annoy, irritate, rile, nettle, gall, irk, anger.

ransack v search, scour, comb, rummage, rifle, raid, sack, strip, despoil, ravage, loot, plunder, pillage.

ransom n price, money, payment, pay-off, redemption, deliverance, rescue, liberation, release. ◇ v buy off, redeem, deliver, rescue, liberate, free, release.

rant v shout, cry, yell, roar, bellow, declaim, bluster, rave.

rap v 1 KNOCK, hit, strike, tap, thump. 2 (sl) REPROVE, reprimand, criticize, censure. ◇ n 1 KNOCK, blow, tap, thump. 2 (sl) REBUKE, reprimand, censure, blame, punishment.

rape n violation, assault, abuse, maltreatment. ◇ v violate, assault, abuse, maltreat.

rapid adj swift, speedy, quick, fast, express, lightning, prompt, brisk, hurried, hasty, precipitate, headlong. ⊠ slow, leisurely, sluggish.

rapport n bond, link, affinity, relationship, empathy, sympathy, understanding, harmony.

rapt adj engrossed, absorbed, preoccupied, intent, gripped, spellbound, enthralled, captivated, fascinated, entranced, charmed, enchanted, delighted, ravished, enraptured, transported.

rapture n delight, happiness, joy, bliss, ecstasy, euphoria, exaltation.

rare adj 1 UNCOMMON, unusual, scarce, sparse, sporadic, infrequent. 2 EXQUISITE, superb, excellent, superlative, incomparable, exceptional, remarkable, precious. ☒ 1 common, abundant, frequent.

rarefied adj exclusive, select, private, esoteric, refined, high, noble, sublime.

rarely adv seldom, hardly ever, infrequently, little. ☒ often, frequently.

raring adj eager, keen, enthusiastic, ready, willing, impatient, longing, itching, desperate.

rarity n 1 CURIOSITY, curio, gem, pearl, treasure, find. 2 UNCOMMONNESS, unusualness, strangeness, scarcity, shortage, sparseness, infrequency. ☒ 2 commonness, frequency.

rascal n rogue, scoundrel, scamp, scallywag, imp, devil, villain, good-for-nothing, wastrel.

rash¹ adj reckless, ill-considered, foolhardy, ill-advised, madcap, hare-brained, hot-headed, headstrong, impulsive, impetuous, hasty, headlong, unguarded, unwary, indiscreet, imprudent, careless, heedless, unthinking. ☒ cautious, wary, careful.

rash² n eruption, outbreak, epidemic, plague.

rasp n grating, scrape, grinding, scratch, harshness, hoarseness, croak. ◇ v grate, scrape, grind, file, sand, scour, abrade, rub.

rate n 1 SPEED, velocity, tempo, time, ratio, proportion, relation, degree,

grade, rank, rating, standard, basis, measure, scale. 2 CHARGE, fee, hire, toll, tariff, price, cost, value, worth, tax, duty, amount, figure, percentage. ◇ v 1 JUDGE, regard, consider, deem, count, reckon, figure, estimate, evaluate, assess, weigh, measure, grade, rank, class, classify. 2 ADMIRE, respect, esteem, value, prize. 3 DESERVE, merit.

rather adv 1 MODERATELY, relatively, slightly, a bit, somewhat, fairly, quite, pretty, noticeably, significantly, very. 2 PREFERABLY, sooner, instead.

ratify v approve, uphold, endorse, sign, legalize, sanction, authorize, establish, affirm, confirm, certify, validate, authenticate. ☒ repudiate, reject.

rating n class, rank, degree, status, standing, position, placing, order, grade, mark, evaluation, assessment, classification, category.

ratio n percentage, fraction, proportion, relation, relationship, correspondence, correlation.

ration n quota, allowance, allocation, allotment, share, portion, helping, part, measure, amount. ◇ v apportion, allot, allocate, share, deal out, distribute, dole out, dispense, supply, issue, control, restrict, limit, conserve, save.

rational adj logical, reasonable, sound, well-founded, realistic, sensible, clear-headed, judicious, wise, sane, normal, balanced, lucid, reasoning, thinking, intelligent, enlightened. ☒ irrational, illogical, insane, crazy.

rationale n logic, reasoning, philosophy, principle, basis, grounds, explanation, reason, motive, motivation, theory.

rationalize v 1 JUSTIFY, excuse, vindicate, explain, account for. 2 REORGANIZE, streamline.

rations n food, provisions, supplies, stores.

rattle v clatter, jingle, jangle, clank, shake, vibrate, jolt, jar, bounce, bump. • **rattle off** reel off, list, run through, recite, repeat.

raucous adj harsh, rough, hoarse, husky, rasping, grating, jarring, strident, noisy, loud.

ravage v destroy, devastate, lay waste, demolish, raze, wreck, ruin, spoil, damage, loot, pillage, plunder, sack, despoil.
◇ n destruction, devastation, havoc, damage, ruin, desolation, wreckage, pillage, plunder.

rave v rage, storm, thunder, roar, rant, ramble, babble, splutter.
◇ adj (infml) enthusiastic, rapturous, favourable, excellent, wonderful.

ravenous adj hungry, starving, starved, famished, greedy, voracious, insatiable.

ravine n canyon, gorge, gully, pass.

raving adj mad, insane, crazy, hysterical, delirious, wild, frenzied, furious, berserk.

ravish v enrapture, delight, enchant, charm, captivate, entrance, fascinate.

ravishing adj delightful, enchanting, charming, lovely, beautiful, gorgeous, stunning, radiant, dazzling, alluring, seductive.

raw adj 1 raw vegetables: uncooked, fresh. 2 UNPROCESSED, unrefined, untreated, crude, natural. 3 PLAIN, bare, naked, basic, harsh, brutal, realistic. 4 SCRATCHED, grazed, scraped, open, bloody, sore, tender, sensitive. 5 COLD, chilly, bitter, biting, piercing, freezing, bleak. 6 a raw recruit: new, green, immature, callow, inexperienced, untrained, unskilled.
⊡ 1 cooked, done. 2 processed, refined. 5 warm. 6 experienced, skilled.

ray n beam, shaft, flash, gleam, flicker, glimmer, glint, spark, trace, hint, indication.

raze v demolish, pull down, tear down, bulldoze, flatten, level, destroy.

re prep about, concerning, regarding, with regard to, with reference to.

reach v arrive at, get to, attain, achieve, make, amount to, hit, strike, touch, contact, stretch, extend, grasp.
◇ n range, scope, compass, distance, spread, extent, stretch, grasp, jurisdiction, command, power, influence.

react v respond, retaliate, reciprocate, reply, answer, acknowledge, act, behave.

reaction n response, effect, reply, answer, acknowledgement, feedback, counteraction, reflex, recoil, reciprocation, retaliation.

reactionary adj conservative, right-wing, rightist, die-hard, counter-revolutionary.
⊡ progressive, revolutionary.
◇ n conservative, right-winger, rightist, die-hard, counter-revolutionary.
⊡ progressive, revolutionary.

read v 1 STUDY, peruse, pore over, scan, skim, decipher, decode, interpret, construe, understand, comprehend. 2 RECITE, declaim, deliver, speak, utter. 3 the gauge read zero: indicate, show, display, register, record.

readable adj 1 LEGIBLE, decipherable, intelligible, clear, understandable, comprehensible. 2 INTERESTING, enjoyable, entertaining, gripping, unputdownable (infml).
⊡ 1 illegible. 2 unreadable.

readily adv willingly, unhesitatingly, gladly, eagerly, promptly, quickly, freely, smoothly, easily, effortlessly.
⊡ unwillingly, reluctantly.

reading n 1 STUDY, perusal, scrutiny, examination, inspection, interpretation, understanding, rendering, version, rendition, recital. 2 *a reading from the Bible*: passage, lesson.

ready adj 1 *ready to go*: prepared, waiting, set, fit, arranged, organized, completed, finished. 2 WILLING, inclined, disposed, happy, game (*infml*), eager, keen. 3 AVAILABLE, to hand, present, near, accessible, convenient, handy. 4 PROMPT, immediate, quick, sharp, astute, perceptive, alert.
⊞ 1 unprepared. 2 unwilling, reluctant, disinclined. 3 unavailable, inaccessible. 4 slow.

real adj actual, existing, physical, material, substantial, tangible, genuine, authentic, bona fide, official, rightful, legitimate, valid, true, factual, certain, sure, positive, veritable, honest, sincere, heartfelt, unfeigned, unaffected.
⊞ unreal, imaginary, false.

realistic adj 1 PRACTICAL, down-to-earth, commonsense, sensible, level-headed, clear-sighted, businesslike, hard-headed, pragmatic, matter-of-fact, rational, logical, objective, detached, unsentimental, unromantic. 2 LIFELIKE, faithful, truthful, true, genuine, authentic, natural, real, real-life, graphic, representational.
⊞ 1 unrealistic, impractical, irrational, idealistic.

reality n truth, fact, certainty, realism, actuality, existence, materiality, tangibility, genuineness, authenticity, validity.

realize v 1 UNDERSTAND, comprehend, grasp, catch on, cotton on (*infml*), recognize, accept, appreciate. 2 ACHIEVE, accomplish, fulfil, complete, implement, perform. 3 SELL FOR, fetch, make, earn, produce, net, clear.

really adv actually, truly, honestly, sincerely, genuinely, positively, certainly, absolutely, categorically, very, indeed.

realm n kingdom, monarchy, principality, empire, country, state, land, territory, area, region, province, domain, sphere, orbit, field, department.

rear n 1 BACK, stern, end, tail. 2 RUMP, buttocks, posterior, behind, bottom, backside (*infml*).
⊞ 1 front.
◇ adj back, hind, hindmost, rearmost, last.
⊞ front.
◇ v 1 *rear a child*: bring up, raise, breed, grow, cultivate, foster, nurse, nurture, train, educate. 2 RISE, tower, soar, raise, lift.

reason n 1 CAUSE, motive, incentive, rationale, explanation, excuse, justification, defence, warrant, ground, basis, case, argument, aim, intention, purpose, object, end, goal. 2 SENSE, logic, reasoning, rationality, sanity, mind, wit, brain, intellect, understanding, wisdom, judgement, common sense, gumption.
◇ v work out, solve, resolve, conclude, deduce, infer, think.
• **reason with** urge, persuade, move, remonstrate with, argue with, debate with, discuss with.

reasonable adj 1 SENSIBLE, wise, well-advised, sane, intelligent, rational, logical, practical, sound, reasoned, well-thought-out, plausible, credible, possible, viable. 2 *a reasonable price*: acceptable, satisfactory, tolerable, moderate, average, fair, just, modest, inexpensive.
⊞ 1 irrational. 2 exorbitant.

reasoning n logic, thinking, thought, analysis, interpretation, deduction, supposition, hypothesis, argument, case, proof.

reassure v comfort, cheer,

encourage, hearten, inspirit, brace, bolster.
☒ alarm.

rebate n refund, repayment, reduction, discount, deduction, allowance.

rebel v revolt, mutiny, rise up, run riot, dissent, disobey, defy, resist, recoil, shrink.
☒ conform.
◇ n revolutionary, insurrectionary, mutineer, dissenter, nonconformist, schismatic, heretic.

rebellion n revolt, revolution, rising, uprising, insurrection, insurgence, mutiny, resistance, opposition, defiance, disobedience, insubordination, dissent, heresy.

rebellious adj revolutionary, insurrectionary, insurgent, seditious, mutinous, resistant, defiant, disobedient, insubordinate, unruly, disorderly, ungovernable, unmanageable, intractable, obstinate.
☒ obedient, submissive.

rebirth n reincarnation, renaissance, resurrection, regeneration, renewal, restoration, revival, revitalization, rejuvenation.

rebound v recoil, backfire, return, bounce, ricochet, boomerang.

rebuff v spurn, reject, refuse, decline, turn down, repulse, discourage, snub, slight, cut, cold-shoulder.
◇ n rejection, refusal, repulse, check, discouragement, snub, brush-off (infml), slight, put-down, cold shoulder.

rebuke v reprove, castigate, chide, scold, tell off (infml), admonish, tick off (infml), reprimand, upbraid, rate, censure, blame, reproach.
☒ praise, compliment.
◇ n reproach, reproof, reprimand, lecture, dressing-down (infml), telling-off (infml), ticking-off (infml), admonition, censure, blame.

☒ praise, commendation.

recall v remember, recollect, cast one's mind back, evoke, bring back.

recapitulate v recap, summarize, review, repeat, reiterate, restate, recount.

recede v go back, return, retire, withdraw, retreat, ebb, wane, sink, decline, diminish, dwindle, decrease, lessen, shrink, slacken, subside, abate.
☒ advance.

receipt n 1 VOUCHER, ticket, slip, counterfoil, stub, acknowledgement. 2 RECEIVING, reception, acceptance, delivery.

receipts n takings, income, proceeds, profits, gains, return.

receive v 1 TAKE, accept, get, obtain, derive, acquire, pick up, collect, inherit. 2 receive guests: admit, let in, greet, welcome, entertain, accommodate. 3 EXPERIENCE, undergo, suffer, sustain, meet with, encounter. 4 REACT TO, respond to, hear, perceive, apprehend.
☒ 1 give, donate.

recent adj late, latest, current, present-day, contemporary, modern, up-to-date, new, novel, fresh, young.
☒ old, out-of-date.

recently adv lately, newly, freshly.

receptacle n container, vessel, holder.

reception n 1 ACCEPTANCE, admission, greeting, recognition, welcome, treatment, response, reaction, acknowledgement, receipt. 2 PARTY, function, do (infml), entertainment.

receptive adj open-minded, amenable, accommodating, suggestible, susceptible, sensitive, responsive, open, accessible, approachable, friendly, hospitable, welcoming, sympathetic, favourable, interested.

⊉ narrow-minded, resistant, unresponsive.

recess n 1 BREAK, interval, intermission, rest, respite, holiday, vacation. 2 ALCOVE, niche, nook, corner, bay, cavity, hollow, depression, indentation.

recession n slump, depression, downturn, decline.
⊉ boom, upturn.

recipe n formula, prescription, ingredients, instructions, directions, method, system, procedure, technique.

reciprocal adj mutual, joint, shared, give-and-take, complementary, alternating, corresponding, equivalent, interchangeable.

reciprocate v respond, reply, requite, return, exchange, swap, trade, match, equal, correspond, interchange, alternate.

recital n performance, concert, recitation, reading, narration, account, rendition, interpretation, repetition.

recitation n passage, piece, party piece, poem, monologue, narration, story, tale, recital, telling.

recite v repeat, tell, narrate, relate, recount, speak, deliver, articulate, declaim, perform, reel off, itemize, enumerate.

reckless adj heedless, thoughtless, mindless, careless, negligent, ill-advised, irresponsible, imprudent, indiscreet, rash, hasty, foolhardy, daredevil, wild.
⊉ cautious, wary, careful, prudent.

reckon v 1 CALCULATE, compute, figure out, work out, add up, total, tally, count, number, enumerate. 2 DEEM, regard, consider, esteem, value, rate, judge, evaluate, assess, estimate, gauge. 3 THINK, believe, imagine, fancy, suppose, surmise, assume, guess, conjecture.

• **reckon on** rely on, depend on, bank on, count on, trust in, hope for, expect, anticipate, foresee, plan for, bargain for, figure on, take into account, face.

reckoning n 1 by my reckoning: calculation, computation, estimate. 2 BILL, account, charge, due, score, settlement. 3 JUDGEMENT, retribution, doom.

reclaim v recover, regain, recapture, retrieve, salvage, rescue, redeem, restore, reinstate, regenerate.

recline v rest, repose, lean back, lie, lounge, loll, sprawl, stretch out.

recognition n 1 IDENTIFICATION, detection, discovery, recollection, recall, remembrance, awareness, perception, realization, understanding. 2 CONFESSION, admission, acceptance, acknowledgement, gratitude, appreciation, honour, respect, greeting, salute.

recognize v 1 IDENTIFY, know, remember, recollect, recall, place, see, notice, spot, perceive. 2 CONFESS, own, acknowledge, accept, admit, grant, concede, allow, appreciate, understand, realize.

recollect v recall, remember, cast one's mind back, reminisce.

recollection n recall, remembrance, memory, souvenir, reminiscence, impression.

recommend v advocate, urge, exhort, advise, counsel, suggest, propose, put forward, advance, praise, commend, plug (infml), endorse, approve, vouch for.
⊉ disapprove.

recommendation n advice, counsel, suggestion, proposal, advocacy, endorsement, approval, sanction, blessing, praise, commendation, plug (infml), reference, testimonial.
⊉ disapproval.

recompense n compensation, indemnification, damages, reparation, restitution, amends, requital, repayment, reward, payment, remuneration, pay, wages.

reconcile v reunite, conciliate, pacify, appease, placate, propitiate, accord, harmonize, accommodate, adjust, resolve, settle, square.
🗷 estrange, alienate.

reconciliation n reunion, conciliation, pacification, appeasement, propitiation, rapprochement, détente, settlement, agreement, harmony, accommodation, adjustment, compromise.
🗷 estrangement, separation.

reconnoitre v explore, survey, scan, spy out, recce (sl), inspect, examine, scrutinize, investigate, patrol.

reconstruct v remake, rebuild, reassemble, re-establish, refashion, remodel, reform, reorganize, recreate, restore, renovate, regenerate.

record n 1 REGISTER, log, report, account, minutes, memorandum, note, entry, document, file, dossier, diary, journal, memoir, history, annals, archives, documentation, evidence, testimony, trace.
2 RECORDING, disc, single, CD, compact disc, album, release, LP.
3 break the record: fastest time, best performance, personal best, world record. 4 BACKGROUND, track record, curriculum vitae, career.
◇ v 1 NOTE, enter, inscribe, write down, transcribe, register, log, put down, enrol, report, minute, chronicle, document, keep, preserve.
2 TAPE-RECORD, tape, videotape, video, cut.

recording n release, performance, record.

Types of recording include: album, audiotape, cassette, CD, compact disc, DAT (digital audiotape), digital recording, disc, DVD (digital versatile disk), EP (extended play), 45, gramophone record, long-playing record, LP, magnetic tape, MiniDisc®, mono recording, MP3, podcast, 78, single, stereo recording, tape, tape-recording, telerecording, video, videocassette, videodisc, videotape, vinyl (infml).

recount v tell, relate, impart, communicate, report, narrate, describe, depict, portray, detail, repeat, rehearse, recite.

recoup v recover, retrieve, regain, get back, make good, repay, refund, reimburse, compensate.

recover v 1 recover from illness: get better, improve, pick up, rally, mend, heal, pull through, get over, recuperate, revive, convalesce, come round. 2 REGAIN, get back, recoup, retrieve, retake, recapture, repossess, reclaim, restore.
🗷 1 worsen. 2 lose, forfeit.

recovery n 1 RECUPERATION, convalescence, rehabilitation, mending, healing, improvement, upturn, rally, revival, restoration.
2 RETRIEVAL, salvage, reclamation, repossession, recapture.
🗷 1 worsening. 2 loss, forfeit.

recreation n fun, enjoyment, pleasure, amusement, diversion, distraction, entertainment, hobby, pastime, game, sport, play, leisure, relaxation, refreshment.

recrimination n countercharge, accusation, counter-attack, retaliation, reprisal, retort, quarrel, bickering.

recruit v enlist, draft, conscript, enrol, sign up, engage, take on, mobilize, raise, gather, obtain, procure.
◇ n beginner, novice, initiate,

learner, trainee, apprentice, conscript, convert.

rectify v correct, put right, right, remedy, cure, repair, fix, mend, improve, amend, adjust, reform.

recuperate v recover, get better, improve, pick up, rally, revive, mend, convalesce.
☒ worsen.

recur v repeat, persist, return, reappear.

recurrent adj recurring, chronic, persistent, repeated, repetitive, regular, periodic, frequent, intermittent.

recycle v reuse, reprocess, reclaim, recover, salvage, save.

red adj 1 SCARLET, vermilion, cherry, ruby, crimson, maroon, pink, reddish, bloodshot, inflamed. 2 RUDDY, florid, glowing, rosy, flushed, blushing, embarrassed, shamefaced. 3 red hair: ginger, carroty, auburn, chestnut, Titian.

redden v blush, flush, colour, go red, crimson.

redeem v 1 BUY BACK, repurchase, cash (in), exchange, change, trade, ransom, reclaim, regain, repossess, recoup, recover, recuperate, retrieve, salvage. 2 COMPENSATE FOR, make up for, offset, outweigh, atone for, expiate, absolve, acquit, discharge, release, liberate, emancipate, free, deliver, rescue, save.

reduce v 1 LESSEN, decrease, contract, shrink, slim, shorten, curtail, trim, cut, slash, discount, rebate, lower, moderate, weaken, diminish, impair. 2 DRIVE, force, degrade, downgrade, demote, humble, humiliate, impoverish, subdue, overpower, master, vanquish.
☒ 1 increase, raise, boost.

reduction n decrease, drop, fall, decline, lessening, moderation,

weakening, diminution, contraction, compression, shrinkage, narrowing, shortening, curtailment, restriction, limitation, cutback, cut, discount, rebate, devaluation, depreciation, deduction, subtraction, loss.
☒ increase, rise, enlargement.

redundant adj 1 UNEMPLOYED, out of work, laid off, dismissed. 2 SUPERFLUOUS, surplus, excess, extra, supernumerary, unneeded, unnecessary, unwanted. 3 WORDY, verbose, repetitious, tautological.
☒ 2 necessary, essential. 3 concise.

reel v stagger, totter, wobble, rock, sway, waver, falter, stumble, lurch, pitch, roll, revolve, gyrate, spin, wheel, twirl, whirl, swirl.

refer v 1 SEND, direct, point, guide, pass on, transfer, commit, deliver. 2 refer to a catalogue: consult, look up, turn to, resort to. 3 ALLUDE, mention, touch on, speak of, bring up, recommend, cite, quote. 4 APPLY, concern, relate, belong, pertain.

referee n umpire, judge, adjudicator, arbitrator, mediator, ref (infml).
◇ v umpire, judge, adjudicate, arbitrate.

reference n 1 ALLUSION, remark, mention, citation, quotation, illustration, instance, note. 2 TESTIMONIAL, recommendation, endorsement, character. 3 RELATION, regard, respect, connection, bearing.

refine v process, treat, purify, clarify, filter, distil, polish, hone, improve, perfect, elevate, exalt.

refined adj civilized, cultured, cultivated, polished, sophisticated, urbane, genteel, gentlemanly, ladylike, well-bred, well-mannered, polite, civil, elegant, fine, delicate, subtle, precise, exact, sensitive, discriminating.
☒ coarse, vulgar, rude.

refinement n 1 MODIFICATION,

alteration, amendment, improvement. 2 CULTIVATION, sophistication, urbanity, gentility, breeding, style, elegance, taste, discrimination, subtlety, finesse.
⊠ 1 deterioration. 2 coarseness, vulgarity.

reflect v 1 MIRROR, echo, imitate, reproduce, portray, depict, show, reveal, display, exhibit, manifest, demonstrate, indicate, express, communicate. 2 THINK, ponder, consider, mull over, deliberate, contemplate, meditate, muse.

reflection n 1 IMAGE, likeness, echo, impression, indication, manifestation, observation, view, opinion. 2 THINKING, thought, study, consideration, deliberation, contemplation, meditation, musing.

reform v change, amend, improve, ameliorate, better, rectify, correct, mend, repair, rehabilitate, rebuild, reconstruct, remodel, revamp, renovate, restore, regenerate, reconstitute, reorganize, shake up (infml), revolutionize, purge.
◇ n change, amendment, improvement, rectification, correction, rehabilitation, renovation, reorganization, shake-up (infml), purge.

refrain v stop, cease, quit, leave off, renounce, desist, abstain, forbear, avoid.

refresh v 1 COOL, freshen, enliven, invigorate, fortify, revive, restore, renew, rejuvenate, revitalize, reinvigorate. 2 refresh one's memory: jog, stimulate, prompt, prod.
⊠ 1 tire, exhaust.

refreshing adj cool, thirst-quenching, bracing, invigorating, energizing, stimulating, inspiring, fresh, new, novel, original.

refreshment n sustenance, food, drink, snack, revival, restoration,

renewal, reanimation, reinvigoration, revitalization.

refuge n sanctuary, asylum, shelter, protection, security, retreat, hideout, hideaway, resort, harbour, haven.

refugee n exile, émigré, displaced person, fugitive, runaway, escapee.

refund v repay, reimburse, rebate, return, restore.
◇ n repayment, reimbursement, rebate, return.

refusal n rejection, no, rebuff, repudiation, denial, negation.
⊠ acceptance.

refuse¹ v reject, turn down, decline, spurn, repudiate, rebuff, repel, deny, withhold.
⊠ accept, allow, permit.

refuse² n rubbish, waste, trash, garbage, junk, litter.

refute v disprove, rebut, confute, give the lie to, discredit, counter, negate.

regain v recover, get back, recoup, reclaim, repossess, retake, recapture, retrieve, return to.

regal adj majestic, kingly, queenly, princely, imperial, royal, sovereign, stately, magnificent, noble, lordly.

regard v consider, deem, judge, rate, value, think, believe, suppose, imagine, look upon, view, observe, watch.
◇ n care, concern, consideration, attention, notice, heed, respect, deference, honour, esteem, admiration, affection, love, sympathy.
⊠ disregard, contempt.

regarding prep with regard to, as regards, concerning, with reference to, re, about, as to.

regardless adj disregarding, heedless, unmindful, neglectful, inattentive, unconcerned, indifferent.
⊠ heedful, mindful, attentive.
◇ adv anyway, nevertheless,

nonetheless, despite everything, come what may.

regime n government, rule, administration, management, leadership, command, control, establishment, system.

regimented adj strict, disciplined, controlled, regulated, standardized, ordered, methodical, systematic, organized.
🖢 free, lax, disorganized.

region n land, terrain, territory, country, province, area, district, zone, belt, sector, neighbourhood, range, scope, expanse, domain, realm, sphere, field, division, section, part, place.

Types of geographical region include: basin, belt, coast, continent, country, desert, forest, grassland, heath, hemisphere, interior, jungle, lowlands, marshland, outback, pampas, plain, prairie, savannah, scrubland, seaside, steppe, subcontinent, tract, tropics, tundra, veld, wasteland, wilderness, woodland.

Types of social region include: commuter belt, development area, ghetto, ghost town, inner city, metropolis, new town, reservation, resort, riviera, satellite town, shanty town, suburb, township.

register n roll, roster, list, index, catalogue, directory, log, record, chronicle, annals, archives, file, ledger, schedule, diary, almanac.
◇ v **1** RECORD, note, log, enter, inscribe, mark, list, catalogue, chronicle, enrol, enlist, sign on, check in. **2** SHOW, reveal, betray, display, exhibit, manifest, express, say, read, indicate.

regret v rue, repent, lament, mourn, grieve, deplore.
◇ n remorse, contrition, repentance,

compunction, self-reproach, shame, sorrow, grief, disappointment, bitterness.

regretful adj remorseful, rueful, repentant, contrite, penitent, conscience-stricken, ashamed, sorry, apologetic, sad, sorrowful, disappointed.
🖢 impenitent, unashamed.

regrettable adj unfortunate, unlucky, unhappy, sad, disappointing, upsetting, distressing, lamentable, deplorable, shameful, wrong, ill-advised.
🖢 fortunate, happy.

regular adj **1** ROUTINE, habitual, typical, usual, customary, time-honoured, conventional, orthodox, correct, official, standard, normal, ordinary, common, commonplace, everyday. **2** PERIODIC, rhythmic, steady, constant, fixed, set, unvarying, uniform, even, level, smooth, balanced, symmetrical, orderly, systematic, methodical.
🖢 **1** unusual, unconventional.
2 irregular.

regulate v control, direct, guide, govern, rule, administer, manage, handle, conduct, run, organize, order, arrange, settle, square, monitor, set, adjust, tune, moderate, balance.

regulation n rule, statute, law, ordinance, edict, decree, order, commandment, precept, dictate, requirement, procedure.
◇ adj standard, official, statutory, prescribed, required, orthodox, accepted, customary, usual, normal.

rehearsal n practice, drill, exercise, dry run, run-through, preparation, reading, recital, narration, account, enumeration, list.

rehearse v practise, drill, train, go over, prepare, try out, repeat, recite, recount, relate.

reign n rule, sway, monarchy,

empire, sovereignty, supremacy, power, command, dominion, control, influence.
◇ *v* rule, govern, command, prevail, predominate, influence.

reimburse *v* refund, repay, return, restore, recompense, compensate, indemnify, remunerate.

reinforce *v* strengthen, fortify, toughen, harden, stiffen, steel, brace, support, buttress, shore, prop, stay, supplement, augment, increase, emphasize, stress, underline.
⊠ weaken, undermine.

reinforcements *n* auxiliaries, reserves, back-up, support, help.

reinstate *v* restore, return, replace, recall, reappoint, reinstall, re-establish.

reject *v* refuse, deny, decline, turn down, veto, disallow, condemn, despise, spurn, rebuff, jilt, exclude, repudiate, repel, renounce, eliminate, scrap, discard, jettison, cast off.
⊠ accept, choose, select.
◇ *n* failure, second, discard, cast-off.

rejection *n* refusal, denial, veto, dismissal, rebuff, brush-off, exclusion, repudiation, renunciation, elimination.
⊠ acceptance, choice, selection.

rejoice *v* celebrate, revel, delight, glory, exult, triumph.

rejoicing *n* celebration, revelry, merrymaking, festivity, happiness, gladness, joy, delight, elation, jubilation, exultation, triumph.

relapse *v* worsen, deteriorate, degenerate, weaken, sink, fail, lapse, revert, regress, backslide.
◇ *n* worsening, deterioration, setback, recurrence, weakening, lapse, reversion, regression, backsliding.

relate *v* 1 LINK, connect, join, couple, ally, associate, correlate. 2 REFER, apply, concern, pertain,

appertain. 3 *relate an anecdote*: tell, recount, narrate, report, describe, recite. 4 IDENTIFY, sympathize, empathize, understand, feel for.

related *adj* kindred, akin, affiliated, allied, associated, connected, linked, interrelated, interconnected, accompanying, concomitant, joint, mutual.
⊠ unrelated, unconnected.

relation *n* 1 LINK, connection, bond, relationship, correlation, comparison, similarity, affiliation, interrelation, interconnection, interdependence, regard, reference. 2 RELATIVE, family, kin, kindred.

relations *n* 1 RELATIVES, family, kin, kindred. 2 RELATIONSHIP, terms, rapport, liaison, intercourse, affairs, dealings, interaction, communications, contact, associations, connections.

relationship *n* bond, link, connection, association, liaison, rapport, affinity, closeness, similarity, parallel, correlation, ratio, proportion.

relative *adj* comparative, proportional, proportionate, commensurate, corresponding, respective, appropriate, relevant, applicable, related, connected, interrelated, reciprocal, dependent.
◇ *n* relation, family, kin.

relax *v* slacken, loosen, lessen, reduce, diminish, weaken, lower, soften, moderate, abate, remit, relieve, ease, rest, unwind, veg out (*infml*), chill out (*infml*), calm, tranquillize, sedate.
⊠ tighten, intensify.

relaxation *n* 1 REST, repose, refreshment, leisure, recreation, fun, amusement, entertainment, enjoyment, pleasure. 2 SLACKENING, lessening, reduction, moderation, abatement, let-up (*infml*), détente, easing.

⊞ **2** tension, intensification.

relaxed adj informal, casual, laid-back (infml), easy-going (infml), carefree, happy-go-lucky, cool, calm, composed, collected, unhurried, leisurely.
⊞ tense, nervous, formal.

relay n **1** BROADCAST, transmission, programme, communication, message, dispatch. **2** work in relays: shift, turn.
◇ v broadcast, transmit, pass on, communicate, send, spread, carry, supply.

release v **1** LOOSE, unloose, unleash, unfasten, extricate, free, liberate, deliver, emancipate, acquit, absolve, exonerate, excuse, exempt, discharge. **2** ISSUE, publish, circulate, distribute, present, launch, unveil.
⊞ **1** imprison, detain, check.
◇ n **1** FREEDOM, liberty, liberation, deliverance, emancipation, acquittal, absolution, exoneration, exemption, discharge. **2** ISSUE, publication, announcement, proclamation.
⊞ **1** imprisonment, detention.

relent v give in, give way, yield, capitulate, unbend, relax, slacken, soften, weaken.

relentless adj unrelenting, unremitting, incessant, persistent, unflagging, ruthless, remorseless, implacable, merciless, pitiless, unforgiving, cruel, harsh, fierce, grim, hard, punishing, uncompromising, inflexible, unyielding, inexorable.
⊞ merciful, yielding.

relevant adj pertinent, material, significant, germane, related, applicable, apposite, apt, appropriate, suitable, fitting, proper, admissible.
⊞ irrelevant, inapplicable, inappropriate, unsuitable.

reliable adj unfailing, certain, sure, dependable, responsible, trusty, trustworthy, honest, true, faithful,

constant, staunch, solid, safe, sound, stable, predictable, regular.
⊞ unreliable, doubtful, untrustworthy.

reliance n dependence, trust, faith, belief, credit, confidence, assurance.

relic n memento, souvenir, keepsake, token, survival, remains, remnant, scrap, fragment, vestige, trace.

relief n reassurance, consolation, comfort, ease, alleviation, cure, remedy, release, deliverance, help, aid, assistance, support, sustenance, refreshment, diversion, relaxation, rest, respite, break, breather (infml), remission, let-up (infml), abatement.

relieve v reassure, console, comfort, ease, soothe, alleviate, mitigate, cure, release, deliver, free, unburden, lighten, soften, slacken, relax, calm, help, aid, assist, support, sustain.
⊞ aggravate, intensify.

religion

Religions include: Christianity, Church of England (C of E), Church of Scotland, Baptists, Catholicism, Methodism, Protestantism, Presbyterianism, Anglicanism, Congregationalism, Calvinism, evangelicalism, Free Church, Jehovah's Witnesses, Mormonism, Quakerism, Amish; Baha'ism, Buddhism, Confucianism, Hinduism, Islam, Jainism, Judaism, Shintoism, Sikhism, Taoism, Zen, Zoroastrianism, voodoo, druidism, paganism.

Religious festivals include:
Buddhist: Buddha Purnima;
Christian: Christmas, Easter, Whitsuntide (or Pentecost), Ascension; *Hindu*: Diwali, Dusserah, Holi, Onam; *Islamic*: Id al-Adha, Id al-Fitr, Mawlid; *Jewish*: Hanukkah, Passover, Purim, Rosh Hashanah, Shavuot, Yom Kippur;

Pagan: Samhain, Yule (or Winter Solstice), Imbolc (or Candlemas), Ostara (or Spring Equinox), Beltane (or May Day), Litha (or Summer Solstice), Lughnasadh (or Lammas), Mabon (or Autumn Equinox).

Sacred writings include: Bible, Old Testament, New Testament, Torah, Talmud, Koran, Bhagavad Gita, Mahabharata, Ramayana, Vedas, Adi Granth, Zend-Avesta.

religious *adj* 1 SACRED, holy, divine, spiritual, devotional, scriptural, theological, doctrinal. 2 *a religious person*: devout, godly, pious, God-fearing, church-going, reverent, righteous.
☒ 1 secular. 2 irreligious, ungodly.

relinquish *v* let go, release, hand over, surrender, yield, cede, give up, resign, renounce, repudiate, waive, forgo, abandon, desert, forsake, drop, discard.
☒ keep, retain.

relish *v* like, enjoy, savour, appreciate, revel in.
◇ *n* 1 SEASONING, condiment, sauce, pickle, spice, piquancy, tang.
2 ENJOYMENT, pleasure, delight, gusto, zest.

reluctant *adj* unwilling, disinclined, indisposed, hesitant, slow, backward, loth, averse, unenthusiastic, grudging.
☒ willing, ready, eager.

rely *v* depend, lean, count, bank, reckon, trust, swear by.

remain *v* stay, rest, stand, dwell, abide, last, endure, survive, prevail, persist, continue, linger, wait.
☒ go, leave, depart.

remainder *n* rest, balance, surplus, excess, remnant, remains.

remaining *adj* left, unused, unspent, unfinished, residual, outstanding, surviving, persisting, lingering, lasting, abiding.

remains *n* rest, remainder, residue, dregs, leavings, leftovers, scraps, crumbs, fragments, remnants, oddments, traces, vestiges, relics, body, corpse, carcase, ashes, debris.

remark *v* comment, observe, note, mention, say, state, declare.
◇ *n* comment, observation, opinion, reflection, mention, utterance, statement, assertion, declaration.

remarkable *adj* striking, impressive, noteworthy, surprising, amazing, strange, odd, unusual, uncommon, extraordinary, phenomenal, exceptional, outstanding, notable, conspicuous, prominent, distinguished.
☒ average, ordinary, commonplace, usual.

remedy *n* cure, antidote, countermeasure, corrective, restorative, medicine, treatment, therapy, relief, solution, answer, panacea.
◇ *v* correct, rectify, put right, redress, counteract, cure, heal, restore, treat, help, relieve, soothe, ease, mitigate, mend, repair, fix, solve.

remember *v* 1 RECALL, recollect, summon up, think back, reminisce, recognize, place. 2 MEMORIZE, learn, retain.
☒ 1 forget.

remind *v* prompt, nudge, hint, jog one's memory, refresh one's memory, bring to mind, call to mind, call up.

reminder *n* prompt, nudge, hint, suggestion, memorandum, memo, souvenir, memento.

reminiscence *n* memory, remembrance, memoir, anecdote, recollection, recall, retrospection, review, reflection.

reminiscent *adj* suggestive, evocative, nostalgic.

remit *v* send, transmit, dispatch,

post, mail, forward, pay, settle.
◇ *n* brief, orders, instructions, guidelines, terms of reference, scope, authorization, responsibility.

remittance *n* sending, dispatch, payment, fee, allowance, consideration.

remnant *n* scrap, piece, bit, fragment, end, offcut, leftover, remainder, balance, residue, shred, trace, vestige.

remorse *n* regret, compunction, ruefulness, repentance, penitence, contrition, self-reproach, shame, guilt, bad conscience, sorrow, grief.

remote *adj* **1** DISTANT, far, faraway, far-off, outlying, out-of-the-way, inaccessible, god-forsaken, isolated, secluded, lonely. **2** DETACHED, aloof, standoffish, uninvolved, reserved, withdrawn. **3** *a remote possibility*: slight, small, slim, slender, faint, negligible, unlikely, improbable.
⊞ **1** close, nearby, accessible.
2 friendly.

remove *v* detach, pull off, amputate, cut off, extract, pull out, withdraw, take away, take off, strip, shed, doff, expunge, efface, erase, delete, strike out, get rid of, abolish, purge, eliminate, dismiss, discharge, eject, throw out, oust, depose, displace, dislodge, shift, move, transport, transfer, relocate.

remuneration *n* pay, wages, salary, emolument, stipend, fee, retainer, earnings, income, profit, reward, recompense, payment, remittance, repayment, reimbursement, compensation, indemnity.

render *v* **1** *they rendered it harmless*: make, cause to be, leave. **2** GIVE, provide, supply, tender, present, submit, hand over, deliver. **3** TRANSLATE, transcribe, interpret, explain, clarify, represent, perform, play, sing.

renew *v* **1** RENOVATE, modernize,

refurbish, refit, recondition, mend, repair, overhaul, remodel, reform, transform, recreate, reconstitute, re-establish, regenerate, revive, resuscitate, refresh, rejuvenate, reinvigorate, revitalize, restore, replace, replenish, restock. **2** REPEAT, restate, reaffirm, extend, prolong, continue, recommence, restart, resume.

renounce *v* abandon, forsake, give up, resign, relinquish, surrender, discard, reject, spurn, disown, repudiate, disclaim, deny, recant, abjure.

renovate *v* restore, renew, recondition, repair, overhaul, modernize, refurbish, refit, redecorate, do up, remodel, reform, revamp, improve.

renown *n* fame, celebrity, glory, stardom, acclaim, eminence, illustriousness, distinction, note, mark, esteem, reputation, honour.
⊞ obscurity, anonymity.

renowned *adj* famous, well-known, celebrated, acclaimed, famed, noted, eminent, distinguished, illustrious, notable.
⊞ unknown, obscure.

rent *n* rental, lease, hire, payment, fee.
◇ *v* let, sublet, lease, hire, charter.

repair *v* mend, fix, patch up, overhaul, service, rectify, redress, restore, renovate, renew.
◇ *n* mend, patch, darn, overhaul, service, maintenance, restoration, adjustment, improvement.

repartee *n* banter, badinage, jesting, wit, riposte, retort.

repay *v* refund, reimburse, compensate, recompense, reward, remunerate, pay, settle, square, get even with, retaliate, reciprocate, revenge, avenge.

repeal *v* revoke, rescind, abrogate, quash, annul, nullify, void, invalidate,

cancel, countermand, reverse, abolish.
⊞ enact.

repeat v restate, reiterate, recapitulate, echo, quote, recite, relate, retell, reproduce, duplicate, renew, rebroadcast, reshow, replay, rerun, redo.
◇ n repetition, echo, reproduction, duplicate, rebroadcast, reshowing, replay, rerun.

repeatedly adv time after time, time and (time) again, again and again, over and over, frequently, often.

repel v 1 DRIVE BACK, repulse, check, hold off, ward off, parry, resist, oppose, fight, refuse, decline, reject, rebuff. 2 DISGUST, revolt, nauseate, sicken, offend.
⊞ 1 attract. 2 delight.

repent v regret, rue, sorrow, lament, deplore, atone.

repentance n penitence, contrition, remorse, compunction, regret, sorrow, grief, guilt, shame.

repentant adj penitent, contrite, sorry, apologetic, remorseful, regretful, rueful, chastened, ashamed.
⊞ unrepentant.

repercussion n result, backlash, consequence, reverberation, echo, rebound, recoil.

repetition n restatement, reiteration, recapitulation, echo, return, reappearance, recurrence, duplication, tautology.

repetitive adj recurrent, monotonous, tedious, boring, dull, mechanical, unchanging, unvaried.

replace v 1 replace the lid: put back, return, restore, make good, reinstate, re-establish. 2 SUPERSEDE, succeed, follow, supplant, oust, deputize, substitute.

replacement n substitute, stand-

in, understudy, fill-in, supply, proxy, surrogate, successor.

replenish v refill, restock, reload, recharge, replace, restore, renew, supply, provide, furnish, stock, fill, top up.

replica n model, imitation, reproduction, facsimile, copy, duplicate, clone.

reply v answer, respond, retort, rejoin, react, acknowledge, return, echo, reciprocate, counter, retaliate.
◇ n answer, response, retort, rejoinder, riposte, repartee, reaction, comeback, acknowledgement, return, echo, retaliation.

report n article, piece, write-up, record, account, relation, narrative, description, story, tale, gossip, hearsay, rumour, talk, statement, communiqué, declaration, announcement, communication, information, news, word, message, note.
◇ v state, announce, declare, proclaim, air, broadcast, relay, publish, circulate, communicate, notify, tell, recount, relate, narrate, describe, detail, cover, document, record, note.

reporter n journalist, correspondent, columnist, newspaperman, newspaperwoman, hack, newscaster, commentator, announcer.

represent v stand for, symbolize, designate, denote, mean, express, evoke, depict, portray, describe, picture, draw, sketch, illustrate, exemplify, typify, epitomize, embody, personify, appear as, act as, enact, perform, show, exhibit, be, amount to, constitute.

representation n 1 LIKENESS, image, icon, picture, portrait, illustration, sketch, model, statue, bust, depiction, portrayal, description, account, explanation. 2 PERFORMANCE, production, play, show, spectacle.

representative n delegate, deputy, proxy, stand-in, spokesperson, spokesman, spokeswoman, ambassador, commissioner, agent, salesman, saleswoman, rep (*infml*), traveller.
◇ *adj* typical, illustrative, exemplary, archetypal, characteristic, usual, normal, symbolic.
🖃 unrepresentative, atypical.

repress v inhibit, check, control, curb, restrain, suppress, bottle up, hold back, stifle, smother, muffle, silence, quell, crush, quash, subdue, overpower, overcome, master, subjugate, oppress.

repression n inhibition, restraint, suppression, suffocation, gagging, censorship, authoritarianism, despotism, tyranny, oppression, domination, control, constraint, coercion.

repressive *adj* oppressive, authoritarian, despotic, tyrannical, dictatorial, autocratic, totalitarian, absolute, harsh, severe, tough, coercive.

reprieve v pardon, let off, spare, rescue, redeem, relieve, respite.
◇ *n* pardon, amnesty, suspension, abeyance, postponement, deferment, remission, respite, relief, let-up (*infml*), abatement.

reprimand n rebuke, reproof, reproach, admonition, telling-off (*infml*), ticking-off (*infml*), lecture, talking-to (*infml*), dressing-down (*infml*), censure, blame.
◇ v rebuke, reprove, reproach, admonish, scold, chide, tell off (*infml*), tick off (*infml*), lecture, criticize, slate (*infml*), censure, blame.

reprisal n retaliation, counter-attack, retribution, requital, revenge, vengeance.

reproach v rebuke, reprove,
reprimand, upbraid, scold, chide, reprehend, blame, censure, condemn, criticize, disparage, defame.
◇ *n* rebuke, reproof, reprimand, scolding, blame, censure, condemnation, criticism, disapproval, scorn, contempt, shame, disgrace.

reproachful *adj* reproving, upbraiding, scolding, censorious, critical, fault-finding, disapproving, scornful.
🖃 complimentary.

reproduce v 1 COPY, transcribe, print, duplicate, mirror, echo, repeat, imitate, emulate, match, simulate, recreate, reconstruct. 2 BREED, spawn, procreate, generate, propagate, multiply.

reproduction n 1 COPY, print, picture, duplicate, facsimile, replica, clone, imitation. 2 BREEDING, procreation, generation, propagation, multiplication.
🖃 1 original.

reproductive *adj* procreative, generative, sexual, sex, genital.

reproof n rebuke, reproach, reprimand, admonition, upbraiding, dressing-down (*infml*), scolding, telling-off (*infml*), ticking-off (*infml*), censure, condemnation, criticism.
🖃 praise.

reprove v rebuke, reproach, reprimand, upbraid, scold, chide, tell off (*infml*), reprehend, admonish, censure, condemn, criticize.
🖃 praise.

reptile

Reptiles include: adder, puff adder, grass snake, tree snake, asp, viper, rattlesnake, sidewinder, anaconda, boa constrictor, cobra, king cobra, mamba, python; lizard, frilled lizard, chameleon, gecko, iguana, skink, slowworm; turtle, green turtle, hawksbill turtle, terrapin, tortoise, giant tortoise; alligator, crocodile.

---

repugnance n reluctance, distaste, dislike, aversion, hatred, loathing, abhorrence, horror, repulsion, revulsion, disgust.
⊞ liking, pleasure, delight.

repulsive adj repellent, repugnant, revolting, disgusting, nauseating, sickening, offensive, distasteful, objectionable, obnoxious, foul, vile, loathsome, abominable, abhorrent, hateful, horrid, unpleasant, disagreeable, ugly, hideous, forbidding.
⊞ attractive, pleasant, delightful.

reputable adj respectable, reliable, dependable, trustworthy, upright, honourable, creditable, worthy, good, excellent, irreproachable.
⊞ disreputable, infamous.

reputation n honour, character, standing, stature, esteem, opinion, credit, repute, fame, renown, celebrity, distinction, name, good name, bad name, infamy, notoriety.

reputed adj alleged, supposed, said, rumoured, believed, thought, considered, regarded, estimated, reckoned, held, seeming, apparent, ostensible.
⊞ actual, true.

request v ask for, solicit, demand, require, seek, desire, beg, entreat, supplicate, petition, appeal.
◊ n appeal, call, demand, requisition, desire, application, solicitation, suit, petition, entreaty, supplication, prayer.

require v 1 NEED, want, wish, desire, lack, miss. 2 *you are required to attend*: oblige, force, compel, constrain, make, ask, request, instruct, direct, order, demand, necessitate, take, involve.

requirement n need, necessity,

essential, must, requisite, prerequisite, demand, stipulation, condition, term, specification, proviso, qualification, provision.

requisite adj required, needed, necessary, essential, obligatory, compulsory, set, prescribed.

requisition v request, put in for, demand, commandeer, appropriate, take, confiscate, seize, occupy.

rescue v save, recover, salvage, deliver, free, liberate, release, redeem, ransom.
⊞ capture, imprison.
◊ n saving, recovery, salvage, deliverance, liberation, release, redemption, salvation.
⊞ capture.

research n investigation, inquiry, fact-finding, groundwork, examination, analysis, scrutiny, study, search, probe, exploration, experimentation.
◊ v investigate, examine, analyse, scrutinize, study, search, probe, explore, experiment.

resemblance n likeness, similarity, sameness, parity, conformity, closeness, affinity, parallel, comparison, analogy, correspondence, image, facsimile.
⊞ dissimilarity.

resemble v be like, look like, take after, favour, mirror, echo, duplicate, parallel, approach.
⊞ differ from.

resent v grudge, begrudge, envy, take offence at, take umbrage at, take amiss, object to, grumble at, take exception to, dislike.
⊞ accept, like.

resentful adj grudging, envious, jealous, bitter, embittered, hurt, wounded, offended, aggrieved, put out, miffed (*infml*), peeved (*infml*), indignant, angry, vindictive.
⊞ satisfied, contented.

resentment n grudge, envy,

jealousy, bitterness, spite, malice, ill-will, ill feeling, animosity, hurt, umbrage, pique, displeasure, irritation, indignation, vexation, anger, vindictiveness.
⊠ contentment, happiness.

reservation n 1 DOUBT, scepticism, misgiving, qualm, scruple, hesitation, second thought. 2 PROVISO, stipulation, qualification. 3 RESERVE, preserve, park, sanctuary, homeland, enclave. 4 BOOKING, engagement, appointment.

reserve v 1 SET APART, earmark, keep, retain, hold back, save, store, stockpile. 2 reserve a seat: book, engage, order, secure.
⊠ 1 use up.
◇ n 1 STORE, stock, supply, fund, stockpile, cache, hoard, savings. 2 SHYNESS, reticence, secretiveness, coolness, aloofness, modesty, restraint. 3 RESERVATION, preserve, park, sanctuary. 4 REPLACEMENT, substitute, stand-in.
⊠ 2 friendliness, openness.

reserved adj 1 BOOKED, engaged, taken, spoken for, set aside, earmarked, meant, intended, designated, destined, saved, held, kept, retained. 2 SHY, retiring, reticent, unforthcoming, uncommunicative, secretive, silent, taciturn, unsociable, cool, aloof, standoffish, unapproachable, modest, restrained, cautious.
⊠ 1 unreserved, free, available. 2 friendly, open.

reservoir n 1 LAKE, pond, pool, loch. 2 TANK, cistern, vat, basin, container, receptacle. 3 STORE, stockpile, stock, supply, source, reserves, accumulation, fund, holder, bank, repository (fml), reservatory (fml).

reside v live, inhabit, dwell, lodge, stay, sojourn, settle, remain.

residence n dwelling, habitation, domicile, abode, seat, place,
home, house, lodgings, quarters, hall, manor, mansion, palace, villa, country house, country seat.

resident n inhabitant, citizen, local, householder, occupier, tenant, lodger, guest.
⊠ non-resident.

residual adj remaining, leftover, unused, unconsumed, net.

resign v stand down, leave, quit, abdicate, vacate, renounce, relinquish, forgo, waive, surrender, yield, abandon, forsake.
⊠ join.
• **resign oneself** reconcile oneself, accept, bow, submit, yield, comply, acquiesce.
⊠ resist.

resignation n 1 STANDING-DOWN, abdication, retirement, departure, notice, renunciation, relinquishment, surrender. 2 ACCEPTANCE, acquiescence, submission, non-resistance, passivity, patience, stoicism, defeatism.
⊠ 2 resistance.

resigned adj reconciled, philosophical, stoical, patient, unprotesting, unresisting, submissive, defeatist.
⊠ resistant.

resilient adj 1 resilient material: flexible, pliable, supple, plastic, elastic, springy, bouncy. 2 STRONG, tough, hardy, adaptable, buoyant.
⊠ 1 rigid, brittle.

resist v oppose, defy, confront, fight, combat, weather, withstand, repel, counteract, check, avoid, refuse.
⊠ submit, accept.

resistant adj 1 OPPOSED, antagonistic, defiant, unyielding, intransigent, unwilling. 2 PROOF, impervious, immune, invulnerable, tough, strong.
⊠ 1 compliant, yielding.

resolute adj determined, resolved, set, fixed, unwavering, staunch, firm,

steadfast, relentless, single-minded, persevering, dogged, tenacious, stubborn, obstinate, strong-willed, undaunted, unflinching, bold.
⊜ irresolute, weak-willed, half-hearted.

resolution n **1** DETERMINATION, resolve, willpower, commitment, dedication, devotion, firmness, steadfastness, persistence, tenacity, perseverance, doggedness, zeal, courage, boldness. **2** DECISION, judgement, finding, declaration, proposition, motion.
⊜ **1** half-heartedness, uncertainty, indecision.

resolve v decide, make up one's mind, determine, fix, settle, conclude, sort out, work out, solve.

resort v go, visit, frequent, patronize, haunt.
◇ n recourse, refuge, course (of action), alternative, option, chance, possibility.
• **resort to** turn to, use, utilize, employ, exercise.

resound v resonate, reverberate, echo, re-echo, ring, boom, thunder.

resounding adj **1** RESONANT, reverberating, echoing, ringing, sonorous, booming, thunderous, full, rich, vibrant. **2** a resounding victory: decisive, conclusive, crushing, thorough.
⊜ **1** faint.

resource n **1** SUPPLY, reserve, stockpile, source, expedient, contrivance, device. **2** RESOURCEFULNESS, initiative, ingenuity, inventiveness, talent, ability, capability.

resourceful adj ingenious, imaginative, creative, inventive, innovative, original, clever, bright, sharp, quick-witted, able, capable, talented.

resources n materials, supplies, reserves, holdings, funds, money, wealth, riches, capital, assets, property, means.

respect n **1** ADMIRATION, esteem, appreciation, recognition, honour, deference, reverence, veneration, politeness, courtesy. **2** in every respect: point, aspect, facet, feature, characteristic, particular, detail, sense, way, regard, reference, relation, connection.
⊜ **1** disrespect.
◇ v **1** ADMIRE, esteem, regard, appreciate, value. **2** OBEY, observe, heed, follow, honour, fulfil.
⊜ **1** despise, scorn. **2** ignore, disobey.

respectable adj **1** HONOURABLE, worthy, respected, dignified, upright, honest, decent, clean-living. **2** ACCEPTABLE, tolerable, passable, adequate, fair, reasonable, appreciable, considerable.
⊜ **1** dishonourable, disreputable. **2** inadequate, paltry.

respectful adj deferential, reverential, humble, polite, well-mannered, courteous, civil.
⊜ disrespectful.

respective adj corresponding, relevant, various, several, separate, individual, personal, own, particular, special.

respond v answer, reply, retort, acknowledge, react, return, reciprocate.

response n answer, reply, retort, comeback, acknowledgement, reaction, feedback.
⊜ query.

responsibility n fault, blame, guilt, culpability, answerability, accountability, duty, obligation, burden, onus, charge, care, trust, authority, power.

responsible adj **1** GUILTY, culpable, at fault, to blame, liable, answerable, accountable. **2** a responsible citizen: dependable, reliable, conscientious,

trustworthy, honest, sound, steady, sober, mature, sensible, rational. **3** IMPORTANT, authoritative, executive, decision-making.
⊟ **2** irresponsible, unreliable, untrustworthy.

rest[1] *n* **1** LEISURE, relaxation, repose, lie-down, sleep, snooze, nap, siesta, idleness, inactivity, motionlessness, standstill, stillness, tranquillity, calm. **2** BREAK, pause, breathing-space, breather (*infml*), intermission, interlude, interval, recess, holiday, vacation, halt, cessation, lull, respite. **3** SUPPORT, prop, stand, base.
⊟ **1** action, activity. **2** work.
◇ *v* **1** PAUSE, halt, stop, cease. **2** RELAX, repose, sit, recline, lounge, laze, lie down, sleep, snooze, doze. **3** DEPEND, rely, hinge, hang, lie. **4** LEAN, prop, support, stand.
⊟ **1** continue. **2** work.

rest[2] *n* remainder, others, balance, surplus, excess, residue, remains, leftovers, remnants.

restaurant *n* eating-house, bistro, steakhouse, grill room, dining room, snack bar, buffet, cafeteria, café, diner.

restful *adj* relaxing, soothing, calm, tranquil, serene, peaceful, quiet, undisturbed, relaxed, comfortable, leisurely, unhurried.
⊟ tiring, restless.

restless *adj* fidgety, unsettled, disturbed, troubled, agitated, nervous, anxious, worried, uneasy, fretful, edgy, jumpy, restive, unruly, turbulent, sleepless.
⊟ calm, relaxed, comfortable.

restore *v* **1** REPLACE, return, reinstate, rehabilitate, re-establish, reintroduce, re-enforce. **2** *restore a building*: renovate, renew, rebuild, reconstruct, refurbish, retouch, recondition, repair, mend, fix. **3** REVIVE, refresh, rejuvenate, revitalize, strengthen.
⊟ **1** remove. **2** damage. **3** weaken.

restrain *v* **1** HOLD BACK, keep back, suppress, subdue, repress, inhibit, check, curb, bridle, stop, arrest, prevent, restrict, regulate, control, govern. **2** BIND, tie, chain, fetter, manacle.
⊟ **1** encourage. **2** liberate.

restrained *adj* moderate, temperate, mild, subdued, muted, quiet, soft, low-key, unobtrusive, discreet, tasteful, calm, controlled, steady, self-controlled.
⊟ unrestrained.

restraint *n* **1** MODERATION, inhibition, self-control, self-discipline, hold, grip, check, curb, rein, bridle, suppression, restriction, control, constraint, limitation, tie, hindrance, prevention. **2** CONFINEMENT, bonds, chains, fetters.
⊟ **2** liberty.

restrict *v* limit, bound, demarcate, control, regulate, confine, contain, cramp, constrain, impede, hinder, hamper, handicap, tie, restrain, curtail.
⊟ broaden, free.

restriction *n* limit, bound, confine, limitation, constraint, handicap, check, curb, restraint, ban, embargo, control, regulation, rule, stipulation, condition, proviso.
⊟ freedom.

result *n* effect, consequence, sequel, repercussion, reaction, outcome, upshot, issue, end-product, fruit, score, answer, verdict, judgement, decision, conclusion.
⊟ cause.
◇ *v* follow, ensue, happen, occur, issue, emerge, arise, spring, derive, stem, flow, proceed, develop, end, finish, terminate, culminate.
⊟ cause.

resume *v* restart, recommence, reopen, reconvene, continue, carry on, go on, proceed.
⊟ cease.

resumption n restart, recommencement, reopening, renewal, resurgence, continuation.
⊜ cessation.

resurrect v restore, revive, resuscitate, reactivate, bring back, reintroduce, renew.
⊜ kill, bury.

resurrection n restoration, revival, resuscitation, renaissance, rebirth, renewal, resurgence, reappearance, return, comeback.

resuscitate v revive, resurrect, save, rescue, reanimate, quicken, reinvigorate, revitalize, restore, renew.

retain v 1 KEEP, hold, reserve, hold back, save, preserve. 2 *retain information*: remember, memorize. 3 EMPLOY, engage, hire, commission.
⊜ 1 release. 2 forget. 3 dismiss.

retaliate v reciprocate, counter-attack, hit back, strike back, fight back, get one's own back, get even with, take revenge.

retaliation n reprisal, counter-attack, revenge, vengeance, retribution.

reticent adj reserved, shy, uncommunicative, unforthcoming, tight-lipped, secretive, taciturn, silent, quiet.
⊜ communicative, forward, frank.

retire v leave, depart, withdraw, retreat, recede.
⊜ join, enter, advance.

retirement n withdrawal, retreat, solitude, loneliness, seclusion, privacy, obscurity.

retiring adj shy, bashful, timid, shrinking, quiet, reticent, reserved, self-effacing, unassertive, modest, unassuming, humble.
⊜ bold, forward, assertive.

retort v answer, reply, respond, rejoin, return, counter, retaliate.
◊ n answer, reply, response,

rejoinder, riposte, repartee, quip.

retract v take back, withdraw, recant, reverse, revoke, rescind, cancel, repeal, repudiate, disown, disclaim, deny.
⊜ assert, maintain.

retreat v draw back, recoil, shrink, turn tail (*infml*), withdraw, retire, leave, depart, quit.
⊜ advance.
◊ n 1 WITHDRAWAL, departure, evacuation, flight. 2 SECLUSION, privacy, hideaway, den, refuge, asylum, sanctuary, shelter, haven.
⊜ 1 advance, charge.

retrieve v fetch, bring back, regain, get back, recapture, repossess, recoup, recover, salvage, save, rescue, redeem, restore, return.
⊜ lose.

retrograde adj retrogressive, backward, reverse, negative, downward, declining, deteriorating.
⊜ progressive.

retrospect n hindsight, reflection, afterthought, re-examination, review, recollection, remembrance.
⊜ prospect.

return v 1 COME BACK, reappear, recur, go back, backtrack, regress, revert. 2 GIVE BACK, hand back, send back, deliver, put back, replace, restore. 3 *return a favour*: reciprocate, requite, repay, refund, reimburse, recompense.
⊜ 1 leave, depart. 2 take.
◊ n 1 REAPPEARANCE, recurrence, comeback, home-coming.
2 REPAYMENT, recompense, replacement, restoration, reinstatement, reciprocation.
3 REVENUE, income, proceeds, takings, yield, gain, profit, reward, advantage, benefit.
⊜ 1 departure, disappearance.
2 removal. 3 payment, expense, loss.

reveal v expose, uncover, unveil, unmask, show, display, exhibit,

manifest, disclose, divulge.
⊞ hide, conceal, mask.

revelation n 1 UNCOVERING,
unveiling, exposure, unmasking,
show, display, exhibition,
manifestation, disclosure.
2 CONFESSION, admission, giveaway,
leak.

revel in v enjoy, relish, savour,
delight in, thrive on, bask in, glory
in, lap up, indulge in, wallow in,
luxuriate in.

revelry n celebration, festivity, party,
merrymaking, jollity, fun, carousal,
debauchery.
⊞ sobriety.

revenge n vengeance, satisfaction,
reprisal, retaliation, requital,
retribution.
◇ v avenge, repay, retaliate, get one's
own back.

revenue n income, return, yield,
interest, profit, gain, proceeds,
receipts, takings.
⊞ expenditure.

reverberate v echo, re-echo,
resound, resonate, ring, boom,
vibrate.

revere v respect, esteem, honour,
pay homage to, venerate, worship,
adore, exalt.
⊞ despise, scorn.

reverence n respect, deference,
honour, homage, admiration, awe,
veneration, worship, adoration,
devotion.
⊞ contempt, scorn.

reverent adj reverential, respectful,
deferential, humble, dutiful, awed,
solemn, pious, devout, adoring,
loving.
⊞ irreverent, disrespectful.

reversal n negation, cancellation,
annulment, nullification, revocation,
countermanding, rescinding, repeal,
reverse, turnabout, turnaround, U-
turn, volte-face, upset.

⊞ advancement, progress.

reverse v 1 BACK, retreat, backtrack,
undo, negate, cancel, annul,
invalidate, countermand, overrule,
revoke, rescind, repeal, retract,
quash, overthrow. 2 TRANSPOSE, turn
round, invert, up-end, overturn,
upset, change, alter.
⊞ 1 advance, enforce.
◇ n 1 UNDERSIDE, back, rear, inverse,
converse, contrary, opposite,
antithesis. 2 MISFORTUNE, mishap,
misadventure, adversity, affliction,
hardship, trial, blow, disappointment,
setback, check, delay, problem,
difficulty, failure, defeat.
◇ adj opposite, contrary, converse,
inverse, inverted, backward, back,
rear.

revert v return, go back, resume,
lapse, relapse, regress.

review v 1 CRITICIZE, assess, evaluate,
judge, weigh, discuss, examine,
inspect, scrutinize, study, survey,
recapitulate. 2 review the situation:
reassess, re-evaluate, re-examine,
reconsider, rethink, revise.
◇ n 1 CRITICISM, critique, assessment,
evaluation, judgement, report,
commentary, examination, scrutiny,
analysis, study, survey, recapitulation,
reassessment, re-evaluation, re-
examination, revision. 2 MAGAZINE,
periodical, journal.

revise v 1 revise one's opinion:
change, alter, modify, amend,
correct, update, edit, rewrite,
reword, recast, revamp, reconsider,
re-examine, review. 2 STUDY, learn,
swot up (infml), cram (infml).

revival n resuscitation, revitalization,
restoration, renewal, renaissance,
rebirth, reawakening, resurgence,
upsurge.

revive v resuscitate, reanimate,
revitalize, restore, renew, refresh,
animate, invigorate, quicken, rouse,
awaken, recover, rally, reawaken,
rekindle, reactivate.

☞ weary.

revoke v repeal, rescind, quash, abrogate, annul, nullify, invalidate, negate, cancel, countermand, reverse, retract, withdraw.
☞ enforce.

revolt n revolution, rebellion, mutiny, rising, uprising, insurrection, putsch, coup (d'état), secession, defection.
◇ v 1 REBEL, mutiny, rise, riot, resist, dissent, defect. 2 DISGUST, sicken, nauseate, repel, offend, shock, outrage, scandalize.
☞ 1 submit. 2 please, delight.

revolting adj disgusting, sickening, nauseating, repulsive, repellent, obnoxious, nasty, horrible, foul, loathsome, abhorrent, distasteful, offensive, shocking, appalling.
☞ pleasant, delightful, attractive, palatable.

revolution n 1 REVOLT, rebellion, mutiny, rising, uprising, insurrection, putsch, coup (d'état), reformation, change, transformation, innovation, upheaval, cataclysm. 2 ROTATION, turn, spin, cycle, circuit, round, circle, orbit, gyration.

revolutionary n rebel, mutineer, insurgent, anarchist, revolutionist.
◇ adj 1 REBEL, rebellious, mutinous, insurgent, subversive, seditious, anarchistic. 2 revolutionary ideas: new, innovative, avant-garde, cutting-edge, different, drastic, radical, thoroughgoing.
☞ 1 conservative.

revolve v rotate, turn, pivot, swivel, spin, wheel, whirl, gyrate, circle, orbit.

revulsion n repugnance, disgust, distaste, dislike, aversion, hatred, loathing, abhorrence, abomination.
☞ delight, pleasure, approval.

reward n prize, honour, medal, decoration, bounty, pay-off, bonus, premium, payment, remuneration,

recompense, repayment, requital, compensation, gain, profit, return, benefit, merit, desert, retribution.
☞ punishment.
◇ v pay, remunerate, recompense, repay, requite, compensate, honour, decorate.
☞ punish.

rewarding adj profitable, remunerative, lucrative, productive, fruitful, worthwhile, valuable, advantageous, beneficial, satisfying, gratifying, pleasing, fulfilling, enriching.
☞ unrewarding.

rhetoric n eloquence, oratory, grandiloquence, magniloquence, bombast, pomposity, hyperbole, verbosity, wordiness.

rhetorical adj oratorical, grandiloquent, magniloquent, bombastic, declamatory, pompous, high-sounding, grand, high-flown, flowery, florid, flamboyant, showy, pretentious, artificial, insincere.
☞ simple.

rhyme n poetry, verse, poem, ode, limerick, jingle, song, ditty.

rhythm n beat, pulse, time, tempo, metre, measure, movement, flow, lilt, swing, accent, cadence, pattern.

rhythmic adj rhythmical, metric, metrical, pulsating, throbbing, flowing, lilting, periodic, regular, steady.

rich adj 1 WEALTHY, affluent, moneyed, prosperous, well-to-do, well-off, loaded (sl). 2 PLENTIFUL, abundant, copious, profuse, prolific, ample, full. 3 FERTILE, fruitful, productive, lush. 4 rich food: creamy, fatty, full-bodied, heavy, full-flavoured, strong, spicy, savoury, tasty, delicious, luscious, juicy, sweet. 5 rich colours: deep, intense, vivid, bright, vibrant, warm. 6 EXPENSIVE, precious, valuable, lavish, sumptuous, opulent, luxurious,

splendid, gorgeous, fine, elaborate, ornate.
☞ **1** poor, impoverished. **3** barren. **4** plain, bland. **5** dull, soft. **6** plain.

riches n wealth, affluence, money, gold, treasure, fortune, assets, property, substance, resources, means.
☞ poverty.

rickety adj unsteady, wobbly, shaky, unstable, insecure, flimsy, jerry-built, decrepit, ramshackle, broken-down, dilapidated, derelict.
☞ stable, strong.

rid v clear, purge, free, deliver, relieve, unburden.

riddle[1] n enigma, mystery, conundrum, brain-teaser, puzzle, poser, problem.

riddle[2] v **1** PERFORATE, pierce, puncture, pepper, fill, permeate, pervade, infest. **2** SIFT, sieve, strain, filter, mar, winnow.

ride v sit, move, progress, travel, journey, gallop, trot, pedal, drive, steer, control, handle, manage.
◇ n journey, trip, outing, jaunt, spin, drive, lift.

ridicule n satire, irony, sarcasm, mockery, jeering, scorn, derision, taunting, teasing, chaff, banter, badinage, laughter.
☞ praise.
◇ v satirize, send up, caricature, lampoon, burlesque, parody, mock, make fun of, jeer, scoff, deride, sneer, tease, rib (infml), humiliate, taunt.
☞ praise.

ridiculous adj ludicrous, absurd, nonsensical, silly, foolish, stupid, contemptible, derisory, laughable, farcical, comical, funny, hilarious, outrageous, preposterous, incredible, unbelievable.
☞ sensible.

rife adj abundant, rampant, teeming, raging, epidemic, prevalent,

widespread, general, common, frequent.
☞ scarce.

rift n **1** SPLIT, breach, break, fracture, crack, fault, chink, cleft, cranny, crevice, gap, space, opening. **2** DISAGREEMENT, difference, separation, division, schism, alienation.
☞ **2** unity.

rig n equipment, kit, outfit, gear, tackle, apparatus, machinery, fittings, fixtures.
• **rig out** equip, kit out, outfit, fit out, supply, furnish, clothe, dress (up).

right adj **1** the right answer: correct, accurate, exact, precise, true, factual, actual, real. **2** PROPER, fitting, seemly, becoming, appropriate, suitable, fit, admissible, satisfactory, reasonable, desirable, favourable, advantageous. **3** FAIR, just, equitable, lawful, honest, upright, good, virtuous, righteous, moral, ethical, honourable. **4** RIGHT-WING, conservative, Tory.
☞ **1** wrong, incorrect. **2** improper, unsuitable. **3** unfair, wrong. **4** left-wing.
◇ adv **1** CORRECTLY, accurately, exactly, precisely, factually, properly, satisfactorily, well, fairly. **2** right to the bottom: straight, directly, completely, utterly.
☞ **1** wrongly, incorrectly, unfairly.
◇ n **1** PRIVILEGE, prerogative, due, claim, business, authority, power. **2** JUSTICE, legality, good, virtue, righteousness, morality, honour, integrity, uprightness.
☞ **2** wrong.
◇ v rectify, correct, put right, fix, repair, redress, vindicate, avenge, settle, straighten, stand up.
• **right away** straight away, immediately, at once, now, instantly, directly, forthwith, without delay, promptly.
☞ later, eventually.

rightful adj legitimate, lawful, legal,

just, bona fide, true, real, genuine, valid, authorized, correct, proper, suitable, due.
⊠ wrongful, unlawful.

rigid adj stiff, inflexible, unbending, cast-iron, hard, firm, set, fixed, unalterable, invariable, austere, harsh, severe, unrelenting, strict, rigorous, stringent, stern, uncompromising, unyielding.
⊠ flexible, elastic.

rigorous adj strict, stringent, rigid, firm, exact, precise, accurate, meticulous, painstaking, scrupulous, conscientious, thorough.
⊠ lax, superficial.

rile v annoy, irritate, nettle, pique, peeve (infml), put out, upset, irk, vex, anger, exasperate.
⊠ calm, soothe.

rim n lip, edge, brim, brink, verge, margin, border, circumference.
⊠ centre, middle.

rind n peel, skin, husk, crust.

ring¹ n 1 CIRCLE, round, loop, hoop, halo, band, girdle, collar, circuit, arena, enclosure. 2 GROUP, cartel, syndicate, association, organization, gang, crew, mob, band, cell, clique, coterie.
◇ v surround, encircle, gird, circumscribe, encompass, enclose.

ring² v 1 CHIME, peal, toll, tinkle, clink, jingle, clang, sound, resound, resonate, reverberate, buzz.
2 TELEPHONE, phone, call, ring up.
◇ n 1 CHIME, peal, toll, tinkle, clink, jingle, clang. 2 PHONE CALL, call, buzz (infml), tinkle (infml).

rinse v swill, bathe, wash, clean, cleanse, flush, wet, dip.

riot n insurrection, rising, uprising, revolt, rebellion, anarchy, lawlessness, affray, disturbance, turbulence, disorder, confusion, commotion, tumult, turmoil, uproar, row, quarrel, strife.
⊠ order, calm.

◇ v revolt, rebel, rise up, run riot, run wild, rampage.

rip v tear, rend, split, separate, rupture, burst, cut, slit, slash, gash, lacerate, hack.
◇ n tear, rent, split, cleavage, rupture, cut, slit, slash, gash, hole.
• **rip off** (sl) overcharge, swindle, defraud, cheat, diddle, do (infml), fleece, sting (sl), con (infml), trick, dupe, exploit.

ripe adj 1 RIPENED, mature, mellow, seasoned, grown, developed, complete, finished, perfect.
2 READY, suitable, right, favourable, auspicious, propitious, timely, opportune.
⊠ 2 untimely, inopportune.

ripen v develop, mature, mellow, season, age.

rise v 1 GO UP, ascend, climb, mount, slope (up), soar, tower, grow, increase, escalate, intensify. 2 STAND UP, get up, arise, jump up, spring up. 3 ADVANCE, progress, improve, prosper. 4 ORIGINATE, spring, flow, issue, emerge, appear.
⊠ 1 fall, descend. 2 sit down. 3 decline.
◇ n 1 ASCENT, climb, slope, incline, hill, elevation. 2 INCREASE, increment, upsurge, upturn, advance, progress, improvement, advancement, promotion.
⊠ 1 descent, valley. 2 fall.

risk n danger, peril, jeopardy, hazard, chance, possibility, uncertainty, gamble, speculation, venture, adventure.
⊠ safety, certainty.
◇ v endanger, imperil, jeopardize, hazard, chance, gamble, venture, dare.

risky adj dangerous, unsafe, perilous, hazardous, chancy, uncertain, touch-and-go, dicey (infml), tricky, precarious.
⊠ safe.

risqué adj indecent, improper,

indelicate, suggestive, coarse, crude, earthy, bawdy, racy, naughty, blue.
☒ decent, proper.

ritual n custom, tradition, convention, usage, practice, habit, wont, routine, procedure, ordinance, prescription, form, formality, ceremony, ceremonial, solemnity, rite, sacrament, service, liturgy, observance, act.
◇ adj customary, traditional, conventional, habitual, routine, procedural, prescribed, set, formal, ceremonial.
☒ informal.

rival n competitor, contestant, contender, challenger, opponent, adversary, antagonist, match, equal, peer.
☒ colleague, associate.
◇ adj competitive, competing, opposed, opposing, conflicting.
☒ associate.
◇ v compete with, contend with, vie with, oppose, emulate, match, equal.
☒ co-operate.

rivalry n competitiveness, competition, contest, contention, conflict, struggle, strife, opposition, antagonism.
☒ co-operation.

river n waterway, watercourse, tributary, stream, brook, beck, creek, estuary.

road n roadway, motorway, bypass, highway, thoroughfare, street, avenue, boulevard, crescent, drive, lane, track, route, course, way, direction.

roam v wander, rove, range, travel, walk, ramble, stroll, amble, prowl, drift, stray.
☒ stay.

roar v, n bellow, yell, shout, cry, bawl, howl, hoot, guffaw, thunder, crash, blare, rumble.
☒ whisper.

rob v steal from, hold up, raid,

burgle, loot, pillage, plunder, sack, rifle, ransack, swindle, rip off (sl), do (infml), cheat, defraud, deprive.

robbery n theft, stealing, larceny, hold-up, stick-up (sl), heist (sl), raid, burglary, pillage, plunder, fraud, embezzlement, swindle, rip-off (sl).

robot n automaton, machine, android, zombie.

robust adj strong, sturdy, tough, hardy, vigorous, powerful, muscular, athletic, fit, healthy, well.
☒ weak, feeble, unhealthy.

rock¹ n boulder, stone, pebble, crag, outcrop.

Rocks include: basalt, breccia, chalk, coal, conglomerate, flint, gabbro, gneiss, granite, lava, limestone, marble, marl, obsidian, porphyry, pumice stone, sandstone, schist, serpentinite, shale, slate.

rock² v **1** SWAY, swing, tilt, tip, shake, wobble, roll, pitch, toss, lurch, reel, stagger, totter. **2** news that rocked the nation: shock, stun, daze, dumbfound, astound, astonish, surprise, startle.

rocky¹ adj stony, pebbly, craggy, rugged, rough, hard, flinty.
☒ smooth, soft.

rocky² adj unsteady, shaky, wobbly, staggering, tottering, unstable, unreliable, uncertain, weak.
☒ steady, stable, dependable, strong.

rod n bar, shaft, strut, pole, stick, baton, wand, cane, switch, staff, mace, sceptre.

rodent n

Rodents include: agouti, beaver, black rat, brown rat, cane rat, capybara, cavy, chinchilla, chipmunk, cony, coypu, dormouse, fieldmouse, gerbil, gopher, grey squirrel, groundhog, guinea pig, hamster, hare, harvest mouse, jerboa, kangaroo rat, lemming, marmot, mouse, muskrat, musquash, pika, porcupine, prairie dog, rabbit, rat, red squirrel, sewer rat, squirrel, vole, water rat, water vole, woodchuck.

rogue n scoundrel, rascal, scamp, villain, miscreant, crook (*infml*), swindler, fraud, cheat, con man (*infml*), reprobate, wastrel, ne'er-do-well.

role n part, character, representation, portrayal, impersonation, function, capacity, task, duty, job, post, position.

roll v 1 ROTATE, revolve, turn, spin, wheel, twirl, whirl, gyrate, move, run, pass. 2 WIND, coil, furl, twist, curl, wrap, envelop, enfold, bind. 3 *the ship rolled*: rock, sway, swing, pitch, toss, lurch, reel, wallow, undulate. 4 PRESS, flatten, smooth, level. 5 RUMBLE, roar, thunder, boom, resound, reverberate.
◇ n 1 ROLLER, cylinder, drum, reel, spool, bobbin, scroll. 2 REGISTER, roster, census, list, inventory, index, catalogue, directory, schedule, record, chronicle, annals. 3 ROTATION, revolution, cycle, turn, spin, wheel, twirl, whirl, gyration, undulation. 4 RUMBLE, roar, thunder, boom, resonance, reverberation.
• **roll up** (*infml*) arrive, assemble, gather, congregate, convene.
⊞ leave.

romance n 1 LOVE AFFAIR, affair, relationship, liaison, intrigue, passion. 2 LOVE STORY, novel, story, tale, fairy tale, legend, idyll, fiction, fantasy. 3 ADVENTURE, excitement, melodrama, mystery, charm, fascination, glamour, sentiment.
◇ v lie, fantasize, exaggerate, overstate.

romantic adj 1 IMAGINARY, fictitious, fanciful, fantastic, legendary, idyllic, fairytale, utopian, idealistic, quixotic, visionary, starry-eyed, dreamy, unrealistic, impractical, improbable, wild, extravagant, exciting, fascinating. 2 SENTIMENTAL, loving, amorous, passionate, tender, fond, lovey-dovey (*infml*), soppy, mushy, sloppy.
⊞ 1 real, practical. 2 unromantic, unsentimental.
◇ n sentimentalist, dreamer, visionary, idealist, utopian.
⊞ realist.

room n space, volume, capacity, headroom, legroom, elbow-room, scope, range, extent, leeway, latitude, margin, allowance, chance, opportunity.

Types of room include: attic, loft, box room, bedroom, boudoir, spare room, dressing-room, guest-room, nursery, playroom, sitting room, lounge, front room, living room, drawing room, salon, reception room, dining room, study, den (*infml*), library, kitchen, kitchenette, breakfast-room, larder, pantry, scullery, bathroom, en suite bathroom, wet room, toilet, lavatory, rest room (*N Am*), WC, loo (*infml*), cloakroom, utility room, hall, landing, conservatory, sun lounge, cellar, basement; classroom, music room, laboratory, office, sickroom, dormitory, workroom, studio, workshop, storeroom, waiting room, anteroom, foyer.

---

roomy adj spacious, capacious, large, sizable, broad, wide, extensive, ample, generous.
⊞ cramped, small, tiny.

root[1] n 1 TUBER, rhizome, stem. 2 ORIGIN, source, derivation, cause, starting point, fount, fountainhead, seed, germ, nucleus, heart, core,

nub, essence, seat, base, bottom, basis, foundation.
◇ *v* anchor, moor, fasten, fix, set, stick, implant, embed, entrench, establish, ground, base.
• **root out** unearth, dig out, uncover, discover, uproot, eradicate, extirpate, eliminate, exterminate, destroy, abolish, clear away, remove.

root² *v* dig, delve, burrow, forage, hunt, rummage, ferret, poke, pry, nose.

roots *n* beginning(s), origins, family, heritage, background, birthplace, home.

rope *n* line, cable, cord, string, strand.
◇ *v* tie, bind, lash, fasten, hitch, moor, tether.
• **rope in** enlist, engage, involve, persuade, inveigle.

roster *n* rota, schedule, register, roll, list.

rostrum *n* platform, stage, dais, podium.

rot *v* decay, decompose, putrefy, fester, perish, corrode, spoil, go bad, go off, degenerate, deteriorate, crumble, disintegrate, taint, corrupt.
◇ *n* **1** DECAY, decomposition, putrefaction, corrosion, rust, mould. **2** (*infml*) NONSENSE, rubbish, poppycock (*infml*), drivel, claptrap.

rotary *adj* rotating, revolving, turning, spinning, whirling, gyrating.
☒ fixed.

rotate *v* revolve, turn, spin, gyrate, pivot, swivel, roll.

rotation *n* revolution, turn, spin, gyration, orbit, cycle, sequence, succession, turning, spinning.

rotten *adj* **1** DECAYED, decomposed, putrid, addled, bad, off, mouldy, fetid, stinking, rank, foul, rotting, decaying, disintegrating. **2** INFERIOR, bad, poor, inadequate, low-grade, lousy, crummy (*sl*), ropy (*sl*), mean,

nasty, beastly, dirty, despicable, contemptible, dishonourable, wicked. **3** (*infml*) ILL, sick, unwell, poorly, grotty (*sl*), rough (*infml*).
☒ **1** fresh. **2** good. **3** well.

rough *adj* **1** UNEVEN, bumpy, lumpy, rugged, craggy, jagged, irregular, coarse, bristly, scratchy. **2** HARSH, severe, tough, hard, cruel, brutal, drastic, extreme, brusque, curt, sharp. **3** APPROXIMATE, estimated, imprecise, inexact, vague, general, cursory, hasty, incomplete, unfinished, crude, rudimentary. **4** *rough sea*: choppy, agitated, turbulent, stormy, tempestuous, violent, wild. **5** (*infml*) ILL, sick, unwell, poorly, off-colour, rotten (*infml*).
☒ **1** smooth. **2** mild. **3** accurate. **4** calm. **5** well.

round *adj* **1** SPHERICAL, globular, ball-shaped, circular, ring-shaped, disc-shaped, cylindrical, rounded, curved. **2** ROTUND, plump, stout, portly.
◇ *n* **1** CIRCLE, ring, band, disc, sphere, ball, orb. **2** CYCLE, series, sequence, succession, period, bout, session. **3** BEAT, circuit, lap, course, routine.
◇ *v* circle, skirt, flank, bypass.
• **round off** finish (off), complete, end, close, conclude, cap, crown.
☒ begin.
• **round on** turn on, attack, lay into, abuse.
• **round up** herd, marshal, assemble, gather, rally, collect, group.
☒ disperse, scatter.

roundabout *adj* circuitous, tortuous, twisting, winding, indirect, oblique, devious, evasive.
☒ straight, direct.

rouse *v* wake (up), awaken, arouse, call, stir, move, start, disturb, agitate, anger, provoke, stimulate, instigate, incite, inflame, excite, galvanize, whip up.
☒ calm.

rout *n* defeat, conquest, overthrow,

beating, thrashing, flight, stampede.
⊜ win.
◇ v defeat, conquer, overthrow, crush, beat, hammer (*infml*), thrash, lick, put to flight, chase, dispel, scatter.

route n course, run, path, road, avenue, way, direction, itinerary, journey, passage, circuit, round, beat.

routine n 1 PROCEDURE, way, method, system, order, pattern, formula, practice, usage, custom, habit. 2 *comedy routine*: act, piece, programme, performance.
◇ adj customary, habitual, usual, typical, ordinary, run-of-the-mill, normal, standard, conventional, unoriginal, predictable, familiar, everyday, banal, humdrum, dull, boring, monotonous, tedious.
⊜ unusual, different, exciting.

row¹ n line, tier, bank, rank, range, column, file, queue, string, series, sequence.

row² n 1 ARGUMENT, quarrel, dispute, controversy, squabble, tiff, slanging match (*infml*), fight, brawl. 2 NOISE, racket, din, uproar, commotion, disturbance, rumpus, fracas.
⊜ 2 calm.
◇ v argue, quarrel, wrangle, bicker, squabble, fight, scrap.

rowdy adj noisy, loud, rough, boisterous, disorderly, unruly, riotous, wild.
⊜ quiet, peaceful.

royal adj regal, majestic, kingly, queenly, princely, imperial, monarchical, sovereign, august, grand, stately, magnificent, splendid, superb.

rub v apply, spread, smear, stroke, caress, massage, knead, chafe, grate, scrape, abrade, scour, scrub, clean, wipe, smooth, polish, buff, shine.
• **rub out** erase, efface, obliterate, delete, cancel.

rubbish n 1 REFUSE, garbage, trash, junk, litter, waste, dross, debris, flotsam and jetsam. 2 NONSENSE, drivel, claptrap, twaddle, gibberish, gobbledegook, balderdash, poppycock (*infml*), rot (*infml*), cobblers (*sl*).
⊜ 2 sense.

ruddy adj red, scarlet, crimson, blushing, flushed, rosy, glowing, healthy, blooming, florid, sunburnt.
⊜ pale.

rude adj 1 IMPOLITE, discourteous, disrespectful, impertinent, impudent, cheeky (*infml*), insolent, offensive, insulting, abusive, ill-mannered, ill-bred, uncouth, uncivilized, unrefined, unpolished, uneducated, untutored, uncivil, curt, brusque, abrupt, sharp, short. 2 *a rude joke*: obscene, vulgar, coarse, dirty, naughty, gross.
⊜ 1 polite, courteous, civil. 2 clean, decent.

rudimentary adj primary, initial, introductory, elementary, basic, fundamental, primitive, undeveloped, embryonic.
⊜ advanced, developed.

rudiments n basics, fundamentals, essentials, principles, elements, ABC, beginnings, foundations.

rugged adj 1 ROUGH, bumpy, uneven, irregular, jagged, rocky, craggy, stark. 2 STRONG, robust, hardy, tough, muscular, weather-beaten.
⊜ 1 smooth.

ruin n destruction, devastation, wreckage, havoc, damage, disrepair, decay, disintegration, breakdown, collapse, fall, downfall, failure, defeat, overthrow, ruination, undoing, insolvency, bankruptcy, crash.
⊜ development, reconstruction.
◇ v spoil, mar, botch, mess up (*infml*), damage, break, smash, shatter, wreck, destroy, demolish,

raze, devastate, overwhelm, overthrow, defeat, crush, impoverish, bankrupt.
≢ develop, restore.

rule n 1 REGULATION, law, statute, ordinance, decree, order, direction, guide, precept, tenet, canon, maxim, axiom, principle, formula, guideline, standard, criterion. 2 REIGN, sovereignty, supremacy, dominion, mastery, power, authority, command, control, influence, regime, government, leadership. 3 CUSTOM, convention, practice, routine, habit, wont.
◇ v 1 *rule a country*: reign, govern, command, lead, administer, manage, direct, guide, control, regulate, prevail, dominate. 2 JUDGE, adjudicate, decide, find, determine, resolve, establish, decree, pronounce.
• **as a rule** usually, normally, ordinarily, generally.
• **rule out** exclude, eliminate, reject, dismiss, preclude, prevent, ban, prohibit, forbid, disallow.

ruler

Titles of rulers include: Aga, begum, Caesar, caliph, consul, emir, emperor, empress, governor, governor-general, head of state, kaiser, khan, king, maharajah, maharani, mikado, monarch, nawab, nizam, Pharaoh, president, prince, princess, queen, rajah, rani, regent, shah, sheikh, shogun, sovereign, sultan, sultana, suzerain, tsar, viceroy.

ruling n judgement, adjudication, verdict, decision, finding, resolution, decree, pronouncement.
◇ adj reigning, sovereign, supreme, governing, commanding, leading, main, chief, principal, dominant, predominant, controlling.

rumour n hearsay, gossip, talk, whisper, word, news, report, story,

grapevine, bush telegraph.

run v 1 SPRINT, jog, race, career, tear, dash, hurry, rush, speed, bolt, dart, scoot, scuttle. 2 GO, pass, move, proceed, issue. 3 FUNCTION, work, operate, perform. 4 *run a company*: head, lead, administer, direct, manage, superintend, supervise, oversee, control, regulate. 5 COMPETE, contend, stand, challenge. 6 LAST, continue, extend, reach, stretch, spread, range. 7 FLOW, stream, pour, gush.
◇ n 1 JOG, gallop, race, sprint, spurt, dash, rush. 2 DRIVE, ride, spin, jaunt, excursion, outing, trip, journey. 3 SEQUENCE, series, string, chain, course.
• **run after** chase, pursue, follow, tail.
≢ flee.
• **run away** escape, flee, abscond, bolt, scarper (*sl*), beat it (*infml*), run off, make off, clear off (*infml*).
≢ stay.
• **run down** 1 CRITICIZE, belittle, disparage, denigrate, defame. 2 RUN OVER, knock over, hit, strike. 3 TIRE, weary, exhaust, weaken. 4 *run down production*: reduce, decrease, drop, cut, trim, curtail.
≢ 1 praise. 4 increase.
• **run into** meet, encounter, run across, bump into, hit, strike, collide with.
≢ miss.
• **run out** expire, terminate, end, cease, close, finish, dry up, fail.

runaway n escaper, escapee, fugitive, absconder, deserter, refugee.
◇ adj escaped, fugitive, loose, uncontrolled.

rundown n 1 REDUCTION, decrease, decline, drop, cut. 2 SUMMARY, résumé, synopsis, outline, review, recap, run-through.

runner n jogger, sprinter, athlete, competitor, participant, courier, messenger.

running adj successive,

consecutive, unbroken, uninterrupted, continuous, constant, perpetual, incessant, unceasing, moving, flowing.
⊠ broken, occasional.
◇ *n* **1** ADMINISTRATION, direction, management, organization, co-ordination, superintendency, supervision, leadership, charge, control, regulation, functioning, working, operation, performance, conduct. **2** *out of the running*: contention, contest, competition.

runny *adj* flowing, fluid, liquid, liquefied, melted, molten, watery, diluted.
⊠ solid.

run-of-the-mill *adj* ordinary, common, everyday, average, unexceptional, unremarkable, undistinguished, unimpressive, mediocre.
⊠ exceptional.

rupture *n* split, tear, burst, puncture, break, breach, fracture, crack, separation, division, schism, rift.
◇ *v* split, tear, burst, puncture, break, fracture, crack, sever, separate, divide.

rural *adj* country, rustic, pastoral, agricultural, agrarian.
⊠ urban.

rush *v* hurry, hasten, quicken, accelerate, speed (up), press, push, dispatch, bolt, dart, shoot, fly, tear, career, dash, race, run, sprint, scramble, stampede, charge.
◇ *n* hurry, haste, urgency, speed, swiftness, dash, race, scramble, stampede, charge, flow, surge.

rust *n* corrosion, oxidation.
◇ *v* corrode, decay, rot, oxidize, tarnish, deteriorate, decline.

rustic *adj* **1** PASTORAL, sylvan, bucolic, countrified, country, rural. **2** PLAIN, simple, rough, crude, coarse, rude, clumsy, awkward, artless, unsophisticated, unrefined, uncultured, provincial, uncouth, boorish, oafish.
⊠ **1** urban. **2** urbane, sophisticated, cultivated, polished.

rustle *v, n* crackle, whoosh, swish, whisper.

rusty *adj* **1** CORRODED, rusted, rust-covered, oxidized, tarnished, discoloured, dull. **2** UNPRACTISED, weak, poor, deficient, dated, old-fashioned, outmoded, antiquated, stale, stiff, creaking.

ruthless *adj* merciless, pitiless, hard-hearted, hard, heartless, unfeeling, callous, cruel, inhuman, brutal, savage, cut-throat, fierce, ferocious, relentless, unrelenting, inexorable, implacable, harsh, severe.
⊠ merciful, compassionate.

Ss

sabotage v damage, spoil, mar, disrupt, vandalize, wreck, destroy, thwart, scupper, cripple, incapacitate, disable, undermine, weaken.
◇ n vandalism, damage, impairment, disruption, wrecking, destruction.

sack v dismiss, fire, discharge, axe (*infml*), lay off, make redundant.
◇ n dismissal, discharge, one's cards, notice, the boot (*infml*), the push (*infml*), the elbow (*infml*), the axe (*infml*), the chop (*infml*).

sacred adj holy, divine, heavenly, blessed, hallowed, sanctified, consecrated, dedicated, religious, devotional, ecclesiastical, priestly, saintly, godly, venerable, revered, sacrosanct, inviolable.
⊞ temporal, profane.

sacrifice v surrender, forfeit, relinquish, let go, abandon, renounce, give up, forgo, offer, slaughter.
◇ n offering, immolation, slaughter, destruction, surrender, renunciation, loss.

sacrilege n blasphemy, profanity, heresy, desecration, profanation, violation, outrage, irreverence, disrespect, mockery.
⊞ piety, reverence, respect.

sacrosanct adj sacred, hallowed, untouchable, inviolable, impregnable, protected, secure.

sad adj 1 UNHAPPY, sorrowful, tearful, grief-stricken, heavy-hearted, upset, distressed, miserable, low-spirited, downcast, long-faced, crestfallen, glum, dejected, downhearted,

despondent, melancholy, depressed, low, gloomy, dismal. 2 *sad news*: upsetting, distressing, painful, depressing, touching, poignant, heart-rending, tragic, grievous, lamentable, regrettable, sorry, unfortunate, serious, grave, disastrous.
⊞ 1 happy, cheerful. 2 fortunate, lucky.

sadden v upset, distress, grieve, depress, dismay, discourage, dishearten.
⊞ cheer, please, gratify, delight.

saddle v burden, encumber, lumber, impose, tax, charge, load (*infml*).

sadistic adj cruel, inhuman, brutal, savage, vicious, merciless, pitiless, barbarous, bestial, unnatural, perverted.

safe adj 1 HARMLESS, innocuous, non-toxic, non-poisonous, uncontaminated. 2 UNHARMED, undamaged, unscathed, uninjured, unhurt, intact, secure, protected, guarded, impregnable, invulnerable, immune. 3 UNADVENTUROUS, cautious, prudent, conservative, sure, proven, tried, tested, sound, dependable, reliable, trustworthy.
⊞ 1 dangerous, harmful. 2 vulnerable, exposed. 3 risky.

safeguard v protect, preserve, defend, guard, shield, screen, shelter, secure.
⊞ endanger, jeopardize.
◇ n protection, defence, shield, security, surety, guarantee, assurance, insurance, cover, precaution.

safekeeping n protection, care, custody, keeping, charge, trust, guardianship, surveillance, supervision.

safety n protection, refuge, sanctuary, shelter, cover, security, safeguard, immunity, impregnability, safeness, harmlessness, reliability, dependability.
⊞ danger, jeopardy, risk.

sag v bend, give, bag, droop, hang, fall, drop, sink, dip, decline, slump, flop, fail, flag, weaken, wilt.
⊞ bulge, rise.

sail v 1 *sail for France*: embark, set sail, weigh anchor, put to sea, cruise, voyage. 2 CAPTAIN, skipper, pilot, navigate, steer. 3 GLIDE, plane, sweep, float, skim, scud, fly.

sailor n seafarer, mariner, seaman, marine, rating, yachtsman, yachtswoman.

saintly adj godly, pious, devout, God-fearing, holy, religious, blessed, angelic, pure, spotless, innocent, blameless, sinless, virtuous, upright, worthy, righteous.
⊞ godless, unholy, wicked.

sake n benefit, advantage, good, welfare, wellbeing, gain, profit, behalf, interest, account, regard, respect, cause, reason.

salary n pay, remuneration, emolument, stipend, wages, earnings, income.

sale n selling, marketing, vending, disposal, trade, traffic, transaction, deal, auction.

salesperson n sales assistant, salesman, saleswoman, shop assistant, shop-boy, shop-girl, shopkeeper, representative, rep (*infml*).

salient adj important, significant, chief, main, principal, striking, conspicuous, noticeable, obvious, prominent, outstanding, remarkable.

sallow adj yellowish, pale, pallid, wan, pasty, sickly, unhealthy, anaemic, colourless.
⊞ rosy, healthy.

salt n seasoning, taste, flavour, savour, relish, piquancy.

salty adj salt, salted, saline, briny, brackish, savoury, spicy, piquant, tangy.
⊞ fresh, sweet.

salubrious adj sanitary, hygienic, health-giving, healthy, wholesome, pleasant.

salutary adj good, beneficial, advantageous, profitable, valuable, helpful, useful, practical, timely.

salute v greet, acknowledge, recognize, wave, hail, address, nod, bow, honour.
◇ n greeting, acknowledgement, recognition, wave, gesture, hail, address, handshake, nod, bow, tribute, reverence.

salvage v save, preserve, conserve, rescue, recover, recuperate, retrieve, reclaim, redeem, repair, restore.
⊞ waste, abandon.

salvation n deliverance, liberation, rescue, saving, preservation, redemption, reclamation.
⊞ loss, damnation.

salve n ointment, lotion, cream, balm, liniment, embrocation, medication, preparation, application.

same adj identical, twin, duplicate, indistinguishable, equal, selfsame, very, alike, like, similar, comparable, equivalent, matching, corresponding, mutual, reciprocal, interchangeable, substitutable, synonymous, consistent, uniform, unvarying, changeless, unchanged.
⊞ different, inconsistent, variable, changeable.

sample n specimen, example, cross-section, model, pattern, swatch, piece, demonstration, illustration,

instance, sign, indication, foretaste.
◇ v try, test, taste, sip, inspect,
experience.
◇ adj representative, specimen,
demonstrative, demo (infml),
illustrative, dummy, trial, test, pilot.

sanctify v hallow, consecrate, bless,
anoint, dedicate, cleanse, purify,
exalt, canonize.
🄴 desecrate, defile.

sanctimonious adj self-righteous,
holier-than-thou, pious, moralizing,
smug, superior, hypocritical,
pharisaic(al).
🄴 humble.

sanction n authorization,
permission, agreement, OK (infml),
approval, go-ahead, ratification,
confirmation, support, backing,
endorsement, licence, authority.
🄴 veto, disapproval.
◇ v authorize, allow, permit,
approve, ratify, confirm, support,
back, endorse, underwrite, accredit,
license, warrant.
🄴 veto, forbid, disapprove.

sanctions n restrictions, boycott,
embargo, ban, prohibition, penalty.

sanctity n holiness, sacredness,
inviolability, piety, godliness,
religiousness, devotion, grace,
spirituality, purity, goodness,
righteousness.
🄴 unholiness, secularity,
worldliness, godlessness, impurity.

sanctuary n 1 CHURCH, temple,
tabernacle, shrine, altar. 2 ASYLUM,
refuge, protection, shelter, haven,
retreat.

sand n beach, shore, strand, sands,
grit.

sane adj normal, rational, right-
minded, all there (infml), balanced,
stable, sound, sober, level-headed,
sensible, judicious, reasonable,
moderate.
🄴 insane, mad, crazy, foolish.

sanitary adj clean, pure,

uncontaminated, unpolluted, aseptic,
germ-free, disinfected, hygienic,
salubrious, healthy, wholesome.
🄴 insanitary, unwholesome.

sanity n normality, rationality,
reason, sense, common sense,
balance of mind, stability, soundness,
level-headedness, judiciousness.
🄴 insanity, madness.

sap v bleed, drain, exhaust, weaken,
undermine, deplete, reduce,
diminish, impair.
🄴 strengthen, build up, increase.

sarcasm n irony, satire, mockery,
sneering, derision, scorn, contempt,
cynicism, bitterness.

sarcastic adj ironical, satirical,
mocking, taunting, sneering, derisive,
scathing, disparaging, cynical,
incisive, cutting, biting, caustic.

sardonic adj mocking, jeering,
sneering, derisive, scornful, sarcastic,
biting, cruel, heartless, malicious,
cynical, bitter.

sash n belt, girdle, cummerbund,
waistband.

satanic adj satanical, diabolical,
devilish, demonic, fiendish, hellish,
infernal, inhuman, malevolent,
wicked, evil, black.
🄴 holy, divine, godly, saintly,
benevolent.

satire n ridicule, irony, sarcasm, wit,
burlesque, skit, send-up, spoof, take-
off, parody, caricature, travesty.

satirical adj ironical, sarcastic,
mocking, irreverent, taunting,
derisive, sardonic, incisive, cutting,
biting, caustic, cynical, bitter.

satirize v ridicule, mock, make fun
of, burlesque, lampoon, send up,
take off, parody, caricature, criticize,
deride.
🄴 acclaim, honour.

satisfaction n 1 GRATIFICATION,
contentment, happiness, pleasure,
enjoyment, comfort, ease, wellbeing,

fulfilment, self-satisfaction, pride.
2 SETTLEMENT, compensation,
reimbursement, indemnification,
damages, reparation, amends,
redress, recompense, requital,
vindication.
🔁 **1** dissatisfaction, displeasure.

satisfactory adj acceptable,
passable, up to the mark, all right,
OK (infml), cushty (sl), fair, average,
competent, adequate, sufficient,
suitable, proper.
🔁 unsatisfactory, unacceptable,
inadequate.

satisfy v **1** GRATIFY, indulge, content,
please, delight, quench, slake, sate,
satiate, surfeit. **2** satisfy requirements:
meet, fulfil, discharge, settle, answer,
fill, suffice, serve, qualify. **3** ASSURE,
convince, persuade.
🔁 **1** dissatisfy. **2** fail.

saturate v soak, steep, souse,
drench, waterlog, impregnate,
permeate, imbue, suffuse, fill.

sauce

Types of sauce, dip and dressing
include: sauces: gravy, tartare,
Worcestershire, béchamel, white,
brown, barbecue, tomato ketchup,
hollandaise, Tabasco®, apple,
mint, cranberry, horseradish, pesto;
dips: fondue, guacamole, hummus,
salsa, taramasalata; dressings:
mayonnaise, French dressing, olive
oil, balsamic vinegar, salad cream.

saucy adj cheeky (infml),
impertinent, impudent, insolent,
disrespectful, pert, forward,
presumptuous, flippant.
🔁 polite, respectful.

saunter v stroll, amble, mosey
(infml), mooch (infml), wander,
ramble (sl), meander.
◇ n stroll, walk, constitutional,
ramble.

savage adj wild, untamed,
undomesticated, uncivilized,

primitive, barbaric, barbarous,
fierce, ferocious, vicious, beastly,
cruel, inhuman, brutal, sadistic,
bloodthirsty, bloody, murderous,
pitiless, merciless, ruthless, harsh.
🔁 tame, civilized, humane, mild.
◇ n brute, beast, barbarian.
◇ v attack, bite, claw, tear, maul,
mangle.

save v **1** ECONOMIZE, cut back,
conserve, preserve, keep, retain,
hold, reserve, store, lay up, set aside,
put by, hoard, stash (infml), collect,
gather. **2** RESCUE, deliver, liberate,
free, salvage, recover, reclaim.
3 PROTECT, guard, screen, shield,
safeguard, spare, prevent, hinder.
🔁 **1** spend, squander, waste,
discard.
◇ n economy, thrift, discount,
reduction, bargain, cut, conservation,
preservation.
🔁 expense, waste, loss.

savings n capital, investments, nest
egg, fund, store, reserves, resources.

saviour n rescuer, deliverer,
redeemer, liberator, emancipator,
guardian, protector, defender,
champion.
🔁 destroyer.

savour n taste, flavour, smack, smell,
tang, piquancy, salt, spice, relish,
zest.
◇ v relish, enjoy, delight in, revel in,
like, appreciate.
🔁 shrink from.

savoury adj **1** TASTY, appetizing,
delicious, mouthwatering, luscious,
palatable. **2** savoury pancakes: salty,
spicy, aromatic, piquant, tangy.
🔁 **1** unappetizing, tasteless, insipid.
2 sweet.

say v **1** SPEAK, express, phrase, put,
render, utter, voice, articulate,
enunciate, pronounce, deliver,
quote, recite. **2** ANSWER, reply,
respond, rejoin, retort. **3** STATE,
comment, remark, observe, mention,
announce, declare, assert, affirm,

maintain, point out, claim, profess, relate, reveal, disclose, divulge. **4** COMMUNICATE, convey, intimate, suggest, imply, signify. **5** TELL, instruct, command, order. **6** GUESS, estimate, reckon, judge, imagine, suppose, surmise.

Ways of saying include: accuse, babble, bark, bawl, beg, bellow, blurt, boast, complain, confide, croak, cry, curse, drawl, echo, emphasize, enquire, exclaim, expostulate, gasp, groan, growl, grumble, grunt, howl, implore, jeer, joke, laugh, lecture, lie, mimic, moan, mumble, murmur, mutter, nag, plead, protest, question, rant, rebuke, remonstrate, request, roar, scoff, scold, scream, screech, shout, shriek, snap, snarl, squeak, stammer, storm, stutter, swear, taunt, tease, thunder, urge, whine, whisper, yell.

saying n adage, proverb, dictum, precept, axiom, aphorism, maxim, motto, slogan, phrase, expression, quotation, statement, remark.

scale¹ n ratio, proportion, measure, degree, extent, spread, reach, range, scope, compass, spectrum, gamut, sequence, series, progression, order, hierarchy, ranking, ladder, steps, gradation, graduation, calibration, register.
◇ v climb, ascend, mount, clamber, scramble, shin up, conquer, surmount.

scale² n encrustation, deposit, crust, layer, film, lamina, plate, flake, scurf.

scamp n rogue, rascal, scallywag, monkey, imp, devil.

scamper v scuttle, scurry, scoot, dart, dash, run, sprint, rush, hurry, hasten, fly, romp, frolic, gambol.

scan v **1** EXAMINE, scrutinize, study, search, survey, sweep, investigate,
check. **2** SKIM, glance at, flick through, thumb through.
◇ n screening, examination, scrutiny, search, probe, check, investigation, survey, review.

scandal n outrage, offence, outcry, uproar, furore, gossip, rumours, smear, dirt, discredit, dishonour, sleaze (infml), disgrace, shame, embarrassment, ignominy.

scandalize v shock, horrify, appal, dismay, disgust, repel, revolt, offend, affront, outrage.

scandalous adj shocking, appalling, atrocious, abominable, monstrous, unspeakable, outrageous, disgraceful, shameful, disreputable, infamous, improper, unseemly, defamatory, scurrilous, slanderous, libellous, untrue.

scanty adj deficient, inadequate, insufficient, short, scant, little, limited, restricted, narrow, poor, meagre, insubstantial, thin, skimpy, sparse, bare.
⊜ adequate, sufficient, ample, plentiful, substantial.

scar n mark, lesion, wound, injury, blemish, stigma.
◇ v mark, disfigure, spoil, damage, brand, stigmatize.

scarce adj few, rare, infrequent, uncommon, unusual, sparse, scanty, insufficient, deficient, lacking.
⊜ plentiful, common.

scarcely adv hardly, barely, only just.

scarcity n lack, shortage, dearth, deficiency, insufficiency, paucity, rareness, rarity, infrequency, uncommonness, sparseness, scantiness.
⊜ glut, plenty, abundance, sufficiency, enough.

scare v frighten, startle, alarm, dismay, daunt, intimidate, unnerve, threaten, menace, terrorize, shock, appal, panic, terrify.

⊟ reassure, calm.
◇ n fright, start, shock, alarm, panic, hysteria, terror.
⊟ reassurance, comfort.

scared adj frightened, fearful, nervous, anxious, worried, startled, shaken, panic-stricken, terrified.
⊟ confident, reassured.

scary adj frightening, alarming, daunting, intimidating, disturbing, shocking, horrifying, terrifying, hair-raising, bloodcurdling, spine-chilling, chilling, creepy, eerie, spooky (infml).

scathing adj sarcastic, scornful, critical, trenchant, cutting, biting, caustic, acid, vitriolic, bitter, harsh, brutal, savage, unsparing.
⊟ complimentary.

scatter v disperse, dispel, dissipate, disband, disunite, separate, divide, break up, disintegrate, diffuse, broadcast, disseminate, spread, sprinkle, sow, strew, fling, shower.
⊟ gather, collect.

scatterbrained adj forgetful, absent-minded, airheaded (infml), empty-headed, feather-brained, dizzy (infml), scatty (infml), flaky (US infml), ditsy (US infml), careless, inattentive, thoughtless, unreliable, irresponsible, frivolous.
⊟ sensible, sober, efficient, careful.

scattering n sprinkling, few, handful, smattering.
⊟ mass, abundance.

scavenge v forage, rummage, rake, search, scrounge.

scenario n outline, synopsis, summary, résumé, storyline, plot, scheme, plan, programme, projection, sequence, situation, scene.

scene n 1 PLACE, area, spot, locale, site, situation, position, whereabouts, location, locality, environment, milieu, setting, contact, background, backdrop, set, stage. 2 LANDSCAPE, panorama, view, vista, prospect, sight, spectacle, picture, tableau, pageant. 3 EPISODE, incident, part, division, act, clip. 4 don't make a scene: fuss, commotion, to-do (infml), performance, drama, exhibition, display, show.

scenery n landscape, terrain, panorama, view, vista, outlook, scene, background, setting, surroundings, backdrop, set.

scenic adj panoramic, picturesque, attractive, pretty, beautiful, grand, striking, impressive, spectacular, breathtaking, awe-inspiring.
⊟ dull, dreary.

scent n 1 PERFUME, fragrance, aroma, bouquet, smell, odour. 2 follow the scent: track, trail.
⊟ 1 stink.
◇ v smell, sniff (out), nose (out), sense, perceive, detect, discern, recognize.

scented adj perfumed, fragrant, sweet-smelling, aromatic.
⊟ malodorous, stinking.

sceptic n doubter, unbeliever, disbeliever, agnostic, atheist, rationalist, questioner, scoffer, cynic.
⊟ believer.

sceptical adj doubting, doubtful, unconvinced, unbelieving, disbelieving, questioning, distrustful, mistrustful, hesitating, dubious, suspicious, scoffing, cynical, pessimistic.
⊟ convinced, confident, trusting.

scepticism n doubt, unbelief, disbelief, agnosticism, atheism, rationalism, distrust, suspicion, cynicism, pessimism.
⊟ belief, faith.

schedule n timetable, programme, agenda, diary, calendar, itinerary, plan, scheme, list, inventory, catalogue, table, form.
◇ v timetable, time, table, programme, plan, organize, arrange, appoint, assign, book, list.

schematic *adj* diagrammatic, representational, symbolic, illustrative, graphic.

scheme *n* 1 PROGRAMME, schedule, plan, project, idea, proposal, proposition, suggestion, draft, outline, blueprint, schema, diagram, chart, layout, pattern, design, shape, configuration, arrangement. 2 INTRIGUE, plot, conspiracy, device, stratagem, ruse, ploy, shift, manoeuvre, tactic(s), strategy, procedure, system, method.
◇ *v* plot, conspire, connive, collude, intrigue, machinate, manoeuvre, manipulate, pull strings, mastermind, plan, project, contrive, devise, frame, work out.

schism *n* 1 DIVISION, split, rift, rupture, break, breach, disunion, separation, severance, estrangement, discord. 2 SPLINTER GROUP, faction, sect.

scholar *n* pupil, student, academic, intellectual, egghead (*infml*), authority, expert.
🅴 dunce, ignoramus.

scholarly *adj* learned, erudite, lettered, academic, scholastic, school, intellectual, highbrow, bookish, studious, knowledgeable, well-read, analytical, scientific.
🅴 uneducated, illiterate.

scholarship *n* 1 ERUDITION, learnedness, learning, knowledge, wisdom, education, schooling. 2 *a scholarship to a public school*: grant, award, bursary, endowment, fellowship, exhibition.

school *n* college, institute, institution.

Schools, colleges and universities include: kindergarten, nursery school, infant school, primary school, middle school, secondary school, secondary modern, upper school, high school, comprehensive, grammar school, grant-maintained school, foundation school, city academy, faith school, preparatory school, public school, private school, boarding school, sixth-form college, polytechnic, technical college, university, academy, seminary, finishing school, Sunday school, convent school, summer school.

◇ *v* educate, teach, instruct, tutor, coach, train, discipline, drill, verse, prime, prepare, indoctrinate.

schooling *n* education, book-learning, teaching, instruction, tuition, coaching, training, drill, preparation, grounding, guidance, indoctrination.

science *n* technology, discipline, specialization, knowledge, skill, proficiency, technique, art.

Sciences include: acoustics, aerodynamics, aeronautics, agricultural science, anatomy, anthropology, astronomy, astrophysics, behavioural science, biochemistry, biology, biophysics, botany, chemistry, chemurgy, climatology, computer science, cybernetics, dynamics, earth science, ecology, electrodynamics, electronics, engineering, entomology, environmental science, genetics, geochemistry, geography, geology, geophysics, hydraulics, information technology, inorganic chemistry, life science, linguistics, mathematics, mechanical engineering, mechanics, medical science, metallurgy, meteorology, microbiology, mineralogy, morphology, natural science, nuclear physics, organic chemistry, ornithology, pathology, pharmacology, physics, physiology, psychology, radiochemistry, robotics, sociology, space technology, telecommunications, thermodynamics, toxicology, ultrasonics, veterinary science, zoology.

scientific *adj* methodical, systematic, controlled, regulated, analytical, mathematical, exact, precise, accurate, scholarly, thorough.

scintillating *adj* sparkling, glittering, flashing, bright, shining, brilliant, dazzling, exciting, stimulating, lively, animated, vivacious, ebullient, witty.
⊞ dull.

scoff[1] *v* mock, ridicule, poke fun, taunt, tease, rib (*sl*), jeer, sneer, pooh-pooh, scorn, despise, revile, deride, belittle, disparage, knock (*infml*).
⊞ praise, compliment, flatter.

scoff[2] *v* eat, consume, devour, put away (*infml*), gobble, guzzle, wolf (*infml*), bolt, gulp.
⊞ fast, abstain.

scold *v* chide, tell off (*infml*), tick off (*infml*), reprimand, reprove, rebuke, take to task, admonish, upbraid, reproach, blame, censure, lecture, nag.
⊞ praise, commend.

scolding *n* castigation, telling-off, ticking-off (*infml*), dressing-down, reprimand, reproof, rebuke, lecture, talking-to, earful (*infml*).
⊞ praise, commendation.

scoop *n* 1 LADLE, spoon, dipper, bailer, bucket, shovel. 2 EXCLUSIVE, coup, inside story, revelation, exposé, sensation, latest (*infml*).
◇ *v* gouge, scrape, hollow, empty, excavate, dig, shovel, ladle, spoon, dip, bail.

scope *n* 1 RANGE, compass, field, area, sphere, ambit, terms of reference, confines, reach, extent, span, breadth, coverage. 2 *scope for improvement*: room, space, capacity, elbow-room, latitude, leeway, freedom, liberty, opportunity.

scorch *v* burn, singe, char, blacken, scald, roast, sear, parch, shrivel, wither.

scorching *adj* burning, boiling, baking, roasting, sizzling, blistering, sweltering, torrid, tropical, searing, red-hot.

score *n* 1 RESULT, total, sum, tally, points, marks. 2 SCRATCH, line, groove, mark, nick, notch.
◇ *v* 1 RECORD, register, chalk up, notch up, count, total, make, earn, gain, achieve, attain, win, have the advantage, have the edge, be one up. 2 SCRATCH, scrape, graze, mark, groove, gouge, cut, incise, engrave, indent, nick, slash.

scorn *n* contempt, scornfulness, disdain, sneering, derision, mockery, ridicule, sarcasm, disparagement, disgust.
⊞ admiration, respect.
◇ *v* despise, look down on, disdain, sneer at, scoff at, deride, mock, laugh at, slight, spurn, refuse, reject, dismiss.
⊞ admire, respect.

scornful *adj* contemptuous, disdainful, supercilious, haughty, arrogant, sneering, scoffing, derisive, mocking, jeering, sarcastic, scathing, disparaging, insulting, slighting, dismissive.
⊞ admiring, respectful.

scour[1] *v* scrape, abrade, rub, polish, burnish, scrub, clean, wash, cleanse, purge, flush.

scour[2] *v* search, hunt, comb, drag, ransack, rummage, forage, rake.

scourge *n* 1 AFFLICTION, misfortune, torment, terror, bane, evil, curse, plague, penalty, punishment. 2 WHIP, lash.
⊞ 1 blessing, godsend, boon.
◇ *v* 1 AFFLICT, torment, curse,

plague, devastate, punish, chastise, discipline. 2 WHIP, flog, beat, lash, cane, flail, thrash.

scout v spy out, reconnoitre, explore, investigate, check out, survey, case (sl), spy, snoop, search, seek, hunt, probe, look, watch, observe.
◇ n spy, reconnoitrer, vanguard, outrider, escort, lookout, recruiter, spotter.

scowl v, n frown, glower, glare, grimace, pout.
🖭 smile, grin, beam.

scraggy adj scrawny, skinny, thin, lean, lanky, bony, angular, gaunt, undernourished, emaciated, wasted.
🖭 plump, sleek.

scramble v 1 CLIMB, scale, clamber, crawl, shuffle, scrabble, grope. 2 RUSH, hurry, hasten, run, push, jostle, struggle, strive, vie, contend.
◇ n rush, hurry, race, dash, hustle, bustle, commotion, confusion, muddle, struggle, free-for-all, mêlée.

scrap¹ n bit, piece, fragment, part, fraction, crumb, morsel, bite, mouthful, sliver, shred, snippet, atom, iota, grain, particle, mite, trace, vestige, remnant, leftover, waste, junk.
◇ v discard, throw away, jettison, shed, abandon, drop, dump, ditch (sl), cancel, axe, demolish, break up, write off.
🖭 recover, restore.

scrap² n fight, scuffle, brawl, dust-up (infml), quarrel, row, argument, squabble, wrangle, dispute, disagreement.
🖭 peace, agreement.
◇ v fight, brawl, quarrel, argue, fall out, squabble, bicker, wrangle, disagree.
🖭 agree.

scrape v grate, grind, rasp, file, abrade, scour, rub, clean, remove, erase, scrabble, claw, scratch, graze, skin, bark, scuff.

scrappy adj bitty, disjointed, piecemeal, fragmentary, incomplete, sketchy, superficial, slapdash, slipshod.
🖭 complete, finished.

scratch v claw, gouge, score, mark, cut, incise, etch, engrave, scrape, rub, scuff, graze, gash, lacerate.
◇ n mark, line, scrape, scuff, abrasion, graze, gash, laceration.

scrawny adj scraggy, skinny, thin, lean, lanky, angular, bony, underfed, undernourished, emaciated.
🖭 fat, plump.

scream v, n shriek, screech, cry, shout, yell, bawl, roar, howl, wail, squeal, yelp.

screen v 1 screen a film: show, present, broadcast. 2 SHIELD, protect, safeguard, defend, guard, cover, mask, veil, cloak, shroud, hide, conceal, shelter, shade. 3 SORT, grade, sift, sieve, filter, process, evaluate, gauge, examine, scan, check, vet.
🖭 2 uncover, expose.
◇ n partition, divider, shield, guard, cover, mask, veil, cloak, shroud, concealment, shelter, shade, awning, canopy, net, mesh.

screw v fasten, adjust, tighten, contract, compress, squeeze, extract, extort, force, constrain, pressurize, turn, wind, twist, wring, distort, wrinkle.

scribble v write, pen, jot, dash off, scrawl, doodle.

scribe n writer, copyist, amanuensis, secretary, clerk.

script n 1 a film script: text, lines, words, dialogue, screenplay, libretto, book. 2 WRITING, handwriting, hand, longhand, calligraphy, letters, manuscript, copy.

scrounge v cadge, beg, sponge.

scrounger n cadger, sponger, parasite.

scrub v 1 *scrub the floor*: rub, brush, clean, wash, cleanse, scour. 2 (*infml*) ABOLISH, cancel, delete, abandon, give up, drop, discontinue.

scruffy adj untidy, messy, unkempt, dishevelled, bedraggled, run-down, tattered, shabby, disreputable, worn-out, ragged, seedy, squalid, slovenly. ⊜ tidy, well-dressed.

scruple n reluctance, hesitation, doubt, qualm, misgiving, uneasiness, difficulty, perplexity.
◇ v hesitate, think twice, hold back, shrink.

scruples n standards, principles, morals, ethics.

scrupulous adj 1 PAINSTAKING, meticulous, conscientious, careful, rigorous, strict, exact, precise, minute, nice. 2 PRINCIPLED, moral, ethical, honourable, honest, upright. ⊜ 1 superficial, careless, reckless. 2 unscrupulous, unprincipled.

scrutinize v examine, inspect, study, scan, analyse, sift, investigate, probe, search, explore.

scrutiny n examination, inspection, study, analysis, investigation, inquiry, search, exploration.

scuff v scrape, scratch, graze, abrade, rub, brush, drag.

scuffle v fight, scrap, tussle, brawl, grapple, struggle, contend, clash.
◇ n fight, scrap, tussle, brawl, fray, set-to, rumpus, commotion, disturbance, affray.

sculpt v sculpture, carve, chisel, hew, cut, model, mould, cast, form, shape, fashion.

scum n froth, foam, film, impurities, dross, dregs, rubbish, trash.

scurrilous adj rude, vulgar, coarse, foul, obscene, indecent, salacious, offensive, abusive, insulting, disparaging, defamatory, slanderous,

libellous, scandalous.
⊜ polite, courteous, complimentary.

scurry v dash, rush, hurry, hasten, bustle, scramble, scuttle, scamper, scoot, dart, run, sprint, trot, race, fly, skim, scud.

sea n 1 OCEAN, main, deep, briny (*infml*). 2 *a sea of faces*: multitude, abundance, profusion, mass.
◇ adj marine, maritime, ocean, oceanic, salt, saltwater, aquatic, seafaring.
⊜ land, air.
• **at sea** adrift, lost, confused, bewildered, baffled, puzzled, perplexed, mystified.

seafaring adj sea-going, ocean-going, sailing, nautical, naval, marine, maritime.

seal v 1 *seal a jar*: close, shut, stop, plug, cork, stopper, waterproof, fasten, secure. 2 SETTLE, conclude, finalize, stamp.
⊜ 1 unseal.
◇ n stamp, signet, insignia, cachet, authentication, assurance, attestation, confirmation, ratification.
• **seal off** block up, close off, shut off fence off, cut off, segregate, isolate, quarantine.
⊜ open up.

seam n 1 JOIN, joint, weld, closure, line. 2 *coal seam*: layer, stratum, vein, lode.

seamy adj disreputable, sleazy, sordid, squalid, unsavoury, rough, dark, low, nasty, unpleasant.
⊜ respectable, wholesome, pleasant.

sear v burn, scorch, brown, fry, sizzle, seal, cauterize, brand, parch, shrivel, wither.

search v seek, look, hunt, rummage, rifle, ransack, scour, comb, sift, probe, explore, frisk (*sl*), examine, scrutinize, inspect, check, investigate, inquire, pry.
◇ n hunt, quest, pursuit, rummage,

probe, exploration, examination, scrutiny, inspection, investigation, inquiry, research, survey.

searching *adj* penetrating, piercing, keen, sharp, close, intent, probing, thorough, minute.
⊠ vague, superficial.

seaside *n* coast, shore, beach, sands.

season *n* period, spell, phase, term, time, span, interval.
◇ *v* 1 *season food*: flavour, spice, salt. 2 AGE, mature, ripen, harden, toughen, train, prepare, condition, treat, temper.

seasonable *adj* timely, well-timed, welcome, opportune, convenient, suitable, appropriate, fitting.
⊠ unseasonable, inopportune.

seasoned *adj* mature, experienced, practised, well-versed, veteran, old, hardened, toughened, conditioned, acclimatized, weathered.
⊠ inexperienced, novice.

seasoning *n* flavouring, spice, condiment, salt, pepper, relish, sauce, dressing.

seat *n* 1 CHAIR, bench, pew, stool, throne. 2 *country seat*: residence, abode, house, mansion. 3 PLACE, site, situation, location, headquarters, centre, heart, hub, axis, source, cause, bottom, base, foundation, footing, ground.
◇ *v* sit, place, set, locate, install, fit, fix, settle, accommodate, hold, contain, take.

seating *n* seats, chairs, places, room, accommodation.

secluded *adj* private, cloistered, sequestered, shut away, cut off, isolated, lonely, solitary, remote, out-of-the-way, sheltered, hidden, concealed.
⊠ public, accessible.

seclusion *n* privacy, retirement, retreat, isolation, solitude, remoteness, shelter, hiding, concealment.

second¹ *adj* duplicate, twin, double, repeated, additional, further, extra, supplementary, alternative, other, alternate, next, following, subsequent, succeeding, secondary, subordinate, lower, inferior, lesser, supporting.
◇ *n* helper, assistant, backer, supporter.
◇ *v* approve, agree with, endorse, back, support, help, assist, aid, further, advance, forward, promote, encourage.

second² *n* minute, tick (*infml*), moment, instant, flash, jiffy (*infml*).

secondary *adj* subsidiary, subordinate, lower, inferior, lesser, minor, unimportant, ancillary, auxiliary, supporting, relief, back-up, reserve, spare, extra, second, alternative, indirect, derived, resulting.
⊠ primary, main, major.

second-hand *adj* used, old, worn, hand-me-down, borrowed, derivative, secondary, indirect, vicarious.
⊠ new.

second-rate *adj* inferior, substandard, second-class, second-best, poor, low-grade, shoddy, cheap, tawdry, mediocre, undistinguished, uninspired, uninspiring.
⊠ first-rate.

secrecy *n* privacy, seclusion, confidentiality, confidence, covertness, concealment, disguise, camouflage, furtiveness, surreptitiousness, stealthiness, stealth, mystery.
⊠ openness.

secret *adj* 1 PRIVATE, discreet, covert, hidden, concealed, unseen, shrouded, covered, disguised, camouflaged, undercover, furtive, surreptitious, stealthy, sly,

underhand, under-the-counter, hole-and-corner, cloak-and-dagger, clandestine, underground, backstairs, back-door. **2** CLASSIFIED, restricted, confidential, hush-hush (*infml*), unpublished, undisclosed, unrevealed, unknown. **3** CRYPTIC, mysterious, occult, arcane, recondite, deep. **4** SECRETIVE, close, retired, secluded, out-of-the-way.
✍ **1** public, open. **2** well-known.
◇ *n* confidence, mystery, enigma, code, key, formula, recipe.

secretary *n* personal assistant, PA, typist, stenographer, clerk.

secrete¹ *v* hide, conceal, stash away (*infml*), bury, cover, screen, shroud, veil, disguise, take, appropriate.
✍ uncover, reveal, disclose.

secrete² *v* exude, discharge, release, give off, emit, emanate, produce.

secretion *n* exudation, discharge, release, emission.

secretive *adj* tight-lipped, close, cagey (*infml*), uncommunicative, unforthcoming, reticent, reserved, withdrawn, quiet, deep, cryptic, enigmatic.
✍ open, communicative, forthcoming.

sect *n* denomination, cult, division, subdivision, group, splinter group, faction, camp, wing, party, school.

sectarian *adj* factional, partisan, cliquish, exclusive, narrow, limited, parochial, insular, narrow-minded, bigoted, fanatical, doctrinaire, dogmatic, rigid.
✍ non-sectarian, cosmopolitan, broad-minded.

section *n* division, subdivision, chapter, paragraph, passage, instalment, part, component, fraction, fragment, bit, piece, slice, portion, segment, sector, zone, district, area, region, department, branch, wing.
✍ whole.

sector *n* zone, district, quarter, area, region, section, division, subdivision, part.
✍ whole.

secular *adj* lay, temporal, worldly, earthly, civil, state, non-religious, profane.
✍ religious.

secure *adj* **1** SAFE, unharmed, undamaged, protected, sheltered, shielded, immune, impregnable, fortified, fast, tight, fastened, locked, fixed, immovable, stable, steady, solid, firm, well-founded, reliable, dependable, steadfast, certain, sure, conclusive, definite. **2** CONFIDENT, assured, reassured.
✍ **1** insecure, vulnerable. **2** uneasy, ill at ease.
◇ *v* **1** OBTAIN, acquire, gain, get. **2** FASTEN, attach, fix, make fast, tie, moor, lash, chain, lock (up), padlock, bolt, batten down, nail, rivet.
✍ **1** lose. **2** unfasten.

security *n* **1** SAFETY, immunity, asylum, sanctuary, refuge, cover, protection, defence, surveillance, safekeeping, preservation, care, custody. **2** *security for a loan*: collateral, surety, pledge, guarantee, warranty, assurance, insurance, precautions, safeguards. **3** CONFIDENCE, conviction, certainty, positiveness.
✍ **1** insecurity.

sedate *adj* staid, dignified, solemn, grave, serious, sober, decorous, proper, seemly, demure, composed, unruffled, serene, tranquil, calm, quiet, cool, collected, imperturbable, unflappable (*infml*), deliberate, slow-moving.
✍ undignified, lively, agitated.

sedative *adj* calming, soothing, anodyne, lenitive, tranquillizing, relaxing, soporific, depressant.
✍ rousing.
◇ *n* tranquillizer, sleeping-pill, narcotic, barbiturate.

sedentary *adj* sitting, seated, desk-bound, inactive, still, stationary, immobile, unmoving.
⊞ active.

sediment *n* deposit, residue, grounds, lees, dregs.

sedition *n* agitation, rabble-rousing, subversion, disloyalty, treachery, treason, insubordination, mutiny, rebellion, revolt.
⊞ calm, loyalty.

seduce *v* entice, lure, allure, attract, tempt, charm, beguile, ensnare, lead astray, mislead, deceive, corrupt, dishonour, ruin.
⊞ repel.

seduction *n* enticement, lure, attraction, temptation, come-on (*infml*), corruption, ruin.

seductive *adj* enticing, alluring, attractive, tempting, tantalizing, inviting, come-hither (*infml*), flirtatious, sexy, provocative, beguiling, captivating, bewitching, irresistible.
⊞ unattractive, repulsive.

see *v* **1** PERCEIVE, glimpse, discern, spot, make out, distinguish, identify, sight, notice, observe, watch, view, look at, mark, note. **2** IMAGINE, picture, visualize, envisage, foresee, anticipate. **3** *I see your point*: understand, comprehend, grasp, fathom, follow, realize, recognize, appreciate, regard, consider, deem. **4** DISCOVER, find out, learn, ascertain, determine, decide. **5** LEAD, usher, accompany, escort, court, go out with, date. **6** VISIT, consult, interview, meet.
• **see to** attend to, deal with, take care of, look after, arrange, organize, manage, do, fix, repair, sort out.

seed *n* pip, stone, kernel, nucleus, grain, germ, sperm, ovum, egg, ovule, spawn, embryo, source, start, beginning.

seedy *adj* **1** SHABBY, scruffy, tatty, mangy, sleazy, squalid, grotty (*infml*), crummy (*sl*), run-down, dilapidated, decaying. **2** UNWELL, ill, sick, poorly, ailing, off-colour.
⊞ **2** well.

seek *v* look for, search for, hunt, pursue, follow, inquire, ask, invite, request, solicit, petition, entreat, want, desire, aim, aspire, try, attempt, endeavour, strive.

seem *v* appear, look, feel, sound, pretend to be.

seeming *adj* apparent, ostensible, outward, superficial, surface, quasi-, pseudo, specious.
⊞ real.

seep *v* ooze, leak, exude, well, trickle, dribble, percolate, permeate, soak.

seethe *v* **1** BOIL, simmer, bubble, effervesce, fizz, foam, froth, ferment, rise, swell, surge, teem, swarm. **2** RAGE, fume, smoulder, storm.

see-through *adj* transparent, translucent, sheer, filmy, gauzy, gossamer(y), flimsy.
⊞ opaque.

segment *n* section, division, compartment, part, bit, piece, slice, portion, wedge.
⊞ whole.

segregate *v* separate, keep apart, cut off, isolate, quarantine, set apart, exclude.
⊞ unite, join.

segregation *n* separation, isolation, quarantine, apartheid, discrimination.
⊞ unification.

seize *v* grab, snatch, grasp, clutch, grip, hold, take, confiscate, impound, appropriate, commandeer, hijack, annex, abduct, catch, capture, arrest, apprehend, nab (*infml*), collar (*infml*).
⊞ let go, release, hand back.

seizure *n* **1** FIT, attack, convulsion, paroxysm, spasm. **2** TAKING, confiscation, appropriation, hijack,

annexation, abduction, capture, arrest, apprehension.
⊞ **2** release, liberation.

seldom *adv* rarely, infrequently, occasionally, hardly ever.
⊞ often, usually.

select *v* choose, pick, single out, decide on, appoint, elect, prefer, opt for.
◇ *adj* selected, choice, top, prime, first-class, first-rate, hand-picked, élite, exclusive, limited, privileged, special, excellent, superior, posh (*infml*).
⊞ second-rate, ordinary, general.

selection *n* choice, pick, option, preference, assortment, variety, range, line-up, miscellany, medley, pot-pourri, collection, anthology.

selective *adj* particular, choosy (*infml*), careful, discerning, discriminating.
⊞ indiscriminate.

self *n* ego, personality, identity, person.

self-centred *adj* selfish, self-seeking, self-serving, self-interested, egotistical, narcissistic, self-absorbed, egocentric.
⊞ altruistic.

self-confident *adj* confident, self-reliant, self-assured, assured, self-possessed, cool, fearless.
⊞ unsure, self-conscious.

self-conscious *adj* uncomfortable, ill at ease, awkward, embarrassed, shamefaced, sheepish, shy, bashful, coy, retiring, shrinking, self-effacing, nervous, insecure.
⊞ natural, unaffected, confident.

self-control *n* calmness, composure, cool, patience, self-restraint, restraint, self-denial, temperance, self-discipline, self-mastery, willpower.

self-denial *n* moderation, temperance, abstemiousness,

asceticism, self-sacrifice, unselfishness, selflessness.
⊞ self-indulgence.

self-esteem *n* ego, self-respect, self-regard, self-assurance, self-confidence, pride, self-pride, dignity, amour-propre.
⊞ inferiority complex.

self-evident *adj* obvious, manifest, clear, undeniable, axiomatic, unquestionable, incontrovertible, inescapable.

self-government *n* autonomy, independence, home rule, democracy.
⊞ subjection.

self-indulgent *adj* hedonistic, dissolute, dissipated, profligate, extravagant, intemperate, immoderate.
⊞ abstemious.

selfish *adj* self-interested, self-seeking, self-serving, mean, miserly, mercenary, greedy, covetous, self-centred, egocentric, egotistical.
⊞ unselfish, selfless, generous, considerate.

selfless *adj* unselfish, altruistic, self-denying, self-sacrificing, generous, philanthropic.
⊞ selfish, self-centred.

self-respect *n* pride, dignity, self-esteem, self-assurance, self-confidence.

self-righteous *adj* smug, complacent, superior, goody-goody (*infml*), pious, sanctimonious, holier-than-thou, pietistic, hypocritical, pharisaic(al).

self-sacrifice *n* self-denial, self-renunciation, selflessness, altruism, unselfishness, generosity.
⊞ selfishness.

self-satisfied *adj* smug, complacent, self-congratulatory, self-righteous.
⊞ humble.

self-styled *adj* self-appointed, professed, so-called, would-be.

self-supporting *adj* self-sufficient, self-financing, independent, self-reliant.
⊞ dependent.

sell *v* barter, exchange, trade, auction, vend, retail, stock, handle, deal in, trade in, traffic in, merchandise, hawk, peddle, push, advertise, promote, market.
⊞ buy.

seller *n* vendor, merchant, trader, dealer, supplier, stockist, retailer, shopkeeper, salesman, saleswoman, agent, representative, rep (*infml*), traveller.
⊞ buyer, purchaser.

semblance *n* appearance, air, show, pretence, guise, mask, front, façade, veneer, apparition, image, resemblance, likeness, similarity.

send *v* 1 POST, mail, e-mail, text, dispatch, consign, remit, forward, convey, deliver. 2 TRANSMIT, broadcast, communicate. 3 PROPEL, drive, move, throw, fling, hurl, launch, fire, shoot, discharge, emit, direct.
• **send for** summon, call for, request, order, command.
⊞ dismiss.
• **send up** satirize, mock, ridicule, parody, take off, mimic, imitate.

send-off *n* farewell, leave-taking, departure, start, goodbye.
⊞ arrival.

senile *adj* old, aged, doddering, decrepit, failing, confused.

senior *adj* older, elder, higher, superior, high-ranking, major, chief.
⊞ junior.

seniority *n* priority, precedence, rank, standing, status, age, superiority, importance.

sensation *n* 1 FEELING, sense, impression, perception, awareness, consciousness, emotion. 2 *the report caused a sensation*: commotion, stir, agitation, excitement, thrill, furore, outrage, scandal.

sensational *adj* 1 EXCITING, thrilling, electrifying, breathtaking, startling, amazing, astounding, staggering, dramatic, spectacular, impressive, exceptional, excellent, wonderful, marvellous, smashing (*infml*). 2 SCANDALOUS, shocking, horrifying, revealing, melodramatic, lurid.
⊞ 1 ordinary, run-of-the-mill.

sense *n* 1 FEELING, sensation, impression, perception, awareness, consciousness, appreciation, faculty. 2 REASON, logic, mind, brain(s), wit(s), wisdom, intelligence, cleverness, understanding, discernment, judgement, intuition. 3 MEANING, significance, definition, interpretation, implication, point, purpose, substance.
⊞ 2 foolishness. 3 nonsense.
◇ *v* feel, suspect, intuit, perceive, detect, notice, observe, realize, appreciate, understand, comprehend, grasp.

senseless *adj* 1 FOOLISH, stupid, unwise, silly, idiotic, mad, crazy, daft (*infml*), ridiculous, ludicrous, absurd, meaningless, nonsensical, fatuous, irrational, illogical, unreasonable, pointless, purposeless, futile. 2 UNCONSCIOUS, out, stunned, anaesthetized, deadened, numb, unfeeling.
⊞ 1 sensible, meaningful. 2 conscious.

sensible *adj* wise, prudent, judicious, well-advised, shrewd, far-sighted, intelligent, level-headed, down-to-earth, commonsense, sober, sane, rational, logical, reasonable, realistic, practical, functional, sound.
⊞ senseless, foolish, unwise.

sensitive *adj* 1 SUSCEPTIBLE, vulnerable, impressionable, tender, emotional, thin-skinned,

temperamental, touchy, irritable, sensitized, responsive, aware, perceptive, discerning, appreciative.
2 DELICATE, fine, exact, precise.
⊡ **1** insensitive, thick-skinned.
2 imprecise, approximate.

sensual *adj* self-indulgent, voluptuous, sultry, worldly, physical, animal, carnal, fleshly, bodily, sexual, erotic, sexy, lustful, randy (*infml*), lecherous, lewd, licentious.
⊡ ascetic.

sensuous *adj* pleasurable, gratifying, voluptuous, rich, lush, luxurious, sumptuous.
⊡ ascetic, plain, simple.

sentence *n* judgement, verdict, decision, condemnation, ruling, pronouncement, decree, order.
◇ *v* judge, pass judgement on, condemn, doom, punish, penalize.

sentiment *n* **1** THOUGHT, idea, feeling, opinion, view, judgement, belief, persuasion, attitude.
2 EMOTION, sensibility, tenderness, soft-heartedness, romanticism, sentimentality, mawkishness.

sentimental *adj* tender, soft-hearted, emotional, gushing, touching, pathetic, tear-jerking, weepy (*infml*), maudlin, mawkish, nostalgic, romantic, lovey-dovey (*infml*), slushy, mushy, sloppy, schmaltzy, soppy, corny (*infml*).
⊡ unsentimental, realistic, cynical.

sentry *n* sentinel, guard, picket, watchman, watch, lookout.

separable *adj* divisible, detachable, removable, distinguishable, distinct.
⊡ inseparable.

separate *v* divide, sever, part, split (up), divorce, part company, diverge, disconnect, uncouple, disunite, disaffiliate, disentangle, segregate, isolate, cut off, abstract, remove, detach, withdraw, secede.
⊡ join, unite, combine.

◇ *adj* single, individual, particular, independent, alone, solitary, segregated, isolated, apart, divorced, divided, disunited, disconnected, disjointed, detached, unattached, unconnected, unrelated, different, disparate, distinct, discrete, several, sundry.
⊡ together, attached.

separation *n* division, severance, parting, leave-taking, farewell, split-up, break-up, divorce, split, rift, gap, divergence, disconnection, disengagement, dissociation, estrangement, segregation, isolation, detachment.
⊡ unification.

septic *adj* infected, poisoned, festering, putrefying, putrid.

sequel *n* follow-up, continuation, development, result, consequence, outcome, issue, upshot, pay-off, end, conclusion.

sequence *n* succession, series, run, progression, chain, string, train, line, procession, order, arrangement, course, track, cycle, set.

serene *adj* calm, tranquil, cool, composed, placid, untroubled, undisturbed, still, quiet, peaceful.
⊡ troubled, disturbed.

series *n* set, cycle, succession, sequence, run, progression, chain, string, line, train, order, arrangement, course.

serious *adj* **1** IMPORTANT, significant, weighty, momentous, crucial, critical, urgent, pressing, acute, grave, worrying, difficult, dangerous, grim, severe, deep, far-reaching.
2 UNSMILING, long-faced, humourless, solemn, sober, stern, thoughtful, pensive, earnest, sincere.
⊡ **1** trivial, slight. **2** smiling, facetious, frivolous.

sermon *n* address, discourse, lecture, harangue, homily, talking-to (*infml*).

serrated *adj* toothed, notched, indented, jagged.
☒ smooth.

servant *n* domestic, maid, valet, steward, attendant, retainer, hireling, lackey, menial, skivvy (*infml*), slave, help, helper, assistant, ancillary.
☒ master, mistress.

serve *v* **1** WAIT ON, attend, minister to, work for, help, aid, assist, benefit, further. **2** *serve a purpose*: fulfil, complete, answer, satisfy, discharge, perform, act, function. **3** DISTRIBUTE, dole out, present, deliver, provide, supply.

service *n* **1** EMPLOYMENT, work, labour, business, duty, function, performance. **2** USE, usefulness, utility, advantage, benefit, help, assistance. **3** SERVICING, maintenance, overhaul, check. **4** *church service*: worship, observance, ceremony, rite.
◇ *v* maintain, overhaul, check, repair, recondition, tune.

serviceable *adj* usable, useful, helpful, profitable, advantageous, beneficial, utilitarian, simple, plain, unadorned, strong, tough, durable, hard-wearing, dependable, efficient, functional, practical, convenient.
☒ unserviceable, unusable.

servile *adj* obsequious, sycophantic, toadying, cringing, fawning, grovelling, bootlicking, slavish, subservient, subject, submissive, humble, abject, low, mean, base, menial.
☒ assertive, aggressive.

session *n* sitting, hearing, meeting, assembly, conference, discussion, period, time, term, semester, year.

set *v* **1** PUT, place, locate, situate, position, arrange, prepare, lodge, fix, stick, park, deposit. **2** SCHEDULE, appoint, designate, specify, name, prescribe, ordain, assign, allocate, impose, fix, establish, determine, decide, conclude, settle, resolve.

3 ADJUST, regulate, synchronize, co-ordinate. **4** *the sun sets*: go down, sink, dip, subside, disappear, vanish. **5** CONGEAL, thicken, gel, stiffen, solidify, harden, crystallize.
☒ **4** rise.
◇ *n* batch, series, sequence, kit, outfit, compendium, assortment, collection, class, category, group, band, gang, crowd, circle, clique, faction.
◇ *adj* scheduled, appointed, arranged, prepared, prearranged, fixed, established, definite, decided, agreed, settled, firm, strict, rigid, inflexible, prescribed, formal, conventional, traditional, customary, usual, routine, regular, standard, stock, stereotyped, hackneyed.
☒ movable, free, spontaneous, undecided.

• **set about** begin, start, embark on, undertake, tackle, attack.

• **set aside 1** PUT ASIDE, lay aside, keep (back), save, reserve, set apart, separate, select, earmark. **2** ANNUL, abrogate, cancel, revoke, reverse, overturn, overrule, reject, discard.

• **set back** delay, hold up, slow, retard, hinder, impede.

• **set off 1** LEAVE, depart, set out, start (out), begin. **2** DETONATE, light, ignite, touch off, trigger off, explode. **3** DISPLAY, show off, enhance, contrast.

• **set on** set upon, attack, turn on, go for, fall upon, lay into, beat up (*infml*).

• **set out 1** LEAVE, depart, set off, start (out), begin. **2** LAY OUT, arrange, display, exhibit, present, describe, explain.

• **set up** raise, elevate, erect, build, construct, assemble, compose, form, create, establish, institute, found, inaugurate, initiate, begin, start, introduce, organize, arrange, prepare.

setback *n* delay, hold-up, problem, snag, hitch, hiccup, reverse,

misfortune, upset, disappointment, defeat.
⊠ boost, advance, help, advantage.

setting n mounting, frame, surroundings, milieu, environment, background, context, perspective, period, position, location, locale, site, scene, scenery.

settle v 1 ARRANGE, order, adjust, reconcile, resolve, complete, conclude. 2 SINK, subside, drop, fall, descend, land, alight. 3 CHOOSE, appoint, fix, establish, determine, decide, agree, confirm. 4 COLONIZE, occupy, populate, people, inhabit, live, reside. 5 *settle a bill*: pay, clear, discharge.

settlement n 1 RESOLUTION, agreement, arrangement, decision, conclusion, termination, satisfaction. 2 PAYMENT, clearance, clearing, discharge. 3 COLONY, outpost, community, kibbutz, camp, encampment, hamlet, village.

settler n colonist, colonizer, pioneer, frontiersman, frontierswoman, planter, immigrant, incomer, newcomer, squatter.
⊠ native.

set-up n system, structure, format, organization, arrangement, business, conditions, circumstances.

sever v cut, cleave, split, rend, part, separate, divide, cut off, amputate, detach, disconnect, disjoin, disunite, dissociate, estrange, alienate, break off, dissolve, end, terminate.
⊠ join, unite, combine, attach.

several adj some, many, various, assorted, sundry, diverse, different, distinct, separate, particular, individual.

severe adj 1 STERN, disapproving, sober, strait-laced, strict, rigid, unbending, harsh, tough, hard, difficult, demanding, arduous, punishing, rigorous, grim, forbidding, cruel, biting, cutting, scathing,

pitiless, merciless, oppressive, relentless, inexorable, acute, bitter, intense, extreme, fierce, violent, distressing, serious, grave, critical, dangerous. 2 PLAIN, simple, unadorned, unembellished, functional, restrained, austere, ascetic.
⊠ 1 kind, compassionate, sympathetic, lenient, mild.
2 decorated, ornate.

sew v stitch, tack, baste, hem, darn, embroider.

sex n 1 GENDER, sexuality.
2 SEXUAL INTERCOURSE, intercourse, sexual relations, copulation, coitus, lovemaking, fornication, reproduction, union, intimacy.

sexual adj sex, reproductive, procreative, genital, coital, venereal, carnal, sensual, erotic.

sexy adj sensual, voluptuous, nubile, beddable (*infml*), seductive, inviting, flirtatious, arousing, provoking, provocative, titillating, pornographic, erotic, salacious, suggestive.
⊠ sexless.

shabby adj 1 RAGGED, tattered, frayed, worn, worn-out, mangy, moth-eaten, scruffy, tatty, disreputable, dilapidated, run-down, seedy, dirty, dingy, poky. 2 *a shabby trick*: contemptible, despicable, rotten, mean, low, cheap, shoddy, shameful, dishonourable.
⊠ 1 smart. 2 honourable, fair.

shack n hut, cabin, shanty, hovel, shed, lean-to.

shade n 1 SHADINESS, shadow, darkness, obscurity, semi-darkness, dimness, gloom, gloominess, twilight, dusk, gloaming. 2 AWNING, canopy, cover, shelter, screen, blind, curtain, shield, visor, umbrella, parasol. 3 COLOUR, hue, tint, tone, tinge. 4 TRACE, dash, hint, suggestion, suspicion, nuance, gradation, degree, amount, variety. 5 GHOST,

spectre, phantom, spirit, apparition, semblance.
◇ v shield, screen, protect, cover, shroud, veil, hide, conceal, obscure, cloud, dim, darken, shadow, overshadow.

shadow n 1 SHADE, darkness, obscurity, semi-darkness, dimness, gloom, twilight, dusk, gloaming, cloud, cover, protection. 2 SILHOUETTE, shape, image, representation. 3 TRACE, hint, suggestion, suspicion, vestige, remnant.
◇ v 1 OVERSHADOW, overhang, shade, shield, screen, obscure, darken. 2 FOLLOW, tail, dog, stalk, trail, watch.

shadowy adj dark, gloomy, murky, obscure, dim, faint, indistinct, ill-defined, vague, hazy, nebulous, intangible, unsubstantial, ghostly, spectral, illusory, dreamlike, imaginary, unreal.

shady adj 1 SHADED, shadowy, dim, dark, cool, leafy. 2 (infml) DUBIOUS, questionable, suspect, suspicious, fishy (infml), dishonest, crooked, unreliable, untrustworthy, disreputable, unscrupulous, unethical, underhand.
⊜ 1 sunny, sunlit, bright. 2 honest, trustworthy, honourable.

shaft n 1 HANDLE, shank, stem. 2 BEAM, ray.

shaggy adj hairy, long-haired, hirsute, bushy, woolly, unshorn, dishevelled, unkempt.
⊜ bald, shorn, close-cropped.

shake v 1 WAVE, flourish, brandish, wag, waggle, agitate, rattle, joggle, jolt, jerk, twitch, convulse, heave, throb, vibrate, oscillate, fluctuate, waver, wobble, totter, sway, rock, tremble, quiver, quake, shiver, shudder. 2 the news shook her: upset, distress, shock, frighten, unnerve, intimidate, disturb, discompose, unsettle, agitate, stir, rouse.

• **shake off** get rid of, dislodge, lose, elude, give the slip, leave behind, outdistance, outstrip.

shake-up n reorganization, rearrangement, reshuffle, disturbance, upheaval.

shaky adj 1 TREMBLING, quivering, faltering, tentative, uncertain. 2 UNSTABLE, unsteady, insecure, precarious, wobbly, rocky, tottery, rickety, weak. 3 DUBIOUS, questionable, suspect, unreliable, unsound, unsupported.
⊜ 2 firm, strong.

shallow adj superficial, surface, skin-deep, slight, flimsy, trivial, frivolous, foolish, idle, empty, meaningless, unscholarly, ignorant, simple.
⊜ deep, profound.

sham n pretence, fraud, counterfeit, forgery, fake, imitation, simulation, hoax, humbug.
◇ adj false, fake, counterfeit, spurious, bogus, phoney (infml), pretended, feigned, put-on, simulated, artificial, mock, imitation, synthetic.
⊜ genuine, authentic, real.
◇ v pretend, feign, affect, put on, simulate, imitate, fake, counterfeit.

shame n disgrace, dishonour, discredit, stain, stigma, disrepute, infamy, scandal, ignominy, humiliation, degradation, shamefacedness, remorse, guilt, embarrassment, mortification.
⊜ honour, credit, distinction, pride.
◇ v embarrass, mortify, abash, confound, humiliate, ridicule, humble, put to shame, show up, disgrace, dishonour, discredit, debase, degrade, sully, taint, stain.

shamefaced adj ashamed, conscience-stricken, remorseful, contrite, apologetic, sorry, sheepish, red-faced, blushing, embarrassed, mortified, abashed, humiliated, uncomfortable.

⊠ unashamed, proud.

shameful adj 1 a shameful waste of money: disgraceful, outrageous, scandalous, indecent, abominable, atrocious, wicked, mean, low, vile, reprehensible, contemptible, unworthy, ignoble. 2 EMBARRASSING, mortifying, humiliating, ignominious. ⊠ 1 honourable, creditable, worthy.

shameless adj 1 UNASHAMED, unabashed, unrepentant, impenitent, barefaced, flagrant, blatant, brazen, brash, audacious, insolent, defiant, hardened, incorrigible. 2 IMMODEST, indecent, improper, unprincipled, wanton, dissolute, corrupt, depraved. ⊠ 1 ashamed, shamefaced, contrite. 2 modest.

shape n 1 FORM, outline, silhouette, profile, model, mould, pattern, cut, lines, contours, figure, physique, build, frame, format, configuration. 2 APPEARANCE, guise, likeness, semblance. 3 in good shape: condition, state, form, health, trim, fettle.

Geometrical shapes include: polygon, circle, semicircle, quadrant, oval, ellipse, crescent, triangle, equilateral triangle, isosceles triangle, scalene triangle, quadrilateral, square, rectangle, oblong, rhombus, diamond, kite, trapezium, parallelogram, pentagon, hexagon, heptagon, octagon, nonagon, decagon; polyhedron, cube, cuboid, prism, pyramid, tetrahedron, pentahedron, octahedron, cylinder, cone, sphere, hemisphere.

◇ v form, fashion, model, mould, cast, forge, sculpt, carve, whittle, make, produce, construct, create, devise, frame, plan, prepare, adapt, adjust, regulate, accommodate, modify, remodel.

shapeless adj formless, amorphous,

unformed, nebulous, unstructured, irregular, misshapen, deformed, dumpy.

share v divide, split, go halves, partake, participate, share out, distribute, dole out, give out, deal out, apportion, allot, allocate, assign.
◇ n portion, ration, allowance, quota, allocation, allotment, lot, part, division, proportion, percentage, cut (infml), dividend, due, contribution, whack (infml).

sharp adj 1 a sharp needle: pointed, keen, edged, knife-edged, razor-sharp, cutting, serrated, jagged, barbed, spiky. 2 CLEAR, clear-cut, well-defined, distinct, marked, crisp. 3 QUICK-WITTED, alert, shrewd, astute, perceptive, observant, discerning, penetrating, clever, crafty, cunning, artful, sly. 4 SUDDEN, abrupt, violent, fierce, intense, extreme, severe, acute, piercing, stabbing. 5 PUNGENT, piquant, sour, tart, vinegary, bitter, acerbic, acid. 6 TRENCHANT, incisive, cutting, biting, caustic, sarcastic, sardonic, scathing, vitriolic, acrimonious.
⊠ 1 blunt. 2 blurred. 3 slow, stupid. 4 gentle. 5 bland. 6 mild.
◇ adv punctually, promptly, on the dot, exactly, precisely, abruptly, suddenly, unexpectedly.
⊠ approximately, roughly.

sharpen v edge, whet, hone, grind, file.
⊠ blunt.

shatter v break, smash, splinter, shiver, crack, split, burst, explode, blast, crush, demolish, destroy, devastate, wreck, ruin, overturn, upset.

sheath n 1 SCABBARD, case, sleeve, envelope, shell, casing, covering. 2 CONDOM, rubber (sl), French letter (sl).

shed[1] v cast (off), moult, slough, discard, drop, spill, pour, shower, scatter, diffuse, emit, radiate, shine, throw.

shed² *n* outhouse, lean-to, hut, shack.

sheen *n* lustre, gloss, shine, shimmer, brightness, brilliance, shininess, polish, burnish.
☒ dullness, tarnish.

sheepish *adj* ashamed, shamefaced, embarrassed, mortified, chastened, abashed, uncomfortable, self-conscious, silly, foolish.
☒ unabashed, brazen, bold.

sheer *adj* 1 UTTER, complete, total, absolute, thorough, mere, pure, unadulterated, downright, out-and-out, rank, thoroughgoing, unqualified, unmitigated. 2 *a sheer drop*: vertical, perpendicular, precipitous, abrupt, steep. 3 THIN, fine, flimsy, gauzy, gossamer, translucent, transparent, see-through.
☒ 2 gentle, gradual. 3 thick, heavy.

sheet *n* cover, blanket, covering, coating, coat, film, layer, stratum, skin, membrane, lamina, veneer, overlay, plate, piece, panel, slab, pane, expanse, surface.

shelf *n* ledge, mantelpiece, sill, step, bench, counter, bar, bank, sandbank, reef, terrace.

shell *n* covering, hull, husk, pod, rind, crust, case, casing, body, chassis, frame, framework, structure, skeleton.
◇ *v* 1 *shell nuts*: hull, husk, pod. 2 BOMB, bombard, barrage, blitz, attack.

shelter *v* cover, shroud, screen, shade, shadow, protect, safeguard, defend, guard, shield, harbour, hide, accommodate, put up.
☒ expose.
◇ *n* cover, roof, shade, shadow, protection, defence, guard, security, safety, sanctuary, asylum, haven, refuge, retreat, accommodation, lodging.
☒ exposure.

sheltered *adj* covered, shaded, shielded, protected, cosy, snug, warm, quiet, secluded, isolated, retired, withdrawn, reclusive, cloistered, unworldly.
☒ exposed.

shelve *v* postpone, defer, put off, suspend, halt, put aside, pigeonhole, put on ice, mothball.
☒ expedite, implement.

shield *n* buckler, escutcheon, defence, bulwark, rampart, screen, guard, cover, shelter, protection, safeguard.
◇ *v* defend, guard, protect, safeguard, screen, shade, shadow, cover, shelter.
☒ expose.

shift *v* change, vary, fluctuate, alter, adjust, move, budge, remove, dislodge, displace, relocate, reposition, rearrange, transpose, transfer, switch, swerve, veer.
◇ *n* change, fluctuation, alteration, modification, move, removal, displacement, rearrangement, transposition, transfer, switch.

shifty *adj* untrustworthy, dishonest, deceitful, scheming, contriving, tricky, wily, crafty, cunning, devious, evasive, slippery, furtive, underhand, dubious, shady (*infml*).
☒ dependable, honest, open.

shimmer *v* glisten, gleam, glimmer, glitter, scintillate, twinkle.
◇ *n* lustre, gleam, glimmer, glitter, glow.

shine *v* 1 BEAM, radiate, glow, flash, glare, gleam, glint, glitter, sparkle, twinkle, shimmer, glisten, glimmer. 2 POLISH, burnish, buff, brush, rub. 3 *shine at athletics*: excel, stand out.
◇ *n* 1 LIGHT, radiance, glow, brightness, glare, gleam, sparkle, shimmer. 2 GLOSS, polish, burnish, sheen, lustre, glaze.

shining *adj* 1 BRIGHT, radiant, glowing, beaming, flashing,

gleaming, glittering, glistening, shimmering, twinkling, sparkling, brilliant, resplendent, splendid, glorious. **2** *a shining example*: conspicuous, outstanding, leading, eminent, celebrated, distinguished, illustrious.
🔁 **1** dark.

shiny *adj* polished, burnished, sleek, sheeny, lustrous, glossy, bright, gleaming, glistening.
🔁 dull, matt.

ship *n* vessel, craft, liner, steamer, tanker, trawler, ferry, boat, yacht.

shirk *v* dodge, evade, avoid, duck (*infml*), shun, slack, skive (*infml*).

shiver *v* shudder, tremble, quiver, quake, shake, vibrate, palpitate, flutter.
◇ *n* shudder, quiver, shake, tremor, twitch, start, vibration, flutter.

shock *v* disgust, revolt, sicken, offend, appal, outrage, scandalize, horrify, astound, stagger, stun, stupefy, numb, paralyse, traumatize, jolt, jar, shake, agitate, unsettle, disquiet, unnerve, confound, dismay.
🔁 delight, please, gratify, reassure.
◇ *n* fright, start, jolt, impact, collision, surprise, bombshell, thunderbolt, blow, trauma, upset, distress, dismay, consternation, disgust, outrage.
🔁 delight, pleasure, reassurance.

shocking *adj* appalling, outrageous, scandalous, horrifying, disgraceful, deplorable, intolerable, unbearable, atrocious, abominable, monstrous, unspeakable, detestable, abhorrent, dreadful, awful, terrible, frightful, ghastly, hideous, horrible, disgusting, revolting, repulsive, sickening, nauseating, offensive, distressing.
🔁 acceptable, satisfactory, pleasant, delightful.

shoddy *adj* inferior, second-rate, cheap, tawdry, tatty, trashy, rubbishy, poor, careless, slipshod, slapdash.

🔁 superior, well-made.

shoe

Types of shoes and boots include: court shoe, brogue, casual, lace-up (*infml*), slip-on (*infml*), slingback, sandal, mule, espadrille, stiletto heel, kitten heel, platform heel, wedge heel, moccasin, Doc Martens®, DMs (*infml*), slipper, flip-flop (*infml*), jelly shoe, bootee, wellington boot, welly (*infml*), galosh, gumboot, football boot, rugby boot, tennis-shoe, plimsoll, pump, sneaker, trainer, running shoe, rock boot, snowshoe, ballet shoe, clog, sabot.

shoot *v* **1** FIRE, discharge, launch, propel, hurl, fling, project. **2** DART, bolt, dash, tear, rush, race, sprint, speed, charge, hurtle. **3** HIT, kill, blast, bombard, gun down, snipe at, pick off.
◇ *n* sprout, bud, offshoot, branch, twig, sprig, slip, scion.

shop

Types of shop include: bazaar, market, farmers' market, indoor market, mini-market, corner shop, charity shop, shopping mall, department store, supermarket, superstore, hypermarket, cash-and-carry, online shop; butcher, baker, grocer, greengrocer, fishmonger, dairy, delicatessen, health-food shop, fish and chip shop, takeaway, off-licence, tobacconist, sweet shop, confectioner, tuck shop; bookshop, bookstore (*N Am*), newsagent, stationer, chemist, pharmacy, tailor, outfitter, dress shop, boutique, milliner, shoe shop, haberdasher, draper, florist, jeweller, toyshop, hardware shop, ironmonger, computer shop, phone shop, video shop, bookmaker, pawnbroker, post office.

shore¹ n seashore, beach, sand(s), shingle, strand, waterfront, front, promenade, coast, seaboard, lakeside, bank.

shore² v support, hold, prop, stay, underpin, buttress, brace, strengthen, reinforce.

short adj 1 BRIEF, cursory, fleeting, momentary, transitory, ephemeral, concise, succinct, terse, pithy, compact, compressed, shortened, curtailed, abbreviated, abridged, summarized. 2 BRUSQUE, curt, gruff, snappy, sharp, abrupt, blunt, direct, rude, impolite, discourteous, uncivil. 3 SMALL, little, low, petite, diminutive, squat, dumpy. 4 INADEQUATE, insufficient, deficient, lacking, wanting, low, poor, meagre, scant, sparse.
⊞ 1 long, lasting. 2 polite. 3 tall. 4 adequate, ample.

shortage n inadequacy, insufficiency, deficiency, shortfall, deficit, lack, want, need, scarcity, paucity, poverty, dearth, absence.
⊞ sufficiency, abundance, surplus.

shortcoming n defect, imperfection, fault, flaw, drawback, failing, weakness, foible.

shorten v cut, trim, prune, crop, dock, curtail, truncate, abbreviate, abridge, reduce, lessen, decrease, diminish, take up.
⊞ lengthen, enlarge, amplify.

shortly adv soon, before long, presently, by and by.

short-sighted adj 1 MYOPIC, near-sighted. 2 IMPROVIDENT, imprudent, injudicious, unwise, impolitic, ill-advised, careless, hasty, ill-considered.
⊞ 1 long-sighted, far-sighted.

shot n 1 BULLET, missile, projectile, ball, pellet, slug (infml), discharge, blast. 2 (infml) ATTEMPT, try, effort,

endeavour, go (infml), bash (infml), crack (infml), stab (infml), guess, turn.

shoulder v 1 PUSH, shove, jostle, thrust, press. 2 ACCEPT, assume, take on, bear, carry, sustain.

shout n, v call, cry, scream, shriek, yell, roar, bellow, bawl, howl, bay, cheer.

shove v push, thrust, drive, propel, force, barge, jostle, elbow, shoulder, press, crowd.

shovel n spade, scoop, bucket.
◇ v dig, scoop, dredge, clear, move, shift, heap.

show v 1 REVEAL, expose, uncover, disclose, divulge, present, offer, exhibit, manifest, display, indicate, register, demonstrate, prove, illustrate, exemplify, explain, instruct, teach, clarify, elucidate. 2 show him out: lead, guide, conduct, usher, escort, accompany, attend.
⊞ 1 hide, cover.
◇ n 1 OSTENTATION, parade, display, flamboyance, panache, pizzazz (infml), showiness, exhibitionism, affectation, pose, pretence, illusion, semblance, façade, impression, appearance, air. 2 DEMONSTRATION, presentation, exhibition, exposition, fair, display, parade, pageant, extravaganza, spectacle, entertainment, performance, production, staging, showing, representation.
• **show off** parade, strut, swagger, brag, boast, swank (infml), flaunt, brandish, display, exhibit, demonstrate, advertise, set off, enhance.
• **show up 1** (infml) ARRIVE, come, turn up, appear, materialize (infml). 2 HUMILIATE, embarrass, mortify, shame, disgrace, let down. 3 REVEAL, show, expose, unmask, lay bare, highlight, pinpoint.

showdown n confrontation, clash, crisis, climax, culmination.

shower n rain, stream, torrent, deluge, hail, volley, barrage.
◇ v spray, sprinkle, rain, pour, deluge, inundate, overwhelm, load, heap, lavish.

show-off n swaggerer, braggart, boaster, exhibitionist, peacock, poser, poseur, egotist.

showy adj flashy, flamboyant, ostentatious, gaudy, garish, loud, tawdry, fancy, ornate, pretentious, pompous, swanky (infml), flash (infml).
⊜ quiet, restrained.

shred n ribbon, tatter, rag, scrap, snippet, sliver, bit, piece, fragment, jot, iota, atom, grain, mite, whit, trace.

shrewd adj astute, judicious, well-advised, calculated, far-sighted, smart, clever, intelligent, sharp, keen, acute, alert, perceptive, observant, discerning, discriminating, knowing, calculating, cunning, crafty, artful, sly.
⊜ unwise, obtuse, naive, unsophisticated.

shriek v, n scream, screech, squawk, squeal, cry, shout, yell, wail, howl.

shrill adj high, high-pitched, treble, sharp, acute, piercing, penetrating, screaming, screeching, strident, ear-splitting.
⊜ deep, low, soft, gentle.

shrink v 1 CONTRACT, shorten, narrow, decrease, lessen, diminish, dwindle, shrivel, wrinkle, wither.
2 RECOIL, back away, shy away, withdraw, retire, balk, quail, cower, cringe, wince, flinch, shun.
⊜ 1 expand, stretch. 2 accept, embrace.

shrivel v wrinkle, pucker, wither, wilt, shrink, dwindle, parch, dehydrate, desiccate, scorch, sear, burn, frizzle.

shroud v wrap, envelop, swathe, cloak, veil, screen, hide, conceal, blanket, cover.
⊜ uncover, expose.
◇ n winding-sheet, pall, mantle, cloak, veil, screen, blanket, covering.

shrub

Shrubs include: azalea, berberis, broom, buddleia, camellia, cotoneaster, daphne, dogwood, euonymus, firethorn, forsythia, fuchsia, heather, hebe, holly, honeysuckle, hydrangea, japonica, jasmine, laburnum, laurel, lilac, magnolia, mock orange, peony, privet, rhododendron, rose, spiraea, viburnum, weigela, witch hazel. see also **flower**; **plant**.

shudder v shiver, shake, tremble, quiver, quake, heave, convulse.
◇ n shiver, quiver, tremor, spasm, convulsion.

shuffle v 1 MIX (UP), intermix, jumble, confuse, disorder, rearrange, reorganize, shift around, switch.
2 shuffle across the room: shamble, scuffle, scrape, drag, limp, hobble.

shun v avoid, evade, elude, steer clear of, shy away from, spurn, ignore, cold-shoulder, ostracize.
⊜ accept, embrace.

shut v close, slam, seal, fasten, secure, lock, latch, bolt, bar.
⊜ open.
• shut down close, stop, cease, terminate, halt, discontinue, suspend, switch off, inactivate.
• shut in enclose, box in, hem in, fence in, immure, confine, imprison, cage.
• shut off seclude, isolate, cut off, separate, segregate.
• shut out 1 EXCLUDE, bar, debar, lock out, ostracize, banish. 2 HIDE, conceal, cover, mask, screen, veil.
• shut up 1 SILENCE, gag, quiet, hush up, pipe down (infml), hold one's tongue, clam up (infml). 2 CONFINE, coop up, imprison, incarcerate, jail,

intern.

shy *adj* timid, bashful, reticent, reserved, retiring, diffident, coy, self-conscious, inhibited, modest, self-effacing, shrinking, hesitant, cautious, chary, suspicious, nervous.
⊜ bold, assertive, confident.

sick *adj* **1** ILL, unwell, indisposed, laid up, poorly, ailing, sickly, under the weather, weak, feeble. **2** VOMITING, queasy, bilious, seasick, airsick. **3** *sick of waiting*: bored, fed up (*infml*), tired, weary, disgusted, nauseated.
⊜ **1** well, healthy.

sicken *v* nauseate, revolt, disgust, repel, put off, turn off (*sl*).
⊜ delight, attract.

sickening *adj* nauseating, revolting, disgusting, offensive, distasteful, foul, vile, loathsome, repulsive.
⊜ delightful, pleasing, attractive.

sickly *adj* **1** UNHEALTHY, infirm, delicate, weak, feeble, frail, wan, pallid, ailing, indisposed, sick, bilious, faint, languid. **2** NAUSEATING, revolting, sweet, syrupy, cloying, mawkish.
⊜ **1** healthy, robust, sturdy, strong.

sickness *n* **1** ILLNESS, disease, malady, ailment, complaint, affliction, ill health, indisposition, infirmity. **2** VOMITING, nausea, queasiness, biliousness.
⊜ **1** health.

side *n* **1** EDGE, margin, fringe, periphery, border, boundary, limit, verge, brink, bank, shore, quarter, region, flank, hand, face, facet, surface. **2** STANDPOINT, viewpoint, view, aspect, angle, slant. **3** TEAM, party, faction, camp, cause, interest.
◇ *adj* lateral, flanking, marginal, secondary, subsidiary, subordinate, lesser, minor, incidental, indirect, oblique.
• **side with** agree with, team up with, support, vote for, favour, prefer.

sidestep *v* avoid, dodge, duck, evade, elude, skirt, bypass.
⊜ tackle, deal with.

sidetrack *v* deflect, head off, divert, distract.

sideways *adv* sidewards, edgeways, laterally, obliquely.
◇ *adj* sideward, side, lateral, slanted, oblique, indirect, sidelong.

sidle *v* slink, edge, inch, creep, sneak.

sieve *v* sift, strain, separate, remove.
◇ *n* colander, strainer, sifter, riddle, screen.

sift *v* **1** SIEVE, strain, filter, riddle, screen, winnow, separate, sort. **2** EXAMINE, scrutinize, investigate, analyse, probe, review.

sigh *v* breathe, exhale, moan, complain, lament, grieve.

sight *n* **1** VISION, eyesight, seeing, observation, perception. **2** VIEW, look, glance, glimpse, range, field of vision, visibility. **3** APPEARANCE, spectacle, show, display, exhibition, scene, eyesore, monstrosity, fright (*infml*).
◇ *v* see, observe, spot, glimpse, perceive, discern, distinguish, make out.

sightseer *n* tourist, visitor, holidaymaker, tripper, excursionist.

sign *n* **1** SYMBOL, token, character, figure, representation, emblem, badge, insignia, logo. **2** INDICATION, mark, signal, gesture, evidence, manifestation, clue, pointer, hint, suggestion, trace. **3** NOTICE, poster, board, placard. **4** PORTENT, omen, forewarning, foreboding.
◇ *v* autograph, initial, endorse, write.
• **sign up** enlist, enrol, join (up), volunteer, register, sign on, recruit, take on, hire, engage, employ.

signal *n* sign, indication, mark, gesture, cue, go-ahead, password, light, indicator, beacon, flare, rocket,

alarm, alert, warning, tip-off.
◇ v wave, gesticulate, gesture, beckon, motion, nod, sign, indicate, communicate.

signature n autograph, initials, mark, endorsement, inscription.

significance n importance, relevance, consequence, matter, interest, consideration, weight, force, meaning, implication, sense, point, message.
⊞ insignificance, unimportance, pettiness.

significant adj 1 IMPORTANT, relevant, consequential, momentous, weighty, serious, noteworthy, critical, vital, marked, considerable, appreciable. 2 MEANINGFUL, symbolic, expressive, suggestive, indicative, symptomatic.
⊞ 1 insignificant, unimportant, trivial. 2 meaningless.

signify v 1 MEAN, denote, symbolize, represent, stand for, indicate, show, express, convey, transmit, communicate, intimate, imply, suggest. 2 MATTER, count.

silence n quiet, quietness, hush, peace, stillness, calm, lull, noiselessness, soundlessness, muteness, dumbness, speechlessness, taciturnity, uncommunicativeness, reticence, reserve.
⊞ noise, sound, din, uproar.
◇ v quiet, quieten, hush, mute, deaden, muffle, stifle, gag, muzzle, suppress, subdue, quell, still, dumbfound.

silent adj inaudible, noiseless, soundless, quiet, peaceful, still, hushed, muted, mute, dumb, speechless, tongue-tied, taciturn, mum, reticent, reserved, tacit, unspoken, unexpressed, understood, voiceless, wordless.
⊞ noisy, loud, talkative.

silhouette n outline, contour, delineation, shape, form, configuration, profile, shadow.

silky adj silken, fine, sleek, lustrous, glossy, satiny, smooth, soft, velvety.

silly adj foolish, stupid, imprudent, senseless, pointless, idiotic, daft (infml), ridiculous, ludicrous, preposterous, absurd, meaningless, irrational, illogical, childish, puerile, immature, irresponsible, dizzy (infml), scatterbrained, airheaded (infml).
⊞ wise, sensible, sane, mature, clever, intelligent.

silt n sediment, deposit, alluvium, sludge, mud, ooze.
• **silt up** block, clog, choke.

similar adj like, alike, close, related, akin, corresponding, equivalent, analogous, comparable, uniform, homogeneous.
⊞ dissimilar, different.

similarity n likeness, resemblance, similitude, closeness, relation, correspondence, congruence, equivalence, analogy, comparability, compatibility, agreement, affinity, homogeneity, uniformity.
⊞ dissimilarity, difference.

simmer v boil, bubble, seethe, stew, burn, smoulder, fume, rage.
• **simmer down** calm down, cool down, control oneself, collect oneself.

simple adj 1 a simple question: easy, elementary, straightforward, uncomplicated, uninvolved, clear, lucid, plain, understandable, comprehensible. 2 a simple child: unsophiscated, natural, innocent, artless, guileless, ingenuous, naive, green, foolish, stupid, silly, idiotic, halfwitted, simple-minded, feeble-minded, backward.
⊞ 1 difficult, hard, complicated, intricate. 2 sophisticated, worldly, artful, clever.

simplicity n simpleness, ease, straightforwardness, clarity, purity,

plainness, restraint, naturalness.
⊞ difficulty, complexity, intricacy,
sophistication.

simplify v disentangle, untangle,
decipher, clarify, paraphrase,
abridge, reduce, streamline.
⊞ complicate, elaborate.

simplistic adj superficial, shallow,
oversimplified, sweeping, facile,
simple, naive.
⊞ analytical, detailed.

simply adv **1** MERELY, just, only,
solely, purely, utterly, completely,
totally, wholly, absolutely, quite,
really, undeniably, unquestionably,
clearly, plainly, obviously. **2** EASILY,
straightforwardly, directly, intelligibly.

simulate v pretend, affect, assume,
put on, act, feign, sham, fake,
counterfeit, reproduce, duplicate,
copy, imitate, mimic, parrot, echo,
reflect.

simultaneous adj synchronous,
synchronic, concurrent,
contemporaneous, coinciding,
parallel.
⊞ asynchronous.

sin n wrong, offence, transgression,
trespass, misdeed, lapse, fault, error,
crime, wrongdoing, sinfulness,
wickedness, iniquity, evil, impiety,
ungodliness, unrighteousness, guilt.
◇ v offend, transgress, trespass,
lapse, err, misbehave, stray, go astray,
fall, fall from grace.

sincere adj honest, truthful, candid,
frank, open, direct, straightforward,
plain-spoken, serious, earnest,
heartfelt, whole-hearted, real,
true, genuine, pure, unadulterated,
unmixed, natural, unaffected, artless,
guileless, simple.
⊞ insincere, hypocritical, affected.

sincerity n honour, integrity,
probity, uprightness, honesty,
truthfulness, candour,
frankness, openness, directness,
straightforwardness, seriousness,

earnestness, whole-heartedness,
genuineness.
⊞ insincerity.

sinewy adj muscular, brawny,
strong, sturdy, robust, vigorous,
athletic, wiry, stringy.

sinful adj wrong, wrongful, criminal,
bad, wicked, iniquitous, erring,
fallen, immoral, corrupt, depraved,
impious, ungodly, unholy, irreligious,
guilty.
⊞ sinless, righteous, godly.

sing v chant, intone, vocalize, croon,
serenade, yodel, trill, warble, chirp,
pipe, whistle, hum.

singe v scorch, char, blacken, burn,
sear.

singer n vocalist, songster,
songstress, chanteuse, warbler.

Singers include: balladeer,
minstrel, troubadour, opera singer,
diva, prima donna, soloist,
precentor, choirboy, choirgirl,
chorister, chorus, folk-singer, pop
star, crooner, carol-singer; soprano,
coloratura soprano, castrato, tenor,
treble, contralto, alto, baritone,
bass.

single adj one, unique, singular,
individual, particular, exclusive,
sole, only, lone, solitary, separate,
distinct, free, unattached, unmarried,
celibate, unshared, undivided,
unbroken, simple, one-to-one, man-
to-man.
⊞ multiple.
● **single out** choose, select, pick,
hand-pick, distinguish, identify,
separate, set apart, isolate, highlight,
pinpoint.

single-handed adj, adv solo,
alone, unaccompanied, unaided,
unassisted, independent(ly).

single-minded adj determined,
resolute, dogged, persevering,
tireless, unwavering, fixed,

unswerving, undeviating, steadfast, dedicated, devoted.

sinister *adj* ominous, menacing, threatening, disturbing, disquieting, unlucky, inauspicious, malevolent, evil.
🔁 auspicious, harmless, innocent.

sink *v* 1 DESCEND, slip, fall, drop, slump, lower, stoop, succumb, lapse, droop, sag, dip, set, disappear, vanish. 2 DECREASE, lessen, subside, abate, dwindle, diminish, ebb, fade, flag, weaken, fail, decline, worsen, degenerate, degrade, decay, collapse. 3 FOUNDER, dive, plunge, plummet, submerge, immerse, engulf, drown. 4 *sink a well*: bore, drill, penetrate, dig, excavate, lay, conceal.
🔁 1 rise. 2 increase. 3 float.

sinner *n* wrongdoer, miscreant, offender, transgressor, trespasser, backslider, reprobate, evil-doer, malefactor.

sinuous *adj* lithe, slinky, curved, wavy, undulating, tortuous, twisting, winding, meandering, serpentine, coiling.
🔁 straight.

sip *v* taste, sample, drink, sup.
◇ *n* taste, drop, spoonful, mouthful.

sit *v* 1 SETTLE, rest, perch, roost, brood, pose. 2 SEAT, accommodate, hold, contain. 3 MEET, assemble, gather, convene, deliberate.

site *n* location, place, spot, position, situation, station, setting, scene, plot, lot, ground, area.
◇ *v* locate, place, position, situate, station, set, install.

sitting *n* session, period, spell, meeting, assembly, hearing, consultation.

situation *n* 1 SITE, location, position, place, spot, seat, locality, locale, setting, scenario. 2 STATE OF AFFAIRS, case, circumstances, predicament, state, condition, status, rank, station, post, office, job, employment.

sizable *adj* large, substantial, considerable, respectable, goodly, largish, biggish, decent, generous.
🔁 small, tiny.

size *n* magnitude, measurements, dimensions, proportions, volume, bulk, mass, height, length, extent, range, scale, amount, greatness, largeness, bigness, vastness, immensity.
● **size up** gauge, assess, evaluate, weigh up, measure.

sizzle *v* hiss, crackle, spit, sputter, fry, frizzle.

skeleton *n* bones, frame, structure, framework, bare bones, outline, draft, sketch.

sketch *v* draw, depict, portray, represent, pencil, paint, outline, delineate, draft, rough out, block out.
◇ *n* drawing, vignette, design, plan, diagram, outline, delineation, skeleton, draft.

sketchy *adj* rough, vague, incomplete, unfinished, scrappy, bitty, imperfect, inadequate, insufficient, slight, superficial, cursory, hasty.
🔁 full, complete.

skilful *adj* able, capable, adept, competent, proficient, deft, adroit, handy, expert, masterly, accomplished, skilled, practised, experienced, professional, clever, tactical, cunning.
🔁 inept, clumsy, awkward.

skill *n* skilfulness, ability, aptitude, facility, handiness, talent, knack, art, technique, training, experience, expertise, expertness, mastery, proficiency, competence, accomplishment, cleverness, intelligence.

skilled *adj* trained, schooled, qualified, professional, experienced, practised, accomplished, expert, masterly, proficient, able, skilful.
🔁 unskilled, inexperienced.

skim v 1 BRUSH, touch, skate, plane, float, sail, glide, fly. 2 SCAN, look through, skip. 3 CREAM, separate.

skimp v economize, scrimp, pinch, cut corners, stint, withhold.
⊡ squander, waste.

skin n hide, pelt, membrane, film, coating, surface, outside, peel, rind, husk, casing, crust.
◇ v flay, fleece, strip, peel, scrape, graze.

skinny adj thin, lean, scrawny, scraggy, skeletal, skin-and-bone, emaciated, underfed, undernourished.
⊡ fat, plump.

skip v 1 HOP, jump, leap, dance, gambol, frisk, caper, prance. 2 skip a page: miss, omit, leave out, cut.

skirmish n fight, combat, battle, engagement, encounter, conflict, clash, brush, scrap, tussle, set-to, dust-up (infml).

skirt v circle, circumnavigate, border, edge, flank, bypass, avoid, evade, circumvent.

Types of skirt include: miniskirt, dirndl, pencil skirt, pinafore skirt, culottes, kilt, sarong.

skit n satire, parody, caricature, spoof, take-off, sketch.

skulk v lurk, hide, prowl, sneak, creep, slink.

sky n space, atmosphere, air, heavens, blue.

slab n piece, block, lump, chunk, hunk, wodge (infml), wedge, slice, portion.

slack adj 1 LOOSE, limp, sagging, baggy. 2 LAZY, sluggish, slow, quiet, idle, inactive. 3 NEGLECTFUL, negligent, careless, inattentive, remiss, permissive, lax, relaxed, easy-going (infml).
⊡ 1 tight, taut, stiff, rigid. 2 busy.

3 diligent.
◇ n looseness, give, play, room, leeway, excess.
◇ v idle, shirk, skive (infml), neglect.

slacken off v loosen, release, relax, ease, moderate, reduce, lessen, decrease, diminish, abate, slow (down).
⊡ tighten, increase, intensify, quicken.

slacker n idler, shirker, skiver (infml), dawdler, clock-watcher, good-for-nothing, layabout.

slam v 1 BANG, crash, dash, smash, throw, hurl, fling. 2 (infml) CRITICIZE, slate (infml), pan (infml).

slander n defamation, calumny, misrepresentation, libel, scandal, smear, slur, aspersion, backbiting.
◇ v defame, vilify, malign, denigrate, disparage, libel, smear, slur, backbite.
⊡ praise, compliment.

slanderous adj defamatory, false, untrue, libellous, damaging, malicious, abusive, insulting.

slang n cant, jargon, argot, patois, patter, cockney, cockney rhyming slang, vulgarism, doublespeak, gobbledygook, colloquialism, informal expressions, lingo (infml), mumbo-jumbo (infml).

slant v 1 TILT, slope, incline, lean, list, skew, angle. 2 DISTORT, twist, warp, bend, weight, bias, colour.
◇ n 1 SLOPE, incline, gradient, ramp, camber, pitch, tilt, angle, diagonal. 2 BIAS, emphasis, attitude, viewpoint.

slanting adj sloping, tilted, oblique, diagonal.

slap n smack, spank, cuff, blow, bang, clap.
◇ v 1 SMACK, spank, hit, strike, cuff, clout, bang, clap. 2 DAUB, plaster, spread, apply.

slash v cut, slit, gash, lacerate, rip,

tear, rend.
◇ *n* cut, incision, slit, gash, laceration, rip, tear, rent.

slate *v* scold, rebuke, reprimand, berate, censure, blame, criticize, slam (*infml*).
⊞ praise.

slaughter *n* killing, murder, massacre, extermination, butchery, carnage, bloodbath, bloodshed.
◇ *v* kill, slay, murder, massacre, exterminate, liquidate, butcher.

slave *n* servant, drudge, vassal, serf, villein, captive.
◇ *v* toil, labour, drudge, sweat, grind, slog.

slaver *v* dribble, drivel, slobber, drool, salivate.

slavery *n* servitude, bondage, captivity, enslavement, serfdom, thraldom, subjugation.
⊞ freedom, liberty.

slavish *adj* 1 UNORIGINAL, imitative, unimaginative, uninspired, literal, strict. 2 SERVILE, abject, submissive, sycophantic, grovelling, cringing, fawning, menial, low, mean.
⊞ 1 original, imaginative.
2 independent, assertive.

sleek *adj* shiny, glossy, lustrous, smooth, silky, well-groomed.
⊞ rough, unkempt.

sleep *v* doze, snooze, slumber, kip (*sl*), doss (down) (*sl*), hibernate, drop off, nod off, rest, repose.
◇ *n* doze, snooze, nap, forty winks, shut-eye (*infml*), kip (*sl*), slumber, hibernation, rest, repose, siesta.

sleepless *adj* unsleeping, awake, wide awake, alert, vigilant, watchful, wakeful, restless, disturbed, insomniac.

sleepy *adj* drowsy, somnolent, tired, weary, heavy, slow, sluggish, torpid, lethargic, inactive, quiet, dull, soporific, hypnotic.
⊞ awake, alert, wakeful, restless.

slender *adj* 1 SLIM, thin, lean, slight, svelte, graceful. 2 *a slender chance*: faint, remote, slight, inconsiderable, tenuous, flimsy, feeble, inadequate, insufficient, meagre, scanty.
⊞ 1 fat. 2 appreciable, considerable, ample.

slice *n* piece, sliver, wafer, rasher, tranche, slab, wedge, segment, section, share, portion, helping, cut (*infml*), whack (*infml*).
◇ *v* carve, cut, chop, divide, segment.

slick *adj* 1 GLIB, plausible, easy, deft, adroit, sharp, dexterous, skilful, professional. 2 SMOOTH, sleek, glossy, shiny, polished.

slide *v* slip, slither, skid, skate, ski, toboggan, glide, plane, coast, skim.

slight *adj* 1 MINOR, unimportant, insignificant, negligible, trivial, paltry, modest, small, little, inconsiderable, insubstantial. 2 SLENDER, slim, diminutive, petite, delicate.
⊞ 1 major, significant, noticeable, considerable. 2 large, muscular.
◇ *v* scorn, despise, disdain, disparage, insult, affront, offend, snub, cut, cold-shoulder, ignore, disregard, neglect.
⊞ respect, praise, compliment, flatter.
◇ *n* insult, affront, slur, snub, rebuff, rudeness, discourtesy, disrespect, contempt, disdain, indifference, disregard, neglect.

slim *adj* 1 SLENDER, thin, lean, svelte, trim. 2 SLIGHT, remote, faint, poor.
⊞ 1 fat, chubby. 2 strong, considerable.
◇ *v* lose weight, diet, reduce.

slimy *adj* 1 MUDDY, miry, mucous, viscous, oily, greasy, slippery.
2 SERVILE, obsequious, sycophantic, toadying, smarmy, oily, unctuous.

sling *v* 1 THROW, hurl, fling, catapult, heave, pitch, lob, toss, chuck (*infml*).
2 HANG, suspend, dangle, swing.

slink *v* sneak, steal, creep, sidle, slip,

prowl, skulk.

slinky adj close-fitting, figure-hugging, clinging, skin-tight, sleek, sinuous.

slip¹ v slide, glide, skate, skid, trip, stumble, fall, slither, slink, sneak, steal, creep.
◇ n mistake, error, slip-up (*infml*), bloomer (*infml*), blunder, fault, indiscretion, boob (*infml*), omission, oversight, failure.

slip² n piece, strip, voucher, chit, coupon, certificate.

slippery adj 1 SLIPPY, icy, greasy, glassy, smooth, dangerous, treacherous, perilous. 2 *a slippery character*: dishonest, untrustworthy, false, duplicitous, two-faced, crafty, cunning, devious, evasive, smooth, smarmy.
⊞ 1 rough. 2 trustworthy, reliable.

slipshod adj careless, slapdash, sloppy, slovenly, untidy, negligent, lax, casual.
⊞ careful, fastidious, neat, tidy.

slit v cut, gash, slash, slice, split, rip, tear.
◇ n opening, aperture, vent, cut, incision, gash, slash, split, tear, rent.

slither v slide, slip, glide, slink, creep, snake, worm.

sliver n flake, shaving, paring, slice, wafer, shred, fragment, chip, splinter, shiver, shard.

slobber v dribble, drivel, slaver, drool, salivate.

slogan n jingle, motto, catchphrase, catchword, watchword, battle-cry, war cry.

slop v spill, overflow, slosh, splash, splatter, spatter.

slope v slant, lean, tilt, tip, pitch, incline, rise, fall.
◇ n incline, gradient, ramp, hill, ascent, descent, slant, tilt, pitch, inclination.

sloppy adj 1 WATERY, wet, liquid, runny, mushy, slushy. 2 *sloppy work*: careless, hit-or-miss, slapdash, slipshod, slovenly, untidy, messy, clumsy, amateurish. 3 SOPPY, sentimental, schmaltzy, slushy, mushy.
⊞ 1 solid. 2 careful, exact, precise.

slot n hole, opening, aperture, slit, vent, groove, channel, gap, space, time, vacancy, place, spot, position, niche.
◇ v insert, fit, place, position, assign, pigeonhole.

slouch v stoop, hunch, droop, slump, lounge, loll, shuffle, shamble.

slovenly adj sloppy, careless, slipshod, untidy, scruffy, slatternly, sluttish.
⊞ neat, smart.

slow adj 1 LEISURELY, unhurried, lingering, loitering, dawdling, lazy, sluggish, slow-moving, creeping, gradual, deliberate, measured, plodding, delayed, late, unpunctual. 2 STUPID, slow-witted, dim, thick (*infml*). 3 PROLONGED, protracted, long-drawn-out, tedious, boring, dull, uninteresting, uneventful.
⊞ 1 quick, fast, swift, rapid, speedy. 2 clever, intelligent. 3 brisk, lively, exciting.
◇ v brake, decelerate, delay, hold up, retard, handicap, check, curb, restrict.
⊞ speed, accelerate.

sluggish adj lethargic, listless, torpid, heavy, dull, slow, slow-moving, slothful, lazy, idle, inactive, lifeless, unresponsive.
⊞ brisk, vigorous, lively, dynamic.

slump v 1 COLLAPSE, fall, drop, plunge, plummet, sink, decline, deteriorate, worsen, crash, fail. 2 DROOP, sag, bend, stoop, slouch, loll, lounge, flop.
◇ n recession, depression, stagnation, downturn, low, trough, decline, deterioration, worsening,

fall, drop, collapse, crash, failure.
⊡ boom.

sly *adj* wily, foxy, crafty, cunning,
artful, guileful, clever, canny, shrewd,
astute, knowing, subtle, devious,
shifty, tricky, furtive, stealthy,
surreptitious, underhand, covert,
secretive, scheming, conniving,
mischievous, roguish.
⊡ honest, frank, candid, open.

smack *v* hit, strike, slap, spank,
whack (*infml*), thwack (*infml*), clap,
box, cuff, pat, tap.
◇ *n* blow, slap, spank, whack (*infml*),
thwack (*infml*), box, cuff, pat, tap.
◇ *adv* bang, slap-bang, right, plumb,
straight, directly, exactly, precisely.

small *adj* 1 LITTLE, tiny, minute,
minuscule, short, slight, puny,
petite, diminutive, pint-size(d)
(*infml*), miniature, mini, pocket,
pocket-sized, young. 2 PETTY, trifling,
trivial, unimportant, insignificant,
minor, inconsiderable, negligible.
3 INADEQUATE, insufficient, scanty,
meagre, paltry, mean, limited.
⊡ 1 large, big, huge. 2 great,
considerable. 3 ample.

small-minded *adj* petty, mean,
ungenerous, illiberal, intolerant,
bigoted, narrow-minded, parochial,
insular, rigid, hidebound.
⊡ liberal, tolerant, broad-minded.

smarmy *adj* smooth, oily, unctuous,
servile, obsequious, sycophantic,
toadying, ingratiating, crawling,
fawning.

smart *adj* 1 *smart clothes*: elegant,
stylish, chic, fashionable, modish,
neat, tidy, spruce, trim, well-
groomed. 2 CLEVER, intelligent, bright,
sharp, acute, shrewd, astute.
⊡ 1 dowdy, unfashionable, untidy,
scruffy. 2 stupid, slow.
◇ *v* sting, hurt, prick, burn, tingle,
twinge, throb.

smarten *v* neaten, tidy, spruce up,
groom, clean, polish, beautify.

smash *v* 1 *smash a window*: break,
shatter, shiver, ruin, wreck, demolish,
destroy, defeat, crush. 2 CRASH,
collide, strike, bang, bash, thump.
◇ *n* accident, crash, collision, pile-
up.

smattering *n* bit, modicum,
dash, sprinkling, basics, rudiments,
elements.

smear *v* 1 DAUB, plaster, spread,
cover, coat, rub, smudge, streak.
2 DEFAME, malign, vilify, blacken,
sully, stain, tarnish.
◇ *n* 1 STREAK, smudge, blot, blotch,
splodge, daub. 2 DEFAMATION, slander,
libel, mudslinging, muck-raking.

smell *n* odour, whiff, scent, perfume,
fragrance, bouquet, aroma, stench,
stink, pong (*infml*).
◇ *v* sniff, nose, scent, stink, reek,
pong (*infml*).

smelly *adj* malodorous, pongy
(*infml*), stinking, reeking, foul, bad,
off, fetid, putrid, high, strong.

smile *n*, *v* grin, beam, simper, smirk,
leer, laugh.

smoke *n* fumes, exhaust, gas,
vapour, mist, fog, smog.
◇ *v* fume, smoulder, cure, dry.

smoky *adj* sooty, black, grey, grimy,
murky, cloudy, hazy, foggy.

smooth *adj* 1 LEVEL, plane, even,
flat, horizontal, flush. 2 STEADY,
unbroken, flowing, regular, uniform,
rhythmic, easy, effortless. 3 SHINY,
polished, glossy, silky, glassy, calm,
undisturbed, serene, tranquil,
peaceful. 4 SUAVE, agreeable, smooth-
talking, glib, plausible, persuasive,
slick, smarmy, unctuous, ingratiating.
⊡ 1 rough, lumpy. 2 irregular,
erratic, unsteady. 3 rough, choppy.
◇ *v* 1 IRON, press, roll, flatten, level,
plane, file, sand, polish. 2 EASE,
alleviate, assuage, allay, mitigate,
calm, mollify.
⊡ 1 roughen, wrinkle, crease.

smother *v* suffocate, asphyxiate,

strangle, throttle, choke, stifle,
extinguish, snuff, muffle, suppress,
repress, hide, conceal, cover, shroud,
envelop, wrap.

smoulder v burn, smoke, fume,
rage, seethe, simmer.

smudge v blur, smear, daub, mark,
spot, stain, dirty, soil.
◇ n blot, stain, spot, blemish, blur,
smear, streak.

smug adj complacent, self-satisfied,
superior, holier-than-thou, self-
righteous, priggish, conceited.
☒ humble, modest.

snack n refreshment(s), bite, nibble,
titbit, elevenses (infml).

snag n disadvantage, inconvenience,
drawback, catch, problem, difficulty,
complication, setback, hitch,
obstacle, stumbling-block.
◇ v catch, rip, tear, hole, ladder.

snap v 1 the twig snapped: break,
crack, split, separate. 2 BITE, nip,
bark, growl, snarl, retort, crackle,
pop. 3 SNATCH, seize, catch, grasp,
grip.
◇ n break, crack, bite, nip, flick,
fillip, crackle, pop.
◇ adj immediate, instant, on-the-
spot, abrupt, sudden.

snappy adj 1 SMART, stylish, chic,
fashionable, modish, trendy (infml).
2 QUICK, hasty, brisk, lively, energetic.
3 CROSS, irritable, edgy, touchy,
brusque, quick-tempered, ill-natured,
crabbed, testy.
☒ 1 dowdy. 2 slow.

snare v trap, ensnare, entrap, catch,
net.
◇ n trap, wire, net, noose, catch,
pitfall.

snarl[1] v growl, grumble, complain.

snarl[2] v tangle, knot, ravel, entangle,
enmesh, embroil, confuse, muddle,
complicate.

snatch v grab, seize, kidnap, take,
nab (infml), pluck, pull, wrench,
wrest, gain, win, clutch, grasp,
grip.

sneak v 1 CREEP, steal, slip, slink,
sidle, skulk, lurk, prowl, smuggle,
spirit. 2 TELL TALES, split (sl), inform on,
grass on (sl).
◇ n tell-tale, informer, grass (sl).

sneaking adj private, secret, furtive,
surreptitious, hidden, lurking,
suppressed, grudging, nagging,
niggling, persistent, worrying,
uncomfortable, intuitive.

sneer v scorn, disdain, look down
on, deride, scoff, jeer, mock, ridicule,
gibe, laugh, snigger.
◇ n scorn, disdain, derision, jeer,
mockery, ridicule, gibe, snigger.

snide adj derogatory, disparaging,
sarcastic, cynical, scornful, sneering,
hurtful, unkind, nasty, mean, spiteful,
malicious, ill-natured.
☒ complimentary.

sniff v breathe, inhale, snuff, snuffle,
smell, nose, scent.

snigger v, n laugh, giggle, titter,
chuckle, sneer.

snip v cut, clip, trim, crop, dock, slit,
nick, notch.

snippet n piece, scrap, cutting,
clipping, fragment, particle, shred,
snatch, part, portion, segment,
section.

snobbery n snobbishness,
superciliousness, snootiness (infml),
airs, loftiness, arrogance, pride,
pretension, condescension.

snobbish adj supercilious,
disdainful, snooty (infml), stuck-
up (infml), toffee-nosed (infml),
superior, lofty, high and mighty,
arrogant, pretentious, affected,
condescending, patronizing.

snoop v spy, sneak, pry, nose,
interfere, meddle.

snooze v nap, doze, sleep, kip (sl).
◇ n nap, catnap, forty winks, doze,
siesta, sleep, kip (sl).

snub v rebuff, brush off, cut, cold-shoulder, slight, rebuke, put down, squash, humble, shame, humiliate, mortify.
◇ n rebuff, brush-off, slight, affront, insult, rebuke, put-down, humiliation.

snug adj cosy, warm, comfortable, homely, friendly, intimate, sheltered, secure, tight, close-fitting.

soak v wet, drench, saturate, penetrate, permeate, infuse, bathe, marinate, souse, steep, submerge, immerse.

soaking adj soaked, drenched, sodden, waterlogged, saturated, sopping, wringing, dripping, streaming.
⊜ dry.

soar v fly, wing, glide, plane, tower, rise, ascend, climb, mount, escalate, rocket.
⊜ fall, plummet.

sob v cry, weep, bawl, howl, blubber, snivel.

sober adj 1 TEETOTAL, temperate, moderate, abstinent, abstemious. 2 SOLEMN, dignified, serious, staid, steady, sedate, quiet, serene, calm, composed, unruffled, unexcited, cool, dispassionate, level-headed, practical, realistic, reasonable, rational, clear-headed. 3 sober dress: sombre, drab, dull, plain, subdued, restrained.
⊜ 1 drunk, intemperate. 2 frivolous, excited, unrealistic, irrational. 3 flashy, garish.

so-called adj alleged, supposed, purported, ostensible, nominal, self-styled, professed, would-be, pretended.

sociable adj outgoing, gregarious, friendly, affable, companionable, genial, convivial, cordial, warm, hospitable, neighbourly, approachable, accessible, familiar.
⊜ unsociable, withdrawn,

unfriendly, hostile.

social adj communal, public, community, common, general, collective, group, organized.
◇ n party, do (infml), get-together, gathering.

socialize v mix, mingle, fraternize, get together, go out, entertain.

society n 1 COMMUNITY, population, culture, civilization, nation, people, mankind, humanity. 2 CLUB, circle, group, association, organization, company, corporation, league, union, guild, fellowship, fraternity, brotherhood, sisterhood, sorority. 3 FRIENDSHIP, companionship, camaraderie, fellowship, company. 4 UPPER CLASSES, aristocracy, gentry, nobility, élite.

soft adj 1 YIELDING, pliable, flexible, elastic, plastic, malleable, spongy, squashy, pulpy. 2 soft colours: pale, light, pastel, delicate, subdued, muted, quiet, low, dim, faint, diffuse, mild, bland, gentle, soothing, sweet, mellow, melodious, dulcet, pleasant. 3 FURRY, downy, velvety, silky, smooth. 4 LENIENT, lax, permissive, indulgent, tolerant, easy-going (infml), kind, generous, gentle, merciful, soft-hearted, tender, sensitive, weak, spineless.
⊜ 1 hard. 2 harsh. 3 rough. 4 strict, severe.

soften v 1 MODERATE, temper, mitigate, lessen, diminish, abate, alleviate, ease, soothe, palliate, quell, assuage, subdue, mollify, appease, calm, still, relax. 2 MELT, liquefy, dissolve, reduce. 3 CUSHION, pad, muffle, quicken, lower, lighten.

soft-hearted adj sympathetic, compassionate, kind, benevolent, charitable, generous, warm-hearted, tender, sentimental.
⊜ hard-hearted, callous.

soggy adj wet, damp, moist, soaked, drenched, sodden, waterlogged, saturated, sopping, dripping, heavy, boggy, spongy, pulpy.

soil[1] n earth, clay, loam, humus, dirt, dust, ground, land, region, country.

soil[2] v dirty, begrime, stain, spot, smudge, smear, foul, muddy, pollute, defile, besmirch, sully, tarnish.

solace n comfort, consolation, relief, alleviation, support, cheer.

soldier n warrior, fighter, serviceman, servicewoman.

Types of soldier include: cadet, private, sapper, NCO, orderly, officer, gunner, infantryman, trooper, fusilier, rifleman, paratrooper, sentry, guardsman, marine, commando, tommy, dragoon, cavalryman, lancer, hussar, conscript, recruit, regular, Territorial, GI (US), mercenary, legionnaire, guerrilla, partisan, centurion. see also **armed services**.

---

sole adj only, unique, exclusive, individual, single, singular, one, lone, solitary, alone.
☒ shared, multiple, several.

solemn adj 1 a solemn expression: serious, grave, sober, sedate, sombre, glum, thoughtful, earnest, awed, reverential. 2 GRAND, stately, majestic, ceremonial, ritual, formal, ceremonious, pompous, dignified, august, venerable, awe-inspiring, impressive, imposing, momentous.
☒ 1 light-hearted. 2 frivolous.

solicit v ask, request, seek, crave, beg, beseech, entreat, implore, pray, supplicate, sue, petition, canvass, importune.

solicitor n lawyer, advocate, attorney, barrister, QC.

solicitous adj caring, attentive, considerate, concerned, anxious, worried.

solid adj 1 HARD, firm, dense, compact, strong, sturdy, substantial,

sound, unshakable. 2 a solid white line: unbroken, continuous, uninterrupted. 3 RELIABLE, dependable, trusty, worthy, decent, upright, sensible, level-headed, stable, serious, sober. 4 REAL, genuine, pure, concrete, tangible.
☒ 1 liquid, gaseous, hollow. 2 broken, dotted. 3 unreliable, unstable. 4 unreal.

solidarity n unity, agreement, accord, unanimity, consensus, harmony, concord, cohesion, like-mindedness, camaraderie, team spirit, soundness, stability.
☒ discord, division, schism.

solidify v harden, set, jell, congeal, coagulate, clot, cake, crystallize.
☒ soften, liquefy, dissolve.

solitary adj sole, single, lone, alone, lonely, lonesome, friendless, unsociable, reclusive, withdrawn, retired, sequestered, cloistered, secluded, separate, isolated, remote, out-of-the-way, inaccessible, unfrequented, unvisited, untrodden.
☒ accompanied, gregarious, busy.

solitude n aloneness, loneliness, reclusiveness, retirement, privacy, seclusion, isolation, remoteness.
☒ companionship.

solution n 1 ANSWER, result, explanation, resolution, key, remedy. 2 MIXTURE, blend, compound, suspension, emulsion, liquid.

solve v work out, figure out, puzzle out, decipher, crack, disentangle, unravel, answer, resolve, settle, clear up, clarify, explain, interpret.

sombre adj dark, funereal, drab, dull, dim, obscure, shady, shadowy, gloomy, dismal, melancholy, mournful, sad, joyless, sober, serious, grave.
☒ bright, cheerful, happy.

someday adv sometime, one day, eventually, ultimately.
☒ never.

sometimes *adv* occasionally, now and again, now and then, once in a while, from time to time.
⊞ always, never.

song *n* tune, melody, number, ditty.

Types of song include: air, anthem, aria, ballad, barcarole, blues, calypso, cantata, canticle, cantilena, canzone, canzonet, carol, chanson, chansonette, chant, chorus, descant, dirge, ditty, elegy, folk song, gospel song, hymn, jingle, lay, lied, love-song, lullaby, madrigal, ode, plainchant, plainsong, pop song, psalm, recitative, requiem, roundelay, serenade, shanty, spiritual, torch song, wassail, yodel.

---

soon *adv* shortly, presently, in a minute, before long, in the near future.

soothe *v* alleviate, relieve, ease, salve, comfort, allay, calm, compose, tranquillize, settle, still, quiet, hush, lull, pacify, appease, mollify, assuage, mitigate, soften.
⊞ aggravate, irritate, annoy, vex.

sophisticated *adj* **1** URBANE, cosmopolitan, worldly, worldly-wise, cultured, cultivated, refined, polished. **2** *sophisticated technology*: advanced, highly-developed, complicated, complex, intricate, elaborate, whizzy (*infml*), delicate, subtle.
⊞ **1** unsophisticated, naive.
2 primitive, simple.

soporific *adj* sleep-inducing, hypnotic, sedative, tranquillizing, sleepy, somnolent.
⊞ stimulating, invigorating.

soppy *adj* sentimental, lovey-dovey (*infml*), weepy (*infml*), sloppy, slushy, mushy, corny (*infml*), mawkish, cloying, soft, silly, daft (*infml*).

sorcery *n* magic, black magic, witchcraft, wizardry, necromancy, voodoo, spell, incantation, charm, enchantment.

sordid *adj* dirty, filthy, unclean, foul, vile, squalid, sleazy, seamy, seedy, disreputable, shabby, tawdry, corrupt, degraded, degenerate, debauched, low, base, despicable, shameful, wretched, mean, miserly, niggardly, grasping, mercenary, selfish, self-seeking.
⊞ pure, honourable, upright.

sore *adj* **1** PAINFUL, hurting, aching, smarting, stinging, tender, sensitive, inflamed, red, raw. **2** ANNOYED, irritated, vexed, angry, upset, hurt, wounded, afflicted, aggrieved, resentful.
⊞ **2** pleased, happy.
◇ *n* wound, lesion, swelling, inflammation, boil, abscess, ulcer.

sorrow *n* sadness, unhappiness, grief, mourning, misery, woe, distress, affliction, anguish, heartache, heartbreak, misfortune, hardship, trouble, worry, trial, tribulation, regret, remorse.
⊞ happiness, joy.

sorry *adj* **1** APOLOGETIC, regretful, remorseful, contrite, penitent, repentant, conscience-stricken, guilt-ridden, shamefaced. **2** *in a sorry state*: pathetic, pitiful, poor, wretched, miserable, sad, unhappy, dismal. **3** SYMPATHETIC, compassionate, understanding, pitying, concerned, moved.
⊞ **1** impenitent, unashamed.
2 happy, cheerful. **3** uncaring.

sort *n* kind, type, genre, ilk, family, race, breed, species, genus, variety, order, class, category, group, denomination, style, make, brand, stamp, quality, nature, character, description.
◇ *v* class, group, categorize, distribute, divide, separate, segregate, sift, screen, grade, rank, order, classify, catalogue, arrange, organize, systematize.

• **sort out** resolve, clear up, clarify, tidy up, neaten, choose, select.

soul n 1 SPIRIT, psyche, mind, reason, intellect, character, inner being, essence, life, vital force. 2 INDIVIDUAL, person, man, woman, creature.

sound¹ n noise, din, report, resonance, reverberation, tone, timbre, tenor, description.
◊ v 1 RING, toll, chime, peal, resound, resonate, reverberate, echo. 2 ARTICULATE, enunciate, pronounce, voice, express, utter, say, declare, announce.

sound² adj 1 FIT, well, healthy, vigorous, robust, sturdy, firm, solid, whole, complete, intact, perfect, unbroken, undamaged, unimpaired, unhurt, uninjured. 2 VALID, well-founded, reasonable, rational, logical, orthodox, right, true, proven, reliable, trustworthy, secure, substantial, thorough, good.
⊡ 1 unfit, ill, shaky. 2 unsound, unreliable, poor.

sound³ v measure, plumb, fathom, probe, examine, test, inspect, investigate.

soup

Types of soup include: bouillabaisse, borsch, broth, gumbo, cock-a-leekie, consommé, gazpacho, goulash, minestrone, vegetable soup, vichyssoise.

sour adj 1 TART, sharp, acid, pungent, vinegary, bitter, rancid. 2 EMBITTERED, acrimonious, ill-tempered, peevish, crabbed, crusty, disagreeable.
⊡ 1 sweet, sugary. 2 good-natured, generous.

source n 1 ORIGIN, derivation, beginning, start, commencement, cause, root, rise, spring, fountainhead, wellhead, supply, mine. 2 ORIGINATOR, authority, informant.

souvenir n memento, reminder, remembrance, keepsake, relic, token.

sovereign n ruler, monarch, king, queen, emperor, empress, potentate, chief.
◊ adj ruling, royal, imperial, absolute, unlimited, supreme, paramount, predominant, principal, chief, dominant, independent, autonomous.

sow v plant, seed, scatter, strew, spread, disseminate, lodge, implant.

space n 1 ROOM, place, seat, accommodation, capacity, volume, extent, expansion, scope, range, play, elbow-room, leeway, margin. 2 BLANK, omission, gap, opening, lacuna, interval, intermission, chasm.

spacious adj roomy, capacious, ample, big, large, sizable, broad, wide, huge, vast, extensive, open, uncrowded.
⊡ small, narrow, cramped, confined.

span n spread, stretch, reach, range, scope, compass, extent, length, distance, duration, term, period, spell.
◊ v arch, vault, bridge, link, cross, traverse, extend, cover.

spank v smack, slap, wallop (infml), whack (infml), thrash, slipper, cane.

spare adj reserve, emergency, extra, additional, leftover, remaining, over, unused, surplus, superfluous, supernumerary, unwanted, free, unoccupied.
⊡ necessary, vital, used.
◊ v 1 PARDON, let off, reprieve, release, free. 2 GRANT, allow, afford, part with.

sparing adj economical, thrifty, careful, prudent, frugal, meagre, miserly.
⊡ unsparing, liberal, lavish.

spark n flash, flare, gleam, glint, flicker, hint, trace, vestige, scrap, atom, jot.
◊ v kindle, set off, trigger, start,

cause, occasion, prompt, provoke, stimulate, stir, excite, inspire.

sparkle v 1 TWINKLE, glitter, scintillate, flash, gleam, glint, glisten, shimmer, coruscate, shine, beam. 2 EFFERVESCE, fizz, bubble.
◇ n twinkle, glitter, flash, gleam, glint, flicker, spark, radiance, brilliance, dazzle, spirit, vitality, life, animation.

sparse adj scarce, scanty, meagre, scattered, infrequent, sporadic.
🗷 plentiful, thick, dense.

spartan adj austere, harsh, severe, rigorous, strict, disciplined, ascetic, abstemious, temperate, frugal, plain, simple, bleak, joyless.
🗷 luxurious, self-indulgent.

spasm n burst, eruption, outburst, frenzy, fit, convulsion, seizure, attack, contraction, jerk, twitch, tic.

spasmodic adj sporadic, occasional, intermittent, erratic, irregular, fitful, jerky.
🗷 continuous, uninterrupted.

spate n flood, deluge, torrent, rush, outpouring, flow.

speak v talk, converse, say, state, declare, express, utter, voice, articulate, enunciate, pronounce, tell, communicate, address, lecture, harangue, hold forth, declaim, argue, discuss.

speaker n lecturer, orator, spokesperson, spokesman, spokeswoman.

special adj 1 a special occasion: important, significant, momentous, major, noteworthy, distinguished, memorable, remarkable, extraordinary, exceptional.
2 DIFFERENT, distinctive, characteristic, peculiar, singular, individual, unique, exclusive, select, choice, particular, specific, unusual, precise, detailed.
🗷 1 normal, ordinary, usual.
2 general, common.

specialist n consultant, authority, expert, master, professional, connoisseur.

speciality n strength, forte, talent, field, pièce de résistance.

specific adj precise, exact, fixed, limited, particular, special, definite, unequivocal, clear-cut, explicit, express, unambiguous.
🗷 vague, approximate.

specification n requirement, condition, qualification, description, listing, item, particular, detail.

specify v stipulate, spell out, define, particularize, detail, itemize, enumerate, list, mention, cite, name, designate, indicate, describe, delineate.

specimen n sample, example, instance, illustration, model, pattern, paradigm, exemplar, representative, copy, exhibit.

spectacle n show, performance, display, exhibition, parade, pageant, extravaganza, scene, sight, curiosity, wonder, marvel, phenomenon.

spectacular adj grand, splendid, magnificent, sensational, impressive, striking, stunning, staggering, amazing, remarkable, dramatic, daring, breathtaking, dazzling, eye-catching, colourful.
🗷 unimpressive, ordinary.

spectator n watcher, viewer, onlooker, looker-on, bystander, passer-by, witness, eye-witness, observer.
🗷 player, participant.

spectre n ghost, phantom, spirit, wraith, apparition, vision, presence.

speculate v wonder, contemplate, meditate, muse, reflect, consider, deliberate, theorize, suppose, guess, conjecture, surmise, gamble, risk, hazard, venture.

speculative adj conjectural, hypothetical, theoretical, notional, abstract, academic, tentative, risky, hazardous, uncertain, unpredictable.

speech n 1 DICTION, articulation, enunciation, elocution, delivery, utterance, voice, language, tongue, parlance, dialect, jargon. 2 *make a speech*: oration, address, discourse, talk, lecture, harangue, spiel (*sl*), conversation, dialogue, monologue, soliloquy.

speechless adj dumbfounded, thunderstruck, amazed, aghast, tongue-tied, inarticulate, mute, dumb, silent, mum.
⊞ talkative.

speed n velocity, rate, pace, tempo, quickness, swiftness, rapidity, celerity, alacrity, haste, hurry, dispatch, rush, acceleration.
⊞ slowness, delay.
◊ v race, tear, belt (*infml*), zoom, career, bowl along, sprint, gallop, hurry, rush, hasten, accelerate, quicken, put one's foot down (*infml*), step on it (*infml*).
⊞ slow, delay.

speedy adj fast, quick, swift, rapid, nimble, express, prompt, immediate, hurried, hasty, precipitate, cursory.
⊞ slow, leisurely.

spell¹ n period, time, bout, session, term, season, interval, stretch, patch, turn, stint.

spell² n charm, incantation, magic, sorcery, witchery, bewitchment, enchantment, fascination, glamour.

spellbound adj transfixed, hypnotized, mesmerized, fascinated, enthralled, gripped, entranced, captivated, bewitched, enchanted, charmed.

spend v 1 *spend money*: disburse, pay out, fork out (*infml*), shell out (*infml*), invest, lay out, splash out (*infml*), waste, squander, fritter, expend, consume, use up, exhaust.
2 PASS, fill, occupy, use, employ,

apply, devote.
⊞ 1 save, hoard.

spendthrift n squanderer, prodigal, profligate, wastrel.
⊞ miser.
◊ adj improvident, extravagant, prodigal, wasteful.

sphere n 1 BALL, globe, orb, round. 2 DOMAIN, realm, province, department, territory, field, range, scope, compass, rank, function, capacity.

spherical adj round, rotund, ball-shaped, globe-shaped.

spicy adj 1 PIQUANT, hot, pungent, tangy, seasoned, aromatic, fragrant. 2 RACY, risqué, ribald, suggestive, indelicate, improper, indecorous, unseemly, scandalous, sensational.
⊞ 1 bland, insipid. 2 decent.

spike n point, prong, tine, spine, barb, nail, stake.
◊ v impale, stick, spear, skewer, spit.

spill v overturn, upset, slop, overflow, disgorge, pour, tip, discharge, shed, scatter.

spin v turn, revolve, rotate, twist, gyrate, twirl, pirouette, wheel, whirl, swirl, reel.
◊ n 1 TURN, revolution, twist, gyration, twirl, pirouette, whirl, swirl. 2 COMMOTION, agitation, panic, flap (*infml*), state (*infml*), tizzy (*infml*). 3 DRIVE, ride, run.
● **spin out** prolong, protract, extend, lengthen, amplify, pad out.

spindle n axis, pivot, pin, rod, axle.

spine n 1 BACKBONE, spinal column, vertebral column, vertebrae. 2 THORN, barb, prickle, bristle, quill.

spineless adj weak, feeble, wimpy (*infml*), irresolute, ineffective, cowardly, faint-hearted, lily-livered, yellow (*sl*), soft, wet, submissive, weak-kneed.
⊞ strong, brave.

spiral adj winding, coiled,

corkscrew, helical, whorled, scrolled, circular.
◇ *n* coil, helix, corkscrew, screw, whorl, convolution.

spire *n* steeple, pinnacle, peak, summit, top, tip, point, spike.

spirit *n* **1** SOUL, psyche, mind, breath, life. **2** GHOST, spectre, phantom, apparition, angel, demon, fairy, sprite. **3** LIVELINESS, vivacity, animation, sparkle, vigour, energy, zest, fire, ardour, motivation, enthusiasm, zeal, enterprise, resólution, willpower, courage, backbone, mettle. **4** *the spirit of the law*: meaning, sense, substance, essence, gist, tenor, character, quality. **5** MOOD, humour, temper, disposition, temperament, feeling, morale, attitude, outlook.

spirited *adj* lively, vivacious, animated, sparkling, high-spirited, vigorous, energetic, active, ardent, zealous, bold, courageous, feisty (*infml*), mettlesome, plucky.
⊞ spiritless, lethargic, cowardly.

spiritual *adj* unworldly, incorporeal, immaterial, otherworldly, heavenly, divine, holy, sacred, religious, ecclesiastical.
⊞ physical, material.

spit *v* expectorate, eject, discharge, splutter, hiss.
◇ *n* spittle, saliva, slaver, drool, dribble, sputum, phlegm, expectoration.

spite *n* spitefulness, malice, venom, gall, bitterness, rancour, animosity, ill feeling, grudge, malevolence, malignity, ill nature, hate, hatred.
⊞ goodwill, compassion, affection.
◇ *v* annoy, irritate, irk, vex, provoke, gall, hurt, injure, offend, put out.

spiteful *adj* malicious, venomous, catty, bitchy, snide, barbed, cruel, vindictive, vengeful, malevolent, malignant, ill-natured, ill-disposed, nasty.

⊞ charitable, affectionate.

splash *v* **1** BATHE, wallow, paddle, wade, dabble, plunge, wet, wash, shower, spray, squirt, sprinkle, spatter, splatter, splodge, spread, daub, plaster, slop, slosh, plop, surge, break, dash, strike, buffet, smack. **2** PUBLICIZE, flaunt, blazon, trumpet.
◇ *n* **1** SPOT, patch, splatter, splodge, burst, touch, dash. **2** PUBLICITY, display, ostentation, effect, impact, stir, excitement, sensation.

splendid *adj* brilliant, dazzling, glittering, lustrous, bright, radiant, glowing, glorious, magnificent, gorgeous, resplendent, sumptuous, luxurious, lavish, rich, fine, grand, stately, imposing, impressive, great, outstanding, remarkable, exceptional, sublime, supreme, superb, excellent, first-class, wonderful, marvellous, admirable.
⊞ drab, ordinary, run-of-the-mill.

splendour *n* brightness, radiance, brilliance, dazzle, glow, gleam, lustre, glory, resplendence, magnificence, richness, grandeur, majesty, solemnity, pomp, ceremony, display, show, spectacle.
⊞ drabness, squalor.

splice *v* join, unite, wed, marry, bind, tie, plait, braid, interweave, interlace, intertwine, entwine, mesh, knit, graft.

splinter *n* sliver, shiver, chip, shard, fragment, flake, shaving, paring.
◇ *v* split, fracture, smash, shatter, shiver, fragment, disintegrate.

split *v* divide, separate, partition, part, disunite, disband, open, gape, fork, diverge, break, splinter, shiver, snap, crack, burst, rupture, tear, rend, rip, slit, slash, cleave, halve, slice up, share, distribute, parcel out.
◇ *n* **1** DIVISION, separation, partition, break, breach, gap, cleft, crevice, crack, fissure, rupture, tear, rent, rip, rift, slit, slash. **2** SCHISM, disunion, dissension, discord, difference,

divergence, break-up.
◇ adj divided, cleft, cloven, bisected, dual, twofold, broken, fractured, cracked, ruptured.
• **split up** part, part company, disband, break up, separate, divorce.

spoil v 1 MAR, upset, wreck, ruin, destroy, damage, impair, harm, hurt, injure, deface, disfigure, blemish.
2 *spoil a child*: indulge, pamper, cosset, coddle, mollycoddle, baby, spoon-feed. 3 DETERIORATE, go bad, go off, sour, turn, curdle, decay, decompose.

spoils n plunder, loot, booty, haul, swag (*sl*), pickings, gain, acquisitions, prizes, winnings.

sponge v 1 WIPE, mop, clean, wash.
2 CADGE, scrounge.

sponger n cadger, scrounger, parasite, hanger-on.

spongy adj soft, cushioned, yielding, elastic, springy, porous, absorbent, light.

sponsor n patron, backer, angel (*infml*), promoter, underwriter, guarantor, surety.
◇ v finance, fund, bankroll, support, subsidize, patronize, back, promote, underwrite, guarantee.

spontaneous adj natural, unforced, untaught, instinctive, impulsive, unpremeditated, free, willing, unhesitating, voluntary, unprompted, impromptu, extempore.
⊠ forced, studied, planned, deliberate.

sporadic adj occasional, intermittent, infrequent, isolated, spasmodic, erratic, irregular, uneven, random, scattered.
⊠ frequent, regular.

sport n 1 GAME, exercise, activity, pastime, amusement, entertainment, diversion, recreation, play. 2 FUN, mirth, humour, joking, jesting, banter, teasing, mockery, ridicule.

Sports include: badminton, fives, lacrosse, squash, table tennis, tennis; American football, Australian rules football, baseball, basketball, billiards, boules, bowls, cricket, croquet, football, golf, handball, hockey, netball, pelota, pétanque, polo, pool, rounders, Rugby, snooker, soccer, tenpin bowling, volleyball; athletics, cross-country running, decathlon, discus, high jump, hurdling, javelin, long jump, marathon, pentathlon, pole vault, running, shotput, triple jump; angling, aqua aerobics, canoeing, diving, fishing, jet skiing, rowing, sailing, skin-diving, surfing, swimming, synchronized swimming, water polo, water-skiing, windsurfing, yachting; bobsleigh, curling, ice hockey, ice-skating, ringette, cross-country skiing, downhill racing, skeleton bob, slalom, snowboarding, speedskating, tobogganing, luging; aerobics, fencing, gymnastics, jogging, keep fit, roller-skating, trampolining; archery, darts, quoits; boxing, judo, ju-jitsu, karate, tae kwon do, weight-lifting, wrestling; climbing, mountaineering, Nordic walking, rock-climbing, walking, orienteering, potholing; cycle racing, drag-racing, go-karting, motor racing, speedway racing, stock car racing, greyhound-racing, horse-racing, showjumping, hunting, shooting, clay pigeon shooting; gliding, paragliding, sky-diving. see also **martial art**.

◇ v wear, display, exhibit, show off.

sporting adj sportsmanlike, gentlemanly, decent, considerate, fair.
⊠ unsporting, ungentlemanly, unfair.

sporty adj 1 ATHLETIC, fit, energetic, outdoor. 2 STYLISH, trendy (*infml*), jaunty, natty (*infml*), snazzy (*infml*), showy, loud, flashy, casual, informal.

spot *n* **1** DOT, speckle, fleck, mark, speck, blotch, blot, smudge, daub, splash, stain, discoloration, blemish, flaw, pimple. **2** PLACE, point, position, situation, location, site, scene, locality. **3** (*infml*) PLIGHT, predicament, quandary, difficulty, trouble, mess.
◇ *v* see, notice, observe, detect, discern, identify, recognize.

spotless *adj* immaculate, clean, white, gleaming, spick and span, unmarked, unstained, unblemished, unsullied, pure, chaste, virgin, untouched, innocent, blameless, faultless, irreproachable.
⊠ dirty, impure.

spotted *adj* dotted, speckled, flecked, mottled, dappled, pied.

spotty *adj* pimply, pimpled, blotchy, spotted.

spouse *n* husband, wife, partner, mate, better half (*infml*).

spout *v* jet, spurt, squirt, spray, shoot, gush, stream, surge, erupt, emit, discharge.
◇ *n* jet, fountain, geyser, gargoyle, outlet, nozzle, rose, spray.

sprawl *v* spread, straggle, trail, ramble, flop, slump, slouch, loll, lounge, recline, repose.

spray¹ *v* shower, spatter, sprinkle, scatter, diffuse, wet, drench.
◇ *n* **1** MOISTURE, drizzle, mist, foam, froth. **2** AEROSOL, atomizer, sprinkler.

spray² *n* sprig, branch, corsage, posy, bouquet, garland, wreath.

spread *v* **1** STRETCH, extend, sprawl, broaden, widen, dilate, expand, swell, mushroom, proliferate, escalate, open, unroll, unfurl, unfold, fan out, cover, lay out, arrange. **2** SCATTER, strew, diffuse, radiate, disseminate, broadcast, transmit, communicate, promulgate, propagate, publicize, advertise,

publish, circulate, distribute.
⊠ **1** close, fold. **2** suppress.
◇ *n* **1** STRETCH, reach, span, extent, expanse, sweep, compass. **2** *the spread of disease*: advance, development, expansion, increase, proliferation, escalation, diffusion, dissemination, dispersion.

spree *n* bout, fling, binge, splurge, orgy, revel.

sprightly *adj* agile, nimble, spry, active, energetic, lively, spirited, vivacious, hearty, brisk, jaunty, cheerful, blithe, airy.
⊠ doddering, inactive, lifeless.

spring¹ *v* **1** JUMP, leap, vault, bound, hop, bounce, rebound, recoil. **2** ORIGINATE, derive, come, stem, arise, start, proceed, issue, emerge, emanate, appear, sprout, grow, develop.
◇ *n* **1** JUMP, leap, vault, bound, bounce. **2** SPRINGINESS, resilience, give, flexibility, elasticity, buoyancy.

spring² *n* **1** SOURCE, origin, root, beginning, cause, fountainhead, wellspring. **2** FOUNT, geyser, spa.

springy *adj* bouncy, resilient, flexible, elastic, stretchy, rubbery, spongy, buoyant.
⊠ hard, stiff.

sprinkle *v* shower, spray, spatter, scatter, strew, dot, pepper, dust, powder.

sprint *v* run, race, dash, tear, belt (*infml*), dart, shoot.

sprout *v* shoot, bud, germinate, grow, develop, come up, spring up.

spruce *adj* smart, elegant, neat, trim, dapper, well-dressed, well-turned-out, well-groomed, sleek.
⊠ scruffy, untidy.
• **spruce up** neaten, tidy, smarten up, groom.

spur *v* goad, prod, poke, prick, stimulate, prompt, incite, drive, propel, impel, urge, encourage,

motivate.
⊵ curb, discourage.
◇ *n* incentive, encouragement, inducement, motive, stimulus, incitement, impetus, fillip.
⊵ curb, disincentive.

spurious *adj* false, fake, counterfeit, forged, bogus, phoney (*infml*), mock, sham, feigned, pretended, simulated, imitation, artificial.
⊵ genuine, authentic, real.

spurn *v* reject, turn down, scorn, despise, disdain, rebuff, repulse, slight, snub, cold-shoulder, ignore, disregard.
⊵ accept, embrace.

spurt *v* gush, squirt, jet, shoot, burst, erupt, surge.
◇ *n* burst, rush, surge, spate, fit, access.

spy *n* secret agent, undercover agent, double agent, mole (*infml*), fifth columnist, scout, snooper.
◇ *v* spot, glimpse, notice, observe, discover.

squabble *v* bicker, wrangle, quarrel, row, argue, dispute, clash, brawl, scrap, fight.

squad *n* crew, team, gang, band, group, company, brigade, troop, force, outfit.

squalid *adj* dirty, filthy, unclean, foul, disgusting, repulsive, sordid, seedy, dingy, untidy, slovenly, unkempt, broken-down, run-down, neglected, uncared-for, low, mean, nasty.
⊵ clean, pleasant, attractive.

squander *v* waste, misspend, misuse, lavish, blow (*sl*), fritter away, throw away, dissipate, scatter, spend, expend, consume.

square *v* settle, reconcile, tally, agree, accord, harmonize, correspond, match, balance, straighten, level, align, adjust, regulate, adapt, tailor, fit, suit.
◇ *adj* 1 QUADRILATERAL, rectangular,

right-angled, perpendicular, straight, true, even, level. 2 FAIR, equitable, just, ethical, honourable, honest, genuine, above-board, on the level (*infml*).

squash *v* 1 CRUSH, flatten, press, squeeze, compress, crowd, trample, stamp, pound, pulp, smash, distort. 2 SUPPRESS, silence, quell, quash, annihilate, put down, snub, humiliate.
⊵ 1 stretch, expand.

squat *adj* short, stocky, thickset, dumpy, chunky, stubby.
⊵ slim, lanky.
◇ *v* crouch, stoop, bend, sit.

squawk *v, n* screech, shriek, cry, croak, cackle, crow, hoot.

squeak *v, n* squeal, whine, creak, peep, cheep.

squeal *v, n* cry, shout, yell, yelp, wail, scream, screech, shriek, squawk.

squeamish *adj* queasy, nauseated, sick, delicate, fastidious, particular, prudish.

squeeze *v* 1 PRESS, squash, crush, pinch, nip, compress, grip, clasp, clutch, hug, embrace, enfold, cuddle. 2 *squeeze into a corner*: cram, stuff, pack, crowd, wedge, jam, force, ram, push, thrust, shove, jostle. 3 WRING, wrest, extort, milk, bleed, force, lean on (*infml*).
◇ *n* 1 PRESS, squash, crush, crowd, congestion, jam. 2 HUG, embrace, hold, grasp, clasp.

squirt *v* spray, spurt, jet, shoot, spout, gush, ejaculate, discharge, emit, eject, expel.
◇ *n* spray, spurt, jet.

stab *v* pierce, puncture, cut, wound, injure, gore, knife, spear, stick, jab, thrust.
◇ *n* 1 ACHE, pang, twinge, prick, puncture, cut, incision, gash, wound, jab. 2 (*infml*) TRY, attempt, endeavour, bash (*infml*).

stability n steadiness, firmness, soundness, constancy, steadfastness, strength, sturdiness, solidity, durability, permanence.
☒ instability, unsteadiness, insecurity, weakness.

stable adj steady, firm, secure, fast, sound, sure, constant, steadfast, reliable, established, well-founded, deep-rooted, strong, sturdy, durable, lasting, enduring, abiding, permanent, unchangeable, unalterable, invariable, immutable, fixed, static, balanced.
☒ unstable, wobbly, shaky, weak.

stack n heap, pile, mound, mass, load, accumulation, hoard, stockpile.
◊ v heap, pile, load, amass, accumulate, assemble, gather, save, hoard, stockpile.

staff n 1 member of staff: personnel, workforce, employees, workers, crew, team, teachers, officers.
2 STICK, cane, rod, baton, wand, pole, prop.

stage n point, juncture, step, phase, period, division, lap, leg, length, level, floor.
◊ v mount, put on, present, produce, give, do, perform, arrange, organize, stage-manage, orchestrate, engineer.

stagger v 1 LURCH, totter, teeter, wobble, sway, rock, reel, falter, hesitate, waver. 2 SURPRISE, amaze, astound, astonish, stun, stupefy, dumbfound, flabbergast (infml), shake, shock, confound, overwhelm.

stagnant adj still, motionless, standing, brackish, stale, sluggish, torpid, lethargic.
☒ fresh, moving.

stagnate v vegetate, idle, languish, decline, deteriorate, degenerate, decay, rot, rust.

staid adj sedate, calm, composed, sober, demure, solemn, serious, grave, quiet, steady.
☒ jaunty, debonair, frivolous, adventurous.

stain v 1 MARK, spot, blemish, blot, smudge, discolour, dirty, soil, taint, contaminate, sully, tarnish, blacken, disgrace. 2 DYE, tint, tinge, colour, paint, varnish.
◊ n mark, spot, blemish, blot, smudge, discoloration, smear, slur, disgrace, shame, dishonour.

stake¹ n post, pole, standard, picket, pale, paling, spike, stick.

stake² n bet, wager, pledge, interest, concern, involvement, share, investment, claim.
◊ v gamble, bet, wager, pledge, risk, chance, hazard, venture.

stale adj 1 stale bread: dry, hard, old, musty, fusty, flat, insipid, tasteless. 2 OVERUSED, hackneyed, clichéd, stereotyped, jaded, worn-out, unoriginal, trite, banal, commonplace.
☒ 1 crisp. 2 new.

stalemate n draw, tie, deadlock, impasse, standstill, halt.
☒ progress.

stalk¹ v track, trail, hunt, follow, pursue, shadow, tail, haunt.

stalk² n stem, twig, branch, trunk.

stall v temporize, play for time, delay, hedge, equivocate, obstruct, stonewall.

stalwart adj strong, sturdy, robust, rugged, stout, strapping, muscular, athletic, vigorous, valiant, daring, intrepid, indomitable, determined, resolute, staunch, steadfast, reliable, dependable.
☒ weak, feeble, timid.

stamina n energy, vigour, strength, power, force, grit, resilience, resistance, endurance, indefatigability, staying power.
☒ weakness.

stammer v stutter, stumble, falter, hesitate, splutter.

stamp v 1 TRAMPLE, crush, beat,

pound. **2** IMPRINT, impress, print, inscribe, engrave, emboss, mark, brand, label, categorize, identify, characterize.

◇ *n* **1** PRINT, imprint, impression, seal, signature, authorization, mark, hallmark, attestation. **2** BRAND, cast, mould, cut, form, fashion, sort, kind, type, breed, character, description.

stampede *n* charge, rush, dash, sprint, flight, rout.

◇ *v* charge, rush, dash, tear, run, sprint, gallop, shoot, fly, flee, scatter.

stance *n* position, posture, deportment, carriage, bearing, standpoint, viewpoint, angle, point of view, attitude.

stand *v* **1** PUT, place, set, erect, up-end, position, station. **2** *I can't stand it*: bear, tolerate, abide, endure, suffer, experience, undergo, withstand, weather. **3** RISE, get up, stand up.

◇ *n* base, pedestal, support, frame, rack, table, stage, platform, place, stall, booth.

• **stand by** support, back, champion, defend, stick up for, uphold, adhere to, hold to, stick by.

⊜ let down.

• **stand down** step down, resign, abdicate, quit, give up, retire, withdraw.

⊜ join.

• **stand for** represent, symbolize, mean, signify, denote, indicate.

• **stand in for** deputize for, cover for, understudy, replace, substitute for.

• **stand out** show, catch the eye, stick out, jut out, project.

• **stand up for** defend, stick up for, side with, fight for, support, protect, champion, uphold.

⊜ attack.

• **stand up to** defy, oppose, resist, withstand, endure, face, confront, brave.

⊜ give in to.

standard *n* **1** NORM, average, type,

model, pattern, example, sample, guideline, benchmark, touchstone, yardstick, rule, measure, gauge, level, criterion, requirement, specification, grade, quality. **2** FLAG, ensign, pennant, pennon, colours, banner.

◇ *adj* normal, average, typical, stock, classic, basic, staple, usual, customary, popular, prevailing, regular, approved, accepted, recognized, official, orthodox, set, established, definitive.

⊜ abnormal, unusual, irregular.

standardize *v* normalize, equalize, homogenize, stereotype, mass-produce.

⊜ differentiate.

standards *n* principles, ideals, morals, ethics.

standoffish *adj* aloof, remote, distant, unapproachable, unsociable, uncommunicative, reserved, cold.

⊜ friendly.

standpoint *n* position, station, vantage point, stance, viewpoint, angle, point of view.

standstill *n* stop, halt, pause, lull, rest, stoppage, jam, log-jam, hold-up, impasse, deadlock, stalemate.

⊜ advance, progress.

staple *adj* basic, fundamental, primary, key, main, chief, major, principal, essential, necessary, standard.

⊜ minor.

star *n* celebrity, personage, luminary, idol, lead, leading man, leading lady, superstar, megastar.

Types of star include: nova, supernova, pulsar, red giant, supergiant, white dwarf, red dwarf, brown dwarf, neutron star.

---

stare *v* gaze, look, watch, gape, gawp, gawk, goggle, glare.

◇ *n* gaze, look, glare.

stark *adj* **1** *stark landscape*: bare,

barren, bleak, bald, plain, simple, austere, harsh, severe, grim, dreary, gloomy, depressing. **2** UTTER, unmitigated, total, consummate, absolute, sheer, downright, out-and-out, flagrant, arrant.

start v **1** BEGIN, commence, originate, initiate, introduce, pioneer, create, found, establish, set up, institute, inaugurate, launch, open, kick off (*infml*), instigate, activate, trigger, set off, set out, leave, depart, appear, arise, issue. **2** JUMP, jerk, twitch, flinch, recoil.
☒ **1** stop, finish, end.
◇ n **1** BEGINNING, commencement, outset, inception, dawn, birth, break, outburst, onset, origin, initiation, introduction, foundation, inauguration, launch, opening, kick-off (*infml*). **2** JUMP, jerk, twitch, spasm, convulsion, fit.
☒ **1** stop, finish, end.

startle v surprise, amaze, astonish, astound, shock, scare, frighten, alarm, agitate, upset, disturb.
☒ calm.

starvation n hunger, famine, undernourishment, malnutrition.
☒ plenty, excess.

starve v hunger, fast, diet, deprive, refuse, deny, die, perish.
☒ feed, gorge.

starving adj hungry, underfed, undernourished, ravenous, famished.

state v say, declare, announce, report, communicate, assert, aver, affirm, specify, present, express, put, formulate, articulate, voice.
◇ n **1** CONDITION, shape, situation, position, circumstances, case.
2 NATION, country, land, territory, kingdom, republic, government.
3 (*infml*) PANIC, flap (*infml*), tizzy (*infml*), bother, plight, predicament.
4 POMP, ceremony, dignity, majesty, grandeur, glory, splendour.
◇ adj national, governmental, public, official, formal, ceremonial,

pompous, stately.

stately adj grand, imposing, impressive, elegant, majestic, regal, royal, imperial, noble, august, lofty, pompous, dignified, measured, deliberate, solemn, ceremonious.
☒ informal, unimpressive.

statement n account, report, bulletin, communiqué, announcement, declaration, proclamation, communication, utterance, testimony.

static adj stationary, motionless, immobile, unmoving, still, inert, resting, fixed, constant, changeless, unvarying, stable.
☒ dynamic, mobile, varying.

station n place, location, position, post, headquarters, base, depot.
◇ v locate, set, establish, install, garrison, post, send, appoint, assign.

stationary adj motionless, immobile, unmoving, still, static, inert, standing, resting, parked, moored, fixed.
☒ mobile, moving, active.

statue n figure, head, bust, effigy, idol, statuette, carving, bronze.

status n rank, grade, degree, level, class, station, standing, position, state, condition, prestige, eminence, distinction, importance, consequence, weight.
☒ unimportance, insignificance.

staunch adj loyal, faithful, hearty, strong, stout, firm, sound, sure, true, trusty, reliable, dependable, steadfast.
☒ unfaithful, weak, unreliable.

stay v **1** LAST, continue, endure, abide, remain, linger, persist. **2** RESIDE, dwell, live, settle, sojourn, stop, halt, pause, wait.
☒ **1** go, leave.
◇ n visit, holiday, stopover, sojourn.

steady adj stable, balanced, poised, fixed, immovable, firm,

settled, still, calm, imperturbable, equable, even, uniform, consistent, unvarying, unchanging, constant, persistent, unremitting, incessant, uninterrupted, unbroken, regular, rhythmic, steadfast, unwavering. ⊜ unsteady, unstable, variable, wavering.
◇ v balance, stabilize, fix, secure, brace, support.

steal v 1 *steal a car*: thieve, pilfer, filch, pinch (*infml*), nick (*infml*), take, appropriate, snatch, swipe, shoplift, poach, embezzle, lift, plagiarize. 2 CREEP, tiptoe, slip, slink, sneak. ⊜ 1 return, give back.

stealthy adj surreptitious, covert, clandestine, secret, unobtrusive, secretive, quiet, furtive, sly, cunning, sneaky, underhand. ⊜ open.

steam n vapour, mist, haze, condensation, moisture, dampness.

steep adj 1 *a steep slope*: sheer, precipitous, headlong, abrupt, sudden, sharp. 2 (*infml*) EXCESSIVE, extreme, stiff, unreasonable, high, exorbitant, extortionate, overpriced. ⊜ 1 gentle, gradual. 2 moderate, low.

steer v pilot, guide, direct, control, govern, conduct.

stem[1] n stalk, shoot, stock, branch, trunk.

stem[2] v stop, halt, arrest, stanch, staunch, block, dam, check, curb, restrain, contain, resist, oppose. ⊜ encourage.

stench n stink, reek, pong (*infml*), smell, odour.

step n 1 PACE, stride, footstep, tread, footprint, print, trace, track. 2 MOVE, act, action, deed, measure, procedure, process, proceeding, progression, movement, stage, phase, degree. 3 RUNG, stair, level, rank, point.
◇ v pace, stride, tread, stamp, walk,

move.
• **step down** stand down, resign, abdicate, quit, leave, retire, withdraw.
⊜ join.
• **step up** increase, raise, augment, boost, build up, intensify, escalate, accelerate, speed up.
⊜ decrease.

stereotype n formula, convention, mould, pattern, model.
◇ v categorize, pigeonhole, typecast, standardize, formalize, conventionalize, mass-produce.
⊜ differentiate.

sterile adj 1 GERM-FREE, aseptic, sterilized, disinfected, antiseptic, uncontaminated. 2 INFERTILE, barren, arid, bare, unproductive, fruitless, pointless, useless, abortive.
⊜ 1 septic. 2 fertile, fruitful.

sterilize v disinfect, fumigate, purify, clean, cleanse.
⊜ contaminate, infect.

stern adj strict, severe, authoritarian, rigid, inflexible, unyielding, hard, tough, rigorous, stringent, harsh, cruel, unsparing, relentless, unrelenting, grim, forbidding, stark, austere.
⊜ kind, gentle, mild, lenient.

stew v boil, simmer, braise, casserole.

stick[1] v 1 THRUST, poke, stab, jab, pierce, penetrate, puncture, spear, transfix. 2 GLUE, gum, paste, cement, bond, fuse, weld, solder, adhere, cling, hold. 3 ATTACH, affix, fasten, secure, fix, pin, join, bind. 4 PUT, place, position, set, install, deposit, drop.
• **stick at** persevere, plug away (*infml*), persist, continue.
⊜ give up.
• **stick out** protrude, jut out, project, extend.
• **stick up for** stand up for, speak up for, defend, champion, support, uphold.

⊞ attack.

stick² n branch, twig, wand, baton, staff, sceptre, cane, birch, rod, pole, stake.

sticky adj **1** ADHESIVE, gummed, tacky, gluey, gummy, viscous, glutinous, gooey (infml). **2** (infml) a sticky situation: difficult, tricky, thorny, unpleasant, awkward, embarrassing, delicate. **3** HUMID, clammy, muggy, close, oppressive, sultry.
⊞ **1** dry. **2** easy. **3** fresh, cool.

stiff adj **1** RIGID, inflexible, unbending, unyielding, hard, solid, hardened, solidified, firm, tight, taut, tense. **2** FORMAL, ceremonious, pompous, standoffish, cold, prim, priggish, austere, strict, severe, harsh. **3** DIFFICULT, hard, tough, arduous, laborious, awkward, exacting, rigorous.
⊞ **1** flexible. **2** informal. **3** easy.

stiffen v harden, solidify, tighten, tense, brace, reinforce, starch, thicken, congeal, coagulate, jell, set.

stifle v smother, suffocate, asphyxiate, strangle, choke, extinguish, muffle, dampen, deaden, silence, hush, suppress, quell, check, curb, restrain, repress.
⊞ encourage.

stigma n brand, mark, stain, blot, spot, blemish, disgrace, shame, dishonour.
⊞ credit, honour.

still adj stationary, motionless, lifeless, stagnant, smooth, undisturbed, unruffled, calm, tranquil, serene, restful, peaceful, hushed, quiet, silent, noiseless.
⊞ active, disturbed, agitated, noisy.
◇ v calm, soothe, allay, tranquillize, subdue, restrain, hush, quieten, silence, pacify, settle, smooth.
⊞ agitate, stir up.
◇ adv yet, even so, nevertheless, nonetheless, notwithstanding, however.

stilted adj artificial, unnatural, stiff, wooden, forced, constrained.
⊞ fluent, flowing.

stimulate v rouse, arouse, animate, quicken, fire, inflame, inspire, motivate, encourage, induce, urge, impel, spur, prompt, goad, provoke, incite, instigate, trigger off.
⊞ discourage, hinder, prevent.

stimulus n incentive, impetus, encouragement, inducement, spur, goad, provocation, incitement.
⊞ discouragement.

sting v **1** bees sting: bite, prick, hurt, injure, wound. **2** SMART, tingle, burn, pain.
◇ n bite, nip, prick, smart, tingle.

stingy adj mean, miserly, niggardly, tight-fisted (infml), parsimonious, penny-pinching.
⊞ generous, liberal.

stink v smell, reek, pong (infml), hum (sl).
◇ n smell, odour, stench, pong (infml), niff (sl).

stint n spell, stretch, period, time, shift, turn, bit, share, quota.

stipulate v specify, lay down, require, demand, insist on.

stipulation n specification, requirement, demand, condition, proviso.

stir v **1** MOVE, budge, touch, affect, inspire, excite, thrill, disturb, agitate, shake, tremble, quiver, flutter, rustle. **2** MIX, blend, beat.
◇ n activity, movement, bustle, flurry, commotion, ado, fuss, to-do (infml), uproar, tumult, disturbance, disorder, agitation, excitement, ferment.
⊞ calm.
• **stir up** rouse, arouse, awaken, animate, quicken, kindle, fire, inflame, stimulate, spur, prompt, provoke, incite, instigate, agitate.

⊞ calm, discourage.

stock n 1 GOODS, merchandise, wares, commodities, capital, assets, inventory, repertoire, range, variety, assortment, source, supply, fund, reservoir, store, reserve, stockpile, hoard. 2 PARENTAGE, ancestry, descent, extraction, family, line, lineage, pedigree, race, breed, species, blood. 3 LIVESTOCK, animals, cattle, horses, sheep, herds, flocks.
◇ adj standard, basic, regular, routine, ordinary, run-of-the-mill, bog-standard (infml), usual, customary, traditional, conventional, set, stereotyped, hackneyed, overused, banal, trite.
⊞ original, unusual.
◇ v keep, carry, sell, trade in, deal in, handle, supply, provide.
• **stock up** gather, accumulate, amass, lay in, provision, fill, replenish, store (up), save, hoard, pile up.

stocky adj sturdy, solid, thickset, chunky, short, squat, dumpy, stubby.
⊞ tall, skinny.

stoical adj patient, long-suffering, uncomplaining, philosophical, resigned, indifferent, impassive, unemotional, phlegmatic, dispassionate, cool, calm, imperturbable.
⊞ excitable, anxious.

stolid adj slow, heavy, dull, bovine, wooden, blockish, lumpish, impassive, phlegmatic, unemotional.
⊞ lively, interested.

stomach n tummy (infml), tum (infml), gut, insides, belly, abdomen, paunch, pot.
◇ v tolerate, bear, stand, abide, endure, suffer, submit to, take.

stony adj 1 BLANK, expressionless, hard, cold, frigid, icy, indifferent, unfeeling, heartless, callous, merciless, pitiless, inexorable, hostile. 2 stony beach: pebbly, shingly, rocky.

⊞ 1 warm, soft-hearted, friendly.

stoop v 1 HUNCH, bow, bend, incline, lean, duck, squat, crouch, kneel. 2 stoop to blackmail: descend, sink, lower oneself, resort, go so far as, condescend, deign.

stop v 1 HALT, cease, end, finish, conclude, terminate, discontinue, suspend, interrupt, pause, quit, refrain, desist, pack in (sl). 2 PREVENT, bar, frustrate, thwart, intercept, hinder, impede, check, restrain. 3 SEAL, close, plug, block, obstruct, arrest, stem, stanch.
⊞ 1 start, continue.
◇ n 1 STATION, terminus, destination. 2 REST, break, pause, stage. 3 HALT, standstill, stoppage, cessation, end, finish, conclusion, termination, discontinuation.
⊞ 3 start, beginning, continuation.

stoppage n stop, halt, standstill, arrest, blockage, obstruction, check, hindrance, interruption, shutdown, closure, strike, walk-out, sit-in.
⊞ start, continuation.

stopper n cork, bung, plug.

store v save, keep, put aside, lay by, reserve, stock, lay in, deposit, lay down, lay up, accumulate, hoard, salt away, stockpile, stash (infml).
⊞ use.
◇ n 1 STOCK, supply, provision, fund, reserve, mine, reservoir, hoard, cache, stockpile, accumulation, quantity, abundance, plenty, lot. 2 STOREROOM, storehouse, warehouse, repository, depository.
⊞ 1 scarcity.

storey n floor, level, stage, tier, flight, deck.

storm n 1 TEMPEST, squall, blizzard, gale. 2 OUTBURST, uproar, furore, outcry, row, rumpus, commotion, tumult, disturbance, turmoil, stir, agitation, rage, outbreak, attack, assault.
⊞ 2 calm.

Kinds of storm include: buran, cyclone, dust devil, dust storm, electrical storm, haboob, hailstorm, hurricane, monsoon, rainstorm, sandstorm, snowstorm, thunderstorm, tornado, typhoon, whirlwind. see also **wind¹**.

◇ v charge, rush, attack, assault, assail, roar, thunder, rage, rant, rave, fume.

stormy adj tempestuous, squally, rough, choppy, turbulent, wild, raging, windy, gusty, blustery, foul.
▣ calm.

story n 1 TALE, legend, fiction, yarn, anecdote, episode, plot, narrative, history, chronicle, record, account, relation, recital, report, article, feature. 2 LIE, falsehood, untruth.

Types of story include: adventure story, bedtime story, blockbuster (infml), children's story, comedy, black comedy, crime story, detective story, fable, fairy tale, fantasy, folk-tale, ghost story, love-story, mystery, myth, novelization, parable, romance, saga, science fiction, sci-fi (infml), short story, spine-chiller, spy story, tall story, thriller, western, whodunnit (infml).

stout adj 1 FAT, plump, fleshy, portly, corpulent, overweight, heavy, bulky, big, brawny, beefy, hulking, burly, muscular, athletic. 2 stout packaging: strong, tough, durable, thick, sturdy, robust, hardy, vigorous. 3 BRAVE, courageous, valiant, plucky, fearless, bold, intrepid, dauntless, resolute, stalwart.
▣ 1 thin, lean, slim. 2 weak.
3 cowardly, timid.

stow v put away, store, load, pack, cram, stuff, stash (infml).
▣ unload.

straight adj 1 a straight line: level, even, flat, horizontal, upright,

vertical, aligned, direct, undeviating, unswerving, true, right. 2 TIDY, neat, orderly, shipshape, organized. 3 HONOURABLE, honest, law-abiding, respectable, upright, trustworthy, reliable, straightforward, fair, just. 4 FRANK, candid, blunt, forthright, direct. 5 straight whisky: undiluted, neat, unadulterated, unmixed.
▣ 1 bent, crooked. 2 untidy.
3 dishonest. 4 evasive. 5 diluted.
◇ adv directly, point-blank, honestly, frankly, candidly.
● **straight away** at once, immediately, instantly, right away, directly, now, there and then.
▣ later, eventually.

straighten v unbend, align, tidy, neaten, order, arrange.
▣ bend, twist.
● **straighten out** clear up, sort out, settle, resolve, correct, rectify, disentangle, regularize.
▣ confuse, muddle.

straightforward adj 1 EASY, simple, uncomplicated, clear, elementary. 2 HONEST, truthful, sincere, genuine, open, frank, candid, direct, forthright.
▣ 1 complicated. 2 evasive, devious.

strain¹ v 1 PULL, wrench, twist, sprain, tear, stretch, extend, tighten, tauten. 2 SIEVE, sift, screen, separate, filter, purify, drain, wring, squeeze, compress, express. 3 WEAKEN, tire, tax, overtax, overwork, labour, try, endeavour, struggle, strive, exert, force, drive.
◇ n stress, anxiety, burden, pressure, tension, tautness, pull, sprain, wrench, injury, exertion, effort, struggle, force.
▣ relaxation.

strain² n 1 STOCK, ancestry, descent, extraction, family, lineage, pedigree, blood, variety, type. 2 TRAIT, streak, vein, tendency, trace, suggestion, suspicion.

strained *adj* forced, constrained, laboured, false, artificial, unnatural, stiff, tense, unrelaxed, uneasy, uncomfortable, awkward, embarrassed, self-conscious.
☒ natural, relaxed.

strait-laced *adj* prudish, stuffy, starchy, prim, proper, strict, narrow, narrow-minded, puritanical, moralistic.
☒ broad-minded.

strand *n* fibre, filament, wire, thread, string, piece, length.

stranded *adj* marooned, high and dry, abandoned, forsaken, in the lurch, helpless, aground, grounded, beached, shipwrecked, wrecked.

strange *adj* **1** ODD, peculiar, funny (*infml*), curious, queer, weird, bizarre, eccentric, abnormal, irregular, uncommon, unusual, exceptional, remarkable, extraordinary, mystifying, perplexing, unexplained. **2** NEW, novel, untried, unknown, unheard-of, unfamiliar, unacquainted, foreign, alien, exotic.
☒ **1** ordinary, common. **2** well-known, familiar.

stranger *n* newcomer, visitor, guest, non-member, outsider, foreigner, alien.
☒ local, native.

strangle *v* throttle, choke, asphyxiate, suffocate, stifle, smother, suppress, gag, repress, inhibit.

strap *n* thong, tie, band, belt, leash.
◇ *v* **1** BEAT, lash, whip, flog, belt. **2** FASTEN, secure, tie, bind.

stratagem *n* plan, scheme, plot, intrigue, ruse, ploy, trick, dodge, manoeuvre, device, artifice, wile, subterfuge.

strategic *adj* important, key, critical, decisive, crucial, vital, tactical, planned, calculated, deliberate, politic, diplomatic.
☒ unimportant.

strategy *n* tactics, planning, policy, approach, procedure, plan, programme, design, scheme.

stray *v* wander (off), get lost, err, ramble, roam, rove, range, meander, straggle, drift, diverge, deviate, digress.
◇ *adj* **1** LOST, abandoned, homeless, wandering, roaming. **2** RANDOM, chance, accidental, freak, odd, erratic.

streak *n* line, stroke, smear, band, stripe, strip, layer, vein, trace, dash, touch, element, strain.
◇ *v* **1** BAND, stripe, fleck, striate, smear, daub. **2** SPEED, tear, hurtle, sprint, gallop, fly, dart, flash, whistle, zoom, whizz, sweep.

stream *n* **1** RIVER, creek, brook, beck, burn, rivulet, tributary. **2** CURRENT, drift, flow, run, gush, flood, deluge, cascade, torrent.
◇ *v* issue, well, surge, run, flow, course, pour, spout, gush, flood, cascade.

streamer *n* ribbon, banner, pennant, pennon, flag, ensign, standard.

streamlined *adj* aerodynamic, smooth, sleek, graceful, efficient, well-run, smooth-running, rationalized, time-saving, organized, slick.
☒ clumsy, inefficient.

strength *n* toughness, robustness, sturdiness, lustiness, brawn, muscle, sinew, power, might, force, vigour, energy, stamina, health, fitness, courage, fortitude, spirit, resolution, firmness, effectiveness, potency, concentration, intensity, vehemence.
☒ weakness, feebleness, impotence.

strengthen *v* reinforce, brace, steel, fortify, buttress, bolster, support, toughen, harden, stiffen, consolidate, substantiate, corroborate, confirm, encourage, hearten, refresh, restore, invigorate, nourish, increase,

heighten, intensify.
⊞ weaken, undermine.

strenuous *adj* **1** *strenuous work*:
hard, tough, demanding, gruelling,
taxing, laborious, uphill, arduous,
tiring, exhausting. **2** ACTIVE, energetic,
vigorous, eager, earnest, determined,
resolute, spirited, tireless,
indefatigable.
⊞ **1** easy, effortless.

stress *n* **1** PRESSURE, strain, tension,
worry, anxiety, weight, burden,
trauma, hassle (*infml*). **2** EMPHASIS,
accent, accentuation, beat, force,
weight, importance, significance.
⊞ **1** relaxation.
◇ *v* emphasize, accentuate, highlight,
underline, underscore, repeat.
⊞ understate, downplay.

stretch *n* **1** EXPANSE, spread, sweep,
reach, extent, distance, space, area,
tract. **2** PERIOD, time, term, spell, stint,
run.
◇ *v* pull, tighten, tauten, strain, tax,
extend, lengthen, elongate, expand,
spread, unfold, unroll, inflate, swell,
reach.
⊞ compress.
• **stretch out** extend, relax, hold out,
put out, lie down, reach.
⊞ draw back.

strict *adj* **1** *a strict teacher*: stern,
authoritarian, no-nonsense, firm,
rigid, inflexible, stringent, rigorous,
harsh, severe, austere. **2** EXACT,
precise, accurate, literal, faithful,
true, absolute, utter, total, complete,
thoroughgoing, meticulous,
scrupulous, particular, religious.
⊞ **1** easy-going (*infml*), flexible.
2 loose.

strident *adj* loud, clamorous,
vociferous, harsh, raucous, grating,
rasping, shrill, screeching, unmusical,
discordant, clashing, jarring, jangling.
⊞ quiet, soft.

strife *n* conflict, discord, dissension,
controversy, animosity, friction,
rivalry, contention, quarrel, row,

wrangling, struggle, fighting,
combat, battle, warfare.
⊞ peace.

strike *n* **1** INDUSTRIAL ACTION, work-
to-rule, go-slow, stoppage, sit-in,
walk-out, mutiny, revolt. **2** HIT, blow,
stroke, raid, attack.
◇ *v* **1** STOP WORK, down tools, work to
rule, walk out, protest, mutiny, revolt.
2 HIT, knock, collide with, slap,
smack, cuff, clout, thump, wallop
(*infml*), beat, pound, hammer, buffet,
raid, attack, afflict. **3** IMPRESS, affect,
touch, register. **4** FIND, discover,
unearth, uncover, encounter, reach.
• **strike out** cross out, delete, strike
through, cancel, strike off, remove.
⊞ add.

striking *adj* noticeable, obvious,
conspicuous, salient, outstanding,
remarkable, extraordinary,
memorable, impressive, dazzling,
arresting, astonishing, stunning.
⊞ unimpressive.

string *n* **1** *a piece of string*: twine,
cord, rope, cable, line, strand, fibre.
2 SERIES, succession, sequence, chain,
line, row, file, queue, procession,
stream, train.
◇ *v* thread, link, connect, tie up,
hang, suspend, festoon, loop.

stringent *adj* binding, strict, severe,
rigorous, tough, rigid, inflexible,
tight.
⊞ lax, flexible.

strip[1] *v* **1** PEEL, skin, flay. **2** DENUDE,
divest, deprive, undress, disrobe,
unclothe, uncover, expose, lay bare,
bare. **3** EMPTY, clear, gut, ransack,
pillage, plunder, loot.
⊞ **2** dress, clothe, cover.

strip[2] *n* ribbon, thong, strap, belt,
sash, band, stripe, lath, slat, piece,
bit, slip, shred.

stripe *n* band, line, bar, chevron,
flash, streak, fleck, strip, belt.

strive *v* try, attempt, endeavour,
struggle, strain, work, toil, labour,

fight, contend, compete.

stroke n 1 CARESS, pat, rub. 2 BLOW, hit, knock, swipe. 3 SWEEP, flourish, movement, action, move, line.
◇ v caress, fondle, pet, touch, pat, rub, massage.

stroll v saunter, amble, dawdle, ramble, wander.
◇ n saunter, amble, walk, constitutional, turn, ramble.

strong adj 1 TOUGH, resilient, durable, hard-wearing, heavy-duty, robust, sturdy, firm, sound, lusty, strapping, stout, burly, well-built, beefy, brawny, muscular, sinewy, athletic, fit, healthy, hardy, powerful, mighty, potent. 2 INTENSE, deep, vivid, fierce, violent, vehement, keen, eager, zealous, fervent, ardent, dedicated, staunch, stalwart, determined, resolute, tenacious, strong-minded, strong-willed, self-assertive. 3 HIGHLY-FLAVOURED, piquant, hot, spicy, sharp, highly-seasoned, pungent, undiluted, concentrated. 4 strong argument: convincing, persuasive, cogent, effective, telling, forceful, weighty, compelling, urgent.
⊜ 1 weak, feeble. 2 indecisive. 3 mild, bland. 4 unconvincing.

stronghold n citadel, bastion, fort, fortress, castle, keep, refuge.

structure n construction, erection, building, edifice, fabric, framework, form, shape, design, configuration, conformation, make-up, formation, arrangement, organization, set-up.
◇ v construct, assemble, build, form, shape, design, arrange, organize.

struggle v strive, work, toil, labour, strain, agonize, fight, battle, wrestle, grapple, contend, compete, vie.
⊜ yield, give in.
◇ n 1 DIFFICULTY, problem, effort, exertion, pains, agony, work, labour, toil. 2 CLASH, conflict, strife, fight, battle, skirmish, encounter, combat, hostilities, contest.

⊜ 1 ease. 2 submission, co-operation.

stub n end, stump, remnant, fag-end (infml), dog-end (infml), butt, counterfoil.

stubborn adj obstinate, stiff-necked, mulish, pigheaded, obdurate, intransigent, rigid, inflexible, unbending, unyielding, dogged, persistent, tenacious, headstrong, self-willed, wilful, refractory, difficult, unmanageable.
⊜ compliant, flexible, yielding.

stuck adj 1 FAST, jammed, firm, fixed, fastened, joined, glued, cemented. 2 BEATEN, stumped (infml), baffled.
⊜ 1 loose.

stuck-up adj snobbish, toffee-nosed (infml), supercilious, snooty (infml), haughty, high and mighty, condescending, proud, arrogant, conceited, bigheaded (infml).
⊜ humble, modest.

student n undergraduate, postgraduate, scholar, schoolboy, schoolgirl, pupil, disciple, learner, trainee, apprentice.

studied adj deliberate, conscious, wilful, intentional, premeditated, planned, calculated, contrived, forced, unnatural, overelaborate.
⊜ unplanned, impulsive, natural.

studio n workshop, workroom.

studious adj scholarly, academic, intellectual, bookish, serious, thoughtful, reflective, diligent, hard-working, industrious, assiduous, careful, attentive, earnest, eager.
⊜ lazy, idle, negligent.

study v read, learn, revise, cram, swot (infml), mug up (infml), read up, research, investigate, analyse, survey, scan, examine, scrutinize, peruse, pore over, contemplate, meditate, ponder, consider, deliberate.
◇ n 1 READING, homework, preparation, learning, revision, cramming, swotting (infml), research, investigation, inquiry, analysis,

examination, scrutiny, inspection, contemplation, consideration, attention. **2** REPORT, essay, thesis, paper, monograph, survey, review, critique. **3** OFFICE, den (*infml*).

stuff *v* **1** PACK, stow, load, fill, cram, crowd, force, push, shove, ram, wedge, jam, squeeze, compress. **2** GORGE, gormandize, overindulge, guzzle, gobble, sate, satiate. ⊜ **1** unload, empty. **2** nibble. ◇ *n* **1** MATERIAL, fabric, matter, substance, essence. **2** (*infml*) BELONGINGS, possessions, things, objects, articles, goods, luggage, paraphernalia, gear (*infml*), clobber (*infml*), kit, tackle, equipment, materials.

stuffing *n* padding, wadding, quilting, filling.

stuffy *adj* **1** *a stuffy room*: stale, musty, airless, unventilated, suffocating, stifling, oppressive, heavy, close, muggy, sultry. **2** STAID, strait-laced, prim, conventional, old-fashioned, pompous, dull, dreary, uninteresting, stodgy. ⊜ **1** airy, well-ventilated. **2** informal, modern, lively.

stumble *v* **1** TRIP, slip, fall, lurch, reel, stagger, flounder, blunder. **2** STAMMER, stutter, hesitate, falter. • **stumble on** come across, chance upon, happen upon, find, discover, encounter.

stumbling-block *n* obstacle, hurdle, barrier, bar, obstruction, hindrance, impediment, difficulty, snag.

stump *n* end, remnant, trunk, stub. ◇ *v* (*infml*) defeat, outwit, confound, perplex, puzzle, baffle, mystify, confuse, bewilder, flummox (*infml*), bamboozle (*infml*), dumbfound. ⊜ assist. • **stump up** (*infml*) pay, hand over, fork out (*infml*), shell out (*infml*), donate, contribute, cough up (*infml*). ⊜ receive.

stun *v* amaze, astonish, astound, stagger, shock, daze, stupefy, dumbfound, flabbergast (*infml*), overcome, confound, confuse, bewilder.

stunning *adj* beautiful, lovely, gorgeous, ravishing, dazzling, brilliant, striking, impressive, spectacular, remarkable, wonderful, marvellous, great, sensational. ⊜ ugly, awful.

stunt[1] *n* feat, exploit, act, deed, enterprise, trick, turn, performance.

stunt[2] *v* stop, arrest, check, restrict, slow, retard, hinder, impede, dwarf. ⊜ promote, encourage.

stupefy *v* daze, stun, dumbfound, numb, shock, stagger, amaze, astound.

stupendous *adj* huge, enormous, gigantic, colossal, vast, prodigious, phenomenal, tremendous, breathtaking, overwhelming, staggering, stunning, amazing, astounding, fabulous, fantastic, superb, wonderful, marvellous. ⊜ ordinary, unimpressive.

stupid *adj* **1** SILLY, foolish, ill-advised, irresponsible, indiscreet, foolhardy, rash, senseless, mad, lunatic, brainless, halfwitted, idiotic, imbecilic, moronic, feeble-minded, simple-minded, slow, dim, dull, dense, thick, dumb, dopey, crass, inane, puerile, mindless, futile, pointless, meaningless, nonsensical, absurd, ludicrous, ridiculous, laughable. **2** DAZED, groggy, stupefied, stunned, sluggish, semiconscious. ⊜ **1** sensible, wise, clever, intelligent. **2** alert.

stupor *n* daze, stupefaction, torpor, lethargy, inertia, trance, coma, numbness, insensibility, unconsciousness. ⊜ alertness, consciousness.

sturdy *adj* strong, robust, durable,

well-made, stout, substantial, solid, well-built, powerful, muscular, athletic, hardy, vigorous, flourishing, hearty, staunch, stalwart, steadfast, firm, resolute, determined.
⊯ weak, flimsy, puny.

stutter *v* stammer, hesitate, falter, stumble, mumble.

style *n* **1** APPEARANCE, cut, design, pattern, shape, form, sort, type, kind, genre, variety, category. **2** ELEGANCE, smartness, chic, flair, panache, stylishness, taste, polish, refinement, sophistication, urbanity, fashion, vogue, trend, mode, dressiness, flamboyance, affluence, luxury, grandeur. **3** *style of working*: technique, approach, method, manner, mode, fashion, way, custom. **4** WORDING, phrasing, expression, tone, tenor.
⊯ **2** inelegance, tastelessness.
◇ *v* **1** DESIGN, cut, tailor, fashion, shape, adapt. **2** DESIGNATE, term, name, call, address, title, dub, label.

stylish *adj* chic, fashionable, à la mode, modish, in vogue, voguish, trendy (*infml*), snappy, natty (*infml*), snazzy (*infml*), dressy, smart, elegant, classy (*infml*), polished, refined, sophisticated, urbane.
⊯ old-fashioned, shabby.

suave *adj* polite, courteous, charming, agreeable, affable, soft-spoken, smooth, unctuous, sophisticated, urbane, worldly.
⊯ rude, unsophisticated.

subconscious *adj* subliminal, unconscious, intuitive, inner, innermost, hidden, latent, repressed, suppressed.
⊯ conscious.

subdue *v* overcome, quell, suppress, repress, overpower, crush, defeat, conquer, vanquish, overrun, subject, subjugate, humble, break, tame, master, discipline, control, check, moderate, reduce, soften, quieten, damp, mellow.
⊯ arouse, awaken.

subdued *adj* **1** SAD, downcast, dejected, crestfallen, quiet, serious, grave, solemn. **2** QUIET, muted, hushed, soft, dim, shaded, sombre, sober, restrained, unobtrusive, low-key, subtle.
⊯ **1** lively, excited. **2** striking, obtrusive.

subject *n* **1** TOPIC, theme, matter, issue, question, point, case, affair, business, discipline, field. **2** NATIONAL, citizen, participant, client, patient, victim.
⊯ **2** monarch, ruler, master.
◇ *adj* **1** LIABLE, disposed, prone, susceptible, vulnerable, open, exposed. **2** SUBJUGATED, captive, bound, obedient, answerable, subordinate, inferior, subservient, submissive. **3** DEPENDENT, contingent, conditional.
⊯ **1** vulnerable. **2** free, superior. **3** unconditional.
◇ *v* expose, lay open, submit, subjugate, subdue.

subjection *n* subjugation, defeat, captivity, bondage, chains, shackles, slavery, enslavement, oppression, domination, mastery.

subjective *adj* biased, prejudiced, personal, individual, idiosyncratic, emotional, intuitive, instinctive.
⊯ objective, unbiased, impartial.

sublime *adj* exalted, elevated, high, lofty, noble, majestic, great, grand, imposing, magnificent, glorious, transcendent, spiritual.
⊯ lowly, base.

submerge *v* submerse, immerse, plunge, duck, dip, sink, drown, engulf, overwhelm, swamp, flood, inundate, deluge.
⊯ surface.

submerged *adj* submersed, immersed, underwater, sunk, sunken, drowned, swamped, inundated, hidden, concealed, unseen.

submission n 1 SURRENDER, capitulation, resignation, acquiescence, assent, compliance, obedience, deference, submissiveness, meekness, passivity. 2 PRESENTATION, offering, contribution, entry, suggestion, proposal.
⊞ 1 intransigence, intractability.

submissive adj yielding, unresisting, resigned, patient, uncomplaining, accommodating, biddable, obedient, deferential, ingratiating, subservient, humble, meek, docile, subdued, passive.
⊞ intransigent, intractable.

submit v 1 YIELD, give in, surrender, capitulate, knuckle under, bow, bend, stoop, succumb, agree, comply. 2 PRESENT, tender, offer, put forward, suggest, propose, table, state, claim, argue.
⊞ 1 resist. 2 withdraw.

subordinate adj secondary, auxiliary, ancillary, subsidiary, dependent, inferior, lower, junior, minor, lesser.
⊞ superior, senior.
◇ n inferior, junior, assistant, attendant, second, aide, dependant, underling (infml).
⊞ superior, boss.

subscribe v 1 subscribe to a theory: support, endorse, back, advocate, approve, agree. 2 GIVE, donate, contribute.

subscription n membership fee, dues, payment, donation, contribution, offering, gift.

subsequent adj following, later, future, next, succeeding, consequent, resulting, ensuing.
⊞ previous, earlier.

subside v sink, collapse, settle, descend, fall, drop, lower, decrease, lessen, diminish, dwindle, decline, wane, ebb, recede, moderate, abate, die down, quieten, slacken, ease.
⊞ rise, increase.

subsidiary adj auxiliary, additional, supplementary, ancillary, assistant, supporting, contributory, secondary, subordinate, lesser, minor.
⊞ primary, chief, major.
◇ n branch, offshoot, division, section, part.

subsidize v support, back, fund, underwrite, sponsor, finance, aid, promote.

subsidy n grant, allowance, assistance, help, aid, contribution, sponsorship, finance, support, backing.

subsistence n living, survival, existence, livelihood, maintenance, support, keep, sustenance, nourishment, food, provisions, rations.

substance n 1 MATTER, material, stuff, fabric, essence, pith, entity, body, solidity, concreteness, reality, actuality, ground, foundation. 2 SUBJECT, subject matter, theme, gist, meaning, significance, force.

substandard adj second-rate, inferior, imperfect, damaged, shoddy, poor, inadequate, unacceptable.
⊞ first-rate, superior, perfect.

substantial adj large, big, sizable, ample, generous, great, considerable, significant, important, worthwhile, massive, bulky, hefty, well-built, stout, sturdy, strong, sound, durable.
⊞ small, insignificant, weak.

substantiate v prove, verify, confirm, support, corroborate, authenticate, validate.
⊞ disprove, refute.

substitute v 1 CHANGE, exchange, swap, switch, interchange, replace. 2 STAND IN, fill in (infml), cover, deputize, understudy, relieve.
◇ n reserve, stand-by, temp (infml), supply, locum, understudy, stand-in, replacement, relief, surrogate, proxy, agent, deputy, makeshift, stopgap.
◇ adj reserve, temporary, acting,

surrogate, proxy, replacement, alternative.

subterfuge n trick, stratagem, scheme, ploy, ruse, dodge, manoeuvre, machination, deviousness, evasion, deception, artifice, pretence, excuse.
⊜ openness, honesty.

subtle adj 1 DELICATE, understated, implied, indirect, slight, tenuous, faint, mild, fine, nice, refined, sophisticated, deep, profound.
2 ARTFUL, cunning, crafty, sly, devious, shrewd, astute.
⊜ 1 blatant, obvious. 2 artless, open.

subtract v deduct, take away, remove, withdraw, debit, detract, diminish.
⊜ add.

suburbs n suburbia, commuter belt, residential area, outskirts.
⊜ centre, heart.

subversive adj seditious, treasonous, treacherous, traitorous, inflammatory, incendiary, disruptive, riotous, weakening, undermining, destructive.
⊜ loyal.
◇ n seditionist, terrorist, freedom fighter, dissident, traitor, quisling, fifth columnist.

succeed v 1 TRIUMPH, make it, get on, thrive, flourish, prosper, make good, manage, work. 2 winter succeeds autumn: follow, replace, result, ensue.
⊜ 1 fail. 2 precede.

succeeding adj following, next, subsequent, ensuing, coming, to come, later, successive.
⊜ previous, earlier.

success n 1 TRIUMPH, victory, luck, fortune, prosperity, fame, eminence, happiness. 2 CELEBRITY, star, somebody, winner, bestseller, hit, sensation.
⊜ 1 failure, disaster.

successful adj 1 VICTORIOUS, winning, lucky, fortunate, prosperous, wealthy, thriving, flourishing, booming, moneymaking, lucrative, profitable, rewarding, satisfying, fruitful, productive.
2 a successful writer: famous, well-known, popular, leading, bestselling, top, unbeaten.
⊜ 1 unsuccessful, unprofitable, fruitless. 2 unknown.

succession n sequence, series, order, progression, run, chain, string, cycle, continuation, flow, course, line, train, procession.

successive adj consecutive, sequential, following, succeeding.

succinct adj short, brief, terse, pithy, concise, compact, condensed, summary.
⊜ long, lengthy, wordy, verbose.

succulent adj fleshy, juicy, moist, luscious, mouthwatering, lush, rich, mellow.
⊜ dry.

succumb v give way, yield, give in, submit, knuckle under, surrender, capitulate, collapse, fall.
⊜ overcome, master.

suck v draw in, imbibe, absorb, soak up, extract, drain.

sudden adj unexpected, unforeseen, surprising, startling, abrupt, sharp, quick, swift, rapid, prompt, hurried, hasty, rash, impetuous, impulsive, snap (infml).
⊜ expected, predictable, gradual, slow.

sue v prosecute, charge, indict, summon, solicit, appeal.

suffer v 1 HURT, ache, agonize, grieve, sorrow. 2 BEAR, support, tolerate, endure, sustain, experience, undergo, go through, feel.

suffering n pain, discomfort, agony, anguish, affliction, distress, misery, hardship, ordeal, torment, torture.

⊞ ease, comfort.

sufficient *adj* enough, adequate, satisfactory, effective.
⊞ insufficient, inadequate.

suffocate *v* asphyxiate, smother, stifle, choke, strangle, throttle.

suggest *v* 1 PROPOSE, put forward, advocate, recommend, advise, counsel. 2 IMPLY, insinuate, hint, intimate, evoke, indicate.

suggestion *n* 1 PROPOSAL, proposition, motion, submission, recommendation, idea, plan. 2 IMPLICATION, insinuation, innuendo, hint, intimation, suspicion, trace, indication.

suggestive *adj* 1 EVOCATIVE, reminiscent, expressive, meaning, indicative. 2 *a suggestive remark*: indecent, immodest, improper, indelicate, off-colour, risqué, bawdy, dirty, smutty, provocative.
⊞ 1 inexpressive. 2 decent, clean.

suit *v* 1 SATISFY, gratify, please, answer, match, tally, agree, correspond, harmonize. 2 FIT, befit, become, tailor, adapt, adjust, accommodate, modify.
⊞ 1 displease, clash.
◇ *n* outfit, costume, dress, clothing.

Types of suit include: dress suit, evening suit, tuxedo, business suit, lounge suit, trouser suit, catsuit, jump suit, safari suit, track suit, shell suit, zoot suit.

suitable *adj* appropriate, fitting, convenient, opportune, suited, due, apt, apposite, relevant, applicable, fit, adequate, satisfactory, acceptable, befitting, becoming, seemly, proper, right.
⊞ unsuitable, inappropriate.

sulk *v* mope, brood, pout.

sulky *adj* brooding, moody, morose, resentful, grudging, disgruntled, put

out, cross, bad-tempered, sullen, aloof, unsociable.
⊞ cheerful, good-tempered, sociable.

sullen *adj* 1 SULKY, moody, morose, glum, gloomy, silent, surly, sour, perverse, obstinate, stubborn. 2 DARK, gloomy, sombre, dismal, cheerless, dull, leaden, heavy.
⊞ 1 cheerful, happy. 2 fine, clear.

sully *v* dirty, soil, defile, pollute, contaminate, taint, spoil, mar, spot, blemish, besmirch, stain, tarnish, disgrace, dishonour.
⊞ cleanse, honour.

sultry *adj* hot, sweltering, stifling, stuffy, oppressive, close, humid, muggy, sticky.
⊞ cool, cold.

sum *n* total, sum total, aggregate, whole, entirety, number, quantity, amount, tally, reckoning, score, result.
• **sum up** summarize, review, recapitulate, conclude, close.

summarize *v* outline, précis, condense, abridge, abbreviate, shorten, sum up, encapsulate, review.
⊞ expand (on).

summary *n* synopsis, résumé, outline, abstract, précis, digest, condensation, compendium, abridgement, summing-up, review, recapitulation.
◇ *adj* short, succinct, brief, cursory, hasty, prompt, direct, unceremonious, arbitrary.
⊞ lengthy, careful.

summit *n* top, peak, pinnacle, apex, point, crown, head, zenith, acme, culmination, height.
⊞ bottom, foot, nadir.

summon *v* call, send for, invite, bid, beckon, gather, assemble, convene, rally, muster, mobilize, rouse, arouse.
⊞ dismiss.

sumptuous *adj* luxurious, plush,

lavish, extravagant, opulent, rich, costly, expensive, dear, splendid, magnificent, gorgeous, superb, grand.
⊟ plain, poor.

sunbathe v sun, bask, tan, brown, bake.

sunburnt adj brown, tanned, bronzed, weather-beaten, burnt, red, blistered, peeling.
⊟ pale.

sundry adj various, diverse, miscellaneous, assorted, varied, different, several, some, a few.

sunken adj submerged, buried, recessed, lower, depressed, concave, hollow, haggard, drawn.

sunny adj 1 FINE, cloudless, clear, summery, sunshiny, sunlit, bright, brilliant. 2 CHEERFUL, happy, joyful, smiling, beaming, radiant, light-hearted, buoyant, optimistic, pleasant.
⊟ 1 sunless, dull. 2 gloomy.

sunrise n dawn, crack of dawn, daybreak, daylight.

sunset n sundown, dusk, twilight, gloaming, evening, nightfall.

superb adj excellent, first-rate, first-class, superior, choice, fine, exquisite, gorgeous, magnificent, splendid, grand, wonderful, marvellous, admirable, impressive, breathtaking.
⊟ bad, poor, inferior.

superficial adj surface, external, exterior, outward, apparent, seeming, cosmetic, skin-deep, shallow, slight, trivial, lightweight, frivolous, casual, cursory, sketchy, hasty, hurried, passing.
⊟ internal, deep, thorough.

superfluous adj extra, spare, excess, surplus, remaining, redundant, supernumerary, unnecessary, needless, unwanted, uncalled-for, excessive.

⊟ necessary, needed, wanted.

superintend v supervise, oversee, overlook, inspect, run, manage, administer, direct, control, handle.

superior adj 1 EXCELLENT, first-class, first-rate, top-notch (infml), top-flight (infml), high-class, prime, exclusive, quality, choice, select, fine, de luxe, admirable, distinguished, exceptional, unrivalled, par excellence. 2 BETTER, preferred, greater, higher, senior. 3 HAUGHTY, lordly, pretentious, snobbish, snooty (infml), supercilious, disdainful, condescending, patronizing.
⊟ 1 inferior, average. 2 worse, lower. 3 humble.
◇ n senior, elder, better, boss (infml), chief, principal, director, manager, foreman, supervisor.
⊟ inferior, junior, assistant.

superiority n advantage, lead, edge, supremacy, ascendancy, pre-eminence, predominance.
⊟ inferiority.

superlative adj best, greatest, highest, supreme, transcendent, unbeatable, unrivalled, unparalleled, matchless, peerless, unsurpassed, unbeaten, consummate, excellent, outstanding.
⊟ poor, average.

supernatural adj paranormal, unnatural, abnormal, metaphysical, spiritual, psychic, mystic, occult, hidden, mysterious, miraculous, magical, phantom, ghostly.
⊟ natural, normal.

supersede v succeed, replace, supplant, usurp, oust, displace, remove.

superstition n myth, old wives' tale, fallacy, delusion, illusion.

superstitious adj mythical, false, fallacious, irrational, groundless, delusive, illusory.
⊟ rational, logical.

supervise v oversee, watch over,

look after, superintend, run, manage, administer, direct, conduct, preside over, control, handle.

supervision n surveillance, care, charge, superintendence, oversight, running, management, administration, direction, control, guidance, instruction.

supervisor n overseer, inspector, superintendent, boss (infml), chief, director, administrator, manager, foreman, forewoman.

supplant v replace, supersede, usurp, oust, displace, remove, overthrow, topple, unseat.

supple adj flexible, bending, pliant, pliable, plastic, lithe, graceful, loose-limbed, double-jointed, elastic.
⊜ stiff, rigid, inflexible.

supplement n addition, extra, insert, pull-out, addendum, appendix, codicil, postscript, sequel.
◇ v add to, augment, boost, reinforce, fill up, top up, complement, extend, eke out.
⊜ deplete, use up.

supplementary adj additional, extra, auxiliary, secondary, complementary, accompanying.

supplier n dealer, seller, vendor, wholesaler, retailer.

supplies n stores, provisions, food, equipment, materials, necessities.

supply v provide, furnish, equip, outfit, stock, fill, replenish, give, donate, grant, endow, contribute, yield, produce, sell.
⊜ take, receive.
◇ n source, amount, quantity, stock, fund, reservoir, store, reserve, stockpile, hoard, cache.
⊜ lack.

support v 1 BACK, second, defend, champion, advocate, promote, foster, help, aid, assist, rally round, finance, fund, subsidize, underwrite. 2 HOLD UP, bear, carry, sustain,

brace, reinforce, strengthen, prop, buttress, bolster. 3 MAINTAIN, keep, provide for, feed, nourish. 4 support a statement: endorse, confirm, verify, authenticate, corroborate, substantiate, document.
⊜ 1 oppose. 3 live off. 4 contradict.
◇ n 1 BACKING, allegiance, loyalty, defence, protection, patronage, sponsorship, approval, encouragement, comfort, relief, help, aid, assistance. 2 PROP, stay, post, pillar, brace, crutch, foundation, underpinning.
⊜ 1 opposition, hostility.

supporter n fan, follower, adherent, advocate, champion, defender, seconder, patron, sponsor, helper, ally, friend.
⊜ opponent.

supportive adj helpful, caring, attentive, sympathetic, understanding, comforting, reassuring, encouraging.
⊜ discouraging.

suppose v assume, presume, expect, infer, conclude, guess, conjecture, surmise, believe, think, consider, judge, imagine, conceive, fancy, pretend, postulate, hypothesize.
⊜ know.

supposed adj alleged, reported, rumoured, assumed, presumed, reputed, putative, imagined, hypothetical.
⊜ known, certain.
• **supposed to** meant to, intended to, expected to, required to, obliged to.

supposition n assumption, guess, presumption, conjecture, theory, speculation, hypothesis, idea, notion.
⊜ knowledge.

suppress v crush, stamp out, quash, quell, subdue, stop, silence, censor, stifle, smother, strangle, conceal, withhold, hold back, contain, restrain, check, repress, inhibit.
⊜ encourage, incite.

supreme *adj* best, greatest, highest, top, crowning, culminating, first, leading, foremost, chief, principal, head, sovereign, pre-eminent, predominant, prevailing, world-beating, unsurpassed, second-to-none, incomparable, matchless, consummate, transcendent, superlative, prime, ultimate, extreme, final.
🖝 lowly, poor.

sure *adj* **1** CERTAIN, convinced, assured, confident, decided, positive, definite, unmistakable, clear, accurate, precise, unquestionable, indisputable, undoubted, undeniable, irrevocable, inevitable, bound.
2 SAFE, secure, fast, solid, firm, steady, stable, guaranteed, reliable, dependable, trustworthy, steadfast, unwavering, unerring, unfailing, infallible, effective.
🖝 **1** unsure, uncertain, doubtful.
2 unsafe, insecure.

surface *n* outside, exterior, façade, veneer, covering, skin, top, side, face, plane.
🖝 inside, interior.
◇ *v* rise, arise, come up, emerge, appear, materialize, come to light.
🖝 sink, disappear, vanish.

surly *adj* gruff, brusque, churlish, ungracious, bad-tempered, cross, crabbed, grouchy, crusty, sullen, sulky, morose.
🖝 friendly, polite.

surpass *v* beat, outdo, exceed, outstrip, better, excel, transcend, outshine, eclipse.

surplus *n* excess, remainder, residue, balance, superfluity, glut, surfeit.
🖝 lack, shortage.
◇ *adj* excess, superfluous, redundant, extra, spare, remaining, unused.

surprise *v* startle, amaze, astonish, astound, stagger, flabbergast (*infml*), bewilder, confuse, nonplus, disconcert, dismay.

◇ *n* amazement, astonishment, incredulity, wonder, bewilderment, dismay, shock, start, bombshell, revelation.
🖝 composure.

surprised *adj* startled, amazed, astonished, astounded, staggered, flabbergasted (*infml*), thunderstruck, dumbfounded, speechless, shocked, nonplussed.
🖝 unsurprised, composed.

surprising *adj* astonishing, amazing, astounding, staggering, jaw-dropping (*infml*), stunning, incredible, extraordinary, remarkable, startling, unexpected, unforeseen.
🖝 unsurprising, expected.

surrender *v* capitulate, submit, resign, concede, yield, give in, cede, give up, quit, relinquish, abandon, renounce, forgo, waive.
◇ *n* capitulation, resignation, submission, yielding, relinquishment, renunciation.

surreptitious *adj* furtive, sly, stealthy, covert, veiled, hidden, secret, clandestine, underhand, unauthorized.
🖝 open, obvious.

surround *v* encircle, ring, girdle, encompass, envelop, encase, enclose, hem in, besiege.

surrounding *adj* encircling, bordering, adjacent, adjoining, neighbouring, nearby.

surroundings *n* neighbourhood, vicinity, locality, setting, habitat, environment, background, milieu, ambience.

survey *v* view, contemplate, observe, supervise, scan, scrutinize, examine, inspect, study, research, review, consider, estimate, evaluate, assess, measure, plot, plan, map, chart, reconnoitre.
◇ *n* review, overview, scrutiny, examination, inspection, study, pull,

appraisal, assessment, measurement.

survive v outlive, outlast, endure, last, stay, remain, live, exist, withstand, weather.
☒ succumb, die.

susceptible adj liable, prone, inclined, disposed, given, subject, receptive, responsive, impressionable, suggestible, weak, vulnerable, open, sensitive, tender.
☒ resistant, immune.

suspect v 1 DOUBT, distrust, mistrust, call into question. 2 *I suspect you're right*: believe, fancy, feel, guess, conjecture, speculate, surmise, suppose, consider, conclude, infer.
◇ adj suspicious, doubtful, dubious, questionable, debatable, unreliable, iffy (*sl*), dodgy (*infml*), fishy (*infml*).
☒ acceptable, reliable.

suspend v 1 HANG, dangle, swing. 2 ADJOURN, interrupt, discontinue, cease, delay, defer, postpone, put off, shelve. 3 EXPEL, dismiss, exclude, debar.
☒ 2 continue. 3 restore, reinstate.

suspense n uncertainty, insecurity, anxiety, tension, apprehension, anticipation, expectation, expectancy, excitement.
☒ certainty, knowledge.

suspension n adjournment, interruption, break, intermission, respite, remission, stay, moratorium, delay, deferral, postponement, abeyance.
☒ continuation.

suspicion n 1 DOUBT, scepticism, distrust, mistrust, wariness, caution, misgiving, apprehension. 2 TRACE, hint, suggestion, soupçon, touch, tinge, shade, glimmer, shadow. 3 IDEA, notion, hunch.
☒ 1 trust.

suspicious adj 1 DOUBTFUL, sceptical, unbelieving, suspecting, distrustful, mistrustful, wary, chary,

apprehensive, uneasy. 2 DUBIOUS, questionable, suspect, irregular, shifty, shady (*infml*), dodgy (*infml*), fishy (*infml*).
☒ 1 trustful, confident.
2 trustworthy, innocent.

sustain v 1 NOURISH, provide for, nurture, foster, help, aid, assist, comfort, relieve, support, uphold, endorse, bear, carry. 2 MAINTAIN, keep going, keep up, continue, prolong, hold.

sustained adj prolonged, long-drawn-out, protracted, steady, continuous, constant, perpetual, unremitting.
☒ broken, interrupted, intermittent, spasmodic.

sustenance n nourishment, food, provisions, fare, maintenance, subsistence, livelihood.

swagger v bluster, boast, crow, brag, swank (*infml*), parade, strut.
◇ n bluster, show, ostentation, arrogance.

swallow v 1 CONSUME, devour, eat, gobble up, guzzle, drink, quaff, knock back (*infml*), gulp, down (*infml*). 2 ENGULF, enfold, envelop, swallow up, absorb, assimilate, accept, believe.

swamp n bog, marsh, fen, slough, quagmire, quicksand, mire, mud.
◇ v flood, inundate, deluge, engulf, submerge, sink, drench, saturate, waterlog, overload, overwhelm, besiege, beset.

swap, swop v exchange, transpose, switch, interchange, barter, trade, traffic.

swarm n crowd, throng, mob, mass, multitude, myriad, host, army, horde, herd, flock, drove, shoal.
◇ v 1 STREAM, flock, flood, mass, congregate, crowd, throng.
2 *swarming with tourists*: teem, crawl, bristle, abound.

swarthy adj dark, dark-skinned,

dark-complexioned, dusky, black, brown, tanned.
⊜ fair, pale.

sway v 1 ROCK, roll, lurch, swing, wave, oscillate, fluctuate, bend, incline, lean, divert, veer, swerve. 2 INFLUENCE, affect, persuade, induce, convince, convert, overrule, dominate, govern.

swear v 1 VOW, promise, pledge, avow, attest, asseverate, testify, affirm, assert, declare, insist. 2 CURSE, blaspheme.

swear-word n expletive, four-letter word, curse, oath, imprecation, obscenity, profanity, blasphemy, swearing, bad language.

sweat n 1 PERSPIRATION, moisture, stickiness. 2 ANXIETY, worry, agitation, panic. 3 TOIL, labour, drudgery, chore.
◇ v perspire, swelter, exude.

sweaty adj damp, moist, clammy, sticky, sweating, perspiring.
⊜ dry, cool.

sweep v 1 sweep the floor: brush, dust, clean, clear, remove. 2 PASS, sail, fly, glide, scud, skim, glance, whisk, tear, hurtle.
◇ n 1 ARC, curve, bend, swing, stroke, movement, gesture. 2 SCOPE, compass, range, extent, span, stretch, expanse, vista.

sweeping adj general, global, all-inclusive, all-embracing, blanket, across-the-board, broad, wide-ranging, extensive, far-reaching, comprehensive, thoroughgoing, radical, wholesale, indiscriminate, oversimplified, simplistic.
⊜ specific, narrow.

sweet adj 1 SUGARY, syrupy, sweetened, honeyed, saccharine, luscious, delicious. 2 PLEASANT, delightful, lovely, attractive, beautiful, pretty, winsome, cute, appealing, lovable, charming, agreeable, amiable, affectionate,

tender, kind, treasured, precious, dear, darling. 3 FRESH, clean, wholesome, pure, clear, perfumed, fragrant, aromatic, balmy. 4 sweet music: melodious, tuneful, harmonious, euphonious, musical, dulcet, soft, mellow.
⊜ 1 savoury, salty, sour, bitter. 2 unpleasant, nasty, ugly. 3 foul. 4 discordant.
◇ n 1 CONFECTION, bonbon, candy. 2 DESSERT, pudding, afters (infml).

Sweets include: barley sugar, bull's-eye, butterscotch, caramel, chocolate, fondant, Creme Egg®, fruit pastille, fudge, gobstopper, gumdrop, humbug, jelly baby, jellybean, liquorice, liquorice allsort, lollipop, M & M®, Mars bar®, marshmallow, Milky Way®, nougat, peppermint, praline, rock, Smartie®, toffee, toffee apple, truffle, Turkish delight.

---

sweeten v sugar, honey, mellow, soften, soothe, appease, temper, cushion.
⊜ sour, embitter.

swell v expand, dilate, inflate, blow up, puff up, bloat, distend, fatten, bulge, balloon, billow, surge, rise, mount, increase, enlarge, extend, grow, augment, heighten, intensify.
⊜ shrink, contract, decrease, dwindle.
◇ n billow, wave, undulation, surge, rise, increase, enlargement.

swelling n lump, tumour, bump, bruise, blister, boil, inflammation, bulge, protuberance, puffiness, distension, enlargement.

sweltering adj hot, tropical, baking, scorching, stifling, suffocating, airless, oppressive, sultry, steamy, sticky, humid.
⊜ cold, cool, fresh, breezy, airy.

swerve v turn, bend, incline, veer, swing, shift, deviate, stray, wander, diverge, deflect, sheer.

swift adj fast, quick, rapid, speedy, express, flying, hurried, hasty, short, brief, sudden, prompt, ready, agile, nimble, nippy (infml).
🔁 slow, sluggish, unhurried.

swimsuit n swimming costume, bathing-costume, bathing-suit, bikini, trunks.

swindle v cheat, defraud, diddle, do (infml), overcharge, fleece, rip off (sl), trick, deceive, dupe, con (infml), bamboozle (infml).
◊ n fraud, fiddle, racket, sharp practice, double-dealing, trickery, deception, con (infml), rip-off (sl), scam (infml).

swindler n cheat, fraud, impostor, con man (infml), trickster, shark, rogue, rascal.

swing v hang, suspend, dangle, wave, brandish, sway, rock, oscillate, vibrate, fluctuate, vary, veer, swerve, turn, whirl, twirl, spin, rotate.
◊ n sway, rock, oscillation, vibration, fluctuation, variation, change, shift, movement, motion, rhythm.

swingeing adj harsh, severe, stringent, drastic, punishing, devastating, excessive, extortionate, oppressive, heavy.
🔁 mild.

swipe v 1 HIT, strike, lunge, lash out, slap, whack (infml), wallop (infml), sock (sl). 2 (infml) STEAL, pilfer, lift, pinch (infml).
◊ n stroke, blow, slap, smack, clout, whack (infml), wallop (infml).

swirl v churn, agitate, spin, twirl, whirl, wheel, eddy, twist, curl.

switch v change, exchange, swap, trade, interchange, transpose, substitute, replace, shift, rearrange, turn, veer, deviate, divert, deflect.
◊ n change, alteration, shift, exchange, swap, interchange, substitution, replacement.

swivel v pivot, spin, rotate, revolve, turn, twirl, pirouette, gyrate, wheel.

swollen adj bloated, distended, inflated, tumid, puffed up, puffy, inflamed, enlarged, bulbous, bulging.
🔁 shrunken, shrivelled.

swoop v dive, plunge, drop, fall, descend, stoop, pounce, lunge, rush.
◊ n dive, plunge, drop, descent, pounce, lunge, rush, attack, onslaught.

swop see swap.

sword n blade, foil, rapier, sabre, scimitar.

swot v study, work, learn, memorize, revise, cram, mug up (infml), bone up (sl).

syllabus n curriculum, course, programme, schedule, plan.

symbol n sign, representation, token, mark, emblem, badge, character, ideograph, figure, image.

Symbols include: coat of arms, crest, hieroglyph, icon, ideogram, insignia, logo, logogram, monogram, motif, pictograph, trademark, watermark; ampersand, asterisk, at sign, caret, dagger, double-dagger, hash, obelus, emoticon, smiley.

symbolic adj symbolical, representative, emblematic, token, figurative, metaphorical, allegorical, meaningful, significant.

symbolize v represent, stand for, denote, mean, signify, typify, exemplify, epitomize, personify.

symmetrical adj balanced, even, regular, parallel, corresponding, proportional.
🔁 asymmetrical, irregular.

symmetry n balance, evenness, regularity, parallelism, correspondence, proportion, harmony, agreement.

⊞ asymmetry, irregularity.

sympathetic *adj* understanding, appreciative, supportive, comforting, consoling, commiserating, pitying, interested, concerned, solicitous, caring, compassionate, tender, kind, warm-hearted, well-disposed, affectionate, agreeable, friendly, congenial, like-minded, compatible.
⊞ unsympathetic, indifferent, callous, antipathetic.

sympathize *v* understand, comfort, commiserate, pity, feel for, empathize, identify with, respond to.
⊞ ignore, disregard.

sympathy *n* 1 UNDERSTANDING, comfort, consolation, condolences, commiseration, pity, compassion, tenderness, kindness, warmth, thoughtfulness, empathy, fellow-feeling, affinity, rapport. 2 AGREEMENT, accord, correspondence, harmony.
⊞ 1 indifference, insensitivity, callousness. 2 disagreement.

symptom *n* sign, indication, evidence, manifestation, expression, feature, characteristic, mark, token, warning.

symptomatic *adj* indicative, typical, characteristic, associated, suggestive.

synonymous *adj* interchangeable, substitutable, the same, identical, similar, comparable, tantamount, equivalent, corresponding.
⊞ antonymous, opposite.

synopsis *n* outline, abstract, summary, résumé, précis, condensation, digest, abridgement, review, recapitulation.

synthesize *v* unite, combine, amalgamate, integrate, merge, blend, compound, alloy, fuse, weld, coalesce, unify.
⊞ separate, analyse, resolve.

synthetic *adj* manufactured, man-made, simulated, artificial, ersatz, imitation, fake, bogus, mock, sham, pseudo.
⊞ genuine, real, natural.

system *n* 1 METHOD, mode, technique, procedure, process, routine, practice, usage, rule. 2 ORGANIZATION, structure, set-up, systematization, co-ordination, orderliness, methodology, logic, classification, arrangement, order, plan, scheme.

systematic *adj* methodical, logical, ordered, well-ordered, planned, well-planned, organized, well-organized, structured, systematized, standardized, orderly, businesslike, efficient.
⊞ unsystematic, arbitrary, disorderly, inefficient.

Tt

tab *n* flap, tag, marker, label, sticker, ticket.

table *n* 1 BOARD, slab, counter, worktop, desk, bench, stand. 2 DIAGRAM, chart, graph, timetable, schedule, programme, list, inventory, catalogue, index, register, record.

Types of table include: dining table, gateleg table, refectory table, lowboy, side table, coffee table, card-table, dressing-table.

◇ *v* propose, suggest, submit, put forward.

taboo *adj* forbidden, prohibited, banned, proscribed, unacceptable, unmentionable, unthinkable.
⊞ permitted, acceptable.
◇ *n* ban, interdiction, prohibition, restriction, anathema, curse.

tacit *adj* unspoken, unexpressed, unvoiced, silent, understood, implicit, implied, inferred.
⊞ express, explicit.

taciturn *adj* silent, quiet, uncommunicative, unforthcoming, reticent, reserved, withdrawn, aloof, distant, cold.
⊞ talkative, communicative, forthcoming.

tack *n* 1 NAIL, pin, drawing-pin, staple. 2 COURSE, path, bearing, heading, direction, line, approach, method, way, technique, procedure, plan, tactic, attack.
◇ *v* add, append, attach, affix, fasten, fix, nail, pin, staple.

tackle *n* 1 *a rugby tackle*: attack, challenge, interception, intervention,

block. 2 EQUIPMENT, tools, implements, apparatus, rig, outfit, gear, trappings, paraphernalia.
◇ *v* 1 BEGIN, embark on, set about, try, attempt, undertake, take on, challenge, confront, encounter, face up to, grapple with, deal with, attend to, handle, grab, seize, grasp. 2 INTERCEPT, block, halt, stop.
⊞ 1 avoid, sidestep.

tact *n* tactfulness, diplomacy, discretion, prudence, delicacy, sensitivity, perception, discernment, judgement, understanding, thoughtfulness, consideration, skill, adroitness, finesse.
⊞ tactlessness, indiscretion.

tactful *adj* diplomatic, discreet, politic, judicious, prudent, careful, delicate, subtle, sensitive, perceptive, discerning, understanding, thoughtful, considerate, polite, skilful, adroit.
⊞ tactless, indiscreet, thoughtless, rude.

tactic *n* approach, course, way, means, method, procedure, plan, stratagem, scheme, ruse, ploy, subterfuge, trick, device, shift, move, manoeuvre.

tactical *adj* strategic, planned, calculated, artful, cunning, shrewd, skilful, clever, smart, prudent, politic, judicious.

tactics *n* strategy, campaign, plan, policy, approach, line of attack, moves, manoeuvres.

tactless *adj* undiplomatic, indiscreet, indelicate, inappropriate, impolitic, imprudent, careless,

clumsy, blundering, gauche, insensitive, unfeeling, hurtful, unkind, thoughtless, inconsiderate, rude, rough, impolite, discourteous.
⊞ tactful, diplomatic, discreet.

tag *n* label, sticker, tab, ticket, mark, identification, note, slip, docket.
◇ *v* **1** LABEL, mark, identify, designate, term, call, name, christen, nickname, style, dub. **2** ADD, append, annex, adjoin, affix, fasten.
• **tag along** follow, shadow, tail, trail, accompany.

tail *n* end, extremity, rear, rear end, rump, behind (*infml*), posterior (*infml*), appendage.
◇ *v* follow, pursue, shadow, dog, stalk, track, trail.
• **tail off** decrease, decline, drop, fall away, fade, wane, dwindle, taper off, peter out, die (out).
⊞ increase, grow.

tailor *n* outfitter, dressmaker.
◇ *v* fit, suit, cut, trim, style, fashion, shape, mould, alter, modify, adapt, adjust, accommodate.

tailor-made *adj* made-to-measure, custom-built, bespoke, ideal, perfect, right, suited, fitted.
⊞ unsuitable.

taint *v* contaminate, infect, pollute, adulterate, corrupt, deprave, stain, blemish, blot, smear, tarnish, blacken, dirty, soil, muddy, defile, sully, harm, damage, blight, spoil, ruin, shame, disgrace, dishonour.
◇ *n* contamination, infection, pollution, corruption, stain, blemish, fault, flaw, defect, spot, blot, smear, stigma, shame, disgrace, dishonour.

take *v* **1** SEIZE, grab, snatch, grasp, hold, catch, capture, get, obtain, acquire, secure, gain, win, derive, adopt, assume, pick, choose, select, accept, receive. **2** REMOVE, eliminate, take away, subtract, deduct, steal, filch, purloin, nick (*infml*), pinch (*infml*), appropriate, abduct, carry off. **3** NEED, necessitate, require,

demand, call for. **4** *take me home*: convey, carry, bring, transport, ferry, accompany, escort, lead, guide, conduct, usher. **5** BEAR, tolerate, stand, stomach, abide, endure, suffer, undergo, withstand.
⊞ **1** leave, refuse. **2** replace, put back.
• **take aback** surprise, astonish, stun, astound, stagger, startle, disconcert, bewilder, dismay, upset.
• **take apart** take to pieces, dismantle, disassemble, analyse.
• **take back** reclaim, repossess, withdraw, retract, recant, repudiate, deny, eat one's words.
• **take down 1** DISMANTLE, disassemble, demolish, raze, level, lower. **2** NOTE, record, write down, put down, set down, transcribe.
• **take in 1** ABSORB, assimilate, digest, realize, appreciate, understand, comprehend, grasp, admit, receive, shelter, accommodate, contain, include, comprise, incorporate, embrace, encompass, cover.
2 DECEIVE, fool, dupe, con (*infml*), mislead, trick, hoodwink, bamboozle (*infml*), cheat, swindle.
• **take off 1** REMOVE, doff, divest, shed, discard, drop. **2** LEAVE, depart, go, decamp, disappear. **3** IMITATE, mimic, parody, caricature, satirize, mock, send up.
• **take on 1** ACCEPT, assume, acquire, undertake, tackle, face, contend with, fight, oppose. **2** *take on staff*: employ, hire, enlist, recruit, engage, retain.
• **take up 1** OCCUPY, fill, engage, engross, absorb, monopolize, use up. **2** *take up a hobby*: start, begin, embark on, pursue, carry on, continue. **3** RAISE, lift. **4** ACCEPT, adopt, assume.

take-off *n* imitation, mimicry, impersonation, parody, caricature, spoof, send-up, travesty.

takeover *n* merger, amalgamation, combination, incorporation, coup.

takings *n* receipts, gate, proceeds, profits, gain, returns, revenue, yield, income, earnings, pickings.

tale *n* **1** STORY, yarn, anecdote, spiel (*sl*), narrative, account, report, rumour, tall story, old wives' tale, superstition, fable, myth, legend, saga. **2** LIE, fib, falsehood, untruth, fabrication.

talent *n* gift, endowment, genius, flair, feel, knack, bent, aptitude, faculty, skill, ability, capacity, power, strength, forte.
⊞ inability, weakness.

talented *adj* gifted, brilliant, well-endowed, versatile, accomplished, able, capable, proficient, adept, adroit, deft, clever, skilful.
⊞ inept.

talk *v* speak, utter, articulate, say, communicate, converse, chat, gossip, natter (*infml*), chatter, discuss, confer, negotiate.
◇ *n* **1** CONVERSATION, dialogue, discussion, conference, meeting, consultation, negotiation, chat, chatter, natter (*infml*), gossip, hearsay, rumour, tittle-tattle. **2** *give a talk*: lecture, seminar, symposium, speech, address, discourse, sermon, spiel (*sl*). **3** LANGUAGE, dialect, slang, jargon, speech, utterance, words.
• **talk into** encourage, coax, sway, persuade, convince, bring round, win over.
⊞ dissuade.
• **talk out of** discourage, deter, put off, dissuade.
⊞ persuade, convince.

talkative *adj* garrulous, voluble, vocal, communicative, forthcoming, unreserved, expansive, chatty, gossipy, verbose, wordy.
⊞ taciturn, quiet, reserved.

talking-to *n* lecture, dressing-down (*infml*), telling-off (*infml*), ticking-off (*infml*), scolding, reprimand, rebuke, reproof, reproach, criticism.
⊞ praise, commendation.

tall *adj* high, lofty, elevated, soaring, towering, big, great, giant, gigantic.
⊞ short, low, small.

tally *v* **1** AGREE, concur, tie in, square, accord, harmonize, coincide, correspond, match, conform, suit, fit. **2** ADD (UP), total, count, reckon, figure.
⊞ **1** disagree, differ.
◇ *n* record, count, total, score, reckoning, account.

tame *adj* **1** *a tame rabbit*: domesticated, broken in, trained, disciplined, manageable, tractable, amenable, gentle, docile, meek, submissive, unresisting, obedient, biddable. **2** DULL, boring, tedious, uninteresting, humdrum, flat, bland, insipid, weak, feeble, uninspired, unadventurous, unenterprising, lifeless, spiritless.
⊞ **1** wild, unmanageable, rebellious. **2** exciting.
◇ *v* domesticate, house-train, break in, train, discipline, master, subjugate, conquer, bridle, curb, repress, suppress, quell, subdue, temper, soften, mellow, calm, pacify, humble.

tamper *v* interfere, meddle, mess (*infml*), tinker, fiddle, fix, rig, manipulate, juggle, alter, damage.

tang *n* sharpness, bite, piquancy, pungency, taste, flavour, savour, smack, smell, aroma, scent, whiff, tinge, touch, trace, hint, suggestion, overtone.

tangible *adj* touchable, tactile, palpable, solid, concrete, material, substantial, physical, real, actual, perceptible, discernible, evident, manifest, definite, positive.
⊞ intangible, abstract, unreal.

tangle *n* knot, snarl-up, twist, coil, convolution, mesh, web, maze, labyrinth, mess, muddle, jumble, mix-up, confusion, entanglement, embroilment, complication.
◇ *v* entangle, knot, snarl, ravel, twist, coil, interweave, interlace,

intertwine, catch, ensnare, entrap, enmesh, embroil, implicate, involve, muddle, confuse.
🔁 disentangle.

tangled adj knotty, snarled, messy, matted, tousled, dishevelled, muddled, jumbled, confused, twisted, convoluted, tortuous, involved, complicated, complex, intricate.

tangy adj sharp, biting, acid, tart, spicy, piquant, pungent, strong, fresh.
🔁 tasteless, insipid.

tank n container, reservoir, cistern, aquarium, vat, basin.

tantalize v tease, taunt, torment, torture, provoke, lead on, titillate, tempt, entice, bait, balk, frustrate, thwart.
🔁 gratify, satisfy, fulfil.

tantamount adj as good as, equivalent, commensurate, equal, synonymous, the same as.

tantrum n temper, rage, fury, storm, outburst, fit, scene, paddy (infml).

tap¹ v hit, strike, knock, rap, beat, drum, pat, touch.
◇ n knock, rap, beat, pat, touch.

tap² n 1 STOPCOCK, valve, faucet, spigot, spout. 2 STOPPER, plug, bung.
◇ v use, utilize, exploit, mine, quarry, siphon, bleed, milk, drain.

tape n 1 BAND, strip, binding, ribbon. 2 VIDEO, cassette.
◇ v 1 RECORD, video. 2 BIND, secure, stick, seal.

taper v narrow, attenuate, thin, slim, decrease, reduce, lessen, dwindle, fade, wane, peter out, tail off, die away.
🔁 widen, flare, swell, increase.
◇ n spill, candle, wick.

target n aim, object, end, purpose, intention, ambition, goal, destination, objective, butt, mark, victim, prey, quarry.

tariff n price list, schedule, charges, rate, toll, tax, levy, customs, excise, duty.

tarnish v discolour, corrode, rust, dull, dim, darken, blacken, sully, taint, stain, blemish, spot, blot, mar, spoil.
🔁 polish, brighten.

tart¹ n pie, flan, pastry, tartlet, patty.

tart² adj sharp, acid, sour, bitter, vinegary, tangy, piquant, pungent, biting, cutting, trenchant, incisive, caustic, astringent, acerbic, scathing, sardonic, sarcastic.
🔁 bland, sweet.

task n job, chore, duty, charge, imposition, assignment, exercise, mission, errand, undertaking, enterprise, business, occupation, activity, employment, work, labour, toil, burden.

taste n 1 FLAVOUR, savour, relish, smack, tang. 2 SAMPLE, bit, piece, morsel, titbit, bite, nibble, mouthful, sip, drop, dash, soupçon. 3 a taste for adventure: liking, fondness, partiality, preference, inclination, leaning, desire, appetite. 4 DISCRIMINATION, discernment, judgement, perception, appreciation, sensitivity, refinement, polish, culture, cultivation, breeding, decorum, finesse, style, elegance, tastefulness.
🔁 1 blandness. 3 distaste.
4 tastelessness.
◇ v 1 SAVOUR, relish, sample, nibble, sip, try, test, differentiate, distinguish, discern, perceive. 2 EXPERIENCE, undergo, feel, encounter, meet, know.

tasteful adj refined, polished, cultured, cultivated, elegant, smart, stylish, aesthetic, artistic, harmonious, beautiful, exquisite, delicate, graceful, restrained, well-judged, judicious, correct, fastidious, discriminating.
🔁 tasteless, garish, tawdry.

tasteless adj 1 FLAVOURLESS, insipid, bland, mild, weak, watery, flat, stale, dull, boring, uninteresting, vapid. 2 INELEGANT, graceless, unseemly, improper, indiscreet, crass, rude, crude, vulgar, kitsch, naff (sl), cheesy (sl), cheap, tawdry, flashy, gaudy, garish, loud.
🖅 1 tasty. 2 tasteful, elegant.

tasty adj luscious, palatable, appetizing, mouthwatering, delicious, flavoursome, succulent, scrumptious (infml), yummy (sl), tangy, piquant, savoury, sweet.
🖅 tasteless, insipid.

tattered adj ragged, frayed, threadbare, ripped, torn, tatty, shabby, scruffy.
🖅 smart, neat.

tatters n rags, shreds, ribbons, pieces.

taunt v tease, torment, provoke, bait, goad, jeer, mock, ridicule, gibe, rib (sl), deride, sneer, insult, revile, reproach.
◇ n jeer, catcall, gibe, dig, sneer, insult, reproach, taunting, teasing, provocation, ridicule, sarcasm, derision, censure.

taut adj tight, stretched, contracted, strained, tense, unrelaxed, stiff, rigid.
🖅 slack, loose, relaxed.

tautological adj repetitive, superfluous, redundant, pleonastic, verbose, wordy.
🖅 succinct, economical.

tautology n repetition, duplication, superfluity, redundancy, pleonasm.

tawdry adj cheap, vulgar, tasteless, fancy, showy, flashy, gaudy, garish, tinselly, glittering.
🖅 fine, tasteful.

tax n levy, charge, rate, tariff, customs, contribution, imposition, burden, load.

Taxes include: capital gains tax, capital transfer tax, community charge, corporation tax, council tax, customs, death-duty, estate duty, excise, income tax, inheritance tax, pay-as-you-earn (PAYE), poll tax, property tax, rates, surtax, tithe, toll, value-added tax (VAT).

◇ v 1 LEVY, charge, demand, exact, assess, impose. 2 BURDEN, load, strain, stretch, try, tire, weary, exhaust, drain, sap, weaken.

tea n infusion, tisane, char (sl).

Types of tea include: black tea, green tea, oolong; pekoe, orange pekoe; Assam, Ceylon, China, Darjeeling, Earl Grey, English Breakfast, Indian, jasmine, Keemun, lapsang souchong, rooibos, Russian; chai, decaffeinated tea, fruit tea, herbal tea, iced tea, lemon tea, mint tea.

teach v instruct, train, coach, tutor, lecture, drill, ground, verse, discipline, school, educate, enlighten, edify, inform, impart, inculcate, advise, counsel, guide, direct, show, demonstrate.
🖅 learn.

teacher n schoolteacher, master, schoolmaster, mistress, schoolmistress, educator, pedagogue, tutor, lecturer, professor, don, instructor, trainer, coach, adviser, counsellor, mentor, guide, guru.
🖅 pupil.

teaching n 1 INSTRUCTION, tuition, training, grounding, schooling, education, pedagogy, indoctrination. 2 DOGMA, doctrine, tenet, precept, principle.

team n side, line-up, squad, shift, crew, gang, band, group, company, stable.
• **team up** join, unite, couple, combine, band together, co-operate, collaborate, work together.

tear v 1 RIP, rend, divide, rupture, sever, shred, scratch, claw, gash, lacerate, mutilate, mangle. 2 PULL, snatch, grab, seize, wrest. 3 *tear down the street*: dash, rush, hurry, speed, race, run, sprint, fly, shoot, dart, bolt, belt (*infml*), career, charge.
◊ n rip, rent, slit, hole, split, rupture, scratch, gash, laceration.

tearful adj crying, weeping, sobbing, whimpering, blubbering, sad, sorrowful, upset, distressed, emotional, weepy (*infml*).
🖃 happy, smiling, laughing.

tears n crying, weeping, sobbing, wailing, whimpering, blubbering, sorrow, distress.

tease v taunt, provoke, bait, annoy, irritate, aggravate (*infml*), needle (*infml*), badger, worry, pester, plague, torment, tantalize, mock, ridicule, gibe, banter, rag (*sl*), rib (*sl*).

technical adj mechanical, scientific, technological, electronic, computerized, specialized, expert, professional.

technique n method, system, procedure, manner, fashion, style, mode, way, means, approach, course, performance, execution, delivery, artistry, craftsmanship, skill, facility, proficiency, expertise, know-how (*infml*), art, craft, knack, touch.

tedious adj boring, monotonous, uninteresting, unexciting, dull, dreary, drab, banal, humdrum, tiresome, wearisome, tiring, long-winded, laborious, long-drawn-out.
🖃 lively, interesting, exciting.

teeming adj swarming, crawling, alive, bristling, seething, full, packed, brimming, overflowing, bursting, replete, abundant, fruitful, thick.
🖃 lacking, sparse, rare.

teenage adj teenaged, adolescent, young, youthful, juvenile, immature.

teenager n adolescent, youth, boy, girl, minor, juvenile.

teetotal adj temperate, abstinent, abstemious, sober, on the wagon (*sl*).

telepathy n mind-reading, thought transference, sixth sense, ESP, clairvoyance.

telephone n phone, handset, receiver, blower (*infml*), cellphone, mobile phone.
◊ v phone, ring (up), call (up), dial, buzz (*infml*), contact, get in touch.

telescope v contract, shrink, compress, condense, abridge, squash, crush, shorten, curtail, truncate, abbreviate, reduce, cut, trim.

television n TV, receiver, set, telly (*infml*), the box (*infml*), goggle-box (*infml*), idiot box (*infml*), small screen.

tell v 1 INFORM, notify, let know, acquaint, impart, communicate, speak, utter, say, state, confess, divulge, disclose, reveal. 2 *tell a story*: narrate, recount, relate, report, announce, describe, portray, mention. 3 ORDER, command, direct, instruct, authorize. 4 DIFFERENTIATE, distinguish, discriminate, discern, recognize, identify, discover, see, understand, comprehend.
• **tell off** (*infml*) scold, chide, tick off (*infml*), upbraid, reprimand, rebuke, reprove, lecture, berate, dress down (*infml*), carpet (*infml*), reproach, censure.

temerity n impudence, cheek (*infml*), impertinence, gall, nerve (*infml*), audacity, boldness, daring, rashness, recklessness, impulsiveness.
🖃 caution, prudence.

temper n 1 MOOD, humour, nature, temperament, character, disposition, constitution. 2 ANGER, rage, fury, passion, tantrum, paddy (*infml*), hissy fit (*sl*), annoyance, irritability, ill-humour. 3 CALM, composure, self-control, cool (*sl*).

⊞ 2 calmness, self-control. 3 anger, rage.
◇ *v* 1 MODERATE, lessen, reduce, calm, soothe, allay, assuage, palliate, mitigate, modify, soften. 2 HARDEN, toughen, strengthen.

temperament *n* nature, character, personality, disposition, tendency, bent, constitution, make-up, soul, spirit, mood, humour, temper, state of mind, attitude, outlook.

temperamental *adj* 1 MOODY, emotional, neurotic, highly-strung, sensitive, touchy, irritable, impatient, passionate, fiery, excitable, explosive, volatile, mercurial, capricious, unpredictable, unreliable. 2 NATURAL, inborn, innate, inherent, constitutional, ingrained.
⊞ 1 calm, level-headed, steady.

temperance *n* teetotalism, prohibition, abstinence, sobriety, abstemiousness, continence, moderation, restraint, self-restraint, self-control, self-discipline, self-denial.
⊞ intemperance, excess.

temperate *adj* 1 *temperate climate*: mild, clement, balmy, fair, equable, balanced, stable, gentle, pleasant, agreeable. 2 TEETOTAL, abstinent, abstemious, sober, continent, moderate, restrained, controlled, even-tempered, calm, composed, reasonable, sensible.
⊞ 2 intemperate, extreme, excessive.

tempestuous *adj* stormy, windy, gusty, blustery, squally, turbulent, tumultuous, rough, wild, violent, furious, raging, heated, passionate, intense.
⊞ calm.

temple *n* shrine, sanctuary, church, tabernacle, mosque, pagoda.

tempo *n* time, rhythm, metre, beat, pulse, speed, velocity, rate, pace.

temporal *adj* secular, profane, worldly, earthly, terrestrial, material, carnal, fleshly, mortal.
⊞ spiritual.

temporary *adj* impermanent, provisional, interim, makeshift, stopgap, temporal, transient, transitory, passing, ephemeral, evanescent, fleeting, brief, short-lived, momentary.
⊞ permanent, everlasting.

tempt *v* entice, coax, persuade, woo, bait, lure, allure, attract, draw, seduce, invite, tantalize, provoke, incite.
⊞ discourage, dissuade, repel.

temptation *n* enticement, inducement, coaxing, persuasion, bait, lure, allure, appeal, attraction, draw, pull, seduction, invitation.

tenable *adj* credible, defensible, justifiable, reasonable, rational, sound, arguable, believable, defendable, plausible, viable, feasible.
⊞ untenable, indefensible, unjustifiable.

tenant *n* renter, lessee, leaseholder, occupier, occupant, resident, inhabitant.

tend¹ *v* incline, lean, bend, bear, head, aim, lead, go, move, gravitate.

tend² *v* look after, care for, cultivate, keep, maintain, manage, handle, guard, protect, watch, mind, nurture, nurse, minister to, serve, attend.
⊞ neglect, ignore.

tendency *n* trend, drift, movement, course, direction, bearing, heading, bias, partiality, predisposition, propensity, readiness, liability, susceptibility, proneness, inclination, leaning, bent, disposition.

tender¹ *adj* 1 KIND, gentle, caring, humane, considerate, compassionate, sympathetic, warm, fond, affectionate, loving, amorous, romantic, sentimental, emotional, sensitive, tender-

hearted, soft-hearted. **2** YOUNG, youthful, immature, green, raw, new, inexperienced, impressionable, vulnerable. **3** SOFT, succulent, fleshy, dainty, delicate, fragile, frail, weak, feeble. **4** SORE, painful, aching, smarting, bruised, inflamed, raw.
⊞ **1** hard-hearted, callous. **2** mature. **3** tough, hard.

tender² v offer, proffer, extend, give, present, submit, propose, suggest, advance, volunteer.
◇ n **1** *legal tender*: currency, money. **2** OFFER, bid, estimate, quotation, proposal, proposition, suggestion, submission.

tense adj **1** TIGHT, taut, stretched, strained, stiff, rigid. **2** NERVOUS, anxious, worried, jittery, uneasy, apprehensive, edgy, fidgety, restless, jumpy, overwrought, keyed up. **3** STRESSFUL, exciting, worrying, fraught.
⊞ **1** loose, slack. **2** calm, relaxed.
◇ v tighten, contract, brace, stretch, strain.
⊞ loosen, relax.

tension n **1** TIGHTNESS, tautness, stiffness, strain, stress, pressure. **2** NERVOUSNESS, anxiety, worry, uneasiness, apprehension, edginess, restlessness, suspense.
⊞ **1** looseness. **2** calm(ness), relaxation.

tent n tepee, wigwam, marquee, big top.

tentative adj experimental, exploratory, speculative, hesitant, faltering, cautious, unsure, uncertain, doubtful, undecided, provisional, indefinite, unconfirmed.
⊞ definite, decisive, conclusive, final.

tenuous adj thin, slim, slender, fine, slight, insubstantial, flimsy, fragile, delicate, weak, shaky, doubtful, dubious, questionable.
⊞ strong, substantial.

tepid adj lukewarm, cool, half-hearted, unenthusiastic, apathetic.
⊞ cold, hot, passionate.

term n **1** WORD, name, designation, appellation, title, epithet, phrase, expression. **2** TIME, period, course, duration, spell, span, stretch, interval, space, semester, session, season.
◇ v call, name, dub, style, designate, label, tag, title, entitle.

terminal adj **1** LAST, final, concluding, ultimate, extreme, utmost. **2** *terminal illness*: fatal, deadly, lethal, mortal, incurable.
⊞ **1** initial.

terminate v finish, complete, conclude, cease, end, stop, close, discontinue, wind up, cut off, abort, lapse, expire.
⊞ begin, start, initiate.

terminology n language, jargon, phraseology, vocabulary, words, terms, nomenclature.

terminus n **1** END, close, termination, extremity, limit, boundary, destination, goal, target. **2** DEPOT, station, garage, terminal.

terms n **1** *on good terms*: relations, relationship, footing, standing, position. **2** CONDITIONS, specifications, stipulations, provisos, provisions, qualifications, particulars. **3** RATES, charges, fees, prices, tariff.

terrain n land, ground, territory, country, countryside, landscape, topography.

terrestrial adj earthly, worldly, global, mundane.
⊞ cosmic, heavenly.

terrible adj bad, awful, frightful, dreadful, shocking, appalling, outrageous, disgusting, revolting, repulsive, offensive, abhorrent, hateful, horrid, horrible, unpleasant, obnoxious, foul, vile, hideous, gruesome, horrific, harrowing, distressing, grave, serious, severe, extreme, desperate.

⊜ excellent, wonderful, superb.

terribly adv very, much, greatly, extremely, exceedingly, awfully, frightfully, decidedly, seriously.

terrific adj 1 EXCELLENT, wonderful, marvellous, super, smashing (infml), outstanding, brilliant, magnificent, superb, fabulous (infml), fantastic (infml), sensational, amazing, stupendous, breathtaking. 2 HUGE, enormous, gigantic, tremendous, great, intense, extreme, excessive.
⊜ 1 awful, terrible, appalling.

terrify v petrify, horrify, appal, shock, terrorize, intimidate, frighten, scare, alarm, dismay.

territory n country, land, state, dependency, province, domain, preserve, jurisdiction, sector, region, area, district, zone, tract, terrain.

terror n fear, panic, dread, trepidation, horror, shock, fright, alarm, dismay, consternation, terrorism, intimidation.

terrorize v threaten, menace, intimidate, oppress, coerce, bully, browbeat, frighten, scare, alarm, terrify, petrify, horrify, shock.

terse adj short, brief, succinct, concise, compact, condensed, pithy, epigrammatic, incisive, snappy, curt, brusque, abrupt, laconic.
⊜ long-winded, verbose.

test v try, experiment, examine, assess, evaluate, check, investigate, analyse, screen, prove, verify.
◇ n trial, try-out, experiment, examination, assessment, evaluation, check, investigation, analysis, proof, probation, ordeal.

testify v give evidence, depose, state, declare, assert, swear, avow, attest, vouch, certify, corroborate, affirm, show, bear witness.

testimonial n reference, character, credential, certificate, recommendation, endorsement,

commendation, tribute.

testimony n evidence, statement, affidavit, submission, deposition, declaration, profession, attestation, affirmation, support, proof, verification, confirmation, witness, demonstration, manifestation, indication.

tether n chain, rope, cord, line, lead, leash, bond, fetter, shackle, restraint, fastening.
◇ v tie, fasten, secure, restrain, chain, rope, leash, bind, lash, fetter, shackle, manacle.

text n words, wording, content, matter, body, subject, topic, theme, reading, passage, paragraph, sentence, book, textbook, source.

texture n consistency, feel, surface, grain, weave, tissue, fabric, structure, composition, constitution, character, quality.

thank v say thank you, be grateful, appreciate, acknowledge, recognize, credit.

thankful adj grateful, appreciative, obliged, indebted, pleased, contented, relieved.
⊜ ungrateful, unappreciative.

thankless adj unrecognized, unappreciated, unrequited, unrewarding, unprofitable, fruitless.
⊜ rewarding, worthwhile.

thanks n gratitude, gratefulness, appreciation, acknowledgement, recognition, credit, thanksgiving, thank-offering.
• **thanks to** because of, owing to, due to, on account of, as a result of, through.

thaw v melt, defrost, defreeze, de-ice, soften, liquefy, dissolve, warm, heat up.
⊜ freeze.

theatrical adj 1 DRAMATIC, thespian. 2 MELODRAMATIC, histrionic, mannered, affected, artificial, pompous, ostentatious, showy, extravagant, exaggerated, overdone.

theft *n* robbery, thieving, stealing, pilfering, larceny, shoplifting, kleptomania, fraud, embezzlement.

theme *n* subject, topic, thread, motif, keynote, idea, gist, essence, burden, argument, thesis, dissertation, composition, essay, text, matter.

theorem *n* formula, principle, rule, statement, deduction, proposition, hypothesis.

theoretical *adj* hypothetical, conjectural, speculative, abstract, academic, doctrinaire, pure, ideal.
☒ practical, applied, concrete.

theorize *v* hypothesize, suppose, guess, conjecture, speculate, postulate, propound, formulate.

theory *n* hypothesis, supposition, assumption, presumption, surmise, guess, conjecture, speculation, idea, notion, abstraction, philosophy, thesis, plan, proposal, scheme, system.
☒ certainty, practice.

therapeutic *adj* remedial, curative, healing, restorative, tonic, medicinal, corrective, good, beneficial.
☒ harmful, detrimental.

therapy *n* treatment, remedy, cure, healing, tonic.

therefore *adv* consequently, so, then, as a result.

thesis *n* **1** *doctoral thesis*: dissertation, essay, composition, treatise, paper, monograph. **2** SUBJECT, topic, theme, idea, opinion, view, theory, hypothesis, proposal, proposition, premise, statement, argument, contention.

thick *adj* **1** WIDE, broad, fat, heavy, solid, dense, impenetrable, close, compact, concentrated, condensed, viscous, coagulated, clotted. **2** FULL, packed, crowded, chock-a-block,

swarming, teeming, bristling, brimming, bursting, numerous, abundant. **3** (*infml*) STUPID, foolish, slow, dull, dim-witted, brainless, simple.
☒ **1** thin, slim, slender, slight. **2** sparse. **3** clever, brainy (*infml*).

thicken *v* condense, stiffen, congeal, coagulate, clot, cake, gel, jell, set.
☒ thin.

thicket *n* wood, copse, coppice, grove, spinney.

thickness *n* **1** WIDTH, breadth, diameter, density, viscosity, bulk, body. **2** LAYER, stratum, ply, sheet, coat.
☒ **1** thinness.

thick-skinned *adj* insensitive, unfeeling, callous, tough, hardened, hard-boiled.
☒ thin-skinned, sensitive.

thief *n* robber, bandit, mugger, pickpocket, shoplifter, burglar, housebreaker, plunderer, poacher, stealer, pilferer, filcher, kleptomaniac, swindler, embezzler.

thin *adj* **1** LEAN, slim, slender, narrow, attenuated, slight, skinny, bony, skeletal, scraggy, scrawny, lanky, gaunt, spare, underweight, undernourished, emaciated. **2** *thin fabric*: fine, delicate, light, flimsy, filmy, gossamer, sheer, see-through, transparent, translucent. **3** SPARSE, scarce, scattered, scant, meagre, poor, inadequate, deficient, scanty, skimpy. **4** WEAK, feeble, runny, watery, diluted.
☒ **1** fat, broad. **2** thick, dense, solid. **3** plentiful, abundant. **4** strong.
◇ *v* **1** NARROW, attenuate, diminish, reduce, trim, weed out. **2** WEAKEN, dilute, water down, rarefy, refine.

thing *n* **1** ARTICLE, object, entity, creature, body, substance, item, detail, particular, feature, factor, element, point, fact, concept, thought. **2** DEVICE, contrivance, gadget, tool, implement, instrument, apparatus, machine, mechanism. **3** ACT, deed, feat, action, task, responsibility, problem. **4** CIRCUMSTANCE, eventuality, happening, occurrence, event, incident, phenomenon, affair, proceeding. **5** (*infml*) OBSESSION, preoccupation, fixation, fetish, phobia, hang-up (*infml*).

things *n* belongings, possessions, effects, paraphernalia, stuff (*infml*), goods, luggage, baggage, equipment, gear (*infml*), clobber (*infml*), odds and ends, bits and pieces.

think *v* **1** BELIEVE, hold, consider, regard, esteem, deem, judge, estimate, reckon, calculate, determine, conclude, reason. **2** CONCEIVE, imagine, suppose, presume, surmise, expect, foresee, envisage, anticipate. **3** *think it over*: ponder, mull over, chew over, ruminate, meditate, contemplate, muse, cogitate, reflect, deliberate, weigh up, recall, recollect, remember.
• **think up** devise, contrive, dream up, imagine, conceive, visualize, invent, design, create, concoct.

thinker *n* philosopher, theorist, ideologist, brain, intellect, mastermind.

thinking *n* reasoning, philosophy, thoughts, conclusions, theory, idea, opinion, view, outlook, position, judgement, assessment.
◇ *adj* reasoning, rational, intellectual, intelligent, cultured, sophisticated, philosophical, analytical, reflective, contemplative, thoughtful.

third-rate *adj* low-grade, poor, bad, inferior, mediocre, indifferent, shoddy, cheap and nasty.
⊡ first-rate.

thirst *n* **1** THIRSTINESS, dryness, drought. **2** DESIRE, longing, yearning, hankering, craving, hunger, appetite, lust, passion, eagerness, keenness.

thirsty *adj* **1** DRY, parched (*infml*), gasping (*infml*), dehydrated, arid. **2** *thirsty for knowledge*: desirous, longing, yearning, hankering, craving, hungry, burning, itching, dying, eager, avid, greedy.

thorn *n* spike, point, barb, prickle, spine, bristle, needle.

thorough *adj* full, complete, total, entire, utter, absolute, perfect, pure, sheer, unqualified, unmitigated, out-and-out, downright, sweeping, all-embracing, comprehensive, all-inclusive, exhaustive, thoroughgoing, intensive, in-depth, conscientious, efficient, painstaking, scrupulous, meticulous, careful.
⊡ partial, superficial, careless.

though *conj* although, even if, notwithstanding, while, allowing, granted.
◇ *adv* however, but, nevertheless, nonetheless, yet, still, even so, all the same, for all that.

thought *n* **1** THINKING, attention, heed, regard, consideration, study, scrutiny, introspection, meditation, contemplation, cogitation, reflection, deliberation. **2** IDEA, notion, concept, conception, belief, conviction, opinion, view, judgement, assessment, conclusion, plan, design, intention, purpose, aim, hope, dream, expectation, anticipation. **3** THOUGHTFULNESS, consideration, kindness, care, concern, compassion, sympathy, gesture, touch.

thoughtful *adj* **1** PENSIVE, wistful, dreamy, abstracted, reflective, contemplative, introspective, thinking, absorbed, studious, serious, solemn. **2** CONSIDERATE, kind, unselfish, helpful, caring, attentive, heedful, mindful, careful, prudent, cautious, wary.
⊡ **2** thoughtless, insensitive, selfish.

thoughtless *adj* **1** INCONSIDERATE, unthinking, insensitive, unfeeling, tactless, undiplomatic, unkind,

selfish, uncaring. **2** CARELESS, absent-minded, inattentive, heedless, mindless, foolish, stupid, silly, rash, reckless, ill-considered, imprudent, negligent, remiss.
🗷 **1** thoughtful, considerate.
2 careful.

thrash v **1** PUNISH, beat, whip, lash, flog, scourge, cane, belt, spank, clobber, wallop (*infml*), lay into.
2 DEFEAT, beat, trounce, hammer (*infml*), slaughter (*infml*), crush, overwhelm, rout. **3** THRESH, flail, toss, jerk.
• **thrash out** discuss, debate, negotiate, settle, resolve.

thread n **1** COTTON, yarn, strand, fibre, filament, string, line. **2** COURSE, direction, drift, tenor, theme, motif, plot, storyline.

threadbare adj **1** *threadbare clothes*: worn, frayed, ragged, moth-eaten, scruffy, shabby. **2** HACKNEYED, overused, old, stale, tired, trite, commonplace, stock, stereotyped.
🗷 **1** new. **2** fresh.

threat n menace, warning, omen, portent, presage, foreboding, danger, risk, hazard, peril.

threaten v menace, intimidate, browbeat, pressurize, bully, terrorize, warn, portend, presage, forebode, foreshadow, endanger, jeopardize, imperil.

threatening adj menacing, intimidatory, warning, cautionary, ominous, inauspicious, sinister, grim, looming, impending.

threshold n doorstep, sill, doorway, door, entrance, brink, verge, starting point, dawn, beginning, start, outset, opening.

thrift n economy, husbandry, saving, conservation, frugality, prudence, carefulness.
🗷 extravagance, waste.

thrifty adj economical, saving, frugal, sparing, prudent, careful.

🗷 extravagant, profligate, prodigal, wasteful.

thrill n excitement, adventure, pleasure, stimulation, charge, kick, buzz (*sl*), hit (*sl*), sensation, glow, tingle, throb, shudder, quiver, tremor.
◇ v excite, electrify, galvanize, exhilarate, rouse, arouse, move, stir, stimulate, flush, glow, tingle, throb, shudder, tremble, quiver, shake.
🗷 bore.

thrive v flourish, prosper, boom, grow, increase, advance, develop, bloom, blossom, gain, profit, succeed.
🗷 languish, stagnate, fail, die.

throb v pulse, pulsate, beat, palpitate, vibrate, pound, thump.
◇ n pulse, pulsation, beat, palpitation, vibration, pounding, thumping.

throttle v strangle, choke, smother, asphyxiate, suffocate, stifle, gag, silence, suppress, inhibit.

through prep **1** BETWEEN, by, via, by way of, by means of, using.
2 *all through the night*: throughout, during, in. **3** BECAUSE OF, as a result of, thanks to.
◇ adj **1** FINISHED, ended, completed, done. **2** *through train*: direct, express, non-stop.

throw v **1** HURL, heave, lob, pitch, chuck (*infml*), sling, cast, fling, toss, launch, propel, send. **2** *throw light*: shed, cast, project, direct.
3 BRING DOWN, floor, upset, overturn, dislodge, unseat, unsaddle, unhorse.
4 (*infml*) PERPLEX, baffle, confound, confuse, disconcert, astonish, dumbfound.
◇ n heave, lob, pitch, sling, fling, toss, cast.
• **throw away 1** DISCARD, jettison, dump, ditch (*sl*), scrap, dispose of, throw out. **2** WASTE, squander, fritter away, blow (*sl*).
🗷 **1** keep, preserve, salvage, rescue.
• **throw off** shed, cast off, drop,

abandon, shake off, get rid of, elude.
• **throw out 1** EVICT, turn out, expel,
turf out (*infml*), eject, emit, radiate,
give off. **2** REJECT, discard, dismiss,
turn down, jettison, dump, ditch (*sl*),
throw away, scrap.
• **throw up 1** (*infml*) VOMIT, spew,
regurgitate, disgorge, retch, heave.
2 ABANDON, renounce, relinquish,
resign, quit, leave.

thrust *v* push, shove, butt, ram, jam,
wedge, stick, poke, prod, jab, lunge,
pierce, stab, plunge, press, force,
impel, drive, propel.
◇ *n* **1** PUSH, shove, poke, prod, lunge,
stab. **2** DRIVE, impetus, momentum.

thud *n*, *v* thump, clump, knock,
clunk, smack, wallop (*infml*), crash,
bang, thunder.

thug *n* ruffian, tough, robber, bandit,
mugger, killer, murderer, assassin,
gangster, hooligan.

thump *n* knock, blow, punch, clout,
box, cuff, smack, whack (*infml*),
wallop (*infml*), crash, bang, thud,
beat, throb.
◇ *v* hit, strike, knock, punch, clout,
box, cuff, smack, thrash, whack
(*infml*), wallop (*infml*), crash, bang,
thud, batter, pound, hammer, beat,
throb.

thunder *n* boom, reverberation,
crash, bang, crack, clap, peal,
rumble, roll, roar, blast, explosion.
◇ *v* boom, resound, reverberate,
crash, bang, crack, clap, peal,
rumble, roll, roar, blast.

thunderous *adj* booming,
resounding, reverberating, roaring,
loud, noisy, deafening, ear-splitting.

thus *adv* so, hence, therefore, then,
consequently, accordingly, like this,
in this way, as follows.

thwart *v* frustrate, foil, stymie,
defeat, hinder, impede, obstruct,
block, check, baffle, stop, prevent,
oppose.
⊡ help, assist, aid.

tick *n* **1** CLICK, tap, stroke, tick-tock.
2 (*infml*) *wait a tick*: moment, instant,
flash, jiffy (*infml*), second, minute.
◇ *v* **1** MARK, indicate, choose, select.
2 CLICK, tap, beat.
• **tick off** (*infml*) scold, chide,
reprimand, rebuke, reproach,
reprove, upbraid, tell off (*infml*).
⊡ praise, compliment.

ticket *n* pass, card, certificate, token,
voucher, coupon, docket, slip, label,
tag, sticker.

tickle *v* excite, thrill, delight, please,
gratify, amuse, entertain, divert.

ticklish *adj* sensitive, touchy,
delicate, thorny, awkward, difficult,
tricky, critical, risky, hazardous,
dodgy (*infml*).
⊡ easy, simple.

tide *n* current, ebb, flow, stream,
flux, movement, course, direction,
drift, trend, tendency.

tidy *adj* **1** NEAT, orderly, methodical,
systematic, organized, clean, spick
and span, shipshape, smart, spruce,
trim, well-kept, ordered, uncluttered.
2 (*infml*) *a tidy sum*: substantial,
large, sizable, considerable, good,
generous, ample.
⊡ **1** untidy, messy, disorganized.
2 small, insignificant.
◇ *v* neaten, straighten, order,
arrange, clean, smarten, spruce up,
groom.

tie *v* **1** KNOT, fasten, secure, moor,
tether, attach, join, connect, link,
unite, rope, lash, strap, bind.
2 RESTRAIN, restrict, confine, limit,
hamper, hinder.
◇ *n* **1** KNOT, fastening, joint,
connection, link, liaison,
relationship, bond, affiliation,
obligation, commitment, duty,
restraint, restriction, limitation,
hindrance. **2** DRAW, dead heat,
stalemate, deadlock.
• **tie up 1** MOOR, tether, attach,
secure, rope, lash, bind, truss, wrap
up, restrain. **2** CONCLUDE, terminate,

wind up, settle. **3** OCCUPY, engage, engross.

tier n floor, storey, level, stage, stratum, layer, belt, zone, band, echelon, rank, row, line.

tight adj **1** TAUT, stretched, tense, rigid, stiff, firm, fixed, fast, secure, close, cramped, constricted, compact, snug, close-fitting. **2** SEALED, hermetic, -proof, impervious, airtight, watertight. **3** (infml) MEAN, stingy, miserly, niggardly, parsimonious, tight-fisted (infml). **4** tight security: strict, severe, stringent, rigorous.
⊟ **1** loose, slack. **2** open.
3 generous. **4** lax.

tighten v tauten, stretch, tense, stiffen, fix, fasten, secure, narrow, close, cramp, constrict, crush, squeeze.
⊟ loosen, relax.

tight-fisted adj mean, stingy, miserly, mingy (infml), niggardly, penny-pinching, sparing, tight (infml), parsimonious, grasping.
⊟ generous, charitable.

till v cultivate, work, plough, dig, farm.

tilt v slope, incline, slant, pitch, list, tip, lean.
◇ n slope, incline, angle, inclination, slant, pitch, list.

timber n wood, trees, forest, beam, lath, plank, board, log.

time n **1** SPELL, stretch, period, term, season, session, span, duration, interval, space, while. **2** TEMPO, beat, rhythm, metre, measure. **3** MOMENT, point, juncture, stage, instance, occasion, date, day, hour. **4** AGE, era, life, lifetime, generation, heyday, peak.

Periods of time include: eternity, eon, era, age, generation, epoch, millennium, century, decade, year, quarter, month, fortnight, week, mid-week, weekend, long weekend, day, today, tonight, yesterday, tomorrow, morrow, weekday, hour, minute, second, moment, instant, millisecond, microsecond, nanosecond; dawn, sunrise, sunup, the early hours, wee small hours (infml), morning, morn, a.m., daytime, midday, noon, high noon, p.m., afternoon, teatime, evening, twilight, dusk, sunset, nightfall, bedtime, night, night-time; season, spring, summer, midsummer, autumn, fall (N Am), winter, midwinter.

◇ v clock, measure, meter, regulate, control, set, schedule, timetable.

timeless adj ageless, immortal, everlasting, eternal, endless, permanent, changeless, unchanging.

timely adj well-timed, seasonable, suitable, appropriate, convenient, opportune, propitious, prompt, punctual.
⊟ ill-timed, unsuitable, inappropriate.

timetable n schedule, programme, agenda, calendar, diary, rota, roster, list, listing, curriculum.

timid adj shy, bashful, modest, shrinking, retiring, nervous, apprehensive, afraid, timorous, fearful, cowardly, faint-hearted, spineless, irresolute.
⊟ brave, bold, audacious.

tinge n tint, dye, colour, shade, touch, trace, suggestion, hint, smack, flavour, pinch, drop, dash, bit, sprinkling, smattering.
◇ v tint, dye, stain, colour, shade, suffuse, imbue.

tingle v sting, prickle, tickle, itch, thrill, throb, quiver, vibrate.
◇ n stinging, prickling, pins and needles, tickle, tickling, itch, itching, thrill, throb, quiver, shiver, gooseflesh, goose-pimples.

tinker v fiddle, play, toy, trifle,

potter, dabble, meddle, tamper.

tint n dye, stain, rinse, wash, colour, hue, shade, tincture, tinge, tone, cast, streak, trace, touch.
◇ v dye, colour, tinge, streak, stain, taint, affect.

tiny adj minute, microscopic, infinitesimal, teeny (infml), small, little, slight, negligible, insignificant, diminutive, petite, dwarfish, pint-size(d) (infml), pocket, miniature, mini (infml).
🗷 huge, enormous, immense.

tip¹ n end, extremity, point, nib, apex, peak, pinnacle, summit, acme, top, cap, crown, head.
◇ v cap, crown, top, surmount.

tip² v lean, incline, slant, list, tilt, topple over, capsize, upset, overturn, spill, pour out, empty, unload, dump.
◇ n dump, rubbish heap, refuse heap.

tip³ n 1 CLUE, pointer, hint, advice, suggestion, warning, tip-off, information, inside information, forecast. 2 GRATUITY, gift, perquisite.
◇ v 1 ADVISE, suggest, warn, caution, forewarn, tip off, inform, tell. 2 tip the driver: reward, remunerate.

tire v weary, fatigue, wear out, exhaust, drain, enervate.
🗷 enliven, invigorate, refresh.

tired adj 1 WEARY, drowsy, sleepy, flagging, fatigued, worn out, exhausted, dog-tired, drained, jaded, fagged (sl), bushed (infml), whacked (infml), shattered (infml), beat (infml), dead-beat (infml), all in (infml), knackered (infml). 2 tired of waiting: fed up, bored, sick. 3 STALE, overused, jaded, unoriginal, hackneyed.
🗷 1 lively, energetic, rested, refreshed. 3 new, original.

tireless adj untiring, unwearied, unflagging, indefatigable, energetic, vigorous, diligent, industrious, resolute, determined.
🗷 tired, lazy.

tiresome adj troublesome, trying, annoying, irritating, exasperating, wearisome, dull, boring, tedious, monotonous, uninteresting, tiring, fatiguing, laborious.
🗷 interesting, stimulating, easy.

tiring adj wearying, fatiguing, exhausting, draining, demanding, exacting, taxing, arduous, strenuous, laborious.

tissue n 1 SUBSTANCE, matter, material. 2 FABRIC, stuff, gauze. 3 a tissue of lies: web, mesh, network, structure, texture.

titbit n morsel, scrap, appetizer, snack, delicacy, dainty, treat.

titillate v stimulate, arouse, turn on (sl), excite, thrill, tickle, provoke, tease, tantalize, intrigue, interest.

title n 1 NAME, appellation, denomination, term, designation, label, epithet, nickname, pseudonym, rank, status, office, position. 2 HEADING, headline, caption, legend, inscription. 3 RIGHT, prerogative, privilege, claim, entitlement, ownership, deeds.
◇ v entitle, name, call, dub, style, term, designate, label.

titter v laugh, chortle, chuckle, giggle, snigger, mock.

titular adj honorary, formal, official, so-called, nominal, token.

toast v grill, brown, roast, heat, warm.
◇ n drink, pledge, tribute, salute, compliment, health.

together adv jointly, in concert, side by side, shoulder to shoulder, in unison, as one, simultaneously, at the same time, all at once, collectively, en masse, closely, continuously, consecutively, successively, in succession, in a row, hand in hand.
🗷 separately, individually, alone.

toil n labour, hard work, donkey-work, drudgery, sweat, graft (infml),

industry, application, effort, exertion, elbow grease.
◇ *v* labour, work, slave, drudge, sweat, grind, slog, graft (*infml*), plug away (*infml*), persevere, strive, struggle.

toilet *n* lavatory, WC, loo (*infml*), bog (*sl*), bathroom, cloakroom, washroom, rest room (*N Am*), public convenience, Ladies (*infml*), Gents (*infml*), urinal, convenience, powder room.

token *n* **1** SYMBOL, emblem, mark, sign, representation, indication, manifestation, demonstration, expression, evidence, proof, clue, warning, reminder, memorial, memento, souvenir, keepsake. **2** *gift token*: voucher, coupon, counter, disc.
◇ *adj* symbolic, emblematic, nominal, minimal, perfunctory, superficial, cosmetic, hollow, insincere.

tolerable *adj* bearable, endurable, sufferable, acceptable, passable, adequate, reasonable, fair, average, all right, OK (*infml*), not bad, mediocre, indifferent, so-so (*infml*), unexceptional, ordinary, run-of-the-mill.
⊞ intolerable, unbearable, insufferable.

tolerance *n* **1** TOLERATION, patience, forbearance, open-mindedness, broad-mindedness, magnanimity, sympathy, understanding, lenity, indulgence, permissiveness.
2 VARIATION, fluctuation, play, allowance, clearance. **3** RESISTANCE, resilience, toughness, endurance, stamina.
⊞ **1** intolerance, prejudice, bigotry, narrow-mindedness.

tolerant *adj* patient, forbearing, long-suffering, open-minded, fair, unprejudiced, broad-minded, liberal, charitable, kind-hearted, sympathetic, understanding,

forgiving, lenient, indulgent, easy-going (*infml*), permissive, lax, soft.
⊞ intolerant, biased, prejudiced, bigoted, unsympathetic.

tolerate *v* endure, suffer, put up with, bear, stand, abide, stomach, swallow, take, receive, accept, admit, allow, permit, condone, countenance, indulge.

toll¹ *v* ring, peal, chime, knell, sound, strike, announce, call.

toll² *n* charge, fee, payment, levy, tax, duty, tariff, rate, cost, penalty, demand, loss.

tomb *n* grave, burial-place, vault, crypt, sepulchre, catacomb, mausoleum, cenotaph.

tone *n* **1** *tone of voice*: note, timbre, pitch, volume, intonation, modulation, inflection, accent, stress, emphasis, force, strength. **2** TINT, tinge, colour, hue, shade, cast, tonality. **3** AIR, manner, attitude, mood, spirit, humour, temper, character, quality, feel, style, effect, vein, tenor, drift.
◇ *v* match, co-ordinate, blend, harmonize.
• **tone down** moderate, temper, subdue, restrain, soften, dim, dampen, play down, reduce, alleviate, assuage, mitigate.

tongue *n* language, speech, discourse, talk, utterance, articulation, parlance, vernacular, idiom, dialect, patois.

tongue-tied *adj* speechless, dumbstruck, inarticulate, silent, mute, dumb, voiceless.
⊞ talkative, garrulous, voluble.

tonic *n* cordial, pick-me-up, restorative, refresher, bracer, stimulant, shot in the arm (*infml*), boost, fillip.

too *adv* **1** ALSO, as well, in addition, besides, moreover, likewise.
2 EXCESSIVELY, inordinately, unduly, over, overly, unreasonably,

ridiculously, extremely, very.

tool n 1 IMPLEMENT, instrument, utensil, gadget, device, contrivance, contraption, apparatus, appliance, machine, means, vehicle, medium, agency, agent, intermediary. 2 PUPPET, pawn, dupe, stooge, minion, hireling.

Types of tool include: crowbar, jackhammer, jointer, mattock, pick, pickaxe, sledgehammer; clamp, drill, hacksaw, jack, pincers, pliers, punch, sander, socket wrench, soldering iron, spray gun, vice; auger, awl, brace-and-bit, bradawl, chisel, file, fretsaw, hammer, handsaw, jack plane, jigsaw, mallet, plane, rasp, saw, screwdriver, tenon saw; billhook, chainsaw, chopper, dibble, fork, hoe, pitchfork, pruning knife, pruning shears, rake, scythe, secateurs, shears, shovel, sickle, spade, trowel; needle, scissors, pinking shears, bodkin, forceps, scalpel, tweezers, tongs, cleaver, gimlet, pestle, paperknife, stapler, pocket knife, penknife.

---

top n 1 HEAD, tip, vertex, apex, crest, crown, peak, pinnacle, summit, acme, zenith, culmination, height. 2 LID, cap, cover, cork, stopper. 3 JUMPER, sweater, jersey.
⊜ 1 bottom, base, nadir.

Types of top include: cardigan, fleece, polo neck, turtleneck, guernsey, pullover, twinset, shirt, dress-shirt, sweat-shirt, tee shirt, T-shirt, hoodie, waistcoat, blouse, smock, tabard, tunic.

◇ adj highest, topmost, upmost, uppermost, upper, superior, head, chief, leading, first, foremost, principal, sovereign, ruling, pre-eminent, dominant, prime, paramount, greatest, maximum, best, finest, supreme, crowning, culminating.

⊜ bottom, lowest, inferior.
◇ v 1 TIP, cap, crown, cover, finish (off), decorate, garnish. 2 BEAT, exceed, outstrip, better, excel, best, surpass, eclipse, outshine, outdo, surmount, transcend. 3 HEAD, lead, rule, command.

topic n subject, theme, issue, question, matter, point, thesis, text.

topical adj current, contemporary, up-to-date, up-to-the-minute, recent, newsworthy, relevant, popular, familiar.

topple v totter, overbalance, tumble, fall, collapse, upset, overturn, capsize, overthrow, oust.

torment v tease, provoke, annoy, vex, trouble, worry, harass, hound, pester, bother, bedevil, plague, afflict, distress, harrow, pain, torture, persecute.
◇ n provocation, annoyance, vexation, bane, scourge, trouble, bother, nuisance, harassment, worry, anguish, distress, misery, affliction, suffering, pain, agony, ordeal, torture, persecution.

torrent n stream, volley, outburst, gush, rush, flood, spate, deluge, cascade, downpour.
⊜ trickle.

tortuous adj twisting, winding, meandering, serpentine, zigzag, circuitous, roundabout, indirect, convoluted, complicated, involved.
⊜ straight, straightforward.

torture v pain, agonize, excruciate, crucify, rack, martyr, persecute, torment, afflict, distress.
◇ n pain, agony, suffering, affliction, distress, misery, anguish, torment, martyrdom, persecution.

toss v 1 FLIP, cast, fling, throw, chuck (infml), sling, hurl, lob. 2 ROLL, heave, pitch, lurch, jolt, shake, agitate, rock, thrash, squirm, wriggle.
◇ n flip, cast, fling, throw, pitch.

total n sum, whole, entirety, totality,

all, lot, mass, aggregate, amount.
◇ *adj* full, complete, entire, whole,
integral, all-out, utter, absolute,
unconditional, unqualified, outright,
undisputed, perfect, consummate,
thoroughgoing, sheer, downright,
thorough.
⊡ partial, limited, restricted.
◇ *v* add (up), sum (up), tot (up), count
(up), reckon, amount to, come to.

totter *v* stagger, reel, lurch, stumble,
falter, waver, teeter, sway, rock,
shake, quiver, tremble.

touch *n* **1** FEEL, texture, brush, stroke,
caress, pat, tap, contact. **2** *a touch
of garlic*: trace, spot, dash, pinch,
soupçon, suspicion, hint, suggestion,
speck, jot, tinge, smack. **3** SKILL, art,
knack, flair, style, method, manner,
technique, approach.
◇ *v* **1** FEEL, handle, finger, brush,
graze, stroke, caress, fondle, pat,
tap, hit, strike, contact, meet, abut,
adjoin, border. **2** MOVE, stir, upset,
disturb, impress, inspire, influence,
affect, concern, regard. **3** REACH,
attain, equal, match, rival, better.
• **touch on** mention, broach, speak
of, remark on, refer to, allude to,
cover, deal with.

touched *adj* **1** MOVED, stirred,
affected, disturbed, impressed.
2 MAD, crazy, deranged, disturbed,
eccentric, dotty (*infml*), daft (*infml*),
barmy (*infml*).

touching *adj* moving, stirring,
affecting, poignant, pitiable, pitiful,
pathetic, sad, emotional, tender.

touchy *adj* irritable, irascible, quick-
tempered, bad-tempered, grumpy,
grouchy, crabbed, cross, peevish,
captious, edgy, over-sensitive.
⊡ calm, imperturbable.

tough *adj* **1** STRONG, durable,
resilient, resistant, hardy, sturdy,
solid, rigid, stiff, inflexible, hard,
leathery. **2** *tough criminal*: rough,
violent, vicious, callous, hardened,
obstinate. **3** HARSH, severe, strict,

stern, firm, resolute, determined,
tenacious. **4** ARDUOUS, laborious,
exacting, hard, difficult, puzzling,
perplexing, baffling, knotty, thorny.
⊡ **1** fragile, delicate, weak, tender.
2 gentle, soft. **3** gentle. **4** easy,
simple.
◇ *n* brute, thug, bully, ruffian,
hooligan, lout, yob (*sl*).

tour *n* circuit, round, visit,
expedition, journey, trip, outing,
excursion, drive, ride, course.
◇ *v* visit, go round, sightsee, explore,
travel, journey, drive, ride.

tourist *n* holidaymaker, visitor,
sightseer, tripper, excursionist,
traveller, voyager, globetrotter.

tournament *n* championship,
series, competition, contest, match,
event, meeting.

tow *v* pull, tug, draw, trail, drag, lug,
haul, transport.

towards *prep* **1** TO, approaching,
nearing, close to, nearly, almost.
2 *his feelings towards her*: regarding,
with regard to, with respect to,
concerning, about, for.

tower *n* fortification, bastion,
citadel, fort, fortress, castle.

Types of tower include: barbican,
bastille, belfry, bell-tower,
belvedere, campanile, church
tower, column, demi-bastion,
donjon, gate-tower, high-rise
building, keep, lookout tower,
martello tower, minar, minaret,
mirador, pagoda, peel-tower,
skyscraper, spire, steeple, tower
block, turret, watchtower, water
tower.

Famous towers include: Bastille,
Blackpool Tower, Eiffel Tower,
Leaning Tower of Pisa, Tower of
Babel, Tower of London.

◇ *v* rise, rear, ascend, mount, soar,

loom, overlook, dominate, surpass, transcend, exceed, top.

towering *adj* soaring, tall, high, lofty, elevated, monumental, colossal, gigantic, great, magnificent, imposing, impressive, sublime, supreme, surpassing, overpowering, extreme, inordinate.
🗷 small, tiny, minor, trivial.

town *n* borough, municipality, burgh, market town, county town, new town, city, suburbs, outskirts, conurbation, metropolis, urban district, settlement, township, pueblo.
🗷 country.

toxic *adj* poisonous, harmful, noxious, unhealthy, dangerous, deadly, lethal.
🗷 harmless, safe.

toy *n* plaything, game, doll, knick-knack.
◇ *v* play, tinker, fiddle, sport, trifle, dally.

trace *n* trail, track, spoor, footprint, footmark, mark, token, sign, indication, evidence, record, relic, remains, remnant, vestige, shadow, hint, suggestion, suspicion, soupçon, dash, drop, spot, bit, jot, touch, tinge, smack.
◇ *v* **1** COPY, draw, sketch, outline, delineate, depict, mark, record, map, chart. **2** FIND, discover, detect, unearth, track (down), trail, stalk, hunt, seek, follow, pursue, shadow.

track *n* footstep, footprint, footmark, scent, spoor, trail, wake, mark, trace, slot, groove, rail, path, way, route, orbit, line, course, drift, sequence.
◇ *v* stalk, trail, hunt, trace, follow, pursue, chase, dog, tail, shadow.
• **track down** find, discover, trace, hunt down, run to earth, sniff out, ferret out, dig up, unearth, expose, catch, capture.

tract *n* stretch, extent, expanse, plot, lot, territory, area, region,

zone, district, quarter.

trade *n* **1** COMMERCE, traffic, business, dealing, buying, selling, shopkeeping, barter, exchange, transactions, custom. **2** OCCUPATION, job, business, profession, calling, craft, skill.
◇ *v* traffic, peddle, do business, deal, transact, buy, sell, barter, exchange, swap, switch, bargain.

trademark *n* brand, label, name, sign, symbol, logo, insignia, crest, emblem, badge, hallmark.

trader *n* merchant, tradesman, broker, dealer, buyer, seller, vendor, supplier, wholesaler, retailer, shopkeeper, trafficker, peddler.

tradition *n* convention, custom, usage, way, habit, routine, ritual, institution, folklore.

traditional *adj* conventional, customary, habitual, usual, accustomed, established, fixed, long-established, time-honoured, old, historic, folk, oral, unwritten.
🗷 unconventional, innovative, new, modern, contemporary.

traffic *n* **1** VEHICLES, shipping, transport, transportation, freight, passengers. **2** TRADE, commerce, business, dealing, trafficking, barter, exchange. **3** COMMUNICATION, dealings, relations.
◇ *v* peddle, buy, sell, trade, do business, deal, bargain, barter, exchange.

tragedy *n* adversity, misfortune, unhappiness, affliction, blow, calamity, disaster, catastrophe.

tragic *adj* sad, sorrowful, miserable, unhappy, unfortunate, unlucky, ill-fated, pitiable, pathetic, heartbreaking, shocking, appalling, dreadful, awful, dire, calamitous, disastrous, catastrophic, deadly, fatal.
🗷 happy, comic, successful.

trail *v* **1** DRAG, pull, tow, droop, dangle, extend, stream, straggle,

dawdle, lag, loiter, linger. **2** TRACK,
stalk, hunt, follow, pursue, chase,
shadow, tail.
◇ *n* track, footprints, footmarks,
scent, trace, path, footpath, road,
route, way.

train *v* **1** TEACH, instruct, coach,
tutor, educate, improve, school,
discipline, prepare, drill, exercise,
work out, practise, rehearse. **2** POINT,
direct, aim, level.
◇ *n* **1** *train of events*: sequence,
succession, series, progression, order,
string, chain, line, file, procession,
convoy, cortège, caravan. **2** RETINUE,
entourage, attendants, court,
household, staff, followers, following.

trainer *n* teacher, instructor, coach,
tutor, handler.

training *n* teaching, instruction,
coaching, tuition, education,
schooling, discipline, preparation,
grounding, drill, exercise,
working-out, practice, learning,
apprenticeship.

trait *n* feature, attribute, quality,
characteristic, idiosyncrasy,
peculiarity, quirk.

traitor *n* betrayer, informer,
deceiver, double-crosser, turncoat,
renegade, deserter, defector,
quisling, collaborator.
⊠ loyalist, supporter, defender.

tramp *v* walk, march, tread, stamp,
stomp, stump, plod, trudge, traipse,
trail, trek, hike, ramble, roam, rove.
◇ *n* vagrant, vagabond, hobo, down-
and-out, dosser (*sl*).

trample *v* tread, stamp, crush,
squash, flatten.

trance *n* dream, reverie, daze,
stupor, unconsciousness, spell,
ecstasy, rapture.

tranquil *adj* calm, composed,
cool, imperturbable, unexcited,
placid, sedate, relaxed, laid-back
(*infml*), serene, peaceful, restful,
still, undisturbed, untroubled,

quiet, hushed, silent.
⊠ agitated, disturbed, troubled,
noisy.

tranquillizer *n* sedative, opiate,
narcotic, barbiturate.

transaction *n* deal, bargain,
agreement, arrangement, business,
negotiation, affair, matter, proceeding,
enterprise, undertaking, deed, action,
execution, discharge.

transcend *v* surpass, excel,
outshine, eclipse, outdo, outstrip,
beat, surmount, exceed, overstep.

transcribe *v* write out, copy,
reproduce, rewrite, transliterate,
translate, render, take down, note,
record.

transcript *n* transcription,
copy, reproduction, duplicate,
transliteration, translation, version,
note, record, manuscript.

transfer *v* change, transpose, move,
shift, remove, relocate, transplant,
transport, carry, convey, transmit,
consign, grant, hand over.
◇ *n* change, changeover, move,
transposition, shift, removal,
relocation, displacement,
transmission, handover, transference.

transfix *v* **1** FASCINATE, spellbind,
mesmerize, hypnotize, paralyse.
2 IMPALE, spear, skewer, spike, stick.

transform *v* change, alter, adapt,
convert, remodel, reconstruct,
transfigure, revolutionize.
⊠ preserve, maintain.

transformation *n* change,
alteration, mutation, conversion,
metamorphosis, transfiguration,
revolution.
⊠ preservation, conservation.

transient *adj* transitory, passing,
flying, fleeting, brief, short, short-
lived, momentary, ephemeral,
temporary, short-term.
⊠ lasting, permanent.

transit *n* passage, journey, travel,

movement, transfer, transportation, conveyance, carriage, haulage, shipment.

transition n passage, passing, progress, progression, development, evolution, flux, change, alteration, conversion, transformation, shift.

transitional adj provisional, temporary, passing, intermediate, developmental, changing, fluid, unsettled.
🠪 initial, final.

translate v interpret, render, paraphrase, simplify, decode, decipher, transliterate, transcribe, change, alter, convert, transform, improve.

translation n rendering, version, interpretation, gloss, crib, rewording, rephrasing, paraphrase, simplification, transliteration, transcription, change, alteration, conversion, transformation.

transmission n 1 BROADCASTING, diffusion, spread, communication, conveyance, carriage, transport, shipment, sending, dispatch, relaying, imparting, transfer. 2 a live transmission: broadcast, programme, show, signal.
🠪 1 reception.

transmit v communicate, impart, convey, carry, bear, transport, send, dispatch, forward, relay, transfer, broadcast, radio, disseminate, network, diffuse, spread.
🠪 receive.

transparency n slide, photograph, picture.

transparent adj 1 transparent plastic: clear, see-through, translucent, sheer. 2 PLAIN, distinct, clear, lucid, explicit, unambiguous, unequivocal, apparent, visible, obvious, evident, manifest, patent, undisguised, open, candid, straightforward.
🠪 1 opaque. 2 unclear, ambiguous.

transplant v move, shift, displace, remove, uproot, transfer, relocate, resettle, repot.
🠪 leave.

transport v convey, carry, bear, take, fetch, bring, move, shift, transfer, ship, haul, remove, deport.
◇ n conveyance, carriage, transfer, transportation, shipment, shipping, haulage, removal.

transpose v swap, exchange, switch, interchange, transfer, shift, rearrange, reorder, change, alter, move, substitute.

transverse adj cross, crosswise, transversal, diagonal, oblique.

trap n snare, net, noose, springe, gin, booby trap, pitfall, danger, hazard, ambush, trick, wile, ruse, stratagem, device, trickery, artifice, deception.
◇ v snare, net, entrap, ensnare, enmesh, catch, take, ambush, corner, trick, deceive, dupe.

trash n rubbish, garbage, refuse, junk, waste, litter, sweepings, offscourings, scum, dregs.

trauma n injury, wound, hurt, damage, pain, suffering, anguish, agony, torture, ordeal, shock, jolt, upset, disturbance, upheaval, strain, stress.
🠪 healing.

traumatic adj painful, hurtful, injurious, wounding, shocking, upsetting, distressing, disturbing, unpleasant, frightening, stressful.
🠪 healing, relaxing.

travel v journey, voyage, go, wend, move, proceed, progress, wander, ramble, roam, rove, tour, cross, traverse.
🠪 stay, remain.
◇ n travelling, touring, tourism, globetrotting.

traveller n 1 TOURIST, explorer, voyager, globetrotter, holidaymaker, tripper (infml), excursionist, passenger, commuter, wanderer, rambler, hiker, wayfarer, migrant, nomad, gypsy, itinerant, tinker, vagrant. **2** SALESMAN, saleswoman, representative, rep (*infml*), agent.

travelling *adj* touring, wandering, roaming, roving, wayfaring, migrant, migratory, nomadic, itinerant, peripatetic, mobile, moving, vagrant, homeless.
⊞ fixed.

travels *n* voyage, expedition, passage, journey, trip, excursion, tour, wanderings.

travesty *n* mockery, parody, take-off, send-up, farce, caricature, distortion, sham, apology.

treacherous *adj* **1** TRAITOROUS, disloyal, unfaithful, faithless, unreliable, untrustworthy, false, untrue, deceitful, double-crossing, backstabbing. **2** *treacherous roads*: dangerous, hazardous, risky, perilous, precarious, icy, slippery.
⊞ **1** loyal, faithful, dependable. **2** safe, stable.

treachery *n* treason, betrayal, disloyalty, infidelity, falseness, duplicity, double-dealing, backstabbing.
⊞ loyalty, dependability.

tread *v* walk, step, pace, stride, march, tramp, trudge, plod, stamp, trample, walk on, press, crush, squash.
◇ *n* walk, footfall, footstep, step, pace, stride.

treason *n* treachery, perfidy, disloyalty, duplicity, subversion, sedition, mutiny, rebellion.
⊞ loyalty.

treasonable *adj* traitorous, perfidious, disloyal, false, subversive, seditious, mutinous.
⊞ loyal.

treasure *n* fortune, wealth, riches, money, cash, gold, jewels, hoard, cache.
◇ *v* prize, value, esteem, revere,

worship, love, adore, idolize, cherish, preserve, guard.
⊞ disparage, belittle.

treat *n* indulgence, gratification, pleasure, delight, enjoyment, fun, entertainment, excursion, outing, party, celebration, feast, banquet, gift, surprise, thrill.
◇ *v* **1** DEAL WITH, manage, handle, use, regard, consider, discuss, cover. **2** TEND, nurse, minister to, attend to, care for, heal, cure. **3** PAY FOR, buy, stand, give, provide, entertain, regale, feast.

treatise *n* essay, dissertation, thesis, monograph, paper, pamphlet, tract, study, exposition.

treatment *n* **1** HEALING, cure, remedy, medication, therapy, surgery, care, nursing. **2** MANAGEMENT, handling, use, usage, conduct, discussion, coverage.

treaty *n* pact, convention, agreement, covenant, compact, negotiation, contract, bond, alliance.

tree *n* bush, shrub.

Trees include: acacia, alder, almond, apple, ash, aspen, balsa, bay, beech, birch, blackthorn, box, cedar, cherry, chestnut, coconut palm, cypress, date-palm, dogwood, ebony, elder, elm, eucalyptus, fig, fir, gum, hawthorn, hazel, hickory, holly, hornbeam, horse chestnut, larch, laurel, lime, linden, mahogany, maple, monkey puzzle, mountain ash, oak, palm, pear, pine, plane, plum, poplar, pussy willow, redwood, rowan, rubber tree, sandalwood, sequoia, silver birch, spruce, sycamore, teak, walnut, weeping willow, whitebeam, willow, witch-hazel, yew, yucca; bonsai, conifer, deciduous, evergreen, fruit, hardwood, ornamental, softwood.

---

trek *n* hike, walk, march, tramp,

journey, expedition, safari.
◇ *v* hike, walk, march, tramp, trudge, plod, journey, rove, roam.

tremble *v* shake, vibrate, quake, shiver, shudder, quiver, wobble, rock.
◇ *n* shake, vibration, quake, shiver, shudder, quiver, tremor, wobble.
☒ steadiness.

tremendous *adj* wonderful, marvellous, stupendous, sensational, spectacular, extraordinary, amazing, incredible, terrific, impressive, huge, immense, vast, colossal, gigantic, towering, formidable.
☒ ordinary, unimpressive.

tremor *n* shake, quiver, tremble, shiver, quake, quaver, wobble, vibration, agitation, thrill, shock, earthquake.
☒ steadiness.

trend *n* 1 COURSE, flow, drift, tendency, inclination, leaning. 2 CRAZE, rage (*infml*), fashion, vogue, mode, style, look.

trespass *v* invade, intrude, encroach, poach, infringe, violate, offend, wrong.
☒ obey, keep to.
◇ *n* invasion, encroachment, intrusion, poaching, infringement, violation, wrong, contravention, offence, sin, misdemeanour, transgression.

trespasser *n* intruder, poacher, offender, criminal.

trial *n* 1 LITIGATION, lawsuit, hearing, inquiry, tribunal. 2 EXPERIMENT, test, examination, check, dry run, dummy run, practice, rehearsal, audition, contest. 3 AFFLICTION, suffering, grief, misery, distress, adversity, hardship, ordeal, trouble, nuisance, vexation, tribulation.
☒ 3 relief, happiness.
◇ *adj* experimental, test, pilot, exploratory, provisional, probationary.

tribe *n* race, nation, people, clan,

family, house, dynasty, blood, stock, group, caste, class, division, branch.

tribute *n* 1 PRAISE, commendation, compliment, accolade, homage, respect, honour, credit, acknowledgement, recognition, gratitude. 2 PAYMENT, levy, charge, tax, duty, gift, offering, contribution.

trick *n* fraud, swindle, deception, deceit, artifice, illusion, hoax, practical joke, joke, leg-pull (*infml*), prank, antic, caper, frolic, feat, stunt, ruse, wile, dodge, subterfuge, trap, device, knack, technique, secret.
◇ *adj* false, mock, artificial, imitation, ersatz, fake, forged, counterfeit, feigned, sham, bogus.
☒ real, genuine.
◇ *v* deceive, delude, dupe, fool, hoodwink, beguile, mislead, bluff, hoax, pull someone's leg (*infml*), cheat, swindle, diddle, defraud, con (*infml*), trap, outwit.

trickery *n* deception, illusion, sleight of hand, pretence, artifice, guile, deceit, dishonesty, cheating, swindling, fraud, imposture, double-dealing, monkey business, funny business (*sl*), chicanery, skulduggery, hocus-pocus.
☒ straightforwardness, honesty.

trickle *v* dribble, run, leak, seep, ooze, exude, drip, drop, filter, percolate.
☒ stream, gush.
◇ *n* dribble, drip, drop, leak, seepage.
☒ stream, gush.

tricky *adj* 1 *a tricky problem*: difficult, awkward, problematic, complicated, knotty, thorny, delicate, ticklish. 2 CRAFTY, artful, cunning, sly, wily, foxy, subtle, devious, slippery, scheming, deceitful.
☒ 1 easy, simple. 2 honest.

trifle *n* 1 LITTLE, bit, spot, drop, dash, touch, trace. 2 TOY, plaything, trinket, bauble, knick-knack, triviality, nothing.

◇ *v* toy, play, sport, flirt, dally, dabble, fiddle, meddle, fool.

trifling *adj* small, paltry, slight, negligible, unimportant, insignificant, minor, trivial, petty, silly, frivolous, idle, empty, worthless.
⊟ important, significant, serious.

trigger *v* cause, start, initiate, activate, set off, spark off, provoke, prompt, elicit, generate, produce.
◇ *n* lever, catch, switch, spur, stimulus.

trim *adj* 1 NEAT, tidy, orderly, shipshape, spick and span, spruce, smart, dapper. 2 SLIM, slender, streamlined, compact.
⊟ 1 untidy, scruffy.
◇ *v* 1 CUT, clip, crop, dock, prune, pare, shave. 2 DECORATE, ornament, embellish, garnish, dress, array, adjust, arrange, order, neaten, tidy.
◇ *n* condition, state, order, form, shape, fitness, health.

trimmings *n* 1 GARNISH, frills, decorations, ornaments, extras, accessories. 2 CUTTINGS, clippings, parings, ends.

trinket *n* bauble, jewel, ornament, knick-knack.

trio *n* threesome, triad, triumvirate, trinity, triplet, trilogy.

trip *n* outing, excursion, tour, jaunt, ride, drive, spin, journey, voyage, expedition, foray.
◇ *v* stumble, slip, fall, tumble, stagger, totter, blunder.

triple *adj* treble, triplicate, threefold, three-ply, three-way.
◇ *v* treble, triplicate.

trite *adj* banal, commonplace, ordinary, run-of-the-mill, stale, tired, worn, threadbare, unoriginal, hackneyed, overused, stock, stereotyped, clichéd, corny (*infml*).
⊟ original, new, fresh.

triumph *n* 1 WIN, victory, conquest, walk-over, success, achievement, accomplishment, feat, coup,

masterstroke, hit, sensation.
2 EXULTATION, jubilation, rejoicing, celebration, elation, joy, happiness.
⊟ 1 failure.
◇ *v* win, succeed, prosper, conquer, vanquish, overcome, overwhelm, prevail, dominate, celebrate, rejoice, glory, gloat.
⊟ lose, fail.

triumphant *adj* winning, victorious, conquering, successful, exultant, jubilant, rejoicing, celebratory, glorious, elated, joyful, proud, boastful, gloating, swaggering.
⊟ defeated, humble.

trivial *adj* unimportant, insignificant, inconsequential, incidental, minor, petty, paltry, trifling, small, little, inconsiderable, negligible, worthless, meaningless, frivolous, banal, trite, commonplace, everyday.
⊟ important, significant, profound.

triviality *n* unimportance, insignificance, pettiness, smallness, worthlessness, meaninglessness, frivolity, trifle, detail, technicality.
⊟ importance, essential.

troop *n* contingent, squadron, unit, division, company, squad, team, crew, gang, band, bunch, group, body, pack, herd, flock, horde, crowd, throng, multitude.
◇ *v* go, march, parade, stream, flock, swarm, throng.

troops *n* army, military, soldiers, servicemen, servicewomen.

trophy *n* cup, prize, award, souvenir, memento.

tropical *adj* hot, torrid, sultry, sweltering, stifling, steamy, humid.
⊟ arctic, cold, cool, temperate.

trot *v* jog, run, scamper, scuttle, scurry.

trouble *n* 1 PROBLEM, difficulty, struggle, annoyance, irritation, bother, nuisance, inconvenience, misfortune, adversity, trial, tribulation, pain, suffering, affliction,

distress, grief, woe, heartache, concern, uneasiness, worry, anxiety, agitation. **2** UNREST, strife, tumult, commotion, disturbance, disorder, upheaval. **3** *back trouble*: disorder, complaint, ailment, illness, disease, disability, defect. **4** EFFORT, exertion, pains, care, attention, thought.
⊞ **1** relief, calm. **2** order. **3** health.
◇ *v* annoy, vex, harass, torment, bother, inconvenience, disturb, upset, distress, sadden, pain, afflict, burden, worry, agitate, disconcert, perplex.
⊞ reassure, help.

troublemaker *n* agitator, rabble-rouser, incendiary, instigator, ringleader, stirrer, mischief-maker.
⊞ peacemaker.

troublesome *adj* **1** ANNOYING, irritating, vexatious, irksome, bothersome, inconvenient, difficult, hard, tricky, thorny, taxing, demanding, laborious, tiresome, wearisome. **2** UNRULY, rowdy, turbulent, trying, unco-operative, insubordinate, rebellious.
⊞ **1** easy, simple. **2** helpful.

trough *n* gutter, conduit, trench, ditch, gully, channel, groove, furrow, hollow, depression.

trousers *n* pants, bags (*infml*), breeches, shorts.

Types of trousers and shorts include: jeans, Levis®, denims, cargo pants, chinos, slacks, cords, flannels, drainpipes, bell-bottoms, dungarees, leggings, Capri pants, pedal-pushers, plus-fours, jodhpurs, Bermuda shorts, hot pants.

---

truancy *n* absence, absenteeism, shirking, skiving (*infml*).
⊞ attendance.

truant *n* absentee, deserter, runaway, idler, shirker, skiver (*infml*), dodger.

◇ *adj* absent, missing, runaway.

truce *n* ceasefire, peace, armistice, cessation, moratorium, suspension, stay, respite, let-up (*infml*), lull, rest, break, interval, intermission.
⊞ war, hostilities.

truck *n* lorry, van, wagon, trailer, float, cart, barrow.

trudge *v* tramp, plod, clump, stump, lumber, traipse, slog, labour, trek, hike, walk, march.
◇ *n* tramp, traipse, slog, haul, trek, hike, walk, march.

true *adj* **1** REAL, genuine, authentic, actual, veritable, exact, precise, accurate, correct, right, factual, truthful, veracious, sincere, honest, legitimate, valid, rightful, proper. **2** FAITHFUL, loyal, constant, steadfast, staunch, firm, trustworthy, trusty, honourable, dedicated, devoted.
⊞ **1** false, wrong, incorrect, inaccurate. **2** unfaithful, faithless.

truism *n* truth, platitude, commonplace, cliché.

truly *adv* very, greatly, extremely, really, genuinely, sincerely, honestly, truthfully, undeniably, indubitably, indeed, in fact, in reality, exactly, precisely, correctly, rightly, properly.
⊞ slightly, falsely, incorrectly.

trumpet *n* bugle, horn, clarion, blare, blast, roar, bellow, cry, call.
◇ *v* blare, blast, roar, bellow, shout, proclaim, announce, broadcast, advertise.

truncate *v* shorten, abbreviate, curtail, cut, lop, dock, prune, pare, clip, trim, crop.
⊞ lengthen, extend.

trunk *n* **1** CASE, suitcase, chest, coffer, box, crate. **2** TORSO, body, frame, shaft, stock, stem, stalk.

truss *v* tie, strap, bind, pinion, fasten, secure, bundle, pack.
⊞ untie, loosen.
◇ *n* binding, bandage, support, brace, prop, stay, shore, strut, joist.

trust n 1 FAITH, belief, credence, credit, hope, expectation, reliance, confidence, assurance, conviction, certainty. 2 CARE, charge, custody, safekeeping, guardianship, protection, responsibility, duty.
☒ 1 distrust, mistrust, scepticism, doubt.
◇ v 1 BELIEVE, imagine, assume, presume, suppose, surmise, hope, expect, rely on, depend on, count on, bank on, swear by. 2 ENTRUST, commit, consign, confide, give, assign, delegate.
☒ 1 distrust, mistrust, doubt, disbelieve.

trusting adj trustful, credulous, gullible, naive, innocent, unquestioning, unsuspecting, unguarded, unwary.
☒ distrustful, suspicious, cautious.

trustworthy adj honest, upright, honourable, principled, dependable, reliable, steadfast, true, responsible, sensible.
☒ untrustworthy, dishonest, unreliable, irresponsible.

truth n 1 TRUTHFULNESS, veracity, candour, frankness, honesty, sincerity, genuineness, authenticity, realism, exactness, precision, accuracy, validity, legitimacy, honour, integrity, uprightness, faithfulness, fidelity, loyalty, constancy. 2 tell the truth: facts, reality, actuality, fact, axiom, maxim, principle, truism.
☒ 1 deceit, dishonesty, falseness. 2 lie, falsehood.

truthful adj veracious, frank, candid, straight, honest, sincere, true, veritable, exact, precise, accurate, correct, realistic, faithful, trustworthy, reliable.
☒ untruthful, deceitful, false, untrue.

try v 1 ATTEMPT, endeavour, venture, undertake, seek, strive. 2 HEAR, judge. 3 EXPERIMENT, test, sample, taste, inspect, examine, investigate,

evaluate, appraise.
◇ n 1 ATTEMPT, endeavour, effort, go (infml), bash (infml), crack (infml), shot (infml), stab (infml). 2 EXPERIMENT, test, trial, sample, taste.

trying adj annoying, irritating, aggravating (infml), vexatious, exasperating, troublesome, tiresome, wearisome, difficult, hard, tough, arduous, taxing, demanding, testing.
☒ easy.

tub n bath, basin, vat, tun, butt, cask, barrel, keg.

tube n hose, pipe, cylinder, duct, conduit, spout, channel.

tuck v 1 INSERT, push, thrust, stuff, cram. 2 FOLD, pleat, gather, crease.
◇ n fold, pleat, gather, pucker, crease.

tuft n crest, beard, tassel, knot, clump, cluster, bunch.

tug v pull, draw, tow, haul, drag, lug, heave, wrench, jerk, pluck.
◇ n pull, tow, haul, heave, wrench, jerk, pluck.

tuition n teaching, instruction, coaching, training, lessons, schooling, education.

tumble v fall, stumble, trip, topple, overthrow, drop, flop, collapse, plummet, pitch, roll, toss.
◇ n fall, stumble, trip, drop, plunge, roll, toss.

tumult n commotion, turmoil, disturbance, upheaval, stir, agitation, unrest, disorder, chaos, pandemonium, noise, clamour, din, racket, hubbub, hullabaloo, row, rumpus, uproar, riot, fracas, brawl, affray, strife.
☒ peace, calm, composure.

tumultuous adj turbulent, stormy, raging, fierce, violent, wild, hectic, boisterous, rowdy, noisy, disorderly, unruly, riotous, restless, agitated, troubled, disturbed, excited.
☒ calm, peaceful, quiet.

tune *n* melody, theme, motif, song, air, strain.
◇ *v* pitch, harmonize, set, regulate, adjust, adapt, temper, attune, synchronize.

tuneful *adj* melodious, melodic, catchy, musical, euphonious, harmonious, pleasant, mellow, sonorous.
⊞ tuneless, discordant.

tunnel *n* passage, passageway, gallery, subway, underpass, burrow, hole, mine, shaft, chimney.
◇ *v* burrow, dig, excavate, mine, bore, penetrate, undermine, sap.

turbulent *adj* rough, choppy, stormy, blustery, tempestuous, raging, furious, violent, wild, tumultuous, unbridled, boisterous, rowdy, disorderly, unruly, undisciplined, obstreperous, rebellious, mutinous, riotous, agitated, unsettled, unstable, confused, disordered.
⊞ calm, composed.

turmoil *n* confusion, disorder, tumult, commotion, disturbance, trouble, disquiet, agitation, turbulence, stir, ferment, flurry, bustle, chaos, pandemonium, bedlam, noise, din, hubbub, row, uproar.
⊞ calm, peace, quiet.

turn *v* 1 REVOLVE, circle, spin, twirl, whirl, twist, gyrate, pivot, hinge, swivel, rotate, roll, move, shift, invert, reverse, bend, veer, swerve, divert. 2 MAKE, transform, change, alter, modify, convert, adapt, adjust, fit, mould, shape, form, fashion, remodel. 3 *turn cold*: go, become, grow. 4 RESORT, have recourse, apply, appeal. 5 SOUR, curdle, spoil, go off, go bad.
◇ *n* 1 REVOLUTION, cycle, round, circle, rotation, spin, twirl, twist, gyration, bend, curve, loop, reversal. 2 CHANGE, alteration, shift, deviation. 3 *it's your turn*: go, chance,

opportunity, occasion, stint, period, spell. 4 ACT, performance, performer.
• **turn away** reject, avert, deflect, deviate, depart.
⊞ accept, receive.
• **turn down** 1 *turn down an offer*: reject, decline, refuse, spurn, rebuff, repudiate. 2 LOWER, lessen, quieten, soften, mute, muffle.
⊞ 1 accept. 2 turn up.
• **turn in** 1 GO TO BED, retire. 2 HAND OVER, give up, surrender, deliver, hand in, tender, submit, return, give back.
⊞ 1 get up. 2 keep.
• **turn off** 1 BRANCH OFF, leave, quit, depart from, deviate, divert. 2 SWITCH OFF, turn out, stop, shut down, unplug, disconnect. 3 (*sl*) REPEL, sicken, nauseate, disgust, offend, displease, disenchant, alienate, bore, discourage, put off.
⊞ 1 join. 2 turn on. 3 turn on (*sl*).
• **turn on** 1 SWITCH ON, start (up), activate, connect. 2 (*sl*) AROUSE, stimulate, excite, thrill, please, attract. 3 HINGE ON, depend on, rest on. 4 ATTACK, round on, fall on.
⊞ 1 turn off. 2 turn off (*sl*).
• **turn out** 1 HAPPEN, come about, transpire, ensue, result, end up, become, develop, emerge. 2 SWITCH OFF, turn off, unplug, disconnect. 3 APPEAR, present, dress, clothe. 4 PRODUCE, make, manufacture, fabricate, assemble. 5 EVICT, throw out, expel, deport, banish, dismiss, discharge, drum out, kick out, sack (*infml*). 6 *turn out the attic*: empty, clear, clean out.
⊞ 2 turn on. 5 admit. 6 fill.
• **turn over** 1 THINK OVER, think about, mull over, ponder, deliberate, reflect on, contemplate, consider, examine. 2 HAND OVER, surrender, deliver, transfer. 3 OVERTURN, upset, up-end, invert, capsize, keel over.
• **turn up** 1 ATTEND, come, arrive, appear, show up (*infml*). 2 AMPLIFY, intensify, raise, increase. 3 DISCOVER, find, unearth, dig up, expose,

disclose, reveal, show.
☒ **1** stay away. **2** turn down.

turning n turn-off, junction, crossroads, fork, bend, curve, turn.

turning-point n crossroads, watershed, crux, crisis.

turnout n **1** ATTENDANCE, audience, gate, crowd, assembly, congregation. **2** APPEARANCE, outfit, dress, clothes.

tussle v struggle, battle, wrestle, fight, scrap, brawl.
◇ n struggle, battle, fight, scrap, scuffle, brawl, fracas.

tutor n teacher, instructor, coach, educator, lecturer, supervisor, guide, mentor, guru, guardian.
◇ v teach, instruct, train, drill, coach, educate, school, lecture, supervise, direct, guide.

tweak v, n twist, pinch, squeeze, nip, pull, tug, jerk, twitch.

twiddle v turn, twirl, swivel, twist, wiggle, adjust, fiddle, finger.

twig ¹ n branch, sprig, spray, shoot, offshoot, stick, wattle, whip, ramulus (fml).

twig ² v understand, see, grasp, get, comprehend, fathom, rumble, catch on (infml), cotton on (infml), tumble to (infml).

twilight n dusk, half-light, gloaming, gloom, dimness, sunset, evening.

twin n double, look-alike, likeness, duplicate, clone, match, counterpart, corollary, fellow, mate.
◇ adj identical, corresponding, matching, symmetrical, parallel, matched, paired, double, dual, duplicate, twofold.
◇ v match, pair, couple, link, join.

twine n string, cord, thread, yarn.
◇ v wind, coil, spiral, loop, curl, bend, twist, wreathe, wrap, surround, encircle, entwine, plait, braid, knit, weave.

twinge n pain, pang, throb, spasm, throe, stab, stitch, pinch, prick.

twinkle v sparkle, glitter, shimmer, glisten, glimmer, flicker, wink, flash, glint, gleam, shine.
◇ n sparkle, scintillation, glitter, shimmer, glisten, glimmer, flicker, wink, flash, glint, gleam, light.

twirl v spin, whirl, pirouette, wheel, rotate, revolve, swivel, pivot, turn, twist, gyrate, wind, coil.
◇ n spin, whirl, pirouette, rotation, revolution, turn, twist, gyration, convolution, spiral, coil.

twist v **1** TURN, screw, wring, spin, swivel, wind, zigzag, bend, coil, spiral, curl, wreathe, twine, entwine, intertwine, weave, entangle, wriggle, squirm, writhe. **2** twist one's ankle: wrench, rick, sprain, strain. **3** CHANGE, alter, garble, misquote, misrepresent, distort, contort, warp, pervert.
◇ n **1** TURN, screw, spin, roll, bend, curve, arc, curl, loop, zigzag, coil, spiral, convolution, squiggle, tangle. **2** CHANGE, variation, break. **3** PERVERSION, distortion, contortion. **4** SURPRISE, quirk, oddity, peculiarity.

twisted adj warped, perverted, deviant, unnatural.
☒ straight.

twit n idiot, fool, simpleton, blockhead, clown, nincompoop (infml).

twitch v jerk, jump, start, blink, tremble, shake, pull, tug, tweak, snatch, pluck.
◇ n spasm, convulsion, tic, tremor, jerk, jump, start.

twitter v chirp, chirrup, tweet, cheep, sing, warble, whistle, chatter.

two-faced adj hypocritical, insincere, false, lying, deceitful, treacherous, double-dealing, devious, untrustworthy.
☒ honest, candid, frank.

tycoon n industrialist, entrepreneur, captain of industry, magnate, mogul, baron, supremo, capitalist, financier.

type n 1 SORT, kind, form, genre, variety, strain, species, breed, group, class, category, subdivision, classification, description, designation, stamp, mark, order, standard. 2 ARCHETYPE, embodiment, prototype, original, model, pattern, specimen, example. 3 PRINT, printing, characters, letters, lettering, face, fount, font.

typhoon n whirlwind, cyclone, tornado, twister (*infml*), hurricane, tempest, storm, squall.

typical adj standard, normal, usual, average, conventional, orthodox, stock, model, representative, illustrative, indicative, characteristic, distinctive.
⊠ atypical, unusual.

typify v embody, epitomize, encapsulate, personify, characterize, exemplify, symbolize, represent, illustrate.

tyrannical adj dictatorial, despotic, autocratic, absolute, arbitrary, authoritarian, high-handed, domineering, overbearing, imperious, magisterial, ruthless, harsh, severe, oppressive, overpowering, unjust, unreasonable.
⊠ liberal, tolerant.

tyranny n dictatorship, despotism, autocracy, absolutism, authoritarianism, imperiousness, ruthlessness, harshness, severity, oppression, injustice.
⊠ democracy, freedom.

tyrant n dictator, despot, autocrat, absolutist, authoritarian, bully, oppressor, slave-driver, taskmaster.

Uu

ubiquitous *adj* omnipresent, ever-present, everywhere, universal, global, pervasive, common, frequent.
⊞ rare, scarce.

ugly *adj* **1** UNATTRACTIVE, plain, unsightly, unprepossessing, ill-favoured, hideous, monstrous, misshapen, deformed. **2** UNPLEASANT, disagreeable, objectionable, nasty, horrid, offensive, disgusting, revolting, repulsive, vile, frightful, terrible.
⊞ **1** attractive, beautiful, handsome, pretty. **2** pleasant.

ulterior *adj* secondary, hidden, concealed, undisclosed, covert, secret, private, personal, selfish.
⊞ overt.

ultimate *adj* final, last, closing, concluding, eventual, terminal, furthest, remotest, extreme, utmost, greatest, highest, supreme, superlative, perfect, radical, fundamental, primary.

ultimately *adv* finally, eventually, at last, in the end, after all.

umpire *n* referee, linesman, judge, adjudicator, arbiter, arbitrator, mediator, moderator.
◇ *v* referee, judge, adjudicate, arbitrate, mediate, moderate, control.

umpteen *adj* a good many, numerous, plenty, millions, countless, innumerable.
⊞ few.

unabashed *adj* unashamed, unembarrassed, brazen, blatant, bold, confident, undaunted, unconcerned, undismayed.
⊞ abashed, sheepish.

unable *adj* incapable, powerless, impotent, unequipped, unqualified, unfit, incompetent, inadequate.
⊞ able, capable.

unacceptable *adj* intolerable, inadmissible, unsatisfactory, undesirable, unwelcome, offensive, objectionable, unpleasant.
⊞ acceptable, satisfactory.

unaccompanied *adj* alone, lone, unescorted, unattended, solo, single-handed.
⊞ accompanied.

unaccountable *adj* inexplicable, unexplainable, unfathomable, impenetrable, incomprehensible, baffling, puzzling, mysterious, astonishing, extraordinary, strange, odd, peculiar, singular, unusual, uncommon, unheard-of.
⊞ explicable, explainable.

unaccustomed *adj*
1 *unaccustomed to such luxury*: unused, unacquainted, unfamiliar, unpractised, inexperienced.
2 STRANGE, unusual, uncommon, different, new, unexpected, surprising, uncharacteristic, unprecedented.
⊞ **1** accustomed, familiar.
2 customary.

unaffected *adj* **1** UNMOVED, unconcerned, indifferent, impervious, untouched, unchanged, unaltered. **2** UNSOPHISTICATED, artless, naive, ingenuous, unspoilt, plain, simple, straightforward, unpretentious, unassuming, sincere, honest, genuine.
⊞ **1** moved, influenced. **2** affected,

pretentious, insincere.

unalterable adj unchangeable, invariable, unchanging, immutable, final, inflexible, unyielding, rigid, fixed, permanent.
⊞ alterable, flexible.

unanimity n consensus, unity, agreement, concurrence, accord, like-mindedness, concord, harmony, unison, concert.
⊞ disagreement, disunity.

unanimous adj united, concerted, joint, common, as one, in agreement, in accord, harmonious.
⊞ disunited, divided.

unapproachable adj inaccessible, remote, distant, aloof, standoffish, withdrawn, reserved, unsociable, unfriendly, forbidding.
⊞ approachable, friendly.

unarmed adj defenceless, unprotected, exposed, open, vulnerable, weak, helpless.
⊞ armed, protected.

unashamed adj shameless, unabashed, impenitent, unrepentant, unconcealed, undisguised, open, blatant.

unasked adj uninvited, unbidden, unrequested, unsought, unsolicited, unwanted, voluntary, spontaneous.
⊞ invited, wanted.

unassuming adj unassertive, self-effacing, retiring, modest, humble, meek, unobtrusive, unpretentious, simple, restrained.
⊞ presumptuous, assertive, pretentious.

unattached adj unmarried, single, free, available, footloose, fancy-free, independent, unaffiliated.
⊞ engaged, committed.

unattended adj ignored, unguarded, disregarded, unwatched, unsupervised, unaccompanied, unescorted, alone.
⊞ attended, escorted.

unauthorized adj unofficial, unlawful, illegal, illicit, illegitimate, irregular, unsanctioned.
⊞ authorized, legal.

unavoidable adj inevitable, inescapable, inexorable, certain, sure, fated, destined, obligatory, compulsory, mandatory, necessary.
⊞ avoidable.

unaware adj oblivious, ignorant, unconscious, uninformed, unknowing, unsuspecting, unmindful, heedless, blind, deaf.
⊞ aware, conscious.

unbalanced adj 1 INSANE, mad, crazy, lunatic, deranged, disturbed, demented, irrational, unsound.
2 an unbalanced report: biased, prejudiced, one-sided, partisan, unfair, unjust, unequal, uneven, asymmetrical, lopsided, unsteady, unstable.
⊞ 1 sane. 2 unbiased.

unbearable adj intolerable, unacceptable, insupportable, insufferable, unendurable, excruciating.
⊞ bearable, acceptable.

unbeatable adj invincible, unconquerable, unstoppable, unsurpassable, matchless, supreme, excellent.

unbecoming adj unseemly, improper, unsuitable, inappropriate, unbefitting, ungentlemanly, unladylike, unattractive, unsightly.
⊞ suitable, attractive.

unbelief n atheism, agnosticism, scepticism, doubt, incredulity, disbelief.
⊞ belief, faith.

unbelievable adj incredible, inconceivable, unthinkable, unimaginable, astonishing, staggering, extraordinary, impossible, improbable, unlikely, implausible, unconvincing, far-fetched, preposterous.

⊒ believable, credible.

unborn adj embryonic, expected, awaited, coming, future.

unbounded adj boundless, limitless, unlimited, unrestricted, unrestrained, unchecked, unbridled, infinite, endless, immeasurable, vast.
⊒ limited, restrained.

unbreakable adj indestructible, shatterproof, toughened, resistant, proof, durable, strong, tough, rugged, solid.
⊒ breakable, fragile.

unbridled adj immoderate, excessive, uncontrolled, unrestrained, unchecked.

unbroken adj 1 INTACT, whole, entire, complete, solid, undivided. 2 UNINTERRUPTED, continuous, endless, ceaseless, incessant, unceasing, constant, perpetual, progressive, successive. 3 unbroken record: unbeaten, unsurpassed, unequalled, unmatched.
⊒ 1 broken. 2 intermittent, fitful.

uncalled-for adj gratuitous, unprovoked, unjustified, unwarranted, undeserved, unnecessary, needless.
⊒ timely.

uncanny adj weird, strange, queer, bizarre, mysterious, unaccountable, incredible, remarkable, fantastic, extraordinary, unnatural, unearthly, supernatural, eerie, creepy, spooky (infml).

uncaring adj unconcerned, unmoved, unsympathetic, inconsiderate, unfeeling, cold, callous, indifferent, uninterested.
⊒ caring, concerned.

unceasing adj ceaseless, incessant, unending, endless, never-ending, non-stop, continuous, unbroken, constant, perpetual, continual, persistent, relentless, unrelenting, unremitting.
⊒ intermittent, spasmodic.

uncertain adj 1 UNSURE, unconvinced, doubtful, dubious, undecided, ambivalent, hesitant, wavering, vacillating. 2 INCONSTANT, changeable, variable, erratic, irregular, shaky, unsteady, unreliable. 3 UNPREDICTABLE, unforeseeable, undetermined, unsettled, unresolved, unconfirmed, indefinite, vague, insecure, risky, iffy (sl).
⊒ 1 certain, sure. 2 steady. 3 predictable.

uncertainty n doubt, scepticism, irresolution, dilemma, hesitation, misgiving, confusion, bewilderment, perplexity, puzzlement, unreliability, unpredictability, insecurity.
⊒ certainty.

unchanging adj unvarying, changeless, steady, steadfast, constant, perpetual, lasting, enduring, abiding, eternal, permanent.
⊒ changing, changeable.

uncharitable adj unkind, cruel, hard-hearted, callous, unfeeling, insensitive, unsympathetic, unfriendly, mean, ungenerous.
⊒ kind, sensitive, charitable, generous.

uncharted adj unexplored, undiscovered, unplumbed, foreign, alien, strange, unfamiliar, new, virgin.
⊒ familiar.

uncivilized adj primitive, barbaric, savage, wild, untamed, uncultured, unsophisticated, unenlightened, uneducated, illiterate, uncouth, antisocial.
⊒ civilized, cultured.

unclean adj dirty, soiled, filthy, foul, polluted, contaminated, tainted, impure, unhygienic, unwholesome, corrupt, defiled, sullied.
⊒ clean, hygienic.

unclear adj indistinct, hazy, dim, obscure, vague, indefinite, ambiguous, equivocal, uncertain,

unsure, doubtful, dubious.
🔁 clear, evident.

uncomfortable adj 1 CRAMPED, hard, cold, ill-fitting, irritating, painful, disagreeable. 2 AWKWARD, embarrassed, self-conscious, uneasy, troubled, worried, disturbed, distressed, disquieted, conscience-stricken.
🔁 1 comfortable. 2 relaxed.

uncommon adj rare, scarce, infrequent, unusual, abnormal, atypical, unfamiliar, strange, odd, curious, bizarre, extraordinary, remarkable, notable, outstanding, exceptional, distinctive, special.
🔁 common, usual, normal.

uncommunicative adj silent, taciturn, tight-lipped, close, secretive, unforthcoming, unresponsive, curt, brief, reticent, reserved, shy, retiring, withdrawn, unsociable.
🔁 communicative, forthcoming.

uncompromising adj unyielding, unbending, inflexible, unaccommodating, rigid, firm, strict, tough, hard-line, inexorable, intransigent, stubborn, obstinate, die-hard.
🔁 flexible.

unconcealed adj open, patent, obvious, evident, manifest, blatant, conspicuous, noticeable, visible, apparent.
🔁 hidden, secret.

unconcerned adj indifferent, apathetic, uninterested, nonchalant, carefree, relaxed, complacent, cool, composed, untroubled, unworried, unruffled, unmoved, uncaring, unsympathetic, callous, aloof, remote, distant, detached, dispassionate, uninvolved, oblivious.
🔁 concerned, worried, interested.

unconditional adj unqualified, unreserved, unrestricted, unlimited, absolute, utter, full, total, complete, entire, whole-hearted,

thoroughgoing, downright, outright, positive, categorical, unequivocal.
🔁 conditional, qualified, limited.

unconnected adj 1 IRRELEVANT, unrelated, unattached, detached, separate, independent.
2 DISCONNECTED, incoherent, irrational, illogical.
🔁 1 connected, relevant.

unconscious adj 1 STUNNED, knocked out, out, out cold, out for the count, concussed, comatose, senseless, insensible.
2 UNAWARE, oblivious, blind, deaf, heedless, unmindful, ignorant. 3 an unconscious reaction: involuntary, automatic, reflex, instinctive, impulsive, innate, subconscious, subliminal, repressed, suppressed, latent, unwitting, inadvertent, accidental, unintentional.
🔁 1 conscious. 2 aware.
3 intentional.

uncontrollable adj ungovernable, unmanageable, unruly, wild, mad, furious, violent, strong, irrepressible.
🔁 controllable, manageable.

uncontrolled adj unrestrained, unbridled, unchecked, rampant, wild, unruly, undisciplined.
🔁 controlled, restrained.

unconventional adj unorthodox, alternative, different, offbeat, eccentric, idiosyncratic, individual, original, odd, unusual, irregular, abnormal, bizarre, way-out (sl).
🔁 conventional, orthodox.

unconvincing adj implausible, unlikely, improbable, questionable, doubtful, dubious, suspect, weak, feeble, flimsy, lame.
🔁 convincing, plausible.

unco-ordinated adj clumsy, awkward, ungainly, ungraceful, inept, disjointed.
🔁 graceful.

uncouth adj coarse, crude, vulgar, rude, ill-mannered, unseemly,

improper, clumsy, awkward, gauche, graceless, unrefined, uncultivated, uncultured, uncivilized, rough.
☒ polite, refined, urbane.

uncover v unveil, unmask, unwrap, strip, bare, open, expose, reveal, show, disclose, divulge, leak, unearth, exhume, discover, detect.
☒ cover, conceal, suppress.

uncritical adj undiscerning, undiscriminating, unselective, unquestioning, credulous, accepting, trusting, gullible, naive.
☒ discerning, discriminating, sceptical.

uncultivated adj fallow, wild, rough, natural.
☒ cultivated.

uncultured adj unsophisticated, unrefined, uncultivated, uncivilized, rough, uncouth, boorish, rustic, coarse, crude, ill-bred.
☒ cultured, sophisticated.

undaunted adj undeterred, undiscouraged, undismayed, unbowed, resolute, steadfast, courageous, brave, fearless, bold, intrepid, dauntless, indomitable.
☒ discouraged, timorous.

undecided adj uncertain, unsure, in two minds, ambivalent, doubtful, hesitant, wavering, irresolute, uncommitted, indefinite, vague, dubious, debatable, moot, unsettled, open.
☒ decided, certain, definite.

undemonstrative adj aloof, distant, remote, withdrawn, reserved, reticent, uncommunicative, stiff, formal, cool, cold, unemotional, restrained, impassive, phlegmatic.
☒ demonstrative, communicative.

undeniable adj irrefutable, unquestionable, incontrovertible, sure, certain, undoubted, proven, clear, obvious, patent, evident, manifest, unmistakable.
☒ questionable.

under prep below, underneath, beneath, lower than, less than, inferior to, subordinate to.
☒ over, above.
• **under way** moving, in motion, going, in operation, started, begun, in progress, afoot.

undercover adj secret, hush-hush (infml), private, confidential, spy, intelligence, underground, clandestine, surreptitious, furtive, covert, hidden, concealed.
☒ open, unconcealed.

undercurrent n undertone, overtone, hint, suggestion, tinge, flavour, aura, atmosphere, feeling, sense, movement, tendency, trend, drift.

underestimate v underrate, undervalue, misjudge, miscalculate, minimize, belittle, disparage, dismiss.
☒ overestimate, exaggerate.

undergo v experience, suffer, sustain, submit to, bear, stand, endure, weather, withstand.

underground adj 1 an underground passage: subterranean, buried, sunken, covered, hidden, concealed. 2 SECRET, covert, undercover, revolutionary, subversive, radical, experimental, avant-garde, alternative, unorthodox, unofficial.

undergrowth n brush, scrub, vegetation, ground cover, bracken, bushes, brambles, briars.

underhand adj unscrupulous, unethical, immoral, improper, sly, crafty, sneaky, stealthy, surreptitious, furtive, clandestine, devious, dishonest, deceitful, deceptive, fraudulent, crooked (infml), shady (infml).
☒ honest, open, above board.

underline v mark, underscore, stress, emphasize, accentuate, italicize, highlight, point up.
☒ play down, soft-pedal.

underlying *adj* basic, fundamental, essential, primary, elementary, root, intrinsic, latent, hidden, lurking, veiled.

undermine *v* erode, wear away, weaken, sap, sabotage, subvert, vitiate, mar, impair.
⊟ strengthen, fortify.

underprivileged *adj* disadvantaged, deprived, poor, needy, impoverished, destitute, oppressed.
⊟ privileged, fortunate, affluent.

underrate *v* underestimate, undervalue, belittle, disparage, depreciate, dismiss.
⊟ overrate, exaggerate.

undersized *adj* small, tiny, minute, miniature, pygmy, dwarf, stunted, underdeveloped, underweight, puny.
⊟ oversized, big, overweight.

understand *v* **1** *I don't understand*: grasp, comprehend, take in, follow, get (*infml*), cotton on (*infml*), fathom, penetrate, make out, discern, perceive, see, realize, recognize, appreciate, accept. **2** SYMPATHIZE, empathize, commiserate. **3** BELIEVE, think, know, hear, learn, gather, assume, presume, suppose, conclude.
⊟ **1** misunderstand.

understanding *n* **1** GRASP, knowledge, wisdom, intelligence, intellect, sense, comprehension, judgement, discernment, insight, appreciation, awareness, impression, perception, belief, idea, notion, opinion, interpretation. **2** AGREEMENT, arrangement, pact, accord, harmony. **3** SYMPATHY, empathy.
◇ *adj* sympathetic, compassionate, kind, considerate, sensitive, tender, loving, patient, tolerant, forbearing, forgiving.
⊟ unsympathetic, insensitive, impatient, intolerant.

understate *v* underplay, play down, soft-pedal, minimize, make light of, belittle, dismiss.
⊟ exaggerate.

understood *adj* accepted, assumed, presumed, implied, implicit, inferred, tacit, unstated, unspoken, unwritten.

understudy *n* stand-in, double, substitute, replacement, reserve, deputy.

undertake *v* **1** PLEDGE, promise, guarantee, agree, contract, covenant. **2** BEGIN, commence, embark on, tackle, try, attempt, endeavour, take on, accept, assume.

undertaking *n* **1** ENTERPRISE, venture, business, affair, task, project, operation, attempt, endeavour, effort, job. **2** PLEDGE, commitment, promise, vow, word, assurance.

undertone *n* hint, suggestion, whisper, murmur, trace, tinge, touch, flavour, feeling, atmosphere, undercurrent.

undervalue *v* underrate, underestimate, misjudge, minimize, depreciate, disparage, dismiss.
⊟ overrate, exaggerate.

underwater *adj* subaquatic, undersea, submarine, submerged, sunken.

underwear *n* underclothes, undergarments, lingerie, undies (*infml*), smalls (*infml*).

Types of underwear include: bra, brassière, Wonderbra®, body stocking, camisole, liberty bodice, corset, girdle, garter, suspender-belt, suspenders, shift, slip, petticoat, teddy, basque, bustier, briefs, pants, panties, thong, G-string, French knickers, camiknickers, pantihose, tights, stockings; underpants, boxer shorts, boxers (*infml*), Y-fronts, vest, string vest, singlet.

---

underweight *adj* thin, undersized, underfed, undernourished, half-starved.
⊞ overweight.

underwrite *v* endorse, authorize, sanction, approve, back, guarantee, insure, sponsor, fund, finance, subsidize, subscribe, sign, initial, countersign.

undesirable *adj* unwanted, unwelcome, unacceptable, unsuitable, unpleasant, disagreeable, distasteful, repugnant, offensive, objectionable, obnoxious.
⊞ desirable, pleasant.

undignified *adj* inelegant, ungainly, clumsy, foolish, unseemly, improper, unsuitable, inappropriate.
⊞ dignified, elegant.

undisguised *adj* unconcealed, open, overt, explicit, frank, genuine, apparent, patent, obvious, evident, manifest, blatant, naked, unadorned, stark, utter, outright, thoroughgoing.
⊞ secret, concealed, hidden.

undisputed *adj* uncontested, unchallenged, unquestioned, undoubted, indisputable, incontrovertible, undeniable, irrefutable, accepted, acknowledged, recognized, sure, certain, conclusive.
⊞ debatable, uncertain.

undistinguished *adj* unexceptional, unremarkable, unimpressive, ordinary, run-of-the-mill, everyday, banal, indifferent, mediocre, inferior.
⊞ distinguished, exceptional.

undivided *adj* solid, unbroken, intact, whole, entire, full, complete, combined, united, unanimous, concentrated, exclusive, whole-hearted.

undo *v* 1 UNFASTEN, untie, unbuckle, unbutton, unzip, unlock, unwrap, unwind, open, loose, loosen, separate. 2 ANNUL, nullify, invalidate, cancel, offset, neutralize, reverse, overturn, upset, quash, defeat, subvert, undermine, mar, spoil, ruin, wreck, shatter, destroy.
⊞ 1 fasten, do up.

undoing *n* downfall, ruin, ruination, collapse, destruction, defeat, overthrow, reversal, weakness, shame, disgrace.

undone *adj* 1 UNACCOMPLISHED, unfulfilled, unfinished, uncompleted, incomplete, outstanding, left, omitted, neglected, forgotten. 2 UNFASTENED, untied, unlaced, unbuttoned, unlocked, open, loose.
⊞ 1 done, accomplished, complete. 2 fastened.

undoubted *adj* unchallenged, undisputed, acknowledged, unquestionable, indisputable, incontrovertible, undeniable, indubitable, sure, certain, definite, obvious, patent.

undress *v* strip, peel off (*infml*), disrobe, take off, divest, remove, shed.

undressed *adj* unclothed, disrobed, stripped, naked, stark-naked, nude.
⊞ clothed.

undue *adj* unnecessary, needless, uncalled-for, unwarranted, unreasonable, disproportionate, excessive, immoderate, inordinate, extreme, extravagant, improper.
⊞ reasonable, moderate, proper.

unduly *adv* too, over, excessively, immoderately, inordinately, disproportionately, unreasonably, unjustifiably, unnecessarily.
⊞ moderately, reasonably.

unearth *v* dig up, exhume, disinter, excavate, uncover, expose, reveal, find, discover, detect.
⊞ bury.

unearthly *adj* 1 SUPERNATURAL, ghostly, eerie, uncanny, weird, strange, spine-chilling. 2 *at this unearthly hour*: unreasonable, outrageous, ungodly.

⊜ **2** reasonable.

uneasy adj uncomfortable, anxious, worried, apprehensive, tense, strained, nervous, agitated, shaky, jittery, edgy, upset, troubled, disturbed, unsettled, restless, impatient, unsure, insecure.
⊜ calm, composed.

uneducated adj unschooled, untaught, unread, ignorant, illiterate, uncultivated, uncultured, philistine, benighted.
⊜ educated.

unemotional adj cool, cold, unfeeling, impassive, indifferent, apathetic, unresponsive, undemonstrative, unexcitable, phlegmatic, objective, dispassionate.
⊜ emotional, excitable.

unemployed adj jobless, out of work, laid off, redundant, unwaged, on the dole (infml), idle, unoccupied.
⊜ employed, occupied.

unending adj endless, never-ending, unceasing, ceaseless, incessant, interminable, constant, continual, perpetual, everlasting, eternal, undying.
⊜ transient, intermittent.

unenviable adj undesirable, unpleasant, disagreeable, uncongenial, uncomfortable, thankless, difficult.
⊜ enviable, desirable.

unequal adj different, varying, dissimilar, unlike, unmatched, uneven, unbalanced, disproportionate, asymmetrical, irregular, unfair, unjust, biased, discriminatory.
⊜ equal.

unequivocal adj unambiguous, explicit, clear, plain, evident, distinct, unmistakable, express, direct, straight, definite, positive, categorical, incontrovertible, absolute, unqualified, unreserved.
⊜ ambiguous, vague, qualified.

unethical adj unprofessional, immoral, improper, wrong, unscrupulous, unprincipled, dishonourable, disreputable, illegal, illicit, dishonest, underhand, shady (infml).
⊜ ethical.

uneven adj **1** uneven ground: rough, bumpy. **2** ODD, unequal, inequitable, unfair, unbalanced, one-sided, asymmetrical, lopsided, crooked. **3** IRREGULAR, intermittent, spasmodic, fitful, jerky, unsteady, variable, changeable, fluctuating, erratic, inconsistent, patchy.
⊜ **1** flat, level. **2** even, equal. **3** regular.

uneventful adj uninteresting, unexciting, quiet, unvaried, boring, monotonous, tedious, dull, routine, humdrum, ordinary, commonplace, unremarkable, unexceptional, unmemorable.
⊜ eventful, memorable.

unexceptional adj unremarkable, unmemorable, typical, average, normal, usual, ordinary, indifferent, mediocre, unimpressive.
⊜ exceptional, impressive.

unexpected adj unforeseen, unanticipated, unpredictable, chance, accidental, fortuitous, sudden, abrupt, surprising, startling, amazing, astonishing, unusual.
⊜ expected, predictable.

unfair adj unjust, inequitable, partial, biased, prejudiced, bigoted, discriminatory, one-sided, unbalanced, partisan, arbitrary, undeserved, unmerited, unwarranted, uncalled-for, unethical, unscrupulous, unprincipled, wrongful, dishonest.
⊜ fair, just, unbiased, deserved.

unfaithful adj disloyal, treacherous, false, untrue, deceitful, dishonest, untrustworthy, unreliable, fickle, inconstant, adulterous, two-timing, duplicitous, double-dealing, faithless,

unbelieving, godless.
≠ faithful, loyal, reliable.

unfamiliar adj strange, unusual, uncommon, curious, alien, foreign, uncharted, unexplored, unknown, different, new, novel, unaccustomed, unacquainted, inexperienced, unpractised, unskilled, unversed.
≠ familiar, customary, conversant.

unfashionable adj outmoded, dated, out-of-date, out, passé, old-fashioned, antiquated, obsolete.
≠ fashionable.

unfasten v undo, untie, loosen, unlock, open, uncouple, disconnect, separate, detach.
≠ fasten.

unfavourable adj inauspicious, unpromising, ominous, threatening, discouraging, inopportune, untimely, unseasonable, ill-suited, unfortunate, unlucky, disadvantageous, bad, poor, adverse, contrary, negative, hostile, unfriendly, uncomplimentary.
≠ favourable, auspicious, promising.

unfeeling adj insensitive, cold, hard, stony, callous, heartless, hard-hearted, cruel, inhuman, pitiless, uncaring, unsympathetic, apathetic.
≠ sensitive, sympathetic.

unfinished adj incomplete, uncompleted, half-done, sketchy, rough, crude, imperfect, lacking, wanting, deficient, undone, unaccomplished, unfulfilled.
≠ finished, perfect.

unfit adj 1 UNSUITABLE, inappropriate, unsuited, ill-equipped, unqualified, ineligible, untrained, unprepared, unequal, incapable, incompetent, inadequate, ineffective, useless. 2 UNHEALTHY, out of condition, flabby, feeble, decrepit.
≠ 1 fit, suitable, competent. 2 healthy.

unfold v 1 DEVELOP, evolve. 2 REVEAL, disclose, show, present, describe, explain, clarify, elaborate. 3 unfold

a map: open, spread, flatten, straighten, stretch out, undo, unfurl, unroll, uncoil, unwrap, uncover.
≠ 2 withhold, suppress. 3 fold, wrap.

unforeseen adj unpredicted, unexpected, unanticipated, surprising, startling, sudden, unavoidable.
≠ expected, predictable.

unforgettable adj memorable, momentous, historic, noteworthy, notable, impressive, remarkable, exceptional, extraordinary.
≠ unmemorable, unexceptional.

unforgivable adj unpardonable, inexcusable, unjustifiable, indefensible, reprehensible, shameful, disgraceful, deplorable.
≠ forgivable, venial.

unfortunate adj 1 UNLUCKY, luckless, hapless, unsuccessful, poor, wretched, unhappy, doomed, ill-fated, hopeless, calamitous, disastrous, ruinous. 2 REGRETTABLE, lamentable, deplorable, adverse, unfavourable, unsuitable, inappropriate, inopportune, untimely, ill-timed.
≠ 1 fortunate, happy. 2 favourable, appropriate.

unfounded adj baseless, groundless, unsupported, unsubstantiated, unproven, unjustified, idle, false, spurious, trumped-up, fabricated.
≠ substantiated, justified.

unfriendly adj unsociable, standoffish, aloof, distant, unapproachable, inhospitable, uncongenial, unneighbourly, unwelcoming, cold, chilly, hostile, aggressive, quarrelsome, inimical, antagonistic, ill-disposed, disagreeable, surly, sour.
≠ friendly, amiable, agreeable.

ungainly adj clumsy, awkward, gauche, inelegant, gawky, unco-

ordinated, lumbering, unwieldy.
☒ graceful, elegant.

ungodly adj **1** UNREASONABLE,
outrageous, intolerable, unearthly,
unsocial. **2** IMPIOUS, irreligious,
godless, blasphemous, profane,
immoral, corrupt, depraved, sinful,
wicked.

ungrateful adj unthankful,
unappreciative, ill-mannered,
ungracious, selfish, heedless.
☒ grateful, thankful.

unguarded adj **1** in an unguarded
moment: unwary, careless,
incautious, imprudent, impolitic,
indiscreet, undiplomatic, thoughtless,
unthinking, heedless, foolish,
foolhardy, rash, ill-considered.
2 UNDEFENDED, unprotected, exposed,
vulnerable, defenceless.
☒ **1** guarded, cautious. **2** defended,
protected.

unhappy adj **1** SAD, sorrowful,
miserable, melancholy, depressed,
dispirited, despondent, dejected,
downcast, crestfallen, long-faced,
gloomy. **2** UNFORTUNATE, unlucky,
ill-fated, unsuitable, inappropriate,
inapt, ill-chosen, tactless, awkward,
clumsy.
☒ **1** happy. **2** fortunate, suitable.

unharmed adj undamaged, unhurt,
uninjured, unscathed, whole, intact,
safe, sound.
☒ harmed, damaged.

unhealthy adj **1** UNWELL, sick,
ill, poorly, ailing, sickly, infirm,
invalid, weak, feeble, frail, unsound.
2 UNWHOLESOME, insanitary,
unhygienic, harmful, detrimental,
morbid, unnatural.
☒ **1** healthy, fit. **2** wholesome,
hygienic, natural.

unheard-of adj **1** UNTHINKABLE,
inconceivable, unimaginable,
undreamed-of, unprecedented,
acceptable, offensive, shocking,
outrageous, preposterous.

2 UNKNOWN, unfamiliar, new,
unusual, obscure.
☒ **1** normal, acceptable. **2** famous.

unheeded adj ignored, disregarded,
disobeyed, unnoticed, unobserved,
unremarked, overlooked, neglected,
forgotten.
☒ noted, observed.

unhesitating adj immediate,
instant, instantaneous, prompt,
ready, automatic, spontaneous,
unquestioning, unwavering,
unfaltering, whole-hearted, implicit.
☒ hesitant, tentative.

unholy adj **1** IMPIOUS, irreligious,
sinful, iniquitous, immoral, corrupt,
depraved, wicked, evil. **2** (infml)
an unholy mess: unreasonable,
shocking, outrageous, ungodly,
unearthly.
☒ **1** holy, pious, godly. **2** reasonable.

unhurried adj slow, leisurely,
deliberate, easy, relaxed, calm, easy-
going (infml), laid-back (infml).
☒ hurried, hasty, rushed.

unidentified adj unknown,
unrecognized, unmarked, unnamed,
nameless, anonymous, incognito,
unfamiliar, strange, mysterious.
☒ identified, known, named.

uniform n outfit, costume, livery,
insignia, regalia, robes, dress, suit.
◇ adj same, identical, like, alike,
similar, homogeneous, consistent,
regular, equal, smooth, even, flat,
monotonous, unvarying, unchanging,
constant, unbroken.
☒ different, varied, changing.

unify v unite, join, bind, combine,
integrate, merge, amalgamate,
consolidate, coalesce, fuse, weld.
☒ separate, divide, split.

unimaginable adj inconceivable,
mind-boggling (infml), unbelievable,
incredible, impossible, fantastic,
undreamed-of, unthinkable,
unheard-of.

unimaginative adj uninspired,

unoriginal, predictable, hackneyed, banal, ordinary, dull, boring, routine, matter-of-fact, dry, barren, lifeless, unexciting, tame.
🗷 imaginative, creative, original.

unimportant adj insignificant, inconsequential, irrelevant, immaterial, minor, trivial, trifling, petty, slight, negligible, worthless.
🗷 important, significant, relevant, vital.

unimpressive adj unspectacular, undistinguished, unexceptional, unremarkable, uninteresting, dull, average, commonplace, indifferent, mediocre.
🗷 impressive, memorable, notable.

uninhabited adj unoccupied, vacant, empty, deserted, abandoned, unpeopled, unpopulated.

uninhibited adj unconstrained, unreserved, unselfconscious, liberated, free, unrestricted, uncontrolled, unrestrained, abandoned, natural, spontaneous, frank, candid, open, relaxed, informal.
🗷 inhibited, repressed, constrained, restrained.

unintelligible adj incoherent, incomprehensible, inarticulate, double Dutch, garbled, scrambled, jumbled, muddled, indecipherable, illegible.
🗷 intelligible, comprehensible, clear.

unintentional adj unintended, accidental, fortuitous, inadvertent, unplanned, unpremeditated, involuntary, unconscious, unwitting.
🗷 intentional, deliberate.

uninterested adj indifferent, unconcerned, uninvolved, bored, listless, apathetic, unenthusiastic, blasé, impassive, unresponsive.
🗷 interested, concerned, enthusiastic, responsive.

uninteresting adj boring, tedious, monotonous, humdrum,

dull, drab, dreary, dry, flat, tame, uneventful, unexciting, uninspiring, unimpressive.
🗷 interesting, exciting.

uninterrupted adj unbroken, continuous, non-stop, unending, constant, continual, steady, sustained, undisturbed, peaceful.
🗷 broken, intermittent.

uninvited adj unasked, unsought, unsolicited, unwanted, unwelcome.
🗷 invited.

union n alliance, coalition, league, association, federation, confederation, confederacy, merger, combination, amalgamation, blend, mixture, synthesis, fusion, unification, unity.
🗷 separation, alienation, estrangement.

unique adj single, one-off, sole, only, lone, solitary, unmatched, matchless, peerless, unequalled, unparalleled, unrivalled, incomparable, inimitable.
🗷 common.

unison n concert, co-operation, unanimity, unity.

unit n item, part, element, constituent, piece, component, module, section, segment, portion, entity, whole, one, system, assembly.

unite v join, link, couple, marry, ally, co-operate, band, associate, federate, confederate, combine, pool, amalgamate, merge, blend, unify, consolidate, coalesce, fuse.
🗷 separate, sever.

united adj allied, affiliated, corporate, unified, combined, pooled, collective, concerted, one, unanimous, agreed, in agreement, in accord, like-minded.
🗷 disunited.

unity n agreement, accord, concord, harmony, peace, consensus, unanimity, solidarity, integrity, oneness, wholeness, union, unification.

⊠ disunity, disagreement, discord, strife.

universal adj worldwide, global, all-embracing, all-inclusive, general, common, across-the-board, total, whole, entire, all-round, unlimited.

universe n cosmos, world, nature, creation, firmament, heavens, macrocosm (fml).

unjust adj unfair, inequitable, wrong, partial, biased, prejudiced, one-sided, partisan, unreasonable, unjustified, undeserved.

⊠ just, fair, reasonable.

unjustifiable adj indefensible, inexcusable, unforgivable, unreasonable, unwarranted, immoderate, excessive, unacceptable, outrageous.

⊠ justifiable, acceptable.

unkempt adj dishevelled, tousled, rumpled, uncombed, ungroomed, untidy, messy, scruffy, shabby, slovenly.

⊠ well-groomed, tidy.

unkind adj cruel, inhuman, inhumane, callous, hard-hearted, unfeeling, insensitive, thoughtless, inconsiderate, uncharitable, nasty, malicious, spiteful, mean, malevolent, unfriendly, uncaring, unsympathetic.

⊠ kind, considerate.

unknown adj unfamiliar, unheard-of, strange, alien, foreign, mysterious, dark, obscure, hidden, concealed, undisclosed, secret, untold, new, uncharted, unexplored, undiscovered, unidentified, unnamed, nameless, anonymous, incognito.

⊠ known, familiar.

unlawful adj illegal, criminal, illicit, illegitimate, unconstitutional, outlawed, banned, prohibited, forbidden, unauthorized.

⊠ lawful, legal.

unlikely adj 1 IMPROBABLE, implausible, far-fetched, unconvincing, unbelievable, incredible, unimaginable, unexpected, doubtful, dubious, questionable, suspect, suspicious. 2 SLIGHT, faint, remote, distant.

⊠ 1 likely, plausible.

unlimited adj limitless, unrestricted, unbounded, boundless, infinite, endless, countless, incalculable, immeasurable, vast, immense, extensive, great, indefinite, absolute, unconditional, unqualified, all-encompassing, total, complete, full, unconstrained, unhampered.

⊠ limited.

unload v unpack, empty, discharge, dump, offload, unburden, relieve.

⊠ load.

unlock v unbolt, unlatch, unfasten, undo, open, free, release.

⊠ lock, fasten.

unloved adj unpopular, disliked, hated, detested, unwanted, rejected, spurned, loveless, uncared-for, neglected.

⊠ loved.

unlucky adj unfortunate, luckless, unhappy, miserable, wretched, ill-fated, ill-starred, jinxed, doomed, cursed, unfavourable, inauspicious, ominous, unsuccessful, disastrous.

⊠ lucky.

unmanageable adj 1 UNWIELDY, bulky, cumbersome, awkward, inconvenient, unhandy. 2 UNCONTROLLABLE, wild, unruly, disorderly, difficult.

⊠ 1 manageable. 2 controllable.

unmarried adj single, unwed, celibate, unattached, available.

⊠ married.

unmask v unveil, uncloak, uncover, bare, expose, reveal, show, disclose, discover, detect.

⊠ mask, conceal.

unmentionable adj unspeakable,

unutterable, taboo, immodest, indecent, shocking, scandalous, shameful, disgraceful, abominable.

unmistakable adj clear, plain, distinct, pronounced, obvious, evident, manifest, patent, glaring, explicit, unambiguous, unequivocal, positive, definite, sure, certain, unquestionable, indisputable, undeniable.
☒ unclear, ambiguous.

unmoved adj unaffected, untouched, unshaken, dry-eyed, unfeeling, cold, dispassionate, indifferent, impassive, unresponsive, unimpressed, firm, adamant, inflexible, unbending, undeviating, unwavering, steady, unchanged, resolute, resolved, determined.
☒ moved, affected, shaken.

unnatural adj 1 ABNORMAL, anomalous, freakish, irregular, unusual, strange, odd, peculiar, queer, bizarre, extraordinary, uncanny, supernatural, inhuman, perverted. 2 AFFECTED, feigned, artificial, false, insincere, contrived, unspontaneous, laboured, stilted, forced, strained, self-conscious, stiff.
☒ 1 natural, normal. 2 sincere, fluent.

unnecessary adj unneeded, needless, uncalled-for, unwanted, non-essential, dispensable, expendable, superfluous, redundant, tautological.
☒ necessary, essential, indispensable.

unnerve v daunt, intimidate, frighten, scare, discourage, demoralize, dismay, disconcert, upset, worry, shake, rattle (infml), confound, fluster.
☒ nerve, brace, steel.

unnoticed adj unobserved, unremarked, unseen, unrecognized, undiscovered, overlooked, ignored, disregarded, neglected, unheeded.
☒ noticed, noted.

unobtrusive adj inconspicuous, unnoticeable, unassertive, self-effacing, humble, modest, unostentatious, unpretentious, restrained, low-key, subdued, quiet, retiring.
☒ obtrusive, ostentatious.

unoccupied adj uninhabited, vacant, empty, free, idle, inactive, workless, jobless, unemployed.
☒ occupied, busy.

unofficial adj unauthorized, illegal, informal, off-the-record, personal, private, confidential, undeclared, unconfirmed.
☒ official.

unorthodox adj unconventional, nonconformist, heterodox, alternative, fringe, irregular, abnormal, unusual.
☒ orthodox, conventional.

unpaid adj 1 unpaid bills: outstanding, overdue, unsettled, owing, due, payable. 2 unpaid work: voluntary, honorary, unsalaried, unwaged, unremunerative, free.
☒ 1 paid.

unpalatable adj 1 UNAPPETIZING, distasteful, insipid, bitter, uneatable, inedible. 2 UNPLEASANT, disagreeable, unattractive, offensive, repugnant.
☒ 1 palatable. 2 pleasant.

unparalleled adj unequalled, unmatched, matchless, peerless, incomparable, unrivalled, unsurpassed, supreme, superlative, rare, exceptional, unprecedented.

unpleasant adj disagreeable, ill-natured, nasty, objectionable, offensive, distasteful, unpalatable, unattractive, repulsive, bad, troublesome.
☒ pleasant, agreeable, nice.

unpopular adj disliked, hated, detested, unloved, unsought-after, unfashionable, undesirable, unwelcome, unwanted, rejected, shunned, avoided, neglected.

⊉ popular, fashionable.

unprecedented adj new, original, revolutionary, unknown, unheard-of, exceptional, remarkable, extraordinary, abnormal, unusual, freakish, unparalleled, unrivalled.
⊉ usual.

unpredictable adj unforeseeable, unexpected, changeable, variable, inconstant, unreliable, fickle, unstable, erratic, random, chance.
⊉ predictable, foreseeable, constant.

unprepared adj unready, surprised, unsuspecting, ill-equipped, unfinished, incomplete, half-baked, unplanned, unrehearsed, spontaneous, improvised, ad-lib, off the cuff.
⊉ prepared, ready.

unpretentious adj unaffected, natural, plain, simple, unobtrusive, honest, straightforward, humble, modest, unassuming, unostentatious.
⊉ pretentious.

unproductive adj infertile, sterile, barren, dry, arid, unfruitful, fruitless, futile, vain, idle, useless, ineffective, unprofitable, unremunerative, unrewarding.
⊉ productive, fertile.

unprofessional adj amateurish, inexpert, unskilled, sloppy, incompetent, inefficient, casual, negligent, lax, unethical, unprincipled, improper, unseemly, unacceptable, inadmissible.
⊉ professional, skilful.

unprotected adj unguarded, unattended, undefended, unfortified, unarmed, unshielded, unsheltered, uncovered, exposed, open, naked, vulnerable, defenceless, helpless.
⊉ protected, safe, immune.

unqualified adj 1 UNTRAINED, inexperienced, amateur, ineligible, unfit, incompetent, incapable, unprepared, ill-equipped. 2 ABSOLUTE,

categorical, utter, total, complete, thorough, consummate, downright, unmitigated, unreserved, whole-hearted, outright, unconditional, unrestricted.
⊉ 1 qualified, professional.
2 conditional, tentative.

unravel v unwind, undo, untangle, disentangle, free, extricate, separate, resolve, sort out, solve, work out, figure out, puzzle out, penetrate, interpret, explain.
⊉ tangle, complicate.

unreal adj false, artificial, synthetic, mock, fake, sham, imaginary, visionary, fanciful, make-believe, pretend (infml), fictitious, made-up, fairytale, legendary, mythical, fantastic, illusory, immaterial, insubstantial, hypothetical.
⊉ real, genuine.

unrealistic adj impractical, idealistic, romantic, quixotic, impracticable, unworkable, unreasonable, impossible.
⊉ realistic, pragmatic.

unreasonable adj 1 UNFAIR, unjust, biased, unjustifiable, unjustified, unwarranted, undue, uncalled-for.
2 IRRATIONAL, illogical, inconsistent, arbitrary, absurd, nonsensical, far-fetched, preposterous, mad, senseless, silly, foolish, stupid, headstrong, opinionated, perverse.
3 unreasonable prices: excessive, immoderate, extravagant, exorbitant, extortionate.
⊉ 1 reasonable, fair. 2 rational, sensible. 3 moderate.

unrecognizable adj unidentifiable, disguised, incognito, changed, altered.

unrefined adj raw, untreated, unprocessed, unfinished, crude, coarse, vulgar, unsophisticated, uncultivated, uncultured.
⊉ refined, finished.

unrelated adj unconnected,

unassociated, irrelevant, extraneous, different, dissimilar, unlike, disparate, distinct, separate, independent.
$\boxminus$ related, similar.

unrelenting adj relentless, unremitting, uncompromising, inexorable, incessant, unceasing, ceaseless, endless, unbroken, continuous, constant, continual, perpetual, steady, unabated, remorseless, unmerciful, merciless, pitiless, unsparing.
$\boxminus$ spasmodic, intermittent.

unreliable adj unsound, fallible, deceptive, false, mistaken, erroneous, inaccurate, doubtful, unconvincing, implausible, uncertain, untrustworthy, unstable, fickle, irresponsible.
$\boxminus$ reliable, dependable, trustworthy.

unrepentant adj impenitent, unapologetic, unabashed, unashamed, shameless, incorrigible, confirmed, hardened, obdurate.
$\boxminus$ repentant, penitent, ashamed.

unrest n protest, rebellion, turmoil, agitation, restlessness, dissatisfaction, dissension, disaffection, worry.
$\boxminus$ peace, calm.

unrestricted adj unlimited, unbounded, unopposed, unhindered, unimpeded, unobstructed, clear, free, open, public, unconditional, absolute.
$\boxminus$ restricted, limited.

unripe adj unripened, green, immature, undeveloped, unready.
$\boxminus$ ripe, mature.

unrivalled adj unequalled, unparalleled, unmatched, matchless, peerless, incomparable, inimitable, unsurpassed, supreme, superlative.

unruffled adj undisturbed, untroubled, collected, composed, cool, calm, tranquil, serene, peaceful, smooth, level, even.
$\boxminus$ troubled, anxious.

unruly adj uncontrollable,

unmanageable, ungovernable, intractable, disorderly, wild, rowdy, riotous, rebellious, mutinous, lawless, insubordinate, disobedient, wayward, wilful, headstrong, obstreperous.
$\boxminus$ manageable, orderly.

unsafe adj dangerous, perilous, risky, hazardous, treacherous, unreliable, uncertain, unsound, unstable, precarious, insecure, vulnerable, exposed.
$\boxminus$ safe, secure.

unsatisfactory adj unacceptable, imperfect, defective, faulty, inferior, poor, weak, inadequate, insufficient, deficient, unsuitable, displeasing, dissatisfying, unsatisfying, frustrating, disappointing.
$\boxminus$ satisfactory, pleasing.

unscathed adj unhurt, uninjured, unharmed, undamaged, untouched, whole, intact, safe, sound.
$\boxminus$ hurt, injured.

unscrupulous adj unprincipled, ruthless, shameless, dishonourable, dishonest, crooked (infml), corrupt, immoral, unethical, improper.
$\boxminus$ scrupulous, ethical, proper.

unseemly adj improper, indelicate, indecorous, unbecoming, undignified, unrefined, disreputable, discreditable, undue, inappropriate, unsuitable.
$\boxminus$ seemly, decorous.

unseen adj unnoticed, unobserved, undetected, invisible, hidden, concealed, veiled, obscure.
$\boxminus$ visible.

unselfish adj selfless, altruistic, self-denying, self-sacrificing, disinterested, noble, magnanimous, generous, liberal, charitable, philanthropic, public-spirited, humanitarian, kind.
$\boxminus$ selfish.

unsentimental adj realistic, practical, pragmatic, hard-headed,

tough, unromantic, level-headed.
≠ sentimental, idealistic.

unsettle v disturb, upset, trouble, bother, discompose, ruffle, fluster, unbalance, shake, agitate, rattle (*infml*), disconcert, confuse, throw.

unsettled adj 1 DISTURBED, upset, troubled, agitated, anxious, uneasy, tense, edgy, flustered, shaken, unnerved, disoriented, confused. 2 UNRESOLVED, undetermined, undecided, open, uncertain, doubtful. 3 *unsettled weather*: changeable, variable, unpredictable, inconstant, unstable, insecure, unsteady, shaky. 4 UNPAID, outstanding, owing, payable, overdue.
≠ 1 composed. 2 certain. 3 settled. 4 paid.

unshakable adj firm, well-founded, fixed, stable, immovable, unassailable, unwavering, constant, steadfast, staunch, sure, resolute, determined.
≠ insecure.

unsightly adj ugly, unattractive, unprepossessing, hideous, repulsive, repugnant, off-putting, unpleasant, disagreeable.
≠ attractive.

unskilled adj untrained, unqualified, inexperienced, unpractised, unprofessional, inexpert, amateurish, incompetent.
≠ skilled.

unsociable adj unfriendly, aloof, distant, standoffish, withdrawn, introverted, reclusive, retiring, reserved, taciturn, unforthcoming, uncommunicative, cold, chilly, uncongenial, unneighbourly, inhospitable, hostile.
≠ sociable, friendly.

unsolicited adj unrequested, unsought, uninvited, unasked, unwanted, unwelcome, uncalled-for, gratuitous, voluntary, spontaneous.

≠ requested, invited.

unsophisticated adj artless, guileless, innocent, ingenuous, naive, inexperienced, unworldly, childlike, natural, unaffected, unpretentious, unrefined, plain, simple, basic, straightforward, uncomplicated, uninvolved.
≠ sophisticated, worldly, complex.

unsound adj 1 *unsound reasoning*: faulty, flawed, defective, ill-founded, fallacious, false, erroneous, invalid, illogical. 2 UNHEALTHY, unwell, ill, diseased, weak, frail, unbalanced, deranged, unhinged. 3 UNSTABLE, unsteady, wobbly, shaky, insecure, unsafe.
≠ 1 sound. 2 well. 3 stable.

unspeakable adj unutterable, inexpressible, indescribable, awful, dreadful, frightful, terrible, horrible, shocking, appalling, monstrous, inconceivable, unbelievable.

unspoilt adj preserved, unchanged, untouched, natural, unaffected, unsophisticated, unharmed, undamaged, unimpaired, unblemished, perfect.
≠ spoilt, affected.

unspoken adj unstated, undeclared, unuttered, unexpressed, unsaid, voiceless, wordless, silent, tacit, implicit, implied, inferred, understood, assumed.
≠ stated, explicit.

unstable adj 1 CHANGEABLE, variable, fluctuating, vacillating, wavering, fitful, erratic, inconsistent, volatile, capricious, inconstant, unpredictable, unreliable, untrustworthy. 2 UNSTEADY, wobbly, shaky, rickety, insecure, unsafe, risky, precarious, tottering, unbalanced.
≠ 1 stable. 2 steady.

unsteady adj unstable, wobbly, shaky, rickety, insecure, unsafe, treacherous, precarious, tottering, unreliable, inconstant, irregular,

flickering.
⊠ steady, firm.

unsuccessful adj failed, abortive, vain, futile, useless, ineffective, unavailing, fruitless, unproductive, sterile, luckless, unlucky, unfortunate, losing, beaten, defeated, frustrated, thwarted.
⊠ successful, effective, fortunate, winning.

unsuitable adj inappropriate, inapt, unsuited, unfit, unacceptable, improper, unseemly, unbecoming, incompatible, incongruous.
⊠ suitable, appropriate.

unsung adj unhonoured, unpraised, unacknowledged, unrecognized, overlooked, disregarded, neglected, forgotten, unknown, obscure.
⊠ honoured, famous, renowned.

unsure adj uncertain, doubtful, dubious, suspicious, sceptical, unconvinced, unpersuaded, undecided, hesitant, tentative.
⊠ sure, certain, confident.

unsurpassed adj surpassing, supreme, transcendent, unbeaten, unexcelled, unequalled, unrivalled, unparalleled, incomparable, matchless, superlative, exceptional.

unsuspecting adj unwary, unaware, unconscious, trusting, trustful, unsuspicious, credulous, gullible, ingenuous, naive, innocent.
⊠ suspicious, knowing.

unsympathetic adj unpitying, unconcerned, unmoved, unresponsive, indifferent, insensitive, unfeeling, cold, heartless, soulless, hard-hearted, callous, cruel, inhuman, unkind, hard, stony, hostile, antagonistic.
⊠ sympathetic, compassionate.

untangle v disentangle, extricate, unravel, undo, resolve, solve.
⊠ tangle, complicate.

unthinkable adj inconceivable, unimaginable, unheard-of,

unbelievable, incredible, impossible, improbable, unlikely, implausible, unreasonable, illogical, absurd, preposterous, outrageous, shocking.

unthinking adj thoughtless, inconsiderate, insensitive, tactless, indiscreet, rude, heedless, careless, negligent, rash, impulsive, instinctive, unconscious, automatic, mechanical.
⊠ considerate, conscious.

untidy adj messy, cluttered, disorderly, muddled, jumbled, unsystematic, chaotic, topsy-turvy, scruffy, dishevelled, unkempt, slovenly, sloppy, slipshod.
⊠ tidy, neat.

untie v undo, unfasten, unknot, unbind, free, release, loose, loosen.
⊠ tie, fasten.

untimely adj early, premature, unseasonable, ill-timed, inopportune, inconvenient, awkward, unsuitable, inappropriate, unfortunate, inauspicious.
⊠ timely, opportune.

untiring adj unflagging, tireless, indefatigable, dogged, persevering, persistent, tenacious, determined, resolute, devoted, dedicated, constant, incessant, unremitting, steady, staunch, unfailing.
⊠ inconstant, wavering.

untold adj countless, uncounted, unnumbered, unreckoned, incalculable, innumerable, uncountable, infinite, measureless, boundless, inexhaustible, undreamed-of, unimaginable.

untouched adj unharmed, undamaged, unimpaired, unhurt, uninjured, unscathed, safe, intact, unchanged, unaltered, unaffected.
⊠ damaged, affected.

untrained adj unskilled, untaught, unschooled, uneducated, unqualified, inexperienced, amateur, unprofessional, inexpert.
⊠ trained, expert.

untried *adj* untested, unproved, experimental, exploratory, new, novel, innovative, innovatory.
☒ tried, tested, proven.

untrue *adj* **1** FALSE, fallacious, deceptive, misleading, wrong, incorrect, inaccurate, mistaken, erroneous. **2** UNFAITHFUL, disloyal, untrustworthy, dishonest, deceitful, untruthful.
☒ **1** true, correct. **2** faithful, honest.

untrustworthy *adj* dishonest, deceitful, untruthful, disloyal, unfaithful, faithless, treacherous, false, untrue, capricious, fickle, fly-by-night, unreliable, untrusty.
☒ trustworthy, reliable.

untruth *n* lie, fib, whopper (*infml*), porkie (*infml*), story, tale, fiction, invention, fabrication, falsehood, lying, untruthfulness, deceit, perjury.
☒ truth.

untruthful *adj* lying, deceitful, dishonest, crooked (*infml*), two-faced, hypocritical, insincere, false, untrue.
☒ truthful, honest.

unused *adj* leftover, remaining, surplus, extra, spare, available, new, fresh, blank, clean, untouched, unexploited, unemployed, idle.
☒ used.

unusual *adj* uncommon, rare, unfamiliar, strange, odd, curious, queer, bizarre, unconventional, irregular, abnormal, extraordinary, remarkable, exceptional, different, surprising, unexpected.
☒ usual, normal, ordinary.

unveil *v* uncover, expose, bare, reveal, disclose, divulge, discover.
☒ cover, hide.

unwanted *adj* undesired, unsolicited, uninvited, unwelcome, outcast, rejected, unrequired, unneeded, unnecessary, surplus, extra, superfluous, redundant.
☒ wanted, needed, necessary.

unwarranted *adj* unjustified, undeserved, unprovoked, uncalled-for, groundless, unreasonable, unjust, wrong.
☒ warranted, justifiable, deserved.

unwary *adj* unguarded, incautious, careless, imprudent, indiscreet, thoughtless, unthinking, heedless, reckless, rash, hasty.
☒ wary, cautious.

unwelcome *adj* **1** UNWANTED, undesirable, unpopular, uninvited, excluded, rejected. **2** *unwelcome news*: unpleasant, disagreeable, upsetting, worrying, distasteful, unpalatable, unacceptable.
☒ **1** welcome, desirable. **2** pleasant.

unwell *adj* ill, sick, poorly, off-colour, indisposed, ailing, sickly, unhealthy.
☒ well, healthy.

unwieldy *adj* unmanageable, inconvenient, awkward, clumsy, ungainly, bulky, massive, hefty, weighty, ponderous, cumbersome.
☒ handy, dainty.

unwilling *adj* reluctant, disinclined, indisposed, resistant, opposed, averse, loath, slow, unenthusiastic, grudging.
☒ willing, enthusiastic.

unwind *v* **1** UNROLL, unreel, unwrap, undo, uncoil, untwist, unravel, disentangle. **2** (*infml*) RELAX, wind down, calm down, chill out (*infml*).
☒ **1** wind, roll.

unwitting *adj* unaware, unknowing, unsuspecting, unconscious, involuntary, accidental, chance, inadvertent, unintentional, unplanned.
☒ knowing, conscious, deliberate.

unworldly *adj* spiritual, transcendental, metaphysical, otherworldly, visionary, idealistic, impractical, unsophisticated, inexperienced, innocent, naive.

worldly, materialistic, sophisticated.

unworthy *adj* undeserving, inferior, ineligible, unsuitable, inappropriate, unfitting, unbecoming, unseemly, improper, unprofessional, shameful, disgraceful, dishonourable, discreditable, ignoble, base, contemptible, despicable.
worthy, commendable.

unwritten *adj* verbal, oral, word-of-mouth, unrecorded, tacit, implicit, understood, accepted, recognized, traditional, customary, conventional.
written, recorded.

upbraid *v* reprimand, admonish, rebuke, reprove, reproach, scold, chide, castigate, berate, criticize, censure.
praise, commend.

upbringing *n* bringing-up, raising, rearing, breeding, parenting, care, nurture, cultivation, education, training, instruction, teaching.

update *v* modernize, revise, amend, correct, renew, renovate, revamp.

upgrade *v* promote, advance, elevate, raise, improve, enhance.
downgrade, demote.

upheaval *n* disruption, disturbance, upset, chaos, confusion, disorder, turmoil, shake-up (*infml*), revolution, overthrow.

uphill *adj* hard, difficult, arduous, tough, taxing, strenuous, laborious, tiring, wearisome, exhausting, gruelling, punishing.
easy.

uphold *v* support, maintain, hold to, stand by, defend, champion, advocate, promote, back, endorse, sustain, fortify, strengthen, justify, vindicate.
abandon, reject.

upkeep *n* maintenance, preservation, conservation, care, running, repair, support, sustenance, subsistence, keep.
neglect.

upper *adj* higher, loftier, superior, senior, top, topmost, uppermost, high, elevated, exalted, eminent, important.
lower, inferior, junior.

uppermost *adj* highest, loftiest, top, topmost, greatest, supreme, first, primary, foremost, leading, principal, main, chief, dominant, predominant, paramount, pre-eminent.
lowest.

upright *adj* 1 VERTICAL, erect, perpendicular, straight. 2 RIGHTEOUS, good, virtuous, upstanding, noble, honourable, ethical, principled, incorruptible, honest, trustworthy.
1 horizontal, flat. 2 dishonest.

uprising *n* rebellion, revolt, mutiny, rising, insurgence, insurrection, revolution.

uproar *n* noise, din, racket, hubbub, hullabaloo, pandemonium, tumult, turmoil, turbulence, commotion, confusion, disorder, clamour, outcry, furore, riot, rumpus.

uproot *v* pull up, rip up, root out, weed out, remove, displace, eradicate, destroy, wipe out.

upset *v* 1 DISTRESS, grieve, dismay, trouble, worry, agitate, disturb, bother, fluster, ruffle, discompose, shake, unnerve, disconcert, confuse, disorganize. 2 TIP, spill, overturn, capsize, topple, overthrow, destabilize, unsteady.
◇ *n* 1 TROUBLE, worry, agitation, disturbance, bother, disruption, upheaval, shake-up (*infml*), reverse, surprise, shock. 2 *stomach upset*: disorder, complaint, bug (*infml*), illness, sickness.
◇ *adj* distressed, grieved, hurt, annoyed, dismayed, troubled, worried, agitated, disturbed, bothered, shaken, disconcerted, confused.

upshot n result, consequence, outcome, issue, end, conclusion, finish, culmination.

upside down adj inverted, upturned, wrong way up, upset, overturned, disordered, muddled, jumbled, confused, topsy-turvy, chaotic.

up-to-date adj current, modern, contemporary, fashionable, trendy (infml), latest, recent, new.
🗷 out-of-date, old-fashioned, oldfangled (infml).

upturn n revival, recovery, upsurge, upswing, rise, increase, boost, improvement.
🗷 downturn, drop.

urban adj town, city, inner-city, metropolitan, municipal, civic, built-up.
🗷 country, rural.

urge v advise, counsel, recommend, advocate, encourage, exhort, implore, beg, beseech, entreat, plead, press, constrain, compel, force, push, drive, impel, goad, spur, hasten, induce, incite, instigate.
🗷 discourage, dissuade, deter, hinder.
◇ n desire, wish, inclination, fancy, longing, yearning, itch, impulse, compulsion, impetus, drive, eagerness.
🗷 disinclination.

urgency n hurry, haste, pressure, stress, importance, seriousness, gravity, imperativeness, need, necessity.

urgent adj immediate, instant, top-priority, important, critical, crucial, imperative, exigent, pressing, compelling, persuasive, earnest, eager, insistent, persistent.
🗷 unimportant.

usable adj working, operational, serviceable, functional, practical, exploitable, available, current, valid.
🗷 unusable, useless.

usage n 1 TREATMENT, handling, management, control, running, operation, employment, application, use. 2 TRADITION, custom, practice, habit, convention, etiquette, rule, regulation, form, routine, procedure, method.

use v utilize, employ, exercise, practise, operate, work, apply, wield, handle, treat, manipulate, exploit, enjoy, consume, exhaust, expend, spend.
◇ n utility, usefulness, value, worth, profit, advantage, benefit, good, avail, help, service, point, object, end, purpose, reason, cause, occasion, need, necessity, usage, application, employment, operation, exercise.
• **use up** finish, exhaust, drain, sap, deplete, consume, devour, absorb, waste, squander, fritter.

used adj second-hand, cast-off, hand-me-down, nearly new, worn, dog-eared, soiled.
🗷 unused, new, fresh.

useful adj handy, convenient, all-purpose, practical, effective, productive, fruitful, profitable, valuable, worthwhile, advantageous, beneficial, helpful.
🗷 useless, ineffective, worthless.

useless adj futile, fruitless, vain, unproductive, idle, unavailing, hopeless, pointless, worthless, unusable, broken-down, clapped-out (sl), unworkable, impractical, ineffective, inefficient, incompetent, weak.
🗷 useful, helpful, effective.

usher n usherette, doorkeeper, attendant, escort, guide.
◇ v escort, accompany, conduct, lead, direct, guide, show, pilot, steer.

usual adj normal, typical, stock, standard, regular, routine, habitual, customary, conventional, accepted, recognized, accustomed, familiar, common, everyday, general,

ordinary, unexceptional, expected, predictable.
≢ unusual, strange, rare.

usually adv normally, generally, as a rule, ordinarily, typically, traditionally, regularly, commonly, by and large, on the whole, mainly, chiefly, mostly.
≢ exceptionally.

usurp v take over, assume, arrogate, seize, take, annex, appropriate, commandeer, steal.

utensil n tool, implement, instrument, device, contrivance, gadget, apparatus, appliance.

utility n usefulness, use, value, profit, advantage, benefit, avail, service, convenience, practicality, efficacy, efficiency, fitness, serviceableness.

utmost adj 1 with the utmost care: extreme, maximum, greatest, highest, supreme, paramount. 2 FARTHEST, furthermost, remotest, outermost, ultimate, final, last.

◇ n best, hardest, most, maximum.

utter[1] adj absolute, complete, total, entire, thoroughgoing, out-and-out, downright, sheer, stark, arrant, unmitigated, unqualified, perfect, consummate.

utter[2] v speak, say, voice, vocalize, verbalize, express, articulate, enunciate, sound, pronounce, deliver, state, declare, announce, proclaim, tell, reveal, divulge.

utterance n statement, remark, comment, expression, articulation, delivery, speech, declaration, announcement, proclamation, pronouncement.

utterly adv absolutely, completely, totally, fully, entirely, wholly, thoroughly, downright, perfectly.

U-turn n about-turn, volte-face, reversal, backtrack.

Vv

vacancy *n* opportunity, opening, position, post, job, place, room, situation.

vacant *adj* **1** EMPTY, unoccupied, unfilled, free, available, void, not in use, unused, uninhabited. **2** BLANK, expressionless, vacuous, inane, inattentive, absent, absent-minded, unthinking, dreamy.
⊠ **1** occupied, engaged.

vacate *v* leave, depart, evacuate, abandon, withdraw, quit.

vacuum *n* emptiness, void, space, nothingness, vacuity, chasm, gap.

vague *adj* **1** ILL-DEFINED, blurred, indistinct, hazy, dim, shadowy, misty, fuzzy, nebulous, obscure. **2** INDEFINITE, imprecise, unclear, uncertain, undefined, undetermined, unspecific, generalized, inexact, ambiguous, evasive, loose, woolly.
⊠ **1** clear. **2** definite.

vain *adj* **1** *a vain attempt*: useless, worthless, futile, abortive, fruitless, pointless, unproductive, unprofitable, unavailing, hollow, groundless, empty, trivial, unimportant. **2** CONCEITED, proud, self-satisfied, arrogant, self-important, egotistical, bigheaded (*infml*), swollen-headed (*infml*), stuck-up (*infml*), affected, pretentious, ostentatious, swaggering.
⊠ **1** fruitful, successful. **2** modest, self-effacing.

valiant *adj* brave, courageous, gallant, fearless, intrepid, bold, dauntless, heroic, plucky, indomitable, staunch.
⊠ cowardly, fearful.

valid *adj* **1** LOGICAL, well-founded, well-grounded, sound, good, cogent, convincing, telling, conclusive, reliable, substantial, weighty, powerful, just. **2** OFFICIAL, legal, lawful, legitimate, authentic, bona fide, genuine, binding, proper.
⊠ **1** false, weak. **2** unofficial, invalid.

valley *n* dale, vale, dell, glen, hollow, cwm, depression, gulch.

valuable *adj* **1** *valuable necklace*: precious, prized, valued, costly, expensive, dear, high-priced, treasured, cherished, estimable. **2** *valuable suggestions*: helpful, worthwhile, useful, beneficial, invaluable, constructive, fruitful, profitable, important, serviceable, worthy, handy.
⊠ **1** worthless. **2** useless.

value *n* **1** COST, price, rate, worth. **2** WORTH, use, usefulness, utility, merit, importance, desirability, benefit, advantage, significance, good, profit.
◇ *v* **1** PRIZE, appreciate, treasure, esteem, hold dear, respect, cherish. **2** EVALUATE, assess, estimate, price, appraise, survey, rate.
⊠ **1** disregard, undervalue, neglect.

vanish *v* disappear, fade, dissolve, evaporate, disperse, melt, die out, depart, exit, fizzle out, peter out.
⊠ appear, materialize.

vanity *n* **1** CONCEIT, conceitedness, pride, arrogance, self-conceit, self-love, self-satisfaction, narcissism, egotism, pretension, ostentation, affectation, airs, bigheadedness (*infml*), swollen-headedness (*infml*).

2 WORTHLESSNESS, uselessness, emptiness, futility, pointlessness, unreality, hollowness, fruitlessness, triviality.
⊜ **1** modesty. **2** worth.

vapour *n* steam, mist, fog, smoke, breath, fumes, haze, damp, dampness, exhalation.

variable *adj* changeable, inconstant, varying, shifting, mutable, fitful, unpredictable, fluctuating, unstable, unsteady, wavering, vacillating, temperamental, fickle, flexible.
⊜ fixed, invariable, stable.

variance *n* **1** VARIATION, difference, discrepancy, divergence, inconsistency, disagreement.
2 DISAGREEMENT, disharmony, conflict, discord, division, dissent, dissension, quarrelling, strife.
⊜ **1** agreement. **2** harmony.

variation *n* diversity, variety, deviation, discrepancy, change, diversification, alteration, difference, departure, modification, modulation, inflection, novelty, innovation.
⊜ monotony, uniformity.

varied *adj* assorted, diverse, miscellaneous, mixed, various, sundry, heterogeneous (*fml*), different, wide-ranging.
⊜ standardized, uniform.

variegated *adj* multicoloured, many-coloured, parti-coloured, varicoloured, speckled, mottled, dappled, pied, streaked, motley.
⊜ monochrome, plain.

variety *n* **1** ASSORTMENT, miscellany, mixture, collection, medley, pot-pourri, range. **2** DIFFERENCE, diversity, dissimilarity, discrepancy, variation, multiplicity. **3** SORT, kind, class, category, species, type, breed, brand, make, strain.
⊜ **2** uniformity, similitude.

various *adj* different, differing, diverse, varied, varying, assorted, miscellaneous, heterogeneous (*fml*),

distinct, diversified, mixed, many, several.

varnish *n* lacquer, glaze, resin, polish, gloss, coating.

vary *v* **1** CHANGE, alter, modify, modulate, diversify, reorder, transform, alternate, permutate.
2 DIVERGE, differ, disagree, depart, fluctuate.

vast *adj* huge, immense, massive, gigantic, enormous, great, colossal, extensive, tremendous, sweeping, unlimited, fathomless, immeasurable, never-ending, monumental, monstrous, far-flung.

vault¹ *v* leap, spring, bound, clear, jump, hurdle, leap-frog.

vault² *n* **1** CELLAR, crypt, strongroom, repository, cavern, depository, wine cellar, tomb, mausoleum. **2** ARCH, roof, span, concave.

veer *v* swerve, swing, change, shift, diverge, deviate, wheel, turn, sheer, tack.

vegetable

Vegetables include: artichoke, asparagus, aubergine, baby corn, bean, beetroot, bok choy, broad bean, broccoli, Brussels sprout, butter bean, cabbage, calabrese, capsicum, carrot, cassava, cauliflower, celeriac, celery, chicory, courgette, cress, cucumber, daikon, edamame, eggplant (*N Am*), endive, fennel, French bean, garlic, Jerusalem artichoke, kale, kohlrabi, leek, lentil, lettuce, mangetout, marrow, mibuna, mizuna, mung bean, mushroom, okra, onion, parsnip, pea, pepper, petits pois, potato, pumpkin, radish, romanesco, runner bean, shallot, soya bean, spinach, spring onion, squash, swede, sweetcorn, sweet potato, turnip, water chestnut, watercress, yam, zucchini (*N Am & Aust*). *see* *also* **mushroom**.

Vegetable dishes include: bhaji, onion bhaji, bubble and squeak, cauliflower cheese, champ, chillada, colcannon, coleslaw, couscous, crudités, dal, dolma, felafel, gado-gado, gnocchi, guacamole, hummus, latke, macaroni cheese, mushy peas, nut cutlet, pease pudding, pilau, polenta, ratatouille, raita, rösti, salad, Waldorf salad, sauerkraut, stuffed marrow, stuffed mushroom, succotash, tabbouleh, tzatziki, vegetable chilli, vegetable curry, vegetarian goulash.

vegetate *v* stagnate, degenerate, deteriorate, rusticate, go to seed, idle, rust, languish.

vehement *adj* impassioned, passionate, ardent, fervent, intense, forceful, emphatic, heated, strong, powerful, urgent, enthusiastic, animated, eager, earnest, forcible, fierce, violent, zealous.
🗷 apathetic, indifferent.

vehicle *n* **1** CONVEYANCE, transport. **2** MEANS, agency, channel, medium, mechanism, organ.

Vehicles include: plane, boat, ship, car, taxi, cab, hackney carriage, bicycle, bike (*infml*), tandem, tricycle, penny-farthing, motorcycle, motorbike, scooter, quad bike, minimoto, bus, omnibus, minibus, double-decker (*infml*), coach, charabanc, caravan, caravanette, camper, train, sleeper, tube, tram, monorail, trolleybus; van, Transit®, lorry, truck, juggernaut, pantechnicon, trailer, tractor, tank, wagon; bobsleigh, sled, sledge, sleigh, toboggan, troika; barouche, brougham, dogcart, dray, four-in-hand, gig, hansom, landau, phaeton, post chaise, stagecoach, sulky, surrey, trap; rickshaw, sedan chair, litter.
see also **aircraft**; **boat**; **car**.

veil *v* screen, cloak, cover, mask, shadow, shield, obscure, conceal, hide, disguise, shade.
🗷 expose, uncover.
◇ *n* cover, cloak, curtain, mask, screen, disguise, film, blind, shade, shroud.

vein *n* **1** STREAK, stripe, stratum, seam, lode, blood vessel. **2** MOOD, tendency, bent, strain, temper, tenor, tone, frame of mind, mode, style.

Veins and arteries include: aorta, axillary, brachial, carotid, femoral, frontal, gastric, hepatic, iliac, jugular, portal, pulmonary, radial, renal, saphena, subclavian, superior, temporal, tibial.

vendetta *n* feud, blood-feud, enmity, rivalry, quarrel, bad blood, bitterness.

veneer *n* front, façade, appearance, coating, surface, show, mask, gloss, pretence, guise, finish.

venerable *adj* respected, revered, esteemed, honoured, venerated, dignified, grave, wise, august, aged, worshipped.

venerate *v* revere, respect, honour, esteem, worship, hallow (*fml*), adore.
🗷 despise, anathematize.

vengeance *n* retribution, revenge, retaliation, reprisal, requital, tit for tat.
🗷 forgiveness.

venom *n* **1** POISON, toxin. **2** RANCOUR, ill-will, malice, malevolence, spite, bitterness, acrimony, hate, virulence.

venomous *adj* **1** POISONOUS, toxic, virulent, harmful, noxious. **2** MALICIOUS, spiteful, vicious, vindictive, baleful, hostile, malignant,

rancorous, baneful.
⊞ 1 harmless.

vent n opening, hole, aperture, outlet, passage, orifice, duct.
◇ v air, express, voice, utter, release, discharge, emit.

ventilate v 1 *ventilate a room*: air, aerate, freshen. 2 *ventilate one's feelings*: air, broadcast, debate, discuss.

venture v 1 DARE, advance, make bold, put forward, presume, suggest, volunteer. 2 RISK, hazard, endanger, imperil, jeopardize, speculate, wager, stake.
◇ n risk, chance, speculation, hazard, gamble, undertaking, project, adventure, endeavour, enterprise, operation, fling.

verbal adj spoken, oral, verbatim, unwritten, word-of-mouth.

verbatim adv word for word, exactly, literally, to the letter, precisely.

verbose adj wordy, garrulous, long-winded, prolix, loquacious, diffuse, circumlocutory.
⊞ succinct, brief.

verdict n decision, judgement, conclusion, finding, adjudication, assessment, opinion, sentence.

verge n border, edge, margin, limit, rim, brim, brink, boundary, threshold, extreme, edging.
• **verge on** approach, border on, come close to, near.

verify v confirm, corroborate, substantiate, authenticate, bear out, prove, support, validate, testify, attest.
⊞ invalidate, discredit.

vernacular adj indigenous, local, native, popular, vulgar, informal, colloquial, common.
◇ n language, speech, tongue, parlance, dialect, idiom, jargon.

versatile adj adaptable, flexible, all-round, multipurpose, multifaceted, adjustable, many-sided, general-purpose, functional, resourceful, handy, variable.
⊞ inflexible.

verse n poetry, rhyme, stanza, metre, doggerel, jingle.

versed adj skilled, proficient, practised, experienced, familiar, acquainted, learned, knowledgeable, conversant, seasoned, qualified, competent, accomplished.

version n 1 RENDERING, reading, interpretation, account, translation, paraphrase, adaptation, portrayal. 2 TYPE, kind, variant, form, model, style, design.

vertical adj upright, perpendicular, upstanding, erect, on end.
⊞ horizontal.

vertigo n dizziness, giddiness, light-headedness.

verve n vitality, vivacity, animation, energy, dash, élan, liveliness, sparkle, vigour, enthusiasm, gusto, life, relish, spirit, force.
⊞ apathy, lethargy.

very adv extremely, greatly, highly, deeply, truly, terribly (infml), really, majorly (sl), remarkably, excessively, exceedingly, acutely, particularly, absolutely, noticeably, unusually.
⊞ slightly, scarcely.
◇ adj actual, real, same, selfsame, identical, true, genuine, simple, utter, sheer, pure, perfect, plain, mere, bare, exact, appropriate.

vestige n trace, suspicion, indication, sign, hint, evidence, whiff, inkling, glimmer, token, scrap, remains, remainder, remnant, residue.

vet v investigate, examine, check, scrutinize, scan, inspect, survey, review, appraise, audit.

veteran n master, past master, old hand, old stager, old-timer, pro

(*infml*), warhorse.
⊞ novice, recruit.
◇ *adj* experienced, practised, seasoned, long-serving, expert, adept, proficient, old.
⊞ inexperienced.

veto *v* reject, turn down, forbid, disallow, ban, prohibit, rule out, block.
⊞ approve, sanction, ratify.
◇ *n* rejection, ban, embargo, prohibition, thumbs-down (*infml*).
⊞ approval, assent.

vex *v* irritate, annoy, provoke, pester, trouble, upset, worry, bother, put out (*infml*), harass, hassle (*infml*), aggravate (*infml*), needle (*infml*), disturb, distress, agitate, exasperate, torment, fret.
⊞ calm, soothe.

vexed *adj* **1** IRRITATED, annoyed, provoked, upset, troubled, worried, nettled, put out, exasperated, bothered, confused, perplexed, aggravated (*infml*), harassed, hassled (*infml*), ruffled, riled, disturbed, distressed, displeased, agitated.
2 *a vexed question*: difficult, controversial, contested, disputed.

viable *adj* feasible, practicable, possible, workable, usable, operable, achievable, sustainable.
⊞ impossible, unworkable.

vibrant *adj* **1** ANIMATED, vivacious, vivid, bright, brilliant, colourful, lively, responsive, sparkling, spirited, sensitive. **2** THRILLING, dynamic, electrifying, electric.

vibrate *v* quiver, pulsate, shudder, shiver, resonate, reverberate, throb, oscillate, tremble, undulate, sway, swing, shake.

vice *n* **1** EVIL, evil-doing, depravity, immorality, wickedness, sin, corruption, iniquity (*fml*), profligacy (*fml*), degeneracy. **2** FAULT, failing, defect, shortcoming, weakness, imperfection, blemish, bad habit,

besetting sin.
⊞ **1** virtue, morality.

vicinity *n* neighbourhood, area, locality, district, precincts, environs, proximity.

vicious *adj* **1** WICKED, bad, wrong, immoral, depraved, unprincipled, diabolical, corrupt, debased, perverted, profligate (*fml*), vile, heinous. **2** MALICIOUS, spiteful, vindictive, virulent, cruel, mean, nasty, slanderous, venomous, defamatory. **3** SAVAGE, wild, violent, barbarous, brutal, dangerous.
⊞ **1** virtuous. **2** kind.

victim *n* sufferer, casualty, prey, scapegoat, martyr, sacrifice, fatality.
⊞ offender, attacker.

victimize *v* **1** OPPRESS, persecute, discriminate against, pick on, prey on, bully, exploit. **2** CHEAT, deceive, defraud, swindle (*infml*), dupe, hoodwink, fool.

victorious *adj* conquering, champion, triumphant, winning, unbeaten, successful, prize-winning, top, first.
⊞ defeated, unsuccessful.

victory *n* conquest, win, triumph, success, superiority, mastery, vanquishment, subjugation, overcoming.
⊞ defeat, loss.

vie *v* strive, compete, contend, struggle, contest, fight, rival.

view *n* **1** OPINION, attitude, belief, judgement, estimation, feeling, sentiment, impression, notion.
2 SIGHT, scene, vision, vista, outlook, prospect, perspective, panorama, landscape. **3** SURVEY, inspection, examination, observation, scrutiny, scan. **4** GLIMPSE, look, sight, perception.
◇ *v* **1** CONSIDER, regard, contemplate, judge, think about, speculate.
2 OBSERVE, watch, see, examine, inspect, look at, scan, survey,

witness, perceive.

viewer n spectator, watcher, observer, onlooker.

viewpoint n attitude, position, perspective, slant, standpoint, stance, opinion, angle, feeling.

vigilant adj watchful, attentive, alert, observant, on one's guard, on the lookout, cautious, wide awake.
⊒ careless.

vigorous adj energetic, active, lively, healthy, strong, strenuous, robust, lusty, sound, vital, brisk, dynamic, forceful, forcible, powerful, stout, spirited, full-blooded, effective, efficient, enterprising, flourishing, intense.
⊒ weak, feeble.

vigour n energy, vitality, liveliness, health, robustness, stamina, strength, resilience, soundness, spirit, verve, gusto, activity, animation, power, potency, force, forcefulness, might, dash, dynamism.
⊒ weakness.

vile adj **1** a vile wretch: base, contemptible, debased, depraved, degenerate, bad, wicked, wretched, worthless, sinful, miserable, mean, evil, impure, corrupt, despicable, disgraceful, degrading, vicious, appalling. **2** a vile meal: disgusting, foul, nauseating, sickening, repulsive, repugnant, revolting, noxious, offensive, nasty, loathsome, horrid.
⊒ **1** pure, worthy. **2** pleasant, lovely.

villain n evil-doer, miscreant (fml), scoundrel, rogue, malefactor (fml), criminal, reprobate, rascal.

villainous adj wicked, bad, criminal, evil, sinful, vicious, notorious, cruel, inhuman, vile, depraved, disgraceful, terrible.
⊒ good.

vindicate v **1** CLEAR, acquit, excuse, exonerate, absolve, rehabilitate. **2** JUSTIFY, uphold, support, maintain, defend, establish, advocate, assert,

verify.

vindictive adj spiteful, unforgiving, implacable, vengeful, relentless, unrelenting, revengeful, resentful, punitive, venomous, malevolent, malicious.
⊒ forgiving.

vintage n year, period, era, epoch, generation, harvest, crop.
◇ adj choice, best, fine, prime, select, superior, rare, mature, old, ripe, classic, venerable, veteran.

violate v **1** CONTRAVENE, disobey, disregard, transgress, break, flout, infringe. **2** OUTRAGE, debauch, defile, rape, ravish, dishonour, desecrate, profane, invade.
⊒ **1** observe.

violence n **1** FORCE, strength, power, vehemence, might, intensity, ferocity, fierceness, severity, tumult, turbulence, wildness. **2** BRUTALITY, destructiveness, cruelty, bloodshed, murderousness, savagery, passion, fighting, frenzy, fury, hostilities.

violent adj **1** INTENSE, strong, severe, sharp, acute, extreme, harmful, destructive, devastating, injurious, powerful, painful, agonizing, forceful, forcible, harsh, ruinous, rough, vehement, tumultuous, turbulent. **2** CRUEL, brutal, aggressive, bloodthirsty, impetuous, hot-headed, headstrong, murderous, savage, wild, vicious, unrestrained, uncontrollable, ungovernable, passionate, furious, intemperate, maddened, outrageous, riotous, fiery.
⊒ **1** calm, moderate. **2** peaceful, gentle.

virgin n girl, maiden, celibate, vestal.
◇ adj virginal, chaste, intact, immaculate, maidenly, pure, modest, new, fresh, spotless, stainless, undefiled, untouched, unsullied.

virile adj man-like, masculine, male, manly, macho (infml), robust,

vigorous, potent, lusty, red-blooded, forceful, strong, rugged.
🔁 effeminate, impotent.

virtual *adj* effective, essential, practical, implied, implicit, potential.

virtually *adv* practically, in effect, almost, nearly, as good as, in essence.

virtue *n* 1 GOODNESS, morality, rectitude, uprightness, worthiness, righteousness, probity (*fml*), integrity, honour, incorruptibility, justice, high-mindedness, excellence. 2 QUALITY, worth, merit, advantage, asset, credit, strength.
🔁 1 vice, sleaze.

virtuoso *n* expert, master, maestro, prodigy, genius.

virtuous *adj* good, moral, righteous, upright, worthy, honourable, irreproachable, incorruptible, exemplary, unimpeachable, high-principled, blameless, clean-living, excellent, innocent.
🔁 immoral, vicious.

virulent *adj* 1 POISONOUS, toxic, venomous, deadly, lethal, malignant, injurious, pernicious, intense. 2 HOSTILE, resentful, spiteful, acrimonious, bitter, vicious, vindictive, malevolent, malicious.
🔁 1 harmless.

visible *adj* perceptible, discernible, detectable, apparent, noticeable, observable, distinguishable, discoverable, evident, unconcealed, undisguised, unmistakable, conspicuous, clear, obvious, manifest, open, palpable, plain, patent.
🔁 invisible, indiscernible, hidden.

vision *n* 1 APPARITION, hallucination, illusion, delusion, mirage, phantom, ghost, chimera, spectre, wraith. 2 IDEA, ideal, conception, insight, view, picture, image, fantasy, dream, daydream. 3 SIGHT, seeing, eyesight, perception, discernment, far-sightedness, foresight, penetration.

visionary *adj* idealistic, impractical, romantic, dreamy, unrealistic, utopian, unreal, fanciful, prophetic, speculative, unworkable, illusory, imaginary.
◇ *n* idealist, romantic, dreamer, daydreamer, fantasist, prophet, mystic, seer, utopian, rainbow-chaser, theorist.
🔁 pragmatist.

visit *v* call on, call in, stay with, stay at, drop in on (*infml*), stop by (*infml*), look in, look up, pop in (*infml*), see.
◇ *n* call, stay, stop, excursion, sojourn (*fml*).

visitor *n* caller, guest, company, tourist, holidaymaker.

vista *n* view, prospect, panorama, perspective, outlook, scene.

visualize *v* picture, envisage, imagine, conceive.

vital *adj* 1 CRITICAL, crucial, important, imperative, key, significant, basic, fundamental, essential, necessary, requisite, indispensable, urgent, life-or-death, decisive, forceful. 2 LIVING, alive, lively, life-giving, invigorating, spirited, vivacious, vibrant, vigorous, dynamic, animated, energetic, quickening (*fml*).
🔁 1 inessential, peripheral. 2 dead.

vitality *n* life, liveliness, animation, vigour, energy, vivacity, spirit, sparkle, exuberance, go (*infml*), strength, stamina.

vitriolic *adj* bitter, abusive, virulent, vicious, venomous, malicious, caustic, biting, sardonic, scathing, destructive.

vivacious *adj* lively, animated, spirited, high-spirited, effervescent, ebullient, cheerful, sparkling, bubbly, light-hearted.

vivid *adj* 1 BRIGHT, colourful, intense, strong, rich, vibrant, brilliant,

glowing, dazzling, vigorous, expressive, dramatic, flamboyant, animated, lively, lifelike, spirited. **2** MEMORABLE, powerful, graphic, clear, distinct, striking, sharp, realistic.
⊞ **1** colourless, dull. **2** vague.

vocal adj **1** SPOKEN, said, oral, uttered, voiced. **2** ARTICULATE, eloquent, expressive, noisy, clamorous, shrill, strident, outspoken, frank, forthright, plain-spoken.
⊞ **1** unspoken. **2** inarticulate.

vocation n calling, pursuit, career, métier, mission, profession, trade, employment, work, role, post, job, business, office.

vociferous adj noisy, vocal, clamorous, loud, obstreperous, strident, vehement, thundering, shouting.
⊞ quiet.

vogue n fashion, mode, style, craze, popularity, trend, prevalence, acceptance, custom, fad (infml), the latest (infml), the rage (infml), the thing (infml).

voice n **1** SPEECH, utterance, articulation, language, words, sound, tone, intonation, inflection, expression, mouthpiece, medium, instrument, organ. **2** SAY, vote, opinion, view, decision, option, will.
◇ v express, say, utter, air, articulate, speak of, verbalize, assert, convey, disclose, divulge, declare, enunciate.

void adj **1** EMPTY, emptied, free, unfilled, unoccupied, vacant, clear, bare, blank, drained. **2** ANNULLED, inoperative, invalid, cancelled, ineffective, futile, useless, vain, worthless.
⊞ **1** full. **2** valid.
◇ n emptiness, vacuity, vacuum, chasm, blank, blankness, space, lack, want, cavity, gap, hollow, opening.

volatile adj changeable, inconstant, unstable, variable, erratic,

temperamental, unsteady, unsettled, fickle, mercurial, unpredictable, capricious, restless, giddy, flighty, up and down (infml), lively.
⊞ constant, steady.

volley n barrage, bombardment, hail, shower, burst, blast, discharge, explosion.

voluble adj fluent, glib, articulate, loquacious (fml), talkative, forthcoming, garrulous.

volume n **1** BULK, size, capacity, dimensions, amount, mass, quantity, aggregate, amplitude, body. **2** BOOK, tome, publication.

voluminous adj roomy, capacious, ample, spacious, billowing, vast, bulky, huge, large.

voluntary adj **1** FREE, gratuitous, optional, spontaneous, unforced, willing, unpaid, honorary.
2 CONSCIOUS, deliberate, purposeful, intended, intentional, wilful.
⊞ **1** compulsory. **2** involuntary.

volunteer v offer, propose, put forward, present, suggest, step forward, advance.

voluptuous adj **1** SENSUAL, licentious, luxurious. **2** EROTIC, shapely, sexy (infml), seductive, provocative, enticing.

vomit v be sick, bring up, heave, retch, throw up (infml), puke (infml).

voracious adj insatiable, greedy, hungry, gluttonous, acquisitive, avid, devouring, ravenous, ravening, uncontrolled, unquenchable, edacious (fml), omnivorous, prodigious, rapacious.

vortex n whirlpool, maelstrom, eddy, whirlwind, whirl.

vote n ballot, poll, election, franchise, referendum.
◇ v elect, ballot, choose, opt, plump for, declare, return.

vouch for v guarantee, support, back, endorse, confirm, certify, affirm, assert, attest to, speak for, swear to, uphold.

vow v promise, pledge, swear, dedicate, devote, profess, consecrate, affirm.
◇ n promise, oath, pledge.

voyage n journey, trip, passage, expedition, crossing.

vulgar adj 1 TASTELESS, flashy, gaudy, tawdry, cheap and nasty (infml). 2 UNREFINED, uncouth, coarse, common, crude, ill-bred, impolite, indecorous. 3 INDECENT, suggestive, risqué, rude, indelicate. 4 ORDINARY,

general, popular, vernacular.
🗷 1 tasteful. 2 correct. 3 decent.

vulgarity n 1 CRUDENESS, indecency, crudity, dirtiness, rudeness, ribaldry, coarseness. 2 TASTELESSNESS, tawdriness, gaudiness, showiness, ostentation, garishness.
🗷 1 decency, politeness. 2 tastefulness.

vulnerable adj unprotected, exposed, defenceless, susceptible, weak, sensitive, wide open.
🗷 protected, strong.

Ww

wad *n* chunk, plug, roll, ball, wodge (*infml*), lump, hunk, mass, block.

waddle *v* toddle, totter, wobble, sway, rock, shuffle.

waffle *v* jabber, prattle, blather, rabbit (on) (*infml*), witter (on) (*infml*).
◇ *n* blather, prattle, wordiness, padding, nonsense, gobbledegook (*infml*), hot air (*infml*).

waft *v* drift, float, blow, transport, transmit.
◇ *n* breath, puff, draught, current, breeze, scent, whiff.

wag *v* shake, waggle, wave, sway, swing, bob, nod, wiggle, oscillate, flutter, vibrate, quiver, rock.

wage *n* pay, fee, earnings, salary, wage packet, payment, stipend, remuneration, emolument (*fml*), allowance, reward, hire, compensation, recompense.
◇ *v* carry on, conduct, engage in, undertake, practise, pursue.

waif *n* orphan, stray, foundling.

wail *v* moan, cry, howl, lament, weep, complain, yowl (*infml*).
◇ *n* moan, cry, howl, lament, complaint, weeping.

wait *v* delay, linger, hesitate, hold back, pause, hang around, hang fire, remain, rest, stay.
⊠ proceed, go ahead.
◇ *n* hold-up, hesitation, delay, interval, pause, halt.

waive *v* renounce, relinquish, forgo, resign, surrender, yield.

wake¹ *v* **1** RISE, get up, arise, rouse, come to, bring round. **2** STIMULATE, stir, activate, arouse, animate, excite, fire, galvanize.
⊠ **1** sleep.
◇ *n* funeral, deathwatch, vigil, watch.

wake² *n* trail, track, path, aftermath, backwash, wash, rear, train, waves.

walk *v* **1** STEP, stride, pace, proceed, advance, march, plod, tramp, traipse, trek, trudge, saunter, amble, stroll, tread, hike, promenade, move, hoof it. **2** ACCOMPANY, escort.
◇ *n* **1** *he has an odd walk*: carriage, gait, step, pace, stride. **2** *go for a walk*: stroll, amble, ramble, saunter, march, hike, tramp, trek, traipse, trudge, trail. **3** *a tree-lined walk*: footpath, path, walkway, avenue, pathway, promenade, alley, esplanade, lane, pavement, sidewalk.

walker *n* pedestrian, rambler, hiker.

walk-out *n* strike, stoppage, industrial action, protest, rebellion, revolt.

walk-over *n* pushover (*infml*), doddle (*infml*), child's play, piece of cake (*infml*), cinch (*infml*).

wall *n* **1** PARTITION, screen, panel, divider, fence, hedge, enclosure, membrane, bulkhead. **2** FORTIFICATION, barricade, rampart, parapet, stockade, embankment, bulwark, palisade. **3** OBSTACLE, obstruction, barrier, block, impediment.

wallow *v* **1** *wallow in mud*: loll, lie, roll, wade, welter, lurch, flounder, splash. **2** *wallow in nostalgia*: indulge, luxuriate, relish, revel, bask, enjoy, glory, delight.

wand n rod, baton, staff, stick, sprig, mace, sceptre, twig.

wander v 1 ROAM, rove, ramble, meander, saunter, stroll, prowl, drift, range, stray, straggle. 2 DIGRESS, diverge, deviate, depart, go astray, swerve, veer, err. 3 RAMBLE, rave, babble, gibber.
◇ n excursion, ramble, stroll, saunter, meander, prowl, cruise.

wanderer n itinerant, traveller, voyager, drifter, rover, rambler, stroller, stray, straggler, ranger, nomad, gypsy, vagrant, vagabond, rolling stone (infml).

wane v diminish, decrease, decline, weaken, subside, fade, dwindle, ebb, lessen, abate, sink, drop, taper off, dim, droop, contract, shrink, fail, wither.
⊡ increase, wax.

wangle v manipulate, arrange, contrive, engineer, fix, scheme, manoeuvre, work, pull off, manage, fiddle (infml).

want v 1 DESIRE, wish, crave, covet, fancy, long for, pine for, yearn for, hunger for, thirst for. 2 NEED, require, demand, lack, miss, call for.
◇ n 1 DESIRE, demand, longing, requirement, wish, need, appetite. 2 LACK, dearth, insufficiency, deficiency, shortage, inadequacy. 3 POVERTY, privation, destitution.

wanting adj 1 ABSENT, missing, lacking, short, insufficient. 2 INADEQUATE, imperfect, faulty, defective, substandard, poor, deficient, unsatisfactory.
⊡ 1 sufficient. 2 adequate.

wanton adj malicious, immoral, shameless, arbitrary, unprovoked, unjustifiable, unrestrained, rash, reckless, wild.

war n warfare, hostilities, fighting, battle, combat, conflict, strife, struggle, bloodshed, contest, contention, enmity.

⊡ peace, ceasefire.

Types of war include: biological warfare, chemical warfare, civil war, cold war, germ warfare, guerrilla warfare, holy war, hot war, jihad, jungle warfare, limited war, nuclear war, private war, total war, trade war, turf war, war of attrition, war of nerves, world war.

Famous wars include: American Civil War (Second American Revolution), American Revolution (War of Independence), Boer War, Crimean War, Crusades, English Civil War, Falklands War, Franco-Prussian War, Gulf War, Hundred Years War, Indian Wars, Iran-Iraq War, Iraq War, Korean War, Mexican War, Napoleonic Wars, Opium Wars, Peasants' War, Russo-Finnish War (Winter War), Russo-Japanese War, Russo-Turkish Wars, Seven Years War, Six-Day War, Spanish-American War, Spanish Civil War, Thirty Years War, Vietnam War, War of 1812, War of the Pacific, Wars of the Roses, World War I (the Great War), World War II.

◇ v wage war, fight, take up arms, battle, clash, combat, strive, skirmish, struggle, contest, contend.

ward n 1 ROOM, apartment, unit. 2 DIVISION, area, district, quarter, precinct, zone. 3 CHARGE, dependant, protégé(e), minor.
• **ward off** avert, fend off, deflect, parry, repel, stave off, thwart, beat off, forestall, evade, turn away, block, avoid.

warden n keeper, custodian, guardian, warder, caretaker, curator, ranger, steward, watchman, superintendent, administrator, janitor.

warder n jailer, keeper, prison

officer, guard, wardress, custodian.

wardrobe n 1 CUPBOARD, closet.
2 CLOTHES, outfit, attire.

warehouse n store, storehouse,
depot, depository, repository,
stockroom, entrepot.

wares n goods, merchandise,
commodities, stock, products,
produce, stuff.

warfare n war, fighting, hostilities,
battle, arms, combat, strife, struggle,
passage of arms, contest, conflict,
contention, discord, blows.
⊞ peace.

warlike adj belligerent, aggressive,
bellicose, pugnacious, combative,
bloodthirsty, warmongering,
militaristic, hostile, antagonistic,
unfriendly.
⊞ friendly, peaceable.

warm adj 1 HEATED, tepid, lukewarm.
2 ARDENT, passionate, fervent,
vehement, earnest, zealous. 3 warm
colours: rich, intense, mellow,
cheerful. 4 FRIENDLY, amiable, cordial,
affable, kindly, genial, hospitable,
hearty, sympathetic, affectionate,
tender. 5 FINE, sunny, balmy,
temperate, close.
⊞ 1 cool. 2 indifferent. 3 cold.
4 unfriendly. 5 cool.
◇ v 1 HEAT (UP), reheat, melt, thaw.
2 ANIMATE, interest, please, delight,
stimulate, stir, rouse, excite.
⊞ 1 cool.

warmth n 1 WARMNESS, heat.
2 FRIENDLINESS, affection, cordiality,
tenderness. 3 ARDOUR, enthusiasm,
passion, fervour, zeal, eagerness.
⊞ 1 coldness. 2 unfriendliness.
3 indifference.

warn v caution, alert, admonish,
advise, notify, counsel, put on one's
guard, inform, tip off .

warning n 1 CAUTION, alert,
admonition, advice, notification,
notice, advance notice, counsel, hint,
lesson, alarm, threat, tip-off. 2 OMEN,

augury, premonition, presage, sign,
signal, portent.

warp v twist, bend, contort, deform,
distort, kink, misshape, pervert,
corrupt, deviate.
⊞ straighten.
◇ n twist, bend, contortion, kink,
deformation, distortion, bias,
irregularity, turn, defect, deviation,
quirk, perversion.

warrant n authorization, authority,
sanction, permit, permission, licence,
guarantee, warranty, security, pledge,
commission, voucher.
◇ v 1 GUARANTEE, pledge, certify,
assure, declare, affirm, vouch for,
answer for, underwrite, uphold,
endorse. 2 AUTHORIZE, entitle,
empower, sanction, permit, allow,
license, justify, excuse, approve, call
for, commission, necessitate, require.

wary adj cautious, guarded,
careful, chary, on one's guard, on
the lookout, prudent, distrustful,
suspicious, heedful, attentive, alert,
watchful, vigilant, wide awake.
⊞ unwary, careless, heedless.

wash v 1 CLEAN, cleanse, launder,
scrub, swab down, rinse, swill.
2 BATHE, bath, shower, douche,
shampoo.
◇ n 1 CLEANING, cleansing, bath,
bathe, laundry, laundering, scrub,
shower, shampoo, washing, rinse.
2 FLOW, sweep, wave, swell.

wash-out n failure, disaster,
disappointment, fiasco, flop (infml),
debacle.
⊞ success, triumph.

waste v 1 SQUANDER, misspend,
misuse, fritter away, dissipate, lavish,
spend, throw away, blow (infml).
2 CONSUME, erode, exhaust, drain,
destroy, spoil.
⊞ 1 economize. 2 preserve.
◇ n 1 SQUANDERING, dissipation,
prodigality, wastefulness,
extravagance, loss. 2 MISAPPLICATION,
misuse, abuse, neglect. 3 RUBBISH,

refuse, trash, garbage, leftovers, debris, dregs, effluent, litter, scrap, slops, offscourings, dross.
◇ *adj* **1** USELESS, worthless, unwanted, unused, leftover, superfluous, supernumerary, extra. **2** BARREN, desolate, empty, uninhabited, bare, devastated, uncultivated, unprofitable, wild, dismal, dreary.

wasted *adj* **1** UNNECESSARY, needless, useless. **2** EMACIATED, withered, shrivelled, shrunken, gaunt, washed-out, spent.
⊟ **1** necessary. **2** robust.

wasteful *adj* extravagant, spendthrift, prodigal, profligate, uneconomical, thriftless, unthrifty, ruinous, lavish, improvident.
⊟ economical, thrifty.

wasteland *n* wilderness, desert, barrenness, waste, wilds, void.

watch *v* **1** OBSERVE, see, look at, regard, note, notice, mark, stare at, peer at, gaze at, view. **2** GUARD, look after, keep an eye on, mind, protect, superintend, take care of, keep. **3** PAY ATTENTION, be careful, take heed, look out.
◇ *n* **1** TIMEPIECE, wristwatch, clock, chronometer. **2** VIGILANCE, watchfulness, vigil, observation, surveillance, notice, lookout, heed, attention, alertness, inspection, supervision.
• **watch out** notice, be vigilant, look out, keep one's eyes open.
• **watch over** guard, protect, stand guard over, keep an eye on, look after, mind, shield, defend, shelter, preserve.

watchdog *n* **1** GUARD DOG, house-dog. **2** MONITOR, inspector, scrutineer, vigilante, ombudsman, guardian, custodian, protector.

watcher *n* spectator, observer, onlooker, looker-on, viewer, lookout, spy, witness.

watchful *adj* vigilant, attentive,

heedful, observant, alert, guarded, on one's guard, wide awake, suspicious, wary, chary, cautious.
⊟ unobservant, inattentive.

watchman *n* guard, security guard, caretaker, custodian.

water *n* rain, sea, ocean, lake, river, stream.
◇ *v* wet, moisten, dampen, soak, spray, sprinkle, irrigate, drench, flood, hose.
⊟ dry out, parch.
• **water down** dilute, thin, water, weaken, adulterate, mix, tone down, soften, qualify.

waterfall *n* fall, cascade, chute, cataract, torrent.

watertight *adj* **1** WATERPROOF, sound, hermetic. **2** IMPREGNABLE, unassailable, airtight, flawless, foolproof, firm, incontrovertible.
⊟ **1** leaky.

watery *adj* **1** LIQUID, fluid, moist, wet, damp. **2** WEAK, watered-down, diluted, insipid, tasteless, thin, runny, soggy, flavourless, washy, wishy-washy (*infml*).
⊟ **1** dry.

wave *v* **1** BECKON, gesture, gesticulate, indicate, sign, signal, direct. **2** BRANDISH, flourish, flap, flutter, shake, sway, swing, waft, quiver, ripple.
◇ *n* **1** BREAKER, roller, billow, ripple, tidal wave, wavelet, undulation, white horse (*infml*). **2** SURGE, sweep, swell, upsurge, groundswell, current, drift, movement, rush, tendency, trend, stream, flood, outbreak, rash.

waver *v* **1** VACILLATE, falter, hesitate, dither, fluctuate, vary, seesaw. **2** OSCILLATE, shake, sway, wobble, tremble, totter, rock.
⊟ **1** decide.

wavy *adj* undulating, rippled, curly, curvy, ridged, sinuous, winding, zigzag.

wax *v* grow, increase, rise, swell,

develop, enlarge, expand, magnify, mount, fill out, become.
🔁 decrease, wane, diminish.

way n 1 METHOD, approach, manner, technique, procedure, means, mode, system, fashion. 2 CUSTOM, practice, habit, usage, characteristic, idiosyncrasy, trait, style, conduct, nature. 3 DIRECTION, course, route, path, road, channel, access, avenue, track, passage, highway, street, thoroughfare, lane.
• **by the way** incidentally, in passing.

wayward adj wilful, capricious, perverse, contrary, changeable, fickle, unpredictable, stubborn, self-willed, unmanageable, headstrong, obstinate, disobedient, rebellious, insubordinate, intractable, unruly, incorrigible.
🔁 tractable, good-natured.

weak adj 1 FEEBLE, frail, infirm, unhealthy, sickly, delicate, debilitated, exhausted, fragile, flimsy. 2 VULNERABLE, unprotected, unguarded, defenceless, exposed. 3 POWERLESS, impotent, spineless, cowardly, indecisive, ineffectual, irresolute, poor, lacking, lame, inadequate, defective, deficient, inconclusive, unconvincing, untenable. 4 FAINT, slight, low, soft, muffled, dull, imperceptible. 5 INSIPID, tasteless, watery, thin, diluted, runny.
🔁 1 strong. 2 secure. 3 powerful. 4 strong. 5 strong.

weaken v 1 ENFEEBLE, exhaust, debilitate, sap, undermine, dilute, diminish, lower, lessen, reduce, moderate, mitigate, temper, soften (up), thin, water down. 2 TIRE, flag, fail, give way, droop, fade, abate, ease up, dwindle.
🔁 1 strengthen.

weakness n 1 FEEBLENESS, debility, infirmity, impotence, frailty, powerlessness, vulnerability. 2 FAULT, failing, flaw, shortcoming, blemish,

defect, deficiency, foible. 3 LIKING, inclination, fondness, penchant, passion, soft spot (infml).
🔁 1 strength. 2 strength. 3 dislike.

wealth n 1 MONEY, cash, riches, assets, affluence, prosperity, funds, mammon, fortune, capital, opulence, means, substance, resources, goods, possessions, property, estate. 2 ABUNDANCE, plenty, bounty, fullness, profusion, store.
🔁 1 poverty.

wealthy adj rich, prosperous, well-off, affluent, moneyed, opulent, comfortable, well-heeled, well-to-do, flush (infml), loaded (sl), rolling in it (infml).
🔁 poor, impoverished.

weapon
___

Weapons include: gun, airgun, pistol, revolver, automatic, Colt®, Luger®, Magnum®, Mauser, six-gun, six-shooter, rifle, air rifle, carbine, shotgun, blunderbuss, musket, elephant gun, machinegun, kalashnikov, submachine-gun, Uzi, tommy gun, sten gun, Bren gun, cannon, field gun, gatling gun, howitzer, mortar, turret gun; knife, bowie knife, flick-knife, stiletto, dagger, dirk, poniard, sword, épée, foil, rapier, sabre, scimitar, bayonet, broadsword, claymore, lance, spear, pike, machete; bomb, atom bomb, H-bomb, cluster bomb, depth charge, incendiary bomb, Mills bomb, mine, landmine, napalm bomb, time bomb; bow and arrow, longbow, crossbow, blowpipe, catapult, boomerang, sling, harpoon, bolas; rocket, bazooka, ballistic missile, cruise missile, Exocet®, Scud, torpedo, hand grenade, flame-thrower; battle-axe, poleaxe, halberd, tomahawk, cosh, cudgel, knuckleduster, shillelagh, truncheon; gas, CS gas, mustard gas, tear gas.

wear v 1 DRESS IN, have on, put on, don, sport, carry, bear, display, show. 2 DETERIORATE, erode, corrode, consume, fray, rub, abrade, waste, grind.
◇ n 1 CLOTHES, clothing, dress, garments, outfit, costume, attire. 2 DETERIORATION, erosion, corrosion, wear and tear, friction, abrasion.
• **wear off** decrease, abate, dwindle, diminish, subside, wane, weaken, fade, lessen, ebb, peter out, disappear.
⊞ increase.
• **wear out 1** EXHAUST, fatigue, tire (out), enervate, sap. 2 DETERIORATE, wear through, erode, impair, consume, fray.

wearing adj exhausting, fatiguing, tiresome, tiring, wearisome, trying, taxing, oppressive, irksome, exasperating.
⊞ refreshing.

weary adj tired, exhausted, fatigued, sleepy, worn out, drained, drowsy, jaded, all in (infml), done in (infml), fagged out (infml), knackered (infml), dead-beat (infml), dog-tired (infml), whacked (infml).
⊞ refreshed.

wearying adj tiring, fatiguing, exhausting, wearisome, wearing, taxing, trying.
⊞ refreshing.

weather n climate, conditions, temperature.

Types of weather include: breeze, wind, squall, tornado, typhoon, monsoon, cyclone, cloud, mist, dew, fog, smog, rain, drizzle, shower, sunshine, heat wave, haze, drought, storm, thunder, lightning, frost, hoar frost, hail, sleet, snow, snowstorm, ice, black ice, thaw.

◇ v 1 ENDURE, survive, live through, come through, ride out, rise above, stick out, withstand, surmount, stand, brave, overcome, resist, pull through, suffer. 2 EXPOSE, toughen, season, harden.
⊞ 1 succumb.

weave v 1 INTERLACE, lace, plait, braid, intertwine, spin, knit, entwine, intercross, fuse, merge, unite. 2 CREATE, compose, construct, contrive, put together, fabricate. 3 WIND, twist, zigzag, criss-cross.

web n network, net, netting, lattice, mesh, webbing, interlacing, weft, snare, tangle, trap.

wedding n marriage, matrimony, nuptials (fml), wedlock, bridal.
⊞ divorce.

wedge n lump, block, chunk, wodge, chock.
◇ v jam, cram, pack, ram, squeeze, stuff, push, lodge, block, thrust, crowd, force.

weedy adj thin, skinny, puny, scrawny, undersized, weak, feeble, frail, weak-kneed, insipid, wet (infml), wimpish (infml), wimpy (infml).
⊞ strong.

weep v cry, sob, moan, lament, wail, mourn, grieve, bawl, blubber, snivel, whimper, blub (infml).
⊞ rejoice.

weigh v 1 BEAR DOWN, oppress. 2 CONSIDER, contemplate, evaluate, meditate on, mull over, ponder, think over, examine, reflect on, deliberate.
• **weigh down** oppress, overload, load, burden, bear down, weigh upon, press down, get down (infml), depress, afflict, trouble, worry.
⊞ lighten, hearten.
• **weigh up** assess, examine, size up, balance, consider, contemplate, deliberate, mull over, ponder, think over, discuss, chew over (infml).

weight n 1 HEAVINESS, gravity, burden, load, pressure, mass, force, ballast, tonnage, poundage.

2 IMPORTANCE, significance, substance, consequence, impact, moment, influence, value, authority, clout (*infml*), power, preponderance, consideration.
1 lightness.
◇ *v* **1** LOAD, weigh down, oppress, handicap. **2** BIAS, unbalance, slant, prejudice.

weighty *adj* **1** HEAVY, burdensome, substantial, bulky. **2** IMPORTANT, significant, consequential, crucial, critical, momentous, serious, grave, solemn. **3** DEMANDING, difficult, exacting, taxing.
1 light. **2** unimportant.

weird *adj* strange, uncanny, bizarre, eerie, creepy, supernatural, unnatural, ghostly, freakish, queer, mysterious, grotesque, spooky (*infml*), far-out (*infml*), way-out (*infml*).
**normal, usual.

welcome *adj* acceptable, desirable, pleasing, pleasant, agreeable, gratifying, appreciated, delightful, refreshing.
**unwelcome.
◇ *n* reception, greeting, salutation (*infml*), acceptance, hospitality, red carpet (*infml*).
◇ *v* greet, hail, receive, salute, meet, accept, approve of, embrace.
**reject, snub.

weld *v* fuse, unite, bond, join, solder, bind, connect, seal, link, cement.
**separate.

welfare *n* wellbeing, health, good, prosperity, happiness, benefit, advantage, interest, profit, success.

well[1] *n* spring, wellspring, fountain, fount, source, reservoir, wellhead, waterhole.
◇ *v* flow, spring, surge, gush, stream, brim over, jet, spout, spurt, swell, pour, flood, ooze, run, trickle, rise, seep.

well[2] *adv* rightly, correctly, properly, skilfully, ably, expertly, successfully, adequately, sufficiently, suitably, easily, satisfactorily, thoroughly, greatly, fully, completely, agreeably, pleasantly, happily, kindly, favourably, splendidly, substantially, considerably, comfortably, readily, carefully, clearly, highly, deeply, justly.
**badly, inadequately, incompetently, wrongly.
◇ *adj* **1** HEALTHY, in good health, fit, able-bodied, sound, robust, strong, thriving, flourishing. **2** SATISFACTORY, right, all right, good, pleasing, proper, agreeable, fine, lucky, fortunate.
1 ill. **2** bad.

well-balanced *adj* **1** RATIONAL, reasonable, level-headed, well-adjusted, stable, sensible, sane, sound, sober, together (*sl*). **2** SYMMETRICAL, even, harmonious.
1 unbalanced. **2** asymmetrical.

wellbeing *n* welfare, happiness, comfort, good.

well-bred *adj* well-mannered, polite, well-brought-up, mannerly, courteous, civil, refined, cultivated, cultured, genteel.
**ill-bred.

well-dressed *adj* smart, well-groomed, elegant, fashionable, chic, stylish, neat, trim, spruce, tidy.
**badly dressed, scruffy.

well-known *adj* famous, renowned, celebrated, famed, eminent, notable, noted, illustrious, familiar.
**unknown.

well-off *adj* rich, wealthy, affluent, prosperous, well-to-do, moneyed, thriving, successful, comfortable, fortunate.
**poor, badly-off.

well-thought-of *adj* respected, highly regarded, esteemed, admired, honoured, revered.
**despised.

well-worn adj time-worn, stale, tired, trite, overused, unoriginal, hackneyed, commonplace, stereotyped, threadbare, corny (infml).
⊜ original.

wet adj 1 DAMP, moist, soaked, soaking, sodden, saturated, soggy, sopping, watery, waterlogged, drenched, dripping, spongy, dank, clammy. 2 RAINING, rainy, showery, teeming, pouring, drizzling, humid. 3 (infml) WEAK, feeble, weedy, wimpish (infml), wimpy (infml), spineless, soft, ineffectual, namby-pamby, irresolute, timorous.
⊜ 1 dry. 2 dry. 3 strong.
◇ n wetness, moisture, damp, dampness, liquid, water, clamminess, condensation, humidity, rain, drizzle.
⊜ dryness.
◇ v moisten, damp, dampen, soak, saturate, drench, steep, water, irrigate, spray, splash, sprinkle, imbue, dip.
⊜ dry.

whack v hit, strike, smack, thrash, slap, beat, bash (infml), bang, cuff, thump, box, buffet, rap, wallop (infml), belt (infml), clobber (infml), clout (infml), sock (infml).
◇ n smack, slap, blow, hit, rap, stroke, thump, cuff, box, bang, clout (infml), bash (infml), wallop (infml).

wharf n dock, quay, quayside, jetty, landing-stage, dockyard, marina, pier.

wheedle v cajole, coax, persuade, inveigle, charm, flatter, entice, court, draw.
⊜ force.

wheel n turn, revolution, circle, rotation, gyration, pivot, roll, spin, twirl, whirl.
◇ v turn, rotate, circle, gyrate, orbit, spin, twirl, whirl, swing, roll, revolve, swivel.

wheeze v pant, gasp, cough, hiss, rasp, whistle.

whereabouts n location, position, place, situation, site, vicinity.

whet v 1 SHARPEN, hone, file, grind. 2 STIMULATE, stir, rouse, arouse, provoke, kindle, quicken, incite, awaken, increase.
⊜ 1 blunt. 2 dampen.

whiff n breath, puff, hint, trace, blast, draught, odour, smell, aroma, sniff, scent, reek, stink, stench.

whim n fancy, caprice, notion, quirk, freak, humour, conceit, fad, vagary, urge.

whimper v cry, sob, weep, snivel, whine, grizzle, mewl, moan, whinge (infml).
◇ n sob, snivel, whine, moan.

whimsical adj fanciful, capricious, playful, impulsive, eccentric, funny, droll, curious, queer, unusual, weird, odd, peculiar, quaint, dotty (infml).

whine n 1 CRY, sob, whimper, moan, wail. 2 COMPLAINT, grumble, grouse, gripe (infml), grouch (infml).
◇ v 1 CRY, sob, whimper, grizzle, moan, wail. 2 COMPLAIN, carp, grumble, whinge (infml), gripe (infml), grouch (infml).

whip v 1 BEAT, flog, lash, flagellate, scourge, birch, cane, strap, thrash, punish, chastise, discipline, castigate (fml). 2 PULL, jerk, snatch, whisk, dash, dart, rush, tear, flit, flash, fly. 3 GOAD, drive, spur, push, urge, stir, rouse, agitate, incite, provoke, instigate.
◇ n lash, scourge, switch, birch, cane, horsewhip, riding-crop, cat-o'-nine-tails.

whirl v swirl, spin, turn, twist, twirl, pivot, pirouette, swivel, wheel, rotate, revolve, reel, roll, gyrate, circle.
◇ n 1 SPIN, twirl, twist, gyration, revolution, pirouette, swirl, turn, wheel, rotation, circle, reel, roll. 2 CONFUSION, daze, flurry, commotion, agitation, bustle,

hubbub, hurly-burly, giddiness, tumult, uproar.

whirlwind *n* tornado, cyclone, vortex.
◇ *adj* hasty, impulsive, quick, rapid, speedy, swift, lightning, headlong, impetuous, rash.
☒ deliberate, slow.

whisk *v* 1 WHIP, beat. 2 DART, dash, rush, hurry, speed, hasten, race. 3 BRUSH, sweep, flick, wipe, twitch.

whisper *v* 1 MURMUR, mutter, hiss, mumble, breathe, rustle, sigh. 2 HINT, intimate, insinuate, gossip, divulge.
☒ 1 shout.
◇ *n* 1 MURMUR, undertone, sigh, hiss, rustle. 2 HINT, suggestion, suspicion, breath, whiff, rumour, report, innuendo, insinuation, trace, tinge, soupçon, buzz.

white *adj* 1 PALE, pallid, wan, ashen, colourless, anaemic, pasty. 2 LIGHT, snowy, milky, creamy, ivory, hoary, silver, grey. 3 PURE, immaculate, spotless, stainless, undefiled.
☒ 1 ruddy. 2 dark. 3 defiled.

whiten *v* bleach, blanch, whitewash, pale, fade.
☒ blacken, darken.

whittle *v* 1 CARVE, cut, scrape, shave, trim, pare, hew, shape. 2 ERODE, eat away, wear away, diminish, consume, reduce, undermine.

whole *adj* 1 COMPLETE, entire, integral, full, total, unabridged, uncut, undivided, unedited. 2 INTACT, unharmed, undamaged, unbroken, inviolate, perfect, in one piece, mint, unhurt. 3 WELL, healthy, fit, sound, strong.
☒ 1 partial. 2 damaged. 3 ill.
◇ *n* total, aggregate, sum total, entirety, all, fullness, totality, ensemble, entity, unit, lot, piece, everything.
☒ part.
• **on the whole** generally, mostly, in general, generally speaking, as a rule, for the most part, all in all, all things considered, by and large.

whole-hearted *adj* unreserved, unstinting, unqualified, passionate, enthusiastic, earnest, committed, dedicated, devoted, heartfelt, emphatic, warm, sincere, unfeigned, genuine, complete, true, real, zealous.
☒ half-hearted.

wholesale *adj* comprehensive, far-reaching, extensive, sweeping, wide-ranging, mass, broad, outright, total, massive, indiscriminate.
☒ partial.

wholesome *adj* 1 *wholesome food*: healthy, hygienic, salubrious, sanitary, nutritious, nourishing, beneficial, salutary, invigorating, bracing. 2 *wholesome entertainment*: moral, decent, clean, proper, improving, edifying, uplifting, pure, virtuous, righteous, honourable, respectable.
☒ 1 unhealthy. 2 unwholesome.

wholly *adv* completely, entirely, fully, purely, absolutely, totally, utterly, comprehensively, altogether, perfectly, thoroughly, all, exclusively, only.
☒ partly.

wicked *adj* 1 EVIL, sinful, immoral, depraved, corrupt, vicious, unprincipled, iniquitous, heinous, debased, abominable, ungodly, unrighteous, shameful. 2 BAD, unpleasant, harmful, offensive, vile, worthless, difficult, dreadful, distressing, awful, atrocious, severe, intense, nasty, injurious, troublesome, terrible, foul, fierce. 3 NAUGHTY, mischievous, roguish.
☒ 1 good, upright. 2 harmless.

wide *adj* 1 BROAD, roomy, spacious, vast, immense. 2 DILATED, expanded, full. 3 EXTENSIVE, wide-ranging, comprehensive, far-reaching, general. 4 LOOSE, baggy. 5 OFF-TARGET, distant, remote.
☒ 1 narrow. 3 restricted. 5 near.

◇ *adv* **1** ASTRAY, off course, off target, off the mark. **2** FULLY, completely, all the way.
⊞ 1 on target.

widen *v* distend, dilate, expand, extend, spread, stretch, enlarge, broaden.
⊞ narrow.

widespread *adj* extensive, prevalent, rife, general, sweeping, universal, wholesale, far-reaching, unlimited, broad, common, pervasive, far-flung.
⊞ limited.

width *n* breadth, diameter, compass, thickness, span, scope, range, measure, girth, beam, amplitude, extent, reach.

wield *v* **1** *wield a weapon*: brandish, flourish, swing, wave, handle, ply, manage, manipulate. **2** *wield power*: have, hold, possess, employ, exert, exercise, use, utilize, maintain, command.

wife *n* partner, spouse, mate, better half (*infml*), bride.

wild *adj* **1** UNTAMED, undomesticated, feral, savage, barbarous, primitive, uncivilized, natural, ferocious, fierce. **2** UNCULTIVATED, desolate, waste, uninhabited. **3** UNRULY, unrestrained, unmanageable, violent, turbulent, rowdy, lawless, disorderly, riotous, boisterous. **4** STORMY, tempestuous, rough, blustery, choppy. **5** UNTIDY, unkempt, messy, dishevelled, tousled. **6** RECKLESS, rash, imprudent, foolish, foolhardy, impracticable, irrational, outrageous, preposterous, wayward, extravagant. **7** MAD, crazy (*infml*), frenzied, distraught, demented.
⊞ 1 civilized, tame. **2** cultivated. **3** restrained. **4** calm. **5** tidy. **6** sensible. **7** sane.

wilderness *n* desert, wasteland, waste, wilds, jungle.

wiles *n* trick, stratagem, ruse,

ploy, device, contrivance, guile, manoeuvre, subterfuge, cunning, dodge (*infml*), deceit, cheating, trickery, fraud, craftiness, chicanery.
⊞ guilelessness.

wilful *adj* **1** DELIBERATE, conscious, intentional, voluntary, premeditated. **2** SELF-WILLED, obstinate, stubborn, pigheaded, obdurate, intransigent, inflexible, perverse, wayward, contrary.
⊞ 1 unintentional. **2** good-natured.

will *n* **1** VOLITION, choice, option, preference, decision, discretion. **2** WISH, desire, inclination, feeling, fancy, disposition, mind. **3** PURPOSE, resolve, resolution, determination, willpower, aim, intention, command.
◇ *v* **1** WANT, desire, choose, compel, command, decree, order, ordain. **2** BEQUEATH, leave, hand down, pass on, transfer, confer, dispose of.

willing *adj* disposed, inclined, agreeable, compliant, ready, prepared, consenting, content, amenable, biddable, pleased, well-disposed, favourable, happy, eager, enthusiastic.
⊞ unwilling, disinclined, reluctant.

wilt *v* droop, sag, wither, shrivel, flop, flag, dwindle, weaken, diminish, fail, fade, languish, ebb, sink, wane.
⊞ perk up.

wily *adj* shrewd, cunning, scheming, artful, crafty, foxy, intriguing, tricky, underhand, shifty, deceitful, deceptive, astute, sly, guileful, designing, crooked, fly (*infml*).
⊞ guileless.

win *v* **1** BE VICTORIOUS, triumph, succeed, prevail, overcome, conquer, come first, carry off, finish first. **2** GAIN, acquire, achieve, attain, accomplish, receive, procure, secure, obtain, get, earn, catch, net.
⊞ 1 fail, lose.
◇ *n* victory, triumph, conquest, success, mastery.
⊞ defeat.

• **win over** persuade, prevail upon, convince, influence, convert, sway, talk round, charm, allure, attract.

wind[1] *n* air, breeze, draught, gust, puff, breath, air current, blast, current.

Types of wind include:
anticyclone, austral wind, berg wind, bise, bora, Cape doctor, chinook, cyclone, east wind, El Niño, etesian, Favonian wind, föhn, gale, gregale, harmattan, hurricane, khamsin, levanter, libeccio, mistral, monsoon, north wind, nor'wester, pampero, prevailing wind, samiel, simoom, sirocco, southerly, trade wind, tramontana, westerly, whirlwind, williwaw, willy-willy, zephyr, zonda. *see also* **storm**.

---

wind[2] *v* coil, twist, turn, curl, curve, bend, loop, spiral, zigzag, twine, encircle, furl, deviate, meander, ramble, wreath, roll, reel.
• **wind down 1** SLOW (DOWN), slacken off, lessen, reduce, subside, diminish, dwindle, decline. **2** RELAX, unwind, quieten down, ease up, calm down.
⊜ **1** increase.
• **wind up 1** CLOSE (DOWN), end, conclude, terminate, finalize, finish, liquidate. **2** END UP, finish up, find oneself, settle. **3** (*infml*) ANNOY, irritate, disconcert, fool, trick, kid (*infml*).
⊜ **1** begin.

windfall *n* bonanza, godsend, jackpot, treasure-trove, stroke of luck, find.

window *n* pane, light, opening, skylight, rose window, casement, oriel, dormer, astragal.

windy *adj* breezy, blowy, blustery, squally, windswept, stormy, tempestuous, gusty.
⊜ calm.

wine

Types of wine include: alcohol-free, dry, brut, sec, demi-sec, sweet, sparkling, table wine, house wine; red wine, house red (*infml*), white wine, house white (*infml*), rosé, blush wine, fortified wine, mulled wine, tonic wine, vintage wine, plonk (*infml*); sherry, dry sherry, fino, medium sherry, amontillado, sweet sherry, oloroso; port, ruby, tawny, white port, vintage port.

Varieties of wine include: Asti, Auslese, Beaujolais, Beaune, Bordeaux, Burgundy, Cabernet Sauvignon, Carmenère, cava, Chablis, Chambertin, champagne, chardonnay, Chianti, claret, Côtes du Rhône, Dão, Fitou, frascati, Gewörztraminer, Graves, Grenache, hock, Kabinett, Lambrusco, Liebfraumilch, Mâcon, Madeira, Malaga, Malbec, Marsala, Médoc, Merlot, Moselle, Muscadet, muscatel, nebbiolo, Niersteiner, Piesporter, retsina, Riesling, Rioja, Sangiovese, Sauternes, Sekt, semillon, Shiraz, Soave, Spätlese, Tarragona, Valpolicella, vinho verde, Vouvray, Zinfandel.

---

wing *n* branch, arm, section, faction, group, grouping, flank, circle, coterie, set, segment, side, annexe, adjunct, extension.

wink *v* blink, flutter, glimmer, glint, twinkle, gleam, sparkle, flicker, flash. ◇ *n* **1** BLINK, flutter, sparkle, twinkle, glimmering, gleam, glint. **2** INSTANT, second, split second, flash.

winner *n* champion, victor, prizewinner, medallist, title-holder, world-beater, conqueror.
⊜ loser.

winning *adj* **1** CONQUERING,

triumphant, unbeaten, undefeated, victorious, successful. **2** WINSOME, charming, attractive, captivating, engaging, fetching, enchanting, endearing, delightful, amiable, alluring, lovely, pleasing, sweet.
⊞ **1** losing. **2** unappealing.

winnow v sift, separate, screen, divide, cull, select, part, fan.

wintry adj cold, chilly, bleak, cheerless, desolate, dismal, harsh, snowy, frosty, freezing, frozen, icy.

wipe v **1** RUB, clean, dry, dust, brush, mop, swab, sponge, clear. **2** REMOVE, erase, take away, take off.
• **wipe out** eradicate, obliterate, destroy, massacre, exterminate, annihilate, erase, expunge, raze, abolish, blot out, efface.

wiry adj muscular, sinewy, lean, tough, strong.
⊞ puny.

wisdom n discernment, penetration, sagacity, reason, sense, astuteness, comprehension, enlightenment, judgement, judiciousness, learning, understanding, knowledge, intelligence, erudition, foresight, prudence.
⊞ folly, stupidity.

wise adj **1** DISCERNING, sagacious, perceptive, rational, informed, well-informed, understanding, erudite, enlightened, knowing, intelligent, clever, aware, experienced. **2** WELL-ADVISED, judicious, prudent, reasonable, sensible, sound, long-sighted, shrewd.
⊞ **1** foolish, stupid. **2** ill-advised.

wish v **1** DESIRE, want, yearn, long, hanker, covet, crave, aspire, hope, hunger, thirst, prefer, need. **2** ASK, bid, require, order, instruct, direct, command.
◇ n **1** DESIRE, want, hankering, aspiration, inclination, hunger, thirst, liking, preference, yearning, urge, whim, hope. **2** REQUEST, bidding, order, command, will.

wisp n shred, strand, thread, twist, piece, lock.

wispy adj thin, straggly, frail, fine, attenuated, insubstantial, light, flimsy, fragile, delicate, ethereal, gossamer, faint.
⊞ substantial.

wistful adj **1** THOUGHTFUL, pensive, musing, reflective, wishful, contemplative, dreamy, dreaming, meditative. **2** MELANCHOLY, sad, forlorn, disconsolate, longing, mournful.

wit n **1** HUMOUR, repartee, facetiousness, drollery, banter, jocularity, levity. **2** INTELLIGENCE, cleverness, brains, sense, reason, common sense, wisdom, understanding, judgement, insight, intellect. **3** HUMORIST, comedian, comic, satirist, joker, wag.
⊞ **1** seriousness. **2** stupidity.

witch n sorceress, enchantress, occultist, magician, hag.

witchcraft n sorcery, magic, wizardry, occultism, the occult, wicca, the black art, black magic, enchantment, necromancy, voodoo, spell, incantation, divination, conjuration.

withdraw v **1** RECOIL, shrink back, draw back, pull back. **2** RECANT, disclaim, take back, revoke, rescind, retract, cancel, abjure, recall, take away. **3** DEPART, go (away), absent oneself, retire, remove, leave, back out, fall back, drop out, retreat, secede. **4** DRAW OUT, extract, pull out.

withdrawal n **1** REPUDIATION, recantation, disclaimer, disavowal, revocation, recall, secession, abjuration. **2** DEPARTURE, exit, exodus, retirement, retreat. **3** EXTRACTION, removal.

withdrawn adj **1** RESERVED, unsociable, shy, introvert, quiet,

retiring, aloof, detached, shrinking, uncommunicative, unforthcoming, taciturn, silent. 2 REMOTE, isolated, distant, secluded, out-of-the-way, private, hidden, solitary.
☒ 1 extrovert, outgoing.

wither v shrink, shrivel, dry, wilt, droop, decay, disintegrate, wane, perish, fade, languish, decline, waste.
☒ flourish, thrive.

withering adj 1 DESTRUCTIVE, deadly, death-dealing, devastating. 2 SCORNFUL, contemptuous, scathing, snubbing, humiliating, mortifying, wounding.
☒ 2 encouraging, supportive.

withhold v keep back, retain, hold back, suppress, restrain, repress, control, check, reserve, deduct, refuse, hide, conceal.
☒ give, accord.

withstand v resist, oppose, stand fast, stand one's ground, stand, stand up to, confront, brave, face, cope with, take on, thwart, defy, hold one's ground, hold out, last out, hold off, endure, bear, tolerate, put up with, survive, weather.
☒ give in, yield.

witness n 1 TESTIFIER, attestant, deponent (fml). 2 ONLOOKER, eye-witness, looker-on, observer, spectator, viewer, watcher, bystander.
◇ v 1 SEE, observe, notice, note, view, watch, look on, mark, perceive. 2 TESTIFY, attest, bear witness, depose (fml), confirm, bear out, corroborate. 3 ENDORSE, sign, countersign.

witty adj humorous, amusing, comic, sharp-witted, droll, funny, whimsical, original, brilliant, clever, ingenious, lively, sparkling, facetious, fanciful, jocular.
☒ dull, unamusing.

wizard n 1 SORCERER, magician, warlock, enchanter, necromancer, occultist, witch, conjurer. 2 (infml)

EXPERT, adept, virtuoso, ace, master, maestro, prodigy, genius, star (infml), whiz (infml), hotshot (infml).

wizened adj shrivelled, shrunken, dried up, withered, wrinkled, gnarled, thin, worn, lined.

wobble v shake, oscillate, tremble, quake, sway, teeter, totter, rock, seesaw, vibrate, waver, dodder, fluctuate, hesitate, dither, vacillate, shilly-shally.

wobbly adj unstable, shaky, rickety, unsteady, wonky (infml), teetering, tottering, doddering, doddery, uneven, unbalanced, unsafe.
☒ stable, steady.

woman n female, lady, girl, maid, maiden, matriarch, lass, chick (sl).

womanly adj feminine, female, ladylike, womanish.

wonder n 1 MARVEL, phenomenon, miracle, prodigy, sight, spectacle, rarity, curiosity. 2 AWE, amazement, astonishment, admiration, wonderment, fascination, surprise, bewilderment.
◇ v 1 MEDITATE, speculate, ponder, ask oneself, question, conjecture, puzzle, enquire, query, doubt, think. 2 MARVEL, gape, be amazed, be surprised.

wonderful adj 1 MARVELLOUS, magnificent, outstanding, excellent, superb, admirable, delightful, phenomenal, sensational, stupendous, tremendous, super (infml), terrific (infml), brilliant (infml), great (infml), fabulous (infml), fantastic (infml). 2 AMAZING, astonishing, astounding, startling, surprising, extraordinary, incredible, remarkable, staggering, strange.
☒ 1 appalling, dreadful. 2 ordinary.

woo v 1 (fml) woo a lover: court, chase, pursue. 2 woo custom: encourage, cultivate, attract, look for, seek.

wood n 1 TIMBER, lumber, planks.

2 FOREST, woods, woodland, trees, plantation, thicket, grove, coppice, copse, spinney.

Types of wood include: timber, lumber (*N Am*), hardwood, softwood, heartwood, sapwood, seasoned wood, green wood, brushwood, cordwood, firewood, kindling, matchwood, plywood, pulpwood, whitewood, chipboard, deal, hardboard, wood veneer; ash, balsa, beech, bitterwood, cedar, cherry, chestnut, ebony, elm, iroko, mahogany, African mahogany, maple, oak, pine, redwood, rosewood, rubberwood, sandalwood, satinwood, sheesham, teak, walnut, willow. *see also* **tree**.

---

wooded *adj* forested, timbered, woody, tree-covered, sylvan (*fml*).

wooden *adj* **1** TIMBER, woody. **2** EMOTIONLESS, expressionless, awkward, clumsy, stilted, lifeless, spiritless, unemotional, stiff, rigid, leaden, deadpan, blank, empty, slow. ⊠ **2** lively.

wool *n* fleece, down, yarn.

woolly *adj* **1** WOOLLEN, fleecy, downy, shaggy, fuzzy, frizzy. **2** UNCLEAR, ill-defined, hazy, blurred, confused, muddled, vague, indefinite, nebulous. ⊠ **2** clear, distinct. ◇ *n* jumper, sweater, jersey, pullover, cardigan.

word *n* **1** NAME, term, expression, designation, utterance, vocable (*fml*). **2** CONVERSATION, chat, talk, discussion, consultation. **3** INFORMATION, news, report, communication, notice, message, bulletin, communiqué, statement, dispatch, declaration, comment, assertion, account, remark, advice, warning. **4** PROMISE, pledge, oath, assurance, vow, guarantee. **5** COMMAND, order,

decree, commandment, go-ahead (*infml*), green light (*infml*). ◇ *v phrase*, express, couch, put, say, explain, write.

words *n* **1** ARGUMENT, dispute, quarrel, disagreement, altercation, bickering, row, squabble. **2** LYRICS, libretto, text, book.

wordy *adj* verbose, long-winded, loquacious (*fml*), garrulous, prolix, rambling, diffuse, discursive. ⊠ concise.

work *n* **1** OCCUPATION, job, employment, profession, trade, business, career, calling, vocation, line, métier, livelihood, craft, skill. **2** TASK, assignment, undertaking, job, chore, responsibility, duty, commission. **3** TOIL, labour, drudgery, effort, exertion, industry, slog (*infml*), graft (*infml*), elbow grease (*infml*). **4** CREATION, production, achievement, composition, opus. ⊠ **1** play, rest, hobby. ◇ *v* **1** BE EMPLOYED, have a job, earn one's living. **2** LABOUR, toil, drudge, slave. **3** FUNCTION, go, operate, perform, run, handle, manage, use, control. **4** BRING ABOUT, accomplish, achieve, create, cause, pull off (*infml*). **5** CULTIVATE, farm, dig, till. **6** MANIPULATE, knead, mould, shape, form, fashion, make, process. ⊠ **1** be unemployed. **2** play, rest. **3** fail.

● **work out 1** SOLVE, resolve, figure out, calculate, puzzle out, sort out, understand, clear up. **2** DEVELOP, evolve, go well, succeed, prosper, turn out, pan out (*infml*). **3** PLAN, devise, arrange, contrive, invent, construct, put together. **4** ADD UP TO, amount to, total, come out.

● **work up** incite, stir up, rouse, arouse, animate, excite, move, stimulate, inflame, spur, instigate, agitate, generate.

worker *n* employee, labourer, working man, working woman, artisan, craftsman, tradesman, hand, operative, wage-earner, breadwinner, proletarian.

workforce n workers, employees, personnel, labour force, staff, labour, workpeople, shop floor.

working n functioning, operation, running, routine, manner, method, action.
◇ adj 1 FUNCTIONING, operational, running, operative, going. 2 EMPLOYED, active.
⊟ 1 inoperative. 2 idle.

workmanship n skill, craft, craftsmanship, expertise, art, handicraft, handiwork, technique, execution, manufacture, work, finish.

works n 1 FACTORY, plant, workshop, mill, foundry, shop. 2 ACTIONS, acts, doings. 3 PRODUCTIONS, output, oeuvre, writings, books. 4 MACHINERY, mechanism, workings, action, movement, parts, installations.

workshop n 1 WORKS, workroom, atelier, studio, factory, plant, mill, shop. 2 STUDY GROUP, seminar, symposium, discussion group, class.

world n 1 EARTH, globe, planet, star, universe, cosmos, creation, nature. 2 EVERYBODY, everyone, people, human race, humankind, humanity. 3 SPHERE, realm, field, area, domain, division, system, society, province, kingdom. 4 TIMES, epoch, era, period, age, days, life.

worldly adj 1 TEMPORAL, earthly, mundane, terrestrial, physical, secular, unspiritual, profane. 2 WORLDLY-WISE, sophisticated, urbane, cosmopolitan, experienced, knowing, streetwise (infml). 3 MATERIALISTIC, selfish, ambitious, grasping, greedy, covetous, avaricious.
⊟ 1 spiritual, eternal. 2 unsophisticated.

worn adj 1 SHABBY, threadbare, worn-out, tatty, tattered, frayed, ragged. 2 EXHAUSTED, tired, weary, spent, fatigued, careworn, drawn, haggard, jaded.
⊟ 1 new, unused. 2 fresh.
• **worn-out** 1 SHABBY, threadbare, useless, used, tatty, tattered, on its last legs, ragged, moth-eaten, frayed, decrepit. 2 TIRED (OUT), exhausted, weary, done in (infml), all in (infml), dog-tired (infml), knackered (infml).
⊟ 1 new, unused. 2 fresh.

worried adj anxious, troubled, uneasy, ill at ease, apprehensive, concerned, bothered, upset, fearful, afraid, frightened, on edge, overwrought, tense, strained, nervous, disturbed, distraught, distracted, fretful, distressed, agonized.
⊟ calm, unworried, unconcerned.

worry v 1 BE ANXIOUS, be troubled, be distressed, agonize, fret. 2 IRRITATE, plague, pester, torment, unsettle, upset, annoy, bother, disturb, vex, tease, nag, harass, harry, perturb, hassle (infml). 3 ATTACK, go for, savage.
⊟ 1 be unconcerned. 2 comfort.
◇ n 1 PROBLEM, trouble, responsibility, burden, concern, care, trial, annoyance, irritation, vexation. 2 ANXIETY, apprehension, unease, misgiving, fear, disturbance, agitation, torment, misery, perplexity.
⊟ 2 comfort, reassurance.

worsen v 1 EXACERBATE, aggravate, intensify, heighten. 2 GET WORSE, weaken, deteriorate, degenerate, decline, sink, go downhill (infml).
⊟ improve.

worship v venerate, revere, reverence, adore, exalt, glorify, honour, praise, idolize, adulate, love, respect, pray to, deify.
⊟ despise, hate.
◇ n veneration, reverence, adoration, devotion(s), homage, honour, glory, glorification, exaltation, praise, prayer(s), respect, regard, love, adulation, deification, idolatry.

worst v beat, defeat, get the better of, overcome, overpower, overthrow, conquer, crush, master, subdue, drub (*infml*), whitewash, best, subjugate, vanquish (*fml*).

worth n worthiness, merit, value, benefit, advantage, importance, significance, use, usefulness, utility, quality, good, virtue, excellence, credit, desert(s), cost, rate, price, help, assistance, avail.

⊞ worthlessness.

worthless adj 1 VALUELESS, useless, pointless, meaningless, futile, unavailing, unimportant, insignificant, trivial, unusable, cheap, poor, rubbishy, trashy, trifling, paltry. 2 CONTEMPTIBLE, despicable, good-for-nothing, vile.

⊞ 1 valuable. 2 worthy.

worthwhile adj profitable, useful, valuable, worthy, good, helpful, beneficial, constructive, gainful, justifiable, productive.

⊞ worthless.

worthy adj praiseworthy, laudable, creditable, commendable, valuable, worthwhile, admirable, fit, deserving, appropriate, respectable, reputable, good, honest, honourable, excellent, decent, upright, righteous.

⊞ unworthy, disreputable.

would-be adj aspiring, budding, striving, endeavouring, ambitious, enterprising, keen, eager, hopeful, optimistic, wishful, longing.

wound n 1 INJURY, trauma, hurt, cut, gash, lesion, laceration, scar. 2 HURT, distress, trauma, torment, heartbreak, harm, damage, anguish, grief, shock. ◇ v 1 DAMAGE, harm, hurt, injure, hit, cut, gash, lacerate, slash, pierce. 2 DISTRESS, offend, insult, pain, mortify, upset, slight, grieve.

wrangle n argument, quarrel, tiff, dispute, controversy, squabble, row (*infml*), bickering, disagreement, clash, altercation, contest, slanging

match (*infml*), set-to (*infml*).

⊞ agreement.

◇ v argue, quarrel, disagree, dispute, bicker, altercate, contend, fall out (*infml*), row (*infml*), squabble, scrap, fight, spar.

⊞ agree.

wrap v envelop, fold, enclose, cover, pack, shroud, wind, surround, package, muffle, cocoon, cloak, roll up, bind, bundle up, immerse.

⊞ unwrap.

• **wrap up 1** WRAP, pack up, package, parcel. **2** (*infml*) CONCLUDE, finish off, end, bring to a close, terminate, wind up, complete, round off.

wrapper n wrapping, packaging, envelope, cover, jacket, dust jacket, sheath, sleeve, paper.

wrath n anger, bitterness, rage, fury, exasperation, indignation, irritation, annoyance, temper, resentment, passion, displeasure, spleen, choler, ire (*fml*).

⊞ calm, pleasure.

wreak v inflict, exercise, create, cause, bring about, perpetrate, vent, unleash, express, execute, carry out, bestow.

wreath n garland, coronet, chaplet, festoon, crown, band, ring.

wreathe v encircle, surround, enfold, entwine, twine, twist, wind, coil, wrap, envelop, crown, adorn, shroud, enwrap, festoon, intertwine, interweave.

wreck v destroy, ruin, demolish, devastate, shatter, smash, break, spoil, play havoc with, ravage, write off.

⊞ conserve, repair.

◇ n ruin, destruction, devastation, mess, demolition, ruination, write-off, disaster, loss, disruption.

wreckage n debris, remains, rubble, ruin, fragments, flotsam, pieces.

wrench v yank, wrest, jerk, pull, tug, force, sprain, strain, rick, tear, twist, wring, rip, distort.

wrestle v struggle, strive, fight, scuffle, grapple, tussle, combat, contend, contest, vie, battle.

wretch n scoundrel, rogue, villain, good-for-nothing, ruffian, rascal, vagabond, miscreant, outcast.

wretched adj 1 ATROCIOUS, awful, deplorable, appalling. 2 UNHAPPY, sad, miserable, melancholy, depressed, dejected, disconsolate, downcast, forlorn, gloomy, doleful, distressed, broken-hearted, crestfallen. 3 PATHETIC, pitiable, pitiful, unfortunate, sorry, hopeless, poor. 4 CONTEMPTIBLE, despicable, vile, worthless, shameful, inferior, low, mean, paltry.
🗷 1 excellent. 2 happy. 3 enviable. 4 worthy.

wriggle v squirm, writhe, wiggle, worm, twist, snake, slink, crawl, edge, sidle, manoeuvre, squiggle, dodge, extricate, zigzag, waggle, turn.
◇ n wiggle, twist, squirm, jiggle, jerk, turn, twitch.

wring v 1 SQUEEZE, twist, wrench, wrest, extract, mangle, screw. 2 EXACT, extort, coerce, force. 3 DISTRESS, pain, hurt, rack, rend, pierce, torture, wound, stab, tear.

wrinkle n furrow, crease, line, fold, gather, pucker, crumple, corrugation.
◇ v furrow, crease, fold, crinkle, shrivel, gather, pucker, corrugate, crumple.

write v pen, inscribe, record, jot down, set down, take down, transcribe, scribble, scrawl, correspond, communicate, draft, draw up, copy, compose, create.
• **write off 1** DELETE, cancel, cross out, disregard. 2 WRECK, destroy, crash, smash up.

writer n author, scribe, wordsmith, hack, penpusher (infml), scribbler.

Writers include: annalist, autobiographer, bard, biographer, blogger (infml), chronicler, clerk, columnist, contributor, copyist, copywriter, correspondent, court reporter, diarist, dramatist, editor, essayist, fiction writer, ghost-writer, historian, journalist, leader-writer, lexicographer, librettist, lyricist, novelist, playwright, poet, poet laureate, reporter, rhymer, satirist, scriptwriter, secretary, short story writer, sonneteer, stenographer, technical writer, web author.

writhe v squirm, wriggle, thresh, thrash, twist, wiggle, toss, coil, contort, struggle.

writing n 1 HANDWRITING, calligraphy, script, penmanship, scrawl, scribble, hand, print. 2 DOCUMENT, letter, book, composition, literature, work, publication.

Types of writing instrument include: pen, ballpoint, Biro®, calligraphy pen, cartridge pen, dip pen, eraser pen, felt-tip pen, fountain pen, marker pen, rollerball pen, writing brush; pencil, chinagraph pencil, coloured pencil, crayon, ink pencil, lead pencil, propelling pencil; board marker, laundry marker, permanent marker, highlighter; cane pen, quill, reed, steel pen, stylus; brailler, typewriter, word-processor.

wrong adj 1 INACCURATE, incorrect, mistaken, erroneous, false, fallacious, in error, imprecise. 2 INAPPROPRIATE, unsuitable, unseemly, improper, indecorous, unconventional, unfitting, incongruous, inapt. 3 UNJUST, unethical, unfair, illicit, unlawful, immoral, illegal, dishonest, criminal, crooked (infml), reprehensible, blameworthy, guilty,

to blame, bad, wicked, sinful, iniquitous, evil. **4** DEFECTIVE, faulty, out of order, amiss, awry.
⏏ **1** correct, right. **2** suitable, right. **3** good, moral.
◇ *adv* amiss, astray, awry, inaccurately, incorrectly, inexactly, wrongly, mistakenly, faultily, badly, erroneously, improperly.
⏏ right.
◇ *n* sin, misdeed, offence, crime, immorality, sinfulness, transgression, wickedness, wrongdoing, trespass (*fml*), injury, grievance, abuse, injustice, iniquity, inequity, infringement, unfairness, error.
⏏ right.
◇ *v* abuse, ill-treat, mistreat, maltreat, injure, ill-use, hurt, harm, discredit, dishonour, misrepresent, malign, oppress, cheat.

wrongdoer *n* offender, law-breaker, transgressor, criminal, delinquent, felon, miscreant, evil-doer, sinner, trespasser, culprit.

wrongful *adj* immoral, improper, unfair, unethical, unjust, illegal, illegitimate, illicit, dishonest, criminal, blameworthy, dishonourable, wrong, reprehensible, wicked, evil.
⏏ rightful.

wry *adj* **1** *wry humour*: ironic, sardonic, dry, sarcastic, mocking, droll. **2** TWISTED, distorted, deformed, contorted, warped, uneven, crooked.
⏏ **2** straight.

Yy

yank *v, n* jerk, tug, pull, wrench, snatch, haul, heave.

yap *v* **1** BARK, yelp. **2** (*infml*) CHATTER, jabber, babble, prattle, natter, jaw (*infml*).

yardstick *n* measure, gauge, criterion, standard, benchmark, touchstone, comparison.

yarn *n* **1** THREAD, fibre, strand. **2** STORY, tale, anecdote, fable, fabrication, tall story, cock-and-bull story (*infml*).

yawning *adj* gaping, wide, wide open, huge, vast, cavernous.

yearly *adj* annual, per year, per annum, perennial.
◇ *adv* annually, every year, once a year, perennially.

yearn for *v* long for, pine for, desire, want, wish for, crave, covet, hunger for, hanker for, ache for, languish for, itch for.

yell *v* shout, scream, bellow, roar, bawl, shriek, squeal, howl, holler (*infml*), screech, squall, yelp, yowl, whoop.
⊜ whisper.
◇ *n* shout, scream, cry, roar, bellow, shriek, howl, screech, squall, whoop.
⊜ whisper.

yelp *v* yap, bark, squeal, cry, yell, yowl, bay.
◇ *n* yap, bark, yip, squeal, cry, yell, yowl.

yield *v* **1** SURRENDER, renounce, abandon, abdicate, cede, part with, relinquish. **2** GIVE WAY, capitulate, concede, submit, succumb, give (in),

admit defeat, bow, cave in, knuckle under, resign oneself, go along with, permit, allow, acquiesce, accede, agree, comply, consent. **3** PRODUCE, bear, supply, provide, generate, bring in, bring forth, furnish, return, earn, pay.
⊜ **1** hold. **2** resist, withstand.
◇ *n* return, product, earnings, harvest, crop, produce, output, profit, revenue, takings, proceeds, income.

yoke *n* **1** HARNESS, bond, link. **2** BURDEN, bondage, enslavement, slavery, oppression, subjugation, servility.
◇ *v* couple, link, join, tie, harness, hitch, bracket, connect, unite.

young *adj* **1** YOUTHFUL, juvenile, baby, infant, junior, adolescent. **2** IMMATURE, early, new, recent, green, growing, fledgling, unfledged, inexperienced.
⊜ **1** adult, old. **2** mature, old.
◇ *n* offspring, babies, issue, litter, progeny, brood, children, family.

youngster *n* child, boy, girl, toddler, youth, teenager, kid (*infml*).

youth *n* **1** ADOLESCENT, youngster, juvenile, teenager, kid (*infml*), boy, young man. **2** YOUNG PEOPLE, the young, younger generation. **3** ADOLESCENCE, childhood, immaturity, boyhood, girlhood.
⊜ **3** adulthood.

youthful *adj* young, boyish, girlish, childish, immature, juvenile, inexperienced, fresh, active, lively, well-preserved.
⊜ aged.

Zz

zany *adj* comical, funny, amusing, eccentric, droll, crazy (*infml*), clownish, loony (*infml*), wacky (*infml*).
⊟ serious.

zeal *n* ardour, fervour, passion, warmth, fire, enthusiasm, devotion, spirit, keenness, zest, eagerness, earnestness, dedication, fanaticism, gusto, verve.
⊟ apathy, indifference.

zealot *n* fanatic, extremist, bigot, militant, partisan.

zealous *adj* ardent, fervent, impassioned, passionate, devoted, burning, enthusiastic, intense, fanatical, militant, keen, eager, earnest, spirited.
⊟ apathetic, indifferent.

zenith *n* summit, peak, height, top, pinnacle, apex, high point, climax, optimum, culmination, acme, meridian, vertex.
⊟ nadir.

zero *n* nothing, nought, nil, nadir, bottom, cipher, zilch (*infml*), duck, love.

zest *n* **1** GUSTO, appetite, enthusiasm, enjoyment, keenness, zeal, exuberance, interest. **2** FLAVOUR, taste, relish, savour, spice, tang, piquancy.
⊟ **1** apathy.

zigzag *v* meander, snake, wind, twist, curve.
◇ *adj* meandering, crooked, serpentine, sinuous, twisting, winding.
⊟ straight.

zodiac

The signs of the zodiac (with their symbols) are: Aries (Ram), Taurus (Bull), Gemini (Twins), Cancer (Crab), Leo (Lion), Virgo (Virgin), Libra (Balance), Scorpio (Scorpion), Sagittarius (Archer), Capricorn (Goat), Aquarius (Water Bearer), Pisces (Fishes).

zone *n* region, area, district, territory, section, sector, belt, sphere, tract, stratum.

zoo *n* zoological gardens, safari park, wildlife park, animal park, aquarium, aviary, menagerie.

zoom *v* race, rush, tear, dash, speed, fly, hurtle, streak, flash, shoot, whirl, dive, buzz, zip.